Psychotherapy

by James J. Walsh

Copyright © 8/27/2015
Jefferson Publication

ISBN-13: 978-1517090043

Printed in the United States of America

Contents

PSYCHOTHERAPY

INTRODUCTION

To physicians who are students not alone of the manifestations of disease but also of the workings of human nature, there are few chapters in the history of medicine more interesting than those which record the welcome by each generation of the supposed advances in the treatment of disease. Each generation announced its cures for diseases, provided its remedies to relieve symptoms, and invented methods of treatment that seemed to put off the inevitable tendency toward dissolution. Yet few of these inventions and discoveries maintain their early reputations, and succeeding generations invariably abandon most of this supposed medical progress in favor of ideas of their own, which later suffer a like fate. Plausible theories have not been lacking to support the successive remedies and methods of treatment, but the general acceptance of them was always founded far less upon theory than upon actual observation of their supposed efficacy. Certain remedies were given and the patients began to improve. Patients who did not have the remedies continued to suffer, and sometimes the course of their disease led to a fatal termination. Even with the best remedies death sometimes took place, but that was easily accounted for on the ground that the disease had secured so firm a hold that it could not be dislodged, even by a good remedy. The connection of cause and effect between the administration of the remedy and the improvement and eventual cure of the patient seemed to be demonstrated.

The archives of old-time medicine disprove the notion that clinical learning and teaching—that is, observation and demonstration at the bedside—were not part of medical education until quite modern times. The medical books of the thirteenth, fourteenth and fifteenth centuries are full of descriptions of actual cases, while, over a millenium before, one of Martial's epigrams tells of a patient who dreaded the coming of his physician because he brought with him so many students, whose cold hands gave chills to the poor victim.

Coincidence and Consequence.—In spite of the opportunities for careful observation thus afforded and the facilities for training clinical observers in medicine, many remedies came into vogue, were enthusiastically applied, and then, after a time, went out of use and were heard of no more. Sometimes they were subsequently revived and had even a greater vogue than when originally brought out. But most of these remedies eventually went forever into the lumber room of disused treatments. Of the many thousands of remedies which had the approval and the praise of past generations, two score at most hold a place in the pharmacopeia of to-day.

There are many reasons for this initial success and eventual failure; but the most important explanation lies not so much in reason as in coincidence. In the majority of human ills there is a definite tendency to get better, and almost anything that is given to the patient will be followed by relief and {2} improvement. The recovery is not, however, on account of the remedy, but occurs only after a definite succession of events that would have taken place either with or without the remedy.

Mental Influence.—What the old physicians did not, as a rule, appreciate, or at least failed to value at its true significance, was the effect upon the patient's mind of the taking of a remedy. Because of the confidence with which it was given, the patient, having full faith in the physician who gave it, became impressed with the idea that now he must get well. The very presence of the physician and his assurance that the illness was not serious and that many symptoms that were sources of dread to the patient were only concomitant conditions of the ailment, naturally to be expected under the circumstances, relieved the patient from worry, and so gave his nervous energy a chance to exert itself in bringing about improvement. In other words, the suggestive elements of the presence of the physician and the taking of his remedy were important therapeutic factors which enabled what was an absolutely inefficient remedy, as the event proved when closer observations of it had been made, to relieve even serious symptoms, or helped a weak remedy to accomplish good results by strengthening the patient's resistive vitality.

In recent years we have come to study much more closely this suggestive element and to appreciate better its true value. Suggestion has always been an important factor in therapeutics, but has been used indeliberately and indirectly rather than with careful forethought. Not that the great thinkers in medicine have not known its value and have not used it deliberately on appropriate occasions, but that the profession generally has been so much occupied with the merely material means of curing that practitioners have not realized the influence for good of the psychotherapeutic factors they were unconsciously employing.

The history of the phases of psychotherapy brings out clearly how much it has always meant in the curing of human ills.

Constancy of Psychotherapy in Medicine.—Though we are prone to think of it as coming to attention in our time, psychotherapy has played an important role in every phase of the history of medicine. It has always been at work, though usually under other names, and has been effectively used without conscious direction. Germs and their pernicious activity were not recognized before our time, yet many definite precautions against them, such as cooking of food and the keeping of perishable goods on ice, which now seem to be the direct result of our knowledge of bacteriology, were commonly practiced. The influence of the mind on the body exerted itself quite apart from man's recognition of its place or appreciation of its power. When employed unconsciously it was in many ways even more effective than it will be when a consciousness of the means by which it is applied becomes more general. For most people are unwilling to confess that their minds exercise as much influence as now proves to be the case, and that over-solicitude means so much in inhibiting the curative powers of nature, and that it is this which is favorably affected by psychotherapy.

The great physicians employed psychotherapy very commonly, and on that account many of their disciples were inclined to think that they were neglectful of medication and other remedial measures. At all times physicians have had to be large-minded and have had to recognize the limitations of medicine in {3} their own time, to turn to other agents and to appreciate how much their own influence on the patient and that of the patient on himself meant for the relief of symptoms and the increase of resistive vitality.

Some of the phases of indeliberate psychotherapy, however, are even more interesting than this chapter of the history of genuine and deliberate psycho-therapeutics. Not a few of the remedies recommended, even by distinguished physicians, were utterly inert, yet accomplished good through their effect upon the patient's mind. If we were to omit all reference to certain favorite prescriptions that passed down from generation to generation, sometimes for centuries, yet eventually proved to be quite inefficient for the purpose for which they were employed, what a large lacuna would be left in the history of medical treatment! Galen's *theriac* is a typical example of this. Still more strikingly the role of psychotherapy is seen in the many remedies that were recommended at various times for such self-limited diseases as erysipelas, ordinary coughs and colds, pneumonia and typhoid fever. Anything that was administered just before the change for the better came in these diseases, or that was persistently taken until that change came, was proclaimed as curative.

An even more interesting chapter in the positive history of psychotherapy is that which shows how the value of genuine remedies was exaggerated by suggestion, and how these remedies became therapeutic fads, and sometimes almost seemed to be cure-alls. What a large place antimony holds in medical history, though it is now entirely discredited! How beneficent has venesection seemed, though it is now frankly confessed that it has but a narrow usefulness for a very circumscribed set of ills! Calomel in large doses has a history very like that of antimony. Alcohol in various forms, now so strikingly losing its hold in therapeutics, must also be placed in this category.

Psychotherapy has perhaps had its most fruitful field of potency in connection with discoveries in the physical sciences. Whenever a discovery has been made in any science, an application of it to medicine has been mooted by some fertile mind, though as a rule it eventually proved to have no place in medicine. One might ordinarily expect that the suggestion would be latent only when the discovery was in one of the sciences allied to medicine, but this relation has not been necessary. Discoveries in astronomy even, in light, in electricity, in every department of physical science, have each been given their opportunity to affect patients' minds favorably, and have succeeded.

Irregular Phases of Psychotherapy.—The quack has always been a psycho-therapeutist *par excellence*. His main stock in trade has been his knowledge of men and his power to convince them that he was able to do them good, so that he could tap all the sources of energy that were in the patient, some of them quite latent, yet of great efficiency. Often what the quack and the nostrum vender did for their patients was calculated to do harm rather than good, yet the mental energy aroused by the appeal to the patients' minds was sufficient not only to neutralize the evil, but to release curative powers that otherwise would not have been called out. The advertisements of the nostrum maker have proved especially effective, and printer's ink, properly administered, has been a most potent remedy.

Drug Therapeutics.—Many of the newer phases of mental healing pretend to do away with drugs. Nothing is farther from my purpose than to condemn drugs: I am simply pointing out how much supposed drug efficacy has been {4} due to the mental influence on the patient of the suggestion that went with the drugs. There has been no thought at all of pushing drugs out of the extremely valuable place they occupy in medicine, for I yield to no one in my thorough conviction of their usefulness. But the efficacious element in the administration of many drugs has been entirely the confidence of the physician in them, which confidence was communicated to the patient's mind. Undoubtedly many highly recommended drugs have in themselves tended to do harm rather than good, and have been useful only because of this psycho-therapeutic element. Dr. Oliver Wendell Holmes' famous expression, that if all the drugs that had ever been used had been thrown into the sea instead of put into patients' bodies the human race might have been the better for it, should not be taken to mean that a great many drugs are not efficacious. Above all, it leaves out the most important consideration, that patients, while taking drugs that are either inert or at times even slightly harmful, have had their mental attitude towards themselves and their ills so favorably modified by the repeated suggestion that the result has been distinctly beneficial.

There are probably two score of drugs that are simply invaluable—magnificent auxiliaries in times of physical and mental distress. To realize and appreciate the place of these drugs, their limitations, how they should be administered, and what they can do under varying circumstances, has taken us centuries. When to these drugs there is intelligently attached the influence that psychotherapy has over the patient, their efficacy is probably doubled. Without that influence nature often works against the drug and lowers its efficiency. That is the reason why physicians, when themselves patients, do not respond well to drugs. Familiarity has bred contempt for some of the old-fashioned remedies, but the contempt that comes from familiarity is often quite undeserved, and many of the things that we thus undervalue because of accustomedness have a power that should be respected. People in a dynamite factory become so familiar with danger as to despise it at times, but that does not lessen the energy of the dynamite when occasion arises. When the physician himself is ill he is likely to remember his failures with drugs rather than his successes. That is, however, only the tendency of human nature to a certain pessimistic outlook where we ourselves are concerned.

There is another class in whom familiarity with drugs has become a serious matter. They are the patients who have made the rounds of physicians, have learned to read prescriptions, have looked up the significance of the various remedies that they have seen prescribed, have heard doctors talk about them, and remember only what is depreciatory, and who critically examine a prescription and conclude that the remedies recommended are not likely to do them good. Every physician knows the hopeless condition such patients are in. Mental attitude will greatly help drugs, and it can utterly undo the effect of all drugs except those which have certain drastic mechanical effects. Drug failure in these cases is another illustration of how much psychotherapy means in connection with drug treatment.

Not only is there no intent, then, to lessen respect for drugs in this textbook of psychotherapeutics, but the one thing that the author would like to emphasize is the necessity for giving drugs in sufficient doses. Recommendations in text-books of medicine are often vague in their indications as to dosage, and surprisingly small doses are, in consequence, sometimes prescribed. {5} Practically the only remedial element of such small doses is the mental effect on the patient, whereas a combination of pharmaceutic and psychotherapeutic factors would be much more efficacious. It is not unusual to find that the patient who is supposed to be taking nux vomica as an appetizer or a muscle tonic, or in order to produce heart equilibrium in the cardiac neuroses, is getting five drops, two and a half minims, three times a day, when he should be getting at least twenty drops with the same frequency. I have known a physician to prescribe ten grains of bromid where thirty to sixty grains should have been prescribed, and such valuable pharmaceutic materials as bismuth and pepsin are often given in doses so small that they preclude all possibility of benefit except by mental influence.

With therapeutic nihilism or skepticism of the power of drugs I have no sympathy. As a teacher of medicine I have for years emphasized the necessity of the use not of conventional doses of drugs for every patient, but of doses proportioned to the body weight. It seems to me quite absurd to give the same amount of a drug to a woman who weighs a hundred pounds and to a man who weighs two hundred and fifty pounds of solid muscular tissue. I believe in using drugs well up to their physiological effects if the drugs are really indicated.

With regard to other modes of treatment the same thing is true. Where they are indicated, balneo-therapy, hydro-therapy, mechano-therapy, electro-therapy, massage, and all the forms of external treatment, should be used rationally and not merely conventionally. The individual and not his affection must be treated. In all of these methods there is a psychotherapeutic element, and for the benefit of the patient this, too, must be recognized and used to its fullest extent.

Supposed Novelties in Mind Healing.—We hear much of mental healing, of absent treatment, of various phases of suggestion, and of the marvelous therapeutic efficiency of complete denial of the existence of evil, and sometimes we wonder whether all these things are not offshoots of our recent growth in the knowledge of psychology. It is possible, however, to find, masquerading under the head of the efficacy of nostrums in the past, the equivalents for all the activities of mental healing of the present. It all depends on what is the scientific fad of the hour. If it is electricity, then some mode of electrical treatment serves the purpose of suggesting cure, and relief of symptoms follows. If drug treatment of any particular kind is attracting much attention, then the suggestion is most effective that is founded on this basis. Perkins' tractors or the Leyden jar are effective at one time, radium or the X-rays at another, sarsaparilla or dilute alcohol at another, while a generation that is much interested in psychology may find, as ours does to a noteworthy degree, quite sufficient favorable suggestion for the cure of many ills in purely psychic influences, either direct or indirect, deliberate or unconscious.

Men and women do not change, their ills are about the same, and except for certain definite scientific remedies it is only the superficial mode of treatment that differs very much. Psychotherapy has always been an important element in most of the therapeutics of history. With so much accomplished in the past by indirection, there can be no doubt but that important advances in psychotherapeutics must result from the extension of its deliberate use.

We have not yet reached a point in our knowledge of the mode of the {6} influence of the mind on the body that will enable us to treat this large subject in a scientific manner. What has been written is set down rather as suggestive than conclusive. There is almost nothing that the human mind cannot do, its power ranging from the ability to delay death for hours or even days to causing sudden or unlooked for death under strong emotional strain. But we are as yet without definite data as to the possibilities of the immense power for good, and also for ill, that lie unrevealed in this domain. Anything that makes for observations by a large body of trained observers in a large number of cases will almost surely serve to bring about a development of this subject of valuable practical application.

Psychotherapy is open to large abuse. It will happen that men who are not trained in diagnosis will occasionally try to use psychotherapeutic means when what is needed is the knife, the actual cautery, a good purge, some strong drug, or other efficient remedy whose value has been demonstrated and which any trained physician can use. It will also happen that men who lack tact will occasionally disturb patients' minds still further by what they say to them in a mistaken attempt at psychotherapy, and will sometimes suggest other symptoms and make sufferers worse by their clumsy attempts to remove symptoms that are already present. Every good thing, however, is open to the same objection. Even good food is abused. The use of drugs has been so abused that the abuse has done much to discredit medicine at many periods. There is a Latin proverb which says: "From the abuse of a thing no argument against its use can be drawn." We cannot prevent liability to abuse, and psychotherapy is sure to meet that fate. It has been abused in the past, and is abused now, and always will be abused, but formal study of psychotherapy and its deliberate employment will do more than anything else to limit the inevitable abuse.

If its place in history and in medicine is definitely set forth, its problems squarely faced and their solutions definitely suggested, it is much less likely to be misused. At least, then, the whole subject is open for free and frank discussion and for such additions and subtractions as may make this department of therapeutics as important, or at least in a measure as valuable, as climato-therapy or balneo-therapy or mechano-therapy or electro-therapy. The development of each of these subjects has proved helpful. It is true that each specialist has, in the eyes of his colleagues in general practice, exaggerated the significance of his own department. This is true in all specialties, however, and psychotherapy deserves quite as much as any of the subjects we have mentioned to have a place among the text-books of medicine; and so this one is committed to the judgment of clinical observers. Long ago Horace said:

Si quid novisti rectius his candidus imperti
Si non his utere mecum.

{7}

HISTORY OF PSYCHOTHERAPEUTICS

SECTION I

PSYCHOTHERAPY IN THE HISTORY OF MEDICINE

CHAPTER I

GREAT PHYSICIANS IN PSYCHOTHERAPY

"The real physician is the one who cures: the observation which does not touch the art of healing is not that of a physician, it is that of a naturalist."

Psychotherapy is as old as the history of medicine and may be traced to the earliest ages. The great physicians of all time have recognized its value, have used it themselves and commended its use to their disciples, though realizing its mysterious side and appreciating its limitations.

FIRST PHYSICIAN

The first physician of whom we have any record was I-em-Hetep, who lived in the reign of King Tcsher of the third dynasty of Egypt, probably before 4000 B. C. Among his titles, besides that of Master of Secrets, was Bringer of Peace. He was looked up to as one who, when not able to cure physical ailments, did succeed in consoling and reassuring patients so as to make their condition much more bearable. Like others of the great early physicians, he was after his death worshiped as a god, a tribute which probably signifies that those who had been benefited by his ministrations felt that he must have been more than mortal.

The extent of the Egyptians' admiration for him will be appreciated from the fact that the step pyramid at Sakkara is said to have been built in his honor, though, as a rule, pyramids were erected only to honor kings or the very highest nobility. The extant statue of I-em-Hetep shows a placid-looking man with an air of beneficent wisdom, seated with a scroll on his knees. It produces the distinct impression, as may be seen from the illustration, that his patients must have trusted him thoroughly, since this is the memory of his personality that was transmitted to posterity. While he came to be looked upon as the medical divinity of the Egyptians, he was never represented with a beard, which is the token of the gods, or of mortals who have been really apotheosized. Evidently his devotees felt that it was the divine in his humanity which was the most prominent feature that they wished to honor. Among the Greeks AEsculapius, who had been merely a successful physician, came to be honored as a deity. When we recall the condition of therapeutics at that {8} time, it is evident that man's appreciation of his power to console, even though he might not be able to heal, of his influence over men's minds in the midst of their sufferings, and the confidence that his presence inspired, were the real sources of their grateful recognition.

PSYCHOTHERAPY IN EGYPT

Among the Egyptians the first great development of medicine came among the priests. The two professions, the medical and priesthood, were one, and the temples were the hospitals of the time. We have stories of people traveling long distances to certain temples in the early days of Egypt and also of Greece. Often the sick slept in the temples and dreamed of ways by which they would be cured. The stories make one feel that somehow the sleep which came over them was not entirely natural and spontaneous, but must have been something like hypnotic sleep. As for the dreams, the suggestions of modern time given in the hypnotic condition seem to be the best indication that we have of what happened in those old days. Certain it is that the persuasion of the patient that he would get better, the influence of the diversion of mind consequent upon his journey and the regulation of life under new circumstances in the temple, with the repeated suggestions of the priests and of their various remedial measures, as well as those due to the fact that other patients around him were improving, all plainly show the place of psychotherapy at this time.

Much of the old-time therapy was in association with dreams supposed to have been in some way inspired. This was true at Epidaurus, at Kos, at Rome, at Lebene, at Athens, and at every place we know of where cures were worked in the olden times. To the modern mind it seems impossible that dreams should come so apropos unless they were in some way directed. The only explanation seems to be the use of suggestion, with the probable production of sleep resembling our modern hypnotic trance. Apparently the patient's attention was little directed to the origin of the suggestions received, but he remembered and benefited by them.

The most explicit testimony that we have to the antiquity of psychotherapeutics and to the employment of the influence of the minds of patients over their ailments in the olden time is in Pinel's "Nosographie philosophique" and in his "Traité médico-philosophique sur l'alienation mentale."

Pinel himself will be remembered as the great French psychiatrist who, confident that he could control most of them by mental influence, first dared to strike the chains from the insane in the asylums of Paris, at the end of the eighteenth century, when for more than a century they had been treated more barbarously than ever before in history. The passage makes clear that the writer himself, over a hundred years ago, was persuaded of the significance of the patient's mental attitude and of the value of mental treatment for many nervous and mental diseases:

An intimate acquaintance with human nature and with the character in general of melancholics must always point out the urgent necessity of forcibly agitating the system, of interrupting the chain of their gloomy ideas, and of engaging their interest by powerful and continuous impressions on their external senses. Wise regulations of this nature are considered as having constituted in part the celebrity and utility of the priesthood of ancient Egypt. Efforts of industry and of art, scenes of magnificence and of grandeur, the varied pleasures of sense, and {9} the imposing influences of a pompous and mysterious superstition, were perhaps never devoted to a more laudable purpose. At both extremities of ancient Egypt, a country which was at that time exceedingly populous and flourishing, were temples dedicated to Saturn, whither melancholics resorted in crowds in quest of relief. The priests, taking advantage of their credulous confidence, ascribed to miraculous powers the effects of natural means exclusively. Games and recreations of all kinds were instituted in these temples. Beautiful paintings and images were everywhere exposed to public view. The most enchanting songs, and sounds the most melodious "took prisoner the captive sense." Flowery gardens and groves, disposed with taste and art, invited them to refreshment and salubrious exercise. Gaily decorated boats sometimes transported them to breathe, amidst rural concerts, the pure breezes of the Nile. Sometimes they were conveyed to its verdant Isles, where, under the symbols of some guardian deity, new and ingeniously contrived entertainments were prepared for their reception. Every moment was devoted to some pleasurable occupation, or rather a system of diversified amusements, enhanced and sanctioned by superstition. An appropriate and scrupulously observed regimen, repeated excursions to the holy places, preconcerted fêtes at different stages to excite and keep up their interest on the road, with every other advantage of a similar nature that the experienced priesthood could invent or command, were, in no small degree, calculated to suspend the influence of pain, to calm the inquietudes of a morbid mind, and to operate salutary changes in the various functions of the system.

The Temple at Epidaurus as a Health Resort

This gives some slight idea of the magnificent arrangement of this famous health resort of the Greeks in which every possible care was taken to influence the mind of the patient favorably and bring about his cure. The buildings of the Hieron or medical institution of Epidaurus were beautifully situated about six miles from the town of Epidaurus in picturesque scenery and the most healthful surroundings. There were a series of bathing houses for hydropathy. The abatons, lofty and airy sleeping chambers with their southern sides and open colonnade, are singularly like the open balconies of our tuberculosis sanatoria. Every occupation of mind was provided. There was a theatre that would seat over 10,000 people. Here the great classic Greek plays were given with fullest effect. There was a stadium seating about 12,000 people in which athletic events were witnessed, finally there was a hippodrome for alt sorts of amusements in which animals shared. Then there were the walks through the country, sheltered paths around the grounds for inclement weather, even tunnels for passage from one building to another and all the influence of religion, of suggestion, of contact with cultured priests thoroughly accustomed to dealing with all manner of patients. No wonder the place was popular and many cures effected.

11

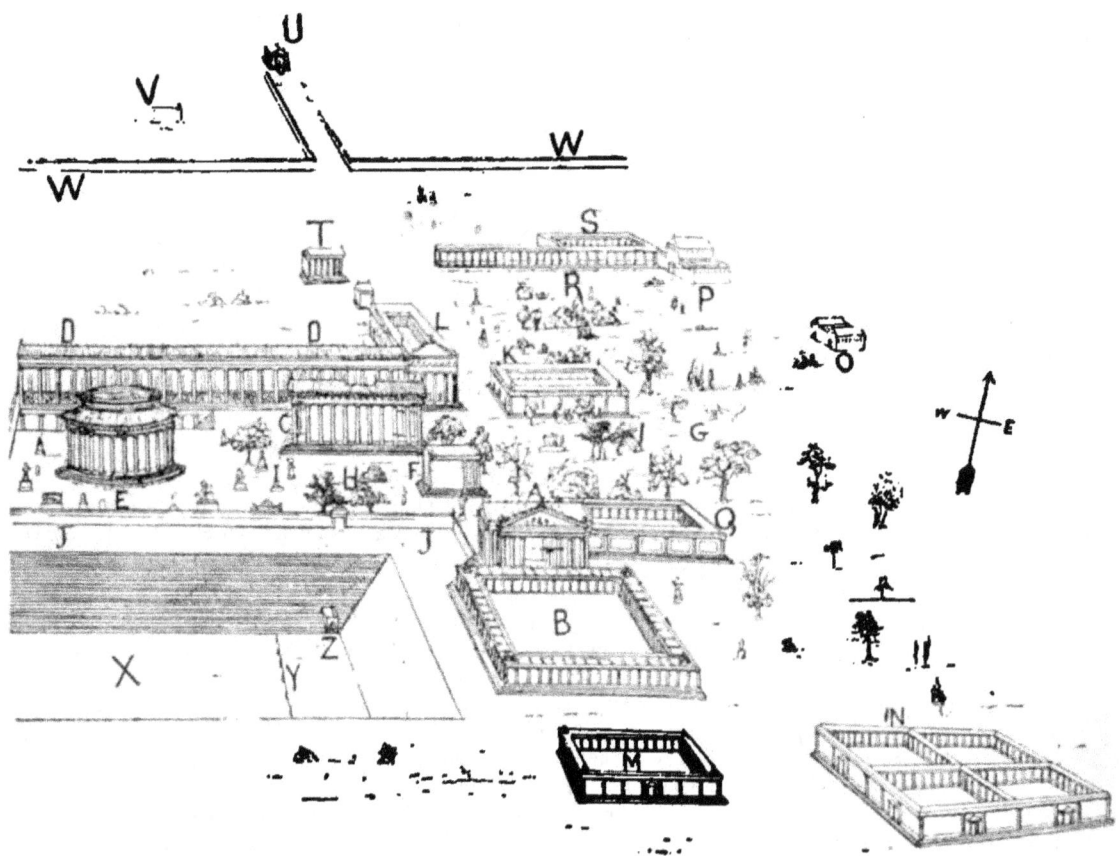

THE TEMPLE AT EPIDAURUS AS A HEALTH RESORT

A, South Propylaea; B, Gymnasium; C, Temple of Esculapius; DD, East and West Abatons (temple enclosures); E, Pholos; F, Temple of Artemis; G, Grove; H, Small Altar; I, Large Alter; J, South Boundary; K, Square (building); L, Baths of Esculapius; M, Gymnasium and Hostel; N, Four Quadrangles (for promenade and exercise); O, Roman Building; P, Roman Bath; Q, Portico of Cotys; R, Northeastern Colonnade; S, Northeastern Quadrangle; T, Temple of Aphrodite (?); U, Northern Propylaea, on the Road to Epidaurus; V, Roman Building; W, Northern Boundary; X, Stadium; Y, Goal or Starting Line; Z, Tunnel between Temple and Stadium. (Caton.)

There are other phases of Egyptian medicine which serve to show us how early many of the psychological ideas that we now are trying to adopt and adapt in medicine had come to the thinkers in medicine of long ago. There is, for instance, now in the Berlin museum an interesting papyrus of the Middle Kingdom, the date of which is about 2500 B. C, in which there are many modern ideas. It is a dialogue which attempts the justification of suicide. The principal speaker, a man weary of life, has made up his mind to suicide, but is hesitant. The others who speak in the dialogue are his *secondary personalities*. The Egyptians considered that there were several of these interior persons with whom the man himself might have communication. A man could play draughts with his *ba* somewhat as we play solitaire. He could talk to and exchange gifts with his *ka*. He could argue and remain at variance, but more often come to an agreement, with his *khou*. This last was his luminous immortal *ego*, which, according to the then generally received Egyptian conception, formed a complete and independent personality. The whole scene thus outlined is typically modern in certain phases of its psychology, and presents the only known treatment for the tendency to suicide. While we have but this instance, there seems no doubt that the same system of persuasion must have been employed for the cure of other mental conditions than that which predisposes to suicide.

What is described in our quotation from Pinel as the most ancient form of psychotherapy has all down the centuries been the rule of life for patients at institutions similar to those of Egypt. We know more of Greece than of other countries; there the shrines of AEsculapius were in many ways what we now call sanatoria. They were spacious buildings pleasantly situated, the hours of rising and of rest were definitely regulated, the patients' minds were occupied with the details of the cure, they met pleasant companions from distant places, they had all the advantages of diversion of mind, simple diet, long hours in the open air and abundance of rest away from the ordinary worries of life. Besides, there had usually been some weeks or months of {10} preparation during a lengthy journey and all the diversion of mind which that implies. No wonder that these institutions acquired a reputation for cures of symptoms which the physician had been unable to accomplish while the patient was at home in the midst of his daily cares and worries of life.

The temples in Egypt, in Assyria, in Greece, were much like the health institutions—"cure houses," as the expressive German phrase calls them—of our day. Pictures of the temple of AEsculapius at Epidaurus show a magnificent building with beautiful grounds, ample bathing facilities, and evidently many opportunities for a quiet, easy life far from the worries and bustle of the world and with everything that would suggest to the patient that he must get well. This phase of psychotherapy in the olden time is not only interesting in itself, but furnishes a valuable commentary on corresponding modern institutions, since it shows that it is not so much the physical influences, which have differed markedly at different periods, as the mental attitude so constantly influenced at these institutions which was the real therapeutic factor.

Now our sanatoria are nearly all founded on some special principle of therapeutics. Some of them have dietetic fads and no food out of which the life has been cooked is eaten. Some of them are absolutely vegetarian. Some of them depend on wonderful springs in their neighborhoods, others on certain forms of exercise, still others give the rest cure. All succeed in relieving many symptoms. No one who has analyzed the cures effected will think for a moment that it is the special therapeutic fad of the institution that accomplishes all the good done for patients suffering from so many different complaints. Similar ills often are affected quite differently, and, while some are relieved, others are not. Those who fail to be cured at one will, however, often be relieved at another. It depends on how much influence of mind is secured over the patient and how much diversion from thoughts of self is provided.

MIND HEALING IN GREECE

When Greece awoke to the great literary and scientific discussion of human thought that gave us such philosophic and scientific thinkers as Hippocrates, Plato and Aristotle, then psychotherapy, in the formal sense of caring for the mind of the patient as well as for his body, came to be explicitly recognized as having therapeutic value. Hippocrates insisted that medicine was an art rather than a science, that personality had much to do with it, and that the patient must be optimistically influenced in every way. The first of his aphorisms is well known, but few realize all of its significance. Hippocrates declares that "life is short and art long, the occasion fleeting, experience fallacious and judgment difficult. The physician must not only be prepared to do what is right himself, *but also to make the patient, the attendants and externals coöperate."* No one emphasized more than he the necessity for differentiating the individual patient, and to him we owe, in foundation at least, the aphorism that it is more important to know what sort of an individual has a disease than what sort of a disease the individual has, for the chances of cure greatly depend on favorable individuality.

Perhaps Hippocrates' most striking direct contribution to psychotherapy is his aphorism with regard to pain. He said: "Of two pains occurring together in different parts of the body, the stronger weakens the other." When {11} the attention is distracted from pain, then it is lessened. Of two pains, then, only the one that attracts the most attention is much felt, and, if a slight pain is succeeded by a severe pain in another part of the body, the lesser pain will apparently become trivial, or, indeed, not be felt at all.

In Plato we find the direct philosophic expression of the value of psychotherapy. There had been during the preceding century a great increase in information with regard to the facts of physical nature, and especially the sciences relating to the human body, and so men had come, as they are prone to at such eras—our own, for instance—to think too much of the body and too little of the mind that rules it. Accordingly, we have from Plato a deliberate, emphatic assertion of this great truth under circumstances which make us realize how keenly he appreciated its significance for the art of medicine and for humanity.

Professor Osier, in his address, "Physic and Physicians as Depicted in Plato," tells a story which shows clearly how much the great Greek philosopher appreciated the place of psychotherapy.

Charmides had been complaining of a headache, and Critias had asked Socrates to make believe that he could cure him of it. Socrates said that he had a charm which he had learnt, when serving with the army, of one of the physicians of the Thracian king. Zamolxis. This physician had told Socrates that the cure of a part should not be attempted without treatment of the whole, and, also, that no attempt should be made to cure the body without the soul, "and, therefore, if the head and body are to be well, you must begin by curing the mind; that is the first thing. And he who taught me the cure and the charm added a special direction. 'Let no one,' he said, 'persuade you to cure the head until he has first given you his soul to be cured. *For this,'* he said, *'is the great error of our day in the treatment of the human body, that physicians separate the soul from the body.'"*

Because it anticipates so much that is thought to be recent in the treatment of certain affections this paragraph is interesting from many standpoints. Headache is typically one of the ills that in the modern time has often been cured by suggestion. Critias knew how much confidence Charmides had in Socrates, whom he looked upon as his master, and that, therefore, Socrates' declaration of his power to cure would probably be sufficient to relieve his disciple. Critias shrewdly suggests, however, that Socrates possessed a charm which he had learned from a distinguished royal physician. Cures in the modern time of any kind are likely to be much more effective if they come from a distance and, above all, if they have some connection with royalty, or have been tried with favorable results upon distinguished personages.

ALEXANDRIAN PSYCHOTHERAPY

When the center of interest in Greek medicine was transferred from Greece itself to Egypt, and the Alexandrian school represented what was best in medical thinking and investigation, we find evidence once more of wise physicians realizing the influence of the mind on the body and of what seemed to physicians of lesser experience the cure of physical ills by mental means. One of the most distinguished physicians of all time is Erasistratos, who, with Herophilus, made the fame of the great medical school at Alexandria, {12} the first university medical school in the world's history. Both practiced dissection with assiduity, and, while it is Herophilus' name that is associated with the *torcular* within the skull, and it was he who gave the name *calamus scriptorius* to certain appearances in the fourth ventricle, and otherwise stamped his personality on the study of the brain, it is to Erasistratos that we have to turn for a typical example of the mental physician. Erasistratos, about 300 B. C, recognized the valves of the heart, gave them the names tricuspid and sigmoid, and, like his great colleague, studied particularly the nervous system. He seems to have distinguished the nerves of motion from those of sensation, recognized their different functions and the different directions in which they carried impulses, and thought the brain the most important organ in the body.

The story is told that he was summoned in consultation to see the son of Seleukos, surnamed Nikator, the Macedonian general of Alexander the Great, who became ruler of Babylonia. The illness of this son, Antiochos, had baffled the skill of the court physicians. While Erasistratos was feeling his patient's pulse, the stepmother of the young prince entered the room. She, the second wife of his father, was young and handsome, and Erasistratos noted that there was great perturbation of the pulse as soon as the stepmother came in. He correctly surmised that the young man was in love with the lady and that his illness had been occasioned by the feeling that his love was hopeless. The very sharing of his secret seems to have started the young man's cure, and Erasistratos' wisdom and medical skill became a proverb throughout the East.

PSYCHOTHERAPY AT ROME

Galen.—Galen, whom we are prone to think of as a Latin because so much of his work was done at Rome, but whose works have come to us in Greek, and who was a disciple of the Greek school of medicine, brought up under Greek influence in his native town of Pergamos, re-echoed Hippocrates' expressions as to the necessity for securing the patient's confidence and setting his mind at ease. The story in the "Arabian Nights" of his experience with the quack, which is known to most people, shows clearly how the place of mental influence in the relief of human ills must have been brought home to him. For nearly fifteen centuries his works continued to be the most read of medical documents. Nine tenths of all the physicians of education and influence, confidently looking to him as their master, kept copies of his works constantly near them, and turned to them for medical guidance as they would to the Bible for spiritual aid.

The book of Galen which is usually placed first among his collected works shows how much more important is the mind than the body for human happiness, and insists on mental interests as making life worth while. In it he describes the good physician, and says that to be a good physician a man must also be a good philosopher. When he comes to talk of the different sects in medicine—for even in his time there were groups of men who founded their medical practice on very different principles—he points out that the members of the different medical sects, while all employing practically the same remedies, do so on quite different principles, and yet get about the same {13} results. This concept comes as near to being a conscious reflection as to the place that the patient's mental reaction had in therapeutics as might well be expected at that early date.

Alexander of Tralles.—After Galen, medicine suffered an eclipse because the Romans became too devoted to luxury to permit of its development, and later the descent of the barbarians from the North disturbed silence and culture. In spite of the disturbance, however, there is evidence during the succeeding centuries of the deliberate use of mental influence and even of direct suggestion in the cure of disease.

Alexander of Tralles (sixth century A. D.) was not judiciously critical in his selection of remedies. Often he has quite ridiculous therapeutic suggestions, and yet we have at least two stories with regard to him which clearly indicate his employment of mental influence. One of his patients is said to have been suffering from the delusion that his head had been cut off by order of the tyrant, but he was cured as soon as the doctor hit on the interesting expedient of making him wear a leaden hat, which eradicated his delusion and made him think his head had been restored.

It is also in Alexander Trallianus, as he is sometimes called, that we have the original of the story which has been often told, many writers giving it as an experience of their own. A woman was sure that she had swallowed a snake, and that it continued to exist in her stomach, devouring much of her food and causing acute pain whenever large quantities of food were not provided for it. All sorts of remedies had been tried without result. At last Alexander gave her an emetic and then slipped into the basin into which she was vomiting a snake resembling as closely as possible that which she thought she had swallowed. The ruse effected a complete cure. Usually in latter-day variants of this story the cure is only temporary, for the patient after a time has the same symptoms as before and then is sure that during the time of its residence in the stomach the snake has given birth to young.

Paul of AEgina.—In the seventh century Paul of AEgina collected all that had been written on insanity by physicians of olden times, and many of his directions and prescriptions for treatment show that he appreciated the value of mental influence. He recommends that those who are suffering from mental disease should be placed in a quiet institution, should be given baths, and that an important portion of the treatment should consist of mental recreations.

ARABIAN MENTAL MEDICINE

The Arabian physicians who succeeded to the traditions of Greek medicine preserved also those relating to psychotherapy. Rhazes, the first of the great Arabian physicians, has a number of aphorisms that show his interest in and recognition of the value of mental healing. He insisted that "doctors ought to console their patients even though the signs of death are impending. For the bodies of men follow their spirits." He believed that the most important function of the physician was "to strengthen the natural vitality for, if you add to that you will remove a great many ills, but if you lessen it by the drugs which you employ you add to the patient's danger." "Truth in medicine," he said, "is a goal which cannot be absolutely reached, and the art of {14} healing, as it is described in books, is far beneath the practical experience of a skillful, thoughtful physician." Manifestly he realized the importance of the influence of the physician over the individual patient.

His greatest successor among the Arab physicians, Avicenna (eleventh century), "the Hippocrates and the Galen of the Arabians," as Whewell called him, has some striking tributes to what he recognized as the influence of the mind on the body. He appreciated that not only might the mind heal or injure its own body, but that it might influence other bodies, through their minds, for weal or woe. He says: "The imagination of man can act not only on his own body, but even on other and very distinct bodies. It can fascinate and modify them, make them ill or restore them to health." In this, of course, he is yielding to the dominant mystical belief that man can work harm to others, which subsequently, under the name of witchcraft, came to occupy so prominent a place for ill in European history. But at the same time it is evident that his opinions are founded on his knowledge of the influence of mind on body, as he had seen its action in medicine. From him we have the expression: "At times the confidence of the patient in the physician has more influence over the disease than the medicine given for it."

MEDIEVAL MIND-HEALING

During the Middle Ages faith was one of the things most frequently appealed to, and even the physicians made use of religious belief to secure a favorable attitude of the patient's mind toward the remedies. One of the men who particularly realized the importance of this was Mondeville, the great French surgeon.

Pagel has called attention to Mondeville's insistence on preparing the patient's mind properly for venesection. The patient should be made to feel that this procedure was sure to do him good, and various reasons should be given him why the removal of a certain amount of blood carried with it poisons from the body, and so gave a better opportunity to nature to conquer the disease. If the patients were unfavorably disposed towards venesection, Mondeville thought that it should not be performed, as it was not likely to do good. It was not that he felt that the mental influence was the more important of the two therapeutic factors, but that a combination of the remedial force of blood-letting with a favorable state of the patient's mind meant so much more than could be accomplished by venesection alone that it was worth while to take pains to have the combination of the two. We in modern times realize that in most cases blood-letting rather did physical harm than good. It continued to hold a place in medicine because patients were so much impressed by it that they were given renewed vigor after its use.

MENTAL HEALING IN THE RENAISSANCE

What is exemplified in medieval medicine in this matter remains true during the Renaissance. In the fifteenth century Petrus Pomponatius, well known as a thinker and writer on borderland subjects related to medicine, came to the conclusion that men might very well be cured of certain ailments {15} by influence from the minds of others, and that such treatment, undertaken by physicians appropriately endowed, produced wonderful effects. He said:

Some men are specially endowed with eminently curative faculties; the effects produced by their touch are wonderful: but even touch is not always necessary; their glances, their mere intention of doing good are efficient for the restoration of health. The results, however, are due to natural causes.

PSYCHOTHERAPY AND MODERN MEDICINE

Paracelsus.—Paracelsus, the great physician of the first half of the sixteenth century, who may well be considered the father of modern pharmaceutics, had no illusions with regard to the exclusive power of drugs over disease. He recognized that mental influence was extremely important, and often lent a power not otherwise possessed to many remedies. He said:

Imagination and faith can cause and remove diseases. Confidence in the virtue of amulets is the whole secret of their efficacy. It is from faith that imagination draws its power. Anyone who believes in the secret resources of Nature receives from Nature according to his own faith; let the object of your faith be real or imaginary, you will in an equal degree obtain the same results.

Personal magnetism, in the sense in which we now use it, a transference of the idea from the science of magnetics as related to the phenomena of the magnet, seems to have originated with Paracelsus. He was sure that the influence exerted over certain patients by certain physicians was due to a force very like that exerted by the magnet over iron. He was even inclined to think that magnets themselves might exert a strong potency over diseased conditions, and he found them to be useful in epilepsy. Doubtless in many cases of supposed epilepsy successfully treated the ailment was really of an hysterical nature. In these cases the strong suggestion which the use of the magnets gave for many centuries acted favorably.

Agrippa.—The writings of Cornelius Agrippa, a contemporary of Paracelsus, and, like him, a student of alchemy and of the secrets of nature, contain corresponding passages which serve to show how much of interest there was in mental influence during the Renaissance. All of these men were, of course, a little outside of the ordinary medical tradition, intent on getting to realities, not being satisfied either with words or assumptions, refusing to accept many thing that the physicians of their time completely credited. Agrippa in a characteristic passage said:

Our mind doth effect divers things by faith (which is a firm adhesion, a fixed intention, and a vehement application of the worker or receiver) in him that coöperates in anything, and gives power to the work which we intend to do. So that there is made in us, as it were, the image of the virtue to be received, and the thing to be done in us, or by us. We must, therefore, in every work and application of things, affect vehemently, imagine, hope and believe strongly, for that will be a great help.

Van Helmont.—At the end of the sixteenth century Van Helmont, who carried on the work in pharmaceutics begun by Paracelsus, and to whom we owe the discovery of a number of substances commonly used, as well as the invention of the word "gas," was a thorough believer in the influence of mind over body and, indeed, in the existence in human beings of storehouses {16} of latent energy ordinarily unemployed, but that might under special circumstances be tapped to produce wonderful effects. Indeed, some passages remind us of Prof. James' expressions in his discussion of the law of human energy. Van Helmont said:

All magical power lies dormant in man, and requires to be excited. (Compare Prof. James's "Law of Mental Energy" in the chapter on Mental Influence). This (need for excitation) is particularly the case if the subject upon whom we wish to operate is not in the most favorable disposition; if his internal imagination does not abandon itself entirely to the impression we wish to make upon him; or if he towards whom the action is directed possesses more energy than he who operates. But when the patient is well disposed or weak, he readily yields to the magnetic influence of him who operates upon him through the medium of his imagination. In order to operate powerfully, it is necessary to employ some medium; but this medium is nothing unless accompanied by internal action.

Sydenham.—In the more modern period the deliberate use of the influence of the mind on the body is quite as clear. Undoubtedly the greatest of modern physicians, who well deserves the name of the English Hippocrates, is Sydenham. How much Sydenham realized that many of his patients' ailments could only be cured by occupying their minds with other things is seen in his writings. There is a characteristic story told by Dr. Paris in his "Pharmacologia" which illustrates this well and is a striking anticipation of what we are prone to think of as very modern views in these matters:

This great physician, Sydenham, having long attended a gentleman of fortune with little or no advantage, frankly avowed his inability to render him any further service, at the same time adding, that there was a physician of the name of Robertson, at Inverness, who had distinguished himself by the performance of many remarkable cures of the same complaint as that under which his patient labored, and expressing a conviction that, if he applied to him, he would come back cured. This was too encouraging a proposal to be rejected; the gentleman received from Sydenham a statement of his case, with the necessary letter of introduction, and proceeded without delay to the place in question. On arriving at Inverness, and anxiously inquiring for the residence of Dr. Robertson, he found, to his utter dismay and disappointment, that there was no physician of that name, nor ever had been in the memory of any person there. The gentleman returned, vowing eternal hostility to the peace of Sydenham, and on his arrival, at home indignantly expressed his indignation at having been sent on a Journey of so many hundred miles for no purpose. "Well," replied Sydenham, "are you better in health?" "Yes, I am now quite well; but no thanks to you." "No," says Sydenham, "but you may thank Dr. Robertson for curing you. I wished to send you on a journey with some object of interest in view; I knew it would be of service to you: in going, you had Dr. Robertson and his wonderful cures in contemplation; and in returning, you were equally engaged in thinking of scolding me."

Morgagni.—In the century following Sydenham we have a number of examples cited by Morgagni, the father of pathology, in which his recognition of the value of the mind as a curative agent and of the harm that may be done by over-occupation of the mind is set forth at its proper value. Benjamin Ward Richardson in his "Disciples of AEsculapius" tells of two incidents in which this phase of Morgagni's very practical application of knowledge to medical practice is exemplified:

{17}

In other examples, where the symptoms are due to mental oppression, he pursued a course of treatment that was of soothing nature. A distinguished professor of physic at Bologna happened to discover that his pulse was intermittent, and being extremely anxious about it was incessantly feeling his pulse, to discover that the evil was daily increasing. Morgagni's advice to his patient was to take his finger off his wrist and not to inquire too anxiously about his condition. The advice was followed, and the result was a complete removal of the disturbance.

It is a very singular truth that in describing the action of the nervous system on the circulation Morgagni shows that he was cognizant of the fact that the circulation may be disturbed by two sets of nervous irritations, one inflicted through the pneumogastrics, the other "through those nerves which are subservient to the arteries"—the vaso-motor system which is readily disturbed by the mind. In one patient he observed great perturbations of the pulse in both wrists as the result of mental anxiety. But a day or two later the pulse derangement was confined to the left side altogether. The pulse of the right arm was quite regular, while that of the left arm still showed the inequality. When the mental distress was relieved, this pulse also became equal.

Morgagni cites Sydenham's contemporary, Lancisi, the great Italian physician, as recognizing the influence of the emotions on the heart. Examples of similar convictions as to mental influence in medicine are also found in the works of Morgagni's great contemporaries, Boerhaave and Van Swieten, and the great physicians of the seventeenth and eighteenth centuries were closely imitated in their recognition of the value of the influence of mind over body in medicine by their successors in the profession.

John Hunter.—Wise old John Hunter recognized the influence of the mind on the body very clearly. He said, for instance, "There is not a natural action in the body, whether voluntary or involuntary, that may not be influenced by the peculiar state of mind at the time." He lays it down as a law that "every part of the body sympathizes with the mind, for whatever affects the mind, the body is affected in proportion." He said further, "as a state of the mind is capable of producing a disease, another state of it may affect a cure." He called attention to the fact that the touch of a corpse produced wonderful effects upon the minds of patients. He said, "Even tumors have yielded to the stroke of a dead man's hand." He observes that "while we should naturally expect that diseases connected with the nerves—and those in which their alteration is in the action of parts not in their structure—would be most affected by the imagination, we find that there are other diseases in which they appear to have little connection that are much affected by the state of mind."

German Mind Healing.—In his monograph on "Psychotherapy in Its Scientific Aspects" Dr. Berthold Kern calls attention to a forgotten book of the German physician Scheidemantel, published in 1787. Its title was "The Emotions as Remedies." It seems to be very rare since even our Surgeon General's Library has no copy of it. The author treated psychotherapy systematically. He insisted that man was a unit in which body and soul mutually influenced each other. Scheidemantel blamed the moralists for considering the soul exclusively and the physicians for thinking only of the body. He thought that this was a serious mistake for both sides and he seems to have anticipated much of our recent discussion on the influence of the body and {18} of things physical generally in what is called crime and various divagations from law. On the other hand, he thought that the influence of the mind on the body was one of the most important elements in therapeutics.

Reil, after whom the Island of Reil is named, and who taught us much with regard to brain anatomy, was also interested in the influence of mind on body. He was the professor of anatomy at Berlin in the early part of the nineteenth century and had great influence over the medical science of the time. He insisted on the recognition and development of psychotherapy and hoped to give it a place beside the medical and surgical treatment of human ills. He did much to create a current of thought in German medicine which culminated in Johann Müller's very definite expressions with regard to the power of the mind over the body.

Very probably the most striking expression of the influence of mind upon body is in that wonderful old book, Johann Müller's text-book of physiology, issued in an English edition (London, 1842) under the title "Elements of Physiology." The subject, a favorite study, is set forth very clearly, and evidently from personal knowledge. He recognized that the mind might influence every organ and function of the body. The influence of expectancy he emphasized particularly:

The influence of ideas upon the body gives rise to a very great variety of phenomena which border on the marvelous. It may be stated as a general fact that any state of the body, which is conceived to be approaching and which is expected with perfect confidence and certainty of its occurrence, will be very prone to ensue as the mere result of that idea, if it do not lie without the bounds of possibility. The case mentioned by Pictet, in his observations on nitrous oxide, may be adduced as an illustration of such phenomena. A young lady, Miss B., wished to inspire this intoxicating gas; but in order to test the power of the imagination, common atmospheric air was given to her, instead of the nitrous oxide. She had scarcely taken two or three inspirations of it, when she fell into a state of syncope, which she had never suffered previously; she soon recovered. The influence of the ideas, when they are combined with a state of emotion, generally extends in all directions, affecting the senses, motions and secretions. But even simple ideas, unattended with a disturbed state of the passions, produce most marked organic effects in the body.

With regard to the influence of the mind over the body in the matter of fatigue Müller is especially emphatic. He states just as clearly two generations ago the Law of Reserve Energy as James stated it in recent years. Of course, Müller was far beyond his time in everything, but then men who really think always are, and even Müller's accurate expression only represents what had been in the minds of thinking men in many previous generations. He says:

The idea of our own strength gives added strength to our movements. A person who is confident of effecting anything by muscular efforts, will do it more easily than one not so confident in his own power. The idea that a change is certainly about to take place in the actions of the nervous system, may produce such a change in the nervous energy, that exertions hitherto impossible become possible. This is still more likely to be the case, if the individual is at the time in a state of mental emotion.

Even this necessarily fragmentary and rather disjointed sketch of the main features of psychotherapeutics, as we see them recognized by the great {19} physicians of the past, serve to show that mental influence has always been appreciated as an important element in the care of the individual patient.

The times when special attention has been paid to psychotherapy have certain special characteristics. Usually the periods have come just after a signal advance in medicine made through devotion to physical science. Great attention is given to the advances and for a time the individual patient is forgotten in the hope that at last physical science is going to solve the problems of the physical man. With the disappointment that always follows there is a reversion of feeling and men realize once more how important is the mental state of the patient, even in physical diseases. Then there comes an emphatic expression of the value of psychotherapy. We are at present in the midst of one of these periods, hence the widespread interest in the subject.

CHAPTER II

UNCONSCIOUS PSYCHOTHERAPEUTICS

The great authorities in medicine, the men whose thought counted for most in the development of not only the science but the art of medicine, the men to whom we look back as having been great practicing physicians, have always used this remedial measure deliberately and have suggested to others that it should be so used. But the smaller minds have been satisfied to think that their drugs, their external remedies and applications, have been the sole sources of the benefit that accrued to the patient. Such smaller men are prone to think that they have specifics for disease, while the larger men hesitate and recognize that coincidence plays a large role and that the suggestive factors in therapeutics often deceive us as to the real efficacy of drugs and remedies.

All physicians have at all times used, though often unconsciously, the suggestive factor in therapeutics, and mental influence has had everywhere a large role in the treatment of disease. Only in recent years have we come to appreciate how many diseases are self-limited. In the treatment of these self-limited diseases all sorts of drugs and therapeutic methods achieved a reputation. Some of them were looked upon by generations as specifics, though we know now that they are almost, if not completely, useless so far as any direct influence upon the disease is concerned. Indeed, at times they were, *per se*, harmful rather than beneficial, and the patient literally got well in spite of the treatment, though the repeated suggestion of betterment often more than overcame the ill effect and helped in recovery.

REMEDIES PLUS SUGGESTION

Prof. Richet, the head of the department of physiology, University of Paris, quotes the expression of a French critic of medicine: "Hurry up and take the new remedy while it still cures. After a time it will lose its power." The power that is lost as remedies grow familiar is the suggestive element that accompanied them at the beginning. They were announced with a flourish of trumpets as a discovery in therapeutics, a number of cases treated with them {20} were much benefited (because of the feeling that they must do good), and it was only after a great many cases had been treated, many of them under circumstances where patients knew nothing of the claims made for the remedies, and where physicians had little or no previous confidence in them, that their true place in therapeutics was revealed. Every physician of experience has seen the popularity of remedies wax and wane as a consequence of the attention called to them. We have new therapeutic discoveries every week. Enthusiastic articles are written about them, many of them in perfect good faith, and then after a time no more is heard of them, or they sink back into the long list of dubious remedies that may be tried when others have failed, but have no special claim upon us, in spite of the fact that some physicians continue to think them wonder-working.

"Time is short and art is long, the occasion is fleeting, experience fallacious and judgment difficult," as Hippocrates bemoaned 2400 years ago, and conditions in medicine continue the same. With suggestions and coincidence ever at work, it is still practically impossible to determine the intrinsic value of any remedy until after a prolonged trial. In the olden time it was still more difficult because there had been no such accumulation of experience as we have to guide us, and so it is not surprising to find striking examples of even great physicians recommending remedies whose main therapeutic influence must have been the element of suggestion.

Galen's Theriac.—Perhaps the most striking instance of suggestive therapeutics is Galen's famous *theriac*, various prescriptions for which have come down to us, some of them much more complex than others, so Galen is probably not responsible for all its absurdities. This remedy contained a host of ingredients, some of which neutralized others, and all of which taken together could have had but little effect save by a strong suggestion to the patient that as he was taking so many drugs he surely must be benefited.

Bernard's Theriac.—Almost in our own time another *theriac* came prominently before the public. In his younger years Claude Bernard, the French physiologist, worked in a little drug store in a country place not far from the farm on which he was born. There he found that the most called for remedy was a *theriac*. It was good for most of the ills that flesh is heir to and was bought in quantities by the old women of the neighborhood, who administered it on every occasion. The remedy was made in large quantities, but the secret of its composition in this particular pharmacy was what interested Bernard. Whenever any compound was for any reason spoiled in the drug store, the rule was, "Put that aside for the *theriac*." This much sold remedy then consisted of the most heterogeneous drugs. It was so diluted that it could do no harm, though it had quite sufficient taste and odor to make every one who took it realize that without doubt they were taking a strong medicine.

The effect of the knowledge of the composition of this wonderful remedy on Claude Bernard was the best that could have been anticipated. He resolved to study the physiological effects of drugs so that they could be given scientifically, and not in the hit or miss fashion that made possible the success of the *theriac*.

The custom of Bernard's country drug store, however, was not different from that of most country drug stores of the time. Unconscious psychotherapeutics we may well call it, because the main therapeutic factor was {21} suggestion, renewed as often as the mixture was taken, that the patient ought to feel better, until finally whatever symptoms were due to over-attention and to concentration of mind on

18

feelings of discomfort were diverted. Just as soon as the inhibition exercised by this over-attention ceased its hampering effect nature completed the cure.

Suggestion in Colds.—Many remedies acquired a reputation for breaking up coughs and colds. It is, however, extremely doubtful whether any one has ever aborted a cold, or any other infection, that had gained a hold on the patient. We now know that this common affliction is not due to cold but to absorption of infectious material. Nansen spent two winters near the North Pole without catching any cold, and his men were as healthy as himself. He had been back in civilization scarcely a week before he and his men were confined to bed with a grippy cold. In the far north, and high on mountains where the temperature is low, colds are not as common as they are in crowded cities and especially among those who are much in crowds. Cold weather only predisposes to the infection, and after it has occurred it is sure to run its course. That course may be longer or shorter. The cold is usually preceded by chilly feelings. Every one knows it is possible to have chilly feelings that seem to portend a cold, yet be well the next day. If in the meantime any remedy is taken, credit will be given to the remedy. When a cold was supposed to be merely a disturbance of circulation or a congestion, one might expect to break it up. Now that we know that it is a microbic infection, and know further that microbic diseases are usually cured by a definite reaction on the part of the body, we are not so likely to think of breaking them up. There are still physicians who think they can abort a threatened pneumonia or abbreviate typhoid fever, but they are not those who know most about the science of medicine.

We have the story, then, of a series of remedies used with great confidence in coughs and colds, some of them physically beneficial, many of them, especially those containing opium, often physically harmful, yet taken with such confidence that undoubtedly the patient was helped through his mind if not otherwise. What is thus true for this class of diseases can also be said of other minor affections. Many internal remedies have been used for boils and styes and other external infections and have often had wide vogue. The reason for their acceptance as remedies has been that the giving of anything produces a more hopeful attitude in the mind of the patient and this, by bettering the general health, sometimes overcomes the tendency that may exist to a repetition of such infectious processes.

Erysipelas.—The medical history of erysipelas is just a succession of remedies recommended, each claimed to be almost infallible, yet abandoned after a time for another for which like exaggerated claims were made. The doctrine of signatures played a large rôle in the treatment of erysipelas, and, strange as it may seem, still survives. According to the doctrine of signatures, erysipelas, being a disease involving intense redness of the skin, red things in nature would be likely to do it good. Red pepper, for instance, was suggested for it over and over again, both internally and externally. Various red remedies have been favorites at different times in history. At present, in many country places, a poultice made of cranberries is supposed to be most efficacious. For many years I lived in a small town where one of the grocers {22} put in a large stock of cranberries each fall, though the people of the neighborhood used them but little on the table, because during the winter there were many calls for them for the making of poultices for erysipelas. People who have had erysipelas, especially if it has occurred on unexposed portions of the body, are supposed to be protected against its recurrence—for there is a distinct liability to its recurrence—by the wearing of red flannels!

There is scarcely any drug that has not at some time been recommended as almost a specific for erysipelas. Anything that was given on the third or fourth day, and it was only at this time as a rule that patients came to physicians to be treated, seemed to bring about the alleviation of symptoms that occurred on the fifth or sixth day.

Erysipelas, because of the sudden irruption of fever which accompanies it, the intense redness which characterizes it, and the discomfort which is often present, is an affection that disturbs patients very much. For them, then, the presence of the physician and his assurance that their affection is not likely to be severe, and his prompt relief of certain conditions, all act by suggestion on the patient's mind and strengthen the natural curative reaction.

In country places where physicians were not near, erysipelas was one of the affections that continued almost down to our own day to be treated by incantations. I have known in a little American country town of a woman making a "charm," as it was called, for erysipelas.

Pneumonia.—Pneumonia is another of these sharply self-limited diseases that give opportunity to many remedies for the acquisition of a reputation as cures. Croupous pneumonia is so disturbing in its onset, so rapid in its progress, yet so strictly self-limited in the previously strong and healthy, that in the old days there were many remedies that were supposed to bring about the crisis. The old text-books contain so many cures that it is surprising pneumonia should have continued to be the fatal disease it has been at all times. Almost any remedy that is used for three or four days in pneumonia will be followed by the crisis with, in most cases, a favorable termination. The crisis takes place some time from the seventh to the tenth or eleventh day, and often we do not see a pneumonia patient until the second or third day of the disease. Just before the crisis the patient runs into a series of acute and more or less alarming symptoms. Often there is much restlessness, difficulty of breathing with complaint of heaviness, and perhaps prostration. The pulse and temperature are high, the skin hot and dry. Then in the midst of this the patient sleeps, there is a critical sweat, the temperature drops, the patient wakes up feeling quite well, there is little difficulty in breathing, and he feels that recovery is sure to come. The change is so great that it is natural that it should have been attributed to all sorts of remedies which had been used immediately preceding the crisis.

I once heard an old physician declare at a meeting of a large and important medical society that calomel in divided doses was practically a specific for pneumonia. He said he waited forty-eight hours to be sure that the affection was pneumonia, and also that it had reached that diffusion in the lungs beyond which it was not likely to go, then he gave the calomel. He said that, almost as a rule, during the next forty-eight hours the crisis came—and he attributed it to the calomel. We have had other remedies just as curious as this recommended and taken quite seriously. Some years ago a {23} Russian physician, who had been treating soldiers in the Russian army for the pneumonia which occurs so commonly after exposure on the Steppes, announced that he had found in digitalis almost a specific. He pushed the tincture up to twenty drops three times a day, beginning it just as soon as the pneumonia was detected, and the rate of mortality among his patients was about one per cent. According to his theory, it was the failure of the heart in pneumonia that made the disease fatal.

19

Apparently the character of the patients in whom his pneumonias occurred was forgotten. They were absolutely the most favorable cases that could be selected. Most of them were young men between twenty and twenty-five. At this age no one who is given a reasonable amount of fresh air should die of pneumonia. If the patient had a serious heart lesion, or a crippled kidney from nephritis after scarlet fever, or crippled lungs because of a previous attack of tuberculosis, then the pneumonia might be fatal—indeed, almost inevitably would be, or, in the last-mentioned case, would end by lysis and not crisis. It really matters little what remedy is given to young, otherwise healthy, adults; they will get better, barring serious complications. The use of digitalis lessened the chances of recovery by stimulating too early in the case the heart that later had to bear one of the most serious strains that the organ can stand. But doubtless this harm was more than overcome by the patient's knowledge that he was taking a new and powerful remedy, supposed to be particularly calculated to cure him.

Moreover, the special interest of the physician in these cases, and his administration of a remedy with confidence which inspired the patient, undoubtedly did much good. Pneumonia is one of those diseases in which the patient is likely to be greatly depressed unless he is surrounded by favorable mental influences, and is encouraged to believe that he is going to get well. Every physician has probably had cases in which patients died, not because of the severity of the disease, but because they gave up the struggle in fright. If several of a man's friends have died of pneumonia during the year or two before he gets it, he is likely to conclude, especially if he is of the worrying kind, that his doom is sealed as soon as the diagnosis of pneumonia is made. If this thought persists hardly anything will save him. He must be assured that pneumonia is not necessarily serious, that there are remedies that influence it, and that his own case is particularly likely to respond favorably to them.

We now realize that nursing is the most important element in the treatment of pneumonia. Such attention to the patient as will treat symptoms so as to prevent them from disturbing him, will secure him against discouragement, will arouse his resistive vitality by assuring him of a favorable termination. This will above all prevent the patient from feeling that he is attacked by a fatal disease. The presence of the doctor and his general directions make the patient realize how thoroughly the course of the disease is understood and therefore how likely it is that a favorable termination will be brought about. We know how much the mind may interfere with the breathing if allowed to dwell on it, and therefore if the patient becomes over-solicitous about the condition of his lungs he seriously hampers his recovery. In pneumonia the physician has always brought relief, and he has usually attributed his success to his drugs, though he has felt, too, that the confidence inspired {24} by him meant much for his patient. It would have been better had he exaggerated the mental influence rather than the drug power.

Typhoid Fever.—Typhoid fever is another affection for which we have many therapeutic suggestions, with wide vogue, that are nevertheless almost directly opposed to what we know about the pathology and etiology of the disease. Typhoid fever runs its course in from between twenty to thirty days. The majority of people who take the affection and who give in to it early enough, so as not to wear themselves out, come through successfully. Complications may carry them off, but we expect uncomplicated cases to recover. The longer course of typhoid has made the action of drugs appear less striking than in pneumonia and erysipelas, but a number of remedies have been proclaimed to shorten its course, to make it less dangerous, to cure, and sometimes actually to abort it. So often have these come and gone that the physician who knows the history of therapeutics is likely to be suspicious of them. Even at present there are certain remedies supposed to have this effect, but one does not find them used in hospitals where large numbers of cases are seen and where there are opportunities for comparative observation. They are used only by physicians who see a few cases every year, and to whom coincidences may mean much more than they are likely to when extensive statistics of the disease are made.

As a rule, these remedies are founded on some real or supposed scientific principle. The antiseptic treatment of typhoid, for instance, was based on the supposition that if one can kill the microbes in the intestine the disease will run a shorter course. The principle apparently fails to note that any remedy likely to kill microbes is still more likely to kill cells of other kinds, and above all human cells lessened in their resistive vitality by disease. The advocates of this remedy also forget that typhoid is now recognized as a general disease with only a local manifestation in the intestines, and that the treatment of this local manifestation is no more likely to affect the course of the disease than the treatment of the symptoms of typhoid would be likely to do. But the giving of remedies with the thoroughgoing confidence that awakens trust is in itself an excellent therapeutic agent, and patients thus treated are sure to be benefited in so far as they share the physician's confidence. Just the same effect, however, can be produced by careful nursing and by making the patient realize that even though typhoid fever runs a definite course, which we cannot abbreviate nor probably influence, we can by nursing so prevent complications as to make a fatal termination almost impossible.

Whooping Cough.—Perhaps none of the common affections illustrate the influence of psychotherapy better than it is exemplified in the history of the therapeutics of whooping cough. We have had all sorts of remedies suggested for it, and most of them have been introduced by those who had found them of great service in shortening the course of the disease, and in making the "whoop" disappear much sooner than would otherwise be the case. There have been internal and external remedies, inhalations and inunctions, as well as many less likely methods of treatment. Practically none has maintained itself. Whooping cough is likely to run a rather long course. We know now that as a consequence of the strain upon the lungs tuberculosis not infrequently develops. Whenever this is true the tendency to cough is likely to be {25} prolonged far beyond the natural period, and from habit ingrained upon the nervous system the "whoop" is likely to continue, though there is no necessity for it. It is this secondary period of the affection that the remedies have succeeded in shortening either apparently or in fact.

Practically anything that is done for children is likely to instil the persuasion that the "whoop" should disappear. Anything impressive will arouse this favorable attitude of mind toward the affection, and hence the remedies have obtained a reputation. In the interior of many countries draughts of sea water are a popular remedy for whooping cough. Sea water, it is said, loses its efficacy if carried long distances from the shore, so the children must be brought to the seaside. In mining regions children are taken down into the mines. The experience is enough of itself, especially when talked over a good deal in the family, and when the occasion is often the first outing that the child has had for months, to bring with it such improvement in health as will enable it to suppress the whoop. If the exposure to the mine air does not bring improvement, it is said to be either because the child was not taken deep enough, or because there was no gas in the air, or the wrong sort of mine was chosen, or some other plausible excuse is advanced.

The development of scientific medicine, or at least what we are pleased to think of as more scientific therapeutics than they had in the past, has not kept us from having many and varied remedies for whooping cough, which, after being introduced on apparently good authority and apparently accomplishing many good results, have eventually been allowed to drop into innocuous desuetude. Whenever the administration of any such remedy was accompanied by strong suggestion—when the internal remedies were particularly distasteful, or the inhalations rather trying or at least sure to attract the attention of the sufferers—then good results followed. But the cures were due to the mental influences at work. In recent years various serums, including diphtheria serum, have been tried with reported good results. The giving of the injection is one of those little operations that is likely to impress itself forcibly upon the child's mind, and when given in connection with the promise, implied or explicit, of improvement it is easy to understand that there will be a tendency to lessening the frequency of the whoop, at least during the secondary periods of the disease.

CHAPTER III

GENUINE REMEDIES AND SUGGESTIVE EXAGGERATION

The story of the suggestive use of drugs shows us many suggestions employed even by distinguished physicians, men whose work is eminently rational and has lived long after their time. In fact, very few, even of the most distinguished physicians, have failed to extol remedies which later proved to be quite ineffectual. Hippocrates felt quite sure that an external application of snake skin was a cure for all forms of that chronic skin manifestation, lichen. Pythagoras declared that anise seed held in the hand was an excellent remedy for epilepsy. These are only examples which serve to show how much suggestion has been used unconsciously by the medical profession. The sensation {26} produced by the touch of the viper's skin was sufficient in some patients to bring about a change in the circulation in the skin, or perhaps a distinct modification of the nerve impulses on which trophic conditions in the skin depend, and this may have produced some cures on which Hippocrates founded his recommendation. We know that the skin can be unfavorably affected directly through the nervous system, and there is no good reason for thinking that it may not also be affected favorably. In our own day we have seen the suggestive influence of an operation act as a remedy in epilepsy and have lauded it for a time. It is, therefore, not surprising that Pythagoras saw, as he thought, the strong scent of the anise seed act favorably. Both of these conclusions as to the causative agency at work were wrong, because it was suggestion and not the operation in most cases, nor the anise in any case, which caused the improvement.

THERAPEUTIC PERSUASION

It is not only in the distant past, however, but also in quite modern times that these therapeutic persuasions have existed among physicians, and as a result physicians have frequently recommended and employed remedies that we now know not only to have been quite useless, but sometimes even harmful. A typical example of this is the use of antimony, originally discovered and studied by Basil Valentine, an alchemist who had busied himself much with the nature of substances, vegetable and mineral, and with their action as remedies for disease. Sir Michael Foster hailed him as the first of pharmacologists, and said: "The old monk did not care for the problem of the body; all he sought to understand was how the constituents of the soil and of plants might be treated so as to be available for healing the sick and how they produced their effect."

Suggestion and Antimony.—This was an eminently scientific research. It brought the father of pharmacology to certain supposed discoveries which continued to occupy men's minds for centuries, yet ultimately proved to be utter misunderstandings of drug action, because suggestion played so large a role that it vitiated all the conclusions. The best known of Basil Valentine's books is the "Triumphal Chariot of Antimony," which contains many interesting scientific observations that were probably new at the time and which show their author's investigating spirit and his interest in scientific research.

In spite of his scientific advances, however, Valentine was wholly mistaken with regard to antimony. He used it in various diseases, and, of course, it always produced very definite effects on the bowels. These effects the physician could easily foretell. It was for the patient a proof that the physician knew much, both about his disease and his remedies, since he could prophesy the results. After the antimony had exerted its influence the patient was much more ready to think that he must get better, and the influence of this suggestion worked strongly in all cases where the affection was not serious, and undoubtedly helped the patient's resistive vitality to throw off disease. In weak patients its physical effect was lamentable. It still further reduced vitality, and when used by thoughtless physicians must have done great harm. In spite of this, however, antimony continued to be used for centuries. Shortly {27} after the middle of the seventeenth century, when it was beginning to be neglected, antimony received a new lease of life as a consequence of its employment in a lingering illness of Louis XIV. The French king was attacked by what has since been recognized as typhoid fever. Many remedies were tried, but all in vain; the fever continued. When the fever had nearly run its course and the physicians were on the point of acknowledging that they could do nothing, and when a fatal termination seemed near, it was decided at a consultation to follow the advice of an old practitioner and use the old-fashioned remedy, antimony. Almost immediately the king began to get better. His improvement was quite naturally attributed to the last drug that he had taken, and antimony regained and held its remedial reputation for the next two centuries.

Such stories have always worked wonders in producing popular faith and even professional confidence in drugs. When great personages seem to be cured by certain remedies, ordinary logic ceases to act, and the strong power of suggestion comes in to strengthen whatever remedial influence there may be.

Calomel and Suggestion.—Such mistaken notions as to therapeutic efficiency are not confined to centuries before our own. During much of the nineteenth century calomel was employed as extensively as antimony had been in preceding centuries. Calomel was often given in doses which produced effects resembling those of antimony. Even in the small doses we now employ, it is apt to be a thorough purgative. In the twenty and forty grain doses, commonly administered by the country doctors of two generations ago at the beginning of practically every ailment, it was purgative—and worse. Its effects could, of course, be very strikingly seen, and what patients wanted were just such visible results of the doctor's prescription. Undoubtedly, then, the calomel did good, but not by its effect upon the patients' bodies, but upon their minds. Calomel is still used in ways that partake more of the old-fashioned ideas than we care to confess. Some of its supposed effects in stimulating the flow of bile have been placed in doubt by modern investigation, but we still use it empirically, and undoubtedly its effectiveness is partly due to the fact that many patients see the results in the purgation in dark coloration of the stools and are confident that improvement must follow—and it does. Perhaps at a subsequent operation we find the bile ducts effectively blocked and then learn for certain that the stool coloration observed was not biliary but due to a chemical reaction of the calomel itself.

Venesection and Its Suggestiveness.—Between the periods of antimony and calomel popularity venesection was the favorite remedy of physicians. It is hard to understand now the extent to which this practice was carried by the medical profession. People were bled for nearly every combination of symptoms. In severe cases the amount of bleeding practiced was almost incredible. Mirabeau, the great French orator, suffering from angina pectoris, was bled some eighty ounces in the course of forty-eight hours. In spite of this heroic treatment, which his physicians thought ought to have cured him, he died. We find it hard to understand how he lived so long. This, of course, was an exceptional case at the very height of the venesection furor, but it helps us to realize how convinced physicians were of the curative power of the practice.

{28}

Thoughtful physicians like Morgagni did not accredit it, or at least refused to allow it to be practiced on themselves, but its acceptance was practically universal. Probably no remedial measure ever generally used was calculated to be so effective as bleeding in producing a strong mental influence. The rather sacrificial preparations for it, the sight and the prick of the lancet, then the sight of the blood, the languor that followed, the reaction on nature's part to reproduce the lost material, all united to impress the patient's mind so deeply that it is easy to understand that all the reserve of mental force was now directed toward helping nature in the cure of whatever disease was present. Venesection itself in nine out of ten cases probably did more physical harm than good, but all the good came from its suggestion.

We are now apt to think of venesection as consisting only in the removal of some blood from a favorably situated vein, but we must not forget that in the olden time they bled from many veins, and that a particular vein was picked out because it was supposed to be connected in some way with the seat of the special trouble under treatment, and as a result there was a particular appeal to mental influence. A vein on the forehead was opened for the treatment of migraine and diseases of the eyes, on the nose in case of discharge from the eyes, back of the ears in chronic headache and in stuporous conditions, or beneath the chin when there was pain in the eyes, or in the nose, or in the jaws. The cephalic vein was opened for headache and for certain affections of the eyes and ears. Altogether there were thirty different veins opened for as many maladies. It was thought extremely important in the drawing of blood from the arm that that arm should be chosen which, for some anatomical or other reason, was supposed to be the more intimately connected with the affected part of the trunk or head. The psychotherapeutic factors at work in these cases are easy to understand, and their beneficial effects gave the practice a firm foothold in medicine.

Quinine and Suggestion.—Whenever any drug has secured a reputation its use has always been extended to many other diseases besides that for which it was definitely indicated. Quinine is a typical example. It is a specific for malaria and, properly administered in suitable doses, breaks up the fever—not because of any action upon the febrile condition itself, but because it kills the *Plasmodium malariae* whose reproduction in the blood brings about the paroxysms of fever. It was argued, however, that since quinine was good for one kind of fever it would probably be good in others, and all sorts of theories were invented and supported by supposed observations of the effect of quinine on various organs and tissues, even on the white blood cells, by which its efficacy in fever was supposed to be explained. Quinine was used in all sorts and conditions of fever, and acquired a reputation as a remedy that had the power even to abort conditions leading to all fevers. It was used in large doses for such conditions as cold, incipient pneumonia, or indeed any disease with a chill at the beginning, and was supposed to be a powerful prophylactic.

Now it is settled that while quinine in small doses is an excellent tonic, it has no effect at all upon fevers in themselves nor upon fever-producing conditions. Yet it is still administered by many who have not quite abandoned the old teachings as if it were a general febrifuge. In the meantime, the use of quinine as a prophylactic of colds and other minor febrile conditions has {29} spread so that many people make themselves very uncomfortable by taking a large dose of quinine and whiskey whenever they fear they are going to have a cold. As a consequence they feel dull and heavy the next day, but assume that they would have been much worse than they are had they not taken the potent remedy the night before. Undoubtedly some of them are enabled by the suggestive value of the remedy and the continued suggestion of its unpleasant effects to throw off the lassitude that comes from some minor infection and are encouraged to get out into the air, when they might otherwise have stayed in the house. This enables them to get rid of their colds sooner than would be the case if they allowed themselves to be confined. Most of them, however, are harmed rather than benefited, and the cold runs its course, unaffected except that the patient is more miserable and depressed for the first day or two than he would otherwise have been. There are physicians who still use quinine as a febrifuge in typhoid and other essential fevers, and doubtless its bitter taste helps their patients because of the suggestive value of an unpleasant medicine.

St. John Long's Liniment.—An interesting exemplification of the power of mystery in adding to the curative value of a commonplace remedy is found in the story of the famous St. John Long liniment. St. John Long was a well-known quack in London in the early part of the nineteenth century. Like all quacks at all times, his specialty was chronic diseases. He claimed to be able by means of external applications to cure the pains and aches to which the old are so likely to be subject. St. John soon acquired an immense reputation. He gave a liniment with a secret formula that was literally a miracle worker. People who used it found after a few times that they were free from, or at least greatly relieved of, aches that had bothered them for years. It was good for sprains and for internal pains of all kinds, as well as for the so-called chronic rheumatisms, which have as their principal symptom pains and aches around joints. So great a reputation, indeed, was acquired by the remedy that an agitation was begun to have Parliament buy the secret from its inventor in order to present it to the British nation. The proposition was actually carried through the legislative chambers and a considerable amount of money, still larger in those days because of the comparatively greater value of money, was voted to St. John Long.

His liniment had a place in the British Pharmacopeia under his name for many years afterwards. It proved to be only a simple old-fashioned remedy, the basis of which was turpentine, and one of the principal ingredients was the white of egg. Just as soon as the secret was known the power of the remedy began to decline. So long as it remained mysterious and unknown, discovered by a man who supposedly had made a special study for many years of these conditions, and had finally worked out the external applications necessary for them, it accomplished wonders. Just as soon as it was known to be a combination of familiar turpentine and egg it lost its power. The remedy is, of course, an excellent counter-irritant, and the gentle rubbing undoubtedly did much good. The most important element, however, was the mental influence, the feeling that now things must be better, which thought distracted attention from the aches and pains and caused the unfavorable influence of over-concentration of mind on the part to cease, for the vaso-motor system is particularly under mental influence. Every now and then since that time some {30} liniment or oil containing nearly the same ingredients as that of St. John Long's acquires a reputation as a consequence of a campaign of advertising. It is the printers ink that counts, however, and just as soon as the advertising ceases to attract attention the remedy fails in efficiency.

Alcohol Plus Suggestion.—Alcohol has been employed in medicine with the persuasion that it is a remedy for many states of exhaustion, though we have gradually gotten away from its use to a great extent, because we realize that subsequent physical ill consequences outweigh, in most cases, the physical good it may do. Its use was undoubtedly due to the confidence of physicians communicated to patients, and the sense of good feeling which it gives and which proves a further strong suggestion to the patient. This sense of well-being is illusory, for it is sure to be followed by a longer period of dejection, which more than counteracts it unless the dose of alcohol can be maintained for some time.

A generation ago few physicians would have cared to treat exhausting diseases, the continued fevers for instance, without liberal doses of alcohol. Practically the only treatment for pyemia and septicemia on which any stress was laid, and in which there was any general confidence, was the administration of alcohol in large quantities. In the septicemia consequent upon puerperal infection it was the common teaching to give alcohol by the tablespoonful or more every hour, or oftener, until its effects began to be noticed, and ordinarily large quantities were required, so that sometimes nearly a quart was taken in the twenty-four hours. Undoubtedly these septic conditions were accompanied by great mental prostration, and this was emphasized by the knowledge that they are often fatal. So patients were usually depressed into a state of mind in which their resistive vitality was much lowered. Alcohol, then, by producing a sense of well-being as well as by stimulating hope in other ways and suggesting possibilities of recovery, undoubtedly exerted a powerful and favorable influence on the mind. Its use in these cases nearly always did good, in spite of its inevitable depressive reaction, for the course of these infections was rapid and the dosage of alcohol could be maintained until there was a change for the better or the fatal termination was in sight.

Alcohol was frequently used in many other conditions of a similar nature, and above all in the septic conditions so common in hospitals before the days of antisepsis and asepsis. When it is recalled that amputations yielded a mortality from sepsis of at least one in four, the extensive use of alcohol in hospital practice two generations ago will be readily understood. We have changed that, however, and Sir Frederick Treves, at a meeting of the British Medical Association at Toronto, five years ago, called particular attention to the statistics of the use of alcohol in British hospitals. During the last forty years milk and alcohol have exactly changed places in the London hospitals. Between 1860 and 1870 about four times as much was spent for alcohol as for milk in these hospitals; during the last decade about four times as much was spent for milk as for alcohol.

A corresponding change has taken place in many other phases of treatment in which alcohol was commonly used. The physician of fifty years ago would have thought that one of his most efficient remedies had been taken from him if he could not use alcohol freely in tuberculosis. There are practically no well-known specialists in tuberculosis now who recommend the use {31} of alcohol. On the contrary, most of them point out the dangers from its use and consider that the depression which follows even a moderate dose is likely to do much more harm than the temporary and fleeting stimulation which it gives can do good. In the treatment of phthisis in recent years milk has done much more than take the place of alcohol: it has displaced it entirely. The medical profession realizes now that what the consumptive needs is not more stimulation—for more of that than is good for him is forced upon him by the toxins of the disease—but more nutrition to enable him to resist the progress of the disease and raise his resistive vitality against its toxemia. The one stimulant that is of service in the affection is oxygen, and even that should be given in nature's dosage rather than by artificial means.

Alcohol in Pneumonia.—A corresponding change has taken place in the professional attitude towards the use of alcohol in pneumonia. There was a time not so very long ago when alcohol was considered the sheet anchor of our therapeutics for pneumonic conditions, especially those in which from the beginning a fatal termination seemed inevitable, because of the age of the patient or some complication. There were physicians who said that if they had to choose between all the drugs of the pharmacopeia on the one hand without whiskey and whiskey without all drugs whatsoever, for the treatment of pneumonia, they would make the latter choice. We are not as yet entirely away from the point of view that attributes a certain value to alcohol in pneumonia, though even those who still employ alcohol are less emphatic in their advocacy of it. Any one who has seen the result of the fresh air for pneumonia patients will think less and less of alcohol. One well-known clinical authority declares that the very best place to treat pneumonia in our cities would be beneath the trees in the parks. Our patients are being treated at the ends of wards with the windows up, on the balconies, and on the roofs, and the death rate is much reduced and the necessity for any other than oxygen stimulation seems much less.

Alcohol in Vague Affections.—The suggestive influence of the effect of alcohol is unconsciously obtained in a number of vague and rather chronic affections. Among these the most noteworthy are women's diseases. Various alcoholic home remedies, gin and whiskey, usually disguised by some bitter, used to be popular. But the known presence of alcohol in these discredited them. Then the nostrum vendors proceeded to supply something just as good. They were, in fact, the same things under another name. Many of the much-advertised remedies that are supposed to cure the ills the weaker sex is liable to, have been found to be little more than dilute whiskey, for in alcoholic strength they were about equal to whiskey diluted once with water, and the other substances were added only to disguise the taste and the odor of this principal ingredient. Many of these remedies have elicited innumerable flattering testimonials and not all of these were fraudulent or obtained by questionable means, but many of them were given because of results secured through the remedies. The alcohol gave the well-known sense of well-being, and the suggestive influence of this increased the appetite, tempted the patient to move around more, and to get more into the air than before, and the consequence was an improvement in the general health, in the midst of which many symptoms that seemed to the excited imaginations of run-down individuals to be serious were relieved. In a great many cases, however, the result was the {32} formation of a whiskey habit; hence the crusade which has discredited these remedies.

Other patent medicines, and, indeed, some of the proprietary preparations, commonly recommended as nutrients and the like, and supposed to be ethical, are found to owe whatever efficiency they have to their alcoholic content. Here once more the suggestive elements were the more important, and enabled substances of little physical efficiency to produce effects that seemed to indicate the presence of powerful energizing materials.

Whiskey in Snake-Bites.—A typical example of a remedy which owes its efficacy to mental influence over the patient is the use of whiskey for snake-bites. It is generally recognized that whiskey is not only of no special beneficial effect for snake-bite, but that when taken in the large quantities usual in such cases it probably produces an ill effect by disturbing the patient's general condition and lowering his resistive vitality. I have no doubt, however, that its use in considerable quantities has in these cases proved of value because of the mental effect upon the patient. Ordinarily a snake-bite is followed by a sense of extreme terror and prostration that lowers the resistive vitality. This is overcome by the temporary stimulation of the alcohol. The generally accepted idea that whiskey is almost a specific remedy for snake-bite takes away from most people this dread and consequent depression, and does this especially at a time when the acuter symptoms of the venom are making themselves felt. Only about one in six even of those bitten by large rattlesnakes are likely to die. Many circumstances are in their favor. The bite is not likely to be fatal unless the full contents of the poison sac is injected—which will not be done if the sac has been emptied in the preceding twenty-four hours—and if there are any obstacles, such as clothing or even hair, on the part struck by the snake. Most people, however, would almost die from fright, and such a thing is quite possible, if they thought there was no remedy. The fact that they understand that alcohol is an almost infallible remedy gives them courage, and as soon as they receive some whiskey and it begins to take effect this intense depression is relieved.

It would be better if the knowledge we now have as to snake-bites were more generally used, and if people understood that only rarely is such an accident fatal. In this way there would be no necessity for an appeal to mental influence through whiskey. It is probable, however, that alcohol will still be used for many years, at least in the country districts, because the supposed knowledge is too widely diffused for a correction to come soon, and then other modes of treatment have not that persuasive mental influence which whiskey has as the result of the long tradition. There are many other popular remedies for snake-bite not quite so inefficient as whiskey, but that will continue to enjoy a reputation and really have a certain efficacious result as a consequence of the expectant attitude evoked by the fact that for as long as the patient has heard anything about these things this particular remedy has been mentioned always as the one thing sure to do good.

Other Cures.—Fontana, toward the end of the eighteenth century, was sure that he had discovered in caustic potash an absolute specific for snake poisoning. He had had a series of cases, and felt that he had actually observed this substance following the snake poison into the system and neutralizing it. Its active effect on the external tissues proved eminently suggestive for {33} the patient and good results followed. We have had many specifics since, and yet we are not quite sure how much any of them avail unless recent biological remedies prove lasting in their effects and are really of therapeutic efficiency.

Antidotes and Suggestion.—For many other poisons beside snake venom there have been announced supposed antidotes of all kinds. The literature of the antidotes used for opium is extremely interesting and even in recent times contains many disillusions. Twenty years ago our medical journals contained any number of cases in which a solution of potassium permanganate seemed to have proved effective in neutralizing not only opium itself but its alkaloids and derivatives. Not only was it efficacious, then, if taken while the opium was still in the stomach but, just as with Fontana's caustic potash and the snake venom, it followed the opium into the tissues and at least blunted its action. Numbers of cases were reported in which potassium permanganate was supposed to have had this desirable effect. The effect of alcohol in neutralizing carbolic acid attracted as much attention as did potassium permanganate for opium. Here there was no doubt that alcohol immediately after the external application of carbolic acid did prevent its corrosive action. It was supposed to do the same thing in the stomach and even, as some enthusiastic observers thought, followed the carbolic acid into the tissues. Here once more the claim is not proven and it is evident that the influence on patients' minds when small doses of carbolic acid were taken, was the real therapeutic factor at work.

Poultices in Suggestive Therapeutics.—Poultices represent another phase of the value of suggestion in medicine and surgery, though for many centuries those who used them were sure that the reasons for their employment were entirely physical and not psychic. All sorts of poultices have been used and each was supposed to do specific curative work. New forms of poultice material have been introduced, and physicians and patients have been certain that each worked wonders of its own. The drawing power of the poultice was extolled until patients dwelt on the idea that this external application was literally engaged in extracting from them, even from distant portions of their anatomy, virulent material that would do harm if allowed to remain in them. Poultices in suitable cases, because they represent moist heat, do good by counter irritation, by bringing about the expulsion of gas, by diverting internal hyperemia to external tissues, but most of their supposed efficacy has been really due to the bother required to prepare and apply them, the discomfort of having them on, and the feeling that now something had been done and the aches and pains must get better. They are still used, but to a much less degree than before. Now the ordinary teaching is that a hot water bag wrapped in dry flannel, if dry heat is the agent desired, and in moist flannel, if moist heat is the desideratum, is much more efficient. It takes but a few minutes for a poultice, no matter how hot when applied—and occasionally in the olden time they were applied so warm as to burn or scald—to decrease in temperature to that of the body. After that they represent only a moist compress.

It is easy to understand that the suggestive influence of poultices might serve for an age that knew less about the realities of the efficacy of external applications than ours. As a matter of fact, we have, nevertheless, shown ourselves to be quite as credulous and ready to receive analogous remedies as the past generation. With the waning of the popularity of the poultice, not {34} only among the profession, but also among the people generally, there came into use various plasters which were supposed to have even more wonderful efficacy than the poultice of the olden time. These required a good deal of trouble to apply and once applied remained on for hours, and so continued to produce a definite curative effect on patients' minds. When first introduced, exaggerated claims were made for their therapeutic value and a regular crusade to diffuse correct information regarding them had to be made, in order to set them in their proper place as mere wet compresses, without any therapeutic efficiency beyond that of cloths wrung out in water and kept in touch with the skin.

Poultices and the Doctrine of Signatures.—There was a general impression in the past that the indication of the ailment for which substances are medically useful has been set on them by nature, either through the color, or the form of the plant, or other qualities. In general, the law of similars is supposed to hold in the doctrine of signatures—like cures like. Hence the cornmeal poultice for light jaundice, the flax-seed meal poultice for darker jaundiced conditions and for tendencies to gangrene. The charcoal poultice was employed for this same purpose with no better reason, though some of its efficacy may have been due to oxygen present in the pores of the charcoal. I have already spoken of the appeal to the patient's mind in the use of the cranberry for erysipelas, and various other berries were used in like manner on the doctrine of signatures.

Deterrent Materials and Suggestion.—Another basic principle in the making of poultices was the use of deterrent, repulsive materials, because these were more effective on the patient's mind. All the ordures were so employed. Goose and chicken excrement was supposed to be particularly efficacious for many of the purposes for which we now use iodine. It was applied over sprains and bruises on the unbroken skin. Cow-dung was employed as a poultice for sprains of the larger joints, especially on the feet and legs, but to be efficacious it had to be applied fresh. I have known, within twenty years, of physicians in two so supposedly cultured parts of the country as Pennsylvania and Maryland, to employ such ordure poultices for the cure of sprains and dislocations, and these physicians had a great reputation among the people of their countryside. They were known especially as good bone doctors, and their use of such deterrent materials instead of decreasing their practices rather added to them.

Ointments.—In the Middle Ages ointments made of the most far-fetched materials were employed even by distinguished surgeons. That, indeed, is the one serious flaw in the surgery of the thirteenth and fourteenth centuries, when they did everything else so well. These ointments contained all manner of materials that were likely to impress patients and make them feel that something wonderful was being done for them. Crushed insects of all kinds were employed for external lesions. Here the doctrine of similars seems once more to have been in play. Insects gave creepy feelings, and whenever such feelings, or the paresthesiae generally, were complained of, a poultice or ointment made of insects seemed to be the natural remedy. The more repellent the materials, the more efficient they were likely to be. Many of the paresthesiae are due to neurotic conditions and it is not surprising that when an ointment of crushed lice—these insects being collected from barnyard {35} fowls or from hogs—was used, the suggestive influence was strong. Another important ingredient in ointments were portions of dead bodies. A bit of a mummy from the East was supposed to be particularly efficacious. Portions of the bodies of men who had been hanged, or of the moss that grew on the skulls of malefactors whose bodies had been long exposed in chains to the air, were also favorite ingredients. Plants and shrubs gathered in graveyards, especially in the dark of the moon, because on account of the terror of the place they were then harder to get, also had a great reputation.

CHAPTER IV

SIGNATURES AND PSYCHOTHERAPY

Similia similibus curantur, like is cured by like, is a very old idea. According to the doctrine of signatures nature had put an external natural marking or a symbolical appearance or characteristic upon a plant, mineral or other object, to indicate its special usefulness for the treatment of certain diseases or for affections of certain organs. Sir Robert Boyle, sometimes spoken of as the father of chemistry, said, "Chymists observe in the book of nature that those simples that wear the figure or resemblance, by them termed signature, of a distempered part, are medicinal for that part or that infirmity whose signature they bear." On this principle yellow flowered plants were good for jaundice, because they resembled it in color. The blood stone was good for hemorrhage, and plants of certain forms were good for the organs or parts of man which they resembled. Certain plants were named with this idea. Kidneywort, liverwort, are typical examples. Scorpion grass, our familiar forget-me-not of the *genus myosotis*, was so-called because its spike resembled a scorpion's tail and was, therefore, good against the scorpion's sting, or against pains similar to that produced by such a sting. Some of the resemblances were extremely far-fetched, but in spite of the defect of nature's signature on them, they seem to have been effective in therapeutics. The plant, sometimes called Jew's ear, which can by an effort of the imagination be made to bear resemblance to the human ear, was, for instance, supposed to be a successful cure for diseases of that organ.

We know now that there is no significance in this doctrine of signatures. It represented one phase of pseudo-science. But the idea of itself was enough to help people to throw off many symptoms, to relieve discouragement, to encourage them with the thought that they ought to get better; accordingly they took new heart, ate better, went out more, and as a result naturally slept better, and then nature did the rest. Signatures are an exquisite example of pure psychotherapy, as the initial agent and natural curative methods accomplishing the cure.

Signature Details.—Some of the details of the doctrine of signatures are amusing. For a considerable period nuts were supposed to be a good brain food, and some traces of this idea are still extant, although there does not seem to be any better reason for it than the fact that many nuts have an arrangement of their lobes which resembles the conformation of the brain. On the same principle the Chinese use ginseng-root as a general tonic. The extract is not {36} of any special significance in medicine, though it has come to be much advertised in recent years, and the Chinese continue to pay high prices for it. The reason is that the root of the ginseng plant often resembles the human body. The more nearly this resemblance can be traced, the more virtue there is for the Chinese in the particular specimen of ginseng. The signature is on the roots. It is good for man because it looks like man, just as the nuts are good for the brain because they look like the brain. In modern times we are likely to think that we are far away from any such self-deception. But our deceptions have a more appealing pseudo scientific element in them. Fish was for some time considered a good brain food because fish has phosphorus in it and so has the brain. The two reasons have as much connection as that between nuts and the brain; or ginseng and man.

Astrological ideas came in to help out ignorance and foster supposed knowledge. The sun and the stars were favorable planets and the moon unfavorable. If anything about a plant reminded the gatherer of the sun or the stars, then that plant was sure to be beneficial, especially in chronic diseases. If anything reminded him of the moon, however, then it could be expected to be maleficent in influence. Though childish, this had yet its power to help.

The use of nitrate of silver, which in the old days was called lunar caustic, because it had, in a fresh state, a silvery, moon-like sheen, was largely a matter of signatures. The signature went both by similitude and by contrary. Since the lunar caustic supposedly had a moon quantity, therefore it would be good for moon-struck people—the lunatics of the old time and of our own time. As a consequence nitrate of silver was used in many obscure nervous and mental diseases. In epilepsy it was commonly employed. Even in our own times, entirely on empiric grounds, it was used for such severe organic nervous diseases as locomotor ataxia and sometimes to such an extent as to produce argyria. Undoubtedly, its use, with confidence on the part of the physician and suggestion and persuasion on the part of the patient, did much to relieve sufferers from discouragement and from such psychic disturbance of their general health as would have made their condition seem worse.

Wines as Remedies.—How much suggestibility means in the choice of remedies that of themselves are more or less indifferent, may be well judged from the recommendations with regard to various wines that have been made by physicians. At one time and place it is red wine, at another it is white wine that is particularly effective. For certain nations the stronger wines, as Port or some of the Hungarian wines, have appeared to exercise specific effects. Except for the tastiness of these various brands or for other trivial accessories, it is probable that the therapeutic efficacy of the wine depends entirely on the alcohol and the effect of this upon the patient. In his "Memories of My Life," Francis Galton relates that Robert Frere, one of his fellow pupils with Prof. Partridge, who became through marriage in later years a managing partner in a very old and eminent firm of wine merchants, told him that the books of the firm for one hundred and fifty years showed that every class of wine had in its turn been favored by the doctors.

In prescribing wine the doctrine of signatures probably had more to do with the special choice than anything else. Red wines were recommended for anemic people, because somehow the coloring was supposed to affect the {37} patient in such a way as to make up for the lack of coloring in the blood. On the other hand, the light, and especially the straw-colored wines, were recommended for liver troubles, because of their relation in color to the yellow of bile. Light wines were best for people who had more color than normal. Some wines are much stronger than others, and the alcohol, as in so many of our patent medicines, had a stimulating tonic effect, but in olden times this was supposed to constitute only the smallest portion of the efficiency of the wine, while the ingredients that made its color and taste were extremely important. The taking of red wine by anemic patients often proved suggestively valuable, and the alcoholic stimulation led them to eat more freely and look at things more hopefully and, consequently, to improve in health more rapidly than would have been the case had they not had the feeling that somehow they were actually consuming elements that would make their blood red.

Precious Stones.—The doctrine of signatures applied particularly to precious stones, and many of the popular medical superstitions with regard to precious stones were founded on it. The blood stone was said to be efficient as a tonic: it stimulated people: it made the anemic stronger and ruddier if it were worn on the fingers. The torquise turned pale when its owner was in poor health. It was the stone that was an index of what has been called "the blues" or what one modern writer has dignified by the title "splanchnic neurasthenia." Dr. Donne wrote of:

A compassionate turquoise that doth tell
By looking pale, the owner is not well.

It is probable that the pallor of the patient's hands as the background to the stone made the difference in its appearance thus noted. It became deeper in hue, as it were, when people were in ruddy health. The suggestive influence of such beliefs is easy to understand. It is even possible that the wearing of an amethyst did help to keep people from indulging in liquor to excess, for that is the traditional effect of the wearing of this stone, though its virtue seems to be founded on nothing better than the supposed derivation of the name from the Greek *a* privative and *methuo*, "I get drunk," suggesting strongly to the wearer that he should not get drunk.

The jacinth superinduced sleep and doubtless the strong suggestion of this supposed influence helped many sufferers from so-called insomnia to get sleep. The single fixed idea that now they must get to sleep would greatly help them. Pillows in the olden time were occasionally set with bits of jacinth, and there is even the record of bed-linen embroidered with it. This would probably be quite as effective as are hop-pillows in the modern time, for their main influence, as is also true of pine pillows, seems to be through suggestion. Some other traditions with regard to precious stones are harder to understand, yet may be explained. The owner of a diamond was supposed to be invincible. Diamonds represented money and money meant power. It is harder to explain the tradition that the possession of an agate made a man able and eloquent.

The wide acceptance of the doctrine of signatures, and of allied ideas, as to the effect of precious stones and metal and jewelry upon disease, makes {38} it clear that the acceptance of a mental persuasion with the changes in habits that follow, may serve as the basis of a successful system of therapeutics. The materials associated with the idea had absolutely no more physical influence than does the carrying of a horse chestnut or a potato in the pocket serve to keep off rheumatism.

CHAPTER V

PSEUDO-SCIENCE AND MENTAL HEALING

An interesting phase of psychotherapy is found in the history of the applications of new scientific discoveries to medicine. The development of every physical science has been followed by an attempt to apply its new principles and discoveries to the treatment of disease. Such applications have nearly always been followed by excellent results at the beginning. But almost without exception, the medical significance of these discoveries has, after a time, been found to be *nil*. When these discoveries were made they became the center of public attention. The announcement of their application to medicine then seemed natural and produced a feeling that another great therapeutic principle had been discovered. Sometimes wonderful therapeutic effects were noted. The chronic diseases particularly were helped for some time, at least, and practically all the affections that have mainly subjective symptoms were greatly relieved, or actually cured. After a time, however, when the novelty of the discovery wore off, its suggestive power was lessened and then the remedy lost its therapeutic power.

ASTROLOGY

Astrology is the typical example of pseudo-science in medicine. The stars, and particularly the planets and the moon, were supposed to have great influence on human destiny, human health, and human constitutions. Astrology was an organized body of knowledge over 3,000 years ago. Mr. Campbell Thompson has recently translated a series of 300 inscriptions from the cuneiform tablets in the British Museum, and Professor Südhoff of Leipzig has compiled all the references to medicine in these. The latter's studies show the extent which star influence was supposed to have over human health. A halo round the moon, an obscuration of the constellation of Cancer, the pallor of a planet in opposition to the moon, the conjunction of Mars and Jupiter, and other movements and phenomena of heavenly bodies were supposed to foretell the approach of disease for man and beast.

As a consequence of this application of astrological knowledge to medicine, operations were performed only on certain favorable days or under favorable conjunctions of planets. An ailment that occurred at an unfavorable time, because of an unpropitious state of the heavens, would not be relieved until the motions of the stars brought a more benign conjunction. Observations seemed clearly to indicate that the stars actually had such influences. Even Hippocrates, though he insisted that "the medical art requires no basis of vain presumption, such as the existence of distant and doubtful factors, the {39} discussion of which, if it should be attempted, necessitates a hypothetic science of supra-terrestrial of subterrestrial belief," could not entirely get away from astrology. In his treatise on "Air, Water and Locality" he writes: "Attention must be paid to the rise of the stars, especially to that of Sirus as well as the rise of Arcturus, and after these to the setting of the Pleiades, for most diseases in which crises occur develop during these periods." In the second chapter he writes: "If anyone would be of the opinion that these questions belong solely in the realm of astrology, he will soon change his opinion as he learns that astrology is not of slight, but of very essential importance in medical art." (Personally I doubt the Hippocratean authorship of these passages, but they are surely very old.)

The influence of the suggestions derived from astrology on human patients continued until almost the nineteenth century. There were many protests, especially from the Doctors of the Church, that the applications of astrology to medicine were false, but the practice continued. Both Kepler and Galileo drew horoscopes for patrons, and while Kepler doubted their value, he felt that in making them he was justified by custom. Galileo drew up the horoscope of the Grand Duke of Tuscany during an illness, and declared that the stars foretold a long life, but the Duke died two weeks later. But incidents of this kind did not disturb either popular faith or medical confidence in astrology as helpful, in prognosis, at least, if not also in diagnosis. Even so late as 1766 Mesmer was graduated at the University of Vienna, when it was doing the best medical work in Europe, with a thesis on "The Influence of the Stars on Human Constitutions."

Later Astrology.—Few now realize that the curious figure printed at the beginning of most of our almanacs down to the present day is a relic of the time when physicians believed in the influence of the constellations over the various portions of the body. Even yet this idea has not entirely gone out of the popular mind, and hence its retention as something more than a symbol in our little weather books. Man was considered as a little world, a microcosm, and the universe, as men knew it—the sun, the moon and the planets together—constituted a macrocosm. It was observed that the bodies constituting the universe were circumscribed in their movements and never went out of a particular zone in the heavens which was called the zodiac. This zodiac was divided into twelve equal parts called signs or constellations. Similarly man's body was divided into twelve parts, of which each one was governed by a sign of the zodiac or by the corresponding constellation. The ram governed the head; the bull the neck; the twins the paired portions, shoulders, arms and hands; the crab the chest; the lion the stomach, and so on. The old surgical rule, as quoted by Nicaise in his edition of Guy de Chauliac's "Grande Chururgie," was that the surgeon ought not make an incision, or even a cauterization, of a part of the body governed by a particular sign or constellation on the day when the moon was in that particular portion of the heavens, for the moon was supposed to be the bringer of ill-luck and to have untoward influences. The incision should not be made at these unfavorable periods for fear of too great effusion of blood which might then ensue. Neither should an incision be made when the sun was in the constellation governing a particular member, because of the danger and peril that might be occasioned thereby.

{40}

Such rules were supposed to be founded on observation. Patients were influenced by them mainly because they were assured that the surgical treatment was undertaken under the most favorable influence of the stars and that all unfavorable influences had been carefully observed and eliminated. It is hard for us to understand how such ideas could have been maintained for so long in the minds of men whose other attainments clearly show how thorough they were in observing and how profoundly intelligent in reaching conclusions. We should, however, have very little censure for them, since from some other standpoint we find every generation, down to and including our own, jumping at conclusions just as absurd and just as inconsequential. And the practice of astrology was not without its value, for the reassurance given patients by the consciousness that the stars were favorable did much to relieve their anxiety as to the consequences of surgery, lessened shocks, hastened convalescence, and favored recovery.

HERBAL MEDICINE

What is thus exemplified in astronomy and astrology can be found in the story of every other science. After the knowledge of the stars, the next organized branch of information that might deserve the name of science related to plants. This, too, was introduced into medicine, and with more justification than astrology. Most of what was accomplished by early herbal medicine was, however, due to the influence produced on the mind rather than to any physical influence tending to correct pathological conditions. The shape and color of plants, their form, the appearance of their leaves, were all supposed to indicate medical applications for human ailments. The reason for their acceptance was entirely the ideas associated with the plants and not any definite therapeutic effect. Whatever good nine-tenths of all the herbal medication accomplished certainly was by means of the influence on the mind. We have abandoned the use of most herbal remedies in recent years, even many that are still retained in the pharmacopeia, because we have realized their physical incapacity for good.

ALCHEMY

When chemistry, under the old name of alchemy, began to develop, its first study was of minerals, and just as soon as a body of knowledge was acquired chemistry was applied to medicine. All the investigators were engaged in searching for the philosopher's stone, the substance by means of which it was hoped to change base metals into precious. It was generally believed that when this substance was found, it would have wonderful applications to human diseases and would transmute diseased tissues into healthy tissues in the same way that it transformed metals. It was felt that the philosopher's stone would be an elixir of life as well as a master of secrets for wealth. This would seem amusingly childish to us were it not for the fact that in radium we, too, seem to have discovered a philosopher's stone—a substance that transmutes elements. For some years after its discovery {41} we were inclined to think that it must have some wonderful application in medicine and in surgery, and we actually secured many good results until its suggestive value wore off.

The fact that much had been learned about chemicals persuaded men that they must be beneficial to human beings. Thus they were taken with confidence and produced good results. When our modern chemistry developed out of alchemy a great variety of drugs began to be used, and long, complex, many-ingredient prescriptions were written. Polypharmacy became such an abuse that the time was ripe for Hahnemann, whose principles, if carried to their legitimate conclusions, would require his disciples to give practically nothing to patients and treat them entirely by suggestion.

MATHEMATICAL MEDICINE

When mathematics developed, applications of that science were made to physiology and to medicine. Under the influence of Borelli, the school of Iatro-Mathematical medicine developed and it flourished long after him. Foster, in his "History of Physiology," says:

Borelli was so successful in his mechanical solutions of physiological problems that many coming after him readily rushed to the conclusion that all such problems could be solved by the same methods. Some of his disciples proposed to explain all physiological phenomena by mathematical formulas and hypotheses concerning forces and the shapes and sizes of particles.

MAGNETISM

Magnetism occupied a large place in the minds of the great thinkers of the sixteenth and seventeenth centuries. There is no doubt that Paracelsus accepted, quite literally, what we embody in figurative expressions with regard to magnetism. To him the attraction of sex was magnetic. People had personal magnetism because they possessed physical powers by which they attracted others. He considered that these powers of attraction were expressions in human beings of the power of the magnet in the physical world, and that the two were literally equivalents. Kepler, one of the deepest thinkers of his time, evidently entertained the idea that the magnet represented the soul of the physical world, and that the planets were held in connection with the sun and their satellites with the planets, by magnetic attraction. We now call it the attraction of gravitation. We understand the force no better than before, but have changed the terms. Descartes theorized much along magnetic lines, and felt that by the use of certain expressions he was adding to knowledge, though he was really only multiplying terms.

Human Magnetism.—How seriously the question of human magnetism was taken will perhaps be best appreciated from one old fallacy. For a long period it was supposed that human beings were so highly magnetic that if a man were exposed in an open boat, in perfectly calm weather, in the open sea, where no currents would disturb him, his face would turn to the north, under the same magnetic influences as caused the needle to point to the north! Many studies of magnetism were made at this time, so that the subject {42} attracted widespread attention. Columbus had made some rather startling observations on his voyage to America with regard to the declination of the magnetic needle, and, during the century following, Norman and Gilbert made interesting studies in the same subject. Father Kircher wrote two books on magnetism and there were a number of others written by university professors. Advantage was taken of this thoroughly scientific interest in magnetism to erect a whole body of pseudo-scientific medicine supposed to be founded on magnetic principles. The same theories were also applied to supposed explanations of various psychological phenomena.

During the sixteenth and seventeenth centuries the application of magnets was a favorite treatment for a great many diseases. Especially were they useful in the treatment of muscular pains and aches and the chronic diseases which so disturbed men's minds. Many of the joint troubles of the aged, the muscular pains and aches that develop from the wrong use of muscles, and the vague internal discomforts which often disturb men so seriously, were cured by the application of magnets. Perkins' success with his tractors shows how much can be accomplished in this way.

ELECTROTHERAPY

The great development of pseudo-science in medicine remained for the era following the scientific investigation of electricity. With the discovery of the Leyden jar and its startling spark, a new and marvelous healing agent seemed to be at hand. It is quite amusing to read the accounts of the influence of the spark of the Leyden jar on the well and on the ailing. In my "Catholic Churchmen in Science" (Dolphin Press, Phila., 1909) I summed up the situation.

Winckler of Leipzig said that the first time he tried the jar, he found great convulsions by it in his body; it put his blood into great agitation; he was afraid of an ardent fever, and was obliged to use refrigerating medicines. He felt a heaviness in his head as if a stone lay upon it. Twice it gave him a bleeding at the nose. After the second shock his wife could scarcely walk, and, though a week later, her curiosity stronger than her fears, she tried it once more, it caused her to bleed at the nose after taking it only once. Many men were terrified by it, and even serious professors describe entirely imaginary symptoms. The jar was taken around Europe for exhibition purposes, and did more to awaken popular interest than all the publications of the learned with regard to electricity, in all the preceding centuries.

The extent to which the curative power of electric sparks from the Leyden jar was supposed to go is best appreciated from a list of the affections that one distinguished electro-therapeutist claimed could be not only benefited, but absolutely cured by its employment. It included pulmonic fever, under which title practically all the more or less acute diseases of the chest were included, and some at least of the sub acute; dropsy, by which was meant every effusion into the abdominal cavity no matter what its cause; dysentery, under which was included at that time not only the specific dysenteries but many of the summer complaints and some typhoid fevers; diarrhea, including all the intestinal diseases not already grouped under dysentery; putrid and bilious fever, under which category were assembled the worst cases of typhoid; typhus {43} fever, and all the other continued fevers, and any febrile condition reasonably severe for which no other term could be used; epidemic diseases, pest, anthrax, small-pox, cancer, gravel, diseases of the bladder and of the brain and spinal cord. The Leyden jar had no real effect on any of these affections, but doubtless the mental effect of this new remedy was quite sufficient to be of distinct therapeutic value in the milder forms of many of them.

With Galvani's discovery of the twitching of the muscles of the frog there came a new impetus to the exploitation of electricity in medicine. Many felt that now it was beyond doubt that electrical energy bore some definite relation to vital energy—that one might be made to replace the other if indeed they were not more or less the same thing. This led to many applications of electricity in medicine. Students of physiology were convinced that they were getting close to the solution of the mystery of life, and their persuasion was readily carried over to the people of the time, so that electricity literally worked wonders on them.

When the various electrical machines were invented and their use popularized, pseudo-science proceeded to exploit them, and succeeded, because the mechanical shock of the electric current proved a suggestive therapeutic stimulant. Gordon in the eighteenth century made the first practical frictional electrical machine, and soon some men were observing wonderful effects with it, though the charge was so small that it could actually accomplish little. Just after the invention of the voltaic pile in 1800 it came to be used in medicine with wonderful results. We are prone to think that electrotherapy is modern, but when electrical machines were quite crude, current strength small and potential low, old-time electro-therapeutists were recording their wonderful results and were getting just as marvelous effects as are reported now by enthusiasts. Considerable electro-medical literature existed a century ago when next to nothing was known of electricity. When, later, high potency currents came in and the Wimshurst and other powerful machines were invented, there was revealed at each novel invention a new horizon in electro-therapy and wondrous cures were reported. These continue to occur in the practice of a few favored individuals, though the general profession secures only some ordinary mechanico-muscular effects, which demand much time for real good to be accomplished and have nothing at all of the marvelous about them.

The power of the pseudo-scientific aspect of electricity to influence patients, far from being lost in our time, has rather been increased. Our newspapers make their readers eminently suggestible because they constantly furnish suggestions, and nothing so strengthens a function of any kind as exercise of it. All sorts of electrical contrivances and apparatuses are advertised to cure various pains and aches. Many of them actually seem to relieve long-standing discomfort, though it is not through any electrical power that they do so, but entirely through their influence on the patient's mind. A museum of the electrical contrivances of various kinds for which absurdly high prices are paid at the present time and which people recommend to others because of having been benefited by them would be interesting. There are belts of many kinds, and rings, and medallions, and plates to be worn on the back and on the chest, and curiously shaped poles or "polar plates" resembling various organs, and pendants and armlets and anklets and insoles of many, many kinds, usually {44} going in pairs, one made in zinc and the other in copper, and worth exactly as much as the weight of copper and zinc in them, yet curing chronic ailments by suggestion, or at least bringing relief from many pains and aches complained of.

LIGHT AND PSYCHOTHERAPY

Just as electricity has always been therapeutically abused by those who have taken advantage of the suggestive influence of its marvelous energy, so each new discovery in light has been the source of pseudo-scientific applications to medicine. When the explanation of photography was first made, shortly after the middle of the nineteenth century, and it was demonstrated that it was the blue light, or at least that end of the spectrum, and even some of the rays beyond the visible violet, which were the most active in this regard, applications of this fact to popular medicine became the order of the day. We had a wave of "blue light therapy" that wandered over this country and sold tons of blue glass. People simply sat beneath the blue glass as the sun shone through it and were supposed to absorb the actinic rays and acquire new life. According to many who had tried them, the ultra-violet rays were quite equal in their power to heal and restore new vigor to old frames to the fabled elixir of life of the olden time. "Rheumatism (that universal ill of the unthinking) in all its hydra-headed forms disappeared," as one enthusiast declared, "before the blue light, like the mists of the morning before the sun." All this, though it is said that the movement had no more serious foundation than the desire of a manager of a glass factory, who found himself stocked up with blue glass through a mistake, to dispose of his surplus stock. He not only did so, but many other manufacturers turned special attention to the new product because of the demand for it. The newspaper advertising was through the reading columns. The results were heard of on every side.

THE X-RAY

That happened two generations ago, and it might be supposed that in the meantime there had been so much advance in popular education, and particularly in the diffusion of scientific knowledge, that such a self-deception on the part of scientists, and blind following by the people, could not take place in our time. Just as soon as Roentgen discovered the X-ray, however, we began to have applications of that wonderful agent to curative purposes. About 1900, scarcely five years after Roentgen's discovery, there was hardly an ailment that some one did not claim to have seen treated successfully by the X-rays. Especially was this true for the chronic and hitherto supposedly incurable diseases. All the forms of malignant disease were treated by the new agent, and some supposedly marvelous cures were reported. Everything chronic was favorably affected—lupus, rodent ulcer, eczema, acne rosacea, even tuberculosis of the lungs. At the time I was on the staff of a medical journal, and the favorable reports came in so thick and fast that it really looked for a time as though the surgery of the future was to be much simplified. It took but a year or two to show us how little of lasting therapeutic benefit there was {45} in the X-ray, in spite of the fact that it is a marvelous agent in its action upon living tissues. At the present moment it is used comparatively little, and its use is gradually diminishing, except for very special limited affections.

RADIUM AND RADIO-ACTIVITY

When radium was discovered, though it came so soon after the discovery of the X-ray and our disappointment with it, the old story of another pseudo-scientific medical application was told. For a time it looked as though radium might accomplish all that had been promised for the X-ray, though that promise had been so lamentably broken. Then, besides radium, we had brought home to us the whole class of radio-active substances, and their possibilities. The internal administration of radio-active liquids was one of the hopes of therapeutics. We had found it difficult to explain how many of the mineral waters produced the beneficial action credited to them when taken at the spring. We knew that artificially made waters of exactly the same chemical composition, so far as we could determine, did not have the same effect, nor even the waters themselves when taken at a distance from the spring.

With the discovery of the radio-active principle there came the suggestion that possibly the main virtue of mineral waters at the spring was due to radio-activity. This would not be present in artificial water and would disappear from the natural water during shipment. This new idea was alluring, and it captured many. Radium seemed to be the new panacea. But we are discovering its limitations. It is of little avail in surgery; it is probably of less avail in medicine. As yet, however, we cannot say absolutely and must wait until results are determined. In the mean time many zealous advocates of the marvelous power of radio-activity to cure are exploiting it, apparently getting results and certainly making money. In the case of the mineral waters, also, the most important therapeutic element is probably the mental influence, which is strongest at the spring itself, where the suggestion of efficiency is repeated many times a day, and where the very atmosphere breathes confidence in the results to be obtained.

SUGGESTION AND PSEUDO-SCIENCE

These applications of science, or rather of supposed science, illustrate the influence of suggestion. The succession of events in each case is about as follows: The definite attitude of mental expectancy is created in the popular mind. As a consequence, with the application of the new scientific principle, patients cease inhibiting the recovery that would have come spontaneously before, only that they were self-centered and had their nervous energies short-circuited. Some are benefited by the habits of life that are established as a consequence of the belief that they are about to be cured, while before this they had been largely confining themselves to their houses, and had been refusing to take recreation or get diversion because of the conviction that they were ill. Finally, many of them had no real physical ills, but were suffering from mental ailments brought on by dreads and by a concentration {46} of attention on certain portions of the body which interfered with the normal physiologic action of those parts. Whenever strong mental impressions are produced, from any cause, results will surely follow, some of them marvelous. The supposed causes of these results will seem quite absurd to those who study them afterwards, but they were living realities to the sufferers. Nothing is more calculated to produce a strong mental impression than a newly discovered scientific fact with some supposedly wonderful application to humanity. The subsequent history of the application of scientific discoveries to medicine has been as invariably the same as the primary enthusiasm over each new therapeutic agent. After a time some people were not benefited. Physicians lost confidence in the power of the new remedial measure, whatever it might be. Patients were no longer impressed by the assurance that they would be benefited, and then the new application has either completely disappeared from our list of remedies, or has remained only to be used by a few, who still report good results from it. In spite of the constancy of this succession of events, we are still quite ready to take up with enthusiasm new discoveries in science and their applications to medicine. We have not yet lost the feeling, common in earlier centuries, that all science was meant for man and that every new scientific development must have some special reference to him.

CHAPTER VI

QUACKERY AND MIND CURES

Not less interesting than the therapeutic results obtained by men who in good faith were using inert remedies that they thought effective, are the cures obtained by men who had good reason to know that the therapeutic methods they were using were quite inefficient. Their good results, often loudly proclaimed by healed patients, are obtained entirely through the patients' minds. Usually these men are supposed to possess some wonderful therapeutic secret, which they have obtained by a fortunate discovery, or by long years of study, though usually their discovery is a myth and their long years of study a fable. So long as people can be brought to believe in their powers many cures are sure to follow their ministrations. The real secret is their knowledge of human nature. They induce people to tap new sources of vital energy in themselves, and somehow they succeed in bringing to their aid this law of reserve energy. Besides, in many cases the real reasons why patients continue to have certain symptoms once they have been initiated, is that their worry about themselves inhibits their natural curative power. This inhibition is prevented or obliterated by the change of mind produced by the quack, and then the *vis medicatrix naturae* brings about a cure.

Probably the oldest story that we have of a quack in our modern sense of the word is found in the Arabian Nights, some of the stories of which were old even in the time of Herodotus. One day Galen, famous for his work at Rome in the second century after Christ, found a wandering healer pursuing his avocation in his front yard. He found also that this man succeeded in relieving certain patients for whom he had been unable to do anything. He {47} found that the medicines prescribed were likely to do harm rather than good, yet many of the patients were benefited.

Galen succeeded in winning the man's confidence, who told him his story. He had been a weaver, but his wife thought he was not making money enough to support her properly, so she had advised him to become a leech. After taking lessons from a wandering quack, he set up for himself. When Galen inquired as to his method of making a diagnosis, he found that he did it entirely by his knowledge of human nature. He was even able to tell what was the matter with patients at a distance when friends came to demand medicine for them.

We think that such ready deception was possible only in earlier times, when education was not widely diffused and when belief in superstitions was fostered. Any such idea completely ignores the modern status of the quack and the success that he meets among even the more intelligent members of the community. Indeed, with the diffusion of information in modern times the quack has secured a wider audience. Superficial ideas of science are disseminated by the newspapers and by the magazines, people think that they understand all about it, and then these ideas are turned to their own advantage by the irregular practitioners of medicine. We have quacks by the score in all the centers of population, making a livelihood by exploiting the ailing, and serving to no small extent to create a feeling of popular discontent towards the physician, because that serves the purpose of quackery. Indeed, it is during the past century or a little more that some of the most striking examples of quackery have occurred.

Cagliostro.—Cagliostro, whose story is told in Dumas' "Memoirs of a Physician," and an excellent account of whose life may be found in Carlyle's "Miscellanies," is one of the great quacks and humbugs of history. He began his supposed medical work at Strasburg by the modest claim that during his travels in the East he had found a series of remedies which made old people young. In proof of his power to do this he exhibited his wife. She was a handsome young woman of very shady reputation whom he had married on his travels. She professed to be sixty years of age, though she was really under thirty and looked it, but she claimed that she had a son who had served for many years in the Dutch army. This imposition was so effective that in Strasburg, and subsequently in Paris, the charming pair collected large sums from wealthy old persons, especially from women on whom the marks of time had begun to show, and who expected, as the result of the treatment, to be shortly as young and as handsome-looking as Madame Cagliostro herself.

We might think that it is quite impossible for any such a deception as this supposed renewal of youth to be practiced in our more enlightened day when popular education is so widely diffused. We must not forget, however, that the newspapers bring us evidence every month of some old person who is quite sure that something that was being done for him was, if not renewing his youth, at least giving him back much of his pristine vigor, healing his aches and pains, and enabling him to take up his work once more. In treating the ravages of old age, which would seem to be altogether beyond any influence of psychotherapy, some of the most striking results are obtained. New therapeutic methods for the old come into vogue every year. As they grow older, {48} people become discouraged and so do not exert even the natural energy that they have for the maintenance of health and the keeping up of strength. Their discouragement keeps them from exercising enough, and this decreases appetite and sleep, and as a consequence there are many disturbances of function. All of this disappears as soon as they feel encouraged. Brown Sequard and his extract of testicular tissues is a typical example of how strong suggestion may influence the old and make them think that they are renewing their vigor and strength, and even their youth.

Perkins, Prince of Quacks.—Shortly after Cagliostro an American succeeded in using a very simple idea to gain world fame and at the same time to make an immense amount of money. He was a Connecticut Yankee with the typical name, Elisha Perkins. Dr. Perkins must have been born under a lucky star; at least he lived in fortunate circumstances for his purposes. Galvani's discovery of the twitchings that occur in the frog's legs when a nerve-muscle preparation or its equivalent was touched by metals in contact, had aroused world-wide discussion as to the place of electricity and magnetism in biology. Volta's brilliant experiments, which led to the invention of the Voltaic Pile, still further increased men's interest in this subject. It was then that Dr. Perkins came to exploit these electrical and magnetic ideas in medicine by means of a very simple invention. It was indeed the simplicity of his apparatus that made its appeal even more wide than would otherwise have been the case, and, be it said, left a larger measure of profit for the inventor.

Oliver Wendell Holmes in his "Medical Essays" has told the story of what may be called the rise and fall of tractoration. Any physician who wants to appreciate the real significance of cured cases should read Holmes' essay. We quote:

Dr. Elisha Perkins was born at Norwich, Connecticut, in the year 1740. He had practiced his profession with a good local reputation for many years, when he fell upon a course of experiments, as it is related, which led to his great discovery. He conceived the idea that metallic substances might have the effect of removing diseases, if applied in a certain manner; a notion probably suggested by the then recent experiments of Galvani, in which muscular contractions were found to be produced by the contact of two metals with the living fiber. It was in 1796 that Perkins' discovery was promulgated in the shape of the Metallic Tractors, two pieces of metal, one apparently iron and the other brass, about three inches long, blunt at one end and pointed at the other. These instruments were applied for the cure of different complaints, such as rheumatism, local pains, inflammations, and even tumors, by drawing them over the affected parts very lightly for about twenty minutes. Dr. Perkins took out a patent for his discovery, and traveled about the country to diffuse the new practice.

Just what the tractors were composed of may be found in the description of them filed with an application for a patent in the Rolls Chapel Office in London. They were not simply two different metals, but a combination of many metals, with even a little of the precious metals in them, partly because {49} of the appeal that this would make to the multitude, as chloride of gold did to our own generation, but doubtless mainly because the claim of precious metals entering into the composition enabled the inventor to sell his tractors at a better price.

Dr. Holmes continues:

Perkins soon found numerous advocates of his discovery, many of them of high standing and influence. In 1798 the tractors had crossed the Atlantic, and were publicly employed in the Royal Hospital at Copenhagen. About the same time the son of the inventor, Mr. Benjamin Douglass Perkins, carried them to London where they soon attracted attention. The Danish physicians published an account of their cases in a respectable octavo volume, containing numerous instances of alleged success. In 1804 an establishment, honored with the name of the Perkinean Institution, was founded in London. The transactions of this institution were published in pamphlets, the Perkinean Society had public dinners at the Crown and Anchor, and a poet celebrated their medical triumphs.

Miss Watterson tells how he attracted attention. Like all successful quacks, he had an inborn genius for advertising.

He lived in the house once occupied by John Hunter , and in 1804 the Perkinean Institute was opened, but by the end of 1802, 5,000 cases had already been treated. Lord Rivers was president. Sir William Barker, Vice-President Twenty-one physicians, nineteen surgeons, and the leading veterinaries succumbed to the influence of the magic tractors. One "eminent physician" who had had 30 guineas from a country patient and had done him no good was very angry when the sick man took to Perkinism.

"Why, I could have cured you in the same way with my old brick-bat or tobacco pipe, or even my fingers."

"Then why, sir," answered the patient in a stern voice (Perkins quotes this), "did you dishonorably pick my pocket when you had the means of restoring me to health?"

In some 176 pages young Perkins gives us the pick of 2,000 cases who had, of course, been foolish enough at first to put faith in the ordinary physician and his drugs.

In Bath, particularly, where aristocratic London went, as they do to-day, to repair the damage wrought by a season in town, the Tractor Cure was the talk of the place. But an enemy dwelt there, a Dr. Haygarth, an unbeliever. He, with a certain Dr. Falconer, fabricated a pair of false tractors. Five cases of gout and rheumatism were operated on by the conspirators, who discussed in a light tone the wonders of magnetism as they described circles, squares and triangles with the sham tractors. "We were almost afraid to look each other in the face lest an involuntary smile should remove the mask from our faces," says Haygarth, but the two assistant doctors, unaware of what was being done, were almost converted to Perkinism when they saw the five patients slowly mending under the treatment. One man experienced such burning pain that he begged to wait till the next day.

So rapid, and so many were the hospital cures wrought by these two doctors, that patients crowded to them and they could hardly spare five minutes to eat. They amused themselves inventing other instruments made of common nails and sealing wax, and effected with them cures, while they sent a pair of false tractors {50} to Sir William Watson in London and Dr. Moncriffe in Bristol, who operated with them with wonderful results.

It must not, however, be thought that the uneducated, or the unskilled, or even merely unoccupied, were the only ones taken in by the supposed power of Perkins' Tractors. As we have seen, many physicians did not hesitate to avow themselves publicly as believers in this new and marvelous application of magnetism to human healing. It is true that the only thing we know about the men who became advocates of this new instrumental therapeusis, is their connection with it. The attention of the scientific world was rather cleverly managed. Dr. Perkins presented a pair of his tractors and the book that he had written about their use to the Royal Society. The custom of that learned body was to accept such presentations by a formal letter of thanks and place the objects and books on their shelves. No formal investigation of the claims to scientific consideration of such presentations was made. All possible advantage was taken of the fact that the Royal Society had accepted the new invention and had publicly thanked the discoverer for it.

How characteristically recent this old story is; it is renewed on every possible occasion and wears all the familiar aspect of modern devices for securing recognition and obtaining the apparent approbation or recommendation of some scientific society or institution. We had an example of it a few years ago when a nostrum exploiter signed the register of an International Congress immediately after a great medical investigator and then used a photograph of the names for advertising purposes.

How did the tractors secure the vogue they enjoyed? Those who believed in them did so not because of the scientific theory that animal magnetism or magnetic influence was behind them, nor because of the plausible ways of the Connecticut Yankee, but because of the unquestioned and unquestionable facts of actual healing that they saw in connection with the use of the tractors. Every one of these applications of science to medicine that has proved to be pseudo-scientific after enthusiasm subsides has made its appeal through the cures effected by it. Cures are what Eddyism advances to support its claims, cured patients are presented as their most effective argument by the osteopaths, cured symptoms are the proofs for Hahnemannism, but none of these systems of treatment ever cured as many cases in a corresponding time as did Perkins' tractors. They cured all sorts of physical ills, but their only effect was exerted through the mind.

Holmes wrote:

Let us now look at the general tenor of the arguments addressed by believers to sceptics and opponents. Foremost of all, blazoned at the head of every column, loudest shouted by every triumphant disputant, held up as paramount to all other considerations, stretched like an impenetrable shield to protect the weakest advocate of the great cause against the weapons of the adversary, was that omnipotent monosyllable which has been the patrimony of cheats and the currency of dupes from time Immemorial—Facts! Facts! FACTS! First came the published cases of the American clergymen, brigadier-generals, almshouse governors, representatives, attorneys and esquires. Then came the published cases of the surgeons of Copenhagen. Then followed reports of about one hundred and fifty cases, published in England, "demonstrating the efficacy of the metallic practice" in a variety of complaints, both upon the human body and on horses, etc. But the progress of facts in Great Britain did not stop here. Let those who rely upon the numbers {51} of their testimonials, as being alone sufficient to prove the soundness and stability of a medical novelty digest the following from the report of the Perkinistic Committee. "The cases published (in Great Britain) amounted, in March last, the date of Mr. Perkins' last publication, to about five thousand. Supposing that not more than one cure in three hundred, which the tractors have performed, has been published, and the proportion is probably much greater, it will be seen that the number, to March last, will have exceeded one million five hundred thousand!"

It is not surprising that with such "facts" behind them the tractors attracted deep and wide attention. A contemporary tells of it and the fate of the inventor:

A gentleman in Virginia sold a plantation and took the pay for it in tractors. Nothing was more common than to sell horses and carriages to buy them. But the worst (or the best) of it was, yellow fever was raging in New York, and Perkins thought he could cure the fever with the tractors and fell a victim to the fever himself.

Success of Quackery.—Always in the history of quackery and, indeed, in the history of all therapeutics, the appeal is to the cures that have been effected. This is the only evidence, of course, that can be adduced for the development of therapeutics, and yet the history of medicine makes it clear how carefully supposed cures must be analyzed if they are really to mean anything. Mesmer could adduce thousands of cured cases. Perkins could do the same. Every quack in history, from Galen's weaver, who became a leech, down to the last street corner nostrum vendor, does the same thing. When on the strength of supposed cures, then, a new system of therapeutics is introduced, it is much more likely than not that there is no foundation for the claims made. We have had ever so many more experiences of disappointment after the introduction of remedies which cured at the beginning of their history, than we have had of remedies that maintain themselves after prolonged experience. It is the attitude of scepticism and suspended judgment until after a remedy or method of treatment has been tried on many different kinds of cases in varying circumstances that constitutes the only efficient safeguard against repeating the unfortunate errors of old times in the matter of drugs and remedial measures. If the public could be made to realize this, they would be much less easily taken in.

What the quacks cure are not always imaginary ills, but often ills that are very real, at least to the patients, and the symptoms of which are relieved by the confidence aroused in the new remedy and the representations of the supposed discoverer, who, in spite of the exaggerated claims which he makes, somehow succeeds in catching the trust of patients. Very often this process initiated by the quack is really only the beginning of the cure.

In most people a vicious circle of pathological subsidiary causes is formed when anything becomes the matter. Patients are persuaded that a serious illness is ahead of them. This keeps them from exercising as much as before. Becoming overcareful of their diet, they reduce it below the normal limit for healthy activity. This causes them to have less energy for work and disturbs their sleep. Then a host of minor symptoms, supposed to be due to the disease, whatever it is or they think it is, but really consequent upon the unhealthy habits that have formed, begin to develop. Just as soon as confidence in their power to regain health is restored to these people, a virtuous circle, {52} to use the Latin word virtue in its etymological sense, of strength and courage, is formed. Everything conspires to stimulate the patients; they live more naturally, the subsidiary symptoms consequent upon their bad habits disappear and the disappearance of each one of them means for the patients a new assurance of triumph over disease. They attribute every improvement to the remedy they happen to be taking, though most of them are due to the changes in their habits, their diversion of mind, and the new energy released by their sense of encouragement.

An excellent example of how some of these mental persuasions in quackery act, and of how the cure is often really due to the physician who previously treated the case, though it is credited to the quack, may be found in the story that Hilton tells in his "Rest and Pain":

When this patient was first seen by a surgeon, he was thought to be laboring under some disease of the bladder and kidneys, for he had severe lumbago, pain over the bladder, and offensive urine. There had been no suspicion of anything wrong as regards the spine. He was a master painter and a house decorator, and was monstrously conceited, thinking himself right and everybody else wrong. When I explained to him, after careful examination, that the spine was the cause of the symptoms, he was not satisfied with my opinion and without my knowledge consulted Sir Benjamin Brodie, who also assured him that his spine was diseased and told him that he must rest it by lying down. To this he then assented. As he could not be controlled in his own house, I persuaded him to go to Guy's Hospital, where he had got nearly well; but he was very impatient, and would not remain long enough under my care to be quite cured. He returned home, gradually improved, and was getting quite well when some pseudo friend advised hydropathy and homeopathy—it did not matter which of the two—

as "the thing" to cure him. After a few months he was perfectly restored, not by either hydropathy or homeopathy, but, no doubt, by nature. The man, however, feels convinced that hydropathy and homeopathy cured him. It so happens, gentlemen, that sometimes we do not get the degree of credit which perhaps belongs to us.

To Mr. Hilton's reflections one is tempted to add that many of these patients, after having been seriously ill, cannot bring themselves to think that they will gradually get well by the forces of nature. Even after they have improved very much they are still inclined to think that that improvement is illusory or will relapse because they have not been "cured," that is, actively treated, in some way so that a "cure" should result. When they are nearly well, because of properly directed rest and nursing, someone recommends some irregular form of treatment. They take it up and this gives them confidence that they are being cured. This state of mind makes the ultimate steps of their recovery more rapid than it otherwise would be. As a consequence, the irregular gets the credit. Immediately after this case Mr. Hilton tells the story of another case in which a "rubber" got all the credit for the cure. It is evident that the modern osteopath has only somewhat systematized what had been in existence generations ago.

All this tendency of human nature to respond to anything that is done for it, provided the promise of cure goes with it, is taken advantage of by the quack, sometimes unconsciously, for his own purposes. Results, as a rule, are secured, in spite of the remedies that he suggests, which in most cases do harm rather than good. Of the thousands of remedies that have been introduced by quacks, not one now remains, though every one of them produced {53} wonderful cures on a great many patients at some time or other. It is the duty of the physician to secure just as good results honestly. He must influence the patient's mind favorably so as to bring about a modification of habits and a hopeful outlook on life, in spite of whatever ailment there may be. If he can do so he will have in his hands the best therapeutic measure that has been employed in all the history of medicine. It is the most universally applicable. It will cure, that is help, all forms of disease. It will relieve many of the symptoms of even incurable diseases. It will occasionally arouse the resistive vitality of the patient to such an extent that even apparently incurable diseases will be overcome. This is the lesson that the modern student of medicine must draw from the history of quackery.

CHAPTER VII

NOSTRUMS AND THE HEALING POWER OF SUGGESTION

A striking illustration of the power of the mind to bring about the cure of ailments and symptoms of every sort is found in the history of the many nostrums and remedies that have worked wonders for a time and later proved to be inert or even harmful. The ordinary definition of a nostrum includes the idea of secrecy. At all times in the world's history fortunes have been made out of such remedies. They appeal not only to the uneducated, but also to those who are supposed to be well informed, and this in spite of the fact that generally the remedies are claimed to do good for nearly every form of disease, and it must be evident to anyone, after a moment's serious thought, that the one idea of their inventor is not to benefit patients, but to make money.

With the multiplication of newspapers and magazines, there has been a great increase in these secret remedies and of their users. Apparently all that is needed for many people who are ailing, or think they are ailing, is to be told in a more or less impressive way that some remedy will cure, and then it proceeds to do them good. There is a general impression abroad that some of these remedies represent great discoveries in medicine, and the feeling of most of those who take them is that the inventor has found a new and wonderful remedy. During all the centuries such secret remedies have come and gone, and not one of them has proved to be of lasting value. Just as soon as its composition is no longer a secret it begins to fail. It is, therefore, evident that its effect was entirely due to influence on the mind and not at all to any influence on the body.

The stories of the origin of these remedies bear a striking similarity. There are two variants on the theme: either the inventor is supposed to be an earnest student of science, devoting himself to profound research for many years and finally finding some wonderful secret of nature hitherto hidden from men; or else the remedy has been discovered by happy accident, and some chronic sufferer pronounced by the most eminent physicians to be hopelessly incurable has in despair turned to the now method, caring little really, so discouraged is he, whether it does good or ill, and wakes up to find that he is on the high road to recovery, apparently having been directed by Providence in the use of the remedy in question. Overflowing with gratitude, he {54} wants to share the heaven-sent blessing with all mankind—for a valuable consideration.

The Weapon Ointment.—Among the most famous nostrums, and a striking example of the great rôle played in therapeutics by mental influence and coincidence, is the Unguentum Armariam or Weapon Ointment. This famous remedy would cure any wound made by a weapon, if it could only be employed before the fatal effects were absolutely manifest. There was an abundance of evidence that it stopped the pain, checked the bleeding and initiated the restoration of the patient to health. We know the remedy not from traditions of its use among the uneducated, but from descriptions that we have by men who were among the best educated of their time, and that by no means an era of dullards. The story of this infallible remedy is all the more surprising because it was not applied to the wound itself, nor indeed to the sufferer at all, but *to the weapon which inflicted the wound.* Nay, it was well authenticated that, where the weapon could not be secured for inunction, if the ointment were applied to a wooden model of the weapon, the cure followed with almost, though, it was confessed by some, not quite so much assurance as in the fortunate case of the weapon being available.

The story has been so well told by Oliver Wendell Holmes in his "Medical Essays" that it seems best to retell it in abstracts from his "Homeopathy and Its Kindred Delusions." He says:

Fabricius Hildanus, whose name is familiar to every surgical scholar, and Lord Bacon, who frequently dipped a little into medicine, are my principal authorities for the few circumstances I shall mention regarding it. The Weapon Ointment was a preparation used for the healing of wounds, but instead of its being applied to them, the injured part was washed and bandaged, and the weapon with which the wound was inflicted was carefully anointed with the unguent. Empirics, ignorant barbers, and men of that sort are said to have especially employed it. *Still there was not wanting some among the more respectable members of the medical profession who supported its claims.* The composition of this ointment was complicated, in the different formulas given by different authorities; but some substances addressed to the imagination, rather than the wound or weapon, entered into all. Such were portions of mummy, of human blood and of moss from the skull of a thief hung in chains.

Hildanus was a wise and learned man, one of the best surgeons of his time. He was fully aware that a part of the real secret of the Unguentum Armarium consisted in the washing and bandaging the wound and then letting it alone. But he could not resist the solemn assertions respecting its efficacy; he gave way before the outcry of facts (!), and therefore, instead of denying all their pretensions, he admitted and tried to account for them upon supernatural grounds.

Holmes says further:

Lord Bacon speaks of the weapon ointment, in his Natural History, as having in its favor the testimony of men of credit, though, in his own language, he himself "as yet is not fully inclined to believe it." His remarks upon the asserted facts respecting it show a mixture of wise suspicion and partial belief. He does not like the precise directions given as to the circumstances under which the animals from which some of the materials were obtained were to be killed, for he thought it looked like a provision for an excuse in case of failure, by laying the fault to the omission of some of these circumstances. But he likes well that "they do not observe the confecting of the Ointment under any certain constellation; which is commonly the excuse of magical medicines, when they fail, that they {55} were not made under a fit figure of heaven." It was pretended that if the offending weapon should not he had, it would serve the purpose to anoint a wooden one made like it. "This," says Lord Bacon, "I should doubt to be a device to keep this strange form of cure in request and use, because many times you cannot come by the weapon itself." And in closing his remarks on the statements of the advocates of the ointment, he says, "Lastly, it will cure a beast as well as a man, which I like best of all the rest, because it subjecteth the matter to an easy trial." It is worth remembering that more than 200 years ago, when an absurd and fantastic remedy was asserted to possess wonderful power, and when sensible persons ascribe its pretended influence to imagination, it was boldly answered that the cure took place when the wounded party did not know of the application made to the weapon, and even when the brute animal was the subject of the experiment, and that this assertion, lie as we all know it was, came in such a shape as to shake the incredulity of the keenest thinker of his time.

It is interesting to follow up some of the controversies among scientific men with regard to the weapon ointment, for they serve to show how the remedy came to maintain its prominence for so long. Podmore, in his "Mesmerism and Christian Science" (London, 1909), tells the story of the controversy between Goclenius, a professor of medicine at the University of Marburg, who published as the Inaugural Thesis for his professorship, a treatise on the "Weapon Salve," and Father Roberti, a Jesuit scientist and philosopher, whose final treatise in the controversy was entitled after the lengthy fashion of titles in that day, "Goclenius Corrected Out of His Own Mouth; or, The Downfall of the Magnetic Cure and the Weapon Salve." The decision of the controversy was eventually referred to the great physician of the time. Van Helmont, who decided that both disputants were partly wrong, the Jesuit erring most, but that above all Goclenius should distinguish between the cases when the weapon had blood on it and when it had not. When there is blood on the weapon, he held, then the salve is always effective; when there is not, then much stronger remedies were required. In both cases, of course, the salve or ointment was applied to the weapon.

In the midst of this discussion of the points at issue, it is interesting to note Van Helmont's opinion with regard to many curious things used in medicine at that time. He insists that Goclenius makes a mistake in attributing therapeutic power alone to the moss taken from the skull of a condemned criminal who had been hung in chains. This material, under the name of *usnea*, was apparently quite popular in prescriptions for various chronic ills, and especially those that we now recognize as prolonged neurotic affections. Van Helmont emphasizes the fact that the experience of all physicians shows that material taken from the heads of condemned criminals executed in other ways, as, for instance, those broken on the wheel, may be just as effective. Van Helmont conceived of the magnetic and sympathetic feeling as a natural process. All the force of the stars might be concentrated in objects that had been beneath their beams for a long time, and this might be communicated in some wonderful way to patients so as to supply defects of vitality. Such defects of vitality Van Helmont's prescriptions actually were compensating, but the source was in the patients themselves—that reservoir of surplus energy which remains unused unless some strong suggestion brings it out.

Sympathetic Powder.—After the weapon ointment, the best known of the nostrums of older times is probably Sir Kenelm Digby's famous Sympathetic {56} Powder, which Dr. Holmes talks of as even better known than its great therapeutic predecessor. This, too, was a wonderworker. Unlike the Unguentum Armarium, however, its composition was simple. It was nothing else than copper sulphate which had been allowed to deliquesce to a white powder. This powder would cure any injury as infallibly as the weapon ointment. It, too, was not applied to the wound, but to the *bloodstained* garments (Van Helmont's distinctions between the bloody and the bright weapon should be recalled) of the wounded person. The patient did not need to be present at the time the application was made. He might be far away and yet its efficacy was, according to many very intelligent and highly educated persons, quite assured.

For the sympathetic powder we have one of the stories of far-fetched discovery that have since become so familiar. A missionary, traveling in the East, was said to have brought the recipe to Europe about the middle of the seventeenth century. The Grand Duke of Tuscany, in whose dominions the missionary took up his residence, heard of the cures performed by him and tried by offers of money and favor to obtain the missionary's secret, but without success. Sir Kenelm Digby, however, who was traveling in Italy, happened by good fortune to do a favor for the missionary, and put him under such deep obligations that he felt the only way he could properly repay his benefactor was to confide to him the composition of this wonderful remedy. Sir Kenelm Digby was at this time one of the best known of English scholars. After having reached distinction in the English navy, he had devoted himself to literature, to philosophy, and to politics. He had devoted much time to the old books of alchemy. Therefore, the offer of this precious piece of information especially appealed to him. On his return to England he proceeded to use it for the benefit of his friends, and it created a sensation. The French dictionary of the Medical Sciences tells the story of the application of the powder for the first time in England and of the subsequent use of it, especially on the nobility of England:

An opportunity soon presented itself to try the powers of the famous powder. A certain Mr. Howell, having been wounded in endeavoring to part two of his friends who were fighting a duel, submitted himself to a trial of the sympathetic powder. Four days after he received his wounds, Sir Kenelm dipped one of Mr. Howell's garters in a solution of the powder, and immediately, it is said, the wounds, which were very painful, grew easy, although the patient, who was conversing in a corner of the chamber, had not the least idea of what was doing with his garter. He then returned home leaving his garter in the hands of Sir Kenelm, who had hung it up to dry, when Mr. Howell sent his servant in a great hurry to tell him that his wounds were paining him horribly; the garter was therefore replaced in the solution of the Powder, and the patient got well after five or six days of its continued immersion.

King James I, his son, afterwards Charles I, the Duke of Buckingham, then Prime Minister, and all the principal personages of the time were cognizant of this fact; and James himself, being curious to know the secret of this remedy, asked it of Sir Kenelm, who revealed it to him, and his majesty had the opportunity of making several trials of its efficacy, *which all succeeded in a surprising manner*.

Tar Water and Therapeutic Faith.—One further story of an old nostrum deserves to be told because of the distinction of its chief promoter, who did not, however, as do most of the nostrum promoters, make a fortune by it. {57} This is the incident of Bishop Berkeley and his tar water. Berkeley was one of the leaders of thought of the eighteenth century. At one time he came to America with the idea of enlightening the ignorance of the colonists and of founding a school of philosophy. Besides being one of the most learned men of his time, he was one of the best. He was known for his gentleness, his unselfishness, and his lack of pretension. Yet all of these virtues were unable to save him from falling a victim to a medical delusion. One of his essays is on the value of tar water in medicine, and is entitled "Siris, a Chain of Philosophical Reflections and Inquiries Concerning the Virtues of Tar Water," etc.

Tar water was prepared by stirring a gallon of water with a quart of tar, letting it stand for several days, and then pouring off the clear water. It, in fact, retained scarcely more of the tar than the odor. According to the great philosopher, this not only cured, but prevented diseases. The list is, indeed, so long that it is hard to understand how the claims for it could have received any credence. They did, however, and Berkeley himself, and many of his friends, were cured of many and various ills, and were protected from many more by its frequent use. The odor was the factor that proved of suggestive value and set free the springs of vital energy.

Sarsaparilla.—It might be thought that such deception of self and others as has been illustrated in the weapon salve and sympathetic powder would be impossible in our enlightened day. Anyone who thinks so forgets certain incidents of recent times. The story of sarsaparilla is a striking illustration. Few drugs have been more popular in the last half century, and it is even yet popularly supposed to be a wonderful tonic, a cure for many diseases. During the first half of the nineteenth century, when the humoral theory of the causation of diseases was generally accepted, certain German physicians thought they observed that a decoction of sarsaparilla was a sovereign remedy for various ailments having their origin in the blood. The blood was at that time supposed to become impure for many reasons, and the possibility of neutralizing such impurity by medical measures was seriously attempted. As Virchow used to insist, the humoral pathology still holds its ground in popular estimation, and so blood purifiers are favorite remedies, and will doubtless continue to be for at least another generation, until cellular pathology secures a hold on the popular mind.

Sarsaparilla came in, then, as a great blood purifier, and was used for ten years by many of the physicians of the world, confident that they were obtaining excellent results from its use. After a time, however, further study of the drug showed that it was inert. Gradually the employment of sarsaparilla as a remedial agent ceased, though it continued to be used as an elegant vehicle in the prescription of nauseating remedies.

Only after it had been thus abandoned by the regular profession, was it taken up extensively by others who advertised its virtues widely and secured a great clientele for it. Probably more money has been spent on sarsaparilla during the last fifty years than on any other single drug. Many millions were every year appropriated by rival concerns to advertise its virtues. It has been possible at any time during the last half century to secure any number of people who were willing and ready to declare   and most of them convinced of the truth of what they said—that various preparations of {58} sarsaparilla had cured them of long-standing ills, and that they considered it a life-saving remedy.

The efficient ingredient in the sarsaparilla, so far as any of its various preparations have seemed to do good, has not been anything that was in the bottle, but the printer's ink that was absorbed from the outside of it. People were persuaded that they would get better, and, as far as most of them were concerned, this was of itself quite sufficient to turn the scale in favor of improvement that led to the obliteration of symptoms. So long as these symptoms were a source of worry and trouble to them, they continued to be quite incurable. Just as soon as the inhibition of nervous energy, due to worry and over-attention to their sensations, stopped, then the natural force of the body was sufficient to remove the sources of complaint.

Psychology, Old and New, of Remedies.—Men have always known how to take advantage of the possibility of influencing patients' minds by wondrous claims for remedies. Anyone is sadly deceived who thinks that it is only in recent times that men have learned to make their advertisements of nostrums suggestive by the promises made or that we have developed the psychology of advertising to such a degree as to appeal to the ailing more forcibly and surely than was done in the past. Here is the announcement that went with a remedy in old Irish medicine more than 1,000 years ago. It was, according to its inventor, "a preservative from death, a restorative for the want of sinews (strength), for the tongue-tied, a cure for swelling in the head, and of wounds from iron and of burning by fire, and of the bite of the hound; it preventeth the lassitude of old age, cures the decline, the rupture of the blood vessels, takes away the virulence of the festering sore, the fever of the blood, the poignancy of grief—he to whom it shall be applied shall be made whole." The announcement ended up with the panegyric "extolled be the elixir of life bequeathed by Diancecht to his people; by which everything to which it is applied is made whole." When it is noted that, besides death and loss of muscle power and aphasia and wounds and burns and bites, it also cures old age and consumption (for that is what is meant by decline) and hemorrhages, and probably aneurysms, and fevers and also grief, there are not many modern panaceas that exceed it in power.

Always, as in this Irish announcement of the olden time, the climax of the advertisement is a note of exultant praise for the inventor who has brought such a magnificent blessing to mankind. The ways of the nostrum vender are ever the same.

Roman Nostrums.—How old are all these methods, and how little human nature has changed through all the centuries! The patent medicine men of Rome in the early Christian eras made use of just the same methods that are employed to-day. Friedländer, in his "Roman Life and Manners Under the Early Roman Empire," tells the story well. Many remedies were known by special arbitrary names, instead of descriptive names recalling the ingredients. Sometimes they were named after famous physicians who had used them, or were said to have done so; again, the preparations were named after persons of distinction who actually, or supposedly, were cured thereby, much as, in our own day, cigars are named after poets, statesmen and pugilists. The titles of some of these preparations, for instance, were "Ointment for Gout, Made for Patroculus, Imperial Freedman—Safe Cure"; "Ointment for {59} Aburnius Valens" (probably the famous jurist) called the "Expensive Ointment"; "Eye Salve with Which Florus Cured Antonia, the Wife of Drusus (the Emperor's son) After the Other Doctors had Nearly Blinded Her." Many of these remedies were labeled "instantaneous," "safe," "sure cure," "Harmless remedy," and the like. Frequently euphonious names, sometimes from the Greek, were chosen: Ambrosia, Anicetum, Nectarium, for the promoters evidently knew the satisfying effect, on both patient and physician, of a mystifying foreign name.

Proprietary Remedies.—A corresponding abuse very like that of our own time was with reference to proprietary medicines. Physicians, instead of compounding their own, accepted those made by others with the exaggerated claims for them, used them on patients, transferring their own confidence in them to the patients, thus producing cures which, after a time, proved to be due entirely to the influence on the patient's mind. Pliny, the elder, complains that physicians of his time (the first century after Christ) often bought their remedies so as to avoid the trouble of preparation. He evidently refers to compounds supposed to be curative for various affections; for Friedländer says that "often the physicians did not know the exact ingredients of the compounds that they used and should they desire to make up written prescriptions, would be cheated by the salesmen." Both Galen and Pliny complain that physicians used ready-made medicines, instead of original prescriptions carefully prepared by or under the supervision of the physicians themselves. It is evident that the proprietary remedy had come into existence thus early, and that various drug manufacturers made specialties which physicians, following the line of least resistance, found it easy to prescribe, though men like Pliny and Galen realized that this was an abdication of one of the most important functions of their profession, which was bound to work harm in the end both to themselves and to their patients.

How curious it is to find exactly the same state of affairs recurring in our time, with absolutely similar results. Simple remedies that are well known combinations of ordinary drugs receive high-sounding names, usually derivatives from the Greek or the like, and are claimed to work just as many wonders as the old-fashioned nostrums. Even imitations of the old-fashioned poultices, when thus exploited, give a new lease of life to the exploded idea of the drawing-out power of external applications.

Common Ailments and Nostrums.—Certain ailments are particularly the subject of exploitation by the manufacturers of remedies. Rheumatism is one of these, neuralgia is another, catarrh is a third, and headache a fourth. Then there are various forms of indigestion and all the pains and aches associated with it. All of these ailments are rather vague and are in some cases at least, due to the insistent dwelling of the patient's mind on some symptom of very little significance. Others are real pains and aches, relieved by some simple anodyne drugs, doubly efficient when taken with the suggestion that they represent a wonderful discovery, which came only after long years of study and investigation, and are said to represent a new departure in medicine. Another favorite field for the nostrum vender is the series of pains and aches associated with the menstrual condition. Many of these nostrums are used by hundreds of thousands, and yet an analysis shows that probably the only active substance in them is the alcohol in which certain of the drug {60} principles are dissolved. This makes the patient feel better by the exaltation that comes from the dose of alcohol and the rest is merely suggestion, though there is no doubt that symptoms which have failed to be cured by physicians are sometimes relieved by these remedies. It is a cure by faith, not by medicine.

Cured Cases as Evidence.—As all of the nostrums, and indeed all the therapeutic movements supposedly medical or physical or religious, secure their vogue on the strength of reported cures, this would seem to be the best possible evidence for the efficacy of a remedy. But unless the cases supposed to be cured are critically examined and analyzed, and above all, followed for some time afterwards, such evidence is open to all sorts of errors. Is it any wonder, then, that the physician, familiar with the history of medicine in this regard, asks for the careful study and analysis of these cases. We know that it was on the strength of cures effected by it, that the weapon ointment became possible throughout Europe. We know that portions of the body of executed criminals and the touch of the hanged cured as many cases as, let us say, osteopathy or Eddyism. The sympathetic powder and its advocates appealed to the many cures that followed its use. Every other nostrum from the beginning of time has made this same appeal.

CHAPTER VIII

AMULETS, TALISMANS, CHARMS

Amulets, talismans, charms—these words are commonly used with something of the same significance, and for our purpose all three may be treated in common.

Prophylactic Objects.—From the earliest ages men have worn amulets, that is, objects often resembling jewelry, though sometimes the remains of animals or even of men, with the idea that they would ward off illness, or cure it when present. Rings of many sorts, brooches, various objects suspended around the neck, ear-rings, head-bands, belts for the waist, and rings for the wrists and the ankles, ornamented bracelets and anklets, have at all times had a medicinal power attached to them in some minds. Earrings are still worn by many with the idea that they are helpful in affections of the eyes. I have known children's ears to be pierced and earrings inserted because the little ones were suffering from headache. Precious stones were supposed to have this power when worn. The amethyst protected its wearer from drunkenness; the bloodstone cured anemia; while the opal was supposed to portend evil. Occasionally such gems were ground up and used as internal or external remedies, because of the power supposed to be attached to them. Their influence upon the mind, at least, can be readily understood. The earliest prescription we have in America is at the Metropolitan Museum, New York, among the curiosities from Egypt (about 1500 B.C.). It calls for the use of ground up precious stones in fumigations, probably for an hysterical person.

The precious metals were used also as powerful cures. Chaucer says, "for {61} gold in physick is a cordial." Some think that our own use of chloride of gold a few years ago for many chronic ills had little more reason than the preciousness of gold impressing itself on patients. Inscriptions were made on the metals, and these were supposed to add to their healing or preservative quality. Famous among these was the abracadabra. It had to be written in a particular triangular form, and was then very powerful. Here the amulet invades the sphere of the charm. Prayers were written on parchment, or on paper, or on papyrus, in the old time in Egypt, Babylon and Assyria, and when worn about the body were supposed to do great good. It is surprising to us now how many physicians and scientists placed confidence in these things because they thought that they had seen good results. Alexander of Tralles recommends a number of them. Robert Boyle, the father of chemistry, says that he was cured of a severe ague, that the doctors could not benefit, by the application of an amulet to his wrists. Burton, in the "Anatomy of Melancholy," has a series of references that show how much he, himself, and the educated men of his time, believed in the power of amulets to help in illnesses and Boyle, particularly, has a number of references to precious stones and their curative virtue.

Rings in Therapy.—Under Faith Cures I mention the cramp rings blest by the Queen of England and effective against abdominal pains. Other kinds of therapeutic rings were used rather commonly. All through the Middle Ages iron rings were worn, which were good for colic and biliousness and also for rheumatic pains. There are literally thousands of such rings worn now, here in the United States, and by quite intelligent people. Personally, I know of more than a dozen cases where they have been worn for years. The wearers faithfully take them off each day, rub off the rust which collects on the inside, call their own and others' attention to the fact that all this material has been drawn out of the body through the supposed electrical power of the ring, and then they replace them. Here is pseudo science obtruding itself. Usually these rings are of polished steel and look a little like silver. They may, however, be obtained in gold plate, and then are supposed to be quite as efficacious. The iron or steel rings cost two dollars each; gold-plated rings cost five to ten dollars, according to the ability of the patient to pay, for metallotherapy has as one of its effects the lessening of congestion of the purse. Those who wear them would not part with them, because they feel the benefits derived. These rings are supposed to be particularly good for vague, painful conditions in the joints, especially the so-called rheumatic pains.

In old times these rings were sometimes engraved with a legend that was itself a strong suggestive element. The rings of the Middle Ages that were supposed to be a cure for biliousness were engraved with a command to the bile to go and take possession of a bird. Occasionally rings were supposed to be valuable because of their origin. Epileptic fits, for instance, were rendered much less frequent and less severe if a ring made of money that had been given in the church were worn. The condition was that the sufferer should stand at the church door asking a penny from every unmarried man who passed in or out. After sufficient alms had been thus collected the money was exchanged for silver money that had been contributed to the church, and from this the ring was made. It was to have a cross and sometimes a verselet from Scripture, or an exorcism, or a prayer, engraved on it. It is {62} easy to understand that all of this represents strong suggestive influence and that the standing at the church door begging alms might well represent an enforced prolonged opportunity to get rest and air, for many unmarried men do not go to church, and so there were also physical factors at work in the cure noted.

Precious Stones as Preservatives.—Pettigrew, in his "Superstitions Connected with Medicine and Surgery," mentions a number of the precious stones and their power to heal. Garnet hung about the neck relieves sorrow and refreshes the heart; chrysolite is the wisdom stone, the enemy of folly; heliotrope staunches blood and acts as an antidote; sapphire is good for ague and gout, and also gives its wearer courage; it also stops bleeding at the nose and was an antidote; the topaz was good for lunatics; the carnelian cured bloody fluxes and also fluxes of anger and passion. Jasper, hematite and similar stones had certain general powers of doing good. The Bezoar stone had a great reputation against melancholy; the smaragdum was infallible against epilepsy; the onyx was good for sleep; the sardonyx prevented bad dreams. The most wonderful stone, however, was the agate; taken in liquid it was good for any disease. It made the skin healthy. It preserved against snakebite, and against all poisons, and it prevented the devil from injuring one who wore it or drank it, and also preserved him from being struck by lightning. Considering how common agates were and how readily they could be obtained, it is rather surprising that we should have so many stories of illness and deaths by lightning and from poison and from venomous serpents in the old days when its curative value was rated so high.

Amulets.—The coin given by the kings of England when they healed the scrofulus or epileptic came to be, in one sense, an amulet. The sight and the touch of this acted as an ever recurrent suggestion tending to make these patients better, and undoubtedly the coin was of great service by its renewal of the mental influence of the touch of the king. There are traditions, also, that these coins healed others who touched them, and sometimes for generations they were kept in families as representing a fountain of healing and of preservation of health. Any object that thus became invested with reverence produced healing effects. Virchow, in the introduction to Schliemann's "Troas," tells of going to a long distance for water, during the time when he was present at the excavations, in order to be sure that the water would be absolutely pure. The natives had heard that he was a great physician from the West. They concluded that the reason why he went to this particular distant spring for water, in spite of the trouble involved, was that it must have some wonderful healing virtues. Accordingly a tradition of healing grew up around it, and people came from long distances, drank from it and were cured.

There are still people who carry horse chestnuts for rheumatism, and occasionally a farmer carries a potato for the same purpose. The feeling is, if they do no good, at least they can do no harm. Doubtless in the Middle Ages the same feeling prevailed as to other favorite objects. At present, among the better informed classes, various pendants supposed to have some connection with electricity are popular. I have seen a medal made of alternate discs of copper and zinc, and confidently believed to be strongly electrical, worn even by an otherwise sensible merchant in a country town. Electric belts still are {63} extremely common—and expensive. Supposed electric insoles, one made of copper, the other of zinc, are sold in great numbers and at good prices, though, quite needless to say, they are absolutely inert electrically. Various electric contrivances, small batteries, and the like, really are of the nature of amulets. People have a faith in them that is not justified by anything in science, but that faith helps them in their ills. Most of the supposed medicinal plasters are in the same class. As a rule, sufficient curative material cannot be incorporated in a plaster to be of any service, and most of them, though widely advertised, are scarcely more than rubber adhesive plaster. They do good partly by their mechanical effect, because they actually support muscles, but mainly because of faith in their efficacy. Whenever a particular discomfort occurs the feeling that a plaster is covering the spot gives the patient assurance that he or she must soon be better. In all of these effects there is no manifestation of any physical or marvelous supernormal power, but simply and solely of the influence of the mind on the body.

CHAPTER IX

DETERRENT THERAPEUTICS

In the history of therapy a peculiar phase was the use of all sorts of materials, intensely repugnant to human nature and deterrent to all the finer feelings, but which, nevertheless, proved curative of many ills. We know now that there was absolutely nothing remedial in these substances or methods of treatment, but only the effect produced upon the patient's mind. If the patient makes sufficient effort to overcome the intense repugnance, that enables him to release hitherto latent vital energies, or to correct hampering inhibitions which have prevented curative reactions. The more the patient had to conquer himself, or herself, the more surely did the remedy produce a good effect. It was effective, however, not only among the poor and the uneducated, but often also among the better informed, provided the patients became persuaded of its efficiency. Persuasion in these matters is usually best secured by the reports of cured cases. It is easy to obtain "cures" from almost anything. They are set up as confident proofs of the remedial virtue of methods of treatment. They have been, in the history of medicine, more often the indexes of action upon mind than upon body. Real remedies help patients to get better. Supposed remedies, that afterwards prove quite inert, *cure*.

Portions of Corpses.—One of the ingredients of the famous Unguentum Armarium (see chapter on Nostrums) was, as has been said, moss scraped from the skull of a man who had been hanged. It was declared to be particularly efficacious against so-called dead members, such as the blanched fingers of Raynaud's disease, or the hysterical palsies, and other functional paralytic conditions of the limbs. The real therapeutic factor was not the gruesome material itself, but the potent suggestions awakened by it. It is probable that the quacks and witch doctors who gave out the formula of their remedies as containing such material often did not take the trouble to collect them, and that their salves and ointments were really quite inoffensive preparations.

{64}

Touch of the Hanged.—Some of the traditions which gather round the effect of contact with the body of a hanged person are curiously interesting from the standpoint of psychotherapy. This form of execution seems to have had a much more potent influence in producing therapeutic elements in the bodies of the victims than any other. We do not hear much of the touch of a beheaded person's body nor of any place in medicine for portions of the victims of execution by shooting, though Van Helmont claims curative properties for these in lesser degree. All sorts of ailments were, however, supposed to be cured by the touch of a hanged person. Thomas Hardy in his "Wessex Tales" tells of a young woman in his time suffering from a paralyzed arm, apparently a form of paralysis due to a functional nervous condition, who was recommended by an old "conjure" doctor to touch her bared arm, as soon after the execution as possible, to the purple mark of the rope around the neck of a man who had been hanged. The doctor assured her this was the only means by which she could be cured. We would not be surprised to hear of her cure under such circumstances.

Hardy has carefully collected his material regarding the traditions of the southern part of England, and he makes the hangman say, when the woman applies to him for permission to touch the body of the victim, that such a request had not been made for some years, but that there used to be many applicants when he was a younger man. He adds, moreover, that it was the custom to apply to the governor of the prison and that usually this application was made by the physician of the patient who accompanied him or her on the visit to the corpse. There is no doubt that physicians did, in many cases, have recourse to such methods, and that the reasons for their belief in the efficacy of the touch of the dead was that they had seen the cure in this way of many puzzling diseased conditions, which their skill in wortcraft and herbal medicines had not enabled them to relieve. The touch of the corpse was supposed to bring about a "turning of the blood," and this produced the good effects. Occasionally the patients fainted from terror, yet afterwards were found to be able to use limbs that had been quite beyond their control before. The story is typical of what happened in country districts all over Europe for centuries.

Mummies.—How little distant we are from the use of such material for therapeutic purposes will be appreciated from the fact that mummy was used in medicine down nearly to the end of the eighteenth century. The first edition of the "Encyclopedia Brittanica" (1768) said:

We have two different substances preserved for medicinal use under the name of mummy, though both in some degree of the same origin. The one is the dried and preserved flesh of human bodies, embalmed with myrrh and spices; the other is the liquor running from such mummies, when newly prepared, or when affected by great heat or damps. The latter is sometimes in a liquid, sometimes of a solid form, as it is preserved in vials well stopped, or suffered to dry and harden in the air. The first kind of mummy is brought to us in large pieces, of a lax and friable texture, light and spongy, of a blackish brown color, and often damp and clammy on the surface: it is of a strong but disagreeable smell. The second kind of mummy, in its liquid state, is a thick, opaque, and viscous fluid, of a blackish color, but not disagreeable smell. In its indurated state, it is a dry solid substance, of a fine shining black color, and close texture, easily broken, and of a good smell; very inflammable, and yielding a scent of myrrh and aromatic ingredients while burning. This, if we cannot be content without medicines from our own bodies, ought {65} to be the mummy used in the shops; but it is very scarce and dear; while the other is so cheap, that it will always be most in use.

All these kinds of mummy are brought from Egypt. But we are not to imagine, that anybody breaks up the real Egyptian mummies, to sell them in pieces to the druggists, as they may make a much better market of them in Europe whole, when they can contrive to get them. What our druggists are supplied with, is the flesh of executed criminals, or of any other bodies the Jews can get, who fill them with the common bitumen so plentiful in that part of the world; and adding a little aloes, and two or three other cheap ingredients, send them to be baked in an oven, till the juices are exhaled, and the embalming matter has penetrated so thoroughly that the flesh will keep and bear transportation into Europe. Mummy has been esteemed resolvent and balsamic: but whatever virtues have been attributed to it, seem to be such as depend more upon the ingredients used in preparing the flesh, than in the flesh itself; and it would surely be better to give those ingredients without so shocking an addition.

Serpents in Therapeutics.—Snakes and portions of snakes have been prominent features of deterrent therapeutics at all times. Headaches were cured by wrapping a dead snake around the head, or by the touch of a snake's skin, and sore throat by wearing a snake's skin around the throat at night. This seems one degree better than the custom, still common, of wrapping the stocking, that has been worn during the day, around the neck. In the chapter on Graves Disease, the use of the touch of a snake, or of a snake's skin worn around the neck, is mentioned. Girdles made of snake's skin or snakes themselves, were supposed to be good for colic and for various internal troubles, and were sometimes, among barbarous peoples, a sovereign remedy for the ills of pregnancy and assured the woman a safe delivery and an easy labor. Undoubtedly they lessened dreads by suggestion and the effort necessary to overcome repugnance. Some of the symptoms of the menopause have been cured in the same way. Rattlesnake oil has had a special reputation among mountainous people, where the snakes abounded, for the pains and aches of the old, and the vague joint discomfort, sometimes spoken of as rheumatic, but really due to various individual conditions. It is probable that in most cases the oil thus employed was not extracted from the rattlesnake, but was some ordinary oil palmed off under that name, and having its special effectiveness because of the thought associated with it.

Various portions of serpents are still in use, sometimes in the hands of physicians, though usually in popular medicine. I knew a physician in a small inland city who had a great local reputation for curing external eye troubles, and who owed not a little of it to the fact that the people in his neighborhood thought that he used rattlesnake oil as one of the ingredients for his strongest prescriptions. He was supposed to be able to dissolve even cataract by his remedies, and there is no doubt that in many cases of chronic indolent ulcer of the eye he was able to bring about a cure sooner, and have it last longer, than those of the regular profession who had not the advantage of this popular faith. He was careful to buy rattlesnakes from certain of the mountain people, who killed and brought them to him and who advertised the fact that they had such commissions from him. The stories were made all the more interesting by the fact that the doctor would not purchase dead rattlesnakes. They must be brought to him alive, since the therapeutic virtues can only be extracted immediately after death. A mountaineer with a couple of live rattlesnakes with him is always an interesting object and a fine {66} advertisement. One would like to know what the doctor did with the snakes—that is, how he disposed of them without suspicion. Homeopathic physicians still have lachesis-viper venom in their pharmacopeia. Their remedies, however, if they really follow the dilution principle of their founder, can have an effect only on the mind, so that the use of lachesis is not surprising.

Repugnant Remedial Measures.—Quite in keeping with the use of deterrent remedies of various kinds are the recommendations to do certain things that involve great self-control, and the overcoming of repugnance, or fright, or the like. A favorite mode of preparing remedies in the Middle Ages was to gather the particular herbs for the prescription in a graveyard in the dark of the moon. The patient himself was supposed to gather them and to be alone when doing so, if they were to be effective. How much occupation of mind and diversion of thought would be afforded for timid people by the effort to overcome themselves to this extent! The occupation of mind alone and the concentration of thought necessary for the ordeal would be quite sufficient to divert many people from the centralization of attention on themselves, which is responsible for so many of their symptoms, or for that exaggeration of symptoms that aggravates the ailment.

Ordures as Remedies.—Among all primitive peoples we have the story of the use, as remedies, of ordures of various kinds, of repugnant portions of animals, of ground insects, of animal excrement and urine, and even of human excretions, of the blood of serpents, or eels, or carrion feeding birds, and the like. Ground lice and insects of various kinds are very common as prescriptions in the history of primitive medicine. They turn up here and there through the Middle Ages, and they are said to be still used in China. The more one knows about side-tracks in medicine, the more does one find of far-fetched repugnant materials vaunted as wonderful cures. Some of the substances employed are so disgusting that one does not care to mention, much less discuss, them. I have had a man tell me that, in a severe epidemic of diphtheria, he saved his children's lives when they were attacked by the disease, and the children of others were dying all around him, by blowing the dried excrement of dog down their throats.

There are certain popular medical practices that are related to these old traditions of deterrent therapeutics. In many manufacturing establishments, in spite of progress with regard to sepsis and antisepsis and the diffusion of information as to first aid to the injured, it is still the custom to put spittle on wounds. I am sure that every doctor has seen quids of tobacco used in this way. Even native-born Americans, who are not illiterate, are sometimes found using some deterrent material. I have known such a man use his own urine as an eye-wash for sore eyes, and the use of children's urine for such purposes is much commoner than might be thought. After all, it is only a generation since physicians used to taste urine in order to determine whether it contained sugar or not, and I have seen a country doctor even take between his finger and his thumb a little of the excrement of a child and apply his tongue to it, pretending of course that he obtained very valuable information this way.

Excretions and Secretions.—All the human excretions have formed the basis of vaunted remedies. Tears, on the principle that like cures like, were used for melancholia; nasal secretion to lessen respiratory difficulty through {67} the nose; sputum for various mouth affections, but also as an application to external abrasions, and to the eyes, the ears, and the like. Undoubtedly patients were helped by many of these, not because of any physical effect, but because they felt easier as a consequence of the satisfaction of having something done for them, and the consequent freedom from solicitude which allowed nature to produce her curative reaction without interference. The greater the effort he has to make, apparently the more efficiently does he control this disturbing state of mind. This is the secret of many cures now as well as in the olden time.

Whatever good effect is produced in such cases comes, of course, from the persuasion that these substances will do good, and there must be a strong suggestion to that effect before the repugnance can be overcome. While we are prone to think the older peoples who used such materials commonly are to be condemned for ignorance and superstition, it is well to recall that human nature has not changed, and is still ready to be influenced in the same way. Brown Sequard's extract of testicular substance came in this category. We had a wave of organotherapy a few years ago, and we know now that whatever benefits patients derived from taking heart substance for heart troubles, and brain substance for brain troubles, and kidney for renal diseases, was entirely due to mental influence. The cannibal who eats the heart of his enemy, thinking that the vigor and courage of the other will pass into him, undoubtedly has for a time a power of accomplishment greater than before. Nothing acts so powerfully as suggestion of this kind to give renewed vigor and to enable us to tap sources of energy that we were not aware of in ourselves, and that enable us to accomplish what before seemed quite impossible, and even to bring about curative reactions.

Diseases Benefited.—Observe the classes of disease that were particularly relieved by deterrent therapeutics. Headache was one of these. All sorts of things were cures for headaches—the touch of the hangman's rope, or of an executed criminal, or some herb gathered in the graveyard in the dark of the moon, or pills made of the excrement of various animals. The forms of headache thus relieved would be those in which over-attention to self, rather than real headache, produced queer feelings in the head, though concentration of attention might exaggerate this into an ache. Foot troubles were cured by deterrent therapeutics. To wear the shoes of a dead person, especially of a murderer who had been hanged, would cure them. Colic was cured by pills of excrementitious materials, and by all sorts of other deterrent remedies. For instance, one well-known remedy was to wash the feet and drink the wash-water. The wash-water of little babies was a favorite remedy for the vague abdominal pains of old maids, and for the symptoms due to the menopause.

Deterrent Pain.—A striking illustration of a strong mental influence helping out a slight amount of therapeutic efficiency is found in the use of the actual cautery for medical affections. At a number of times in history most of the chronic pains and aches, the arthritises, the so-called gouty tendencies when localized, the rheumatic affections and especially the chronic rheumatisms, have been treated by means of the cautery. All of the neuralgias, many of the neuroses, all of the neuritises and a certain number of so-called palsies and paralyses, were treated successfully by this means. It is a very suggestive remedy producing a deep impression that now relief must be in sight. It {68} became popular over and over again, though after a time it always lost its influence, and ceased to have the beneficial effects that it had at the beginning of its reintroduction.

During the second half of the eighteenth and the beginning of the nineteenth century the cautery became very popular. It was applied particularly in the form of the moxa. A cylinder of cotton was employed for this purpose, being set on fire and allowed to burn on the skin of the patient, producing a deep wound. The mental effect of this can be readily understood. Baron Larrey, one of the most eminent surgeons of the time, thought the moxa one of the best aids that he had in the treatment of many affections where the knife was not indicated. There were large groups of diseases in which it was almost a specific. Larrey employed it in affections of vision, of smell, of taste, of hearing and of speech. In many paralytic affections of the muscular system, in all chronic affections of the head, among which he enumerates non-traumatic affections, hydrocephalus, chronic headaches and many other affections supposed to be seated in the cranium. In asthma he was particularly successful with the moxa. Old catarrhal affections yielded to it. Consumption was frequently benefited by it. Most of the chronic affections of the uterus were benefited, as were also similar affections of the stomach. He considered that the moxa must be admitted, without contradiction, to be the remedy *par excellence* against rachitis. In Pott's disease, which he called dorsal consumption, it worked wonders. In sacrocoxalgia, in cocygodynia and femero-coxalgia he had excellent results with the moxa.

A glance at this list shows exactly the class of cases in which suggestion has always played a large role, and for which there has been, at various times, a series of specific remedies, medicinal, manipulative and surgical. Others extended the value of the moxa beyond these affections. Ponto found it valuable in gout, and in the various chronic affections which are sometimes grouped under the name chronic rheumatism. He insisted that the moxa could be placed on almost any part of the body, though the contra indications he suggests show how far the men of his time went with its use. Only these portions named might not have a moxa applied to them. It must not be used on the skull, on the eyelids, on the ears, on the mamme, on the larynx and on the genitals, though it might be applied to the perineum or the perineal body.

Deterrent Taste and Smell.—The disturbing effects produced by other senses besides those of sight have been used in the same way for the production of definite therapeutic suggestive effects. A number of the ill-tasting, almost nauseating drugs of the olden time prove to have very little real therapeutic efficiency in the light of modern clinical careful observation. This is particularly true of the herbs and simples. Many a disgusting preparation apparently owed all of its' good effects on the patient to the effort that was required to swallow it, producing such a favorable influence upon the mind, by *contrecoup* as it were, that the patient got better. A little girl said that cough medicines were nasty things they gave you in order to keep you from catching cold again. The sense of smell has been used in the same way. Valerian is probably an efficient drug in certain respects, but undoubtedly its efficiency is materially increased by its intensely repulsive odor. For many of the psycho-neuroses and neurotic conditions generally the ammonium valerianate is likely to be much more efficient than the strychnin valerianate, though probably the {69} latter should be considered as more physically efficacious in its tonic properties. Asafetida, musk and some preparations of the genital organs of animals that used to be in the pharmacopeia, owed most, if not all, of their power, whatever it was, to the mental effect of their odor and the feeling of deterrence that had to be overcome before they were taken.

There is a precious therapeutic secret in this use of deterrent, repugnant, frightful materials which patients use to advantage under certain circumstances. It illustrates the influence of the mind over the body, and emphasizes the fact that such influence can be exerted in the full only when a deep impression is produced upon the patient. Whether this can be imitated without deceit, and without the use of undignified methods, must depend on the physician himself and his personality. There can be no doubt that there is a wonderful power here to be employed. It must be the physician's business to find out in each individual case, according to his own personal equation, just how he may be able to use at least some of it. It is well worth studying and striving for, because nothing is more potent for psychoneurotic conditions, and for neuroses on the borderland of the physical, than which no ailments are more obstinate to treatment.

CHAPTER X

INFLUENCE OF THE PERSONALITY IN THERAPEUTICS

Though it has seldom been fully realized and has probably never been appreciated as in our time, one of the most important factors in therapeutics, in every period of the history of medicine, has been the personal influence of the physician. Therapeutic fashions have come and gone, new drugs have been introduced, have had their day and then been relegated to the limbo of worn-out ideas. At all times, however, physicians have succeeded in doing good, or at least using, with apparent success, the therapeutic means of their own time, however crude and inadequate these afterwards proved to be. They have succeeded in shortening the progress of disease as well as increasing the patient's resistive vitality and thus enabled him not infrequently to survive where otherwise a fatal termination might have occurred. All unsuspected during most of the time, it was the personal influence of the physician that counted for most in all of the historical vicissitudes of therapeusis. It mattered not that the means he employed might seem absurd to the second succeeding generation, as was so often, indeed almost invariably, the case, his personal influence has at all times overshadowed his available therapeutic auxiliaries. In spite of all our advance in scientific medicine, to a considerable degree this remains true even at the present time, and to fail properly to use this important auxiliary is to cripple medical practice.

Place of Personal Influence.—When the antitoxins and directly curative serums seemed about to make for themselves a place in therapeusis, it looked for a time as though this personal element might be entirely superseded. It seemed that all other therapeutic factors must give way to definitely accurate doses of antitoxic principles, directly opposed to the toxins of disease and {70} capable of conquering it. With the success of diphtheria serum, the prospects for scientific therapeutics from the biological standpoint became very promising. Unfortunately, our further experience with antitoxins and therapeutic sera of various kinds has not been satisfactory, and now the medical world is looking elsewhere for progress in therapeutics.

This throws us back once more on the old-time therapeutics, and we have to learn to use all their elements. One of the most important of these, if not, as we have suggested, absolutely the most important, the one that in all the many variations of therapeusis has maintained itself, is the personal influence of the physician by which he is able to soothe the patient's fears, allay his anxieties, make him face the situation calmly so that he may not use up any of his vital force in useless worry, but on the contrary employ all his available psychic energy in helping nature to overcome whatever disturbance there is within the organism. This personal influence was for several centuries spoken of as personal magnetism, not merely in the figurative sense in which we now employ that term, but in a literal sense. The implication was that some men possessed within themselves a reservoir of superfluous energy, vital in character, but thought to be related to the force exhibited by the magnet, when it attracted bodies to itself, and made metals for a time magnetic like itself, and which actually passed over from the physician to his patient. We have gotten away from the idea of any physical force flowing from physician to patient, but we know very well that certain physicians are much more capable than others of arousing the vital energies of the patient, sometimes to the extent of making him feel, after treatment, that he has more force than before. The patient feels that something must have been added to his natural powers, though he has only been brought into a state of mind where he can better use his own powers.

It is the men whose presence created this impression in patients, an impression that is justified by the fact that somehow he enabled them to vitalize themselves better than before, who have been most successful in the treatment of patients. In all ages the men of reputation for healing have had this. A careful study of their lives shows that this counted for more in many of the experiences of their healing than the drugs and remedies which they employed. The men who have been the most sought by patients have not as a rule left us great therapeutic secrets; on the contrary, they have only employed the conventional remedies of their times with reasonable common-sense and have added to them their own personal influences. On the other hand, the men who have made discoveries in therapeutics, and in medicine, have not always been popular as physicians. They have known too much of their own lack of knowledge to be quite confident in their use of remedies, and this has hurt something of their personal influence over patients.

IMPRESSIVE PERSONALITY

As a matter of fact, it is easy to comprehend, even from the comparatively scanty details that we have of habits and methods of the great physicians, that their effect upon their patients was always largely a matter of impressive personality. Any one who, from a pharmaceutical standpoint, knows how {71} inefficient were many of the remedies that great physicians depended on, yet how effective they seemed to be to their patients, and even to themselves, will appreciate the factor of personal magnetism that entered into their employment. It is not alone in the olden time that great physicians have been almost worshiped. For their patients they have at all times been men of exalted knowledge, masters of secrets and comforters of the afflicted, just as was the first great physician of whom we have any account, I-em-Hetep, in Egypt nearly six thousand years ago. Such men as Hippocrates, as Galen, as Sydenham and Boerhaave, and Van Swieten, accomplished curative results far beyond the therapeutics of their time. The loving admiration of patients and of their disciples shows how strong were their personalities and gives us, almost better than the writings they have left to us, the secret of their successes as practitioners of medicine.

A Great Modern Physician's Influence.—It is interesting to study in the lives of great physicians the details which illustrate their personal influence, their consciousness of it and how deliberately they used it. A typical example very close to us, whose reputation was still fresh while I was at the University of Paris, was Professor Charcot. He had made great discoveries in nervous pathology. To a great extent he had revolutionized our knowledge of nervous diseases and added many new chapters to this rather obscure department of medicine. Far from making the treatment of nervous diseases easier than before, or giving more assurance to the physician who dealt with them, his discoveries, however, had just the opposite effect. His work emphasized that practically all of the so-called nervous diseases were due to degenerations in the central nervous system, which no medicine could be expected to relieve in any way, and which nothing short of the impossible re-creation of damaged parts could ever cure. His studies included organic degenerations of other organs, and in his treatise on "Diseases of the Old" it is made clear that many of the symptoms of old age are due to organic lesions for which no cure can ever be expected. This would seem to discourage treatment, yet somehow Charcot became a great practicing physician as well as a medical scientist and pathologist.

His success was due to his personal influence over his patients. In spite of the unfavorable prognosis that he had to give in so many cases, he was able by suggestion to help many patients with regard to their course of life, and to reassure them, so that many adventitious neurotic symptoms not due to their underlying nervous disease, but to their solicitude about themselves, disappeared. Very few people who came to him went away without feeling that his advice had been very valuable to them and without experiencing, as a rule, after they had followed his advice, that they were much better than they had been before. It was for the neurotic conditions associated with nervous affections that Charcot's personal influence over patients was of the greatest therapeutic significance.

He himself recognized this and did not hesitate to use it to its fullest extent. Towards the end of his life, the method by which his patients were presented to him was calculated to make their relation to him, above all, a very personal one, and to give his influence the fullest weight. Nervous patients who came to see him, were each in his turn invited from the general waiting-room into a small ante-room just outside of Charcot's office and {72} there, in silence and dim light, asked to await the summons of the physician himself. When the time came for him to call them in, the folding doors between the rooms opened and he stood in a blaze of light inviting them to enter. Many a neurotic patient despairing of relief for symptoms that had lasted long in spite of the treatment of many other physicians, felt at once that here, in this kindly, gentle-voiced man standing so prominently in the light, was surely the long looked-for physician who would heal whatever ills there were. They came fully impressed with his power to heal, and all the valuable influence of auto-suggestion was enlisted on the side of their physician.

What is true in the regular practice of medicine can be seen much more clearly in the history of those who were not physicians, but who, nevertheless, by personal magnetism, succeeded in curing various ills, or at least in lifting up patients so that they used their own natural powers of recovery to much better advantage than would have been possible if left unaided.

Every successful healer has had this same personal influence, personal magnetism, call it what we will, which his patients have thought helpful to them through some direct communication, but which he himself, if he seriously studied it, and which every other thorough student of the question must realize, was due only to his power to call out the latent vitality of his patients. The mystery is not one of teledynamics, a transfer of energy from the operator, but one of awakening dormant faculties in the subject. Just why they should be dormant, since the patient so much wants to use them if he only could, is hard to understand. They do, however, lie dormant until the call of another strong personality wakens them to activity. Many people are so constituted that they cannot do effective work except under the direction of others. They lack initiative, though they may fill secondary places very well, indeed, much better often than the man of initiative who so frequently lacks capacity for details. In the same way many people are not able to bring out to the full all their own energies, even for their own bodily needs, unless under the guidance and influence of others; hence the stories of the healers that we have all down the centuries, and who have a definite place in the history of humanity and of medicine.

A Modern Healer.—A typical instance of the really marvelous power of mental influence over the minds of sufferers from many kinds of ills, is found in the career of the well-known Father Kneipp. For more than twenty-five years he had attracted the attention of Europe, and had made the little town of Woerishofen well known all over the world because of the cures effected there by him. The exactly proper phrase is effected *by him* because it is clear to anyone who has studied the therapeutic methods he employed, that it was not these, or at least not these alone, that enabled him to cure so many ailments which had resisted the efforts of some of the best physicians in Europe. It was his magnetic personality which won patients to the persuasion that they must get better because he said so, and then to the following out of certain very simple natural rules of life, and certain quite as simple remedial measures, which acted as alteratives and enabled patients to tap reservoirs of vitality, of which they themselves were unconscious, but which, supplying energies to overcome tendencies to various symptomatic conditions, brought about cures.

{73}

Pfarrer Kneipp had himself suffered from consumption, had been practically given up and then, as is the case of many another, had taken himself in hand, had secured much more outdoor air than before, and more abundant nutrition, until gradually his ailment was overcome. It is true that he used various hydrotherapeutic measures, some of them, as he confessed afterwards, to an excess, both as regards the temperature of water and the length of the application of it, that might have seriously hurt him if he had been less robust, but it was not so much his hydrotherapy as his own determination to get better and to live a little closer to nature that led to his cure. Then he became the apostle of cold water and of many natural remedial measures, and as a consequence, healer of all forms of ills in the many thousands who flocked to consult him in the little South German town. He made his patients get up early in the morning, get out in the air shortly after rising, the excuse, or, as he declared it, the reason being that they were to walk with bare feet in the dewy grass. After this he had them eat heartily of simple food, of such variety and in such quantity as relieved them of constipation, made them use water, internally and externally, in abundance, and after a time, sent most of them on their way rejoicing that they had been cured from chronic ills.

Some of the highest in Europe came to him; the Empress of Austria was his patient, and he was asked to prescribe for the Pope; reigning princes and all the lesser order of the nobility were included among his patients. Several of the Rothschild family went to him and where they went, of course, others flocked. Very few failed to be benefited. People less educated, and less rich in the world's goods than these, came also, and went away relieved. After a time Kneipp societies were founded all over Europe and even spread through America. These consisted of organizations of men and women who encouraged each other to keep up the Kneipp practices. With his death there has come a decline in interest in Kneipp methods. He, himself, was sure that his remedies and recommendations were the important curative factors. Now it has become clear that it was mainly his forceful personality, his power to lift patients above their ills, and enable them to use mental resources or vital forces that they could not use until encouraged by him with the thought that they would surely get better. In the atmosphere he thus created, they seemed to borrow something of his overmastering personality. It can not be too often repeated that this is the secret of the success of the great world healers. They do not transfer force to others, but they enable others to use their *own* forces more successfully.

An Ancient Healer.—Let us compare some of the details of the career of Father Kneipp with the story we have of one Aristides, who, as the result of dreams that came to him while practicing the cult of AEsculapius and the injunctions contained in these dreams, was cured of many ills, and afterward delivered a series of sacred orations. Aristides is one of the first of the large group of literary men, much interested in their own health and their own ills, whose writings have been preserved for us. He was intensely proud of the number and variety of his ills, and he was perhaps conceited about the curious ways in which some of them had been cured. Traveling in the winter time he caught a chill; then he suffered from earache and in the midst of a storm developed fever, asthma and toothache. Arrived in Rome, he had severe internal sufferings, shivering fits and want of breath. Treatment by the Roman {74} doctor only aggravated his sufferings. A stormy voyage home made him worse. When, at last, he arrived in Smyrna, the doctors gathered round him, and were astonished at the manifold nature of the disease. They could do nothing for him.

Suffering from all these ills (which remind one of a modern literary man who has got his mind on his stomach and his body on his mind), Aristides went to a number of the old temple hospitals and received suggestions in sleep from AEsculapius. These he has described in what are called his sacred orations. In them we have every phase of modern therapy that has the strong element of suggestion in it. Like Pfarrer Kneipp, he tried very cold baths and was benefited by them. Walking in the dewy grass in his bare feet was another recommendation that had come to him in a dream. Occasionally he would run rapidly for a considerable distance, and then when heated plunge into a cold bath. We have many complaints of his fever and stomach troubles. Mud-baths were also recommended to him and, of course, tried with benefit for a time. Sand baths later proved to be beneficial. For rheumatism a cold bath, after running almost naked in the cold north wind, proved

45

successful when other remedies failed. Aristides wrote out his experiences, and his writings had great influence over generations of patients and maintained the influence of the old Greek temples as cure houses long after the general acceptance of Christianity. As the result of his writings, no matter how bizarre a dream might be, some interpretation of a therapeutic nature was found from it.

Constancy of the Law of Personal Influence.—Indeed, there has apparently never been a time when some strong character, full of religious enthusiasm and of high purpose, strong in the confidence of men, has not succeeded in accomplishing wonderful curative results by the reassurance that comes from a renewal of faith in the goodness of Providence. There are, for instance, a number of stories which show John Wesley's power to help men to tap the reservoir of surplus energy that all of us have within us, but that somehow we do not succeed in making use of, unless some strong mental influence is brought to bear on us. Practically every religious man who has had the love and the veneration and the respect of those around him has succeeded in accomplishing the cures that many people in recent years have been prone to regard as rather novel phenomena in the history of psychology. Men like St. Philip Neri, St. Francis Xavier, and St. Francis of Assisi, and St. Bernard, have many stories told of them which show how much they were able to help fellow mortals by enabling them to make use, even in a physical way, of their own highest and best powers. Their lives show how much more they did.

Nor is this power confined to men. In nearly every century we have the story, also, of wonderfully strong women, leaders of their time, who inspired the profound confidence and veneration of those around them, and who were enabled, by their own strength of character, to help people physically as well as morally. The Life of St. Catherine of Siena is full of such instances. She spent her life mainly in caring for the sick and the distressed at the hospital in Siena, and the beautiful hospital there was completed largely as a monument to her. During her lifetime marvelous cures occurred that in many cases were evidently due to her power over the minds of people. The {75} life of St. Teresa has a number of similar examples, and Joan of Arc, in her lifetime, lifted many a dispirited man into vigorous strength because of her own abounding personality and the physical reaction which contact with her enthusiasm brought.

Modern Examples.—Nor did such occurrences come only in older and less sophisticated centuries than ours. John Wesley is close enough to our time to negative any such impression, but there are many other examples. There is Pastor Gassner, whose cures remind Prof. Münsterberg of the Emanuel movement at the present time, but there are also a number of strong, religious characters whose influence was exercised in the alleviation of physical ills during the nineteenth century. The name of Father Matthew, the Irish "Apostle of Temperance," as he was called, is mainly connected with wonderful cures of the worst forms of alcoholic addiction. Physicians know how difficult such cases are to cure, yet there are many thousands of what were apparently hopeless cases to Father Matthew's credit. It may be remarked that this is one of the ills that modern mental treatment claims most success with. Besides these morbid habits there are, however, other cases, told in detail, in which Father Matthew's influence enabled people to shake off headaches, to get rid of illusions, to overcome hysteria, and even to relieve other and much more physical affections. Animal magnetism was the subject of much thought in his lifetime (nineteenth century), so that it is not surprising that Mr. John Francis McGuire, a member of the English Parliament, who wrote Father Matthew's life in 1864, declared that "Father Matthew possessed in a large degree the power of animal magnetism, and great relief was afforded by him to people suffering from various affections; and in some cases I was satisfied that permanent good was effected by his administrations."

Another strong man of this same kind was Prince Alexander of Hohenlohe. Though a prince he had become a clergyman and spent his life in the service of the poor. Shortly after he became a priest he went through a great epidemic, fearlessly caring for his poor people, and as a consequence inspired them with so much confidence that ever after they came to him with all their ills. He was able to help, not only the poor, but also many of the nobility. Some of the things reported as accomplished through his influence show extraordinary power. His usual method was to endeavor to inspire in the people who came to him a faith in their cure, and then after a time the cure was actually accomplished.

During the recent troubles in Russia, attention was called to the fact that the famous Father John of Cronstadt, the hero of Bloody Sunday, was looked up to with so much respect and veneration that many people found themselves helped physically by contact with him. There are a number of interesting stories of cures of ills of various kinds, some of them exclusively mental, but many of them fundamentally physical, which took place as a consequence of the new spirit of hope infused into people because of their confidence in Father John. His subsequent history seems to indicate that this was evidently due to the forceful personality of the man rather than to any special religious influence. His influence was not limited to the ignorant masses in Russia, for some of the cures reported occurred in families of the better class, thoroughly capable of judging the character of the man apart from his religion.

{76}

SUCCESS IN HEALING

We have any number of examples, then, of this power of the healer in history. Over and over again we find that it was the personality of the man and the suggestive value of the means that he employed that enabled patients to cure themselves, that is, to use all the vital force which they had for curative purposes. This force had hitherto been inhibited by their own doubts of themselves and their doubts of the value of all ordinary means of cure which had been previously employed in their cases. This is the secret of the success of the healer, and this secret is much more valuable for therapeusis than any remedy which has come down to us from the olden time. It has, unfortunately, been neglected, and thus an important benefit to humanity has been lost. Now that we are able to review frankly and deliberately the conditions that obtained in the past, it is time to set about making use of this oldest secret in medicine, now no longer a secret, as a strong factor in the treatment not of disease but of patients.

Healers are at all times strong characters who are helpful to others because of their own superabundant strength. The world is made up of two classes of people, lifters and leaners, and the leaners constitute by far the larger class. Most men and women are the subjects of doubts and dreads and difficulties with regard to their health, and the more time they have for introspection, the more are they likely to suffer. Unable to overcome them by themselves, they need the help of others. What they need, above all, is the reassurance that a trained strong mind can give them. The exercise of this mental influence over them, is only what corresponds to leadership in all the affairs of life. Most people need to be led and to be guided. The place of the physician is that of guide and director. The family physician of the olden time had a precious amount of influence that accrued to him from his character, and it was used to magnificent purpose. Most of his drug treatment would be looked upon as quite absurd at the present time, yet he did a great good work by lifting people up to their own highest possibilities of resistive vitality. That means more for the conquest of disease, even now, in most cases, than any remedies we possess.

Often men do not realize how much their personal influence counts for. They think it is their method of treatment, or some new discovery in drugs or remedial measures, or some new phase of psychology they have hit upon, that is producing results. This makes it difficult to determine, in given cases, just what are the actual influences at work. Many men supposing themselves to be discoverers of some novel force, are merely exploiting that old-time influence of one mind over another that can be observed all down the centuries.

It is interesting to study the careers of men who thought they were employing on their patients some new psychological method, when all they were exploiting was the old-fashioned influence of suggestion from a stronger personality to a weaker. A dozen times in history hypnotism has been announced as a wonderful curative agent. At present no one thinks it so, but, on the contrary, if used frequently, we think that it is much more likely to do harm than good. We went through a phase of interest in hypnotism a quarter of {77} a century ago and there are now signs of the possibility of its return in another form. In recent years we have heard much of psycho-analysis, of dominant ideas, of the auto-suggestion that comes from this, and how much benefit can be conferred on the patient by removing such ideas or revealing their unfavorable influence and so neutralizing them.

The patients that come for treatment and to whom psychotherapy is of special benefit, are not, as a rule, those suffering from acute diseases or injuries, though even in these cases the attitude of mind is always an important therapeutic factor. The patients are mainly those suffering from chronic ailments, and from minor affections which, while they do not confine them to bed, often prove the source of such serious disturbance as makes them very miserable. The suffering in the world is out of all proportion to the actual disease. Many people who have little disease suffer a great deal, partly from over-sensitiveness, partly from concentration of mind on their ailments, and partly from such ignorance of whatever pathological condition is present that they grow discouraged and morbid over it. The rôle of psychotherapy is particularly to help patients of this kind. This does not mean that its main purpose is to treat imaginary disease, or disease which exists only in the mind of patients, for in nearly all of these cases there is a definite physical element in the affection. Even where the disease is quite imaginary, though that term has been so sadly abused that it is perhaps better to speak of affections as purely mental in origin, psychotherapy is important. As has been well said, a patient not having something physical the matter who thinks that there is something the matter, is in a worse state than one who really has something the matter. There are a great many such cases. If the principles of psychotherapy can relieve them and cure many of them, then it has a large place in human life.

In order that the individual patient may be benefited, a thorough understanding must be established between physician and patient. This must take on the character of a personal relationship. The patient must feel that the physician has a personal interest in him—that there are certain individual features in his ailment which make his case mean something much more than ordinary to his physician. Some physicians have the power to make their patients feel this personal relationship to a marked degree. They are the eminently successful practitioners of medicine. Their patients sound their praises, and even though they may not be distinguished scientists, they acquire a large practice. Some of them are thoroughly scientific men. All of us know them and, while we may not be able to understand just how it is done, we recognize their power.

CHAPTER XI

FAITH CURES

The series of phenomena that may be grouped under the term "faith cures" represent the oldest, the most frequent, universal, and constantly recurring examples of the influence of the mind over the body for the healing of ills. Whenever men have believed deeply and with conviction that some other being {78} was able to help them, many of their ills, or at least the conditions from which they suffered severely, have dropped from them and their complaints, real or imaginary have disappeared. This was true whether it was the touch of another human being supposed to have some wonderful power that was the agent, or some persuasion of the interference of the supernatural that appealed to them. Religions of all kinds have always had their cures, and one of the main reasons why men have accepted the various religions has nearly always been because of the weight of these healing phenomena. Apparently it does not matter how debased the form of religion may be, whether it is exercised by the medicine man of a savage tribe with methods that appeal only to barbarous instincts, or by a highly cultured priest of a form of religion appealing to the loftiest feeling and the profoundest intellectuality, cures take place whenever devotees have complete and absolute faith in the possibility of divine or supernatural interference in their behalf. The very earliest history that we have tells us of such cures, and the daily papers bring us reports of them from all quarters among the high and the low, the educated and the uneducated.

The phenomenon is universal and we come logically to the belief that the Supreme Being intended that confidence in Him, and above all recognition of the fact that somehow the world with all its ills has a meaning for good, should be rewarded. The argument that religion is a natural revelation should then apparently be extended to include also the thought of a healing power in connection with it. Many of the founders of religions that have meant much for uplift to mankind, have made healing a principal portion of their message to man—the proof of their missions. Indeed, there actually seems to be an extension of power, above what is natural, to those who in profound confidence in Divinity, turn to this source of strength for relief from the ills that flesh is heir to. In any of these cases, definite inquiry as to the significance of the particular incident is needed, and not any general principle of either acceptance or rejection. Faith healing is a fact, its meaning is of the greatest importance for psychotherapy and its phenomena deserve that specific study which alone can give any certainty in the matter.

Accessories of Faith Cures.—From the earliest dawn of history we have definite records of faith cures. It is true that they were usually associated with certain physical factors besides the mere act of the mind. In ancient Egypt the physicians were also priests, and while they administered various remedies, these had the added advantage of being supposed to be the result of divine inspiration, or suggestion, or to be in some way connected with religion. Among these men there were many strong personalities, contact with whom brought healing. Dreams and premonitions and hallucinations all had a definite place in their therapeutics because of their supposed connection with religion, or at least with the beings of another world. Spiritualism, itself a form of religion, is very old, and communications from spirits, real or supposed, were easily thought to have therapeutic significance.

Miracles.—In most cases of faith healing, faith acts through the definite conviction that there is to be a direct interference with the ordinary course of nature in the patient's behalf. Some of the evidence for such direct interference on the part of Providence is so strong as to carry conviction even to serious and judicious and judicial minds. When the circumstances are such {79} that an exception to the laws of nature would not involve an absurdity, there is no good reason why its occurrence should be absolutely put out of the question. It may well be urged that we know so little about the laws of nature that we cannot determine absolutely what are and what are not exceptions to those laws. There is in itself, however, no absurdity in what is called a miracle, and unless one is ready to reject Christianity entirely, or to declare it absolutely impossible that the God who made the universe should have any personal care for it, or above all any interest in particular individuals in it, their possibility must be admitted. The attitude of utter negation and incredulity often assumed at the present day is only a reflection of a certain ignorance of philosophy, and too great dependence on a superficial knowledge of physical science, so characteristic of narrowly trained minds. After a visit to Lourdes and careful study of *"La clinique de Lourdes,"* I am convinced that miracles happen there. There is more than natural power manifest.

In a great many cases it is easy to see that the agents involved in the faith cures, and the circumstances surrounding them, are quite unworthy of any supposition that the Deity should have interfered. Where there is anything irrational, or sordid, or eminently selfish about the faith-healing, then any appeal to a supposed interference from on high is absurd. Horace said in another matter, but it will bear application here: "Nec deus intersit nisi dignus vindice nodus." Do not let a god intervene unless there is a set of circumstances worthy of him. In many of the faith-healing phenomena claimed to be connected with religion there are a number of absurdities. It may be suggested that any one person must not set himself up as the judge of such absurdity. When it is evident, however, that the ailing are being exploited for the benefit of one or of a few persons, or when there are certain manifestly irrational conditions in the circumstances of healing, then it is fair to conclude that what we have to do with are only examples of healing by means of strong mental influence. But it would be quite wrong on account of these abuses to dismiss the whole subject of miracle healing as all imposture or merely mental influence.

The Royal Touch.—Probably the most interesting chapter in the history of faith cures is that of the touch of the King of England for scrofula, or, as it was known, the King's Evil. His touch was also supposed to be efficacious in epilepsy. English historians usually trace the origin of the custom to Edward the Confessor. Aubrey remarks that "the curing of the King's Evil by the touch of the King does much puzzle our philosophers, for whether our Kings were of the house of York or Lancaster, it did the cure for the most part."

Even the change of religion in the time of Henry VIII and Elizabeth made no difference. Some people who hesitated about submitting to Elizabeth as queen lost their hesitancy when they heard that the queen's touch was successful in curing. James I wanted to drop it, but was warned not to, as it was a prerogative of the crown with which he had no right to interfere. Charles I was particularly successful. Charles II, whose licentious life apparently would quite unfit him for the exercise of any such power, was perhaps the English king who devoted most time to healing. While he was in exile in the Netherlands, many people crossed over to the Low Countries in order to be touched by him, and they returned cured of many different diseases. {80} This effectively prepared the minds of many for his return. Under scrofula were included most of the wasting diseases, and under epilepsy many neurotic conditions as well as many organic disturbances. It is easy to understand how great was the room for the successful employment here of mental influence.

Queen Anne continued the practice, and many cures were reported in her time as late as the eighteenth century. William of Orange, when he ascended the throne with Mary, refused to believe that there was any special power for good in his touch. On one occasion he touched a person who came to him, saying as he did so: "God give you better health and more sense." In spite of this skeptical attitude his touch is said to have healed that particular person. In the next reign, however. Queen Anne resumed the practice, and Dr. Samuel Johnson, as a boy of five, was touched by her with some hundreds of others in 1712. No cure was effected in his case, but as the gruff old doctor lived to a round age in rather sturdy health, doubtless some would raise the question as to whether, if he had early scrofula, it was not greatly modified for the better.

The circumstances connected with the royal touch were all calculated to be curative of the affections for which this practice had a therapeutic reputation. There were certain times in the year, particularly in the spring after Easter, when the king touched people for their ills. Ordinarily preparations would be made for some time before, and the patients would have all the benefit of expectancy. Then there came the journey to London to the king's presence, and as it was usually known that these ailing folks were on their way to the king, they received particular care from the people of the towns through which they passed. Then came the day of the touch itself, and the presentation of a coin, the so-called coin of the king's touch, which the patient was supposed to preserve. On the way home they were once more subjects of solicitude, and they had the royal coin to assure them every now and then that they had been touched by the king's hand,

and that they ought to get well—for had not many others been thus cured? All this favorable suggestion, with the outing and the better food, was eminently calculated to cure the so-called scrofular conditions, under which term was grouped many vague forms of malnutrition and the milder epilepsies and pseudo epilepsies, for the cure of which the touch was famous.

Cramp Rings.—Scarcely less famous than the king's touch for nutritional and neurotic conditions were the "cramp rings," which were blessed by the Queens of England and were supposed to cure all sorts of cramps. The power attached to them for this form of ailment was similar to that which the king's touch had for scrofula or the king's evil. Cramps seemed to be the "queen's evil." Whenever a queen died there was a great demand for these rings, because no more could be obtained until a new queen was crowned. The efficiency of these and the cures which they performed can be readily understood. Many of the hysterical conditions within the abdomen are cramplike in character. Hysteria will imitate nearly every form of cramp, including even those due to gallstone and kidney calculus. Any strong mental influence will do more for hysterical pain than our strongest medicines. On the other hand, many of the cramplike conditions within the abdomen may be relieved by concentration of mind on some distracting thought, and feelings of discomfort in the intestines may thus be relieved.

{81}

Mental Healers.—When the king was absent from England during Cromwell's time, the touching for the king's evil was sadly missed. If Cromwell himself had announced that he would touch for the diseases that used to come to the king, a number of cures would undoubtedly have been reported. As it was, Greatrakes, the Irish soldier adventurer, dreamt that he was commissioned from on high to touch for the same diseases as formerly had gone to the king, and, having begun it, cures followed until probably many more came to him every year than usually went to the sovereign in the olden times. He worked at least as great a proportion of cures. Greatrakes had many imitators, some of them doubtless quite sincere, but they were people of more or less deranged intellect, the kind who easily get the idea that they are commissioned for some purpose that sets them above the common people. Indeed, the story of the mental healers is probably, more than anything else, a chapter in the history of insanity, and the power of those with delusions to lead others to share their delusions. This is not a slur upon human nature, and especially upon some of the inspirations and aspirations that lift it up to do great things, but a literal statement of the view of these phenomena that seems forced upon us by modern advances in the knowledge of the psychology of mental influence and of psychic contagion.

Most of the influence that was acquired by men who in the course of history claimed to have a heavenly mission has been due, as with healers heretofore referred to, to reputed cures made by them. Trace the story of this among the Eastern nations in the old time. The pseudo-Messiahs of the Jews always advanced as one evidence their healing power, but so did the founders of religions among all the other nations of antiquity. It must be borne in mind, however, that many of the queer religions of after times were founded by men who claimed to have a Messiahship, and put forth, as the evidence of a divine commission, their power to cure the afflicted. Sometimes the men who made these claims were good men. In many cases they were apparently self-deceived. Very often, however, they had no claim to goodness in the commonly accepted meaning of that term, for they counseled the violation of moral precepts, made exceptions, for their own benefit, to general laws, and exploited their followers for selfish reasons. Provided their followers had confidence in them, however, they continued to work cures, so that even reasonable people were likely to be led to the thought that there must be something supernatural about their activities. In every century there have been two or three men who have thus secured a following, and apparently healed many diseases.

The phenomena of faith-healing as the result of belief in the heavenly mission of special men, are as common now as at any time. Dr. Cutten in his "Three Thousand Years of Mental Healing" (*Scribners*, 1911) has a chapter on "Healers of the Nineteenth Century," which shows how many phenomena of faith-healing can be studied in recent generations. Some of the men and the women who are mentioned secured wide reputations throughout our own country.

These faith-healing movements have particularly affected the New England portion of our population, and many of our most prominent healers have been born in the New England States. Wherever the new cults flourished, it is usually found that some of the most prominent members are descendants of {82} the old New Englanders. It has been suggested that this is due to the gradual loss of belief in great religious truths by New Englanders, and a definite tendency toward reaction against this loss of the religious sense, which, as is usual with reactions, easily becomes exaggerated. From lack of belief they jump to excess of belief. Men without trust in Providence find the trials of life hard to bear, and they dread the development of physical ill so much that they exaggerate their feelings, or even create symptoms. Men are happier with the feeling that the supernatural powers surrounding them are interested in them directly and personally, and that somehow things, even in an incomprehensible world, are arranged, if not for the best, at least for such good as makes ills stepping-stones to new benefits. Whenever they are led far away from that thought, there is likely to be an exaggerated reaction back to it. The stronger minded apparently can get on without religion, but to the great mass of men a strong religious sense is needed to enable them to overcome the lack of self-confidence that is the root of dreads, doubts, difficulties of many kinds, and which is also the source of many symptoms as well as the cause of the exaggeration of many ailments.

As a rule, modern healers have been founders of new religions, or at least they have broken away from old-established sects, and have formed congregations for themselves. They have sprung up in every part of the country. East, North, South, West, and among all the differing nationalities of our population. We cannot console ourselves with the idea that they affect especially the foreigners, for the native-born people have proved to be quite as susceptible to them. These healers have, as a rule, abused the medical profession and the use of drugs, and have taught that disease, if it really existed at all, was from the devil: that what one needed, in order to secure relief from pains and ills, was faith in God—but always through *them*. Many of these men and women have probably been serious and earnest and have deceived themselves first. Most of them have undoubtedly been more or less disequilibrated, though they have practically all exhibited the power to accumulate large amounts of money from their followers. The people who have gone to them have not been the ignorant among our population, but particularly those who read the newspapers, and who look upon themselves as well informed. The intelligence of the disciples of these healers, as we ordinarily estimate intelligence, has been a little above the average, rather than below it.

Schlatter and Dowie.—Probably the most disillusioning phenomena with regard to the complacent idea that the diffusion of information prevents manifestations of superstition are stories of the healers Schlatter and Dowie. At the end of the nineteenth century both of them attracted widespread attention. Schlatter was probably not quite sane. He wandered through the deserted portions of the Southwest, hatless, unkempt, with clothing torn and without shoes. In July, 1895, he first attracted attention as a public healer in New Mexico. After a reputed forty-day fast he went to Denver, where people flocked from all parts of the country to him. Files of people formed—sometimes five or six thousand—to be touched, and healed, by him. His reputation was due to the cures that were reported. Dowie was another of these healers. Just at the beginning of the twentieth century he organized a great new church of his own, and announced himself as Elijah, the prophet, returned to life. {83} Nearly 20,000 persons are claimed to have been healed during the first ten years of his healing career. Toward the end of his life he declared that he treated, and cured, over 50,000 a year. An abundance of crutches, canes and every form of surgical appliance for the ailing hung on the walls of his church at Zion City, Chicago, left by people who, having been healed, had no further use for them.

{84}

GENERAL PSYCHOTHERAPEUTICS

SECTION II

GENERAL CONSIDERATIONS

CHAPTER I

INFLUENCE OF MIND ON BODY

The power of mind over body for the relief of symptoms has been recognized, not only by physicians, but by the generality of men at all times. Every one has had experiences of aches, or actual pains, or discomfort quite annoying while one is alone, but that disappear while in pleasant company or occupied in some absorbing occupation. Many a headache that was painful enough to disturb us seriously while we tried to apply ourselves to something of little interest, and became almost unbearable if we tried to do something disagreeable, and actually intolerable if the occupation of the moment was a drudgery, disappeared, at least for the time, when we turned to a pleasant game of cards or indulged in some other favorite pastime. Our relief was not, however, from an imaginary ill, for the symptoms usually reasserted themselves when we got through with the pleasant occupation, showing that they have been there all the time and that we have only turned our mind away from them, and hence have ceased to feel them. This is so familiar it seems almost too commonplace to repeat, yet it constitutes the special phenomenon that lies at the base of psychotherapeutics, or the mental healing of physical ills.

It is not alone the slighter, more or less negligible aches or pains, nor the vague discomforts that thus disappear when our attention is occupied, but even quite severe and otherwise unbearable pain may be modified to a great extent. A toothache that is bearable, though it nags at us constantly and never lets us forget its presence while we are occupied with many other things during the evening, may become a positive torture when we get to bed. This is not only because of physical conditions modifying the pain, for there seems no doubt that the warmth induced by the preliminaries for sleep and the bed-covering have a tendency to increase congestion, but it is mainly because as we doze off we are able, less and less, to inhibit our attention, or divert it from the pain that is present, and so this is emphasized until we have to do something for it or lose hours of sleep. This lack of inhibition, which characterizes the dozing hours, represents the state of mind in which people are who have no interest in their occupations, and who have ceased to find recreation in the ordinary pleasures of life, when pain of any kind comes to them.

Cabanis, at the beginning of the nineteenth century, under the title of {85} "The Influence of the Moral on the Physical," discusses what we would now call mental influence on the body. He says:

The great influence of what one may call the moral or mental on what may be called the physical is an incontestible fact. Examples without end confirm it every day. Every man capable of making observations finds proofs of it thousands of times in himself. Many physiologists and psychologists as well as moralists, have collected the evidence that brings out clearly this power of the intellectual operations and emotions on the different organs and the diverse functions of the living body. All of us could add new illustrations to these collections. Men who are rude and credulous talk of the effect of the imagination, and if they are not themselves its playthings and its victims, at least they know how to observe its effects In others.

As a matter of fact, the action of our organs can be in turn excited, suspended, or totally inhibited, according to the state of mind, the change of ideas, the affections and the emotions.

A vigorous, healthy man has just made a good meal. In the midst of the feeling of satisfaction which diffuses itself over all his body, his food is digested with energy and without any bother. The digestive juices perform their work steadily and without causing any annoyance. But let such a man receive some bad news; let some sudden emotion come to excite him, and especially to shock him into profound sadness, and at once his stomach and intestines cease to act upon the food which they inclose, or they at best perform their functions badly. The digestive juices, by which the food materials were gradually being dissolved, are suddenly stricken with inactivity. What might seem to be a stupor comes over the digestive tract, and while the nervous influence which determines digestion ceases entirely, that which tends to bring about the expulsion of material from the digestive tract may become more active and all the material contained in the digestive viscera may, in a short time, be expelled.

Relief in Severe Injuries.—Even extremely severe injuries, which inflict serious organic lesions that ordinarily would produce shock and collapse, quite apart from the pain induced, may at moments of excitement pass unnoticed. A soldier often does not know that he is wounded until the flow of blood calls his attention to it, or perhaps a friend points it out to him, or loss of blood causes him to faint. The prostrating effects of even fatal wounds may thus be overcome for a considerable time in the excitement of battle, or because of a supreme occupation by a surpassing sense of duty. There is the well-known story of the young corporal detailed to make a report to Napoleon at a very important crisis of one of his great battles, who made the report with such minute accuracy that it called forth a compliment from Bonaparte, for it involved a very special exercise of memory for details, yet who was actually on the verge of death when he delivered the message. As his duty was accomplished the Emperor, noticing his extreme pallor, said: "But you are wounded, my lad." The young soldier replied, as if, now that duty was done, the consciousness of his wound had just come to him, "No, Sire, I am killed," dropping dead at the Emperor's feet as he uttered the words.

In all of the great theater fires examples of this kind are recorded. A woman who barely escaped with her life from a theater fire some years ago had an ear torn off, very probably by some one grasping it in the crowd. She knew nothing of this until it was called to her attention after she got out of the theater, and then she promptly fainted from the pain and shock. Under such circumstances men walk with broken legs or limp even with dislocations, utterly unconscious that anything serious has happened to them. Men have been known to be unaware of a broken bone or even more serious conditions, {86} ordinarily quite painful and disabling, while laboring to help others in an accident.

Suppression of Reaction.—This side of the influence of the mind on the body is so interesting that its effects have often been noted and studied. While we do not quite understand the mechanism by which it accomplishes its marvels of anesthesia and even of motility under apparently impossible conditions, there is no doubt that severe pain may utterly fail to reach the consciousness, though the nervous system is uninterruptedly carrying the messages just as it did before. The lack of attention suppresses the ordinary effect upon the personality. Evidently the messages originate and are carried to the nerve centers, but find no attention available for them, and so pass unnoticed. The study of phases of this phenomenon of suppression of reaction forms a good basis for the use of mental influence, and shows its marvelous power to overcome disturbing physical factors.

Amputation Stump Aches.—An interesting example of the influence of mind over body, when circumstances favor its exercise or emphasize it, and at the same time a striking illustration of the potency of suggestion in the cure of discomfort, is found in the stories that are so common of cases of pains in amputation stumps. Any number of weird tales are told of men who complain of feeling cramps in the toes of an amputated limb after this portion of their body had been buried. The discomfort is common enough. In the special stories, however, the limbs have been dug up, the toes straightened out—according to the story, they were always found cramped in some way—and then the patient is at once restored to ease. In the good old times they probably believed in some direct connection between the straightening out of the toes of the amputated member and subsequent relief of pain. For us it is but an example of the power of suggestion. It is not the sort of suggestion that one likes to think of employing, though it has a certain dramatic quality which adds efficiency to suggestion.

The Mind and Motility.—We have spoken thus far almost exclusively of painful conditions as relieved by suggestion or mental influence, but disturbance of motor function may also be favorably affected. There are any number of cases on record in which patients who had been utterly unable to walk were restored to motility by a shock. Many such patients have, in the midst of the excitement of a fire, or the scare caused by the presence of a burglar, got up and walked quite as well as ever, though sometimes they have been for years previously confined to bed. The San Francisco earthquake is said to have exerted such an effect on a number of patients, and, while such unusual disturbances cannot often be provided for the cure of these ailments, there can be no doubt at all of the power of a shock to the mind to overcome functional incapacity that has resisted every possible form of treatment.

Ailments of this kind, which involve inability of the will to control, or rather to initiate, movements of the body, receive their best explanation on the neuron or neuroglia theory. (See the chapter on the Mechanism of Suggestion.) The central neurons become either quite separated from certain of the peripheral neurons, or at least the connections are not made with that nice adjustment necessary for the proper passage of nerve impulses. The shock communicated to the nervous system by fright is sufficient, however, to restore these connections, and consequently to enable the patient once more to exercise motor functions that have been in abeyance for some time.

{87}

Astasia-abasia.—Any one who has had to deal with the cases for which the French have invented the rather impressive Greek name of astasia-abasia—how much better it would be to call the condition simply what we know it to be, nervous inability to stand or walk!—appreciates how almost a miracle is needed to improve them. The incapacity for station or movement to which the disease owes its name is so complete in many cases, and the patients' lack of confidence in self so absolute, that no ordinary remedial measure is capable of doing

51

any good. These cases are usually a severe trial to the patients' friends. Indeed, the patients themselves maintain their nutrition so well and, as a rule, enjoy such good health, or, as has been said, enjoy their bad health so well, that it is for their attendants the physician feels most commiseration. Yet generally he is quite unable to do anything. It is certain, however, that with care and authoritative suggestion there would not need to be an earthquake, or a fire, or even a burglary, as a therapeutic measure in these cases. As a matter of fact, their cure when it occurs is always brought about by some strong mental influence.

Mental Influence on Organs.—*The Heart.*—The influence of mind can be noted on practically every organ of the body in a concrete way. It might be thought that the heart, the first living thing in the animal being, the pulsations of which begin before there is any sign of the nervous system, might be free from this influence. On the contrary, the heart is so readily affected by mental states that, taking effect for cause, the old popular, and even scientific idea with regard to it, was that it was the organ of the emotions. The heart is stimulated more by favoring circumstances, and suffers more from depression, than almost any other organ. In the melancholic states it usually beats less frequently and is sluggish. When individuals are tired out and the heart has become weakened in its action, new courage will first be noted as having its effect upon the heart action. As the whole muscular system is much influenced by the mental state and, as the control of the arterial system depends on the muscles in the arteries, it is easy to understand how much the general bodily condition may by mental influence be modified for good and ill.

Digestive Tract.—The stomach and intestines, though their functions might be presumed to be dependent entirely on physical conditions, are almost completely under the control of the mental state. At moments of depression, just after bad news has been received, the appetite is absent, or is very slight and digestion itself proceeds slowly and unsatisfactorily. On the other hand, when there is mental good feeling appetite is vigorous and digestion is usually quite capable of disposing of all that is eaten. If after a period of rejoicing in the midst of which food is taken abundantly bad news is brought, the mental influence on digestion can be seen very well. It is not alone that depression interferes with digestive processes, but apparently some favorable factors for digestion consequent upon the previous state of mind are withdrawn, and now what would have been a proper amount of food proves to be an excess and the digestive organs find it difficult to deal with it.

Nervous Inhibition.—The mind can actually inhibit certain of the involuntary processes of the body by thinking about them, and, above all, by dwelling on the thought that they are going wrong. This becomes easier to understand when we recall how, in the same way, we may disturb many habitual and more or less unconscious actions that we have grown accustomed to. There {88} are any number of actions requiring careful attention to details which become so habitual that we do not have to think of them at all. Not infrequently it happens when we try to explain to others how we do them, we disturb the facility of performance and have to repeat the acts several times before we succeed in performing successfully what a moment before we did without any thought. The story of the centipede who was asked how he walked with all his hundred legs, and who tried to describe how easy it was and got so mixed up that he was unable to move at all, is a whimsical symbol of conscious attention disturbing actions which go on quite well of themselves if only we do not allow ourselves to think consciously of each and every phase of them.

How much the mind may influence the body under certain conditions when trance-like states either assert themselves or are brought on, has often been noted. Lombroso in his book "After Death What?" says of Eusapia Paladino the "medium," that "when she is about to enter the trance state the frequency of the respiratory movements is lessened just as is the case with the Indian fakirs. Before the trance she will have been breathing eighteen to twenty times a minute; as the trance begins the number of respirations is gradually reduced to fifteen; when the trance is fully developed she breathes twelve times a minute or less. On the other hand, at the same time the heart beats increase. Normally her pulse is about seventy, but during the early trance stage it rises to ninety, while during the course of a deep trance, it may go as high even as one hundred and twenty. The passing from a more or less rigid state to that of active somnambulism is marked by yawns and sobs and spontaneous perspiration on the forehead." The observation of these phenomena is, of course, entirely apart from any theory one may hold with regard to mediumistic manifestations, and it provides evidence of mental influence that is very striking.

Imaginary Drug Effects.—Drug effects may be produced through the imagination. Physicians know that when patients are persuaded that certain effects are to be expected from a particular medicine, the effects may follow all the same in sensitive, imaginative people, if that medicine is replaced by some inert compound. Many a physician who has used bread pills or other placebos to replace a drug that he did not want the patient to acquire a habit for, has thus been able to allow good effects to go on without interruption, where the stoppage of medicine had previously interfered with the continuance of the good habit that had been formed. Very few physicians have not seen the effect of a hypodermic of pure water when a hypodermic of morphine is demanded, and when the patient would not sleep without having the hypodermic injection. Sleeping powders of various kinds can sometimes with distinct advantage be replaced by inert materials, because the patient's mind is fixed upon the idea of sleep coming after a certain time and they, in consequence, compose themselves to rest.

The Nerves and Tissues.—Cases occur where disturbances of vitality are noted as a consequence of nervous affections, though no gross lesion of the nervous system is demonstrated. Certain nervous people suffer from ulcerative conditions of their hands, and it is evident that in some the nervous impulses {89} that would ordinarily keep the skin surface in good, healthy condition are insufficient. Some people who use a typewriter have no difficulty at all with the ends of their fingers, while others are subject even to loss of skin or ulcerative conditions that make it almost impossible for them to go on with their work. In some this is true in the winter, in others in the summer. There are a number of skin conditions which are due to nervous factors and these evidently point to the influence of the central nervous system in keeping the forces of our body in such health, and resistive vitality, as will enable us to carry on whatever work we may wish to. This is, of course, a very individual matter. Some people chap very easily, some suffer from chilblains, or are frost-bitten even on slight exposure, and these peculiarities are evidently dependent on the intensity of the nervous impulses as well as the tone of the circulation, which itself depends on the nerves to a great extent.

It is evident that some of these disturbances are not enduring, but are only temporary and therefore are due to functional disturbances of the nervous system. Physicians often see hysterical patients suffering from intense pain that requires an injection of morphine, yet after a series of such incidents, the physician is able to give an injection of plain water and produce just as good an anodyne effect. In these cases some influence of the will is enough to correct the painful disturbances. Occasionally a single member loses sensation, or motion, or both, yet the fact that its nutrition does not suffer shows that there is only disturbance in the motor connections between it and the central nervous system and not in the sensory nor trophic tracts, and that this functional defect may be restored by some favorable influence.

Nerve Supply and Health.—We know now that when a part of the body is cut off from its connections with the central nervous system, it begins at once to be lowered in vitality and gradually tends to dissolution. This will be true in spite of the fact that the circulation continues as actively as before. It is not necessary, indeed, that the nerve trunk to a part should be cut, if it is sufficiently compressed its function is stopped and various disturbances begin to appear in the vitality of the part which it supplies. A typical example is to be seen in certain fractures of the clavicle, where a fragment presses on one of the nerves leading to the arm. After a time pains develop in the arm, a burning feeling is noticed in the skin, which becomes shiny and cold and of distinctly lowered vitality. Even a slight injury to the arm will now produce a serious ulcerative condition. There are evidently important influences for life that flow down through the nerves from the central nervous system, quite as important in their way as the nutritional elements which flow through the blood.

How these influences of the mind on the body are accomplished is a portion of that larger mystery of the influence of mind, or soul, or principle of life, on the material elements of which our body is composed. Why a man receives a shock of lightning or a charge of electricity at high voltage, and without a mark on his body or a change in any cell that we can make out, be dead, though he was living an instant before, is another of these mysteries too familiar for discussion. There is no change in the weight of the body, nothing physical has happened, but what was living matter with the power to accomplish the functions of living things is now simply dead material, unable to resist the invasion of saprophytic micro-organisms which will at once, {90} unhampered, proceed to tear it down, though the preceding moment resistive vitality was completely victorious. The mystery remains, but the mechanism of the influence can now at least be studied with much more satisfaction than was the case a few years ago.

Death and the Mind.—The extent to which the mind can be made to influence the body is apparently without limit. While the doctor is frequently disturbed by the fact that death occurs when there is no adequate physical reason for it, just because the patient has looked forward to it with complete preoccupation of mind, there is no doubt that occasionally death may be put off in the same way. We talk about people living on their wills. This is a literal expression of what actually occurs in certain cases. On the other hand, without the will to live, it is sometimes extremely difficult to keep alive patients who are in a run down condition. If one of an old married couple dies when the other is ill, we conceal the sad news very carefully from the survivor. This is done not alone to put off the shock and sorrow for a time, but because often, under such circumstances, there will be no will to live.

When the vital forces have run down to such a degree that it seems impossible, so far as ordinary medical reason goes, to look for anything but dissolution, patients still cling to life if there is some reason why they want to live until a definite time. It does not happen so much with the acute diseases but is quite common in chronic cases. Patients will live on expectant of seeing a friend who is known to be hurrying to them, or for some other purpose on which they very strongly set their minds. In the life of Professor William Stokes, the Irish physician, to whom we owe the introduction of the stethoscope to the English medical world, and many other important contributions to medicine, there is a striking story that illustrates this power of the will to maintain life until a definite moment.

An old pensioner, a patient of Stokes' in the Meath Hospital whose life was despaired of, and whose death was hourly expected, was one morning distressed and disappointed at observing that Stokes, who believing that the man was unconscious at the time, and that it was useless to attempt anything further as his condition was hopeless, was passing by his bed. The patient cried out: "Don't pass me by, your honor, you must keep me alive for four days." "We will keep you as long as we can, my poor fellow," answered Stokes; "but why for four days particularly?" "Because," said the other, "my pension will be due then, and I want the money for my wife and children; don't give me anything to sleep for if I sleep I'll die." On the third day after this, to the amazement of Stokes and all the class, the patient was still breathing. On the morning of the fourth day he was found still breathing and quite conscious, and on Stokes' coming into the ward, he saw the patient holding the certificate which required the physician's signature in his hand. On Stokes approaching him, the dying man gasped out. "Sign, sign!" This was done, the man sank back exhausted, and in a few minutes after crossed both hands over his breast and said, "The Lord have mercy on my soul," and then passed quietly away.

Dread and Death.—Dr. Laurent in his little book, "La Médecine des Âmes," has a story of similar kind but from a very different motive:

They brought to the prison infirmary one day an old burglar, an incorrigible offender, who was undergoing a long sentence. He was suffering from cancer of the stomach, and was already in a very advanced stage of the affection. The poor devil seemed to realize his condition very well, and felt that it was only a question of a short time until he should die. He had made up his mind to that with the {91} resignation which so often characterizes people of this kind. Only one thing put him out very much, and that was the fear of dying in prison.

"I know well that I have to pass in my checks," he said over and over again; "but I do not want to die here. I do not want to be cut up after I am dead."

53

He still had two months of his sentence to undergo. Every day the disease made notable progress. His cachexia became more profound. Life was passing from him drop by drop. At the end of five weeks he was scarcely more than a living skeleton. Every morning we expected to find him dead, or at least in his last agony. Nevertheless, every morning, by an effort, he was able to recognize me and a little life shone out of his sharp, small eyes that seemed like those of a bird of prey.

One morning he said to me: "Oh! you need not watch me. You shall not have my carcass. I do not want to die in prison. I shall not die here." He lived on till the end of his sentence. The morning of his freedom he said to me, "I told you that I did not want to die here, and that I would not die here."

By an effort of his will he aroused himself enough so that his friends were able to take him out of the prison. It was the last bit of energy he had, however. His will power was at an end. A few hours after his arrival in the house of his son he went off into a profound depression, and would not talk even to his own. Then his death agony came on, and he died that same evening. The strange and surprising struggle of this man against death, the marvelous force of physiological resistance which the fear of autopsy, if he died, gave him, struck me vividly at the time. What intimate and mysterious bond connects mind and matter that the one is able to react in so much energy upon the other. How wonderful to think that the fear, lest his abandoned body should be cut up, should actually keep body and mind together until after the danger of that dreaded event was passed.

Suggestion and Death.—On the other hand, there are many stories that show us how the giving up of hope of life seems to even hasten death. We have many stories of the death on the same day of husband and wife, or of brothers and sisters who thought very much of each other. Some of these are mere coincidences, but there are too many to be all explained on the score of coincidence. It seems clear that the living one, on hearing of the death of the other, feels that now there is nothing more to live for, and gives up the struggle. Hence the important rule in medical practice that a seriously ill patient should not be told of an accident, and, above all, of the death of a near relative.

On the other hand, strong expectation of death at a definite time, especially if accompanied by suggestions with some physical signs, may bring about actual dissolution. We have a number of well authenticated stories to illustrate this.

Renewal of Hope.—How much energy even the slightest hope may furnish, when apparently all power of effort is exhausted, is well illustrated by what happens to men who are lost at sea or in a desert. After the lapse of a certain length of time human nature seems utterly incapable of further effort and they sink down exhausted. The appearance of a light at a distance, a hail, any communication that gives them even the slightest hope will renew their energy and enable them to draw on unsuspected stores of vitality after the end seemed inevitable. It may be said that the exhaustion in these cases is more apparent than real, that discouragement prevents the release of even the energy that is present, and might be used under more favorable circumstances, but that is exactly the argument which favors the deliberate employment of psychotherapeutic motives to enable patients to use the energies which they possess. In the midst of disease, or the struggle for life, when vitality is {92} being sapped, hope is lost or obscured, just as it is when a man is alone in the desert or struggling far from help on the ocean. If we can prevent this discouragement from sapping his powers there will always be a prolongation of life, and often this will be sufficient to enable vital resistance to overcome exhausting disease.

Law of Reserve Energy.—Prof. William James called particular attention to the law of reserve energy which recent studies in psychology have emphasized. This law of reserve energy is a conclusion from certain facts which are very familiar to men and have been observed as long as the memory of man runs, yet the full significance of which has never been read quite aright. Applied to a very limited range of actions, it has been applied only half-heartedly in ordinary life, and to its full extent only under the pressure of absolute necessity. This law holds out the best promise to psychotherapy. It shows that there are reservoirs of surplus energy in man which, if they can be successfully tapped, present possibilities of resistance to fatigue and fatigue in many more ways than we used to think resembles disease. Besides, this law represents a very wonderful capacity for withstanding pains and aches and conquering disinclination that would otherwise seem impossible. If it can be made to apply to ordinary life as well as it does to extraordinary events, then the conscious deliberate use of psychotherapy or mental suggestion should prove to have wonderful remedial power. Prof. James said:

Everyone knows what it is to start a piece of work, either intellectual or muscular, feeling stale—or "cold," as an Adirondack guide once put it to me. And everybody knows what it is to warm up to his job. The process of warming up gets particularly striking in the phenomena known as second wind. On usual occasions we make a practice of stopping an occupation as soon as we meet the first effective layer (so to call it) of fatigue. We have then walked, played, or worked enough, so we desist. That amount of fatigue is an efficacious obstruction on this side of which our usual life is cast.

But if an unusual necessity forces us to press onward, a surprising thing occurs. The fatigue gets worse up to a certain critical point, when gradually it passes away, and we are fresher than before. We have evidently tapped a level of new energy, masked until then by the fatigue obstacle usually obeyed. There may be layer after layer of this experience. A third and fourth wind may supervene. Mental activity shows the phenomenon as well as physical, and in exceptional cases we may find, beyond the very extremity of fatigue distress, amounts of ease and power that we never dreamed ourselves to own—sources of strength habitually not taxed at all, because habitually we never push through the obstruction, never pass those early critical points.

He then states what has come to be called the law of reserve energy.

It is evident that our organism has stored up reserves of energy that are ordinarily not called upon, but that may be called upon; deeper and deeper strata of combustion or explosible material, discontinuously arranged, but ready for use for any one who probes so deep, and repairing themselves by rest as well as do the superficial strata.

There is, then, a marvelous reserve power in men and women which can be used in emergencies and in times of severe strain, to enable men and women to accomplish what looks impossible and which has often contradicted the prognosis of the physician. History is full of applications of this law which, however, does not come into action, unless especially called. Men and women {93} may die simply because they give up the struggle. Men and women who *will not give up* seem able to overcome severe illness that would take away ordinary people. It has often been said that tuberculosis takes only the quitters and that men of character constitute the typically favorable patients for tuberculosis sanatoria. Psychology is now getting at the explanation of many events that were formerly quite inexplicable. The science has come to recognize the reservoir of reserve energy in human nature which may be tapped under special favoring circumstances. The physicians of the past have often succeeded in tapping it deliberately as well as unconsciously. There is large room, however, for the further development of medicine along this line, to the great advantage of therapeutics and probably the most promising field at the present time in view in therapy lies in this direction. Hence the necessity for more deliberate conscious use of it in every possible suitable form.

CHAPTER II

UNFAVORABLE MENTAL INFLUENCE

Much as may be accomplished by psychotherapeutics through favorable mental influence—the modifying of the mental attitude towards disease, diversions of mind from aches and pains, concentration of attention on subjects apart from ailments—much more may be done by removing any unfavorable mental influence. This of itself produces symptoms either by interfering with normal processes through surveillance of them, or by so exaggerating, through attention to them, slight symptoms that may be present that patients are made quite miserable, though there is no adequate physical cause for their condition. Perhaps the most striking example that we have of unfavorable mental influence as productive of the persuasion that disease is present, is familiar to every physician who is close to medical students when they are first introduced to the symptoms of disease. It is almost a rule that certain members of the class immediately conclude that they are suffering from one or more of the symptoms which they are studying, and that, therefore, they must have the diseases with which the symptoms are associated. If at this time they walk on the shady side of a street on an autumn day and have a little shivery feeling, or when they get into the sun they feel a glow, these two very normal feelings are exaggerated into chilliness and fever, and the student has to go to his professor to have his mental malaria or typhoid treated. To the student, his symptoms are for the moment very real, and unless someone in whom he has confidence reassures him, his discomfort will probably continue for some time.

Pathological Suggestion.—In a word, suggestions of disease are much easier to take than is usually imagined, and if people read or hear much about diseases they are likely to jump to the conclusion that they are sufferers. Under present conditions there are many more such sinister suggestions put before people than used to be the case. The newspapers are constantly reporting curious cases and rare diseases, and usually those of absolutely unfavorable prognosis and inevitably fatal termination are particularly dilated on. Pathology has become a source of many sensations, until the community {94} generally has come to eke out the thrills of the day's news by reading about fatal diseases and fatal injuries, whenever murder and suicide sensations fail. As a consequence, many become persuaded that they are suffering from forms of disease of which they have not a symptom, and, not infrequently, the wonderful cures that are reported in the newspapers consist of nothing more than recoveries from these imaginary ills into which people have suggested themselves as the result of reading about morbid states.

A typical illustration of the power of the mind to influence the body unfavorably is recognized in many of the comic stories that have had a vogue in recent years. Their underlying thought is that if a man is only told often enough, and by a number of different people, that he does not look well, or if he is even asked a little solicitously as to whether he feels well or not, he will almost invariably begin to persuade himself that there must be something the matter with him. After a time, under the influence of this unfavorable suggestion, he begins to feel tired and is likely to think that he cannot go on with his work. When meal time comes his appetite fails him. A victim has been even known to go home and send for the doctor, persuaded that there is something the matter, simply because a series of friends, for a joke, or sometimes through a mistake, have insisted on asking him questions that called attention to his state of health. Few men are strong enough to stand the influence of unfavorable suggestion of this kind, if it is frequently repeated. More direct forms of suggestion of disease have, of course, even greater effects. Many a man goes to a quack only feeling a little out of sorts and wanting to reassure himself, but easily becomes persuaded that there is something serious the matter with him.

Unfavorable Suggestion in Ancient Times.—This unfavorable influence of the mind on the body, even to the extent of the production of disease by means of suggestion, was recognized by the ancients. They knew and wrote of hypochondriasis and, indeed, they invented the term. In many of these cases the seat of auto-suggestion is supposed to be the digestive organs and the localization of the discomfort is in the hypochondria, that is, in the upper abdominal region. The Grecian writers seemed to recognize clearly that the symptoms were the result of thinking over much about self and concentration of attention upon unfavorable suggestions.

Plato, in the "Republic," says:

In former days the guild of Asclepius did not practice our present system of medicine, which may be said, he declares, to educate diseases. He cites the example of Herodicus who, "being a trainer (of gymnasts) and himself of a sickly constitution, by a happy combination of training and doctoring, came to the invention of lingering death; for he had a mortal disease, which he perpetually tended, and, as recovery was out of question, he passed his entire life as a valetudinarian." Plato, finishing the description, makes us recognize the hypochondriac when he says: "He could do nothing but attend upon himself, and he was in constant torment whenever he departed in anything from his usual regimen, and so dying hard, by the help of science he struggled on to old age."

The picture of the neurasthenic, or hypochondriac, who has educated himself, as Plato says, into disease, is an interesting parallel to modern conditions in this matter.

Nowhere more than in this matter of knowledge of disease, can weight {95} be attached to Pope's dictum that a little knowledge is a dangerous thing, and that one must drink deep or touch not the Pierian Spring of medical information. The teaching of pathology under the guise of physiology, now so common in our schools, is likely to do more harm than good. Various pathological conditions, such as those produced by alcohol and tobacco, have been emphasized to such an extent as to produce unfavorable suggestions in the pupils' minds with regard to the untoward events that may happen in their insides, and the serious lasting pathological changes that may occur, though all unconsciously, to the sufferer as the result of indiscretions. The study of the morbid changes produced in the mucous membranes of the digestive tract by the use of stimulants, impresses ideas on the mind that are readily transferred to other abuses in eating or drinking. The rather vivid pictures and descriptions of the pathological conditions that may develop, become a portion of the acquired consciousness as to internal conditions, and this consciousness acts as an unfavorable suggestive factor whenever there are any digestive symptoms.

Bacteriphobia.—The development of bacteriology has had a similar effect, especially because periodicals and newspapers like to take up only the sensational side of biological discoveries. Most physicians who have had anything to do with nervous diseases have seen cases of misophobia, the fear of dirt, which in our day has taken on the special character of fear of microbes. Those who are sensitive to the possibility of contamination learn of the almost sacrificial precautions that surgeons take to avoid wound infection, and conclude that practically everything they handle must fairly reek with microbes. They hesitate about touching the door knob or latch, and invent all sorts of excuses to wait for a moment outside the door in order to have someone else open it. Especially are they timorous about touching the door knobs of a physician's residence, or the chairs in his waiting room, or even to shake hands with him. Hospital walls and doors become an abomination to them. These cases emphasize how much of unfavorable suggestion there has been in the present spread of popular knowledge with regard to microbes.

A writer on popular science once said that every time we spread a piece of bread of the size of the hand with butter, we scatter over its surface as many microbes as there are inhabitants in the United States. The expression has gone the rounds, producing its effect on sensitive people, occasionally causing even a disgust for so important an article of diet as butter, more often giving rise to an extreme sensitiveness with regard to any special savor that butter may have, and it may have many according to the prevailing food of the cow. There has been much emphasis laid on the potentialities for harm of the microbes, and very little on the important part which they play in the production of many forms of food materials. Most people know and dread the fact that microbes produce disease. Very few seem to realize that while we know many thousands of different kinds of microbes, scarcely more than a score of them are known to be seriously pathogenic, while all the others are either indifferent or, as we know of very many, are actually benefactors of mankind.

People have heard much of the flora of the digestive tract, until they have come to think with anxiety of the almost infinite number and multitudinous variety of the minute plant life that finds a habitat in the human intestine. Most people think that all of these are, in tendency at least, {96} harmful, and are only kept from being positively dangerous by the overwhelming vital activity of the mucous membrane and the secretions which keep them from exerting their malign activity. Very few appreciate the fact that the intestinal flora, far from being a disturbing factor, are often an aid to digestion, and that the equilibrium established among them favors many biological and chemical processes which help in the preparation of food and in the breaking up of waste products that might be dangerous if reabsorbed during their stay in the intestinal tract. Microbes we have always with us and always will have, and men have lived to round old age, not only in spite of them, but very probably partially because of them. They are part of that beneficent mystery of nature of which as yet, in spite of scientific progress, we know comparatively little.

Opposing Favorable Suggestion,—A recent striking change of sentiment with regard to one form of food material furnishes a good example of how little we know about the real effect of bacterial life within the digestive tract. There was a time, not so long since, when sour milk was supposed to be especially harmful, or at least only likely to do good to those of particularly strong digestive vitality. Metchnikoff's work on the influence of sour milk on the digestive tract, however, has brought a complete reversal of opinion in this matter. Now most physicians are convinced that the bacillus of sour milk, acts in the intestinal tract to inhibit the reproduction and growth of other, and possibly more disturbing, bacterial agents. Sour milk is looked upon as one of the things that, by neutralizing certain unfortunate bacterial processes in the digestive tract, lead to longevity. There seems no doubt at all, that those who consume a great deal of it, live longer lives than the average, and many old men have taken to its use with a consequent amelioration of digestive annoyances.

The popularization of bacteriology, then, has been one of those moments of unfavorable suggestion that have affected a large number of people. Such influences do not mean much for people of phlegmatic temperament. For others, however, they have a weighty significance and make every symptom, or more properly every sensation, that is at all unusual in the digestive tract, seem of ominous import. Certain sensations inevitably accompany digestion. The peristaltic movements are usually said to be unfelt, but even a slight exaggeration brings them into the sphere of sensation. Where attention is given to the abdominal region and its contents, feelings that ordinarily are not noticed at all come to be perceived. With the unfavorable suggestion derived from the unfortunate diffusion of a superficial knowledge of pathology and of bacteriology instead of hygiene and the science of beneficent microbiology, these feelings produce a bad effect upon the individual.

Familiar Examples of Unfavorable Suggestion.—There are many familiar examples of the discomfort that may be produced by the mental persuasion that something will disagree with us, or that certain feelings have a significance quite beyond that which ought to be attributed to them. Everyone knows how qualmy may be the feeling produced by being told that something eaten with a relish contained some unusual material, or was cooked under unclean conditions. Food that agrees quite well with people, so long as they do not know too much about it, often fails to be beneficial after they see how it has been prepared. It is often said that people would not relish the food {97} placed before them if they were aware how lacking in cleanliness was the place of its preparation, and how negligent those who had charge of it. Occasionally a peep at the kitchen of a boarding house effectually takes away appetite, or disturbs the equanimity with which food must be taken, if there is to be that undisturbed digestion which makes for healthy nutrition.

It is, indeed, with regard to digestion that the influence of the mind on the body, favorable as well as unfavorable is, perhaps, most effectively exercised. Unfortunately the unfavorable influence is even more pronounced than its opposite. Some people are much more sensitive than others in this respect, and even the thought of certain defects in the preparation of their food seriously disturbs them. Everyone has had the experience of seeing sensitive persons leave the table because some one insisted on telling a nauseating tale. Anyone who has seen the effect of talking of blood sausage or fried brains with black butter sauce at a table on shipboard, when some practical joker was exercising his supposed wit, knows how much the imagination can disturb, not only appetite but digestion. The attitude of mind means much, and especially are such unfavorable suggestions likely to produce serious effects in inhibiting digestion.

Suggestion and Seasickness.—Seasickness illustrates the place of unfavorable suggestion in digestion. The nausea, consequent upon the movement of a vessel at sea, is due to a disturbance of the circulation within the skull, and particularly of the circulation in the semi-circular canals. The organ of direction of the body is disturbed by the over-function demanded of it, consequent upon the continuous movement of the vessel. This is, however, only a predisposing element. A strong additional factor is the firm persuasion many people have that they will suffer from nausea and seasickness, and the unfavorable expectancy thus aroused. Most people have to give their dole to Neptune. Those who for weeks before have been expecting and dreading it usually pay a heavy tribute. Probably the best remedy for seasickness is the suggestion that there is no necessity for losing more than a meal or two, if even that much, provided there is simplicity of diet and proper predisposition of body by gentle opening of the bowels, and lack of the over-feeding that sometimes comes from dinners given before departure. I have known many people who, after suffering severely not in one but in many voyages, have, by means as simple as this, been saved from days of seasickness even in rough weather.

Most of the cures for seasickness that have been suggested have depended principally on the suggestive element. For instance, there is no doubt that many people are relieved by wearing dark glasses, and this remedy does good for train sickness and other afflictions of a similar kind. There is, however, no good physical reason why wearing dark glasses should help except through their constant physical suggestion. A simple remedy that has helped many through seasickness is the wearing of a sheet of glazed paper, usually some heavy writing-paper, immediately over the skin of the abdominal region. This of itself has no physical effect, but the sensation of its presence constantly obtrudes itself, and by making people feel that they must be better because a great many other people have declared that they were bettered by this remedy, they actually suffer less from nausea and vomiting. Many of the internal remedies employed for seasickness are directed to the stomach and intestines. {98} As the seat of the difficulty is not here but within the skull, the reputation which these remedies have acquired has been due largely to the suggestive effect of taking them rather than to any physical qualities they possessed, though of course they have served to set at rest stomachs disturbed by unfavorable expectancy.

Disease Groups and Suggestion.—Labeling groups of ailments with a single term gives rise to many unfortunate conclusions and dreads with regard to what a particular condition really is. The word "indigestion" is commonly used for any stomach discomfort or disturbance, especially that occurring after eating, from the slight distress because too much has been eaten, or the uncomfortable feeling of fullness because too much liquid has been taken, or the discomfort due to an unsuitable mixture of food materials, to such serious conditions as develop when there is motor insufficiency of the stomach, followed by dilatation, with delay of the food for long periods and with consequent fermentation, distress and bad breath. Whenever the word "indigestion" is mentioned, the patient may think of the worst cases that he has seen or heard of with this label, and concludes that while his ailment may not be very serious just now, it is only a question of time until it becomes so, and that unless he can get rid of his uncomfortable feeling he is destined to have one of the forms of "indigestion" that are productive of such serious discomfort, with probably ever increasing torment, until some fatal complication develops. The initial symptoms of gastric ulcer and cancer have been labeled indigestion, and people, often recalling the serious consequences that followed in such cases, fear for themselves.

Fearing the Worst.—This looseness of terms is noted with regard to many other forms of disease. Rheumatism calls up the picture of advanced arthritis deformans, with the awful deformed joints and bed-riddenness, which should not bear the term rheumatism at all, but which the patient has heard called so. Catarrh is the simplest of inflammatory processes, meaning merely an increase of secretion, functional in character and without any serious disturbance of an organic character beneath it, but many people have heard the foul-smelling ozena called catarrh, at least popularly, and so the mental picture of such a repulsive progressive process as beginning in them is suggested. It is important, therefore, when using words that have such wide connotation as these, to explain exactly what is meant, and perhaps, better still, not to use the words, but to employ some more specific term that does not carry a cloud of dreads with it. Indigestion can be a very simple passing set of symptoms, but once certain people get the notion that they are troubled with indigestion, their minds dwell on it to such an extent that they are likely to limit their eating more than they should, and to disturb digestive processes by thinking about them and using up in worry nervous energy that should be allowed to flow down to actuate digestion.

So-called Incurability.—Patients are likely to hear entirely too much of the incurability of disease. To the doctor and patient this word, incurability, often has an entirely different meaning. The doctor means only that the diseased tissues cannot be restored to their previous condition by any of our known remedies, and that the effects of the deterioration are likely to be felt to some degree for the rest of the patient's life. To the patient it means, as a rule, not only that the doctor can do nothing for him, which is usually {99} quite untrue, for much can be done for his symptoms even though the underlying disease may be intractable, but also that the symptoms are to grow constantly worse. This is often quite without foundation, for nature's compensatory powers are very wonderful and seldom fail to afford relief. In a great many cases fatal termination comes, not from the original affection, but through intercurrent disease. Above all, incurable means to many patients that finally the victim is to become more and more subject to the pains and ills of his "incurable" ailment until he becomes perhaps a pitiable object. Incurability, when we recall that patients are so likely to mistranslate this term in the way indicated, must be a word little used. Etymologically it is never true, for *cura* means care, and we can always care for and relieve the patient. In every chronic case there is room for hope of much relief through accustomedness, various remedies, nature's compensatory methods, and, above all, the modification of the state of mind.

There is probably no incurable disease that is ever quite as serious as it is pictured by its victim when he first hears this word pronounced. When we recall the chances of life, and that in any given case, almost as a rule, the patient will live to hear of the deaths of men and women who were in perfect good health when his ailment was pronounced incurable, there is much of consolation to be derived from conditions as they are. It seldom happens that a physician sees a sufferer from tuberculosis, whose affection is running a somewhat chronic course, without being able to find out that since the first symptoms of the disease manifested itself, one or more of the patient's near relatives have died because of exposure incident to their abounding health. Pneumonia, appendicitis, typhoid fever, accidents of various kinds, take off the healthy relatives, while the tuberculous patient, constantly obliged to care for his health, lives on, and often is able to accomplish a good deal of work. It is important to impress facts of this kind upon these "incurable" cases, for they represent the light in the desert, or the shout, or the whistle at sea, that give renewed energy when nature seems about to give up the struggle.

Thinking Health.—Hudson in "The Law of Mental Medicine" suggests that we should think health and talk health on all suitable occasions, remembering that under the law of suggestion health, as well as disease, may be made contagious. This expression probably represents an important element for the prophylaxis of disease under all conditions. Under present conditions people talk entirely too much about disease and have too many suggestions of pathological possibilities constantly thrown around them by our newspapers, our magazines and by popular lecturers as well as by our free public libraries. People have learned to think and talk disease rather than health. This predisposes them to exaggerate the significance of their feelings, if it does not actually, on occasion, lower their resistive vitality because of solicitude. The medical student torments himself with the thought that he is suffering from the diseases that he studies, and we cannot expect that the general public will be even as sensible as he is in this matter. On the contrary, people generally are much more liable to exaggerate the significance of their feelings, hence the necessity for healthy suggestions rather than innuendoes of disease.

In recent years, to paraphrase Plato's expression, people are much more {100} inclined to educate themselves in disease than in health. The result has been a storehouse of unfavorable suggestion, from which ideas are constantly being taken to make whatever symptoms that may be present seem unduly important. Consequently people look for the worst, and suggest themselves into conditions where not only are they exaggerating their symptoms, but they are absolutely preventing the flowing down of such nervous impulses as will enable them to overcome affections that are present. Whenever anything turns up that lessens their tendency to unfavorable auto-suggestion, their health improves. Hence the taking, with confidence, of any quack medicine, no matter what its constituents, cures them; hence the success of the numerous and very varied forms of mental treatment. New Thought, Eddyism, osteopathy, and the like, attain most of their successes because of the removal of unfavorable suggestions, and the setting up in their stead of favorable suggestion. In psychotherapy the first duty of the physician is to undo all the unfavorable suggestion at work, and, if successful in that, great therapeutic triumphs are possible.

CHAPTER III

THE INFLUENCE OF BODY ON MIND

While trying to take advantage of the influence of the mind on the body for therapeutics, it is important to remember that the body has a great influence on the mind. There are many states of mind that are dependent on states of body, and that can be modified only by first modifying the body. Body changes can at least greatly help. In order to use the mind in the therapeutics of conditions in which it would help in the awakening of such vitality as is necessary for the cure, particularly of many of the chronic affections, it is necessary first to dispose the body so that it will not constantly be adding to, or at least emphasizing, an unfavorable state of mind. For this purpose it is important to study definitely and practically the influence that various attitudes, expressions and external manifestations may have in changing the internal feelings. This factor seems trivial when viewed from the standpoint of health, but it is one of the trifles that are very helpful in the predisposition of the patient to get better. Alteratives in medicine, while we have not been able to say just what their effect was, have done much for us, and the influence of body on mind is just such an alterative.

Even those who have insisted most strenuously on the independence of mind from body have always recognized not only the influence of the mind on the body, but also of the body on the mind. Perhaps the most familiar example of this is the well-known liability to dream after eating things that disturb digestion and seem to interfere, probably by congestive tendencies, with the circulation of the brain during sleep. It has always been recognized that mental operations are sluggish for some time after eating, and that a period of depression is likely to follow any excess. The Romans feared the consequences of indigestion so much that, occasionally after they had surfeited themselves with rich food, they took such direct mechanical means as a feather or a finger in the throat to relieve their overloaded stomach, in order that they {101} might not suffer the after consequences, but especially the depression and irritability of mind.

Disposition and Digestion.—The relation of the body to the mind in many other besides the purely animal digestive functions has always been realized. It has always been felt that the disposition of an individual depended to a great extent on his nutrition. Men were not usually approached for favors before their meals, and especially after a long fast, but, as far as possible, requests were made shortly after meals. It has always been recognized that the best time for men to get together in council is, at least so far as amiability goes, shortly after meals. Tiredness was also felt to be an important element in affecting the mind. The tired man, even though he may be hungry, can only eat a hearty meal at the risk of serious disturbance of digestion, for, as a consequence of the fatigue of the body being communicated to the mind, the mental influence which predisposes to good digestion is lacking, and it is easy for serious digestive disturbances to be set up. In a word, body and mind are inextricably involved in all that concerns not only health but good feeling, and these two terms are practically convertible.

Feeling and Expression.—In nothing is the influence of the body on the mind more clear than in the influence of expression upon the disposition. Actors know that if they want to well express a certain feeling, they must arouse that feeling deeply, and the easiest, surest and most direct method of doing so is to fix the features in the expressions that would ordinarily indicate the presence within of these feelings. If we insist on putting our features into the shape which ordinarily expresses sadness, that will be reflected internally, and we shall become as sad as our expression. On the other hand, if the features are drawn, even by force of will, into the state that ordinarily expresses joy or lightness of heart, we shall be tempted more and more to feel that way, until at last even internal melancholy may be dissipated. In the oldest book in the world, "The Instruction of Ptah Hotep," written about 3,000 years before Christ, the old father giving advice to his sons says: "Let thy face be bright what time thou livest," and the literature of every time since then emphasizes the same idea.

This influence of the expression on the mind is an extremely important element in psychotherapy. Men and women must be taught to shake off inner sadness, and over-occupation of mind, by training their facial muscles of expression as far as possible to occupy positions expressive of good feeling, but above all not to let them be fixed in positions indicative of ill feeling. It makes a great difference for the mental state whether a man has the corners of his mouth drawn down or up, or whether they are pulled straight across the face to give the severe, austere expression that some people seem to cultivate. If the corners of the mouth are allowed to droop the glumness and depression is likely to grow deeper. If the lips are curled upward and smile, even though it may be a forced smile, the inner feeling will soon yield to it. Actors are able to counterfeit the reality, but much more than this, as we have said, they realize that, by imitating the externals of the feeling, they awaken the feeling itself within them. This is true for anger and loathing, and for many of the more serious dispositions as well as for those that might be thought more superficial, and hence more controlled by the external muscles.

{102}

The Mouth.—It is interesting to realize how different are the expressions of the face as a consequence merely of control of the sphincter of the mouth and its associated muscles. Physiological psychologists have often called attention to the fact that only a few lines are necessary to picture the characteristic human expressions of sadness, joy and severity. If a little droop is given to the line that represents the lips, melancholy is at once expressed, while the upward curve expresses joy, and the straight line severity. These types of human expression are easy to control, and the internal effect of each is soon felt where there is deliberate, or indeliberate, perseverance in its maintenance.

Fig. 1.

Fig. 1. Three abstract faces.

The Eyes.—A typical example of the influence of the mind on the body is to be found in the use of the eye muscles, especially the oblique muscles. Of definite and important use for many purposes, they are especially employed to attract attention by means of the eyes. Coquetry has used them to express various phases of sex attraction. We all know the picture of the young woman who "makes eyes." It is interesting, however, to set solemn people imitating these exercises of the oblique eye muscles. For most people it is practically impossible to use these muscles without a corresponding quasi-demure setting of the features, commonly associated with those who use them most. There is even likely to be a certain attitude of mind aroused corresponding to the setting of the features in a particular way. While this is true for almost any other expressive state of the countenance, it is not so easy to demonstrate as is this.

The use of the superior recti muscles has also a definite effect upon the disposition. One of the pleasures of walking in a well-kept forest where the trees meet high overhead, is that the eyes are inevitably attracted upward to range among them, and there is a corresponding

59

elevation of feeling. Bernard Shaw once said that it was impossible to enter a Gothic church without an elevation of the spirit, because the eyes were surely attracted upward by the height of the nave, and a corresponding uplift of feeling ensued. During a period of glumness it is apparently impossible to keep the eyes raised. People who are depressed and "cast down," as the expression is, invariably keep their eyes downward, and just as soon as a man "looks up and not down" there is a lifting of the depression. Even such apparently trivial muscular actions as this may influence the mind, and thus react upon the physical system generally.

Wrinkles.—Many influences of the body on the mind group themselves in the muscles of expression around the eyes. Wrinkles, for instance, are originally a habit of mind, and then the emphasis of this, in the muscles of the face, is reflected back to deepen still further the dejection or nervous unrest that originally causes them. It is surprising to see what an influence it has on patients who go round much with wrinkled foreheads, to have them give over the practice and discipline themselves to appear with uncorrugated superciliary muscles. St. Ignatius Loyola, the founder of the Jesuits, and one of {103} the wisest managers of men that ever lived, has emphasized in one of his rules that "wrinkles on the forehead and still more on the nose" are a sign of interior disquiet and must not be seen. He realized that the interior feelings could be influenced by suggestion at least, by having those who indulged in wrinkles keep their foreheads and noses smooth. Most of the expression of the face is concerned with the eyebrows and neighboring regions, and people should occasionally be asked to look at themselves in the glass, so as to rid themselves of habits of expression indicative of a disturbed mind, for this will do much to help to relieve the mental disturbance.

Attitudes and the Mind.—With regard to the influence of the body on the mind, and the stimulating mental reaction that follows even a pose of well-being and good feeling, perhaps nothing affords more striking evidence than the effect of assuming the expressions and attitudes usually associated with various states of mind and then noting the results. If a man throws his shoulders back, and takes in long breaths of air, expanding his chest and stimulating his circulation, his whole body as well as his mind feels the effect. A slow walk with bowed shoulders and head, while one moodily turns over all the possibilities for ill in the life around, does very little good, while a brisk walk with head thrown back, shoulders erect, brings a man home with mind and body both ready to throw off temporary obstacles of all kinds, and in addition to the fact that the mental depression has disappeared, to some extent at least, all the physical functions will be accomplished better than before.

Tears and Feeling.—Some of the usual translations of the meaning of external expressions are not justified by what we know of their actual purpose and effects. For instance, tears are supposed to be a sign of deep grief. Except in the very young they are not, as a rule, to be thus understood. As we grow older they are much more frequently a sign of deep feeling that is usually quite pleasurable. It is almost impossible for a human being to be touched deeply without a glistening of the eyes that readily runs over into tears. A mother who is proud of something that her children have done is quite sure to have tears in her eyes. If she is present at a successful musical or dramatic performance given by a son or a daughter, especially where there is something of a triumph for them, she is sure to have tears in her eyes. There are few mothers who fail to be moved in this way when their children take prizes, or when some one writes to tell them how well their children are doing. Tears, indeed, far from being a sign of sadness, usually in adults indicate profound joy.

Tears, then, instead of being discouraged, should rather be encouraged, unless when indulged in to excess. We realize how trying to health and strength is the stony grief that does not melt into tears. The mother who faints over the sudden death of her child, and who wakes to silent consciousness, is in a dangerous condition until the solace of tears comes to her. Until there are tears, we fear for the effect upon her mind of the grief. The sufferer from melancholia is sad, but a good outburst of tears will, indeed, often mean the end of a prolonged period of melancholia. In the trials of life tears are a consolation rather than an addition to sorrow. In the olden times men wept as well as women, and Homer's heroes thought it not at all beneath their dignity to be seen in tears. Over and over again, the physician learns that while people have been going to "shows" that were supposed to make them {104} laugh and so divert their minds, the best possible effect is derived not from trivial laughter, but from a serious play that touches the heart deeply and makes all who go to it melt a little. Many nervous patients never feel better than after they have had a good quiet cry.

The influence of the serious things of life in producing favorable states of mind is not sufficiently appreciated, or at least has come to be neglected in our day. There is a seeking far and wide for pleasure and diversion that should be obtained near home, through the simple joys of domestic life or intimate contact with others who need us in some way. As has been well said, it is not far-fetched pleasure, but simple joys that are more needed in our time. Nothing so enables the patient to get his, and above all her, mind off self as care for others. This must be expressed, however, in external acts accomplished by ourselves for others to have any deep effect. Doing things for other people deepens the feeling of sympathy, and so makes the mind much more ready to respond to increase of these feelings so profoundly as to displace selfish considerations. Exercise is valuable, but exercise undertaken for a worthy motive, constantly before the mind during the time it is taken, means ever so much more in awakening all the sources of energy that there are in men and women to make life worth living for themselves and others.

Application of Principles.—The best possible source of relief from that combination of mental despondency, and the lack of bodily vitality which so often accompanies it, and which, if not interrupted, may lead to a serious breakdown of mental health, is the discipline of work; above all, work for the benefit, of others, to which one forces one's self gradually but persistently, not with, long intervals, but day after day. The discipline of the asylum and the sanatorium is probably the most efficient curative agent when these cases are at their worst. When the symptoms are beginning, a discipline of a milder character, yet resembling that of the institution, but appealing to higher motives and leading to frequently repeated actions for the benefit of others, will undoubtedly do much to prevent worse developments or make the future condition of the patient less serious than it would otherwise be. Undoubtedly some of the old monastic regulations were efficient in preventing the more serious developments of despondency when the danger to himself and others of the melancholic was not so well recognized as at present.

Laughing Cures.—Every now and then the newspapers announce that some physician has invented a laughing cure, or a smiling cure, or something of the kind. Sometimes these reports are founded on actual occurrences; oftener, perhaps, they are the invention of a reporter suffering from a dearth of news. There is, however, no doubt that a smiling cure will do much to make people, even those who have serious reasons to be depressed, feel better. Every physician knows that if melancholic patients of the milder type can be amused quietly, their depression is modified for the better. Accordingly, we advise them to see farces or lively comedy, and we try to pick out cheerful nurses for them. The depression consequent upon some serious illness can be better relieved in this way than by any tonics or stimulants. For the depression, for instance, that so often follows a stroke of apoplexy, the employment of a nurse with a good human sense of humor and a large sympathy with the humorous side of things in life will do more to arouse a man from the lethargy into which he settles than almost anything else.

{105}

With regard to laughing, there is, of course, another element that must be remembered. A hearty laugh moves the diaphragm up and down vigorously, empties and ventilates the lungs, stimulates the heart mechanically by its action upon the intra-thoracic viscera, and is one of the best tonics that we have for the circulation in the abdominal cavity, and probably also for the important nervous mechanisms centered there. Its action upon the lungs is readily recognized. Its influence upon the heart is usually not so much thought of, but deserves even a more prominent place. It is now well known that when patients have gone into coma or the apneic condition that sometimes follows shock, or the administration of an anesthetic, when the heart ceases to beat, the only effectual means of resuscitation is by directly irritating the organ. It has been suggested that if the abdominal cavity is open the surgeon's hands should be passed up and should squeeze the heart through the diaphragm. It has even been proclaimed that tapping on the chest vigorously over the precordium may arouse a heart that has for the moment stopped beating. It is easy to understand, then, that a hearty laugh, by stirring up all the intra-thoracic viscera, stimulates the heart mechanically and sets it beating more vigorously than before. This is one of the reasons why people feel so well after a hearty laugh.

Even slight swallows of water act as a distinct heart stimulant. When people have fainted, a succession of swallows of water, each of them acting as a heart tonic, is one of the best methods that we have of stimulating the heart's action. It is usually said that this action is a consequence of the reflex from the terminal filaments of the vagus nerve running back and reflected down again to the heart. To me it has always seemed that the swallowing action had a direct mechanical effect upon the heart, because the esophagus passes so close to it in the thoracic cavity.

Man is the only animal that laughs, and, as the old philosophers point out, he might very well be defined as *animal risibile* with just as much truth as by the words *animal rationale*. It requires reason in order to have a sense of humor. The higher the reason, the more the humor. Peasants and the uneducated have, as a rule, a very undeveloped sense of humor. It is the highly educated man of deep intellectual powers who catches all the humor of a situation, and, though his expression of it may not be loud, it is deep and helpful at moments of depression. Humor is, of course, very different from wit, which is biting and which seems almost to be shared by the animals, if we can judge from the fact that they appear, occasionally, to play practical jokes upon one another.

It seems almost absurd that a physician should tell patients that it will do them good to practice smiling, to take every possible opportunity to laugh, and even to take frequent glances into a looking glass, to see that they are not pulling long faces. The difference between a feeling of melancholy and one of gladness consists mainly in the position of the outer angles of the mouth. The putting into practice of the maxim, not to let the sad lines dominate the countenance, but to insist on keeping the others there as far as possible, means much for the correction of internal feelings of depression and discouragement that may be badly interfering with the flow of nerve impulses from the brain to the body.

Mouth Breathing.—Since Meyer's discovery of the overgrowth of the {106} lymphoid tissue in the pharynx, we have learned to appreciate how important is mouth breathing, even for the intellectual life. We all knew before, and indeed from time immemorial it was well understood, that, as a rule, people who went around with their mouths open were of low grade intelligence. All sorts of methods were used to teach these young people to keep their mouths shut. They were reminded of it at home, they were told about it at school, and, if they married, their wives tried to keep them from this apparent manifestation of lack of intelligence. Of course, they were not, as a rule, able to carry out the well-meant intentions of their friends and advisors. The mouths were kept open because they could not breathe normally through their noses, and so respiration had to be accomplished by the only other available avenue. As a consequence of the open mouth, the lips were inclined to roll out somewhat, and certain indications of the human physiognomy were supposed to be associated with these thick lips.

Now we know the real meaning of the condition. Mouth breathing is possible, but it is inadequate. Insufficient respiration leads to insufficient oxidation of tissues, and to lowered vitality in all structures, and this is particularly notable in the brain, as well as in certain other higher structures. It is not because the individuals are lacking in intelligence that their mouths are open, but because the same reason that compels the open mouth also affects their intellectual activity. The blocking of nasal respiration lowers vital activity of all kinds. Hence the lowered intellectual vitality. The thick lips, which are supposed to be characteristic of a certain passionateness of nature, and which usually are associated with a lack of thorough control over animal inclinations, probably owe their significance to the fact that this special peculiarity of feature usually accompanies mouth breathing, and that the individual who labors under this deficient respiration, is likely to lack control to at least some degree. There is even a question whether the deficient oxidation is not likely to be much more notable in its effect upon the higher faculties than on the lower, and as a consequence the latter develop somewhat to the detriment of the former.

These studies in physiognomy may, indeed, be correlated in many ways with distinct physical conditions instead of as formerly with the general constitution of the individual. For instance, large protruding eyes used to be said to be characteristic of nervous, timid, sensitive

61

individuals, easily scared, and not well able to take up the harder parts of the battle of life. Now we know that this feature is usually associated with an excess of secretion of the thyroid gland, and that the nervousness is not a matter of character so much as it is due to the disturbance of internal metabolism consequent upon this interference with the proper function of an important organ. It might well be called a slight thyroid intoxication. In large amounts it produces all the symptoms of Graves' disease.

Bodily Conditions and Stupidity.—We have many illustrations of the influence of the body on the mind, when purely physical causes work rather serious results on disposition and character and energy. A typical example was the so-called tropical anemia which existed in Porto Rico when the Americans took possession of the island. There were so many cases of it that out of about 25,000 deaths reported in 1903, nearly 6,000 were from so-called anemia. Investigation of the conditions soon revealed the real cause. It had been {107} thought to be due to a combination of the climate, malaria and the lack of nutrition on the part of the country people. The people were absolutely without ambition, they had no energy, they seemed scarcely able to keep body and soul together, and they cared for nothing except to get just enough to supply them with a meager sustenance. Of incentive to lift themselves up, there was none. This was largely attributed by the first Americans who went to the island to the conditions which had existed under Spanish rule, as the Spaniards had not encouraged manufactures or industries in the island, and had left the people without any incentives to the awakening of enterprise or initiative.

Hook-Worm Disease.—Before long it was found that the real reason for the anemia of the Porto Ricans was the presence in their intestines in large numbers of the so-called hook-worm. These worms exhausted the vitality of the sufferers and left them without surplus energy and, indeed, with scarcely enough life to care whether or not life itself continued. It was not a moral condition, but a very definite physical cause that was at work. Shortly afterwards it was found that the same disease existed in our Southern states among the so-called "poor whites." Before this, these people had been supposed to be a characterless, unambitious, lazy people, who cared not to get on, who had sunk to about the lowest depths possible for civilized people, and who were quite satisfied to remain there. The discovery of hook-worm disease among them, however, soon made it clear that their laziness was the result of the drain upon their systems due to the presence of thousands of hook-worms. When these were removed, if nature was not already exhausted, the "poor whites" became normal human beings once more with ambition and initiative.

This story of pathology influencing racial qualities is not new in the history of the world. It is not improbable that even certain periods of decadence in Egyptian history which have ordinarily been attributed to the so-called running out of particular ruling races or families, or to the degeneration of the people consequent upon luxury, were really the result of the spread of the hook-worm disease through certain portions of Egypt. Dr. Sandwith, who has studied the disease very carefully in Egypt, is sure that it has existed there for at least four thousand years, and that the descriptions of certain affections which occurred in Egypt in historic times were really due to the same cause as now is known to produce the so-called Egyptian chlorosis, the name that was used for hook-worm disease in Egypt. Workers in soil, and in mines and in tunnels, are especially likely to be affected by it, and whenever it is neglected it spreads rather widely, as is seen in the mines of Germany and Hungary at the present time. As the cause was unrecognized in the olden time, it is possible that periods of supposed lassitude among the people were really due to infection by this parasite.

Malaria and Degeneration.—In recent years it has come to be generally recognized that the decadence of Greece, for instance, was not due to moral causes so much, perhaps, as to physical reasons. During the classic periods in Greece there are no traces of malaria. After the invasion of Sicily, the expedition against Syracuse and other attempts on the part of the cities of Greece to spread their dominion, malaria seems to have been introduced among her people, and as the *anopheles* mosquito was already there, the malaria spread widely, and in the course of a century affected so many of the people that their energy and ambition and initiative were to a great extent destroyed. {108} It is well known that these effects often occur as a consequence of malaria, and as generation after generation is affected by the disease, are emphasized more and more. The relaxing effect of tropical climates, of which we have heard so much, and which is supposed after a time to bring about the inevitable production of a race eminently lazy and careless of the future, is probably much more due to certain affections, such as malaria and those consequent upon animal parasites, than to any constitutional change that has taken place in the body, or any profound corresponding change in the mind. It is a case of the body influencing the mind and producing an apparently different race from that which existed before, though all this may be changed for the better by some even slight amelioration of bodily conditions.

In any attempt, then, to influence the human mind in order to use its power and its reserve energy for therapeutic purposes, the place of the body and its influence upon the mind must always be remembered. It is quite impossible to lift people up to enable them to use their mental reserve force if they are living in discouraging physical conditions, which use up so much of energy as to make it impossible to have any to spare. Many of the phases of mental discouragement and lack of initiative which are reflected in what we call lowered resistive vitality and lack of immunity to infection, are really consequent upon physical states representing a drain upon the system that can be removed, or at least greatly improved, if they are discovered and properly treated. Victims of chronic malaria and of hook-worm disease cannot be lifted up by psychotherapy. Neither can sufferers from other forms of chronic physical debility. After the removal of the debilitating cause, however, mental influence may be brought to bear to encourage them to rise to their opportunities, to literally take on new life, and gradually accumulate reserve energy that will enable them to accomplish, not only the average work of mankind, but even better, in the reaction that comes with the new feeling of physical energy. And what is thus true in these extreme cases is even more true of minor ailments and conditions.

CHAPTER IV

THE MECHANISM OF THE INFLUENCE OF MIND ON BODY

The question as to how mind influences body, and body mind, has always proved a riddle to all but those with a special theory in the matter. The facts of the mutual influence of mind on body are so obtruded on observation that they could never be missed, but it is quite another thing to reach a satisfactory explanation of them. How the will initiates motion continues in spite of all our advance in psychology, to be as much a mystery as ever. Just how sensation is transformed into ideas is a parallel mystery. Since the mind is able to influence motion, it is not surprising that it should be capable of modifying secretion or inhibiting other kinds of functions. Any of these various activities is scarcely more mysterious than the other. Since the transformation of sensation into thought takes place, it is comparatively easy to conclude that the mental processes are able to exclude, or to some extent inhibit, sensation. All these activities have actually been observed. How does this mutual influence of mind on body take place? What principles underlie it?

{109}

At present, it would be futile to hope to outline the absolute principles on which the mechanism of mental influence or suggestion depends, but we can discuss recent explanations that have been offered, and this will help us to understand, not the mystery itself, but just where the mystery lies and what the physical mechanism connected with it is.

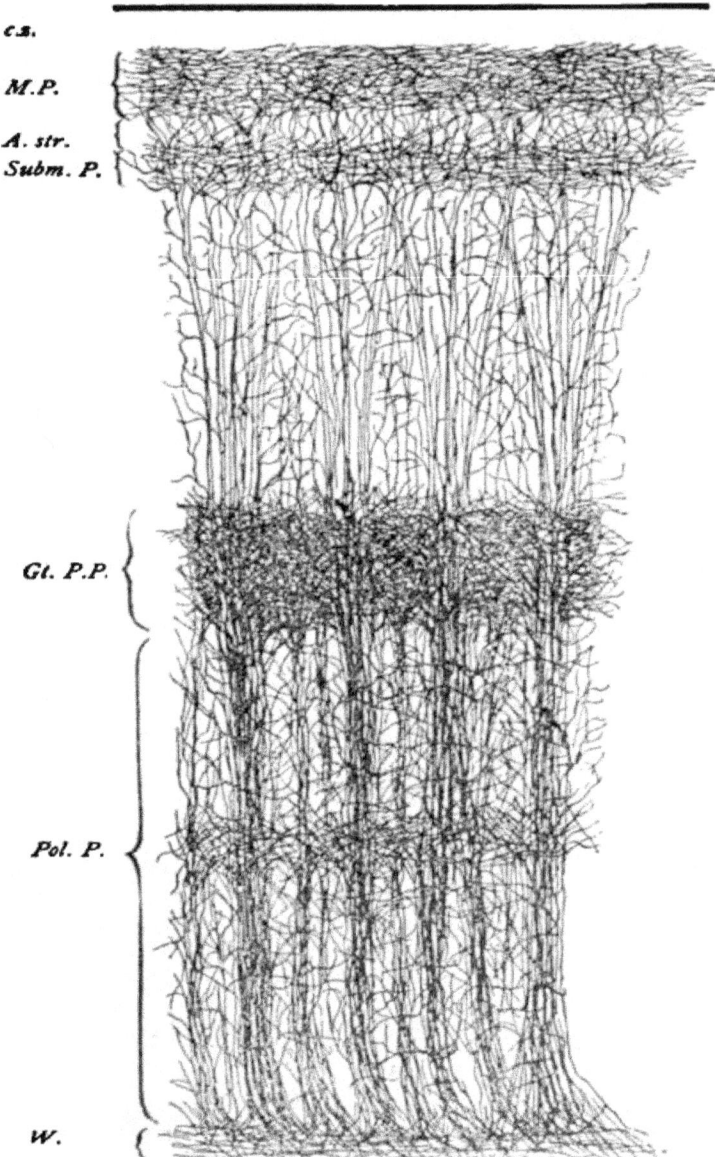

FIG. 2.—CORTEX OF HUMAN BRAIN ILLUSTRATING COMPLEXITY OF THE SYSTEMS AND PLEXUSES OF NERVE FIBERS (Combination of the methods of Weigert and Golgi—after Andriezen). *c. z.*, clear zone free from nerve fibers; *M. P.*, Exner's plexus in the molecular layer; *A. str.*, ambiguous cell stratum; *Subm. P.*, sub-molecular plexus; *Gt. P. P.*, great pyramidal plexus; *Pol. P.*, polymorphic plexus; *W.*, white matter. (Barker.)

Fig. 2.—CORTEX OF HUMAN BRAIN ILLUSTRATING COMPLEXITY OF THE SYSTEMS AND PLEXUSES OF NERVE FIBERS (Combination of the methods of Weigert and Golgi—after Andriezen). *c, z.*, clear zone free from nerve fibers; *M.P.*, Exner's plexus in the molecular layer; *A. str.*, ambiguous cell stratum; *Subm, P.*, sub-molecular plexus; *Gt. P. P.*, great pyramidal plexus; *Pol. P.*, polymorphic plexus; *W.*, white matter. (Barker.)

{110}

These explanations are as yet only theoretic, but theories have often helped students in science to make their thoughts more concrete and their investigations more practical. It would be a mistake to conclude that because some of the theories advanced are very plausible, we have, therefore, reached definite truth with regard to the mechanics of the brain that underlie suggestion and mental influence.

Brain Complexity.—The most interesting feature of the discoveries in brain anatomy during the past generation, has been that the central nervous system is of even greater complexity than had been thought. Because of this, these new discoveries, instead of solving the biological mystery they subtend, or even helping very much to solve it, have made it still harder to understand just how we succeed in controlling and directing this immensely complex machine, of whose details we are utterly unconscious, yet which we learn to use with such discriminating nicety of adjustment and accomplishment. The discoveries of Golgi and of Ramon y Cajal show us that the brain consists of nerve cells with a number of ramifying fibers connecting each cell and each group of cells with other simple and compound elements of the brain, and sending down connecting fibers to every organ and every part of the body. Dr. Ford Robertson calculates that in an average human brain there are at least three billions of cells. Without knowing anything of their existence, much less anything of the infinite detail of their structure and mode of operation, we have learned to use these for many purposes.

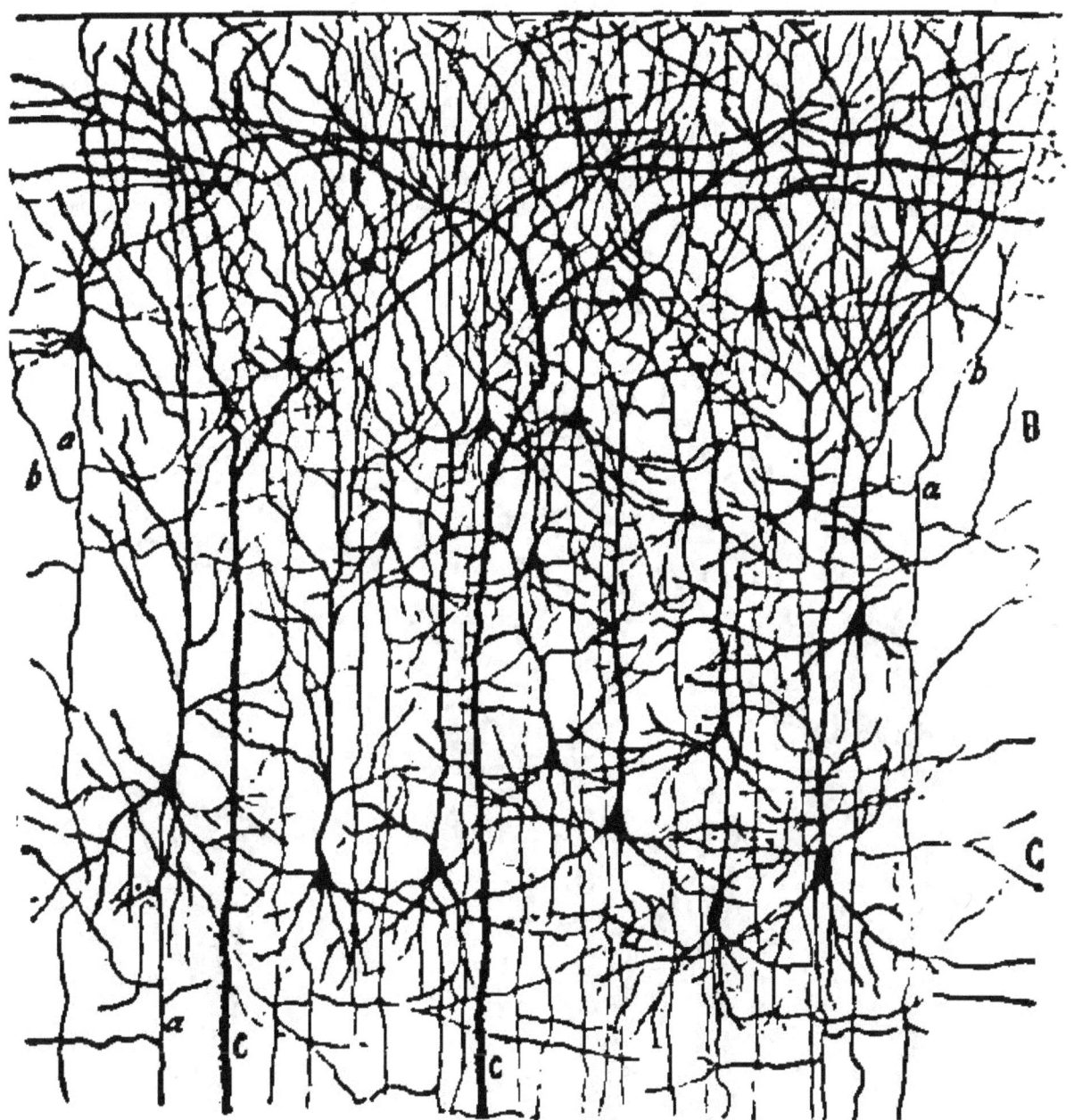

FIG. 3.—SMALL AND MEDIUM-SIZED PYRAMIDAL CELLS OF THE VISUAL CORTEX OF A CHILD TWENTY DAYS OLD. Section taken from the neighborhood of the calcarine fissure. A. plexiform layer; B, layer of the little pyramid; C, layer of the medium sized pyramid; a, descending axis cylinders; b, ascending or centripetal collaterals; c, stems of the giant pyramidal cells. (Ramon y Cajal.)

(This and the next three illustrations illustrate the complexity of the central nervous system as observed in the very young child where the development does not as yet obscure the interesting details of dentritic branching. They serve to emphasize the much more pronounced condition which develops in the adult.)

Nerve Impulses.—We do not know even how nerve impulses travel. Probably they do so by a mode of vibration, just as heat and light and electricity are transmitted as modes of motion. The similarity that used to be thought to exist between the transmission of nerve impulses and of electrical energy is now known definitely to be only an analogy, and not to represent anything closer. Waves of nervous energy travel at a different rate of speed from electrical waves, and there are other notable differences. Such phases as molecular action, or motion, or vibration are only cloaks for our ignorance, A generation ago Huxley declared that "the forces exerted by living matter are either identical with those existing in the inorganic world or are convertible into them." He instanced nervous energy as the most recondite of all, and {111} yet as being in some way or other associated with the electrical processes of living beings. As Prof, Forel said in his "Hygiene of the Nerves," "the neurokym cannot be a simple physical wave, such as electricity, light or sound; if it were its exceedingly fine weak waves would soon exhaust themselves without causing the tremendous discharges which they actually call forth in the brain."

Law of Avalanche.—How great is the power of the nervous system or the energy of it that may be set loose by some very simple reflex, as suggested by Forel, is illustrated by what Ramon y Cajal calls the Law of Avalanche. A single peripheral nerve ending is represented in many different portions of the brain. An ocular nerve ending, for instance, probably has direct connection with four or more portions of each hemisphere. Each of these portions of the brain has association fibers connecting it with other parts and so the stirring of a single nerve ending may disturb many thousands, perhaps hundreds of thousands, of brain cells; at least it affects them in some way or other. The older psychologists used to insist on the similarity, or analogy, between the cosmos ol the universe and the microcosmos that man is. The English poet of the nineteenth century told us that there is no moving of a flower without the stirring of a star, so intimately connected by the laws of gravitation is the universe. In the microcosm something of this same thing is true and a titillation of even the most trivial nerve ending may produce, in Ramon y Cajal's phrase, "an avalanche" of cell disturbances in the central nervous system which may seriously disturb the whole system.

What is thus true for the brain is true, also, for the cord, and the complexity of spinal cells needs to be seen to be properly realized.

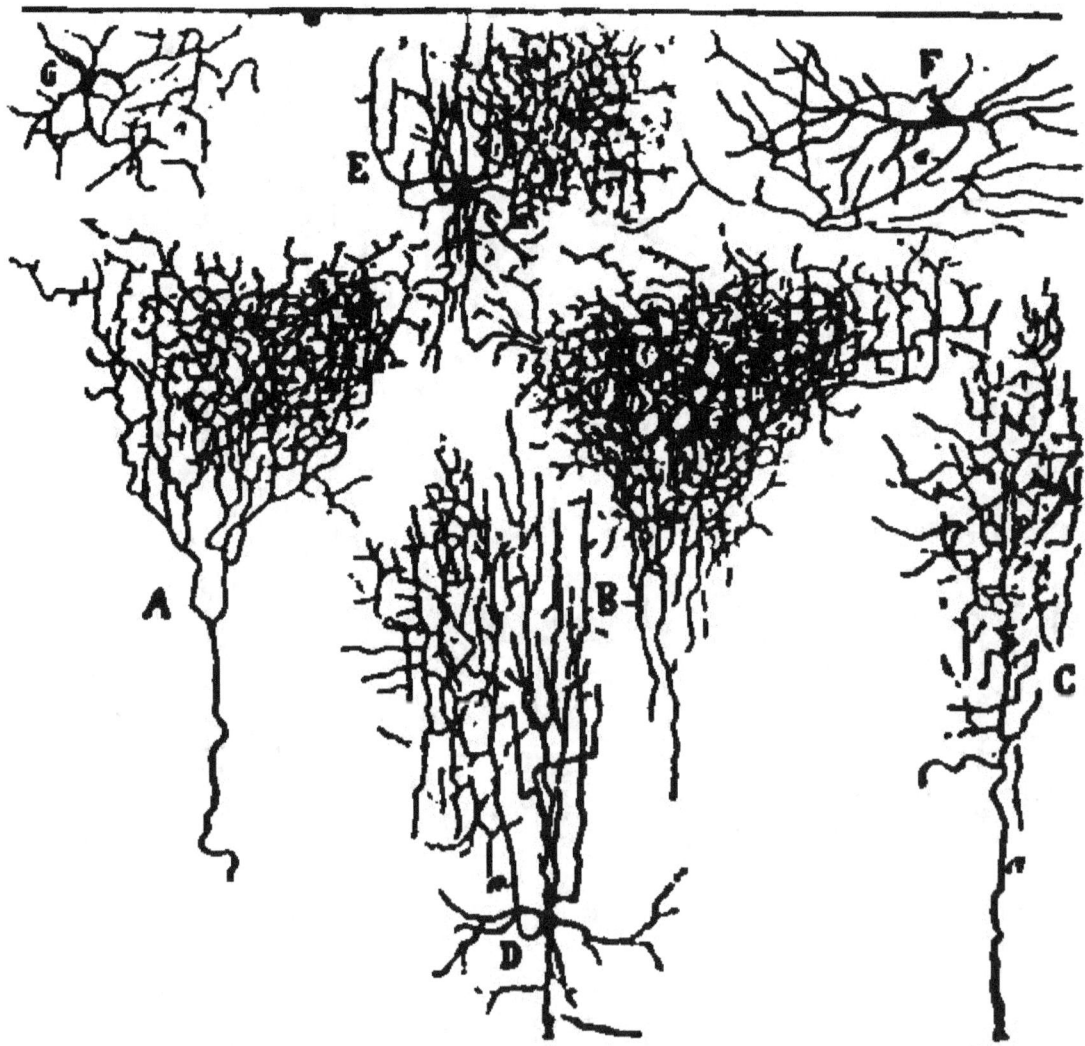

Fig. 4.—SERIES OF SECTIONS SHOWING THE FINE NERVE ENDINGS AND BRANCHINGS OF THE FIRST AND SECOND LAYER OF THE VISUAL CORTEX OF A CHILD FIFTEEN DAYS OLD. A and B, very thick nerve plexus of the layer in which the little pyramids are contained; C, a plexus containing a series of branches that is less thick and intricate; D, small cells whose ascending axis-cylinders have resolved themselves into a set of similar branches; E, arachnoid star cells whose axis cylinders produce a thick plexus in the first layer; F and G, small cells with short axis cylinders that have very few branches. (Ramon y Cajal.)

Psychic States.—There are a number of human states representing extremes of sensory and intellectual conditions in man, that have always attracted attention, and in recent years have been special objects of investigation by physiologists. Natural sleep is one of these; the unconsciousness of narcotism or anesthesia is another. Hypnotism is allied to both of these, and would seem to lie on a plane between them. Then there are various states of exaltation in which sensations fail to produce their usual effect. Those {112} escaping from a fire, or passing through a severe panic of any kind may sustain all manner of injuries without being aware of them. Martyrs, for all manner of causes, are able to withstand suffering with such equanimity, and sometimes even joy, that it is evident that they cannot feel, as would people under ordinary conditions, the pain that is being inflicted on them.

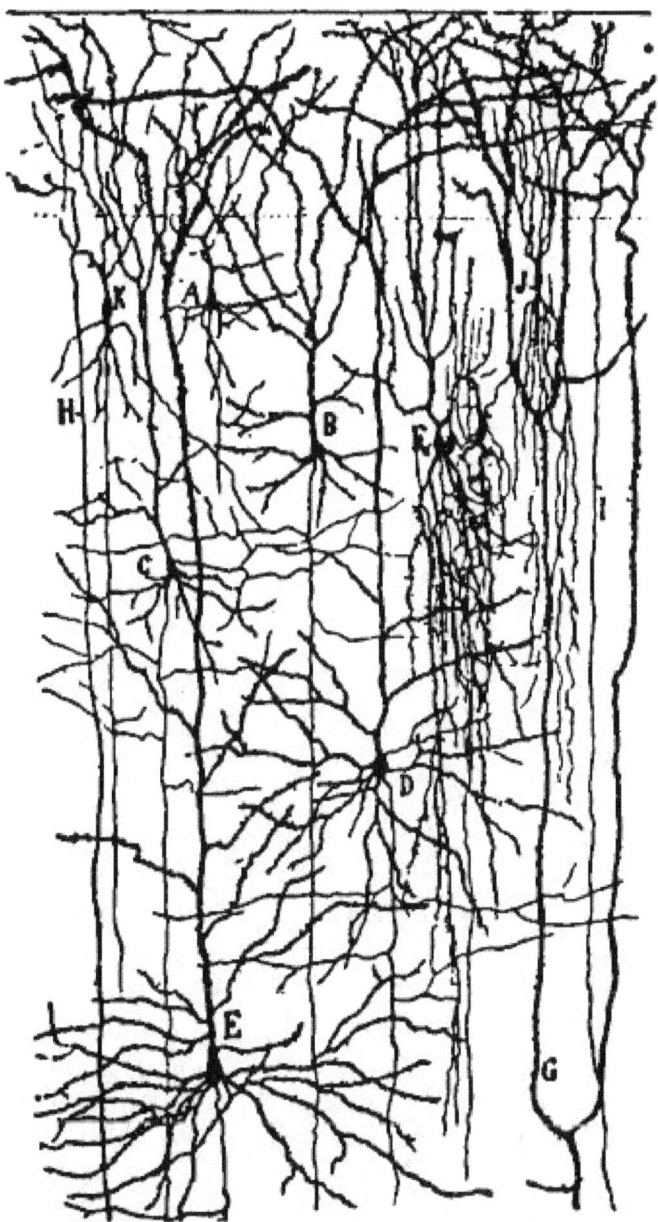

Fig. 5.—FIRST, SECOND AND THIRD LAYER OF THE ANTERIOR CENTRAL CONVOLUTION (THAT IS, OF THE ASCENDING FRONTAL CONVOLUTION) OF THE BRAIN OF A CHILD ONE MONTH OLD. A, B, and C, little pyramids; D and E, medium-sized pyramids; F, cells with two sets of tufts; their axis cylinders resolved into end tufts; G, protoplasmic layer that comes from one of the large pyramids of the fourth layer; H and I, fine dentrites of the cells of the sixth and seventh layer; J, small cells with two end tufts; K, spindle cells with long axis cylinder. (Raymon y Cajal.)

67

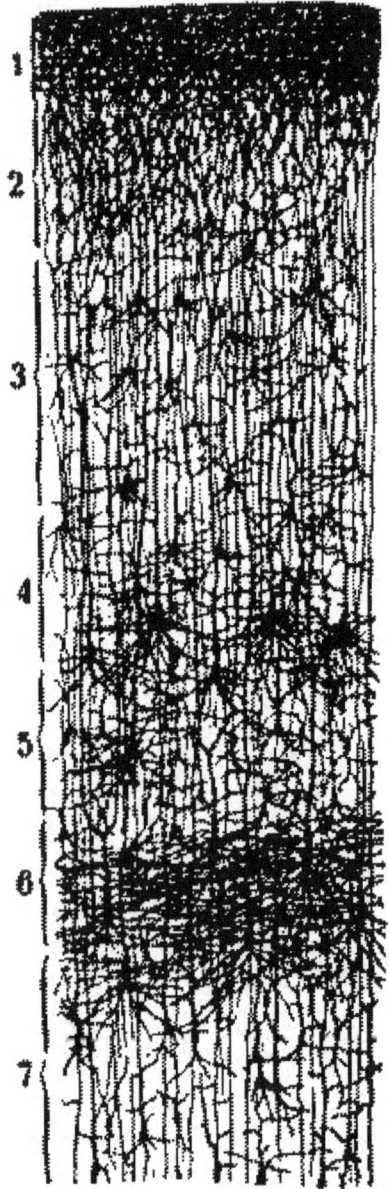

FIG. 6.—LAYERS OF THE POSTERIOR CENTRAL OR ASCENDING PARIETAL CONVOLUTION OF A NEWBORN CHILD. 1. plexiform layer; 2. small pyramids; 3. medium-sized pyramids; 4. external large pyramids; 5. small pyramids and star shaped cells; 6, deep layer of large pyramids; 7, spindle and triangular shaped cells. (Raymon y Cajal.)

In the midst of intense mental preoccupation one may hold so cramped a position as would be quite impossible for the same length of time with the faculties normally engaged. There are pathological conditions, like hysteria, in which the pain and fatigue sense may, for a time at least, be quite in abeyance.

{113}

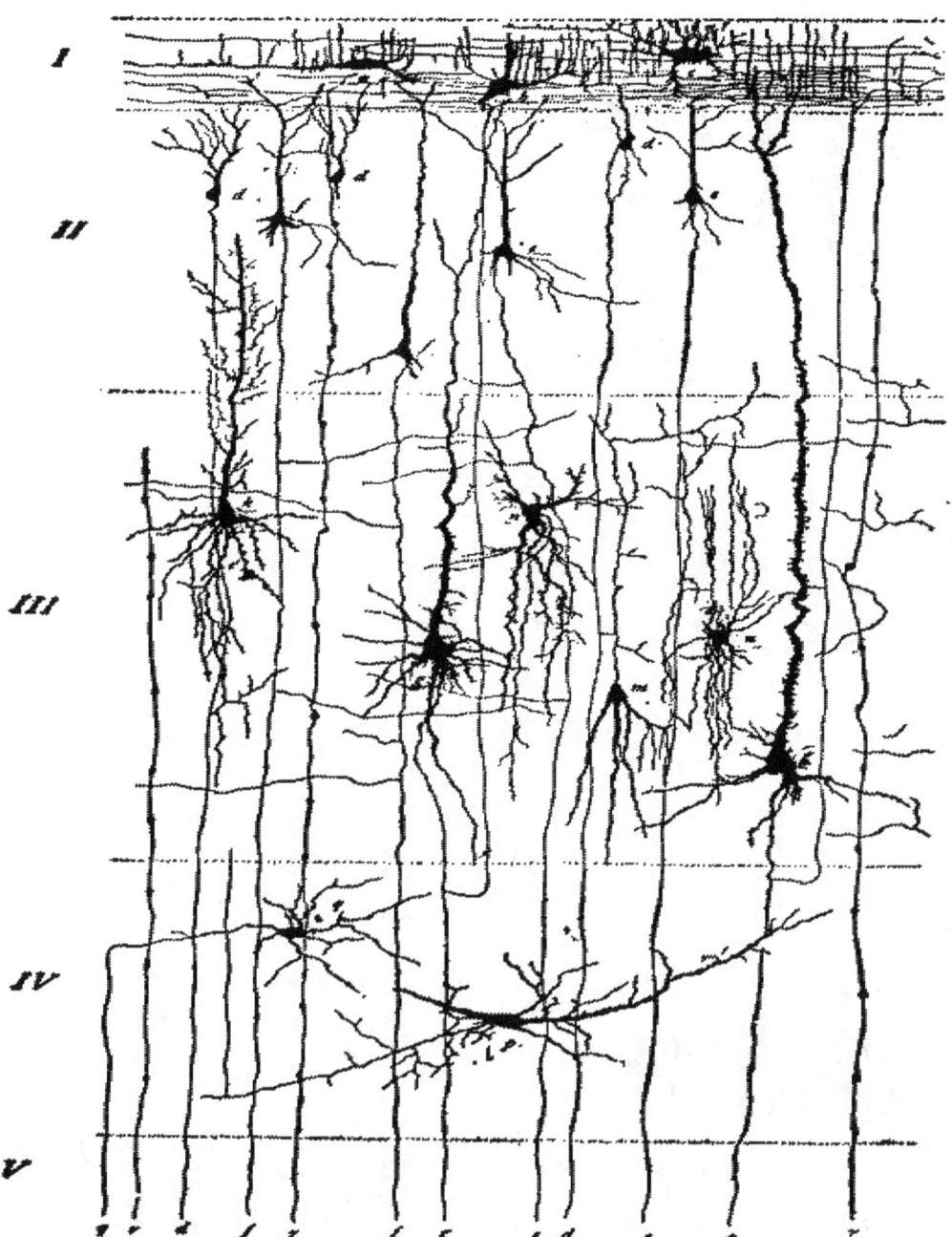

FIG. 7.—DIAGRAM OF CELLS OF CEREBRAL CORTEX (after Starr, Strong and Leaming). I, superficial layer; a, fusiform; b, triangular; c, polygonal cells of Ramon y Cajal; II, layer of small pyramids; d, smallest; e, small; f, medium-sized pyramidal cells with axones descending to the white matter and giving off collaterals in their course; III, layer of large pyramidal cells; g, largest (giant) pyramidal cells; k, large pyramidal cells with very numerous dendrites; all pyramidal cells are seen to send long apical dendrites up to I; m, Martinotti cell with descending dendrites and ascending axone; n, polygonal cells; IV, deep layer; p, fusiform cell; q, polygonal cell; V, the white matter containing the axones from the pyramidal cells, d, e, f, g, and from a cell of the deep layer q; r, neuroglia fibers. (Barker.)

{114}

69

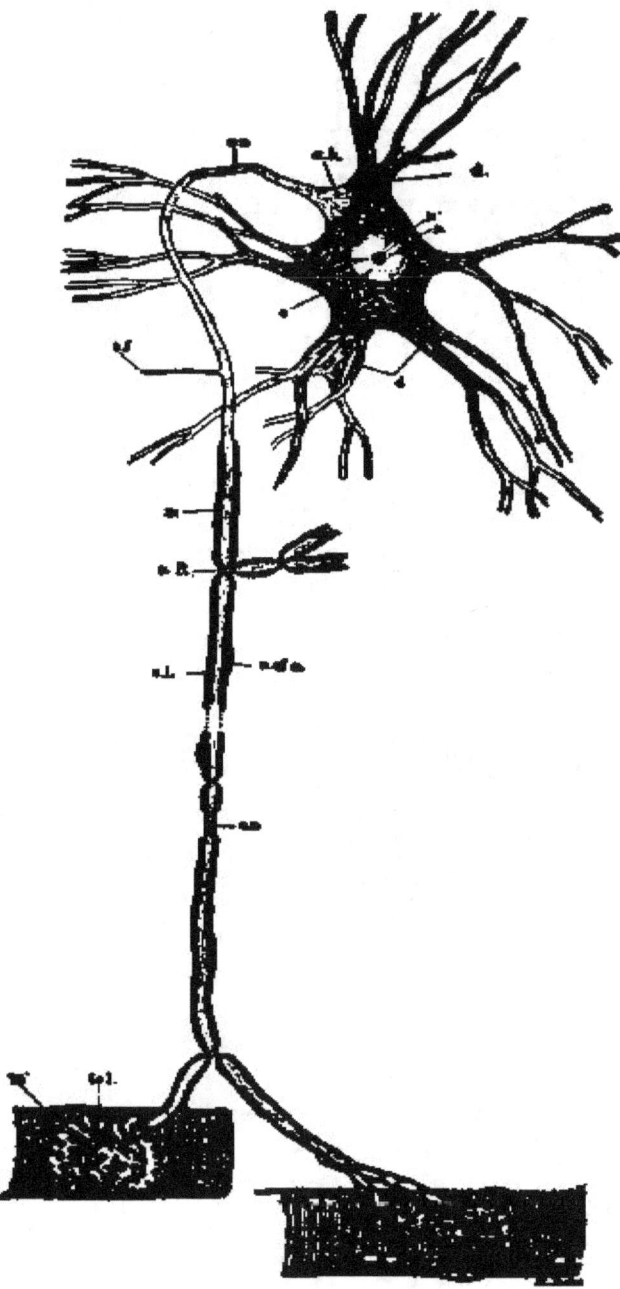

FIG. 8.—SCHEME OF LOWER MOTOR NEURON. The motor-cell body, with protoplasmic processes, axis cylinder, side fibrils or collaterals, and end ramifications, represents parts of a neuron. a. h., axon hillock devoid of Nissl bodies, showing fibrillation; ax., axon. This process near the cell body becomes surrounded by myelin, m., and a cellular sheath, the neurilemma (not an integral part of the neuron); c, cytoplasm showing Nissl bodies and lighter ground substance; d, protoplasmic processes (dendrites) containing Nissl bodies; n., nucleus; n., nucleolus: n. r., node of Ranvier; s. f., side fibril; n. of n., nucleus of neurilemma; tel., motor end plate or telodendrion; m., striped muscle fiber; s. l., segmentation of Lautermann. (Barker.)

Neurons.—With the advance in our knowledge of brain anatomy, various explanations for these curious conditions have been suggested. The discovery that the central nervous system is composed of a large number of separate units, and not of a feltwork of continuous fibers with cells here and there, revolutionized all previous attempts at explanation of these conditions. We know now that it is not fibers but cells that are the most important components of the brain and spinal-cord substance, and that, indeed, the fibers are only prolongations of cells. The central nervous system is made up of nerve cells with various appendages, and each one of these cells and its appendages is called a neuron. These appendages are of two kinds, one the axon, the long conducting fiber which transmits the nerve force of the cell, the other the dendrons or connecting elements by which the cell is linked with the axon of another cell. The contact of the axon of one neuron with the dendrons of another is called a synapse. Each neuron does not extend to and from the brain and the periphery, but series of neurons connect the surface of the body with the brain. There is usually a group of neurons in the path from the surface to the brain cortex. The peripheral neuron for sensation runs from the surface of the body to the spinal cord, while for motion it runs in the opposite direction. There is a secondary neuron in each chain that runs up or down the spinal cord to and from the base of the brain. A third—sometimes, perhaps, a fourth—neuron connects in the two directions, afferent and efferent, the cortex and the base of the brain.

Neuronic Movement.—Duval, the French anatomist and histologist, suggested the possibility of voluntary and involuntary movement in the neurons or nerve cells themselves, thus making and breaking connections.

{115}

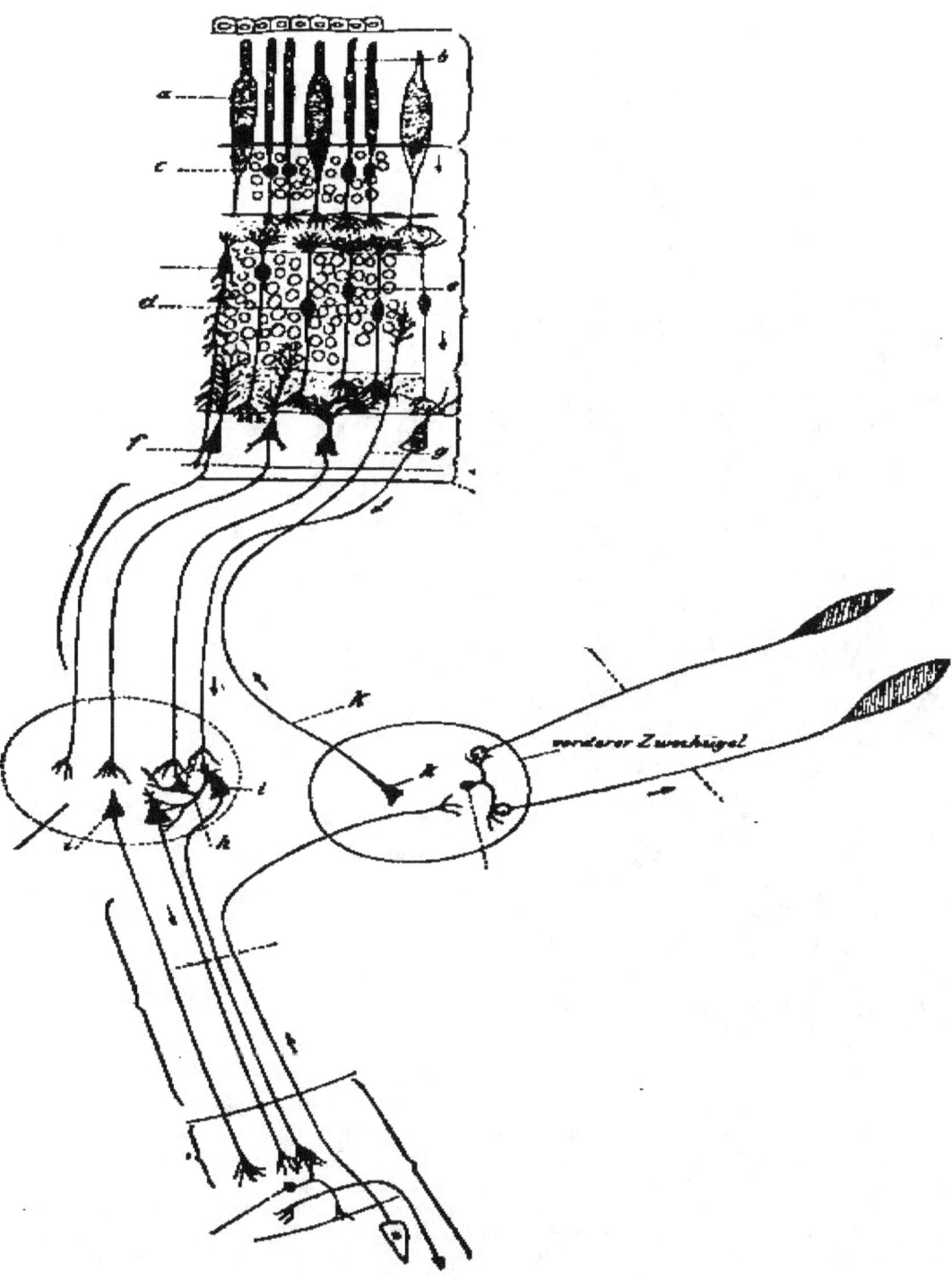

FIG. 9.—SCHEME OF THE VISUAL CONDUCTION PATHS (after C. von Monakow). a, rods and cones; b, rods; c, nuclei of rods; d, bipolar cells for the cones; e, bipolar cells for the rods; f, large multipolar ganglion cells giving rise to the axons of the N. opticus; g, centrifugal axon of a neuron, the cell body of which is situated in the collieulus superior, its telodendron being situated in the retina; h,

71

Golgi cell of Type II, or dendraxon in the corpus geniculatum laterale; i, neuron connecting the corpus geniculatum laterale with the lobus occipitalis, its axon running in the radiato occipito-thalamica (Gratioleti). The visual impulses are indicated by the arrow. (Barker)

{116}

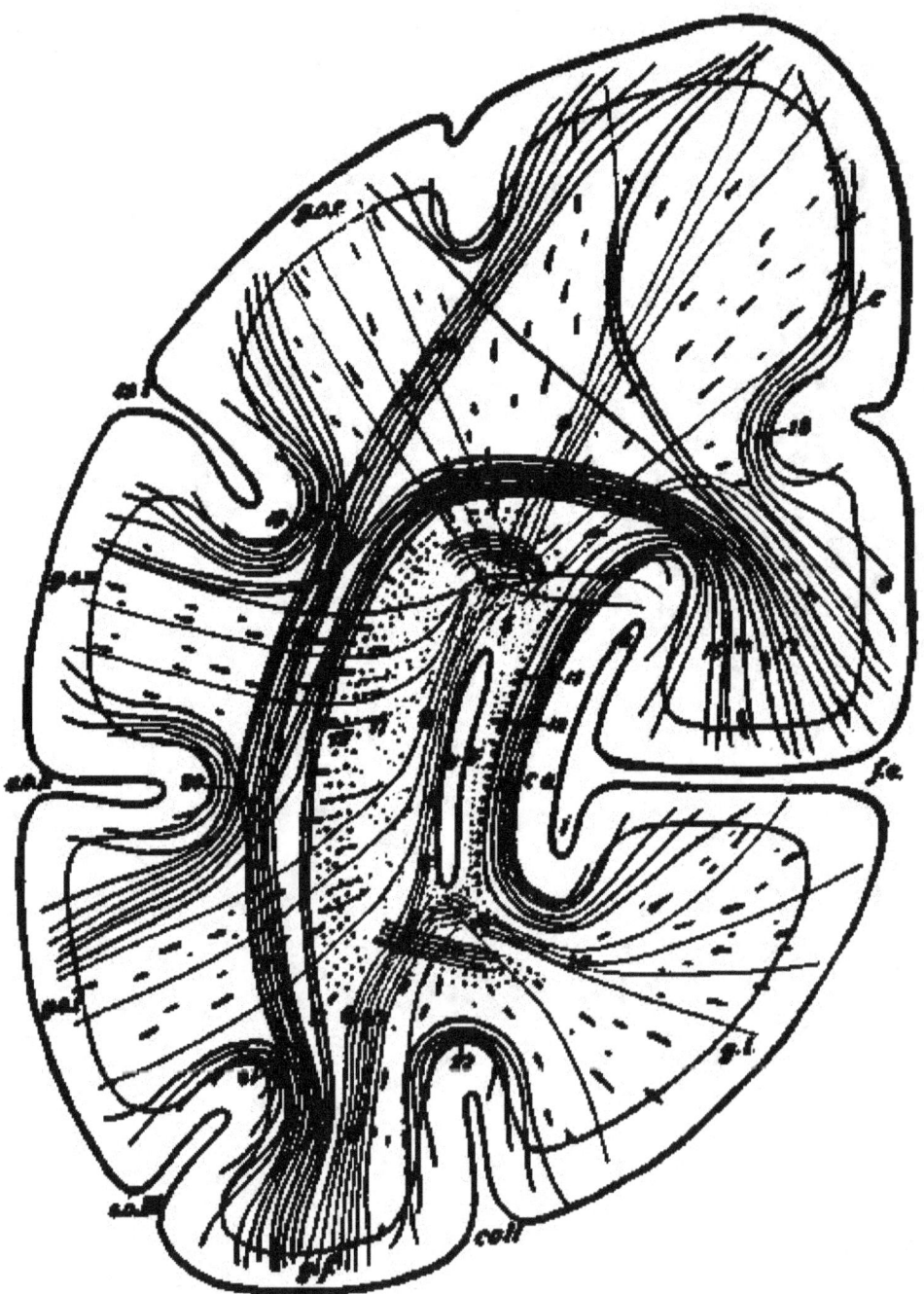

FIG. 10.—SCHEMATIC FRONTAL SECTION THROUGH THE OCCIPITAL LOBE ILLUSTRATING MANIFOLD CONNECTIONS IN A SINGLE LOBE (after H. Sachs), v, cornu posterius ventriculi lateralis; f. c, fissura calcarina; b, upper division: i, lower division; coll, sulcus collateralis; s. o. I, sulcus occipitalis superior (fissura interparietalis); s. o. II, sulcus occipitalis medius; s. o. III, sulcus occipitalis inferior; c. a., calcar avis; g. l., gyrus lingualis; g. f., gyrus fusiformis; g. o. s., gyrus occipitalis superior; g. o. m., gyrus occipitalis medius; g. o. i.. gyrus occipitalis inferior; c, cuneus; 1-10, forceps; 11-14, stratum sagittale internum: 15, stratum sagittale externum; 16, stratum calcarinum; 17, stratum cunei transversum; 18, stratum proprium cunei; 19, stratum proprium s. o. I; 20, stratum proprium s. o. II; 21, stratum proprium. s. o. III; 22, stratum proprium, s. coll.; 23, stratum profundum convexitatis. (Barker.)

According to his suggestion, sleep would be due to a separation of the neurons that run from the surface of the body to the brain cortex, because the various neurons had become too tired for further function. As a consequence of fatigue, their terminal filaments would fall away from one another, external sensations would no longer be communicated to the brain, because the peripheral neuron was not connected with the next in the chain. As a further result, the brain, undisturbed by sensations, would be left at rest so far as the body was concerned. Within the brain certain connections through which flow thoughts that would keep us awake, are also supposed on this theory to be broken, and consequently all the nerve cells have a chance to rest, except, of course, those concerned with such very vital functions as heart movement, respiration and peristalsis.

{117}

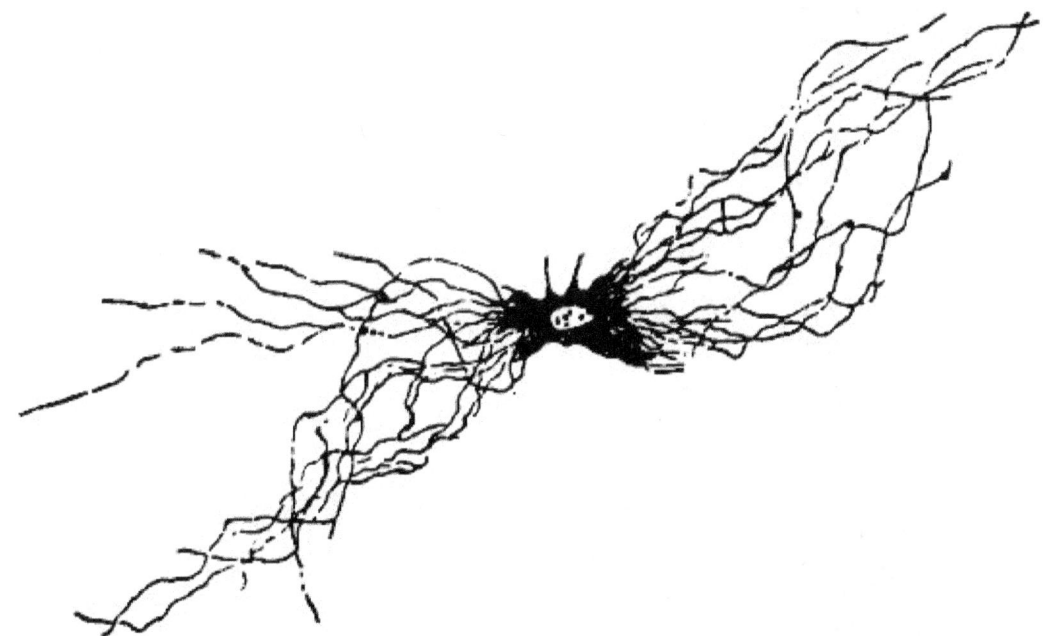

FIG. 11.—ISOLATED CELL FROM HUMAN SPINAL CORD (Obersteiner).

Somehow, these vital neurons obtain their rest in the intervals between the impulses which they send down, just as cardiac cells do between heart beats.

Neurons in Psychic States.—This same explanation would serve for narcosis, that is, for anesthesia, due to chloroform or ether, or any other drug. As a consequence of the effect of the narcotic upon the central neuron, they are brought into a condition resembling fatigue, at least to the extent of breaking their connections with other neurons so long as they are under the influence of the drug. While sensory nerves at the periphery, then, are being stimulated by the cutting of tissues to which they are attached, the message from them does not reach the brain because of a disturbance of the connections in the chain of neurons. Drunkenness illustrates the same phenomenon in a less degree. The effect of the intoxicant upon the central neurons disturbs sensation because it makes the connection much less complete than before, and so it is easy to understand the familiar occurrence of even severe injuries to drunken men without their being aware of them, or at least without their suffering nearly so much as would be the case if they were not intoxicated.

Hypnotism.—The same theory would also hold for the phenomena observed in hypnotism. After all, the best explanation of hypnotism that we have is that there is a turning inward of the patient's attention, so that only those sensations are allowed to reach the brain to which mental attention has already been called by suggestion. Hypnotism usually begins with a certain fatigue of peripheral neurons until these do not act normally, and then the cerebral neurons become, as it were, short-circuited on themselves with a consequent internal concentration of attention. The anesthesia so often noted in hypnotic or hysterical states is explained by the same theory. For the time being, at least, the connection between the peripheral neurons and the central neurons is broken or but imperfectly made, and conduction does not take place, or is hampered. There may be loss of motion as well as of sensation, or of motion without sensation. In all these cases, the discontinuity of the nervous system enables us to understand more readily the mechanism by which these curious phenomena occur. Exaltation or intense interest or profound preoccupation may so concentrate nervous energy within the nerve centers themselves as to inhibit the flow of sensory impulses from without and thus enable {118} people to stand pain and fatigue that would otherwise seem quite unbearable.

Unconsciousness.—The unconsciousness due to apoplexy, or to a blow on the head, would be comparatively easy of explanation on the same theory. The hemorrhage would actually push certain neurons apart within the skull, or the intracranial pressure produced by it would keep them from making proper connections. A blow on the head may readily be supposed to jar neuronic terminal filaments so severely that it would be some time before connections could be made, and the injury might be serious enough to prevent certain cells from ever again coming in contact in such a way as to allow the passage of nerve impulses from one to the other. Concussion of the brain would, on this theory, mean that neurons were so shaken apart as to produce some confusion in their terminal filaments and consequent serious

73

disturbances of consciousness, if not its complete loss, and corresponding disturbance of the power to move. In a word, this theory would seem to afford a reasonably satisfactory explanation for most of the extraordinary phenomena of mental life and, therefore, might also be expected to be applicable to the ordinary phenomena, though these are so elusive that it is difficult to satisfactorily apply theories to them.

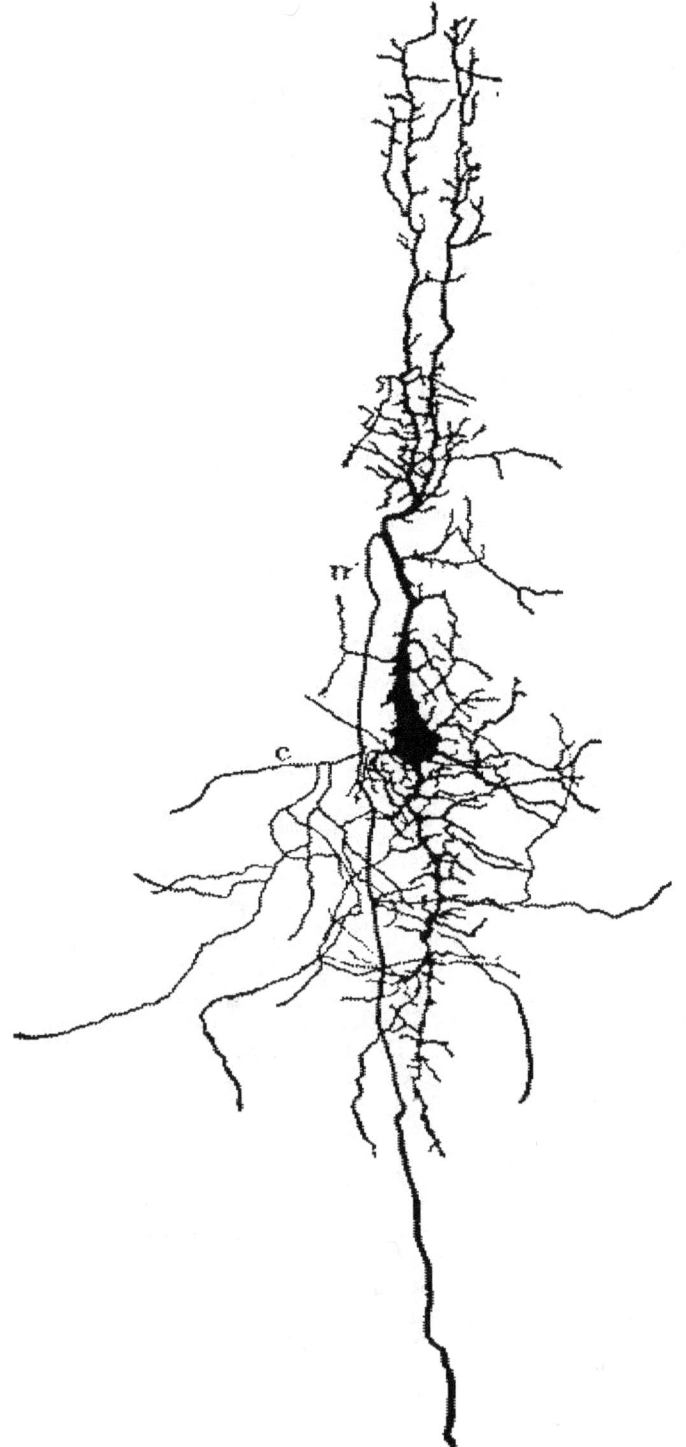

FIG. 12.—NEURON FROM THE OPTIC LOBE OF THE EMBRYO CHICK (after Kölliker). The axon n runs toward the center, giving off in its course several collaterals. One of these, c, is much branched. (Barker.)

Tired States.—When fatigued, it becomes extremely difficult for us to follow a train of thought, especially if it is somewhat intricate. It becomes easy to forget things, even such as under ordinary circumstances would be readily remembered. Names are much more likely to be forgotten. Facts and, above all, dates, refuse to come as they do under normal conditions. Efforts in the direction of recalling details are eminently unsatisfactory. The command goes forth, but there is {119} evidently hesitation about obedience. Other thoughts intrude themselves. Ideas come unbidden. The connection of thought is readily broken, and is hard to get at again. There may have been very little mental work, but somehow the fatigue of the general physical system is reflected through our central nervous system on the mind as well as the body. The early morning hours are the best for mental work, not, it seems, because the mind is fresher after its rest, but rather because the physical factors that are important for mental action are in good condition. Later they become disturbed by the fatigues of the day. The delicate cells of the brain become fatigued by sympathy with the somatic cells and it is harder to secure those nervous connections necessary for thought.

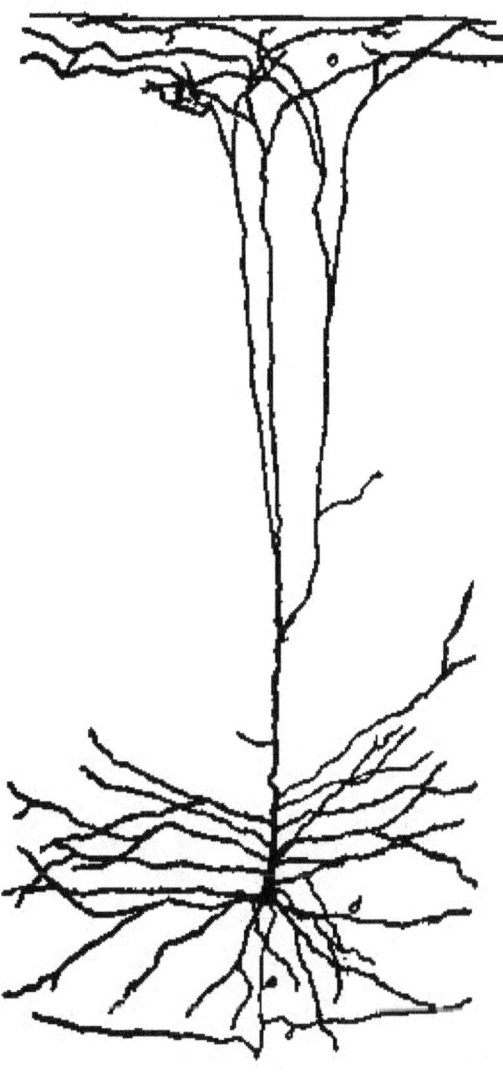

FIG. 13.—DEEP LAYER OF GIANT PYRAMIDAL CELLS OF THE POSTERIOR CENTRAL OR ASCENDING PARIETAL, CONVOLUTION OF A CHILD THIRTY DAYS OLD. a, axis-cylinder; c, collateral branch; d, long basilar dendrites; e, end tuft. (Ramon y Cajal.)

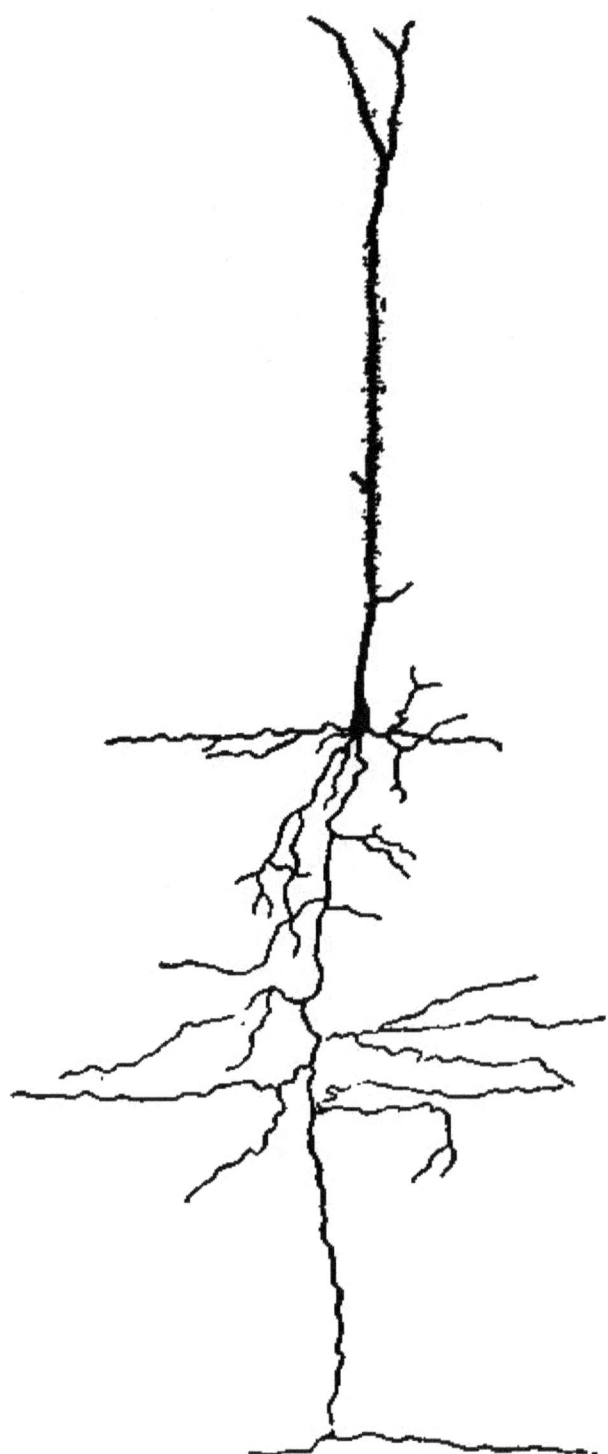

Voluntary Neuron Motion.—This theory of Duval's supposes that to some extent the neurons or nerve cells are possessed of voluntary movement. At least during certain states of the mind, they are moved and seem to have an inherent, if not quite voluntary, power {120} of motion. There are many objections urged against the theory because of this neuronic motion. It has been said that the movement of neurons has been observed in certain of the *Medusae*. The observation has been doubted and it lacks confirmation. In higher animals, of course, the observation is impossible because an investigation of the nervous system for this purpose would necessarily bring about the death of the animal and the cessation of spontaneous mobility. Whether it occurs or not, therefore, is a theoretic problem. So many objections tell against Duval's theory that it is now only discussed because of its subjective value.

Neuroglia Theory.—Ramon y Cajal elaborated a second theory of explanation for the mechanism of the nervous system that has seemed to many authorities in brain physiology much more satisfactory than Duval's theory of the actual motion of the neurons themselves. The Spanish nervous histologist had made a special study of the neuroglia or connective tissue cells in the central nervous system. These are very small in size but very numerous. Ramon y Cajal suggested that it was because the terminal filaments of these neuroglia cells inserted themselves between the neuronic filaments, thus insulating one from another, somewhat as if an insulating plug were inserted between two portions of an electric circuit, that the interruption of nervous currents took place. This explanation is free from many of the objections urged against Duval's theory.

The small size of the neuroglia cells makes it easy to understand how movement may take place in them sufficient to bring about separation of neurons. It would not be surprising if they should be more or less actively contractile. Whenever they contract, neuronic filaments which they have been holding apart, come together so as to permit the passage of nervous impulses, if any are flowing at the time. When the neuroglia cells become fatigued or seriously disturbed, they refuse any longer to obey the will in any way, or at least gradually get beyond control, and in their relaxation becoming prolonged, push neurons apart. When a man is very tired it gradually becomes impossible for him to keep awake. This is partly because poisons, produced in the course of fatigue, exhaust the vitality of the neuroglia cells and also of the neurons, so that less energy is required to push these latter apart.

It is easy to understand that the neuroglia cells might well become affected by the various narcotics and intoxicants in such a way as to produce the phenomena of anesthesia and drunkenness. The rapid recovery from anesthetics seems to indicate that it is not neurons, or essential nerve cells, that are so deeply affected, but some extraneous, and less important, mechanism within the brain. The neuroglia theory explains this very well and does away with the difficulty. Certain curious phenomena of hysteria are easily explained on this theory. When there is anesthesia in a member because of hysteria, this anesthesia does not follow the distribution of certain nerves, but is limited by a line in the shape of a cuff drawn round the limb. This indicates that the trouble is not peripheral but central, and that owing to psychic disturbance, all the neurons that receive sensory impulses from a particular portion of the body are so affected by a psychic condition that they are no longer capable of receiving impulses from the periphery. The neuroglia cells in a particular area have passed from the control of the will and, relaxing themselves, have {121} inserted their processes between the terminal filaments of neurons, thus preventing conduction.

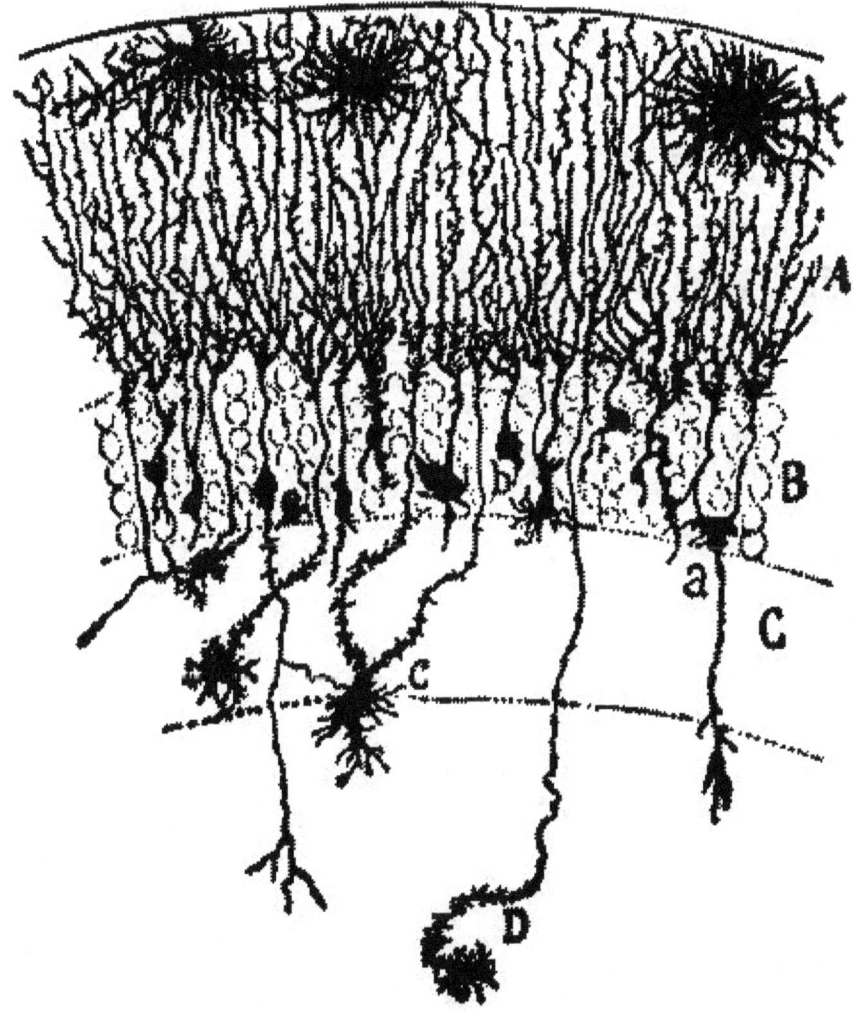

FIG. 15.—NEUROGLIA CELLS OR THE FASCIA DENTATA; IN THE NEW-BORN RABBIT (method of Golgi). A, molecular layer; B, granular layer; C, layer of polymorphis cells; D. horn of ammon; a. neuroglia cell furnished with a descending appendage; b, another neuroglia cell; piroform; c. a cell more deeply situated; d, spider cell; e, fusiform neuroglia cell. (Ramon y Cajal.)

Varieties of Neuroglia.—The connective tissue cells are of many kinds, each probably exercising a special function. Ramon y Cajal has described and pictured a special kind of neuroglia cells for the gray and another for the white matter. In his description of these cells he has pointed out many interesting diversities of form, and probably also of function. He has also described particularly a special form of neuroglia cells which lie close to the blood vessels. These he calls perivascular cells, and they seem to have an important function in regulating the amount of blood that goes to a particular part of the brain. He has written so clearly and yet so concisely with regard to these that it seems better to cite his own words:

Under the term neuroglia are included at least three kinds of cells,—those of the white brain substance, those of the gray substance, and the perivascular cells, which have been described by Golgi. The neuroglia cells of the white brain material are easily recognizable, being large and with rather prominent, smooth, and sharply outlined processes. As my brother seems to have shown, their object appears to be to furnish an insulating, or, at least, a badly conducting, substance to serve as an interrupter of nerve-currents. They certainly do not represent interstices of true nerve substance through which lymphatic fluid can conveniently find its way.

The neuroglia cells of the gray matter present a very special and highly characteristic appearance. They are of manifold form,—at times star-shaped, at times {122} like a comet drawn out in length. These are the tall cells of von Retzius. They have very numerous prolongations, with a large number of short branched collaterals which give the whole cell the appearance of having feathers projecting from its periphery. These cells have been observed in two different conditions. One is that of relaxation, and the picture is that given above. The other is that of contraction, during which the cell body has more protoplasm in it, and the processes become shorter and thicker, and some of the secondary branches disappear entirely. These cells resemble, in certain ways at least, the pigment cells which occur in the skin of some animals. By means of their contractility, these pigment cells can stretch out their processes while in a state of contraction. It must be remembered that this form of neuroglia cells is most abundantly present in those parts of the brain in which it might be expected that a number of nerve currents would frequently come together. They occur, for example, with special frequency in the molecular layer of the cerebral cortex, where the bundle of pyramidal fibers, with their immense number of terminal nerve-endings, come in contact with one another.

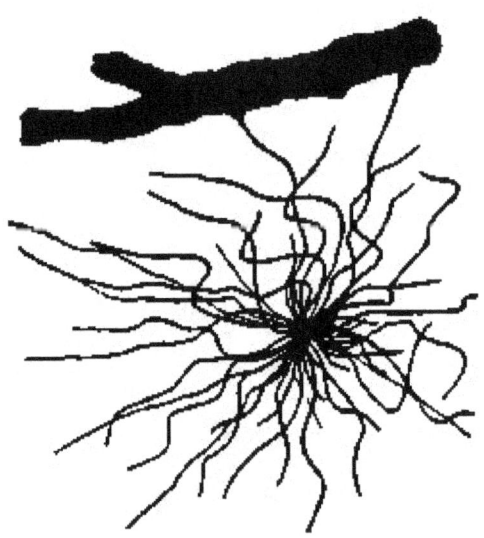

FIG. 16.—NEUROGLIA CELL FROM THE SUBCORTICAL LAYER OF THE CEREBRUM FROM WHICH TWO PROCESSES GO TO A BLOOD VESSEL (Obersteiner).

FIG. 17.—NEUROGLIA CELLS FROM THE SPINAL CORD. Longitudinal section (Obersteiner).

The third form of neuroglia cells consists of those known as the perivascular cells. They are found only in the neighborhood of the capillaries of the gray matter and they send one or more firm prolongations to the outer surface of the endothelium of the blood vessels.

These processes are inserted in the walls of the blood vessels. Every capillary has thousands of these little pseudopod prolongations, and from the vessel the cell reaches out in a number of directions. The object of these cells undoubtedly is by contraction of the prolongations to bring about local dilatation of the blood vessels. This dilatation of the blood vessels causes greater or less intensity of the psychical processes in certain parts of the brain, because of the greater or less congestion of the circulation in a part which it produces.

With the exception of these last cells the object of the neuroglia cells is to insulate nerve fibrils and cells from one another. When the cells are relaxed, the passage of a nerve current is either entirely prevented or rendered much less easy than before. It is in this way that the true nature of intellectual rest is explained. Sleep—not only natural sleep, but also artificial narcosis, such as is produced by narcotics, hypnotics or hypnotization—is evidently the result of the same conditions.

During the state of contraction the pseudopod of the neuroglia cells are drawn in; that is to say, the protoplasm of the cells absorbs the processes, and so the true nerve cells and nerve fibrils which were separated from each other by the interposition of neuroglia come into contact. By this mechanism the brain passes from the condition of rest into one of activity. These neuroglia contractions may, particularly in certain parts of the brain, occur automatically. Often, however, they are produced by the action of the will, which, in this manner is able to influence {123} the definite groups of neuroglia cells. As the result of this influence of the will the association of intellectual operations can be guided in various directions. The unusual course that the association of ideas sometimes takes, the flow of words and of thoughts at certain moments, the passing difficulty of speech, the recurrence of tormenting thoughts, the disappearance of expressions or ideas from the memory, even the increase of mental activity and of every kind of motor reaction as well as many other phenomena of intellection, can be satisfactorily explained on this hypothesis. It is only necessary to suppose that in certain parts of the brain the neuroglia cells are at rest, while at other parts they are in a condition of active contraction.

To put it all in a few words, the neuroglia cells of the gray substance of the brain represent an insulating and switching apparatus for nerve currents. They are an insulation apparatus when in a state of contraction, a switching and insulating apparatus when in a state of rest. It is to be remarked, then, that according to this theory the contraction of brain cells does not take place, as in Duval's theory, during intellectual rest, but, on the contrary, during the state of activity of the cerebral cortex. It is much more probable that the action of cells coincides with the active stage of intellection than that brain cellular activity—that is, contraction—should correspond with psychic rest.

The application of some of these theories enables us to understand just how short-circuiting may come about, how many of the curious phenomena of memory happen, and what are the effects, as well as the causes, of attention and distraction of attention and of diversion of mind. It is particularly the latter portion of Ramon y Cajal's theory, with regard to attention and the more or less voluntary though unconscious and usually indeliberate control of blood supply to various portions of the brain, that is of special interest. If the neuroglia cells, whose end plates are attached to blood-vessel walls, become over-contracted or lose their power of relaxation or of contraction, many of the curious phenomena of over-tiredness in neurotic conditions, and the lack of the power of concentration, and sufficient attention to

79

things, can be readily understood. In a word, the theory enables us to translate many expressions that are vague and indefinite, from terms of mind into terms of the physical basis of mind—the anatomy and physiology of the brain.

While I have dwelt on Ramon y Cajal's theory, because for years it has been familiar, of course I must reĕcho his own warning that it is, after all, only a theory. It presupposes an active interposition of the glia cells between the axon of one neuron and the dendrons of another. This cannot be demonstrated. A third theory of mental operations, then, has been suggested, and the English school, so ably led by Sherrington ("Integrative Action of the Nervous System," London, 1903) and McDougal ("Synapse Theory of Fatigue," *Brain*, 1910) has deservedly attracted wide attention. They contend that all the phenomena can be more simply explained without postulating the movement required for the Duval Theory or the glial activity of Ramon y Cajal's hypothesis. They consider that each nerve cell has, as it were, a certain potential energy which it sends forth in nerve impulses. These are transferred from neuron to neuron through the synapse. If what we might call, to borrow a figure from electricity, the voltage of the cell impulse be sufficient to overcome the resistance at the synapse, the impulse passes from neuron to neuron. In fatigue the potential energy of the cell is gradually dissipated. The impulses become feebler till they cease to pass. This occurs in the state we usually experience as tiredness and in analogous states such as sleep, unconsciousness, narcosis and the like. Obviously this {124} theory can be elaborated and applied parallel with the neuroglia theory except that here we are substituting synapse resistance for the hypothetical, undemonstrated action of the glial cells. But, as the latter seems a simpler process upon which to explain the various phenomena, especially to those not familiar with very recent developments in nervous histology and studies in nervous mechanism, and as it merely involves a question of the nature of the resistance and not of its site, I have used it for explanatory purposes without advocating either theory in the present state of our knowledge.

CHAPTER V

BRAIN CELLS AND MENTAL OPERATIONS

While the theories of neuronic action we have discussed do not represent absolute knowledge, they are at least suggestive and helpful in psychotherapy. Whenever there are disturbances of mental operations, patients are likely to become very solicitous, lest these represent organic and incurable changes. The application of Ramon y Cajal's neuroglia theory serves to bring out the fact that most of them can be very well explained as merely functional, due to passing disturbances of activity, and not necessarily to tissue changes. When patients become possessed of the fear that certain nervous symptoms portend definite injuries to the nervous system, this unfavorable suggestion keeps them from using, to its proper and full extent for repair and convalescence, the nervous energy which they possess. This disturbing influence can be counteracted by a straightforward exposition of Ramon y Cajal's or the newer English theory of brain mechanism.

Patients become very much disturbed if they observe a failure of certain faculties in themselves, and are prone to think that such a failure means serious exhaustion or enduring change. The power of attention is one of the faculties often disturbed in neurotic cases and causes patients needless solicitude. Disturbances of memory are the next most alarming elements in these cases. There are then many forms of mental distraction, absorption and preoccupation that sometimes frighten neurotic individuals who have become solicitous about themselves. Though only passing incidents, due to overattention to themselves and their ills, real or fancied, and the consequent lack of concentration of mind on a particular subject, the patients fear serious deterioration of their mental condition, or at least of mental control. The neuroglia theory of mental action throws a light on all these phases of mentality that serves to lessen the solicitude of patients and enable them to understand that, in spite of their fears, there is nothing but functional disturbance. The condition can be readily explained and it admits of complete restoration to health.

ATTENTION

Even more important, perhaps, than any other of the functions attributed to the neuroglia cells, is the rôle they may play in enabling the individual to concentrate attention on a particular subject, or at least to use a particular {125} portion of his brain, by bringing about a more active circulation in that portion than in any other, Ramon y Cajal attributes this power to the perivascular neuroglia cells. Every capillary in the brain has thousands of these little pseudopod prolongations. When the cells in a particular region contract, the blood vessels of the part are pulled wide open and a larger supply of blood flows more freely, stimulating the nerve cells by which it passes and supplying them with nutrition for the expenditure of energy that they may have to make. This is the physical process that underlies attention. When too much, that is, too long-continued attention is paid to any subject, without diversion of mind, the capillaries may easily acquire the habit of being open, and cells the custom of contraction, so that relaxation does not readily take place. Something of this kind is the most important element in the etiology of many functional nervous disorders.

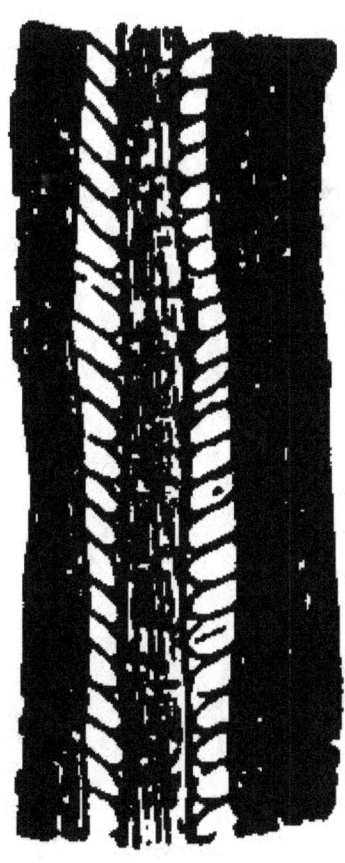

FIG. 18.—AN ARTERY FROM THE CEREBRAL CORTEX.—One can see numerous fine fibers passing over to the brain substance (Obersteiner).

Ease and Pleasure in Mental Operations.—On the other hand this same set of ideas explains many things otherwise difficult of understanding. For instance, we all know that habit enables us to apply ourselves to a particular subject with ever growing ease. What was extremely difficult for us at the beginning, may after a time become comparatively easy, and later even positively pleasant. Study, that is application of mind, is, at the beginning, for most people, not agreeable. If persisted in, it almost inevitably becomes a pleasure. Hard exercise of any kind is, at the beginning, sure to require great energy of purpose, and requires some subsidiary motive of approbation or reward to make us persist in it. But what was a distinct labor at the beginning becomes pleasant after a while. This may be applied to the neuroglia cells apparently as well as to the muscle fibers. On this theory, the reason for the gradual acquirement of an intense pleasure in the intellectual life becomes easy to understand.

Dangers of Over-attention.—The danger of concentration of mind on one's self, quite as much as on any other subject, becomes clearer when this theory is accepted as explaining the physical basis of the mental operations involved in attention. If people allow thoughts of themselves and of their physical processes constantly to occupy their minds, gradually that portion of the brain ruling over these becomes over-fatigued and fails to respond to the calls for relaxation. Insomnia may develop readily as a consequence of continued solicitude and prove to be, as the worst forms of insomnia so often are, quite unamenable to direct drug treatment, because, even during the enforced sleep that comes from drugs, dreams with regard to self and the supposed ills may still occupy the overworked portion of the brain. Nervous people are, most occupied with those parts of the brain which have something to do with the omission and transmission of trophic influence to particular parts of the body. As a consequence of the persistent hyperemia, too many trophic impulses are sent down. These cause an exaggeration of physiological function, in the stomach, the heart, or some other important organ. Hence these organs may become oversensitive.

For all these reasons, this theory of attention, of the great Spanish {126} investigator, deserves to be well known by those who hope to treat neurotic affections, especially functional diseases of the brain, and therefore I prefer once more to give it in his own words.

Ramon y Cajal's Theory of Attention.—Under usual conditions, the motor apparatus of the gray matter suffices for the explanation or the varied course of association of ideas and of the reaction produced by voluntary motion. But as soon as attention is concentrated upon an idea, or a small number of associated ideas, there enters into the problem, besides the active retraction of the neuroglia of the corresponding part of the brain, a new factor—the active congestion of the capillaries of the over-excited region. As a consequence of this, the energy of

81

emotion reaches a maximum. The heat and metabolism of the hyperemic parts is increased, which, of course, makes these parts capable of more work.

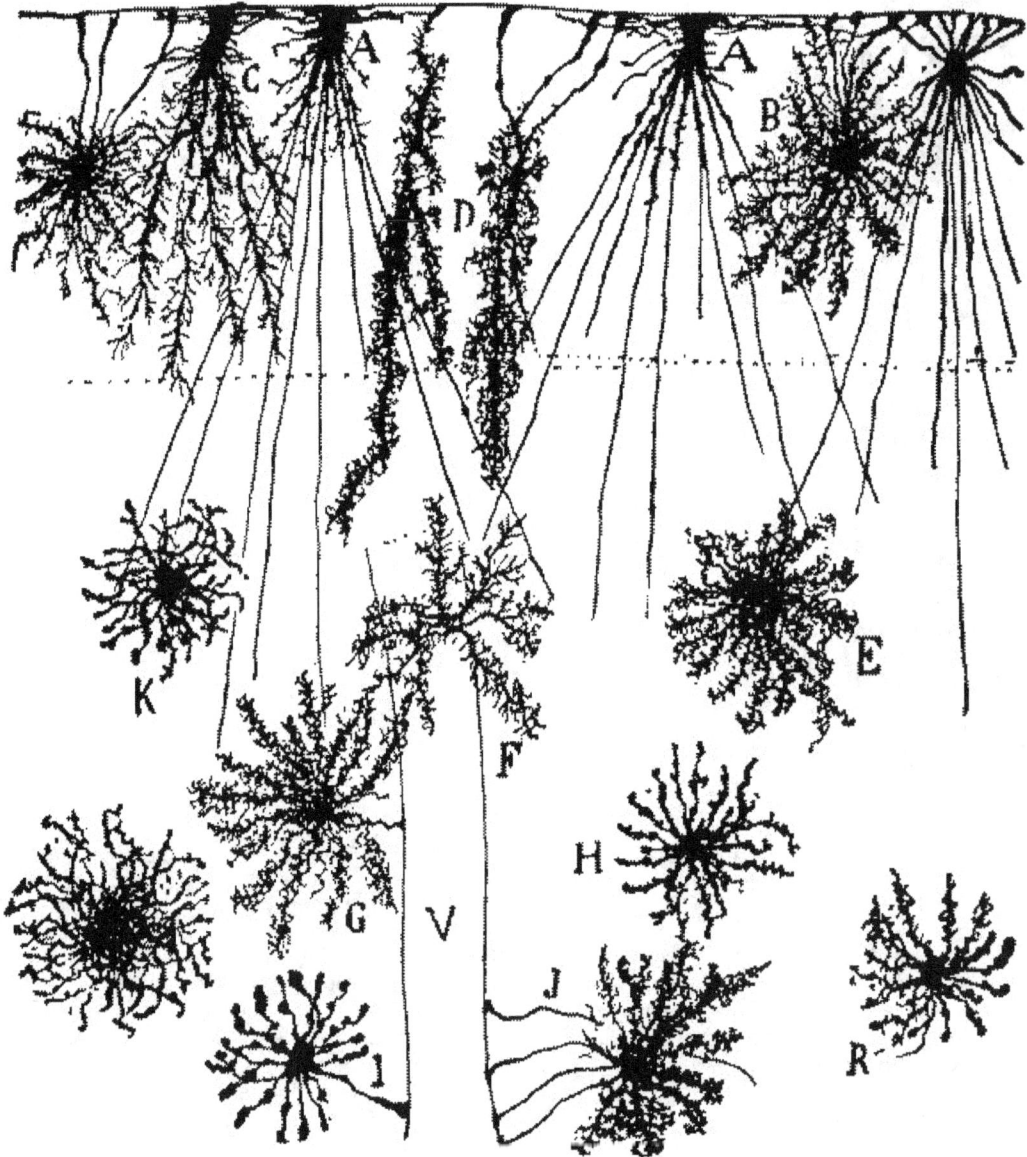

FIG. 19.—NEUROGLIA CELLS OF THE SUPERFICIAL LAYERS OF THE BRAIN FROM AN INFANT AGED TWO MONTHS (method of Golgi). A, B, C, D, neuroglia cells of the plexiform layer; E, F, G, H, K, R, neuroglia cells of the second and third layers; I, J, neuroglia cells with vascular pedicles; V, blood-vessel. (Ramon j Cajal.)

This congestion of various parts of the brain has been experimentally observed {127} by a number of physiologists. It can be best explained by considering that the will has an influence upon the nerves which produce a dilatation of the blood-vessels in different parts of the cerebral cortex. The process of attention, however, by which intellectual activity is concentrated upon a limited number of ideas, seems to be but very little under the control of the sympathetic nerve endings.

As a matter of fact, the capillaries of the brain are wanting in nerves and smooth muscle fibers. Hence they are not under the control of the sympathetic system. Only the relatively large arteries of the pia mater, which possesses a tunica muscularis are under a certain limited control of the sympathetic, which is able to produce in them an incomplete and not very well limited congestion. One of the difficulties of the problem of the activity of the sympathetic is best realized when we recall that vasomotor activity is usually involuntary. The process of attention, however, is entirely conscious and voluntary.

In the hypothesis that we have given, most of the difficulties disappear. Under the influence of the will, the pseudopod branches of the neuroglia cells, which end in the walls of the capillaries, contract. As the result of this, the bloodvessels, all of which are surrounded by lymph spaces, dilate, and this dilatation may proceed to such an extent that the vessels occupy the whole of the lymph spaces. Thus we can easily understand how the very limited congestions which are necessary for the concentration of thought upon a single idea may be brought about.

The perivascular lymph spaces which exist in the brain seem to be for the purpose of making these limited hyperemias easier. At the same time they serve a very useful purpose in preventing pressure or concussion, such as might be caused upon the neighboring nerve cells by too great dilatation of the blood vessels of a part.

It is needless to add that we do not consider the hypothesis that we have advanced to be absolutely without objection. On the contrary we believe that, owing to the difficulty of the problem and our, as yet, extremely slight knowledge of the anatomy and physiology of the nerve protoplasm, any theory as to the special mechanism of psychic processes is sure to be faulty. Rational hypotheses, however, which are supported by well-known facts, are not only justified, but are often fruitful of suggestive ideas. A scientific hypothesis often gives a new direction, suggests an untried method of observation, or hints at new ways of experiment, and, though it may not lead directly to truth, always brings us closer to methods of investigation and of criticism that are invaluable. Even though our further investigations should not confirm our hypothesis, the result will not be less positive. Negative conclusions lessen the number of possible hypotheses and therefore diminish the possibility of error in future investigations.

MEMORY

It is evident that some of the physical mechanisms that are employed for the lower grade mental processes at least can be explained on the neuroglia theory. Memory we share to a great extent with the animals, and for this the physical processes can be rather interestingly studied. We have all had the experience of being unable to recall a word when we wanted it. Commonly the word is a proper name with which there are not many direct connecting ideas, so that, somehow, we seem unable to trace the word to its depository in the brain. Occasionally we are sure that we know the first letter of the word. Sometimes we are able to name this letter, and, if we do so, the rest of the word will usually turn up a moment later. At times, however, the word fails to come and we grope for it. Then if we stop deliberately seeking it, the word will often after a longer or shorter time, come up spontaneously.

This experience is familiar to everyone. It is especially frequent with public speakers. Certain words have a habit of slipping away just when we {128} want them. At times by beginning a sentence confidently, even though there is a feeling that there is a missing word ahead, the word will turn up in time. Often it will not, and then a weak circumlocution must be indulged in. If it is a proper name, a description may have to be substituted, sometimes a confession may have to be made that the name will not come and the audience, unless it is very young, will sympathize with the speaker.

If we accept the idea that the memory has a definite location in the brain, the process is easily understood. Just how we cannot say, but somehow brain cells serve as the media by which our memory processes revert to knowledge that has been previously stored up. If now we assume that the repetition of things known is accomplished by bringing brain cells into connection with one another, and with the organs of speech, it is easy to understand that somehow the connection with a particular cell or set of cells cannot be secured at a given moment. This delay prevents us from being able to repeat things that we know, and know that we know, though we cannot somehow get at them. The will fails to reach the proper insulating plug of a neuroglia cell, which, if acted upon, would put a cell or group of cells in communication with others. As a result the message from it cannot flow down. We feel that we have it on the tip of our tongue, as we say, that a little effort may bring it to us and sometimes that effort succeeds. If there is any disturbance of consciousness by secondary motives, however, as by the excitement of public speaking or the flustering that comes to some people when they try to introduce even old-time friends and forget their names, then we cannot control the brain processes and memory fails. We do not for a moment think of attributing this failure of memory to the faculty of memory itself. We have the feeling that there is some mechanical obstacle. Ramon y Cajal's theory enables us to understand this obstacle better, perhaps, than any other.

An interesting phase of this lapse in memory helping us to a revelation of something of the physical process which underlies the faculty, is the fact that it implies a very intricate machine. Recalling has become such an obvious incident that we do not think of the complexity of action involved. Many things are brought together, and relations of all kinds serve to recall various facts and names and dates. Some of these relations are most bizarre. Particular names recall a definite series of facts. A color will bring up a scene or the memory of an individual. An odor will recall scenes long since apparently forgotten and will set trains of thought at work that are quite unexpected. Sometimes we wake in the morning with a name or a fact on our lips that we have been looking for for several days.

UNCONSCIOUS CEREBRATION

Some people actually learn to depend on unconscious cerebration. A man, for instance, who has to make an address on a particular subject or to write an article, will record that fact on a tablet and after gathering a few basic thoughts in connection with the subject proposed, will put it aside for the time being. He is confident that various illustrations and thoughts in connection with the subject will occur to him at intervals during the next few days, and that he will thus without direct labor accumulate an amount of {129} material for use. In the early morning hours he may find that thoughts on it come to him unbidden. Sometimes he will find these thoughts precious germs, that will develop during the course of the following days, and will be of great help to him. If he is worried and preoccupied with other things very much, this may not happen, but under ordinary circumstances he can continue routine occupations which demand practically all of his time, yet continue to develop the subject selected for his paper or address. The more he has occupied his mind with the subject at the beginning, the more will this unconscious cerebration continue.

ABSTRACTION OF MIND

Features of the mechanism of mental operations are brought out in certain phenomena of abstraction of mind, which show how the attention can be so short-circuited that sensations from the periphery utterly fail to penetrate to the consciousness. Most men have had the experience of taking out their watches, looking at them, and then putting them back. Presently somebody asks what time it is. Unable to recollect what it was that they saw, they have to look again. There is no doubt that they meant to observe the time.

The same thing is true for practically all the senses. A pickpocket takes advantage of our being occupied with many other feelings in the midst of the jostling in a crowd on a car, or before a show window, or he has a confederate add to the sensations already streaming up to us, calling attention particularly to the other side of the body, and then inserts his hand into our pocket and extracts what he finds. Sometimes we have a faint memory of something having happened to that pocket, but our attention was occupied elsewhere.

In hearing we have the same experience. When thoroughly occupied with a book, a person may talk to us or ask us a question and we have no idea of what was said, sometimes utterly failing to hear the voice; sometimes we hear the sound of the voice, but do not comprehend the meaning of the words.

When we are unprepared for a question we nearly always have to have it repeated to us. Sitting in a railroad train, if the person behind us, whom we did not expect to talk to us, asks a question, it is very probable that on the first asking we shall not notice it at all, considering that it is addressed to someone else. On its repetition, it may appeal to us as addressed to ourselves, but even then we readily lose its significance because our attention has not been called to the wording of it soon enough to enable us to comprehend it thoroughly. These experiences, so familiar that we have probably all had them at some time or other, indicate how universal is the power of the mind to concentrate itself upon itself to the extent of neglecting sensations from the outer world, even though they may pass the periphery of the organism and manifestly affect the first neuron of the chain that leads up to our brain and consequently to consciousness. They do not reach the center with sufficient intensity to be understood, and a conscious act of attention must be made before we comprehend their meaning.

{130}

PREOCCUPATION OF MIND

This is true, not only for ordinary sensations, but even for such as would ordinarily be presumed to be so insistent in their call that they could not be neglected. The concentration of mind necessary for this is not common to all mankind; it is possessed only by a few individuals whose intellect represents the larger portion of their personality. Certain of the great investigating scientific geniuses have had the faculty of so concentrating their attention upon the questions with which their intellects were engaged, that even the call of appetite did not make itself felt. Newton was one of these. Over and over again, he was known to neglect to take his meals, even though they were brought to him, and, occasionally, he would entirely forget whether he had taken a meal or not. But Newton is not an extreme exception. Most of the great mathematicians have had experiences of this kind and, indeed, mathematics seems to be that special branch of intellectual work which most readily brings about a preoccupation of mind sufficient to completely shut out the outer world for the time being. Archimedes, the great ancient mathematician, lost his life because of preoccupation with mathematical problems that kept him from telling the Roman soldiers, who had strict orders to spare him, who he was.

Complete absorption of mind to the exclusion of all external sensations is not, however, confined to the mathematicians. Mommsen, the historian, was famous for his fits of mental abstraction. Once he patted a school-boy on the head and asked whose boy he was, to be told rather startlingly, "Yours." Lombroso, the criminal psychologist, was subject to abstraction in almost as great a degree. Men have become so preoccupied in study as not to appreciate the significance of warnings, indicating that a serious accident was about to happen, such as a fire or the fall of some object that they should have avoided, or some other danger to themselves. The tendency to such abstraction is responsible for many accidents on busy city streets. When so preoccupied, painters walk off scaffolds, and such preoccupation of mind is extremely dangerous, not only for the man himself, but for those who are working with him.

Everyone knows that a slight headache frequently disappears in pleasant company. There is sometimes the suspicion, though it is quite unjustified, that because a person has a headache which can be cured by engaging in a favorite occupation, the headache is more imaginary than real. The common experience with toothache shows the falsity of this opinion. There is no imagination in regard to toothache, yet it, too, except in very severe cases, will be so modified as to be quite negligible if the victim has some mental occupation that is very absorbing. Pains of other kinds that are just as real, may be modified in the same way. I have known a boy to suffer enough from the presence of an unsuspected kidney stone to give up play and come into the house, yet he could be made entirely to forget his discomfort by a game of checkers. On account of the ease with which the pain was thus dispelled, the suspicion was harbored that his ache was more imaginary than real. The ache continued and at the end of about a year there was an acute exacerbation which justified an operation, and the stone was removed.

In all these instances there is evidently a question of the unmaking, or at {131} least imperfect making, of connections between the peripheral and central neurons, because of the existence of connections between different portions of the brain itself which take up the attention. This attention to mental things may become exaggerated, and must be guarded against, but it represents a valuable psychotherapeutic remedy. Whenever the peripheral connections are unmade, external sensation is unfelt. Even though the peripheral neuron may be suffering to some extent, this is true. It is this law of attention that must be taken advantage of for psychotherapeutics. People who are liable to be too much concerned with their sensations, must be taught to occupy themselves with interests that will absorb the attention. Central neurons can, except under very serious circumstances, be made to connect with one another so intimately as to bring about the neglect of many bothersome external sensations.

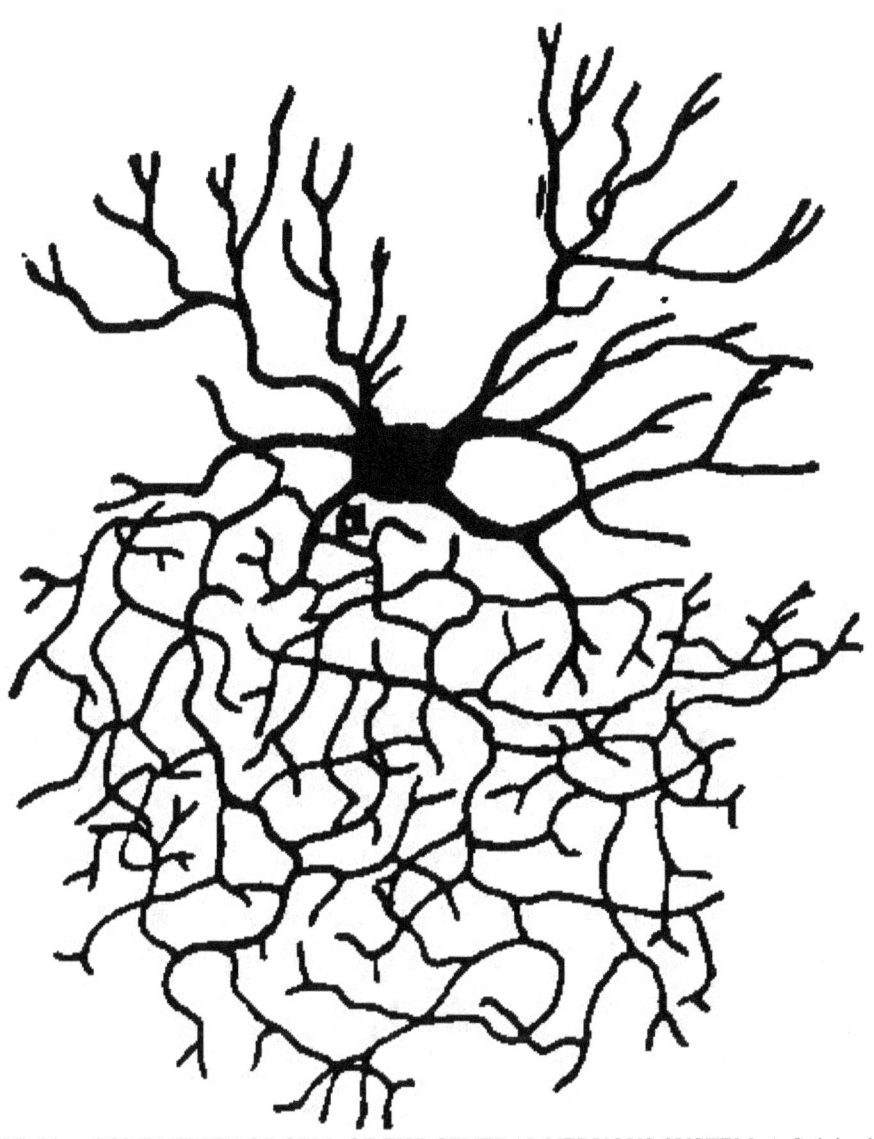

FIG. 20.—COMPLEXITY OF CELL OF THE CENTRAL NERVOUS SYSTEM. A Golgi cell after Andriezen. (Barker.)

On the other hand, when the connections with the periphery are well made, external sensations flow in on us to the exclusion of thought and then even simple sensations may be exaggerated so as to become painful. Anything that attracts our attention so much that we cannot think quietly about it, is likely to be a disturbance rather than a pleasure. Music is distinctly pleasant, yet very loud music becomes painful. The reason is that the peripheral neuron is so much disturbed that these excessive vibrations are communicated to other neurons connected with it and they are unable to occupy themselves with anything except this over-strenuous sensation. A very bright light has something of the same effect, and the same thing is true for all the other senses. A pleasant odor, if over strong, becomes disgusting. A very sweet taste is cloying. This over excitation of neurons may come from without, or may come from within. If the central neuron is so much occupied with itself, and the sensation that is flowing into it, that it is prevented from making such connections as would communicate and distribute the sensations properly, then the sensory phenomenon becomes painful, though it may not be exaggerated in the peripheral neuron.

VITAL ENERGY BEHIND BRAIN CELLS

In all of these phenomena there is something more than brain cells at work. Brain cells are guided, co-ordinated, controlled, and even overseen, in their labors. The same conclusion becomes inevitable with regard to the action of the cells of the body generally. A generation or two ago it was the custom to attempt to explain all the processes in the body by chemical and physical principles. Respiration, for instance, and absorption of gases into the blood in the lungs and the expiration of gases that have been generated within the body during vital processes, were supposed to be entirely explicable on the principle of the diffusion of gases. The absorption of various substances into

85

the body proper from the intestinal tract, and the excretion {132} of various substances from within the body into the excretory organs, as well as the process of secretion, were supposed to be nothing more than varying phenomena of osmosis and exosmosis. There has since been a general recognition of the fact that these principles do not explain many of the incidents within the body in its relations to its surroundings, and that vital processes are something much more than merely manifestations of physics and chemistry.

The lungs are not mere laboratories in which refinements of the laws of the diffusion of gases may be studied, for under varying pressures from without that would vitiate the ordinary laws of diffusion, inspiration and expiration continues. Fishes live at depths where the pressure is so great that expiration would seem to be impossible, yet they succeed in eliminating harmful gaseous material. Prof. Haldane of Cambridge has called attention to many of these processes. Animal stomachs are not test-tubes. Animal excretion, and above all, secretion, is carried on sometimes in accordance with but, almost more often, in defiance of chemical and physical principles. The individual, even in the lower animals, counts for much more than the chemical constituents of the tissues and the physical principles involved.

Besides, all the parts of the organism are co-ordinated, and there are wonderful checks and counterchecks which show that animals are much more than colonies of cells fortuitously growing together and habituated to such common life by many generations of heredity and environment and training. In a word, the old vitalistic principle has become popular once more and even great physiologists have insisted that there is a principle of life which guides and controls and co-ordinates the different portions of the body. Especially does this seem to be true of the brain. We have here an intensely complex machine, composed literally of billions of parts which work together, and in doing so accomplish wonderful results. Of the existence of this machine, much more of the great intricacy of its parts and mechanism, we are quite unconscious. We learn to use it in very early years with an assurance and a perfection that is amazing, considering how complex it is. The less we think about it and its workings, the better does it work and the less disturbance of function is there in its accomplishment.

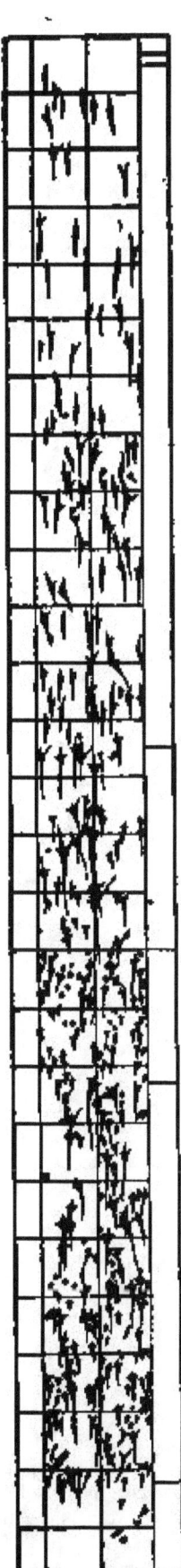

Fig. 21.—SECTION THROUGH THE CORTEX OF THE GYRUS OCCIPITALIS SUPERIOR. (Hammarberg. Barker.)

If a vitalistic principle were needed to enable us to understand the workings of the ordinary body cells, how much more is it required for the workings of brain cells. There is something behind that guides and rules the brain, and through which it accomplishes its work. It is this that brings about an unconscious cerebration accomplishing intellectual results for us even when the brain machine itself is at rest as when asleep, or fails, for some reason, to be in readiness to take up the work that we demand of it. It is this vital principle that coordinates the movements of brain cells which represent {133} the physical processes underlying memory and the nervous elements of the sensitive and motor phenomena of the organism. Reflection on the physical mechanism underlying mental operations of various kinds, demands the vitalistic explanation much more than the physiological phenomena which have converted physiologists to the old way of thinking in our time. Our individuality is probably largely due to the physical basis of our mentality, but there is something more than that required for any theory of mental operations that would satisfy all the questions that come to us. There is, then, actual proof of the existence of a force that is part of us, that constitutes a bit of the essence of our personalities, yet is capable of accomplishing results that we cannot understand, and of managing a machine that transcends any physical powers that we can think of.

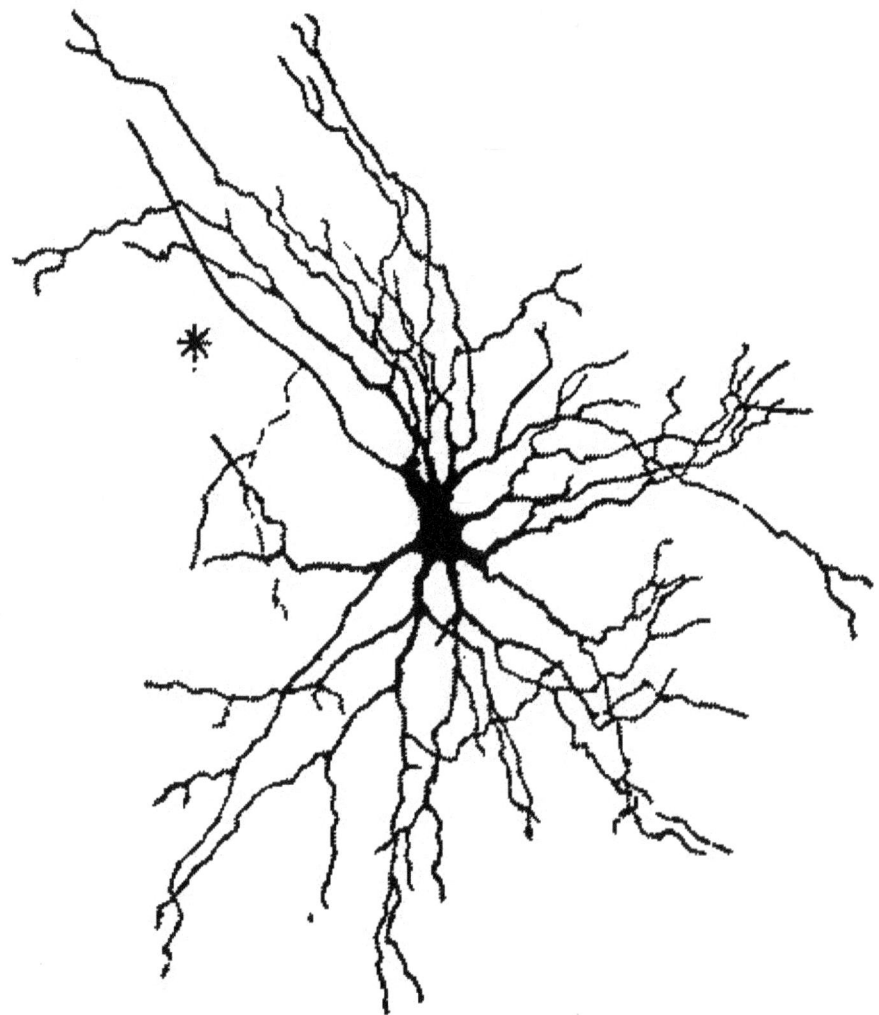

FIG. 22—MOTOR CELL OF VENTRAL HORN OF SPINAL CORD FROM THE HUMAN FETUS, THIRTY CENTIMETERS LONG (method of Golgi; after von Lenhossek. Barker.)

This vital force behind the nervous system contains stores of energy that can be called on for therapeutic purposes. It is the directing, co-ordinating and energizing force which controls the central nervous system, and enables it to accomplish its purposes. It is the disappearance of this force at death which leaves the body without vital activity, though no physical difference between the dead and the living body can be demonstrated. Changes in the body *follow* death; they are not simultaneous. This vital force supplies the energy that we call the will, and underlies the process called "living on the will" which so often serves to maintain existence when there is every reason to think that a fatal termination is due. The amount of energy thus available is limited, {134} but is much more powerful than has been thought. It is of the greatest possible service in preserving health and eliminating disease. Its existence, demonstrated by the complex nervous system which we employ with such confidence, though we know nothing of it, furnishes the best possible basis for confident attempts at rousing the patient to use the vital energy he possesses for the strengthening of weakness, the correction of deficiency and the control of evil tendencies.

CHAPTER VI

UNCONSCIOUS CEREBRATION

Many of the exhausting neurotic and psycho-neurotic affections so common in recent years are largely due to the failure of patients to secure such mental relaxation as will permit complete repair of nervous waste. We are proud of being a generation of specialists. Some men never get completely away from the set of thoughts with which they are occupied in their particular specialty. Waking or sleeping these thoughts are with them. It is almost impossible, then, for cells of the central nervous system to secure such rest as they need. Cells must be put at absolute rest so that nutritional processes may go on entirely undisturbed, and every portion of the cell be renewed in vigor. Re-creation, in its original meaning, is exactly what must be provided for nerve cells.

The trouble is not alone that men occupy a very narrow set of brain cells with their special interest, and make all their energy pass through that set, but among men who are lacking in a certain insulation in the nervous system, this particular set of cells continues to be active, even at times when they think they are resting or diverting themselves. Unconscious cerebration (the occupation of the mind with subjects when we are not deliberately giving our attention to them) is a common phenomenon in human psychology. With the rise of extreme specialization, it has become even more dangerous than before. In the past unconscious cerebration might mean any occupation, with any one of a number of interests. At the present it is likely to mean concentration of thought on a particular subject with which the brain is prone to be occupied more than is good for it, even during the hours of ordinary labor. It seems worth while to discuss at some length, then, the subject of unconscious cerebration, because it constitutes the pathological physiology of many nervous states that we see in modern life.

Frequency of Unconscious Cerebration.—The mind, having been set to work over a given thought, continues at it sub-consciously, even while apparently completely occupied with something else. Most people who devote themselves to the intellectual life have experienced phenomena more striking and going much farther in unconscious cerebration than this. Most writers have a common experience: if they arrange their thoughts on a given subject and then turn aside to something else, they find, when they go over the same subject next day, much more material than came the day before. The thoughts for an article will often gradually accumulate by unconscious cerebration after the process has been consciously started.

{135}

At intervals during the next few days succeeding the determination to write a certain article (at moments when no conscious thought is being given to it), ideas crop up that help to fill out the original scheme of thought, and if these are jotted down, a good deal of intellectual work is accomplished without the necessity for that labor over a desk that most of us scheme to avoid. The more familiar literary work becomes, the more frequent are these experiences, and one occasionally wakes up with a thought that opens up a new vista and adds valuable material to what has already been accumulated. If the subject is a large one, as for a book, then most writers will probably confess that some of their best thoughts have come in this "hit and miss" fashion rather than at the times when they were seriously applying themselves to elaborating their theme.

Inspiration.—Some of the great literary writers have felt that their brain work was so independent of themselves that the word inspiration properly suited what they were accomplishing. Thackeray destroyed sheet after sheet of manuscript, utterly dissatisfied with it until, as the result of keeping at it, inspiration would come. Then he would be able to fill up rapidly many pages with work so finished that it needed little correction or polish. George Eliot, at times, became so absorbed in her writing that it almost appeared to her that some other personality than her own was wielding the pen. Her imaginary characters became real to her, and it was while under the stimulus of this impression of living in an imaginative world with them that she succeeded in accomplishing her best work. Many other authors were, of course, very different. Some of them ridiculed the idea of waiting for inspiration. Most of them, however, found it difficult to begin their task at certain times, yet if they forced themselves to it, and once got their minds going, the line of thought ran on easily and, at the close of the task, they looked back with pleasure and wonder that they were able to accomplish so much.

Illustrations.—This is true not only of literary work, whose main purpose is the arrangement of details of information of various kinds with personal opinions concerning it, but also of original thought of any kind. Many stories of poets are told illustrating this. They wander round with pencils and jot down thoughts that come here and there at what are called moments of inspiration. The poets dream over their subjects, catch fleeting thoughts that, vague at first, sing themselves into musical expression. Music seems to be on the same plane with poetry, for there is the well-known story of the distinguished German musician who, walking with his wife in the park, found himself without paper at the moment when he had an inspiration. He used his own cuffs to write upon, and then finally impressed those of his wife into the service of carrying home the precious musical motifs that he was afraid might not come again if he allowed the favorable moment to pass without recording them.

There are stories of Tennyson finding some of his most perfect lines in the fields, after hours of seclusion and effort in his study had failed to round them out to his satisfaction, or dreaming them into shape, or waking to find one ready made to be written down. The letters of Wordsworth tell how often such incidents happened in his life.

{136}

SLEEP COMMUNICATIONS

Any one who has been thinking much for several days about a problem is likely to wake up with the thought that he has dreamed a solution of it, though unfortunately the solution has not remained in his memory. It seems as if a communication has been made to him during sleep. I have discussed dream life with many men engaged in serious work, and practically all of them confess to such experiences. Preoccupation of mind with a subject during the waking hours leads to at least some occupation of mind with the same subject during sleep. This unconscious occupation must often require rather strenuous attention, exhausting nutrition, using up nerve force and hampering the rest that is so important for tired human nature.

It is interesting both as psychological fact and as showing how, sleeping and waking, his work was ever present with him. He had been for two weeks striving to decipher the somewhat obscure impression of a fossil fish on the stone slab in which it was preserved. Weary and perplexed he put his work aside at last, and tried to dismiss it from his mind. Shortly after, he waked one night persuaded that while asleep he had seen his fish with all the missing features perfectly restored. But when he tried to hold and make fast the image it escaped him. Nevertheless he went early to the Jardin des Plantes, thinking that on looking anew at the impression he should see something that would put him on the track of his vision. In vain—the blurred record was as blank as ever. The next night he saw the fish again, but with no more satisfactory result. When he woke it disappeared from his memory as before. Hoping that the same experience might be repeated, on the third night he placed a pencil and paper beside his bed before going to sleep. Accordingly toward morning the fish reappeared in his dream, confusedly at first, but at last with such distinctness that he had no longer any doubt as to its zoological characters. Still half dreaming, in perfect darkness, he traced these characters on the sheet of paper at the bedside. In the morning he was surprised to see in his nocturnal sketch features which he thought it impossible the fossil itself should reveal. He hastened to the Jardin des Plantes, and, with his drawing as a guide, succeeded in chiseling away the surface of the stone under which the portions of the fish proved to be hidden. When wholly exposed, it corresponded with his drawing, and his dream, and he succeeded in classifying it with ease. He often spoke of this as a good illustration of the well-known fact that when the body is at rest the tired brain will do the work it refused before.

Hilprecht's Sleep Vision.—Quite as surprising a dream was that of Prof. Hilprecht, of the University of Pennsylvania. He had been trying for some time to decipher certain characters on ancient cylinders from the Orient. In spite of much hard mental labor he had been utterly unable to reach definite conclusions. In the midst of work on the subject he dreamt one night that a priest of the olden time appeared to him and read off the inscription that he had in vain been trying to decipher. Immediately after waking he told his wife of his dream and wrote down the interpretation that had thus been given. It was quite different from anything that he himself had obtained any hint of in his previous studies. When he got back to the inscription he found that this interpretation would satisfy the conditions better than any other, and there seemed no doubt that it represented the missing solution.

{138}

Somnambulism.—These curiously vivid dreams are occasionally associated with somnambulistic phenomena. Sometimes very definite purposes, requiring careful adaptation of means to ends, are accomplished in the somnambulistic state, and yet the actions are completely forgotten. I have recently been consulted about a case in which a young woman, on a visit to a family, had been shown some pretty though not expensive jewels. Evidently the guest envied their possession, for she got up during sleep and took the jewels and hid them. There seems no reason to doubt her statement that she remembered nothing at all about the incident. The taking was not attributed to her. There had been previous experiences of the same kind with things belonging to this young woman's sister. Somnambulism represents a degree of unconscious cerebration that may have serious results. Combinations of intellectual work with somnambulism are not infrequent, though many of the stories that are told are exaggerated. Some of them are authenticated. Ribot has a typical example of intellectual accomplishment, in a somnambulistic condition, that shows how far this may go:

A clear case of somnambulism was that of a clergyman, whom his wife saw rise from bed in his sleep, go to a writing table, and write rapidly for some minutes. This done he returned to bed, and slept on until morning. On awaking, he told her that in a dream he had worked out an argument for a sermon, of which he now retained no recollection whatever. She led him to the writing table, and showed him the written sheet upon which he found his argument worked out in the most satisfactory manner.

PATHOLOGICAL SIGNIFICANCE

Unconscious cerebration is not, then, a trivial matter, and not an unusual experience. It probably occurs in every individual to a much greater extent than he thinks, unless he is engaged in analyzing his mental processes and their ways rather carefully. This constitutes one of the dangers of the intellectual life, which must also be guarded against in business life or in any absorbing occupation. When the mind has become intensely occupied with a subject, it is not easy to relinquish it. Even when we turn to something else, mental activity in the old groove continues to some extent, and so will prevent the rest that is necessary for the repair of tissue. Under these conditions the *re-creation* that is so important does not take place quite as well as it should, and even sleep does not relieve us from the burden of mental work. Mental exhaustion will result as a consequence of constant occupation, and so mental relaxation must be secured. Deliberate means and methods must be employed in order that we may not deceive ourselves into thinking we are securing mental recreation, though all the time certain exhausting mental processes continue to be active.

Dual Mental Occupation.—Many are inclined to think that reading, especially the reading of newspapers and magazines, which has become so popular in our time, furnishes an occupation of mind that enables one, for a time at least, to get away from cares and worries. This is probably true when the news is of special interest, or there is some form of excitement, or at the beginning of such reading before one grows accustomed to the usual {139} formula of the magazine stories; but as years go on and cares increase, such reading does not afford an occupation of mind that enables one to throw them off. It helps to pass the time, but the cares and worries keep insistently presenting themselves, and the effort to inhibit them, and at the same time pay some attention to what we are reading, makes a double task. Such reading, then, far from being restful, rather adds to the burden of care and to the labor of the mind, for besides the conscious cerebration, there is the undercurrent of subconscious cerebration disturbing the rest of cells that should be free from labor. The constant renewal of effort to keep one train of thought from interfering with another is itself a waste of nervous energy. This whole matter of reading is coming to occupy a new place in the minds of educators, especially of those who are trying to realize the scientific significance of various phases of education. In his address as the President of the British Association for the Advancement of Science, at the Winnipeg meeting in 1909, Prof. J. J. Thompson, the British physicist, sums up the value of reading as an intellectual exercise in a way that would not be gratifying to those who, in recent years, have apparently accepted the doctrine that in much reading there is much information and, therefore, much education. He says:

It is possible to read books to pass examinations without the higher qualities of the mind being called into play. Indeed, I doubt if there is any process in which the mind is more quiescent than in reading without interest. I might appeal to the widespread habit of reading in bed as a prevention of insomnia as a proof of this.

Social Duties.—So-called social duties are, in this respect, very like reading. When we meet new people who are interesting, we get diversion of mind in their company. When the people with whom we are, however, already familiar, and perhaps most of them a little tiresome, then what is presumed to be a social diversion becomes merely a bore, all the problems of the day obtrude themselves, of real rest there is none, and re-creation can scarcely be possible. Nearly the same thing is true of the present-day theater, after we have become used to its offerings. A serious play, well constructed and with life's problems touched deeply, may grip us and take us out of ourselves, constituting a complete and magnificent diversion. For a limited number of people music accomplishes this purpose. Unfortunately, the number is very limited, and for those for whom music is the greatest diversion, it sometimes constitutes in itself a poignant source of mental exhaustion. Music may be a very trying thing, especially for women, and for those who have souls extremely sensitive to its manifold effects.

Upon these considerations, the importance of unconscious cerebration is brought home to the physician. It is impossible for a great many people to keep their minds inactive, and this is particularly true of two classes of people: those who have superabundant mental energy and those who lack self-control. To both of these classes of men and women, the physician must point out the dangers of unconscious cerebration—the occupation of mind with some subject, even at times while they imagine they are occupied with something else, or even during sleep. Such continuous occupation with a single subject is dangerous. Physicians must emphasize that many supposed {140} mental occupations are really so superficial that they allow other more exhausting processes to continue below them in the sphere of consciousness. As a consequence, the mind, instead of being relaxed, is really more tense than before, because occupied with two sets of thoughts. Very often it would be better for such people to continue with the more serious problem until its solution came, or until they realized that they must divert themselves.

MENTAL RELAXATION

What is important for mental relaxation, apparently, is not that a man shall try to set his mind at absolute rest, for that seems to be impossible, if a man really has a mind; nor that he shall occupy it with trivial things (because his interest will not be caught by them and will revert to the last serious thing that he was doing), but that he shall have an outlet for mental activity in entirely another direction from that to which he usually devotes himself. In other words, it is important that a man shall have a hobby, and that he shall ride that hobby whenever his ordinary business, whatever that may be, will permit him, and the more interesting the hobby, the better.

REMEDIAL MEASURES

The most important general remedy for over-prolonged mental occupation with a single subject, is some outdoor sport or form of exercise that requires all the attention. Horseback exercise is particularly valuable; boating, especially where the man has charge of the boat himself and where he has to have his wits about him, and the various sports. It is particularly important that men should not be alone during the taking of their exercise and diversion of mind. Above all, human interests take a man outside of himself and keep him from disturbing his mental equipoise by too much devotion to a single subject.

CHAPTER VII

DISTANT MENTAL INFLUENCE

There is a very general impression that it is possible, at least under certain circumstances, for one human mind to influence another at a distance without any of the ordinary known means of communication. Many people have had the experience of thinking about a friend whom they have not seen for a long while, and shortly after meeting him. Sometimes it is found that the friend was making up his mind to bring about the meeting just about the time that the thought of him came. Many have had the experience of writing a letter and having it cross in the mails with another from their correspondent, evidently written within a few hours, though there had perhaps been no communication for weeks or months before. There are people who insist that they can, by concentrating the mind and fixing their eyes on the head of a {141} person some distance in front of them in a theater, or a railway car, cause the person to turn around. There are others who say that by thinking strongly of some person in a distant part of a large room, that person can be made to think of them. In general, there are many persons who are quite sure that there is evidence enough to indicate the possibility of distant mental influence, or, as it has come to be called learnedly, telepathy.

Telepathy, from the two Greek words, *tele*, at a distance, and *pathos*, feeling, has been much discussed in recent years. Many people who use the word glibly are inclined to think they know much about it. A long word, however, is not an explanation, and, just here, George Eliot's expression "we map out our ignorance in long Greek names" is worth recalling. There are a number of phenomena that seem to require some such theory as that of telepathy, but the phenomena are still under discussion and their significance is by no means clear. As we understand it, telepathy may mean either thought transference or mind reading, that is, either the active process by which we communicate our thought to someone at a distance, or the passive process by which we receive communications from others. These thoughts include the idea of mental influence at a distance; that is, we can by willing influence the wills, or at least the motives to action, of people at a distance and they may, in turn, influence ours. The further thought has come, that since the mind largely influences the body in matters of health, so mental influence from a distance by affecting mind, may either improve or injure health.

Some sensitive people are disturbed by the thought that they may be influenced from a distance by others, or at least that suggestions that come to them, may be due to telepathic influence. Investigation would probably show that there are at least as many persons disturbed by real or supposed telepathic influences as there are of those who have hallucinations. Sometimes it is said that such persons are not quite sane, but the more experience a physician has with them, the more he dismisses the thought of insanity and proceeds to use contrary suggestion and frank discussion, in order to counteract the mental influences. Insane persons think they are being influenced from a distance just as they hear voices and see visions, but such hallucinations may occur to the sane, as apparent telepathic experiences may also.

Witchcraft.—It used to be a common belief that people could be influenced, even at a distance, by the mere evil wishes or intentions of others. After all, the old beliefs in witchcraft that were so common in Europe and in America until well into the eighteenth century represent the conviction of mankind that at least certain people might, from a distance, seriously influence them for evil. Always the fear of malign influence was uppermost in people's minds and literally hundreds of thousands of witches were prosecuted, and many thousands of them put to death, because of this belief in the possibility of their working evil to others at a distance, merely by willing it. Occasionally some such material auxiliary to malign purpose as an image in wax of the one to whom the evil was to be done was used. Into this the ill wisher stuck pins according to the part that he or she would want to be affected in the enemy, but as a rule the will, and nothing more, was used.

Absent Treatment.—In our own time a system of healing, that has attracted many followers, has taken up the idea of beneficent mental influence at a distance. "Absent treatment" has now become a familiar expression. {142} That those who believe in such favorable influence at a distance should also believe in unfavorable influence seems inevitable. As a matter of fact, we know that the founder of this special sect always insisted on the power for evil over herself and her followers of those who want to exert the injurious influence of animal magnetism—malicious animal magnetism as it is called. A very definite attempt was made to bring a case of this kind before the courts, the subject matter of which exactly resembled some of the old witchcraft trials in New England! And in spite of the insistence and emphatic assertion that no such thing is intended, from the principles that are accepted the necessary logical conclusion is a return to the belief in witchcraft.

Malignant Magnetism.—As a number of persons are likely to fear such evil influence of others upon them, the question of the possibility of it must come up for discussion in order that its status may be clear in the physician's mind, for by just as much as he can make certain to the patient that modern psychology refuses to accept distant influence, will he be able to reassure his patient. Of course, the patients who come with such complaints have usually some element of mental trouble. The alienist sees any number of people who are sure that enemies at a distance are working spells upon them, some by electrical, some by magnetic means, and some by telepathic absent treatment, or absent ill-wishing. Such notions are the delusions of the disequilibrated and these persons often cannot be reasoned with. Yet very often a distinct delusion may be reasoned out of even a subrational person, if it is taken seriously, and some striking expression of its irrationality and of its total disagreement with scientific views can be shown to the patient.

Action Without a Medium.—The medieval scholastic philosophers quoted as an absolutely accepted principle the Latin axiom, *"actio in distans repugnat."* Literally translated this means action at a distance is repugnant to reason. Expressed less technically, the principle declares that any action of one body on another, where there is no medium connecting them, no link that in some way places them in contact with one another, is absurd. The expression *in distans* means that the two bodies are separated from one another and stand in two places having no connection of any kind. This principle would ordinarily seem to preclude the possibility of one person acting on another, unless there is some mode of communication.

Crookes' Theory.—Sir William Crookes, at a meeting of the British Association for the Advancement of Science about ten years ago, in discussing telepathy, directed attention to the fact that there exists by scientific hypothesis, generally accepted, a definite medium of communication by which minds at a distance might influence one another. The medium is the ether which, according to physical theories, besides carrying light, also carries heat and electrical waves, and in recent years is recognized as transmitting the impulses of wireless telegraphy. It is possible that when the cells of certain human minds are stimulated to a particular phase of vibration, they may, even at long distances, affect the cells of other individuals that resemble them, or are attuned to them, that is, have the same moment of vibration. This is the principle which underlies wireless telegraphy. Whether the vibrations of living nerve cells can be made thus to radiate out over the ether and arouse in any way other cells, especially to the extent of communicating ideas, is a matter still open for investigation. The possibility of this occurring {143} cannot be denied. We are, however, still in the presence of a condition and not a theory. The question is whether minds are thus influenced at a distance—whether we have data enough to establish the occurrence of telepathy or mental communications of any kind at a distance.

No Practical Thought Transfer.—At the beginning, it is of the greatest importance to recall that, while many people think there must be something in telepathy and presume that the investigations of recent years have shown not only the possibility of the communication of ideas from mind to mind and of the mental influence of one person over another, even at long distances, but also its actual occurrence, yet all our ordinary life is founded on the absolute negation of any such phenomenon. For instance, our courts of law are conducted in direct contradiction of the possibility of anything like telepathy. Juries are summoned of twelve good men and true who, as far as possible, know nothing about the prisoner and as little as may be about the case. They are supposed to get all their information in the court room. We do not believe that any of them by any wonderful process might be able to know what was going on in the prisoner's mind in spite of his plea. Nor do we think for a moment that they can know what is going on, apart from what he communicates in evidence, in the mind of any witness. Neither is there the slightest presumption that the judge or any of our lawyers can know anything about what is in the minds of any of the persons present, except as they reveal it by outward signs.

A lawyer who could employ telepathy with success would be simply invaluable. Before a month had passed, he would have all the business of the criminal courts in his hands.

Mental Retention.—In answer to this it may be said that these represent conditions in which determined effort is made to keep all possible information that may be in the minds of all concerned from passing to others. Everyone concedes the power of such absolute self retention of our thoughts, when we deliberately wish to keep them from being known to others. When people wish to communicate their thoughts to others, then it may be different. In that case the sending and receiving minds are both active and the conditions for interaction, if it were at all possible, would be favorable. Just this condition obtains in the court room every day. An innocent prisoner wants with all his heart and soul to communicate the idea of his innocence to the judge and jury. Of course, he does not succeed by telepathic means in transferring to them any inkling of the truth. On the contrary, his very nervousness and anxiety to set himself right before them will sometimes actually cause prejudice.

The rule that has thus been exemplified in our courts of law holds for all business transactions. The ordinary customs of business presume that the buyer does not know what the seller paid for the particular article that is being exchanged, and it is on the strength of this that profit becomes possible. A few telepathic merchants or customers would work serious havoc in business life.

What thus holds for important affairs in life is just as strikingly exemplified in the trivial round of social existence and in our intercourse with friends. Suppose one woman knew what another woman thought of her!

That charming, old-fashioned institution "courting" would go entirely by {144} the board, if there were any such thing as real telepathy. In general, social life in all its features would become very, very different to what it is.

How Much Slight External Expression Conveys.—Mrs. Coventry Patmore, the English poet's wife, once told a little story of some people who lived in a distant island where the inhabitants possessed tails. These tails were, as they are on the animals, organs of expression, but of involuntary and quite unconscious expression. It was utterly impossible for the people there to say nice things to one another when they had quite other things in mind, because if they did not like the person their tails hung down behind; if they did like them they wagged rather vigorously, no matter what their owner might be saying. This simple revelation of feelings, so much less than even the slightest

93

degree of telepathy would occasion, was quite enough to work a revolution in the social affairs of this romantic island. It made the people truthful and candid in their relations with one another.

Negation of Telepathy.—There is, perhaps, some evidence of the occurring of telepathy in special cases, but all of our present-day life is organized on a firm basis of complete negation of the existence or occurrence of telepathy to even the slightest degree. Every-day experiences teach us that husbands and wives, even those who have the greatest love and confidence toward each other, do not really know their life partners, for it frequently happens that something turns up which reveals an unsuspected side of character even after many years of intimate union.

We human beings are "infinitely repellent particles," to use the phrase, of Matthew Arnold. We never get close enough to one another to have a real glimpse into the depths of other minds. The information that is supposed to pass by telepathy from one person to another is so often just the kind that we would most sedulously conceal. There is extreme unlikelihood then that any such passage of information takes place. The cases cited, as proof of this transference of thought, are much more likely to be coincidences than any evidence of true telepathy.

Supposed Examples of Telepathy.—In the first place, though there are opportunities for the exhibition of the phenomena of telepathy every day and every hour of existence, the cases in which it is supposed to occur are extremely rare and are distant from one another, both in time and place. Even the people who claim to have had the phenomena of telepathy happen to them once or twice, do not pretend that it is at all a common occurrence with them, and as for the supposed exhibitions of telepathy upon the stage, these have been exposed over and over again as the simplest fakes.

As to the cases of telepathy that have been reported, with careful collection of evidence, to the psychic research societies, and which are few in number, though some of them are very difficult to explain, there is no reason why they should not be striking coincidences rather than startling examples of telepathy. An example will illustrate what I mean:

A few years ago what seemed to be a complete case of telepathy was reported in connection with a railroad accident. A Western man about to take an express train for the East was the object of a good deal of solicitude. There had previously been a series of accidents to this very fast train which he was to take. This fact had been discussed in the family, and did not tend to allay the fears of those who remained at home. During the night the {145} train actually left the track, and the car in which the subject of the story was asleep rolled down the bank.

At the moment his train went down the bank the thought of his wife and daughter came very vividly to his mind. For a moment the awful position in which they would be placed if anything serious happened to him occupied his mind to the exclusion of all other thoughts. As soon as he could, he telegraphed home that he was unhurt, with the understanding that the telegram should not be delivered before the following morning.

During the night mother and daughter sleeping in adjoining rooms were wakened at the same moment, and very seriously disturbed, by something, they knew not quite what. They rose at once to go to each other and met at the door. They felt vaguely that father was in some way connected with their awakening and disturbance of mind. After they received his telegram they were sure that what disturbed them during the night was the telepathic communication of father's danger. Each had, however, deliberately kept from speaking of her impression. When they found that he had passed through the danger unhurt, they were sure that it was a call from him that each had heard.

This bears most of the ear-marks of a genuine case of telepathy. Here are minds whose cells by custom and inheritance are finely attuned to those of a distant mind that is suddenly very much disturbed. If the perturbations of that first mind were carried through the ether by a sort of wireless telegraphy, it would apparently not be very surprising. So carried, they woke the receptive cells of similar minds at a long distance, and mother and daughter felt the thrill at the same instant. Vague though it was, there was a telepathic message.

But there were other passengers in this train who had near and dear relatives, yet none of them received communications. There have been literally hundreds of thousands of other accidents in the past fifty years of railroading in which passengers who have been put in very serious danger, have thought intensely of their loved ones, and yet, there has been at most only a dozen or so examples of vague telepathy of this class. Similar cases to this are extremely rare, though accidents in America are very frequent. At most, then, we are in the presence of a very exceptional case. Such cases would mean nothing as evidence for a scientific law, since they occur so rarely as to aptly exemplify the old adage that the exception proves the rule. The rule evidently is that there is no communication at a distance, hence the surprise when there seems to be some reason for thinking that a communication has actually taken place. Instead of proving that telepathy occurs, such cases make it clear, to the limit of demonstration, that telepathy does not occur unless some extremely special conditions intervene to make it possible.

How much more easy it is to explain such a case on the score of coincidence! Of course, mother and daughter, with father absent, and absent in the midst of what they thought was danger, would go to bed anxiously thinking of him. They would sleep lightly because of the worry. Any slight unusual noise would wake them, and at once the thought of father and his danger would occur to them. If the noise was sudden, and not repeated, and therefore inexplicable to one awakened out of sleep, they would probably be so disturbed that it is easy to understand that they would arise at once and seek each other's company. Their meeting, therefore, in the doorway between their rooms would be readily explicable. Neither would say much {146} about the subject uppermost in her thoughts in order to shield the other. The telegram in the morning would throw a glow of retrospective light on the events and seem to give an entirely new significance to their thoughts. The whole affair, though only a coincidence, would seem to be a demonstration of telepathy.

Even more marvelous instances of coincidence, in which there was no question of anything more than coincidence, have been related. The English Psychical Research Society reported the case of a young man sent to find some trace of his brother who had disappeared mysteriously from a steamer sailing from Plymouth to Lisbon. On board the steamer late at night he stood by the rail thinking of his lost brother and wondering what could possibly have become of him. Suddenly as he looked down into the ocean a body came bobbing up out of the waves almost directly under his gaze. He reported it to the officers of the vessel and it was grappled for and lifted aboard. It proved to be the body of his brother. Is this an example of telepathy, that is, of the mental influence of the perturbed spirit of the live brother upon the dead brother's body floating below the surface? No one would stretch supposed telepathy to that extent. The steamer disturbed the body which had been floating below the surface, as bodies do, gradually developing within themselves the gases of decomposition. After a time any slight disturbance, as, for instance, the booming of a cannon or the passage of even a small boat, will bring a body up. It so happened that the brother was on the spot, and actually thinking of the body, but that was the merest coincidence. There was no connection of cause and effect.

Most of the cases of so-called telepathy can be explained in this way. As we have said, no source of error is so copious as that of concluding that because one thing happens after another therefore the second is caused by the first. People who are so inclined will still continue to accept such a notion of connection of cause and effect, however, and we shall have many cases of supposed telepathy exploited for us on no better grounds than this.

Twins and Telepathy.—There is a definite popular impression that twins are gifted with the power of telepathic communication much more than others. Accepting Sir Wm. Crookes' theory, the possibility of mental reciprocal influence, even at a distance, is greater for them, since their brain cells must be considered as having corresponding moments of vibration. Twins of the same sex, especially those who resemble one another closely, are usually born from a single ovum. The intimate relations of two such beings to each other can be readily understood, so that we have many stories of mental communication at long distances and curious warnings, forebodings and communications of danger, and especially of sickness and death.

Especially does one find stories of wraith-like appearances of one to the other of such persons at the moment of death. A series of these stories, apparently well authenticated, is published by the Psychic Research Society. There are also a number of tales, seemingly well attested, of cloud-like shapes of other persons at the moment of death. As a consequence, there has been developed an idea that there is some evidence of the distinct possibility of such appearances when the soul leaves the body. It, however, seems very doubtful whether these are anything more than a very striking coincidence. Twins are likely to be almost constantly in one another's minds, so there is abundant {147} room for coincidences. But any number of twins have died at a distance from each other without there being any such warning. Occasionally such startling appearances occur in connection with people who are so slightly related, or whose existence bears such slight importance to each other, that it is hard to understand why the appearance may have come. Whether they are anything more than the figment of an excited imagination remains to be seen, for, while we have a little positive evidence, this only emphasizes the possibility of coincidental day-dreaming in nervous persons.

Negative Tests.—We hear much of the possibility of reading minds at a distance, or of getting definite information from sealed documents and the like, but it must not be forgotten that whenever definite conditions have been set down, so that all the actions of the supposed clairvoyant could be controlled, then telepathy has always failed to be manifested. Sir James Simpson, for instance, publicly offered to give a five-hundred-pound note, which he had placed in a safe deposit vault, to anyone who could read its number which he had carefully impressed on his own mind. Needless to say, no one got it. In the days when Bishop, the exhibiting mind reader, was creating such a furore in New York and London by supposedly reading people's minds, Labouchère, the editor of London *Truth*, offered a similar opportunity to Bishop, but advantage of it was not taken. Bishop's power was entirely due to muscle reading. People make involuntary movements of muscles that are very slight, but sufficient for a trained observer to notice, especially if his hand is on the individual experiencing the emotions, and the consequent muscle reflexes. About the middle of the last century, the French Academy made a labored investigation of telepathy and found that whatever there seemed to be in it, when control was not properly kept, it at once was demonstrated to be impossible when conditions were planned so as to prevent deception.

If patients are worried over disturbing influences from others or the reading of their thoughts or telepathic suggestions, a calm review with them of the practical side of this subject, as we have come to know it in the modern time from actual investigation, will do more than anything else to relieve their apprehensions. Most of these patients are unfortunately insane, but the reasoning will help even some of these. There are some quite rational believers in such manifestations who will be greatly benefitted.

CHAPTER VIII

SECONDARY PERSONALITY

So much attention has recently been directed to the subject of secondary personality by the startling phenomena described in numerous books and articles on the subject, that a certain class of "nervous" patients have permitted themselves to be influenced by the auto-suggestion, flattering the vanity, that they, too, have a secondary personality. They even do not hesitate to hint that this condition is responsible for many of the failures on {148} their part to do what they ought to do, or at least what they think they would like to do; but self-control and self-discipline require such constant attention and effort that they fail. Even when these patients have not quite reached the persuasion of a complete secondary personality, they at least think that the subconscious (or their subliminal self) plays a large role in their conduct. As a consequence, they assert, it is more or less beyond their power to control themselves, and their responsibility for certain acts is surely somewhat impaired. This is a rather satisfying doctrine for those who do not feel quite equal to the effort of conquering vicious or unfortunate tendencies. Those who like to have some excuse for self-indulgence take refuge in this supposedly scientific explanation to absolve them from blame, and from the necessity of self-control. The drug habitué, the inebriate, the victim of other habits, sometimes hug this flattering invention to their souls, especially when they are of the class who delight in the study of the abnormal. Reform becomes well-nigh impossible as long as such an auto-suggestion of inherent weakness and lack of will-power is at work.

The Other Self.—From the beginning of written history, man has always been inclined to find some scapegoat for his failings. The story of Adam blaming the first fault on the woman and the woman blaming it on the serpent, is a lively symbol of what their descendants have been doing ever since. The less personal the blame is, the better, and the more it can be foisted over on some inevitable condition of human nature, the more generally satisfying it is. A secondary personality can scarcely resent being blamed for its acts by the primary personality to which it is attached, and so the field of auto-suggestion as to the blameless inevitability of certain acts is likely to widen if it is given a quasi-scientific basis. Long ago St. Paul spoke of the law in his members opposed to the higher authority, and declared that the things he would do he did not, while what he would not do he sometimes did. There is no doubt that there are two natures in the curious personality of man. Everyone at times has the uncanny feeling that there is something within almost apart from himself, leading him in ways that he does not quite understand. Usually the leading is away from what is considered best in us. But those who have dwelt much on the better side of man and have tried to climb above mere selfish aims, have realized that there is also a power within them leading to higher paths. Indeed, some of the greatest thoughts that men think, and the resolves that lift them up to heroic heights, are apparently so far beyond ordinary human powers, that the hero and the poet and even the more ordinary literary man, is quite ready to proclaim inspiration as the source of his best ideas—as if they were breathed into him from without and above.

Personal Responsibility.—For ordinary normal individuals, this question of secondary personality has scant interest. Normal persons go about their work realizing that what they want to do, they may do, and what they do not want to do they can keep from doing, unless some contrary *physical* force intervenes. There are many metaphysical arguments for free will, but none of them is so convincing as the observation that every sane man, with regard to his own actions, has the power to choose between two things that attract him. He may be much drawn to one thing, yet choose another. He may allow himself to be ruled by baser motives; he may sternly follow the {149} dictates of reason, or he may do neither and hold himself inactive. In any case, he realizes his power to choose. While this power may be impaired by many external conditions, his consciousness of its actuality makes him appreciate his responsibility. He realizes that punishment for wrong done is not only a part of the law, but it is also a proper vindication of that consciousness of free will which all men have, and which does not deceive them. The question has been obscured by much talk, but the reality is there, and the common-sense of mankind has proclaimed its truth. All our laws are founded on it. Without it punishment as meted out is an awful injustice and crime is a misnomer.

Hysterical Phenomena.—Most of the cases of secondary personality that have been discussed at greatest length have been in persons who were as desirous of attracting attention, and as pleased over being the subject of special study as were the hysterical patients who used to delight in investigation two generations ago. That most of the phenomena of so-called dual personalities are mainly hysterical seems now to be clear. In a few cases, where the patient has found that the existence of a double personality was of special interest, a definite tendency to the formation of further personalities has been noted. Some triple personalities have been discussed and, in a few cases, a group of personalities, even up to five or more, began to assert themselves. This *reductio ad absurdum*, of the hypothesis of supernumerary personality has revealed the real hysteric character of the phenomena.

The whole story of secondary personality in recent years vividly recalls commonplaces in the older medical literature that gathered around the study of hysteria, and that afford a striking confirmation of the conclusion as to the relation of the conditions ascribed to hysteria. Physicians of a generation or two ago who found their hysterical patients interesting, because of certain marvelous symptoms which they presented, were usually astonished to learn that their patients could, under suggestion, develop still further and more surprising symptoms. Each new visit, especially when other physicians were brought to see the patient, showed the existence of still further symptoms and revealed new depths of interesting disease. Indeed, the soil was found to be inexhaustible in its power to produce ever new and interesting crops of symptoms.

When the real significance of hysteria as a mental condition in which patients devoted themselves to the task of furnishing new symptoms for the physician began to be realized, one of the most potent objections against this explanation was that it would have been impossible for the patients to have studied out their symptoms enough to furnish the new material for study which physicians found so interesting. The patients were supposed to be mentally incapable of fooling the physicians. When, however, a person devotes entire attention to the one subject of making phenomena in themselves appear interesting to others, some very startling results are usually produced.

After having attracted the sensational attention so common with any novel observation and having been exaggerated out of all proportion to its due significance, the phenomenon is now settling down to its proper place—a rather obscure neurotic phenomenon of memory in hysteric individuals.

Other Neurotic Symptoms.—Janet's studies at the Salpetriêre seem to show that the alterations of memory which bring about what we call {150} secondary personality (the forgetting of certain phases of existence and the maintenance for a time of a small portion of consciousness and memory quite apart from the rest) correspond with alterations in the physical basis of memory, that is, in the circulation to certain portions of the brain, and probably also in the modes of association of brain cells. They occur, particularly, in connection with certain phenomena of hystero-epilepsy so-called, or with the deeper forms of epilepsy in which there are various paresthesias, hyperesthesias and anesthesias as a consequence of a disturbance of the circulation in the central nervous system; and probably also of the connections made by neurons and the movements of neuroglia cells in making and breaking these connections. These alterations of memory are represented physically by such cases as those in which patients so lose their consciousness of sensation that they are unable to tell even where their feet are. As they themselves say, "they have lost their legs." In these cases, patients are often very deaf or have a limited auditory power, and their fields of vision are extremely narrowed. In most of these cases, recovery of the original personality takes place after hypnosis. This probably represents a relaxation of that short-circuiting, within the nervous system, which brought about the curious phenomenon studied as secondary personality.

Dual Dispositions.—The studies of secondary personality that we have had seem to show us persons under the influence of some strong suggestion, in what is practically a hypnotic condition. There are many similarities between the actions and the mentality of hypnotics and of those in secondary-personality conditions. The individuals are, for the moment, unable to recall what happened in other states. They may be very different in disposition, gentle and tractable in one state, but morose and difficult to get along with in another. Such differences are, however, only exaggerations of the variations of normal personality. There are times when, under the stress of circumstances, even the mildest of men and women become querulous and difficult. It is often noted that people are much more gentle and careful in their relations with some people than with others. Men who are known in their business relations to be quiet, easy to get along with, are at times bears in their homes. This is a matter of the exercise of inhibition for certain mental qualities, and this inhibition is neglected for some places and persons. An American humorist said not long since that a young girl passing a weekend at the house of a friend, should remember that she is expected to be unselfish, thoughtful for others, and ready to help her hostess to make it pleasant for others, so that the party may be successful. He adds that, of course, as soon as she returns home she should be perfectly natural again.

At least in a limited sense, all of us have buried in us secondary personalities that are due to a lack of control of ourselves, or occasionally to a lack of such initiative as makes possible the best that is in us. The secondary personality of some people, that side of their characters that their friends see only rarely, is the best side of them. Many people, under the demand of some great purpose, rise up to be really heroic in quality, yet in the commonplace relations of life they are quite ordinary. The secondary personality in either of these cases is not something abnormal. It is due to a tapping of deeper levels in personality than most people realize that they possess. When taken in connection with hypnotism and the power of suggestion over {151} susceptible individuals, these adumbrations of the deeper problem of secondary personality as the psychologists have discussed it, furnish the best data for its fuller explanation. Excuses for actions founded on secondary personality must either rest ultimately on insanity, or else on that lack of inhibition which constitutes the source of so many of our actions that we regret.

People who are susceptible to hypnotism may remember absolutely nothing of what occurs to them in the hypnotic condition, though they will recall it without any difficulty if during hypnosis it is suggested to them that they should remember it. This represents the most prominent feature of secondary personality; the individuals who are affected by it do not recall in one state of personality what happens to them in the other. In the two states they are very different in character. These differences have been much emphasized with regard to a few cases that are especially abnormal and have not attracted much attention in cases where the differences are slight. Indeed, in a number of the cases where secondary personality asserted itself, the differences in the character of the individual in the two states were practically nil. The only difference was a lapse of memory for certain important events. Considerations such as these help in the understanding and psychotherapy of what are sometimes puzzling cases of apparent dualism of disposition.

What we have to do with here are the suggestions of secondary personality which neurotic patients have been inclined to make to themselves as a consequence of the interest in the subject in recent years. The investigations of Head and of Gordon Holmes have undoubtedly shown, however, that there are true pathological conditions associated with certain definite and very marked manifestations of dualism of disposition consequent upon lesions in the optic thalamus. These cases so far as can be judged at the present time, at least, are quite rare and at most would account for duality and not for the plurality of personality that has come to be discussed by certain enthusiastic neurologists in recent years. The magnificent work done on this shows how much may yet be accomplished in the elucidation of nervous diseases by faithful study and investigation of selected cases.

CHAPTER IX

HYPNOTISM

Hypnotism is popularly supposed to be a mysterious psychological process by which susceptible subjects are brought under the influence of a person possessing some marvelous power over others' minds and wills. According to this supposition, during the periods in which the subjects are under this influence, they either have some new source of energy transferred to them from the operator's strong personality, or else they share to some extent in the will power possessed by him. In the midst of the sub-consciousness which characterizes the hypnotic condition, then, they are in some way endowed with new strength, which enables them to overcome obstacles to physical or mental health, some of which seemed at least quite insurmountable under their normal condition.

{152}

As a matter of fact, hypnotism is much simpler than this, consisting merely of a state of mental absorption in which all distracting thoughts are for the moment warded off, and only such thoughts as are suggested by the hypnotist reach the consciousness of the patient. The essence of hypnotism is the concentration of mind on one idea or only a few ideas dictated by the hypnotist. This mental concentration produces the effect of greater strength, whether apparent or real, to carry out the purposes connected with those thoughts. It is usually considered that hypnotism involves sleep, and in some cases it does. This is often undesirable. True, therapeutic hypnosis leaves at least certain senses of the subject open to perceive such things as are presented by the hypnotist's suggestion though these senses may be, and usually are, quite closed to all other perceptions. In a great many cases, though there is a real hypnotic condition, a state resembling true sleep does not occur. There is only a more or less complete concentration of attention on the suggestions of the operator, and a complete cessation of all spontaneous thought, or of all suggestions that might come in ordinary ways from the subject's own senses.

Effects of Hypnotism.—Most people have a very erroneous notion with regard to the effects of hypnotism. Some expect that the hypnotic sleep will work miracles. Nothing is more common in the experience of one who is known to employ hypnotism, even occasionally, than to have a patient who is addicted to some habit, alcoholic, drug, or sexual, ask, "Do you hypnotize?" If an affirmative answer is given, the patient proceeds to say that he has heard that one can be hypnotized, and then all the tendency to fall back into the old habit is immediately lost, and he has no further bother from it. This supposed miraculous effect of hypnotism in supplanting the necessity for using the human will has been cultivated very sedulously in the public mind by quacks and charlatans of various kinds and even exploiters of hypnotism who belong to the medical profession. But there is nothing in it. Hypnotism will not change character unless it be for the worse, since the habit of it sometimes leads to dependence on suggestion rather than spontaneous motives. Hypnotism cannot be substituted for weakness of will. The suggestions given in the hypnotic state are practically no stronger than those given in the waking state, if the patient would only equally concentrate his mind to receive them, and would be as ready in response. It is the readiness of response which comes in cumulative fashion, in the midst of the utter abstraction from other thoughts, that characterizes the hypnotic condition.

This is, of course, quite a different valuation of hypnotism from the very strong expressions, with regard to the power of hypnotists to influence the human will, which have at various times been made. These exaggerated claims have been no stronger than those often made for remedies of various kinds that have been long since discredited. I have heard a serious though young professor of psychology declare that he was not sure whether he was justified in using all the power that he possessed by hypnotism to influence men's wills to keep them from indulging in liquor to excess, because after all men had a right to their free will, even in a matter of this kind, and it would be wrong to take it away from them. He added very philosophically that no human being had the right to play the role of Providence in directing others' actions even for good, unless they themselves were perfectly satisfied. {153} If there was any such force in hypnotism as is thus suggested, the reformation of the world, or still more its deformation, at the hands of some of the strong-minded practicers of hypnotism, would be a comparatively easy process. As a matter of fact, however, the hypnotizer has, except as regards abnormally suggestible people, only as much influence over the person hypnotized as the subject permits, and the subject retains all his personality as an individual with all his weaknesses. After he has been helped away from his weaknesses by hypnotism, he is just as likely as ever to yield to them again, unless, during the interval of conquest, he has succeeded in bracing up his will to resist them.

FORMER METHODS OF HYPNOTIZATION

All the methods of hypnotizing, then, are directed to securing this state of concentration of the patient's mind. The hypnotic state is brought about in different ways by different operators, and even the same operator must employ quite different methods to secure hypnotic influence over different subjects. In the old times, mysterious passes and strokings and rubbings of various kinds, and instruments that flashed light, or that made special sounds, were employed. Among the pioneers, each worker invented methods of his own. A review of these will bring out the fact that none of them represents essentials, and that they are only auxiliaries to secure concentration of the patient's mind.

The methods of hypnotism practiced by those most noted in the history of the art were very different from one another, but not more different than are the methods in vogue to-day among individual hypnotizers. Indeed, the practices of the past have come down as a heritage to our own time. Stroking and touching, of which we have hints in the oldest times in Egypt and Babylonia and Greece, have always been prominent features. Valentine Greatrakes dreamt that he heard a voice in his dream telling him that his right hand should be dead and that stroking it with his left should cause it to recover its power once more. After this had happened three times in succession he began to apply this method to the ills of others. Greatrakes seems really to have come in to replace the touching by the king for the King's Evil at a time when there was no king in England, Pastor Gassner, the next worker who attracted attention by hypnotic procedures, used words of command after attracting the profound attention of his patients. Father Hell employed the touch of magnets. Mesmer used music to predispose the mind, but had many of the methods of modern hypnotists.

Mesmer.—While Mesmer undoubtedly attracted attention to certain phases of hypnotism that were to prove valuable, he was by no means the first to do so, and what he did had such a tincture of charlatanism it is no wonder that he was discredited. There was a little truth, but there was a deal of mere pretense in his work. While he undoubtedly obtained results, he did so mainly because of certain mentally impressive methods that he employed in connection with whatever of hypnotism he used. Binet and Feré, who have given us some details of his work, describe his methods in such a way as to make it clear that they smacked largely of quackery:

{154}

Mesmer, wearing a coat of lilac silk, walked up and down amid his agitated throng, accompanied by Dezlon and his associates, whom he chose for their youth and comeliness. Mesmer carried a long iron wand with which he touched the bodies of the patients and especially the diseased parts. Often laying aside the wand, he magnetized the patients with his eyes, fixing his gaze on theirs, or applying his hand to the hypochondriac region and to the abdomen. This application was often applied for hours, and at other times the master made use of passes. He began by placing himself "en rapport" with his subject. Seated opposite to him, foot against foot, knee against knee, Mesmer laid his fingers upon the hypochondriac region and moved them to and fro, lightly touching the ribs. Magnetism, with strong electric currents, was substituted for these manipulations when more energetic results were to be produced. The master, raising his fingers in a pyramidal form, passed his hands all over the patient's body, beginning with the head, and going downward over the shoulders to the feet. He then returned to the head, both back and front, then the belly and the back, and renewed the process again and again until the magnetized person was saturated with the healing fluid and transported with pain or pleasure, both sensations being equally salutary. Young women were so much gratified by the crisis that they wished to be thrown into it anew. They followed Mesmer through the halls and confessed that it was impossible not to be warmly attached to the person of the magnetizer.

De Puysegur and His Successors.—De Puysegur has some definite instructions for hypnotizers, whom he called magnetizers. It is instructive even now to read these, for they emphasize the most important element in all hypnotism, the confidence of the operator in his own power, for this, communicated to the subject, produces the beneficial results:

You are to consider yourself as a magnet; your arms, and particularly your hands, being its poles; and when you touch a patient by laying one of your hands on his back, and the other in direct opposition upon his stomach, you are to imagine that the magnetic fluid has a tendency to circulate from one hand to the other through the body of the patient. You may vary this position by placing one hand on the head and the other on the stomach, still with the same intention, the same desire of doing good. The circulation from one hand to the other will continue, the head and stomach being the parts of the body where the greatest number of nerves converge; these are, therefore, the two centres to which your action ought to be mostly directed. Friction is quite unnecessary; it is sufficient to touch with great attention.

Some of these methods continued to be employed by the successors of Mesmer and De Puysegur, the sense of touch being the principal adjuvant, though Mesmer employed also the sense of hearing. Braid seems to have been the first to realize that the sense of sight could be used effectively, or perhaps that the tiring of the muscle sense might well serve as a point for the concentration of attention. He used the flash of a light from some bright object or tired the eye muscles by having the patient look upward at some object brought near so as to require convergence of vision. His methods were imitated by most of the hypnotizers of the nineteenth century. Liebault and Bernheim, at Nancy, employed them regularly, and they were used in the investigations at the Salpêtrière. It was found, however, that after a patient had been once hypnotized, all that was needed was a word of command or a definite suggestion, and the hypnotic state recurred. Further experience showed also that the original hypnotic phenomena might, in most cases, be secured very simply by word-suggestion to the patient, though some individuals required persistent efforts in the application of several methods {155} to secure the concentration of mind on a single idea or set of ideas that is the essence of hypnotism.

By most serious hypnotists, especially those who use hypnotism for therapeutic purposes, all the rubbings and manipulations are now either completely eliminated, or are used only under special circumstances. The important element of the operator's influence consists in obtaining the complete confidence of the subject in the operator's power to control his intelligence for the time being; getting the subject to resign himself completely, with absolute assurance that his trust will be for his good, and can by no means result in harm. Without this attitude of mind on the part of the subject, anything like real hypnotism is impossible. Even with this, only a slight degree of the hypnotic condition may be secured in certain people, but the majority have a distinct susceptibility to it.

PRESENT DAY METHODS OF HYPNOTIZATION

Though various methods of producing the hypnotic sleep are in use, the rule is now that, in the course of a hypnotizer's experience, less and less external auxiliaries of any kind are needed, and more and more dependence is placed on the bringing about of mental *rapport* between the active and passive agencies in hypnotism by persuasion and command. If the hypnotic sleep has once been obtained, usually all that is necessary is a few gentle words, and then the command to sleep. It is at the initial attempts to hypnotize a particular person somewhat refractory to the condition that auxiliaries are needed. In these cases it is often well to tire the eyes of the patient. This is done by directing them to the fingers of the operator held well above the patient's head. After a minute or two of effort the distinct fatigue which occurs may induce forgetfulness of everything else and cause absorption in the single idea of attending only to the hypnotizer's suggestions. This constitutes the beginning of hypnotism. Occasionally the flash of a bright object, or a revolving mirror, may be used, but these are only adjuncts and may be dispensed with entirely if the operator has the patience and the time to give to the subject.

Accessories.—Some operators use a mirror on which a ray of light is cast for the purpose of concentrating the attention and bringing about tiredness of the eye muscles. In so far as it has a more universal application, sight is certainly the best sense to act upon. Other senses may be appealed to, as I suggest later. Instead of a mirror, a polished match-box or pencil-case may be used, but as a rule the less artificiality enters into it and the simpler the procedure, the better. One of the inconveniences of using the flash of a bright object is that occasionally patients who are very susceptible may, after they have had a number of hypnotic experiences, be thrown into a hypnotic condition by the flash of a light in the street, or by the reflection of light from a mirror in their own homes. These conditions of facile auto-hypnotism constitute one of the serious dangers of the practice on susceptible subjects. Whatever good may be accomplished by hypnotism will probably be reached during the first half dozen seances. To proceed with the treatment beyond this, if it is employed at regular and short intervals, is almost sure to result in harm rather than good.

{156}

Sensations.—Besides sight, sounds have sometimes been used for the purpose of inducing hypnotism. The ticks of a watch, for instance, placed at a little distance and listened to very intently, have been known to assist in securing the hypnotic state. Sometimes the sound of a gong, or an imitation of a cathedral chime, have been used in the same way. Soft music has also been used by operators with decided advantage. It is necessary that the sounds should be of a kind that do not disturb, but only attract attention to one sensation, and then, as concentration on this is secured, the hypnotic condition results. Practically any other sensation may be used in the same way. Touch is often employed. Mesmer stroked his patients gently, and others have used the same process with advantage. Some of the French workers in hypnotism have claimed that there were special portions of the body the stroking of which was likely to produce this favorable effect. They have called these regions zones hypnogenes—areas that give rise to hypnotic conditions. Strokings of the forehead, of the cheeks, of the hands, are favorite locations for these auxiliary touches. In this, as with regard to sound, the main thing is to concentrate attention on some one sensation without producing disturbing thoughts.

Stroking.—Stroking seems to affect many people and to easily induce a sort of hypnoidal condition. It is done very naturally to a child when one wants to console or encourage or admonish slightly but kindly. In older people it is a familiar gesture among those who think much of one another, and represents a very natural tendency. Even in the midst of physical discomfort its effect is quite soothing, and it is evident that something resembling hypnotism is at work. Evidently, what really happens is a concentration of attention on the sensation thus produced, which concentration prevents distracting thoughts from making themselves felt and permits the words of the one who does the stroking to produce a deeper effect on the mind than would ordinarily be possible. This seems to be nature's method of making suggestion more effective. It has been adopted, quite spontaneously, by many of the pioneers in hypnotism as the result of their observations upon its efficacy. Lloyd Tuckey calls attention to an illustration of this practice, which makes clear its effectiveness and at the same time shows how naturally it suggests itself as a mode of using mental influence. He says:

Among the medical men who have come to watch some of my cases was a gentleman who seemed much struck at seeing the method I adopted with a rather refractory subject. I held his hand and stroked his forehead while at the same time suggesting the symptoms of sleep. The gentleman told me afterward the reason why he was so interested. It appears that he had a few months previously been in attendance on a very severe and protracted case of delirium tremens. The patient could get no sleep, and the doctor was afraid of death from exhaustion. On the third evening he resolved to make a strong effort to produce sleep, and, if necessary, to sit up all night with the patient. He told the man that he would not leave him until he slept, and sitting down by the bedside, he took his hand in one of his own, and with the other gently stroked the forehead. At the same time he talked quietly and reassuringly to him. In less than half an hour he was rewarded by seeing the restlessness entirely cease and the man drop off into a quiet sleep. That sleep, the doctor told me, lasted fourteen hours, and the patient awoke out of it weak, but cured. Manipulation about the head has in many persons a most soporific effect, and several persons have told me that they always become drowsy under their barber's hands.

{157}

Drugs.—A number of drugs and related substances have been used as aids to hypnosis, but in nearly all of these cases it is doubtful whether it is true hypnotism that results and whether the suggestions in these states have much therapeutic value. One of the drugs most frequently administered by hypnotists is *cannabis indica*, which has long been used in the East for a similar purpose. After this, chloroform is most popular. Schrenck-Notzing even ventured to employ alcohol as an aid in hypnosis, and claims that he has succeeded at times in making intoxication pass into the true hypnotic condition. Bernheim and many others of the French school have used chloral and morphine. These substances are, however, liable to great abuse. Whenever they have to be employed it means that the patient is but little susceptible to hypnotic influence. These aids are employed only because hypnotists do not want to confess that a very considerable portion of humanity is not directly susceptible to the hypnotic influence.

Serious harm may be done by the employment of these drugs. A physician, who hoped that he would be able to overcome a drug addiction that had been the bane of his existence for a long while, went to a well-known hypnotist physician with the idea that perhaps the miracle of hypnotism would be worked in his case. He was one of these flighty mortals whom it is extremely difficult to have fix their minds upon any one idea for a definite time. As it was impossible to bring him into anything like a hypnotic condition by ordinary means, a large dose of chloral was administered. He already had an idea that his heart had been affected by his previous drug-taking habit, but the chloral was administered to him before he realized what it was. When he came out of the sleep it induced, he was in an agony of solicitude and anxiety lest his heart should have been further hurt by the chloral. He went back for no more doses of that kind of hypnotism.

The use of drugs seems to be a confession of failure to secure true hypnotism, so that it is doubtful whether their employment is justified. Suggestions received while in the more or less comatose state induced by drugs, instead of having a strengthening effect on the patient's will, rather tend to produce the idea of the impossibility of effectively using his own will, or even exercising his will when helped, as he supposes, by the will of the operator. The real value of hypnotism consists in the concentration of mind upon a particular idea without any distractions, which enables the subject to make firm resolutions and then to have his mind help his body as much as possible by directing his energy to the accomplishment of one end. When drugs are employed, they have a diffusive rather than a concentrating influence, so that the real purpose of hypnotism is entirely missed.

PRACTICE OF HYPNOTISM

In the ordinary practice of hypnotism now, the patient is placed sitting on a comfortable chair and the operator on one side facing prepares the mind of the subject by proper assurances. The patient must be brought into a thoroughly assured and comfortable state of mind and must be quite ready to submit to hypnotism. Then in most people, if the finger is held rather close to the patient and well above the line of sight, requiring special effort {158} on the part of the superior recti muscles as well as of the power of convergence, a tired feeling will come over the subject with a tendency of the lids to droop. When this happens the subject is asked to allow the lids to drop and to quietly concentrate the attention on the idea of sleep so as to permit the drowsy feeling gradually to increase. On a first seance this may take ten minutes, subsequently much less time will be needed, and, as a rule, in five minutes the subject is quite predisposed to sleep. In more difficult cases a much longer time may be needed, and repeated efforts may have to be made. Great patience is required. The operator soon learns to adjust himself to certain peculiarities of individuals in predisposing them to the hypnotic condition.

Hypnotism Simple, Natural, Not Mysterious.—The most important thing to know about hypnotism is the fact that any one who wishes can hypnotize. There may be need for favoring circumstances, but there is no need for any special faculty in the operator. If he has confidence in himself so as to take up the question of hypnotizing seriously, if the subjects are reasonably susceptible and if they are persuaded that they may be hypnotized, or even if they are not, so long as they take the operator seriously a hypnotic state will result. Nothing is more surprising to the operator himself, the first time he succeeds, than his success. This at once gives him renewed confidence, and future hypnosis becomes a comparatively simple matter. To have this idea widely diffused would do much good, since it would at once strip the charlatans, who abuse hypnotism, of most of the mystery that surrounds them. The general diffusion of such knowledge would also do good in another way. It would expose the supposed wonderful power that some people are presumed to possess. Hypnotism works no wonders; it is a mere natural manifestation not unlike sleep, and probably not a whit more mysterious.

Stages.—A number of divisions of the hypnotic state have been suggested, but probably the simple division into three stages is the best for ordinary teaching purposes, and helps to the understanding both of the conditions themselves and of many things that are written about hypnotism.

The first stage consists of a subdued, dreamy condition, in which the patient is not asleep and yet not thoroughly awake to all that is going on around him. He has his mind so concentrated on certain thoughts that he is preoccupied, and suggestions are much more efficient than under ordinary circumstances. This is really only a state of intense attention to the suggestions that are being made, with the banishment of all distracting thoughts. It is rather difficult for any one to keep from being distracted, and whenever this is accomplished, the ideas that then enter the mind penetrate more deeply and, above all, seem to affect the will more forcibly than when they are merely superficially considered. This first stage of hypnotism would not be considered hypnotic by most people who associate the idea of sleep with hypnotism.

In recent years it has been found that most of the good that is accomplished, especially for nervous people, by hypnotic suggestion, can be attained almost, if not quite as well, in this first stage, and without the hypnotic trance. The first stage is much less liable to the dangers of hypnotism in many ways, and it represents one of the most interesting phases of psychotherapy.

{159}

The second stage of hypnotism is the hypnotic sleep. The patient loses consciousness of his surroundings, though his senses are still open to suggestion from the operator. Practically all that happens in the room apart from what is brought to the subject through the operator's direction remains unnoticed. If the sleep is very deep, even the suggestions of the operator do not penetrate after a time, so it may be quite difficult to awaken the subject. It may be even some hours before the person hypnotized will come out of the lethargy which has been induced in these cases. Under these circumstances, this second stage partakes somewhat of the nature of the deeper trance condition that characterizes the third stage.

The third stage of hypnotism consists of a profound trance-like condition in which there is catalepsy—that is, firm contracture of muscles all over the body—and as the extensors are stronger than the flexors, this contracture takes place in the extended position. The cataleptic condition is really a nervous spasmodic seizure rather than a true stage of hypnotism. It is probably always harmful for the patient to have it induced. Its occurrence as one manifestation of hysteria, apart from hypnotism, shows its real character. It is with this stage of hypnotism that professional hypnotists, who give exhibitions, make their demonstrations—that is, of course, when their demonstrations are really hypnotic and are not merely, as is often the case, performances by actors trained for the purpose. Catalepsy is entirely pathological; experiment with it then is eminently undesirable, and certainly should not be undertaken except under the most careful precautions and by a physician. One of its dangers was very clearly pointed out by the death of a young man, who in a cataleptic condition was subjected to certain strains upon his thorax which brought about the rupture of an aortic aneurism. Catalepsy never permits of suggestion in such a way as to be helpful to the patient. It always leads to further functional deterioration of the nervous system, and yet it has unfortunately come to mean for many people the most essential characteristic of hypnotism. Its production is supposed to represent the acme of skill in the hypnotist. Nothing could possibly be less true nor be more likely to do harm.

Susceptibility.—As to the number of people who are susceptible to hypnotism, there are great differences of opinion. Liebault declared that practically every one is susceptible in the hands of a patient operator. In a carefully made series of cases his failures were less than three per cent. Van Rentergehem and Van Eeden, in a series of over 1,000 persons, failed only with fifty-eight, or little more than five per cent. Schrenk-Notzing's statistics, collected from many countries, seem to show that only about six per cent. were uninfluenced. Bernheim, at Nancy, was not nearly so successful as Liebault, his master, and his failures amounted to twenty-five per cent. at the beginning and at least twenty per cent. later. I remember that when I was at the Saltpêtrière fifteen years ago, they were inclined to discount the enthusiasm of the Nancy school with regard to the value and significance of hypnotism. They insisted that probably not more than one out of two of the persons presenting themselves at a nervous clinic could be hypnotized to the extent that is ordinarily associated with the word—could be brought beyond the drowsy stage. There are other workers in the subject who have insisted that not more than one out of three ordinary individuals can be so {160} deeply hypnotized as to exhibit the ordinary symptoms. These symptoms consist of complete neglect of surroundings and absolute absorption in the suggestions of the operator.

Some people can be hypnotized to the extent of being thrown into sleep and yet walk and talk under the absolute control of the operator. These are so-called somnambules, the class of persons who are exhibited by professional hypnotizers who want to attract popular attention, and, indeed, the class usually exhibited by physicians before medical societies, and even by professors before their classes. This extreme susceptibility is, however, quite rare. Even the most ardent advocates of hypnotism and of the susceptibility of humanity to it do not claim that more than one in ten of average individuals can be influenced to this degree. There are milder degrees of hypnotism than this, until we reach a state in which all the patients feel is a certain dreamy sense of well-being and a heaviness of the eyes, with a readiness to respond to suggestions. Most people who think of the somnambulistic stage as representing hypnotism would not consider these latter to have been at all subjected to the hypnotic state.

Repeated Efforts.—As to this question of susceptibility, much depends on how often the operator has tried to hypnotize the particular subject, for susceptibility develops with repeated trials, not only where there is a manifest impression at first, but also where there is not. It is not uncommon to find that a patient who cannot be brought at all under the influence of hypnotism in the first or second or third trial, will, at the fifth or sixth trial, yield to the suggestion to go into a hypnotic sleep. A dozen unsuccessful efforts may be followed by the development of a very satisfactory hypnosis. Those who have practiced hypnotism much tell of having tried a score or even two score of times before finally bringing on a hypnotic condition. Dr. J. Milne Bramwell, one of the English authorities on hypnotism, tells the story of having tried sixty or more times to hypnotize patients before finally succeeding. It is this persistence that enables successful hypnotic operators to accomplish results where less confident physicians fail. It is also the frequency of trial that makes all the difference in the statistics as to the susceptibility of patients to hypnotism in the hands of different individuals. There must be the confidence of the patient in the physician's power to hypnotize, but, above all, there must be the physician's own confidence in his power to bring on the hypnotic sleep so that he tries and tries again, even to seventy times.

ANIMAL HYPNOTISM

The hypnotization of animals shows that only a very low grade intelligence is needed for the production of this state. The famous experiment of Father Kircher with the hen, which any one may repeat at any time, is a good illustration. The fascination exerted upon birds by snakes is another familiar example. The bird is paralyzed with terror at the sight of the snake, and so cannot escape from its enemy, fairly glueing its eyes on the terrifying object, and thus loses power to control its wings. Stories of snake {161} fascination are usually told as if the eye of the snake attracted the bird, who thereupon proceeded to approach the snake. These are, however, doubtful stories. The paralysis of motion seems to be the main effect. The rabbit is affected in nearly the same way. There is a tremor of horror in anticipation, and then the animal stands perfectly quiet, though ordinarily he would be quite able to escape, while its enemy approaches. The underlying mechanism is evidently a concentration of attention, which completely precludes the possibility of the exertion of any spontaneous energy except that involved in the one act of watching the awful object.

DANGERS OF HYPNOTISM

There are many and various opinions of the dangers of hypnotism. Some of those who have given it a fair trial have insisted on its dangers. Some of those who have had very large experience have declared emphatically that there is no danger at all. Occasionally it has seemed that such a declaration must be considered as having been dictated by such intensity of interest as sometimes leads men to overlook the darker side of things with which they are much occupied. Certain moral aspects of hypnotism are at least dubious, and, it must be admitted, present opportunities for abuse. There are certain dangers connected with its effect upon nervous patients, and especially with its influence upon character, that have become more and more clear in recent years. Dr. John K. Mitchell, in his "Self Help for Nervous Women," a series of familiar talks on economy in nervous expenditure, has dwelt on certain of these dangers of hypnotism for nervous patients in a passage that deserves to be recalled. As a representative of a school of thought that is worthy of special regard from American physicians his expressions must carry weight:

The greatest danger of all is the use of hypnotism in any form or degree, a two-edged sword, capable indeed of usefulness, but more capable of harm. After years of study, beginning with too easy an approval of it, hypnotism, whether called by that name or by the unsuitable one of suggestion, has been laid aside by the medical profession as a means too dangerous for ordinary use, involving great risk of deterioration of character in the subject if often repeated, and putting a terribly tempting tool in the hands of the user, fascinating in the ease with which it can produce superficial and temporary good results and equally capable of being used for harmful ones.

A susceptible person, once hypnotized, is more and more easily thrown into the hypnotic state until even the slightest hint suffices to bring about the condition. It is not necessary for the hypnotization to go so far as deep sleep; this more advanced stage is indeed seldom required, and to say that persons are not hypnotized because they are not put into a sleep or a trance shows ignorance of the subject.

I am not asserting that very slight degrees of the hypnotic condition are as dangerous as the deeper, but I do say that all degrees of it are dangerous to the integrity and healthy action of the subject's nervous system. The danger of harm increases with every repetition of the hypnotization.

In suggestible, that is, over-susceptible, individuals, who are almost universally neurotic persons, to fix the eyes on a small point, especially a bright one, sometimes even to fix the mind on the one idea of going into the hypnotic state (mild or deep), is enough without further intervention from any one to put them into that state.

{162}

In an article on the "Danger and Uses of Hypnotism" Prof. Forel, of Zurich, twenty years ago, while frankly admitting that hypnotism is by no means a panacea for all nervous affections and unfortunate habits, found it to be an extremely valuable help in the treatment of many forms of functional nervous disease. He suggests that some of its many dangers are due to the fact that hypnotism is practiced by men who are too distrustful of it, and this distrust, unconsciously communicated to the patients, produces an unfortunate effect. On the other hand, fear and distrust on the part of the subjects seriously disturbs the process of hypnotization, interferes with its effect and sometimes leads to unfortunate results.

In some cases it seems that the state of dependence on some one else, at least by suggestion, that had been created during the hypnotic experience, resulted in a diminution of will power and caused a less hopeful state on the patient's part than before. I found personally that suggestion in the waking state might in most cases be used quite as efficiently as hypnosis itself, and that when improvement came under these circumstances, the patient always felt more confidence in himself and less in the operator. Anything that restores self-confidence and gives patients the feeling that they can conquer inclinations, tendencies, even habits, if they only will, merely by firmly resolving to do so, is the best possible mental influence for them. The hypnotic relief is always easier, but nothing that is easy is likely to be of lasting value. The enduring effect of gradual cure by suggestion means much more than the hypnotic miracle that these patients are so prone to crave.

At present there is a very general feeling among those who have had considerable experience with hypnotism, that in spite of the claims of certain votaries for it, there is no justification for its frequent or habitual use. It has a definite place in diagnosis, in certain difficult cases, and at the beginning of the treatment of certain forms of the psycho-neuroses. When repeated frequently it is not therapeutic, but is likely to produce serious results in a certain lack of self-control and tendencies to auto-hypnotization with deterioration of character. There is very seldom need of a repetition of deep hypnosis, and, as a rule, all the diagnostic benefit can be secured in one or two seances. Its continued use only illustrates the tendency noted at all times, in the history of medicine, for the unthinking or unprofessional to persist in the application of supposed remedial measures after they have been shown to be useless or even harmful. The subject well deserves further study, but investigations should be carefully made by men who realize the dangers, and who are not likely to be tempted to exploit patients and curious psychological phenomena for the sake of sensational reputation. The use of hypnotism for exhibition purposes, by men who are not physicians, is an unmixed evil, producing entirely wrong impressions on the public, and doing untold evil to the subjects employed.

{163}

SECTION III

THE INDIVIDUAL PATIENT

CHAPTER I

PSYCHOTHERAPY AND THE INDIVIDUAL PATIENT

The most important element in Psychotherapy is the individual patient. Old Dr. Parry of Bath said a century ago, "It is much more important to know what sort of a patient has a disease, than what sort of a disease a patient has." Mental influence is not of the slightest avail against pneumonia or typhoid fever, nor constipation nor rheumatism as such; mental influence may be, and often is, of the greatest possible help to the patient suffering from any of these diseases.

We recognize frankly now that for most diseases we can do nothing to counteract the disease directly or to cure it specifically. The idea of specifics in medicine has to a large extent disappeared. Two or three of them possibly we have, but even with regard to these, there are certain doubts as to the essential modes of their activity. We have learned, however, to help the patient to overcome disease. We know how to conserve his forces, to increase his vital reaction, to maintain his nutrition without disturbing his general condition, and to secure elimination in such a way as to prevent nature from being interfered with in her curative purposes. To this, psychotherapy would enable us to add such encouragement of the patient as would tap new sources of energy in him according to the law of reserve energy, and would prevent discouragement and the inhibition of favorable nerve impulses that so often follow. The outcome of any disease depends on two factors. One is the condition of the patient at the time the infection was acquired, the other is the virulence of the infection. We can do nothing to modify this latter element, once the disease manifests itself. We can, however, do much to enable the patient to throw off the disease and, above all, by securing a favorable attitude of mind, we can enable him to use his forces to the best advantage.

Anyone who has noted the difference between the patient's state just before and just after his physician has called, though absolutely no physical remedy has been employed, is able to realize very well how much psychotherapy is able to accomplish. One who did not know, would be sure to assume that some potent remedy had been administered—and there has been. This potent remedy is psychotherapy. Whether the personal magnetism necessary to produce therapeutic effects of this kind can be learned or not depends on the individuality of the physician. Undoubtedly, however, everyone can add to whatever of personal influence he has by definitely recognizing its place, by {164} making every effort to employ it, and then by regular systematic effort in securing as much personal information as possible with regard to the patient. This personal relationship of physician and patient makes instruction easier and suggestion more effective.

The securing of personal information is of the utmost importance in determining the affections that psychotherapy will relieve, because very often details of life and habits are discovered that can be so modified by instruction as to bring about a disappearance of unfavorable physical influences. It is indeed surprising to find how many unreasonable things people do from habit, from unfortunate persuasion, or from lack of knowledge. In many of the minor chronic ailments that are the source of so much mental discomfort to patients, the physician finds that a change in the patients' habits, not necessarily of marked degree, may make all the difference between cheerful health and rather despondent low-spirited feeling. Now that epidemic disease has become rarer, a physician's practice, especially among the better classes, is much more taken up with these minor ailments than with the typical classical diseases.

The ordinary history of their ailments, as patients commonly present them, especially when there are neurotic elements, is likely to be meager in what is objective, but consists mostly of the subjective. Such patients have much to say of their sensations, their feelings, their dreads, their surmises, their conclusions as to their particular condition, and especially the hereditary elements in it, but comparatively little of the objective realities of their ills and of their environment. What the physician needs to know about them is their habits of life, their daily routine of existence, just as minutely as it is possible to obtain the information. There is just one way to get the latter details, and that is to inquire particularly with regard to actual happenings. In chronic conditions of many kinds, it is so helpful that it will always be worth the physician's while to get at these details, especially in supposedly puzzling cases for which various forms of treatment have been already tried.

In spite of every precaution in this matter, the physician sometimes finds, after a series of consultations, that some point which when brought to light he considers to be of great importance, has been thought so trivial by the patient that it was never mentioned, in spite of the most careful questioning. In all medical practice the rule is that mistakes of diagnosis are much more due to neglect in eliciting necessary information than either to lack of expertness in diagnosis, or lack of knowledge of the significance of symptoms.

In the affections that can be relieved by psychotherapeutics, the most important element for diagnosis, besides a minute knowledge of the patient's habits, is just as detailed information as possible with regard to his ways and modes of thought as to his ills. Practically every motive, as well as every action of the day, must be scrutinized, and often it will be found that little things mean much for the individual. "Trifles make perfection, but perfection is no trifle," as said by Michelangelo, might well be changed for the physician to, "Trifles make all the difference between health and discomfort, though health is no trifle."

{165}

CHAPTER II

THE MORNING HOURS

In getting the history of patients for diagnostic purposes the safest way is to begin with the getting up in the morning and then to follow out the various actions of the day. The hour and mode of rising should be inquired into. Practically all nervous people, and nearly all those beyond middle life, feel less fit in the morning hours than at any other time in the day. Apparently as a consequence of their will having been allowed to lose its hold during sleep, it does not secure thorough command over the organism for some time. Nervous people, as a rule, wake up with a tired feeling, a dread of the day, wondering whether life is worth living. They dread—for it is a real dread—to get up and tackle the daily round of life once more.

If they have nothing very definite to do, then slight tired feelings or discomfort, even of very minor degree, may lead them to think that they cannot get up. Any yielding in this matter is almost sure to do harm. When there are no objective signs, that is, when there is no fever recognizable by the thermometer and there has been no diarrhea or any physical weakness, nervous patients should get up promptly at a particular hour every morning, because, as a rule, within a half hour after getting up they feel better, and by the time they are washed and have had their breakfast, life has grown not only quite possible but even plausible, and the day's work does not seem such a nightmare as it was at first. It is not advisable to tell people all this as soon as they confess their habit of dawdling in the morning, for they must be gradually brought to discipline themselves. The detail emphasizes the necessity of knowing how they get up as well as when.

Mode of Awaking.—It is often valuable to know how patients awake. Sometimes it will be found that they are anxious and solicitous to be at work at a particular hour, or to catch a train at a particular time, and that as a consequence their sleep is disturbed in the early morning hours. At best it may be fitful and when they awake they fear to go to sleep again lest they oversleep. An alarm clock will sometimes remedy this state of affairs. Better still is an arrangement by which someone, who can be depended on, will wake them at a particular time. Occasionally patients cannot content themselves in spite of the assurance that they will be waked. They dread that the alarm clock may not go off, or that the awakener may make a mistake, and so they go to bed with a dominant idea, which is more or less constantly present in their mind during all their sleeping hours, disturbing sleep and preventing complete rest. It may be necessary to insist on a change of occupation for such persons, or a change of residence that will do away with the necessity for early rising. When this is done, many a neurotic condition that has before proved intractable will disappear.

Amount of Sleep.—It is of cardinal importance to know how long patients sleep. In our large cities most people have too little sleep. A comparison of the hours when they get to bed with those when they get up will often show that at least three or four nights in the week some patients who are complaining of nervous symptoms, especially nervous indigestion, are {166} sleeping less than seven hours. There are but few men, and still fewer women, who will retain their health under such conditions. Some men have been able to do it, but they are comparatively rare. King Alfred's rule of dividing the day into three eight-hour periods—one for sleep, one for work, and the third for bodily necessities and recreation, still remains the best for human nature. Whenever people try to live the strenuous life and get along on less than eight hours of sleep, they are almost sure, sooner or later, to render themselves uncomfortable, to make themselves liable to all sorts of neurotic symptoms and, above all, to detract from their efficiency for whatever work they are engaged in. Whether they sleep or not, they should be in bed for nearly eight hours.

Bathing.—*Morning Bath.*—In our larger cities at least, many of the inhabitants begin the day with a bath. In this matter one finds all sorts of harmful fads that need to be corrected. Many men take a cold bath, and unless they are particularly strong and vigorous, this is rather an exhausting experience for the beginning of the day, when the last nutrition the body absorbed is twelve hours before. On the other hand, large, athletic men who manufacture a great deal of heat, their muscles—the heat-making organs—being well developed, will be benefited by having a cold bath because of the abstraction of heat that it involves. It is not, however, infrequent to find that the man for whom it will be good is not taking it, while the thin, neurotic individual, already exhausting more of his vitality by worry and dieting and in various fads with regard to his health than is good for him, is regularly taking his cold plunge or douche. Unless especially asked about it, few men give particulars in this matter, yet they are extremely important.

Women, on the other hand, are likely to take hot baths more frequently than is good for them. Especially when they have maids to assist in dressing and undressing, it is not unusual to find that women take two, and sometimes even three, hot baths in a day. They take them in the early morning when they first get up, and in the evening before dressing for dinner. I have known cases where some took a third hot bath before going to bed and sometimes even put in a fourth before luncheon in case they had had any exercise in the morning hours—tennis, or horseback riding, or the like—that made them perspire. These are details which the physician will learn only if he asks particularly about them. Until he has actually had the experience of finding that they play an important role in some ailment he is almost sure not to think of it. It is probable that even two hot baths a day are too many. I have known women to begin at once to get better of neurotic symptoms that before had proved quite intractable, when their hot baths were limited or when they were changed for a single warm bath with a cold rub after it in the morning, or sometimes just before dinner.

Bathing is more liable to abuse than is usually thought to be possible. While the habits of modern life call for it often, and many people are quite sure that they would not be healthy without it, the people who live longest, and who have had the best health far beyond three score years and ten, have usually not been noted for bathing proclivities. The human body is composed of nearly seven-eighths water, and so our cells are constantly bathed in it, but the making of the whole organism a marine animal once more, as seems to be the definite tendency of some people, is not nearly so hygienic as {167} it is often thought to be. Enough bathing for thorough cleanliness, but not for luxury, must be the rule for people who have active work and want to retain their health.

Bathing Fads.—While such mistakes are usually made only by the wealthy and leisure classes, the physician will sometimes be surprised to find that women who have no maids for personal service are indulging themselves in these over-frequent bathing practices. They have heard that it softens the skin and renews youth, or they have heard that the Japanese take hot baths and are revivified when they are very fatigued, and so they go to great lengths in bathing. Often this is the main reason for the relaxation of muscle tissue and the sense of prostration that has come over them. Neurotic people are constantly going to extremes. Even delicate women will sometimes be found to take very cold baths which are surely doing them harm. Over frequent washings of hands and face are sometimes responsible for skin lesions, especially if the soap used is one of the varieties so scented that the manufacturer is enabled to conceal the impurities in its ingredients. Some women easily run into what is really a misophobia, an exaggerated morbid fear of dirt, and need to be restrained from washing themselves over frequently. Many a chapped hand would be saved by avoiding unnecessary washings, and especially in warm water just before one goes out, for it leaves the skin without its proper oily protection.

Clothing. Then comes the question of clothing. It is curious how irrationally many people clothe themselves. People complain of cold hands and feet when they are wearing thin cotton undergarments, and who need only to have these changed for wool for their feelings to be at once improved. In the meantime they have been persuaded that they have a defective circulation. The usual excuse for not wearing wool is that it produces hyperemia of the skin with itchy discomfort, but this, as a rule, is only passing and is due to unaccustomedness. The coarser wools should not be worn by the sensitive. A thin cotton garment may, if absolutely necessary, be worn next the skin. There is too little variety in the underclothing that people wear. Some change from light to heavy weight and only that, but there should be a medium weight worn, and occasionally, when there is a spell of mild weather in the winter time, even during the season when heavy weight is usually worn, medium weight should be substituted for comfort's sake.

It is even more common to find that neurotic individuals, who fear to catch cold, wear too much clothing, especially around the chest. Very often they alternate from this during the day to next to nothing in the evening, and by so doing subject themselves to special risks of internal congestions. When the skin is covered with too much clothing it loses the habit of reacting, and the warmth and the irritation of wool keep up an artificial hyperemia which gradually lowers the tone of the peripheral vessels. Many people wear "chest protectors," as is evident from the prominent display of these abominations in the drug-store windows. By leaving certain portions of the chest unprotected

105

while other parts are kept over-warm, these add greatly to the risk of such disturbances of circulatory equilibrium as predispose to the infections grouped under the term "taking cold." It is not heavy clothing that keeps people warm so much as the layers of non-conducting air between the skin and the outer air. It is better, therefore, to wear three thin {168} garments than two heavy ones because of the additional layers of air that are thus confined. A paper vest, if one is driving in the wind, will probably protect better than the heaviest woolen garment worn. The wearing of chamois garments is not, as a rule, advisable because chamois does not permit free access of air and it hampers transpiration.

Before Breakfast.—After dressing comes breakfast, with regard to which it may be advisable to ask many questions. It is well to begin with a query as to whether liquids are taken before breakfast. Many people have taken to the fad of drinking a large quantity of warm water, sometimes as much as a pint, before breakfast. Surely this never does any good and, in most cases, just as surely does harm. Plain water will not dissolve mucus that may have collected in the stomach, and warm water merely dilates that organ, relaxes its fibers, and renders the whole gastric digestive system atonic. If cold water can be borne, it will often be found that a glass of cold water the first thing in the morning stimulates peristalsis, and serves to lessen the necessity for laxatives. Many people complain that cold water is too much of a shock. Usually, if they are reminded that when we want to warm our hands we rub them vigorously with cold water and that the reaction after this gives a healthy glow, the effect of the supposed shock, which was merely an unfavorable suggestion, will disappear. Sometimes delicate people cannot drink cold water. If there is any reason to suspect an accumulation of mucus in the stomach, a small bouillon cup of *very hot water*, just as hot as it can be borne, in which a pinch of salt and a pinch of bi-carbonate of soda have been dissolved will prove an excellent aperitive for the day. This is physiological and appropriately chemical, as well as naturally stimulating. Mucus does not dissolve in ordinary water but dissolves readily in an alkaline salt solution, and this is just what is thus recommended. This drink is quite grateful to the palate. Indeed, it tastes very much like clear soup, and, if the eyes are closed, cannot, as a rule, be distinguished from some of the bouillon commonly served. I have known this cup of hot water to stimulate an appetite when drug tonics had failed.

It is better to take the glass of cold water from fifteen to twenty minutes before the morning meal—say immediately on rising. If, instead, the small cup of hot water is chosen, it should come immediately before eating, and will usually prove an appetizer.

Breakfast.—The exact details of the amount of breakfast taken and how it is eaten should be known. Nervous people eat little breakfast. When ordered to eat, they find it difficult at first, but the habit is easily formed, and then they want their breakfast like anyone else. It is surprising how often physicians will find that nervous persons, who are under weight, are not taking enough breakfast. They will ordinarily say that they are eating breakfast about as other people do and will, perhaps, mention eggs and rolls, but it will be found that their ordinary breakfast consists of a roll and piece of toast and coffee, and only occasionally do they have any of the other things mentioned.

Breakfast is ordinarily the meal which those who work are likely to eat too hurriedly. Those who are neurotically inclined are especially victims of the habit. They lie abed until there is only a few minutes left to get the train so as to reach their place of occupation in time, and thus their breakfast is {169} skimped. Their oatmeal or other soft cereal is fairly shovelled in, coffee is gulped, toast is unchewed, the coffee softening it; if they have creamed potatoes they are swallowed in such large pieces that, as every physician knows, if for some reason they vomit they are surprised, beyond all measure, at the large portions they have been able to pass down into their stomachs. A breakfast thus eaten makes a bad beginning for a nervous man's day, and the more that is so eaten the worse for the victim. With a habit like this, it will be utterly impossible by means of drugs or directions as to diet to relieve the discomfort of neurotic indigestion, or to keep the patient from suffering that stomach discomfort so often complained of in the morning.

Working Women.—Working women are even more prone than are men to take a hurried breakfast, and having, as a rule, less appetite than men, their meal is likely to be deficient. It is not unusual to find that a young woman who is under weight and who needs three meals a day, is taking so little for the first meal that even she hesitates to regard it as a meal. Very often her last previous meal has been taken before seven o'clock the night before, so that she goes out ill prepared for her day's work. Much more than men, women are annoyed in the morning by our transportation systems, and by worry as to whether they will get to the office on time. Suggestions as to the modification of this unfortunate routine, the taking of an earlier train, the using of a quiet local instead of a crowded express, a short walk at least before taking the train, will often help in producing a marked change in the general health.

Home Keeping Women.—For those who really have homes, the morning duties are usually sufficient to rouse their activities and make them begin the day well. For those who live in apartment-hotels, however, and for those who have the luxury of many servants, the morning hours are often a serious problem. Madame does not get up, or if she does, it is only to lie around in dressing gown for most of the morning. Breakfast is easily neglected or may be eaten hurriedly because the head of the house is rushing to business. The lack of an incentive requiring them to rise, and get outside for a time every morning, is probably at the root of more feminine symptoms among leisure class patients than anything else. As we grow older all of us are likely to note the lowered physiological cycle of the morning hours, so that unless there is some sharp reason to compel action, we are rather prone to persuade ourselves that it is better to lie abed, or at least to loll around. This leads to a concentration of attention on self and on one's feelings that easily gives rise to neurotic conditions.

Interest in life.—In my special clientéle I have often found that going to church in the early morning hours was an excellent remedy for many of these patients. It gives them a definite reason for rising promptly, the service provides motives to rouse them to activity, they are likely to think during it of how they shall make their life a little bit more livable for others as the result of their trying to be better, and so the apathy that is so fruitful of ill feeling is shaken off. This can only serve for those who have faith in the service. For others, the old-fashioned going out to market, or the making of appointments at morning hours that will tempt them to regular activity early in the day, is of special significance. It is always ominous for health when a woman can look forward to a whole long day without any particular duties {170} in it until the late afternoon or evening hours. This has become so frequently the case for the women of our large cities, particularly those who live in apartment hotels, it is no wonder that neuroses and psychoneuroses of various kinds have grown in frequency. The best prophylaxis for them is occupation of mind. The cure for them is the securing of many interests and such diversion of mind as will prevent concentration of attention on self.

Mail Before Breakfast.—Many people receive their most important mail in the early morning, and personal mail, in cities especially, is likely to be placed beside the breakfast plate. Not infrequently, letters contain serious matters that are likely to disturb people, and occasionally even important business finds its way to the side of the plate at breakfast time. Authors often find their rejected manuscripts sent back in the morning's mail. Occasionally bad news of other kinds comes in this way, and, as a rule, it is the very worst time for its reception. The human system—it cannot be too often repeated—is at its lowest physiological term in the morning, the temperature is lower than during the rest of the day, all the nervous vitality is below the normal. Half an hour after breakfast the reception of bad news, or the coming of important matters requiring decision, would not make so much difference. Hence, the necessity for knowing whether the mail is ordinarily read in the early morning, in order to know something about people, and about the consumption and digestion of their breakfast.

Company at Breakfast.—Pleasant company during meals is an important factor that makes for good digestion. At the other meals there is much more likelihood of having such pleasant company, while the morning meal is often a solitary, and quite as often as not, a rather glum quarter of an hour, preoccupied with the business cares of the day. As may be readily understood from our discussion of this problem of mental preoccupation during digestion, this may seriously hamper digestive processes. Often men take refuge in their paper. The thoughts aroused by reading the modern newspaper are not the pleasantest in the world and consist, very often, of the following out of details of hideous crimes and scandals. When, as is sometimes the case, these scandals concern relatives, friends or acquaintances in whom we are interested, and with regard to whom we feel poignantly because of the publicity involved, nearly the same effect is produced as when bad news is received in letters, or when business worries are thus brought to the breakfast table.

The best conditions for the eating of breakfast are those in which it becomes like the other meals, a family matter. When father, mother and children eat their breakfast together, nearly always family interests and especially the enlivening effect of the joyousness with which children face a new day is the best possible tonic for a business man in whom a solitary breakfast starts a day of digestive disturbance. Sociability and sufficient time must be insisted on, whether at home or in a boarding house, at breakfast as well as the other meals, and it will often be surprising to find how much difference this makes both as regards the quantity eaten and the digestion of the food.

Morbid Habits.—In matters of diet, it is important to ask for details, for it is surprising what unexpected things may be discovered after weeks of treatment. That was illustrated for me once by a case of persistent acne in a young girl, which all the ordinary remedies failed to cure. I felt sure that {171} I had given her such explicit directions with regard to diet that I knew exactly what she was taking and that nothing could be hoped for from any change. As a last resort, I asked once more with regard to all that she ate and only then discovered that before breakfast every day she ate a baked banana. It had been recommended to her by a friend as a sure cure for constipation, she had formed the habit of taking it as a medicine, and so had not spoken of it. Baked bananas agree with many people well, but just as soon as this was eliminated from her diet her acne began to improve and before long had disappeared almost entirely. The taking of large amounts of warm water, already spoken of, is another of these morbid habits. Then many people take a glass of salt water, or laxative water, and some have curious habits with regard to the eating to excess of salt on cereal or on fruit, or sometimes they eat too great a variety of fruit. All this should be known, but often will not be ascertained unless particularly inquired about.

CHAPTER III

THE DAY'S WORK

Probably even more important than details with regard to the early hours of the day, is detailed information as to the day's work, the kind and character of the occupation and the length of time spent at it, the interruptions that may occur, the habits with regard to luncheon, and, above all, the state of mind in which the occupation is pursued. The physician will only learn these details when he sets before himself a definite schedule of what he wants to know, and then proceeds to secure information with regard to it. With this sufficient can be learned in a short time to ascertain the source of the affection or the symptoms complained of. In some cases it is, however, only when the whole day's occupation is reviewed that proper suggestions can be made.

Getting to Work.—Many a man, especially if he has been accustomed to much exercise in younger years, craves muscular exercise, feels much better whenever he has the opportunity to take it, yet rides down to business every morning and back every evening. On his vacation in the summer time, he gets up early for the sake of a morning walk, but he scarcely has time to take his breakfast and ride to business at other times, though the main reason for his better feeling during his vacation is his exercise. There is usually the story of crowded cars in the busy hours, often with annoying thoughts pestering him that he may not be in time and with a constant call on nervous energy while he stands up in the train, jolted, pushed, crowded, or unable to read his paper with satisfaction, even if he has a seat. The discomfort experienced during a ride in crowded cars to business is about as bad a way to begin a day for a nervous person as could be imagined.

As a rule, it will take more than half an hour to get to business in this way. If an extra twenty minutes were taken, it would be possible to walk the distance. On at least two out of every three days in the year this would give a magnificent opportunity for exercise of the best kind, for fresh air, {172} for diversion of mind, for the route could be frequently changed, and, during the spring and fall, if there are parks on the way, these would provide occasion for pleasant thoughts to replace the annoyances which too intimate contact with over-strenuous humanity in overcrowded cars is likely to occasion.

This seems almost too trivial for a doctor to talk about, but it is on the care of trivialities that good health often depends. It is easy to assume that this amounts to little for health but tempt a dissatisfied patient, whose digestion and sleep are disturbed, to do it, especially in the spring and in the fall, and see what a difference it makes in all his physical functions. If he is not used to walking, he will have to begin by walking only a mile or two, but after a time he will do his four-mile walk in about an hour, with no waste of business time, and with a renewal of energy that will seem little short of marvelous.

Details of the Day's Work.—If patients are to be benefited through mental influence it is extremely important that details as to occupation be completely secured. This must include, especially in cases where there are objective but obscure symptoms, minute information that may seem trivial, and yet which often proves to be of great importance. In recent years there has been profound study of the dangers of trades and occupations. Anyone who wants to treat nervous patients, must know much about these occupations, for otherwise symptoms may be ascribed to old infections, to obscure rheumatic conditions, to intestinal auto-intoxication, or to nervous weakness or exhaustion, when they are really the result of occupation-conditions. The various poisons must be carefully looked for, or affections will be wrongly treated. I have had a series of cases of lead poisoning under most unexpected conditions which have taught me much as to the possibilities of obscure plumbism. Lead poisoning from new lead pipes—with no one else in the household suffering from it, lead poisoning from frequent drinking of carbonated waters, the bottles of which had the old-fashioned lead stoppers, lead poisoning from the painting of a flat by a settlement worker who could not get a painter to do it, show how carefully such things must be looked for.

Dust and Respiratory Affections.—Mechanical conditions connected with trades are especially important. Workers in dusty trades are almost sure to suffer severely from bronchitis at times, and to have the affection oftener than others, to have it "hang on longer," as they say, and eventually to have tuberculosis develop. There are some of the polishing trades in the metal industries in which it is impossible to maintain the ordinary death benefit fund that workmen have in other trades, because the men die so frequently and at such an early age from consumption that the drain on the treasury makes it impossible to maintain the fund. Practically all of the dusty occupations have this same tendency. This is true often in occupations where dust is sometimes not supposed to be much of a factor. Railroad trainmen suffer more frequently from colds than do those in other trades because of the dust to which they are exposed, and a trainman with incipient consumption will be greatly benefited by getting out of the dust during the summer months. Sweepers in large buildings, janitors and janitresses have colds that are often untractable because of the dust in their occupations. It is to be hoped that {173} the new vacuum cleaning system now becoming so popular will obviate these dangers, though like all improvements, it will probably bring its own dangers with it.

Lack of Light.—People who work at occupations that keep them from the light are likely to suffer from lung symptoms and to have quite intractable colds which will not clear up until they get more sunlight. Workers in theaters and like places who do their sweeping where sunlight does not penetrate, are in more danger than others from respiratory disease. Those who work in gloomy lower stories, especially in narrow but busy and dusty streets, suffer the same way. Attendants at moving picture shows who work much in the dark where the frequently changing crowd brings in dust which cannot be well removed, and in quarters where the sun does not penetrate, are almost sure to have persistent repeated respiratory troubles.

Habitual Movements.—After the question of dust comes the mode of the occupation. Many occupations demand certain habitual and repeated movements. When people come complaining of pains in muscles in and around joints, or of achy conditions in the limbs, it is important to know every detail of their occupation movements, if the physician is to appreciate just what pathological causes are at work. It is not enough, for instance, to know that a man is a clerk, or a bookkeeper, but it should be asked whether he stands much at his occupation, or walks considerably, or whether he sits practically all the day. If he stands much, we can expect that he will have various painful conditions in his feet and legs, unless he takes care to change his position frequently, to wear the most comfortable shoes obtainable and, above all, to provide against any yielding of the arch of the foot. Often it will be found that people who complain of discomfort in the feet stand much on a cold, and sometimes damp and draughty floor, and this needs to be corrected or their symptoms, often carelessly called rheumatic, will not disappear. If he sits down always during his occupation, he will need exercise and air or he will suffer from many vague discomforts, over sensitiveness and irritability of nerves, as well as from physical conditions.

Most patients prefer to think that they are suffering from some constitutional condition, rather than from a merely local manifestation due to their occupations. Those who have to stand much can often make such arrangements as will permit their sitting down from time to time. They may, if they are standing at a desk, have a high stool; they may during their hour of lunch sit down restfully, or even to recline for a time, so as to restore the circulation in the legs. For many people who suffer from the achy discomfort connected with varicose veins in the leg, a rest of half an hour in the middle of the day with the feet a little higher than the head, will do more than anything else to make them comfortable. This same thing is true for people with flat-foot, and there are many occupations with regard to which advice of this kind will be appreciated. The well known tendency of many men to sit with their feet higher than their head is not a mere caprice, but is due to the fact that this is an extremely restful posture and thoroughly hygienic for those who have been standing much.

Unfortunately, it is not so easy to secure such relief for working women, but occasionally the advice to lie down during the middle of the day on the couches of the retiring rooms may be the best medical prescription that can {174} be given. This will carry young women over trying periods of the month when everything seems to be going wrong. In women particularly, if there are complaints of the pains in the lower limbs, footwear must be investigated. When the heels are too high those who have to stand much are thrown forward and there is a strain of the muscles of the thighs and on the muscles of the back. Many young women suffer from backache supposed to be due to internal conditions usually of gynecological character, when it is only due to high heels or a combination of high heels and constipation. On the other hand, heels that are too low are not comfortable and women's shoes, in spite of the outcry against them, have been better adapted than men's to prevent them from developing flat foot. Fewer women than men suffer from this affection. Shoes that are too loose are almost as bad, sometimes it would seem worse, than those that are too tight.

Habitual Motions and So-Called Rheumatism.—The habitual movements of various trades are extremely important for the diagnosis of conditions that develop in the muscular system. Much of the so-called rheumatism of the working people is really due to the muscular over-activity demanded by their trades. This affects all kinds of working people. Men who have to work foot-lathes, or women who have to work sewing machines, or men or women who have to use their arms much in repeated vigorous movements, are likely to suffer from achy discomfort. The strong and healthy ones do not suffer, but the delicate do. The suffering is much more prevalent in rainy, damp weather; it is worse during the spring and fall than at other times. It is particularly noticeable whenever the patient is run down physically, is worrying about many things, or, above all, is getting insufficient nutrition. The discomfort is particularly likely to recur in those who do not know how to use their muscles properly, who are naturally awkward, and who perhaps have from nature an insufficient control over opposing and coördinating muscles, so that they do not accomplish movements quite as readily as would be the case if they were normal. The personal element enters largely into these affections. Many patients, however, can be trained to do their habitual movements under the best possible mechanical conditions, whereas very often they are found accomplishing them under the worst possible mechanical conditions.

Men who have to do much writing may have to be taught the application of Gowers' rule, that the forearm should so move as a whole during writing that if a pen were fastened to the elbow it would execute exactly all the movements of a pen held in the hand. The writing must all be done from the shoulder. People who do typewriting may have to be instructed not to allow the machine to be too much above them, nor on the other hand, too much below them when they sit down. Young people particularly who, from long hours of practice on the piano, suffer from neurotic conditions, may have to be instructed to do this under good mechanical conditions.

Men who do much filing of metal will often suffer from painful conditions in the arms. These will be much worse in case the filing is done at a table or workbench so high that pressure has to be brought to bear upon the file by the arms instead of through the weight of the body. This same thing is true for women who iron much. If the ironing board is so high that the additional pressure applied is made by the arms, then painful conditions will {175} almost inevitably develop if the work is long continued. These details are discussed in the chapters on joint and muscular affections.

Night Work.—In a large city there are many workmen who are on night duty. They will be disturbed in many ways in health, unless they make special arrangements to live under conditions that enable them to have full eight hours of sleep every day and, above all, to have their meals regularly. When they come home in the morning they usually have a rather hearty meal. Most of them can sleep very well with this, but very few of them sleep the full eight hours, and all need this amount. Usually they have another full meal about five in the evening. Very often it will be found that the third meal of the day consists of a sandwich, with a glass of milk or a glass of beer, and some cake or some crackers and cheese, or the inevitable pie. Every workman should have three full meals, and a man who is suffering from almost any symptoms will be improved at once if the third good meal is insisted upon. At one time I had occasion to see a number of men whose work began not later than seven in the evening and did not finish until six or seven in the morning. They were sufferers from all sorts of complaints. Most of them were under weight. Not a few were constipated. Some were suffering from severe headaches that came rather frequently, and a few from a headache that was severe but came only every two or four weeks. These patients alternated night and day work, and it was the week after they had been on day work, and first went on to night work, that they suffered from headache.

In every one of these cases instructions with regard to eating and sleeping proved to be the best remedy. Nearly all of them were not eating enough, and were skimping the third meal. Three of them were taking only between four and five hours of sleep. They stayed up after breakfast to read the paper, went to bed about nine and got up about two o'clock. Just as soon as two or three hours was added to their sleep, they began to feel better, and various symptoms, digestive, rheumatic and nervous, of which they complained, began to disappear.

Nearly always night workers are more prone than the ordinary run of workmen to some indulgence in spirituous liquors. Cold and shivery on the way home from work in the early morning, they take a nip of whiskey to brace them up. Alcoholic cirrhosis of the liver is a little more common among sea captains, policemen, printers and night workmen on the railroads than among the average of the population. The reason for it seems to be that undilute whiskey is thrown into the circulation by being taken into the stomach at a time when that viscus is empty and all the cells are craving food and drink. It is carried directly to the liver, and there either produces or predisposes to the bad effects upon liver cells which we know as cirrhosis.

It is usually useless to treat such men for the indigestion and other symptoms that are likely to develop as a consequence of their habits, without getting at their story completely. It is easy, as a rule, to relieve them of certain of their symptoms by ordinary drug therapeutics. Unless their habits are changed, this relief, however, is only temporary. It must not be forgotten that in recent years women have come to do a good deal of work at night that was not usual to them before. In the telephone service of certain cities, as cashiers in restaurants, as ticket sellers in various places of entertainment, {176} as office help at busy seasons of the year, women may be kept occupied either all night or at least until quite late. Not infrequently during times when rehearsals are on, chorus girls are kept until the wee small hours. They are particularly likely to suffer from such variations in normal habits, and no treatment is so effective with them as pointing out how they must live, if they want to preserve their appearance and continue in such exacting occupations. A healthy young woman can burn the candle of life at both ends with less protest from nature at the beginning than man, but she suffers more for it and the suffering begins sooner.

Positions During Occupations.—The question of position during occupation, especially as regards its influence upon digestive processes, has always seemed to me much more important than most people think. Our idea of digestion has been so largely one of digestive secretions, to the neglect of the motor side of the gastric and intestinal functions, that we have missed some important points. If a person leans over a desk shortly after a meal, there is no doubt that the crowding of the abdominal viscera hinders peristalsis, at least to some degree, not of course in the robust and healthy, but in those who already have some irregularity or sluggishness in this region. The old high desks at which many clerks used to stand, at which even proprietors did not hesitate to take their position, had a reason in common sense that has been forgotten in the modern times, and the variation of position thus permitted seems to have been good for the workers.

A good deal of comfort may be obtained by having a suitable desk and chair for business hours. Not infrequently it happens that a desk is too high for comfortable writing. Any discomfort that is continuous and makes itself felt intrusively during occupation with other things, will have an unfortunate effect. Such things seem trivial by contrast with serious disease and may seem safely negligible. Trivial they are, but little things count both in themselves and as to the attitude of mind which they occasion. It is the attitude of mind that we try to modify by psychotherapy, and even the removal of little sources of annoyance help a patient materially to get through life more happily and through work more efficiently and without any more discomfort than is absolutely unavoidable.

Positions After Meals.—While we have talked thus of business people, what is said refers, also, to the positions assumed out of business hours, as, for instance, at home after dinner. A Morris chair that permits of a somewhat reclining position, or a rocking chair that temps one to sit back, pretty well distending the abdomen and giving all due play to the internal viscera, will be found not only much more comfortable than a straight-back chair which tempts a man to lean forward, but also there will be less interference with gastric motility, the most important digestive function of the stomach. Arm-chairs which really support the arms, and therefore tend to keep the shoulders up, have something of the same effect. We naturally assume these positions, though occasionally social usage forbids them. The tendency, for instance, for elbows to be put on the table, especially toward the end of a meal, represents a natural instinct to lift up the shoulders and keep the weight of the upper part of the trunk off the abdominal organs. Children's instincts often curiously guide their postures—as is illustrated by the story of the little boy who, when asked by his grandmother if he could manage {177} another tart, said that he thought he could if he stood up. (See chapter on Position.)

Mental Conditions of Occupations.—While the details of manual occupations have to be learned with great care if we are to modify the conditions so as to prevent certain unfortunate effects, just as much care has to be exercised, with those not employed manually, in finding out details as to mental worries, and the various disturbances consequent upon business conditions. Many a man has not brain enough to run his business and his liver. This is the old English expression, and the liver, as the largest of the abdominal organs, is taken for the physical life generally. Many people have not vital energy enough to waste any of it on worries and then be able to complete their digestion and other physiological functions with success. The preceding mental condition is a predisposing cause of many a purely physical ailment. It used to be said that during a cabinet crisis in England, or rather just after it was over, attacks of gout were most frequent among prominent politicians. Mental influence usually kept the attacks off until the very end of the crisis. Merchants come down with pneumonia or digestive disturbances more frequently during periods of acute business depression. Physicians are attacked by pneumonia, or influenza in bad form, after they have been wearing themselves out in an epidemic and worrying about patients. Just after a mother has nursed a child through a severe ailment she herself is prone to suffer from some acute infection. Such common-place infections as boils, styes, abscesses and even the more serious osteomyelitis are likely to come at these times.

It is important, then, to know as much as possible about a business man's affairs. Any one who has had a series of tuberculous patients (who were getting along quite well in spite of latent or even active lesions) disturbed by anxieties of one kind or another, knows how much worries may mean. Men will lose weight and appetite and weaken in their general condition as a consequence of some serious business incident, while all the time physical conditions are the same as they were when they were improving. And it must not be forgotten that even in those who do no physical labor, there may be physical conditions of their occupation that are important. Many a business man does his work cooped up in a small office, with insufficient ventilation, and sometimes, especially where his business is on the ground floor of a large building, with so little sunlight that his environment is quite unhygienic. The great air purifier is sunlight. Unless sunlight is admitted for hours every day to the rooms in which people live, the dust that is inevitably breathed will contain living germs, active and noxious, though had they been exposed to sunlight these germs would be harmless.

Especially then for people with respiratory defects of any kind, whether these be tuberculous or of chronic bronchitic character, the conditions surrounding the occupation should be carefully inquired into. Once the family physician knew such things as a matter of course. Now he is likely to know very little. The lack of such information may not be important for the more serious conditions that he has to treat at patients' homes, but they usually mean much for the submorbid conditions, so to say, the discomforts and chronic conditions, which come for office treatment. They mean much for comfort in life, and for the conservation of health and strength. They {178} represent that newer medicine which people are asking of us now so much more than before, which shall keep them in good health and prevent them, as much as possible, from suffering even from minor ills.

Business Habits.—The modern idea of having a flat-top business desk, instead of a roll-top desk, and having it thoroughly cleared off every evening, so that each day's work does not accumulate, is an important psychic factor in the strenuous life, which in recent years many corporations have been taking advantage of. It is well for those who are their own masters to realize the value of this principle. Nothing so disturbs the efficiency of work, nor adds so much to the incubus that work may become, as having a number of unfinished things which keep intruding themselves. It is not always possible to dispose of problems, but discipline is necessary to keep us from pushing business matters aside. Then they have to be done in a rush, very often at a moment when other things are also pressing. The result is poor work, but, above all, a waste of nerve force and energy that leads up to nervous symptoms and eventually nervous exhaustion. The orderly man, who has learned to settle things as they come up, or at definite times, can accomplish an immense amount of work. Some men are born orderly, but any one who wants to do much work must have order grafted on his makeup—a habit which can be made a second nature. It may seem that a physician is unwarranted in intruding on a man's business affairs thus to inquire about the ways he does things, but this is the difference between psychotherapy and the regulation of life as compared with cures by more material but less effective means.

Personal Hygiene.—Expert Advice.—For many men who are much occupied with business, the best possible safeguard for health, as well as the best guarantee against nervous or physical breakdown, would be a detailed consultation once a year with a physician regarding their habits of life and their business in relation to their health, present and future. In recent years many a business firm has found it not only expedient but profitable to turn to an expert accountant or auditing company and ask advice with regard to the management of its business. It is often found that certain business customs are causing serious drains, and that there are newer ways of doing things that save time and money. Sometimes a reorganization of the accounting system, or of the method of dealing with credits and debits, or the receiving or shipping department, proves advantageous to the business. Sometimes it is found that the capital invested will not justify the extension of business that is proposed, and not infrequently it is shown that a proposed extension adds to business movement but does not add to profits. Sometimes there are departments that can be dropped to advantage, though they seem to be adding to both business and profit.

All of this may well be transferred to the question of health in its relation to business. Not infrequently it is found that the capital of strength of the business man is not sufficient to justify the extension that he is planning or has already attempted. Sometimes suggestions can be made with regard to the mode of doing business, the hours employed and the hours of relaxation, that will make business less of a drain on the system. Occasionally arrangements for sleep and exercise, as well as for afternoons or special times of diversion, may save a man from that concentration of attention on one thing {179} which frequently leads to nervous breakdown. Not infrequently business men who are of neurotic habit have customs of doing business which add to their nervous irritability, and these might be modified so as to lessen the call on nervous energy. There is need that the physician be looked to as an expert in personal health and its relation to business, just as the expert accountant or auditing firm is looked to for advice with regard to business methods.

CHAPTER IV

THE MIDDLE OP THE DAY

Information regarding the mid-day meal will be of value to the physician in many cases. In cities, luncheon, likely to be rather an apology for a meal, is taken rapidly, and immediately there is a return to work. As a medical student in Vienna, I was much interested in the mid-day meal of the bankers and merchants of the old Austrian capital. At that time—I hope they have not changed the good custom since—the banks closed at 12 o'clock and did not open again until 3 o'clock. This gave time for taking the mid-day meal in comfort, and for a proper interval for digestion. In all the southern countries of Europe, for seven or eight months in the year at least, little is done during the two or three hours in the middle of the day. The people get up earlier and rest at mid-day as a break between the afternoon and morning. It is quite beyond expectation that anything like this will ever again be possible in the great commercial cities. The fact that this was the custom of our European forefathers, however, shows how business has obtruded itself on the habits that man would naturally form for himself. Business men hurry to luncheon, or if they take any time over it, it is because they have invited some one to lunch with them with whom they wish to talk over important matters. This means of saving time recalls the well-known expression of James Jeffrey Roche: "Time is money. Every second saved from your dinner now is a sequin in your doctor's pocket later on in life!"

Hurried Lunch.—The seeds of our frequent American dyspepsia are sown partly at the hurried breakfast and then at the hurried mid-day lunch. When a physician finds this to be the case, then the patient's habits must be reformed. Otherwise there is little prospect of relief from neurotic digestive symptoms, or from those uncomfortable feelings so often supposed to refer to the heart, or other important organ, when digestion is interfered with. There should be pleasant company at luncheon if possible; it should be preceded by fifteen or twenty minutes in the open air, with, as far as possible, complete seclusion from business thoughts so as to allow the stomach to secure its share of blood, and it should be followed by at least half an hour of pleasant occupation that does not call for serious mental work. This may not be possible for every one, and many will complain that this is asking too much in our busy time. We physicians are not here to make the nice customs of medicine courtesy to great kings of finance or to the busy tyrants of the professions, but to tell them what we think should be {180} done in order that nature may not be abused. Men should be advised to take their luncheon in some building different from that in which their offices are located, or, if they eat in the same building, to go out on the street for a while before the meal. In the old days men used to call on one another in order to transact business, and these little trips were often made just before or after luncheons.

Now the telephone and the messenger boy have done away with this, with a great saving of time, but with an increase of intensity of labor that makes for nervous exhaustion. Luncheon clubs are excellent things when men do not talk shop, but they have one fatal defect. Almost invariably they lack simplicity of menu, and, because of the variety supplied and the example of others, there is a tendency to eat to

111

excess. A game of billiards after eating is often excellent, because, when standing, digestion is accomplished with more comfort than when seated. A walk after the lighter midday meal is a good thing, though the old saw said "after dinner sit a while," but that was in reference to the largest meal of the day, and may still hold good for the evening meal, which is likely to be the heaviest one.

Women's Lunch.—Women are very likely to take their mid-day meal, when it is their luncheon, very irregularly. If they have to get it for themselves they are likely to be satisfied with almost anything. If they get it outside the house they are likely to take it rather late, so that if they have breakfast before eight o'clock, this putting off of the next meal causes some disturbance of the economy. When the stomach gets to be empty, either there is a tendency to swallow air, or there is a rumbling sense of fullness that disturbs the appetite, or the appetite itself is capricious, and a headache develops. How many headaches are due to missed meals it would be hard to say, but this is one of the most fruitful causes of the ordinary passing headache. Delicate women, and especially those who work, are likely not to eat enough luncheon. All the details with regard to this meal must be known or the physician will find it hard to get rid of many neurotic symptoms, particularly in working women. The same thing is true for the so-called society woman, since she is likely to have a late breakfast and then skip her mid-day meal. This is permissible if she is so stout as to be able to spare it, but it is all wrong if she is thin and needs every ounce of weight.

Nature of the Noon Meal.—During the last two generations fashion, custom and the increasing demands of business have pushed the hour of taking the principal meal farther and farther away from mid-day. There are, however, cases in which it seems better that the principal meal should be taken in accordance with the old custom, about noon time. For tuberculous patients this is especially important. They often have fever in the afternoon that seriously disturbs appetite. They may eat with comfort and relish a couple of hours before the fever is due. For delicate persons, especially those who have not much appetite for breakfast and who can not be persuaded to eat a sufficient amount early in the morning, a hearty meal at noon is almost a necessity. They should be shown how low their nutrition is during working hours. Their principal meal of the day before was taken between six and seven o'clock. They have had a light breakfast, a meager lunch, and naturally have little reserve force during the afternoon hours. As a consequence they become overtired, this lessens the appetite, they do not eat properly, and, {181} above all, they do not digest as well as they would if their last good meal were not so far away. They are suffering from inanition, and, as is well known, starving people cannot be allowed to eat heartily, because their stomachs have not enough vitality to digest well.

It is often difficult to change the hour of taking the principal meal, but in special cases this can be done with decided advantage. I have seen such a change make all the difference between slow recuperation from bad colds, and have seen it of the greatest possible importance in tuberculosis. The very changing of the hour will sometimes suggestively react to make the patient eat more heartily than usual, the day is broken up better, the reaction against the morning discouragement comes earlier, and the patient's general condition improves. Many people rest better at night if their principal meal is taken at the middle of the day.

CHAPTER V

THE LEISURE HOURS.

Then comes the return from business. Here once more the ordinary method of getting on a crowded train, standing up to be pushed and jammed, to have all sorts of unpleasant things happen, to have the pessimism of one's nature stirred to its depths by the utter disregard for women, the heedless rush of men, the roughness of railroad employees, and the general lack of humanity that characterizes the evening rush from business in a large city, is eminently unsuitable as a preparation for dinner; while a calm walk of three to five miles is ideal. To walk home will probably take twenty minutes or half an hour longer, but not more than this—and it avoids the undesirable features of the usual method.

Gymnastics.—Occasionally one finds that men rush through the last hour of business in order to spend an hour in a gymnasium. Often this is quite undesirable. Exercise within doors, taken in a routine manner and merely for the sake of exercise, with no diversion of mind, is eminently unsuitable for the busy man. What he needs is air much more than exercise. Walking out of doors is the very best thing for him. If he walks at a rapid pace, swinging his arms a little freely and carrying a cane in one hand and perhaps a book in the other, because this exercises his fingers and keeps him from having any unpleasant congestion of the hands when they hang down, then the exercise is almost ideal. Owing to the novelty of it, and the interest that a new occupation arouses, great benefit will at first be derived from the gymnasium. Very often, too, the cold plunge after the exercise does more good than the exercise itself. The plunge is real fun, especially when taken with many others, but the exercise itself is likely to degenerate into the sorriest kind of a task. If the man who walks home will take a bath before dinner, the temperature of the water being made suitable to him and the reaction that comes to his particular nature, there is no need of anything else, and there is nothing better that he could do. The walk must be varied. The course must not always be through the same streets. Occasionally it {182} should even lead one to see some monument or new building, or to go out of the way with a friend, so that variety is introduced.

Work at Home.—There are men who in busy times take some of their work home with them. This is a mistake. And though it is the custom to tell the doctor that they cannot do otherwise, it is practically always a bit of self-deception. When the case is properly put before them, they realize, if they already have any neurotic symptoms, that to continue home work will be a serious risk. Most men who carry business home with them, easily get into the habit of pushing certain details away from them during the day with the idea that they will have more time for that in the evening. They do a certain amount of dawdling over their work. If they really resolved to finish work during business hours they could do it, and do it better than during the evening at home. Six hours of work is about all that a man ought to do with his intellect at high pressure. This should be pretty well divided into two periods of three hours each, with an interval of an hour to an hour and a half between. The nearer a man can come to this arrangement the better for him, and the better, also, for his affairs. If he has assumed obligations that require more of his time and attention than this, he is trying to do too much.

After-Dinner Hours.—The evening hours and their proper occupation are important for the business man, or for anyone who is much occupied during the day. The temptation to let the work of the day run over into the evening must be overcome at all costs, or it will prove serious for the health of most men. It is important as far as possible to get something completely different for men to do at night. Many men settle down to the reading of a newspaper or of a magazine or novel. While this does very well under some circumstances, reading does not provide diversion whenever there is serious worry or solicitude over business matters. A man may think that he is occupying himself with the newspaper, but we all know very well that business cares intrude, that business troubles are often doubled by reading about others. The reading of novels does well for a while, but the serious-minded man tires of them and then, while they may occupy a couple of hours, they have exactly the same objection as the newspaper. A genuine diversion should give the physical basis of mind an opportunity literally to remake itself by storing up new energies.

Amusements.—The fact of the matter is that a man must have, if possible, some other serious interest in life besides his business. He must have a hobby. We have discussed this in the chapter on Diversion of Mind and refer to it here only to indicate the importance of knowing something about a man's recreation as well as his work. It is not a casual occupation but a real interest that he should have. This need not necessarily be a useful employment and, indeed, it may be absolutely useless provided it is absorbing. Card playing is an excellent diversion for many people. When joined with gambling, new worries and feverish excitement usually make it harmful for neurotic persons. Chess is hard work, but of a different kind from that of the day and, therefore, often makes an excellent recreation. Any games are good. Bowling, for instance, is excellent, and billiards, if a man has an interest in it, is a fine sport for evening hours. It has the added advantage of physical exercise. A man does not sit down during billiards, crowding his {183} already well-distended abdominal viscera, but walks around and gives his viscera a better chance for their work and aids rather than retards peristalsis.

Encroachment on Sleep.—There is just one defect about some of the more absorbing recreations—they keep a man up too late. Whenever a so-called recreation takes up such time that a man has less than eight full hours in bed, then a mistake, almost sure to be serious sooner or later, is being made. When the physician tries to limit a man's recreation by suggesting an earlier hour for retirement, he may be told that his patient must have some time for diversion and recreation. But the physician must insist that no form of recreation is as good as sleep, and any other form must be limited in order that sleep may be obtained. A man may easily regulate his affairs so that he shall have eight hours of sleep, and it is only negligence of such regulation that gives him the idea that recreation cannot be obtained except after eleven o'clock at night. Little suppers after the theater are often fine diversions, but whenever they interfere with sleep they must not be allowed except at long intervals. Other diversions that keep a man out of bed after midnight are sure not to do good in the long run, though an occasional lapse in this matter may prove a stimulant rather than a depressant. It is custom that must be regulated; an occasional variant from it is rather good than otherwise.

Leisure of the Working Woman.—A woman's occupation, unlike a man's, holds out little future for her. Her occupation does not arouse her ambition. Daily work is a monotonous grind that must be endured for the sake of the wages that it brings. For a time this serves to occupy attention. After some years, when the prospects of matrimony grow less, and further advance is out of the question, women often need to have some special interest that will grip them. The working woman may then need to be tempted to some occupation of mind, especially with the companionship of others, that will give her renewed interests in life. Clubs, charities in which they are active, friends, serious intellectual interests, must all be appealed to, in different cases, in order to secure diversion. Women must have something to look forward to each week. They must know on Monday that before the following Sunday there is going to be a theater party, a lecture, a visit to friends, something to break the deadliness of weekly routine, which is anticipated with pleasure and then pleasantly remembered. This may seem to be only a slight matter, but it is of importance in many cases.

Feminine Occupations.—The occupations of women who stay at home are even more important than those of women who go out to work. In our time the root of much nervousness, as it is called, neurotic symptoms of various kinds and of many symptoms apparently quite distant from real nervousness, is really a lack of occupation. Many women who live in apartment hotels have almost nothing with which to occupy their minds. They are not obliged to get up in the morning if they do not want to, or, at least, any excuse, however slight, serves to keep them in bed. Very often there are either no children or the mother has nothing to do with her children early in the morning. After the age of three, they go off to kindergarten; later on they go to school. Breakfast is sent up, there may be a nap of an hour or two after the meal, and often a magazine is glanced over lying in bed, and perhaps it will be twelve o'clock before madame gets up. Anyone in a position to do this, and who allows the habit to grow, is sure to be profoundly {184} miserable. Without any real occupation of mind, the mind occupies itself with the body and emphasizes every sensation, evokes new pains and aches, and the consequence is likely to be a highly neurotic state.

113

Such women have nothing serious to think about in the afternoon. At best it is a luncheon engagement with a friend, or attendance at the matinee, or a lecture, or a meeting of a club. For a while, and for a certain few, these things are satisfying, but after they have been indulged in for a time, they pall so completely on most people as to leave them almost helplessly at the mercy of their feelings. These persons may have some favorite charities that occupy part of their time. They may have other interests, but most of these interests are quite amateurish. They create no obligations; they arouse no sense of duty; they are abandoned at a moment for anything else that turns up, and consequently they lack that absorbing power that a real interest gives. It is quite impossible that these people should be either happy or healthy. These ladies of leisure sometimes have fads for physical exercise that keep them from becoming absolutely sluggish, but except in a few cases, these fads pall after a time, and in a few years women of the leisure classes are generally without any interest that will save them from themselves. The root of many a case of nervousness that wanders from physician to physician and then from quack to quack, and from charlatan of one kind to charlatan of another kind, that takes up now this remedy and now that, and advertises each new method of healing—mental, hypnotic, mechanical—is due to nothing more serious than lack of proper occupation of mind.

The Ambition to Have Nothing to Do.—It seems to be the ambition of everyone to reach a place in life so that he can give up work and do nothing. Men and women often envy those whose material situation is such that they are not compelled to work. It is from the leisure classes, however, that our neurotic invalids are mainly recruited. The symptoms these people give will sometimes make one wonder whether they may not be suffering from some serious ailment, but just as soon as the details of their daily occupation are gone into, the real cause for their complaints can be readily seen. Nothing will do them any lasting good until they get interested enough in life to be distracted from themselves. Such men and women are invalids by profession. They are profoundly to be pitied, for they are much more the victims of present-day social conditions than of any special fault of their own. They go from one health resort to another seeking relief and now and again finding it, not because of any special effect of the remedies that they take, but just in proportion to the amount of diversion and occupation of mind they are able to secure in their wanderings. After a time they relapse, then, the old cures having lost novelty, the physician who succeeds in occupying their minds does them good; his brother physician, who does not, fails; but anyone else, however absurd his quackery, who can in any way catch their attention, will benefit them at least for the time being.

Business Anxieties.—The physician should know all that concerns such sources of excitement, worry and anxiety, as are suggested by the words speculation, investment, going on bonds and securities, especially when the person bonded gets into trouble. Fortunately most of these latter sources of worry have been eliminated by the bonding companies of recent years. Details {185} of this kind were given to the old family physician as a matter of course. With the going out of the family physician there has often been no one to replace him in hearing such stories, and it has been harder for some to bear the consequences in solitude. The very telling of many cares lessens the burden of them. The warnings of a medical friend may be more effective in keeping a man from serious loss than those of financial friends. Everyone realizes that the physician's advice is quite unselfish and that what he objects to, even more than the danger and loss of money, is worry and anxiety which may lead to loss of health.

For ordinary therapeutic purposes, the physician may be content to know only the physical signs and symptoms of his patient's affection. For psychotherapeutics, he must, if he would be successful, know every possible source of worry and annoyance and, as nearly as may be ascertained, every slight phase of physical fatigue that may be a disturbing factor in his patient's life. It is surprising how many things the physician will find to correct when he carefully goes over all the actions of the day and ascertains all the possible sources of worry and anxiety his patient may have. It may happen that in many cases he will be unable immediately to remove these sources of worry. But there is relief in telling them, and then, even when they cannot be completely eradicated, they can often be modified. Every improvement of this kind, however slight, is a fountain of favorable suggestion which makes the patient look on the brighter side of life. From every amelioration, however trivial, there is a reaction on the feelings that gives more and more confidence.

{186}

SECTION IV

GENERAL PSYCHOTHERAPEUTICS

CHAPTER I

GENERAL PRINCIPLES OF PSYCHOTHERAPY

In formal, deliberate psychotherapeutics the first and most important principle is the treatment of the individual patient, and not of his disease. It is much more important to know the kind of an individual who has pneumonia, as a rule, than to be able to tell the amount of pulmonary involvement. If heart, kidneys or lungs are affected when the disease declares itself, the outlook is extremely unfavorable. Similar conditions are true of the patient's mind. If he is of the worrying kind, the outlook is serious. If, on the contrary, he faces it bravely, and without after-thought except that of responding to medical treatment, he will probably get well.

Pneumonia is only one example of the part the individual plays in therapeutics. In the popular mind it is supposed that for each disease there is a definite remedy, and that when the physician gives that remedy the patient gets well. This idea of specific remedies has come to the people from the physician, but only the quack now pretends to cure disease, the physician helps the patient to overcome the affection from which he is suffering.

No Incurable Patients.—There are many incurable diseases, but there are no patients to whom a doctor should say with truth, "I can do nothing for you." We may be unable to do anything for the underlying disease. That may be absolutely incurable. In spite of this, there are practically always symptoms for which the patient can be afforded so much relief that he feels better than before. This is the most important attitude of mind for the physician who would use psychotherapy. He can always do something. Prof. Richet said not long since, "Physicians can seldom cure, but they can nearly always relieve and they can always console," and it is the physician's duty to lift up and console the mind as well as to heal the body.

Unfavorable Suggestions.—Patients often have many opinions and conclusions with regard to their ailments which are not confided to their medical attendants, and which constitute the basis of many annoying symptoms. They have mental convictions with regard to the incurableness of their ailments, the supposed progressive character of the disease, and the development of symptoms which will still further annoy them, that are often more serious and harder to bear than the symptoms from which they are actually suffering. Unless the physician has their complete confidence, these patients may suffer much in silence, though the revelation of their state of mind would {187} often be sufficient to afford a good measure of relief, and the correction of false notions would do nearly all the rest. Psychotherapy confers its benefits mainly by securing the most complete *rapport* between the mind of patient and physician. Good advice is often more important than any medicine. The correction of wrong notions will do more to relieve the patient, and make whatever symptoms he has bearable, than most of the anodyne drugs. The stimulation of hope means more than almost anything else in arousing the latent forces of nature and predisposing to recovery. The removal of unfavorable suggestions is but little less efficient.

Study of the Individual.—The great differences in the relations between physicians and their patients is well recognized. To some physicians a patient will present only conventional symptoms, while a follow practitioner will discover the elements of an interesting case. Above all, the painstaking physician, interested in psychology, will find mental and other personal manifestations in his patient that distinctly modify the course of the disease. We must know all that is possible about the patient's attitude of mind toward his malady, and all the ideas that he has acquired with regard to it, either from previous relations with physicians or from what he may have read or heard from others. The removal of many false notions that are thus working harm will reward the medical practitioner who gets at his patient's ideas. The old rule in therapeutics is *non nocere*—to be sure to do no harm. The special rule in psychotherapy is to be sure to remove all the ideas that are doing harm to the patient and making his symptoms mean more to him than they really signify.

Neutralizing Contrary Suggestion.—In the application of psychotherapy, then, the first principle is the neutralization of unfavorable mental influence. In our day men have such a smattering of knowledge about disease, especially about the worst forms of it, that they are likely to be in a frame of mind with regard to many affections that is quite unfavorable. Many patients think disease and not health. Disease means discomfort, and consequent loss of vital energy and disturbance of the resistive vitality that would enable the patient to throw off the affection. Sometimes the physician does not realize what a large part unfavorable suggestions are playing in the affection. Sometimes patients conceal their state of mind lest the doctor should confirm their worst fears. The preliminary to all successful treatment is to remove unfavorable suggestion.

Favorable Suggestion.—The next thing is to set certain favorable suggestions at work. It is possible always to do this. Even in certain of the acute diseases favorable suggestion has its place, and for all chronic cases this form of therapeutics is extremely important. The very presence of the physician, especially if he is thoroughly in control of himself, placid, imperturbed, evidently ready to use all his powers without any excitement, is of itself the strongest kind of favorable suggestion. From the very beginning of medical history the presence of the physician has in most cases meant even more than his medicines.

Münsterberg, in his recent book on Psychotherapy, has emphasized this in a way that deserves to be recalled:

There is one more feature of general treatment which seems almost a matter of course, and yet which is perhaps the most difficult to apply because it cannot {188} simply be prescribed: the sympathy of the psychotherapist. The feelings with which an operation is performed or drugs given do not determine success, but when we build up a mental life, the feelings are a decisive factor. To be sure, we must not forget that we have to deal here with a causal and not with a purposive point of view. Our sympathy is therefore not in question in its moral value, but only as a cause of a desired effect. It is therefore not really our sympathy which counts but the appearance of sympathy, the impression which secures the belief of the patient that sympathy for him exists. The physician who, although full of real sympathy, does not understand how to express it and make it felt will thus be less successful than his colleague who may at heart remain entirely indifferent but has a skillful routine of going through the symptoms of sympathy. The sympathetic vibration of the voice and skillful words and suggestive movements may be all that is needed, but without some power of awakening this feeling of personal relation, almost of intimacy, the wisest psychotherapeutic treatment may remain ineffective. That reaches its extreme in those frequent cases in which social conditions have brought about an emotional isolation of the patient and have filled him with an instinctive longing to break his mental loneliness, or in the still more frequent cases where the patient's psychical sufferings are misunderstood or ridiculed as mere fancies, or misjudged as merely imaginary evils. Again everything depends upon the experience and tact of the physician. His sympathy may easily overdo the intention and further reinforce the patient's feeling of misery, or make him an hypochondriac. It ought to be sympathy with authority and sympathy which always at the same time shows the way to discipline. Under special conditions, it is even advisable to group patients with similar diseases together, and to give them strength through the natural mutual sympathy; yet this too can be in question only where this community becomes a starting point for common action and common effort, not for mere common depression. In this way a certain psychical value may be acknowledged for the social classes of tuberculosis as they have recently been instituted.

Favorable Environment.—After the removal of unfavorable suggestion and the implanting of favorable suggestion, the next point must be the persistent occupation of the patient's mind with thoughts favorable to his condition. A nurse who is inclined to be pessimistic must be taken out of the sick room, and there must be only cheerful faces and cheery people around him. Hence the modern trained nurse, and especially the picked nurse, who does not allow herself to be disturbed, who is not fussy, who is not forcibly cheerful but quietly placid and confident and cheery, means much for the patient's recovery. Relatives are almost sure to exert strong unfavorable suggestions, though time was when the devoted wife or mother might be depended upon to cover up all her personal feelings and give the best possible service for the mental uplift of the patient. When she can thus conceal her own solicitude, a near relative may be the best possible auxiliary in psychotherapeutics.

Natural Relief.—The fourth step in the application of psychotherapeutics is that all the natural modes for the relief of symptoms, the making of patients comfortable in body as well as in mind, must be employed. In acute rheumatism, for instance, a number of small pillows must be at the disposition of the patient so that his limbs can be fixed in those positions in which there is the least discomfort. Every physician should frequently read Hilton's classical volume on "Rest and Pain" because of its unpretentious significance for psychotherapy, as well as its enduring value in the treatment of painful conditions. Just as soon as a patient finds that simple procedures relieve his pain and add to his comfort, his fear of the seriousness of his ailment is lessened, {189} and he begins to get bettor. Cold water in fevers, cold fresh air in pneumonia, all the natural modes of treating disease, thus become active factors in the application of psychotherapy. When fevers were treated by the administration of hot drinks the effect upon the patient's mind must have been quite serious. Freedom to use cold water, just as one wants it and whenever it is craved for, is of itself an excellent suggestion.

Neuroses in Organic Disease.—Fifth, psychotherapy, by suggestion, may alleviate or even completely eradicate neurotic symptoms that develop in connection with organic diseases. Such neurotic symptoms may prove even more bothersome to the patient than the symptoms due to his underlying affection, and may, by interfering with nutrition, hamper recovery. The appetite of a patient who is worrying about a chronic disease will be disturbed, and, as a consequence of insufficient food, constipation and a whole train of attendant evils may ensue. Headache, sleeplessness, worry at slight irritation and exaggerated complaints from slight pain may all be due to this worry and not to the underlying disease. All these, the result of over-solicitude, are attributed by the patient to his chronic ailment. They can be relieved by simple measures after he is saved from his own worry. Until the patient is made to rouse himself and look hopefully at the situation, eating more, getting out more, and relaxing his mind from its constant attention to himself, he cannot get better.

Application of Principles.—It should be pointed out to the patient that there is a constant tendency to exaggerate the significance of disease. This is true in acute as well as in chronic disease, but in acute diseases the necessity for removing unfavorable influences directly is not so urgent, since usually the presence of the physician, with his simple declaration of the meaning of symptoms, is sufficient to neutralize the effect of previous exaggerations.

Secondly, the action of unfavorable suggestions due to imperfect knowledge (everything unknown is magnified, as Cicero said), or to previous medical opinions which the case does not justify, must be stopped. The natural dread which comes to all men in the presence of symptoms of disease must be as far as possible removed.

Thirdly, the favorable elements in the case should be emphasized. This needs to be thoroughly done in order to secure the patient's co-operation, even though the serious possibilities of his ailment may be pointed out to his friends. These friends, however, must be persons who can be absolutely depended on not to reveal by word, or, what is much more important, by their looks or actions, the possible worse prognosis of the case.

Unfortunately, people expect a doctor to tell them the worst, rather than the best. Many physicians seem to have formed the habit of representing the condition of patients as grave as possible, in order, apparently, that they may have more credit when the patient recovers. Not a little of the tendency of ills to hang on in neurotic persons is due to this habit. Over-cautiousness leads some physicians to reveal a case in its worst aspect, lest, by any chance, something unexpected should happen, and the friends of the patient might think that the physician was incompetent because he had not anticipated it. Some of the serious accidents of disease are quite beyond anticipation; but they occur only rarely. For the sake of safeguarding the possible reflection on the physician because of them, it is quite unjustifiable to make bad {190} prognosis habitually, for this acts deterrently on the vital resistance and delays recovery.

Symptoms of Organic Disease.—It is usually considered that psychotherapy is beneficial only in nervous cases; yet we know that all sorts of affections with tissue changes in the skin, in the circulation, and very probably also in the internal organs, may be produced in hysterical affections—ailments dependent on loss of control over the vaso-motor nervous system. Just as ills can be produced, so they may also be cured. As a matter of fact, analysis of the statistics of disease cured by mental influence, shows that it has been more strikingly manifest in organic than in so-called nervous or functional diseases. Neurotic patients often make extremely unsuitable subjects for the exercise of

116

mental influence, because their very nervousness is a manifestation of lack of power properly to control the mind. Cures by mental influence have oftenest been reported in non-neurotic patients. As Dr. Hack Tuke pointed out in "The Influence of the Mind on the Body" as long ago as 1884, it is in such cases as rheumatism, gout and dropsy that benefit was most frequently reported by mental means.

Tuberculosis, certain digestive and intestinal ailments that evidently are associated with tissue changes, have in recent years come particularly into this category of ailments affected by psychotherapy. Dr. Hack Tuke's declaration, made nearly thirty years ago, seems conservative even at the present day: "The only inference which we are justified in drawing from the statistics of the affections cured by mental means is that the beneficial influence of psychotherapeutics is by no means confined to nervous disorders." Many physicians are likely to hold that when cures take place the so-called organic diseases were not actual, but were only *supposed* to exist because of certain obscure symptoms that apparently could not otherwise be explained. But many of the cases have had external symptoms, striking and unmistakable. To assume that physicians of experience and authority were in error in diagnosing them is simply to beg the question. It is more probable that mental influence acted curatively even over tissue changes as it so often does, directly under our observation, in the production of such changes in the skin.

Tissue Changes From Nerves.—Until one recalls how many physical changes may be brought about by mental influences or emotional disturbances, it is not always clear just how mental influence can affect disease favorably or unfavorably. Prof. Forel, of Zurich, in his "Hygiene der Nerven und des Geistes im Gesunden und Kranken Zusande," Zurich, 1905, English translation 1907, brings together into a single paragraph most of these physical and physiological influences of the mind upon the central nervous system:

Through the brain and spinal cord, thoughts can lead to a paralysing or stimulation of the sympathetic ganglion nodes, and consequently to blushing or blanching of certain peripheral parts. Through disturbance of this mechanism, many nervous disorders arise, such as chilblains, sweats, bleeding of the nose, chills and congestions, various disturbances of the reproductive organs, and, if it lasts long enough, nutritional disturbances in the part of the body supplied by the blood vessels affected. In the same way there are peripheral ganglionic mechanisms which superintend glandular secretion, the action of the intestinal muscles, etc. These likewise can be influenced through the brain by ideas and emotions. Thus we can explain how constipation and a vast number of other disturbances of digestion and of menstruation can be produced through the brain, without having their cause in {191} the place in which they appear. It is for the same reason that such disturbances can be cured by hypnotic suggestion.

Health and the Central Nervous System.—Nature has so constituted and ordered the human economy that its health depends to a great extent on conditions in the central nervous system. We discuss elsewhere the return of vitalism in physiology—that is, the reassertion of a principle of life behind the chemical and physical forces of the human organism regulating it, supplying energy, occasionally enabling it to transcend the ordinary laws of osmosis, or the diffusion of gases. The main seat of this principle of life is in the central nervous system and especially in the cerebral cortex. The importance of this portion of the human anatomy can scarcely be exaggerated. In his inaugural address to the Royal Medical Society, delivered at Edinburgh in 1896, Prof. T. S. Clouston, the distinguished English psychiatrist, has a passage on this subject that deserves to be recalled:

I would desire this evening to lay down and to enforce a principle that is, I think, not sufficiently, and often not at all, considered in practical medicine and surgery. It is founded on a physiological basis, and it is of the highest practical importance. The principle is that the brain cortex, and especially the mental cortex, has such a position in the economy that it has to be reckoned with more or less as a factor for good or evil in all diseases of every organ, in all operations and in all injuries. Physiologically, the cortex is the great regulator of all functions, the ever active controller of every organ and the ultimate court of appeal in every organic disturbance.

Psychotherapy in Its Relation to Patient and Physician.—In spite of the present-day fad for psychotherapy, I have no illusions with regard to its popularity among patients, unless practiced with due regard to individuals and with proper tact. Psychotherapy has been most effective in the past when it was cloaked beneath the personality of the physician; when it was felt that there was in him a power to do good that must help the patient. This personal influence has to be maintained if the patient's mind is to be influenced favorably. Very few people are willing to think, and still less to welcome the thought, that they themselves are either bringing about a continuance of their symptoms or are hindering their own recovery. They are quick to conclude that this would be a confession that their ills are imaginary. "Imaginary" has no place in medicine. There are physical ills and mental ills. Mental ills are just as real as physical ills. There are no fancied ills. A person may be ailing because he persuades himself that he is ailing, but in that case his mind is so affecting his body that he is actually ailing physically, though the etiology of the trouble is mental.

It is the duty of the physician to get at these mental causes of physical ills and remove them by persuasion, by reassurance, by changing the mental attitude, by making people understand just how mind influences body, but this must be done tactfully. From the beginning of time we have written our prescriptions in such a way that ninety-nine out of one hundred patients have not been able to understand them. It has often been said that we should change this method of prescription writing, and write directions for the compounding of our medicines in plain vernacular. Besides the many {192} scientific reasons against this, it is better for patients not to know exactly the details of their treatment. Physicians, because of their real or supposed knowledge, are usually the worst patients. If, when a physician is ill, a drug is administered in which he has lost confidence, he will really oppose its action by contrary suggestion, and perhaps neutralize it. Confidence added to the action of the drug itself, makes it much more potent and much more direct. Hence the suggestive value of a prescription the ingredients of which are unknown. Every physician knows of patients who have declared that a drug has been tried on them without avail, when it has only been used in such small quantities as to be quite nugatory in its effect. Such use was enough to prejudice them against it so that when given in physiological doses it failed to work properly.

117

Opium given to a trusting patient, in gradually reduced doses until practically there is nothing but the flavor of the drug in the compound that he takes, will continue to have its effect. But to a patient prejudiced against the drug, even large doses of opium will prove unavailing, because the lack of confidence disturbs the mind, directs attention to whatever discomfort may be present, emphasizes the ill and prevents sleep by preoccupying the mind with the thought that neither the drug nor the dose can accomplish its purpose. In a word, medicine plus mental influence is extremely valuable. Medicine minus mental influence is valuable but sometimes ineffective. Medicine, with mental influence opposed to it, is often without effect because of the strong power the mind has over bodily functions.

Most people would rather be cured by some supposedly wonderful discovery, which presumedly made it clear that they had been suffering from a severe and quite unusual ailment, than by ordinary simple methods. The recent growth of interest in psychotherapy and psychology has, however, somewhat prepared people to accept mental influence as an important factor in therapeutics. The direct and frank use of psychotherapy will be of benefit to these people. But in most cases mental influence will have to be exerted in such a way as to conceal from patients that it is their own energy we want to tap to help them cure themselves. This would be for them quite an unsatisfactory method of being cured. In practically all cases such a combination of methods is needed that the place of mental influence is not over-emphasized. As a rule, mental influence must not be used alone. Its place is that of an adjunct, a precious auxiliary, to other methods of treatment.

Psychotherapy represents one of the important elements in therapeutics, and we must learn to use it in a way suitable to our patients. We have to learn to use our drugs in accordance with the nature and physical make-up of the patient. We have to find out by experience just how to use hydrotherapy for each individual. Varying currents of electricity and varying forms of electrical action are needed for different individuals. Just in the same way, our psychotherapy must be dosed out according to the special need of each individual, the form of the affection and the particular kind of mind that is to be dealt with. To learn the place of mental influence in healing, so that we shall not be attributing to other therapeutic factors what is really due to the mind, will be a great advance in therapeutics. This is the mistake that we have been making in the past.

In brief, the applications of the general principles of psychotherapy {193} include all means, apart from the physical, of influencing patients. Drugs will always have a large place in rational therapy. Many physical remedial measures, hydrotherapy, electrotherapy, climatotherapy and others, must be important adjuncts. To these is now added psychotherapy. It has been used before, as have most of the other forms of therapy, but in our day we are trying to systematize therapeutic modes so as to secure the greatest possible information with regard to their exact application. This is what must be done with regard to psychotherapy also. Just now its importance is being exaggerated by ardent advocates. In every department of therapy this has always been done by enthusiasts. The business of the practicing physician must be to select what is best, and above all what is sure and harmless, from the many suggestions offered, so as to build up a practical body of applied truth.

{194}

SECTION V

ADJUVANTS AND DISTURBING FACTORS

CHAPTER I

SUGGESTION

Under the head of Adjuvants and Disturbing Factors in the psychic treatment of patients come the various phases of life which make for and against such a favorable state of mind as predisposes to the continuance of good health, minimizes inhibition, and adds to favorable suggestion. By modifying the modes of life, an ever renewed set of suggestions is initiated. By definite instruction and advice with regard to exercise, position, training, habit, pain, occupation of mind and diversion of mind, patients may be profoundly influenced, and gradually made to take on an entirely new attitude of mind towards themselves. These chapters, then, while apparently much more concerned with physiotherapy than psychotherapy, are really directions for the use of such physical methods as by frequent repetition make the most valuable suggestions. There is probably nothing more valuable in the ordinary application of psychotherapy than these various auxiliaries, with their power to remove disturbing factors, while, on the other hand, nothing aids more in bringing relief for many conditions than the removal of certain disturbing factors.

There is now a general recognition of the fact that suggestion in the waking state can in most cases be as therapeutically efficient as hypnotism, and is probably even more enduring in its effects when successful, without the dangers and sequelae connected with hypnosis. *Every idea tends to act itself out.* When we crave something, when there are active ideas of desire, there usually are movements of our flexor muscles. These affect the hands especially. At moments of hatred, detestation or abhorrence our extensor muscles are affected, as if we would wave these things away from us. There may even be an involuntary turning of the trunk muscles, as if we would no longer face what is abhorrent, though the repulsive thing may be present only to the mind. It is not far-fetched to argue that, since the voluntary function of muscles is thus influenced, other functions are also touched by emotions, ideas, trains of thought, especially when the mind is much concentrated on them.

Bishop, the so-called mind-reader, whose exhibitions attracted much attention in London and New York some years ago, confessed that his feats were accomplished mainly through muscle reading. He would permit a committee to select a book in a library in a certain house, and even a particular page of {195} that book, and then, blindfolded, sitting with the committee in a carriage with his hand on the forehead and the arm of one of the committee, he would direct just where the carriage should be driven and would, while always continuing his contact with the member of the committee, go to the particular house and room, select the special book, and eventually find the page. There was no opportunity for collusion in some of these feats. The most startling things were often accomplished by the system of forcing a choice which prestidigitateurs use in order to compel the taking of the particular card by suggestion (though all the time they seemed to be leaving absolute liberty of selection to the person), but there was much, besides this, required to accomplish what he did. He said that there were always involuntary muscle movements, little starts and tremors that guided him in his work. Other exhibitors have been able to use this to a considerable extent, though not with Bishop's success. That our thoughts can be read in our muscle system is interesting and valuable confirmation of the unconscious tendency of ideas to affect the body.

When a single idea occupies the consciousness it will, some psychologists insist, necessarily act itself out unless some distracting thought prevents it. We know how difficult it is to stand at the edge of a height, say at the brink of a waterfall or on the cornice of a high building, or to look down a mine or elevator shaft, because the thought comes to us, how dreadful it would be to plunge over. As a consequence of this insistent idea taking possession of our consciousness, we have the sense of falling, we become tremulous and have to withdraw, or we would actually fall, or find in ourselves a tendency to throw ourselves over. There are persons who cannot even sit in the front row of a balcony because of the constant effort required to neutralize the suggestion that they may fall or throw themselves over its railing. Curious sensations become associated with this idea—a feeling of numbness and tingling in the back, sometimes a girdle feeling, sometimes a sense of suffocation. All of these are due to the concentration of attention on a single idea and its suggestions.

Very few men, shaving themselves with an old-fashioned razor, have not, at moments of worry and nervousness, sometimes had the thought of how easy it would be to end existence by drawing the edge of the razor through the important structures in the neck. Some are so affected by this thought that they have to give up shaving themselves. It is a surprise usually to find how otherwise sensible, according to all our ordinary standards, are the individuals who confess to having had annoyance from such thoughts. This illustrates how strongly suggestive the concentration of attention may make an idea, and how much a single idea, when it alone occupies the center of consciousness, tends to work itself out in act, though there is no reason at all for willing in that direction. It is not improbable that in some inexplicable cases of suicide the tendency has actually worked itself out.

The expression, "he is a man of one idea," enshrines in popular language the conclusion of psychologists that if a single idea is present in the mind it will surely work itself out. We all know how much men of one idea accomplish. All their powers, physical and mental, are brought to bear on its development. Obstacles that deter other men, conditions that prevent others from daring even to think of doing the thing, seem as nothing to the man {196} of one idea, and in spite of discouragement, and even apparent failure, he often succeeds, notwithstanding obstacles that seemed insurmountable. What is thus true in the practical world is paralleled, for both good and ill, in the microcosm of the human body. A man who has one idea to urge him on is capable of accomplishing things in spite of pains and aches and all sorts of disturbances of function. On the other hand, if the one idea is unfavorable, then, in spite of a heritage of good physical and mental powers, his efficiency is inhibited. If a man gets an idea that there is something the matter with any organ, and concentrates attention on it, he will surely disturb the function of that organ. Just the opposite, however, will happen in case, even with physical defect, he believes that there is nothing the matter, or only something that can be overcome. This is the power of faith as illustrated in the various forms of faith healing, from mental science to Eddyism and the rest.

This is the power that the physician must learn to use. In *The Lancet* for November, 1905, Dr. J. W. Springthorpe, writing on the "Position, Use and Abuse of Mental Therapeutics," said:

Few indeed are the medical practitioners who daily prescribe suggestion as well as diet, hygiene and drugs. Yet the physician who makes even a minimum effort in this direction often does more for his patient than his more highly qualified confrère, who makes none. To some, and they naturally the most successful, this endeavor comes without conscious search, and improves with experience, but in some measure it may be acquired by all and no one who has become familiar with its powers will henceforward be content to remain without its constant aid.

This power is thoroughly exploited by the irregular practitioner, and the regular practitioner is bound in duty to learn to use it just as thoroughly.

What is true for the lesser faculties is eminently true for our most important faculty, the intellect. We all know how intellectual training enables us to accomplish without difficulty what at first seemed almost impossible. Not only that, but we acquire the power to devote ourselves to a subject that was at first irksome, if not actually forbidding. There are educators who insist that this discipline of mind, by which the power to devote ourselves to what we do not care for is gained, is the principal fruit of genuine education. It has been lost, or at least impaired to a great degree, by educational experiments, especially those related to the elective system which pushed interest, instead of discipline, into the foreground of education. In the same way the power of self-control, and the faculty of self-denial, so precious to the human race, have been lessened by the methods of training which omitted the consideration of these and emphasized the idea of personal comfort. Much can be done to make the unpleasant things that are inevitable in life not only tolerable, but actually to give a satisfaction surpassing selfish pleasure. It is this discipline that is needed in psychotherapy at the present time and the physician must endeavor to encourage it by every means in his power.

The one purpose of the use of suggestion in therapeutics, then, is to secure as far as possible concentration of mind on a single idea. This is what is done in hypnosis, but frequently in such a way as to leave the idea {197} to work out unfavorably associated suggestions. If there could, in the conscious state, be the same absolute concentration of mind on an idea, a great force for good, without accompaniment of ill,

119

would be secured. Experience has shown that with patient effort and definite methods such concentration of attention on a single idea can be secured, at least to such an extent as to make it efficiently therapeutic.

Ordinarily, suggestion accompanies the material remedies that the doctor prescribes. He must emphasize just when and how the medicine is to be taken, and it is well to emphasize the effects that are expected and just about how they will come. If he is prescribing a tonic, he does not merely say before meals. He specifies from ten to twenty minutes before meals, according as he wishes it taken, with a definite amount of water, stating that the taste of it will excite appetite and that only food in reasonably liberal quantities will satisfy the craving produced by it. If he is prescribing a laxative, he states just when it should be taken and when its effects may be expected. The arousing of expectancy does much to relax inhibition and to permit the flow of nervous impulses that may be helpful. If a sleeping potion is given, the patient is directed to compose himself for sleep immediately after it is taken, or to take it just a definite time before he gets into bed, and then to expect its action in the course of twenty minutes or a half hour, designating rather definitely just when it shall have its climax of effect. Two or three things done together, as, for instance, a gentle rubbing with cool water over the body to produce a glow, a warm foot-bath, and then a sleeping potion, will combine to produce a climax of physical and psychical effect.

In many conditions that come for treatment to the modern physician, the physical remedies are much less important than the psychical. This is particularly true for the affections known as psychoneuroses, in which some slight nervous disturbance is exaggerated into an extremely painful condition or a disturbing paralytic state; in the so-called hysteria of the older times; in the drug habits; in the sex habits; in the over-eating and under-eating habits, and then with regard to dreads and other psychic disturbances connected with dreams, premonitions and the like. In all these cases it is important to secure concentration of the patient's mind on a neutralizing suggestion. This must be done deliberately and in such a way as to secure thorough concentration of attention. It is often a time-taking process, but nearly everything worth while requires time, and the results justify the expenditure. Methods mean much in the attainment of this. They must be impressive, the patient must be convinced of the power of the physician to help him, and he must have trust in the efficacy of the mode of treatment.

The patient should be put into a comfortable position, preferably in a large, easy arm-chair, should be asked to compose himself in such a way as to bring about thorough relaxation of muscles, and then to give his whole attention to the subjects in hand. Occasionally the arms should be lifted and allowed to fall, to see whether relaxation is complete, and the knee jerks may be tested, to show the patient that he is not yet allowing himself fully to relax. There should be no lines in the face: the muscles around the mouth, and especially those in the forehead, should relax. It is surprising how {198} much can be done, sometimes by slight touches on the forehead, to secure this. The patient should then be made to feel that the tension in which he has been holding himself, and which makes it so difficult for him to relax, has really been consuming energy that he can use to overcome the tendencies to sensory or motor disturbance, or to supply the lack of will which makes him a victim of a drug or other habit, or takes away from him that mental control that would enable him to at once throw off dreads and doubts and questionings and bothersome premonitions which now, because of the short circuiting on himself through worry and nervousness, he cannot do.

Two or three séances usually show a patient how much better control over himself even a short period of relaxation will give. He comes out of a ten-minute session of relaxation, during which he has been talked to quietly, soothingly, encouragingly, with a new sense of power. Often he feels that there will be no difficulty in overcoming his habit. This may pass, of course, but he has received a new idea of his own resources of energy and self-control.

In most cases it is well, after securing relaxation, to ask the patient to close his eyes gently and to keep them closed till all his muscles are relaxed. Then suggestions may be made to him with regard to his power to control cravings, and to put away doubts and questionings, because, after all, as he sees them himself, they are quite irrational and entirely due to habitual tendencies that he has allowed to grow on him. A concentration of attention on the idea, not only of conquering but of being able to conquer, will be secured. Unless this complete attention can be had, suggestion in the waking state may not prove efficient. There are nervous, excitable people for whom, at the beginning, it will be quite impossible to secure such relaxation and peaceful quiet as will be helpful to them. For these a number of séances may be necessary, but on each occasion a little more of quieting influence is secured.

In recent years, this quiet, peaceful condition, with eyes closed, thorough relaxation and absolute attention, has sometimes been spoken of as the hypnoidal state. If it be recalled that hypnos in Greek means sleep, and that this is a state resembling sleep with the restfulness that sleep gives, the term is valuable in its suggestions. If, however, the word is connected with hypnotism, then there may be an unfortunate connotation. This state is entirely free from the dangers of hypnotism, and instead of making a patient dependent on his physician, teaches him to depend on his own will. It is not a new invention as this term hypnoidal might seem to indicate, but is as old as our history at least.

CHAPTER II

EXERCISE

In recent years a great change has come over the popular mind regarding exercise, especially in the open air. It is well to emphasize at the very beginning the subject of too much exercise, because there is no doubt in the minds of many who study the question, that many Americans, and indeed people of the northern nations generally, take a certain amount of voluntary {199} exercise that is not good for them, though they take it at the cost of considerable effort and sacrifice of time and are firmly persuaded that it is of great benefit.

Sufficient Exercise.—There is a much larger number of persons who do not take sufficient exercise. The amount to be taken is eminently an individual matter. Neurotic patients exaggerate everything in either direction, so that perhaps the state of affairs that exists is not so surprising as it might otherwise seem. Instead of the uncertainty that prompts now to too much exercise, and again to too little, for health's sake there must, as far as possible, be a definite settlement of the needs.

National Customs.—There is a curious difference in the attitude of mind of the various nations towards exercise. Most of the southern nations of Europe do not as a rule take any violent exercise. As is well known, however, they are not for this reason any less healthy than their northern contemporaries, though perhaps they are less strong and muscular. But muscularity and health are not convertible terms, though many people seem to think they are. An excess of any tissue is not good. Our economy should be taxed to maintain only what is useful to it. Nature evidently intended, in cold climates at least, that men should maintain a certain blanket of fat to help them retain their natural heat, but any excess of fat lessens their resistive vitality by lowering oxidation processes. Fat in cold climates can be used to advantage as a retainer of heat. In the warmer climate it would be a decided disadvantage. Muscular tissue is a manufacturer of heat and this is a decided advantage in the colder climates, but in the temperate zone, where the summers are very warm, muscle in over-abundance, unless its energy is consumed by actual physical exercise, may be quite as much of a burden as fat. Muscular people do not stand heat well. They demand exercise to keep muscle energy from being converted into heat, and they require frequent cold baths, and other forms of heat dissipation, in order to be reasonably comfortable.

Exercise in Early Years.—The question of the amount of exercise that is to be taken must be decided at an early age for individuals. Most of the young people of the Celtic and Anglo-Saxon races are tempted by traditions and by social usage to develop considerable muscle during their growing years. In this respect, the difference between the German and the English schoolboy is very striking. The English schoolboy is likely to be as "hard as nails," as the expression is, as a consequence of violent exercise in his various sports, taken often to the uttermost limit of fatigue. The German schoolboy has his walk to and from school, and some other simple methodical exercises, with some mild amusements that make little demand on muscle, but of games in the open he has very few, and of the violent sports he has none at all. A comparison of the health of the two nations will not show that the English boy, who receives a public school and a university education, with all their temptations to exercise, enjoys any better health, and, above all, reaches an average longer life than the German youth, who has gone through a similar educational career in his own country, but without the athletic training that the English schoolboy has had.

As a consequence of the absence of athletics and its diverting interest, the German is apt to have learned more than his English colleague, but a {200} comparison of mortality and morbidity tables would show that his resistive vitality, his power to overcome disease and recover from accident is not lower than that of his colleague from across the North Sea. The German is less strong muscularly, and in a contest of physical effort would as a rule come out second best, but then we have gotten beyond the period when it is important for a man to be able to defend himself by physical force, except in emergencies that may never come. Surely the English time and effort devoted to athletics is not justified by this.

Preparation for a Sedentary Life.—Certainly if a young man is going to live a sedentary life in his after years, it does not seem advisable for him deliberately to devote much time to muscular exercise during his growing years. This only provides him with a set of muscles for which he has no use. Ordinarily it is assumed that muscles are organs for the single purpose of evolving energy. This is not true, since they are important organs for the disposition of certain food materials and for the manufacture of heat for the body. Nature in her economy probably never makes an organ for one function alone, but usually arranges so that each set of organs accomplishes two or three functions, thus saving space and utilizing nutrition to the full. The man with a well-developed muscular system, which he is not using, will have to feed it, and besides will have constantly to exert a controlling power over the heat that it manufactures whenever it is not dissipated by actual exercise. For these reasons he will be constantly nagged by it into taking more exercise than his occupation in life demands, and if he does not do this, his developed musculature is likely to deteriorate so as to be a serious impediment, or to degenerate by fatty metamorphosis into a lower order of tissue that is a clog and not a help to life.

The Germans are more sensible. As students, they live quite sedentary lives, develop their muscles just enough to keep them in reasonably good health, and then, when it comes to living an indoor life, as will be almost inevitable in their chosen professions or occupations, they do not meet with the difficulties that confront the Anglo-Saxon with his burdensome, over-developed muscular system. German professors, as a class, do not find themselves under the necessity of taking systematic daily exercise. They are quite content and quite healthy with an hour or two of sitting in the open air, and a quiet walk from the home to the university or the school. With the ideas that some people have with regard to the value of exercise for health, it might be expected that the German professors would be less healthy than their Anglo-Saxon colleagues. This is notoriously untrue, for the Germans live longer lives on the average, and most of them accomplish much more, and above all are much more content in the accomplishment, than their physically strenuous Anglo-Saxon colleagues. They are not oppressed by the demands of a muscular system that insists on having its functions exercised, since it has been called into being in the formative period. These German professors live to a magnificent old age, requiring very little sleep and often doing a really enormous amount of work. The man with a developed muscular system generally requires prolonged sleep, particularly after exercise, but even without it very seldom is it possible for him to do with less than seven hours, while the Germans often are content and healthy with five hours, or less.

{201}

Our muscular system is our principal heat-making apparatus. It is easy to understand. If we have larger heat-making organs than are necessary for the maintenance of the temperature of the body, and if we have no mode of dissipating our heat by muscular energy, as through exercise, then there will be a constant tendency for our temperature to rise, which must be overcome, at considerable expense of

121

energy, by the heat-regulating mechanism of the body. This heat-regulating mechanism is extremely delicate, yet does not seem to be easily disturbed. With the external temperature at 120° F. or—10°, human temperature is constant. With a heating apparatus entirely too large for its purpose, it is no wonder that irritability of the nervous system ensues because of the constant over-exercise of a function called for from it. It is this state of affairs which seems to me to account for the marked tendency to nervous unrest, and to the presence of many heart and digestive symptoms that often characterize athletes who develop a magnificent muscular system when they are young, and later have no use for it. They must learn the lesson and keep up the practice of using their muscles sufficiently to dissipate surplus heat, so as to prevent this energy from being used up in various ways within the body, with a resulting disturbance of many delicate nervous mechanisms.

Useless Muscles.—Whatever a human being has to carry round as useless can only be expressed by the telling Roman word for the baggage of an army, *impedimenta*. Prof. James, in his "Principles of Psychology," sums up the law very well:

The great thing in all education is to make our nervous system our ally instead of our enemy. It is to fund and capitalize our acquisitions and live at ease upon the interest of the fund. For this we must make automatic and habitual as early as possible as many useful actions as can be and guard against the growing into ways that may be disadvantageous to us as we should guard against the plague.

An over-developed muscular system, with its tendency to manufacture heat and its craving to be used, and the consciousness it is so apt to produce of ability to stand various dangerous efforts, is a disadvantage rather than an advantage.

Useless Fat.—This reminds us very much of the attitude with regard to children in the acquisition of fat. Chubby babies with rolls of fat all over them and deep creases near their joints are considered to be "perfectly lovely." Mothers are proud to exhibit them. They are supposed to be typical examples of abounding good health. Neighborly mothers come in to coo over them and, in general, the main aim of existence for children in their early years would seem to be to make them as fat as possible. Such children, as is brought out in the discussion of the subject in the chapter on obesity, are not healthy in the true sense of the word, are well known to be of lower resistive vitality than thinner infants, and easily succumb to diseases.

Resistive Vitality.—One reason for the early deaths of many athletes is the fact that, confident of their strength, they allow themselves to become so overwhelmed by an infection, before they confess that they are sick and take to bed, that often the cure of their affection is hopeless. Ordinarily neither pneumonia nor typhoid are likely to be fatal diseases for men between twenty and fifty. If a man's heart and kidneys are in good condition during this {202} period, an attack of either of these diseases, while a serious incident, is likely to be only a passing loss of time. Rather frequently, however, strong and healthy men without any organic defect that may be considered responsible for the fatal termination, succumb to these diseases. The reason for the fatality is that they are not willing to admit that they are ill enough to be in bed, they have a large reserve force of strength on which they call and which enables them, for a good while, to resist the weakening influence of disease. Doctors know and dread these cases. A young man in the flower of youth, with magnificent muscular development, comes into the office breathing very rapidly and with a laboring pulse. Almost exhausted, he sinks into a chair, confesses that he is nearly "all in," and wonders what is the matter. At times the physician will find practically a whole lung solidified by pneumonia, and at times both lungs are seriously affected. The wonder is how the young man succeeded in holding out so long. Sometimes the doctor is summoned to see him because he has fainted in his home, or in his office, and his friends are alarmed. These cases are almost invariably fatal. Any one who continues to be up and around until the third or fourth day of pneumonia will have so exhausted his vitality, no matter how great that may be, that he will have no reserve force for the life-struggle that must come before the crisis is reached.

Nearly the same thing is true for typhoid fever in the same class of persons. A young athlete, who considers it babyish to confess to illness, complains of feeling out of sorts but nothing more, until some morning he is literally unable to leave his bed, or has a fainting fit after going up-stairs. He is found by the physician with a temperature of 104°, or near it, and with evident signs of being in the middle of the second week of typhoid fever. The termination of such a case is generally fatal.

The ordinary man knows his limitations better; he recognizes the fact that he may be ill, and gives in quietly and rests, so that nature may employ all her energies in conquering the infection. Most of the long-lived people of history have been rather delicate and have learned young the precious lesson of caring for themselves. This care has not been exaggerated, but it has consisted in avoiding danger, in resting when tired, in not overdoing things, and above all in yielding to the symptoms of disease before these become serious.

Regulation of Exercise.—Each man must be a law unto himself as to the amount of exercise that is necessary for him. He must take enough to use up the energy supplied by the food he eats, just as, on the other hand, he must eat enough food to make up for whatever waste there is in his body. There are many men who eat over-heartily and then have to take exercise to use up this material or else suffer for it. This is one of the compensations that the hearty eater must pay: he overfeeds and becomes obese, or, if he succeeds in keeping down his weight to the normal, it is only by the expenditure of time in securing such muscular action as will use up surplus energy. Many men find it difficult to control their appetites, and prefer to take exercise rather than to deny the appetite which they created during their days of indulgence in athletics. It is for such men to decide just what seems preferable. If the fuel is supplied to the heat engine, which all human beings are, it must be used for the production of energy or else it will exert {203} itself in accumulating certain waste in the tissues, just as over-abundant fuel serves merely to clog up the fire-box of an engine without doing any work.

Air and Exercise.—It is easy to deceive one's self in the matter of exercise. With regard to air such a mistake is almost impossible. As a rule, it is air rather than exercise that people need when they have the restlessness and nervousness which comes from over-abundant nutrition. Fresh, pure air enables the individual to burn up nutritive material to the best advantage by the encouragement of oxidation. It is a surprise to those who are not accustomed to it, to see how tuberculosis patients who come to sanatoria with very little appetite, soon acquire an appetite and are able to consume large quantities of food, to sleep well and become restful—all as the result of living constantly in the open air during the day, and also having an abundance of fresh air at night. This is particularly true if the air in which they live is rather cold, and, above all, if it has a large difference of temperature every day, so that there is an upward and downward swing of the thermometer of from thirty to forty degrees. This varying temperature seems to use up nutritive material, and keeps all the natural processes going.

Gymnastics.—The very opposite to this plan of open air life is that followed by those who take gymnastic exercises for health's sake, with the idea that the use of certain muscles is necessary to keep the bodily economy in equilibrium. Such gymnastics are usually undertaken indoors, sometimes in stuffy quarters, and the movements are commonly repeated with such continued routine that absolutely all interest is lost. That there are many who advocate this form of exercise, it has nearly always seemed to commonsense physicians an entirely wrong solution of the important question of the encouragement of oxidation. It is like running an engine, not for the purpose of having it do something, but simply in order to have it oil itself, and consume the fuel that has been put into its boiler and that must be used up because more will be put in to-morrow. It would be much better, either to limit the amount of fuel or to give the muscular exercise some useful purpose, above all connect it with some interest that furnishes diversion of mind at the same time that the muscles are used. This last is the most important consideration, for, after a time, gymnastics pall in spite of artificial incentive.

Dr. Saleeby, in "Health, Strength and Happiness," has expressed very forcibly what has come to be the feeling of many physicians with regard to gymnastics, especially indoor gymnastics:

The natural spontaneous exercise having been forbidden, and the bad consequences of no exercise having become conspicuous, there has been adopted a system of factitious exercise—gymnastics. That this is better than nothing, we admit; but that it is an adequate substitute for play we deny. . . . The common assumption that, so long as the amount of bodily action is the same, it matters not whether it be pleasurable or otherwise, is a grave mistake. . . . The truth is that happiness is the most powerful of tonics. . . Hence the intrinsic superiority of play to gymnastics. The extreme interest felt by children in their games and the riotous glee with which they carry on their rougher frolics, are of as much importance as the accompanying exertion. And as not supplying these mental stimuli, gymnastics must be radically defective.

Granting, then, as we do, that formal exercises of the limbs are better than nothing—granting further that they may be used with advantage as supplementary aids, we yet contend that they can never serve in place of the exercises prompted by nature. For girls, as well as boys, the sportive activities to which the instincts {204} impel, are essential to bodily welfare. Whoever forbids them, forbids the divinely appointed means to physical development.

Play and Exercise.—There has been a distinct tendency in modern times to think that gymnastic exercise can be a substitute for play for growing young folks. When certain of the instruments and methods of the modern systems of gymnastics which have been introduced into schools, and are supposed to be so wonderfully beneficial, are put to the test of the psychology of exercise, the conclusions are likely to be very different from the theories under which they were introduced. Dr. Saleeby has expressed these differences rather strikingly:

Anyone who will consider for a moment the natural constitution of man and the principles of natural education, must agree that the deplorable thing called a dumb-bell offers an exquisite parody of what exercise should really be. The cat, as she exercises her kittens along the lines of their natural proclivities and needs, never telling them that this is exercise for the sake of exercise, and certainly prepared, if she could, to turn up her nose at any artificial implement we might offer her—should be our model in this respect. It may be imagined that some unfortunate girl, brought up on early Victorian lines, having never been permitted to wear comfortable garments, or to stretch her arms, would welcome and enjoy the dumb-bells when first introduced to them. But any one who has had a natural childhood and who has been taught to play, and who has taken his or her exercise naturally, or incidentally in the course of pursuing some mental interest—any such person may be excused for saying that a pair of dumb-bells should be deposited in our museums as indications of what was understood by exercise even as late as the earlier years of the twentieth century. All exercise for the sake of exercise is a mistake—or, at any rate, a second best. You may do your mind—and body, too—more harm by sheer boredom than you may gain good from the exercise you go through. The dumb-bell symbolizes the fact that the most elementary and obvious truths of psychology are still unrecognized, though the play and games of every natural child—if you object to be instructed by kittens—should be perfectly sufficient to teach us what indeed nature taught us ages ago, if only we would listen to her.

Indoor Sport.—Indoor sport is another thing. In wintry weather it is impossible to play outside conveniently, and indoor games have their place. Unfortunately they are usually associated with dust, and when played before crowds of spectators, the participants suffer also from the disadvantage of rebreathed air containing, too, the emanations of those who are looking on. It must not be forgotten that these two factors are the most prominent predisposing causes of tuberculosis. Those who have any tendency to tuberculosis, by which is meant specifically all those who are associating with tuberculosis patients, whether those patients are related to them or not, or who are more than 20 per cent. under the weight that they should have for their height, should not be allowed to take part in indoor sports where these drawbacks are sure to be encountered.

Sport, because of the diversion of mind involved, is an ideal form of exercise. An exercise that becomes a mere routine and that can be eventually gone through with so mechanically as to leave abundant room for thoughts of business or study or worries of other kinds, loses sight of one of the principal purposes of exercise as nature demands it.

Horseback Biding.—It is because of the complete diversion of mind that is necessarily involved in it, that horseback riding makes such a magnificent exercise for the busy man. The old expression "the outside of a horse is the {205} best thing for the inside of a man" is founded even more on the mental influence of horseback riding than its physical quality. The same amount of exercise in the open air,

123

taken otherwise, often does not accomplish so much good, because a man's thoughts may continue to run on his business or be occupied with his worries, or he may not be able to divert his thoughts from himself and his digestion or his ills. A horseback rider must pay attention to the other animal, rather than himself, and that represents the complete diversion of mind so necessary for the health of most people. Just as soon as man rides an old favorite animal on whose back he can throw down the reins, allowing it to saunter on as it will, while he occupies himself with other things, then horseback riding loses its efficacy and falls back into the class of bicycle riding or carriage riding or walking in the open air unless there is diversion of mind in the scenes, or the necessity for care at street crossings, to banish preoccupation of mind. Unless business troubles and worries are necessarily excluded by its conditions, or are deliberately eliminated from the mind during the course of any exercise, it may even become a renewed source of worrisome thoughts, rather than a renewal of energy, mental and physical.

It is doubtful whether horseback riding should ever be recommended for those who have not been accustomed to it from their youth. To ask a man past forty to learn to ride horseback for the sake of exercise is nearly always a mistake. It becomes a trial rather than a recreation, and may thus do harm rather than good. On the other hand, horseback riding is one of the things that may be, and indeed often is, much abused. The old English fox-hunting squire would never have lived out his life even as long as he did, consuming the amount of proteid material that was his custom, and drinking his three or more quarts of port at dinner every day, but that the excessive drain upon his system by long days of hard riding in the hunting field made calls upon his nutrition which kept even this amount of food and stimulant from doing immediate harm. Just as soon, however, as long spells of severe exercise become excuses for the consumption of big dinners, and exercise is used as a factor to enable one to overeat with more comfort than would otherwise be the case, a vicious circle is formed, and one serious abuse is counterbalanced by another. What many well-to-do people of leisure need is not so much more exercise as less eating.

Walking.—Perhaps the best and most readily available form of exercise for most people is walking. It has one disadvantage. As soon as the walk becomes too much of a routine, and the ground gone over has lost its interest, or is even of such a nature as to permit or, indeed, tempt introspection and occupation with other things, rather than with the surroundings, then walking loses most of its efficacy as a form of exercise. Walking in the country, for instance, becomes monotonous, though at first it is a great source of pleasure. Walking in a large city, however, has little of this objection and as large city life has grown more and more strenuous in recent years, the good effect of walking to and from the office or walking in the busy parts of the city has been increased. Between the trolley and the automobile, and the hustling commercial traffic of the streets, it is impossible for a man to walk through the busier portions of any large American city without keeping his wits thoroughly intent on what he is doing, nor without requiring all of his {206} attention for his transportation. An abstracted man will in the course of a half hour have so many narrow escapes from being run down in a busy quarter that he will either eschew walking in that particular neighborhood, or give up his habits of mental abstraction, or else he will come to himself some day in a hospital.

Besides, the passing show in city life is itself of surpassing interest. It is not things but men that interest us most. There are so many phases of human life to be seen on busy city streets, so many things happen in the course of even a short walk to bring out prominently traits of human nature that, if a man is at all sympathetic, he finds much to occupy his attention, to distract him from his own worries and take him away from his business cares. The long walk to and from the office may thus become an efficacious source of thoughts that are different and of profound pleasure. All depends on the man and his mood. Men who try it whole-heartedly soon find a renewed interest in life. An hour of daily walking in the open air with the distractions of city life all around, provided the walking is done briskly and faithfully, is of infinitely more hygienic value than an hour of gymnasium work. There is only one thing that hampers this form of exercise—there are so many excuses to tempt one not to keep it up. If one gets to a gymnasium there is an instructor or director who keeps tabs on one's hours and so helps a weak human will, and excuses are easier made to one's self than to others.

Massage as Exercise.—This curious tendency of men to take their exercise far more regularly, provided some other is concerned in their taking it so that it cannot be neglected without explanation, is illustrated in many of the experiences of the doctor in modern life. A number of forms of massage have come into vogue as wonderful cure-alls. It is comparatively easy for some men, and above all for many women, to take their exercise by means of massage rather than in some more vigorous way that requires their own initiative. A man who is working hard, and who feels the need of exercise, will not take the easy natural way of getting up half an hour earlier, having his breakfast half an hour sooner and then walking down to his office four or five miles, but he hears of someone who gives vigorous massage and he engages him to come every morning and exercise him for half an hour or an hour. In order to do so, he has to get up an hour earlier, but the fact that he has the engagement with someone else, rather than with himself, makes it more difficult for him to make excuses, and so morning after morning, in spite of the fact that he may have been up late the night before, perhaps to a big dinner, he gets up to be given his exercise. If he is a heavy eater he will, of course, at the end of a week or ten days feel ever so much better for he has been using up material that was clogging his circulation and irritating his nervous system.

At the end of a month he will probably feel so much better that he will conclude that he has found the root of all evil in life, or of all disease, in a failure of circulation that can be removed by means of massage, manipulation and passive movements. When he gets well enough to give it up, he drops straight back into his old troubles, because what he needs is a radical change of life that will adapt his eating to the amount of exercise that he takes, and his exercise to the amount that he eats. If this fails to come, he has had only a temporary benefit that has probably tempted him rather to increase {207} the amount that he eats normally than otherwise and will probably do him harm in the end. This massage brings about a distinct reduction in the weight of women, and as most of them are very desirous of this, the remedy becomes even more precious to them than to men. Here, too, however, it is only a temporary expedient. They are tempted to eat more than before, or at least not to reduce their diet, and the good that is accomplished is only for the moment, while no habits, either of restraint of eating, or of more exercise in the open air which so many of them need, have been formed.

Passive Movements.—The success of osteopathy has been largely founded on this curious peculiarity of human nature. People are not satisfied to regulate their eating and exercise in a sensible way. They prefer to submit to various methods of exercise, manipulations and passive movements which make up for the muscular exertion that should help the circulation within the body, but do not accomplish the purpose nearly so well as the voluntary exercise of muscles. It requires little exercise of will to submit to this treatment, while for many people it requires considerable exertion of will power to exercise their muscles for themselves. The old particularly, who are likely to suffer from achy conditions around joints, always worse on rainy days, which would be expelled by enough exercise to stimulate the circulation in these structures, find the new remedial measures of vicarious exercise of great service to them and consequently osteopathy has gained many votaries. Old members of many a state legislature who have been accustomed to ride for so long that exercise is almost an unknown quantity in their lives, are treated by the osteopath and lose so many vague pains and aches and discomforts of various kinds that it has not been difficult to persuade them that it is a great new discovery in medicine, and so in many of the states the osteopaths have secured legal recognition.

Summary.—Exercise, as exercise, often does harm rather than good. Thin people seldom need exercise, stout people seldom take enough of it. No one should be encouraged to exercise merely that he may be able to use up material that he has eaten, when it is evident that he is eating more than is required for his ordinary occupation. The question can never be settled without taking into consideration all these individual peculiarities of each case. Properly used, exercise is one of the most important therapeutic aids. But it is liable to as many abuses as are drugs, and the patient's attitude of mind toward any particular exercise is always an extremely important factor. If the exercise produces fatigue and disgust, then it will do no good, in spite of all that is hoped from it. If it creates true diversion of mind, it will surely be precious, even though it may, for other reasons, seem unsuitable.

CHAPTER III

POSITION

There are many changes of position that relieve pain, lessen discomfort, aid in excretion, and in the evacuation of material from the body, yet it is often found that very little advantage is taken of this natural method of therapeutic aid. Traditions and habit often rule to such an extent that {208} certain quite unfavorable positions are assumed, modifications of which frequently bring about distinct amelioration of symptoms. Very often patients learn this alone. There are many mechanical principles that can be applied in the treatment of pathological conditions which patients will not use unless definite suggestions are made. Often the physician has to suggest that they should try first one position and then another, in order to determine whether a certain amount of relief may not be afforded by position alterations, and perhaps function encouraged, or at least certain inhibiting factors modified for the better.

Favoring Return Circulation.—For people who have to stand much during the day, position in their resting hours is often extremely important. The caricature of the old-time American exhibited him with his feet on the mantlepiece, or somewhere as high as his head. For thin individuals there is no doubt that the placing the feet about as high as the head often makes a very comfortable position for a time. To those who have been standing much it is particularly restful. This may be easily accomplished lying down, though it must not be forgotten that the tendency to place the feet on a neighboring chair, or over the arm of the chair, so often seen in young folks, is in response to a physiological stimulus that brings relief to the heart by encouraging by means of gravity the return circulation in the veins from dependent portions of the body distant from the heart. For people who have not much exercise, and who have to stand all day, a brisk walk or leg exercises that thoroughly empty their muscles of blood by bringing about active contraction of them is important as a factor in their hours of rest. It makes all the difference in the world between the feeling of intense tiredness due to the sluggish circulation, and a return of vigor in the muscles.

Varicose Veins.—For patients suffering from varicose veins, position is particularly important. When they have to stand much, their limbs get painfully tired. The ache in the sense of fatigue is reflected over the body with the resultant depression. Active exercise, for a time, is not so good for them, and yet it is helpful. The ideal relief from their achy condition is afforded by gentle massage upwards of the limbs. That empties the dilated veins of blood and restores vigor to the circulation. It must not be forgotten, that when the circulation in the lower limbs is rendered sluggish by varicosity, the heart is also affected because it is so much more difficult to secure the return of blood through the tortuous dilated veins. This accounts for the intense general sense of fatigue that many of these patients have. Varicosities have a definite tendency to develop in those who are occupied in standing occupations, waiters, footmen, clerks, and the like, and often they have to continue at these occupations in spite of the varicose condition. It is particularly important for them to have an hour of lying down during the middle of the day so as to break their day's work in two. With a little insistence it can be secured in a great many cases and will afford more relief to the patient than anything else that can be done, even the wearing of rubber stockings, bandages and the like. I have known waiters massage each other at the time they had their period of rest with excellent results.

For the rupture of a varicose vein, position may be one of the most important auxiliaries to prevent serious hemorrhage. I remember as an ambulance surgeon once being called to see a case in which a great deal of blood {209} had been lost because efforts had been used to stop the bleeding by the application of a tourniquet. This shut off the superficial arteries, but not the deep ones and effectually prevented the return of any venous blood into the trunk, while all the time the ruptured varicose veins continued to bleed profusely. Local applications of styptics failed, of course, because the varicose vein itself had nearly the diameter of the little finger. Pressure over the wound did good for the time, but the bleeding was renewed whenever it was let up, and the two physicians in charge, alarmed at the loss of blood, were beginning to lose their heads. The ambulance was summoned to take the patient to the hospital and when it was suggested that if the tourniquet were removed and her foot was elevated the bleeding would probably stop without more ado, the suggestion seemed too simple to be true, but the event showed that that was all that was necessary.

Relief for Flat Foot.—For the achy discomfort of flat-foot, which is usually felt much more in the calf and the knee than in the ankle, some vigorous exercise for the foot, and especially for the calf muscles, at times during the day is likely to give great relief. Ten minutes of vigorous movement of the calf muscles followed by half an hour lying down will save most of them from the intense tiredness that is very discouraging in the late afternoon in many of the standing occupations. This relief removes from patients' minds the common idea that there must be something serious the matter with them. A good many of those who are cured of rheumatism by osteopathy, and of kidney trouble by the advertising specialists, and of various nervous diseases by new thought and irregular mental healing, are only sufferers from conditions such as can be relieved in this way. When flat-footed people sit down they should be advised to cross their feet (not their legs), because this emphasizes the arch of the foot somewhat and helps to strengthen and preserve it.

Abdominal Relaxation.—Many of the discomforts within the abdomen of which patients complain, especially whenever their attention is concentrated on them, can be benefited by suggestions as to position. Many a man who feels very uncomfortable after a hearty meal when sitting curled up beneath a lamp to read the evening paper, does not notice it at all when he stretches out on an easy Morris chair and with head back talks to friends. Many a man who thinks that his discomfort after dinner must mean serious dyspepsia, finds that a game of billiards after dinner will often dissipate almost completely his ill-feeling, unless, of course, it is due to overeating. After meals generally, positions that crowd the abdominal organs should be avoided. It must not be forgotten either that when lying down a full stomach may very well interfere with the heart action and produce marked palpitation. There are many men who cannot lie down within two hours of having eaten a hearty meal without decided heart irregularity, though while they are sitting up or standing quietly, or even moving, there will be no sign of this. Many of the vague discomforts within the abdomen, those due to movable kidney, or even chronic conditions in the biliary or urinary tracts, are only manifest when there is crowding of the organs within the abdomen.

How much the mechanical element may mean in kidney and biliary conditions is well illustrated by the relief often afforded by changes of position when calculi in these organs are giving trouble. Both renal and biliary calculi, which perhaps have been lying quite harmlessly in their positions {210} for years, are especially likely to become productive of discomfort by a jolting ride, or the jar of a fall, or by the influence of changes of position produced by gymnastic efforts of an acrobatic kind, or by a loop-the-loop experience, or something of the kind. In spite of this, only rarely does the physician try to use changes of position for their relief. I have seen a man suffering from excruciating biliary colic get almost immediate relief when put standing on his head alongside of a lounge. He looked upon it as magic. It was only that the stone, in the midst of the relaxation of all abdominal muscles produced by the unusual position, was able to drop back into the gall bladder, where it had been for months perhaps years before without giving any trouble. Similar relief is often afforded from the pain of kidney stones before they become definitely engaged in the ureter.

Raising the Head.—Patients suffering from respiratory difficulties usually learn to accommodate themselves to such changes of position as will afford them the greatest relief. The difficulty of breathing leads to such tossing about that the position easiest for the patient is almost inevitably found. When respiratory difficulties first declare themselves patients may not realize how much relief will be afforded by raising the head, or by the assumption of a sitting position. Often such patients prefer to sit in a chair. It should be borne in mind that, wherever this is compulsory, dispositions can be made so that the chair shall be as comfortable as possible, that its seat edge shall not press upon the underportion of the legs so as to impede blood circulation, nor press upon nerves, and that comfortable arrangements shall be made for the arms. When the patient's head has to be raised in the bed, it is much better to raise the mattress by placing some large properly-shaped object underneath it, so as to secure a gradual slant rather than have the patient's head and upper portion of the thorax bent by pillows. In default of something better, a chair placed so that the mattress lies along its back will be a handy aid. This is a matter of nursing rather than strictly of medical attendance, but unless the physician pays attention to it, it will be neglected, or at least in many cases not used to the best advantage.

Whenever there is difficulty of expectoration, especially when expectoration is abundant as in certain of the chronic bronchitises, and above all in dilatation of the bronchi, the advantage of position should be taken to aid in the expectoration. Patients who have to cough up large amounts in dilatation of the bronchi and who have long severe fits of coughing in the early morning, will often obtain a great measure of relief by leaning out of bed with one hand on the floor, doing their coughing in that position. Gravity helps in the emptying of the pockets of the bronchi and in five minutes they succeed in getting up satisfactorily as much material as would come up, only after severe convulsive efforts for an hour, when gravity was in opposition to their efforts. Children in whooping cough naturally bend over in order to cough. They will cough easiest if placed on a bed with a pillow beneath their chest so as to lift the face from the mattress, or in the case of older children, with the head projecting beyond the edge of the bed. This is only a trifle, but it will often save children severe convulsive efforts. Tuberculous patients who have to cough much, should be encouraged to find for themselves by trial whether certain positions, leaning out of bed, may not be of great service to them. There is often in advanced cases an accumulation of material during {211} the night that must be expectorated, and the patients are severely shaken up by their efforts to bring it up. I have known cases where a considerable measure of relief was afforded by leaning out of bed with the elbow on a pillow, a chair or foot-stool somewhat lower than the level of the bed. The mechanical help of gravity is particularly important where cavities exist and a considerable amount of material has to be emptied out of them.

In modern surgical times one does not often see the emptying of a purulent pleurisy through the bronchi, but I once had an opportunity to see the termination of one of these cases in a very favorable way. When I saw her the patient had already coughed up a cup full of purulent fluid and, altogether, about a quart of pus was thus evacuated. The patient had been so ill that the effort was considerable, but the evacuation was greatly helped by having her lean out of bed whenever material was to be expectorated. The patient is still alive and in good health—fifteen years after the event.

Heart Cases.—Position is also often of very great importance for the relief of the symptoms of patients suffering from heart affections. For organic heart affections, rest in bed is often advised. It must not be forgotten that this does not necessarily mean in a recumbent position. Whenever there is difficulty of breathing in connection with an affection of the heart, the recumbent position is extremely uncomfortable. This is nature's safeguard against the accumulation of fluid in the dependent parts of the lungs at the terminal capillaries of the pulmonary circulation. Most of the natural demands have a definite reason and are prophylactic rather than merely a symptom of aimless discomfort. Patients with heart disease often want to sit up in a chair. Their wish should, as a rule, be yielded to. There is no need of their sitting in a narrow uncomfortable armchair, nor of being incommoded by the position they have to assume. The end of a large lounge, especially one that curves over towards the floor on which pillows can be piled so as to make the patient comfortable, and yet afford many changes of position, is the best.

In general, the arrangements should be such that changes of position can be secured without much difficulty. These prevent hypostatic pneumonia and guard the patient against serious accumulations in the lung tissue because of sluggish circulation. Changes of position can be used as valuable suggestions. Often the main portion of the patient's symptoms consists of the intense fatigue due to one position. This can be relieved and the patient made to feel that, after all, the ailment to which he is suffering must not be so serious since relief can be afforded so simply. Besides, when patients complain, something must be done for them. Medicine cannot be given for every symptom and yet some remedial measure there must be to satisfy them. This satisfaction will often be secured by changes of position, by slight local treatment, by the adjustment of pillows so as to relieve fatigue of particular muscles and parts of the body, and by the movements of the limbs and the head into other positions than those in which they have become fatigued. The experienced nurse is of the greatest possible value in these cases.

Restlessness.—Usually restlessness is considered to be an unfavorable symptom of disease, just as are pain and tenderness. Like these, however, it is really conservative rather than in any sense destructive. Pain prevents serious changes from taking place without our attention being effectively {212} called to them. Restlessness induces the patient to change position frequently and often leads to the discovery of some position in which there is much more comfort than the one that had been assumed. Restlessness, in the recumbent position, is usually nature's protest against the maintenance of a posture in which, owing to failure of circulation, there may be leakage of serum into the lung tissues with dangerous results. Restlessness, in abdominal pain, often leads to such a change of position as affords the best condition for the relief of the discomfort as far as that may be brought about by position of muscles. The man with colic very soon discovers that lying on his stomach may relieve his pain. The drawing up of the knees in peritoneal conditions is the result of a similar reaction. The physician must learn to imitate nature, and recognize what mechanical conditions are likely to be of help. As soon as these afford relief, they act as a strong favorable suggestion, on the patient, and relieve dreads with regard to his affection.

Joint Affections.—In painful joint conditions, position may help much to bring relief or at least considerable mitigation of symptoms. In rheumatism, for instance, of the acute articular type, a number of small pillows can be disposed in various ways, underneath the patient's limbs, between them and in other positions, so as to give as much comfort as possible and will often be of great value. There should be at least half a dozen pillows at the disposal of the patient, besides three or four for the head. In certain relaxed positions of the joints, there is more room within the capsule than others and, almost unconsciously, the patients assume such positions when there is pain from effusion. Occasionally, however, in the midst of fever, or because of apathy, patients may not do this, and then care should be taken to bring them some measure of relief. Generally patients suffering from fever, with delirium of typhoid condition, that is, when there is considerable apathy, should have their positions changed gently from time to time to prevent discomfort developing, and as a prophylactic against skin disturbances from pressure. In children, this is particularly important.

Bladder Evacuation.—In emptying the bladder position may mean much. After childbirth, especially the first, many women are quite unable to empty their bladders while lying down, though if they are allowed to assume the usual position there is little or no difficulty. In certain sensitive men whose power over their bladder is disturbed by self-consciousness, the presence of anyone in the room or near them, makes it impossible for them to urinate, and this is particularly true if they are lying down. In the milder forms of prostatism position occasionally seems to have some influence in helping to empty the bladder. When there is a prostatic bladder pouch behind the prostate, it is quite impossible to empty this in the standing position. It may be emptied in the prone position, that is, lying face downwards, particularly if the pelvis is elevated above the rest of the trunk. Undoubtedly some of the cures reported after operation, when the operation itself effected no reduction in the size of the prostate (as the removal of the testicles or vasectomy), the improvement was brought about partly by the more favorable position in which, for weeks after the operation, the patient emptied his bladder, and also by the greater control gained over it, by the persuasion that the operation would do him good. The same suggestion can be made in connection with the new position for urination with just as good effect.

{213}

Intra-abdominal Conditions.—There are many intra-abdominal conditions in which position is of great importance for the relief of pain. Appendicitis cases are found with the right knee drawn up because this relieves the tension of the abdominal muscles, and probably also of the large muscles that go to the thigh and lie behind the peritoneal cavity. In most cases of intra-abdominal pain flexing of the knees on the abdomen means much in affording relief, and patients usually discover this for themselves. There are certain apathetic patients, however, who need to be helped by suggestions. In certain of the painful conditions, due to intra-pelvic conditions, relaxation of muscles by flexion lessens the pain. Pressure upon the abdomen, as by lying on a pillow, often does this also. Apparently one reason why children

127

with flatulent colic stop crying almost at once, when laid on their stomachs, is because the pressure thus produced tends to bring about a movement of the gas that, collected at one or two places, was causing painful distention.

Importance to the Physician.—There are many other suggestions with regard to position that will occur to thoughtful physicians in particular cases. The one idea is to secure such an alteration of the posture as is likely to bring about mechanically relief of pain. If relief is afforded in this way, as has already been emphasized, a very favorable influence is produced on the patient's mind. Above all, he realizes that his physician not only understands his general condition, but his experience with many patients suffering from the same ailment has given him the power to direct even such slight changes of position as will give comfort. Nothing that I know adds more to the confidence that a patient has in his physician than the realization of this sort of knowledge. Therefore, the necessity for such consideration of each individual case as will enable the physician to recommend such modifications of position to patients. At the same time the patient's mind can be influenced very favorably by attaching definite significance to these alterations, and having them, as it were, repeat their favorable suggestions every time that he thinks about them, and be pleased as to the relief they have afforded. This is the sort of psychotherapy that is particularly likely to be successful, and it needs careful cultivation and development.

CHAPTER IV

TRAINING

One of the most important factors for therapeusis in the sense of the amelioration of defective motor conditions, the relief of disturbing sensory affections and the restoration of or compensation for defective functions of various kinds is training. By this is meant the training of the power of attention and its concentration in such a way that defects are overcome. There are many examples of almost marvelous improvement of function brought about in this way that are familiar, but it is well to recall some of them here in order to illustrate the uses to which this therapeutic mode may be applied. A blind man is able to read by means of his finger tips, and to recognize raised letters that seem quite beyond the possibility of tactile recognition by {214} ordinary individuals gifted with all their senses. The peculiar skill is simply due to the individual being able by concentration of attention upon slight variations in touch sensation to recognize even minute differences readily and so read raised letters with comparative ease and rapidity.

Over and over again it has been shown that neither the congenitally blind nor those whose vision has become defective have any better sense of touch than the average person. With an esthesiometer, their power to recognize the distance between the points of a calipers is shown to be no better than that of an ordinarily sensitive individual. This is illustrated in other ways. Certain blind persons, even those born blind, are known to be able to distinguish colors more or less accurately, that is, at least the three primary colors. Their power to do this is consequent upon a faculty of recognizing differences in heat absorption. The ordinary seeing person going into a room in the dark recognizes at once the difference between a pencil and a piece of metal of the same shape and size by its weight and the greater tendency of the metal to feel colder. When we are not sure whether a pillar in a structure is of stone or an imitation, we determine this by touch, and the fact that stone absorbs heat rapidly while wood and other imitations of stone do not. It is the same faculty for distinguishing specific heat that enables certain blind people to recognize colors. If pieces of cloth of different colors are put over snow when the sun is shining on them, it will be found that black absorbs much more heat than the colored cloths, or white, and consequently that the snow melts faster beneath the black. After black comes red, then green, then blue. It is this difference in the power to absorb heat that the blind recognize and thus distinguish colors after long patient training of themselves.

Obstacle Sense.—An example of the value of training is the so-called obstacle sense which has been rather carefully studied in recent years. By means of it blind people are able to avoid larger obstacles and to know when they are passing an open door or window on a corridor or a building alongside a street. Blind children have been known to play in a garden where there were trees and other obstacles and carefully avoid them even while moving rather rapidly. This sense is disturbed whenever there is loud noise in the vicinity. It is not very active and yet it is of considerable value to the blind. Its disturbance by noise would seem to indicate that it is due to some sense faculty in the tympanum, or ear drum. It exists in everybody, but remains quite undeveloped except in those who need it and therefore learn to make use of it.

Touch and Sight.—The triumph of training is to be seen in the cases of those who are born blind and deaf and who yet are taught to understand through lip and throat reading by the tips of the fingers and taught to talk by being shown patiently the method by which others accomplish it, though the only avenue to their brain is the dull sense of touch which means so little for the ordinary individual. The cases of Laura Bridgeman and of Helen Keller illustrate how a sense that is usually quite neglected can be made to supply the place of both the eyes and the ears by patient, persistent training. Lip reading by sight is, of course, a very interesting example of the same principle that can be learned by anyone who has good sight in a comparatively short time. There are compensations of this kind and powers of development latent in every sense and function of the body that can be {215} employed to make life interesting and to restore usefulness after nearly every form of lesion or defect. Practically all of this compensatory power is mental, hence its place in psychotherapy. We do not increase the power of the sense but by concentration of attention the mind is rendered capable of obtaining definite information from sensory stimuli that are present in every person but that are ordinarily neglected.

Hearing.—One of the most surprising instances of the value of training for cases in which favorable results seemed quite out of the question, is Urbantschitsch's method of training the deaf to hear. After investigating it personally I reported it in the *International Clinics*. Patients who could hear but very little, indeed, only the loudest noises, were trained by means of loud shouting and the hearing of loud notes gradually to catch sounds more and more easily until they invariably they could hear rather well. Sometimes even those who were thought to be absolutely deaf to sound were found to be able to hear very loud sounds and then it was invariably discovered that by practice they could be made to hear much more. The secret of the success consisted not in any increase in the power to hear, but entirely in training the attention to recognize and differentiate sounds so that what seemed at first a confused murmur gradually became intelligible. It is exactly the same process as that by which a man learns to read with his fingers. He is not able to differentiate the letters but after a time it is possible to do so without difficulty.

Equilibrium.—There are typical examples of almost as striking increase of muscle sensation, or rather of ability to distinguish minute differences in muscular sensation, noted in those who train this faculty carefully. Acrobats succeed in developing wonderful control over muscles and marvelous response to slight disturbance of equilibrium. The ordinary individual has comparatively small balancing powers, but the slack-rope performer seems almost to defy the laws of gravity, because he has learned so to coordinate all muscular action as to enable him to maintain his balance. He has trained himself to distinguish every variety of message from his semicircular canals. Of itself neither of these senses gives us very much information, indeed, only as much as we ask for from it, but when we pay careful attention to the minute details of the information that it imparts, we are able to use it to great advantage.

Muscle Training.—It is this power of training to enable us to appreciate minute sensations that forms the basis of the Frenkel treatment of tabes. For the proper guidance of the muscles the muscular sense is all-important, though ordinarily we are quite unconscious of the information it conveys. This is seriously disturbed by the degeneration in tabes. The patient can, however, be taught to use even the slight amount of it that remains to great advantage or else to avail himself of some other compensatory sensations which will enable him to guide his muscles in various motions much better than before.

This same faculty can probably be employed in many other conditions. Frenkel has shown that it is applicable in paralysis agitans and markedly relieves the rigidity that is so annoying a symptom. It gives these patients something to occupy their minds, too, which means a great deal for their {216} general condition, for occupation of attention saves them from neurotic disturbance of themselves.

Sufferers from infantile paralysis can be taught to do many things with their weakened muscles that seem to be quite impossible to them. It requires patience to get results, but they mean so much that the efforts are well worth while. After cerebral incidents, sometimes actual apoplexies, sometimes injuries, occasionally serious effusions due to kidney diseases, there may be disturbance of motor functions. It is surprising how often training will enable the sufferer to use his muscles much better in these cases than at first seemed possible. I have seen a man who had lost most of his power for writing after a cerebral incident regain it as a consequence of being taught to write from his shoulder, instead of from the forearm as had been his custom.

Heart Training.—In recent years we have learned that training is not only good for the external muscles and enables them to do more work without discomfort, but that it is particularly beneficial to the heart muscle whenever that organ can respond to it favorably. At all of the heart cures in recent years, exercise of some kind or another is one of the important features and the failure of physicians generally to secure as good results while pursuing all the other methods followed at these cures, seems to show that exercise was probably the most important factor. Nauheim is the typical heart cure and there, besides the resisted movements in the bath, there is the graduated exercise of the walks around the town, all of which, owing to the situation, lead up hill. Walking up hill, even though it be a gradual ascent, might seem to be the worst possible exercise for heart patients, yet it proves eminently beneficial.

Respiratory Training.—Shortness of breath is often a bothersome symptom, especially for stout people, and prevents them from taking necessary exercise. When it cannot be traced directly to some affection of the heart or of the circulatory apparatus, it is usually due to lack of exercise. Much can be done for it by deliberate training. In the modern time, with elevators so common, people seldom have to walk up-stairs, and consequently one of the modes of exercise that was particularly likely to furnish some training in deep breathing is absent. Any one who has seen the shallow breathing of many of the patients who come to Nauheim and how much it has improved by the gradually increased walks up the hills around the valley, will appreciate how much training in deep breathing means. This exercise of the diaphragm will often give benefit besides in making the bowels more regular, and in getting rid of the accumulation of fat in the abdomen, which is one of the mechanical causes of the interference with the diaphragm and consequent shortness of breath.

Training the Appetite.—Just as training may be used for the sensory and motor systems that are external, so it may also be used for many internal functions analogous to these. There are a great many people who eat too little. They are the nervous, irritable persons with no fund of reserve energy to draw on when anything happens, and who are in their years before middle life likely to be the victims of infectious disease. They suffer much from lack of proper covering in the winter time and from a certain protection that is afforded to the nervous system generally by being up to weight. Often their under-weight is a life-story, and occasionally it is a family matter. When {217} they suffer from neurotic symptoms a gain in weight nearly always does them good. They complain that when they increase their diet they have uncomfortable feelings. This is only what is to be expected, since the muscularis of their stomach—much more important than its secretory function—has not been accustomed to as much exercise as is now being demanded of it.

129

On the other hand, for those who are over-weight, training in eating less is the one important therapeutic factor. If their diet is cut down suddenly, they soon become discouraged. If there is a gradual reduction of food quantities, variety being allowed, so that they may eat practically everything they have been eating before, the system gradually accommodates itself to less and less food. This is the only sensible way of bringing about reduction in weight. It requires constant attention over a long period, but it can be done with excellent success.

In the same way the bowels may be trained to perform their work regularly. Habit means probably more with them than any other factor. Our digestive tract, however, is largely dependent on habit. We get hungry three times a day or twice a day, according to the custom that we have established. Countries differ radically in the matter, and nearly always, when a man goes from one country to another in early years, he changes to the habits of the new country, though if he comes after middle age he usually clings to those that he is used to.

Training to Stand Pain.—There are many painful conditions, especially involving the muscles in the neighborhood of joints, that are worse on rainy days and are spoken of as rheumatism, that can be very much improved by training in the use of muscles. As men grow older and gain in weight, the lack of exercise in their sedentary lives incapacitates their muscles for activities of many kinds. The consequence is that where most strain is put upon them, in the neighborhood of joints, they readily become tender and painful. It is this class of cases particularly that is benefited by irregular practitioners of all kinds. Mental healing, osteopathy, Eddyism, the many liniments, rubbings and manipulations prove beneficial. What is needed is training in the use of muscles so as to enable them to do the work that is required of them without discomforting reaction. This is particularly true for the leg and foot muscles. Exercises that strengthen the muscles of the calf and of the thigh, and particularly such as require free movement of the foot, are almost sure to relieve these patients of many annoying symptoms. Pains around the ankles and in the knee and hip, worse in rainy weather, disappear as a consequence of such gradually increased use of these muscles as gives them increased nutrition and power. This subject is discussed more fully under Foot Troubles and Painful Conditions of the Knee.

There may be a training in bearing discomfort which is of great value to over-sensitive patients. Some nervous patients seem to suffer merely from their ordinary physiological functions. These are the patients who abuse the drugs that are supposed to bring relief. There is just one mode of treatment that is successful with them: they must be told to bear their discomfort for a while without seeking drug relief, but always securing freedom from discomfort by means of attention to other things, until gradually they have succeeded in diverting their minds from the concentration of attention on their functions which is causing their disturbance. The whole programme {218} need not be outlined to them or they will perhaps have a revulsion of feeling against it that will make its accomplishment impossible. They can, however, be made to stand their discomforts for a time with the promise that it is for the best, since there will be eventually an improvement.

Intellectual Faculties.—Nearly every one of our faculties can be trained to do much better work than we have any idea of if we only are willing to take the trouble and give the attention. I have often shown people who came complaining of loss of memory that if they wanted to train themselves to remember they could do so. The memory probably cannot be bettered any more than can the sense of touch in the blind man, but by attention to minute details, in the concentration of the mind on certain subjects, it can accomplish results that seemed quite impossible before. All systems of improving the memory are founded on this method of concentrating attention on what one wishes to remember and connecting it with other things that we know by experience are readily remembered.

CHAPTER V

OCCUPATION OF MIND

Two classes of patients frequently apply to physicians for relief from various discomforts. They are, first, people who have no regular occupation and who often are in what is supposed to be the happy position of being able to do just what they please. The second class consists of those who take their occupations too seriously, so that they never get away from them and, as a consequence, disturb their physical functions. The feelings that these two classes complain of—for, when analyzed, their symptoms prove really to be uncomfortable feelings—can usually be "bothered" away and, if not entirely forgotten, made to disappear when the patients become deeply interested in something other than their usual occupation. The first class of patients needs occupation of mind; the second needs diversion of mind, and that subject will be taken up in another chapter.

Uncomfortable Sensations, Their Location and Causes.—These pains and aches, as patients call them, though it is well to remember that they are only discomforts, senses of unequal pressure, of constriction, or perhaps only unusual feelings, or consciousness of sensation, may occur in every part of the body. Perhaps they are most commonly complained of in the head. Many of the so-called headaches that are more or less continuous consist of these senses of pressure or of constriction over a particular part of the skull. Sometimes there may be a sense of pressure at the back of the eyes. Very often there is a feeling of heaviness at the back of the head that makes the patient feel as if relief would come if the head were allowed to drop forward and if sleep could be thus obtained. Every other portion of the head, however, even within the cavities, may have some of these uncomfortable sensations. In some persons, there is a tightness in the throat. In others, there is a feeling of fullness of one cheek and the dread that they may not be able to use it properly in talking. Sometimes the uncomfortable feeling is within the nose. Not infrequently the discomfort is in the ear.

{219}

All of these may be due to local conditions which need to be corrected, but in most cases nothing is found locally, or at most there is some functional disturbance so slight that, though it is shared by a great many people in our climate, others do not complain of it at all. It seems evident, therefore, that the discomfort must result from the sensitiveness of the individual emphasizing the significance of some slight disturbance.

Every portion of the body may suffer from these discomforts. The upper part of the back, especially below the base of the neck, is a favorite location in men, and particularly in those who bend over a desk. The lower part of the back is affected in such men as tailors and cutters who stoop incessantly at their work. In women, the lower part of the back is likely to suffer, and this is usually attributed to genital conditions, but constipation may play quite as large a role as the genital organs. Some of the stooping occupations of women, at the sewing machine or dressmaking, or even harder occupations, as sweeping, washing, and the like, may also be responsible. The commonest source of discomfort is, perhaps, the upper left-hand quadrant of the abdomen. This seems to be due to the distention of the stomach, either by gas or by liquid. Vague discomforts may occur around the umbilicus, often due to the presence of gas, with or without borborygmi.

Generally the local condition is only an occasion, and the real cause of the complaint is the lack of occupation of mind and consequent concentration of attention on any organ whose function happens to be disturbed sufficiently to make one conscious of its action.

Lack of Occupation.—For all of these cases the most important therapeutic factor is occupation of mind and diversion of attention. In our time, social conditions allow a large number of people to have very little occupation. For instance, many women of the well-to-do classes have absolutely nothing that they must do. Various phases of this are discussed in previous sections.

As a rule, it is useless to try to relieve these discomforts by anodynes. Many an opium habit has been formed by a turning to opium in such cases. The coal tar products are greatly abused here, for they do not bring relief to queer feelings nor to a sense of pressure or discomfort; they rather add to depression. What they are efficacious for is acute pain. The coal tar products relieve even toothache or neuralgia, as well as a real headache, but I have had patients tell me over and over again that the continuous headaches from which they suffered were not relieved in the slightest degree by phenacetin or acetanilid. Occasionally one hears of hyoscine or hyoscyamus suggested for these conditions, but they are quite as useless and as much contraindicated as opium or the coal tar products. As a rule, these headaches are relieved by lying down; they disappear during sleep. The real indication for treatment, however, is found in the fact that all of these vague discomforts are much better or even disappear when the patient is intensely occupied, or at least pleasurably engaged.

What these people need is occupation that really catches their interest and takes attention from themselves. One of the most striking expressions of this truth that we have comes from the poor, sad, mad poet, Cowper:

Absence of occupation is not rest;
A mind quite vacant is a mind distressed.

{220}

And surely poor Cowper, himself the victim of depression, saved from himself only by the suggestion that he should put into poetic form the thoughts that came so abundantly to him, could well understand the depth of wisdom in his couplet. The story of Cowper's life is enough of itself to encourage physician and patient to persevere in the effort to lift depression by occupation, since the fruits of that occupation may prove so valuable.

Mental Short-Circuit.—The minds of these people must do something, and since there is nothing really occupying for them to do, in a very expressive modern phrase, they are doing their possessors. As we suggest elsewhere, the nearest simile is that of the short-circuiting of a dynamo. Mental energy is exerted harmfully within the machine instead of in doing work.

See what happens in these cases when by some chance the women, or the men, who complain almost constantly are suddenly deprived of the means which enabled them to live an aimless life. The physician often has patients who have been in affluence but after a financial panic are in straitened circumstances. It is interesting to note what an excellent tonic effect, in younger people always, in older people very often, the change of life has on these chronic valetudinarians. Sometimes this is attributed to the simpler life which they lead when poorer, occasionally to the lack of responsibility, or other similar reason. Nearly always it is easy to see that the real cause of the improvement in health is the occupation of mind with serious interests outside of self.

Regulation of Life.—In the matter of occupation, and especially occupation of mind, the formation of habits and the training of the will are extremely important. In his book on "The Education of the Will," which was so popular that it went through over thirty editions in France, M. Jules Payot emphasizes the necessity for deliberately arranging the details of life so that time shall not hang heavily on the hands, he reverts to certain rules of life of the old religious orders, and to the habits advised by spiritual directors. He counsels that every one should make an examination of the day's happenings at the end of it, in order to see just where the failures lay and in what accomplishment was made. At the end of this old-fashioned examination of conscience, he counsels that a set of resolutions for the next day be made and an arrangement of work for various times, so that even more may be accomplished.

M. Payot further suggests that a certain time be given up to reflection, or as he calls it, meditation, on the significance of life and on the consideration whether something valuable is being made of it. Without this he insists that it is easy to let one's self slip into habits of life in which absolutely nothing is accomplished for self or others. If there is no real accomplishment, then pleasure soon palls, because pleasure

131

has a place only as an interval in the midst of labor and as a relief from effort. These reversions to the old modes of life and thought of the monastic communities show how little of real advance there is in life, and what excellent conclusions serious men came to even in the distant past. Certainly for many of the leisure class in modern times only the use of periods of reflection and the examination of {221} results obtained will serve to prevent that utter waste of time which leads to the intense dissatisfaction that is often reflected in the general health.

Thought for Others.—After forgetfulness of self, the most important factor in psychotherapeutics is thoughtfulness for others. Ordinary diversions are quite insufficient to occupy most people. One must have a serious occupation that appeals deeply, and then diversions of mind will be useful for purposes of recreation. Pleasure, so-called, if pursued not as an interruption from work but for its own sake and without serious occupation, palls, and after a time its votaries find life is scarcely worth living. The pursuit of pleasure as the sole interest of life is one of the most fruitful resources of depression, discouragement and neurotic symptoms with which modern physicians are brought in contact. The only way to be sure of having compelling interests is to be so much occupied with other people that one forgets self.

Yet mere flippant excitement and superficial entertainment is nothing but a cheap counterfeit of what is needed. Voluntary effort is needed, and this is the field where the psychotherapist must put in his most intelligent effort. There is no one for whom there is not a chance for work in our social fabric. The prescription of work has not only to be adjusted to the abilities, the knowledge, and social conditions, but has to be chosen in such a way that it is full of associations and ultimately of joyful emotions. Useless work can never confer the greatest benefits; mere physical exercises are therefore psychophysically not as valuable as real sport, while physically, of course, the regulated exercises may be far superior to the haphazard work in sport. To solve picture puzzles, even if they absorb the attention for a week, can never have the same effect as a real interest in a human puzzle. There is a chance for social work for every woman and every man, work which can well be chosen in full adjustment to the personal preference and likings. Not everybody is fit for charity work, and those who are may be entirely unfitted for work in the interest of the beautification of the town. Only it has to be work; mere automobiling to charity places or talking in meetings on problems which have not been studied will, of course, be merely another form of the disorganizing superficiality. The hysterical lady on Fifth Avenue and the psychasthenic old maid in the New England country town both simply have to learn to do useful work with a concentrated effort and a high purpose. From a long experience I have to confess that I have seen that this unsentimental remedy is the safest and most important prescription in the prescription book of the psychotherapist.

Care of Children.—Probably the most important therapeutic factor in the cure of the ills which come to unoccupied women is the finding of some occupation that will absorb their hearts as well as their intellects, that is, satisfy their feelings as well as appeal to their intelligence. That very acute observer and kenner of her sex, Mrs. St. Leger Harrison, who is Charles Kingsley's daughter and writes under the pseudonym of "Lucas Malet," said in "Sir Richard Calmady": "Feed their hearts and the rest of the mechanism runs easy. I have known disease to develop in a perfectly healthy woman simply because the heart was starved." For most women the only thing that will entirely satisfy the heart or keep it from hunger is children. Fortunately an interest in other people's children can, under certain circumstances, be almost as satisfying as in one's own.

Interest in Others.—Probably the best possible occupation that a childless woman can have is the care of others. Charity in one form or another satisfies the emotions as well as creates interest and gives varied occupations. Even the frequent disillusions that are encountered in charity work only add variety {222} to the experience, and do not discourage those who have the real charity instinct. For women particularly, as we have said, some charity that brings them much in contact with children is the surest preventive of over-occupation with themselves and over-emphasis on their feelings and sufferings. Many a woman in our large cities owes her freedom from the neurotic symptoms to which her sisters are subject, to her interest in tuberculous children. There is just enough of suffering to arouse all the pity of the visitor, without so much of anguish as would deter the more delicate from being interested in the work.

Touch with Real Suffering,—For patients who think they have much to suffer, yet whose complaints are all of subjective feelings of oppression and depression, there is no better remedy than to come in touch with real suffering. I have known not a few neurotic young women, who were preparing for themselves years of suffering by over-attention to little pains and aches, saved to a life of usefulness and even happiness by having to nurse near relatives through the last stages of fatal cancer. When these neurotic persons are brought intimately in touch with real suffering, have their sympathies aroused, and see how well human nature can bear pain when it has to, and yet not be impatient, nor wish to end it all, then a renewed life comes over them and they cease to be preoccupied with themselves.

Sympathy as a Remedy.—In former days, when hospitals were not so well provided and trained nurses non-existent, all forms of suffering had a wider appeal and aroused more active sympathy than at present. It is true that patients, in both hospitals and homes, suffered from the lack of trained nursing, and that was an even greater disadvantage. But it is, nevertheless, too bad that more actual touch with suffering does not come to people now, for nothing is so sure to make little ills disappear as the sympathy aroused by the sight of real suffering. Certainly, our cancer cases might well be a strong therapeutic factor for many of the neurotic ills of the world. They are, of course, deterrent to many people. It would seem to add needlessly to human suffering for some of the delicate to have to be in contact with what is one of the most awful afflictions that flesh is heir to. If death and suffering were not inevitable, we might try to save people from the suffering which sympathy entails. But there is no avoiding them; soon or late they are sure to come to everyone. The upbuilding of character, consequent upon intimacy with them, is of great value, and really brings so much of contentment to people who are over-worried about little things that it is worth while to recall how valuable this sympathy for suffering is in psychotherapy.

I have spoken of this phase of occupation as if it referred only to women. There are many men of whom one may well say that they need more human sympathy in their lives and that if they had it their supposed ills would drop from them, or seem so slight as to be quite negligible. Over and over again, I have seen men who had become too occupied with themselves lose their pains and aches in an interest in some real charity. Charity, however, not philanthropy, is the secret. The sitting on a board of trustees of a charitable institution may mean little though even this usually has its good effect; but close contact with the poor, intimate personal relations with other human beings who are in suffering, are quite as necessary for men over-occupied with themselves as for women.

{223}

Care of the Incurable.—Mother Lathrop (Hawthorne's daughter) in her cancer work prefers not to take patients suffering from incurable cancer into the homes that she has for them, if they can in any way be cared for reasonably at their own home. Of course, the main reason is because there is so much of cancer in the community (one in thirty of the population now die of it), that it is impossible to take care of all the cases that apply for admission. Another excellent reason is that it would be too bad to take out of a home the opportunity for self-discipline that is afforded by the care of one of these patients, when it does not inflict an intolerable burden on someone already overworked. As a rule, the effect of attendance on such a patient does so much for character upbuilding, and for a proper realization of values in life, that trivial things fall into their right places. Anyone who has seen the development of character, And the growth in amenity of disposition of those who bear such a burden with patience, will realize just what is meant by the expressions used.

Finding Mental Occupation.—For many of his patients the physician simply must find occupation of mind. Not a little racking of brain is needed for this, until experience helps. One form of occupation of mind that seemed quite unpromising at first, but that has in a number of cases proved of value, is the committing to memory of passages in verse. A generation ago it was quite common for people to have their memories stored with fine passages from authors which they could repeat literally. Latin verse particularly was learned by the school boys of fifty years ago. Frenchmen know their classical poets, and some of the Italians also know theirs with wonderful fidelity. It is said that, even in his advanced years, Pope Leo XIII could repeat long passages of Dante and often found a relief from pressing cares of state in the ponderings of the great thoughts recalled by the verses. I have known half a dozen Italian clergymen who could from memory follow up a line of Dante, taken anywhere in the poet's writings, with the rest of the passage.

Such well-stored memories furnished much more abundant food for thought to their possessors than do those of the modern time. Our modern system of education has done away, to a great extent, with learning by heart, but as one of those educated under the older system and who is still able to recall many passages from Pope, or Goldsmith's "Deserted Village," or "The Traveler," or from Virgil or Horace, I feel sure that this is a serious mistake. In some cases I have deliberately tried to make up for it by having people, even well on in years, settle down to memory lessons again. Under disorders of memory I suggest the use of this practice as a valuable training which serves first to dispel the idea that memory is failing when it is only lack of attention and of concentration of mind that is at fault, and secondly, because after a time there can be observed an actual improvement of the memory faculty. Here I would insist on its value as an occupation of mind for those who lack some serious interests. I have found it to be ever so much better as a diversion than reading or the theater. If the interest in it can be awakened, it represents a valuable adjunct in the treatment of some rather difficult cases of mental short-circuiting. Lord Chesterfield, in one of his letters, suggested to his son that even very brief periods during the day—those that are ordinarily used for the fulfillment of bodily necessities—might be employed to store the memory with valuable quotations, great thoughts {224} greatly expressed, and this should be recalled. After a little practice not near so much time is required for memory work as might be imagined, and the effects are excellent.

Much of this may seem too trivial for the physician to occupy himself with and quite apart from his duties as a practitioner of medical science. But it must not be forgotten that medical science is as yet quite imperfect and the practice of medicine is an art. What we have to do, is to treat individual patients rather than cure cases, for that is why medicine is a profession. Each affected individual who comes to us is quite different from any other. In spite of our grouping them under certain heads, the diseases of the race are as distinct from one another as the features of the individuals affected.

CHAPTER VI

DIVERSION OF MIND—HOBBIES

There are two classes for whom diversion is of the utmost value. The first are over-occupied with themselves; and the second group are so occupied with some one interest in life, or with one narrow set of interests, that it becomes an obsession, never leaving them. Constancy of mental occupation with one set of thoughts proves seriously disturbing after a time, especially if the only amusements available are so superficial that they do not really act as a diversion. Many of the so-called neurasthenic or psychasthenic states (I would prefer to call them conditions of nervous weakness and of psychic impotency, because the simpler names carry with them no suggestion of a definite ailment) are really the consequence of this lack of any true diversion. The patients do not get any genuine rest.

The typical example of such lack of diversion is the business man who, contrary to the wisdom of the ages, takes his business home with him. If we accept Ramon y Cajal's theory of attention, by which whenever a particular portion of the brain is occupied with a subject the capillary blood vessels in that particular part are pulled wide open by the contraction of the neuroglia cells, certain of the brain tissues in these cases are constantly in a state of congestion. It is not surprising that such men suffer from insomnia. It is scarcely less to be wondered

133

at if their digestion suffers, since that function is so important that it requires most of the nervous energy that a man can provide at certain times. Besides his brain cells are never really resting. If a man goes to sleep with a thought and wakes with it, even though he may not be quite conscious of the fact, his mind has been occupied with it. Brain cells need definite periods of rest. These cells are not getting such rest—hence the development of many pathological conditions.

I have described the extreme case, but it is not exaggerated. Writers, editors, scientific investigators and generally those whose work does not bring them much in contact with others, are likely to thus suffer. Contact with others, even on business matters, seems to have a relaxing effect. Social amenities and personal interests prevent absolute concentration of mind over long periods. In some people even milder degrees of preoccupation with a {225} single subject may work harm. Some people are able to stand concentration of mind for many hours a day for years. Others cannot. We have come to recognize that more than eight hours a day is a mistake, but there are many people who cannot work more than a four-hour day. The sooner this is recognized and diversion of mind provided, the better for them. This is one of the most important benefits that psychotherapy can confer on many of the so-called neurasthenics.

Possibility of Diversion of Attention from Ills.—The necessity for diversion of attention from one's ills is best realized by considering what happens in the opposite direction. Headache, toothache, and many other uncomfortable feelings, especially discomfort associated with abdominal disturbances, can be entirely banished from the mind by pleasant association with friends, by an interesting play, by a game of cards, or, indeed, by almost anything that takes up the attention completely. It is well understood that the severer forms of pains can not be thus banished, but discomforts that make life miserable for the patient may be entirely relieved for the time being. If this power of mind to divert attention from the ills of the body means so much, it is not hard to understand that if this mental influence be directed in the other way, that is, to emphasize the ailment by attention to it, it will not be long before symptoms become quite unbearable.

Hobbies.—A hobby is the physical salvation for a man who wants to work hard, yet not become so absorbed in his work that it becomes an obsession. Unfortunately, it is not possible to create a hobby for a man or a woman in a short time. It must be a growth for many years until it has become a portion of one's life. It must, as far as possible, be something to which one turns with as much interest as to one's regular occupation, so that the time taken from it, even for the necessary vocation of life, is more or less resented. If a man has two occupations that are intensely interesting, then he gets the best possible rest. Otherwise it will be necessary in many cases for the physician to help him in the choice of another interest in life. It is not enough that there should be a vacation once a year, or a conventional day off on Sunday. There must be much more than this, deliberately planned and faithfully carried out.

Gladstone.—Men with hobbies have done some of the best of the world's work; busy for many hours every day, they have yet lived to be eighty and even ninety years of age, and have been industrious to the end. A typical example in our generation was Gladstone, the great English statesman. Few men had their minds occupied with more serious problems than he for nearly forty years of a busy existence. In spite of this, he found time to make a study of Greek literature and of ecclesiastical writers; He acquired even more authority perhaps in these subjects than in political science, doing the work of several men, yet he lived to be an extremely old man. He welcomed the opportunity to get away from one kind of work in order to devote himself to another, but this occupation of an entirely different set of brain cells gave those that had been previously at work opportunity for complete rest. Very probably, except at times of special crisis or stress of anxiety, his political problems did not disturb his studies of Greek literature, not because he insisted on keeping them away, but because this other interest was so absorbing that it required no special effort to occupy his mind completely with it.

{226}

Virchow.—For more than a year I lived close to the great German pathologist, Virchow, and found that his varied interests were probably the secret of his power to devote himself to work for many hours a day, take only a small amount of sleep and yet live healthily and happily for over eighty years. Frequently he did not leave the Prussian legislature until 1 a. m., or even later, and yet he seldom failed to be at his laboratory before 7:30 o'clock in the morning, though it was several miles from his home and took over half an hour to get there. Besides pathology, he was deeply interested in anthropology and in most of the biological sciences, and his favorite hobby was the practical care of the health of the city of Berlin. From the time when Berlin, just after the Franco-Prussian war, began to grow out of the half-million provincial town that it was, into the great world capital that it became, a transformation that took less than twenty years, Virchow had charge of the health of the men engaged on the sewer farms of the city. Berlin, unlike other great capitals, is not situated on a large stream that will carry off its excreta, and consequently a new problem in sewage disposal had to be met. The sewage was spread over fields outside the city and proved, as might be expected, a magnificent fertilizer. The whole cost of sewage disposal was recouped from the sale of the farm products.

Prophecies of dire disaster of many kinds were made when this system was first proposed. It was said that the men engaged on the farms would suffer from all sorts of disease, especially respiratory and intestinal diseases, that the farm products would be insanitary, and the whole plant would be such a disease producer for the city as to become a nuisance. Virchow was put in charge of the sanitary side of the project, and how well he fulfilled his obligations is shown by the statistics. The people who worked on the farms were healthier than the average inhabitants of Berlin, and were especially free from intestinal disease. Every phase of disease that occurred among the workers on the farms, and there were many thousands of them with their families, was reported to Virchow. Every night, the last thing before he went to bed, he looked over this report and if there were any suspicious cases, made arrangements for the prevention of the spread of disease.

This of itself might seem work enough for one man, but it was only a diversion for Virchow, turning his mind away from his other intellectual work completely during certain hours of the day. His visits to the farms, his planning for the prevention of the spread of disease, his deep interest in the reports and the constant improvement of conditions, instead of hampering his other intellectual activity by wasting brain force, probably proved restful by diverting the blood stream away to the cells that occupied themselves with this other and very different problem, and so proved a benefit, not an evil. Perhaps other men might not have had the store of nervous energy to enable them to

134

carry on work in this way, but for those who have, this is the ideal arrangement. There are many others whose names might be mentioned here. John Bigelow and Pope Leo XIII are typical recent examples. Great workers are usually long livers, barring accident, and all of them have had variety of occupation.

Necessity for Diversity of Occupation.—Even for those of lesser intellectual capacity, it is advisable to have, in a lower order of intellectual occupation, two very different things in which there is intense interest. The blasé {227} attitude in which the individual finds no interest in anything and nothing worth doing, makes it impossible to secure such relaxation as will give relief from worry. So long as nothing happens to call for special resistive vitality, such people may go on nursing their unhappiness. It is from this class, however, that the suicides come. The mind becomes occupied with the worries that it cannot get away from, sleep is interfered with; the worries become an obsession, and brain exhaustion results. It is usually said that suicides are insane, and to this extent certainly the expression is true. Certain brain cells have so long been occupied with a particular subject, because the mind has no other interest to divert attention and blood supply to other portions, that these cells are overborne and become utterly beyond the control of reason and will.

Intervals in Work.—The old university rule of long ago was that no one should do more than two hours of intellectual work continuously at the same subject. Certain of the monastic orders required scholars and students to take a break from an intellectual occupation for a measured interval at least every two hours. The modern business man, and even the literary man or reporter, would think this preposterous. The rule is, however, founded on good common sense, for it relieves the tension and keeps conditions of strain from inveterating themselves in such a way as to do harm.

As a matter of fact, better work is accomplished if it is done in two-hour intervals, with a break of fifteen minutes to a half-hour between, than if the attempt is made to work longer. This may not be true for certain forms of creative literary work, where, when the mood is on, it is easier to finish things than if a break occurs, but these are exceptional cases, and even here there may be serious abuse. Many of the men who work late at night eventually get into habits that seriously impair their sleep. This system of rest prevents such a strain from being put upon the physical organs underlying attention as will prevent them from promptly relaxing when the call upon them has ceased.

There are, of course, men for whom no such rules as these seem to be needed, because they apparently thrive on work. These are exceptions, however, that prove the rule. They will usually be found on investigation to have been men who lived very simply and permitted themselves very little excitement. There is great danger in imitating them because most of them had a superabundant vitality which expressed itself in longevity as well as in a noteworthy capacity for work. They had superabundant brain power to run their business (even though it was deeply intellectual), but then, too, these men were careful not to throw extra burdens upon their digestive organs, nor to abuse stimulants, nor to permit a regular routine of work to be disturbed. When symptoms of nerve weakness begin to show themselves, even the exceptional men must be warned of the danger. The causes of the exhaustion of nervous vitality should be pointed out, and an improvement of habits insisted upon.

Amusement and the Mind.—The theater, as it is at the present time, affords very little opportunity for mental relaxation. Most of our theatricals are mere show that occupies the eye but does not seriously catch the attention, especially after a certain number of types of these performances have been attended. The humor of the comedians of our musical comedy may, for {228} a certain number of people, mean something as a diversion of mind, but it does not last. Unfortunately, practically all their humor runs along the same line, most of it is extremely superficial, much of it is borrowed and wears signs of its origin, not a little of it is mere horse-play, which may divert children but not grown men, and so the theater as a mental relaxation has lost nearly all of its effect. Other diversions are sometimes more hopeful. For baseball enthusiasts, attendance at a game may be such a complete occupation of mind as to furnish thorough relaxation.

The kind of work that provides mental relaxation for others often proves exhausting to those who do it. Humorists, especially those who have to grind out paragraphs or columns of humor every day or every week, are usually melancholy men. The story of Grimaldi illustrates how serious may be the effect of work that seems mere play if pursued too singly. This humorist on one occasion consulted a specialist in mental diseases, for certain symptoms of nervous breakdown and depression that were causing him much annoyance and even more solicitude. The specialist believed in diversion of mind, and, having been to see Grimaldi the night before and enjoyed him hugely, though he did not recognize him off the stage, counseled him to go and see that humorist and have his "blue devils" banished for good. "If Grimaldi won't cure you of your depression," he added, "I don't know anything that will." "My God!" the humorist said, "then don't leave me in despair. Man, I am Grimaldi!"

Sports.—Unfortunately in our modern life we have to a great extent lost the idea of sport. The conventional make-shifts of life in a camp that is really a luxurious country house, or on a luxurious yacht, do not replace the complete diversions that came with real camping, hunting, fishing, sailing and the like. People now go to the country, but take the city with them. They live in country hotels and make five changes of clothing in the day, if not more. If men are interested in hunting and fishing and can go into the forest (unfortunately even the Adirondacks can scarcely be so designated now and we have to go into the Canadian wilderness to get away from the pall of regular life and civilization), complete recreation is secured. This makes a real vacation which does not mean absolute freedom of mind, but freedom from other cares so that one may with complete absorption apply himself to something different. During the year sports for grown-ups are difficult to obtain. Some men continue well on in middle life to play tennis, hand-ball, and certain other games, *O fortunati nimium*, that make the best kind of diversion. Fortunately, in recent years golf has become a favorite and for many makes a genuine diversion.

Children's Diversions.—In recent years we have so interfered with the normal natural development of the child that there is need to emphasize certain details in this matter. The modern child is apt to be precociously occupied with books and adult interests, because he is

135

brought so much into the foreground of family interests. True play for some city-bred children is almost an anomaly. Exercise and air they get. They are conducted solemnly to the park by a nursemaid, who is instructed to see that they do not play with other children unless quite as well dressed as they are themselves, and their dress is often so elaborate that it is quite impossible for them to think of any real play. There is absolutely no recreation for the child in this procedure: on {229} the contrary, a new effort of will is required to walk with the stately propriety that is expected of it. Then the child is preoccupied with the thought of its clothes. Relaxation of mind is often quite out of the question, and yet we wonder why children are nervous and do not sleep well, why they have night terrors and do not digest their food properly, while all the time they are living unnatural lives that give no proper outlet for their energies and little diversion for their mind.

Games are important, but their true spirit has gone out in recent years. There are still a few young people who play for the sake of the sport, but everything now seems to be a preparation for some sort of contest. Only those are engaged in these contests and the preparation for them whose muscular development is such as to suggest that they will help to win. Winning, and not sport, has become the purpose of our games. This makes the participants worry about the games and associate them with dread of errors and ill chances. It is true that the interest for the contestants during the game is sufficient to make up for this and make the game valuable as relaxation; but those who need such relaxation most—the boys and girls who are underdeveloped muscularly—must sit and watch the contests, and this, after one has become accustomed to it, like newspaper reading and the theater, constitutes a poor apology for the complete relaxation of mind and diversion of brain-cell energy that used to come with sports when they were freely indulged, for the sake of the sport and not for the sake of winning.

CHAPTER VII

HABIT

Few people realize how powerful a factor for physical, as well as moral, good and evil is habit. The old expression that habit is second nature is amply illustrated in the most familiar experiences. The child, unable at the beginning to make any but the most ill-directed movements, learns during its first two years to make the most complex co-ordinated movements—first with difficulty, then with ease, and finally with such facility that there is no need for it to pay any but the most perfunctory attention to their execution. Walking requires the co-ordination of a large number of muscles so that the absolute position of every muscle in both the legs and in the trunk, at least as far as the shoulders, must be definitely known and their activity properly directed. Perhaps nothing brings out more clearly the difficulty of walking, though it depends on only one factor, the co-ordination of the two sides of the body, than the story of the Italian Tozzi twins. They were born with two heads and shoulders and with only one pair of legs. It was found that each head ruled the leg on its own side of the body. It was impossible for the creatures to walk. They lived to adolescent life, yet never succeeded in walking. The intimate association of the lower parts of their trunk and the long years of companionship of their brains, did not enable them to accomplish what seems to us so commonplace a co-ordination of movement as walking.

Formation of Habits.—The co-ordination of the two limbs is after all only a small portion of walking. The body must be held erect, the curve of {230} the spine must be managed so that the center of gravity is kept well within the base, and gluteal and femoral and calf muscles must all be co-ordinated with one another. In a few months a child learns to do all this, and in a couple of years it executes all the co-ordinate motions with such certainty that walking becomes not only an easy matter but an absolutely unconscious accomplishment that can be carried on while the mind is occupied with something else or while it becomes so abstracted that surrounding objects are not noticed.

A far more difficult co-ordination is required for talking. It is only when we analyze how nicely adjusted must be every movement, in order to pronounce consonants and vowels properly and to combine them in various ways, that we realize how complex is the mechanism of talking. A difference of a hundredth of an inch in the movement of the tongue, or less than that in the movements of various muscles of the larynx, makes all the differences between clear articulation and a defect of speech. In the course of the years up to seven, the child learns this wonderful co-ordination apparently without difficulty, but really at the cost of constant well-directed effort. There is no time in human existence when the child really learns so much as during the first four years of its existence, even if it learns nothing else except to walk and to talk. The foolishness of obtruding other things, information and study of various kinds, on the child's attention at this time should be manifest.

Unconscious Regulation of Muscles.—What is thus prefigured in early life invades every activity in later years. The boy who learns to ride a bicycle must at first devote all his attention to it, but after a while rides it quite unconsciously, his muscles having learned by habit to accommodate themselves automatically to all the varying positions of his machine. Anything well learned by habit is never forgotten. How hard it is to learn to swim, yet, after years away from the practice of it, the art comes back at once. The same is true of skating, and of the nice adjustments of muscles required in various games. Such is the influence of habit in forming a second nature. It is no wonder that Reid, the Scotch philosopher, should have written:

As without instinct the infant could not live to become a man, so without habit man would remain an infant through life, and would be as helpless, as unhandy, as speechless, and as much a child in understanding at threescore as at three.

Commenting on this Prof. J. P. Gordy, in his "New Psychology," says:

Strong as this statement seems, it is probably an understatement of the truth. Without habit, we should rather say, a man would be as helpless, as speechless, as unhandy at three-score as at birth. Habit is the architect that builds the feeble rudimentary powers of the child into the strong, developed powers of the full-grown man. If a child's vague, purposeless movements give place to definite movements performed for definite purposes, if his sensations become more definite, if his perceptions become clearer, if his memory becomes more accurate, if he reasons more and more correctly and logically, it is because of habit.

Law of Habit.—The law of habit is that every time we perform any action, mental or physical, or allow ourselves to be affected in any way, we have more proneness to, and greater facility in the performance of that action or in {231} experiencing that affection under similar circumstances, than we had before. In the chapter on Tics, I call attention to the fact that all the curious gestures by which we are individualized, are due to the law of habit. It is infinitely amusing to watch a group of people and note the endlessly different habits of which they have become the victims. There are tricks of speech and tricks of gesture eminently characteristic and often quite laughably individualistic. We imitate, especially those of whom we think much. Sometimes it is only when a father's attention is called to them in his sons that he realizes the ludicrousness, or at least laughableness, of some of the things he does, and he proceeds to correct both generations of their faults.

PHYSICAL HABITS

Habit and Food.—Most of our likes and dislikes for food are neither physical nor physiological, but simply habitual. We have become accustomed to certain things, and so we like them. We are unaccustomed to them, and do not care for them. It is amusing when people put forward these lacks of habituation as if they were physiological idiosyncracies. Many thin people do not like butter and milk. The real reason for this is not any peculiarity of digestion, or any gastric incompatibility, at least in 99 cases out of every 100, but the mere fact that they are not habituated to their use. That is one of the reasons why they are thin. Our tastes for curious foreign foods are nearly all deliberately acquired. Not one in ten ordinary Americans likes olives or caviar when first tasted. Nearly every curious article of food is "caviar to the general" at first trial. Later it becomes impossible to understand how we could have had any objection to them. At times, even an actual craving for them asserts itself as a consequence of the habitual use, and then deprivation means positive discomfort.

Slow Eating.—One of the most valuable habits that a man can cultivate, but one of the most difficult to acquire in our time, is that of eating slowly. Most Americans bolt their food to a degree that would be quite appalling to them if they realized what they were doing. Pieces of potatoe as large as the end of the thumb are swallowed. Bread and milk may be eaten so hurriedly as to be as potent a source of digestive disturbance as fried onions. There seems no doubt from what we know of Fletcher's experience and Chittendan and Follin's studies that a man derives more nutrition from food that is masticated properly, that he can get along and do his work on less material and that, above all, there is not the same tendency for him to put on weight that is so common among people after reaching middle age.

Sir Andrew Clarke used to have his patients chew a definite number of times on each bite—say thirty times. Even so great a man as Gladstone submitted to this rule and gradually learned to accustom himself to eating very slowly. Fletcher's system of chewing the food until it passes down the esophagus of itself without any swallowing effort is a better rule. It is a surprise to most people how unconsciously swallowing can be accomplished in this way and how little liquid is needed in order to prepare food to be swallowed. The formation of the habit, however, is not an easy one. Persistence and frequent reminders are needed, or else the beginnings of the habit are soon dissipated and old bolting habits reassert themselves.

{232}

Water Drinking.—In drinking, habit is as supreme as in eating. The majority of people who work outside and perform muscular labor crave and take an abundance of water. Many of those who live indoors, especially in steam-heated houses, may need it quite as much if not more, but get out of the habit of drinking water. As we need about three quarts of water per day for use in our economy, this no water habit often becomes a serious factor in the production of physiological disturbances. We have replaced water drinking and the milk drinking of the olden times by tea and coffee, and as these are stimulants, habits form very readily with regard to them. I have known people who were sure they would be miserable without their half-dozen cups of tea or coffee each day, and who actually would be miserable for a few days, when deprived of it. They were seriously impairing the efficiency of their nervous system by so much stimulation. Unfortunately, it is just those whose nervous systems have least stability, and are already the subjects of more stimulation by conscious introspection than is good for them, that are most likely to form the tea and coffee habits, and who are most harmed by them, though they find it hard to understand the reason therefor.

Air and Exercise Habits.—Habits with regard to exercise and fresh air are particularly important. In this matter it is only habit that can be really helpful. To work at high pressure indoors for several days, and then, when one is quite on edge, to take a lot of severe physical exercise is not good. Every human being should go out between meals. I am not one of those who believe much in exercise for exercise's sake—what is needed is fresh air. Our sanatorium patients who sit out-doors all day have fine appetites. The advice to a busy man that he must form the habit of being out between every two meals for from half an hour to an hour would usually evoke a strenuous protest, but all he needs to do is to get up half an hour earlier and walk down to his office, and if he will walk back in the evening he will have plenty of air and exercise between his meals.

Change of Habits.—Patients do not want to change their habits. They come to a doctor to be treated. They want some medicine that will, without further inconvenience, rid them of certain discomforting symptoms. At the beginning, at least, patients resent interference with their habits. They are quite satisfied, and to modify them requires an effort that must be continued for some time. The changing of old habits and the formation of new habits are most important for the ordinary ills to which mankind is prone. Modifications of habit constitute real hygiene and are not mere corrections of symptoms, permitting the habits that have led up to them to go on.

Patients may conclude that it is too much trouble to change their habits. We all know persons who feel that they can not give up their coffee. As to whether or not the modification of a habit is worth the trouble it involves, the patient must be the judge after the case is put properly before him. It is possible that he may learn to endure the inconvenience given him by his symptoms rather than to stand the inconvenience of changing a nicely settled habit, and forming a new one. The reward should be put very plainly before him, however, and besides, the consequences of his habit in the future should be suggested so that he may realize just what it will lead to.

{233}

MENTAL HABITS

It is evident from the foregoing that physical habits have much to do with making life easier and saving expenditure of nervous energy, but just this same thing holds good for mental states. With care, a proper habit of mind and of the mental attitude towards difficulties in life, can be so cultivated as to ward off many of the discouragements, and most of the causes of depression that weigh heavily on some people. The natural disposition can not be entirely overcome, but habit, as a second nature, can modify the personality so as to make conditions much better than before.

With this wonderful power in habit, it is too bad that its force for good is not used. It is especially important that its force for evil shall not allowed to dominate human actions so as to make them harder of accomplishment. Many people, who are greatly troubled by the inconveniences and discomforts necessarily associated with human life, worry over it to such a degree as to make themselves sick. The expression I have quoted elsewhere of the old man who said, "I have had many troubles but most of them never happened," is a typical example of what the habit of looking at things from a wrong standpoint means to many people. They are confirmed pessimists. Their one consolation, when a small evil happens to them, is that perhaps this may be sufficient to ward off the greater evil that fate surely has in store.

Pessimism.—Pessimism has been defined as sticking one's nose in a dungheap and then asking, "How is it that it smells bad around here?" Some people are always nursing a grievance. No matter how many times they may happen to have been undeceived, still the next time the opportunity occurs they are sure that fate or friends or someone has it in for them and that the worst may happen at any time. In the expressive words of a recent slang phrase, they have a "perennial grouch." This state of mind toward the environment not only prevents the physical and mental good that cheerfulness brings with it, but it unfavorably influences physical conditions within the body. People suffering from indigestion are usually morbid, petulant, and hard to get along with. Many a dyspeptic makes this an excuse for his bad temper. Anyone who has had to study these cases much soon comes to the conclusion that the beginning of the digestive disturbance was the gloomy outlook on life, which flowed inward to disturb the digestion and all the other animal functions.

Depression of Mind and Body.—Patients suffering from melancholia nearly always lose in weight. As a result of their lowered vitality, there is a suppression of the nervous impulses which rule over nutrition, with a consequent loss of weight. In cases where there are only tendencies to depression and gloom, the effect upon the digestive system is not so marked but there is no doubt that there is some effect, and that the indigestion in these cases is more often than not a result of the depressed state of mind, rather than the depression of mind the result of the indigestion.

Moodiness.—The habit of looking at the gloomy side of things is easily formed and, once acquired, it becomes very forceful. Many a man who was quite cheerful when young, becomes moody as he grows older. Nearly everyone permits moods more than is good for him. The attitude of mind that should be cultivated is one in which it is realized that, though there may be {234} many sources of evil in the world there is a preponderance of good even in the worst environment, and that opportunities for making the best of things will be found by any cheerful disposition. *Mrs. Wiggs of the Cabbage Patch* is a typical example in fiction of the optimism that counts. Miss Helen Keller in real life is a typical example of how the most untoward circumstances can not crush the spirit of man if he only wishes to be cheerful—if he only tries to lift himself above his surroundings, no matter how discouraging they may seem to be. No one is without discouragement and causes for unhappiness. "Happy he who has least," the Greek dramatist said.

The difference between the optimistic and the pessimistic point of view is much more a matter of habit than is usually thought to be the case. Indeed, there is good reason for assuming that it is so largely a matter of habit, that other factors count for little. We all know individuals who, after having, been cheery, bright, hopeful and helpful, have had some incident sour them and then they have been just the opposite. This did not come all at once; it was a growth. They felt hurt and aggrieved, and then began to look at things through dark glasses, and after a time could see nothing on its brighter side. Not infrequently, as doctors well know, the growth of such a moody disposition has been the signal for the development of a series of complaints, if not of actual symptoms, and men and women who have not been in the doctor's hands before now become valetudinarians. This new physical condition is often attributed by their friends, by themselves, and even by complacent physicians, to the effect upon them of the trial or disappointment that struck them. Only too often it is wholly due to the cultivation of a habit of pessimism consequent upon a shock that for the moment pushed their cheerfulness into the background. Strong characters will not be thus easily affected, but weaker characters need not suffer such a change of disposition and with it a deterioration of health or well-being unless they so will it.

MANNERS AND DISPOSITION

Habit can modify nature so much as to make what is practically another man. We all know how the dancing master can transform a country gawk into a refined, courteous society man (not gentleman, for that is something else) of graceful carriage and even handsome bearing. He cannot do this for all the pupils that come to him, for it is impossible to make a silk purse out of a sow's ear, but for anyone that comes with good will the revolution in manners is often a revelation to those who have known the man before. When the exterior can be changed so much, the interior attitude toward other people certainly can be greatly modified.

Persons of a melancholic disposition may be surprisingly cheerful, and even gay, with comparative strangers when they make the effort to be so. For many people, meeting with strangers is an excellent remedial measure. It stirs them up to present the best side, and it occupies attention to the exclusion of themselves in a way that is extremely beneficial. If people would only form the habit of being as courteous to their own folks as they are to others, the disposition involved in this would often save them from certain symptoms, and save their physicians from many complaints.

{235}

Happiness is the basis of good health. The phrase is often put the other way: Good health is the basis of happiness. Without health there is no happiness. But every physician knows that many a patient suffering from real organic ills, and having much physical pain to bear, still has many hours of happiness in working for others. This happiness reflected back upon his physical life is not able to cure his ailments, but does so lessen the significance of the symptoms as to make the ailment more bearable.

THERAPEUTIC IMPORTANCE OF HABIT

The most important therapeutic element in the formation of good habits, mental and physical, is that habit does away with the necessity for conscious regulation of many details of life. Without habits of doing things, we have to make numerous decisions and keep on making them under conditions that require special effort and waste of energy. When habit asserts itself, there is little or no difficulty. Habits of living in airy rooms, of taking exercise, of food regulation as to quantity and quality, of methods of taking food as regards mastication, the quantity of fluid ingested, the hours of meals and the like, can all be formed and then followed without effort. Just inasmuch as life can be ruled by habit, nerve force is conserved. This is as true for our attitude towards life, our disposition and consequently our satisfaction with life, as for anything else that we do. Habitual cheerfulness, habitual readiness to make allowance for others and to be helpful to them, habitual self-control—all of these things can be cultivated. Properly cultivated, they save much of the wear and tear of life, and make for contentment and happiness much more than many of the things for which men strive so anxiously because they seem to promise happiness.

CHAPTER VIII

PAIN

Pain, while always a dreaded symptom of disease, seems, with the increase of comfort and the gradual abolition that has come in our time of many of the trials of existence, to have had its terrors increased. Even a slight pain or ache is dreaded, and if continuous or frequently repeated, becomes for many people a trial that is almost impossible to bear. This is all the more to be deplored because ability to stand a certain amount of pain, with reasonable equanimity, is almost a necessary condition of rapid recovery from disease or injury. Placidity of mind favors the flow of nerve impulses for reconstructive purposes, while over-reaction to pain inhibits the natural processes of repair. According to Shakespeare's heroine: "There was never yet philosopher that could endure the toothache patiently." Pain is usually supposed to be an essentially physical phenomena for which mental influence can be of little, if any, benefit. As a matter of fact, however, the mental attitude towards pain modifies it to a considerable degree. I have quoted Hippocrates' declaration that a greater pain drives out a lesser pain. Any strong preoccupation of mind will greatly lessen pain at any time.

{236}

Pain is not, after all, in the nerves, nor in the central nervous system, but in the consciousness. Just as there is no sound unless the waves in the air arouse recognition in the consciousness, so there is no pain unless the disturbance of nerves finds its way above the threshold of consciousness. Nerves may be racked, yet no sensation may be felt. There may be pain in the mind apart from the nerves, and slight nervous affections may produce severe pains. The whole question of the treatment of pain involves the individual much more than it does the affliction which causes the pain. What seems unbearable pain to many may be little more than a passing annoyance to others. What would be, under ordinary circumstances, intolerable torture, especially to sensitive people, may, because of intense preoccupation of mind, remain absolutely unnoticed. Maniacal patients sometimes inflict what would normally be extremely severe pain on themselves by burning or mutilation without any manifestation of pain. In the excitement of a panic men may suffer what would, under other circumstances, be excruciating agony, and yet not know that they are hurt.

To a mind that is without serious interest, even slight pain, if continuous, soon becomes unbearable. The course of pain, where there is no diversion of mind, is an interesting study. While suffering, we seem always able to bear the pain of the present moment, and it is only the cumulative effect of the pain that is past and the anticipation of the discomfort to come, that make the pain unbearable. Nearly, always it is much more the dread of what the pain may mean, and the lack of power to endure which gradually develops as a consequence of suffering, that constitute the worst features of pain. At the beginning of a period of pain we stand it well, as a rule, but its continual nagging debilitates us and heightens our susceptibility until we cannot nerve ourselves to further endurance. If our power of endurance were not thus gradually lessened the pain would not seem severe. There are many neurotic people whose susceptibility to pain has been so much increased by their lack of self-control and their tendency to react easily to pain, that even slight pain becomes a torment. Psychotherapy should gradually train these people to a power of endurance.

Pain from Over-Attention.—Much of what is called pain is really due to such concentration of mind on a particular portion of the body that the ordinary sensations of that part, usually accomplished quite unconsciously, become first a source of uneasy discomfort and then an ache or pain. There may be some slight physical disturbance which calls attention to the part, but there is no really serious pathological condition. While such pains are spoken of as imaginary it must be remembered that this does not mean that they are non-existent. On the contrary they may be much more real to the patient than physical ailments. A pain in the mind is a much more serious condition than having it in the body.

While pain may be thus created by concentration of attention, it must not be forgotten that what the mind can do in increasing pain is even more important than in originating it. Slight discomforts by concentration of attention on them may be made insupportable. It is this element in pain, above all, that the physician requires skill to alleviate. Habits of introspection and the lack of serious occupation of mind of many people leave them the victims of over attention to themselves. In trying to relieve their pain it may be {237} comparatively easy to alleviate their physical condition, but the mental condition, once aroused, may remain, and may easily tempt to the use of habit-forming drugs or others that may do serious harm. The story of the evil effects of headache powders in recent years, and of the opium habits formed in olden times, are a significant commentary on this fact. It is probable that in most of these cases, the discomfort for which remedies were frequently taken was of a kind that should have been treated only partly, if at all, by drugs. It is more important to lessen susceptibility than to try to cure the pain.

The relation of the mind to what is often considered severe physical pain, has come to be generally recognized in recent years. Neuralgias, for instance, have often been reported as recurring after fright, or strong emotion, or worry. It is at moments when patients are much run down in health that pains are particularly likely to be unrelievable, and during periods of emotional strain that anodyne drugs are most called for and are most likely to be abused.

Rest and Pain.—In any study of pain and its relief, one must always recur to that classical contribution to medicine, now in the fiftieth year of its publication and still as important as when it was written, Hilton's "Rest and Pain." He calls attention to the fact that what he wrote was only a development of what many practical physicians had thought long before his time. He quotes a prize essay of the French surgeon, David, written in 1778. Hilton's development of the idea that pain is usually a signal on the part of nature for rest, and that rest will usually enable her to overcome the pathological condition and so relieve the pain without recourse to drugs, is, and ever must be, the basic element in the therapeutics of pain. How many forms rest may take can only be judged by a careful reading of Hilton's book. The oftener one reads it, the better one realizes how much of precious common sense and acute clinical observation there is in it. It is essentially a book of psychotherapy. It treats the patient's mind first and then through that changes his habits, persuades him of the need of rest, directs how that rest should be taken and so leads up to his natural cure.

Every treatment of pain must include rest of mind as well as body. Hilton has particularly dwelt on the rest of body. Rest of mind is just as important. Many pains could be easily borne were it not for the worry that accompanies them. A slight pain becomes greatly annoying because the patient's general condition makes it impossible to stand discomfort with equanimity, and there has been no training in self-control. In spite of all our advance in medicine, we are not likely ever to make life so free from pain that people can go through it without needing self-control. Training in self-control is an important psychotherapeutic prophylactic. If, with a certain amount of capacity to bear discomfort, there goes such rest of mind as does not exaggerate or emphasize the condition, then many of the pains of life lose their power to annoy, all of them are distinctly lessened and the relief of them by accessory physical methods becomes easier.

Pain in Its Relation to Life.—There is an unfortunate tendency to exaggerate the significance of pain. We have cultivated irritability in the physical sense, rather than the power of endurance. Patients should, as far as possible, be lifted out of this condition of over-delicate sensitiveness and put into a state where the idea of pain is not so serious. Only in this way can {238} the more or less inevitable discomforts of life be borne without such reactions as seriously interfere with health. It may be said to be other than the physician's business to secure this magnanimity, but as magnanimity is needed in our patients, and there is no one else to respond, physicians must start its cultivation. The necessity for learning to bear minor discomforts, at least without exaggerated reaction, need not be presented to the patient directly, but can be gradually made a part of the system of treatment. By absorption in other interests, the consciousness of these discomforts disappears without the necessity for recourse to drugs.

Self-Denial.—Many thoughtful people are sure that what is needed to make a large number of our generation more happy, or at least less miserable, is training in self-denial and in self-control. The word self-denial has come to have a very distant sound for most of our generation. From early childhood anything that is unpleasant is shunned and anything that is difficult is likely to be shirked. The head-master of Eton College has recently insisted that too much is being done to please young folks and too little to stimulate them to activity. He declares that, as a rule, any undertaking begins to be useful just where it ceases to be simply pleasant. Unpleasantness is avoided to such a degree that the habit of thinking that it has no part in life comes to be a second nature. As a consequence, the reaction to any continued unpleasantness is likely to be exaggerated and make the subject very miserable, and sometimes disturbs and discourages, whereas it should have the effect of stimulating to reactive efforts, to bring out the best that is in us.

Hinton emphasizes the fact that an ingredient of pain is necessary to all health or pleasure. The fatigue and the hardship associated with mountain climbing is a portion of the essence of the pleasure in it. All healthy, pleasant exercise has an accompaniment of fatigue and some aches and pains. What is needed, then, in our time is the training to do things for the sake of doing them. We should be neglectful of the discomfort that may be associated with them, or we should even consciously rejoice in the fact that this very discomfort is of itself a sign that functions are being used to such an extent, that their limits are being expanded, their limitations overcome.

It may well be said that it is not the physician who, as a rule, should do this; it should be accomplished in the early years by the teachers and trainers of the young. True enough. But physicians can at least help in reforming the tradition in this matter so as to neutralize the present state of mind which seems to look upon pain as an evil. Pain is always either a conservative sensation or an actual stimulus to function. Besides, many of the present generation who come to us, having had no training in the precious qualities of self-denial and self-control under difficulties and discomforts, must have this knowledge supplied for them as far as possible by suggestions of various kinds. It is more difficult to accomplish much in this matter for the adult, but even in apparently hopeless cases of over-attention to self and incapacity to bear discomfort, much can be accomplished by patience and persistence.

The common dread of suffering is quite unwarranted by what we know about the effect of pain. There are many motives that may be adduced to make it seem less terrifying than it now is to many people. The effect of pain upon character is always excellent. The difference between two brothers, as we have said, one of whom has had the discipline of pain or suffering and {239} the development of sympathy that comes with it, and the other who has not had the advantage of this great human experience, is likely to be marked. In the one there is a depth of human nature that enables him to appreciate and even to express the meaning of life better than his apparently more fortunate brother. Practically all the men who have ever got close to the heart of the mystery of life, and expressed it in poetry or other form of literature or art, have gone through suffering as a portion of their training. Even the suffering that comes from ill health is never wasted. Men have gone through it who have thought that the ecstasy of relief following it made the experience worth while.

Men are not deterred from action by the prospect of even severe pain. Probably no greater physical suffering can possibly be invited than is sure to come to those who go on Arctic expeditions, or who undertake prospecting in Alaska. Of course, many of the prospectors find themselves in the bitter cold of the North without having realized what they would have to stand. But Arctic explorers, as a rule, know exactly what they have to expect. Most of of them have been through it all before, yet they deliberately choose to go again for rewards that, to an average man's eyes, seem trivial. The memory of past pain is rather pleasant. Virgil's "Perhaps it will be pleasant to recall these trials at some future time" is not poetic exaggeration.

The Discipline of Pain.—There is only one way to learn how to bear pain, and that is by practice in it. There might be no necessity for this in case life were arranged differently. But all men must die, and death inevitably involves a painful process. Suffering is practically unavoidable for the majority of men. Even in the midst of every possible material comfort, cancer may come with all its hideous connotations. It is important, then, that everyone should be prepared to stand some pain. Certain suggestions help in bearing special pains.

Pain Diffusion.—Pain along one nerve may readily become diffused. This diffusion will sometimes cause discomfort, and even tenderness, at a distance from the original seat of the pain. Such diffusion tends to produce in the patient's mind the idea that the underlying pathological condition is spreading, though it is only a sign that the nervous system is becoming irritable and easily responding to sensory disturbance. Dr. Head's investigations ("Brain," 1893), should be known to physicians, and the conclusions that flow from them should be presented to patients who are sometimes suffering quite as much from their apprehension of the spread of pain, and its significance, as from the discomfort itself. Dr. Head says:

If I have an aching tooth, the pain is at first localized to the tooth affected. The longer the toothache continues the more I become worn out, and the pain is rapidly accentuated by a "neuralgia," that is, a pain in the face. The neuralgia is soon accompanied by distinct cutaneous tenderness over a definite area on the face corresponding to the tooth affected. If I am anemic, or if the pain remains untreated until my bodily health is affected, I no longer have a localized area of tenderness, but the pain, and with it the tenderness, spreads until the whole of one-half of the head and even the neck may be intensely tender. Thus at last the pain of an aching tooth has produced tenderness over areas which bear no relation to the affected organ.

As pain can be suppressed by diversion of mind, or concentration of thought on something that creates great preoccupation, it must not be {240} forgotten that pain may almost be created by concentration of attention on certain areas of the body, or certain nerve tracts. Over-attention will actually make sensations intolerable that are at first quite indifferent, or at least very easy to bear. Sensitive people, in the ordinary meaning of that term, are those who are much given to paying attention to their sensations, and who therefore have much to complain of them. There is much in modern life that has the tendency to produce this sybaritic condition in which even slight discomforts become the sources of almost unbearable annoyance.

Even where there is no good physical reason for the occurrence of pain, thinking may produce discomfort. The one thing that Freud's work has made clear is that in neurotic persons the memory of a mental shock or strain may be transferred to some portion of the body related in some way to the shock, and then prove to be the source of hysterical pains and also of hysterical palsy. The case told by him in which the young woman massaging her father's limbs allows them always to rest on her own lap during the process, and after his death suffers from an hysterical, painful condition in this region, is a typical illustration. Her sympathy for her father, accentuated by his subsequent death, and her sorrow at a time when her nursing efforts made her particularly susceptible, led to an explosion of nervous energy along those nerves which had always felt the impress of his legs. The hysterical condition resulted. This is an extreme case. In milder forms it would be possible to explain many otherwise inexplicable pains and aches in sensitive young people along these same lines.

More than once I have seen young women, who had been asked to rub father or mother with liniment, complain of tingling pains in their fingers which were followed by some redness so that one would be tempted to think of Weir Mitchell's disease, though evidently the pathological cause at work was the slight disturbance of the vasomotor system due to the liniment and the rubbing, emphasized by the sympathetic feelings, and by the over-attention which this brought about. Whenever women have, for a prolonged period, to nurse others in whom they are deeply interested, and have to perform some habitual action that is somewhat fatiguing for them, after the death of the patient there will not infrequently be the development of hysterical or neurotic over-sensitiveness in the parts employed. This may give rise even to an hysterical joint, or to severe neurotic pains. Once these cases are recognized, the attention can be diverted from themselves and they can be made to understand that their grief and sympathy are being concentrated on the part and by transfer are producing physical manifestations. The pain is not imaginary, but the condition will improve as soon as the mind is diverted from it.

Neurotic and Organic Pain.—The distinction between pain due to a neurosis and to a definite lesion is often difficult to make. If there is a definite localization of pain, it is almost surely not neurotic, but organic. If there are certain positions in which pain is felt while it disappears in others, there is some local inflammatory or congestive condition and not mere hypersensitiveness of nerves at the bottom of it. These positions of maximum pain are important. When pain radiates a great deal, even though there may be complaint of a particular region, it is usually neurotic. If patients are asked to tell exactly where their pain is, and they indicate its location by a wave of the hand, it is probable that the condition is neurotic. When there is a definite {241} localized point of tenderness with the pain, even though there may be radiations, usually the condition is based upon some organic trouble. It must not be forgotten, however, that slight local troubles may by concentration of mind on them, become exaggerated and that, in spite of the fact that there is or was at the beginning a definite localization of pain with some tenderness, the neurotic elements may, after a time, become manifest and prove to be much more important than the others.

Pain that is definitely influenced by motion, as by the jarring effect of walking, or by bending and stooping, is practically always organic. The best differential diagnosis between neurotic abdominal conditions and organic trouble can be made by the help of information obtained in this way. If the appendix is inflamed, or the gall bladder infected, or contains a calculus, or if the kidney has a calculus, these are all made worse by movements, by jarring, by stooping as in tying the shoes, by riding on rough roads, and the like. If patients who suffer from obscure abdominal conditions associated with pain of which they complain much, can, at certain times, indulge with impunity in these exercises and motions, it is probable that their attacks are neurotic in character. Especially is this true if the indulgence in these rides and motions is without effect when they are in pleasant, agreeable company, though there may be some complaints when they have to ride alone, or under conditions that are less pleasant. If a hint of this distinction by which the physician differentiates one form of pain from another is given a neurotic patient, the suggestion will serve the purpose of producing complaints whenever the opportunity presents itself. Such patients take such suggestions, as a rule, without wishing to deceive, but they become persuaded that their sufferings are of the character asked for.

{242}

SPECIAL PSYCHOTHERAPY

SECTION VI

THE DIGESTIVE TRACT

CHAPTER I

INFLUENCE OF MIND ON FOOD DIGESTION

With the progress of biological chemistry, digestion came to be considered a purely chemical process. Now we realize that even more important than the chemical factors of digestion is the individual liking for particular kinds of food, and the mental attitude of the patient toward digestion.

Not only may mental factors interrupt or hamper digestive processes generally but, as the investigations of Pawlow at the Imperial Institute of St. Petersburg show, they may modify very materially the chemical processes within the stomach. If, for investigation purposes, a stomach pouch be experimentally segregated in a dog from the rest of the stomach, and the dog be fed food that he has a particular liking for, the gastric juice manufactured will be especially strong and effective. If the food given be less to the dog's liking, the gastric juice is not nearly so efficient in its activity. Finally, if food be consumed for which the dog does not care, but which he takes because hunger compels him, the gastric juice manufactured for its digestion is quite weak and the process of digestion is slow. If this is true for an animal like the dog, whose psyche is comparatively of much less importance than that of human beings, the corresponding influences in men and women will be even more emphasized. This is only what common experience has always shown us. The human stomach is not a test-tube in which mere chemical processes are carried on, but its vital activity is of great importance. That vital activity depends to a large extent on the state of mind, on the relish with which food is eaten, on the individual likes and dislikes, and on the emotional condition during digestion.

Prejudices and Digestion.—Perfectly good food materials may become difficult or impossible of digestion as the result of learning something about their mode of preparation. In the country this is often noted, with regard to butter, milk, and even eggs. The story of the farmer's wife who wanted to trade her own butter for an equivalent amount made by someone else illustrates the influence of mind over relish for food. She was candid enough to say that the reason she wanted to exchange the butter was that a mouse had been seen in the cream, and her children could not, therefore, eat it. She took {243} back home with her exactly the same butter in another crock, and there was no further difficulty, though before this the children would have been actually sick if compelled to eat the butter. I once saw a family of three women who had vomited because they heard that the dishes had been washed in a slop pan, though this proved to be a mistake. Such occurrences emphasize the necessity for properly predisposing the mind, and for removing unfavorable suggestion, if digestion is to proceed properly.

Mental States and the Stomach.—The typical example of the influence of the mind on the digestive tract is to be found in the experiences of Flaubert, the French novelist, while writing "Madame Bovary." When he was writing the scene in which he describes the effects of the arsenic which Madame Bovary takes, he himself suffered from practically all the symptoms due to the drug. In order to describe it faithfully he had studied it carefully. He had the pains, the vomiting, the burning feeling and even the garlicky, metallic taste in his mouth. Such an incident is extremely exceptional, yet its possibility is recognized, and it illustrates how sensitive some people are to the action of mental states upon the body, and how large a role a strongly excited imagination can play in producing definite physical symptoms. There are many more such realistic imaginations than we have, perhaps, been inclined to suspect. It is over these particularly that the psychotherapeutist can exert his influence by helping to modify the cause of their symptoms, the mental attitude which exists, rather than by trying to change the symptoms which are only effects, for diseases must, as far as possible, be treated in their causes.

Disgust and Disturbance of Digestion.—Max Müller's story, told in his book on "Language," to show how language might have been a human invention from imitation of natural sounds, illustrates the influence of an unfavorable state of mind in disturbing digestion. An Englishman, traveling in China, fearful lest he should not be able to obtain food that he cared for, because of his lack of knowledge of the language of the country, was rather surprised on his first day's journey into the interior, to be served with a stew made of some kind of dark meat that tasted very well indeed and with which he was so much pleased that he asked for a second helping. Just as he was about to eat the second portion, he thought it well to ask the waiter what sort of meat it was, as he wished to be able to obtain the same kind at other places. Calling the waiter to him, he said, pointing to the dish of meat with a questioning tone, "Quack, quack?" The waiter at once shook his head and said, "Ugh! bow wow!" The Englishman pushed the second portion away and got up from the table.

Under the same circumstances nearly everybody would feel the same qualmishness—at least all who had been brought up according to our Western notions. Reason has little or nothing to do with it. It is a question of feeling. The dog is much more cleanly in its habits than the hog, but we in the West are used to the idea of eating hog-meat just as they in the East are used to eating dog-meat. The objection, of course, might be urged that the difference between the hog and the dog is that we do not eat carnivorous but only herbivorous animals. But the slop-fed hogs from the neighborhood of our large cities, constituting a goodly portion of those brought to market, eat meat quite ravenously. They certainly are not exclusively herbivorous. There is no {244} principle behind our objection to dog meal then—only the unfamiliarity of the idea of eating it.

The treatment of patients with digestive disturbances requires a careful analysis of the conditions of mind towards foods. If prejudice exists with regard to certain foods, there will be no relish for them, and unless these prejudices can be removed, the foods either will not be taken, though they represent important nutritional elements, or else they must be taken in such small quantities and digested with so much consciousness of their presence and such difficulty as to be a disturbing factor for health. Persuasion, the custom of the country, habit, training, mean much for this modification of mental attitude.

Custom and Food.—In recent years many parts of animals, not generally eaten before, have come to be consumed with a relish because of the removal of prejudices against them. It might be thought that organs like the kidney, the essential function of which is excretory, and through which so much of the offensive waste products of the body pass, could not be a relished article of food. But it has become quite a dainty. The liver, owing to the peculiar nature of its function, its very special flavor, and the staining with bile, might be expected to be objectionable. It is not, but, strange to say, a third organ of the abdominal cavity, the spleen, which has none of the external objectionable features of kidney or liver, is not yet eaten, and most people would probably find it rather difficult to eat it. This difficulty would result, not

143

because of anything in the organic substance itself, but because of the lack of accustomedness to it. There are a number of people who now have trained themselves to eat it. Such apparently impossible portions of the animal as the intestines, even those of the hog, are eaten with relish by a great many people, though there are others who have never been able to get used to them. The dainties of some peoples are utterly repulsive to others. The French like brains and other special portions of animals that are not much eaten by Anglo-Saxons. Fried brains in black butter sauce are enough to turn the stomach of some people by the very thought of it, though it is a highly prized dish in the south of France.

In Italy most visitors eat snail soup with relish before they know what it is. It seems to be a special kind of gumbo soup. Down at Marseilles, gourmets occasionally eat angle-worms and find them to be a very appetizing dish. In all of these things the question of relish and peaceful, happy digestion depends entirely on the attitude of mind. The first men who ate eels must have been looked upon with considerable suspicion by their neighbors as viper eaters, and probably they themselves were not comfortable over the feat. It has been said that the first man who ever swallowed an oyster performed as great a feat as any of our important inventors or discoverers.

Gastric Antipathies.—To the great majority of mankind the idea of eating horseflesh is repulsive. Numbers of people in various parts of Europe have found, however, that after the initial repugnance is conquered, it is quite as pleasant to eat as cow's meat. To my taste, at least, it is much more palatable than venison or bear meat. At the beginning, its sweetish taste has a curious reflex effect. Taken in connection with the thought that this is horse meat, the taste is apt to produce a sensation of nausea. This is readily overcome, though the first time it is necessary to keep constantly inhibiting {245} the mind from acting unfavorably upon the stomach during the course of eating and digestion. Custom, I learned from many, soon made it quite as savory as beef.

Food Varieties and the Mind.—How easy it may be to overcome many prejudices in the matter of food digestion under the stress of necessity and the influence of example, was well illustrated during the siege of Paris. The Parisians, though a most delicate people in the matter of eating, were able to accommodate themselves to the conditions, and practically every kind of animal was eaten with a relish. Before the siege, to most of them it would have seemed quite impossible, that they should sit down with complacency to the dishes which afterwards were so appetizing. At the beginning there was a definite attempt to conceal the eating of rats, mice, cats and dogs under various names, and by various modes of preparation. But it was not long before there was an end of this pretense. The animals in the zoological garden proved a veritable life-saving store of meat. Every one of them was eaten, people were glad to get them, and paid high prices for them. Camel steaks, elephant cutlets, lion and tiger stews, appeared under their own names, even at the banquets of the wealthy.

What is true of the mental attitude for meats influencing not only the relish for them, but their digestion, is also true for many vegetables. There are unfavorable suggestions in the minds of many with regard to the supposed indigestibility of potatoes, turnips, carrots, beans and occasionally with regard to tomatoes, lettuce, or the like. A few definite physiological idiosyncrasies against these vegetables, or certain of them, do actually exist. The attitude of mind, however, is largely responsible for the discomfort that occurs after the consumption of most of them. Patients who ought to consume more starchy substances, or whose bowels need the residual materials that are contained in these vegetables, for the sake of their effect upon peristalsis, should be persuaded to take these vegetables, first in small quantities and then in gradually increasing amounts. Many of them can thus be brought to a diet at once more nutritious and more likely to help out intestinal function. Their objection to them is usually but a fancy.

Genuine Food Idiosyncrasies.—There are certain genuine idiosyncrasies with a physiological basis which prevent the taking of certain kinds of food, or cause disturbance if they are taken, but these are rare. Their presence should never be considered as demonstrated by subjective signs alone for these are eminently fallacious. In certain cases, however, so rare as to be almost always curiosities in medical practice, there are definite objective symptoms of the idiosyncrasy. These consist of urticarial rashes, tendencies to vomiting, or diarrhea, or both. Sometimes these result from the most bland and nutritious of foods. I have notes of the cases of two children—whose father could not eat eggs without vomiting—and to whom fresh eggs fed at the age of two and three years, always produced this same effect. Even small portions of egg would cause it. It mattered not how the egg was prepared, nor even whether it was carefully concealed in custard or in cake provided there was a certain amount of it, the food eaten with it would be vomited. There are many such idiosyncrasies for shell fish, cheese, and such fruits as strawberries, pineapples, pomegranates and the like, but they are demonstrated by objective signs. But by far the greater number of food dislikes are entirely {246} subjective and the subjective feelings can probably always be overcome by habit and training.

Food Dislikes.—*Milk.*—Nothing makes more clear the absolute dominion of the mind over the stomach than the likes and dislikes of people for various kinds of milk. Most Americans can take cow's milk with good relish, though there are a few to whom it is distasteful. In this country we have not had much experience with the milk of other animals. Even goat's milk is not commonly used. The very thought of taking it disturbs many people, and to take it with other food would almost surely produce disturbance of digestion. I have seen people while traveling quite upset over the discovery that goat's milk had been put into their tea or coffee. Mare's milk is commonly used in some parts of Europe and in many parts of Asia, but it would be quite impossible to most of our people. Sheep's milk is used in some places. Ass's milk is commonly used in parts of Asia and may be obtained in Spain and is said to be less likely to disagree with children in summer than cow's milk. Most American mothers would rather not hear of it.

The same thing is true of the milk products. Some people find certain kinds of cheese quite out of the question though other people relish them. It requires special training, not of stomach but of mind, to enable one to eat certain cheese, though once the habit has been acquired such articles are delicious. It is only in recent years that some forms of cheese with greenish tints have become popular in America. To serve them at a dinner a generation ago disgusted many people. Now a dinner does not seem complete without them.

The beverages of various countries illustrate this same principle. The wines the Spaniards care for are not palatable to the Italians, and *vice versa*. Beer, as the result of familiarity, is now drunk everywhere in Europe, but when it was first introduced into Italy from Germany, it was considered impossible to understand how anybody could take it and pretend that its taste was pleasant. The question is said to have been once asked of one of the Congregations at Rome whether it was permissible to take beer on fast days. The Cardinals who tasted it declared that not only did it seem to them permissible but that it was a mortification to drink it and therefore it was proper Lenten exercise.

Eggs.—Many people have a supposed natural repugnance for eggs which they are sure indicates that these are not good for them. As a result, the physician gets all sorts of stories with regard to the supposed effects of eggs. One person tells you that more than two eggs a day makes him bilious. Another will tell you that they are too heavy for him. A third will tell you that they are distinctly constipating. A fourth will tell you that they produce a tendency to diarrhea. Here, as with regard to milk, the experience of the tuberculosis sanatoria has shown that there are but few people who cannot, when properly persuaded and when eggs are given in various forms, take from four to six eggs in the day without injury, and even without inconvenience. In these cases, it is largely a matter of mental attitude towards the food. In many instances, it will be found that the disinclination began in some experience in childhood when an egg was not very good, or when it was served insufficiently cooked, or when, perhaps, eggs always cooked one way were made a staple of the diet for a considerable period. There are over one hundred {247} ways of cooking eggs and this variety of preparation will often make them palatable, and nearly always digestible.

Over and over again I have seen people who had thought that eggs made them bilious, and who accordingly had for long refused to eat them, put in circumstances (from tuberculosis, diabetes, or obesity) where eggs had to form a considerable portion of the diet. Then there was no difficulty about eating and digesting eggs. In three cases in my experience patients with an objection they thought constitutional, developed glycosuria, and then nearly all their desserts were custards, and eggs became a standing dish in their daily diet. In every case not only was there no trouble, but they got to like the eggs and wondered why they should ever have had any prejudice against them. Two of the patients were women, the third a man who had not touched eggs for many years. His wife's comment was: "Eggs always made him bilious when he did not take them, but now that he is taking them freely they no longer make him bilious."

Mental Changes and Digestion.—The change that has come over the public mind with regard to sour milk is a typical illustration of how much a difference in the mental attitude towards a food product may mean for its satisfactory consumption by many people. Sour milk, though many farmers and working people thought it a pleasant acid beverage, was for long looked upon as a product fit at most to be fed to the pigs, if, indeed, there might not be question even of the advisability of this. Only the very poor who craved the nutritious value there was in it, continued to take it to any extent. Even if the milk still tasted sweet, but broke when it went into the tea, that was enough to make it quite impossible for many sensitive stomachs.

Lactic Acid as a Bactericide.—Then came Metchnikoff's announcement that his studies showed sour milk to be an extremely valuable food material, but much more than that, an important auxiliary for the lessening of microbic life in the intestines. He seemed to be able to demonstrate that a great many bacteria, whose products, absorbed from the intestines, hastened that process of deterioration in the tissues that we call old age, were inhibited when sour milk or lactic acid bacteria were present. The general health of the person who took sour milk was, as a consequence, much better. Not only this, but processes of deterioration being lessened, prolonged life and even old age could be promised to those who drank sour milk in sufficient quantities. Metchnikoff had been brought to the study of this question by what he had seen on the Steppes of Russia. Among the nomad tribes a principal part of whose diet consists of soured mare's milk, he found a large proportion of very old people. In looking for the reason for this disproportionate longevity, he came to the conclusion that the sour milk had something to do with it. Then laboratory observations and experiments as to the influence of the bacillus, that causes the souring of the milk, on the growth of other bacteria, and especially such bacteria as are usually found in the human digestive tract, seemed to show that the lactic bacteria had a strong inhibitory effect on nearly all the pathologic flora of the intestines.

As the result of these studies, all the world is now quite willing to take its share of sour milk. We no longer hear the complaint that uncomfortable feelings in the digestive tract are the result of taking milk that was a little sour.

{248}

Since this doctrine of Metchnikoff's has come to be popularly known, fewer patients have insisted that they could not take milk in such quantities as the physician thought desirable for them. Before that, a persuasion with regard to the ease with which milk becomes contaminated with microbes, and the dread that it might thus be a source of disease, or at least of disturbance of digestion, made it very difficult of digestion for many people. Now that they have a good authority who insists that, even if it should become somewhat soured in the ordinary way, this, far from making it a pathological article of diet, rather adds to its value from a therapeutic standpoint, has changed the attitude of mind of these people.

We need a similar feeling with regard to eggs in order that they may be eaten by many people who now refuse them because they fear the possible evil results of taking even a slightly tainted egg. Our recent pure food investigations have shown that the bakers in our large cities have been for many years using canned eggs, and that these would be quite impossible of consumption except disguised as they are in the midst of baker's products. Sometimes these eggs have been kept for several months before being canned. All the cold storage eggs that cannot be disposed of otherwise are thus treated. In spite of the common use of these canned eggs by a large proportion of the city population no serious results have come from them. The change that comes over eggs in time does not apparently spoil their nutritive quality, but only disturbs their taste. The main element in the change is the production of hydrogen sulphide. This gas has a very unpleasing odor, but its presence is not of pathological significance. This gas is a common ingredient in those mineral waters that are known as sulphur waters, and that have a reputation for curing many forms of digestive disturbance, especially chronic cases of nervous indigestion. What is true of sour milk, then, would seem to be true of eggs that have been, to some degree, spoiled, and at least no serious results may be

145

expected from them. If serious results were to be expected, we should have had many evil reports of them in recent years. Whether considerations of this kind will help patients, who need to get over qualminess with regard to eggs, because they are always suspicious lest they should not be fresh, will depend a good deal on the suggestive value of such information as presented by the physician.

Another Organic Acid.—Sauerkraut has shared the fate of sour milk, and because of its acid bacteria has been accepted by Metchnikoff as an ally. Yet sauerkraut used to be thought quite out of the question for invalids, especially those suffering from digestive disturbances. I recall the case of an old German shoemaker who had lived very much on sauerkraut when he was a young man and then, having made money in the manufacture of shoes, had not had much of it for thirty years, pleading with me, when he was old and it was rather hard to get anything to stay on his stomach, that he should be allowed to have sauerkraut. On the principle that what a man craves is usually what does him good, I allowed it. The physician with whom I was in consultation was perfectly sure there would be trouble, and the family were confident that his physicians evidently had given up all hope and were quite ready to yield to his caprices and let him take anything that he cared for. He not only took the sauerkraut without any trouble, though I must confess to some misgivings myself (for I am of those who unfortunately do not care for it and, therefore, {249} was prejudiced), but after having eaten a large plateful of sauerkraut twice a day for several days, he began to crave other things that would not stay down before, retained them well, digested them without difficulty, and got over that attack of indigestion and lived for several years afterwards. His own mental attitude was a better index than our supposed knowledge, though science has now come to confirm his state of mind.

Bacon and a Change in Suggestion,—Another food material with regard to which there has been a complete change of view in recent years, is bacon and hog products generally. Pork in all forms used to be considered quite indigestible, and was one of the first things that people suffering from indigestion—or the fear of it—eliminated from their diet. Now we know how valuable a food product it is, especially for those inclined to suffer from constipation, or who are under weight. Many people still look surprised when advised to eat it regularly. Here we have a typical example of the change in the mental attitude toward a particular article of food bringing about a corresponding difference as regards not only the appetite for it, but also its digestibility. Many persons, who used to have no appetite for breakfast, now find that after eating a crisp piece or two of bacon, they develop an appetite for other foods. Bacon has become a fetish for some people and is considered a help, not a detriment to digestion.

I recall a case in which I had very nearly the same experience with bacon as I related with regard to sauerkraut. The patient was an elderly woman, probably nearly ninety years of age, who, because of a crippling deformity, had not been able to get outside of the house for many years. She sat in a wheel chair, transported herself from one end of an apartment to another, spent most of her time by the window, but was very helpful in many little things about the house and occupied her hands with knitting and sewing. In spite of her condition, she was cheerful, pleasant, happy, and all her life had had a good digestion, her only trouble being a tendency to asthma as she grew old. I came back to the city after a summer vacation to find that she was not expected to live because nothing would stay on her stomach. She was sinking, and the end seemed not far off. I was asked to see her more because I had been her regular physician for some years, and it was thought that it would console her to see me than with any real hope of betterment. It had been extremely hot weather and this seemed to be an unfortunate circumstance. At my visit, I asked her if there was anything that she cared for. She shook her head and yet there seemed a hesitancy. I urged her to tell me if there was anything that she wanted, but only after considerable urging did she venture to say that there was something, only that she knew that she could not have it. Putting her thumb on the top of her little finger, she said, "Oh, I would like so much to have just a teenie-weenie bit of bacon." I said that she should certainly have it. Then taking courage, she asked if she could not have a little cabbage with it. I said, "Certainly." Her friends thought that it was just a yielding to one of the last wishes of an invalid with the idea that nothing could much harm her, since she was so near the end. She had eaten cabbage and bacon all her life; she ate it again with a relish, and in spite of the heat kept it down and digested it well. She had bacon and cabbage next day, and for several days; she gradually got strong and lived several more years of her happy contented life.

{250}

CHAPTER II

INDIGESTION AND UNFAVORABLE STATES OF MIND

Indigestion is the characteristic disease of our time. There are few men or women over thirty who have not suffered from it. The working classes are spared the most, but with the frequent suggestions in the newspapers and the introspection which has become so common, indigestion is often complained of even among them. Sedentary occupations, involving mental work and little physical effort, seem especially to predispose to some form of indigestion. Few of those who live what is called the intellectual life escape suffering from some of its symptoms. Not infrequently men have been hale and hearty specimens of muscular manhood when they took up some profession which compels them to be indoors, yet before long, they begin to complain of discomfort after eating, of tendencies to constipation, of headaches, of depression, of incapacity for mental effort after meals, and all these symptoms are attributed to the almost universal disease, indigestion.

It is possible for the general attitude of mind to have a great effect on digestive processes, and the symptom-complex which is called indigestion, or dyspepsia, is probably much more dependent on the mind than on any other factor. In many cases it is primarily due to over-concentration of attention on digestion. In others it is due to over-occupation with business, worry, or serious thought at times when the digestive processes need all the energy. In many cases so-called dyspepsia is due to an unfavorable state of mind toward digestive processes in general, because of unfavorable auto-suggestion. Normally, stomachic sensations reach our consciousness only under special circumstances. When, however, much attention is paid to them, even the slight sensations that occur with normal digestion may rise above the threshold of consciousness and become subjects of solicitude. If they do so, then the increased attention likely to be paid to them surely interferes with function and changes what may be merely physiological into pathological processes.

Disease Suggestions.—An unfortunate state of the public mind with regard to indigestion in general has been cultivated by many publications on the subject. People dread its occurrence, and fear that the first sign of discomfort in their gastric region is a signal of the beginning of a progressive affection. They fear the worst, and the consequence is a reaction quite out of proportion to the gravity of the ailment. So much has been said particularly of mistakes in diet that just as soon as they feel, or often rather think they feel, the first symptom of beginning dyspepsia they begin to study how to modify their diet so as to prevent its progress. They begin to eliminate various supposedly indigestible foods. Usually among the first things that are greatly reduced in quantity, or are entirely eliminated, are the fats and certain of the starchy vegetables. Because of expressions heard and read as to its harmfulness, the fearful ones also are usually timorous about taking fluid at meal times. As this is about the only time when they are likely to take fluid, unless it be summer, they soon suffer for lack of it. Eating only food that {251} leaves little residue and taking insufficient fluid leads to constipation. This reacts still further to disturb digestion, and to interfere with appetite.

This leads to further reduction in the amount and variety of food, with the consequence that insufficient nutrition to supply energy for bodily needs is taken. The digestive system gives up to the body as much as it possibly can, not only of the food materials to be consumed, but of its own substance. Thus it weakens its own vitality, with a lessening of appetite and of digestive power. Hence, a vicious circle of change is instituted, the consequences of which are easy to see. After a time the patient is taking only the blandest foods, constipation has become an important element in the case, and the mind is constantly occupied with solicitude over the digestion and the choice of materials at meals.

Contrary Suggestion and Digestion.—Hudson, in "The Law of Mental Medicine," insisted on the necessity for not suggesting to children the possibility of indigestion of various substances, for that is almost sure to disturb digestive functions. Children sometimes hear the remark that father or mother cannot take a certain article of food because it disagrees with them. The imitative faculty of the child is sure to be aroused, with the consequence that this particular food is not eaten with relish nor given a fair show for digestion, and will be the source of some stomach disturbance. Not infrequently substances thus spoken of are among those that are especially likely to do children good, such as milk or eggs, or occasionally butter. The harm done by the remark may, therefore, even be serious, for these foods should constitute a large proportion of the child's diet. Indeed, an excellent prophylactic in the matter of indigestion is to prevent as far as possible all conversation at table about the indigestibility of food. Unfortunately, this has, in late years particularly, become a favorite subject of table conversation.

Transferred Feelings.—Professor Cohnheim called attention to the fact that many uncomfortable feelings are likely to be mistranslated because they are referred to organs with which there is nothing wrong. Whenever this function is hampered in any way, there are many uncomfortable feelings associated with the digestion of food. The custom has been to refer the origin of all these to the stomach. Cohnheim thinks that it is much more likely that they really originate in the intestines, though the rule has been to take the patient's feelings as an indication and to treat the stomach. It is not an unreasonable thing for patients to be deceived as to the exact location of discomfort. Even in so acute a process as toothache it is possible to mistake the particular tooth that is giving trouble, and, as dentists know, a perfectly quiescent tooth is sometimes blamed for pain that is coming from another. Fillings have been removed, teeth have been treated, good teeth have been extracted, because patients insisted on the significance of their feelings in such cases. The stomach must not always be blamed. Sometimes the only source of supposed gastric discomfort is the constipation present which is usually easy to relieve.

Gastric Reflexes.—While the mind may serve to disturb digestion and produce gastric discomfort by over-attention, there are many reflexes that center in the digestive tract, the origin of which may be in distant organs. Fright often produces a sensation as of cold at the pit of the stomach. Looking down from a height has the same effect in some persons. Discordant noises {252} have the same effect on people of sensitive hearing and certain reactions to touch may be similarly reflected. There are a number of affections which produce uncomfortable reflex sensations in the gastric region. This is the hypochondrium of the olden time. Whenever feelings were complained of, for which there was no actual basis in the hypochondriac region, it came to be spoken of as hypochondriasis, a word that has an innuendo of imaginativeness about it. Dr. Head's studies with regard to the transfer of sensations from one portion of the body to the other, show us that there is a good physical reason in reflexes for many of these complaints. An explanation of this to patients will often relieve their minds greatly and make their discomfort seem much less serious. Dr. Head said:

With orchitis or prostatitis, we also occasionally find that the patient complains of a pain at the epigastrium, representing the stomach area. This is put down to hypochondriasis and if it occurs in a woman as a consequence of ovaritis, she is said to be hysterical. But this phenomena is no more "hysterical," whatever that may mean, than is the reference of the pain and the tenderness of an aching tooth to the back of the head or the shoulder.

This is the phenomenon I have been accustomed to call "generalization" of visceral pain and tenderness, and is of such common occurrence as to form a very important factor in the clinical picture of many diseases.

The order in which generalization takes place, leads one to speak of the relative "specific resistance" of the centers for the sensory impulses from various organs. No very definite rule can be laid down to govern every case, but each case must be considered on its merits. However, the area which appears most easily on a woman, as a secondary affection, is the tenth dorsal; then, perhaps the sixth dorsal, or inframammary, and then the various gastric areas, beginning first with the ensiform or seventh dorsal. In a man the tenth dorsal appears rather less readily while the ensiform appears with great ease.

Affections of other organs within the abdomen may produce like reflexes. A chronic appendicitis, for instance, will often be reflected in the stomach area. So will the presence of gallstones, or of disturbances of the biliary mucosa. Loose kidney often produces stomach reflexes. Any disturbance of the intestinal function will produce gastric irritation and inhibition of digestion. Most of the other primary conditions are more serious. Often the patient is aware of their existence, and it is a relief to him to find that the stomach symptoms are not the index of further pathological development, but only reflex conditions. This of itself does much to make the condition more bearable.

Patients who are suffering from symptoms of indigestion often have areas of their skin surface that are at least very sensitive, if not actually tender. They feel the pressure of their clothing over a particular portion of the body, usually on the left side of the abdomen somewhat above, though at times also below the umbilicus. Though not painful, as a rule, it is decidedly uncomfortable and produces a constant desire to loosen the clothing, or lift it from the part. Mere loosening, it is soon found, does no good, because the clothing continues to touch the skin and it is not the constriction or pressure but the contact that produces the discomfort. Sometimes there is a distinct lesion of the stomach. This cutaneous hyperasthesia may, indeed, rise to the height of extreme tenderness in cases of gastric ulcer, or the like. But there is no {253} doubt that a certain amount of this sensation is present with all functional disturbances of the stomach and that the reflex sensitiveness of superficial nerves is only what might be expected from what we now know of this subject.

Discomfort and Digestion.—Just as certain food materials disagree because of the state of mind, so certain feelings in the gastric region, even in the skin surface, sometimes disturb digestion and lead to changes of the diet unwarranted by the condition. Patients conclude that, if the skin is so tender, then the underlying organs, the disturbance of which causes this tenderness, must be in a serious condition. For these patients the explanation of the present state of our knowledge as to reflex disturbance of sensory nerves will be of therapeutic value. They must be taught that pain is reflected from one nerve branch to another, and is not communicated by continuity of tissue, or by sympathetic affection from the stomach mucous membrane through the stomach wall, and then from the abdominal wall to the skin surface. This knowledge will prove reassuring.

Division of Energy.—After this mental occupation with digestion itself, which by consuming nervous energy lessens the amount available for digestive purposes, probably the most common factor in the production of indigestion is the concentration of mind on serious subjects, while digestion is proceeding. An old English maxim is that some people have not enough brains to run their liver and their business. The liver in old-time pathology was considered the most important of the abdominal organs and was taken by metathesis for them all. Most of us have only a limited amount of vital energy and, usually, we can accomplish only one thing well at a time. If we try to do intellectual work while digestion is going on, both the intellectual work and the digestion suffer. If we persist in attempting to do both, we will surely disturb the digestive organs and we may bring about grave neurotic disturbances in the central nervous system. We may be able for a time to accomplish the two things at the same time, but it will not be long before evil results will be seen. Nervous, high-strung people should be reminded of Lincoln's anecdote of the little steamboat on the Mississippi which had not steam enough to blow its whistle and run its paddle wheels at the same time, so that whenever the engineer wanted to blow the whistle he stopped the boat.

Indeed, much of the indigestion that we see is due to this dissipation of energy through the attempt to do two things at the same time. Those who live the intellectual life are the most frequent sufferers. Worries and anxieties that are allowed to trouble the mind during digestion time are sure to disturb digestion eventually because they use up energy that is needed for physical purposes.

A change of environment that takes us away from the ordinary cares of life, is often sufficient to make all the difference between ease of digestion and extremely uncomfortable dyspepsia. By worry the mind apparently becomes short-circuited on itself and uses up a large amount of the available energy in nervous impulses that do not find their way outside the central nervous system at all, but are used in disturbing associated nerve cells. Just as soon as a change of scene and occupation calls for a different set of thoughts and other feelings, energy is released for work outside the central nervous system itself, digestion begins to improve, and in a comparatively short time what seemed to be a serious gastric disturbance, disappears almost completely.

{254}

Lack of Sleep Repair.—In my own experience one of the most characteristic stigmata of these cases of indigestion which are due to exhaustion through other channels of vital energy, is that they feel much better in the evening than in the morning. They are, therefore, tempted to stay up late and so do not get the necessary rest. Their excuse for late hours is that they need recreation. To that excuse I have no objection. They do need more recreation; they need more hours during which their minds are absolutely free from business cares; but these hours must not be taken from their sleep, for they need rest even more than recreation.

Worries and Irritations During Meals.—The presence of worries or irritation during meals or shortly after, as well as unfavorable states of mind towards digestion itself, and occupation of mind with serious affairs during digestion, are likely to be sources of serious disturbance of digestion. A fright, a fit of anger, nagging, irritation, or any disturbing emotions, may hamper digestion. An experiment that is sometimes performed in the physiological laboratory on the cat nicely illustrates this. If the laboratory cat is fed some dainty that it likes, mixed with bismuth in order that its stomach and intestines may be made opaque to the x-rays, and then be examined by means of the fluoroscope, the peristaltic processes of digestion by which food is mixed in the stomach, passed out into the intestines, and by which intestinal digestion is stimulated, may be seen to go on very interestingly. If, now, the cat is made to arch its back, and manifest the usual signs of extreme irritation, the process of digestion is interrupted, and will not be resumed till some time after the cat quiets down. The lesson is obvious.

CHAPTER III

PSYCHIC TREATMENT OF DIGESTIVE CONDITIONS

If discouragement and solicitude make a healthy stomach digest imperfectly, the same mental factors will play an even more serious role with a diseased stomach. Certainly without the mind's aid, there can be little hope of such a reactive vital resistance as will enable the organ to recover from the organic ailment.

So many cases of indigestion are due to mental persuasion alone, that after a time there is danger that the physician may be over-confident in his diagnosis, and may occasionally overlook serious organic lesions. Before attempting psychotherapy in these cases, the physician must assure himself that no organic lesion is present. This is particularly true for cancer in the middle-aged and ulcer in young women. At times these lesions are latent except for certain vague digestive symptoms. After careful consideration it is generally possible to make a definite decision, and then the indications are clear. Even when an organic lesion is present, a modification of the mental attitude will often be of great service to the patient. Suggestion will even make a cancer patient gain in weight, though one must be careful of that very fact because the apparent improvement may occasion delay until the case becomes inoperable.

Once the presence of these serious organic lesions of the stomach can be {255} excluded, the bringing of influence to bear on the patient's mind for the improvement of his digestion is indicated. It is true that there are certain reflex disturbances of the digestive tract consequent upon affections of other abdominal organs. Chronic lesions of the appendix may produce stomach symptoms as will also pathological conditions of the biliary tract. A floating kidney, various affections of the pelvic organs, especially in women, and of the urinary organs in men are sometimes said to produce seriously depressing effects upon the stomach. Where this occurs, the first indications undoubtedly are to put the patient into as good condition as possible before making any decision. Where a lesion of the stomach itself exists suggestions with regard to the increase of diet may do harm. They will not do harm in the reflex conditions, and so patients can be brought into better physical condition. As a consequence of this, their symptoms in other organs will often disappear. In case the symptoms do not disappear the patients are in better condition to stand and react from operative intervention.

Before concluding as to the character of the stomach symptoms we must make sure that other important organs are not affected. Most cases of tuberculosis begin with stomach symptoms, which often make their appearance before there is cough or any definite localizing symptom of the disease. Often there is only a disturbance of pulse, and perhaps a slightly increased range of temperature. If the patient has been exposed to tuberculosis, a careful investigation of the lungs should be made. Any disturbance of the liver or pancreas (especially cancer) will almost surely give rise to stomach symptoms. Latent cancer in any part of the body, however, will, by its depressing toxemia, produce loss of appetite, consequent loss of weight, and a number of symptoms that are sure to be referred to the stomach. I have seen cancer of the prostate, without disturbing urination, produce such symptoms for months before it was recognized. I have seen cancer of the rectum in a comparatively young woman treated as piles, without an examination, the development of the piles being attributed to the gastro-intestinal symptoms which were consequent upon the presence of the cancer.

MENTAL INFLUENCE IN DYSPEPSIA AND INDIGESTION

It is often said that this teaching as to the effect of the mind on digestion and its eminent usefulness for the treatment of dyspeptic conditions, is due to the attention that has been attracted to this subject as a consequence of the prominence of Eddyism, New Thought, Mental Healing, and the like. There are absolutely no good grounds for any such assertion. Here in America, more than twenty-five years ago, before there was any question of the modern mental healing movements, our greatest medical clinician, Dr. Austin Flint, expressed himself very emphatically with regard to mental influence over digestion, and to solicitude of mind as one of the most frequent etiological factors in dyspepsia.

Dr. Flint was thoroughly scientific in his medical observations, was no seeker after notoriety, and he was reading his paper before the older physicians of the period, and all of those who took part in that first meeting of the New York Medical Association strove to make their papers of scientific value. His words, then, must carry great weight:

{256}

Dyspepsia formerly prevailed chiefly among those who adopted, to a greater or less extent, the foregoing maxims . It was comparatively rare among those who did not live in accordance with dietetic rules. The affection is much less prevalent now than heretofore, because these maxims are much less in vogue. The dyspeptics of the present day are chiefly those who undertake to exemplify more or less of these maxims. It seems to me, therefore, a fair inference, that dyspepsia may result from an attempt to regulate diet by rules which have for their object the prevention of the affection which they actually produce. It is to be added that an important causative element involved in the practical adoption of these rules is the attention thereby given to digestion. It is by introspection and constant watchfulness of the functions of the stomach, that the mind exerts a direct influence in the causation of this affection.

149

Dietetic Rules of a Former Day.—In order to make definite just what were the views of the olden times which he deprecates, he stated them briefly and forcibly:

The views generally entertained, at the time to which I have referred, largely by physicians and almost universally by non-medical sanitarians, may be summed up in a few maxims as follows: Eat only at stated periods, twice or thrice daily, and never between meals, no matter how great may be the desire for food. Never eat late in the evening or shortly before bedtime. In the choice of articles of diet, carefully select those which reason and personal experience have shown to be best digested; and never yield to the weakness of eating any article of food simply because it is acceptable to the palate. In order to avoid the temptation of overeating, let the articles of food be coarse rather than attractive, and eschew all the devices of the cuisine. Always leave the table hungry. Study personal idiosyncrasies, and never indulge in kinds of food which, although wholesome for most persons, are injurious to a few who are peculiarly organized. With reference to this last maxim, bear in mind that "what is one man's meat is another man's poison." In order to secure, as effectually as possible, a proper restriction in the quantity of food, it was recommended by some physicians and to some extent practiced, that every article be carefully weighed at meal times, and that a certain quantity by weight be never exceeded. Vegetarianism or Grahamism was advocated and practiced by many. Total abstinence from drink was considered by a few as a good sanitary measure, compelling the body to derive the needed fluids exclusively from fruits, vegetables, and other solid articles of diet. Restriction in the amount of drink, as far as practicable with regard to the power of endurance, was very generally deemed important, so as not to dilute the gastric juice.

When to his question, "Do you regulate your diet," the patient answered promptly and often emphatically in the affirmative, Dr. Flint insisted always: "This is a good reason for your having dyspepsia; I never knew a dyspeptic get well who undertook to regulate his diet." When the patient asks then, "How am I to be guided," the reply is, "Not by theoretical views of alimentation and indigestion, no matter how much they appear to be in accord with physiological and pathological doctrines, but by the appetite, the palate and common sense." He then goes on to answer certain other objections that patients are wont to urge, and says:

But the patient will be likely to say, "Am I not to be guided by my own experience and avoid articles of food which I have found to disagree with my digestion?" The answer is, that personal experience in dietetics is extremely fallacious. An article of diet which may cause inconvenience of indigestion to-day may be followed by a sense of comfort and will be readily digested to-morrow. A variety of circumstances may render the digestion of any article of food taken at a {257} particular meal labored or imperfect. As a rule articles which agree with most persons do not disagree with any, except from casual or accidental circumstances, and from the expectation, in the mind of the patient, that they will disagree. Without denying that there are dietetic idiosyncrasies, they are vastly fewer than is generally supposed; and, in general, it is fair to regard supposed idiosyncrasies as purely fanciful. Patients not infrequently cherish supposed idiosyncrasies with gratification. The idea is gratifying to egotism, as evidence that Providence has distinguished them from the common herd by certain peculiarities of constitution.

Dietetic Instructions.—Finally Dr. Flint has a series of instructions for those suffering from indigestion:

Do not adopt the rule of eating only at stated periods, twice or thrice daily. Be governed in this respect by appetite; and eat whenever there is a desire for food. Eat in the evenings or at bedtime, if food be desired. *Insomnia is often attributable to hunger* . In the choice of articles of diet, be distrustful of past personal experience, and consider it to be a trustworthy rule that those articles will be most likely to be digested without inconvenience which are most acceptable to the palate. As far as practicable, let the articles of diet be made acceptable by good cooking. As a rule, the better articles of food are cooked, the greater the comfort during digestion. Never leave the table with an unsatisfied appetite. Be in no haste to suppose that you are separated from the rest of mankind by dietetic idiosyncrasies, and be distrustful of the dogma that another man's meat is a poison to you. Do not undertake to estimate the amount of food which you take. In this respect different persons differ very widely, and there is no fixed standard of quantity, which is not to be exceeded. Take animal and vegetable articles of diet in relative proportions as indicated by instinct. In the quantity of drink, follow nature's indication; namely, thirst. Experience shows abundantly that, with a view of comfortable digestion, there need be no restriction in the ingestion of liquids.

Removal of Solicitude as a Remedial Measure.—Many dyspeptics have no subject that they occupy themselves with more seriously than their digestion, and they thus divert blood needed for digestive purposes as well as nervous energy that would help in it from the stomach to the brain, in order to exercise surveillance over the process. As has been well said, "Probably much more than half of the indigestion is really above the neck." This does not mean that there are not cases that need definite stomachic treatment, or even that patients who have succeeded in functionally disturbing their digestion by thinking over much about it, will not need gastric remedies.

The explanation of the many fads and remedies that *cure* indigestion, real or supposed, is exactly this tendency of the suggestive influence of such remedial measures to lessen the patient's solicitude about digestion. Any change in diet that carries with it the persuasion that for any reason digestion ought to be better, will, because of this, make digestion better. Any habit of taking warm or cold water before meals, or of chewing in a particular way, or of taking a particular kind of food different from what is usually taken—exclusively cereal, uncooked, largely fruit, vegetarian, etc.—will lift the concentration of attention on the digestive process, and so give the stomach a chance to do its work without interference from the brain.

Du Bois has quoted some striking testimony in this matter from Baras, who wrote on the "Gastralgias and Nervous Affections of the Stomach and the Intestines" as early as 1820. Baras had himself been a sufferer from {258} gastric discomfort, fullness after eating, eructations of gas, constipation, and general depression. He consulted most of the distinguished medical practitioners of his time. With one exception they were convinced that he was a sufferer from chronic gastro-enteritis. They added more and more to his concern about his stomach, and furnished him with numerous sources of autosuggestion. In spite of all that they did for him, his condition grew worse and worse, he lost in weight, and was sure that his case was hopeless. He was cured in a single day. His daughter was attacked with consumption, and "in the moment my attention," says Baras, "was centered entirely upon my child, I thought no more of myself, and I was cured."

Brain Workers and Indigestion.—Perhaps the best proof of how necessary it is that people should not continue to occupy their intellect seriously during the time when digestion is going on, is to be found in the frequency with which complaints of indigestion occur in literary folk. The complaints are heard most from literary folk because they are more likely to tell their stories. They have their work, and thoughts of it, always with them. So there is a constant call for nervous and mental activity and for much blood in the brain tissues. This subtracts from the nervous energy necessary for digestion, and makes it impossible to conduct it with that perfection which comes naturally to people who banish all other thoughts and keep their minds free for the pleasures of the table and social intercourse at meal time.

Nervous indigestion is so common among literary folk, teachers and scientific workers, that various causes have been suggested for it. Dr. George Gould, in his "Biographic Clinics," calls attention to it and suggests that the cause is probably the need of properly fitted spectacles. In our own time, when we are much more careful in the matter of eyeglasses, and when most writers and professors wear scientifically adapted glasses, the complaints still continue. The reason is evidently something associated with the almost continuous work that they do. Such people, too, are much more self-conscious than others. They think more about their digestion and what they eat. They often think that they differ from other people and have special idiosyncrasies for food. These thoughts are sure to culminate in nervous indigestion.

Food Faddists.—Literary folk and people who live the intellectual life are very prone to take up with fads of various kinds and find surcease from their sorrows in all sorts of out of the way dietaries, modes of eating, food limitations and specializations. They constitute a majority of the food faddists. Some of them—sure that they should not eat meat—are strenuous vegetarians. Others confine themselves entirely to food the life of which has not been completely destroyed by cooking. They are fruit faddists, nut faddists, milk-product faddists, and the like. Some of them try to persuade the world that it eats too much; others that it eats too frequently. Some of them take but a single real meal a day and have apologies for the other meals. All want to lead people to their particular mode of life, as if all the world had been wrong until they came to set it right. Some want the rest of the world to chew seventy-times-seven before they swallow and to adopt other exaggerations of attention to eating that are quite contrary to instinct, the most precious guide that we have in the matter of food choice and food consumption.

These intellectuals are always improved by their fads, no matter what they {259} may be. The reason is apparent. Their original digestive disturbance was due to over-occupation with intellectual work. Then they began to worry about their digestion and feared that nearly everything they ate would disagree with them. This fear and solicitude still further interfered with digestion. Next they acquired the new fad. They became persuaded that they could eat certain things in certain ways. They no longer disturb their digestion by anxiety about it, but, on the contrary, help it by favorable suggestion. Now under the new regime everything will surely go on well. Besides, they usually learn the lesson of not doing intellectual work close to their meals, and of spacing their work better. They learn to do a daily stint of work and no more. One of the fads that goes with most food fashions is abundant outdoor air. This always does good. Between the favorable mental influence, the lessened work, especially just after meals, and the increased outdoor air they get better and then they attribute it all to their special fad about food. The *"cure"* is due to psychotherapy and common sense, and not in any way to the special fad.

Worry.—Worry of any kind will have the same effect as the over-attention of the literary man or teacher to his work. Anyone who brings his business home with him is likely to suffer and, unless he has a superabundant supply of energy, will impair his digestive function as a consequence of attempting to do business after dinner, perhaps also stealing some of it in before and during breakfast.

PREVENTION AND CORRECTION

The important rule with regard to the mental attitude of the patient toward uncomfortable feelings due to digestion must be, first to correct all other possible sources of the trouble, and only after these have been proved not to be factors in the case, should there be any question of modification of diet. This is just the opposite rule from that which obtains, and by which patients begin to meddle with their diet at the slightest symptom, or supposed symptom, of indigestion. My custom is to tell patients at once that there is probably something else besides their diet at fault. It is not that they eat too much, nor too great a variety, but that perhaps they eat too rapidly. Without reducing their diet, and above all without eliminating supposedly indigestible things from it, there should be formed a habit of eating more slowly. This will usually result in the reduction of the quantity eaten, but the variety of food should be the same, and the patient should not be permitted to limit his diet to a few supposedly bland, unirritating materials. In that event, constipation will assert itself, particularly if there is limitation of the amount of fluid taken.

Longevity of Dyspeptics.—There is one consolation that may be given to nervous dyspeptics, though in the midst of their worst symptoms they may not be sure whether it is a genuine consolation or not. It has been noted that many of those who live to extreme age tell the story of having suffered from nervous dyspepsia in middle-life. Their solicitude about themselves makes them safe against over-indulgences of many kinds in food or drink that might prove hurtful to them. Much of their discomfort is indeed due to the fact that they do not eat quite enough. If they succeed in avoiding the {260} pitfalls of the infectious diseases, and especially tuberculosis during their earlier years, and most of them are likely to because of the great care they take of themselves, they often live to old age. Certainly of two men, one of whom eats very heartily and the other very sparingly, the latter is much the more likely to attain old age. There are those who declare that the valetudinarian life, "half dead and alive," which even Plato satirized nearly 2,500 years ago, ever renews the question as to whether life is worth living or not. It is particularly dyspeptics who seriously discuss this question—yet with all their complaints, they actually do live longer lives.

Pharmaceutic Remedies.—This insistence on the importance of mind in the treatment of indigestion does not imply that tonic remedies, and especially such substances as strychnin, which stimulate appetite and add tone to the muscles of the stomach, should not be used when duly indicated. They are always helpful. Alone, these remedies give but temporary relief and after a short time the system becomes accustomed to them. If prescribed in connection with changes in the patient's habits, and especially such as divert his attention from his digestive tract, and from wrong persuasions as to food taking, the good they accomplish will be lasting. Nervous people usually have an increase of acidity. They are liable to overdo everything, and even the stomach overdoes its acid forming function. For this, alkaline remedies such as rhubarb and soda will do good. But, just as with strychnin, the benefit is but temporary unless the patient's habits and attitude of mind are modified so as to eliminate their solicitude as a constantly disturbing factor.

Circumstantial Suggestions.—There are many changes of habits that are of great value in the treatment of nervous and allied forms of indigestion. These changes often make a great difference in the general health of the patient and thus help to improve digestion. Besides their influence as alteratives, they are valuable from the mental influence which they exercise. It requires a definite exertion of will many times, perhaps, each day to bring about the omission or performance of certain actions, and this act of the will is accompanied by the repeated suggestion that this will cause improvement in the digestion. Many of the cures effected by special diet. Habits of exercise, health resort regimes and the like, owe their efficacy to this accompanying repeated suggestion of acts for the formation of new habits or the breaking of old ones.

Physiological Measures.—There are, of course, certain details with regard to digestion in which the patient's mental attitude needs to be changed by instruction rather than persuasion, by knowledge of physiology rather than by psychology. In the taking of food itself, chewing is, of course, the most important consideration after its good preparation by the cook. If patients are told to chew their food carefully, however, without further directions than this, it will usually be found that they begin to chew their meat a great deal and their vegetables scarcely more than before. It is, however, vegetables that must be chewed particularly. The meat-eating animals bolt their food. They have only cutting and tearing teeth. Their instinct is correct, for the saliva has nothing to do with the digestion of meat, and therefore no chewing is necessary. On the other hand, the vegetable-eating, and especially the grain-eating animals, chew carefully. Most of them are ruminants, that is, after a preliminary thorough chewing of their food, they swallow it, and then {261} afterwards at their leisure bring it up once more into the mouth and chew it again.

Mastication and the Stomach.—If food is not chewed well, and occurs in large masses in the stomach, not only is it not dissolved easily, but the work of passing it out to the intestine is delayed. The reflex which brings about the opening of the stomach and the ejection of food into the intestine is best brought about by the liquefaction of the stomach contents. During the mixing process all the food, as far as possible, becomes fluid and then is passed on. Large pieces of any kind are delayed, however, hamper the emptying of the stomach and interfere with stomach motility. The stomach is only a thin-walled membranous viscus which finds difficulty in dealing with food in lumps. It is different from the stomach of the hen, which, having no teeth, swallows grains of all kinds without chewing, but also by instinct swallows small stones which, in its thick-walled, muscular gizzard, are used for grinding up the food.

Exercise.—The taking of exercise is an important habit that needs to be changed in the case of dyspeptics. Many of those who live a sedentary life, and are much occupied with intellectual or business matters, are almost sure to take little or no exercise. If earlier in life they were accustomed to take much, the lack of it leads to serious disturbances of nutrition. They have formed certain habits as to the amount of food they eat, and these continue, so that they consume more heat-making material than they can use. In the process of dissipating it, there is likely to be much nervous energy wasted, usually to the discomfort of the patient. This is likely to be eventually reflected back to the stomach, with disturbance of appetite and digestion.

We now know that the motor function of the stomach is much more important than its secretory function. Its main purpose is to mix the food and pass it on in small quantities, at intervals, to the intestines. When patients have a sense of uncomfortable fullness in the gastric region after a hearty meal, or of discomfort after the taking of food, especially if much liquid is taken with it, they are prone to attribute these feelings to imperfect secretion not completing digestion as it should, and permitting fermentation with a production of gas and consequent stomach distention. The real reason for their discomfort is not secretory, but motor. It is due to a delay in passing on the food and to stomach distention because the gastric muscle is not in good tone.

People who have been used to taking exercises have their muscular system in good tonic condition. This includes the involuntary muscles, as well as the voluntary, and if they are neglecting air and exercise, the whole muscular system becomes flabby. Hence the uncomfortable sense of distention, because the stomach walls do not contract readily for the expulsion of food. A second important factor is also present—the muscles of the abdomen. Ordinarily they support the abdominal organs without any sense of effort. If by lack of exercise they have diminished in tone, however, when a hearty meal is eaten, the abdominal muscles have to support this additional weight since the stomach itself sags, and the consequence is a feeling of pressure on the left side of the abdomen about the level of the umbilicus. To relieve this feeling the tendency of the patient is almost always to lessen the amount eaten. If he is not distinctly overweight this will do harm rather than good. Instead he {262} needs to take sufficient exercise to tone abdominal muscles and reflexly also tone even involuntary muscles, and with them the gastric muscularis.

Air.—Almost more important than exercise is an abundance of fresh air, and without this muscles soon fail to respond to voluntary or involuntary impulses. If people do not spend two or three hours in the air every day, they are likely to develop an over-sensitive condition in which all nervous sensations are exaggerated. The reason men and women differ so markedly in their reaction to pains, aches and discomforts, is mainly that their habits of being out in the air differ correspondingly. Men are out much and, as a rule, stand discomfort better. Women are out little and are more sensitive to pains and aches. The more a man is out, the less is he likely to notice discomforts and aches that he would otherwise complain about.

Sleep.—Another important factor is the amount of sleep. Over and over again I have found that patients who were beginning to complain of discomfort, which they associated with the word indigestion, were taking too little sleep, and as soon as I persuaded them to add an hour or more to their sleep their gastric symptoms began to improve. It is easy in our large cities to acquire the habit of shortening the hours of rest. This is sometimes done so gradually that the individual scarcely realizes how much he has cut into his sleeping period. Some people who have to get up at seven or half-past seven in the morning go to bed about twelve, but really do not get settled for sleep until nearly one o'clock. Sometimes people read interesting books just before going to bed, or while in bed, and it is nearly two o'clock when they get to sleep.

Many people have the habit of reading themselves to sleep. This may be an excellent way to get rid of bothersome thoughts, provided the reading selected is not of too absorbing a character, and provided also as soon as sleepiness comes its call is heeded. Some write letters late at night. Writing always keeps one awake, though reading may be helpful for sleep. If this abbreviation of sleep becomes habitual, the first organs in the body to set up an objection is the digestive tract. It is one of the hardest worked systems in the body, having to dispose of its quantum of food three times every day, and if the organism does not receive due rest, the digestive tract suffers first. People who get insufficient sleep often have no appetite in the morning, and suffer from uncomfortable feelings in the gastric region. What they are too prone to do is to meddle with their diet, and this practice always does harm.

CHAPTER IV

APPETITE

Two classes of patients come to the physician complaining of lack of appetite. The first and more important class consists of those who are eating too little, who are consequently under weight, and who must be made to eat more. The other class consists of those who eat enough but complain that they do not relish their food. Careful questioning usually elicits sufficient information to enable one to decide that most of these latter are eating too {263} much, or unsuitable food, and at too frequent intervals. They are usually overweight, and there is need to reduce the amount they eat. In both of these classes the physician is tempted to conclude that medicines should form the principal part of the treatment. We have a number of tonics and stimulants that undoubtedly initiate a desire for food, or at least so increase the circulation in the stomach that patients feel much more inclined to eat than they otherwise would. There are a number of remedies, also, the so-called anti-fat group, which produce a disinclination for food.

Power of Mind Over Appetite.—Appetite, whether in deficiency or in excess, is best regulated through the patient's mind. Patients frequently state that they cannot eat more than they do, that they have no inclination for food, and yet, after a little persuasion, they can be made to increase the amount they have been eating, and then that can be gradually raised until they are taking what is for them a normal quantity. There are many things that we swallow without caring for them. Most medicines we not only do not like, but positively dislike. We put them down, they accomplish their purpose, and food will act nearly in the same way. There are few cases where food is positively rejected. Patients can be persuaded to eat more, and after a time will be surprised to find that their desire for food increases with the habit of taking it. On the other hand, patients can be made to see that they are taking too much food really to enjoy its consumption. Their appetites are perpetually cloyed, and to them food has none of the pleasant flavor that exists when it is taken in moderation.

The Will to Eat.—In various parts of this book there is emphasized the necessity for the exercise of the human will in order to aid in the accomplishment of even physical functions. The basis of many nervous symptoms is a lack of sufficient nutrition to steady the nervous system. Some people not only lack will power, but also judgment in the matter of eating; they prefer to err on the side of insufficiency lest they should over-eat. For these people the important remedial measure is to dictate the amount that they shall eat, and gradually to increase it until they are eating enough for their nutritional purposes.

When this advice is given to patients, they are willing to agree that a gain in weight would be good for them, but they cannot understand how they can eat more since they are now eating all they can, or certainly all they care to. Appetite grows by what it feeds on, and increase in appetite is a function of the habit of eating.

But some patients, after having tried the prescription of eating more, are still in the same condition, and find that they cannot put on weight. What is needed in such cases is an inquiry into all the conditions of the daily life, their habits of eating and the amount of time that they take for their meals. They are probably eating one good meal a day, their dinner in the evening—but they confess that the other meals are not satisfactory. If their habits are rearranged, the will to eat does the rest. Sometimes they complain of uncomfortable feelings after eating and this makes them eat less at the next meal. There are various mental elements that disturb the efficacy of the will to eat, consequently these patients do not get on. What they need is emphatic insistence on the necessity for persistent effort in regular eating day after day, meal after meal, and it is not long before improvement comes not {264} only in weight, but also in appetite. I have known patients to gain five or six pounds a week after having tried weeks in vain to gain a single pound.

Sitophobia.—Many people read much of the possibilities of evil in overeating, and they conclude that a limitation of diet would be better for them. After a time some of these people of nervous constitution acquire an actual dread of over-eating and develop what has been called sitophobia, or dread of food. Before anything can be done with them, this dread must be removed. The problem is discussed more fully in the chapter on Weight and Good Feeling, but here it seems necessary to emphasize that it is often quite impossible by ordinary medical means to produce an appetite in these patients. Their mental persuasion with regard to food must first be removed. If it cannot be removed, improvement is usually out of the question. No medicines are sufficiently powerful to overcome a fixed unfavorable idea with regard to food. The same is true as to sleep, or any other natural function—it comes and must go through the mind.

Disturbance of Mind and Its Influence on Appetite.—The basis of the psychotherapy of the digestive tract is the fact that appetite is a function of the state of mind rather than of the state of body. We all know how easy it is to lose the appetite by emotional disturbance. We may come into the house after a brisk walk, when we know that dinner is going to be better than usual, quite ready to anticipate the pleasure we are to have in eating it and with appetite craving that dinner shall not be delayed, we find a telegram announcing the death of a friend or the illness of a relative or some other bad news, and in an instant our appetite has disappeared. It makes no difference to us for hours whether we eat or not. What we eat gives us no satisfaction. It will be taken entirely from a sense of duty and without pleasure and will digest slowly, even if it does not produce discomfort.

Feelings and Appetite.—There is no need for a serious stomach condition to develop, to diminish, or eliminate appetite. The sight of an accident on the street, especially if blood is shed, will entirely take away the appetite of many persons. Now that suicide beneath the wheels of subway trains has become a rather frequent way of going out of life, physicians note that nervous patients who happen to see these sad affairs have no appetite, not alone for the next meal, but sometimes for several days. Some people have no appetite at all if there is a dead body in the house where they live. I have known people who felt it almost a desecration to eat under such circumstances. Even much less than this may serve to diminish appetite. An offensive odor of almost any kind is quite sufficient to take away the appetite of many people. For some the odor of cooking food, if they have been in it for some time, is almost sure to cloy any desire for food.

Cooks suffer from loss of appetite for this reason. The sight of a disagreeable stain on a tablecloth, or of a waiter's thumb in the soup, or of some unpleasant characteristic of the waiter, may be quite enough seriously to disturb the appetite of sensitive people.

We know all this very well, and yet we are prone to think of appetite as something regulated by instinct, and representing the real needs of the organism in its cravings and the limitations of the necessity of food by its satisfaction. In our sophisticated modern life instinct will often fail entirely to fulfill these purposes. Appetite for those who live much indoors is a question of {265} habit and regulation rather than of instinct. It has to be voluntary to a large extent, not only as regards the quality but also the quantity of food. We eat the things that we care for, but how much of them we shall eat is another matter. That depends on how we happen to be disposed at the moment, and whether there is any good reason for eating more or less at the given time.

Appetizers.—There is a whole group of substances recommended as appetizers, most of which are effective, but their effect is likely to be temporary, and to fail particularly in those cases where an appetite is most needed. Anything that will increase the circulation in the stomach will usually add to appetite; consequently warm drinks, alcoholic liquors and spices of various kinds have this effect. In vigorous people, a dash of cold on any portion of the body, is followed by a strong reaction of the circulation. Cold drinks, therefore, will sometimes serve as an appetizer, especially in hot weather. Almost anything that has a certain peculiarity of taste, and that is taken with the definite suggestion that it will produce an appetite, will almost surely have that effect. All sorts of articles of diet have in various countries acquired a reputation as appetizers. Fermented mare's milk is effective in central Europe; a glass of buttermilk in Ireland; some very hot soup with one of the strong spiced sauces in it in England; and various curious combinations of fruit and other materials in the shape of what are called cocktails, in America. Anything that stimulates the stomach a little unusually, and is accompanied by the idea that it is likely to increase the taste for food, almost surely adds to appetite.

This question of appetizers is as yet a mystery to us. It is eminently individual and yet much depends on racial customs, the habits, the environments and the family training. It is surprising what curious materials serve to excite the appetite. Caviar, in spite of the distaste of "the general," is undoubtedly a good appetizer for many people. Bismarck herring, or kippered herring, acts in the same way. In the old days men used to take what were called red herrings and undoubtedly found in the eating of them a renewal of desire for food, when there had been absence of appetite. There are some people in whom a little taste of cheese serves the same purpose. Bitter tastes usually increase appetite. Salt under certain circumstances has a similar effect. Acid fruits sometimes stimulate a jaded desire for food. Nearly always the effect of these various appetizers is increased by the attitude of expectancy. They have the reputation of being appetizers and so, though often at first somewhat disagreeable, they eventually prove to be helpful stimulants.

Appetite and Habit.—For those who live an indoor life, and have that nervous disposition that disturbs instinct, the only safeguard for nutrition is a definite formula for eating which must be followed strictly, especially by those who are below the normal in nutrition. In the chapter on Weight and Good Feeling I discuss the failure of appetite following a diminution of the amount of food. The stomach may be described as unselfish, and in times of scarcity it gives up to other organs more of the nutrition that comes to it than it should. As a consequence, it is not so well able to fulfill its functions of digestion and of craving for food, which is part of its function, as it would otherwise be. It is the people who are eating a proper amount and have been eating it, whose digestive tracts are in a condition to crave the proper {266} amount of food. Those whose habits have unfortunately led them into eating amounts too small, also suffer in not having the proper desire for food.

Nervous people particularly are likely to lack appetite in the early morning. Those who are under weight will almost invariably confess that they take little breakfast. Their reason for so doing is that they have no appetite. For most of them what is really true is that in the early hours of the day their will has not yet taken properly hold of their economies and everything is in a depressed state. These patients usually confess that they wake feeling not rested but tired, fearing the day, and wondering now they will be able to get through it. Only toward the middle of the day do they feel like themselves, while towards evening they wonder how they could have been so depressed in the morning. What these people need is the rousing into activity of their functions. Occasionally, especially in summer, a cold sponge on rising in a room into which an abundance of air is admitted will do much for them. Often a walk of even ten minutes before breakfast will make all the difference between appetite and lack of it. Above all, however, they should be made to feel that if they want to eat they can eat—if they want to they can reestablish the habit of taking breakfast, and then it will be a pleasure instead of a burden.

Food and Caprice.—Those complaining of lack of appetite should learn not to let caprice rule them in the matter of eating. There are people who by habit eat too much. What they must do, as pointed out in the chapter on Obesity, is to unlearn the habit of overeating, and that is almost as hard to break as the habit of taking stimulants. Most nervous people undereat, but they must take themselves in hand, eat three meals a day, and reestablish the habit of taking as much at these meals as they ought. What each one should consume is eminently individual, depending altogether on the sort of heat engine that each one is. Family traits mean much in this. Some must eat much more than others to keep up their weight and strength, because they are wasteful heat engines. As a rule, tall, thin people must eat more in proportion to their weight than shorter individuals of stout build. They expose more surface for heat dissipation. In this each person must learn for himself his own necessities. When there is a question of regulating eating by reason, the rule must be remembered that there is a tendency in people living indoors to take too little rather than too much.

Appetite and Food Preparation.—There are many curious things with regard to the formation of the habit of eating that show how easily the appetite or instinct is vitiated. Women, for instance, are nearly always prone not to eat enough if they have to prepare their own meals. When a mother and daughter or two sisters live together, they usually prepare one good meal, but the other two meals are likely to be picked up any way. The presence of a man in the household makes all the difference in the world. Meals are prepared regularly for men. Even for a boy of five to fifteen, meals are regularly prepared, and, as a rule, the presence of a child makes for regularity in eating.

Habit of Overeating.—On the other hand, it is easy to form habits of eating that go quite beyond appetite and vitiate the desire for food quite as seriously in the opposite direction. Many stout people take snacks between meals; women, already too heavy, indulge in the afternoon tea habit with a surprising amount of substantial food taken with the tea; many a stout man {267} takes a glass of beer occasionally and never fails to take something to eat at the same time, mainly with the idea, as he says to himself, that by taking something to eat the beer will be less likely to do him harm. Stout children are likely to form the habit of eating too frequently. When they come home from school they have a piece of something; before they go to bed they have a glass of milk, and a piece of cake, and sometimes are encouraged in these bad habits by their parents. Any child who is more than ten per cent. above weight, should be kept strictly to its regular meal times, and should not be allowed to put on additional weight, for this will be very hard to get off in adult life. To carry more than ten per cent. of over-weight is a burden, and not a benefit.

Frequent Eating as an Appetizer.—Thin people should be encouraged to indulge in some of these between-meal privileges. Very often a thin person who has been accustomed to take comparatively small amounts at meal times, will find it easier to gain in weight by indulging in luncheons between meals than by increasing the amount of each meal. Large meals on stomachs unaccustomed to them, and somewhat less vigorous than they ought to be because of lack of nutrition, may be the cause of considerable discomfort if abundant meals are taken where small ones have been habitual. In this case, multiple feeding at shorter intervals will gradually increase tissue strength. After the patient has come up to normal weight, regular intervals between meals may be determined and sufficient quantities taken at each meal. Nearly all thin people sleep better, and are more comfortable if they take something shortly before going to bed. Most people will eat their breakfast better after such an indulgence than if fourteen hours elapse between the evening and the morning meal.

Nervous Loss of Appetite.—Nervous patients often say they have no appetite, that, even though they eat, their food has no taste. Such people have often lost their eating instinct to a certain degree. They eat merely from routine, or because food is placed before them. They would usually just as soon not eat and they have no instinctive directions as to quantity. If a number of courses are presented to them, they eat such as they care for and take a conventional amount of each kind of food presented, but they have no particular feeling to guide them in the matter of quantity. There are moods in which these patients care to eat. There are others in which eating seems a hard task. If they are in reasonably poor circumstances and have not to prepare a meal for others they are likely to neglect the preparation of one for themselves, take almost anything that happens to be at hand, and then consider that they have eaten.

Instinct and Natural Life.—If one expects the natural guidance of one's instincts then one must give these instincts a proper opportunity. Instinct is a part of our animal nature, and unless other portions of our animal nature are given rather free play, or at least the opportunities for their natural life, we cannot depend on any single one of the instincts to be a safe guide. Man was meant to live much

155

outside. He was meant to take considerable exercise and to have to get his food by severe exertion. We have changed this. We live indoors to a great extent in an equable temperature, we very seldom tire ourselves by exercise, and it is not to be wondered at if we have not that craving for food that comes to the man who lives a more animal existence. The {268} Scotch surgeon, Abernethy, once said that the best possible tonic for the appetite was "to live on a shilling a day and earn it"—of course, he meant by manual labor. He talked at a time when the English workmen got but three shillings a day for fourteen hours of work.

Application of Principles.—What is needed for the mental treatment of patients with defective appetite, is that they should be made to realize that appetite is a function of habit, rather than of absolute natural craving in the conditions in which men and women live at the present time. The most important physical factor for appetite is not exercise, as has often been thought, because this, by consuming material, is naturally supposed to increase the craving for material to renew the tissue, but air, for it is oxidation processes that stimulate metabolism and make the call for a fresh supply of tissue-building material. People without an appetite must be made to understand that they should spend a considerable portion of the time between meals in the open air. Sitting in the open air is often even more effective than exercise under similar conditions, especially in weak people. The reason is exercise exhausts energy, and sometimes does not leave enough vitality for digestion, or even for the craving for food. Exercise is, of course, excellent for those of stronger constitution, and especially those who have been accustomed to it.

Those who need to eat more, must keep constantly before their minds the suggestion that if they want to eat they can, and that if they actually do eat more, satisfaction with eating grows, and appetite is restored to its normal place of influence. This is as true for those who are convalescing from some ailment, or who are in the midst of some progressive disease such as tuberculosis, as it is for the merely nervous persons whose lack of will and inefficiency of judgment have disturbed their eating habits. The will to eat is the most important appetizer that we have. The old Scotch physician's rule that if food stayed down it would do good, and that if the residue of it passed through the intestinal tract there was nothing very serious the matter with the patient, applies to the majority of patients who come to be treated for obscure ailments, especially of a chronic character, whenever they are associated with or developed on a basis of lack of normal weight.

CHAPTER V

CONSTIPATION

To judge by the frequency of advertisements for laxatives of various kinds, constipation must be an extremely common affection. At least one out of every three city dwellers suffers, it is said, from constipation. Proper regard for the taking of food calculated to help this important function, the formation of appropriate habits, and the proper disposition of the mind so as to relieve worry and anxiety, will cure the majority of these patients. There are some who need additional treatment, pharmacal or mechanical, but these are few. Undoubtedly the mind plays the most important role in the therapeutics of the affection. It is influenced partly through instruction, {269} partly by the modification of unfortunate auto-suggestion, and partly through auxiliary favorable suggestions of one kind or another.

Prophylaxis.—What is needed in most cases is such instruction as will lead to a better observance of certain common-sense laws of health, rather than the addition of remedies which eventually only complicate conditions.

Many people believe that unless they have an ample movement of the bowels every day all sorts of serious results are likely to follow. If they do not have the expected movement before noon, they suffer during the afternoon from headache that is probably due more to worry than to any physical cause. Ordinarily it is quite out of the question that the retention of the contents of the lower bowel for a few hours should produce any such serious effects as these patients immediately begin to feel. Especially is this true when on the day previous there has been, as is often the case, a sufficient movement of the bowels, due to the use of medicine. Some people have become so anxious in the matter that they foster the development of feelings of discomfort both in their abdominal and intracranial regions.

This over-anxiety is all the more important because recent observations have made it clear that over-occupation of mind actually hampers peristaltic movements of the intestines, and thus prevents the muscular action which would gradually pass the excrementitious material on to the lower bowel, to be evacuated in the normal way. *It cannot be too often repeated that nature resents too close surveillance of her functions and operations.* Just as soon as the over-anxiety is relieved, and patients are made to appreciate that if they do not have a movement to-day they may wait without serious solicitude till they have one to-morrow, the amount of medicine required to bring about movements of the bowels is at once reduced.

The Mind and Peristalsis.—Analogous to Pawlow's ingenious experiments, with regard to digestive secretion in the stomach, are Kronecker's experiments at Berne upon the motor function of the intestinal tract. Pawlow showed that the appetite depended, not on physical conditions so much as on the mental state of the animal and its desire for a particular kind of food. Kronecker, by isolating a loop of intestine in which a metal ball was placed, showed that it was possible to modify peristalsis very materially by affecting the psychic condition of the animal. There was a distinct difference in the movements of the intestine, in the passage of a metal ball, when the animal was called and expected to go for a walk with its master, than when it was threatened with punishment or rendered depressed for some other reason. In animals, the psyche plays a very subordinate role in inhibition and stimulation compared to that exercised by man's higher nervous system, since in him this portion of the organism is so much better developed than in the animal. The condition of the human mind in its possibilities of unfavorable influence over the intestinal function, is, therefore, extremely important.

The more one knows about the curious power of the mind even over so material a function as intestinal peristalsis and movement, the more is one convinced of the necessity for a properly disposed mind toward intestinal function, if it is to be accomplished with regularity and without disturbance. Many persons thoroughly under hypnotic influence, who are told that they will have a movement of the bowels at a certain hour the next day will have it. Indeed, this constitutes one way of treating certain forms of constipation in nervous, {270} preoccupied people. There are many stories that illustrate the influence of auto-suggestion upon the bowels. We have already mentioned Flaubert's suffering as a consequence of realistic absorption in "Madame Bovary's" poisoning by arsenic when he was writing that scene in the book. Boris Sidis has told the story of a man who used to have a disturbance of the bowels at every new moon, as the result of his memory, acting unconsciously, reminding him of his mother's habit of giving him a purgative about that time. These may be and doubtless are exceptional cases, yet they illustrate the influence of mind and show how much it must be the effort of the physician to use this effective adjuvant just as much as possible in this very common and often obstinate affection in which drugs so often fail, or are unsatisfactory.

So-called Intestinal Auto-intoxication.—Those who are anxiously interested in the subject are likely to have read so much of intestinal auto-intoxications, of which a great deal has been written in recent years, that they will be quite sure the slightest delay in intestinal evacuation may be serious, or at least may profoundly disturb their economy. As a consequence, just as soon as the hour at which they should have a movement passes, they begin to worry about it. In a couple of hours they feel tingly all over, and they know that there most be poisonous substances in their circulation. After two or three more hours, they begin to have a headache. Then they have to give up work, and still more devote themselves to concentration of attention on the disturbed condition. Their sleep will be disturbed, perhaps will be delayed; they wake unrested and fearful of the awful effects of intestinal auto-intoxication. In most people this state of feeling is entirely due to suggestion.

So much has been said in recent medical literature of the influence of absorption of poisonous substances from the intestinal tract—the so-called intestinal auto-intoxication—that it is a surprise to learn how little we know, definitely and absolutely, about this subject, and how many theories have come and gone. Arthur Hertz, in his "Constipation and Allied Intestinal Disorders" (Oxford Medical Publications, 1909), reviews the whole subject very interestingly but shows that we are entirely without any definite conclusive evidence for what has been talked about so much. The idea had often occurred, and been expressed vaguely, in medical literature in the old time, but began to have its great vogue when the high-sounding Greek term copremia (literally "excrementitious-substances-in-the-blood") was invented, toward the end of the first quarter of the nineteenth century. Naturally this had a strong suggestive effect. Bouchard took it up a generation later, and then intestinal auto-intoxication, another mouth-filling term, came to occupy much attention as an explanation for various vague conditions, and especially nervous discomforts of many kinds. Bouchard's method of proving his theory by showing how much toxic material was reabsorbed from the intestines, using the urine for injection into animals, was open to many objections. Now it has been quite discredited.

Bouchard's disciples exaggerated and theorized even beyond their master, until intestinal auto-intoxication became the same sort of a refuge for the puzzled physicians of our time—like rheumatism or the uric acid diathesis, for those of a score of years ago. Various methods of demonstrating the toxicity of substances absorbed had a vogue for a time, but they have now lost their significance. There are only a limited number of people who seem to suffer {271} from the symptoms attributed to such reabsorption. Some people who are quite constipated have none of the symptoms at all, while a delay of an hour or two in the evacuation seems to affect other people very much. These latter are especially nervous persons. It now seems very clear that the liver acts as a safeguard against the absorption of poisonous materials from the intestinal tract, and that neither degenerate proteid materials, nor bacterial toxins, are allowed to affect the system to any serious degree. After all our study, as Dr. Hertz insists, we have as yet no evidence that poisons are absorbed.

Reassurance as an Element in Treatment.—The most important element in the rational treatment of constipation is to make patients understand that under ordinary circumstances the symptoms of auto-intoxication, of which so much is said, do not develop until there has been long-continued accumulation of excrementitious material and under conditions favoring absorption. Even then nature learns to protect herself against untoward conditions. We have some very striking examples of good health in spite of even very rare movements of the bowels.

Examples of Intestinal Tolerance.—There is the famous case of the French army officer who, from his earliest years, did not have regular movements of the bowels, but secured evacuations of them by artificial aid once every two months or more. He lived to the age of past fifty, and then died from an intercurrent disease not connected with his intestinal condition, having in the meantime enjoyed good health. He was able to accomplish his duties as an officer without any special allowances, and he was on the sick list much less than many brother officers whose intestinal condition left nothing to be desired. This remarkable man succeeded in doing his life work without his condition being known by others to any extent, and it was only inconvenience, and not serious illness, that he suffered from. After his death, it was found that certain folds of the lower bowel were so large as to meet across the lumen of the bowel, making shelves and pouches in which fecal material gathered, preventing the movement of all material above.

In the Orient, it is said that many people, especially of the better class, do not expect to have movements of their bowels every day. Some of them, indeed, do not encourage intestinal evacuations oftener than once a week, sometimes even more seldom. As their diet is more largely vegetable than ours, this is all the more surprising. This custom does not contribute to their good odor, but this they compensate for by using various Eastern perfumes. The average length of life of such people is not much below the Occidentals and the difference is

157

probably accounted for to a great extent by other unhygienic practices, rather than this failure to have regular movements of their bowels. In the meantime, they do not suffer any particular inconvenience, and live life quite as free from the ordinary pains and aches as do the people of the West. Of course, in such cases the custom has been established early, and nature has grown accustomed to it. Nature seems to be able to stand almost anything, if she can only survive it long enough to neutralize its effects by some of her marvelous means of compensation.

A case under my observation some years ago deeply impressed upon me how thoroughly the human system can learn to get along in spite of extremely unfavorable conditions in the matter of intestinal evacuation. The case was that of a young woman suffering from some internal trouble and there was {272} a possibility of the growth of a tumor. Some charitable people had been interested in her case, and the question had arisen whether the tumor might not be physiological. Her story was a very curious one. She and her sister worked in a mill. They came from a family that had been reduced in circumstances, and were much more sensitive, as regards the decencies of life, than were their fellow workers. In order to get to the toilet, the working girls had to pass a window of an office where a number of men were at work. The other girls did not seem to mind it, but these two girls were so sensitive that they preferred not to use the toilet room at the factory. They had to leave home shortly after six o'clock in the morning. They did not get home until nearly seven. For a time, they succeeded in accomplishing their intestinal functions during the hours of their stay at home. Gradually, however, this habit was broken, and at first they went two or three days without an evacuation, then four or five days, and finally a week. It then became their custom to take a large dose of epsom salts on Saturday night and spend most of the day on Sunday getting rid of the accumulated excrementitious material of the whole week.

They taught Sunday School in the afternoons, and as the elimination of the accumulation of week-long material interfered with this, they gradually acquired the habit of doing their Sunday School work on alternate Sundays, each taking the other Sunday for evacuation purposes. It might be expected that this serious abuse of function would soon lead delicate girls, compelled to work full eleven hours a day, into rapid serious breakdown. But it did not. This state of affairs continued for more than a year. Then finally one Sunday, the more delicate of the two girls found it impossible to open her bowels at the end of two weeks, and though she stayed at home the next Sunday found it likewise impossible. Had not the directress of the Sunday School, who had become interested in them, succeeded in gaining their confidence, it is possible that they would not have consulted physicians even for some time longer, though about three weeks had passed without an evacuation.

Probably every physician in active practice has women patients who have been constipated for successive periods of three or four days at a time, for several months, without much disturbance of the general condition. While, then, there are many nervous persons who are quite sure that they begin to notice definite symptoms within a few hours from the failure to have a motion of the bowels at the time when they had been expecting it, it seems certain that this is generally rather the result of anxiety and nervous worry than consequent upon any actual absorption of toxic materials—intestinal auto-intoxication—as these patients, with a naïve liking for nice long names, find such satisfaction in describing their condition. A simple explanation of the complete lack of inconvenience that is found in so many cases of constipation, will neutralize the unfavorable auto-suggestion that exists, and make these people much less likely to suffer.

Individual Variation.—Another suggestive item of information that should be given those who are over-sensitive and anxious in the matter, is that different individuals vary very much in the need for intestinal evacuation. Perfectly healthy people have lived long and happy lives, having an intestinal evacuation only once every two days. Whether it may not in exceptional cases be rarer than this without serious injury, immediate or remote, {273} experience has not definitely settled. Many of these people with infrequent intestinal movements, have gone on utterly unconscious of the frequency or infrequency of the calls of nature, paying no attention at all to the matter until by some chance remark or a newspaper health item, it is brought forcibly to their notice. They have not had a symptom before of any kind, but now they begin to note all sorts of symptoms because they try to order their lives after the supposed rule that they have heard or read.

Anatomical Peculiarities.—On the other hand, some people normally have two evacuations a day, and seem to require them if they are to remain in the best physical condition. While daily evacuation is to be considered normal, individual departures from it in either direction must be respected as quite within the bounds of good health. Sometimes there are anatomical reasons, as the capacity of the large intestine. Sometimes there are physiological factors, as the amount of food taken, or the fullness or rapidity of function in the digestive tract.

Amount of Food as a Causative Factor.—Frequency, or infrequency, of bowel movements seems to depend to a great degree on the amount eaten. It is well known that two men of the same weight and doing the same work often seem to require quite different amounts of food to enable them to accomplish their tasks. This is what might be expected, since it holds true also for the consumption of fuel in heat machines. Engines built in exactly the same way often require quite different amounts of fuel in order to release the same amount of energy. Where men are large eaters, the amount of excrementitious material left will usually provoke, if not actually demand, more frequent evacuation than where the amount eaten is small. Variety of food also has an important bearing. Men who live largely on beef, milk, eggs and food materials that do not leave much residue, do not require, indeed they cannot have, frequent evacuations. Those who live almost exclusively on vegetables, with large amounts of residue, will require more frequent evacuation of the bowels. Certain other dietetic habits, as the amount of fluid taken with the meal, or whether food is eaten in the solid state or cooked into purees, stews and the like, make a decided difference, the reasons for which are obvious.

Habit in Treatment.—For the regulation of the bowels and the proper treatment of constipation in nearly all cases, more weight must be given to the directions laid down for the patient's attitude of mind and habits of life than to drug treatment. The patient must be made to realize that the directions given to him are much more important for the effective relief of his condition, than is the medicine prescribed. As a rule, medicine is meant only to afford relief from immediate inconvenience, in the hope that after a short time new habits will be formed which will remove the habitual constipation by correcting certain hampering conditions that have unfortunately become established.

Habitual Evacuations.—By far the most important element in the treatment is to make the patient realize that habit plays the largest role in the regular evacuation of the bowels. A child, even under two years, can, by tempting it at certain times to evacuate its bowels, be gradually brought to establish a habit that will save much inconvenience for nurses and the family. This has actually been done for most human beings now alive, and this same thing can be done at all stages of life. If a particular time be chosen, and the {274} individual habitually goes to the toilet at that time, results may be confidently expected. It is rather important that the time chosen be one when there is not much hurry nor anxiety, and when it is reasonably certain that the same time can be taken every day. It is surprising how much so simple a bit of advice as this will do for many people who have considered that they have been suffering great discomfort from habitual constipation. Between the persuasion that an occasional failure to have a movement is not serious and the definite habit of journeying to the toilet room at a particular time, whether the desire is felt or not, many cases of habitual constipation will disappear with, perhaps, only the necessity for the administration of such drugs as will prove laxative to a slight degree during the first two or three weeks.

Ingestion of Fluids an Important Influence.—After the suggestion of a habit and its extremely efficient influence, the most important idea that a patient suffering from constipation must be made to grasp, is the necessity for fluids. That there shall be easy movement of excrementitious material in the digestive tract, there must be fluid enough ingested to keep the residue, after digestion, thoroughly moist, so as not to allow it to become dry and compact. To secure this, a reasonable amount of liquids must be taken. So much has been said in recent years about the actual and possible harm of taking much fluid with meals, because of the danger of diluting the gastric juice, dilating the stomach and the like, that many persons who eat under the control of their reasons rather than their instincts, have very materially lessened the amount of liquids taken at meal time. This is undoubtedly one of the reasons why constipation has become more common in the last half century. In the olden time considerable quantities of fluid were taken at meals. With people in our time deliberately diminishing the quantity, there is often not enough fluid ingested to keep the human economy in proper working order. Prof. Hawk's work shows how utterly wrong was this limitation.

The ordinary excretion of water through the kidneys should be at least three pints, another pint is exhaled from the lungs—the quantity is even more than this in steam-heated houses where no provision for moistening inhaled air is made—and probably still another pint is needed for other purposes, perspiration, nasal and ocular secretion, and the like. Two quarts and a half to three quarts of liquid must be daily ingested then, and unless special care is taken to see that this amount is consumed the system may have to get on with much less, but as can readily be understood, not without difficulty. The ordinary glass of water does not contain half a pint; the ordinary tea cup probably holds not more than from four to six ounces. A glass of water and a cup of tea or coffee is about the limit of consumption of fluids at meals for ordinary people, and some take even less. Except in hot weather, comparatively few regularly take any fluids between meals. At the most, then, three or four pints of liquid is taken, instead of five or six, and the consequence is that the intestinal contents are deprived of their fluids by the call of the system for more liquids. Peristalsis has, therefore, to overcome the sluggish movement of the excrementitious material, which usually does not contain as much liquid as would make its movement easy and normal.

Residual Material.—The next most important consideration after the amount of fluid in the intestines, is the amount of the residuum which the lower bowel has to move. Evacuation of the intestines is to a great degree {275} a mechanical arrangement. When sufficient material is contained in the lower bowel, it pushes on ahead of it the matter that has been gathered there during the immediately preceding time, and so leads to an accumulation in the rectum that brings about reflex evacuation. It is only indigestible material that is thus excreted. If sufficient indigestible material is not taken with the food, there will not be sufficient residue left after digestion to call for the exercise of the evacuant function of the intestines, and the consequence will be sluggishness and failure to bring about daily movements. Originally nature provided food materials so arranged that the amount of indigestible material was sufficient for the exercise of peristaltic function; or rather perhaps, the regularity of peristaltic movement is of itself a development from the habits that were gradually formed in moving the residue that is normally left from food materials in the state in which they are produced by nature.

Food materials are no longer taken to any great extent in the form in which they are provided by nature. We have learned to eliminate the coarser indigestible portions. Bread used to be made of the whole wheat, and of rather coarse flour, leaving a large residue for peristalsis to exercise itself on. Now only fine white flour is used, leaving a minimum undigested. Vegetables used to be taken with much more waste material attached to them than is the case now. After being baked, potatoes were often eaten with the skins on, apples and other fruits were eaten unpared and many of the coarser vegetables, turnips, carrots, beets, and greens of various kinds that leave large proportions of waste were much more commonly used. Movements of the bowels depend on this residue. If it is not present the bowel movements will not take place with the regularity observed when food with more residue is consumed.

Diet.—Prof. Otto Cohnheim, in his lecture before The Harvey Society in New York, December, 1909, emphasized the necessity for a mixed diet. The less vegetables are taken, the less cellulose remains undigested to stimulate peristalsis. Liquids find their way through the intestines by a system of percolation, and do not excite peristaltic movements. Meat, if well digested, is almost entirely dissolved in the stomach and becomes a fluid. Vegetables are passed on to the intestines as a rather thick paste. Occasionally, in the midst of this paste there are portions of food of good size. Those excite peristalsis; hence the necessity for vegetables in the diet, if peristaltic movements and regular evacuations are to take place. This physiological law is poorly understood. Patients have heard so much about the indigestibility of starches, that whenever they have any uncomfortable feelings in their abdominal region, supposed to be due to indigestion, they commonly eliminate vegetables from their dietary with the consequence that their disturbed condition is likely to be emphasized rather than improved.

Limitation of Diet.—Just as soon as a patient's attention is attracted forcibly to any tendency to constipation, he is almost sure to conclude that this is a symptom of indigestion and he proceeds to put into practice all the rules which he has heard and read for the treatment of indigestion. The first of these is elimination from the diet of all indigestible food products, including most of the vegetables. The result is a vicious circle of cause and effect by which constipation is rendered worse than before. This needs {276} to be explained to intelligent patients in order to make them understand that some of the new habits which they have been forming and which they are prone to think highly hygienic, of cutting off all food containing indigestible material, are really important factors in the causation of further intestinal disturbance. It will often be found that the real reason for patients' inability to have daily evacuations of the bowels, is that they have become persuaded that various forms of food are either indigestible on general principles, or else are indigestible for them. For this reason they have eliminated from their diet most of nature's ordinary and quite natural provocations to intestinal evacuation, only to have to substitute artificial means to the same end in the form of the various laxatives.

It is important to talk this matter over with patients; otherwise the true cause of their constipation may be missed. For instance, from the very beginning of human life an excess of fat acts as a lubricant of the intestine, and as a material by means of which other and more concentrated objectionable matter that needs to be eliminated is carried out with as little friction as possible. Mother's milk contains from one-fourth to one-third more fat than the baby can use in its economy. This is meant to furnish a lubricant for the large intestine. It is a residue that will aid in securing movements of the bowels at regular intervals.

Fats.—Many people who come to their physicians complaining of habitual constipation have been told, or have read, that fat is rather indigestible, and, as a consequence, they have eliminated from their dietary all fatty materials. Even butter they use but sparingly, and they exchange the cream in their tea or coffee for plain milk; they carefully remove as much as possible of the fat of meat and they abstain from all sauces in which fat is employed. Such practices make normal, natural, regular evacuations of the bowels extremely difficult.

Sugars.—Another food material that is a valuable aid to nature for the stimulation of peristalsis is sugar. In its digestion, a certain amount of fermentation takes place, and the gas from this stimulates peristalsis. Of course, there may be excessive fermentation, and then harm rather than good, is done. Ordinarily a certain amount of sugar is demanded by nature and practically all the food materials, even the meats, contain it. All the starches from vegetables have, as the end products of their digestion, various forms of sugary material. These are just the classes of foods that many nervous persons, suffering from constipation and anxious about their digestion, eliminate from their diet under the mistaken notion that they are indigestible, or are productive of undesirable fermentations. When they do so, it is not surprising that their constipation should be emphasized and that they should have to ingest other irritant materials, laxatives, to replace the sugars. It is probable that where constipation exists in the bottle-fed infant, the addition of a little brown sugar to the water with which the milk is diluted, is the safest and most natural way of correcting the sluggishness of the intestines.

Supposed Idiosyncrasies.—The physician will in many cases meet with the objection that some of these materials that he is recommending disagree with his patient. Most of the presumed idiosyncrasies in the matter of food are founded on extremely insufficient evidence.

Not infrequently young persons who are thin and inclined to be {277} constipated, and who need to take fats plentifully, do not care at all for butter. Sometimes this is founded on nothing more than the fact that at some time or other the butter provided for them was rather poor, and they got out of the habit of eating it. Now they assume that their disinclination is physiological. In this regard, as with milk, a little careful persistence will usually convince the person that there is no natural obstacle and no good reason why they should not partake, in moderate quantities at least, of this extremely valuable article of food.

Often the supposed idiosyncrasy against a food is due to no better reason than that on a single occasion it disagreed, owing to its preparation, the circumstances under which it was eaten, or the materials with which it was associated. An aversion, for instance, to so nutritious and so valuable a food-stuff as hog-meat will be acquired for no better reason than that fried ham or bacon disagreed with the patient on one or more occasions. Such people when told that ham, boiled so thoroughly that it crumbles in the fingers, is a favorite mode of giving meat to convalescents in European hospitals and that it agrees very well with them, will often be tempted to try it. Then they find they have been harboring an illusion as to their supposed idiosyncrasy for hog-meat. Nearly the same thing is true of bacon. A trial or two of crisp bacon, with the fat so thoroughly cooked out of it that it may be eaten out of the fingers without soiling them, will often convince those who doubt of their ability to eat it, how tasty a nutriment it is. Bacon is one of the most precious dietetic adjuvants in the treatment of constipation.

Exercise.—There is always a serious difficulty in the treatment of constipation in stout people. To counsel fats and starches and liquids in the quantities necessary to bring about regular natural movements of the bowels, through the mechanical presence of a sufficient amount of residue, will often add greatly to their weight. For them, exercises are needed. Not exercise in general, for many a man who takes abundant exercise may be constipated. I have patients with this complaint who are letter carriers, expressmen, even stevedores, and the like. The mere absence of a sedentary occupation will not guarantee against constipation. Motormen and conductors not infrequently suffer from it. What is needed particularly is exercise directed to the strengthening of the abdominal muscles, and the increase of peristalsis.

For this certain leg exercises that can be readily and easily done in less than five minutes each day will be found useful. A patient may be directed to lie on his back, lift up the leg as high as possible in the extended position, and do that with each leg an increasing number of times every day. At the end of a month he is able to lift each leg up forty or fifty times at each trial. This exercise twice a day, morning and evening, just before and after sleep, will usually relieve the constipation. The bringing up of the thigh on the abdomen as far as possible, not only acts as a sort of massage upon the abdomen itself, but the bellying of the large muscles within the pelvic and abdominal regions mechanically helps the movement of the intestinal contents. If, in addition to this, the patient gradually accustoms himself to rise to a sitting from a lying position, the constipation will almost invariably yield. In stout people, the presence of fat in the abdominal wall seems to weaken the muscles so that the intestines are not compressed as they should be in ordinary conditions, and peristalsis seems to be thus interfered with.

{278}

A heavy wooden (bowling) ball rolled on the surface of the abdomen, beginning low down in the right lower quadrant up towards the liver, across just above the umbilicus, and then down on the left is often advised. It is a good remedy but not better than the simple exercises of the leg and abdominal muscles suggested. The use of the ball has the advantage of novelty, and of distinctly adding to the suggestive value of the exercise treatment. It is particularly valuable for women. All of these exercises have a distinct value from their suggestive side. If thus twice a day for three minutes people are made to recall while doing the exercises the necessity for taking an abundance of fluid, forming a habit with regard to movements of the bowels and eating so as to encourage peristalsis, a definite good effect will be produced. In the treatment of stout people particularly, it is important to remember that the use of sufficient salt, and then of certain of the natural salts, as Carlsbad or Hunyadi Janos, may be of distinct advantage for their obesity. If taken regularly in small amounts, that is, just enough to help to a movement of the bowels, and if varied from time to time and occasionally interrupted while some other form of laxative is taken, much good may be done. It is as well to take simple irritants of this kind as some of the irritant foods that will have a tendency to add to their accumulation of fat, though they may increase peristalsis.

Influence of Position.—Little things may mean much in the matter of the regular movements of the bowels. In my student days in France, our little hotel in the Quartier had the old-fashioned water-closets consisting of a hole in the floor in one corner, and a place to put one's feet properly beside it, thus reverting to the old-fashioned natural method of bowel evacuation. Some of the American students found it an uncomfortable proceeding at the beginning, but, on the other hand, some of them who had suffered from constipation in America were no longer troubled that way. I have found in quite a few cases of younger men that the suggestion to revert to this natural mode of evacuation helped in the formation of the habit of having bowel movements at a regular time. How much of the effect was physical and how much was mental seemed hard to decide. The suggestion was particularly valuable in my experience with patients of the better educated classes.

CHAPTER VI

NEUROTIC INTESTINAL AFFECTIONS

There is a whole series of intestinal affections dependent on nerve influence that get worse and better under stress of emotion or relief from it. Probably the commonest of these is constipation, which is dealt with in a separate chapter. Often these nervous intestinal conditions are associated with other neurotic manifestations. On the other hand, patients are seen who are absolutely without any other sign of the neurotic habit, and have nothing like hysteria, yet who suffer severely and rather frequently from intestinal neuroses. Most of the people who react symptomatically to the eating of strawberries, or of shellfish, or of pork in any form, or cheese or other milk products, also have a definite tendency to certain skin neuroses and to suffer from intestinal troubles as a consequence of emotional states. It is hard to trace {279} real causation in many of these cases, because it is so easy to accept the patient's expressions that they must have taken cold, or they must have eaten something that disagreed with them.

Neurotic Diarrhea.—But it must not be forgotten that nervousness alone, without any additional factor, may produce a disturbance of the functions of the intestines, and may even increase peristalsis and bring about severe diarrhea. Anyone who has observed students going to examinations has surely seen many examples of this. There are some individuals—fortunately they are rather rare—who always suffer from diarrhea when they have to take a serious examination. Some of these cases are pitiable because the effects are quite beyond control, and make it almost impossible for them to do justice to themselves.

Fright and Loss of Bowel Control.—Severe disturbance, such as fright, may bring on this paralysis of proper regulation of peristalsis, with consequent imperative intestinal evacuation. A classical case in history is that of James II, for whom the Irish soldiers invented a special name because of the tradition that he suffered from an intestinal accident in one of the battles with William of Orange. The imputation of cowardice on the last of the unfortunate Stuarts has been completely wiped out by the investigation of recent historians, and James' character for bravery has been thoroughly vindicated. The fact that the story should have gained credence shows that there is a general persuasion and popular tradition that such intestinal incidents do occur from fright. An incident told of the Franco-German War illustrates this, though I do not vouch for the facts. Wishing to test the bravery of some soldiers whom he was to send on a very dangerous expedition, and above all to try how they would bear up even before the threat of instant death, an officer of the French troops is said to have asked that half a dozen brave men be sent to him. Without a word, he announced that there had been treason in the ranks, and that the army needed an example. They were condemned to be shot. A platoon of soldiers was drawn up, the men were placed with their backs to a wall and they were asked whether they wished to be blindfolded. They refused though they protested that they did not know why they were being put to death. Then the word fire was given. All of the men, excepting one, fell down, though the guns of the firing party had been

161

loaded with blank cartridges. The one who remained standing was told that he was the man who would be selected to go on the expedition, which, though perilous, was also of great glory for himself and profit for his country. He said that he was ready to go, but he asked permission to be allowed to change his clothing, as he had not been able to keep as good control over his intestinal muscles, as he had over his muscles of station.

Fright often has this effect in children. These stories and traditions illustrate the influence of the mind and of deep emotions over the intestines, and while only profound mental disturbance will produce the most serious effects, there seems no doubt that lesser emotions do interfere with normal function. This phase of the subject serves to strengthen the contention that over-attention to the bowels may bring about constipation by causing increased inhibition of peristalsis, just as severe emotional disturbance may paralyze inhibition and so bring about increased peristalsis with consequent diarrheal symptoms.

{280}

Habitual Diarrhea.—There are certain forms of chronic diarrhea, usually considered most intractable, that owe their origin and continuance to neurotic conditions of the intestine, rather than to any gross organic lesion. In these cases the bowels acquire the habit of emptying themselves two or three or more times a day, and the stools are seldom formed. All sorts of physical treatment are employed for these conditions, usually without avail, but whenever the patient's mind can be set at rest, and his attention distracted from his bowels by thorough occupation with some interesting work, the intestinal disturbance gradually becomes less annoying. Ordinarily, when stools have been frequent for a prolonged period, the case is considered more or less unamenable to treatment. So far as ordinary drug remedies go, this is true. What is needed is attention to the patient's mind, to his habits of life, and to his worries, and the way that he takes them. The illustrations given of the influence of the mind over the bowels should make it clear that this therapeutic principle can be of far-reaching significance and must be applied deliberately and with confidence in the results.

Worry as a Factor.—Very often it will be found that the diarrhea is particularly bothersome on days when the patient is worried. In a clergyman friend and patient who was building a church, the approach of days on which bills and notes became due, was always the signal for a diminished control over his bowels, and there were frequently three or four stools in the day. On his vacations, when eating unusual things, drinking unaccustomed water, exposed to changes of temperature, all the factors that give many people diarrhea, he was perfectly regular because the worries had been lifted from his mind. In another case, where for fifteen or twenty years a writer living much indoors had had tendencies to diarrhea, always made worse by worries, self-discipline and the refusal to let troubles occupy him by always turning to something else, did him so much good that he considered himself cured. In his case the return of a manuscript from a magazine would always affect his bowels unfavorably. If, as sometimes happened, he found that the manuscript had been returned only for some corrections, there would be an immediate relief of his condition.

Change of Mode of life and Intestinal Control.—An interesting phase of the neurotic or mechanical disturbance of peristalsis is found in the interference with regular movements of the bowels when persons are aboard trains for long distances, or for more than twenty-four hours. There are very few people who are not bothered in some way by such a journey. Those of a nervous temperament are likely to suffer from diarrhea. This is usually attributed to catching cold because of drafts, but in recent years, when well guarded Pullmans eliminate drafts to a great extent, the bowel disturbance continues. For the majority of people, however, constipation results. The cause of it seems to be due to a disturbance of peristalsis in the line of inhibition because of the vibration and jolting of the train. The more or less conscious assumption of definite positions of the muscles of the abdominal region in order to save the body from the action of the unsteady movement of the train, seems to be reflected in the sphere of peristalsis with consequent constipation. There are other features, such as a lessened consumption of food and water and absence of exercise, that seem also to have an influence. If the journey is for several days patients should be advised to walk out during the longer stops.

{281}

Mental Influence and Indifferent Remedies.—The best evidence that we have of the influence of mind upon the intestinal tract, and the importance of employing that factor for therapeutic purposes, is found in the number of cases of various intestinal disturbances, often apparently chronic in character, which have been cured by the administration of quite indifferent remedies. Dr. Hack Tuke in his "Influence of the Mind on the Body" reports a number of cases in which bread pills were used with good effect. *Pillulae micarum panis* were not an infrequent prescription in preceding generations. They are usually supposed to have been effective only against the curious symptoms that develop in hysterical women, but it must not be forgotten that neurotic manifestations connected with the abdominal region may occur very freely in men, and that treatment by suggestion in connection with some remedy, real or supposed, is the most efficient cure. The "British and Foreign Medical Review" for January, 1847, has a series of cases among naval officers which were reported by a surgeon of long standing and wide experience. These cases include painful intestinal psycho-neuroses, occasionally accompanied by diarrhea, and sometimes by constipation and sometimes even by dysenteric movements, all cured by bread pills when these were administered in certain definite ways, and the patient's attention concentrated on their expected effects. Bismuth lost its effect in one case of repeated colic, opium was beginning to lose its effect. The patient was then told that on the next attack he would be put under a medicine which was generally believed to be most effective, but which was rarely used on account of its dangerous qualities, and that would not be used unless he gave his consent. At the first sign of his next attack, a powder containing four grains of ground biscuit was administered every seven minutes while within the hearing of the patient the greatest anxiety was expressed lest too much should be given. The fourth dose caused an entire cessation of pain. On four other occasions, the same remedy was employed with equal success for the same sort of attack. In a seaman who was suffering from obstinate constipation which resisted even the strongest purgatives, including Croton oil, pills consisting of two grains of bread were administered every seven minutes, and the patient watched with very apparent anxiety lest an overdose should be given. Within two hours he began to have nausea at his stomach, which had been foretold as one of the symptoms to be expected, and his bowels were freely open almost immediately after. Apparently the administration of the bread pills eventually cured his constipation.

162

Skin and Intestinal Sympathy.—Curious intestinal conditions are, as I have said, often associated with neurotic manifestations of other kinds. Attacks of hives and other neurotic skin disturbances are common in association with nervous diarrhea. Sometimes the attack of hives precedes the intestinal disturbance; sometimes it accompanies it. Soon after eating the offending material, the skin manifestations may begin and other symptoms follow. Only a few minutes elapse, even when the patient does not know that the offending material has been eaten, because it is concealed in some combination, yet the reaction takes place evidently not from digestive absorption, but from intestinal reflex. Very often there is vomiting, as well as diarrhea. It is not hard to understand that in these cases there is produced an irritation of the intestinal mucosa, corresponding to that seen in the skin. Whenever {282} this occurs, it is not surprising that there should be evacuation of the contents of the digestive tract in every way that nature has provided for removing irritating material. The simple nervous diarrhea is often spoken of as an "intestinal blush," as the neurotic disturbance of the bladder which causes frequent urination is spoken of as a "vesical blush." Blushing is certainly the external manifestation that corresponds most closely to the disturbance that is probably the basis of these curious manifestations.

Urticaria and Diarrhea.—Patients who suffer from urticaria readily are almost sure to have other neurotic disturbances, and their intestines seldom escape. On the other hand, those who have an idiosyncrasy for certain kinds of food are almost sure to have other nervous neurotic disturbances, which emphasize the fact that these curious idiosyncrasies are of reflex nervous origin, rather than due to any chemical irritation.

Some of these lesions of the intestinal tract related to urticaria may affect, either primarily or secondarily, the biliary structures. Under these circumstances there may be symptoms resembling true biliary colic with some jaundice and pain that radiates toward the right shoulder. Whether these bile symptoms are due to the occurrence of actual urticarial lesions in the bile duct, or so close to the papilla of entrance of the gall passages into the intestine as to occlude it, is doubtful. Practically all the symptoms of the presence of biliary calculus may be thus simulated. The differential diagnosis can only be made by the rapid clearing up of the symptoms, and by the history of the case. As a rule, where there is the story of repeated attacks of neurotic intestinal disturbance, the physician and especially the surgeon, should be slow to conclude as to the presence of a serious pathological condition anywhere in the intestinal tract, unless the symptoms are absolute. This is all the more necessary because now, in patients' minds, the words appendicitis or biliary calculus are associated with the thought of operation. This thought sometimes gives rise to so much dread as to seriously disturb the appetite and still further predispose the patient to the repetition of neurotic intestinal trouble.

In the chapter on Abdominal Discomfort, the necessity for absolute assurance of some definite lesion before there is any question of operation, is insisted on. Here the disturbing mental influence of suggestion, with regard to certain serious abdominal conditions, may be emphasized. Many painful conditions in the abdomen are either primarily or secondarily due to appendicitis. Most of these are quite acute, and practically all amenable to definite diagnosis. There is, however, a tendency to exaggerate the place that this organ holds in the pathology of chronic cases. Many women who suffer from nothing more than hysterical abdominal conditions are told by someone that they have recurrent attacks of appendicitis, though there is nothing except their suggestive complaints of pain on which to found such a diagnosis, and then it becomes extremely difficult to remove this idea from their minds, and contrary suggestion applied over a long period is the only therapeutics that favorably affects them.

Intestinal Idiosyncrasies.—I have had the opportunity to see a series of cases of intestinal idiosyncrasy in a family that has been an interesting study for many years. One of the members has the most exquisite case of susceptibility to various articles of food that I think I have ever seen or heard of. {283} Even the eating of a little unrecognized pork in sausage will give rise to a diarrhea so intense that there is no peace for hours, and slight movements take place every few minutes. Towards the end of the attack, there is always considerable blood in the stools. Often the attack is preceded by vomiting. While in most people the idiosyncrasy is limited to one article of food, this patient has it for all of the articles that are usually the subjects of idiosyncrasy. Besides pork, shell-fish will produce vomiting and diarrhea within a few minutes, strawberries act detrimentally at once, and cheese produces an almost immediate reaction.

The most interesting feature of this case is that occasionally an attack of diarrhea that is extremely severe, will occur merely as a consequence of a strong emotional stress. Any great anxiety will have this effect. The knowledge that someone has a telegram for her whose contents she can not ascertain for a time, will act as a cathartic. She also has other neurotic manifestations, especially of an urticarial character, that are equally interesting. On a number of occasions, when she has particularly prepared for some special event such as a wedding or reception, for which a new gown has been provided and preparations made with considerable solicitude to the end that she shall appear at her best, she has suffered from a severe attack of angio-neurotic edema affecting either her lips or her eye-lids so that it was absolutely impossible for her to be present at the social engagement. This has happened to her over and over again. On the first two occasions, one eye was closed completely by the edema. In each case she attributed it to the sting of an insect. There was no sign of any sting, there was no itching or inflammation, the condition presented all the signs of angio-neurotic edema, had come without warning, and disappeared in from 36 to 48 hours without leaving any mark or trace of its origin.

There is absolutely not a sign of hysteria in this individual, nor is there any tendency to what would be called an emotional neurotic condition. On the contrary, she is lively and sensible, the life of her friends when they are ill, their consolation when they are in trouble, and she herself has shown the power to bear trials and difficulties. It is only the peripheral circulation in the intestinal mucosa, and in the skin, that passes from under her control. She neither laughs nor cries without reason and she has no other exaggerated nerve reactions. Even more interesting is the fact that the angio-neurotic condition can be traced in the preceding generation, while the tendency to an intestinal neurosis complicated by diarrhea exists in a sister in this generation. Examinations are always a source of grave distress to the sister. Although she is a bright intelligent woman she does not do justice to herself because of her nervousness. Usually she has a vomiting spell in the morning before the examination, and rather serious intestinal disturbance during the day. That this is entirely neurotic is clear from its constant disappearance immediately afterwards, and its constant reappearance whenever there is this form of emotional stress.

163

In certain of these cases of supposed neurotic, intestinal troubles, one cause of the condition sometimes fails of recognition. Many of these people are found on inquiry to be taking much more salt than usual. It is hard to understand how this occurs, but I have seen it in a number of cases, sometimes in men, but much more frequently in women. Some sort of a vicious {284} circle has been formed: probably their original tendency to diarrhea led to a craving for salt, because of the excessive serous evacuations. Somehow, then, the habit of taking more salt was formed and its presence reacted to produce irritative conditions in the patient, which, combined with neurotic tendencies, produced the intestinal disturbance. I have seen chronic diarrhea, mucous diarrhea, and even mucous colitis, associated with the over-free taking of salt. When salt was eliminated from the diet the cases at once improved. We now realize the value of a salt-free diet for many conditions disturbing osmosis, and the presence of serum where it should not be. It is probable that most people take more salt than is good for them.

Intestinal Troubles Due to Air.—One of the most annoying intestinal troubles due to a neurosis is the passage of air from the intestines, or in some people a rumbling through them, which is distinctly of neurotic origin. It is increased under emotional stress or whenever there is anxiety with regard to it. This is much more common in the old than in the young, as if relaxation of tissues had much to do with it. Old men seldom complain of it to their physicians, but for obvious conventional reasons, we are rather often asked to control it in older women, and are occasionally asked to treat poignant cases of it in young women. The older women are often stout, of flabby constitution, and one has almost to accept the conclusion that the real trouble is such a relaxation of the intestinal walls that the empty intestines do not fall together as they used to, but rather tend to lie apart from one another with the production of spaces into which gases, perhaps by diffusion from the blood, find their way and are expelled. Usually these patients were stouter than they now are.

Often after these patients have walked outside for some time, especially if they have become quite tired, and then sit down inside and become warm, the expansion of the air in the intestines leads to some rumbling and the production of flatus. This experience is so common with elderly people, when they come in in cold weather, that they do not feel quite right unless it actually happens. The odor of the flatus is seldom offensive.

Air Swallowing.—There seems to be no doubt that a certain amount of air is swallowed, that it finds its way along the intestines, and then, with the change of temperature on coming into the house, expansion takes place and the air finds its way out. In certain patients the habit of swallowing air may grow, and the necessity for its evacuation, either by eructation or flatus, may be a source of great discomfort. The latter form of relief may be impossible owing to conditions, though it is quite as natural as other forms of the evacuation of the bowels, and it must not be considered pathological unless it becomes too frequent. People of other civilizations than ours are not so sensitive in this matter. A late distinguished Chinese Ambassador to this country relieved himself of an accumulation of gas in his lower bowel quite as indifferently as he would have of gas in his stomach—but without so much as "by your leave" and evidently without a thought of anything unseemly in the act—apparently to his own great satisfaction, though sometimes to the consternation of the bystanders. Utterly failing to understand why he should not permit himself this satisfaction, he peremptorily refused to conform to our Western refinements in this matter.

In many of these cases habit may add to the necessity for relief of this {285} kind, and habit may require considerable self-discipline and training of organs to overcome it. To attempt to control this form of intestinal trouble by ordinary intestinal remedies, and especially by carminatives, is almost sure to increase it rather than do any good. It is the patient's mental attitude toward the affection that must be modified, and the intestinal bad habit must be brought under control.

Intestinal Uneasiness.—In young women the cases are much more serious, for the presence of gas in the intestines sometimes leads to such dread of physical events over which they fear they may have no control, that it makes it impossible for them to carry on their ordinary occupations, hinders their conformance with social usages, or even their association with any but very near friends. The cases are not frequent, but are poignant when they occur. Many young women suffer from rumblings in the intestines whenever more than four hours have passed since their last meal. This phenomenon is not likely to manifest itself unless they are nervous, excited and worried over something, but is particularly likely to be troublesome when they are with persons whom they are most solicitous to impress favorably. The manifestation is undoubtedly associated with emptiness of the intestines and relief will usually be afforded by taking something to eat, even something so simple as a glass of milk and some crackers, shortly before the time when the rumblings are usually heard. Dread of this annoyance plays a large role in it, and it is due to an exaggeration of peristalsis with the consequent crowding into larger masses of small quantities of air that ordinarily would find their way much more slowly along the intestinal tract. Milk of bismuth will do more than anything else, though the presence of a certain quantity of food is probably the best prophylactic and remedy.

Besides these cases, there are some that are even more annoying. These occur in young women who have all the symptoms of an approaching intestinal evacuation, and then find when they have excused themselves that there is nothing but gas to be passed. This gas is nearly always quite inoffensive, and is evidently air that has been present in the intestines for some time, and has in the midst of the excitement of peristalsis been forced on into the rectum and gives the sensation of an approaching stool. These cases are coming into notice much more commonly since young women have taken up business occupations. The symptoms are worse in those who are constipated, though sometimes in these cases there are recurring attacks of diarrhea showing that the normal function of the intestine is disturbed. It is more annoying just before and during menstruation than at any other time.

Physical Basis.—Whenever the patients are run down in weight there is a distinct exaggeration of the condition. Whether the loss of weight, by removing fat from within the abdomen, does not tend to make the intestines more ready to take up air and to produce these manifestations is a question worth considering. The most annoying cases that I have seen were in people who had lost considerable weight and though there had been some tendency to the condition before they lost weight, it was doubtful whether the symptoms were greater than those often seen and which are not productive of special annoyance except in very sensitive people. In three of these cases that have been under my observation in recent years, improvement came promptly when weight was put on. The presence of an abundance of fat in {286} the abdominal cavity seemed properly to balance the intestines and to dampen peristalsis.

Reassurance, absence of worry, occupation of mind with interests that keep it from putting such surveillance on the intestinal tract as will surely be resented, must be the chief care of the physician. Without these any relief afforded will be only temporary. With psychotherapy relapses will occur, for these individuals are in a state of unstable intestinal equilibrium, but practically all the successful remedies of the past have been founded on it and its effect may be renewed over and over again under various forms.

CHAPTER VII

MUCO-MEMBRANOUS COLITIS

Probably the severest, certainly the most interesting of the neurotic conditions of the intestines, is muco-membranous colitis. The only lesions discovered are those which point to a functionally increased secretion of tenacious mucus from the lower bowel. No definite pathological changes are known. The colic seems to be due to nothing more than the effort of the large intestine to push off the thick mucus which has been secreted, and which in many cases clings to the bowel walls. This may be of such consistency that it is passed from the bowel in the shape of tubular casts. These casts have often been seen in place in the lower bowel. While the word membranous used in connection with the disease has produced the impression that this might be a form of diphtheritic affection, it is now known that it is only due to an abnormally increased function, and not to any structural pathological condition or infection of the lower bowel. The membranous material is often gelatinous, and so the casts may hang together in long pieces.

Neurotic Etiology.—It might be thought that such a cast could not be formed, remain in situ in the lower bowel for a considerable period, and then be passed as a whole, or in quite long portions, without causing serious tissue disturbance in the mucous membrane. As Sir William Osler says, in spite of the apparent improbability, the separation may and usually does take place without any lesion even of the surface of the mucous membrane. The epithelium seems to be left intact. Owing to the curious nature of the stools, the disease has been recognized for a long time and the descriptions of this disease by the older authors are very interesting. Muco-membranous colitis occurs mainly in nervous individuals, and is much more frequent in women than in men, but it is not limited to women. Some of the severest cases have occurred in men, and Woodward, in the second volume of "The Medical and Surgical Reports of the Civil War," has an exhaustive description of the disease as it occurred among soldiers. It is particularly those who are worried and run down from overwork and excitement who are likely to suffer from it, but it occurs typically in people who, *faute de mieux*, worry about themselves. Most of its victims are self-centered, though not hysterical.

Recent Increase in Number of Cases.—According to all the authorities, there has been a considerable increase in the number of cases in recent years. {287} At one watering place in France, Plombiêres, which has acquired the reputation for relieving, or even curing the disease, about 400 cases had been under treatment during the course of about two years. This increase was attributed by Boas of Berlin to two causes. First the struggle for life has become much more intense in our day, and the nervous conditions which are practically always the basis of muco-membranous colitis, have as a consequence become more frequent. Not only this, but mild cases that were not called to the attention of physicians in the past, have become so emphasized by the nervous worries of the strenuous life that now they seldom escape the physician's attention. Besides our generation is getting away from the old-fashioned idea of patiently standing many pains and aches, and refusing to call in a physician unless the condition persists or seems to be producing serious results. There are more cases of the disease, but physicians also see more of the cases than formerly because patients come for treatment for slighter causes.

Dr. Boas considered that, besides the strenuous life, there was another prominent factor in the increase of the disease. This is the abuse of laxatives and purgatives. Many of these have their principal effect on the lower bowel. In consequence the nervous mechanism of this structure has been irritated to a point where occasionally explosions of nerve force take place. This causes an increase of the secretion, and a tendency to cramp-like contractions. While there is undoubtedly much of truth in this, there is no doubt that the most important factor in the disease is the patient's nervous condition. Only those who are inclined to be introspective, to worry much about themselves, and who are constantly examining their stools for the presence of mucus, suffer severely from the affection.

Very few cases have been seen among the working classes. Most of the cases have hypochondriacal symptoms that sometimes go to the extent of real melancholia and the full persuasion that they have an incurable disease, a visitation on them for some real or fancied lapse from the laws of health in earlier years. The affection usually lasts a long time, or has been in existence for some years when the physician is asked to see it, and patients are made most miserable by it.

Unfavorable Suggestion and Over-attention.—The pathological physiology of this disease, for, as has been said, it has no pathology in the proper sense of the word, is in many cases a problem of mental influence. For some reason, the patient gets his or her lower bowel on his or her mind. There is so much talk of constipation and its evil effects in the newspapers, in advertisements and by suggestion from bill-boards and in the magazines as well as, sad to relate, in parlors, drawing-rooms and even dining-rooms, that it is easy for those who are introspective and nervous about themselves, and who have some little tendency to constipation already, to become much worried about it. If, then, as was suggested by Boas, they take laxatives in profusion, the irritation set up further fixes the attention on this portion of the body. After a while, in these people, a goodly portion of the waking hours are spent in thoughts with regard to the lower bowel. The morning thought is the possibility of a stool to-day, followed by conjecture as to its character. After the stool has taken place, if there seems anything abnormal about it, comes a morbid dread of the consequences of having such stools.

{288}

This constant attention sends down a lot of impulses to the lower bowel. Anyone who has studied the psychology of attention knows how much influence can be exerted on the skin, or on the mucous surface by mental influence. Hyperemia is produced, and this leads to over-action of the glands of the large intestine. These glands secrete a glairy mucus which is necessary to protect the bowel from the offensive material that is always present, and from the hardened material that is so often there when there is a tendency to constipation. This mucus is secreted in large quantities, while at the same time a hyperemia of the colon tends to interfere with peristalsis and consequently to delay the passage of contents and to keep the mucus in place. An accumulation goes on for some time, until irritation is set up by the presence of such a large quantity of material in the intestine, and then colicky efforts for its removal are occasioned. All of this process is accompanied by suggestive reactions upon the mind that further complicate the case. This story of the affection points out the indications for treatment. Unless the patient's mind can be diverted from its constant attention to the lower bowel, the possibility of cure is distant, and even after such diversion any return of attention is likely to bring on a relapse.

Treatment.—The treatment of this affection emphasizes its neurotic origin. We have had any number of cures for it and each one has actually relieved many patients. The more trouble the cure involves, and the greater the impression produced on the patient's mind the more likely is there to be a relief of symptoms. All sorts of drugs have been employed. Many of them have for a time been heralded as more or less specific. The important thing, however, was that the patients should come predisposed to believe that they were going to be improved, and then that suggestion should be made at frequent intervals—a combination of auto-suggestion through the administration at regular intervals for a long period of simple remedies with the confident suggestion of the physician that the patient will get better. Local treatment of various kinds has been reported to bring about improvement. The more difficult this is, and the longer it takes, as well as the more bother it involves for the patient and the attendant, the better the response to it is likely to be. Long rectal tubes were found beneficial in many cases, though they failed in many others, and most physicians have seen relapses occur in spite of the continuance of the treatment that at first did much good. High injections of water containing various drugs, and of olive oil sometimes bring improvement though they afford no guarantee against a relapse. Mineral waters do good only in the suggestive environment of the spring.

Surgery and Suggestion.—The symptoms have sometimes been so severe and the complaints of the patients have been so great that even surgery of serious character has been recommended and tried in some of these cases. The making of an artificial anus in the right inguinal region, so that for a time the feces are not allowed to pass over the colon mucous membrane has been tried. This gives decided relief from the symptoms, but when the artificial anus is allowed to close, recurrences often take place. It has been suggested, therefore, that the artificial anus should be allowed to stay open for months, but even this seems to afford no guarantee against a relapse. In recent years the appendix has been taken out through the opening in the right inguinal region, and a portion of it allowed to remain through which, when {289} fastened to the abdominal wall, injections might be made into the colon. In these cases ice-water has been found probably of more effect than any drug solutions. This rather serious surgical procedure is, however, as yet on trial, and we do not know enough about the after-course of the cases to be sure that it has any permanent effect.

A strong suggestion is involved in the removal of the appendix, and the use of the stump of it as an irrigating tube. When the treatment consists of something that is so strongly excitant of feeling as ice-water, applied directly to the colon, it is easy to understand that suggestion reaches the limit of its possibilities. No wonder these cases improve, though we are not sure as yet what happens after the appendix opening is allowed to close, or is deliberately sutured. I should expect a recurrence of symptoms, if ever a time came when the patient was run down in weight and worried by external conditions, introspection, and above all by concentration of attention on the intestines.

Direct Suggestion.—The question is whether suggestion can be used to advantage in these cases without employing any of the radical measures that have been suggested. There is no doubt that at certain watering places where a specialty is made of this disease, and to which patients go, sure that they are going to be much better than before, and where they see patients all round them who are improving, they often get complete relief. This is only what might be expected. Whether a similar effect can be produced by simple suggestion when the patient is thoroughly convinced that the physician understands the case, and that if they will respond he can cure it, remains to be seen. I know that mild cases improve rapidly under simple hygienic measures, with a renewal of confidence in the possibility of relief, and with the diversion of the patient's mind from the intestinal difficulty. This is the most important factor in the treatment, as it is the most important factor in pathology. If the patient's nerve centers can be kept from sending down impulses causing exaggerated action of the glands, then there is some hope of relief. A habit has been formed in the matter, and a habit can only be broken by a series of acts, just as it was formed. It is not effort for a few days nor a week that counts in these cases, but diversion of mind for long periods, until normal function is restored. It is usually quite impossible to keep up this improvement constantly in nervous patients. There are setbacks, but then this is true in every form of nervous affection. It is, then, that the renewed suggestion of the physician is needed.

Resort Cures and Suggestion.—Physicians often tell patients that muco-membranous colitis is incurable, or at least emphasize strongly that it is very refractory to treatment, and that it is prone to relapse even after improvement. After a certain number of physicians have insisted on these points, it is inevitable that patients should not respond readily to treatment, and that they should be solicitous about themselves, even when improvement does come.

It is most important then to bring about the neutralization of these unfavorable suggestions. This is what is particularly accomplished at the health resorts where muco-membranous colitis is successfully treated. At these the patients see other sufferers from the disease who proclaim how much better they are and some at least who are entirely cured. The waters {290} used at these health resorts are not nearly so efficient when used at a distance because of this lack of additional suggestion.

The most efficacious treatment of muco-membranous colitis then is to bring the patient up to normal weight, for they are often thin people, quiet their solicitude about themselves, give them a bland and irritating diet and get them away from worries or anxieties about themselves or others. I know cases in physicians where the effect of worry of any kind can be traced very clearly in the increased symptoms of their colitis and the greater frequency of attacks. It is particularly important not to give habit-forming drugs in these cases for they always do harm. Where the pain is much complained of the coal-tar anodynes are useful, but ice in the rectum or even suppositories of gluten, or of cocoa butter without any medication often prove useful. Most of these patients watch prescriptions that are given them rather carefully and make up their mind beforehand whether they are likely to do them good or not and the event usually follows their premonition. They often have habits of self-drugging which must be stopped and always carefully inquired into for they will sometimes continue to take things for themselves in spite of being under the doctor's care. If they have heard of surgical treatment for their affection they are likely to think that they will have to come to it eventually and this prevents a favorable attitude of mind towards their affection. Unless this is secured no treatment will prove efficient. With it almost anything that keeps up the suggestion will greatly relieve and often will actually cure the condition.

CHAPTER VIII

OBESITY

Obesity, popularly considered to be an over-accumulation of fat, is sometimes thought to exist only when there is the large development of abdomen which is more properly designated corpulency. In its strictly scientific sense it represents excessive over-weight, that is, above twenty per cent. more of weight than is normal for the height of the particular individual. (See table of weight for height in chapter Weight and Good Feeling.) The Latin derivation of the word gives also its etiology. Ob-ese means having eaten too much. It is a question of failure of due proportion between the taking of nutrition and the oxidation processes within the body. More food being taken than is needed, there is an accumulation of it in the form of fat, and this is deposited by natural preference in certain places, such as the abdomen, the breasts and in the *panniculus adiposus* beneath the skin. The fats and starches are most readily converted into this fat, but under certain circumstances proteid material may be turned into fat, and then a true pathological condition develops resembling diabetes in certain ways.

The metabolism of fat is rather simple, but this may be disturbed by bad habits. When such large quantities of sugar-making materials are taken that they are beyond the power of the normal metabolism to dispose of, they are excreted in the urine with the production of what is known as physiological {291} glycosuria. In the same way, the eating of a superabundance of fat-forming food leads to the deposition of fat in the tissues where, when in excess, it is just as much wasted as if it were excreted. Physiological glycosuria is, however, usually considered to be dangerous, inasmuch as its frequent occurrence may disturb the normal metabolism of sugar, and lead to diabetes. In the same way, the over-consumption of fat-forming materials may disturb the fatty metabolism, and lead even to the changing of proteid materials into fat. This represents a real disease requiring careful management, while ordinary obesity needs only the exercise of the patient's will to secure such proportion between the amount of food taken, and the amount of exercise and fresh air, as will not only prevent accumulation of fat but will lead to the reduction of any accumulation that may, through neglect of this care, already have taken place.

Over-eating.—The putting on of weight depends on the individual's craving for food, and his satisfaction of his appetite. While it is not ordinarily looked at from this standpoint, this craving for food and the habit of satisfying it which is developed, is not very different from the craving for stimulants and the habit that forms with regard to them. People insist that they can not eat less—that their appetite simply requires them to eat. We have all heard this story over and over again from the man who craves alcoholic stimulation. Usually the obese can be persuaded more easily than the inebriate to break off their habit, but they relapse into it even more easily than he does. It is comparatively easy to limit the appetite, or rather to forego the satisfaction of eating abundantly, for a week or two weeks or even a month, but the effort finally becomes appalling and the consequence is a relapse. If the patient really wants to lose weight, in nine cases out of ten it is a comparatively simple matter. The trouble is that they want to lose in weight without giving up the satisfaction of eating.

Under Exercise.—The second factor in obesity—lack of sufficient exercise, is even more important than the habit of over-eating. This is illustrated very well by the cases of certain animals who, without any tendency to fat accumulation by nature, but rather the contrary, acquire fat to a marked degree, owing to the habits that are forced on them by their relations to human beings. A typical example is the pet dog. Dogs living their natural active lives, have little tendency to put on superfluous flesh. Kept in the house in cities, they practically always put on weight until, after some years, many of them are quite incapable of moving except in an awkward waddle, often comically symbolizing their mistresses in this respect. Besides the inactivity, the dog is subject to the influence of the other cause of obesity, the over-eating of fat producing material. Another typical example, and one that provides evidence of the pathological tendency to fat accumulation, is found in the Strasburg geese from whom the fatty goose livers for *pates de foie gras* are obtained. Geese are placed in a warm underground room, in a mass of cement that gradually hardens round their feet keeping them almost completely inactive, and then they are fed abundantly with fat-forming materials. The absence of light and air, and the immobility, leads to the production of the fatty changes, eventually producing the enlarged fatty livers, which delight the gourmet's palate.

What is true of the dog and the goose is exemplified in the lives of all other {292} animals. The fattening process is well understood by butchers—keep the animal inactive and supply an abundance of fattening food. The inactivity is even more important than the food.

Prophylaxsis.—Of course, if obesity is to be successfully treated, cases must be seen early and before there has been a large accumulation of fat. When people are more than 10 per cent. over weight they are in the danger zone, and with 20 per cent. above the normal, decrease must come or the condition becomes inveterate. It is between these two points and not when they are forty or fifty pounds over weight that they need the advice of a physician and the careful institution of regular life to prevent further fat accumulation. After the body has carried thirty or forty pounds over weight for some time, it has acquired the habit of accumulating fat, rather than using it, and this, once acquired, is hard to break. Every additional pound tempts to the formation of lazy or sluggish habits because of the additional weight that has to be carried around. Everyone knows how hard it is to walk a few blocks a little briskly carrying a suit case that weighs thirty pounds. Even twenty pounds soon proves to be a burden. Fat in the tissues, though it seems to be a portion of the individual, is really quite outside of him and consists of extra food material that the body is carrying round, having accumulated it for the purpose, apparently, of using it at some time when it should be necessary. While carrying this burden, people have little inclination to an active life. Inactivity lowers oxidation processes and leaves them with an additional tendency to fat accumulation because of lack of oxidation. In a word, a vicious circle of cause and effect is formed. Accumulation of fat prevents the taking of proper exercise, and lack of exercise leads to further accumulation of fat!

Not only should the treatment of obesity begin early in a particular case, but, in families where there is a recognized tendency to take on fat, it should begin early in life.

Children should not be so fed that they become mere specimens, illustrative of how early fat accumulation may occur, and to what a degree it may go. Just as soon as baby shows signs of an accumulation of fat above its normal weight for age and size, there should be just such a regulation of its diet as would be considered necessary if it were an older person, and showed the same unfortunate tendency. This is particularly important if the parental relatives on either or both sides of the house show tendencies to fat accumulation. We are sure that in diabetes the over-eating of starchy and sugary substances produces what is, at the beginning, an alimentary or so-called physiological glycosuria, though it is doubtful whether any glycosuria is ever absolutely physiological. This may lead to a pathological glycosuria and the production of a true diabetes. So, also, the tendency to accumulation of fat, as the result of what might be called alimentary obesity, may lead eventually to the production of an essential obesity in which even the proteid materials of the food may be changed into fats, just as in the case of diabetes they are changed to sugar. This fat is then stored up in the tissues though there is no need at all for such an accumulation, and the food stuff is wasted quite as much as in diabetes.

The Will in Treatment.—The important element in the treatment of obesity is the readiness of the patient to follow directions. Nine out of every {293} ten stout people are thoroughly able to control the accumulation of fat and even to bring themselves down to about normal weight, if only they *will* to do so. This is no easy matter. It is not an affair of a few weeks, or even a few months. Just as in the case of over-indulgence in alcohol, it will probably be a life struggle. It is well worth the while, however, for life is longer and is larger without the accumulation of fat, which is not only so uncosmetic, but is so preventive of real enjoyment of life. Unfortunately, the cosmetic side of it, that is, the absurdity of going round among one's friends with a very prominent abdomen, or with noticeable protuberances, is the particular motive that appeals to most people. While women may be quite ready to stand many discomforts for cosmetic effect when dictated by fashion, they are not ordinarily persistent enough in their efforts to prevent fat accumulation to be successful in this much more important purpose.

Such patients make the rounds from physician to physician, and from quack to quack, and go from patent medicine to patent medicine, to find something that will enable them to lose weight without the necessity for their taking any trouble. It is the old, old story that the nerve specialist who is known occasionally to treat his patients by hypnotism has so often presented to him. Patients who are sufferers from alcoholism, or drug addiction, or some other vicious habit, present themselves and ask if they cannot be hypnotized and then lose their tendency to fall back into the old habit. There is no possibility of this. If they are willing to cooperate, all of these habits may be overcome, but a constant effort will be required and, even after the habit is broken, there always remains a distinct danger of relapse. Patients suffering from obesity want to transfer the burden of working it off to someone else's shoulders, or they want some specific remedy that will bring about reduction in weight yet permit them to indulge in all the pleasures of their artificially excited appetite. They follow directions for a few weeks, often half-heartedly, and then give up the struggle.

Food Temptations.—With obesity, as with indulgence in alcohol, the main difficulty is the occasion. Most of these fat people are placed in circumstances in which tempting food passes them three times a day, and it is hard to refuse it. If a hot punch or a fragrant cocktail were several times every day passed under the nose of a man with a tendency to inebriety it would be beyond the bounds of reason to hope that he should withstand his craving. Just as soon as those who want to reduce in weight are put in conditions in which only simple food, though there may be a reasonably good variety of it, is presented to them, the difficulty of limiting the amount they eat is comparatively easy. This necessitates, as a rule, refusing invitations to dinner at friends' houses, especially at the beginning of a reduction cure, avoiding hotel *menus* and giving up various social functions. It may even involve changing home customs from those of luxury back to simplicity. The question is whether this is worth while or not. When a husband is likely to indulge over much in alcoholic liquors a wife is apt to consider it easy to deny herself the privilege of such liquors on her table and of avoiding places where he is likely to be tempted. The rest of the family are usually quite satisfied to stand some self-denial so that unfortunate results may not follow.

Where father or mother are suffering from obesity this same thing may be necessary with regard to rich and highly seasoned foods. This would be a {294} hardship to inflict on the family were it not for the fact that the health of all the members will be distinctly benefited and a return to simple food, nutritious and with a variety that makes it eminently wholesome, will be good for them as a prophylactic measure.

Motives for Self-Control.—The task of keeping the weight down is so difficult that very few people with a tendency to over-weight are equal to it. They need the help of every motive possible for encouragement. It is well to make these persons realize that over-weight, according to the statistics carefully gathered and collated by the large insurance companies in recent years, is a serious bar to great expectancy of life. In a large series of cases it was found that not a single individual recorded as being more than twenty per cent. over the normal weight that he should have for height, died of old age. Furthermore no one of over-weight attained the age of eighty years, though 44 under-weights passed this age, and two of them even reached the age of ninety. Death from nearly every known cause is more frequent among the over-weights than in the normal population, except in the single instance of tuberculosis.

What was thus demonstrated from statistics, carefully gathered in modern times, has been a commonplace in medicine since the earliest days. Hippocrates summed up Greek experience in the aphorism "persons who are naturally very fat are apt to die earlier than those who are slender." Practically all the commentators since his time have agreed with him. In early years thinness may be quite as dangerous.

If there were no other reason but the greater frequency of *diabetes* among the obese, this of itself would be sufficient to act as a strong deterrent motive. It may well be used as such, especially in families where a tendency to diabetes has been manifest. Diabetes figures as a cause of death in life insurance statistics five times more frequently among those who are over-weight than in the general population. Those who are under-weight suffer from the disease in fatal form less than one-half as frequently as the average. Hence, obesity and diabetes are evidently closely related. As we have suggested, the disturbance of metabolism due to the failure to use sugar properly in the system and to its consequent elimination, corresponds in some, as yet not well understood, way to the other metabolic disturbance by which unnecessary fat is accumulated in the system. It is probable that the over-eating of starchy foods and fats which leads to obesity, causes in some people a breakdown of metabolism in the matter of the proper disposal of sugar, and this initiates diabetes which becomes a pathological condition, after a time quite beyond control.

Sleep and Exercise.—After the reduction of diet, the most important feature of any successful treatment of obesity must consist of an increase in the amount of exercise. Both of these can be accomplished only through the patient's will, and by frequently repeated suggestion, and auto-suggestion, of the necessity for constant surveillance in both these matters. Any form of exercise that is pursued faithfully is beneficial. Exercise in the open air, because it encourages oxidation, is preferable to gymnastic exercises, but the care of a trained instructor, the influence of example, the habit of taking it at regular hours, make gymnastic exercise of value in this condition. A regular walk every day is invaluable if it can be secured. Women can be tempted {295} to walk even three or four miles, if the habit is gradually formed, and if they realize the necessity for it. It is important that too much sleep should not be indulged in. One of the difficulties with pet animals is that they sleep so much more in domesticity than in the state of nature. Sleep must be absolutely regulated for the obese. The old monastic rule "seven hours for a man, eight hours for a woman and nine hours for a hog" must be emphasized.

Heredity.—There always remains in these cases the influence of heredity. Many people are sure that because they come from families with the tendency to obesity, it is impossible for them to overcome this assumed heredity, and that the only thing for them is to bear the affliction with equanimity. They usually do this while indulging their taste for the luxuries of the table rather freely. This question of heredity, however, has come in recent years to occupy a very different position in the minds of biologists from that which it held a generation ago. We know now that the evidence for acquired characters being transmitted is so trivial as to be quite negligible.

The children of stout parents are likely to acquire their parents' habits as to the consumption of food, in such quantity and quality as will almost inevitably put fat on them. It is this habit much more than any hereditary element, which is the underlying cause of the obesity. There may be some influence of heredity, but it is much less than has been thought, and even where it exists, it is not so inevitable as has been considered. There are cases in every physician's experience where the children of stout parents who, for some reason, have been brought to habits of spare eating, have been thin all their lives. On the other hand, anyone who has seen the change that has come over the sons of spare, lanky farmers, in whom both father and mother were of the thin type, yet who in the midst of the luxury of city life have taken on weight, will be convinced that personal habits mean much more than any influence of heredity in the production of obesity.

Where there is normal occupation of mind and body with strict regulation of the hours of sleep, and simple though abundant food, there is little tendency for people to become obese, even though there may seem to be hereditary tendencies. In a considerable experience with religious communities I have often noted that the member of a family who enters a religious order often goes but slightly above normal weight, even though other members of the family may become distinctly fat. This is not because of rigid self-denial in the matter of food, that is to such an extent as to take less food than is necessary, for most members of the religious communities work too hard for this to be possible, but because they live the regular active life and have the simple food of the community. This is true in spite of the fact that their indoor life would seem to predispose them to the accumulation of fat. After fifty most of them put on weight because this is the physiological accompaniment of that period of life, but it is not this form of fat accumulation that the physician is called upon to treat as a rule, but that in people between the ages of twenty and forty.

If the prevention of over-weight is taken up in time, if habits are broken before they become tyrannous, if proper self-control is cultivated early in life, there are very few people that need fear the oncoming of obesity. There are some pathologically obese families in which this will not be true, but they are as rare as diabetic families. The most important element in any {296} treatment is the rousing of the patient's mind and his will to take up seriously the task of unlearning habits of overeating and not allowing sluggishness of life to gain control. This can be done best, not by removing all sorts of articles for which there is special taste from the diet, but by a general reduction in the quantity of food eaten, by the introduction of food material that does not put on weight yet satisfies the craving, by the replacing of many of

169

the starchy vegetables by greens of various kinds, by replacing many of the desserts by gelatine products and cheese, and by additions to the exercise. But there must be no extremes in the reduction of food or the taking up of exercise. Patients should not be permitted to lose five pounds a week—at most two or three pounds—and they should be made to understand that it is a life work and the formation of lasting habits that they have before them. They should be made to understand, also, after a time the satisfaction that comes from a more active life will give them even more pleasure than the satisfaction of their appetite did before.

Principles of Treatment.—Many systems of treatment of obesity have been invented. All of them are supported by cured cases. Some of them are founded on a reduction in the amount of fluids, some on a reduction of the amount of vegetables eaten, in some cases going to the extreme of an almost exclusively meat diet. Most of them modify the diet very extensively. It is doubtful, however, whether any of these systems, when successful, have owed their success so much to the physical effect as to the suggestive influence exercised on the patient's mind, that he must at the same time limit his eating and increase his exercise. In the matter of fluids particularly, some of the systems are absolutely contradictory of one another, yet success follows their application. There is one serious difficulty in the application of these systems. After a time the patient becomes very tired of the monotony of diet suggested, and growing discouraged, relapse into old habits. If suggestion can be used with as much force without such extreme modifications of diet, the results are as good, and are always more lasting. The important factor is a reduction in the amount eaten, without necessarily denying any but the very rich foods. In this way patients can very soon be induced to take half portions of what they have been previously eating and thus secure a prompt reduction in weight.

It is important that the bowels of obese patients be kept freely open. Tendencies to constipation seem to disturb metabolism in the direction of fat deposition, and even fatty degeneration. Many of the cures at watering places include the taking of laxative salts, or waters of various kinds, and undoubtedly this is helpful at the beginning. But the continuance of such treatment may seriously disturb peristalsis so that it is important to have intervals of rest for the bowels, during which, while there is a regular daily evacuation, there are no tendencies to diarrhea. The suggestive influence of the taking of salts has meant much for a great many so-called obesity cures. They should be employed carefully, but must not be abused.

For fat already accumulated, only exercise will serve as a sure remedy. For fat within the abdomen, the various leg exercises which may be gone through in bed, and the trunk movements, especially those of sitting up from a lying position, when frequently repeated, will soon serve to dissipate accumulated fat. They will also encourage the taking of outdoor exercises, as {297} well as relieve the patient from many muscular discomforts, difficulties of breathing and heart palpitation, which were not only annoying before, but discouraged the taking of exercise.

CHAPTER IX

WEIGHT AND GOOD FEELING

Probably the most important single condition for the maintenance of good health and *good feeling* is the carrying of weight normal for the height and age of the individual, or slightly in excess of normal. Popular expressions contain many proofs of this. The proverb "laugh and grow fat" is undoubtedly due to the recognition by all the world that stout people are nearly always laughers, and as a consequence, perhaps placing the effect for the cause, laughing has been regarded as a factor in putting on flesh. There is no doubt that the exercise for the diaphragm afforded by hearty laughing, with the stimulation of the intra-abdominal circulation consequent upon vigorous diaphragmatic movements, is an important element in producing a healthy state of the important organs of the human economy contained within the abdominal cavity. Dr. Abrams in his book, "The Blues, Causes and Cure," attributes this disturbing condition of depression so familiar to those who have much to do with nervous patients, to a disordered blood and nerve circulation in the splanchnic area, and calls it scientifically, splanchnic neurasthenia. This undoubtedly sums up one important element in the causation of a great many depressive conditions. Most of them are banished by frequent hearty laughter which, with its exercise of the diaphragm, tends to stimulate splanchnic blood vessels and nerves.

Thinness and Discontent.—In general, it is well understood that thin people are likely to be more gloomy and discontented than those of stouter build. The pessimists of the world have usually been lank and lean. Shakespeare, in "Julius Caesar," has the great Roman declare that he likes not "the lean and hungry Cassius," and that "discontent is bred in such bodies." The issue shows his prophetic power. Discontent with life is much more likely in thin people than in stout. Most suicides are under-weight. Where nutrition is under the normal, digestion is sure to be poor because the digestive organs themselves suffer even more than others from lack of food, apparently giving up some of their own substance at the call of other tissues; sleep is nearly always disturbed, constipation is almost the rule, and muscular action becomes distasteful. While in our day we hear much of people overeating, the nervous specialist finds that many of his patients are undereating. {298} These patients grow out of many discomforts, dreads, and symptoms that often seem, even to the physician, to be due to organic change, when they take on enough weight to relieve them from the incessant calls for more nutrition to which insufficient food has made them subject.

Physical Disadvantages of Thinness.—There are many dangers that go with thinness besides the tendency to that irritability of the nervous system which we have come to associate with neurotic symptoms. It has long been known that a person who is under weight is much more likely to contract tuberculosis than a normal individual. From carefully selected statistics, the large insurance companies have determined, that it is far more dangerous to insure a man who is twenty pounds under weight and who has no family heredity of tuberculosis than to insure a man with a family history of tuberculosis on both sides of the house, provided he is well up to or above the normal weight, and is not living in special conditions of danger from contagion. It is contagion and not heredity that plays the most important role in tuberculosis, and the element that is still more important is that of vital resistance. Every adult of thirty years or over has probably at some time had tuberculosis, for traces of its presence are found in the bodies of all adults who come to autopsy. Seven-eighths of the human race are, however, able to resist, and among these seven-eighths by far the greater proportion are those who are above normal weight.

Of course, this matter of the relation of normal weight to good health did not escape the acute observation of the old physicians. Hippocrates, to take the first and greatest of them, realized that while excessive eating and drinking was serious, there were many people who suffered from not eating enough. One of his aphorisms runs, "A slender and restricted diet is generally more dangerous than one a little more liberal." He appreciated, too, the fact that while the old may restrict their diet with more or less impunity, this practice may be, and indeed is likely to be, more serious in young people. He has marshaled the ages and stated the effects of a low diet on them very definitely:

Old persons endure fasting most easily, next adults; young persons not nearly so well, and infants least of all, especially those who are of a particularly lively disposition.

Discomfort Due to Lack of Fat.—Many of the vague discomforts of the internal organs seem to be due to a lack of fat cushions round them, and fat blankets to keep them from being too much subjected to the vicissitudes of external temperature. Anyone who has noted in a series of cases the difference between the condition of patients suffering from a slightly movable kidney when they are well up to weight, and when, on the other hand, they are considerably reduced in weight, will have the significance of the first of these conditions brought home very clearly. Most of the people who suffer much from cold in winter are greatly benefited, as might be expected, by a blanket of fat. It is rather easy to grow accustomed to carrying ten additional pounds of fat when ten additional pounds of clothes would be an insupportable burden. Some fat people are prone to complain of the cold. These are not the plethoric but the anemic. This latter class often have a sluggish circulation, besides a lack of hemoglobin. As a consequence of this their {299} oxidation processes are slow and imperfect, and this is one of the reasons for the over-accumulation of fat. The healthy individual with normal heart and normal blood-making apparatus will always be ever so much more comfortable with a reasonable panniculus adiposus and fat cushions and coverings for the internal organs.

Muscular Weakness and Discomfort.—There are a number of pains and aches occurring in lean persons that are due to nothing else than the weakness of muscle consequent upon the poor nutrition of their muscular tissues. Muscles which do not receive as much nourishment as they should, must necessarily be weak, and if asked to do much work they will resent it. Ordinarily it is not realized how much work is required even for such common muscular efforts as those that are needed to hold the body erect, or to keep it in a stooping position at a definite angle, or to move around on the feet.

I have seen patients lose their aches and pains, and become quite capable of standing weather changes and ordinary hard muscular labor without discomfort, simply as the result of a decided gain in weight. All that was needed was the persuasion to eat more, and especially to eat a full breakfast, the meal likely to be neglected. In some persons, appetite will only return after the correction of constipation and insistence on a certain amount of outdoor air every day, not necessarily exercise—for bus riding or the open cars are excellent appetizers.

Eating Enough.—It is very difficult to persuade some people to eat enough! They have all sorts of excuses. They rather pride themselves on the fact that they do not eat much. Persons who are twenty pounds under weight will calmly tell you that they do not need more than they eat. They are actually in debt to that extent to their tissues, yet they are persuaded that they are paying nature's claims in full. Sometimes the excuse is that they have heard, or read, of how much harm is done by overeating; they have taken to heart the phrase that people are digging their graves with their teeth, and so they are actually cultivating the habit of undereating instead of allowing their instinct for food to manifest itself. Many are found to be following the good old saw of getting up from the table hungry. The inventor of it is not known, but quite unlike the inventor of sleep, it would have been a great blessing if he had kept it to himself by patent right.

After a time habit for these people becomes second nature, and it is hard to get them to eat enough. When people undereat it is the digestive organs that, in my experience, always suffer the most. As a consequence, the appetite decreases because of gradually acquired lack of vitality in the digestive system, its nutrition having been lowered by drafts upon it from other portions of the body. Quite contrary to what is told in the old fable, the stomach apparently is not selfish and does not keep the lion's share for itself. The decrease in the amount of food brings on a decrease in digestive power.

Weight for Height.—The physician who wants to help patients by suggestion must keep before him weight tables for height, as they have been determined by statistics. When people are under weight, it matters not what they may be suffering from, improvement will come if they are made to gain in weight. To be able to show them that they are considerably below the normal and to point out what this probably means in lack of surplus energy, suffices of itself to make many people understand the necessity for {300} effort in the matter and to give them a strong suggestion as to probable relief of their symptoms. The following tables are the best-known averages for men and women:

ADJUSTED TABLE OF WEIGHTS FOR INSURED WOMEN, BASED ON 58,855 ACCEPTED LIVES

171

	15-19	20-24	25-29	30-34	35-39	40-44	45-49	50-54	55-59	60-64	Combined Ages
4' 11"	111	113	115	117	119	119	122	125	128	126	118
5' 0"	113	114	117	119	122	122	125	128	130	129	120
5' 1"	115	116	118	121	124	124	128	131	133	132	122
5' 2"	117	118	120	123	127	127	132	134	137	136	125
5' 3"	120	122	124	127	131	131	135	138	141	140	128
5' 4"	123	125	127	130	134	134	138	142	145	144	131
5' 5"	125	128	131	135	139	139	143	147	149	148	135
5' 6"	128	132	135	139	143	143	146	151	153	152	139
5' 7"	132	135	139	143	147	147	150	154	157	155	143
5' 8"	136	140	143	147	151	151	155	158	161	160	147
5' 9"	140	144	147	151	155	155	159	163	166	165	151
5' 10"	144	147	151	155	159	159	163	167	170	169	155
Combined Heights	123	126	129	132	136	136	139	142	145	142	133

The average shoes of the average woman will raise her about 1-1/2 to 1-3/4 inches.

DR. SHEPHERD'S TABLE OF HEIGHT AND WEIGHT FOR MEN AT DIFFERENT AGES

	15-24	25-29	30-34	35-39	40-44	45-49	50-54	55-59	60-64	65-69
5' 0'	120	125	128	131	133	134	134	134	131	
5' 1'	122	126	129	131	134	136	136	136	134	
5' 2'	124	128	131	133	136	138	138	138	137	
5' 3'	127	131	134	136	139	141	141	141	140	140
5' 4'	131	135	138	140	143	144	145	145	144	143
5' 5'	134	138	141	143	146	147	149	149	148	147
5' 6'	138	142	145	147	150	151	153	153	153	151
5' 7'	142	147	150	152	155	156	158	158	158	156
5' 8'	146	151	154	157	160	161	163	163	163	162
5' 9'	150	155	159	162	165	166	167	168	168	168
5' 10'	154	159	164	167	170	171	172	173	174	174
5' 11'	159	164	169	173	175	177	177	178	180	180
6' 0'	165	170	175	179	180	183	182	183	185	185
6' 1'	170	177	181	185	186	189	188	189	189	189
6' 2'	176	184	188	192	194	196	194	194	192	192
6' 3'	181	190	195	200	203	204	201	198		

Correction of Underweight.—Underweight is undesirable for many reasons, and gain in weight is often the solution of many problems in ill feeling. It is well to bear in mind that most patients who are under weight can be made to gain in weight by an appeal to their reason and by proper directions and care in seeing that those directions are carried out. Patients have told me that they could not eat more and yet I have been able to persuade them that they must eat more, and they have done so. Anyone who has much to do with tuberculous patients knows that utter repugnance for food can be overcome by will-power, when it is once made clear to the patient that they {301} must eat if they want to live. The most interesting event in the process is that with the increase in the amount of food taken, instead of the appetite becoming more and more satiated, as patients are likely to anticipate, and instead of the repugnance for food growing, the appetite grows stronger, and the repugnance gradually disappears. There is only one way to gain in weight; that is by eating more than one has been accustomed to eat. Persons who are twenty pounds under weight ought easily to gain three pounds a week, half a pound a day, if seriously intent on doing so, but in order to do this they will probably have to increase the amount they eat by double this quantity. That means that a solid additional pound of food, quite apart from the watery elements of the food, must be taken every day.

In the correction of under-weight details are all-important. Patients must be given specific directions as to what and how much of the various foods they should take. With regard to supposed idiosyncrasies against such nutritious substances as eggs, milk and butter, enough is said elsewhere to make it clear that, as a rule, these are merely pet notions, beginning in some unfortunate incident and cherished until they have become a mental persuasion strong enough to disturb the digestion of these substances. What is true for quality of food is true also for quantity. People must be made to understand that the amount of food is to be increased. The results attained by this method are well worth the efforts required for it. Of course, the bitter tonics, especially strychnin and cinchona, will do much to help. Just as soon as patients begin to gain in weight many of their neurotic symptoms leave them. Their tired feelings are no longer complained of and when they are up to normal weight they are quite other individuals, both in good humor and efficiency.

If for years patients have been eating less than they should, then they will have discomfort when they begin to eat more. They will have no more discomfort, however, than would be occasioned if they took more exercise than they had been accustomed to. The stomach and intestines must be gradually accustomed to the new task of disposing of more food. Unfortunately, the usual impression among these patients is that discomfort in the abdominal region, by which they mean any sense of fullness, proceeds from indigestion, and indigestion signifies developing dyspepsia with all the horrors that are supposed to go with it. In reality the slight discomfort which comes from increased eating is usually not manifest whenever the patients are occupied with something reasonably interesting. After a time the organs will become accustomed to it, and then the discomfort will cease.

Nervous Patients.—One of the strongest suggestions that we have in our power for thin nervous patients, suffering from many and various ills, is to have them gain in weight. Many of them will be found to be distinctly under weight for their height. They insist that they cannot eat more, that they are eating as much as they care to, and that they have no appetite, that when they eat more they have discomfort, etc. It must be made clear to them that their one easy road to health is to gain in weight. If they are under weight this makes a very definite purpose to put before their minds. The objection so often urged, that they come from a thin family, must not be listened to. The unalterable purpose to make them gain in weight must be insisted upon. If they can be made to eat more than they have been {302} eating before, they will surely gain in weight. To see themselves gaining in weight is a daily renewal of the suggestion that they will be better when they get up to their normal weight. It is much better than electricity or the rest cure, or anything else that I know; it is perfectly natural and, above all, because it may be made an auto-suggestion, it does not leave the patient after a time dependent on anyone else.

CHAPTER X

VAGUE ABDOMINAL DISCOMFORTS—LOOSE KIDNEY

After the vague pains around joints so commonly called rheumatic, and which occur so frequently that probably there is no one over forty who is quite ready to confess that he has not had rheumatism, the most important source of vague discomfort is the abdominal region. This occurs particularly in people who are engaged in a sedentary occupation which prevents much exercise, keeps them indoors, and gives them abundant opportunity as a rule for introspection and dwelling upon their sensations. There are few people who live the intellectual life who have not suffered from some of this abdominal discomfort, which they presumed must mean some definite lesion, or portend some serious development, and yet, as a rule, they have lived for years afterward without any of their fears proving true.

Physicians are not spared from this source of worry and discomfort. They suffer from it even a little more than others. Their knowledge of the possibilities of serious pathological developments within the abdomen, especially after the age of forty, makes them a little more concerned as to the significance of these vague discomforts.

At least half a dozen times a year, for the last ten years, I have heard physicians say that they were sure that some organ or other within was not performing its function properly, and that there was probably some organic lesion. The thought has usually been in their minds for months, sometimes for years, and they have come to be thoroughly examined. Sometimes they rather expect to be told that they should go to a surgeon. They are usually half concealing a question as to how soon they should set about putting their affairs to rights and how serious the outlook is. As a rule, I am able to dismiss them without any further treatment than the injunction not to think so persistently about certain obscure feelings which they are allowing to occupy their consciousness. Sometimes I know they take the advice—even oftener, perhaps, I know they do not. Once it has got hold of us, it is hard to get away from morbid introspection, and I sometimes hear of them consulting others. All of these patients are improved for a time after their consultation by the reassurance that so long as they have a good appetite—which is the case with all of them—and their bowels are regular—which unfortunately is not the case with most of them—and so long as they sleep well and have no acute pain, there is little likelihood of any serious latent abdominal condition.

Such reassurance cannot be given until the abdominal region is carefully palpated, and especially the right side explored as thoroughly as possible. {303} Here lies the appendix, the head of the colon, which is sometimes the seat of trouble not necessarily originating in the appendix. Just above them one may find a loose kidney, for the right kidney is more likely to be movable than the left, because of the overhanging liver, and finally the gall-bladder, and the bile passages, so likely to be the seat of serious trouble. If none of these organs are tender on deep palpation, if the kidney does not come down when the patient is examined in the standing position, if there are no serious derangements of digestion, except such as can be attributed to nervous indigestion, and if there is no dilatation of the stomach, and no enlargement of the spleen, there is no reason why one should do anything but try to get the patient's mind off himself.

There is always the danger of overlooking an abdominal cancer, in these eases, though with the care in diagnosis I have suggested this is minimal. The best therapeutic test that I know to determine this, if there should be any doubt, is to put the patient on an increased diet and watch the scales. If he is able to digest the added food well, and without trouble, and if he proceeds promptly to gain in weight, there is much less than one chance in a hundred that he is the subject of latent cancer in the abdominal region. The old farmer's maxim is: "A sick hog don't get fat." When human beings properly respond to increased feeding, it is probable, not only that there is nothing serious the matter with them, but that the symptoms of which they complained before may very likely have been due to lack of nutrition. The digestive organs not having enough to occupy them, were tempted to digest themselves, or at least to have their function disturbed by the short circuiting of nervous energy looking for something to do.

I have seen a number of these cases that had been operated on for vague discomfort—some whose appendices had been removed, some whose kidneys had been fastened up because they were slightly movable, some whose gall passages had been examined for adhesions that were supposed to exist, or perhaps for a stone that it was thought might be found there, and except where some actual organic lesion was found and relieved, none of them was materially improved when seen several years after operation. I have heard reports of cures of these cases by surgeons who felt that the removal of an appendix presumed to show a catarrhal process, or a hyperemia, or an adhesion at its tip, had meant the cure of vague abdominal discomfort which had continued for many years and made the patient profoundly miserable. But these reports were founded on the patient's condition at the end of convalescence after the operation, and not on the condition that established itself some months, or perhaps a year, later. Operations on the abdomen, except for very definite indications, have, in my experience, always done more harm than good, and I have seen serious conditions—hernia, displacement of organs and disturbance of the peristalsis of the intestines—develop subsequent to them.

I have in mind two typical cases. One was a physician whom I had seen on a number of occasions, and who complained of vague discomfort, mainly in the right side of the abdomen, though never acute, never accompanied by fever, nor even by any disturbance of pulse when he was not in an excitable mood. His bowels were not always regular, and he had had some disturbance of circulation as the result of thrombosis of veins on that side after an {304} attack of typhoid fever. My opinion was that his discomfort was entirely due to the disturbance of circulation. There was probably some interference with the normal full circulation to the large intestine, in its ascending portion, that gave him a feeling of uneasiness, or of consciousness of its function. Eventually he became convinced that he was suffering from a chronic form of appendicitis. After considerable persuasion he convinced a surgeon friend that his appendix should be removed, and the operation was done. I saw his appendix afterwards. It was supposed to be thickened, but considering the normal limits of size of the appendix, I could not think that it was beyond them in any marked way. At most there was but a slight catarrhal inflammation.

For a time after operation he was much improved. He felt confident that all his trouble has disappeared, and he took some pains to impress me with the supposed fact that in these vague cases of discomfort there was always some underlying organic lesion that needed surgical treatment. During convalescence he had gained in weight, and was looking very well. When I met him a year and a half later he said that some of his discomfort had returned. He had grown thinner and was feeling discouraged. Six months later he was about to submit to another operation, this time for the breaking up of adhesions in the neighborhood of his gall-bladder. He had become convinced that this must be the seat of the difficulty. After this operation he was sure, beyond peradventure, that his trouble was gone never to return. Two years later I found him preparing to have his right kidney sewed up. I had known that his right kidney was slightly movable, but it did not move sufficiently to cause any disturbance of kidney function, and certainly not enough to justify serious surgical intervention.

After this operation I met him once casually and he assured me that now everything was surely all right. I have since heard that he submitted to an operation either for the breaking up of some adhesions around his stomach or in order to tuck up that organ for ptosis. It had not been quite decided whether an adhesion caused a slight hour-glass constriction of the stomach, with some dilatation of the splenic end of the fundus, or whether there had been some actual sagging. I am sure that after this operation, as after preceding ones, with the strong suggestion that he ought to be better and an increase of weight during convalescence, he lost his vague abdominal discomfort for a time, though I have no doubt that it either has or will return. When he gets something to so occupy his mind that he does not dwell too much on his discomfort, he will not increase it to the extent that makes it intolerable. Then he will remember that most people have some discomfort, and he will learn to distract his mind, rather than allow it to dwell on the thought of his particular ailment until it becomes intolerable.

It has taken twelve years or more to develop this case to the point where it is as instructive as it now is, and it is a typical example of what may happen even to a physician. There are other cases in my notes that are quite as instructive, two of them occurring in thoroughly educated men, clergymen who were of good intellectual capacity, but who became too much occupied with themselves. One of these had more operations done on him than my friend the physician. He first had his appendix removed, and was better for a time. Then his kidney was fastened up, and improvement once more took place. After this he lost in weight considerably and suffered so much {305} from headaches that a friendly surgeon suggested that there must be adhesions between his dura and his brain. Accordingly a trephining was done, and these adhesions, real or supposed, were broken up. For a time he seemed to be better. Then he had some urinary trouble. A long prepuce, though one that was never tight or adherent, and only required a little attention to cleanliness to keep it from giving bother, was removed. Some disturbance of his appetite led him to limit his eating for a time, and then he suffered from constipation. This was diagnosed by a specialist in rectal troubles as due to abnormally developed valves in his rectum, and these were cut. He still complained very much of abdominal discomfort at times. This was diagnosed as ptosis of his organs, and an operation was done to tuck these up. After this he developed a large ventral hernia, which had to be relieved by a subsequent operation.

I had followed the case carefully during many years, seeing him at times, and I was always opposed to the idea of operation and fully confident that none of the operations were really needed. He could not be persuaded that what his case needed most was occupation of mind with something besides his condition. Whenever I could persuade him of this I had seen him gain in weight, get into much better spirits and be almost able to take up his work again. Then he would become discouraged, and before long I would hear of another operation that was planned, or was about to be performed. During the course of one of his many progressive losses in weight as a consequence of depression of mind, he developed tuberculosis. He resisted this very well, but eventually died rather suddenly of an empyema. A careful autopsy showed nothing but the traces of former operations, and no reason why they should have been done.

Another case: A friend, also a clergyman, had three operations done, one of them circumcision, the second an appendectomy and the third on a supposed floating kidney. None were indicated, so far as I could see, by any definite symptoms, or justified by his condition. He had vague abdominal discomfort, and this continued to bother him in spite of treatment by various specialists, and his mind became so much occupied with it that he was ready to submit to anything in order to be rid of his burden of discomfort. At no time was it an ache, nor did he ever speak of it as a pain. He had some tendency to dilatation of the stomach and at times, when much occupied with indoor work and neglecting muscular exercise, there was probably some delay of digestion. His appetite was good whenever he would let it be; his bowels were regular whenever he was eating sufficient to stimulate them to normal function; he slept well, except when unnerved by something, but the presence of this abdominal discomfort disturbed most of his waking hours. He could stand it so far as it had gone, but he was sure that it would become so much worse in the future that it would be unbearable. He dreaded that cancer or some other awful development would come after a time.

As a matter of fact, the main portion of the discomfort in these cases is the dread of what may happen. It is a dread, just as misophobia or claustrophobia or acrophobia or any of the other dreads that we discuss in the chapter on that subject. The constant occupation with this dread apparently inhibits to some degree the flow of nerve impulses to the abdominal organs, and digestion, already disturbed, is still more impaired. Indeed, the whole {306} of the discomfort seems to be a consciousness of stomach and intestinal function rather than anything more serious. The stomach will take two or three pounds or even more of mingled liquids and solids at a meal and pass them on to the intestines without forcing itself into the field of our consciousness. Anyone who is aware what a thin-walled membranous bag the human stomach is—what it most nearly resembles is perhaps the familiar bladder of the cow—may well be surprised that, though it is supplied with many sensitive nerves, it gives so little sign of the load that is often placed in it. It may, however, be brought rather poignantly into the sphere of consciousness by concentration of attention on it.

The intestines function usually with the same lack of reflex. They proceed to pass on this quantity of food, store up two or three days' rations, digest what is nutritious and eliminate what must be rejected, without rising into consciousness. If either stomach or intestines once begin to attract attention, then it will be difficult, unless care is exercised to distract the mind from them, to replace and keep them back in the sphere of the unconscious once more. Peristaltic movements are constantly taking place in the digestive tract. Various things may interfere with peristalsis, and the disturbance of it will almost surely cause some sensation. It may not be serious, and digestive processes may continue, yet there may be discomfort. If there is delay in the passage of food, gas accumulates in the stomach, presses up against the diaphragm and interferes with the heart action. This will give rise to many bothersome sensations, some of which are felt in the heart region itself; others much lower down on the left side, where it is rather hard to recognize just what the real seat of them may be. A good deal of the abdominal discomfort of which people complain, is due to such functional disturbances, emphasized by the fact that digestive action has come into the sphere of consciousness and now attention is being concentrated on it, to the detriment of digestion itself, as well as to the increase of the annoyance which the discomfort may occasion.

Operations for abdominal discomfort are quite contra-indicated, unless there are very definite localizing symptoms of some pathological lesion that can surely be relieved by operative intervention. To operate on general principles is sure to emphasize the patient's concentration of attention on his abdominal discomfort, if it does not relieve it, and in most of these cases it utterly fails. The strong suggestion of an operation will relieve for the time being, just as operations for epilepsy seemed to relieve when that procedure was first introduced, though now, unless there are definite localizing signs, there is no question of such an operation.

Toxic Factors.—*Tea.*—A very interesting phase of abdominal discomfort seems to be associated with the taking of nerve stimulants. I have frequently found that patients who complained of vague abdominal uneasiness, sometimes rising particularly at night to the height of colicky feelings but always on the left side, were indulging to excess in tea or coffee. In one case, a woman was taking, she thought, about a dozen cups of tea a day. Just how much more than this she actually was taking I do not know, for it is almost incredible the amount of tea that middle-aged women who are alone may take. I once found by actual count made for me, that a woman was taking almost a score of cups of tea in each twenty-four hours.

{307}

Just as soon as there is a reduction in the amount of tea taken in these cases, relief is afforded the patient. This relief will not, however, be absolutely satisfactory because the craving for the tea stimulation makes the patients irritable, and it takes but very little to cause them to complain that they still have their old discomfort. In the course of three or four days they realize that the root of the trouble has been reached. If the discomfort has continued for a good while, a sort of habit seems to be formed, and the attention of the mind gives a sense of uneasiness, if not discomfort, in the left abdominal region. Usually it is in the upper left quadrant and seems to be stomachic in origin. The discomfort is apparently due to the presence of air, or gas, which is not properly expelled because of some lack of co-ordination of muscles, and then the warmth of a room or of the bed at night, or the presence of some slightly irritant substance makes the discomfort more noticeable. In the patient's over-stimulated condition, there is inability to withstand it patiently. In none of these cases is there a fever, though in all there is some disturbance of the pulse as if the heart's action were interfered with and the organ resented it.

Coffee.—In some cases the same vague abdominal discomfort occurs as a consequence of taking too much coffee. This is seen in men more than in women. The tea topers are nearly all women, though my attention was first called to this vague discomfort, that made life miserable for a tea tester, who spent most of his day tasting tea, though drinking very little of it. With regard to coffee, individual idiosyncrasy is an extremely important matter. Some men seem to be able to take five, six or even more cups of coffee in the day without inconvenience; some cannot take even a small cup of coffee after six o'clock at night without being kept awake for several hours; others cannot take a large cup of coffee in the morning without having considerable discomfort, which is usually attributed to indigestion. I have

175

known large, strong men, who were much better for not taking any coffee, or at the most a tablespoonful of it in a cup of milk in the morning to satisfy the taste.

Loose Kidney.—Movable kidney is responsible for many of these cases of abdominal discomfort. Where it exists to a marked degree it may be relieved by operation. It occurs much more frequently in women than in men because, for physiological reasons, the kidneys are normally more movable in women and this is particularly true of the right kidney, which would otherwise perhaps be injured by pressure between the pregnant uterus and the liver. It is probable that many of the cases of the kidney of pregnancy are really due to an abnormal fixity of the kidney to a particular place, so that the growing uterus interferes by pressure with its circulation and its function. Slight movability of the kidney, then, should not be considered pathological.

I have seen a number of these cases. They seem to occur particularly in women who have lost weight. The fat around the kidney is somewhat absorbed during the course of loss in weight, and this leaves this organ more movable and also less protected and consequently more liable to irritation. One sees it rather frequently in many unmarried women who have some strenuous occupation. Many of these young women come back from their vacation at the end of the summer having gained fifteen or twenty pounds in weight. If there has been any kidney sensitiveness or movability before, {308} both have usually disappeared. The kidney is well held in place because there is much more fat within the abdomen, all the organs are better cushioned, yet without any interference with their function.

During the course of the year these patients, school-teachers, stenographers, and daily workers of various kinds, lose in weight. When they have lost ten pounds the kidney begins to be sensitive again and somewhat movable. By the time they have lost fifteen to twenty pounds there is serious complaint in the right upper quadrant of their abdomen extending at times over toward the navel, and the kidney becomes quite movable. At this time the treatment must consist in holding the kidney as firmly in place as possible, for dragging downward will be followed by reflex symptoms in the stomach and intestines. Disinclination to food, loss of appetite, and even the occurrence of some nausea, as well as some constipation, are easily traced to kidney reflexes. During the night there is no trouble, because while the patient is lying down the kidney falls into its proper position. On arising in the morning the kidney drops down out of place. If a corset is put on at this time the kidney may be forced still further out of place, giving rise, after a couple of hours, to considerable discomfort. New shoes can be borne at first, but after a time the pressure they produce shuts off circulation and causes intolerable discomfort. To a less degree this happens to the kidney if thus compressed and this explains the course of symptoms in many cases.

Mechanical Treatment.—If the corset is adjusted before the patient rises, and fits reasonably snugly, but not too tight, the contents of the abdomen will all be kept in place, and the kidney will maintain its normal position. When the corset is not sufficient to retain the kidney in place, a simple pad, a towel or a napkin or, if there is much sensitiveness, something more elaborate, especially adapted to conditions, can be placed over the kidney, and when held firmly by the corset will keep the kidney in its place. At first the kidney is usually sensitive to this on account of having been pressed upon during the preceding weeks or months. The patient must bear some little inconvenience at first, must get accustomed to the new conditions in which the kidney is kept in place, and must not expect complete relief at once. Any improvement must be considered a step forward, and further amelioration can be confidently promised. As in all other cases of the use of apparatus or mechanical aids—spectacles, false teeth or crutches—the patient must be content to grow used to the new order of things, before expecting satisfying relief.

This is the palliative treatment. The natural treatment of many of these cases is to have the patient maintain such weight as will hold the kidney in place, because of the fat within the abdomen, without any necessity for external aids. This can be done more readily than is often thought to be possible. These patients insist that they lose their appetite when they settle down to work, but what they really lose is the habit of eating a definite amount at stated intervals. Very often it will be found that breakfast, which they took abundant time to eat during vacation, is rushed. The luncheon suffers in the same way and is small in quantity. They take only one good meal, and one good meal is not sufficient to maintain normal weight.

Question of Operation.—When a kidney is so movable as to deserve the adjective "floating," so that it moves considerably from its place and, perhaps, even sags and may be felt in the subumbilical region, it should be fastened up {309} by surgical means. There is a choice between two evils. The fastening of the kidney in the loin does not restore the normal condition, but puts it in an artificial condition. The kidney supports are of such a kind that it was evidently meant to be slightly movable. When it is fastened firmly in the loin, it is likely to feel every jar, and certain post-operative cases that I have seen, in which firm adhesions had supposedly taken place, complained considerably of the discomfort occasioned by this. In a certain number of cases, even after the operation, the kidney is still somewhat movable, because the adhesions yield and some of the old distress returns. All this must be realized before there is any question of an operation. There must be not merely a little discomfort, but enough of actual ache and of reflex disturbance that can be traced directly to the kidney to warrant the operation.

No floating kidney should be operated upon in a patient who has lost much in weight and has developed a sensitiveness of the kidney since the reduction of weight. Definite efforts should first be made to bring about increase in weight, so as to see whether this will not restore the previous condition of reasonable comfort. At times it is said that the disturbance of the stomach, that is reflex to such a floating kidney, prevents the patient from taking and assimilating enough food to restore normal weight. This will be true if attention has been called to the condition very seriously, and if the patient is persuaded that this is the reason why there is no appetite and poor digestion. Ordinary palliative measures, such as a binder, or a specially made corset, will be sufficient to prevent the kidney from producing reflex disturbance of the stomach, and will exert a strong suggestion to this effect under the influence of which the patient will usually gain in weight.

Intermittent Discomfort.—The discomfort that comes with a loose kidney may be quite intermittent. I have known patients to be bothered by it for months, and then quite free from it for several years, only to have their discomfort renewed so that they become quite worried. Some definite local or mechanical condition can generally be found for these variations in feeling.

In thin people a jolting ride over a rough road or stepping off a car will occasionally be the beginning of the trouble, and as this also is likely to cause a stone in the kidney to give its first manifestations, there may be serious suspicion of a more grave pathological condition than is really present. If this discomfort continues only the X-ray can absolutely decide the question.

Once the mechanical conditions which cause the discomfort are understood by the patient, the actual ache becomes much more easy to bear. Apprehension makes it almost intolerable. Attention exaggerates it, and makes diversion of mind difficult. Understanding helps all the conditions and lessens the pain, not actually but mentally, until after a time very little attention is paid to it.

{310}

SECTION VII

CARDIOTHERAPY

CHAPTER I

THE HEART AND MENTAL INFLUENCE

The heart is an organ so vitally important that we might expect it to be carefully protected by nature from any interference with its action through mental influence, emotional conditions, or voluntary or involuntary feelings. As a matter of fact, it is extremely susceptible to mental influence, stimulant or depressive, and to emotions of all kinds. Psychotherapy, that is, the removal of inhibiting influences originating in the mind, and the suggestion of favorable mental influences, is probably more important for the heart than for any other organ in the body. The law of reserve energy has its most noteworthy applications with regard to it. When we are apparently so completely fatigued that we cannot do anything more, a purely mental stimulus may so enliven the heart as to give the body a new supply of strength and energy. A man wandering through a desert, or swimming for his life at sea, may be so exhausted as to be quite ready to give up entirely, and be brought to the conviction that he has absolutely no strength left for further effort, when a flash in the distance, or a sound that indicates that help is near, or some other mental incitement, will give renewed energy. It is probably through the heart that there comes to us most of our power to accomplish things when we are already so tired as to seem exhausted. On the other hand, it is the failure of circulation in muscles, because of a slacking heart, that produces the sense of exhaustion. Muscular work is easy or even pleasant when we are in good spirits, while, whenever exertion is undertaken in the midst of discouragement, we cannot accomplish nearly so much as when conditions are so framed as to give stimulus and encouragement.

If a perfectly normal heart can be so affected by mental conditions and emotions as to be seriously disturbed in its work on the one hand, or greatly stimulated into new activity on the other, it is to be expected that a heart affected by disease will be similarly affected and probably even to a greater degree. It is clear, then, that our cardiac patients have to be guarded against unfavorable mental conditions, and have to have all their reserve energy called out for them by encouragement and by the best possible prognosis for their reflection. This is especially true as regards the removal of the many unfavorable suggestions which, because of ignorance, have in the past gathered round most forms of heart disease.

{311}

Emotion and the Heart.—The mental and emotional influence over the heart's action was the truth that lay at the basis of the old fallacy with regard to the physiology of the heart. The literature of all countries testifies that the heart was long supposed to be the seat and origin of the emotions. Every one has experienced how the heart jumps when something unexpected happens. People have fainted from excess of joy as well as of grief. The physical side of emotion is so generally associated with some modification of the heart beat that it is no wonder that emotions were directly connected with the organ. When people are in depressed states the heart is apt to beat more slowly than usual, while when in states of exhilaration, even those dependent merely on mental factors, the pulse is more rapid. Melancholic states have occasionally been attributed to the slowness of the pulse, but the slow pulse seems to be a symptom connected with the mental condition rather than a causative factor. In the maniacal conditions, the rapidity of the pulse, which is sometimes quite marked, must probably be explained in the same way, as due to the mental excitement under which the patient is laboring.

The Heart and the Nervous System.—Prof. Von Leyden ten years ago recalled attention to the fact that the heart is literally the *primum movens* in man, and that before the central nervous system is laid down, or there is any possible question of impulses flowing from center to periphery, the heart, or at least its embryonic representative, is beating as constantly, regularly, rhythmically, as it is to do during all the

177

subsequent life of the individual. Oliver Wendell Holmes has expressed it poetically by stating that the angel of life sets this heart pendulum going and only the angel of death can break into the case and stop it.

Primitive Heart Action.—The original beating of the heart is entirely automatic, and quite apart from any nervous initiative or stimulus. The original bend in the primal blood vessel, which is to represent the heart in the course of development, begins to pulsate very early in the chick and evidently does the same thing in all other living things. Notwithstanding this fact that the heart is thus easily demonstrated to be the *primum movens*, the first exhibitor of vitality, and might thus seem to be one of the organs or indeed the one which should be safe from any nervous interference, later on powerful connections with the nervous system are made, and heart acceleration and inhibition become familiar phenomena. Every emotion, as we have said, has its influence on the heart and even a certain amount of voluntary control may be acquired. Indian fakirs are said to be able to cause the heart to slow and almost to stop. The curious phenomenon of suspended animation which they sometimes exhibit is said to be due to this. Certain of the well-developed muscular subjects who exhibit themselves at medical clinics are able to cause their hearts to miss a beat, but this is said to be rather a result of will-power over other muscles compressing the thorax, and interfering with the heart, than direct influence upon the heart itself.

Mental Influence over Diseased Hearts.—Worry produces much more serious symptoms in heart patients than in others. Anxiety about the heart itself is often a source of serious detriment to a heart patient. Most people have such a terror of having anything the matter with their hearts that the haunting thought of such calamity is likely to have a definite influence in preventing the development of such compensation as will enable the heart to {312} do its work to the best advantage. It used to be the custom to refrain from telling patients suffering from tuberculosis that they had the disease. On the other hand, people with heart disease were usually informed of that fact. The reason given for the latter course was that heart disease may in many cases be the forerunner of sudden death, and the warning knowledge was supposed to enable a man to get his affairs in order. No worse policy for either disease could well have been imagined. The pulmonary patient should be told at once, the heart patient should, as far as possible, be saved the depressing knowledge of his condition.

Dr. MacKenzie, whose practically illuminating studies of heart disease give him a right to express opinions with regard to it (and when those opinions concern the influence of the mind they are doubly valuable because of the absolute objectivity of his studies), has some rather strong expressions with regard to the importance of modifying the mental state in heart cases. He says:

The consciousness of heart trouble has often a depressing effect on people, whether the trouble be slight or serious. When such people become convinced that the trouble is curable or not serious, their condition at once becomes greatly improved. Cures by faith, whether in drugs, baths, elaborate methods or religion, act by playing upon the mental condition. But our employment of this element in treatment should not be the outcome of blind unreasoning faith in some rite or ceremony, bath or drug, but in the intelligent perception of the nature of the symptoms. The reassurance of the patient of the harmless nature of the complaint goes a great way in curing him. The reassurance that with reasonable care no danger need be feared is extremely helpful. Even in serious cases when there is reasonable hope of recovery or a certain degree of recovery, the encouragement of the patient may and does help forward his improvement.

Heart Remedies and Suggestion.—Probably the best evidence we have for the influence of the mind over the heart in diseased conditions, that is, when there is definite organic change in the heart valves or muscle, is to be found in the history of the many remedies that have come and gone in heart therapeutics during the past generation. Strophanthus, for instance, was very popular a quarter of a century ago, and it seems as though in many cases it not only replaced, but was more efficient than digitalis. How few there are who use it now with confidence, and how general is the impression that it does not affect the heart to any extent! The confidence with which the remedy was given by the physician was conveyed to the patient and he "took heart," as the expression is, and proceeded to get better. Even more striking is the evidence afforded by other remedies. For a while it seemed that cactus provided a heart stimulant and regulator of value. Convalaria also gained a reputation as a heart remedy. Both are now practically abandoned. Here, once more, the real remedy, when these substances were employed, was, undoubtedly, the suggestion to the patient in connection with the regulation of his habits of life, so that his heart got a chance to catch up with its work. There are other remedies with which we had similar experiences.

Even digitalis has had phases of confidence and distrust in it, that are interesting to study in the light of what we now know with regard to the influence of the psyche on the heart. One hears at medical society meetings reports of the favorable action of digitalis within a few hours of its administration. These are not examples of digitalis action, but of mental influence. {313} Any heart patient after the first visit of a physician in whom he has confidence is sure to brighten up at once, heart action is ever so much better and symptoms of mental depression, and even of circulatory disturbance, disappear. It is this that has made the study of even the efficiency of digitalis so difficult. There were times when most physicians employed it in rather large quantities for all forms of heart disease. In some heart cases it is absolutely contra-indicated. Fortunately many of the preparations of digitalis used in the past were quite inert, and so no harm was done. The results obtained were psychotherapeutic.

Cardiac Inhibition.—The importance of the role of the nervous system and of the mental influences which control it in all functions is well illustrated by what we have learned during the last half century with regard to inhibition in the animal organism. We used to think that while the nervous system sent down positive impulses—that is, nervous stimuli which brought about the accomplishment of certain activities—it had nothing to do with the stoppage of those activities. Such interference was supposed always to be due to external influences of various kinds, potent for the time, in the organism. We have learned, however, that inhibition is one of the important functions of the nervous system. The idea has now become so familiar that sometimes we are apt to forget how great is its significance. Lauder Brunton, in his article on "Inhibition," set forth its role as we have come to know it.

The recognition of the part inhibition plays in vital phenomena is undoubtedly one of the most important discoveries which have been made in physiology since Harvey discovered the circulation of the blood. It throws light upon an immense number of phenomena previously inexplicable and enables us to form theories of a satisfactory nature about many vital problems. It offers an explanation of the nature of hypnotic states, which is at least as satisfactory as that we have of the action of many drugs.

The nervous mechanism of the heart affords the best and most commonly cited example of inhibitory action, and here it was first studied by Weber and Claude Bernard in 1848. The cardiac ganglia derived from the sympathetic preside over the movements of the organ, and in response to the stimulus of the intra-ventricular blood-pressure cause rhythmical contraction of the cavities. Their action is, however, controlled by the pneumogastric nerve, through which impulses of an inhibitory nature are constantly traveling and acting as a restraining force.

As noted by Lauder Brunton, the late Professor Czermak had a small glandular tumor in close contact with the right pneumogastric nerve and he was able by pressure on this to compress the nerve to any extent he wished, and either "to completely stop the heart or simply retard it." He often performed this experiment so that it is not nearly so dangerous as might be thought. We have some instances, apparently too well authenticated to be doubted, in which the power of the human will to inhibit heart action has been as strikingly manifested as this mechanical disturbance of Professor Czermak. Sometimes these stories of cardiac inhibition through the will are dismissed as unworthy of credence, and doubtless many of them are mere fiction, or have been exaggerated for sensational purposes, but some of them are very suggestive examples of the power of the will over the heart. If only a modicum of such power were to be employed, it would seriously hamper heart action, and it must be the aim of psychotherapy to prevent such inhibition.

{314}

At least one instance of voluntary heart inhibition was observed by thoroughly trained and properly accredited scientists. A report of it has been published. As a bit of documentary evidence, on a subject that is usually considered so vague as to be scarcely worth considering, Dr. Cheyne's description of the remarkable power of Colonel Tonshend over his heart should be in the hands of those who wish to influence hearts through minds and wills.

He could die or expire when he pleased, and yet by an effort, or somehow, he could come to life again. . . . We all three felt his pulse first: it was distinct, though small and thready, and his heart had its usual beating. He composed himself upon his back and lay in a still posture for some time. While I held his right hand. Dr. Baynard laid his hand upon his heart, and Mr. Skrine held a clean looking-glass to his mouth. I found his pulse sink gradually till at last I could not feel any, by the most exact and nice touch; Dr. Baynard could not feel the least motion in the heart, nor Mr. Skrine discern the least soil of breath on the bright mirror. Then each of us by turns examined his arm, heart and breath, but could not by the nicest scrutiny, discover the least symptom of life in him. We reasoned a long time about this odd appearance, and finding he still continued in that position, we began to conclude that he had indeed carried the experiment too far; and at last we were satisfied that he was already dead, and were just ready to leave him. This continued about half an hour. . . . As we were going away we perceived some motion about the body, and, upon examination, found his pulse and the motion of his heart gradually returning; he began to breathe heavily and speak softly.

Nor must it be thought that the inhibitory faculty can act only in slowing the heart. Normally a certain amount of inhibition is exercised over the heart's action. If by any chance this should be decreased then acceleration of cardiac activity may take place. Lauder Brunton called attention to that in discussing another phase of pneumogastric function. He said:

Paralysis of the pneumogastric, of course, does away with its action. And hence we have among other symptoms of this condition increased rapidity of the contractions of the heart from withdrawal of the inhibitory influence.

If slowing of the heart action can be produced through the mind by this mechanism of inhibition, so also under other circumstances may acceleration occur.

Shock and the Heart.—How large a role emotion plays in disturbing the action of a heart that is already diseased, is illustrated by the story told in serious histories, on what seems good authority, of the dwarf of the French king, who was frightened to death by what he thought were the arrangements for his execution. While we take great pains as a rule to impress upon sufferers from organic heart disease the necessity for their avoiding every kind of over-exertion, or sudden movement of any kind, we do not always impress upon them the even greater necessity for the avoidance of shock and fright, and profound emotions. It must not be thought that emotional shocks have a deleterious effect only in advanced cases of heart trouble. Almost any physician will readily recall examples where emotion had much to do with the break in compensation which indicates that the heart has for a time been overworked.

A case in my own experience illustrates this: The patient, a student, had suffered from severe so-called growing pains, undoubtedly rheumatic, when he was about fourteen, and probably had acquired a heart lesion at that time. {315} It did not, however, disturb him in the slightest degree. The patient had never noticed any fatigue on running up stairs; he had no shortness of breath; there were no symptoms pointing to his heart. One summer while his family were in the country he came into town for the day, and missing the last train out, he went to the family home to sleep, though it had been closed up for the summer. He let himself in without difficulty and was preparing to go to bed when he resolved to get a glass of water. There being no tumbler nearer than the dining-room, he went there. As he entered the dining-room he struck a match. With the flash of the light he found himself looking into the barrel of a revolver and a hoarse voice said, "Hands up!" His hands went up. The next minute he was in the hands of two "plain clothes" policemen who had been watching the neighborhood because of recent burglaries. Noticing the light upstairs, they had made their way in for the purpose of catching what they thought a burglar at work.

The young fellow, who had never before fainted, collapsed almost at once, and was unconscious for some minutes. The next day he was rather prostrated and tired on movement. By resting a good deal for the next week this passed off to a considerable degree, but then his physician found that he was suffering from a serious heart lesion, with a decided break in compensation. I saw him several months later. His heart had never regained its old power, and his mitral valve was quite unable to fulfill its function. Just what the mechanism of the

179

almost sudden break in compensation was after he had been for so long quite immune from any effects of the rheumatism, is hard to say, but the lesson of the case is easy to understand.

Place of Psychotherapy in Treatment.—The role of psychotherapy, then, in heart cases consists in the recognition of the part that the mind, the will and the emotions play in their influence over this important organ. These psychic factors may produce disturbed conditions of various kinds. The more experience the physician has with cardiac cases of all kinds, organic as well as functional, the more powerful does he recognize the influence of the mind over the heart to be. The expression that a man is living on his will is no mere figure of speech. Some cases we have cited seem to show that a favorable attitude of mind keeps up heart action, where an unfavorable attitude would almost surely allow the heart to fail. It is this very potent influence then that must be used to as great advantage as possible in the psychotherapy of cardiac patients.

Undoubtedly the most important phase of it is in prophylaxis. As far as possible we must save our heart patients from emotions. The effect of emotion on the heart is known. When that organ is already crippled, emotion may produce a serious strain on it. It is as important to save heart patients from joyful emotions as from those of contrary nature. Many a son who, after years of absence, thought to surprise a dear old mother by suddenly presenting himself to her, has learned to his cost that an old heart may break from joy, almost as easily as from sorrow, and may be as unfavorably affected by the glad emotions as by terror or fright. We must also save heart patients from the unfavorable influence of a bad prognosis, and of too serious a diagnosis, both of which may be quite unjustified, for the rule is that the longer a man has been studying the heart, the less likely is he to be confident in his diagnosis, or unfavorable in his prognosis.

{316}

The curative place of psychotherapy is in the obtaining, as far as possible, of placid easy lives for these patients. This does not mean that they are to give up their occupations, for very often the internal emotional life, which develops when they have nothing to do but think about themselves, will be more serious in its effect upon the heart than the ordinary vocation. Exciting incidents in life work must, however, be avoided. If men are in occupations that require exposure to excitement, then it may be advisable to change their occupations. Brokers, speculators, actors, sometimes public speakers, on whom appearances in public in spite of apparent placidity are often a severe strain, may have to be guided into quieter paths of life. In general, in every attempt to treat heart disease, and the neurotic symptoms which develop in connection with it, the patient's mind must be considered as one of the most important therapeutic factors.

CHAPTER II

DIAGNOSIS AND PROGNOSIS IN HEART DISEASE

The more carefully heart disease, and particularly individual patients affected by various heart lesions, have been studied in recent years the more it has come to be appreciated that the most important element in the treatment of organic heart disease is the definite recognition of the difficulty of exact diagnosis of most cardiac conditions and the unfortunate tendency to make the prognosis worse than it really is. Many heart affections are quite compatible with long life. In the past both of these problems of diagnosis and prognosis have been only too often solved unfavorably to the patient, to the serious detriment of his power of physical reaction against the ailment. Many a patient has been seriously disturbed and even his power of compensation lessened by having a diagnosis of an organic affection of the heart made with the usual prognosis, or at least strong suggestion of early death that goes with it, when there was no justification for such an unfavorable opinion.

Mental Attitude of Patient.—We do not pretend to cure tuberculosis, but we do relieve its symptoms and bring about a remission in the progress with a shutting in of the lesions. In heart disease something of the same kind can very often be accomplished. This does not mean that in advanced cases of heart disease much good can be accomplished any more than in advanced cases of tuberculosis, though in both a change of the mental attitude may lift the patient from what seems almost a death-bed into renewed activity for a prolonged period. Probably heart disease is more serious in its prognosis than tuberculosis, yet undoubtedly the lives of many patients could be prolonged nearly as much as in the pulmonary affection and a large amount of suffering saved through mental influence. We do not hesitate to change the occupation and the place of abode of the patient suffering from tuberculosis. There is even greater reason for doing this same thing when it seems advisable with patients suffering from heart disease.

With regard to heart disease, the best authorities are now agreed that it is better, as a rule, not to tell the patient himself unless it is absolutely {317} necessary to do so in order to get him to take the precautions that will prevent further deterioration of his cardiac condition. The depression incident to the knowledge that one has a serious heart lesion is not reacted against, and especially not during a threatening break in compensation, and a more favorable time must be waited for to reveal his condition to him. The danger of sudden death in valvular heart disease is much less than is popularly supposed. Only sufferers from aortic heart disease are likely to die without warning, and this form of the disease is comparatively rare. The death of the patient suffering from mitral disease is likely to be lingering. Mitral disease is the commonest form of heart disease, and the prognosis of it in ordinary cases is by no means so grave as is usually supposed. I have seen a patient still alive with a mitral murmur who told the story of having had his affection originally diagnosed as mitral regurgitation by Skoda, the distinguished Vienna diagnostician, over forty years before. This patient at the time I saw him was nearly seventy years of age, still had the mitral murmur, but his apex beat was scarcely if at all displaced and there was neither enlargement of the ventricle nor apparently any degeneration of the auricle.

The Apex Beat and Heart Murmurs.—In this regard an expression of Prof. Carl Gerhardt of Berlin deserves to be recalled. That distinguished clinician used to say that if the apex beat was not displaced there was no good reason for thinking that any heart affection which might be present was serious enough to require active treatment. Heart murmurs have been made entirely of too much significance and any man of considerable experience is likely to have seen a number of patients who, because they had a heart murmur, had been seriously and needlessly disturbed by having a physician tell them that they had heart disease, with an air of finality that seemed to the patients to say that they might prepare for the worst very soon. Patients suffering from diseased hearts have to care specially for themselves, but not to the extent of living such maimed lives as is likely to be the case if they are depressed by an unfortunate exaggeration of the seriousness of their condition.

Our best authorities in heart disease have at all times proclaimed their uncertainty as to the diagnosis of heart conditions from murmurs, while mediocre men of comparatively slight experience have not hesitated to declare their certainty in this difficult matter. It is not an unusual thing to hear of a supposed expert having declared upon the witness stand and under oath that he could tell whether a man had heart disease by *listening* to his heart, and some have even gone the length of making their decisions in this matter while listening for a few moments sometimes even above the clothing of the patient! Needless to say, this is quite unjustifiable in our present knowledge of the status of heart affections and only men of small experience and over-confidence in themselves make any such declarations. The more experience a physician has had in heart disease, the more careful he is not to make positive declarations. One or two examinations may very easily be deceptive unless there are signs quite apart from those in the heart itself. Indeed, it is much more the state of the individual than the state of the heart itself, or anything that can be found out about it, except after a prolonged and repeated study, that enables us to make definite decisions. Probably no one during the nineteenth century had studied hearts more carefully than Prof. William Stokes, whose books on the subject were so widely read. He wrote:

{318}

We read that a murmur with a first sound, under certain circumstances, indicates lesion of the mitral valves. And again, that a murmur with the second sound has this or that value. All this may be very true, but is it always easy to determine which of the sounds is the first, and which is the second? Every candid observer must answer this question in the negative. In certain cases of weakened hearts acting rapidly and irregularly, it is often scarcely possible to determine the point. Again, even where the pulsations of the heart are not much increased in rapidity, it sometimes, when a loud murmur exists, becomes difficult to say with which sound the murmur is associated. The murmur may mask not only the sound with which it is properly synchronous, but also that with which it has no connection, so that in some cases even of regularly acting hearts, with a distinct systolic pulse, and the back stroke with the second sound, nothing is to be heard but one loud murmur.

So great is the difficulty in some cases, that we cannot resist altering our opinions from day to day as to which is the first and which the second sound.

To the inexperienced the detailed descriptions of such phenomena as the intensification of the sounds of the pulmonary valves; of constrictive murmurs as distinguished from non-constrictive; of associations of different murmurs at the opposite sides of the heart; of pre-systolic and post-systolic, pre-diastolic and post-diastolic murmurs, act injuriously—first, by conveying the idea that the separate existence of these phenomena is certain, and that their diagnostic value is established; and secondly, by diverting attention from the great object, which—it cannot be too often repeated—is to ascertain if the murmur proceeds from an organic cause; and again, to determine the vital and physical state of the cavities of the heart. . . .

There are too many cases in which murmurs have no such serious significance as was often attributed to them when first studied, and yet it used to be almost a universal custom among physicians, and the custom still obtains with many, to tell a patient rather emphatically whenever a heart murmur was present, that he had heart disease. Above all, too much significance has been ascribed to murmurs in initial cases of heart disease and these are just the cases that should not be disturbed by unfavorable suggestion. The louder the murmur the less likelihood there is of there being heart disease in the ordinarily accepted sense of the term, that is, that the heart is so affected as to be incapable of doing its work properly, for where loud murmurs are present this is almost never the case. A murmur that may be heard a foot distant is usually associated with perfect compensation.

If this were remembered by those who examine hearts generally, there would be much less disturbance of heart action by unfavorable mental influence. A great many more who are suffering from certain symptomatic conditions of the heart not surely or necessarily dependent on organic lesions, are plunged into depression by unfortunate, premature or exaggerated expressions on the part of their physicians. It is almost a rule to have men and even women patients say that it makes no difference to them, that they should be told the exact truth as to what their condition is. The future has been mercifully hidden from us in most things and there is no doubt that this plan is the better for human comfort and accomplishment generally.

The truth is not easy to find and oftener in these cases lies on the side of favorable prognosis and refusal to think the worst than the opposite. In this there has been a great difference between the German and the Irish schools of medicine. The three great Irish physicians, Graves, Stokes and Corrigan, insisted on the place of the individual and upon how much depends upon the general conditions in pulmonary and cardiac disease. Our teaching in {319} America in this matter has come not from the conservative British schools of medicine, but from the German school, and that has had a notable tendency to exaggerate the significance of heart signs over the general condition.

What a great distinction there is between this mode of looking at these diseases and the German method was pointed out by Prof. Lindwurm of Munich, when he translated Prof. Stokes' work on the heart into German. Prof. Lindwurm said:

181

Thus our modern German works are to a greater or lesser extent only treatises on the physical diagnosis of organic affections of the heart. Stokes, on the contrary, resists this one-sided tendency which bases the diagnosis solely on physical signs and disregards the all-important vital phenomena; he lays less weight on the differential diagnosis of lesions on the several valves and on the situation of a sound than on the condition of the heart in general, and especially on the question as to whether a murmur is organic or inorganic, and whether the disease itself is organic or functional.

Broadbent on Cardiac Diagnosis.—What Stokes taught the English-speaking world so emphatically in the first half of the nineteenth century Sir William Broadbent was just as insistent about in the latter half. It is evident, then, that clinical experience has not changed its viewpoint in these matters in spite of all our study of the heart in the interval. In his paper on "The Conduct of the Heart in the Face of Difficulties" he has many suggestions that will prevent the physician of less experience from taking too pessimistic a view of heart symptoms. He said:

Moreover, the heart has very special relations with the nervous system; it reflects every emotion, beats high with courage, is palsied by fear, throbs rapidly and violently with excitement, and acts feebly under nervous depression; but it is not only through the cerebro-spinal system that the heart is influenced, it is in immediate relation with the vasomotor nervous apparatus, and in a scarcely less degree with the sympathetic system generally. Normally, afferent impulses are constantly flowing from the viscera to the central nervous system and by this reflex process their blood supply is regulated, and their functional activity is governed. These afferent impulses when perverted by functional derangement or disease may become serious disturbing influences.

The nervous system in a large and increasing proportion of people is unduly sensitive and excessively mobile, and the reactions to influences of every kind are exaggerated. In some a little emotional excitement gives rise to palpitation, and a piece of bad news or the bang of a door seems to stop the heart altogether. *There is in such subjects no form or degree of cardiac disease which may not he simulated.* Add a touch of hysteria on the lookout for symptoms and for someone to give ear to the narration of the unparalleled agonies of the sufferer, and the difficulties of the heart, and it may be added of dealing with them, are complete.

Typical Case.—We are prone to think that after the age of seventy the existence of definite heart murmurs with some tendency to blueness of the lips and of the fingers, with coldness of the hands, surely indicates the presence of a serious heart lesion. It is in old people, however, that such symptoms may be most deceptive. The outcome may prove that physical signs ordinarily presumed to be surely indicative of organic disease may be only signs of functional disorder, or at most may represent certain organic affections for which even the old heart is thoroughly capable of compensation. One such instance in my own experience is so striking that I venture to give it in detail.

{320}

This was the case of an old physician friend of some eighty years of age. His son had a summer lodge in the Adirondacks. Though for some sixty years the father had been living at the sea level in New York almost constantly, he went up to visit the son and be with his grandchildren at an elevation of nearly 2,500 feet. His heart began to bother him almost at once and he could not go up or down stairs or take any exercise without considerable discomfort, marked shortness of breath and a tendency to palpitation that was almost alarming. He continued his stay for several months in the hope that he would get used to the altitude, though there were always difficulties of circulation manifested by blue lips and finger nails. He returned to New York and placed himself under the care of a heart specialist who found what appeared to be evident signs of heart deterioration of muscular character complicated by valvular lesions. He consoled, the old gentleman by the reflection that a heart that had served his purposes so well for eighty years could not really be complained of if now it should show some signs of deterioration. He also insisted that any mental work would be almost sure to be injurious because of the calls upon the circulation that it would make.

The old gentleman was ordered South for the following winter with an absolute prohibition of any mental work. He had planned to revise an historical work on which he had been engaged for many years and which had served to keep him in good health perhaps more than anything else. This was put away entirely and he proceeded to try to get well doing nothing. Almost needless to say with nothing to do he did not get well. He had been an extremely busy man all his life, had worked at least twelve to fourteen hours a day for most of the preceding fifty years, and for him to do nothing would be quite as impossible as for a child to be kept in utter physical inactivity. His heart palpitation continued and grew worse. He was waked up at night by starts that seriously disturbed him and usually kept him from sleep for hours. As he said himself, after he had read the morning paper and gone to stool, there was nothing else for him to do all day except eat and sleep, and these incidents had never occupied any of his attention in the past. In spite of the doctor's orders he had his manuscript sent to him and proceeded to work. At once he began to grow better. At the end of three months he was feeling better than he had felt for several years. When I saw him, about his eighty-first birthday, he was looking better than he had for some time.

As he said himself in describing his case, his own experience had taught him that the more fuss a heart made the less likelihood was there of its having anything serious the matter with it, at least of such a character as would terminate life suddenly or unexpectedly. The serious heart lesions are those which give no symptoms, or but very slight ones, and the sudden deaths in heart disease usually come from the development of insidious symptoms that do not betray themselves to the patient until the fatal termination is on them. The more the patient himself has been disturbed by his heart, the less likelihood is there of its giving out suddenly. The subjective symptoms are usually due to the fact that the heart is actively overcoming external interference, or resenting over-attention to it in its work. Certain it is, that the neglect of it, so far as that is consonant with reasonably regular life, is the very best thing and the most important part of any prescription given for symptomatic heart disease, whether organic or functional, is to forget it just as far as possible.

{321}

Heart Symptoms in the Young.—In young people particularly it is important not to suggest the possibility of heart disease until there are definite signs in the circulation apart from the heart which place the diagnosis beyond all doubt. The psychotherapeutics of organic heart disease that is most important is that of prophylaxis. Patients' minds must be guarded as far as possible against disturbance from the thought that they have heart disease, for this of itself adds a new factor which tends to disturb compensation and adds to the heart's labor because worry interferes with the vasomotor mechanism. In this matter it seems advisable to repeat once more that there must be a complete reversal of the customs that have existed until now with regard to tuberculosis and heart disease. Consumptives have from the very nature of their disease a tendency to hopefulness which soon brings about a favorable reaction against the bad news, but heart patients derive no advantage from the announcement and, indeed, if they are of the nervous, worrying kind, the effect of it is likely to be cumulative. A week after being told the worst a consumptive has reacted vigorously and hopefully, and if he has a fair share of immunity, the scare will do good by making him take the precautions necessary to increase his resistive vitality. At the end of the same time a heart patient will be just realizing all the significance of the unfavorable diagnosis and prognosis of his case.

It may be urged that heart patients by knowing their condition will be preserved better from injuring themselves by over-exertion, but what we have said elsewhere about the value of exercise in the treatment of heart cases shows how much patients may be injured by having their exercise too much reduced and their activity inhibited by the dread consequent upon the announcement made to them. It is perfectly easy to insist with them that they shall not do sudden things, or take violent exercise, or overdo activity, without disturbing them by the dread words "heart disease."

CHAPTER III

CARDIAC NEUROSES

If, as all the authorities recognize, the attitude of mind toward organic heart disease is extremely important and when favorable is a most helpful therapeutic factor, it is easy to understand that in neurotic conditions of the heart this is of even more significance. The term "heart disease" is bound up with so many unfortunate and persistently unfavorable suggestions that it seems advisable not to use it with regard to non-organic conditions, even though it may be associated with the epithets functional or neurotic. For these the term cardiac neuroses, which avoids the implication of heart disease in the ordinary sense, seems preferable. Many of the cardiac neuroses are quite trifling. Many of them endure for years without producing any serious effect or disturbance of the general health. Many functional disturbances of the heart action which are extremely annoying may disappear entirely with judicious regulation of life. The one important condition in all of these cases is to be sure that the patient does not worry over the condition, for that {322} hampers heart activity and leads to functional disturbances of other organs which make the heart's work harder.

Varieties.—There are many forms of cardiac neuroses. Indeed, functional heart affections are so individual that it is hard to classify them. In every case it is extremely important to study the individual and recognize just what are the special factors bringing about the disturbance of heart action.

Palpitation.—In a certain number of the cases it will be found, indeed, that there is no real disturbance, but that in some way the heart action has been brought above the threshold of consciousness and has become noticeable to the patient. It must not be forgotten that the heart is an intensely active organ. Several gallons of blood are pumped through it every minute and yet it accomplishes its work, as a rule, with such noiseless, frictionless regularity that most people know nothing about it. When the action of the heart becomes conscious, it is usually spoken of as palpitation. Patients are sure to think that this must mean serious over-action, though, as a rule, no sign of over-action or at most a slight exaggeration of the muscular sounds of the heart will be found.

Missed Beats.—A further stage of this cardiac neurosis is the missing of beats. This occurs particularly in those whose attention has been directed for some time to their heart action by the presence of palpitation. It may be due to nothing more than this over-concentration of attention. It may be due, however, to mechanical disturbances, an over-distended stomach, constipation, or certain nervous factors

Arrhythmia.—A third stage of cardiac neuroses consists of irregularity of the heart action, in which not only are the beats missed occasionally, but there may be certain heart sounds much less vigorous than others and the spaces between the sounds may be very unequal. This condition is usually said to be due to some serious condition of the heart muscles, and undoubtedly it often is. There is no doubt, however, that great irregularity of the heart may occur entirely as a neurotic condition without any organic affection and from factors quite extraneous to the heart itself.

Etiology.—There are three causative conditions for cardiac neuroses that deserve careful study and that can be very much modified by changing the attitude of the patient's mind toward his condition. The first of these is an over-attention to self such as is particularly induced by a life without much exercise and devoted to things intellectual. The direct causation is probably intimately connected with the second etiological factor in the production of cardiac neuroses. This consists of an absence of sufficient exercise for the heart itself, when it actually seems to disturb its own activity because adequate calls for exertion are not made on it to use up accumulated energy. Cardiac neuroses are seen particularly in those who having had considerable exercise in earlier years, have settled down to a sedentary life in which there are few calls made upon their muscular system. The third etiological factor is the most important. It is due to cardiac disturbance from the stomach and intestinal tract; this will be discussed in a separate chapter.

Prognosis.—The prognosis in cardiac neuroses is always worse in the patient's mind than it ought to be. If then the physician shows that he is uncertain as to the real significance of the affection, some hint of this uncertainty will be communicated to the patient with resultant unfavorable suggestion. The {323} more carefully neurotic heart affections have been studied, the better the prognosis becomes. Morgagni in the olden time, Stokes and Corrigan in the early nineteenth century, Broadbent and MacKenzie in our time, have all emphasized the necessity for favorable prognosis. Even extreme irregularity is quite compatible with long life without any symptoms of serious circulatory disturbance. MacKenzie has, in his very careful studies of heart action, shown that extra systoles may cause marked irregularity in many forms without warranting unfavorable prognosis.

Arrhythmia may begin in comparatively early life, persist in spite of treatment, and yet continue up to old age. Sir William Osler tells of the case of the late Chancellor Ferrier of McGill University who died at the age of eighty-seven after having exhibited an extremely irregular heart action for the last fifty years of his life. He has seen several other patients who have had heart irregularity for many years without the slightest disturbance of their general health. His experience is not uncommon, and probably every physician who sees many cases of heart disease can recall a few of them. Ten years ago I saw a man past seventy suffering from distinctly irregular heart action, though he gave the history of having had cardiac irregularity for some years at least, and he is still alive, past eighty, and with his heart irregularity still present. I have a patient over seventy whom I know to have had irregular heart action for fifteen years, and he himself is sure that it has been present since he was about forty, at least. It is cases of this kind, together with MacKenzie's recent studies of the subject, that must be before the physician's mind when he makes his prognosis for these patients. There must be no hesitancy about his declaration. Patients think that physicians are prone to deny the significance of heart trouble so as to avoid disturbing their patients. The slightest hesitation, then, will be surely looked upon as of ominous import.

The Intellectual Life and Cardiac Palpitation.—It is curious how many people who give themselves to intellectual work and live an almost exclusively indoor life have subjective symptoms relating to their hearts. Many of the English literary men and women of the last century had complaints of this kind. Sir Walter Scott described very vividly his sensations as if his heart did not have room to accomplish its functions, and said that he used to feel within his chest a fluttering as if there were a bird there beating its wings against a cage too small for it. Other literary people have told of this sense of overfullness in the chest, as if somehow there were not room for all the organs. This discomfort is mainly referred to the precordial region. In oversensitive, nervous people it may be described as painful, though analysis of what they mean by the word pain will show that they have only a persistent feeling of pressure which is uncomfortable and gives a sense of crowdedness in that region rather than any genuine ache. Where the feeling is much dwelt on, however, it may be exaggerated into pain, as, indeed, will any sensation, however trivial, if attention is concentrated on it. On the other hand, in practically all of these cases, just as soon as the mind is strongly diverted by any pleasant occupation, the sense of discomfort disappears not to reappear again until the patient has time to think about himself.

Heart Surveillance.—Prof. Oppenheim of Berlin has in his usual direct way expressed the power of the mind to influence the heart beat, and he does {324} not hesitate to say that certain nervous people who have been watching their hearts overmuch, and continually thinking about them, are capable of playing all sorts of tricks on themselves and sometimes even on their physicians, by this concentration of mind upon their heart and its action. Prof. Oppenheim in his "Letters to Nervous Patients," writing to a patient complaining of irregular heart action, says:

Whenever you succeed in controlling the action of your heart by means of introspection, there flows from your brain to your heart a current of innervation which disturbs the automatic movement of the organ. You now know what you have to thank for the irregularity in the action of your heart. I have frequently proved this to myself in your case: if I succeeded in feeling your pulse without your becoming aware of it, holding your attention by a conversation which interested you, the action of your heart was always absolutely regular. If, however, I tried it under your control, while your attention was anxiously directed to your heart, its action at once became irregular, and you experienced the very unpleasant sensation of palpitation.

Irritable Heart of Athletes.—A curiously interesting form of heart neuroses has appealed to me very much because I have suffered somewhat from it myself and owing to circumstances I think I have seen a larger number of patients suffering from it than usually come to a single individual. I refer to the tendency to irritability of the heart which is so marked in men who have been athletes when they were younger, and have taken a large amount of exercise during the years between fifteen and twenty-five. If these men later settle down to a sedentary life they almost inevitably suffer from a marked sense of discomfort in the precordial region because of palpitation, and are apparently much more liable than other people to have an intermittent pulse. Just what these symptoms are due to is not always easy to discover, and in different individuals there seem to be different accessory causes at work. I have seen it particularly in professional men who while at college have been on the teams and have played such hard games as handball, hockey on the ice, and the like. I do not refer only to those who have played an occasional game, but who every day of the college year have had some severe muscular exercise.

Whether this irregularity of heart action has not at least been predisposed to by over-exertion remains to be determined. Strenuous athletics produce curious heart symptoms. Missed heart beats and irregular heart action and even leakages at the valves are not unusual even in the best of hearts after severe exertion. A careful examination of the hearts of those who took part in a Marathon run at Harvard some years ago showed that immediately after the race many of them were irregular and some of them had leakages at the mitral valve which lasted from one to twenty-four hours. These were probably due to irregularity in the action of the papillary muscles as a consequence of the fatigue. I had occasion to examine the hearts of some theatrical dancers a few years ago, immediately after they came off the stage. One of them is one of the most successful of modern dancers and is able to occupy the better part of an hour in the severest kind of exertion before an audience. Her heart was not only very rapid immediately after she left the stage, but there were missed beats and a distinct disturbance at the mitral valve. It was hard to determine absolutely, but the sounds at all the valves were impure and there {325} seemed to be imperfect closure or irregularity of action. In another case there was a regular missed beat at every sixth or seventh pulsation. This seemed to be due to an abortive systole. Usually within an hour regularity of heart action is restored and the valve sounds become normal. At times when the patient is run down for any reason, the cardiac disturbance may persist for many hours, or even until after long hours of sleep.

The patients I have mentioned seem to have developed their muscles to a noteworthy degree and have enlarged and strengthened their hearts by this exercise. Later on their occupation in life prevents them from taking any severe exercise, or at least furnishes no opportunity for it, and they often settle down to existence that, beyond a short, quiet walk perhaps once a day, affords no exercise at all. Under these circumstances the muscular development that they secured as young men and which kept them in such magnificent health during their adolescent years seems to prove a positive detriment to good health, or at least to good feeling. The muscular system seems to crave to be kept up. Occasionally I have been sure that the intermittent heart action so often seen in these cases was due to the fact that the appetite, or as I should rather put it, the habit of eating, which they formed while they were accustomed to taking vigorous exercise, remains with them during their sedentary life and as a consequence they overeat, particularly of proteid food materials. The large consumption of these materials gives rise to the presence of substances in the blood which make all the muscles more irritable than usual, and this seems to add particularly to the irritability of the heart.

Dietetic Regulation.—For many of these people a regulation of diet seems to be the best possible remedy. They must be made to eat less substantially, since they do not need the same amount of proteid material to make up for muscle waste, now that there is no longer the old use of muscles. Some of them become very heavy. These, however, are mainly individuals who, besides eating abundantly of proteids, also consume carbohydrates in large quantities. In these there is a distinct disturbance of digestion and a tendency to dilatation of the stomach with gas which interferes with the heart action and brings on the intermittent pulse so often seen in them. In a certain number, however, there are no accessory symptoms of indigestion, but the heart symptoms are most prominent.

Exercise.—For these people the only real relief is afforded by a certain amount of exercise every day. They become ever so much more comfortable just as soon as their physician insists that they shall have an hour's walk at least every morning and every afternoon and that this walk shall be brisk and always have some definite purpose in it, so that there is no mere sauntering or delaying on the way. Most business men to whom this prescription of an hour's walk is given will reply that it is impossible. Most clergymen will say that their duties are such that they cannot arrange their hours for this purpose. As a rule, it is not difficult to show the business man, however, that if instead of riding to his business, he should walk every day, and this will probably only take twenty minutes to a half-hour longer than if he goes by trolley or even by automobile, this walk will provide him with a full hour of brisk exercise in the open air. The walk back from business will provide the other hour, whenever golf or some other diversion cannot be provided instead. In most cities men live from three to five miles away from their {326} business, and it is not too much to ask them to take this walk. The muscular clergyman must be made to understand that there shall be no trolley cars for his ordinary clerical calls, or at least that none are to be taken unless he has had his full two hours of brisk walk.

There is always the fear in the patient's mind that exercise, by calling for heart exertion, is almost sure to make the condition worse. This fear of itself further hampers heart action. When exercise is first increased in those who have been living sedentary lives the heart action for a time is brought more and more into the sphere of consciousness and any irregularity that is present is likely to be emphasized. A little persistence, however, soon shows that what the heart actually was craving was the opportunity to expend some of its energy and it was this pent-up force that was disturbing its action. There is often the fear in physicians' minds lest the advising of exercise should really do harm to the patient. They fear the presence of perhaps a fatty condition, or of some obscure muscular condition, or of some other heart lesion not easy to detect, yet likely to produce serious symptoms. Stokes, who probably knew fatty heart disease better than anyone else in the nineteenth century, outlined his views of the therapy of it as follows:

In the present state of our knowledge the adoption of the following principles in the management of a case of incipient fatty heart disease seems justifiable:

We must train the patient gradually but steadily to the giving up of all luxurious habits. He must adopt early hours, and pursue a system of graduated muscular exercises; and it will often happen that, after perseverance in this system, the patient will be enabled to take an amount of exercise with pleasure and advantage, which at first was totally impossible, owing to the difficulty of breathing which followed exertion. This treatment by muscular exercise is obviously more proper in younger persons than in those advanced in life. The symptoms of debility of the heart are often removable by a regulated course of gymnastics or by pedestrian exercise, even in mountainous countries, such as Switzerland or the Highlands of Scotland or Ireland. We may often observe in such persons the occurrence of what is commonly known as "getting the second wind," that is to say, during the first period of the day, the patient suffers from dyspnea and palpitation to an extreme degree, but by persevering, without over-exertion, or after a short rest, he can finish his day's work and even ascend high mountains with facility. In those advanced in life, however, as has been remarked, the frequent complications with atheromatous disease of the aorta, and affections of the liver and lungs must make us more cautious in recommending the course now specified.

Perhaps the most important therapeutic suggestion which Sir William Broadbent has to make with regard to the cardiac conditions that have come to occupy much of the patient's attention is of a negative character. He says that "patients suffering from these functional derangements of the heart usually make them a pretext for avoiding exercise and often for taking stimulants or drugs, whereas exercise and fresh air are what they need. The best way to prevent the expenditure of superfluous energy on the part of the heart in the form of palpitation is to give it a fair amount of legitimate physiological work to do." Personally I have found that most of the cardiac tonics seem to do harm, in the sense of increasing the subjective symptoms, except in cases where the patient is run down in general health because of failure to take sufficient food, when strychnin seems to be of avail and in the shape of nux vomica acts as an appetizer as well as a heart tonic. Sir William Broadbent has warned particularly with regard to the use of alcohol in these cases. {327} Most patients find that for the moment palpitation is lessened by alcoholic stimulation. They pay for it afterwards, however, by an increased sense of discomfort that sometimes lasts for 24 hours or more. As Sir William Broadbent declared, "To relieve one attack of palpitation or fainting by alcohol is to invite another, while the terrible danger of dropping into alcoholism is incurred."

Lest it should be thought that even Broadbent is a little old-fashioned and not quite to be trusted in the light of our present-day knowledge, and above all lest it might be feared that these older men made a better prognosis or emphasized the value of exercise more than is compatible with our recent discoveries in the physiology and pathology of the heart, it seems well to give MacKenzie's opinion of these cases in full. This is all the more important because, as I have said, the influence of German teaching has led to the formation of rather different opinions in America, especially among our younger physicians. Prof. Martius in this country in his lecture for the Harvey Society gave quite a serious prognosis for practically all heart irregularity. He almost went so far as to lay it down as a rule of diagnosis that whenever a heart beats irregularly there is something the matter with the heart muscle or good reason to suspect a myocardial lesion of some kind. MacKenzie's view is very different to this and he warns particularly against permitting the influence of an unfavorable attitude of mind on the part of these patients. He says:

The most serious thing about these cases is that the consciousness of having an irregularity sometimes makes a patient introspective and depressed. He keeps feeling his pulse, and communicates his doleful tale whenever he find a sympathetic ear.

As the process which gives rise to it in elderly people is the same as that which produces the tortuous temporal arteries, no more significance should be attached to the one symptom than to the other. I have followed cases for many years, and watched them pass through seasons of sickness and of stress, and have seen no reason to attach any serious import to this symptom. In rare instances the heart, from being occasionally irregular, has after many years become continuously irregular for short or long periods, and in a few the permanent establishment of the nodal rhythm has been the means of hastening the end. But this is infrequent, and in cases of cardio-sclerosis has only happened in advanced life, and the patient should on no account be frightened by being warned of the possible occurrence of this unlikely contingency. In younger and neurotic people I have never seen it lead to any bad results. It may appear in serious affections of the heart, as in febrile complaints, but it does not of itself add to the gravity of the condition, though I am not sure that when due to an acute infection of the heart, as in pneumonia and rheumatic fever, it may not be a sign of invasion of the myocardium by the diseased process.

If the patient is aware of the irregularity, he should be assured that there is no cause for alarm. It is useless to attempt to treat the irregularity itself. If in other respects the patient is well, then there is no need of any special treatment. If the patient be suffering from conditions which seem to promote irregularity, such as worry, fatigue, dyspepsia, the treatment should be devoted to the removal of the predisposing cause. In people with temporary high blood pressure, who show extra systoles, I find plenty of healthy exercise in the open air specially beneficial, though until they get trained, the extra systoles may at times become more frequent by the exertion.

This last remark of MacKenzie's is particularly important, for at the beginning of an attempt to relieve the symptoms by insisting on more {328} exercise, the patient is almost sure to be disturbed by this symptom of which he will often be conscious, and it takes a good deal of experience on the part of the physician to reassure him that because of the increased subjective symptoms at the beginning of the treatment by increased exertion, he may not be doing harm rather than good. As a rule, however, it is not long before the good results of the exercise treatment of these cases begin to make themselves felt and the patient is reassured. Regulated exercise of body and occupation of mind are the two important factors even in the treatment of organic heart disease. They are extremely important even in the cases with alarming heart symptoms that occur in the very old, once the acute symptoms have subsided. In all the functional heart affections exercise is the most important therapeutic resource we have. It would seem that in the course of muscular exercise some heart tonic was manufactured, which in all but the cases of absolutely failing hearts is the best possible therapeutic resource for the stimulation and steadying of the heart action. Such an internal secretion would not be surprising in the light of all that we have learned of the physiological nexus of organs in recent years.

Many so-called cures for heart disease probably depend for their good effect much more on the graduated exercise that goes with them than on many of the other remedial measures, though it is these latter that are usually vaunted most highly. We all now recognize how little value there is in the Nauheim bath treatment for heart disease away from Nauheim itself. The reason is because the resisted movements of the early part of the cure and, above all, the graduated exercise of walking up the hills around Nauheim, which are such important parts of the treatment there, cannot be so well given with the baths at a distance.

CHAPTER IV

CARDIAC PALPITATION AND GASTRO-INTESTINAL DISTURBANCE

Morgagni, whom Virchow greeted as the Father of Modern Pathology, made a careful study of the pulse and especially of its irregularities. He had learned from the most careful pathological studies that marked intermission and even more decided irregularity of the heart may be present in life, though there may be absolutely no organic affection of the heart itself, either of the valves or of the muscle, discoverable at autopsy. In his opinion the most frequent cause for such irregularity is flatulency and disturbance of digestion generally. He went still farther, however, and seems to have understood very well that constipation was often one of the most important links in the chain of causes leading up to such heart disturbance, itself either a cause or an effect of other digestive symptoms. This idea deserves to be borne in mind when there is question of the significance of heart symptoms. What Morgagni thus determined by precise studies in pathological anatomy had been clinically observed by many of the distinguished old-time practitioners of medicine, who knew the fatal tendencies of organic heart symptoms, yet recognized that many cardiac cases associated with gastric symptoms did not have an unfavorable prognosis.

{329}

In spite of the recognition of these conditions by old-time medical investigators, there has always been a tendency to fear that heart symptoms in these cases might be due to a cardiac affection. This has invariably been true for patients themselves to whom the heart disturbance became conscious, but has often made physicians hesitate as to the diagnosis and rendered their prognosis more unfavorable than is justified by actual knowledge.

Gastro Cardiac Arrhythmia.—What may be called the gastro-intestinal cardiac neuroses usually run a typical course. As a rule, with young folks, the beginning of cardiac unrest is found in some stomachic symptoms. The distention of the stomach with gas is said to be a mechanical reason for interference with the heart action. Whether this is really gas that has formed within the stomach, or whether it is to a great extent, at least, gas which has been diffused from the vessels of the stomach walls in a disordered viscus, or in some cases at least, air which has been swallowed because of certain gaspy habits of neurotic individuals, is hard to determine. In many cases the absence of all odor of decomposition, or of any disagreeable taste, makes for serious doubt whether the substance is really due to fermentation. Certainly the changes that take place in food in the stomach during the course of an hour or two of digestion are not sufficient to account for the volume of gas that exerts pressure upon the gastric walls and is eructated in large mouthfuls. Fermentative processes are slow gas producers, as anyone with experience in the chemical laboratory knows.

Mechanical Cardiac Interference.—Every physician has seen the young man who is sure that he has heart trouble when he is really suffering from indigestion. Many of the feelings of discomfort accompanied by palpitation and irregularity are really phenomena connected rather with the stomach than the heart itself. The reason for this is not always clear. In many cases there seems to be a mechanical interference with the heart's action. This is due to the presence of gas in the stomach pressing against the diaphragm. In many cases the distention of the stomach by a heavy meal, especially if the heart has been rendered sensitive by the taking of stimulants, will have the same effect. This is particularly noticeable if the patients lie down shortly after the meal, when there is distinct discomfort in the cardiac region and noticeable irregularity of the pulse.

The most frequent phenomenon is a missed beat, or often simply a sense of discomfort in connection with the heart action that makes its beating very noticeable. This palpitation, as it is called, is usually entirely subjective. There is nothing abnormal in the sensation produced on the hand when the heart is palpated, nothing the most delicate finger can detect in the apex beat and nothing uniform in the change in the heart sounds produced in these cases. There is usually a somewhat over-excited action of the heart, but this is not characteristically revealed by either palpation or auscultation. The rhythm is interfered with, but the arrythmia affects only an occasional beat, usually rather regularly spaced, and does not interfere with the heart's rate nor with its action in any way. This represents the most familiar form of cardiac neurosis and may, of course, be due to such substances as tobacco, or coffee, or tea, where these are taken in excess. Excess is always a matter of individual idiosyncrasy.

{330}

Cardiac Reflexes.—It is thought by some that this heart irregularity and palpitation is a reflex action due to irritation of the gastric terminal filaments of the vagus nerve reflected back along this nerve and affecting the heart. The doctrine of reflexes is not as popular, however, as it was, but there can be no doubt of the fact that the vagus nerve has terminal filaments in all the large organs, yet is so extremely important to the heart that it has a definite physiological meaning and doubtless is meant to act in such a way as to stimulate the heart when these important organs are overloaded or are laboring in their functions, and, on the other hand, to depress it or at least to inhibit it somewhat, whenever there is a tendency to send too much blood to these parts. In any case, whether the positive factor in the production of the heart trouble be mechanical, as it surely often is, or whether it be reflex and due to the action upon the vagus, it must not be forgotten that in all cases where heart symptoms occur with considerable intervals of absolute freedom from them and with large subjective elements in the case, the relation of the stomach or the digestive organs in general to the heart may serve as their best explanation.

Gastric Dilatation.—In dilatation of the stomach there is likely to be an associated tendency to a cardiac neurosis. Unfortunately, enough of these cases have not been followed up so as to be sure what the outcome is and whether there may not really have been some affection of the myocardium with a premature breakdown of the heart. As a consequence of the excessive irritation of the terminal filaments of the vagus nerve in the stomach wall, or because of the mechanical interference with the heart's action as a consequence of the dilated stomach pulling upon the esophagus and probably somewhat interfering with the action of the diaphragm, an irregularity of the heart action is established and a sense of discomfort in the precordia develops that is often very marked. These patients sometimes suffer from pseudo-angina and still more frequently from cardiac irregularity. This cardiac irregularity is sometimes quite marked, and yet in 24 hours, as a consequence of the emptying of the stomach, will disappear, so that only slight intermittency remains, which eventually subsides. I have known a heart affected thus to be pronounced absolutely without any lesion when examined by a competent heart specialist within a month after it had been so irregular as to be quite alarming to both patient and physician.

187

Upward Distention.—There is sometimes a tendency for the stomach to distend upward rather than to dilate downward and toward the left. Perhaps this is due to the fact that in certain individuals the gastric ligaments are much stronger and more unyielding than they are in others. One thing is sure—that there are great individual differences in these cases. In some that are without any demonstrable gastric dilatation, except that gastric tympany extends higher than usual, there is marked interference with the heart action. The physician needs to see these cases when they are so irregular that there would seem to be absolutely no doubt of the existence of a myocardial lesion and then to examine them some months afterwards when the stomach had been restored to good conditions, before he is able to realize how much interference with heart action is consonant with complete return in a comparatively short time to the normal, at least so far as heart function goes. This is a very different opinion from that held by many heart specialists and {331} especially certain German authorities, who insist that any irregularity of the heart must be considered as probably representing a muscular lesion; but the evidence of careful observers may be adduced in support of it, and it is an opinion that very much reassures the patients.

Old-time Clinicians—Morgagni, Lancisi.—In this subject it has always seemed to me wise to recur to the opinions of some of the old-time clinicians who noted symptoms very carefully and studied out particularly the connection of symptoms with prognosis.

Morgagni.—Morgagni, for instance, whose clinical remarks are always precious, said:

Now that mention is made of the intermission of the pulse which approaches more nearly to the nature of an asphyxia than even its slenderness or weakness (for what else is the intermission of the pulse but a very short asphyxia, or what is an asphyxia but an intermission which lasts very long?) the causes of this disorder in the pulse are not to be passed over without examination in this place, as the greater part of physicians are very greatly terrified thereby, often with good reason, yet frequently without any; as when there is some cause of it in the stomach or intestines, which may even vanish away of itself, or be easily removed by the physician. For in what manner a palpitation of the heart may sometimes be brought on by flatus distending these parts, and again carried off by the dissipation of such flatus, I have already said; and in the same manner, or one not very dissimilar, it is also evident, that an intermission of the pulse has sometimes generated, and gone off of itself, in many whom I have known. At another time, in these very same viscera, there is a matter which produces the same effect, by irritating their nerves, with which you know how easily the nerves of the heart consent. And this matter is sometimes of such a nature that it may readily be prevented from harboring itself there. Thus I remember, when I attended to the cure of a young girl who had a fever, and an intermission of the pulse was added to the other symptoms contrary to my expectations, I was not at all deterred from giving such a medicine as I had before determined upon, that the stomach and intestines might be well cleansed; and even that I gave it so much the more boldly; and that on the same day after these parts had been deterged, the pulse returned to its former standard. But you will read even in the *Sepulchretum* that Ballonius had not only seen this disorder of the pulse, but also that of a languid and small stroke, removed in the same manner. "According to the degrees to which the purging was carried," says he, "the pulse was restored." And, indeed, there is an intermission of the pulse, that is of a far longer continuance as that with which Lancisi says he had been troubled "for the space of six years"; yet if this intermission should be, as it was in him, "from a consent with the hypochondria," it may be entirely and perfectly taken away, by perfectly restoring those parts.

Lancisi.—Lancisi was another distinguished clinical observer who made special studies in neurotic heart disturbance. These studies are all the more interesting because he himself was a sufferer from this affection for many years. He was inclined to think that his heart intermittency was due to disturbance in his digestive organs and especially those lying in the upper part of the abdomen. He attributes it himself to sympathy with these and said that it came *ex hypochondriorum consensu*, as it were a reflex from his hypochondriac regions. As Lancisi lived to a pretty good age in spite of noting this symptom in early middle life, the significance of it will be well understood. It would be perfectly possible to gather a series of such cases from among the distinguished physicians of history, and as for our contemporaries and colleagues, at least one out of four of them will tell you that at some time he has suffered from an affection of this kind and has been much worried {332} about it, yet has recovered without incident and without any serious development.

English Opinion.—The role of the stomach in disturbing the heart is only less important than that of the nervous system itself. Of course, individual peculiarities, as I have said, are extremely important. Some people seem to suffer very little cardiac disturbance from a distended stomach, while in others all sorts of heart affections may be simulated as the result of the mechanical interference with the heart action by the pushing up of the diaphragm. Sir William Broadbent in the article on "The Conduct of the Heart in the Face of Difficulties," already quoted from, does not hesitate to say that heart symptoms secondary to gastric disturbance probably cause more suffering than does actual heart disease. Expressions of this kind need to be borne in mind when we reassure patients who have all sorts of queer, uncomfortable, often even painful, conditions in their cardiac region, "Heart disease" has been, perhaps, mentioned casually to them and as a consequence worry is adding a nervous element to hamper a heart already seriously disturbed by gastric distention. Sir William Broadbent's own words are given because they carry so much weight in this matter:

The difficulties arising out of flatulent distention of the stomach or colon or intestinal canal generally, will require some attention, since they are the cause of most of the functional derangements to which the heart is subject, and give rise to the heart complaints which occasion in the aggregate perhaps more suffering than does actual heart disease. The heart often tolerates a considerable degree of upward pressure of the diaphragm, and it is not uncommon to meet with stomach resonance as high as the fifth space, and to find the apex beat displaced upwards and outwards to the fourth space and outside the nipple line, without conspicuous symptoms. But the heart behaves very differently in different subjects in the presence of flatulent distention of the stomach. It partakes of the general constitutional condition of the individual; in the strong, therefore, it is vigorous; in the weak it cannot be anything but weak.

Prognosis.—Nothing sends a young person sooner to a physician than this cardiac unrest and functional disturbance. He comes all a-tremble, as if to hear the worst. Even in middle age and in those whose education might be expected to steady them somewhat in the matter, even in physicians of long experience, there is a tendency so to exaggerate the condition and its possibilities of fatality as a consequence of emotion that inhibitory action on the heart becomes noticeable. It is a rule with very few exceptions that in these cases when the heart is complained of by young persons who have no history of rheumatism, the causative condition will be found in the stomach, or at least in the digestive tract.

I know a number of physicians who have suffered in this way and who have been badly frightened about themselves, yet who have had no serious difficulty once they took reasonable care of their diet, and paid attention above all to regularity of meals and slowness in eating. Indeed, it is rare to find a physician of a nervous temperament who has not had some trouble of this kind, and the demands made on a busy professional man foster this. Some of them are sure that if their cardiac uneasiness does not signify an actual heart lesion, valvular or muscular, at least it portends a premature wearing out of the heart. There are many evidences to show that this is {333} not so. I have had a distinguished physician, now well past his seventy-fifth year, tell me of distinct irregularity in his heart action as a young man which had rather alarmed him, and as this had been preceded by an attack of acute articular rheumatism there seemed to be every reason to think that he was a sufferer not from functional but from organic heart disease; yet he has lived well beyond the span of life usually allotted to man, has accomplished an immense amount of work and is now in excellent general health almost at the age of eighty. The case is all the more striking because, while rest and care of the health and regular life and conservation of energy are usually supposed to be essential for these cases, this colleague is noted for having made serious inroads on the hours which should have been devoted to sleep in order to accomplish certain medical literary work while devoting himself to the care of a most exacting practice.

That the good prognosis of these cases which I suggest is not forced and is not over-favorable nor the result of the wish to soothe patients may be judged from recent studies of the heart as well as from the older ones. In discussing extra-systole, MacKenzie in his "Diseases of the Heart," says:

Dyspeptic and neurotic people are often liable . That other conditions give rise to extra-systoles, is also evident from the fact that they may occur in young people in whom there is no rheumatic history and no cardiosclerosis and whose after-history reveals no sign of heart trouble.

It is well to note the frequency of such annoying symptoms in those who have gone through rheumatic fever, and where patients have a history of this it is well to be cautious, but even in these cases he says that the trouble is often entirely neurotic and the one important preliminary to any successful treatment is to get the patient's mind off his condition, improve his general nervous state, and above all relieve as far as possible the gastric symptoms that may be present.

He says further:

Some patients are conscious of a quiet transient fluttering in the chest when an extra-systole occurs; others are aware of the long pause, "as if their hearts had stopped"; while others are conscious of the big beat that frequently follows the long pause. So violent is the effect of this after-beat, that in neurotic persons it may cause a shock, followed by a sense of great exhaustion. Most patients are unconscious of the irregularity due to the extra-systole until their attention is called to it by the medical attendant. Both being ignorant of its origin, and its being characteristic of human nature to associate the unknown with evil, patient and doctor are too often unnecessarily alarmed.

Cardiac Stomach Disturbance.—On the other hand, as a word of warning, it seems necessary to say here that later in life acute conditions manifesting themselves through the stomach are often of cardiac origin. Most physicians have been called to see some old man who had partaken of a favorite dish which did not, however, always agree with him and who suffered as a consequence from what at first was thought to be acute gastritis. The severity of the symptoms and the almost immediate collapse without any question of ptomaine poisoning, however, usually make it clear that some other organ is at {334} fault besides the stomach itself. The real etiological train seems to be that a weakened heart sometimes without any valve lesion but with a muscular or vascular degeneration hampering its activity is further seriously disturbed by the overloading of the stomach. The result is a failure for the moment of circulation in the digestive organs with consequent rejection of the contents of the tract, nature's method of relieving herself of substances that cannot be properly prepared for absorption. Unfortunately, the condition sometimes proves so severe a shock to the weakened heart that it stops beating, and the physician is brought face to face with a death from "heart failure."

In these cases it is important to remember that the gastric disturbance may so mask the heart symptoms as completely to deceive the physician. The prognosis of these cases, however, is most serious. It seems worth while to give a warning with regard to these cases, because anything that we may have to say as to the relations of the stomach and the heart and the possibility of lessening the cardiac depression due to unfavorable mental influence when palpitation occurs as a consequence of gastric distention, has nothing to do with these acute cases in older patients where the condition is serious and the prognosis by no means favorable.

Treatment.—The rôle of psychotherapy in this form of cardiac disturbance associated with gastro-intestinal affections is, after the differentiation of neurotic from serious organic conditions, to give the patient such reassurance as is justified by his condition. It is surprising how many people are worrying about their hearts because their stomachic and intestinal conditions give rise to heart palpitation, that is to such action of the heart as brings it into the sphere of their consciousness, sometimes with the complication of intermittency or even more marked irregularity. The less the experience of the physician the more serious is he likely to consider these conditions and the more likely he is to disturb the patient by his diagnosis and prognosis. Until there is some sign of failing circulation, or of beginning disturbance of compensation, the attachment of a serious significance to these conditions always makes patients worse and removes one of the most helpful forms of therapeusis, that of the favorable influence of the mind on the heart. On the other hand, unless the patients' own

189

unfavorable auto-suggestions as regards the significance of their heart symptoms are corrected, these people not only suffer subjectively, but bring about such disturbance of their physical condition as makes many symptoms objective.

While there are serious affections in which heart and stomach are closely associated, these are quite rare and usually manifest themselves in acute conditions and in old people. In the chapter on Angina Pectoris attention is called to the fact that there are may forms of pseudo-angina due to cardiac neuroses consequent upon gastric disturbance and without heart lesion. Broadbent has not hesitated to say that these forms of angina cause more suffering or at least produce more reaction on the part of the patient and are always the source of more complaint than the paroxysms due to serious cardiac conditions which present the constant possibility of a fatal termination.

Where the stomach is the cause of the cardiac neuroses psychotherapy is an extremely important element in the treatment. The continuance and exaggeration of their symptoms is often due to a disturbance of mind consequent upon the feeling that they have some serious form of heart disease. Without {335} definite reassurance in this matter all the experts in heart disease insist that it is extremely difficult to bring about relief of symptoms in these patients. Whenever the general health of the individual has not suffered from his heart affection, it is quite safe to assume that no organic disease of the heart is present, no matter what the symptoms, for, as Broadbent and many other authorities emphasize, gastric cardiac neuroses can simulate every form of heart disturbance. The older physicians insisted that what they called sympathy with the hypochondriac organs might produce all sorts of heart symptoms. The patient must be told this confidently. The slightest exaggeration of the significance of his symptoms can do no possible good and will always do positive harm.

After reassurance, the most important thing is, of course, regulation of the diet and of the digestive functions generally. Unfortunately, regulation of the diet to many patients and even to many physicians seems to mean the limitation of diet. I have seen sufferers from cardiac symptoms have these increased by excessive limitation of diet. If they are lower than they ought to be in weight they must be made to regain it. Above all, there must be no limitation of meat-eating except in the robust. Very often the heart seems to crave particularly that form of nutrition that comes through meat. It is especially important that the bowels should be regular. Fast eating is very harmful. Occupation with serious business immediately after eating is almost the rule in these cases.

All of these elements of the case need special study in each individual patient. The needed suggestions can then be made. Above all, the patient is made to realize that his case is understood and that it is only the question of a gradual acquirement of certain habits, including proper exercise, that is needed for the restoration of his heart to normal.

CHAPTER V

ANGINA PECTORIS

The two forms of this affection, known commonly as true and false angina, are characterized by pain or anguish in the precordial region with reflected pains in other portions of the body. It used to be said that whenever the precordial pain was accompanied by reflected pains in the neck, or down the arm, or, as they may be occasionally, in the jaw, in the ovary, in the testicle, sometimes apparently in the left loin, this was true angina and the patient was in serious danger of death. We know now that false angina may be accompanied by various reflex pains and that, indeed, a detailed description of the anguish and its many points of manifestation is more likely to be given by a neurotic patient suffering from pseudo-angina than by one suffering from true angina. True angina occurs in most cases as a consequence of hardening of the arteries of the heart or of some valvular lesion that interferes in some way with cardiac nutrition. The definite sign of differentiation is that in practically all cases of true angina, there are signs of arterial degeneration in various parts of the body. Without these, the "breast pang," as the English {336} call it, is likely to be neurotic and is of little significance as regards future health or its effect upon the individual's length of life.

Besides the physical pain that accompanies this affection there is, as was pointed out by Latham, a profound sense of impending death. It used to be said that this was characteristic of the organic lesions causing true angina pectoris. It is now well known, however, that the same feeling or such a good imitation of it that it is practically impossible to recognize the true from the false, occurs in pseudo-angina. It is this special element in these cases that needs most to be treated by psychotherapy and which, indeed, can only be reached in this way. Where there are no signs of arterial degeneration and no significant murmurs in the heart, it should be made clear to these patients that they are not suffering from a fatal disease, but only from a bothersome nervous manifestation. Especially can this reassurance be given if the angina occurs in connection with distention of the stomach or in association with gastric symptoms of any kind. In young patients who are run down in health and above all in young women, the subjective symptoms of angina—the physical anguish and the sense of impending death—are all without serious significance.

Differential Diagnosis of True and False Angina.—In the diagnosis of angina pectoris the main difficulty, of course, lies in the differentiation between the true and false forms, that is, those dependent on an organic affection of the heart muscle or blood vessels and those resulting from a neurosis. The neurotic form is not uncommon in young people and is often due to a toxic condition. Coffee is probably one of the most frequent causes of spurious angina, though the discomfort it produces is likely to be mild compared with the genuine heart pang. It must not be forgotten, however, that neurotic patients exaggerate their pains and describe their distress in the heart region as extremely severe and as producing a sense of impending death, when all they mean is that, because the pain is near their heart it produces an extreme solicitude and that a dread of death comes over them because of this anxiety. Coffee and tea, especially when taken strong and in the quantities in which they are sometimes indulged in, may be sources of similar distress. Tobacco will do the same thing in susceptible individuals, or where there is a family idiosyncrasy, and especially in young persons.

For the differentiation of true and spurious angina Huchard's table as given by Osler is valuable:

TRUE ANGINA	NEUROTIC FORM
Most common between the ages of forty and fifty years.	At every age, even six years.
More common in men. Attacks brought on by exertion.	More common in women. Attacks spontaneous.
Attacks rarely periodical or nocturnal.	Often periodical and nocturnal.
Not associated with other symptoms.	Associated with nervous symptoms.
Vaso-motor form rare. Agonizing pain and sensation of compression by a vice.	Vaso-motor form common. Pain less severe; sensation of distention.
Pain of short duration. Attitude: silence, immobility.	Pain lasts one or two hours. Agitation and activity.
Lesions. Sclerosis of coronary artery.	Neuralgia of nerves and cardioplexus.
Prognosis: grave, often fatal.	Never fatal.
Arterial medication.	Antineuralgic medication.

{337}

True Angina and Psychotherapy.—One of the most frequent occasions for the development of true angina is vehement emotion. The place of psychotherapy then in the affection will at once be recognized. A classical example of the influence of the mind and the emotions in the production of attacks of angina pectoris in those who are predisposed to them by a pre-existing pathological condition, is the case of the famous John Hunter. He was attacked by a fatal paroxysm of the affection in the board room of St. Thomas' Hospital, London, when he was about to begin an angry reply with regard to some matter concerning the medical regulation of the hospital. He had previously recognized how amenable he was to attacks of the disease as a consequence of emotion or excitement, and had even stated to friends that he was at the mercy of any scoundrel who threw him into an attack of anger. Some of the deaths from fright or sorrow at a sudden announcement of the death of a relative, or even the deaths from joy are due to angina pectoris precipitated by the serious strain put upon the heart by the flood of terror or emotion.

Men who are sufferers from what seems to be true angina pectoris must be made to understand without disturbing them any more than is absolutely necessary that strong emotions of any kind—worry, anger, exhibitions of temper, and, above all, family quarrels, must be avoided. Not a few of the serious attacks of angina pectoris which physicians see come as a consequence of family jars, owing to the persistence of a son or daughter in a course offensive to the parent. A part of the prophylaxis, then, consists in impressing this fact on members of the family and making them understand the danger. The disposition that causes the family friction is, however, often hereditary and will, therefore, prove difficult of control. It is one of the typical cases of inheritance of defeats.

Solicitude and Prognosis.—The distinguished French neurologist, Charcot, had several attacks of what seemed to be true angina pectoris. His friends were much disturbed by it. Physicians who saw him during the attack feared that he was suffering from an incurable heart lesion. He himself, as his son, Dr. Charcot, told me, refused to accept this diagnosis, and preferred to believe that what he was suffering from was a cardiac neurosis—and, of course, he had seen many of them. He was unwilling to have a heart specialist examine him very carefully for he did not wish to be persuaded of the worst aspects of his condition.

What he said in effect was, "This is either a neurotic condition, as I think it is, or it is an organic condition. If it is organic, my physicians would be apt to tell me that I must stop working so hard, and I am sure that if I should do that I would do myself more harm than good by having unoccupied {338} time on my hands. I want to go on doing my work. If I am wrong some time I shall be carried off in one of these attacks. That will not be such a serious thing, for after all I must die some time and my expectancy of life cannot normally be very long. I prefer, then, to go on with my work and think the best, for it does not seem that I could do anything that would put off the inevitably fatal issue if I am to die a cardiac death." He was found dead one morning, but he had passed into the valley of death without being seriously disturbed and without any of the neurotic symptoms that so often develop in discouraged patients. Curiously enough, one of our most distinguished heart specialists in this country went through almost the same experience and preferred to live "the brief active life of the salmon rather than the long slow life of the tortoise."

The best possible factor in therapy is secured if patients can be brought to the state of mind of these distinguished physicians who calmly faced the future, refusing to disturb themselves or their work, because they feared that the worry that would come down upon them in inactivity would aggravate their disease. Where men are occupied with some not too exacting occupation, that takes most of their attention and at which they have been for years, it is best to leave them at it, though the harder demands of it must be modified. If they can be brought to persuade themselves, as did the two physicians—though probably only half-heartedly—that their affections may possibly be

191

merely neurotic and not true angina, it will always be better for them. Death may come, and commonly will, suddenly, but, after one has lived a reasonably full life, that is rather a blessing (and not in disguise) than the terror which it is sometimes supposed to be.

Pseudo-Angina.—The neurotic form of angina is quite compatible, not only with continued good health but with long life, and even after a long series of attacks, some of them very disturbing in their apparent severity, there may be complete relief for years, or for the rest of life. Exaggeration of feeling due to concentration of attention plays a large role in these cases, and it is evident that the dread of something the matter with the heart connected with even a slight sense of discomfort may readily become so emphasized as to seem severe pain, though many people have similar feelings without making any complaint.

In spite of reassurances attacks of pseudo-angina are likely to worry both patient and physician. The only working rule is that in younger people discomfort in the heart region, even though it may be accompanied by some sympathetic pain in the arm or in the left side of the neck, is usually spurious angina. Broadbent goes so far as to say that this is true also in many older persons. His method of making the differentiation is interesting because so easy and practical that it deserves to be condensed here. The earlier attacks of true angina are practically always provoked by exertion, while spurious angina is especially liable to come on during repose. Any cardiac symptom or pain that can be walked off may be set down as functional and due to some outside disturbing influence, or to nervous irritability. When palpitation or irregular action of the heart, or intermission of the pulse, or pain in the cardiac region, or a sense of oppression follows certain meals at a given interval, or comes on at a certain hour during the night, there need be little hesitation in attributing the disturbance, whatever it may be, to indigestion in {339} some of its forms. Nightmare from indigestion, Broadbent thought, is not a bad imitation of true angina.

In Broadbent's mind acute consciousness of any heart disturbance lays it in general under the suspicion of being neurotic in origin. He was talking to some of the best clinical practitioners in the world and some of the most careful observers of our generation, when, before the London Medical Society, he said: "The intermission of the pulse of which the patient is conscious and the irregularity of the heart's action—though this can be said with less confidence—which the patient feels very much, is usually temporary and not the effect of organic heart disease." This is particularly true, of course, in people of a neurotic character, and Broadbent went on to say that "speaking generally, angina pectoris in a woman is always spurious, and the more minute and protracted and eloquent the description of the pain, the more certain may one be of the conclusion."

I had the opportunity to follow the case of a young woman who had a series of attacks of angina pectoris some twenty years ago, so severe that a bad prognosis seemed surely justified, and though at times the attacks were rather alarming to herself and friends, nothing serious developed and for the past ten years, since she has gained considerably in weight, they have not bothered her at all. She used to be rather thin and delicate, trying to do a large amount of work and living largely on her nervous energy. At times of stress she was likely to suffer from pain in the precordia running down the left arm and accompanied by an intense sense of the possibility of fatal termination. With reasonably large doses of nux vomica, an increase in appetite came and a steadying of her heart that soon did away with these recurrent attacks. These came back later several times when she neglected her general condition, but there never were any objective symptoms that pointed to an organic lesion. After twenty years she is in excellent health, except for occasional attacks of a curious neurotic indigestion that sometimes produces cardiac disturbances. Of course, such cases are not uncommon in the experience of those who see many cardiac and nervous patients.

For the treatment of pseudo-angina, mental influence is all important. Of course, the conditions which predispose to the mechanical interference with heart action that occasions the discomfort, must be relieved as far as possible. The severity of the symptoms, however, are much more dependent on the patient's solicitude with regard to them, they are much more emphasized by worry about them, than by the physical factors which occasion them. Reassurance is the first step towards cure. After relief has been afforded from the severer attacks, the patient's solicitude as to the future must be allayed and the fact emphasized that there are many cases in which a number of attacks of cardiac discomfort simulating angina pectoris have been followed by complete relief and then by many years of undisturbed life. It is important to make patients understand that, in spite of the fact that their attacks occur during the course of digestion, as is not infrequently the case, this constitutes no reason for lessening the amount of food taken. Nearly always these attacks occur with special frequency among those who are under weight, and disappear rather promptly when there is a gain in weight. Solicitude with regard to the heart must be relieved wherever possible and then with the regaining of general health the heart attacks will disappear.

{340}

CHAPTER VI

TACHYCARDIA

Etymologically tachycardia means rapid heart. There are two forms of rapid heart, that which is constant and that which occurs in periodical attacks. It is for this latter that the term tachycardia has been more particularly used, though occasionally the adjective paroxysmal is attached to it to indicate the intermittent character of the affection. With regard to the persistent type of rapid heart something deserves to be said, however, because patients' minds are often seriously disturbed by them. Often it has existed for years, sometimes is known to be a family trait and probably has existed from childhood, yet the discovery of it may be delayed until some pathological condition develops, calling for the attendance of a physician who may be needlessly alarmed and in turn alarm his patient by his recognition of it. The cause for this persistent rapid pulse is not well known and is difficult to determine. Heredity, as has been suggested, sometimes plays an important role in it. Certain families have one or more members in each generation with rapid hearts. Whenever persistent rapid heart is a family trait the patient can be assured, as a rule, without hesitation, that the general prognosis of the case is that of the lives of the rest of the family. Usually the symptom seems to mean nothing as regards early mortality or any special tendency to morbidity.

Favorable Prognosis.—While a rapid pulse often and indeed usually has some serious significance, it must not be forgotten that it may be an individual peculiarity and be quite compatible with long life and hard work. One of the first patients that I saw as a physician had a pulse between ninety-six and one hundred. As there was a slight tendency to irregular heart action also, I was inclined to think that there must be some cardiac muscle trouble. There was apparently no valve lesion. He told me that a physician ten years before had noted his rapid pulse and had made many inquiries about it which rather seriously disturbed him. He had been an extremely healthy man during his fifty-five years of life and there seemed no reason to conclude, since his rapid pulse had been in existence for ten years, that it meant anything serious. He has now lived well beyond the age of seventy and still has a pulse always above ninety. Contrary to what might be thought, he is an extremely placid, unexcitable individual, who, under ordinary circumstances, will probably live for many years to come. He has no family history of tachycardia, though there is a history of rather nervous irritable hearts in other members for two generations.

An interesting case of this kind came under my observation about fifteen years ago in a clergyman whose pulse was never below ninety, and who on slight excitement, or after a rapid walk, or after a heavy meal, would have a pulse of 120. He knew that it was a family trait, his father having had it yet living to be past seventy. He gave a history of its having been recognized in his own person more than twenty years before. His general health, however, was excellent. He took long walks and, indeed, pedestrian excursions {341} were his favorite exercise. He was able to go up flights of stairs rather rapidly without discomfort. He was the pastor in a tenement house district so he had plenty of opportunity for such exertion. Infections of any kind, colds and the like, disturbed his pulse very much, if the ordinary standard was taken, but it was not irregular and the increase in rapidity was probably only proportionate to the original height of the pulse in his case. After all, as the normal pulse of sixty to seventy rises to between ninety and one hundred even in a slight fever, it is not surprising if a pulse normally above ninety should rise fifty per cent. to one hundred and thirty-five under similar conditions. He is now well past sixty, after over thirty-five known years—and probably longer—of a pulse above ninety, yet he is in excellent general health and promises, barring accident, to live beyond seventy.

Some ten years ago I first saw another of these cases of fast heart, with a family history of the affection in a preceding generation. He was a man who had not taken good care of himself and had been especially over-indulgent in alcohol. This indulgence consisted not in rare sprees but in the persistent daily taking of large quantities of straight whiskey. In spite of warnings, he has not given up this habit; yet at the age of sixty-five he is apparently in good health and is able to fulfill the duties of a rather exacting occupation.

Persistent rapid pulse often occurs in connection with some disturbance of the thyroid gland. The larval forms of Graves' disease occur particularly in young persons, though they are sometimes seen in those beyond middle life. They seem to be due to a lack of development of the thyroid in consonance with the rest of the tissues, though occasionally, especially after the menopause, they seem to be connected with some degenerative process out of harmony for the moment with other forms of degeneration. When they occur in young persons they may, of course, represent the beginning of incipient Graves' disease, but they are often only functional and the symptoms may pass away entirely. The rapid heart action may come and go, though usually the attacks last for some days and oftener for a week or more at a time.

Paroxysmal Tachycardia.—A rapid heart may not only exist continuously in an individual for many years without any impairment of general health or shortening of life, but there may be spasmodic attacks of this condition with the pulse running up so high as to deserve the name of paroxysmal tachycardia; yet the patient may live for many years and die from some affection not connected with his heart. Perhaps the most remarkable case of this kind on record is that reported by Prof. H. C. Wood of Philadelphia. The patient was a physician in his later eighties when he came under Dr. Wood's observation. His first attack of paroxysmal tachycardia came in his thirty-seventh year. These attacks had apparently always been similar to those he then suffered and were abrupt in onset and the pulse would rise rapidly to 200 a minute. The original prognosis had been, of course, very unfavorable. The physician had outlived all the prophets of evil in his case, however. When large numbers of these cases were studied, it was found that they always last more than ten years, and, while heart failure in such cases is reported, it is doubtful if this occurs with more frequency in these patients as the result of strong reflexes than in the general run of patients, for it must not be forgotten that there is a certain average number of deaths from so-called heart failure in people supposed to be in good health.

{342}

In connection with these attacks of paroxysmal tachycardia, there often come intense feelings of depression and even local disturbances of circulation. It is probable that in many cases there is a serious factor at work. MacKenzie has suggested that they are due to nodal rhythm of the heart in which the heart beat does not start at the root of the sinus as is usual, but in some other portion of the musculature and as a consequence there is serious interference with the regular rhythmic action. In a number of cases of heart failure, tachycardia becomes a prominent feature and it is probably due to some such disturbance as this. Such cases often look very serious for a time, yet frequently recover completely after a brief interval. This must not disguise the fact, however, that many of these cases, especially where acute dilatation of the heart can be demonstrated, are extremely dangerous and may end in a sudden fatal termination. The patient seems so much prostrated that occasionally the physician may doubt whether it is worth while to put him to the bother necessary in order to diagnose the acute dilatation of the heart. It always is, however. If it were nothing else but the occupation of the patient's attention with the doctor's manipulations, as far as that is possible, the effect would be good, besides whatever irritation may be caused to the heart muscle itself by percussion of the heart area will probably do mechanical good.

The most important element evidently is that the patient shall not be allowed to lose courage or to think that nothing can be done for him. Something must be done, and a combination of swallowing movements and deep breathing, as far as that is possible, with counter-irritation through the chest wall should be carried out. Drugs also should be employed and the aroma of strong coffee with the irritating effect of ammonia upon the nostrils should be employed. These act upon the vagus so as to stimulate the heart, but above all they act upon the mind, and nothing so stimulates the heart as reawakened hope.

CHAPTER VII

BRADYCARDIA

Bradycardia, or persistent slow pulse, is much rarer than the persistent rapid pulse discussed at the beginning of the chapter on tachycardia. Cases are, indeed, sufficiently rare to be medical curiosities. Prof. Clifford Allbutt has called attention to the fact that the status of bradycardia or brachycardia, as Osler (following Riegel because of the analogue tachycardia) prefers to call it, is very different from that of tachycardia. In the latter, especially, in the specific sense of the term, the symptoms occur paroxysmically, endure for a definite length of time and then there is a return to the normal pulse rate. For this, or at least for the condition known as essential tachycardia, there is no well-defined cause and no definite pathological lesion. Bradycardia or brachycardia, however, is usually present as the result of some known physiologic or pathologic condition; it endures as long as the cause continues to act and then ceases, usually not to return unless the same cause gives rise to it again.

{343}

There are some cases, however, of slow pulse that cannot be traced to any definite lesion and in which the pulse is much slower at certain times than at others, though without its being possible to trace any definite immediate cause. These cases seem to be physiological analogues of tachycardia. In tachycardia there is an irritation of the accelerator nerves to the heart, in brachycardia of the inhibitory nerves.

Depressed Mental States.—Occasionally the reason for this can be found, though it is rather vague. In depressed mental states, for instance, a pulse between fifty and sixty is common. In people who suffer from periodic fits of depression it is not unusual to find that in the early morning the pulse is not more than fifty-five. I have seen patients who were worrying about their hearts present records of early morning pulse before they got up that were always below sixty. This is probably in a certain number of people quite normal. I remember a series of observations made on the attendants in the Charite Hospital in Berlin in which it was clear that the normal German morning temperature at seven a.m. was below 97 F., while the pulses were always below sixty. A reassurance of this kind is helpful to patients who have acquired the bad habit of taking their own pulse and have been disturbed by finding it so much below what they consider normal.

Illustrative Case.—A number of cases of persistent slow pulse seem to be congenital or produced by some definite pathological lesion, yet do not prove serious for the patient. Some years ago I described one of these cases in a paper read before the Section on Medicine of the New York Academy of Medicine and I have had the opportunity to follow it for about fifteen years. Though the patient's pulse is usually below forty and even after a rapid walk does not rise above fifty, she is in reasonably good health and during those years has buried two husbands. When I saw her she was compelled to go up and down stairs frequently and yet did not experience much difficulty. While patients suffering from palpitation would find it impossible, because of the discomfort produced, to make the journeys up and down stairs that she did, she felt only about as much respiratory discomfort as would come to a woman of her size. Her respirations were somewhat hurried—22 to 24 to the minute—but her general health was very good. Her urine was normal, her liver not enlarged, her ordinary organic functions were not disturbed and there was no sign of arterial degeneration.

With the pulse rate as low as this one might expect to find the patient phlegmatic, slow of movement and not readily moved to emotion. On the contrary, she has always been rather nervous and high-strung and inclined to be excitable. Her cardiac condition was first noted just after the first grip epidemic in this country, though her attention was not called to it during the course of the grip. It seems probable that the heart condition was acquired as a consequence of some irritative lesion affecting the inhibitory nerves to the heart that developed at that time. After her heart condition had been discovered she was for a time a skirt dancer and frequently danced for the amusement of her friends. She was always lively and active and after her first husband's death, when it became necessary for her to earn her own living, she was on the stage for a time and danced without any embarrassment of either {344} heart or respiration. As a consequence of running down in weight and general health, owing to conditions since her husband's death, she noticed that dancing proved exhausting to her and she gave it up.

In general, she considered herself quite as capable as any of her friends for the ordinary duties and amusements of life. When I first saw her her digestion had been somewhat disturbed by worries and unsuitable nutrition taken at irregular intervals and this, I think, accounted much more than her heart for her complaint of tiredness on exertion. Later, after her second marriage, when she was in better circumstances, all her symptoms disappeared and even her heart rate rose so that it was seldom below forty, and after exertion always went to fifty. What was needed in her case more than anything was a change of environment, the satisfaction of mind that comes with freedom from worries and the cares of making her own living, and the improvement in digestion due to regular meals of good, simple, nutritious food.

Compatibility with Health and Activity.—The above case is interesting as illustrating mental influence upon such a serious condition as bradycardia. Most people who suffer from it are likely to be over-depressed and this reacts to disturb digestion and also further to disturb the heart itself. What these patients need above all, then, is reassurance with regard to their condition. There are some striking examples in history and in medical literature of bradycardia or persistent slow pulse in persons who are able to accomplish a large amount of work and whose general health and capacity for accomplishment were not at all disturbed by this physical condition. Above all, they were not depressed and did not lack initiative. Napoleon I, whose pulse is said normally to have been about forty, rising during the excitement of battle to fifty, is a typical example. Medical literature records a number of patients with congenital slow pulse without any discernible heart lesion who lived long and successful lives. One of these was a very successful English athlete. The prognosis of these cases is not as bad as it might seem to be and the mental state of the patient is more important than anything else in the treatment.

{345}

SECTION VIII

RESPIRATORY DISEASES

CHAPTER I

COUGHS AND COLDS

Cough under most conditions is so completely a natural reflex due to irritation from material which demands expectoration that to talk of the application of psychotherapeutics to its treatment would seem almost an abuse of words. This is true if we think of the curing of an ordinary catarrhal or bronchitic cough by suggestion. We know now, however, that, as a rule, we do not cure diseases, we only relieve their symptoms and thus enable nature to overcome the affection. The ordinary cough remedies do two things: they cause more liquid to exude into the lung tissues and thus soften and liquefy thick mucous material so as to make it easier to expectorate, or they lessen irritation and soothe the cough by making the nervous system less reactive. This second function of our remedial measures directed against cough can at least be assisted very materially by psychotherapeutics. Direct suggestion may be of great help, while the first function, that of softening the cough by liquefying the sputum, can be materially aided by certain suggestions to the patient of natural means and ways by which his cough may be relieved, its secondary symptoms modified, and its course abbreviated.

Cough and Suggestion.—Much of the coughing indulged in is quite unnecessary and might well be dispensed with. At many of the German sanatoria for consumption there is a rule that patients must not cough at dinner, and no coughing is heard in the refectory. Without such a rule the midday meal, if taken in common by the large number of consumptives present, would be a pandemonium of coughing. Cough is largely influenced by suggestion. Most of the respiratory reflexes follow this same rule. To see another yawn tempts us to yawn; to hear another cough tempts us to cough. In church or in a theater after an interval of interest one cough will be followed by a battery of coughs. People who have colds think they have a right to cough, and so they often cough much more than is at all necessary. Of course, when material accumulates in the lungs it must be coughed up, but not a little of the coughing might easily be dispensed with—it is unproductive coughing. A distinguished German medical authority who is accustomed to talk very plainly once said that it is quite as impolite and injustifiable to cough unproductively as to scratch the head unproductively. Only results justify either procedure.

Dry coughing, when persistent, is greatly a matter of habit acquired by yielding to slight irritation. When children scratch their heads we train them {346} not to, and the same thing should be done with regard to yielding to reactions from slight irritations of their lungs.

Even when material has to be expectorated there is often much more fuss and effort made over it than is needed. Most men a generation ago insisted on their right to expectorate in public because it was better for them to rid themselves of offensive material than to retain it. The difference between men and women in this respect has always been distinctive. Women practically never expectorate in public, men do it frequently, or rather, let us hopefully say, used to. It seems to be thought the exercise of a manly privilege to spit and the boy learns the habit. It seemed almost a necessity in the past, yet now we have come to a point where, by legal regulation, we prohibit spitting in public and it seems likely future generations, not far off, will hold it as a rule that instead of the sexes being essentially different by nature in this respect, the habits formed by the enforcement of recent legal regulations will show their essential similarity and we shall have no "expectorating sex."

Unnecessary Coughing Harmful.—Coughing, unless it is necessary, always does harm. It irritates the mucous membrane, already rendered somewhat hyperemic and tender by the inflammatory process at work, to have the breath pass over it in such an expulsive way. This is one case where nature's indications are not to be followed. It is like itchiness in eczema: it needs to be restrained. The cold will get

195

better sooner, the inflammatory process will run its course with less disturbance and in briefer time than if it was not disturbed in this way or disturbed only as little as possible. This is a point that is not often explained to patients and most sufferers from colds are inclined to think that the more they cough the better, even though the cough, like the scratching in eczema, evidently produces a roughening and sensitizing of inflamed tissue. Of course, this principle of the limitation of cough may be carried to excess and indeed sometimes is when opium is administered to quell coughing. This is not the idea, however, of the suggestion made here, which is only to restrain the cough within the limits necessary for the removal of material that should be evacuated.

The history of most of the tuberculous patients who suffer from hemorrhage for the first time shows that they had been coughing unproductively, and then, after coughing in this way rather severely, there came the flow of blood due to the rupture of a minute artery. In these cases the tuberculosis process has been at work for some time and has prepared the tissue for this arterial rupture, but there is no doubt, however, that the coughing itself, far from doing good, rather helped in the destruction of lung tissue, or at least made it more difficult for natural processes in the lungs to wall off the bacilli and prevent further damage. Practically every adult is in some danger of lighting up an acute tuberculous process in his lungs if he racks them by coughing. There are many similar examples in nosology of this possibility of some habit predisposing to or favoring the development of disease.

After measles and whooping cough tuberculosis is especially likely to develop. In both of these diseases, but especially in the latter, coughing is an element of the affection that probably predisposes to the implantation of the tubercle bacillus so commonly present in the air of our cities. The lesions produced in the extreme expulsive efforts of the paroxysm form favorable niduses for the micro-organism. Children particularly, if at all encouraged, are likely {347} to cough more than is good for them. On the slightest irritation they cough. It is almost impossible to restrain them from scratching when they are suffering from eczema, yet we take rather elaborate means to do so, and quite as much must be done to prevent them from coughing when there is no special reason for it. This does not refer to cases in which material is being abundantly expectorated. Elimination can only be secured by a proper expulsive effort. Very often, however, children notice how much solicitude their little dry cough arouses. They like to be the objects of attention. They are dosed with various cough remedies, more or less pleasant, whenever they cough. Instead of being told that they should restrain their cough except when it is necessary, they are rather encouraged to cough whenever there seems to be the slightest occasion.

Reflex Coughs.—There are a number of coughs that are said to be reflex because they are not induced by any lesion of the lungs or of the larynx, or, indeed, of any of the air passages. In these cases some pathological condition is often found in another organ or set of organs, usually one of those connected with the vagus nerves. The wide distribution of these pharyngo-laryngo-esophago-pulmano-cardio-gastric nerves gives ample opportunity for reflexes. We hear much of reflex cough. There is a stomach cough and an intestinal cough, a uterine cough, an ear cough, etc. These coughs are always dry, though often very irritating to patients, and especially may be a source of dread and disturbance of mind and health because they seem to signify some serious pathological condition. As a rule, these coughs can be restrained to a great degree and frequently suppressed entirely by suggestion and discipline. In many cases there is some temptation to cough consequent upon irritation of nerve endings communicated through some devious paths to the nerve supply of the respiratory tract, but this tendency is not very strong and can be easily overcome. It may be said that this is asking too much of human nature, and that, just as sneezing carries with it a certain satisfaction and so is apparently worth the trouble of indulging in, coughing should be permitted, at least, if not encouraged, but the reasoning is fallacious.

Habit Coughs.—An interesting cough that comes to the physician is that in which there is absolutely no pathological reason to account for it. There is an irritation of the mucous membrane somewhere along the respiratory tract but it is very slight and somehow the habit has been acquired of yielding to the reflex that it occasions. I have seen these coughs in children in cases where I was sure that they were nothing but tics. I have seen so-called hacking coughs in girls of twelve to sixteen that were explained as ovarian, or sometimes as puberty coughs, that were really nothing more than habits. A slight hyperemia of the mucous membrane in the upper respiratory tract due to an ordinary cold began in a very slight degree the irritation, and then the habit of coughing was not given up. Of course, I know the danger of treating such cough as habit coughs. Tuberculosis in its initial stage may exist for a prolonged period before it produces any increase of secretion and at a time when none of the ordinary physical diagnostic signs are present, except possibly a little prolongation of expiration over the affected area. At this stage tuberculosis will sometimes produce gastric disturbance, and, as I have already said, these are spoken of as stomach coughs when there really is something much more serious than them at work. When there has been no running down in {348} weight, and, above all, no special opportunity for contagion, then, if there are no physical signs in the lungs, these coughs will be best treated as habits and gradually be made to stop by suggestion. The limitation of coughing will do good in any case.

Coughs as Tics.—Some coughs are not really due to any difficulty in the respiratory tract, but are caused by nervous irritability. There are certain habits in the matter of clearing the throat that sometimes become pronounced and apparently impossible to stop. As I have said, these are tics rather than true coughs. Many of these neurotic coughs very seriously alarm patients and also their friends. They are dry, as a rule, rather harsh and inclined to be brassy. Occasionally they are only what is known as "hacks," as if the patient were trying to clear the throat of some offending material. Of course, at no time must the significance of cough be made light of unless a careful investigation of the patient's condition has been made.

Diagnosis.—Names for these coughs should not be too readily accepted which, by satisfying legitimate curiosity and lessening proper apprehension with regard to them, will stop further investigations. Besides stomach coughs, one often hears of intestinal and even uterine or ovarian coughs. In many cases the real condition is one of an incipient tuberculous condition and there may be no sign of this except a disturbance of the pulse and perhaps a slight variation of the temperature range for the day (two degrees or more Fahrenheit in the twenty-four hours). Such coughs should always be carefully investigated for the possibility of incipient tuberculosis. At once the patient should be warned about coughing without necessity, since this only tends to disseminate the tuberculous process and may help to break down nature's wall of protective lymph.

Where there is no disturbance of pulse or temperature and the patient is not under weight and there are no signs in the lungs, then the cough is merely a habit and partakes of the nature of a tic. Sometimes these habits are rather difficult to break; always, however, much can be done by suggestion, by a habit of self-control, by self-discipline, and by thorough persuasion of the patient. Drugs are likely to inveterate the condition if not allied with suggestion.

Removing Unfavorable Suggestions.—For the ordinary coughs and colds of the winter time there are many unfavorable suggestions that deserve to be eliminated. For instance, most people are sure that exposure to the air will inevitably make their cold and cough worse. This is a relic of the olden time when the confinement of patients to their rooms was supposed to be the best remedial measure for all respiratory diseases. Tuberculosis patients were kept in and died without any chance. Now these patients, even while running a temperature, or suffering from pleurisy, or the intercostal painful conditions that are often serious complications because of the irritability and discomfort produced, and which are so often supposed to be due to drafts, are put out on the porch, or on the roof of a hospital, or allowed calmly to lie in bed between two open windows, without the slightest hesitation. They begin to improve under such treatment much sooner than if they were confined, and indeed the whole prognosis of tuberculosis has been completely changed by the modification of the old-time habit of confinement to that of perfectly free access of outer air and even cold air that has taken its place.

This principle of treatment must be applied for coughs and colds. While {349} patients are running a temperature they must not take exercise, they must not be allowed to work, above all they must not be allowed to get in crowds nor tire themselves in any way. The room in which they are, however, must be thoroughly aired, the window must be open all night and, if possible, they must sit in the sun for several hours a day. This will cure a cough or a cold quicker than anything else. Many coughs that hang on when treated by remedies of various kinds, yield at once if the patient is given an abundance of fluid diet and gets freely into the air. There is no danger of catching another cold, because a cold is not due to a low outdoor temperature, but to dust and microbes, and is a real infection.

Irrational Remedies.—There are an innumerable number of supposed remedies for colds. Scarcely any one who has reached the age of forty apparently feels that he or she is doing the whole duty to humanity unless they have some remedy for colds to recommend. Most of the popular remedies that are employed probably do as much harm as good and many of those that are very popular and are sometimes recommended even by physicians have no rational standing in present-day therapeutics. Perhaps the most popular is a combination of quinin and whisky. The effect of this is to give patients, who are unaccustomed to whisky and who are susceptible to quinin, about as uncomfortable a twenty-four hours the day after they take the remedies as can be imagined. Quinin now has no possible specific therapeutic significance in the cure of the series of infections called colds. In the days when we did not understand malaria and considered it in some way as an essential fever due to the absorption of miasmatic material, quinin seemed to have a specific influence upon several conditions. Accordingly it was employed in all sorts of fevers and, because it is comparatively harmless, also in that short infectious fever which we call a common cold. No physician now employs it (except in small doses as a general tonic) for febrile conditions, unless in malaria. There we know that it acts by killing the plasmodium and is a real specific. We do not think of it any more, however, as a general febrifuge and there is no justification for its use in the slight infective conditions we know as colds.

As for the whisky, if taken in stiff doses as it often is, the reaction is likely to make the patient quite miserable the next day. It seems to be the rule for him to think that if, notwithstanding the taking of the quinin and whisky, he feels thus ill, he would have been ever so much worse without it. Colds, however, when left untreated so far as drugs go but managed by natural means often run a mild course. Some of the reputation of quinin and whisky is due to the fact that not infrequently persons suffer from chilly feelings that seem to portend a cold and take quinin and whisky and the cold does not develop. The remedies are then supposed to have aborted or to have inhibited the development of the cold. Anyone who has seen a number of these cases treated expectantly, however, knows how often it happens that the chilly feelings that seem to announce the cold pass off without incident after a good night's rest.

Rational Treatment.—The old rule of getting the emunctories at work must be the basis of any rational therapy of colds. A mild opening of the bowels, especially if there is some constipation, a hot drink on going to bed so that there is some sweating and perhaps the use of a mild diuretic will almost surely affect these cases favorably. Patients have to be careful, {350} however, next morning to stimulate the circulation in their skin to activity so that the cutaneous muscles shall react upon the capillaries and the capillaries themselves tonically contract in order that there may not be too much blood near the surface of the body, or the patient may easily be chilled in cold weather. This chilling of the blood when much of it is near the surface seems to lower its vitality and the patient easily reinfects himself or, if he goes into dusty or crowded places, catches a fresh dose of infectious material. This is the process which is called catching a fresh cold.

The removing of the unfavorable suggestions of remedies that do harm rather than good and the giving of favorable suggestions founded on our present-day knowledge of what a cold is and just what we need to do in order to benefit it, is the most important element in the treatment. Above all, however, the patient must sleep in an airy room and must be sure that he is neither breathing his own expired air nor that of anyone else. With thorough ventilation, however, and the stimulating effect of the cold air and the confidence due to proper directions, colds rapidly get better.

There can be only one reason for keeping patients indoors who are suffering from cold. That is, if they are suffering from fever, the being out involves exertion. In that case, of course, patients must rest and must avoid exertion, but there is no reason why they should not have all possible fresh air. The unfavorable state of mind towards fresh air and especially night air in these patients was cultivated by the profession up to a generation or two ago, but is quite unjustified by our present knowledge. Night air is probably a little better than day air because it is freer from dust. It is because of malaria that night air was supposed to be detrimental, but we have found that the only good reason for this was that the mosquito travels at night. There are no other constituents of night air that produce any serious effect.

As a rule, patients suffering from colds need more sleep than other people and above all need more sleep than they ordinarily take, for this will increase their resistive vitality and enable them to throw off the infection. A good rule is to add two hours of sleep to the usual quota. The unfortunate habit of keeping people indoors and of keeping fresh outdoor air away from them, because it is feared they will catch a fresh cold, often seriously disturbs sleep and delays recovery. In a word, many a cold that hangs on does so mainly because of unfortunate suggestions of one kind or another that have come to occupy a place in the supposed therapeutics of the condition. The removal of these and the insistence on just as much recourse as possible to the therapeutic means at nature's command constitute the basis of successful therapy of these very common infections, which probably are the source of more morbidity in the community because of their wide diffusion and frequent recurrence than all the other infectious diseases put together.

CHAPTER II

TUBERCULOSIS

Tuberculosis, in spite of all our efforts against it, remains in Defoe's striking phrase the "captain of the men of death." Pneumonia has preempted its {351} place in the statistics of mortality, but this is to a considerable extent because tuberculosis at the end masquerades as an acute pneumonic exacerbation. Not less than one in eight, probably more, of all those who die, die from tuberculosis. It is the most serious of diseases. In spite of its eminently physical character it probably affords the best possible illustration of the place of mental influence in therapeutics. We have had any number of new cures for tuberculosis, introduced by serious physicians who were sure from the results they had secured that they had found an important new remedy. After a few years each of these cures in succession has been relegated to the limbo of unused remedies because found inefficient. At the beginning they produced a beneficial influence because of the suggestion of therapeutic efficiency that went with them. When this suggestion failed because the physician who administered the remedy lacked confidence, the real place of the supposed specific as merely another mind cure was recognized.

Indeed, many of the remedies that have been introduced have not been merely harmless drugs, but not a few of them have probably had rather a detrimental physical effect than a beneficial influence. In spite of this, the influence on the patient's mind has been sufficient to neutralize whatever of harmfulness there might have been and to arouse new courage and new energy. The consequence of this has always been that the patient was tempted to live more in the open air and to eat more. *These* are the two efficient remedies for tuberculosis. With the additional life in the open air and increase of food his appetite grew, for nothing so adds to appetite as the exercise of it, and with the gain in weight there was a cessation of cough, a reduction of fever, a disappearance of night sweats and a definite increase in resistive vitality which gradually helped to overcome the disease. Manifestly, then, the use of mental influence in tuberculosis is very significant.

PROGNOSIS AND SUGGESTION

The most important element in any treatment of tuberculosis must be the neutralization of unfavorable suggestions which are weighing upon the patient and preventing him from using even the vital forces that he has for resistance against the disease. The popular impression of tuberculosis, happily waning, is that it is an intensely fatal disease.

Though this is true in general, tuberculosis is by no means a necessarily mortal disease in individual cases, and, indeed, a great many more patients recover from tuberculosis than die from it. Papers read at the International Congress on Tuberculosis, in Washington, in 1908, showed from careful autopsy records that practically all adults either actually had had at the moment of death, or had suffered previously from tuberculosis. If there are not active lesions then there are always healed lesions of tuberculosis in the body of almost every human being who has passed the age of thirty. Most people have quite enough resistive vitality to enable them to recover from the disease. It is only those who are placed in very unfavorable circumstances during the initial stage of the disease, or who have some serious drawback against them, who succumb to it. The fact that the bacillus finds a lodgment in so many individual tissues shows that it is not insusceptibility that makes the difference {352} between people, since we are all susceptible, but it is the lack of resistive vitality, and that most of us have, under ordinary circumstances, and all of us can have under favorable conditions, quite sufficient immunizing power to prevent serious developments.

Even in advanced cases it is perfectly possible for the progress of the disease to be stopped and for many years of useful life to be gained. Probably patients who have gone beyond the incipient stage, in whom there has once been a breaking down of pulmonary tissue never are entirely cured, but they may be so much improved that all their symptoms disappear and they are able to follow an ordinary occupation for many years. There is no disease in which the unfavorable prognoses of physicians have been more frequently disappointed than in tuberculosis. In any city hospital dispensary one finds many cases of tuberculosis turning up as relapses of previous conditions, with the story that when they were seriously ill before, some prominent physician, since dead, said they had only a few months to live. The fact that the physician who made the unfavorable prognosis has since died himself adds greatly to the zest with which patients tell their story. Neither the severity of the symptoms nor the amount of lung tissue attacked is quite sufficient to justify an absolutely unfavorable prognosis in the majority of cases of pulmonary tuberculosis.

No Incurable Cases.—Above all, it cannot be insisted on too emphatically that there is never a time in the course of the tuberculosis when a physician is justified in saying to a patient suffering from any form of tuberculosis that his case is hopeless. One is never justified in saying "You are incurable." Practically every town of any size in this country has a number of cases in which patients were told by physicians that there was no hope, and yet they have recovered to chronicle as often as they get the chance the fact that they have outlived their physician. To say that no case of tuberculosis can be confidently declared incurable will seem to many an exaggeration. There are patients in whom the prognosis is so unfavorable as to be almost hopeless. There are never cases of which it should be said there is no hope. When patients are told, as they so often are, that they are incurable, absolutely no good is done and harm is inevitable.

Heredity of Resistance.—When the disease has developed very rapidly in patients in whom there is no previous history of tuberculosis, and in whom there is no history of previous cases in the family, the outlook is always serious. These cases come as near being incurable as any the physician sees. But the most apparently hopeless of these will sometimes recover, contrary to all anticipation. In spite of the opposite impression so commonly accepted, the most helpful element in these cases is the presence of a trace of tuberculosis in the family history. This always means the existence of some immunity against the disease and there may be a turn for the better even when the case looks absolutely hopeless and when it seems to just be verging on its fatal termination. Probably the most discouraging are the cases in which miliary tuberculosis is at work and conditions are about as unfavorable as possible. There are cases of this kind on record, however, with the most startling contradiction of anticipation, in which undoubted miliary tuberculosis produced high fever for weeks and even months, then gave rise to pleurisy, to peritonitis, to various cutaneous abscesses and to abscesses of bone, in which patients lost one-third of {353} their weight or even more, and yet after the external lesions began to discharge freely, recovery occurred.

Slow Cases.—As for slow-running cases in which there is a distinct history of tuberculosis in the family, not even the most experienced physician can state with any certainty that a fatal termination is inevitable and that recovery cannot occur. Some of the most expert diagnosticians have been deceived in these cases. After half a dozen physicians have given a man up, some gleam of hope has buoyed his feelings and a turn for the better has come. Men with cavities in three lobes, even in four lobes and occasionally it is said in all five lobes, have survived acute stages, have recuperated to a considerable degree and have been able to return to work or at least to take up some useful occupation for a time. Where the lung lesion progresses slowly it is surprising how small an amount of healthy lung tissue is needed to support life. Only those familiar with many autopsies on the tuberculous can appreciate this. Ordinarily we are apt to think that when more than half the pulmonary tissue is involved so as to be of little or no use for respiratory purposes, death must be inevitable. On the contrary, one-fourth the ordinary lung capacity will serve and all of one lung may be quite out of commission and only a portion of a single lower lobe be available, yet the patient may survive for a prolonged period.

The Specter of Heredity.—The most serious contrary suggestion that patients suffering from tuberculosis are likely to have is that their affection is hereditary and that, therefore, there is little hope of its cure. It is in the family strain and cannot be obliterated. This idea, fortunately, does not carry the weight it used to. It should, however, have no unfavorable influence at all and this needs to be emphasized. We discuss the subject more fully in the chapter on Heredity. We know very definitely now that the hereditary element in tuberculosis is so small that it is quite negligible. There are good authorities who do not hesitate to say that heredity plays no role in the causation of tuberculosis and does not even produce a predisposition. Some remnant of the old superstition (for superstition, from the Latin, superstare, means a survival from a previous state of thinking, the reasons for which have disappeared) always remains, and predisposition is the last rule of outworn opinion.

We know now that contagion is the important element. The possibilities for contagion vitiate all proofs of the predisposition idea. Especially is this true when we recall that thirty years ago practically no one took proper precautions to prevent the dissemination of tuberculosis, and very few took them even fifteen years ago. Even at the present time many tuberculosis patients cough around the house with open mouth, spreading tubercle bacilli all around them. We are caring for the sputum, but many other avenues for the diffusion of the disease are open. Children acquire the infection, overcome it, but retain the seeds of it in them and then in some crisis in life, as after puberty, or when they are over-working and over-worrying, or during the first pregnancy, an opportunity is given to still living tubercle bacilli to find their way out of sclerotic confinement. Other forms of contagion count in the absence of a case in the immediate family. We can trace the contagion only too easily, even if there is no consumptive member of the home circle. Scrub-women, laundresses, those who are careless in their attendance upon the tuberculous, workers in dusty places or in factories, where there are others who cough, all {354} these get the disease. Predisposition counts for so little that it is a vanishing factor.

Patients can be assured at once then that they need not worry that the hereditary factor will make their affection less curable. On the contrary, our recent careful studies in tuberculosis show just the opposite of the old false impressions. The children of parents who had tuberculosis are much more likely to possess resistive vitality to the disease than those whose parents never had it. As we emphasize in the chapter on Heredity, the nations that have had the disease the longest among them are the most resistant to it. When the affection is newly introduced into a tribe or race it carries off a great many victims. This immunity, however, is not a function of heredity or of the increase of resistive vitality by the inheritance of an acquired character from the preceding generation, but tuberculosis takes the non-resistant, weeds out all those who have not some immunity against it, and consequently those that are left possess some immunizing power. Tubercular heredity, then, instead of being a source of discouragement should rather be a source of hope. It is surprising to note what a relief to many patients' minds is the explanation of this newer view of heredity in tuberculosis; it lifts a burden from many and makes them eat and sleep better for days.

ANNOUNCING THE DIAGNOSIS

Friends and especially near relatives sometimes come to a physician when there is suspicion that a young person is suffering from tuberculosis and ask that, if there is a ground for a positive diagnosis, it shall not be communicated to the patient. They usually urge that they fear the discouragement will kill the patient. The young are not so easily killed and the reaction on being told the truth and the facing of it bravely is such a magnificent help in therapeutics that the physician should always refuse for the patient's sake alone, quite apart from any ethical obligations in the matter, to enter into any such arrangement. The assurance may be given that the patient's condition will be so stated that, far from the patient being discouraged after due consideration, he or she will look forward with confidence to overcoming the affection.

EARLY DIAGNOSIS

Mental treatment is most valuable in the very early stage of incipient cases of tuberculosis. The time is past when the diagnosis of tuberculosis was made only after the recognition of definite physical signs in the lungs and a considerable loss in weight.

In the *Medical News* for April 9, 1904, I called attention to the question of "Early Diagnosis of Tuberculosis" from the pulse and the temperature in these cases, and pointed out that a disturbance of temperature need not necessarily be a febrile temperature of over 100 degrees, but that any increase of the normal daily variation of temperature, usually considered to be about a degree and a half, should suffice to arouse serious suspicion at least. If the morning and evening temperatures differ by two degrees, this would indicate the presence of some pathological condition, usually tuberculosis. If in addition to this and the pulse disturbance there is any localized area of prolongation of {355} expiration, then tuberculosis is almost certainly present, even though there may be no other physical signs, no cough, no tubercle bacilli in the sputum, nor any other signs of an active process.

It is in these cases particularly that patients can be benefited. Very often they have a slight hacking cough, frequently repeated, with some disturbance of appetite and of digestion and sometimes some loss in weight. Indigestion is recognized now as one of the early stages of tuberculosis. The cough in these cases, as has been said, is often spoken of as a stomach cough and is supposed to be due to the nervous reflex from the pneumogastric nerve carrying irritative impulses from the stomach to the lungs. It is much more likely to be due directly to irritation of the terminal filaments of this same nerve in the lungs themselves.

FAVORABLE MENTAL ATTITUDE

The most important element in any cure or successful treatment of the disease is a favorable attitude of the patient's mind. He must be told at once that consumption takes away only the "quitters." People who give up the battle or who, though still hoping, do not hope actively—that is, do not make the exertion necessary to get out into the open air and to eat heartily—inevitably succumb to the disease.

Eating.—Eating is often more a question of exertion than appetite or anything else for consumptive patients. They have no active appetite and they simply must force themselves to chew and swallow. Their fatigue from chewing is, indeed, likely to be so disturbing that it is advisable to furnish patients as far as possible with such food as requires no chewing. Milk and eggs and the thin cereal foods, like gruel, and rather thin puddings are the best for this purpose. Patients must be persuaded that they must take these whether they care for them or not. Occasionally they may cough after a meal and vomit it up. The rule in the German sanatoria for consumptives is that whenever this happens they must, after a short interval, repeat the whole meal. Only rarely does it happen that a tuberculous patient vomits without some such mechanical cause as coughing. They must be made to understand that any food that stays down does them good no matter how they may feel toward it.

The actual state of affairs as regards their future must be put before them. It is a question of eating or of death. They face these two alternatives. Eating is objectionable but, as a rule, death is more so. The kinds of food they do not care for, if they are good for them, must be insisted on. Most people who think that they cannot take milk can do so, if it is only presented to them insistently, with at first such slight modifications of taste as may be produced by a little coffee, or tea, or vanilla, or by some other flavoring extract, which modifies its taste. Butter and the meat fats will be taken quite readily if it is only once made perfectly clear to patients that they must take these or else lose in the conflict with the disease.

It deserves to be repeated here that in many of these cases the disinclination to eat is due to the fact that patients find it almost intolerably wearying to make the effort necessary for mastication. This is particularly true if they are asked to eat meat frequently, and especially if asked to eat underdone beef, {356} which usually requires vigorous chewing. Such meat is excellent for them once a day, but it may be made much easier to take by chopping or scraping so that practically no exertion is required. Besides, it is by no means necessary that these patients should eat much meat nor that they should have to chew laboriously at their food. Raw eggs may be the basis of the diet, especially eggs beaten up, and these will be found not only to be very tasty, but eminently digestible. Their vegetables may be taken in purees, so that they require very little chewing effort, though patients must be warned to mix starchy substances well with saliva so as to facilitate their digestion. Their bread may be taken in the shape of milk toast, or in some other soft form—bread pudding for instance. All this helps, without demanding too much effort, to prevent loss of weight and to regain it when it has been lost.

Air and Comfort.—Next to food, the most important adjuvant is fresh air. Often patients find many objections to this. It is too cold for them; they are shivery and become depressed. Most patients need to be dressed much more warmly than is the custom at present, and hands and feet should be covered with woolen gloves and socks and even a woolen hood worn around the head if necessary. There is usually too much covering worn on the chest and too little on the extremities. With fleecy wool garments next the body and sufficient clothing, properly distributed, many a patient who complains of the cold will at once be more comfortable. They must be made to understand that fresh air is absolutely essential. Every extra hour they spend in the air is that much gained; every hour they spend inside is just that much lost in the curative process. If they are uncomfortable, however, they become discouraged, and a discouraged tuberculous patient never resists the progress of his affection. Not only does he not improve, but he inevitably retrogresses. It must not be forgotten, however, that the thin anemic patients who complain bitterly of the cold, when they first take up the habit of living outside, will grow used to it after a time and then will from habit and the accumulation of a ten-pound blanket of fat be able to stand the cold much better than many healthy persons.

Stimulating Examples.—Tuberculous patients need to have their courage kept up. It is true that the toxin of the tubercle bacillus has the definite effect of stimulating its victims so that they are likely to be hopeful, but very often this hopefulness is vague and does not tempt them to eat and to live in the open air, the two things that make their continued resistance to the disease possible. I find that the knowledge of how bravely and how successfully other sufferers from the disease resisted its invasion and succeeded in doing a good life's work is the very best tonic that sufferers from tuberculosis can have. Needless to say, there are any number of examples of heroes of tuberculosis who put to shame perfectly healthy people in the amount of work they succeeded in accomplishing in spite of the drawbacks of their disease. The unfavorable suggestion of the number of deaths from the disease must be overcome by the contrary suggestion of the brave, busy lives lived by those who suffered even the very severe form of the disease and often accomplished the full term of existence in spite of their handicaps from tuberculosis.

Robert Louis Stevenson.—The best example in recent years is undoubtedly Robert Louis Stevenson. In spite of tuberculosis in severe form which prevented his living in the ordinary climates for the last twenty years of his life, he succeeded in doing an amount of work that is simply marvelous and in {357} influencing his generation more widely than most of the perfectly healthy writers who lived in his time. There are over, 2,000,000 published words to the credit of Stevenson, and, when we recall that most of this, owing to his critical care, had been written over and over many times, some idea of the vast amount of work he accomplished will be realized. Perhaps the climax of his cheerful nature, the utter lack of discouragement in the face of what is usually the most depressing possible incident, is to be found in his famous letter to a friend telling him, as he lies in bed, that he cannot write at any great length now but that he will write a long letter next week if "bluidy Jock," his playful name for hemorrhage from the lungs, would only let him.

One of the most striking illustrations of his insatiable appetite for work and his complete refusal to admit that he was being conquered by the disease has been recently told with regard to his unfinished novel, "St. Ives." He had been suffering from certain severe symptoms and had been forbidden to do anything at all, even to dictate brief notes, or anything else that would make any extra work for his respiratory organs. The ideas for chapters of "St. Ives" were in his head and would work themselves out in spite of the doctor's prohibitions. He would not let the thought of his disease overcome him, and so he dictated these chapters to a secretary in the sign language, which he had learned so as to be able to communicate under such conditions. I know nothing that is more likely to make people realize how a brave spirit can overcome every discouragement of body, and how much such a spirit is its own reward, since it secures for its possessor a prolongation of the life of the body that would surely be worn out by depression, by discouragement, and by worry. Undoubtedly Stevenson's interest in his work literally gave him new life. It did use up some nervous energy, but if his mind had been occupied by thoughts of his disease, and its probably fatal consequences, much more of his precious store of nervous energy would have been exhausted in anxiety and worry.

J. Addington Symonds.—After Stevenson probably the most striking example among modern literary men is John Addington Symonds. Comparatively early in life he found that he could not live in England owing to the inevitable advance of tuberculosis when he tried to do so. He took up his residence then at St. Moritz and other places of rather high altitude in Italy and continued his literary work. When we see the row of books that we owe to Symonds' literary activity it is surprising to think that he, too, like Stevenson, had to watch his temperature, that every now and then there were discouraging developments and incidents in his tuberculosis, and that a return to the ordinary habitations of men away from the friendly altitudes of the Italian Alps was always followed by a recrudescence of his symptoms. Symonds' work was not merely literary, but his books are valuable historical monographs on many subjects requiring much reading and diligent study and consultation of authorities. There are few men in perfect health and with abundant leisure who have succeeded in accomplishing as much as did this hero of tuberculosis.

Thoreau.—There are other distinguished literary men of the nineteenth and twentieth centuries the stories of whose tuberculosis has a special interest and tonic quality. One of these is our own Thoreau, another is Francis Thompson, the English poet, whose recent death has brought him even more publicity than did his great poems while he was alive. Both of them are typical examples of another phase of tuberculosis that is interesting to realize. {358} It is probable that if Thoreau had lived the ordinary, practical, everyday life, which those who lived around him thought he should, he would have died of tuberculosis before he was thirty. He had no use for money beyond his present needs and when he had made enough to keep himself very simply he refused to earn any more. He had not time, as he said, to make money. He wanted to live his life for itself and for the interests higher than the material that there can be in it. Accordingly, he set himself to learn all about the birds and beasts and the trees and plants and the waters and their inhabitants around his country home. He introduced the modern taste for nature study in its most beautiful way. He spent most of his time out of doors.

Undoubtedly this out-of-doors life prolonged existence for many years beyond what would have been his term. His biographers say that probably his being out of doors in all sorts of weather laid the foundations of "the cold which settled on his lungs" and eventually carried him off. Those of us who know anything about tuberculosis, as it has been studied in recent years in the tuberculosis sanatoria, are not likely to agree with such an opinion. Our patients in the Adirondacks live outside ten or twelve hours a day and then sleep with their windows open with the temperature sometimes down to zero during the severest winter weather. Rain and dampness are not allowed to interfere with the open air program. Colds that "settle on the chest" so that people die from consumption are not due to exposure to cold but to the bacillus of tuberculosis. Where this once gains a foothold the one hope of prolongation of life is out-door air and the more cold and stimulating that out-door air is, provided he can stand it without discouragement, the better for the patient. Thoreau is an example of a man whose life was prolonged by his out-door habits and by his refusal to live the humdrum, practical existence of other men, just to be like those other men and measure his supposed success by their standards.

CHARACTER AS A THERAPEUTIC ASSET

Recent interest in tuberculosis has taught us that the best possible asset for a tuberculous patient is character. Resistive vitality in the physical order and character in the moral order seem to be co-ordinate factors. If a man will not give in in the fight, if he insists on struggling on in spite of difficulties, discouragement and an outlook that seems hopeless, then he will almost without exception get over his tuberculosis, if there is any favorable factor in his environment. We talk much of immunity inborn and acquired to the disease, but it seems to go hand in hand with a certain capacity to stand the debilitating symptoms of the disease without allowing one's mind to become depressed or one's disposition rendered despondent by them.

Courage and Constancy.—The career of Dr. Trudeau to whom we owe so much of our knowledge of tuberculosis is a striking example of the power of character to enable even an apparently delicate organization to withstand the ravages of the disease. This is all the more striking because he was an advanced case when he finally reached an environment in which he could make head against the disease. The story of his own personal struggle for life at Saranac, in which he both learned himself and taught others what the modern {359} treatment of tuberculosis should be, is one of the best therapeutic documents of modern times. Under circumstances that were quite apt to be discouraging to anyone of less character than he, with the bitter cold of the Adirondacks around him and quite inadequate heating facilities, so that even old-fashioned lamps were in requisition for heating purposes, he yet succeeded in winning back his own way to health and showing others how it could be done. The struggle had to be kept up for long, it had to be renewed again and again, our greatest American authority on tuberculosis had to learn in his own person all the clinical details of the disease, but in the midst of it all he succeeded in accomplishing a life work that will stand beside that of any man of his generation and will probably mean more in the history of American medicine than that of any of his supposedly more distinguished colleagues in our large cities and large teaching institutions.

This is the sort of man whom tuberculosis does not take in spite of every advantage that the disease may seem to have. Two others of our American authorities on tuberculosis had almost the same experience.

Persistence.—Recently I have been in correspondence with a young man who illustrates the same power quite as strikingly. He went to Florida and soon found that the unfortunate fear of tuberculosis that has so unwarrantably come into many minds in recent years made it extremely difficult—indeed, almost impossible—for him to live under such circumstances as he hoped for when he went there. In any boarding-house he went to just as soon as there was question of his having tuberculosis the landlady would either insist on his leaving at once or else plead with him to take his departure, lest her other boarders should desert her. He was coughing, he had some fever, his disease was advancing in the midst of all this disturbance, physical and mental, and the outlook seemed hopeless. His picture of this selfishness of humanity, scared about nothing (for there is practically no danger if tuberculous patients take reasonable precautions, as even nurses in sanatoria do not acquire the disease, though living in the midst of it), constitutes one of the most poignant indictments of human nature in its worst aspect that I have ever had presented to me.

Finally he made up his mind that there was nothing for him to do but to tent out and live by himself. Fortunately he was able to do that and just as soon as he was settled under circumstances where human nature did not bother him, nature began to do him good. He feared that he would die during the first month in the tent, for he was having fever up to 102-1/2 and sometimes more every afternoon; but he laid in a store of provisions which with the milk and eggs delivered to him every day enabled him to stay in bed for a week, opening up the flap of the tent in the middle of the day. Then he went out and got another stock of provisions and stayed in bed for another week. His thoughts were gloomy enough, he had only some old illustrated newspapers to give him a few fresh thoughts every day, he had no one to visit him, but he hung on and kept up his habit of rest and forced feeding in spite of disinclination. At the end of two weeks he had no temperature in the afternoon. At the end of the third week he made for himself a reclining chair and sat in the sun outside of his tent wrapped in a blanket. At the end of four weeks he had gained five pounds in weight. From that on all was plain sailing. It was his character that conquered his tuberculosis.

{360}

SUGGESTION AS TO SYMPTOMS

Besides the value of suggestion for the general condition in tuberculosis many of its symptoms can be treated best by changing the mental attitude of the patient towards them and giving him a proper appreciation of their significance. Most symptoms are likely to produce exaggerated reactions, especially in patients who are over-solicitous about themselves. Not a few of the symptoms are really nature's attempts at compensation, or the result of conditions which show a natural disposition to bring about a cure. Fever, for instance, produces lassitude and great fatigue on exertion, and patients are prone to think that this means weakness or exhaustion. It is really only an indication of the necessity for rest, and is brought about by nature's refusal to supply all the demands of the muscles for nutrition, at a time when the febrile condition is burning up a lot of extra material. Far from being a disadvantage, weakness is a decided advantage in this condition.

Hemorrhage.—Probably no symptom that occurs in connection with tuberculosis is more influenced by the mental attitude than hemorrhage. It is a most disturbing incident. Even in quite small amounts it upsets the patient seriously and, of course, in large amounts it is a source of profound disturbance even to the most placid of patients. Excitement always adds to it. Probably no physical means that we have at command can be depended on to control it. Ergot used to be popular, but such physiological action as it exerts, so far as we know the drug, would seem to be likely to do as much harm as good.

Other remedies have gradually lost favor in the hands of those who have had most experience with the symptom and gallic acid and supra-renal extract, the older and newer remedy, are now little depended on. Two things are important—to secure lower blood pressure and lessened pulmonary activity. For these opium in some form is undoubtedly the best drug; and then a placid state of mind on the part of the patient must be secured as far as possible. The scare in these cases, in so far as it is relaxing, is rather favorable than unfavorable for the patient. In addition, it is necessary to insist on absolute quiet and silence and then to allay all reactionary excitement. It is important to make patients realize that while hemorrhage is a serious complication, it is by no means so serious as is usually thought.

Many cases of tuberculosis that eventually run a slow course are ushered in by hemorrhage, or have it as a very early manifestation. It is surprising how many people have had hemorrhage as a symptom and live to tell of it thirty or forty years later. This was not due to any mistake of diagnosis, for a generation ago tuberculosis was more likely to be missed when actually present than to be diagnosed when absent. Indeed, this tendency for the cases in which hemorrhage occurred to run not so fatal a course as others was a fact that seemed to an older generation of physicians to require explanation. They suggested that possibly the hemorrhage swept out with it some of the virulent elements from the lungs and so lessoned the infection. From what we now know this is a doubtful explanation, but it seems not unlikely that a frank hemorrhage might reduce the amount of toxins in the circulation and so in an early stage of the disease give nature a fresh start in resistive vitality.

{361}

What is much more likely, however, is that the occurrence of early hemorrhage made it easier for the patients to appreciate the seriousness of the affection and brought them to accept advice as to proper precautions. Under ordinary circumstances it is difficult and used to be even more so in the past to make the patient understand at the beginning of the affection the necessity for giving up indoor occupations and living the outdoor life with the care for nutrition that is so important if the case is to be improved. Hemorrhage scared them into submission. In the old days it was the first positive symptom of consumption. Now we have many others, and instead of following the advice of over-solicitous relatives that we should not tell patients what is the matter with them, we tell them frankly and secure such care of the health as will bring about improvement. Probably nothing illustrates so well the necessity for thus influencing the patients' minds into caring for themselves as the fact that the hemorrhagic cases, as a rule, do better than the others. All of this can be used to make the minds of patients much less disturbed than they would otherwise be by this alarming symptom.

Cough.—In the chapter on Coughs and Colds we have outlined how much coughing may depend on suggestion, or habit, or on the tendency to yield to slight bronchial irritation when there is no real necessity for it. Most tuberculous patients cough much more than is necessary. This is always somewhat dangerous for them since it disturbs their lungs, has a tendency to distribute tubercle bacilli in their lungs, or in the air around them, and may by efforts at expulsion lacerate affected blood vessels and produce hemorrhage. Whenever cough is productive it should be indulged in, for it removes material that should not be allowed to accumulate. Unproductive coughing, however, can usually be controlled by training.

It is particularly at the beginning of phthisis that the control of coughing by suggestion is important. There are many little coughs, "hacks" as they are sometimes called, frequently repeated by those in a very early stage of pulmonary tuberculosis and which are consequent upon irritation either of pulmonary nerves or of pulmonary tissues, but that are quite unnecessary, as a rule, if a little attention is paid to suppressing them. As a warning sign they are excellent, but the patient should be taught not to indulge in them. Coughing tends to prevent nature's curative reaction and the contraction of pulmonary tissues which may take place around a lesion. In beginning consumption, even where there is but slight infiltration, we know from the observation of the movements of the diaphragm either by the X-ray or directly by Litton's method that its excursions on the affected side are shortened. Coughing is in direct opposition to this setting of the lung at rest and therefore should be controlled; however, as our drug remedies are likely to disturb the stomach, whose healthy function is so important in these cases, the use of the mind in the control of the cough is of the greatest value.

Thoracic Discomfort.—Complaints are often made by the tuberculous of pains in the thorax. Ordinarily the discomfort is supposed to be due to the lung condition, and it is assumed that it is either actually in the lung itself or in the pleura, or communicated from them by reflex to the muscles. In most cases, however, patients complain of pain on the side that is either not affected at all or least affected. If they have been told that the other side is suffering most from tuberculosis, they are prone either to think that now the {362} well side is being invaded or else that their physician is making a mistake, and both thoughts are seriously discouraging. The reason for the pains on the well or the better side, however, are easy to understand. As far as possible, as can be readily demonstrated by the X-rays or seen in the observation of the so-called Litten's phenomenon—the excursions of the diaphragm—nature puts the ailing lung at rest and the diaphragm moves much less on that side than on any other. In order to make up for the lack of breathing in this side the other lung does compensatory work. This over-stretches the muscles of the thorax on the well side and causes some over-work in them. The consequence is a tiredness which may become fatigue; in damp weather this may be even painful. Just why damp weather has this particular effect on muscles is not surely known. Muscular action is probably accomplished with more difficulty in damp weather because of the relaxing effect of moisture on tissues and circulation. Reassurances may be given them, then, that will keep them from thinking seriously of the significance of these pains except as an index of nature's compensatory efforts. The painful conditions instead of causing discouragement will, then, be a source of encouragement. It must not be forgotten that rubbing with some gentle stimulant, soap, liniment, or the like, will greatly improve the thoracic muscles in these cases, but the rubbing must be done gently and by someone else beside the patient, for it is only beneficial if done from before, backwards, in order to help the return venous circulation which runs in that direction in the external respiratory muscles.

Altitude.—There is a marked difference between the amount of water which finds its way out through the lungs at varying altitudes. At sea level an ordinary patient will lose during the night about 300 cc, that is, something more than half a pint of water, through his respiratory tract. At an altitude of 5,000 feet, however, this amount is almost doubled, and at 10,000 feet is almost trebled. At 2,000 feet it is half as much again as it is at sea level. This copious giving off of water has a marked effect on the lungs. It constitutes one of the reasons why altitude is a favorable element in the treatment of tuberculosis. Only beginning cases of tuberculosis, however, are able to stand the additional work thus put on them, though a slight elevation, up to 2,000 or even 3,000 feet, rather seems to be of benefit to all cases. How far-reaching the effect of this extra loss of fluid is, is appreciated from the concentration of blood which takes place and which produces a blood count of 8,000,000 red cells at a mile of altitude in patients who, at the sea level, have no more than 4,500,000. Such patients, of course, need much more water and fluids generally to be comfortable than when living lower down.

Suggestion and Treatment.—There are many accessory suggestions with regard to food that serve to confirm the patient in the idea that abundance and variety of food must be taken if the battle with the disease is to be won. To patients who find milk difficult to take, it must be explained that a copious amount of fluid in the system is needed in order to make coughing easier. So milk serves a therapeutic as well as a nutritional purpose. In the same way it may be explained that fats, such as bacon and cream, help to keep the bowels from becoming constipated and constipation inevitably disturbs the appetite.

Explanations as to the advisability of being out of the city and in a portion of country not very thickly populated, in order to avoid the possibilities of secondary infection with other respiratory diseases and bacteria of various {363} kinds, will make a patient understand the necessity for leaving town. It may be helpful, also, to insist on the value of living at some elevation above sea level as an aid to expectoration.

Cough is the symptom that many of these patients fear most, and a promise of any amelioration of it by a simple change of location helps them to make the sacrifice of city life for a while. Some patients who have been benefited by a stay in a sanatorium come back with a relapse of their symptoms. They dread to return to the sanatorium and think they can care for themselves as well at home, since they know what the regulations are, though it may be evident to the physician that they are losing ground in their city environment. It is well worth while to give them a careful explanation of what we know of the effect of altitude upon consumptives who have sufficient reactionary power to stand it.

Negative Suggestions.—Some suggestions are valuable for the prophylaxis of complications. For instance, tuberculous patients must be warned not to indulge in breathing exercises without the express consent of the physician. So much is said in popular literature as to the value of breathing exercises that many a patient suffering from tuberculosis thinks that, not only may they be indulged in with impunity, but that they will surely do good and can do no possible harm. Nothing could be more erroneous. Many localized lesions have been diffused in this way and there is always danger that the strain will cause hemorrhage. Patients must be warned also to avoid any possible condition in which they might have to over-exert themselves. Because of the dust inevitably breathed during automobile riding, this pleasure must be denied to tuberculous patients as a rule, but even when they have recovered sufficiently so that this may be permitted they must be warned not to take long rides into the country lest the breaking down of the machine should place them under the necessity of walking a long distance. This idea should also be emphasized for rowing excursions, or trips by motor boat, for occasionally they lead to serious and exhausting exposure.

One negative suggestion should be given at the very initial stage to every patient in whom the presence of pulmonary tuberculosis has been recognized. This should be a warning to exercise the greatest care against permitting the development of constipation. Tuberculous patients must never strain at stool. Almost necessarily a certain number of tubercle bacilli are swallowed every day whenever pulmonary tuberculosis is at all active and they are constantly present in the digestive tract. If tuberculous patients then strain at stool, little abrasions of the mucous membrane of the rectum are caused in which tubercle bacilli find a favorable nidus. Ischio-rectal abscesses are common among the tuberculous and rectal fistulas often give much bother. When a tuberculous patient develops such a condition, a period of depression and discouragement will follow, for there is a curious tendency to depression associated with all lesions of the rectum. A pulmonary patient who has been doing well will often fail to make progress for months after the development of even a small ischio-rectal abscess.

{364}

CHAPTER III

NEUROTIC ASTHMA AND COGNATE CONDITIONS

For the consideration of its psychotherapy asthma may be divided into two forms—symptomatic and essential, or neurotic, asthma. Symptomatic asthma is a difficulty of breathing, the result of some interference with the circulation, as by heart disease, or with the oxidizing power of the blood, as by kidney disease, or various blood conditions, or from direct interference with respiration from some pulmonary affection. Essential asthma is not dependent on any organic condition, but is an interference with breathing without any distinct pathological condition in the lungs themselves or in the general circulation. There may be some emphysema, but not enough to account for the respiratory difficulty. It is spoken of as neurotic asthma, and the most careful investigations made of individuals who have died during a seizure has failed to give any sure pathological basis for the affection. Certain accompanying phenomena are worthy of note. The most interesting of these are Curschmann's spirals, which usually occur in the form of translucent pellets very characteristically described by Laennec as pearls. They are evidently formed in the finer bronchioles and show that the affection extends to the terminal portions of the bronchial system. In connection with these the so-called asthma crystals first described by Charcot and Von Leyden and sometimes called by their combined names are often found. Besides, there are a large number of eosinophiles in the sputum itself entangled within the filaments of the spirals and an eosinophila of the blood.

Etiology.—Not only are we ignorant of the reasons for these phenomena but there is even some doubt as regards the mechanism of the respiratory spasm itself. There is a general impression that the paroxysm is due to incapacity to inspire because of a paroxysmal spasm of the respiratory muscles. Gee in his "Medical Lectures and Aphorisms" rather leans towards the explanation that suffering is due not to any inability to fill the lungs but to incapacity to empty them when they have become over-distended with air. He tells the story related by Dean Swift of the old man whose barrel-shaped chest was fixed in spasm so full of air that the patient could not find room for the slightest additional breath. "If I ever get this air that is in me out," the patient declared to the Dean, "I will never take another breath."

It is important to differentiate symptomatic from neurotic or essential asthma. In symptomatic asthma the only assured treatment of the condition must come through amelioration of the organic condition causing the symptoms. Cardiac and renal asthma respond promptly to remedies which relieve critical conditions that may be present in the heart or kidneys. It must not be forgotten, however, that respiration is readily disturbed by mental influences. Where cardiac or renal disease causes interference with respiration this is much emphasized by the patient's unfavorable mental attitude toward it, or much relieved by keeping him from worrying over his condition. Even symptomatic asthma, then, has a definite place in psychotherapeutics, though {365} it would be serious not to recognize the underlying conditions and treat them. If the patient's attitude of mind is one of discouragement, the respiratory difficulties will continue to be a marked symptom of the case, even though the proper remedies for the relief of cardiac or renal conditions are administered.

Symptomatic Picture.—What is likely to be one of the most disturbing experiences of the young physician early in practice, especially if he has not before seen a typical case, is to be called to a patient suffering from a severe attack of asthma. Often the sufferer is sitting up in bed so as to get all the air possible, and, though the windows are wide open, he is gasping for breath, usually pleading for more air with a tense, anxious expression, starting eyes, and the sweat pouring from his forehead, while the accessory muscles of respiration, deeply engaged in moving his thorax to move air enough to keep him from stifling, emphasize his dyspnea. Occasionally a degree of cyanosis develops that is quite startling for the untrained observer. Most of those who see the symptomatic picture for the first time think that death is impending, and the patient himself, if he has not had a series of attacks, will fear a fatal termination. It appears impossible to believe that the next morning, within six or seven hours of this, the patient will, as a rule, be quite well and walking round in the enjoyment of apparent good health.

As a rule, the worse these cases seem in their intensity and the more the patient is anxious, the more surely are they merely of functional nervous origin; above all, the more complaints of lack of air and of fear of impending death that are made, the more likely is the patient to be all right within a few hours. Asthma looks as though it must be due to some serious organic condition. Of course, in many cases of difficult breathing, even with asthma-like attacks, there are underlying serious conditions of heart and kidneys that are extremely dangerous. As a rule, however, these do not produce the woeful pictures of purely neurotic asthma. Even when the basis of the asthma is an emphysema, which of itself is not dangerous and is quite compatible with long life, the attacks, though frequent and severe, are usually not so serious looking as those in which absolutely no pathological condition of the lungs, or heart, or kidneys can be found, and, indeed, in which there is absolutely no organic change to account for the extremely uncomfortable and even terrifying symptoms.

Mental Influence.—In the medical literature of asthma there are abundant proofs that the attitude of mind of the patient towards his affection means very much. There is the story, thoroughly vouched for, of the two friends stopping at a little country hotel late at night. One of them was a neurotic subject, who, whenever he remained for some time in a stuffy atmosphere, was likely to have a severe asthmatic attack. The quarters assigned to them proved to be one of the cramped little rooms with a single small window that occasionally are found in the attics of country inns in England. During the night the patient of asthmatic tendencies had one of his attacks and begged his friend to open the window. The friend, suddenly roused from sleep, did not remember the position of the window and, the night being very dark, he felt for it and finally found it. He could not raise the sash and he could not move it either inward or outward and there seemed no way of getting it open. His friend was insistently clamoring for air with that tone of despair and {366} dread of impending death so characteristic of the young, inexperienced asthma sufferer. Unable to get the window open, the sympathetic companion finally took his shoe and smashed the glass. The relief was immediate. Scarcely had the crash of the broken glass been heard before the patient gave an audible sigh of relief. When his friend went over to him he felt so much better that it was rather easy for the sufferer to persuade him that nothing more would be needed and that he should go back to bed. In the morning, when the friend awoke, his first glance, directed by the sunlight that came streaming into the window, was toward the broken panes of the night before. To his surprise it was not broken. Wondering what had happened, he looked round the room to find that he had smashed two panes in an old bookcase set into the wall, and that it was the breaking of the glass with the suggestion of free ingress of air that it involved and not any real provision of fresh air that had cured his friend's asthma so promptly.

Suggestion.—When much-vaunted cures for asthma are analyzed, many of them are found to depend more on suggestion than on any other element. Various forms of cigarettes are used, comparatively innocuous in themselves, and certainly of no strong therapeutic action, yet they work marvels in loosening the spasm that comes over the lungs in asthmatic attacks. Any sort of a cigarette will do at the beginning. I have seen dried grape-vine stems work very well in the country, especially in young women to whom the idea of smoking anything was strongly suggestive. Cubebs cigarettes have the same effect on older people. Doubtless there is some relaxing action in the smoke. This is not enough, however, to account for the effect produced without mental influence. After cubebs have been tried for a period and begin to lose their efficacy, then other materials that produce a pungent smoke or have a certain sensory action, as stramonium leaves, may be used, and will also have the marvelous power of cubebs. After a time, however, they, too, lose their efficacy, and, as a rule, each successive cigarette that is tried has less power than the first to control the difficulty of breathing.

The more one hears of cures for asthma, and the longer one has experience with these cases, the clearer does it become that there is a large suggestive element in every successful treatment. If a piece of ordinary blotting paper be dipped in a strong solution of saltpeter and allowed to dry, it will, if touched by a lighted match, burn slowly without flame, but with the production of heavy, thick smoke. The therapeutic elements in this are not very strong, but the suggestive element, when a room gets full of it, is intense and is cumulative. Very probably the thick smoke, rich in nitrites, has some tendency to relax the spasm in the lungs which causes the asthmatic seizure, but after a time the remedy fails and something else has to be tried. In many cases, when first used, it almost works a miracle. This is the simplest type of suggestive treatment for asthma.

Mental Shock.—Any strong mental influence, especially if accompanied by the suggestion of assured relief, is likely to do much for asthma of essentially neurotic character, and indeed is more powerful in dispelling the symptoms of the seizure than almost any other means that we have. Sometimes even things absolutely indifferent which produce a profound mental impression, prove curative. There are many stories of men in the midst of a severe asthmatic seizure being suddenly roused by the cry of fire, or an alarm of some {367} kind near them, having the spasmodic conditions disappear as if by magic. Occasionally where attacks of asthma recurred regularly on successive nights for a considerable period, travel on a railroad train or anything else which occupied the attention much, prolonged the interval between seizures and sometimes put an end to the series of attacks. The more one knows of asthma the more one realizes how much its occurrence depends on mental influences of many kinds in association with various reflex irritations, some of them very distant from the respiratory tract and comparatively trivial in their effects on other people.

Loss of Control.—Occasionally in elderly neurotic people over-fatigue induces an attack of asthma about the time that sleep becomes deep. This usually occurs after the first hour or two of sleep. The inhibitory power of the nervous system over spasmodic contraction of the lung tissues seems lost in deep sleep and then the asthmatic condition develops. The greater the effort to breathe the more intense does the contraction become, until the antispasmodic effect of the presence of a lessened amount of oxygen and an abnormal quantity of carbon dioxide in the blood makes itself felt. In many cases these patients will be relieved of the tendency to such spasm by taking a cup of coffee. This stimulates the general circulation and minimizes the reflex tendency which centers in their respiratory tracts. Such patients after taking an amount of coffee that would keep ordinary people awake all night, sink in the course of half an hour into a quiet, restful sleep and awake quite refreshed. This is not entirely suggestive, but suggestion plays an added role in the relief of all the symptoms.

Treatment.—*Varied Cures.*—We do not mean to say that asthma is entirely amenable to suggestive treatment, but we emphasize the mental influences in its production and its cure. A new and almost infallible cure is announced nearly every year for asthma, as for tuberculosis. Sometimes this is some new treatment for the nose, occasionally it is a novel method of treating the throat, but reflexes from a great many other organs not at all in touch with the respiratory system have also been supposed to be productive of asthma, and their treatment has been followed by relief from this trying condition. Washing out the stomach, for instance, has been followed by prolonged cessation of asthmatic attacks. In children it is claimed that occasionally the correction of eye-strain by the proper glasses has cured neurotic asthma. There are those who have had cases where the relief of long-continued constipation had a like therapeutic result and there are other and even more curious claims for curative effect in this affection.

Negative and Positive Suggestion.—Any condition in the human body that sets nerves in tension and requires constant inhibition may lead to such a cumulative effect of repression that reaction follows and explosion takes place. In particularly susceptible individuals, irritable respiratory centers may be affected with consequent asthmatic seizures. The direct treatment of the respiratory tract to secure ease of respiration often does away with the liability to asthma by direct prevention. If patients, especially young patients, are mouth-breathers the clearing out of the throat and nose so as to insure normal breathing can naturally be expected to lessen any tendency to asthma. In the same way treatment of irritative or degenerative conditions in the throat and larynx, as well as in the nose, may be considered directly curative. On {368} the other hand, there is no doubt that many of the slight ameliorations of intranasal conditions suggested by enthusiastic specialists as curing asthma do not have any direct therapeutic influence but owe their efficacy to the strong suggestion of the operator's assurance on the patient's mind that this treatment has cured asthma in many cases and will surely cure him.

Drugs and Suggestion.—The medicines that are especially effective in asthma of neurotic origin are those which also have a large suggestive influence because of their taste or their effects upon the system. Hoffman's anodyne is an efficient antispasmodic and is wonderfully effective in relieving the tendency to asthma. I have always felt, however, though I have given it freely, that a large element in its effectiveness was its particularly disagreeable taste and odor and then its excretion through the lungs with a certain sense of well-being allied somewhat to the intoxication that comes from the inhalation of ether. I have seen asthmatic tendencies in young women greatly relieved by the use of valerian. Undoubtedly this remedy, like the compound spirits of ether, is antispasmodic in action, yet to a much less degree than Hoffman's mixture, and over and over again I have noted that in pill form, though given in large doses, it was not as effective as if given in liquid form when its nauseating smell added distinctly to its suggestive influence. The drug itself does good but it is distinctly helped by the influence upon the patient's mind of its taste and, above all, of its aroma. The elixir of ammonium valerianate being particularly unpleasant is likely to be more beneficial to these patients.

Climatotherapy and Suggestion.—The climatic treatment of asthma has received much attention. Change of scene and environment nearly always does good. Different patients, however, require very different conditions. Of two cases of neurotic asthma in which no diagnostic differences can be found, one will improve at the seashore or on a sea voyage, while the other will be made worse by such a change though probably the asthma will be improved in the mountains or in some dry climate. Even moving from one part of a city to another has brought great improvement in asthma. Sometimes there were good reasons for this, as, for instance, when an investigation showed that the patient had previously been living above a bakery from which there came a good deal of hot air and flour dust. Some people are actually improved by close contact with human beings in rather crowded quarters. I have known a settlement worker to experience great relief from asthma when living in the slums. Where there is intense occupation of mind, especially if combined with the suggestion that now the asthma ought to be better, seizures will be less frequent and less severe. All sorts of places in the mountains and by the seashore have acquired reputations as relieving asthma which were justified by many cured cases and yet they have lost this reputation. Whenever there are many sufferers together, the expectancy of relief seems to do great good.

CHAPTER IV

DUST ASTHMA, SEASONAL CATARRH, HAY FEVER

Grouped under the term "hay fever" there are probably as many different affections as there are under the term "chronic rheumatism." There are {369} people who, in the springtime, as soon as the weather gets warm, suffer from what is popularly called hay fever. This is often called "spring catarrh" or "rose cold" and seems often to be associated with the pollen of flowers. Then there are people whose hay fever, as it is called, develops about the first of June and continues to be bothersome until the middle of July, when there is a remission of symptoms, though in dry prolonged hot periods after that the affection may recur. It seems as if, at the beginning of the heated term, the warm, dry dusty air irritates their nostrils very much, while after some weeks they gradually become used to this and the reaction is not so violent. Then there are the regular hay-fever patients whose affection occurs principally in haying time, during August and September, though most of them have not been near hay pollen, and the disease is an affection of dwellers in cities rather than in the country, of indoor livers more than of farming people, who might be expected to suffer most from the supposed cause, hay pollen. Even where pollen is directly concerned in its causation it is probably oftener the pollen of the rag weed rather than that of hay that is responsible for it.

There are two elements in the disease apparently of equal importance. One of these is a strictly local condition interfering with respiration in some way, or with the circulation to the mucous membrane of the nose and the lachrymal ducts. The other is an individual over-sensitiveness so that there is an exaggerated reaction to irritation. Some of this is mental, that is, is due to expectancy, or to the persuasion that this reaction is sure to occur under certain circumstances. As a consequence, attacks of hay fever are reported even after a distant view of a hayfield, or of rose cold due to the sight of an artificial rose, and of other recurrences that show the power of the mind to bring about at least a beginning of symptoms.

While the first or physical element in the etiology of dust catarrh can be treated successfully by various means, it is important to get the mind of the individual in a favorable state so as to enable him to obtain better control over his vaso-motor system which is so much influenced by emotions and thoughts. It is this latter element in the causation of the disease that has been successfully treated by the many remedies that for a time have had reported success in the cure of hay fever yet afterwards proved to be of no benefit because they had lost their influence over the patients' minds.

In a review of Morell MacKenzie's book "Hay Fever, with an Appendix on Rose Cold," Dr. J. N. MacKenzie has some paragraphs on hay fever which, though written twenty-five years ago, are worth recalling for a proper understanding of the disease. He preferred to call the disease rhinitis sympathetica or coryza vaso-motoria periodica, names which are much better descriptive terms and have no unsubstantiated suggestions of etiology in them.

207

According to our conception, the so-called nasal reflex neuroses, whether taken singly or collectively, as the cause of the *ensemble* of phenomena known as "hay fever," may be regarded as the protean manifestation of a morbid condition to which we have given the name rhinitis sympathetica, and which is characterized by a hyperesthetic condition of the vaso-motor nerve centers linked to a peculiar excitability of the nasal cavernous tissue. For, if we inquire what condition or conditions is common to them all, and what morbid process is capable of producing them, either singly or in combination; how phenomena apparently {370} so widely different in character and anatomical sphere of operation may be traced to a solitary source, we find the answer in certain more or less clearly defined changes in the nasal apparatus and in a certain exalted state of the sympathetic nervous system, to which latter we instinctively turn as the organ most conspicuously concerned in the evolution of purely reflex acts. In whatever relation the local nasal affection and the condition of the sympathetic stand to each other in the matter of cause and effect, they must both be regarded as inseparable factors in the production of the phenomena under consideration. It matters not to what hypothesis the path of speculation may lead. Of this we can be reasonably sure, that in the production of the characteristic symptoms of this disease, a certain excitability of the nasal passages is necessary, plus an exalted state of the central nervous system.

Dr. MacKenzie calls attention particularly to the erectile character of the tissues mainly involved in all these forms of dust catarrh and dwells on the rôle that mental influence always plays in the phenomena noted in such tissues. This with the vaso-motor elements in the affection which are so largely also under the control of the emotional nature make it clear that the pathology of the affection must be considered from this standpoint and, therefore, its therapy also.

Dr. MacKenzie continues:

From our present knowledge of the disease, it seems difficult to escape the conclusion that its pathology is intimately interwoven with a morbid condition of the vaso-motor sympathetic, and probably a hypersensitive state of the nerve centers themselves. When we recall the fact that in the famous section of the sympathetic in the neck by Claude Bernard, symptoms similar to, or closely allied to, the phenomena of hay fever were produced; when we reflect upon the results reached by Prevost in his experiments on the spheno-palatine ganglion, is there not a clue to lead us through the labyrinth of our difficulties to a rational solution of the question? . . .

. . .In the human body, wherever erectile tissue is found, it is intimately related to reflex or sympathetic acts; there seems to be connected with it a certain receptivity to reflex producing impressions, a certain power of reflex excitability dependent upon its structure and functions. It is thus peculiarly a tissue of sympathy in which we may most satisfactorily study the mechanism of purely reflex or sympathetic acts. Now it seems to us that, as the nasal corpora cavernosa belong to this class of sympathetic tissues, there will be little difficulty in explaining the rôle which they play in the paroxysms of an affection which is probably connected with, if not dependent upon, an excitation of the sympathetic nerve centers, and in more clearly defining the intimate relation which its erection bears to the reflex manifestations of the disease under review.

These considerations explain the heredity of the affection in many cases, since it is dependent on defects that may be family traits, yet they also enable us to understand how slight lesions of the nasal mucous membrane may be the center from which radiate the underlying pathological conditions of the disease.

Railroad Asthma.—There is a form of dust asthma which deserves special attention here because it is due to modern conditions and helps to an understanding of the etiology. It occurs in sensitive persons when they travel on railroad trains in warm weather, particularly if it has been dry for several days and dust is abundant. It has been called railroad asthma or railroad catarrh by the English and the Germans, but the condition has no necessary connection with the railroad. It occurs as a consequence of the infiltration into railroad cars of fine dust during the passage of the train. {371} I have seen it in those who had made long trips over dusty roads in automobiles, though the dust of the railroad seems finer and more penetrating. It develops just as much at the end of a long train as if the passenger spent most of the journey in the car next the engine and apparently it makes no difference whether the engine burns hard or soft coal. They use soft coal almost exclusively in England and Germany, but one sees cases of it here after travel on roads that burn hard coal and are especially cleanly in this respect. Soft coal adds somewhat to the amount of dust and therefore this increases the irritation, but there is nothing specific about coal dust. It is surprising how severe the symptoms may be. I have seen a patient who had traveled continuously for four days across the continent who had so much photophobia when he alighted from the train, that he was almost unable to open his eyes, and it was not until twelve hours had passed that he could open his eyes with any comfort, yet at the end of two days practically all the symptoms had passed off.

Prof. Fraenkel, professor of laryngology and rhinology at the University of Berlin, who was one of the first to classify the condition among the affections related to "hay fever," described certain features of it very well in a clinical lecture reported in *International Clinics*, Vol. II, Ninth Series, 1899. As a rhinologist he insists on the nasal conditions that underlie the affection yet suggests that the nasal hyperemia may be due to reflexes of one kind or another. The basis of these is undoubtedly very often an emotional condition of the patient, a dread of dust, an expectancy of symptoms and a consequent exaggerated reaction. Unorganized dust produces asthma, but organic materials bring more severe and lasting effects, partly because of the mental effect of odors and other sensory conditions in connection with them.

The Personal Element and Power of Suggestion.—The history of these asthmas and other symptoms produced by odors and dust make it clear that the more that is known about the disease the surer it becomes that there is a large personal element, usually dependent on a certain frame of mind, in the cases. Some people are affected by one form of irritant, some by another, some by pollen, others by animal emanations, and not a few by a persuasion of the likelihood of suffering from these things, since occasionally the sight of an artificial product produces a like result. Certain classes suffer much more than others. Those who are much confined to the house and who are especially prone to reflection upon themselves and their feelings form the great majority of the patients. In old days the monks were favorite victims, in modern times literary folk, students, and those who have the time and the inclination for reading and introspection are particularly likely to suffer. How much the mental element may account for in these cases is not clear, but it stands for much more than has been thought and there seems no doubt that more relief of symptoms is afforded by diversion of mind and change of dwelling quite apart from external conditions than in any other way. It is important to remember that no specific dust but almost any kind of dust produces these conditions in sensitive persons.

Dr. MacKenzie describes an interesting case in which all the symptoms were produced by the presence of an artificial rose. The story is so striking and he has told it so well that I prefer to tell it in his own words. I may say, however, that the clinical history of the case was typical. About the end of {372} May or the beginning of June every year the patient suffered from a coryza preceded for a few days by an indefinite sense of general depression with a disagreeable feeling of heaviness in the head. Sometimes there were chilly feelings and general malaise. The catarrhal stage commenced with profuse watery discharge from the nostrils, copious flow of tears with redness of the conjunctiva, itching of the puncta lacrymalia and photophobia. The exterior of the nose, especially at the tip, became intensely red and toward the close of the attack the cuticle desquamated. There was a short, dry, hacking cough relieved by sneezing, an intense tickling sensation in the throat, the voice became husky, the pharynx dry, the ears stopped up and tinnitus occurred. Her attacks continued most of the summer and were always brought on by the pollen of any plant and above all by the smell of a rose. It was, indeed, an example and of the most aggravated form. She was brought to Dr. MacKenzie in consultation and I leave him to tell the rest of the story.

Decidedly skeptical as to the power of pollen to produce a paroxysm in her particular case, I practiced the following deception upon her, which still further confirmed me in that belief. For the purpose of the experiment I obtained an artificial rose of such exquisite workmanship that it presented a perfect counterfeit of the original. To exclude every possible error, each leaf was carefully wiped, so that not a single particle of foreign matter was secreted within the convolutions of the artificial flower. When the patient entered my consultation room, she expressed herself as feeling unusually well. The evening before she attempted to wear some roses, but had been obliged to remove them from her dress, as they had produced a great deal of discomfort. Apart from this incident she had been perfectly comfortable for several days and nights. Her conjunctivae were normal, the nasal passages free, and there was nothing to indicate the presence of her trouble. She conversed with me for some time about her case and on general topics, speaking in the most encouraging manner concerning the progress she was apparently making toward recovery. I proceeded to remove the slight slough from the cautery operation, which lay loose in the nostril, and made an application to the mucous membrane, and all without exciting the slightest tendency to reflex movements. After I felt sure that such tendency was absent, I produced the artificial rose from behind a screen, where it had been secreted, and, sitting before her, held it in my hand, at the same time continuing the conversation. In the course of a minute she said she must sneeze. This sensation was followed almost immediately by a tickling and intense itching in the back of the throat and at the end of the nose. The nasal passages at the same time became suddenly obstructed, and the voice assumed a hoarse nasal tone. In less than two minutes the puncta lacrymalia began to itch violently, the right and afterward the left conjunctiva became intensely hyperemic and photophobia and increased lacrymation supervened. To these symptoms were added, almost immediately, itching in the auditory meatuses and the secretion of a thin fluid in the previously dry nasal passages. In a few minutes the feeling of oppression in the chest began with slight embarrassment of respiration. In other words, in the space of five minutes she was suffering from a severe coryza, the counterpart of that which the presence of natural roses invariably produced in her case. An examination of the throat and nasal passages was then made. The right nostril was completely obstructed by the swollen, reddened, irritable, turbinated structures; the left was only slightly pervious to the air current; both were filled with a serous-looking fluid. The mucous membrane of the throat was also injected, but did not exhibit the same amount of redness and irritability found in the nasal passages. As the discomfort was rapidly increasing, and as I considered the result of the experiment sufficiently satisfactory. I removed the rose and placed it in a distant part of the room. When told that the rose was an artificial one, her amazement was great, and her incredulity on the subject was only removed upon personal examination of the counterfeit {373} flower. She left my office with a severe coryza, but also with the assurance that her disease was not altogether irremediable. A few days later she called to see me again, and on that occasion she buried her nostrils in a large, fragrant specimen of the genuine article and inhaled its pollen without the slightest tendency to the production of reflex acts.

There is but one conclusion that can be drawn from this: that suggestion plays a large rôle in the relief of the symptoms of the disease. If patients once become persuaded that something will do them good, then it surely does. It is true that this good effect will usually not persist, but that is because after a time conditions conspire to make the suggestion fail of its purpose. This does not at all imply that hay fever, or just catarrh as I prefer to call it, is imaginary. The relief of our most serious and fatal diseases with profound pathological lesions, such as tuberculosis, may well be brought about by suggestion. After all, just the same story is told about consumption and its many remedies as of hay fever and its many "cures." However, the most important therapeutic element so far discovered for the treatment of hay fever is evidently suggestion. If the patient's mind can only be brought to a favorable attitude in which the discouragement incident to imperfect oxidation can be greatly lessened, then relief of many of the symptoms will be afforded and under favorable conditions the patient will deem himself cured. Undoubtedly the large amount of attention given to hay fever, the gathering of these patients in particular localities, the repetition of the story of their symptoms to each other, the body of literature that has gathered around hay fever and is read with such avidity by those who are pleased to call themselves its victims, adds to the unfavorable suggestions and inveterates the symptoms, exaggerates the nasal hyperemia and makes the general condition worse.

I am the more positive about the influence of suggestion, favorable and unfavorable, in the affection after having carefully noted the conditions in certain patients from year to year for a number of years. I became interested in it because it is a family affection and several sisters as well as myself are sufferers from it. At the beginning, when the real nature of the trouble is not recognized, there is a year or two of considerable general discomfort, though not much local disturbance. Then comes the realization of what the recurrent affection is and a period of distinct depression during its continuance. Eventually it begins to be appreciated that a number of local applications will lessen the symptoms from day to day and that there need be no apprehension of serious sleep disturbance, or of any lasting effect upon the general health, the affection becomes quite bearable and, while still annoying, is no longer the object of particular solicitude.

209

CHAPTER V

DYSPNEA—CAT AND HORSE ASTHMA

There is a class of cases of difficulty of breathing allied to asthma and often called by that name, the study of which throws light on the origin and the relief of neurotic asthma. These cases are usually accompanied by such a sense of oppression on the chest that breathing becomes labored and, to some {374} extent at least, the accessory muscles of respiration have to be called into play. The most typical cases are connected with the mental influence produced by the presence of some particular animal, the cat being the most frequent and the horse not rare, or with emanations from these animals, when there seems to be some physical nexus between the animal and the symptoms.

Cat Asthma.—The symptoms associated with cats are rather common, and they occur at the sight or touch of the animal, but may be the result only of its presence which in some way the patient is able to recognize without sight of him. Shakespeare's expressions in a number of places, such as "I could endure anything before but a cat" and "some that are mad if they behold but a cat," shows that the affection was commonly recognized at that time and that the reason for it was considered unknowable, for Shakespeare says, "There is no firm reason to be rendered why he cannot abide ... a harmless necessary cat."

Dr. Byron Bramwell in his "Clinical Studies," Vol. I, page 107, has an interesting paragraph with regard to these curious asthmatic conditions which develop in the presence of animals of various kinds. He sums up many of the curious features of this affection as reported by various good observers. Many more people than we would be apt to think are affected by it. He says:

In some persons the smell of a horse or of a cat produces an attack of asthma. Some years ago I repeatedly saw a young gentleman who invariably had an attack of asthma if he went near a stable or a horse. He was so susceptible that he was unable to drive in a cab or a carriage; when traveling from place to place, while sending his traps from the station to the hotel in a cab, he himself was obliged to walk.

Dr. Goodhart mentions a similar instance which occurred in the practice of Prof. Clifford Allbutt. Dr. Goodhart also mentions a remarkable case of "cat asthma":

I have known of two cases of cat asthma. In one of them the existence of cats is the bane of life, for before accepting an invitation she is obliged first to ask, "Is there a cat?" An attack of urticaria and coryza followed by asthma has been noticed to come on within ten minutes of having stroked a cat. At other times, sitting in a room in which there was a cat, without any actual contact with it, was sufficient to produce a bad attack, beginning within ten minutes of entering the room.

There are two forms of this intolerance of a cat. One of them takes on the character of a dread and is discussed in the chapter on Dreads. The other is accompanied by dyspnea or asthma with a sense of discomfort and tightness of the chest that cannot be overcome. It is not merely an imagination, for sometimes even when they cannot see the cat, or at times when friends have been careful to exclude cats from the room, these people become impressed with the idea that a cat is near and a search usually shows that their impression is true, though just what was the means through which they came to know it is difficult to understand.

{375}

Dr. Weir Mitchell's review of the subject of "Cat Asthma and Allied Conditions" in a paper read before the Association of American Physicians brought out many curious details. There is no doubt about the power to recognize the presence of the unseen cat. Besides the respiratory oppression, some patients develop urticarial lesions and occasionally even conjunctivitis and a catarrhal condition of the nasal mucous membrane. These seem to be due to the direct irritant effect of animal emanations. As the symptoms of rose cold or hay fever have sometimes developed after the sight of an artificial rose, or even, it it said, the picture of a hay field, so, in some of these cases, the sight of a picture of a cat has produced at least some of these symptoms. Probably the most interesting feature of the affection is that the large cats, the tiger and the lion, do not have any effect on the patient. There seems to be no doubt, then, that the mind plays an important role in the matter and that relief must be secured through mental influence.

In some of these cases a careful searching of the past of the patient will show that there has been some terrifying incident connected with the cat. In one case in my own experience the patient's earliest recollection, and the first time that death was brought home to her, was when a favorite bird was killed by a cat. Ever after that she had a horror of the animals, the family cat had to be disposed of, and her family never had another. She used to suffer from a severe dyspnea at the sight of a cat and was sure that she could recognize its presence without having seen it. She mentioned a number of occasions on which that had been true. The very idea of living where a cat could come near her was appalling. She was sure that she was even waked by the mere propinquity of a cat if by any chance one got into her room at night, though without any noise.

A change in her material circumstances compelled her to teach in private families. Under these circumstances her cat detestation made difficulties for her. I suggested, since she had had no feeling toward cats before the bird incident, that probably her symptoms were due to suggestion and an acquired habit of mind and that she might by discipline overcome them. She was sure that would be impossible. With determined effort, however, and practice in withstanding her feelings in the presence of cats she finally learned to overcome practically all of her feelings so that though it still requires an effort she can even pick up a cat and stroke it. I have had several other patients with less marked forms of the affection who have by self-discipline overcome their feelings to a great degree. It is always well to search the past of these patients in order to find out whether there may not be a dominant idea derived from some unfortunate experience, which acts as an auto-suggestion in the production of their symptoms of constriction of the chest and sometimes even the recurrence of the swelling of the mucous membrane of the nose that produces difficulty of breathing. Whenever this can be found, contrary suggestion can be given and the patients can be persuaded to try, by frequently repeated auto-suggestion, to relieve themselves of the trouble.

Occasionally these curious manifestations of a catarrhal or asthmatic character in the presence of cats occur in people who like cats. Dr. Taylor in his "Types of Habit Neuro-Psychoses" published in the *Proceedings of the Massachusetts Medical Society*, 1896-98, tells the story of a young woman in whom he saw conjunctivitis developing while she was fondling a cat. In many cases {376} besides the hyperemia of the nose and of the respiratory mucous membrane generally there is marked injections of the ocular conjunctiva. It is rather difficult to understand the phenomena of asthmatic attacks in connection with cats and other animals in terms of a habit formed, because at some time asthmatic or hyperemic manifestations occurred in association with the handling of these animals and that then, somehow, suggestion works to reproduce the same symptoms in the presence of the animals later; but this is undoubtedly the only rational explanation that we have for many of these cases. It represents the most helpful explanation, so far as treatment is concerned, for by means of suggestion either in the waking state or in the first stage of hypnosis, in many cases relief can be brought to these patients. Repeated profound hypnotism is a vaunted remedy for these conditions in the hands of professional hypnotists, but serious physicians who have tried hypnotism do not recommend it. It helps for a time but relapse follows. Only continued suggestion and a carefully cultivated habit of self-discipline and control succeed.

Horse Asthma.—The cases of dyspnea in connection with horses are not less interesting. Occasionally, even when all aversion is absent, emanations from horses are capable of producing a curious effect on certain individuals. How much of this is psychic is not clear. I was once consulted with regard to a patient who suffered from asthma whenever she went to a dance. It mattered not how careful she was in not exposing herself to night air, or in wrapping herself up warmly; invariably a few hours after her return home, she was wakened from sound sleep by an attack of difficult breathing that required the opening of windows and the use of the accessory muscles of respiration in order to satisfy her air hunger, and even then her symptoms were quite alarming to herself and her friends. At first, her asthma was thought to be due to sudden changes of temperature in going out into the air after the dancing, and various devices were tried to lessen the shock of the cold to the respiratory mucous membrane. None of them had any effect. Then it was thought that the dust of the ball-room made the difference and so she was forbidden to dance. After a time it was found, however, that if she went out in the evenings to social functions, whether she danced or not, or though she avoided completely being in dusty rooms or where many people were moving, she still had the attacks a few hours after she returned home.

Finally it was noted that these attacks of asthma also occurred on several occasions after she had been out riding during the day in a carriage. Then one evening after a rather long intermission free from attacks, in spite of directions and her fears, she went to a ball, but owing to circumstances went and returned by trolley instead of, as usual, in the family carriage. That night she had no attack of asthma. Experiments were made then and it was found that whenever she rode behind horses she suffered from an attack of asthma during the following night. The attack was evidently not due to suggestion. The story illustrates the necessity for carefully analyzing all the circumstances of an asthma patient and making sure that some one of these curious and unusual conditions are not at work, for if they are, the only possible curative treatment is by influencing the patient's mind, first by demonstrating the cause of the affection and then by training in self-control to reduce the reaction.

{377}

Recently I have been consulted with regard to a physician who has developed in a rather curious manner a sensitiveness to the presence of horses. As an interne at a hospital during an epidemic of diphtheria he took a dose of diphtheria antitoxin for immunizing purposes. The amount injected was 750 units, the remainder of the dose of 1,500 units contained in the phial being given to the nurse who had charge of the cases. She suffered absolutely no ill effects, so that the manifestations in his case were entirely due to idiosyncrasy and not to anything in the serum itself. Within fifteen minutes after taking the injection the mucous membrane of his nose became so congested as to make it impossible for him to breathe through his nostrils and the mucous membrane of his soft palate was seriously disturbed in the same way. His face became much swollen, the edema affecting particularly his eyelids and his lips and hundreds of wheals appeared all over the body. Fortunately the edema did not affect the larynx, or the issue might have been fatal, or would surely have required intubation. His pulse became extremely rapid and weak, there was marked dyspnea, and whenever the patient sat up there was fainting or a distinct tendency to it.

Under active stimulation and elimination the symptoms rapidly passed off so that the only noticeable edema the next morning was in the eyelids and lips, which, however, also disappeared within twenty-four hours. Up to this time the physician had never been bothered by any tendency to hay fever or to asthma and there is no history of either of these affections in his family. Thereafter, however, though quite without his anticipating it, and, indeed, the first symptoms were incomprehensible, he became extremely sensitive to emanations from horses. When he rides behind a horse for some distance his conjunctivae become injected, the nostrils become congested and difficulty of breathing sets in with a sense of constriction of the chest. These subside as soon as he gets away from the presence of the horse and has washed himself thoroughly. He suggests that he has become sensitized to horse serum and, as it did not exist before his experience with diphtheria serum, he, of course, connects that incident with the present tendency. It is easy for such a case to have its real significance entirely missed and, of course, treatment by prophylaxis, the most efficient form, would then be out of the question.

Other Forms.—Apparently at times human emanations or some peculiarity of odor seems to influence asthmatic conditions. I have been told by a good observer—a physician—of two brothers who had an attack of asthma whenever they visited each other. At first this was attributed to something in the air or some other condition of the visit. After a time it was found to occur under varying circumstances, but that the one essential was the association with each other.

211

Treatment.—The more one knows about asthmatic conditions the more does it become clear that special study of individual cases is extremely important for any definite knowledge of the causation in a particular case. Without a knowledge of the cause the treatment is very unsatisfactory and in the meantime the unfavorable suggestion of the recurrence of the attacks acting upon the patient sometimes disturbs the general health. To remove this unfavorable influence must be the first care of the physician and then if the real cause can be found, favorable suggestion and modifications of the mode of life, with self-discipline and control of the mental attitude and of the {378} nervous system, may greatly aid in the reduction not only of the number of attacks and of the severity of the symptoms, but finally lead to complete eradication of the affection.

Mental control to some degree can be obtained and it has even been suggested that if the emanations from an animal cause physical symptoms, gradually increased dosage of them, beginning with very small amounts, that is, short periods of association with the animals in question, may gradually lead to the production of an immunity to them as it does even to the much more serious results of snake poison. Certainly some patients seem to have succeeded in bringing relief to themselves by this means and it is worth while remembering in the therapy of the affection, if for no other reason than the strong suggestion that goes with it.

{379}

SECTION IX

PSYCHOTHERAPY IN THE JOINT AND MUSCULAR SYSTEM

CHAPTER I

PAINFUL JOINT CONDITIONS—PSEUDO-RHEUMATISM.

Many painful conditions in connection with joints give rise to more or less continuous or frequently repeated discomfort, which often leads patients to think that there are serious pathological factors at work, or that some progressive disease condition has obtained a hold of them. Many of these painful conditions are due entirely to local causes: to over-exertion, to the wrong use of muscles, to the exercise of joints under unfortunate mechanical conditions and the like. Just so long as people are assured that an ailment is local, is not likely to be followed by serious impairment of function, that the discomfort of it is only temporary, and, above all, just as soon as they get rid of the notion of a progressive constitutional malady, they are content to bear even annoying pain without much complaint, and, what is more important, without such discouragement and worry as may impair the general health. Unfortunately, it is the custom to call most of these vague painful conditions "rheumatism," unless there is some other patent cause for them. Especially is this done if the symptoms happen to be worse in rainy weather, or in damp seasons. Rheumatism is always thought of as a progressive constitutional disease, and the very idea of it produces an unfortunate sense of depression.

Exaggeration of Significance.—Toothache, for instance, unless it is allowed to nag for a long time, awakens no dreads and consequently fails to produce the corresponding depression and discouragement, seen so often in connections with conditions much less painful, but associated with the thought of the possibility of serious developments. *"Omne ignotum pro magnifico,"* what is not well understood is always exaggerated, was Cicero's summing up of the tendency of the human mind to make the significance of misunderstood things greater than they really are. It is particularly true of painful {380} conditions of the body, and the tendency must be combated if patients are to be relieved. This must be done not alone because along this way lies relief of suffering, since not a little of the discomfort is due to the mental concentration consequent upon the dread, but because, also, the discouraged state of mind interferes with the trophic influences that go down from the central nervous system to the periphery to keep it in good health and to restore function when there is anything out of order. In a word, the exaggeration of significance so likely to influence such patients for ill must, as far as possible, be removed for their immediate relief as well as ultimate cure.

Rheumatism, Gout, Catarrh.—There are three words in popular medical language which can be made to include more diseases and explain more symptoms than any others. Their meaning has become so indefinite that they now convey very little information, though they are much used—and abused. They are: rheumatism, gout and catarrh. Curiously enough all three of them when their etymology is studied mean the same thing as far as their derivation goes. Catarrh from the Greek word to flow down and rheumatism from the Greek verb to flow are terms that correspond exactly in etymology to gout, which is probably derived from *gutta*, the Latin word for drop—referring to the excess of secretion that is supposed to occur in the disease. All of these have for their basic idea, in etymology at least, an increase of secretion. A generation or two ago, the word rheumatism included a host of disparate painful affections, and was even more sadly abused than now, though its abuse has not ceased. The word catarrh is now at its acme of abuse. Gout has been pushed somewhat into the background by the other two. Any one of these three terms carries with it, in the popular mind, a connotation of progressive constitutional involvement which is not justified by anything that physicians know with regard to these diseases.

The Uric Acid Diathesis.—The usual supposedly scientific explanation of a decade ago for many of these vague pains and aches classed as chronic rheumatism was that they developed on the basis of an excess of uric acid in the system. Advance in chemistry has completely obliterated the significance of the observation on which the theory of a uric acid diathesis, as it was so learnedly called, as an explanation for these conditions was founded. After uric acid there came for a time the theory of an excess of lithic acid, the so-called lithemia or American disease of a few years ago. These are, however, merely pseudo-scientific hypotheses and the more physicians know of chemistry the less they talk about them. Many practitioners, however, continue to accept this universal explanation which makes diagnosis so easy and which is supposed to be so suggestive for treatment. There are various remedies that are claimed to reduce the uric acid content of the blood or the system, and then there are various changes of diet that are supposed to do the same thing. These two systems of treatment and the combination of them have constituted the main therapeutic resource of many physicians for these so-called rheumatic cases, though their success has been anything but what they hoped for.

Diet Tinkering.—Tinkering with diet has been particularly harmful in these cases. Over and over again I have seen patients who had lost considerably in weight because they had had all the supposed acid-forming elements removed from their diet. In many physicians' minds this seems to include most of the starches, as well as the fruits and many meats. Without any {381} potatoes, with only a limited amount of bread, with a warning as to red meats, and occasionally even some distrustful remarks with regard to butter, it is not surprising that the patients lost weight, that muscles became weaker, that painful conditions became severer, and that, above all, the patients' minds became less capable of bearing whatever discomfort is present. Besides, constipation intervenes with its train of consequences and patients become miserable, lose sleep often because of insufficient nutrition and actual clamoring on the part of their gastrointestinal tract for food. I have seen a man who was not much over normal weight to begin with lose twenty-five pounds, nearly one-sixth of his weight, while being dieted for vague pains (worse on rainy days) that were really due to his occupation, but that had been diagnosed as "rheumatic," consequent upon the uric acid diathesis, for which coal tar products were prescribed over a long period and his diet strenuously regulated. This has become as much of an abuse as the old-time purgings and bleedings.

Irregular Treatment.—As we have said, this group of cases constitutes the most frequent and abundant source of profit for quacks and charlatans and irregular practitioners generally. The naturopath, the osteopath, whom we have already mentioned, for to these cases he owes most of his success in appealing to legislatures for recognition, the irregular electropath, many supposed diet specialists, and even the special shoemaker, have reaped a rich harvest from these patients. The reason why they have done so is that, as a rule, they have at once reassured the patients that their condition was not seriously progressive and have promised them certain relief from their ailment. Usually various local measures, such as St. John Long's liniment of one hundred years ago and many of its successors, or the mechanotherapy and the massage and the manipulation of the osteopaths of the present day, have been employed with consequent restoration of circulatory disturbances to normal conditions and, in general, the setting up of better mechanical employment of muscles than was possible before. If so-called chronic rheumatism is to be treated successfully and this opprobrium of medicine, as it has been called, is to be removed, it can only be done by a careful analysis of the ills of each individual patient and a definite determination as to just what local pathological condition is at work and not by a slip-shod diagnosis of rheumatism with immediate recourse to a supposed or assumed theoretic diathesis for the explanation of its etiology.

Differentiation of Joint Conditions.—The local conditions that give rise to painful conditions of joints are most diverse in character. There was a time when all of the infectious joint affections had the term rheumatism applied to them. Even at present it is not unusual to hear of scarlatinal or gonorrheal or influenzal rheumatism. What is meant, of course, is that the microbes of these specific diseases have for some reason found a lowered resistive vitality in one of the joints, or perhaps several of them, and have set up an inflammatory disturbance. These specific arthritises are now definitely separated from the rheumatism group and it seems clear that in the near future we shall have rheumatism itself divided up into a series of diseases. By this I mean that even where there is the redness, the swelling and the fever of true inflammation of joints, it is not always due to one microbe, but to various microbic agents, and so we shall have various forms of rheumatism. At present we are prone to speak of many of the neuritises as rheumatic, but it is probable that {382} here a series of varying microbic infections will be found, some of them much more serious than others, most of them capable of complete cure, though some of them will tend to leave pathological conditions in nerves that are more or less crippling.

Painful Joint Affections.—These pains and aches occur particularly in the old and those who have been hard muscle workers, in those who have been exposed much to the elements and especially in the subjects of old injuries. All of these conditions, one way or another, have left their mark upon tissues so that the nerves do not receive proper nutrition, especially when there is considerable exertion or in rainy weather.

There are a number of reasons why rainy weather produces this effect. The humidity of the atmosphere lessens evaporation. This disturbs heat conditions in the tissues, for evaporation is the most important element in heat dissipation. This leads to the accumulation of heat in the parts and conduces to congestion. Any tissue of lowered vitality will be affected by this and nerves become oversensitive. Besides, it seems probable that the fall in the barometer with the lessened pressure from without makes a difference in the circulation. There is a general feeling of depression in wet weather and apparently the circulation is not so active. It is particularly slow at the surface of the body and in the terminal portions, so that the hands and feet are likely to be cold. Just as soon as the barometer goes up somewhat these

213

conditions cease to be active and there is restoration of the circulation to its previous condition. Besides, it seems not unlikely that dampness produces some relaxation of muscles, so that it is more difficult to make them contract, and consequently they are used at a greater mechanical disadvantage and painful tiredness more readily ensues. All sensitive tissues become more sensitive in rainy weather, though in the case of toothache or neuralgia, for instance, we do not think of connecting this with the word rheumatism.

Classes of Sufferers.—In persons who are over-thin or over-stout complaints of joint discomfort are not uncommon. In the first case they are due to the fact that muscles working around joints are not strong enough to accomplish their normal purposes. In the other cases, owing to the weight of the body, the muscles are overstrained. In a number of stout people the muscles do not increase proportionately to the size of the frame, much of the extra weight being in the shape of adipose tissue that constitutes a grievous burden. In people who run rapidly to either of these conditions of disturbed nutrition—thinness or stoutness—complaints are particularly likely to be heard. Familiar examples are often seen in the tuberculous who have lost weight rapidly or in convalescents from typhoid fever who are much thinner than they were before they took to their beds. On the other hand, those who gain in weight rapidly after typhoid fever or some other such pathological incident, or who, as the result of careful sanatorium treatment, put on twenty pounds in the initial stage of tuberculosis, may have similar discomforts to complain of in and around their joints.

Heredity of Rheumatism.—The strongest unfavorable suggestion which most patients have is that their ailment, whatever it is, is hereditary and therefore not amenable to treatment. Nothing is more amusing to one who knows the present-day status of opinion in biology with regard to heredity than the frequent declaration that rheumatism is hereditary. Probably {383} nothing is commoner than to have a patient who is suffering from some vague, painful condition in muscles or joints, especially if that condition is worse on rainy days, declare that it must be rheumatism because father or mother suffered from rheumatism. I took the trouble to analyze in more than a dozen cases the rheumatism that was supposed to exist in the preceding generation, and found that it consisted of everything from pains due to old injuries and especially dislocations or fractures, through the various deformities connected with flatfoot, up to and including the worst manifestations of arthritis deformans. The condition in the parents supposed to be hereditary is never genuinely rheumatic.

There is just as much sense in talking of hereditary pneumonia as of hereditary rheumatism. Perhaps there is an hereditary lack of resistance in the pulmonary tissues of some people that predisposes them to pneumonia. It must not be forgotten that a century ago, or even less, it was not uncommon to hear that certain people had hereditary tendencies to lung fever. We know now that these were tendencies to tuberculosis and not to true pneumonia. We know, besides, that tuberculosis itself is not hereditary and that probably even the predisposition to it is not specifically hereditary.

As can be readily understood, the question of heredity in rheumatism is extremely important for psychotherapy, since the persuasion that their affection is inherited always produces an unfavorable effect upon patients' minds. In the old days, when tuberculosis was universally considered to be hereditary, a patient was likely to think himself the victim of an hereditary condition which could not be cured and which inevitably led to a fatal termination. Something of the same idea, though the immediate outlook is not so gloomy, is likely to follow the persuasion that rheumatism is hereditary. The question of heredity, of course, is bound up with that of rheumatism being a constitutional disease dependent on hyperacidity or some other pathological condition of the blood. Acute rheumatism, that is, acute arthritis, is an acute, infectious disease due to a microbe. This ought to dispose of any question of heredity in it. Chronic rheumatism is supposed to be related to acute rheumatism and to represent, as it were, a low-grade enduring condition such as in sudden accessions gives rise to acute rheumatism.

So-called Chronic Rheumatism.—In these cases it is always a question whether the condition which causes the pain and discomfort is genuine chronic rheumatism or not. I am one of those who doubt whether we have any genuine, definite symptom-complex that should be termed chronic rheumatism. I have seen many ailments called chronic rheumatism. Any painful condition in the neighborhood of the joint that is worse on rainy days is likely to be labeled rheumatism and, because the salicylates are supposed to be a specific for rheumatism, treated with large doses of these drugs. These relieve the pain, as do any other coal tar products, but it is hard to understand how they are ever supposed to do any good for the underlying pathological conditions. The most noteworthy characteristic of acute rheumatic arthritis is that it leaves no mark upon the joints that were affected by it. These get completely better and the patient has no disability, no deformity, and there usually remains not even the slightest sign of there having been a serious inflammatory condition within the joints.

In this it resembles pneumonia rather strikingly. True lobar pneumonia {384} clears up completely and the man has no symptoms once he has come through the convalescence. There are certain diseases affecting the joints, especially the arthritises in connection with various infectious diseases and the arthritis which accompanies acute arthritis deformans, in which there are serious sequelae and sometimes even complete disorganization of the joint. It is by these after-effects alone that we are sometimes able to differentiate genuine rheumatic arthritis from these other very different affections which resemble it so closely. Just the same thing is true of pneumonia. There are pneumonias that run a course at the beginning strikingly like true lobar pneumonia but which do not have a frank crisis and in which the lungs are seriously affected afterwards. We know now that in these cases it is not an uncomplicated pneumococcus pneumonia that has been at work, but either some other infection or else true pneumonia with a complication. Very often a dormant tuberculosis causes true pneumonia to run a different course from that which it ordinarily follows, and this, as a complication, leaves its serious mark upon the lungs.

Recurrence.—In some cases there seems to be a tendency for the "rheumatic" disease to recur. This also is true of pneumonia. This does not so much indicate, however, any loss of special tissue vitality as a certain loss of vital resistance to a particular microbe. Certainly this tendency is not sufficient to make us think of chronic rheumatism or use that term any more than we would, under similar conditions, talk of chronic pneumonia or of chronic diphtheria, though both of these affections have a tendency to leave a lack of resistive vitality. In a number of cases, subacute rheumatism runs a course that is very bothersome and annoying and that is quite intractable, with relapses and sequelae, but even this is entirely different from the ordinary idea of chronic rheumatism. It is probable that these cases, like the pneumonias that do not end by crises, are complicated by some other condition in the joint that leads to reinfection.

Unclassified Forms.—It is possible that in a certain number of cases for which as yet we have no name but rheumatism, there is a virulence of the microbic factor that brings about some joint disorganization. This, however—and the cases are very rare—is probably an affection to which the name of rheumatic arthritis will not be given when we know more of the disease and its cause. There are probably many forms of acute rheumatic arthritis due to varying microbes which will eventually be divided into groups, as we have made groups in the typhoid series of diseases and in the scarlet fever group and hope to do with other diseases.

The Individual Case and Reassurance.—The main role of psychotherapy in these affections is to set patients' minds at rest as far as possible, by pointing out exactly what is the matter with them and keeping them from worry, discomfort, and even interference with their physical condition by over-solicitude. It is important to know every detail of the patient's occupation, of his habits, of his environment, of his exercise, and, above all, of his individual peculiarities of structure in the neighborhood of joints, so as to decide exactly what is the matter with him, and not be satisfied with the easy but unscientific diagnosis of rheumatism, which may mean much but usually means nothing.

Unless such reassurance is given, and especially if the ordinary drug treatment for so-called chronic rheumatism is persisted in, after a time these {385} patients, unimproved by salicylate treatment, wander off to all sorts of irregular practitioners and form the greater part of the lucrative clientele of quacks and advertising specialists in the cure of chronic diseases. More probably than any other class of cases do they support the irregulars. Osteopathy has particularly appealed to a great many of these patients. It has done it in two ways. The first and most important probably by its effect upon the mind of the patients. Osteopaths immediately proceed to reassure the sufferers that their affection is not rheumatism, but some local condition dependent upon either a subluxation of the vertebra which, according to the founder of osteopathy, constitutes the basis of ninety-five per cent. of all the ills to which human nature is heir or upon some joint or muscle condition which can be corrected by manipulation or massage. These patients have, as a rule, been suffering a good deal before this from the thought that they were afflicted with a progressive constitutional condition which would almost inevitably cripple them. Often they have seen patients who were suffering from arthritis deformans in its worst forms and advanced stages; they have heard this called rheumatism and they have concluded that it was only a question of time when they would be in the same condition. There is no good reason to speak of such conditions as rheumatic. They are entirely local, the hope of relief between attacks is by properly applied massage and passive movements which facilitate the blood supply in the neighborhood, and the best applications at the time of discomfort are the various rubefacients which stimulate the circulation in the parts, call the blood to the surface, and prevent that congestion in the neighborhood of small nerves which is the cause of the aches or pains. These affections take on a much more serious character in the minds of patients as soon as the word rheumatism is mentioned. To tell them that the condition is entirely local, has no tendency to spread, has nothing to do with any constitutional condition, and can be relieved by local measures and the improvement of the general health, will often bring the patient a good measure of relief.

SUGGESTION IN TREATMENT OF SO-CALLED RHEUMATISMS

How much the treatment of these so-called chronic rheumatisms depends on suggestion, in spite of the apparent improbability of anything so materially discomforting being under the influence of the mind, is best appreciated from a consideration of the many inert materials that have been used for the cure of rheumatism. There is, of course, no more virtue in red flannel than in any other colored flannel, but many people suffer from rheumatism or rheumatic discomfort whenever they do not wear red flannel and are sure that it means much for them. Then there are all sorts of supposed electrical contrivances that do not generate an ion of electricity. They are effective only through the appeal they make to the mind. Some men wear electric belts and attribute their freedom from rheumatic pains to them. Others wear so-called electric medals or electric shields or electric insoles. Any number of people in this country wear electric rings on the little finger of one hand and get marvelous relief from it for their chronic rheumatism. Some have noted good results from even less likely objects. There are thousands in this country who carry horsechestnuts as a preventive against rheumatism, and some of {386} them, intelligent men and women, are persuaded it lessens their pains and aches.

In another place I have told the story of the woman who was a sufferer from rheumatism and who found great relief from carrying a horsechestnut. As her husband was also a sufferer, she wanted him to carry one, too, and when he would not, she carried one for him. It is to be hoped that her conjugal tenderness in this matter had as good an effect on him as she was sure the propinquity of the horsechestnut had on her.

The patients' occupations must be regulated by proper advice and detailed directions, and distractions of various kinds must be provided to keep their minds from becoming concentrated on certain portions of their body, emphasizing whatever discomfort is present and preventing nature's curative processes. Finally, local treatment of various kinds must be employed suitable to each individual case, that will remove all mechanical difficulties, disperse congestions, relieve fatigue and over-tiredness, and make conditions favorable for the healthy, normal use of joints and muscles.

Many painful affections of joints, sometimes complicated by immovability, are really psycho-neuroses. Sir Benjamin Brodie once said that four-fifths of the joint troubles that he saw among the better classes were hysterical. Sir James Paget thought this an exaggeration, but

215

confessed that he saw many of them and among all classes of people. One-fifth of those that he saw in hospital and in private practice were entirely neurotic. He emphasized the fact that they must be looked for not only among women but that they are often found in men and that they are by no means confined to those who are nervously inclined, the silly young women or the foolish old women, but that they may be found in special circumstances among the most sensible people. They are often initiated by an injury which makes it quite difficult to differentiate them from real joint affections. Usually, however, there is no redness, nor swelling nor heat with them, though sometimes one of these symptoms at least may occur with the redness. The connection between the trivial accident and the large reaction is usually hard to find and causes a suspicion as to the real process at work. Often, too, there is a delay of several days or sometimes weeks after the accident before the neurosis declares itself. In the meantime it has been getting on the patient's mind.

In general, it must be remembered the patient's attitude of mind in these cases of pain around joints and in muscles is extremely important. They have furnished a goodly proportion of the patients on which quacks and charlatans have fattened. Greatrakes in the seventeenth century, Mesmer and Perkins, St. John Long, the early electrotherapeutists, the blue glass faddists, all the various liniment makers, many of the manufacturers of blood purifiers, and Eddyism and mental healing besides osteopathy in our day have all benefited these sufferers for a time and the patients have often been men and women of education and influence in their communities and have exerted their influence for the benefit of their supposed benefactors. The methods of treatment come and go. The promise of the physician or the healer and the confidence of the patient are the only factors that are common to all the supposed "cures." If people stay at home without the air and exercise they should have, if they nurse their ills and consider that they are sure to get worse, because they labor under hereditary or constitutional ailments, nothing will benefit them. {387} If they are convinced that their disease is only local and begin to go out to see their friends once more, a change comes over the whole aspect of their disease.

CHAPTER II

OLD INJURIES AND SO-CALLED RHEUMATISM

As people advance in years, it is a common experience that tissues injured years before are the source of no little discomfort and are particularly prone to be bothersome during changeable seasons and in rainy weather. A bone broken when the patient was young may twenty or thirty years later continue to give warnings of the approach of change in the weather and be a source of annoyance. A dislocation, especially if complicated in any way by considerable laceration of the tissues in the neighborhood of the luxated joint, is sure to be a source of discomfort of this kind. These painful conditions are generally more noticeable when patients are run down, or when they have been recently affected by exhausting disease of any kind, during convalescence from severe ailments or injuries, or when they are undergoing a special mental strain. These conditions, like nearly all others worse in damp weather, are sometimes grouped under the term rheumatism and have been treated by internal medication. Almost needless to say, such treatment is sure to fail or to be of only temporary anodyne benefit. As rheumatic remedies are usually coal-tar products they may even be distinctly harmful, especially for old patients. It has been shown that the salicylates, for instance, are much less rapidly eliminated in the elderly than in the young, in those with defective circulation or kidney insufficiency than in the well. Their accumulation in the system causes anemic tendencies and disturbs nervous control.

Just what is the underlying pathological condition in these cases is not easy to say. In the case of luxations with laceration of tissues there has undoubtedly been such a disturbance of venous and lymphatic circulation by the break in continuity of tissues and the resultant scar tissue, that lymphatic if not also venous congestion occurs whenever there is any circulatory disturbance. For the maintenance of normal nutrition of nerve endings a constant flow of blood past them and a proper action of the lymphatic channels to carry off waste products is essential. It is easy to understand how much these may be disturbed in the injuries under consideration. When a bone is broken there is usually laceration of the surrounding tissues. Owing to the fixation required to procure proper bony union, the circulation to the part is much more defective than usual and so the repair of torn lymph and venous vessels is not as complete as would otherwise be the case.

This seems to explain why such injuries are especially called to the attention of the patients in damp weather. It is not so much during a rain storm as some hours before it, about the time when the barometer begins to drop, that these old injuries become sensitive. Indeed, it is often said that old persons who have suffered one of these injuries earlier in life carry a barometer around with them.

Not a few of the lesions called sprains, especially those of the ankles and {388} wrists, though also of other joints, are often really breaks of small bones, or at least laceration of ligaments and other structures. These may long afterward prove a source of pain and discomfort, worse always in unsettled weather, or after the feet have been wet, and may seem to be due to some constitutional condition, though they are merely local. These occur more commonly in women than in men and the condition needs careful investigation and must not be put under the vague diagnosis of rheumatism, or the patient will probably not be improved by the treatment suggested. In all these cases the general condition must be looked to, and it must not be forgotten that fat may not mean health, and that increased weight may be a prominent factor in the production of symptoms in these cases, especially when individuals live a sedentary life.

There is an important therapeutic method for the prophylaxis of these conditions that has been attracting attention and yet probably not all the attention it deserves in recent years. Prof. Lucas-Championnière of the University of Paris has pointed out that when fractures and dislocations are treated by the open method with easily removable apparatus and the employment of massage within a few days after the fracture, the subsequent discomfort of these lesions is much lessened.

It seems worth while to emphasize this treatment by manipulations and massage, because it represents a psychotherapeutic factor in the treatment of these injuries. The hiding away of a limb or a joint for days and perhaps weeks, while they wonder whether it is getting better or not is most discouraging to patients. To have the physician see it, to have him declare that it is getting on well, to have the evidence of their own senses that conditions are gradually improving, is of itself a valuable factor for that satisfaction of mind which conduces to the regular functioning of tissues. Repair undoubtedly goes on better under such circumstances. Besides, the lack of constriction or at least its rather frequent periodic relaxation, the airing of the skin, the regulation of the circulation by massage and manipulation, all react upon the mind and prevent it from inhibiting trophic impulses and encourage it to stimulate them in every way.

As to the after-effects of fractures and dislocations as with regard to all this series of vague pains and aches, the patient's attitude of mind is of great importance. As they get older their aches and pains grow worse, partly because circulation is more defective and partly because they are prone to be much more in the house and the nerves of patients who are much within doors are always more sensitive than those of people who are much in the open. If their attention becomes concentrated on their pains and aches, because of lack of diversion of mind, then the condition may become a source of serious annoyance. When these painful conditions develop patients are almost sure to keep much to themselves and to nurse their ills, and consequently to increase their discomfort. The circulation to the affected parts must be stimulated by local treatment, by rubbings, by the milder liniments, by massage and manipulations, and by local hydrotherapy. Douches, as hot as can be borne, on the limb followed by cold, especially if patients are otherwise in good health, will do much to relieve the stagnant circulation.

Active and vigorous movement while the affected part is supported at *skin pressure* (there must be no constriction) is even more valuable than {389} massage, liniments or douches in the treatment of all these painful conditions of joints in which there is any scar-tissue. Wonderful results may be obtained in an old sprain of the wrist, knee and ankle by covering in the part completely (taking care to surround the limb) with strips of adhesive strapping simply laid on at skin pressure, but following exactly every fold or angle of the part, and then with the part completely covered in this way to urge immediate and constant exercise. The maintained pressure prevents any tendency to venous congestion or exudation and favors absorption of fibrous tissue, and exercise, which should be immediate, is now possible through the support furnished by the strapping. The re-assumption of normal active movement molds the old scars, strengthens the muscles and ligaments and improves the patient's general condition. The relief afforded *is immediate*, and the cause of relief, a simple mechanical device, is apparent. Rheumatism is forgotten as the old crutch is discarded and the patient is able to use the limb with confidence.

Recent sprains or bruises treated in this way recover perfectly and do not leave old scar tissue to be a future seat of pain.

CHAPTER III

MUSCULAR PAINS AND ACHES

Whenever exposure to cold causes a period of discomfort in almost any organ, except the teeth and certain definite nerves (for neuralgia has been taken out of the rheumatism group in recent years) we are sure to hear the word rheumatism employed in connection with it. To add to the confusion, the various "specialists" have taken to assuring their patients that local manifestations in the eyes, in the ears, and in the nose, for which they can find no good reason, especially if they are worse in damp weather, are signs of the rheumatic diathesis.

Unfortunately, our supposed knowledge of the uric acid diathesis became widely diffused, and it is not surprising in the light of the widespread acceptance of this theory, that muscular pains of all kinds should have the word rheumatic attached to them, and that patients are sure that the discomfort is only one manifestation of a severe constitutional disease, which they cannot but infer will probably make still more serious trouble for them in years to come, since it seems to be dependent on conditions beyond their control, such as heredity and general constitutional traits and their special mode of nutrition,

Local and Constitutional Conditions.—It cannot be repeated too often that it is this persuasion as to the constitutional character of the disease that has in recent years proved a very unfavorable suggestive element in these cases. Patients think themselves the victims of a serious diathesis, a deep-seated pathological condition, and attribute a host of feelings to it that are sometimes rather seriously disturbing but are really only sensory manifestations of various kinds in the organs and in the skin and muscles, which would be attributed to simple local causes—fatigue, faulty mechanical conditions, etc.—but for the concentration of attention on them.

{390}

Individual Cases.—The careful study of these cases is thus extremely important. They are eminently individual and not to be grouped together. The exact diagnosis of the various conditions from which each patient is suffering is of itself a precious factor in psychotherapeutics. The precise recognition of the condition present is of immediate avail in helping him to dismiss many of his symptoms, or at least to keep him from thinking as much of them as he did before or inevitably will if the older ideas as to the constitutional nature of his affection are allowed to remain.

Nearly every large group of muscles in the body may be the subject of these painful conditions. In recent years, perhaps, the muscles most affected in this way are those that pass around the ankle and give so much discomfort in cases of flatfoot, or beginning flatfoot (euphemistically called weak foot), when the plantar arch is yielding. The manifestations are not only in and around the ankle, but occur in the calf muscles and even above the knee. These painful conditions always develop unless the arch is supported. Until recent years it was rare to discover a bad case of flatfoot in which the patient had not taken many rheumatic remedies and had not come to the conclusion that he was the subject of an incurable and probably hereditary constitutional disease. Flatfoot is likely to cause considerable deformity in the old, the toes becoming bent and twisted up, and the subjects of it complain very much of their feet. Flatfoot runs in families. When the father and mother have complained of what they called rheumatism in their feet which got worse every year, then the son and daughter, when they have their first manifestation, conclude that they are inevitably bound by the stern laws of heredity.

Occupation Aches.—Flatfoot is taken, however, only as an extreme and therefore striking illustration. Whenever a particular group of muscles has to do an excessive amount of work, practically always there is a development of an uncomfortable condition worse on rainy days and therefore likely to be called rheumatic. Over-use of the arm at any occupation, in writing, in the use of a file, at an ironing-board, in sewing, or at anything requiring repeated movements, will produce it almost inevitably. Especially is this true if the occupation is carried on without such careful attention to muscular action as enables the muscles to do their work to the best advantage. These painful conditions are much more likely to occur in run-down individuals of nervous temperament, above all if they have been or are subject to worry. Men who have lost money and now have to do hard physical work, after previously having lived sedentary lives, and women whose previous source of support has been withdrawn and who have to work for a daily wage after former gentle conditions of living, are especially likely to suffer in this way. The conditions develop on a neurotic basis or an exhausted nervous system.

Other groups of muscles may also be the subject of these painful conditions. The large group in the loins, called the lumbar muscles, which are so important for stooping, for the erect posture and for lifting, are so commonly the subject of discomfort that a special name has been applied to their affection—lumbago. In the leg the large group of muscles supplied by the sciatic nerve are likely to be affected, and this affection is so common in men who have to bend the knee and flex the hip at their work that it, too, has received a special name—sciatica. Besides the arm muscles the groups of muscles around the shoulder girdle are often unfavorably affected and though we have not invented {391} a name to cover their conditions, it is so common that we think of it as a separate entity almost in the same manner as we think of lumbago and sciatica. In the neck the group of muscles that rule the movements of the head, especially those at the side may be affected and the special name of torticollis has been given. Practically all of these affections are thought of at times as rheumatic and the ordinary rheumatic treatment is given for them. There is no doubt that the salicylates will relieve the pain almost at once, but so will any other coal-tar product and phenacetin, acetanilid or even antipyrin may be used with good effect. There is no evidence, however, that these drugs make the underlying condition better and, indeed, after patients have tried them for a while, unless the affection is merely passing, they try some other physician and perhaps are treated the same way with a different form of the drug. These are the cases that make their way around to a number of regular practitioners of medicine and then eventually go to some irregular or quack and sometimes obtain relief where the regulars have failed.

When the irregular succeeds it is always because he has done three things. First he has persuaded the patient that it is not rheumatism, with all the unfavorable suggestion that goes with that word, that is, the matter with him; secondly, he has treated the local condition; and, thirdly, he has diverted the patient's mind. Local treatment is often the real secret of his success, though the psychotherapeutic element is not without distinct benefit.

Mode of Occurrence.—These muscular conditions present themselves under two forms, acute and chronic. The acute condition occurs almost suddenly and is accompanied by spasmodic pain and acute discomfort. Muscles go into spasm to avoid the movement that would necessarily bring pain with it. A typical example is found in torticollis in which the patient wakes up some morning to find a stiffness in the muscles of his neck with limitation of movement much more pronounced on one side, and this usually gets worse as movements are attempted during the day. This spasmodic painful condition usually lasts for some days and suggests all sorts of topical applications and often requires anodyne drugs. A similar acute condition may be observed in some cases of lumbago. In this the pain in the loins comes on suddenly, usually during movement, often in the midst of lifting something that one has been able to lift without difficulty before. This pain is so sudden, so unexpected, usually comes entirely without warning and seems so mysterious in its origin, that it is no wonder the Germans speak of it as *Hexenschuss*—"witches' shot"—a remnant of the superstition that a witch, by means of the evil eye or some other maleficent power, or by sticking pins in a wax image of a victim that had previously been devoted to the devil, might produce effects upon the person at the part where the thought was directed or the pin inserted.

These painful conditions, especially when acute, are, as a rule the consequence of exposure to dampness, or to a draft blowing directly on the part, usually in damp and changeable weather, and often when the patient has been sweating just before. The train of events that brings about the painful condition is not difficult to understand. There is a disturbance of the normal smooth-running, indeed almost frictionless, mechanism by which muscles glide over one another. There are practically a series of joints in all muscular groups so as to permit just as free a play as possible of muscles over one another. Each muscle is covered with a glistening membrane so familiar {392} from our dissecting room days, which secretes a substance resembling a synovial fluid, to enable muscles to move upon each other without friction. When, because of exposure to drafts or the evaporation of moisture on the surface, there is a disturbance of the circulation in these intermuscular planes, the secretion which prevents the friction of muscle movements is disturbed. The blood is driven from the surface and some congestion and consequent heat accumulation occurs in the muscles, affecting particularly their contiguous layers. As a result, the muscle surfaces are no longer smooth and the muscles now have not as free play over one another as before. It is not surprising that, owing to this, sensitiveness occurs and some spasm develops. This, however, is thoroughly conservative in character since nature's idea is to set the part at rest so as to allow the normal condition to be restored.

This is the pathological condition that underlies these so-called muscular rheumatisms which develop suddenly. It is important to note, however, that these conditions develop nearly always in people who have been over-using or wrongly using the groups of muscles which become thus affected. The history of a torticollis patient will usually show that there is some contortion of the muscles of the neck familiarly practiced by him. Sometimes it will be found that the patient has the habit of sitting on a particular easy chair in a special relation to the light and that in order to accommodate himself to his chair and the light in his reading, the head has to be placed in such position that the neck muscles are constrained. It is this that predisposes the patient to the development of the condition which seems to be so acute and yet is really only an exacerbation of a chronic condition. Lumbago will develop in men who have been stooping much, especially for heavy lifting, or in women who scrub or have to stoop much while cleaning, dusting and the like.

218

Some interesting muscle pains occur as a consequence of the jostling movements of various modes of transit. They are particularly noticeable if an uncomfortable position has been maintained for a number of hours. People who travel on railroad trains often come with the story that they *must* have caught cold on the trip for they have been sore and achy in many of their muscles since. I have known people who went on a crowded excursion and had to stand for several hours confident that, standing in the drafty aisle of the car on their way home, they had acquired rheumatism. All that had happened was over-tiredness of muscles on the jolting train which required constant balancing and unaccustomed muscular exertion. On board sea-going vessels people often suffer from pains in the loins and in various trunk muscles, due to the roll of the vessel, especially while they are asleep. These, too, are likely to be attributed to drafts, or to some form of rheumatism, or at least to the catching of cold. I have even seen people sure, because of pains in their loins, that they must be developing some kidney trouble. After a time they get used to the swinging motion of the vessel and then their achy muscle tiredness is relieved.

One now sees affections of the same kind in connection with the automobile. People who ride for many hours, especially if the riding is rapid and over a rough road and they are not used to it, are likely to develop pains and aches which they may attribute to the catching of cold or to rheumatism or to something of that kind. The muscles of the trunk are especially likely to {393} suffer. The abdominal muscles may be quite sore and then later the lumbar muscles develop aches. The arms suffer if they are held in unusual positions because of the jolting. The discomfort may be relieved by any of the coal-tar products, though gentle rubbing with a stimulant such as soap liniment, always in the direction of the return circulation in the muscle, will help to relieve the painful condition. The salicylates are often given for these conditions and relieve the discomfort but because of their value as anodynes, which they share with the coal-tar products, and not because of any genuine antirheumatic effect.

Treatment.—Counter-irritation of various kinds, especially the milder forms, always seems to do good. The underlying therapeutic principle seems to be that the attraction of blood to the surface lessens the hyperemia or at least diverts the circulation and permits the restoration of function and encourages the reintegration of normal conditions. Rubbings are especially helpful if accompanied by rather deep pressure from the periphery of the circulation towards the center. The leg muscles must be rubbed upward, the arm muscles upward, the neck muscles downward, the trunk muscles generally in the direction of their return circulation. This would seem to indicate, as might be expected, that it is the venous circulation especially that is disturbed in the tired condition of the muscles, that a venous congestion with interference with the nutrition of nerves accounts for the aches; hence, a mechanical helping of the circulation is of benefit. There are some whose opinion is not to be put aside lightly, who think that the rubbing alone is the most important part of these external treatments and that the liniments and counter-irritants are only of secondary importance. Indeed, some consider that the tingling of the surface is mainly beneficial in making the patient feel that now that part of the body at least *ought* to be better.

Liniments for these conditions, however, though introduced on merely empirical grounds, are very old and have the testimony of many generations as to their therapeutic efficiency. Whenever that is the case, it is a serious question to doubt the conclusions that have been arrived at. The experience of a single generation, and, above all, of a small group or school of men, no matter how learned or how scientific they may be, is often fallacious. The experience of many generations, however, even though no good reason for the benefit derived from the treatment they suggest can be found, is almost inevitably correct. After all, though it is usually forgotten, the use of mercury, of iron, of quinin and of most of the tonics depends on nothing better than empiricism. In our day the liniments have been neglected, more perhaps than was proper, considering how many generations of physicians found them beneficial.

Where it is a neurosis rather than a real disturbance of the circulation, however, that is involved, the use of a counter-irritant, by attracting attention more and more to the part, may really do more harm than good. In nervous people it must be remembered that local neurosis may occur almost anywhere in the body and that subjective discomfort alone in these cases must not be taken to signify a pathological condition, unless the localization is such as to indicate that a particular group of muscles is affected. The differential distinction between a pure neurosis and a discomfort due to a true pathological condition in the intermuscular planes is, that in the one case a group of muscles is affected, while in the other a locality is complained of, and {394} while local tenderness is likely to be a marked source of complaint in the neurosis it is comparatively slight as a rule in the muscular condition.

For the more chronic soreness and discomfort of muscle groups, manipulations with massage are of great importance. Undoubtedly the discomfort and soreness is due in most cases to a disturbance of the venous or lymphatic circulation of the parts. This interferes with the nutrition of nerves and leads to nerve sensitiveness from lack of nutrition, or actual nerve irritation from pressure upon sensitive nerve endings while in a state of congestion. These conditions may be relieved by gentle manipulation and by massage, provided always these measures are not painful. These encourage the circulation and very soon tend to restore functions. Just as soon as the pain of these remedial measures or of any mechano-therapy becomes noticeable, it is not likely that they are doing any good. Pain, of course, must be judged from conditions and not from the patient's complaints, which may be due to fear lest pain should be inflicted.

The main point is that local treatment, gentle, simple, yet directed with the proper therapeutic purpose so as to create a favorable expectancy in the patient's mind, will do much for these conditions, which have in many ways been the opprobrium of modern medicine. The rule has almost been to call them rheumatism, because they were worse in rainy weather. The word rheumatic instinctively calls up in most physicians' minds some cut-and-dried formula of internal medication. So these patients go the rounds of the regular practitioners in medicine taking a series of these formulae in succession and, as a rule, not getting any better. Then they go to an osteopath or to a naturapath, or some other kind of path, have some local massage and manipulations performed, which restores the circulation of the part, to some degree at least, and as a consequence they are encouraged to look for further relief. Not a few of them find the relief they look for, and it is these cured patients that in many parts of the country have insisted on securing for the osteopaths legislative recognition and actually obtained it for them in many cases, just because the regular physicians have neglected methods of cure ready to hand, but not made use of, because drugs are allowed to occupy their attention too exclusively.

Disuse, Atrophy and Pain.—I have seen a striking example of atrophy and pain due entirely to disuse in the upper part of the leg as the consequence of a fall. No bone was broken, the man was laid up for nearly a month from the wrench, and then continued to be somewhat

219

halt for many years. After nearly twenty years his attention became concentrated on this limb and then he spared it more and more in his walking, tilting his pelvis and merely swinging that leg, until there was a difference of nearly two inches between the size of the thighs. Of course, under these circumstances any use of the limb brought fatigue and pain with it. To walk was painful, and he had some twitchings at night. There was no disturbance of sensation, however, anywhere and no reaction of degeneration. His knee jerk was slighter than on the other side, but it was present and the weakness was due to the loss of power in the muscles. It was only weak in proportion to the atrophy of the muscles. This atrophy was not trophic in the sense of any failure of nerve impulses from the central nervous system, but was due to disuse, that is, it did not come from any nervous lesion, central or peripheral, nor from any disturbance of circulation, but from the dwindling of muscles that inevitably {395} comes when they are not employed for their proper purpose. Power to use depends on continuance of function.

All sorts of remedies had been employed in his case, but he did not improve until he was made to understand that there was no bone lesion, no lesion of nerves or muscles, and that what he needed to do was to re-exercise his muscles gently but persistently and confidently back to their normal strength. This was accomplished by exercise and resisted motion, with care never to fatigue the muscles, but at the first sign of tiredness to stop, taking up the exercises at first twice, and then three and four times a day.

As can be readily understood, these curious atrophic muscular conditions from disuse occur more frequently in the legs than in the arms. They may, however, occur in the upper extremities and are noted sometimes in the trunk. After all, certain of the stooping postures of men as they get old are due to lack of use of the large muscles at the back with consequent atrophy of them to the extent that makes standing up straight an effort very fatiguing and even painful. To attempt to straighten an old man by means of braces will lead to the development of painful conditions of tiredness if the correction is emphasized. In the arms the atrophic conditions are not so noticeable because the arms may be used without having to do the hard work required of the trunk and leg muscles in holding the man erect. It is the fear of the strain put upon them by this weight that makes the disuse continue, since there has come into the mind the thought that the muscles cannot be used to bear the weight and the burden is thrown on other muscles with unfortunate results.

Many of these atrophies from disuse are cured by mental influence of one kind or another. They are the best sources of profit and reputation of the "healers." Once the patients become persuaded that they can use a group of muscles if they will, they begin to improve, and it is only a question of six or eight weeks until they are so much better that they persuade themselves that they are as well as ever. It is easy to understand that if a person who has been lame for five to fifteen years, vainly going to physicians of all kinds, is cured by some new form of treatment, all the non-medical world is perfectly sure that there must be much in the new method of treatment.

CHAPTER IV

OCCUPATION MUSCLE AND JOINT PAINS

There is one variety of painful conditions of muscles and joints, often spoken of as muscular rheumatism or as chronic rheumatism and frequently the source of so much discomfort that patients feel that occupations must be given up, even at a great sacrifice. These deserve a special chapter. They occur in persons who have some occupation which requires them to use a particular group of muscles a great number of times during the day. They are most frequent in the arms, but they may be seen in the muscles of the neck, they occur very often in the legs and are not at all infrequent in the muscles of the trunk. Whenever a patient comes complaining of a painful condition in a particular group of muscles, careful inquiry must be made as to his {396} occupation, with details of the movements required. These pains are, of course, as are all human discomforts, worse on rainy days and in damp seasons, so that this has come to be known as rheumatic weather. It is easy to assume without further inquiry that they are rheumatic and this has been done frequently in the past.

There is scarcely any occupation involving frequent and habitual use of muscles which may not be the source of discomfort if the actions necessary for it are done in such a way as not to use the muscles to the best mechanical advantage. In other words, there are a whole group of occupation fatigues which may take on a character of painful discomfort if the individual has not been properly trained in the use of his muscles. This refers not only to the use of muscles in the accomplishment of rather difficult tasks, but especially for those that require nice co-ordination for their accomplishment, though they may not demand the exertion of much muscular energy. In other words, what we have to deal with are rather painful occupation-neuroses than muscular fatigue in its proper sense.

Writers' Ache.—Perhaps the most typical example of these is the painful conditions that may develop in connection with writing. Writers' cramp is well known and consists in a contraction of muscles which makes it increasingly difficult to hold the pen properly for writing and may eventually make it impossible to do so. This is accompanied by a certain amount of distress, but the writer's discomfort that is much more common than writers' cramp does not occur in the fingers, but in the large group of muscles just below the elbow and may extend even to the shoulder. The pain is of a vague achy character and as it is worse on rainy days and in damp weather, the temptation to think of it as rheumatism is very great. It occurs in people who write very much and rapidly, but especially those who write in a bad position. Now that the typewriter has come in much less is heard of it than before among reporters, but it used to be common with them. There is very little hint that it is due to writing, unless one makes careful inquiries.

Gowers' Rule.—Its occurrence can be lessened to a great extent by following Sir Wm. Gowers' directions as to writing. Gowers was a parliamentary reporter before becoming a physician and he learned the difficulties of much writing and studied out the causes of the discomfort as well as of the cramp and of the best methods to avoid it. His rule is to sit on a rather high chair before a rather low table so that the elbow swings free of the table and the writing is what is called free-hand. The extent to which Gowers demands this freedom of the elbow carried may be best appreciated from his direction that the writing must be done in such a way that if a second pen were fastened to the elbow, it would write exactly the same thing that is written by the pen held in the hand. There must not be any movements of the fingers nor of the muscles of the forearm. All the movements required from writing must be accomplished from the shoulder. Just as soon as sufferers from vague aches and discomforts from much writing learn this method of writing, their aches disappear to a great extent. My own experience in the matter, when, as a medical reporter, I often wrote ten thousand words a day, taught me the value of the suggestion. During one winter I suffered so much from discomfort in the shoulder that I was sure that I had a progressive rheumatic affection. Just as soon as I learned to write properly the trouble was minimized to such {397} a degree that I realized that it was merely a question of faulty writing. I have noted over and over again, as is true in my own case, that if there has previously been any injury in the arm, this discomfort is much more likely to develop than otherwise.

Occupation Pains and Habitual Muscle Movements.—What is true for writing is true for any habitual movement of groups of muscles requiring careful co-ordination. I have seen it in marked form in the makers of cigars and the strippers of tobacco. I have seen it in men who do much filing and whose working bench is so high, that pressure direct from their shoulders cannot be brought into play to supply any force that is needed in carrying on the filing process. If such a series of movements as filing is to be accomplished with comfort, then the arms must be held straight, the force being applied from the shoulders and not by the exertion of the muscles of the forearm, which are meant only to guide and not to supply the needed pressure. The Sloyd methods of working at benches are particularly important for workmen if they are not to develop these curious painful conditions which are due to habitual wrong use of muscles, and not to any diathesis. Any and every form of work must be looked at from this standpoint. Women often iron at a table or ironing board placed too high for them, and as a result apply the pressure necessary through their forearm muscles. If they are at all of nervous constitution they will suffer rather serious discomfort from this after a time and this will always be worse in damp weather. I have known women ready to give up because of the discomfort thus occasioned, who found that they could work without muscle discomfort for much longer periods, if the ironing board was placed low enough.

Arm and Shoulder.—The occupation aches and discomforts in the arm and shoulder are very frequent and their variety presents an interesting study in the individual and his history. I remember once having three cases present themselves at a dispensary service of the Polyclinic Hospital on the same day, all presumably suffering from rheumatism. One of them was a motorman suffering from the occupation pains that so often come to those who use their arms overmuch, and the pains seen so frequently, for instance, in baseball pitchers. These pains are always worse on rainy days and in damp weather. There is of course a large individual element as the basis of these. Why can one man pitch nearly every day all season and not suffer with his arm while another man cannot? We can no more tell the reason for this difference than we can tell why one man is right-handed and another left-handed. One individual has a store of nervous energy that serves him very well. Another has a store of nervous energy that serves him well enough for his left hand but not for his right hand. The mystery would seem to be the original endowment of nerve force according to the individual's constitution. The motorman who suffers severely from putting on the brake of a heavy car will probably never be able to continue his occupation with comfort to himself unless his sore arm is due to some temporary condition, easily recognizable.

A second of my patients with rheumatism complained of his shoulder. He had been first easily fatigued, then it was painful when he moved much, most so on rainy days, and finally he had practically lost power in it entirely. His occupation was that of finisher in a molding works. He lifted a heavy hammer many hundreds of times a day with his right arm, striking quick short {398} blows and using mainly his deltoid muscle in the lifting process. It was just his deltoid that was affected and the nerve supply had evidently given out. The third man complained not of his right hand, but of his left and of his forearm, not his shoulder, having lost power especially on the ulnar side of his hand. He was a stonecutter, who held a chisel firmly in his left hand, grasping it mainly with the under or ulnar side of his hand, and consequently overusing the group of muscles supplied by his ulnar nerve, leaving that structure open to pathological conditions.

There was just one feature in the history of all three that was the same. They did not drink alcohol to excess often, but they did take some whiskey straight every day. The easiest explanation seemed to be that there was a neuritis set up in the nerves, which their occupations caused them to use so much, and that, as a consequence, the low grade neuritis finally developed to such a condition as to make further use of the muscle supplied by the affected nerves practically impossible. Just why alcohol will select certain nerves and not others upon which to exercise its deteriorating influence and why lead usually affects an entirely different set we do not know. In the ordinary man of sedentary occupation who walks occasionally, as his only exercise, his most used nerve is his anterior peroneal. Those of us who are not used to walking much, know how soon this nerve complains of fatigue when we take some forced ambulatory effort. It is this nerve then that with most people is affected by alcohol. But any nerve that is overused will apparently be affected the same way, and as many outdoor workers take some whiskey straight pretty regularly, it is not surprising to find that some of them have an idiosyncrasy and develop a low grade alcoholic neuritis.

Alcohol, however, is not the only substance that acts thus insidiously. I was once asked to treat a painter who was suffering from intense tired feelings in his right forearm. They were always worse on rainy days, and he had been treated for rheumatism without avail. He had no signs at all of wrist-drop, there were no suspicious signs on his gums and he had never suffered from constipation or anything like lead colic. It seemed far-fetched, then, to say that his muscles were fatigued mainly because of the irritating presence of lead in the nerves supplying his right forearm. He slipped on the ice, however, and sprained his wrist, and the next day turned up with a typical lead wrist-drop. This fact of having lead poison develop shortly after an accident is not unusual, just as a sprained ankle may sometimes be the signal for an outbreak of alcoholic neuritis in the lower leg which has been preparing for some time, the accident itself being at least partially accounted for in many cases by the awkwardness of muscles with disturbed nerve supply.

221

Leg Occupation Pains.—What is true of the arm is also true of the leg. If a man uses his leg muscles very much and especially at any mechanical disadvantage, he usually suffers painful discomfort that is always worse on rainy days. Before the invention of the electric dental engine, dentists used to suffer from this and the profession talked about the "dentist's limp." This was also more painful in damp weather and many of them were treated for rheumatic conditions, though it was really only over-fatigue.

Neurosis and Neuritis.—There are many cases of painful conditions in the limbs where it becomes difficult to diagnose between a neurosis and a neuritis. The usual differential characteristic of tender points along the course of the {399} nerve cannot be used in many patients with confidence, because they are prone constantly to respond to the question "is that tender" in the affirmative. Besides in a neurosis there always seems to be a hypersensitiveness of the nerves involved that may simulate the tenderness of neuritis. In a number of obscure cases I have felt that the condition was a real neuritis when the development of a corresponding condition on the other side, or relief on one side followed by development on the other, has led to the diagnosis of neurosis. Of course, a double neuritis may well occur in the same nerve on both sides of the body under certain toxic conditions. Double sciatica nearly always indicates glycosuria. Diabetes may cause double neuritis in any other much used pair of nerves. Alcoholic neuritis may manifest itself on both sides. Ordinarily, however, the transference of symptoms or their spread to the other side of the body means a neurotic condition.

In some of these cases where it has been difficult to distinguish between neuritis and neurosis, a change of occupation or some strong diversion of mind for a considerable period or a change of residence has proved the beginning of a cure. I have seen what was considered by experienced physicians to be a chronic low-grade neuritis of quite intractable form clear up completely as the result of the young woman being compelled to take up a wage-earning occupation, when it had always seemed before as though life was going to be smooth and there was no necessity for her to labor. I know of cases of so-called neuritis that had been very obstinate to treatment that were cured by Eddyite treatment. What really happened in these cases was that a group of muscles used considerably more than usual had produced a painful tired condition referred to a particular nerve. Just as soon as the mind's inhibitory action was taken off them by the persuasion that there was nothing the matter with them the patient proceeded to get well, gradually progressive use bringing back the normal trophic condition.

Discomforts of Bursae.—In any consideration of painful conditions in and around joints, especially in connection with occupations, the question of the formation and of the inflammation of bursae must be insisted upon because many of these inflammatory incidents are confused with joint affections and not infrequently treated as if they were due to constitutional disturbance. Practically everybody is familiar with housemaid's knee. Most people know that bunions are inflammations of the bursae which form over the metacarpo-phalangeal joint of the big toe whenever there is pressure and irritation of it. Very few realize, however, that frequently repeated irritations, when pressure is exerted over other joints and bony projections, will produce a bursa, and then, if the irritation continues and an opportunity for infection occurs, there is bursitis. Some of these are mistaken for other conditions and often have been thought by the patient to be serious developments of one kind or another with regard to which there has been much solicitude. An interesting case of this kind in my experience was that of an Italian organ-grinder who suffered from the occupation bursa which so often forms over the anterior superior spine of the ilium because of the frequently repeated rubbing of the hand and arm as it passes this region while turning the handle of his instrument. It had finally become inflamed, and the Italian was much disturbed and he feared that it was appendicitis.

Other bursae are not commonly seen in America. I have seen bursae over {400} the elbows of miners, and in one case saw one of these inflamed so that miner's elbow became a concrete entity. This case had been taken for an acute inflammatory arthritis with the suspicion of tuberculosis.

CHAPTER V

PAINFUL ARM AND TRUNK CONDITIONS

Cervical Ribs.—Some interesting cases with painful conditions of the arms develop as a consequence of the presence of cervical ribs. It would be more or less naturally expected that trouble of this kind would occur early in life, but, as a matter of fact, many of the patients are well on toward thirty or even beyond middle life when the painful symptoms develop. Cases are practically always at the beginning diagnosed as rheumatism because the first symptom is likely to be pain followed by weakness. Even when this quite fruitless diagnosis is not made, the affection is often declared to be rheumatic neuritis, though it is really a traumatic neuritis and entirely a local condition, as are so many of the painful conditions spoken of as rheumatism. Usually the pain is referred to the inside of the arm and is described as resembling slight toothache at first and even severe toothache after a time. It will often be many months or even several years after the first symptoms before wasting of muscles occurs, but this practically always follows after a time and even at this stage some physicians still talk of rheumatic neuritis as affecting the trophic nerve fibers and causing the muscles to waste. Almost a differential diagnostic sign in the case of cervical ribs is that raising the arms above the head nearly always relieves the pain. Patients usually learn this for themselves because they have been tempted to place their arms in many positions in order to get relief. The reason for it is easy to understand as the elevation of the arms changes the relative position of tissues in the neck and so relieves pressure.

The direct reason for the late development of the disease is probably the ossification of the cervical rib and the pressure of this hard, bony substance upon the roots of the brachial plexus. When the disease occurs as early as the age of 30 there is likely, for some reason, to have been a preceding loss of weight. Patients are run down and then, either because there is a precocious calcification as a consequence of deterioration of tissue, or because the loss of substance in the muscles in the neighborhood makes the nerves more likely to be pressed upon, the first symptoms develop. There is only one way definitely to decide the diagnosis. That is to have a careful skiagraph, or, in case of negative results, several of them taken, in order to determine the presence or absence of cervical ribs. Not all the cases of cervical ribs give symptoms and in one recently published series of 26 cases just one-half presented symptoms and the other half did not, but all these vague cases of pain in the arm, especially if any tendency to atrophy manifests itself, should be examined from this standpoint.

Local Conditions.—The subjective symptoms in these cases often include {401} much more than pain. There may be numbness and the hands often feel cold, though they do not become blue. As a rule, indeed, the arms are more affected than the hands, though not infrequently one of the hands becomes more sensitive to injuries than the other and, as a rule, both hands do not heal well after injury. Even scratches take a long time to heal and slight abrasions cause skin lesions that are more or less indolent for some time before healing. Any fresh injury, even of slight degree, puts back healing much more than would ordinarily be the case. In fact, most of the so-called tendency not to heal is local rather than constitutional. When a patient complains that though his or her tissues used to heal rapidly now they are very slow to heal, it is well to think of nephritis or diabetes but it is especially important to know the local conditions.

Pleural Adhesions.—Another interesting cause of pains in the arms is the possible contraction of adhesions of the pleura and surrounding tissues at the apices of the lungs and the spreading by continuity of a low-grade inflammation even to the lower roots of the brachial plexus. A certain number of cases of this kind have been reported in which there seems to be no doubt of the diagnosis. In these, the early symptoms were pains or aches in the arm followed by some weakness of muscles and even some trophic disturbances. Ordinarily the condition has been very acute as, for instance, a pneumonia when the first symptoms were noticed. In the course of the exudation and the contraction of the inflammatory exudate the brachial plexus is interfered with. This, like the cases referred to the presence of a cervical rib, emphasizes the necessity for thoroughly studying local conditions in order to understand the meaning of painful conditions in the arms. It is easy to say the word rheumatism, while it requires time and careful investigation to find the real pathological factor at work; but the difference in the value of the two diagnoses for both patient and physician can be readily understood.

Other Conditions.—Besides these, there are the various conditions discussed in other chapters of this section—old injuries, breaks and dislocations, so-called sprains with laceration of tissues, and any serious pathological condition that has affected the tissues deeply. An old periostitis, for instance, will leave an arm rather easily liable to the development of various painful conditions. Of course, a tuberculous process anywhere in the arm will produce a like effect. An arm that has had a lead neuritis will often be uncomfortable in rainy weather for long after and a crutch palsy may, in the same way, leave the arm sensitive. The musculo-spiral palsies that occur from lying on the arm when drunk, or that are seen sometimes in coachmen who wrap the reins around their arms—a Russian custom—or the nerve conditions seen in patients who have suffered from an anesthetic nerve-pressure disturbance, may all be at the bottom of subsequent painful conditions, worse in rainy weather. The only sure rule is to individualize the cases and make an exact diagnosis. The etiology will probably suggest itself if the history is carefully taken.

In these cases the most important treatment is to disabuse the patient's mind of the idea that there is rheumatism, or any other constitutional ailment present, and to make him realize that the trouble is entirely local. After this, the strengthening of the affected muscles must, as far as possible, be secured by local measures and exercises.

{402}

CHAPTER VI

LUMBAGO AND SCIATICA

Any affection involving discomfort, pain, ache, or disability of the large muscles in the lumbar regions is likely to be called lumbago, not only by patients but by physicians. Any condition that makes it painful to use the upper part of the lower limb and especially the group of large posterior leg muscles just below the nates is called sciatica. These are commonly supposed to be typical "chronic rheumatisms." Anything in this region that is the source of discomfort on rainy days and comes especially to the working man who has been exposed to the elements, or that follows a wetting or the wearing of damp clothes, is confidently classified as a chronic rheumatic condition. Almost needless to say any such conclusion as to the heterogeneous groups of symptoms that occur in these regions, far from adding to our knowledge, rather confuses the situation. There is an assumption that we know something about them when we call these conditions either lumbago or sciatica, but unless each individual case is carefully investigated and its conditions studied so as to get at their true etiology, it is almost impossible to treat them successfully. While the general practitioner of medicine of the regular school often fails in his treatment of them, these affections are among the most fruitful sources of revenue for the irregular practitioners.

It was particularly for pains and aches in the back that St. John Long's liniment proved so efficacious about a century ago. So-called lumbago and sciatica patients were among the most frequent callers on Perkins in the days of the famous tractors and many of them received great relief. In our own time these constitute a class of patients who go from physician to physician and who finally are cured or relieved by some irregular practice which we know contains nothing especially remedial, but the advocates of which somehow succeed in persuading these patients that they must be better than before. Most old people have some aches and pains in either the lumbar muscles or the large muscles at the back of the thigh. Many of them are relieved by massage, but still more of them find relief in the rubbings and manipulations of the osteopaths, and they are great advertisers of the relief that has been afforded them and they have helped much in securing such state recognition as has come to the systems they thought curative in their cases. Eddyism has been helpful to a certain number of them. Fads of various kinds catch still others. Evidently these intractable cases deserve to be studied from the standpoint of what mental influence can do for them.

Conditions Mistaken for Sciatica or Lumbago.—Needless to say, a large number of conditions occur which may be called sciatica or lumbago, but which are due to the most varied causes. An affection of any of the joints in this neighborhood will produce pain to which is often added tenderness and occasionally swelling, and nearly always disability. Disease of the lower part of the lumbar spine due to tuberculosis is often in its earlier stages called lumbago. Indeed, without careful investigation showing that there is a special point of tenderness, some irregular fever and that the muscles are in spasm {403} to protect the underlying joints from use, it is difficult to decide just what is the affection in a particular case. I have seen three physicians diagnose a one-sided tenderness and pain in muscles with disability as lumbago, when the course of the disease proved that it was tuberculosis of the sacro-iliac joint. Any of the bones or joints in this neighborhood may give rise to pain, tenderness and spasm of muscles and it is important not to make the facile diagnosis of lumbago, unless careful investigation has eliminated all underlying organic conditions.

There are other conditions not infrequently mistaken for lumbago or sciatica which are interesting. Needless to say unless they are definitely recognized there will be no relief afforded for any discomfort of a permanent character, though the coal-tar products will give temporary surcease of pain. Occasionally internal hemorrhoids produce an achy discomfort in the lower part of the back that is described as lumbago, and unless the physician is careful to investigate he may tentatively accept that diagnosis. Proper regulation of the bowels and the use of gluten suppositories will often practically cure the condition, though there will be relapses whenever constipation returns. Chronic posterior urethritis sometimes simulates painful conditions very low down in the back or in one hip or the other. Usually in that case there is a chronic inflammatory condition in the seminal vesicle on the side to which the symptoms are referred. Occasionally over-distention of the seminal vesicles, as seen in widowers who have been accustomed for many years to regular evacuation of them, may cause so much pain and disability in the region of the hip on one side as to be mistaken first for lumbago and then even for tuberculous hip joint disease. Artificial emptying of the seminal vesicle by milking through the rectum will usually afford relief. In all of these cases as soon as the exact diagnosis is made, the patient's mind is relieved of a serious burden of anxiety and it is usually not difficult to bring a great measure of relief.

Old Injuries and Discomfort.—Many of the painful conditions described as lumbago are due to old injuries, to wrenches and sprains in this region due especially to heavy lifting and to the laceration of ligaments from over-exertion.

Typhoid Spine.—Protracted cases of typhoid are sometimes followed by pain in the lumbar or sacral regions, developing usually after a slight jar or shock, sometimes after a fall or even following a severe injury, which are really the result of the physical condition of the patient. Stiffness, aching discomfort on movement and sometimes tenderness on pressure are present. Often there are associated neurotic symptoms of various kinds. This used very commonly to be considered rheumatism and occasionally one still sees cases so labeled. On the other hand, much more serious conditions, as Pott's disease, abscess of the liver, or some form of spondylitis, may be suspected. Absence of temperature is almost the rule and usually is the pathognomic differential against these. The whole condition is usually a neurosis though there may be some perispondylitis. The treatment is to increase the patient's nutrition, which has usually suffered to a marked degree, and get the mind off the condition in the back. Concentration of attention on it will make it very uncomfortable, so that even heavy doses of opiates will scarcely relieve the discomfort, and this emphasis of attention will further disturb the mind and develop neurotic {404} symptoms. Diversion of attention, gentle movements, plenty of air, and regulation of the functions of the body will bring about a cure.

Stooping Occupations.—Occupations are especially important in lumbago and people who have to stoop much, above all those who do hard work in a stooping position—lifting, pushing, sawing, planing, and the like—are particularly prone to suffer. Miners working where the height of the vein does not permit them to stand up are commonly subject to it. Any one who has to assume, or has the habit of assuming, a stooping posture for long hours may suffer from lumbago. Constrained position predisposes more than hard work. Tailors, though in a sedentary occupation, often suffer from it.

SCIATICA

Etiology.—What has been said of lumbago applies to a great extent also to sciatica. There are a number of different affections which have come to be grouped under the term sciatica. Here, much more frequently than in the lumbar region, the cause of the pain is a true neuritis. This may be of many forms. Occasionally it is syphilitic in origin; whenever the sciatica is double it commonly develops on a basis of diabetes, while in many cases it is of an infectious nature. There is no special reason to think that there is a rheumatic infection of the nerve, though inasmuch as rheumatic arthritis is probably due to infections by many different kinds of microbes, it may well be that some of these play a role in sciatica. There is no good reason, however, why the word rheumatism or the term chronic rheumatism should be applied either to lumbago or to sciatica. Certainly there is no reason in any definitely known etiology of the affections. Each individual case must be studied carefully. Always these are local and not constitutional conditions, and usually something in the patient's occupation, or in his habits of life, helps us to understand the development of sciatica or lumbago and gives the most valuable hints for treatment.

Men who shovel much and who bend one knee as they stoop in shoveling will often suffer, though more frequently in the leg which they do not bend than in the other. The same thing is true for men who use one foot to run a lathe or a small printing press, or anything of that kind. They must be taught to alternate in the use of their limbs.

Pressure.—Occasionally direct pressure upon the nerve is the cause of the disturbance. I once was asked to see in consultation an elderly lady who had complained very much, first of discomfort and then numbness in her legs, until finally she lost all power in them below the knees. The affection was considered to be some sort of creeping paralysis. I found that her favorite chair, an old-fashioned cushioned easy chair, allowed her to sink down so that the edge of the wood seat frame pressed upon her just where the sciatic nerve comes closest to the surface. As soon as the habit of sitting on this chair was changed her numbness and inability to use her limbs began to disappear.

Alcoholic Neuritis.—In both lumbago and sciatica one underlying factor is often present. This is the consumption of undiluted whiskey in considerable quantities. Outdoor workers are prone to take an occasional glass of whiskey, especially in the winter time, and a copious quantity of malt liquors in the summer. Both of these predispose to the development of a low-grade {405} neuritis in susceptible individuals. Alcohol is said to have an idiosyncrasy for the anterior tibial nerves. That only means, as a rule, however, that these nerves are more frequently affected by alcoholic neuritis than others in the body. The reason for this special location of the affection is that in people who stand and walk much, this constituting their main form of exercise, these nerves are much used. They are probably in such people (that is, if the intensity of impulses that pass through them be taken into account) the most used nerves in the body. It is this that makes them most susceptible to alcohol. In people who stoop much or who have to work hard in stooping postures, the nerves in the lumbar region and those that make up the sciatic trunk are over-used. This makes them more susceptible to pathological influences than others, hence the tendency for neuritis to develop in them.

Intrapelvic Causes.—Sciatica may be due to various pathological conditions within the pelvis. Women with fibroid tumors are particularly likely to suffer from it. Their removal by operation does not always assure against the occurrence of sciatic troubles. I once saw an obstinate case of sciatica in which there was a story of a fibroid having been removed years before and, though there were no signs of any recurrence of the growth of another, there were some adhesions in the region, and there was an obstinate constipation particularly likely to have as one symptom an accumulation of fecal material in the rectum until it was very hard. The keeping of the bowels open meant more than anything else for the relief of the sciatica. This patient subsequently died from what was diagnosed by a well-known French surgeon as rupture of the bowels. This was probably due to the adhesions that occurred after the old operation, done without any regard to the possible development of such a sequela, some twenty years ago. The sciatica was undoubtedly connected with the group of disturbed conditions within the pelvis.

Position at Work.—In this case, as in others that I have seen, the position assumed while at work seemed to have been an appreciable factor in the production of the pain in the limb. The lady made her living by writing and often wrote on a board resting on her knee—a feminine, not a masculine habit. This brought pressure to bear upon the right limb a little more than the other and then, when she crossed her knees in order to put the writing board on top of the knee, this side seemed to be used more than the other.

This question of the position in occupation, even though sedentary, is very important. I have seen a strikingly typical case of the so-called *neuralgia paresthetica*, the achy condition of the outside of the thigh with some anesthesia and paresthesia, occur in an old lady who still retained the girlish habit of sitting on her foot while she did crocheting. I have often seen achiness of muscles of the trunk develop in persons who read much in a cramped position because of the reading light being too low or otherwise wrongly placed for group reading. Whenever a patient has to stand much on one foot while doing something, it is important to remember that there should be alternation in the use of the limbs; otherwise sciatica and lumbar pains will often develop, usually on the side corresponding to the limb that is kept rigid.

Treatment.—*Mental Persuasion.*—The patient must be made to realize that his affection is not rheumatism, but is due to local conditions. Just as soon as a patient's mind is relieved by being made to appreciate that certain habits in his occupation, or certain local conditions that can be corrected, {406} are responsible for much of his discomfort, then that discomfort is much easier to bear. Even in cases where actual neuritis has developed, or where there have been changes in the intermuscular planes bringing considerable disability, the aches caused by these will be much more bearable if the patient's mind is set at rest as to the real significance of the condition. No condition should be called rheumatic unless at some time in the history of it there was an acute inflammatory condition with Galen's classical symptoms—*tumor, color, rubor* and *dolor*. Pain alone is never sufficient to justify the diagnosis. Painful disability is usually due to local causes.

Treatment of Acute Symptoms.—For acute symptoms, the coal tar products may be used and usually afford distinct relief. They include all the old-fashioned salicylates as well as certain more recent compounds, such as aspirin. Phenacetin, however, though usually not thought of in this connection, is an excellent remedy for the discomfort. These drugs should be used freely so as to give relief from the painful condition. The fact that they afford relief, however, should not be taken as an argument that the condition is rheumatic. Rheumatism, as we know it, is an acute infectious disease and there is no reason in the world for saying that the salicylates or cognate drugs are specifics in this affection. They relieve the pain, but just in the same way they would relieve the pain of toothache or of any other painful condition. After the acute symptoms are removed, the condition that remains may be treated in various ways, by massage, by local applications, and by such manipulations as will restore the normal circulation of the part. Care must be taken, however, to distract the patient's mind from the local condition after a time, or mental influence, by interfering with the capillary circulation, may inveterate the symptoms. It is not good to keep patients at rest, though rest, of course, is always indicated if there is much discomfort. Sometimes, however, the discomfort is really due to the fact that muscles have not been used for some time and so are easily fatigued and may ache even under ordinary use. In this case, a gradual restoration of the muscles to normal strength by progressively increased exercise is important.

Counter-Irritation and Its Suggestive Value.—Personally, I have found the use of turpentine particularly efficacious in connection with suggestion. The old-fashioned system of ironing seems to do more good than any ordinary application of turpentine. For this a piece of flannel wrung out in warm water has some turpentine scattered over it and then is placed on the affected loins or back of the thigh and covered by another piece of flannel, and a hot flat-iron is rubbed over it. The physical effect is a considerable hyperemia, but the effect upon the patient's mind is especially interesting, the unusualness of the mode of application adding decidedly to the effect. It must not be forgotten, however, that there are some people who are over-susceptible to the influence of turpentine, and its use is followed by a rash.

Lumbar and Sciatic Psychoneuroses.—Many cases of lumbago and sciatica are really psychoneuroses. They develop exactly as psychoneurotic conditions do in the abdomen or in joints. Not infrequently there is some accident or injury, some sprain or strain, or exposure to dampness or draft, that serves as the occasion. The Germans group all these occasions together under the word "insult." The "insult" produces little physical effect but after some days or sometimes weeks, the slight discomfort present secures the center of {407} attention and then the patient suffers from what seems to be severe pain and often inability to move or use muscles. Even when there is true sciatica or lumbago, that is, a genuine low-grade neuritis of the lumbar or sciatic nerves, most of the symptoms may come from the associated psychoneurosis. This is proved to be so by the fact that such patients are often cured, for the time being at least, by some shock or fright or sudden excitement, that makes them move, forgetful of the pain and inability from which they suffered just before. Besides, such cases are often cured by inert remedies of many kinds, by local applications that have no specific effect, and by various methods of treatment which cannot be responsible for the recovery. The amelioration of the condition is due to the mental influence accompanying the methods of treatment and the reassurance of the patient's mind.

Diversion of Attention.—Almost anything that produces a continuous succession of sensations on the surface of the affected area that attract and hold the attention of the patient may prove a valuable therapeutic suggestion and even eventual relief from symptoms that have proved obstinate to more rational treatment. Liebault, the well-known founder of the Nancy school of hypnotic therapeutics, tells in his "Thérapeutique Suggestive," that he has frequently cured lumbago by the simple recommendation of a rather stiff piece of paper to be applied over the patient's loins. The rationale of this treatment seems to be that the patient's attention is attracted to the skin surface by the sensations constantly produced by it and attention is distracted from other feelings deeper in the muscles. It often happens that after an acute lumbago has run its course, there is left a chronic achiness only partly physical and largely psychoneurotic. Some of it is undoubtedly due to the habit, formed during the acute period, of keeping the muscles quiet, in order to avoid the spasmodic pain that occurs on movement. Patients cannot, as it were, let go of their muscles, and their discomfort is largely due to holding them in a cramped position. The sensation produced by the paper on the cutaneous nerves distracts the attention and brings about relaxation of the muscles with decrease of discomfort and gradual relief of all symptoms.

The paper acts as a constant source of suggestion for the cure of the psychoneuroses when the affection is purely psychoneurotic. The mind has become concentrated on the idea of pain and discomfort in this region and needs another thought to occupy itself with so as to neutralize this. Wearing the paper with the assurance, for instance, that because of its impermeability to air it keeps the part more thoroughly protected from variations of temperature and from such possibilities of transudation as have before been possible, serves to lift patients out of themselves and affords relief. Whenever the sensation produced by the paper is noted, there is a renewal of the suggestion and its curative effects. There are many plasters that have obtained the reputation for curing lumbago. It is doubtful whether any of these have sufficient medicaments on them to be of any serious pharmaceutic significance. They are mostly rubber plaster. The presence of this and the consciousness of the sensation produced by it acts as favorably as does Liebault's sheet of paper.

Mechanical Agents.—It must not be forgotten, however, that a large sheet of adhesive plaster firmly applied may act as a mechanical therapeutic agent, somewhat in the same way that strips of adhesive plaster relieve the pain of pleurisy, or are helpful in a sprained ankle or a knee. The muscles may be {408} held rather firmly together and so there is no necessity for constant attention to prevent spasmodic pain. Undoubtedly some of the newer large-sized adhesive plasters produce an excellent effect in this way. If, besides, the patient has the feeling that they must be doing him good because of materials in their composition, the psychoneurotic elements are more readily relieved. The old idea was that such plasters drew out the pathological elements to the surface whence they were dissipated. There is no truth underlying this thought.

In the old days blisters were applied rather freely to these regions and the actual cautery was often employed. Both of these therapeutic processes are likely to do good in chronic cases, but much more from their psychic than their physical effects. The actual cautery is not used nearly so much as it ought to be in chronic muscular and neurotic conditions, for the mental effect of its application and the distraction of attention to the skin surface while the cauterized areas are healing are excellent remedies.

There are other counter-irritant procedures of the same kind that have been used with reported successes in many cases. Hot needles, for instance, if pushed deeply into the muscles, often have an excellent effect. Some years ago a distinguished surgeon insisted that both lumbago and sciatica might be cured in many cases by the insertion of needles deeply into the muscles. He argued that what happened was that these needles brought about an equilibrium of electricity in the muscular structures which had somehow been disturbed. Deep injections of water into the muscles also do good. Stretching of nerves has been applied with reported success. After a time all of these measures fail, however, because somehow after the novelty of the treatment wears off for the physician, the patient's mind is not sufficiently impressed and then the former results are not secured. Where there are actual neuritic processes present they will almost surely fail. So many of these cases are almost pure psychoneuroses, however, that it is little wonder that anything which produces a strong impression on the mind and leaves after it some condition that attracts attention and so furnishes favorable suggestion will almost surely cure even chronic conditions for which all sorts of physical remedies, employed on rational grounds, have failed.

Anything that modifies the circulation, even to a slight degree, or by causing a reaction in the local vaso-motor state, alters previous conditions, tends to enable the patient to control the affected part. These psychoneurotic conditions in large muscles help us to understand what happens in organic diseases. There is a physical element that must be modified, but unless a strong influence is brought to bear upon the mind so as to arouse all its capacity for control, the cure will not come. Anyone of a dozen things, however, may be used in this way and often when one fails another will succeed. In obstinate cases of lumbago and sciatica if necessary a number of these forms of treatment should be used successively.

Hypnotism.—How much pure psychotherapy may mean for many of these obstinate cases of lumbago and sciatica can be appreciated from the many reports of cures by hypnotism or by suggestion in a light hypnoidal state, or occasionally, under favorable circumstances, even in the waking state. One of these cases, indeed, is responsible to some extent for the French interest in hypnotism which attracted so much attention in the last quarter of the {409} nineteenth century. Prof. Bernheim of the University of Nancy had seen a case of sciatica in which every therapeutic means at his command had failed. As the result of disuse the leg was emaciated and possessed little muscular power. It looked as though the man would never be able to regain the use of it properly. Dr. Liebault succeeded in curing the patient by light hypnotic sleep, in which the suggestion that he would be better was given while the physician stroked the limb. After the first seance the patient was able to use the leg better and the discomfort was greatly decreased. Further seances with Dr. Liebault brought further improvement until finally the condition was cured. Prof. Bernheim, who knew how intractable these cases are, had the case called particularly to his attention and naturally wanted to learn more about the method by which it had been brought about. Liebault's methods had been quite contemned by the regular faculty before. After a series of experiences under Dr. Liebault's direction Prof. Bernheim became enthusiastic over the use of hypnotism as a curative agent and this led to the publication of his well-known work "De la Suggestion et ses Applications dans la Thérapeutique." It was the interest aroused at Nancy that led Charcot to take up hypnotism, and while he came to very different conclusions, there is no doubt that the work at Nancy meant much for our knowledge of suggestion in both waking and hypnotic state in therapeutics.

CHAPTER VII

PAINFUL KNEE CONDITIONS

Most of the painful knee conditions of which patients complain are not directly due to true pathological conditions either of the knee joint itself or of its neighboring structures, but rather to affections of other portions of the leg that set a special strain upon the knee and, above all, to various kinds of foot disturbances. The erect position is maintained principally by a nice balance of nervous and muscular energy in the knee joint and its surrounding structures. Any irregular sensory or motor impulses to the knee-joint or to the muscles of the thigh will disturb the absolute equilibrium of the flexors and extensors and will make standing painful or even impossible. Whenever a morbid condition requires a different use of the muscles and tendons around the knee from that to which they are accustomed, fatigue readily ensues, and aches and even tenderness in muscles and tendons develop as the result of the over-exertion. These collateral conditions must not be overlooked in the diagnosis and treatment of painful knee conditions.

Etiological Factors.—Even a slight sore on one foot will give rise to considerable achy fatigue of the knee of the opposite leg, because, consciously or unconsciously, we stand much more on that leg, use it more in walking, and spare the other because of the pain induced by use of the foot. Above all, throwing more weight on the other leg causes us to use muscles a little abnormally with consequent soreness. This painful fatigue is most likely to be felt around the knee, though it may extend to the hip and even the lumbar {410} region of the well side if the foot continues to be spared for a number of days. Particularly will this be true if there is anything the matter with the big toe, on which so much of the use of the foot depends. An ingrowing toenail will not infrequently give so much discomfort to the well knee and hip as to make the patient sure that there must be some rheumatic or other condition at work in these joints. The serious affection of the joint which the patient apprehends is found to be no more than a sympathetic fatigue induced by having to use his feet, or one of them, a little differently from usual, perhaps because of some condition that leads him to spare them. To call the patient's attention to this is of itself therapeutic.

Inequality of Legs.—The effort required for standing and the accurate balance of the muscles involved in it is such that any mechanical disturbance of the feet or legs or even a trivial pathological condition causes painful fatigue. It must not be forgotten, for instance, that the presumption that human limbs are of exactly the same length is not confirmed by accurate measurements. There is an average difference of probably half an inch in length between the limbs of normal persons, and there may be even a difference of more than an inch before deformity is said to be present. The longer limbs are likely to do more work and are, therefore, more subject to fatigue and consequent complaint. One of the reasons why we can distinguish persons by their gait even at a distance is that the difference in the length of their limbs makes noteworthy characteristics in their walk.

High Heels.—People who are used to walking in a natural manner and who don a pair of high-heeled shoes for the first time are sure to complain of pain in the calf and knee, because the high heels require them to hold the knee more rigid and in a somewhat different position from that required when the persons stand under ordinary circumstances. It is the unusual in muscular effort that gives rise to the extreme fatigue which becomes positive pain if it is allowed to continue. It is curious how small a raising of the heel will cause discomfort. Over and over again I have known the careless putting on of rubber heels to be responsible for pains around the knee, which in damp weather were the source of so much discomfort that it was hard to persuade the patient that he was not suffering from rheumatism or some serious incipient pathological condition.

Unusual Occupations.—Joint pains often develop after the patient has been doing something quite unusual and putting an unaccustomed strain upon his muscles. I have often seen dispensary patients whose knee pains began after there had been a family moving. In the course of the removal of household goods, both men and women are likely to help in hanging pictures, in taking them down, in moving heavy furniture and other occupations of this kind which make them extremely tired. If there is any tendency to relaxation of joint structures the tiredness may manifest itself as a sense of painful discomfort. The knees are particularly likely to suffer if there is a relaxed condition anywhere in the leg. It must be remembered that the laxity of tissue which predisposes a patient to weak or flat feet will have a tendency to produce some looseness of fiber, at least, also in the tissues around the knee. The patient may not have a wabbling knee, nor may he be able to overextend the limb, but still there will usually be some noticeable relaxation of the tissues which will help in the production of the painful condition by {411} making exaggerated calls upon the muscles in order to keep the joint in proper position in spite of the over motion in it.

The disturbance is most frequent in waiters, store clerks, tailors' cutters and fitters, bench men in the trades, and in all those who have to spend much time on their feet. I have seen many such ready to give up their occupations, though they had no other resource and the future looked very blank, indeed, away from their work. It was difficult at first to persuade them that a slight yielding of the arch had so changed mechanical conditions in the use of the muscles of the leg as to produce such pains. But as soon as they were put in a condition where their arch was not allowed to sink, they were at once relieved of their discomfort to a great extent. The question of treatment is discussed more fully in the chapter which follows on Foot Troubles.

An interesting set of painful conditions around the knee develops in a class of people in whom it might least be suspected of being due to over-exertion connected with their occupations. These are lecturers, clergymen, teachers, and others who, for several hours each day, are on their feet in a position from which, as a rule, they do not move, but stand almost perfectly quiet. A distinguished laryngologist has pointed out that not infrequently men who come to be treated for the chronic laryngitis, which is known as clergymen's sore throat, but which is seen so frequently in those who have to talk in the open air, auctioneers, cart-tail orators about election time, and in lecturers to large audiences who do not know how to use the voice, also complain of grievous discomfort from painful knee conditions which often makes the ascent or descent of stairs a painful task. He attributes the simultaneous occurrence of these conditions to some blood dyscrasia, uric acid, or the like, affecting the two most used sets of muscles and organs, the legs and the vocal cords. Whenever I have seen this condition—and circumstances have brought me into intimate personal relations with many clergymen and lecturers—the trouble at the knee has been due to some yielding of the plantar arch, while the laryngeal condition, if present, was due to an erroneous mode of using the voice consequent upon lack of proper training.

Sufferers of this kind must be warned not to stand absolutely immovable while addressing an audience. Some men stand without moving during a whole hour's lecture. This is unfortunate, for it obstructs the return circulation through the tense muscles, for the venous circulation was intended to be helped by muscular contraction. Many a man finds, as he comes down from pulpit or platform, that his knees are stiff and sore, though a moment before he knew nothing about it. The failure to notice any discomfort before is of itself an example of the influence of the mind over the body for the relief of pain.

Associated Lumbar Discomfort.—The painful condition around the knee which develops when high heels are worn is almost sure to be accompanied by pains, or at least a tired feeling, in the back. If we convince the patient that the trouble is due merely to a derangement of the mechanism involved in maintaining the erect posture we shall have scant need of medicine or even of local treatment. But as the pain is much worse on rainy days, owing to the relaxation of the muscles, we must be careful to remove the patient's suspicion that the pain must have a rheumatic origin. The restoration of normal mechanical conditions with the removal of the cause will prevent the {412} recurrence of the affection, and if some discomfort remains, the patient will not worry, and the muscles will gradually grow accustomed to the strain upon them. Of course, these conditions of discomfort are more common in those who are not naturally strong, who are run down, who are under-weight, or whose neurotic tendency will make any irritation seem worse than it is.

Heavy and Light Patients.—Two classes are likely to suffer more than others from these conditions. They are the people who are overweight and the people who are underweight. Those who are overweight exert much more effort to maintain the erect posture than ordinary people, and, besides, in most adipose persons the distribution of weight is such that a disproportionate amount of it is carried forward of the normal center of gravity. High heels cause a further tilting forward that has to be counter-balanced, and that, at least at the beginning, gives rise to muscular discomfort. In people who are underweight the nutrition of the muscles has suffered, and, as a consequence, they are not able to support the frame as well as before. In them the additional effort necessitated by the tilting tendency of high heels is particularly felt because such people are nearly always among the neurotically inclined.

Muscle Disuse.—Sometimes treatment of these conditions seems to lead up to the disuse of certain muscles and the over-use of others. I followed for several years an interesting case of this kind in which the course of the affection was so typical as to deserve to be recalled. A fuller account of the case occurs in my paper on "Rheumatism versus Muscular and Joint Pains" in *The American Journal of the Medical Sciences,* August, 1903.

In that case the joint symptoms caused by the pinching of a loose cartilage within the joint occurred suddenly on two or three occasions, so that a surgeon deemed it wise to put the knee in plaster. As a consequence, some atrophy of the muscles of the leg occurred, and a halt became habitual in the gait. Through this halting gait, the muscles of the back on the same side were also spared and thus became somewhat atrophied. Painful conditions developed in the muscles of the other side of the back from the over-use necessary to compensate for the condition on the less-used side. All of the muscles on the affected side became painful, apparently because of the atrophic condition to which they were reduced.

The young man, though with the best of good will, was utterly unable to conquer the tendency to halt in his gait, and so the muscles remained under-exercised and were used at a mechanical disadvantage, with the usual painful result. He went to at least two prominent orthopedic surgeons, who assured him that all he needed was confidence in himself to walk straight, and that then the normal condition of the muscles and absence of pain would result. But their directions were absolutely without result. He went through the hands of masseurs, of osteopaths, of rubbing quacks of all kinds, and suffered at least two attacks of artificial eczema as a consequence of the use of turpentine liniments, but he remained after it all in what he considered to be an intensely miserable condition. These cases are practically always cured by definite exercise of the muscles of the affected limb so as to bring them back to their normal tone. It requires special attention for this purpose, however, and the patient's mind must be brought to understand that at first the unaccustomed use of muscles will cause discomfort, but that this will disappear after a time. These patients are persuaded that they must be "cured" to get well.

{413}

CHAPTER VIII

FOOT TROUBLES

The more physicians see of affections of the feet and of painful conditions of the legs due to foot troubles the more they realize that the human faculty of the erect position becomes the source of many discomforts unless care is taken of the muscular apparatus of the legs. There are few people engaged in standing occupations who do not suffer from their feet. These achy sensations are especially bothersome if the patient is run down in health, or is in the midst of worry or irritation from physical or mental stress. Even under favorable conditions there are few who reach old age without serious foot troubles or without, at least, some deformity of the feet, which, by preventing or limiting exercise, have an important influence upon the general health. Careful analysis of the conditions that develop will convince an observer that yielding of the joints of the foot has much to do with the deformities and that the wearing of unsuitable shoes rather than any internal pathological condition is responsible for the foot troubles that are so common.

Foot Deformities in All Classes.—An Englishman who visited this country, and who had ample opportunity to observe our people, declared after seeing the bathers at Newport, that there were two interesting peculiarities of American masculine anatomy—the deformity in their feet and the appearance of having swallowed a watermelon whole and retained it within them. The latter condition has doubtless much to do with the causation of the former. Inactive lives, overeating, and the overweighting of flaccid limbs that are not capable of bearing even their normal burden, complicated by tight and ill-fitting shoes, give rise to the deformities of the toes that are so common— hammer toes, over-riding toes, bunched toes, twisted toes, bent toes. Examples of most of these are sure to be seen wherever we observe our men and women bathing. The Englishman's observation was of our so-called better class—at least, our leisure class. Ordinarily, it is assumed that clerks, waiters, and others, who have to stand upon their feet are the principal sufferers from foot deformities. They are, but they are not alone, and a goodly proportion of the population suffers in this way.

Mechanical Factors.—The most important deformity in these cases is a yielding of the arch of the foot with consequent flattening of the instep and lengthening of the foot. This overstretches especially the flexer tendons which run underneath the arch, produces bunions, and gives occasion for the development of corns. The pull upon the flexor longus hallucis which runs along the inside border of the foot, gives rise to the bunion by pulling the big toe outward—in the direction of least resistance. The pressure upon the tendons of the flexor longus digitorum pedis causes the smaller toes to bend somewhat, and this gives rise to projecting angular points on which corns readily form. Besides, the imperfect action of the muscles of the foot consequent upon the fall of the arch gives rise to plantar corns and callouses that are often painful. The living cushion of muscle which is the best protection against injury, while walking or running, has its vitality interfered with by {414} the fall of the arch and the consequent blocking of the return circulation through the thin walled veins. This gives rise to cold feet and, in those who stand much, to the tender feet that are now so much complained of and for which so many foot powders and appliances are advertised.

229

Confusion of Rheumatism and Foot Troubles.—Most foot troubles are reflected up the leg because muscles have to be overused or used at a serious mechanical disadvantage. This combined discomfort of foot and leg is readily referred to rheumatism. Some of the pains produced by yielding of the arch are in the ankle, some are in the calf, some in the tissues around the knee, and some even in the muscles and tendons above the knee. It is much easier to say "rheumatism" than to investigate carefully and differentiate the conditions that may be present. Out of forty successive patients who came to the dispensary of the Polyclinic Hospital of New York complaining of rheumatism, eighteen were suffering from flatfoot. Out of twenty-four who thought they had rheumatism in the feet or legs eighteen proved to be cases of flatfoot. Of the others, one was suffering from that rare disease meralgia paresthetica, two were suffering from sciatic neuritis, one was suffering with sub-acute joint trouble consequent upon pinching of a cartilage within the knee joint, and one had a painful condition consequent upon an old dislocation of the ankle due to a fall, accompanied by considerable laceration of the soft tissues. Analyses of the cases left no room for the so-called chronic rheumatism which had so easily covered all the cases at the beginning.

It was not unusual to see patients who had consulted many physicians and taken all sorts of internal and external remedies for the rheumatism that they supposed was causing their discomfort, yet who had nothing more than flatfoot. Their condition had become so bad that some of them had actually given up occupations that required them to stand. Merely following the advice to wear flatfoot braces in their shoes relieved these patients almost as if by magic. There was no need to measure them particularly; all they needed was an ordinary set of flatfoot braces. Some of them needed only a pair of good shoes, but the metal braces were advised to make sure that there would be a firm support for the arch of the foot. No wonder the "magic shoe-maker" had such success in New York a few years ago.

Nearly always the shoes worn by dispensary patients are of the worst kind, considering the condition. The patients' feet are often cold, and they think this is nature's demand for heavy shoes, so they buy heavy shoes and large sizes so as to be sure they will not hurt their feet. This clumsy footgear allows the arch to drop still further because no proper support is furnished, and the foot-trouble becomes more poignant. Then working people nearly always wear older shoes on rainy days, and this makes two elements for discomfort instead of one. The yielding arch is already a source of discomfort which is more noticeable in rainy weather because any affection around a joint is more bothersome at such times. The support that a new pair of shoes affords to the arch is lacking when what are so aptly termed "sloppy weather shoes" are worn, and the consequence is that the patient is particularly miserable in damp weather.

Unfavorable Disease Suggestions.—Of the cases in my experience of so-called rheumatism in the legs, over one-half are due either to flatfoot or to the incipient yielding of the arch which is called weak foot. Rheumatism is {415} most commonly held accountable for the condition, though gout comes in for its share of blame with quite as little justification. Occasionally some even more serious pathological condition is appealed to. I have seen the tendency to passive congestion in the feet with slight swelling around the ankle consequent upon the yielding of the arch called kidney trouble in spite of the fact that there was nothing in the urine to justify any such diagnosis. I have even known the coldness of the feet, which is likely to be a symptom of the disturbed circulation consequent upon the yielding of the arch, attributed to heart disease. As we shall see, most of the curious deformities of the old that make locomotion so difficult and so painful are due to a breaking down of the arch just after middle life and then to a progressive deformity of the foot. The mechanics of the support of the body are sadly interfered with when the arch yields, for bones are pushed out of place and ligaments and tendons are lengthened in order that the foot may accommodate itself to the new conditions. In nearly all these cases the patients are prone to say that they are sufferers from rheumatism. This diffuses and inveterates the notion which is a source of many unfavorable suggestions, that rheumatism is a curious progressive crippling disease which begins insidiously but advances remorselessly and eventually leaves its victim a prey to deformity.

Gout and Flatfoot.—Bunions consist originally of an enlargement of a bursa over the proximal end and the inner side of the big toe in order to protect the bone and joint from friction. If the irritation is continued, the proximal end of the first phalanx may enlarge, though usually this is preceded by a series of attacks of more or less acute inflammation of the bursa, when the bunion is said to "become sensitive." I have seen these attacks called gout so often that I feel sure that much of the gout reported in this country is nothing more than bunions. There is true gout, and it is probably almost as frequent with us as it is in England, but many of the so-called cases are really flatfoot associated with development of the bunion that so commonly occurs as the arch yields.

I was once asked to see a physician's wife who was thought to be a sufferer from gout. Long ago Oliver Wendell Holmes said that, as the shoemaker's children are likely to wear the worst shoes of the village, so the doctor's family is likely to take the least medicine, that is, be subjected to the least formal medication. The physician had seen the more or less acutely swollen and red enlargement of the base of the big toe, and heard his wife complain of the severe pain associated with it, and had suggested the possibility of gout. After rest in bed and the administration of salicylates and colchicum, the pain subsided and the redness and much of the swelling disappeared. This was a typical illustration of one event following another without causal relation. The succession of events was taken as a therapeutic test of the diagnosis of gout, and the patient was advised to regulate her diet so as to prevent the further accumulation of urates or uric acid in her blood. She was warned about eating red meat, about taking acid fruits, and about the acid fermentation of starchy vegetables. The main result of eating only white meat is apt to be simply a limitation in the amount of meat eaten, because white meat is less savory and after a time palls on the appetite. In the same way fruit was largely eliminated and sweets were taken out of the diet and vegetables were limited.

{416}

As she did not escape recurrent attacks of soreness in her bunion, while at the same time there were achy feelings in her foot, she took up the careful study of the dietary for gouty patients which she found in the books in her husband's library. So many things have seemed possibly deleterious for gouty people that it is not surprising that after a time nearly everything worth eating except a few cereals and milk and eggs had to be eliminated and she began to suffer from inanition. Then, after a time, came constipation, due to the insufficient amount of residue in her intestines, and this, partly by physical action but largely by mental suggestion, still further diminished the appetite for food, and a loss of over twenty pounds in weight was the result. The weakening of the general muscular system consequent upon this loss emphasized the trouble with the foot and the painful condition at the base of the big toe became more marked.

The supposed necessity for more exercise in the open air led her to walk long distances and in order to prevent her feet from hurting her, as she thought, she wore roomy shoes, distinctly too large. This is one of the common mistakes of people whose feet bother them, and it is just the wrong thing to do, since a snug, well-fitting shoe provides both support and protection. It is not surprising that the attacks of sub-acute bursitis became more frequent and more painful.

It was then that I saw her, and, as I feared to disturb the family harmony by suggesting that the whole trouble was a bunion and flatfoot, I compromised by saying that, while there might be some gout, there was undoubtedly flatfoot, and if she would wear the proper sort of shoe and stop limiting her diet so strenuously, and cease suggesting to herself that she had a progressive gouty affection that would lead to deformity and decrepitude, she would soon be much better.

It required tact to make her look favorably on this advice, after all that she had gone through during months of limited diet and enforced exercise. Though not quite convinced, she was ready to try the new method. She began to be better as soon as she was fitted with a pair of shoes that supported her arch and as soon as her increased nutrition began to make itself felt. At the end of two weeks she was able to give up the remedies for constipation that she had been using for nearly a year, while at the end of four weeks she had regained ten pounds of weight and felt much better.

Several years have passed since I saw her professionally and occasionally I hear from her only to be told what a great measure of relief it afforded her and how much better she has been as a consequence of a few simple directions with regard to her feet. I have seen at least a dozen of cases of so-called gout in educated people which followed almost exactly the same course and yielded promptly to the same treatment. The hardest symptom about these cases to cure is the cherished mental conviction that they are the victims of constitutional disease, either gout or rheumatism, to which all their symptoms are attributed. They are cases for psychotherapy more than any other form of therapeutics and need for a considerable period to have repeated assurances of the entirely local character of their affection.

Bunions and Flatfoot.—The etiology and preventive treatment of a bunion has always seemed to me to bear a closer relation to a flat foot than to anything else. The flatfooted man has nearly always a tendency to bunions. The {417} explanation of this is not difficult if one traces the relation between the tendons that run around the arch to the big toe. The usual etiological explanation, however, is that in youth short shoes were worn which initiated a tendency to divert the big toe inward toward the other toes. But there are many reasons against this explanation. Anyone who tries will find that it is practically impossible to wear shoes that are so short that the big toe is crowded back. Women are more apt to shorten their shoes than men, yet women suffer both from flat feet and from bunions much less than men. The reason for this seems to be that the forward position with the elevation of the heel of the shoe supports the arch and gives the shoe a shape more fitted to the normal foot than is found in the masculine flat-heeled shoe. Besides, this form of shoe maintains its shape better, and then, too, women are not so prone to wear old so-called comfortable shoes as are men.

The mechanism of the formation of the bunion in many cases seems to be, that the large toe, instead of lying straight along the inner edge of the foot, is pushed or pulled toward the other toes. If this process began from the wearing of pointed shoes, especially if such shoes did not have a straight line on the inside, conditions within the foot would soon tend to emphasize it. If the adductor hallicis once gets the habit of contracting rather strongly, as it is likely to do through the irritation set up by the yielding of the arch, it will be hard for its opposing muscles to counteract it. More important than this, however, is the fact that the tendon of the flexor longus hallucis runs along the inner border of the foot and is particularly affected by the yielding of the arch. For it works at a decided mechanical disadvantage under the new conditions and is stretched in such a way as to pull forcibly and constantly upon the big toe, necessarily turning it more and more outward as the arch continues to yield. The dropping of the arch makes the distance from the heel to the toe longer than before and the tendon pulls the toe as far outward as possible to compensate for this, as the distance to its insertion is thus made somewhat shorter.

The yielding of the arch lengthens the foot and puts the tendons of all the flexors on the stretch. All of them have a tendency to bend the toes, and as this action is constant, gradually the tendons of the extensors become over-stretched and these muscles are not capable of exerting their full force in overcoming the action of the flexors. The flexor longus digitorum has a tendency to cause a bending of the small toes, and as it also runs across the foot it pulls the toes somewhat inward, that is, toward the big toe. This crowding leads to hammer toes and over-riding. The big toe, however, is maintained in a state of extension by its firm, full contact with the sole of the shoe and with the floor when walking barefoot. The one direction in which it can yield rather readily is outward toward the other toes because this shortens the distance between the end of the toe and the heel. The pressure put upon the flexor longus hallucis will have a tendency to cause this, for it is over-stretched by the yielding of the arch and keeps constantly pulling on the big toe until that member has a distinct flexion outwards.

This makes the metacarpo-phalangeal joint prominent and then nature proceeds to protect it by a water cushion, a special bursa due to the formation between layers of connective tissue of a pocket in which some serum is constantly present. One can scarcely admire enough this provision of nature by {418} which she protects prominent bony points whenever they are subject to much irritation or to such use as would cause injury to important structures below. If continued pressure continues to be irritating, however, the water cushion proves unavailing and an inflammation of the overlying skin occurs with occasionally a spreading of infectious agents from the surface into the serum pocket below. This serum is such a good culture medium that an acute abscess is likely to form—the acute bursitis of the surgeons.

Rarer Foot Troubles.—Besides bunions, a number of other deformities of the feet occur as a consequence of the yielding of the arch. All the toes are likely to bend rather acutely, and the points of them are pressed against the shoe, while the knuckles, so to speak, are made prominent and are more likely to be subject to corns than would otherwise be the case. Besides, the displacement of the big toe toward the little toes leads to a crowding of the toes together, and this gives rise to soft interdigital corns and to a lowered resistive vitality which may be the predisposing factor to slight infections of various kinds that will make the patients miserable. Such affections may appear negligible, a matter for the chiropodist, and not deserving the physician's attention; but they mean so much for the comfort of the patient and the prevention of exercise through sore feet reacts so deleteriously on the general health that these minor ailments become important and merit careful attention. Dr. Emmet tells the story of the old family servant, always grumpy and complaining, who, when he had the many

231

blessings of life pointed out to him, confessed that the Lord had been very good to him, but said, "The Lord knows He takes it out of me in soft corns."

Hammer Toes—Clam Toes.—Nature has provided a wonderful mechanism in the arch of the foot and the anatomical relations of the toes to support the weight of the body firmly, gracefully, and comfortably; yet any yielding of any part of it leads to a disturbance of its delicate mechanical relations and, consequently, to ever-increasing deformity. Hammer toes are typical examples of what such a disturbance may lead to. One of the toes becomes pressed downward between two others. This over-stretches the extensor muscles and tempts the unbalanced flexors to contract. As the extensor muscles become, after a time, unable to work in the constantly bent toes, they atrophy to some extent and then the flexor muscles pull the toe farther and farther down until there is no possibility of its being straightened at all. Now, if the flexor tendons are cut and the toe straightened the atrophic extensor muscles will not hold it in that position, and when the flexors grow together the old condition will reassert itself. In the meantime, muscle changes in the neighboring toes have also taken place. With no resistance on one side of them, they become bent sidewise over the hammer toe, and so their muscles on one side are overstretched and on the other side become contracted. After a time it is impossible to correct this series of deformities which are being constantly increased and emphasized by the weight of the body above.

Present-day Shoes.—In recent years we have heard much more than heretofore about foot troubles. As the old-fashioned shoes were carefully made by skilled shoemakers to fit the feet of one individual and not to conform to some supposed ideal pedal extremity, they supported the feet much better than do the modern cheap machine-made shoes. These custom shoes lasted a long time, and, after they were once molded to the foot, the wearer was not {419} disturbed for many months by the process of having to become accustomed to another shoe. The many advertisements in quite recent times of foot powders and other artificial relief for the foot show that people are suffering much more than before, or, at least, are less able to bear the discomfort. These powders, however, are not likely to do good in the long run, since they tempt the wearers to stand the discomfort against which they do furnish a certain amount of soothing. It is much better, however, for the sufferer to find the cause of the discomfort and to remove it if possible, for otherwise it will lead to constantly growing displacement of bones and muscles and may eventually even bring on actual and ever-increasing deformity.

Prophylaxis.—The most important means of prophylaxis in these cases is to have patients who must assume the standing position for some hours each day, exercise their legs rather vigorously. If teachers, lecturers, and the like, have to stand for a long time, it is important that on the way to and from their occupations they should not have to stand up in cars nor assume cramped and uncomfortable positions. It would be better for them to walk rapidly for several miles rather than ride in a standing or a constrained position. If they are convinced of the necessity for exercise, there is much less likelihood of the development of the severer discomfort that is sometimes very discouraging. It is particularly difficult to make women understand this; yet, once they have found how much relief is afforded by vigorous exercise, they are likely to overdo it and thus run the risk of incurring ills quite as serious as those consequent upon not taking enough. In nervous people the nagging discomfort of a yielding arch will sometimes (just as eye strain does) produce reflex headaches, constipation, lack of appetite, and apparently predispose to the frequent recurrence of migrainous headaches. I have, in not a few cases, seen these conditions relieved by rational treatment of the foot condition.

Circulatory Disturbances Due to Flatfoot.—An interesting direct consequence of flatfoot is the disturbance of the venous circulation, which is likely to bring about some swelling of the feet and nearly always considerable coldness and numbness, particularly in the winter and, above all, on damp days during cold weather. The swelling of the feet makes the patient think—sometimes at the suggestion of his physician—of kidney trouble or heart trouble, and sometimes it is hard to persuade him that there is nothing serious the matter with these important organs. The disturbance of the circulation further leads to numbness, to some anesthesia, and to paresthesia. Corns and especially callouses grow more readily between the toes, and patients who are prone to read about such ailments may conclude that they are suffering from hypesthesia {420} and hyperesthesia due to some serious progressive organic nervous disease. I once had a woman patient discourse learnedly to me about these things who was sure that she had the beginning of some incurable spinal disease. Locomotor ataxia was the least she might expect from her description of her feelings. What I found was flatfoot. Raising her arch cured her.

The cold feet and the numbness, to call them by simple Saxon names which will not disturb patients, may sometimes keep them awake. In the chapter on Insomnia we suggest that the best thing for this is to secure a return of the circulation either by exercises, or by wearing a flatfoot brace during the day, or by putting the feet in water as hot as can be comfortably borne and keeping them there for a quarter of an hour. Of these means exercise is the best. Raising up on the toes after the shoes are off and coming down on the outside of the foot strengthens the muscles, pulls the bones of the arch firmly together and encourages the circulation. For beginning flatfoot this is a curative measure and it is the natural mode of treatment for the coldness and numbness of the feet. Rubbing, also, is good for the feet in order to restore the circulation, but patients are inclined to rub downwards while they should rub upwards in order to help the hampered venous circulation. The thin-walled veins are more likely to be compressed by any disturbance of tissues than are the firm-walled arteries, and it is to help the veins that our remedial measures must be directed.

Secondary Consequences.—The secondary consequences of flatfoot are interesting. It is surprising how many people who frequently suffer from sprains of the ankle have some yielding of the arch as a predisposing factor to that condition. Two classes seem to suffer frequently from sprained ankle—those with yielding arches and those with high insteps. Apparently there is weakness in the excess in both directions. Very flatfooted people apparently do not suffer so frequently from sprained ankles as those in whom there is only an incipient yielding of the arch. They seem to have learned to walk more circumspectly. Perhaps, too, their well-known tendency to toe outward lessens their liability to turning on their ankle. The effects of sprains of the ankle in people with weak foot last, as a rule, longer and leave more weakness after them than they do in ordinary cases. This, of course, might be expected, but it is surprising how often the significance of beginning flatfoot fails to be noticed even by the physician. I have seen rather frequently cases of so-called chronic rheumatism in which there is a series of stories of sprained ankle because of the assumed weakness of the ankle from supposed rheumatism, when the whole case can be summed up in a yielding arch.

Exercises.—If the arch has not yielded much, it is often unnecessary to prescribe flatfoot braces or arch supports of any kind, unless perhaps at first. After the first soreness has passed off, exercises may be employed to strengthen the muscles. As we have said, the patient should rise on his toes and then come down slowly on the outside of his feet. He may be instructed to sit with his feet—not his legs—crossed, the feet resting on their outer edges. He may be shown how even various slight movements of his toes, almost without moving his shoes at all, will strengthen the muscles that pass around the arch, which, thus strengthened, will hold the bones of the arch firmly together and prevent further yielding. There is, at the present day, a tendency to recommend too freely the wearing of flatfoot braces or arches. After all, these are {421} only crutches and should not be worn unless absolutely necessary. If the arch can be strengthened—as it can be in many cases—so as to bear the body weight without discomfort, then this is much the better treatment. If the arch is restored the feet are in a more natural condition, while artificial support leaves the muscles without that exercise which will preserve their functions. Flatfoot braces may be necessary, but only if absolutely necessary should they be advised, and palliative measures, such as exercise, manipulations, and rubbings, should be given a fair trial after the unfavorable suggestions as to his foot condition have been removed from the patient's mind.

Significance of Foot Troubles.—We have devoted much space to foot troubles—more, perhaps, than will seem justified to the minds of many physicians. We have done so, however, because of the firm conviction that the feet are the source of more discouragement and depression of mind than any other part of the body. Life very often takes on another aspect when foot troubles are relieved. In the old, progressive deformities of the feet consequent upon mechanical disturbance are probably the source of more discomfort, and by their interference with exercise and outing, the cause of more ill-feeling and even disturbance of health than any other single factor. Even life may be shortened by the confinement or limitation of movement consequent upon bad feet. Above all, the idea that any constitutional trouble, or hereditary disease, is at the bottom of their affliction must be removed, and then these patients are encouraged to live their lives more fully and with more happiness for themselves and others. Hence this long chapter.

CHAPTER IX

ARTHRITIS DEFORMANS

Arthritis deformans has unfortunately been called by several names besides the descriptive term which, in the present state of our knowledge, is the most suitable for it. We do not know its cause. We do not well understand even the predisposing factors in its causation. Hence, the term arthritis deformans, which declares simply that it is an inflammatory condition of the joints producing deformities, exactly fits it. It has often been spoken of by such names as "rheumatic arthritis," or "rheumatoid arthritis," and, above all, by the unfortunate term "rheumatic gout." Many of the worst suggestions that attach to the word rheumatism are founded on these ill-chosen designations. Arthritis deformans was supposed to be connected with rheumatism or with gout, or perhaps to be due to a combination of the two. In a majority of the cases there is no history of either true gout or rheumatism to be obtained from the patient, and where a rheumatic or gouty history does occur, it is either quite indefinite or it is clear that arthritis deformans developed in a gouty or rheumatic subject, that is, following genuine gout or rheumatism, just as it might develop in any other individual without any causal connection between it and the other affections.

Supposed under the old theory to be a constitutional, probably a blood disease, patients who saw the ugly, crippling deformities produced by it and {422} then heard the word rheumatism used in connection with it were prone to think of this as the terminal stage of all the severe rheumatic conditions. As a matter of fact no evidence that we have shows that the disease has any connection with chemical modifications of nutrition or metabolism; nor, above all, has the so-called uric acid diathesis or any other superacidity of the blood any etiological connection with it. It has always seemed to me to be clearly a nervous arthropathy, as the lesions are almost without exception more or less symmetrically distributed. The joints that suffer are commonly the smaller ones in corresponding positions on opposite sides of the body, and they run a definite atrophic course sometimes with the preceding phase of hypertrophy that is so characteristic of the trophic lesions of an affection produced by a disease or defect of the nervous system. This symmetrical distribution constitutes the best possible evidence that arthritis deformans is not a nutritional disease and, above all, is not due to chemical changes in the blood.

The affection exists in at least three forms and there is a growing persuasion that there are even more varieties of it that will have to be separated by clinical observation.

There is a good study of the three types of the disease in *Guy's Hospital Reports*, Vols. 56-57, London, 1902. The article is entitled "Acute Rheumatoid Arthritis," but there seems no reason for applying the word rheumatoid to the group, especially since there is no proved connection with rheumatism and no similarity, except in the case of acute deforming arthritis in which at the beginning it may be difficult to differentiate the two affections.

HEBERDEN'S NODES

The most familiar form is named Heberden's nodes, from the great English physician who first made a special study of it. The affection is characterized by an enlargement of the sides of the distal phalanges with small, hard nodules, "little hard knobs", as Heberden called them, developing at these points. They are more frequent in women than in men. Evidently neither hard work nor exposure nor excesses in eating or drinking occasions them. They occur in all classes, the poor and rich, manual workers as well as professionals. It is rare to find them on one hand alone, though it is not at all rare to find them affecting solely the little fingers of each hand. I have seen several cases where surgical intervention had been attempted on one little finger because of the deformity produced when the node originally appeared. When I asked if there was not some trace of a similar condition on the other hand I was told there was not, yet I have been able to show that the first signs, at least, of a corresponding growth already existed on the little finger of the other hand. In the two cases in which my attention was called to a slight enlargement on one side before anything developed on the other, my tentative prophecy that corresponding nodosities would grow on the other side was fulfilled during the following years.

While this form of the disease is a true arthritis deformans it seems to be entirely separate from the progressive forms which we shall speak of later. The nodes increase in size and occasionally develop on all of the fingers, but usually never spread beyond the phalangeal joints. There is a tradition in the {423} medical profession of England, where this affection has been observed with care for some two hundred years, that sufferers from these nodes commonly live to long life. This is not founded on any theory, but is an actual observation. There is also a tradition, though I cannot vouch for its truth, that the people who are thus affected have some sort of immunity to tuberculosis, or at least good resistive vitality against a rapidly running tuberculous process.

I have had at least a score of Heberden's nodes cases under observation for more than ten years and some of them for nearly twenty years, and have been surprised at the slowness with which the process develops. A year often makes no change in the size of the nodes, and I have seen cases where after five years the photograph showed no difference. The lesions are often exquisitely symmetrical so that the question of the origin of the affection in the spinal cord constantly crops up, for that is the symmetrical influence in the body. There are, however, no other symptoms that point to involvement of the cord in any way. Most of these patients have suffered more from worry about it than from their affection. It is another case of "having many troubles most of which never happen."

Some of my patients are physicians, and all of them have consulted other, some many other, physicians. As a consequence, many of them have taken to various diets, especially eliminating certain foods and liquids with the idea that this might stop the progress of the disease. I have never known any change of diet or any abstinence from liquids or solids that seemed to make the slightest difference, though I have seen a number of cases that were considerably worse than they would have been if the diet had not been tinkered with to such an extent as seriously to disturb nutrition.

The main disturbing feature of the affection is the dread of the development of serious crippling conditions in the hands or in the large joints.

As a rule, after a time the nodes cease to grow, and then a period of remission sets in that lasts for many years and there may be no recrudescence of the affection. This remission is delayed if the patients allow themselves to run down in general health. It is apparently hastened by getting the patients up to normal weight and removing any factors that disturb their general health. If the patients' minds are properly disposed, the neurotic symptoms that sometimes develop as the result of over-solicitude about their condition are done away with, the patients are more comfortable, and even the progress of the disease is inhibited.

ACUTE PROGRESSIVE ARTHRITIS

The second variety of the affection is a general progressive arthritis which usually begins with fever, redness, and swelling, involving especially the smaller joints. The diagnosis of the disease can almost be made on the fact that its favorite locations are the jaw and the joints of the spine. It is a much more serious affection than Heberden's nodes. In its beginning it often simulates acute rheumatism. It occurs particularly in people who are run down for any reason, in young women who have recently come to the country and are working as domestics, in young men who have recently changed their occupation from indoors to outdoors and are not used to the inclemencies of the weather. On the other hand, it occurs rather often in young persons of {424} both sexes used to living and working out of doors who take up an occupation in a damp interior.

The fever usually runs a lower course than that of genuine acute articular rheumatism, the pain is not favorably affected by salicylates, and the duration of the disease is generally longer. This affection always leaves its marks on the joints and there are always recurrences. It is, indeed, the confusion of this quite distinct disease with acute articular rheumatism that has given the latter affection the bad name it has in many minds as a producer of deformities. Arthritis deformans or general progressive arthritis is always a crippling disease; acute articular rheumatism has for its surest diagnostic sign, when the complete history of the case is known, the fact that it leaves no mark after it except, unfortunately, that so often seen in the heart.

CHRONIC ARTHRITIS DEFORMANS

The third type of arthritis deformans is the chronic slow running type which involves many joints before the process is complete. One form of this, commonly seen in old men, called osteoarthritis, is often confined to the hip joint, and often produces considerable deformity. Another form is more common in women. It begins in middle life by deformities in the terminal joints of the fingers and the carpo-metacarpal joints of the thumbs. Bony outgrowth takes place until the joints become almost or quite useless. It spreads from the joints primarily affected to the elbows, the knees and occasionally involves other joints. The disease has no favorable course, but is progressive, and there is great discomfort, marked disability, aches and pains particularly in rainy weather and, finally, the patient may become quite helpless.

Preliminary Stage.—An early symptom associated with arthritis deformans of chronic character is likely to be a distinct loss of muscle power, which may be the first symptom in cases that have no acute beginning. The patient notices that he is unable to hold a satchel as he did before, or that quite unaccountably it drops from him. There may be a loss of control over muscles and especially small muscles that attracts the patient's attention. He finds that he cannot hold a book as he used to, or that it is difficult to pick up small objects. He finds it hard to turn a door handle or to pull a cork, although the pulling action may be perfect, but the ability to insert the corkscrew is lacking. These symptoms are prone to be intermittent. They are most noticeable when the patient is tired, or after a damp day, or a succession of damp days, when he is not feeling well. It will usually be found that a joint, the affection of which is missed unless it is carefully looked for, that between the radius and ulna has become affected, and as a consequence there is a difficulty in supination. The lesions are different from those which occur in lead poisoning but at the beginning the symptom complexes may easily be confused.

This form of arthritis deformans, in its earlier and its later stages, is a source of unfavorable suggestion as regards other affections. Its first symptoms may be thought neurasthenic, and if it is so called, those who hear the diagnosis and see the later developments will conclude that neurotic symptoms {425} can lead to serious sequelae. On the other hand, the painful tiredness that is always worse in damp weather may be termed rheumatism and be a correspondingly unfavorable suggestion. Patients who develop aches and pains as a consequence of occupations, or through the relaxation of joint tissues, are most uneasy because of the confusion of the later stages of this disease with rheumatism. This must be recalled by the physician if he would be successful in treating such pains and aches; for not a little of the discomfort is due to an exaggerated mental impression of their significance. This of itself often proves sufficient to keep the patients from the exercise that would relieve many of their secondary symptoms, at least, and serve to make their discomfort more bearable.

Course of Chronic Arthritis.—The course of chronic arthritis deformans is always interesting. It is never as serious as the prognosis at the beginning seems to indicate, and it always has intermissions which, in most cases, become favorable remissions with such improvement that the patients feel encouraged, though they never get entirely well. Six rather typical cases have been under my eyes for from five to fifteen years. In all of them the course was slow and the progress of the disease vague at the beginning; and it was difficult to say how the affection began, or what was its cause, and apparently nothing would stop its advance. After a time all of them became discouraged and began to go the rounds. Almost without exception the physicians told them that they were incurable, and nearly all of them received unfavorable prognoses either directly from the physician or from hints sometimes dropped to friends, or from the attitude of the physician toward them. Much of this discouragement proved unjustified by the actual progress of the disease for many years. While they got but scant encouragement from regular physicians, nearly all of them received hopeful suggestions from irregulars and were, as a rule, for the time being, somewhat bettered by the treatments suggested by these, no matter what they were.

Every one of these six cases, as was to be expected under the circumstances, went through a period of intense discouragement, with loss of appetite, partly from confinement to the house, partly from thinking so much about themselves, partly from lack of exercise and, in general, from their morbid mental condition. As a consequence of the loss of appetite, or, at least, of failure to eat in the midst of discouragement, severe constipation developed in five of the six cases and this further complicated the situation. They ran down very much in weight, and this emphasized the apparent size of the hypertrophic nodosities in their joints and weakened their muscles to such an extent that even under good conditions they found it difficult to move. After a time, usually many months, sometimes a couple of years, something happened to make them realize that while they were crippled and were going to be deformed, they still might find much in life that was not to be despised. Then they began to pick up in weight, their muscles got firmer, their nodosities seemed to disappear because the soft tissues around them filled out, though in most cases some of the material previously laid down actually was or seemed to be reabsorbed, perhaps as a consequence of the patient's better metabolism.

Neurotic Additions.—All of these patients are now in much better physical and, above all, in much better dispositional states than they were during the first year or two at the beginning of their disease. While they allowed {426} themselves to run down in weight they were supremely miserable, with many neurotic pains and aches that were extremely hard to relieve, they had tendernesses and sorenesses on rainy days, usually attributed to their rheumatic conditions but really due to intense depression of the nervous system, with a constant tendency to exaggerate slight pains and aches into torments, and in general were invalids, a burden to themselves and others. They have improved to a noteworthy extent so as to become cheerful, reasonably happy in their power to help others, interested in many things and, in at least two of the cases, accomplishing more actual good for those around them than they probably would if their lives had continued to be the conventional existences that they had been before their arthritis came to them. This reminds one of Dean Stanley's famous expression that life looks different when viewed from a horizontal position. He used the expression with reference to fatal illness, but it might well be applied to any ailment that makes people think seriously and keeps them from occupations only with frivolous things. One of these patients is a source of consolation to many friends, who are much better in health than she is, who bring their troubles to her, and who marvel at her power to make the best of things.

The prognosis for cure is extremely unfavorable, but the prognosis for a reasonable amount of happiness and a large amount of usefulness is, in my experience, excellent and though, of course, new habits will have to be formed and new ways of looking at life assumed, if this can be quietly and persuasively made clear to the patient early in the case, much of the more or less inevitable suffering that the patient will have to endure may be lessened.

The older the patient, as a rule, the better the prognosis in these cases. As with regard to diabetes, tuberculosis and many another affection, every year after fifty adds to the prospect that the patient's ordinary span of life will not be much shortened and that the symptoms will not be severe. Occasionally the disease develops in patients who have been extremely healthy until they were well past sixty. I have in mind particularly a patient who did not begin seriously to suffer from the disease until she was sixty-eight. Then for two or three years she was very miserable, mainly because she had been very active and she feared that the disease would cripple her. It did bring about a considerable limitation of her activity. Ten years have passed, however, and she is still able to be about, and, though now well on the way to eighty, in good weather she still attends to various duties that take her outside of her home and occupies herself with many interests.

I was never able to tell her that she would be better. I assured her from the beginning, however, that she would never be so much worse as she imagined, and that she would never be actually crippled. During the early stages of the disease, her discouragement and, above all, the diminution of activity, the lack of exercise and occupation of mind and the over-occupation with herself, made her not only mentally miserable but seriously interfered with many bodily functions.

TREATMENT

In the treatment of arthritis deformans the most important object is the general health of the patient. Owing to the confinement, the pains, which {427} are often worse at night, cause disturbance of sleep which reacts upon the general health. As a result of depression and discouragement, patients are prone to loss of appetite. This is sometimes looked upon as a symptom of the disease, but it is not a direct symptom except during the acute stage when there is fever, and is due rather to the changed conditions in which the patients live and the mental influences that surround them. If the patient loses in weight, as is so often the case, the effects are likely to be more serious, for the remission is delayed and is less complete in its consequences. Above all, it is important not to disturb the diet of the patient in such a way as to interfere with nutrition. Owing to the supposed rheumatic element, meat, or at least red meat, is occasionally taken out of the diet by the recommendation of the physician. Whenever this is done, harm results. There is a definite tendency to anemia, which will be emphasized by an exclusively vegetable diet, especially in those accustomed to eat meat freely. As a rule, there is much more need to encourage the patient to eat than to limit the diet in any way. Patients must rather be advised to take a generous mixed diet and to consume about as much meat and the same varieties as before. Tinkering with the diet has never been known to do any good for arthritis deformans and often does harm. The drinking of large quantities of water seems to do more than almost anything else to help these patients into a better frame of body and mind. Their neurotic symptoms are, as a rule, even more important than their joint symptoms, and if the neurotic symptoms can be cured, as they usually can without much difficulty, the patients feel much better.

Systematic Exercises.—As soon as the acute stage has passed patients should be encouraged to take some systematic exercise in spite of the discomfort that is associated with it. Unless muscles are moved regularly deformities in bad position will result and there will be crippling which can be avoided in most cases. It is sometimes difficult to secure exercises for the small muscles that are involved and definite occupations are better than artificial exercises. For the fingers, for instance, I find that the best thing is knitting. By this I mean using the old-fashioned knitting needles for the making of stockings, wristlets, jackets, and the like. Crocheting is also of some use, but it does not give employment to as many of the small muscles as knitting. If the knitting is done with old-fashioned yarn from which the lanolin has not all been extracted, some of this substance comes off on the fingers during the movements associated with knitting. This seems to do good by rendering the joints more supple and the muscles more easy of movement. At least the suggestion is very helpful to the patients.

Electricity and Mechano-therapy.—Electricity has been much praised, but whatever good it accomplished has always seemed to me to be confined to the exercise afforded the muscles. Its use, however, serves to keep up the patient's hope.

Mechano-therapy often does good and some of the Zander machines are likely to be useful. Pulleys and weights for the shoulders and arms have their place and resisted movements serve to restore muscles to function which they had lost during the time when the joints were worst. Their use helps to bring the joint into the most available conditions.

Something that has distinct hope in it must always be done for these patients. For this local treatment means more than anything else. Unfavorable {428} suggestions keep flowing in upon him from the failure of medicine, and serve to concentrate his attention on his condition and make him think that nothing can benefit him. Often the physician finds that his patient has been to someone else, who did some simple thing that brought relief of symptoms, at least for a time, and restored his confidence to such a degree that he felt much better for a time at least. These ailments are emphasized by advancing years and, though we cannot prevent decay of tissue, we can keep the patient's mind from inhibiting still further the functions of the impaired tissue.

General Condition.—The patient's general condition must be made as good as possible. For this outdoor air is the most important factor. It increases impaired appetite, makes sleep more restful and easy, and gives one of the best occupations of mind that can be obtained. Of course, changes in the weather will bring discomfort. Where it is possible, such patients must be sent to climates as equable as possible. Such a change of climate during December, January and February will often make them very comfortable, and the distraction of mind, with the possibility of getting out in the mild climate, will diminish their sensitiveness and be more powerful factors in the dissipation of their aches and pains than the climate itself. Where people cannot be sent away from home, the securing of corresponding distractions means a great deal. The one thing necessary for the physician is to keep the patient from brooding upon himself and his ills and to find other occupations of mind for him.

CHAPTER X

COCCYGODYNIA

Coccygodynia, or, as it is sometimes called, coccydynia, is a painful affection of the coccyx or bony end of the spinal column. It usually results from trauma, as a fall on the buttocks on an icy pavement, or particularly a fall in coming down stairs in which the main portion of the impact is on the seat. Occasionally it follows horseback riding. It is said to be on the increase among women who ride astride. Occasionally it is reported after severe labor, particularly when the head of the child was very large, or after first labor when the coccyx has been beforehand bent inward somewhat abnormally and is pushed out by the oncoming head. It seems to develop with special frequency in nervous people who have to sit much, particularly if they sit on unsuitable chairs. The chair seat with the ridge in the center which has been introduced in recent years is sometimes blamed. Occasionally, on the other hand, it is said to come from sitting on heavily cushioned chairs, particularly leather chairs which do not allow of much transpiration and cause a feeling of uncomfortable heat.

There are, indeed, so many different causes suggested, sometimes of quite opposite or even contradictory effects, that it seems evident that the main element in the disease is some predisposition to sensitiveness in this region which is exaggerated and emphasized by the cause that is blamed. It occurs particularly in women, though it is occasionally seen in delicate or neurotic men. Sufferers from it sometimes find it impossible to sit for any length of time. {429} Even lying down, especially if they lie on their backs, becomes a source of pain. Various operations, such as the reposition in place of the bent coccyx, or even the removal of the tip of the coccyx, have been suggested. Some reported cures are to be found in the literature. These are mainly surgical cures, however, that is to say, the patient recovered from the operation, was seen for a month or two afterwards, and was then on a fair way to complete recovery. Some of us who have had to treat these cases afterwards for painful conditions apparently due to the scar of the operation, or to a neurotic condition closely corresponding to the old coccygodynia, are not so confident of the value of an operation, though probably in purely traumatic cases surgical intervention is of value.

In most cases the sufferers are women who have little to do, who have much time on their hands to think about themselves, and who usually receive abundant sympathy from friends and relatives. In one case under my observation the death of a husband and the discovery that his estate was much less than had been anticipated, so that his widow had to take up a wage-earning occupation, did more in a short time than all the treatment that had been employed before to relieve her discomfort. She had been quite unable to move around at times, especially in rainy weather, and was something of an invalid during all the winter, but now she was able to go out to work every day and had very little trouble. Her affection originally dated from a fall on an icy sidewalk and her fear to go out in the winter seemed to be dependent on the dread of another fall. She realizes now that practically all her former trouble was due to over-attention to a discomfort which is still present, but which she is now able to forget, except at times when she is alone after there have been worries and troubles that have reduced her power to control her nerves. In young girls an injury to the coccyx by a fall on the buttocks will often leave tenderness for months or even years, but if attention is distracted from this and the patient is not allowed to concentrate her mind on it and does not hear of the awful possibilities of coccygodynia—a mouth-filling Greek name in which we map out our ignorance, and which seems to carry with it such a weight of pathology—she will probably recover completely.

Coccygodynia often resembles hysterical coxalgia or the hysterical arthritises, and seems sometimes to be due to the fact that there is a natural or traumatic abnormal mobility of the coccygeal vertebrae which, owing to concentration of attention, has developed into a neurosis analogous to the corresponding condition in a joint. There are undoubtedly cases in which a real pathological lesion exists, but these are comparatively few. In this, as in other joint and bone affections with vague pains likely to be worse on rainy days, the word rheumatism is often mentioned, but it has no proper place. Treatment that will put the patients into good general condition—never local unless there is objective indication—outdoor air and exercise with reassurance of mind and distraction of the attention are the important therapeutic agents. Patients with much time on their hands do not readily get well, while those who are busily occupied seldom suffer for long.

{430}

SECTION X

GYNECOLOGICAL PSYCHOTHERAPY

CHAPTER I

MENTAL HEALING IN GYNECOLOGY

All physicians are convinced of the good that has been done by the extension of the application of surgery to women's diseases during the pest generation. On the other hand, there are probably very few, except the ultra-specialists, who are not quite sure that there has been too much surgery in gynecology, and that many a woman has been operated on without sufficient reason and without definite indications. In suitable cases surgery is sometimes life-saving and is often the only means of relief for suffering that is seriously disturbing the general conditions and is making life unbearable. Its very possibilities of good, however, have led to abuses. From the abuse of a thing, the old Latins used to say, no argument against its proper use can be derived, and this is eminently true of gynecological surgery. It will not belittle the great benefit that operative work has been to state how much of auxiliary good may be accomplished by the use of psychotherapy in gynecology.

Many a woman who is operated on is benefited only for the time being, and her old symptoms return after a time. Dr. Goodell, one of our first great gynecologists, used to warn his students insistently that women had many organs outside of the pelvis. The individuality in gynecology is extremely important. Some women suffer what they describe as excruciating pain or unbearable torture from pathological conditions that other women do not notice at all. Very often these women either have no real interest in life and are so self-centered that they emphasize their feelings by dwelling on them, or else their attention has been attracted to some sensation not necessarily pathologic and then by concentration of mind on it they so disturb vasomotor conditions and the nutrition of nerves that the condition does become a veritable torture and apparently demands surgical intervention. It is possible to cause a hyperemia in the skin by thinking about certain portions of it, and the genital organs are particularly prone to be influenced by mental states. If for any reason a woman gets her mind on her genital tract and becomes persuaded that there is a pathological condition in it, symptoms will develop until an operation seems inevitable. But the operation will bring relief only for a while, and then her mind will find something else to dwell on and produce similar symptoms.

{431}

Place of Psychotherapy.—To fail to try to sway the mind by all the methods and auxiliaries outlined in the earlier chapters of this work before suggesting an operation to a woman is to neglect a most important means for relief in many gynecological cases. There is scarcely any pathological condition from which women may suffer that does not become worse as the result of the depressing influence of much thinking about it, and that is not made better by a change in their mind that makes them realize the possibility of being well again. The most important preliminary to operation is the promise of complete relief through surgery. The acme of suggestion is reached in the preparation for operation with its constant encouragement and then the congratulations after the operation. Then come the weeks of convalescence during which the same strong suggestion is constantly at work making the patient sure that she must be better. All this serves to add tone to the system, invigorates the appetite and puts patients in the best possible mental attitude to bring about a favorable result. Indeed, the ten or fifteen pounds in weight that such patients gain during their convalescence, especially when they have been under weight before, is often the most beneficial result of their hospital experience.

If the same patients had been given the same promise that they would surely be cured, and then had been removed from depressing home influences and bothersome trials and labors, and been told that what they needed for complete recovery was to gain in weight; if they had then been visited by friends who congratulated them on the fact that now at least they were going to be better and their symptoms were going to disappear, and if they had gained the fifteen pounds that came in convalescence after their operation, most of them would have recovered quite as completely as by the operation from many of their vague gynecological difficulties. This is, of course, true only of cases where there are not very definite indications for surgical intervention. But in a certain number the symptoms are so vague that operation is decided upon rather with the hope than the assurance of benefit; and it is particularly in these that psychotherapy is useful and must be given a thorough trial.

Pain Relief.—It is often set down as a maxim of gynecologic practice, that pain which cannot be relieved except by recourse to dangerous or habit-forming drugs is an indication for operation. Pain, however, is a relative matter and, as we have shown in the chapter on Pain, its intensity depends not a little on the patient's attitude of mind towards it. When there is discouragement and depression, pain becomes insufferable, and what was borne quite well at the beginning may now prove intolerable. Whenever occupation of mind can be secured, however, pain is diminished in intensity.

Reputed Remedies and Suggestion.—Probably the most striking indirect testimony to the value of mental influence and especially of frequently repeated suggestion in gynecology is found in the recent history of various much-advertised remedies that have been sold in enormous quantities for all the ills of women. The composition of these remedies is not, as is popularly supposed, a great mystery. They have all been analyzed and their ingredients are well known. As a rule, they contain only simple tonic drugs that have absolutely no specific effect on the genital organs, but that are stimulating to the general system. There has been much surprise at the definite evidence {432} furnished by expert investigators, that the principal ingredient in most of them—certainly their most active element—is the alcohol they contain, which, until the passage of the pure food and drug law, was in such considerable quantities that practically each tablespoonful of these favorite remedies for women was equal to half an ounce of whisky. No wonder that this gave an immediate sense of well-being which rose in most of those unused to alcohol to a feeling of exaltation. The patient was sure beyond contradiction that she could feel the effects of the medicine! Of the after effects, the less said the better, but there is no doubt that many women acquired the alcohol habit through indulgence in these nostrums.

Illusory as was this sense of well-being, it sufficed in many cases to relieve women of discomfort that had become so serious, to their minds at least, that they feared an operation would be necessary. Undoubtedly many of the testimonials given to such remedies are founded on actual experiences of this kind in which patients were sure that they were cured of serious ills. Where alcohol is not the chief ingredient of these remedies, some other tonic stimulant is employed, and it has proved sufficient to make the patients feel, or at least suggest to themselves, that they must be better. This has given them courage to take more exercise and get more out into the air, and consequently relieves them of many physical symptoms that had developed because they thought they were the subjects of some serious ailment and must be solicitously careful of their health. The idea of care for the health in many persons' minds seems to be to do as little as possible of external, useful work and to occupy themselves principally with their internal concerns. They stay in the house too much and in so doing disturb nearly every physical function. Perfectly well people, if confined with nothing to interest them, become short-circuited on themselves and develop all sorts of symptoms, physical and mental.

The Mind as a Factor in Gynecological Affections.—A gynecologic incident of any kind may become to many women such a center of attention that it is impossible for them to distract their minds from it, and every symptom or feeling that can by any stretch of thought be connected with the genital system becomes greatly exaggerated. Young women, whose menstruation has been perfectly regular, may have it disturbed by fright, grief, a change of environment, getting the feet wet, or something of that kind. At immediately succeeding periods their fear of bad effects will of itself influence unfavorably the conditions in their genital system. They have always had more or less discomfort, but now this discomfort becomes difficult to bear because of the fear that there may be further serious consequences of the disturbing incident in their menstrual life. It occupies all their attention; instead of deliberately trying to disregard it, they fear that, if they should do so, they would be allowing some progressive condition to gain a hold on them which would lead to serious results.

One is apt to see this condition in young married women who have had a miscarriage in their first pregnancy and who fear that there will be serious results from it. If they have been much disturbed by the miscarriage, they may lose in weight, and then a number of subjective symptoms in their genital life will appear. Though their menstruation appears regularly, lasts the usual time, and is neither more scanty nor more profuse than before, and {433} though their physical conditions are normal as ever, they suffer from bearing down pains and feelings and backache just before menstruation begins; their ovarian regions become sensitive and, if they are constipated, their right ovarian region is likely to become tender, and they develop a set of symptoms that seems to call for surgical interference. If, however, they are put in conditions where they have some other occupation besides themselves and their ills, it is surprising how the case will clear up. They gain in weight, their subjective symptoms disappear and especially they lose the persuasion, so common among them, that any betterment of their symptoms is due to their getting used to the pathological condition present and not to any real improvement of it.

Treatment.—In the treatment of gynecological conditions such as are not necessarily indications for operation, the most important consideration is to reassure the patient's mind and secure the discipline of self-control. If patients are under weight this condition must be corrected. If they are in an unfortunate environment it must be modified, as far as possible. If they are without occupation this must be provided for them. Dominant ideas and morbid auto-suggestion must be overcome—not always an easy task, yet always possible if patience, tact, and skill are exercised. They must be made to realize that the women of the past, before the development of modern gynecology, not only lived useful lives without any of the modern gynecological operations, but that most of them were quite happy in so doing. Even though many of them had physical symptoms, the lack of unfavorable suggestion as to the significance of these prevented mental exaggeration, and morbid dwelling on them was not allowed to produce such a deterioration of the physical condition as to emphasize the pathological conditions. This does not mean that women may not have to be operated on, and, when that is necessary, the operation should be determined on and performed with no more delay than is proper to put the patients into suitable physical condition. But many operations that are undertaken without definite indications merely because the women complain, and it is hoped that an operation will somehow prove of relief, would be replaced with much more final satisfaction and relief by properly directed psychotherapy.

There are many minor pathological conditions such as slight cystic enlargements, hyperemias with tenderness, slight displacements of the ovary, slight dislocations of the uterus or twistings of it that can often be successfully treated the same way. After all, what is considered the normal condition of the feminine internal organs is only an average reached from observation and many deviations from this average cannot be considered abnormal. Many a woman living practically without symptoms, or certainly without such symptoms as to justify an operation, has pathological conditions of her internal organs worse than those for which operations are sometimes suggested because over-sensitive women complain of their symptoms. The rule must be first to relieve the over-sensitiveness and then to determine whether an operation is necessary or not. Pain alone, unless it is of a disabling character or reacts upon the physical health, is not a sufficient indication for operation.

{434}

CHAPTER II

PSYCHIC STATES IN MENSTRUATION

One does not need to be a physician to be familiar with the curious psychic states which develop or are accentuated during the menstrual period. Practically all the peculiarities of the individual are emphasized at this time and if there are any special neurotic conditions or psychic anomalies these become quite marked. All the dreads, for instance, are more noticeable at this time. Women who at all times feel uncomfortable on looking down from a height are likely at this time to be quite overcome by fear and be unable to approach any position from which they might look down for a distance. Women who are afraid of horses, yet conquer their dread sufficiently to ride behind them, cannot do so, or only with great difficulty, during the menstrual period, and the same is true of the dread of cats or other animals. Misophobia, the dread of dirt, may be particularly emphasized at this time and servants are puzzled as to what has come over a woman who was not so punctilious in the matter a short time before.

Irritability.—Dr. Charcot, the famous French nerve specialist, used to say that for a day or two before menstruation and during the first day or two of their period many women were not quite responsible. This is not merely an exaggeration of French contempt for women, for Möbius, the distinguished German neurologist, insisted that there is a certain physiological mental disturbance with distinct hampering of the faculty of judgment (Schwachsinn) normally associated with menstruation.

Few physiologists or gynecologists agree with these extreme views, but there is no doubt that many of the troubles which business men experience with women in their employ begin with hasty words spoken at these periods when the real reason for the irritability is not known. The consciousness of this on the part of some women saves them from much undesirable friction by making them more careful at these periods. Many a domestic misunderstanding begins at these times and is unfortunately allowed to continue because the real reason for it—the instability of disposition due to menstruation—is not recognized.

Lack of Inhibition.—There is no doubt that, except in women of the most stable physical and psychic character, a notable lack of inhibition characterizes all their actions at this time. To think that this is universal, however, would be a mistake. Healthy women deeply occupied with something they like often pass through menstruation absolutely undisturbed, and this is particularly true of the mothers of families. In spite of its exaggeration, it is well to keep the great French specialist's expression in mind, for it helps to explain many things that produce much suffering in the world. This is particularly true now that women are working more and more out of their homes at occupations which often make strenuous calls on them just at periods of the month when they should have more rest than usual. The consequence often is the development of a highly neurotic condition in which psychic {435} symptoms are likely to be prominent as well as a tendency to exaggerate the significance of their feelings which is disturbing to the patient and may even disturb the physician.

Exaggeration of Sensitiveness.—The most striking feature of this is the tendency to exaggerate the meaning of physical symptoms which they have often borne with for a good while without much inconvenience, but which now appeal to them as of serious significance. Any uncomfortable feeling is likely to be dwelt on to such an extent as to be called an unbearable ache or even an excruciating pain, and the patient is prone to connect it with some serious pathological process in the region in which it is felt. If a woman has been reading about some special ailment, or, above all, has been listening to the tale, usually neither plain nor unvarnished, of a friend's medical woes, she is almost sure to think that there must be something seriously wrong with herself. Many a supposed chronic indigestion had its origin in nothing more than the uncomfortable feelings in the stomach region during menstruation, which call attention to that organ and then, by morbid introspection, lead to the exaggeration of various sensations that have always been present but have hitherto been disregarded.

It is a good rule to neglect symptoms that develop during the menstrual period and not to treat them directly until it is plainly seen that they persist afterwards; for symptomatic treatment at this time will cause an over-attention to the condition. And we should be careful not to suggest to a woman at this time that her symptoms may be due to some pathological condition in an important organ. Such a suggestion will almost surely be accepted seriously and dwelt on so much as to become an auto-suggestion that may lead to the disturbance of the function of the organ in question because of the surveillance over it. The diagnosis must be put off until menstruation is over in order that the exaggeration of this period may be eliminated. If this were more commonly done and if women were advised to counteract their feelings at this time as far as possible by occupations of interest to them, there would be much less need of medication. As between rest and strenuous work during the menstrual period, work is probably always the better. Rest with nothing to do emphasizes morbid introspection to such a degree as to make even ordinary feelings unbearable.

Symptomatic Conditions.—It is interesting to note how often affections that are always present give symptoms only during the menstrual period or just before it. Many women, however, suffer considerably about the time of the menstrual period from an extremely tired, painful condition of the leg below the knee which is really due to flatfoot. At other times it gives them little annoyance. Old dislocations and sprains are particularly likely to give bother at this time. All the occupation pains and aches are emphasized. Tiredness becomes a torment. This extreme over-sensitiveness extends to physical ills of all kinds, even those that are trivial. For instance, corns and bunions become almost unbearable, especially if there is any change of the weather with moisture in the air about the time of menstruation. Teeth become sensitive and often will ache when there is little that the dentist can find the matter with them. Women are often suffering from teeth that are supposed to be quite intractable because of over-sensitiveness, while in reality it is only at these certain times that the over-sensitiveness is present.

{436}

Over-reactions.—Even habitual actions which are accomplished without much difficulty at other times are likely to be a source of annoyance about this period. If a young woman has to call out figures or read off lists of names, she soon becomes hoarse, her voice becomes husky and it requires more effort to accomplish her work than at other times. Complaint of sore throat is common about this time, and if there have been any recent changes in the weather this is almost sure to be a premonitory symptom of menstruation. Singers and elocutionists are likely to find their occupations particularly trying at this time and actresses are seldom without considerable physical discomfort that makes playing difficult and unsatisfactory. This happens in all occupations requiring frequently repeated use of particular muscles. Piano-players and typewriters find that their fingers become sensitive at this time. This sensitiveness of the ends of the fingers may become so marked as to prevent these usual occupations, or at least may require their limitation.

Physical Basis of Psychic States.—The physical basis of these troubles is probably more responsible for them than has been thought, though the mental state renders the individual more susceptible to annoyances of any and every kind. Careful weighing seems to show that there is a gain in weight amounting sometimes to three to five pounds toward the end of the menstrual month. This is accompanied by a sense of fullness that is perhaps an actual plethora, as if nature were manufacturing a superabundance of blood in anticipation of the loss. This produces a systemic hyperemia. It is well known that hyperemic areas are more sensitive than tissues in ordinary condition and this seems to be the case in menstrual life. This renders the nervous system more active and irritable and the nerve endings more sensitive. With the menstrual loss this physical condition is relieved and then there is a return to normal with a loss of weight only partly due to the actual blood loss and somewhat to increased excretion in perspiration, in transpiration through the lungs and through all the emunctories.

Treatment.—To know that these psychic disturbances are likely to occur at the time of menstruation is to be prepared for them so as to lessen their effect upon one's self and others. They are much relieved by this frank recognition and the patient understands that with the betterment of the psychic condition by such reassurance the physical symptoms are lessened. Many a woman gives up her occupation at such times who would be much better if she bravely clung to it and resisted the temptation to be moodily occupied with her condition. Above all, she needs to be in the air. Oxidizing processes within the body are slower and while much exercise is not beneficial and may be often harmful, riding in the air, sitting in the air, above all, sleeping where there is an abundance of fresh air is all-important. Every form of exertion will be reflected in increased irritability. Shopping, balls and parties will disturb the woman's mental equilibrium and make it more difficult for her to stand whatever physical discomforts she may have, and also make it hard for her to pursue her ordinary occupation if this is somewhat exacting. Even these, however, must not be given up if the sacrifice involves the throwing of the patient back on self and increases introspection. Diversion of mind and temporizing with symptoms are the basis of therapy at the menstrual period.

{437}

CHAPTER III

AMENORRHEA

No feature of menstrual difficulty shows so clearly the influence of the mind over bodily function, and especially over those genital functions that are supposed to be involuntary and spontaneous, as amenorrhea. Almost any kind of mental trouble may produce a cessation of the menstrual functions. Profound grief or a severe fright nearly always does. Every physician of large experience has seen cases of women who have missed their period because they were disturbed by a fire, or a runaway, or an automobile or railroad accident within a short time before their menstruation should normally occur. Even slighter shocks may have a similar effect, and a profound shock of any kind will seriously disturb menstruation. The most frequent effect is to inhibit it, but it may be anticipated or delayed, and where there is a tendency to too profuse a flow, it may produce menorrhagia.

Every physician knows that much less serious mental influences than a profound shock or fright may somewhat disturb menstruation and, in young women at least, this disturbance is nearly always in the direction of lessened flow and amenorrhea. Home-sickness, for instance, will often have this effect. Many of the foreign-born domestics who come to this country have serious disturbances of their menstrual flow, usually a diminution, during the first three or four months after they arrive in America. This may, of course, be due in part to change of climate, change of food and change of habits of life. These girls while in their European homes have often been accustomed to be much more out of doors and to have more exercise in the open air than they have here.

That the mental state has much to do with menstruation may be appreciated from the fact that serious changes of her state of life may be accompanied by amenorrheal symptoms even when the patient stays in the same climate and under conditions not different physically from those under which she has lived. Country girls who come to the city often suffer from such symptoms. Young women who enter convents sometimes have these symptoms for some months, and this is so well recognized as to be expected in a certain number of cases. Indeed, there is danger that it should be attributed too much to the change of mental state, and that other factors, such as incipient tuberculosis, or disease of the ductless glands, or anemic states, which are responsible for it, may fail to be appreciated because of the ready explanation afforded by the mental factor. General experience shows that the attitude of mind of a patient toward menstruation, the expectancy of it at a particular time, and a good general physical condition that predisposes to it, are quite as important for its regularity as the specific physiological conditions which naturally bring it about.

Fright and Amenorrhea.—Fright particularly may disturb menstruation in many ways. Occasionally the disturbance of menstruation consequent upon shock lasts for months or even years. At times when a woman between thirty-five and forty is seriously frightened, especially by terror that endures {438} intensely for some hours, the sort that is said to blanch the hair in a single night—and there are well-authenticated instances—menstruation never recurs or if it does recur it is vicariously from some other portion of the body than the genital tract. Among my notes is a case of a woman frightened by a revolver which a maniac had flourished for hours at her while she dared not make a move nor a sign. Her menstruation stopped completely for a time and then came back irregularly and usually from the ear. The bleeding was from the pierce in the lobule which had been made for earrings, and before it started a large swelling of this would come on in the course of an hour, often not subsiding for days. In another case a woman who was frightened during menstruation by an insane person flourishing a knife near her had for several years after an extremely irregular menstruation, and usually only the molimina in the genital tract, while the bleeding was from the nose. Deep emotion can very seriously affect menstruation.

Pseudocyesis.—The mind may bring about a cessation of menstruation in another way without any other factor interfering and in spite of the fact that physiological conditions would all seem to be favorable to its regular occurrence. We have many cases in medical literature in which married women anxious to have children have concluded that they were pregnant, and have had complete cessation of their menstruation for months with all the symptoms of beginning pregnancy, so as to deceive even careful physicians. The best known historical instance is that of Queen Mary, the eldest daughter of Henry VIII of England, who, nearly forty when she married Philip II of Spain, was very anxious to have children. Not long after her marriage menstruation stopped and all the ordinary symptoms of beginning pregnancy developed. Her condition was widely heralded throughout the kingdom; then, after a time, to the intense disappointment of the Queen and her friends, it proved that she was not pregnant but that her mental attitude had produced the series of symptoms that proved so deceptive. These cases of pseudocyesis are so likely to occur that a physician in dealing with a woman, who being rather well on in years when she marries is anxious to have children, must be on his guard and he must always take into account the possibility of a pseudo-pregnancy and must be careful not to be deceived by symptoms that would ordinarily indicate beyond doubt the beginning of pregnancy. Even experts have been deceived in such cases, and it is in them that accurate rules for the certain detection of pregnancy are most needed.

These symptoms have reference not only to the uterus, but also at times to other organs. They are not merely subjective, but sometimes become so objective as almost to demonstrate the diagnosis of pregnancy, and yet a mental condition is the only source of the changes. For instance, cases of false pregnancy have been reported in which, besides the gradual enlarging of the abdomen with many of the signs of pregnancy accompanying that phenomenon, there has been an enlargement of the breasts and even the secretion of milk. In a few cases the enlargement of the abdomen has been accompanied by pigmentation and the areola of the nipple has also become pigmented. This is not surprising, since corresponding changes take place in connection with fibroid tumors, and the deposit of pigment is not a symptom of pregnancy, but only a result of the congestion which takes place in these structures during their enlargement.

{439}

Amenorrhea from Dread.—In some cases all the symptoms of pregnancy develop, or at least there is complete cessation of menstruation, as a consequence of nervousness and dread of the occurrence of pregnancy. Unmarried women who fear that they may have become pregnant by indiscretion, sometimes become so worried over their condition that, without any physiological reason, they miss one or more periods and thus add to their nervous state and further inhibit menstruation, though usually two months is the limit of such amenorrhea and the menstrual flow commonly makes its reappearance shortly before or after the time of the third period. Occasionally, however, in the case of anxiously expectant married women further symptoms of pregnancy may appear and the case becomes more complicated. Every physician of considerable experience has seen such patients, and doubtless much of the harvest which advertisers reap from drugs that are supposed to produce abortion comes from nervous young women who are not really pregnant, but have inhibited their menstruation by worry, and who take these medicines with confidence and have the menstrual flow restored by trust in their efficacy.

Ductless Gland Disease.—Of course, in many cases of amenorrhea there are serious underlying constitutional conditions which may or may not be amenable to treatment, but the possibilities of which must always be thought of. One case of amenorrhea I saw in recent years proved to be due to a beginning acromegaly. There was no sign of enlargement of the hands, though there had been a coarsening of the face which was attributed to growth and to the fact that the girl was taking much horseback exercise in all weathers. She had a headache for which no remedy seemed to be of any avail, and when the amenorrhea developed it was naturally thought that the headache must be due to gynecologic conditions. Nothing was found on investigation, however, and eventually the gradual development of the symptoms of acromegaly showed what was really the basic cause. Occasionally diseases of other ductless glands, as the thyroid, may have amenorrhea as one of the first symptoms. It is seldom that any serious thyroid condition develops without disturbance of menstruation, but this is less frequently in the direction of diminution than toward profusion and prolongation. In some cases, however, one or more periods is missed in the early development of the disease. In this, however, others of the characteristic tripod of symptoms—rapid heart, tremor, exophthalmes—are sure to be present even though the enlargement of the thyroid is not noticeable.

Tuberculosis.—But more important than these causes of amenorrhea is the early development of tuberculosis. In some cases, even before there is any cough that calls attention to the condition, or when the cough has been considered to be one of those myths now fortunately passing, "a cold that hangs on," the cessation of menstruation may depend entirely on the weakness and anemia due to the growth of tubercle bacilli in the lungs.

Inanition Amenorrhea.—Sometimes indigestion, or what is supposed to be indigestion, may be at the root of the amenorrhea. In many cases it really is not true indigestion that is present, but a disinclination for food which has increased to such a degree as to bring about a lowered state of nutrition. In nervous young women and, above all, in nervous spinsters beyond forty, disturbances of menstruation consequent upon lack of nutrition are not infrequent. Often their indigestion is considered to be a reflex from their genital {440} organs, when, on the contrary, whatever disturbance of their genital organs is present is due to the inanition which has developed because they have not been eating enough. Many of these women literally starve themselves, and they, must be persuaded to eat once more and taught what to eat, and their weight must be watched until it gets up to what is normal for their height.

Psychotherapy and Treatment.—The treatment of amenorrhea on psychotherapeutic principles will be readily understood from the fact that there is a distinct psychic element in practically all the cases touched on in this chapter. This psychic element is generally appreciated and admitted. If a woman is accustomed to connect certain physical incidents with disturbances of menstruation, then those disturbances are almost sure to recur. As a rule, many an incident said to be disturbing to the function would probably have no influence upon it but for the dread connected with it and the anticipation of some interference. In all cases of amenorrhea, then, the patient's mind must be put into a favorable state and suggestions must be made that will lead to the expectancy of menstruation at the next regular period. If the mind can cause menstruation to cease, as is clear from experience, any inhibition from this source must be removed and its power set to bring relief to these patients. Drugs should not be neglected, and general physical conditions must be improved, but if the patient's mind continues to be unfavorably affected towards her menstruation, its satisfactory return will be delayed until somehow mind as well as body are co-ordinates for the resumption of the function.

The best testimony to the value of psychotherapy in amenorrhea is found in the success of many of the remedies used for the condition, which, in the successive phases of medical development, have included all sorts of home treatments, many types of quack medicines, and innumerable proprietary combinations. Many of these have acquired a reputation for efficacy not justified by any direct pharmaceutic effects which we now know them to possess. From the familiar gin and hot water, through the various combinations of aloes and the tonic remedies of a later time, only the most general and obvious effects could have been produced by the medicines, yet apparently specific reactions have followed them in the menstrual cycle. But this was because the mind of the patient was prepared by the taking of the remedies and unfavorable suggestions as to menstruation were removed. Above all, with amelioration of the general health, constipation being relieved, the appetite restored and the whole tone of the system improved, nature became capable of taking up once more the menstrual function. What was accomplished by indirect psychotherapy in the past can now be done much better by direct mental suggestion, when at the same time various remedial measures in other therapeutic departments are employed as auxiliaries. But the physician must be sure that the mind of the patient is properly disposed or remedies may fail and symptoms continue.

CHAPTER IV

DYSMENORRHEA

Practically every woman of menstrual age has more or less discomfort during menstruation. In most cases this does not rise beyond a heavy depressed {441} feeling shortly before menstruation begins, followed by a sense of weight and discomfort in the back and then some sensations more or less acutely uncomfortable due to congestion in the pelvis, which begin to be relieved with the commencement of the flow and then gradually disappear. Even in otherwise healthy women, various achy feelings of distention are often felt in the neighborhood of the ovaries, but these would scarcely be described as pain, unless the patient is over-sensitive. The effect upon the disposition is more marked and more universal. Some women are inclined to be irritable and hard to get along with for a few days before their menstruation and sometimes during the whole of its course. The frank recognition of this fact by them and a consultation of the calendar when they find that everything seems to be going against them and that everybody is lacking in sympathy, usually leads to an appreciation of the fact that the trouble is in themselves rather than in those around them, and their condition becomes more bearable. It is curious, however, to note how often this is forgotten, with consequent give-and-take of irritation in their environment that makes the nervous and mental condition worse and emphasizes the physical symptoms.

The term dysmenorrhea, from the Greek, means difficult menstruation and is usually associated with painful conditions in connection with the menstrual flow. It may be applied, however, to various uncomfortable feelings, to superirritability, to fatigue, to lack of energy, or even to more vague discomforts at this period. The discomforts are usually spoken of as pains, especially after the patient has been dwelling on them for some time and has been reading patent medicine advertisements that tell of how women suffer in silence, but analysis often shows that they are sensations of pressure, of compression, of achy distress at most, and sometimes only of unusual feelings—paresthesiae—that having got over the threshold of consciousness, through concentration of attention upon them, are occupying the center of the stage of mental activity to the exclusion of all serious interests.

The serious difficulties of menstruation are due to definite pathological conditions such as displacements of the uterus, affections of the uterine mucosa and of the ovaries. There are, however, many cases where the trouble is merely functional, dependent on conditions that can be easily corrected without serious surgical or even lengthy medical treatment, and where the patient's attitude of mind towards the trouble is the most important factor in the medical aspect of the case. As a matter of fact, many of the discomforts and even serious pains complained of in connection with menstruation are due rather to the patient's incapacity to bear even slight discomfort with reasonable patience and without exaggerated reaction than to the actual pain inflicted by whatever disturbance of function and tissue may be present. People differ very much in their power to stand discomfort and what seems quite trivial to one becomes unbearable torture to another. With this in mind it is possible to relieve many women who suffer from dysmenorrhea from their discomforts so that they shall only have to bear what is every woman's heritage in the matter. Successful management of these cases will save them from the supposed necessity of being operated on, which is likely to be constantly suggested to them in an age when women so often talk of their operations.

The amount of pain suffered from any cause is dependent on two factors, the pathological condition and the power of the individual to withstand {442} discomfort. When we are irritated, when we are very tired, when we have fever, when we suffer from want of food or lack of sleep or any other condition that exhausts vitality, even slight pains become hard to bear. In relieving pain it is as important to remember this lessened capacity to stand discomfort as it is to get at the cause of the discomfort itself. This habit of standing discomfort with reasonable patience is one of the best remedies for lessening suffering, especially when it is known that the discomfort is only temporary and the end of it is in sight.

Physical Condition.—In the treatment of suffering incident to the menstrual period, then, the correction of all conditions that may increase nervous irritability and make patients less capable of standing pain should be the first care. Young women who are thin and anemic, especially if they are more than ten per cent. under weight, are likely to suffer much at their menstrual periods for two reasons—through their lack of power to withstand discomfort and owing to the fact that their ovaries and the uterus itself are especially sensitive, probably through lack of nutrition consequent upon their general condition. In these cases local treatment is not as necessary as improvement of the patient's general condition and the raising of her general bodily tone.

The bowels must, of course, be regulated, partly for the sake of the general condition and the fact that it is very hard to have a regular appetite unless there is a daily evacuation, and partly also because the presence of an accumulation of fecal material in the lower bowel is likely to produce congestion in the pelvic region. This added to the normal congestion due to the menstrual function may cause undue pressure upon sensitive nerves in the ovaries and uterus. Indeed a regulation of the function of the bowels is immediately followed by a lessening of the menstrual discomfort as well as by a general improvement. Many women find that the taking of a gentle purge a day or two before the menstrual period serves to make that period a source of less discomfort than it would otherwise be, and undoubtedly the suggestive value of such a remedy persuades many women that their discomfort should be lessened.

Professor Goodell's reminder that women have many organs outside of their pelvis is important in dysmenorrhea. Almost any ailment that drains a woman's strength and brings a series of irritations to bear upon her nervous system will be reflected in her genito-urinary system and will cause discomfort during the menstrual period. Over and over again the physician finds that the true source of the menstrual discomfort is not in the essentially feminine organs, but in the digestive organs or occasionally even in such distant organs as the lungs, and that proper attention to these brings relief during the menstrual period. Just as soon as they realize that this is not a new affection but only a reflex from their other ailment, whatever it may be, they stand it with much better spirit and their complaints diminish.

Anyone who has seen the difference between the reaction to menstrual moliminia when patients are in good condition and when they are otherwise run down will realize how much a matter of over-reaction to symptoms dysmenorrhea may be. Teachers who begin the school year, invigorated by their vacations, scarcely notice their periods, but at the end of the course, when run down by months of hard teaching work and especially by the confinement of the winter, they find the strain extremely hard to bear. In many of these cases an examination by a specialist seems to reveal something that might be {443} benefited by operation. There may be various uterine displacements, sensitive ovaries, perhaps slightly enlarged yet often not distinctly pathological, but just as soon as the physical condition is made normal, the symptoms given by these conditions completely disappear. Women who have nothing particular to do, who talk much about themselves and their ills, who have had friends operated on and heard much talk about the subject, are soon convinced that only an operation will do them good. Once *that* suggestion is implanted in their minds, the hypnotic dread of the operation and the morbid attraction of being a center of interest and commiseration will make them exaggerate their symptoms to such a degree that operation becomes almost inevitable.

Moral Fiber.—It is often said that modern women, as the result of civilization, refinement, and city life, are of laxer physical fiber and therefore cannot stand the ills that their grandmothers bore with equanimity and considered as nothing more than what was to be expected in this imperfect existence. Most physicians must feel, however, that the increased laxity is not so much of the physical as of the moral fiber. We have not weaker bodies than our forefathers, but weaker wills. This is especially so with those who have much time to think about themselves, and, therefore, is more true, of women than of men, though in our generation men also have become very introspective. I have seen—and I am sure that my experience is a common one among physicians—delicate women who seemed unable to stand any trial or hardship successfully, placed by unfortunate conditions—such as the sudden death of a husband, or his failure in business—in circumstances that were extremely hard to stand up bravely against. Not only did they stand it, but they had better health, they had less complaint of pains of all kinds, particularly in this matter of dysmenorrhea, than they had before.

Pain and Occupation of Mind.—The more claims a woman has on her attention the less likely is she to be bothered at her monthly periods. If she does not *have* to get up in the morning because there are no insistent obligations upon her, she is likely to lie in bed and worry about herself and by concentrating her attention on her ills will make them worse than they are. But if she has to be up and doing, if household cares cannot be put off, if she has to earn her living by working every day, she not only succeeds in doing it, but often also forgets her ills to a great extent in her occupation. Of course, there are pathological conditions that cannot be put off in this way, and if there are serious uterine changes, or if an infection has spread along the tubes to the ovaries, there will be symptoms that cannot be distracted away. Even where there are minor pathological conditions, however, occupation of mind will make pain less annoying and even make it quite negligible. We know our own experience with toothache. This is a real pain and with a real pathological condition of the most material kind. The congestion of the sensitive dentine or the irritation of an exposed nerve filament causes about as severe pain as it is given to mortals to bear. Even with toothache, however, we can by occupying ourselves with friends, or with a pleasant book, or a game of cards, or the theater, so diminish the annoyance consequent upon the pain as to be comparatively comfortable. If anything completely occupies our attention as, for instance, a fire or an accident, or bad news from a friend, then it may be hours afterwards before we realize that we were suffering from a toothache. Since this will happen with a dental nerve, why should it not {444} happen to branches of the genital nerve? There is no reason why one should be more sensitive than the other, and whatever reason there is is rather in favor of the dental nerve giving more bother, since it is nearer the center of the nervous system and these nerves are usually said to be more sensitive.

Working Women.—With regard to painful menstruation, the habits of many country people, and of the European peasantry generally, furnish valuable indications of the power of work to dissipate discomfort. During my medical student days in Vienna I had the opportunity to know rather well a group of women who were engaged in working on a building. They carried up the bricks and mortar for the men and worked the windlasses by which heavy materials were carried to the different stories, and they mixed the mortar and prepared the building materials generally. These women, living constantly in the air and working very hard, had almost no symptoms of menstrual difficulty. They never laid off at this time except in a few cases in which subinvolution after pregnancies and genital infections had left conditions that made it hard to understand how they worked at all.

I learned in addition from them, for most of them came from the country, that the women who work so commonly in the fields in central Europe have little difficulty with menstruation and practically do not know that it is coming on them until the show indicates its presence. I had known before how true this was for the Irish peasant women. This seems to be the normal healthy condition, and the state of mind of these women aids this satisfactory state of affairs. They rather look down upon women who complain at this time as being of such inferior health as to be despised. Doubtless if they were persuaded, as so many seem to be, that a woman must expect to have a serious time, or at least a great deal of discomfort about this period, they would have it, too. Of course, they have some difference of feeling at this time. They feel more tired in the evenings, and they awake in the morning less rested, but that is no more than the changes in the weather bring to men.

On the coast of Brittany and Normandy many of the women rake for shellfish. Their custom is to wade into the water and, standing with the water often above the knee and waves sometimes washing as high as the waist, to rake all day for the shellfish that they are seeking. They do not lay off from this occupation, as a rule, when their menstruation is on them, but continue as if nothing were the matter, and there are very few complaints of menstrual troubles among them. Such occupation would seem to be positively counter-indicated, but long years of experience have shown them that there is no need of interruptions in their work and as they need every centime that they can obtain in this way for the support of their families, they continue even in very cold weather, when it would seem inevitable that this must produce serious results.

It is not uncommon for a young woman, who, while her family was in good circumstances, was a severe trial to everyone for a week more or less, every month, to become quite free from trouble for herself and others when, owing to a change in the family circumstances, she has had to take up some occupation for a living. I have notes of cases of this kind in which the pain was so severe that, after several years of medication and external applications, it was decided to dilate the cervix uteri in the hope of affording relief. The relief thus afforded, however, was only temporary. A little later in life, {445} however, the necessity of earning a living has in some cases quite freed these young women from the torments that sent them so frequently to their physicians.

We need the report of many more of such gynecological conditions which get better as a consequence of occupation of mind without any other treatment. We have any number of reports of benefits derived from operation, but not infrequently these reports refer only to a few months after the operation, when the strong mental suggestion of the performance of the operation and the general betterment of health consequent upon care during convalescence are still acting upon the patient, and she has the benefit of the gain in weight and strength that usually follows because of hope, appetite, exercise in the air, etc. Not infrequently in these cases there are, later on, sad relapses into painful conditions quite as severe as before, while, on the other hand, some change in the circumstances of the individual, or some intense preoccupation of mind a few years after, brings lasting cure, thus showing that it was the mental state which was at the root of the condition rather than any bodily affection.

Spasmodic Dysmenorrhea.—There are two forms of dysmenorrhea that have been the subject of much study. One of them consists of cramp-like pains which occur some time before menstruation, are relieved if the flow is copious, but continue if it is scanty. This affection has often been attributed to mechanical obstruction. Nearly twenty years ago Dr. Champneys in his Harveian Lectures on Painful Menstruation discussed this subject, and showed that the mechanical explanation while very simple and popular was probably not correct. His conclusion was that the dysmenorrhea was more frequently due to conditions outside of the uterus than in that organ. He recommended plenty of healthy exercise between the periods and especially riding if the patient were not a working woman, regular activity of the bowels with epsom salts as probably the most valuable single remedy, and then a number of drugs such as guiacum and sulphur that are not specifics but have a general effect. In his experience castoreum, a strongly suggestive remedy, gave more relief than anything else. He advised against local treatment unless there was a very definite reason for it and frankly expressed the opinion that the complaints were often due more to an incapacity to stand the slight discomfort that is more or less inevitably associated with the congestive state that precedes menstruation than to any pathological lesion.

Membranous Dysmenorrhea.—This affection like membranous colitis remains one of the mysteries of pathology and etiology. There is no doubt, however, that there are large nervous elements in its production and that it is worse at times of worry, while mental factors of many kinds influence its occurrence and also its relief. In his Harveian Lectures Dr. Champneys discussed the questions connected with it very well and his monograph is a classic on the subject. Many drugs have seemed successful and then have failed. Castoreum has done good in this as in spasmodic dysmenorrhea. A number of gynecological methods of treatment have been successful when first applied, when physician and patient were both confident of their value, and then later has failed. Probably nothing does more good than getting the patient's mind off her condition, securing such occupation as will not permit of introspection to any extent, though of course treating surgically whatever requires operation. It must not be forgotten that while many of those suffering from the disease {446} complain of pain, not a few sufferers from it have no symptoms of this kind and their condition is discovered more or less by accident. After this there is likely to be much more discomfort from it. All this must be borne in mind in its treatment.

Minor Ovarian Lesions.—In many cases there is vague discomfort in the ovarian region about the time of menstruation, and the ovary is found to be somewhat enlarged or perhaps dislocated. In these cases if there is continued complaint of pain, operation will almost surely

245

be advised and frequently cysts are found. This is considered to be justification enough for the removal of the ovaries or at least for their resection. It is doubtful, however, whether ovarian cysts in the majority of cases are really a pathological condition. Those who are engaged in spaying cattle think it almost if not quite normal for cysts to exist in the ovaries. Whether this is not also true of women we have not the data to determine. In a number of the patients who are operated upon for this condition there is a relapse of symptoms, and there seems to be no doubt but that whatever good is accomplished comes from the expectation of relief followed by the weeks of rest and quiet in bed and very often the gain in weight which succeeds the operation. Whether something of this kind would not follow from the simpler procedure of improving the general health is an open question.

It is sometimes insisted that the general health will not improve in gynecological cases unless the offending pathological condition is removed. This is true if the patient is persuaded that there is some pathological condition present which must be corrected or else she will not be better, and if favorable suggestion cannot be used to advantage. If, however, these patients understand from the beginning that probably the local condition, which gives the symptoms, is due rather to their general health than to a definite lesion, there is more probability of improvement. It is surprising how many of these cases are relieved by an improvement of the general health, by the relief of constipation, by the decrease of congestion by laxatives, and by the persuasion that there is nothing which will go on to serious developments (this is the most disturbing of dreads) but only a condition that will probably get no worse and the symptoms from which may yield to general treatment.

The popularity of many so-called remedies for women's diseases is due to their success in lifting the veil of discouragement and, by alcoholic and other tonic stimulation, helping the women into a better general condition and a more favorable frame of mind.

The Individual.—In all cases of dysmenorrhea, then, it is important not to be influenced too much by the complaints (for here, as Broadbent insists with regard to angina pectoris, the more complaint we have the less serious the condition will often be), but to investigate the patient's condition and, where there is not some definite and serious pathological lesion, to analyze the beginning and the development of the individual case and eliminate the neurotic elements. Often the menstrual difficulty is due to suggestion, as the patient has been in contact with others who were sufferers and caught her complaint from them by psychic contagion. Special investigation is needed as to her occupation of mind. This must be provided for her. Nothing else will save her from herself. Travel may do it, exercise may be helpful, but an occupation in which she is deeply interested, especially if it involves {447} association with other people, is the best basis of psychic treatment. Improvement of the general health and the relief of various symptoms are auxiliaries.

Unfavorable Suggestion.—After consulting with many women physicians, with many women who have lived active lives, with many superiors of religious orders in consultation about their religious women, I cannot but conclude that painful menstruation is ever so much oftener a result of mental and nervous states than of organic disturbances. Unfortunately a tradition has now been established that women suffer much at this time, so many of them give in to their feelings, exaggerate their discomfort, dwell on their sensations, affect the blood supply to the genital organs through the sympathetic nervous system, actually produce functionally pathological hyperemia where only physiological was present (the simile of the blush makes this easy to understand), and finally set up a condition that is actually painful, though there was only some discomforting sense of compression and congestion before. We have been educating young girls in disease, not in health. Plato pleaded for the opposite. After these 2,400 years we might take it up seriously.

CHAPTER V

MENORRHAGIA

While the influence of the mind in producing painful menstruation and a much diminished menstrual flow is well recognized, the connection between the mind and an increased menstrual flow is not so generally appreciated. Usually profuse menstruation (especially when it reaches a height where it would properly be called menorrhagia) is considered to be due to some serious pathological condition. Its most frequent cause is undoubtedly subinvolution of the uterus after pregnancy, or an overgrowth of the uterine mucosa because of some pathological condition—usually an infection. While menorrhagia is often attributed to colds or to getting the feet wet (and undoubtedly the disturbance of the circulation consequent upon wet feet is an active factor in the production of an increased menstrual flow) there is no doubt that in most cases there is some more distinctly local cause at work. Another important cause of profuse menstruation is the presence of a fibroid tumor or other neoplasm which brings an increased blood supply to the uterus and a consequent greater elimination at the menstrual epoch.

In most cases of subinvolution a curettage, at least, will have to be done. Often the use of extremely hot douches, that is, just as hot as can be borne, may accomplish much. Such quantities as a quart or two are useless; several gallons should be taken, and that not in the awkward cramped postures in which douching is sometimes done and in which it cannot be expected to accomplish its purpose, but in the reclining position and to be followed by an hour or two of rest with the hips elevated. This treatment will be more effective if women do not get the idea that an operation will surely have to be done on them. Operations are now so much spoken about that some women apparently do not feel that they have had quite all the experience that is coming to them in life unless they have at least one to their credit. If they can be made to realize that, in the past before the days of operative gynecology, most such cases recovered of themselves and that now if courage is {448} resumed, appetite strengthened through the will, constipation relieved, an abundance of outdoor air secured (exercise is not so necessary), recovery will probably be more complete than after an operation, there would be much less need of operations than at present.

The material conditions based upon pathological changes which usually produce menorrhagia hardly seem amenable to influence by the patient's state of mind, yet experience demonstrates that much can be done for these patients by setting their minds at rest, by improving their general condition, by soothing their worry as to what the profuse flow means. Many nervous patients have quite normal menstruation, as regards the length and quantity of flow, until some serious disturbance occurs in their mental state. I have had patients who for months would have a perfectly normal menstrual flow of three to five days to whom a serious mental disturbance always brings a profuse menstruation. The arrest of a woman by mistake just before or at the beginning of her menstrual period will often cause a greatly increased flow and great weakness will follow. Women approaching the menopause already have a tendency to an increased flow though not beyond the bounds of what might be considered normal, and at this time almost any shock will produce profuse menstruation and lead to prostration. If the secondary anemia from this is not overcome during the interval profuse menstruations may succeed each other for many months.

The necessity for reassuring these women, therefore, becomes evident. Most of us have seen women who were worried at having a slightly increased menstruation, and who had been told that they had a fibroid tumor which was producing the increased menstruation, and which would have to be removed if it continued to bring on this serious condition. Such a suggestion inevitably leads to a series of more profuse menstruations during the following months. Such women worry over their state and dread an operation. They do not eat well and, even though they do not lose much in weight, they often become distinctly anemic. This anemia adds to the tendency to a freer flow and as a consequence the menstrual period is lengthened in time and increased in amount. This soon brings them to operation, though very often there has been no increase in size of the fibroid tumor and there is no more reason for operation than there was when they were first examined.

I have had under observation during the last two years a patient in whom the diagnosis of a fibroid brought this unfortunate result. Her menstruation had been profuse and prolonged before but now it became still longer and lasted nearly fifteen days each month. As she lost much in weight, was run down in strength, became self-centered, stayed more at home, and took less exercise, the resultant depression in her general condition emphasized the menorrhagia. As soon as it was made clear to her that her case had but one indication for operation— the loss of blood and that the fibroid was so small that it might well be allowed to remain until after her menopause, when involution would probably prevent further unfavorable action, she took heart, began to exercise, ate more heartily, her marked constipation was relieved, she slept better and in three months her menstruation was almost normal. For many months she had no menorrhagia.

I have seen other cases in which amelioration of symptoms came just as soon as the patient learned that, by improvement in the general health, there {449} was a possibility of lessening the tendency to hemorrhage and thus of putting off the necessity for operation for a time at least, if not until such natural changes occurred in the system as to lessen the danger from the growing tumor. I have in mind the wife of a physician whose menopause was delayed for some ten years as a consequence of a good-sized fibroid growth. She had it when she first came to me, and I watched the case for some seven years, and she absolutely refused to entertain the idea of operation. I set her mind at rest as to the seriousness of the growth provided the bleeding was not injurious and no infective conditions occurred through the intestinal walls to complicate the condition and cause adhesions. Whenever she worked hard, or whenever she was much worried, she would have alarming flooding. Under ordinary circumstances, however, when things did not go awry, she had a menstruation somewhat more profuse than normal and of five or six days in length. This continued from her fiftieth to her fifty-fifth year, and then gradually subsided. She is still alive at the age of sixty and, though she has had many trials and hardships at the end of her life, she is healthy and considers herself much better off than if she had had an operation. I doubt whether this is true, that is, if the operation had been done twenty years ago. But, after watching such a case and realizing that operations on fibroids are more often fatal than any other of the gynecologic operations that do not involve serious conditions, a physician is justified in tiding women over the time to their menopause and then letting nature dispose. Infective incidents pointing to the formation of adhesions are a contraindication to this policy, however.

The sufferer in this case was one of the most patient of women. She had had to suffer much in mind and in body as the result of being left almost destitute after a life of luxury, yet she seldom complained. One might almost think her indifferent to hardship if one did not know her well. She was not at all a stoic but she never allowed her imagination to run away with her, she bore the ills of the day without thinking of what was going to come next week and she worried as little as possible under the circumstances. The ordinary woman, nervous and excitable, would have broken down under the strain that was placed upon her but she promises to live to a good age and her trials have not hurt her vitality nor spoiled her disposition and she looks the world in the face with surprising cheerfulness. This state of mind modifies even fibroid menorrhagia favorably.

Fibroids have been reported "cured" by so many different remedies—local applications, acupuncture, hot needles, electricity in various forms, even internal treatment, which afterwards proved quite unavailing—that it is manifest that the mind plays a large rôle in controlling the symptoms.

Before operation it is important to put the minds of these patients into an attitude of confidence, for operators who make it a point to secure the confidence of their patients, or who for some reason have their full faith, have better results in these cases than others of equal surgical skill.

In unmarried women the development of a small fibroid with its reflex disturbances is sure to be followed by excessive reaction in many ways. Nervous symptoms are likely to be marked and the increase in menstruation is usually much more profuse as a consequence of the solicitude than because of the fibroid. Some of these tumors which, though of small size, are so situated with regard to the nervous and circulatory systems of the uterus as to produce {450} profuse menstruation even in women of phlegmatic disposition. In these patients operations will be necessary whenever the loss of blood makes it clear that the drain on the system is producing serious effects. There are cases, however, in which the menorrhagia is not due directly to the fibroid, but rather to its effect upon the general system and this may be lessened very much by reassurance, by regulation of the general health, by resumption of exercise and toning up of appetite and, above all, by relief of the constipation which so often complicates these cases. Fibroids may or may not continue to grow. The removal of one is no

247

guarantee that others will not form, nor that others are not present in very small form which will develop later. As a rule, there can be no question of the removal of the uterus unless conditions are serious.

If in spite of general treatment and the calming of the patient as far as possible profuse menstruation continues, it is an indication for surgical intervention. Psychotherapy may readily be abused in these cases, but it has a distinct use, and its application is more frequently successful than has been thought; but it must be deliberately employed. When, however, menorrhagia is a symptom of some serious progressive condition, psychotherapy will do harm rather than good. I have known women whose menstruation was stopped and then recurred and even became profuse reassured that this was only a symptom of the menopause when it was the first symptom of a cancer. In such cases there must be no temporizing or reassurance, but a careful determination of the actual condition must be made and immediate operation done if it seems necessary. Psychotherapy may have a place in incurable cancer, but in other cases it has none at all except to calm the patient for operation where surgery may be of service.

CHAPTER VI

THE MENOPAUSE

While the phase of feminine sexual life which involves the cessation of menstruation is physiological and not morbid, it is so commonly associated with physical and mental symptoms difficult to bear that, practically always, it sends the woman to a physician. This is as true of the artificial menopause induced by removal of ovaries as it is of the normal process by which, in the course of time, ovarian function comes to an end and changes are brought about in the system consequent upon the absence of ovarian secretion. The ovaries, like many other organs, have two functions. One, that of ovulation, is so prominent that the other, the internal secretion, has been too much neglected. How important this is, however, may be judged from the change that comes over feminine nature after its cessation. Much of the emotionality of woman disappears, not a few of her special sex qualities are modified and even masculine physical peculiarities may assert themselves. The physical effects of the ovarian internal secretion may be inferred from the definite tendency to grow stout which results from its suppression by the menopause. Certain changes in the organism are inevitable then, and the only hope of therapy is to keep them from disturbing life processes.

Neutralizing Unfavorable Mental Attitude.—Psychotherapy can do more {451} for the troubles of the menopause than any other treatment. The symptoms of the change of life in the long ago, if we can trust traditions, were not so troublesome as they are now. Only rarely did women suffer from it as they are supposed to suffer at the present time. Women are so persuaded that there is to be much suffering, or at least prolonged physical discomfort, as to make it difficult for them to be quite themselves. They are prone to think that their physical symptoms are noted, and that their condition is a subject of remark. This adds to the difficulty of bearing in patience whatever symptoms are present. The introspective attitude of our time has reacted upon such affections as occur in the menopause, and, by creating an abnormal susceptibility of mind, has added much not only to its possibility but also to its actuality of suffering. Drugs or other remedial measures will modify the conditions only partially and temporarily. The mental prophylaxis of suggestion must alter the state of mind both before and during the progress of the condition.

Favorable Suggestion.—After the menopause women are less disturbed by emotional strains and troubles of any kind than before. They settle down into more placid, easy-going lives. They are not subjected to the monthly interruption of their routine of work or amusement, everything comes a little easier to them, and they are not, to use the word in its physiological sense, so irritable—that is, so responsive in reaction. They are not so likely to respond to slight irritations, and are often physically and mentally more content with life. This must be insisted upon, for, at the present time, unfavorable suggestion with regard to the menopause is the universal rule. Women look for the worst from it, and their expectation makes conditions less tolerable than they really are. Most women dread it as if it were the beginning of the end of life, the first descent into old age, while it is often the dawn of a larger and broader life free from sexual and other irritations, and with better possibilities of accomplishment.

Definite Prescriptions.—These patients are best reassured by being told that every woman who has lived to the age of fifty has gone through a similar experience and that they have all, with rare exceptions, revived with health of both body and mind. It is more important to insist on the patients cultivating a certain gaiety of disposition, to plan for regular diversions two or three times a week, to see that they are not too much alone and that they find abundant occupation of mind and body, than to try to combat their manifold symptoms by drugs or local measures. Of course, their physical functions must be kept normal. It is surprising, however, how much improvement can be brought about in the menopause symptoms by definite prescriptions as to the time to be spent in the open air—at least two or three hours a day— with regard to having a definite diversion of some kind in mind two or three days ahead to which they look forward with pleasure, and by convincing them that whenever they allow themselves to dwell much on their condition, their symptoms of discomfort will become so severe as to be intolerable, while when they are occupied with other things they will find them quite easy to bear.

As a rule, mothers of families with many cares and diversions of mind, with little time to think of themselves, do not suffer much at this period, or at least not nearly so much as do those who are without these diversions. The more time a woman has to think about herself at this period, the worse for {452} her. Her irritability of mind will be reflected upon her physical condition and make it worse. In the olden time mothers of families went through it and no one knew about it, or even noticed that there was anything the matter with them except possibly a little increased irritability at certain periods. Neither menstruation nor the menopause is necessarily connected with more than passing discomfort, if the patient is in good health. This is perfectly true if symptoms are not brooded over, if there is not too much expectancy of evils, and the feelings and manifestations which do not deserve the name of symptoms are taken as a matter of course. Best of all, let the woman keep her mind well occupied with many duties—with care for others, the helpless, the ailing, around her, instead of with herself and her passing ills.

Dread of Insanity.—There are few women who go through this period without the hideous thought that possibly they may go crazy. This is especially likely if, as a consequence of the exaggerated desire for seclusion that many women have at this time, they do not get out into the air nor exercise as much as they should. As a consequence, they suffer from constipation, from lack of appetite, and capriciousness of taste for food, and they may have a series of symptoms that, when dwelt on during the hours of solitude, very seriously disturb the good feeling that is so important for the normal accomplishment of physiological functions.

Diversion of Mind.—This tendency to withdraw from social relations with their friends and from the occupations that take them out of doors and which are often a helpful diversion of mind is one of the worst symptoms of this time and must be strenuously combated. It superinduces a series of physical symptoms which are attributed to the menopause but are really due to lack of air, to inactivity, to absence of interest and the consequent opportunity provided for unfortunate auto-suggestion and introspection. These superadded physical symptoms can be readily relieved by directions for rational living and then the genuine menopause symptoms may be so diminished as to be scarcely noticeable. It is impossible for the ordinary human being to stay much in the house, to lie down a large part of the time, eat irregularly and let the bowels become sluggish without having many symptoms of depression.

Summary of Treatment.—The treatment, not of the menopause but of the patients passing through the menopause, then, must consist, first, in putting them in as good physical condition as possible and keeping them in it; second, in maintaining such normal natural habits of life as will enable them to keep up this physical condition without disturbance; thirdly, in putting off solicitude with regard to the menopause and realizing that it is a normal natural process with a definite place in human life and not at all representing a terminal stage of human existence. Nature meant that the mature woman, formed by precious experience, with sympathies broadened by years, should be able to devote herself without sexual irritation to the many things that naturally come to her at this period. There is a place in life for the grandmother and even for the grandaunt, though a French visitor recently declared that he thought there must be no grandmothers in America since all the women seemed to dress in the fashion of the young girl. If this submission to natural conditions is recognized and accepted there are long years of happiness and helpfulness in store for the woman of middle age and the menopause may be welcomed as an important step towards a larger development of life.

{453}

SECTION XI

PSYCHOTHERAPY IN OBSTETRICS

CHAPTER I

SUGGESTION IN OBSTETRICS

In no department of medicine is favorable or unfavorable mental influence more important than in obstetrics. Unfortunately, unfavorable suggestion has here played a serious rôle and must be controlled, modified, neutralized. Suggestion is valuable in its every phase, during the course of pregnancy, in labor itself, in *post-partum* convalescence, and with regard to nursing. Many women in our time are prone to persuade themselves that labor is a more serious incident than it usually proves to be and the consequence is an unfortunate suggestion of pain to come that so exaggerates sensitiveness as to make the actual suffering seem more than it really is. Sympathy expressed for women in pregnancy and in anticipation of their labor is sure to do more harm than good. Pain instead of being lessened by sympathy is increased and capacity to bear it is diminished. Anything that calls attention more particularly to the pain removes distracting conditions that might modify it favorably. Animals have the admirable instinct of withdrawing to some quiet corner when they are in pain, preferring to be alone. In this they follow nature and imitation of them is worthy of consideration, at least so far as the avoidance of opportunities for the expression of sympathy is concerned.

PREGNANCY

Maintenance of Health.—Women must keep up their normal health and strength during pregnancy. By not taking sufficient exercise and by being too much indoors, many women develop a morbid mental state in which every discomfort is less bearable than it was before. Lack of air and of exercise, furthermore, makes them prone to constipation, makes their sleep less restful, and reduces the appetite. For the sake of the being within them, they force themselves to eat, but this often serves only to make them obese, without improving their general health. If a woman in her ordinary condition, who was accustomed to going out-of-doors several hours every day and having reasonable diversion of mind and exercise of body, were to adopt the habits of life that many pregnant women form, she, too, would become morbidly introspective, fearful of the future, irritable over little things, restless at night, and even have certain physical symptoms, such as constipation, tired feelings, loss of {454} appetite, etc. Many of the discomforts and symptoms of which women complain during pregnancy are really due to unfortunate habits and to their mental attitude toward their conditions, rather than to any specific influence of pregnancy on the general health. As a rule, women who live naturally are in somewhat better physical health during pregnancy that at other times.

Obesity and Pregnancy.—It is important that women should not become obese during pregnancy. The woman who is taking too much fat in her diet and accumulating fat is likely to have a fat baby, and with these there is more difficulty in labor itself, and the infants have less resistive vitality than if they were unencumbered with useless adipose tissue. Her will must overcome the tendency to lassitude and the proneness to inactivity that comes over her, and she must feel that labor and her condition after it are dependent on normal, healthy life at this time.

Delayed Labor and Suggestion.—One phase of maternal impressions or of suggestion for the mother's mind that I have always been interested in has been that of the possibility of preventing delay in parturition by frequent suggestion of the time that delivery should be expected. There seems to be no doubt that expectation has some influence on the time of delivery. We do not know just why, after the uterus has tolerated the presence of the fetus for nine calendar months, it should then refuse to do so any longer and contract and expel it. Any number of theories have been suggested and even now our best obstetricians are not agreed as to the reason for this action on the part of the uterus. In some cases this contraction does not take place normally. The due term of labor is past and as a consequence fetuses grow too large within the uterus, greatly increasing the difficulties of parturition and adding to the risk of both mother and child. It is the custom to announce with pride the birth of twelve- and fifteen-pound babies, but it is doubtful whether nature intended that growth to this extent should take place before birth. There is in this, as in other phases of pride with regard to children, a curiously perverted feeling.

Many obstetricians feel that the babies who weigh much more than the average of seven pounds have probably been delayed in the uterus for a lunar month beyond the time when they should, or at least could have been normally born. It is a question whether this delay would have occurred if the mother's expectation of the birth had been directed to a date a month ahead of that on which her mind became fixed as the time of labor. Parturition usually takes place about the period of the recurrence of the menstrual molimina, or at least of that monthly cyclic feeling which many women experience, though there is no flow. It is not always easy to say at which of two monthly periods the birth should be expected. While physicians have warned patients of the possibility of the child being born at the first of the two possible periods, they have been inclined to dwell on the fact that it will probably be delayed until the later term. Women themselves are more prone to take the later than the earlier termination of their pregnancy. Both physician and patient are timorous of the ridicule that may follow if they make premature announcements. Whether we have not in this way created a tradition tending to delay parturition by a lunar month in many cases, is a problem that requires careful study.

The suggestion of as early a period as is compatible with the data provided, so as to create a definite expectancy in the mother's mind, seems well worth {455} deliberate attention. This is a role that psychotherapy has to play in lessening the dangers and the difficulties of parturition. With most healthy women, as indeed with most sensible normal women in life as regards all things, no suggestion is needed and nature will take her course promptly and properly. It is the nervous women, over-anxious about themselves, often of lax physical fiber because of their nervous condition, that need this phase of psychotherapy. It is in them that the unfavorable or mistaken suggestion may be emphasized to such a degree as to delay labor for a lunar month or even more.

Vomiting of Pregnancy.—One of the dreaded complications of pregnancy is serious prolonged vomiting. We know now that this is of two kinds, toxic and neurotic. The toxic variety may be associated with kidney changes, but is more commonly the consequence of certain rare forms of degeneration of the liver. The pathological picture after death is not unlike that of phosphorus poisoning. These cases are due to some serious disturbance of metabolism or to the absorption of some little understood poison. They are probably always fatal. The cases of neurotic vomiting are rather common. They are exaggerations, of the ordinary familiar vomiting of pregnancy which is exhibited by nearly all women at the recurrence of the menstrual times in the early portion of pregnancy. In some of these cases, however, the vomiting is so persistent and so prolonged that the patient's nutrition suffers severely, and there seems to be danger of a fatal termination. The condition has received the unfortunate name of "pernicious vomiting." In these cases there is sometimes question of the advisability of terminating the pregnancy lest the woman should die. Unfortunately this question has been so commonly discussed that most prospective mothers are likely to know something about it, so that when vomiting begins they are fearful lest they should have to lose their child. This becomes an obsession in some minds and an unfavorable suggestion that helps to maintain the vomiting.

A number of remedies have been highly recommended for this at various times. Nearly every alterative drug has had its period of popularity. In the older time nitrate of silver was said to be efficacious. Small doses of ipecac were highly recommended at one time. Small doses of cocain were suggested, and the painting of the back of the throat with cocain. Small doses of morphin had a vogue; codein had its turn after its introduction, and heroin also had a time of popularity. Oxalate of cerium was highly recommended. Any obstetrician of experience will remember many other remedies that have been supposed to be efficacious. Various gynecological procedures have been suggested: the touching of the *cervix uteri* with a mild caustic, with iodin or with nitrate of silver, slight dilatation of the cervix, sometimes the application of a tampon with just enough glycerin to produce a reaction, but not enough to terminate the pregnancy. Occasionally local applications over the stomach region, a mustard leaf, or certain plasters, or finally even a piece of sized paper bound on over this region have been known to be followed by the cessation of the vomiting. When as many different remedies are recommended and seem for a time to be successful and then later prove to be inefficacious, it is reasonably clear that it is not the remedies but the effect produced by these on the mind that is the important therapeutic factor.

Many obstetricians of wide experience now teach that most of these cases of vomiting in pregnancy are merely neurotic and are to be treated entirely {456} as if they were hysterical. The patient's mind is to be distracted from her condition; she is to be assured that even severe vomiting is quite common in pregnancy, that it is annoying, but never serious in its consequences, that it always ends without unfortunate incident for mother or child, and that there need be no solicitude. Above all, no hint of the possibility of the necessity for the termination of the pregnancy, if vomiting continues, should be given. Some physicians are entirely too solicitous in the matter and have by their anxiety made the neurotic condition of their patients worse. Some men see what they call a "pernicious vomiting" in every hundred labors. A well-known obstetrician in New York has had 3,000 births without seeing a single case. He is known for his placidity and lack of over-anxiety. In the great obstetrical clinics in Europe vomiting to the extent that will put mother or child in danger is extremely rare. The greatest obstetrician of the later nineteenth century reports 100,000 obstetrical cases with only one artificial labor.

In foreign obstetrical clinics these cases in recent years have been treated expectantly, without any active interference, especially with pregnancy, and the results have been much more satisfactory than any other method of treatment. There are a number of cases on record now in which pregnant women have lost from twenty to forty pounds as the result of vomiting for weeks, yet after a time the attack has passed and they have carried the child to full term. Where vomiting has occurred and relief has once been afforded by the termination of pregnancy, it is very unlikely that succeeding pregnancies will pass without corresponding conditions in which no remedy will prove effective, except the dreaded obstetrical intervention for the termination of the pregnancy. It is extremely important then that these cases should be treated conservatively and that from the very beginning there should be nothing to arouse the patient's solicitude with regard to herself or above all to give her any hint of the possibility of obstetrical intervention being necessary in her case. For some women the knowledge that a consultation has been held to discuss such a possibility will of itself prove a persistent unfavorable suggestion, that will surely prolong the vomiting.

This may seem a rather strong opinion from one who is not in practical touch with obstetrics. It has been the growing opinion, however, among the great German obstetricians for the last generation. Ahlfeld, in the *Archiv für Gynaekologie* (Band 18 Heft 2 page 310) said that he had seen three cases of so-called pernicious vomiting (*unstillbaren Erbrechen*) in all of which the patients wanted an abortion because they had previously learned the success of this method of treatment, but all of them recovered without incident and carried their children to term. Kronig, ten years ago, in his monograph on "The Significance of Functional Nervous Diseases for Diagnosis and Treatment in Gynaecology" said: "The excessive vomiting of pregnant patients has for a long time seemed to be a genital reflex neurosis. We thought that the growing uterus irritates certain nerve tracts which are connected with the mucous membrane of the stomach. We owe it to Kaltenbach that this opinion was overturned and *hyperemesis gravidarum* set down as the result of a functional neurosis, hysterical in character. A large number of gynaecologists have accepted this opinion in recent {457} years (men of all nations) among others Calderini, Charpentier, Schaeffer, Klein, and Graefe."

Winkel and the leading obstetricians of Germany, especially the directors of obstetrical clinics in the large cities, must be quoted as of the same opinion, since Winkel has collected the statistics of 100,000 pregnancies in the large German clinics in which 6,555 obstetrical operations were performed and in only one case was artificial abortion produced. German opinion is rather strong in the assertion that a number of cases of abortion in the practice of an obstetrician indicates over-hastiness in coming to conclusions as to danger, or leaves him open to the suspicion of yielding too readily to the wishes of mothers who would prefer not to carry their children to term. The suggestion of the possible necessity for abortion has done much to make the hysterical vomiting of these patients continue until this remedy is employed. Insistence from the very beginning that vomiting, though it may injure both mother and child, never necessitates abortion—one out of 100,000 cases is practically never—would be the best possible contrasuggestion.

Kronig thinks that the vomiting of pregnancy is an especially favorable subject for suggestive treatment. He inclines to the opinion that the remedies that have been reported to do good and so many of which have subsequently proved unavailing have really owed whatever success they have had to the suggestion that went with them. Bumm, in his text-book of obstetrics (Grundriss zum Studium der Geburtshülfe von Dr. Ernst Bumm, Wiesbaden, 1902), accepts Kaltenbach's and Ahfeld's conclusions and thinks that the consideration of *hyperemesis* as an hysterical neurosis is well supported by the success and failure of our therapeutics. All sorts of remedies, any number of drugs, all manner of gynecological procedures short of abortion, though also including abortion, have been reported as doing good. All of them even including abortion have failed in a certain number of cases. Evidently suggestion plays a large role. Hypnosis often proves an excellent remedy.

Excessive Salivary Secretion.—Bumm considers that the excess of secretion of saliva which is so often noticed in pregnancy is of the same nature and should be treated rather by suggestion than by any particular remedy, though remedies should be tried because of certain helpful physical effects, and then the psychic element that goes with them. The less importance given to the symptom, the less attention it attracts, the more its passing trivial character is emphasized, the sooner it will subside. Solicitude causes it to persist and even increase.

251

LABOR

Suggestion in Labor.—When the subjects are normal, expectancy has much to do with the severity of labor pains. In recent years so much fuss has been made and so much said and written about woman's burden and travail in the pains of childbirth, that preliminary dread and anxious attention have wrought young women up to such a poignancy of expectation as to make these pains worse than they really are. In the old days child-bearing was as much a matter of course as the husband going out to his daily work, and the taking of the dangers and fatigues of it was a simple matter of duty. Labor was then {458} comparatively easy and, while never pleasant, was also never an over-uncomfortable process. The effect of unfortunate suggestion has been to make it seem ever so much worse than it really is. Multiparae furnish the best proof of this. A healthy woman who has already had more than one child does not dread labor pains very much, or only to a slight degree, because the previous maternities have lessened the physical pain to be experienced, though a healthy woman's tissues are so thoroughly resilient that nature is able to bring about a return to normal conditions so complete that it is not always easy to decide whether a woman has given birth to a child or not. Of course, there are many cases in which tears reveal the former labor, but there are others in which it is not so, and the renewal of the birth process must, therefore, be nearly if not quite as painful as before, especially if it is recalled that succeeding children are usually larger. In spite of this in multiparae, labor has lost most of its terrors because real knowledge of its comparative ease has replaced the previous unfavorable suggestion, and instead there has come a proper appreciation of what will have to be borne, and of the positive pleasure of the relief when it has been borne successfully.

Healthy women of the lower classes have so little difficulty in labor that they are quite frank to confess that it means scarcely more than a few severe muscular pains during an hour or so. Some of them mind it so little that up to within half an hour of the birth of the baby they occupy themselves with other things and succeed effectually in distracting their pains away.

In their article on "Hypnotism and Suggestion in Obstetrics" Drs. Auvard and Secheron suggest that hypnotism can be employed with advantage during labor, but it is more difficult to produce it then than in the normal condition. Its only advantage is anesthesia, and this can be obtained during the preliminary pains in many cases. It is frequently impossible to produce complete anesthesia, however. To replace hypnotism they advise that suggestion in the waking state be used and they even suggest the employment of pseudo-choloroform or other like means. This method they consider more advisable than hypnotism, for there are no inconveniences and many real advantages. The nervous condition of the patient after hypnotism during labor is sometimes far from satisfactory.

Nature's Methods.—In obstetrics and labor we have been finding in recent years that we have not trusted nature enough, have not looked sufficiently to the woman herself for assistance in its difficulties, and have made her too much a passive rather than an active factor. Practically all of the dangers that have accrued to the woman in childbirth, certainly many times more than have come from any other factor, have been due to well-meant but unfortunate attempts to help her while preventing her from helping herself. Before the middle of the nineteenth century most of the puerperal fever was due to infection from over-zealous but unclean attendants. Now men are proudly reporting hundreds of cases of delivery without even a vaginal examination. Above all, we have failed to take advantage of the occupation of mind that could be used to save women much of the anxiety and suffering of labor. If the parturient woman were allowed to change her position, as she does so naturally and frequently in a state of unsophistication, and to help actively, as she can {459} in many postures, in the delivery of her child, it would mean much in diverting her mind from pain which is emphasized by inactivity. The rule of having the woman lie on her back has been unfortunate in many ways and has required much more external interference than if other positions were adopted, while the pains have been more unbearable because that is actually the position in which the woman suffers most and in which she can do least to lessen them.

I was once told by an Irish grandmother the story of nearly one hundred deliveries without accident of any kind, in which the only rule had been not to touch the woman, but to allow her to change her position and, above all, to facilitate her in getting on her knees in a stooping bent-over posture so as to help herself. The upper mattress was doubled over completely and the woman was encouraged to kneel on the lower straw mattress, which was so arranged that it could be changed completely, or destroyed immediately after labor. This seemed old-fashioned and unscientific twenty years ago, when I heard the story, but I have been interested recently in reading Professor King's address on "The Significance of Posture in Obstetrics."

Professor King is sure that there are many advantages in following certain natural inclinations of the mother to change her position and that this helps her in many ways. Above all, as the psychotherapist sees at once, it will occupy her mind, keep down anxiety and lessen pain in many natural ways, besides encouraging concentration of attention on muscular effort instead of on painful sensation. The whole article is well worth reading, for in it he suggests that certain obstetrical operations, even version, would not be so often necessary, if the woman were sometimes allowed to assume the squatting position in the course of birth. His illustrations make very clear the help that changes of position are in the mechanics of many difficulties of labor. The pressure of the patient's thigh on the abdomen, when she was allowed to assume a squatting position, enabled him, in a case in which the woman had been in labor twenty-eight hours, in which ergot had been given by the midwife, in which the waters had been discharged and the uterus was tetanically contracted around its contents, to deliver the child without instrumentation and without further delay. In five minutes the arm (for it was an arm presentation) began to recede, and in twenty minutes the child was delivered, head first, and mother and infant both did well. Other cases with similar results have been reported by obstetricians quite as distinguished as Professor King. Many other experienced obstetrical teachers have expressed themselves to the same purpose in recent years.

Postures after Labor.—Allowing changes of position after labor also has its advantages. There is often retention of urine and this can be relieved by allowing the woman to assume the usual position. It may be impossible owing to the swelling and hyperemia in the neighborhood of her urethra for the woman to pass water, and yet if she is allowed to sit in the usual position upon a commode, she will in most cases pass her water in a few minutes without difficulty and the risks attending catheterization will be obviated. The power to urinate is due in these cases partly to the pressure of the thighs upon the abdomen which helps the bladder to contract and undoubtedly also to the suggestive influence that the position has.

{460}

NURSING

The attitude of mind of a woman toward her milk supply is important, as the flow of milk is closely subject to mental influence. The presence of the child and the consequent exercise of maternal instinct does more to bring about the prompt, healthy flow of milk than anything else. Sometimes women in the later months of their first pregnancy upon seeing a mother nursing her child have felt the flow of milk to their breasts not rarely with such painful overdistention of the milk ducts as to require artificial relief. On the other hand, a fright may stop the flow of milk or make it scanty and a mother's aversion to a child may prevent her being able to nurse it. The sight of the father of the child in a state of intoxication may have a similar result.

How much milk supply may be dependent on the state of mind, or at least the state of the nervous system, can be realized from the animals from which we obtain milk. Any serious disturbance is likely to interfere with the milk supply. When a cow's calf is taken away the animal will often refuse for a time to give milk. If a cow is scared, as by the attack of a wild animal, or by being hit though only slightly injured by an engine, it will often not have milk for several days or even longer. There is an impression prevalent among farmers that if a cow takes a dislike to a particular person they are not likely to "give down" as much milk as would otherwise be the case. This may be only a curious farmer tradition, that has no basis in fact, although it is supported by so many observations reported from many different countries that it is apparently to be taken as of scientific value.

In modern times many fashionable women do not nurse their children because they have not the proper supply of milk. It is easy to see how this can be brought about through suggestion from many sources and the sight of others neglecting their duty in this matter. Most fashionable women would rather not nurse their children, and yet many of them feel a bounden duty in the matter. Some of these, however, having heard that many mothers of the better class are not capable of nursing their children, easily persuade themselves that they come in this category, and so their whole attitude of mind toward nursing is one of extreme doubt. Knowing as we do how the mental state influences nursing we are not surprised when these women prove not to have sufficient milk in the early days of the nursing. If they are to have it they must look forward with confidence to nursing their children and they must be ready and willing to take such food and secure such fresh air as will put them in the best possible condition for this function, always with the thought that nothing can be better for a child than to be nursed by its own mother. Nature has made exactly the form of food suited for the particular child, and it matters not how healthy a wet nurse may be, her milk is not likely to be so suitable. Much depends on the nutrition of the child during this early susceptible period of its life and there is more that passes over with the milk than merely the food elements. It is well recognized now that the reason why nurslings are protected from most of the so-called children's diseases and the contagious diseases generally, is that, as a rule, their mothers {461} have had these diseases, have acquired an immunity to them and this immunity is transferred to the child so long as the nursing process is continued. This has been shown to be true over and over again in animals and holds good for human beings.

Professor Von Leyden, the distinguished professor of medicine at the University of Berlin, points out that we are not quite sure as yet just what may happen to the human race from the very general refusal of mothers to nurse their children and the almost universal substitution of the bovine mother; whether in times to come certain bovine traits, at least as regards susceptibility to disease, may not be stamped upon the human race, cannot be determined until this experiment in ethnology, now being conducted on so large a scale, has been carried to some definite conclusion.

Perhaps this view is groundless, but there is no doubt that milk is more than merely a food and that during the period after birth when the child's nervous system is being formed, the perfectly adapted mother's milk is more likely to be the proper food than anything that human ingenuity can elaborate. We have heard much in recent years of the tendency of education and civilization to lower the birth-rate and to make women less fitted for maternity and for such maternal duties as nursing, but stronger than any deterioration of the physical constitution by the mental development is the unfortunate unfavorable effect of mental suggestion upon such functions, by which the preparation of the organism for their fulfillment is greatly influenced. It is in this respect that the women of to-day differ from the woman of the past much more than in mere physical development.

CHAPTER II

MATERNAL IMPRESSIONS

"Maternal impression" is accepted as a specific designation to signify the real or supposed influence of emotion and especially serious trouble, which may affect the mother's mind during pregnancy and be transferred to the child *in utero*, with the production of deformities or

253

mother's marks. There used to be an almost superstitious belief in the power of the maternal impressions to influence unfavorably the child *in utero*. With the newer developments as to the influence of the subconscious and subliminal there might well occur in some minds an exaggeration of these ideas with the production of much mental suffering at least, if not of more serious results.

Maternal Impressions in Old Literature.—The belief in the influence of maternal impression on the child *in utero* is so strongly fixed that to most people it will seem paradoxical to question the whole subject. The evidence for it, however, is quite trivial, and none of it rises above the grade of what may be explained by coincidence. But there are many apparently insuperable difficulties, from the standpoint of our modern scientific knowledge, with regard to the whole subject. If we take up the medical books and the popular science, or rather pseudo-science, and the folk stories of a century ago we find overwhelming evidence for the belief in maternal impressions. More recent {462} literature has but few examples, and the more the details are studied the less is the evidence of any kind that the mother's mind influences her unborn child. There is really no more reason why a child should he marked within its mother's womb than that it should be marked while nursing at the breast if something should happen to the mother at that time. This latter effect strikes one at once as absurd; the former, as we shall see, is exactly of the same nature.

Many of the older stories of maternal impressions are reported on no better grounds than the vomiting of snakes and the like, even live mice, which used to be found in old-time medical literature. It is true that there was usually no such morbidity about the stories of maternal impressions, but men wanted to find some explanation for the problem of the occurrence of deformities and markings and the maternal impression idea seemed satisfactory and inviting by its very mystery. The belief that animals could live for some time in human stomachs is now relegated to the limbo of old-time credulous traditions. Maternal impressions are on the same path and in twenty-five years they will be as great curiosities in serious medical literature as the gastric fauna of two generations ago. Under these circumstances prospective mothers who are anxious over possibilities and who have dreads of all kinds about their unborn children should be reassured and informed as to the scientific status of this important question.

Mother and Child Distinct Beings.—There is no direct connection between the mother and her unborn babe. No nerves run in the cord and none pass from the uterine tissues to the placenta. It is easy to understand the influence of mind on body under ordinary circumstances, at least the mystery has a rational explanation. The central nervous system rules the nutrition of the body. To cut off the nerve supply has as serious an effect as to cut off the blood supply. Owing to the existence of a chain of neurons, that is, a succession of nervous elements, instead of one continuous nerve fiber from center to periphery, it is possible for one of the neurons of the chain to be so disturbed that the conducting apparatus is interrupted and impulses do not flow. Hence, if a strong impression is produced on the mind with regard to a particular part of the body the neurons leading to it may be so disturbed that trophic nerve impulses do not flow down, the blood supply of the part may be disturbed through the vaso-motor system and consequent changes may take place.

Absence of Circulatory Connection.—Since no nerves pass, as we have said, from mother to babe, disturbances acting on the mother's mind can at most only influence the blood supply to the baby. Most people think that there is a direct blood supply from mother to child and that the mother's blood literally flows in the baby's veins. This is not true. The baby's blood is an entirely independent structure, originating in the child's own body, and always maintaining a distinct and quite different composition from that of the mother. The baby's blood has a higher specific gravity, and it has, in normal condition, nearly double as many red corpuscles to the cubic millimeter as the mother's blood. If the blood supply is disturbed by mental influences, then it is not the baby's blood nor its circulation that is disturbed, but only the circulation through the maternal part of the placenta where an exchange of gases and nutrient elements between mother's and baby's blood takes place. It is {463} impossible to conceive that during this passage through a membrane of nutrient elements, soluble proteids, gases, etc., mental influences should also pass over.

Supposed Examples of Maternal Impression.—The stories that are told would lead us to believe that somehow definite changes in the mother are reproduced in the babe. One case, which in a circle of friends that I knew very well made many a convert to the idea of maternal impressions, was that of a young woman at whom, during an early stage of her first pregnancy, her husband playfully threw a tiny frog. He did not know that she had a mortal dread of frogs. She was seriously frightened and put up her hand to ward off the animal, and as the clammy thing struck her palm she felt a shiver go through her. When her baby was born a curious growth that had some pigment in it and that, by a stretch of the imagination, might be considered to resemble a frog was in the baby's hand—the same hand, by the way, as that which the mother used to ward off the animal. The lack of any nervous connection and of any direct blood connection between mother and child makes the story simply absurd as an illustration of maternal impression.

In recent years such stories have come from more and more distant parts of the country. Kansas was the principal source of them until a generation of great editors arose there. Texas was then their favorite location, but Texas has in recent years become so progressive and so closely connected with the rest of the world that, in spite of its size, it does not produce so many of these wonders. A generation ago the announcement of the birth of six children at once in Austria, or somewhere else in Central Europe, would usually be followed by a report from Texas announcing seven at a birth. Maternal impression stories grew luxuriantly for the benefit of the news-gatherer in dull seasons. A standing type of them is that of the farmer cutting hay on his farm who puts his fingers too far into the hay cutter and has them taken off. His wife binds up the bleeding stump. She is pregnant at the time. When her baby is born—usually two or three months later—just the same fingers are missing on the same hand of the child. Now the mechanism by which such maternal impression could be transferred to the child is incomprehensible. There is no connection between the two, and the old metaphysical axiom (*actio in distans repugnat*) that all action between bodies at a distance from one another, that is without some connecting link between them, is absurd, holds as good in modern times as it did in the Middle Ages. Surely a tendency-to-amputation is not carried over from mother's blood to baby's blood through the membrane in the placenta just as are the gases for respiration and the nutrient elements for food. If it is, we have a greater mystery than ever to solve.

Period of Occurrence.—The infant in the uterus is fully formed before the tenth week of pregnancy and at a time when women are usually almost unconscious of the fact that they are pregnant. Such impressional changes as we have referred to, if produced after this, must be in the nature of backward growth or an inversion of trophic influences or a great perversion of embryonic life. They have nothing to do with the formation of the child, since that is completed. They are as much accidents as if the child should fall after it was born. We know how fetal limbs are amputated through the formation of amniotic bands, but that maternal impressions should influence the formation of these bands is of itself ridiculously absurd. That it should {464} influence them in a directive and selective way so that certain limbs may be amputated at a certain point reaches a climax of absurdity. A distinguished physician of our generation once said that one might as well hope to absorb a pencil case in one's vest pocket by medicine as to try to bring about absorption of fully formed connective tissue by drugs. We cannot think of any mental influence bringing about such absorption, yet to credit maternal impressions with the production of fetal amputations not only supposes the directive formation of connective tissue within the uterus, quite beyond the domain of the influence of the mother's nervous system, but also assumes the direction of the anomalous action of that connective tissue in its mutilating procedures in a very exact and definite way.

Some curious things have been explained on the score of maternal impressions and it is this very exaggeration that is perhaps the best proof of how coincidence, imitation, and other factors play a role that has exaggerated the idea of maternal impressions into a causative factor. A typical illustration is the case cited years ago, half in joke, perhaps, half in earnest, by a distinguished professor of obstetrics. It occurred in the days when the elder Sothern was playing Lord Dundreary to crowded houses and when Dundrearyisms were the current witticisms and Dundreary ties and Dundreary clothes and Dundreary whiskers were all the rage. A young woman who was recently married became much taken with the actor and went to see him over and over again, secured an introduction to him, and showed the liveliest interest in him and the performance. Their acquaintance, however, remained merely that of chance friends. Some months after it began, not more than five or six at the most, a boy was born to her. According to the story this boy, when he began to walk some years later, developed that little skip in his gait which proved so taking to those who crowded the theaters to see Sothern as Lord Dundreary.

By this time the play had lost something of its vogue and most people did not recognize the curious halt in the gait, but it was very clear to the mother and her friends. It was set down as due to a maternal mental impression. Mental transfer seems ludicrous in this case. It is much more likely that the mother was hysterical, and, wishing in a morbid way to attract attention to herself and her child, taught the boy the little skip, or perhaps some curious little skip once taken by the child attracted the mother's attention because of her memory of Sothern, and her surprise at the act impressed the peculiar action upon the boy's mind, who proceeded to attract further attention by repeating it. It is cases like this with their *reductio ad absurdum* of the whole process that have quite discredited the belief in maternal impressions.

Some Figures and Coincidences.—The occurrence of mothers' marks in connection with various external incidents of pregnancy are only coincidences. Most young mothers dread lest something should happen to their children. About once in a thousand times an infant is marked in some way. Nine hundred mothers rejoice over the fact that their baby is not marked in spite of the fact that they feared it might be, ninety-nine of them never gave the matter any thought and one of them finds to her sorrow that her foreboding has come true. Occasionally a mother who has not dreaded such a result finds that her offspring is marked. Then she recalls all the happenings of her pregnancy and picks out something to which she thinks she may attribute the accident. {465} There must be some reason for it and she finds it. Sometimes she begins by saying that it must be because she was frightened at such a time, or fell down at such a place, or saw such a thing, and then a week later she tells the story with circumstantial additions which make it very clear to her friends that she knows exactly the reason and that she had thought about it before and feared it might be so, though the whole matter was hazy until it had been talked over a number of times.

Coincidences have been the most serious detriment in drawing scientific conclusions in every department of medicine. Most of our diseases are self-limited and any medicine that was given being followed by recovery seemed to be the cause of that recovery and the more strictly self-limited a disease the greater the number of remedies. When stories of maternal impressions are analyzed it is found that a great many mothers have had forebodings as to their children being marked and their dreads have not come true. A few have feared and have realized their worst fears. Many women whose children are marked can recall no event in the course of their pregnancy which could have marked their child and they ask the doctor what he thinks must have been the reason. But unintelligent mothers can always find some cause by searching out unpleasant details of their experience during pregnancy.

Intrauterine Nutrition and Nursing.—To explain the occurrence of a frog-like appearance or a mousey patch on a baby as due to its mother having been frightened by one of these little animals while nursing would be the height of absurdity. But it is no more absurd than the supposition that mental impressions in the late months of pregnancy can have the effects that are popularly ascribed to them. If a mother suffers from severe fright, or even if she has a fit of intense anger or other profound mental disturbance, her milk may disagree with her infant. Every physician has seen nursing infants made sick by the change in the milk superinduced by strong mental emotions in the mother. This, however, could have nothing to do with the production of a special lasting physical mark on the outside of the body.

Maternal Solicitude and Superstition.—The wonderful stories that are told are nearly all in the older literature and are much more reasonably explained on the score of coincidence than on that of any possible direct connection of cause and effect. Mothers, then, may be reassured and made to understand that the better their own health, the less they worry about their condition, the more likely is their pregnancy to terminate favorably with a perfectly healthy offspring. This is the source of so much concern in the little world of child-bearing that it is worth while taking it seriously and making mothers understand that the old notions in this matter are but superstitions.

Superstitions are not always nor exclusively religious, they are survivals from a previous state of knowledge, the reasons for which are now known to be false. Maternal impression, that is, the belief in the power of the mother's mind over the unborn child, is a superstition that we must now dismiss.

Favorable Maternal Influences.—Every now and then a sensational newspaper has an article on how mothers will tend to make their children physically handsomer by gazing at beautiful works of art, beautiful scenes in nature, and seeing only handsome (one feels like inserting well-dressed in the category, also) people during pregnancy. The reading of good books {466} containing moral lessons of the highest quality are supposed to have something of the same influence on the child's character. There is no doubt at all that the more carefully and simply and beautifully and healthily the mother lives, and the more her mind possesses itself in peace and happiness, the better will be her own nutrition and consequently that of her offspring, and, all things considered, this will contribute to the perfection of the infant's body and so give the best instrument for the expression of its soul. That these supposed favorable influences have any more direct power than this over the state of the infant that is to be is doubtful. It is worth trying for, but if the indefinite influence for good emphasizes, as it apparently does in many minds, the presumed direct and definite influence for evil, then it is not worth dwelling on.

Etiology of Deformities.—But if these curious deformities and markings are not due to maternal impressions, what, then, is their cause? To the question for many of the minor marks and slight deformities—naevi vascular and pigmentary, extra fingers, slight overgrowths, special peculiarities of bone and soft tissues—no satisfactory answer can be given. We must simply say that as yet we do not know. It is a good thing to say we do not know. Long ago Roger Bacon declared that the principal reason why man did not advance in knowledge more in spite of the amount of their work was that they were afraid to say "I do not know," and accepted inadequate reasons and insufficient authority in order to avoid this humiliating expression. On the other hand, there are many deformities and markings, the reasons for which have been found, and the more important they are the more we know about them, as a rule. Besides, with the advance of our knowledge of embryology we are getting to know more and more about these difficult problems and many things that were mysteries before are now clear. In addition to observation we have experiment and this is making observation more thoroughly scientific.

The more we know of the intricacies of the development of animals and human beings, the greater is our surprise that deformities do not occur even more commonly than they do. All the openings of the human as of the animal body gradually close in with the production of the finished form. The slightest interference with growth in the neighborhood of these openings, which involve nearly all of the front of the body, leaves various deformities. Nature has surrounded the developing embryo with fluid so that it is saved from jars of all kinds and from contact with other tissues that would disturb growth. Cell is laid on cell as brick is laid on brick in the building of a house, and the predetermined plan in the immense majority of cases is followed without accident to the minutest detail. That more mishaps do not occur, considering the delicacy of the process and the perfection of the finished structure, is hard to understand.

There are many factors likely to intrude in every pregnancy that may lead to the production of unfortunate results. Literally millions of cells are growing with apparent freedom from constraint in many portions of the fetus, yet all are directed with definite purpose corresponding to other cells and are destined to meet in due course of time. Each one of them or at least each group seems to be independent in its growth. Each growing cell doubles by dividing every few hours, yet all are co-ordinated to a definite end. We admire the men who begin at the two ends of a tunnel far distant from one another and work without any communication except through the engineer's plans {467} made long before, and yet make two bores that can be depended on to meet with but a few inches of divergence. The bridges of tissue that are built across the openings of the body jut out to meet one another in this way and in more than ninety-nine out of every one hundred cases there is not the slightest divergence. Many things may occur to disturb conditions—not connected with mental influences, but with distinctly physical factors—missteps, trips, jars on stairs or getting off and on cars, on the sidewalk, etc. These, and not the mythical factors that make up so-called maternal impressions, are the causes of deformities and mothers' marks.

{468}

SECTION XII

GENITO-URINARY DISEASES

CHAPTER I

PROSTATISM

It may seem impossible to include prostatic hypertrophy, or the train of symptoms connected with it, among those affections likely to be benefited by mental treatment. The history of this affection, however, and especially of its treatment in recent years since it has come to be the subject of special study, has furnished many examples of the value of suggestion in the relief of many of its symptoms. Many forms of treatment have been exploited for a time, attracting attention because of the cures attributed to them, and have then been relegated to the limbo of unsuccessful remedial measures. A striking example of the place of suggestion came with the development of organo-therapy some fifteen years ago. The succession of events illustrated well how much persuasion and a favorable attitude of mind might mean even in so purely physical an affection as interference with urination by enlargement of the prostate.

It was at a time when thyroid medication for myxedema having proved successful the medical journals were full of reports of other successful phases of organo-therapy. The spleen and the bone marrow were being used in the anemias, the ductless glands in various nutritional diseases and even extract of heart for heart disease. Just on what general principle it was assumed by some German investigator that possibly extract of prostate from animals might be of benefit in the treatment of prostatic hypertrophy is hard to understand. The German physician, however, gave an order to the butcher to send him prostates and as furnished they were administered to the patients. A number of patients began at once to improve on the treatment. They were able to empty their bladders much better than before, the residual urine was decreased, the tendency to fermentation was diminished and, above all, the patients' general symptoms were much improved.

The success was so marked that the German investigator published his cases and, with the public mind interested in organotherapy, they attracted wide-spread attention. He was asked how to obtain the material and only then did he take the trouble to investigate just what the butcher had been sending him. The description furnished the butcher by the doctor was that he wanted an organ lying below and somewhat in front of the bladder of the bull. It was found on careful inquiry that the abattoir attendants following these directions had supplied not prostates but seminal vesicles. As soon as this was found out some of the therapeutic suggestions failed. A number of cases, {469} however, continued to improve. German medical journals made fun of the whole proceeding and most people will consider the ridicule deserved.

Shortly before this time, however, we had had a very similar experience with another pair of organs. In spite of the fact that whatever we know about Graves' disease would seem to indicate that that affection is due to an increased thyroid secretion in the system, at the time of the organo-therapeutic fads, thyroid extract was reported as having been used successfully in the treatment of this affection. The name signed to the report was that of a trustworthy English clinical observer. A few practitioners of medicine got similar results, but most of them failed entirely to get his successes and some of them were sure that their patients were rather harmed than helped by the new medication. An investigation of just what material was being employed in the English cases showed that the butcher was supplying thymus and not thyroid glands. Suggestion did the rest, for thymus has proved to be quite ineffective, and the treatment was entirely expectant but acted on a favorable state of mind. Anyone who has had much experience with Graves' disease knows how amenable to suggestion the patients are. It would seem evident from the foregoing story of organo-therapy for prostatic hypertrophy that sufferers from prostatism are probably as prone to suggestion as patients with Graves' disease. This is all the more surprising as the two affections are so different in their etiology. Graves' disease being undoubtedly a ductless gland disease, while prostatism is due entirely to mechanical obstruction.

We have abundant additional evidence of the role of psychotherapy in prostatism. Some years ago a well-known American surgeon suggested that removal of the testicles would reduce the enlarged prostates. And much improvement was seen after castration in those who previously suffered from prostatism. The subject was carefully studied. Experiments were made on animals and the results seemed to prove that castration in them constantly produced prostatic atrophy. The fallacy probably came from the fact that at the time so little was known about the prostate in comparative anatomy and, above all, with regard to the prostate in dogs, that it was impossible to come to any sure conclusion as to reduction in weight and size after removal of the testicles. A number of prostatic cases were treated by different surgeons and with excellent results. Then after a time the number of supposed successes dwindled or proved to be failures and now no one does the operation. The only explanation that is at all satisfactory in these cases, is that the rest in the hospital, the favorable suggestion of reported cures and of an experimental demonstration on animals led many patients, some of them even physicians, to secure a better control over their bladders.

It took a good deal of persuasion as a rule to bring men, even men well beyond seventy, to consent to the sacrifice of their testicles, but once they did, the sacrifice brought a favorable suggestion to work and so it was not long before they were able to make their bladder act much more efficiently against the obstacles presented to its contraction. Some could be persuaded more easily to sacrifice a single testicle, but in these cases the mental influence was less and the reported cures fewer. After a time the operation of vasectomy was suggested as a substitute for the removal of the testicles. For a time even this in the hands of certain operators gave excellent results. Almost any other operation in the genito-urinary tract performed with the definite persuasion {470} on the part of the patient that he would be better after it would probably have acted just as favorably. The whole story of these series of incidents in the surgery of the last decade of the nineteenth century ought to be a clear demonstration of how valuable for therapeutic purposes is mental influence oven in prostatism, and how much we should try to secure its favorable effects.

Unfavorable Suggestion.—Since enlargement of the prostate has become a familiar subject of discussion and men know and hear much about it every now and then, one has to reassure a man but little beyond fifty that he is not suffering from this affection. Just as soon as a man begins to urinate frequently during the day and to have to got up once at night he begins to wonder how soon he will be likely to suffer from further symptoms of enlarged prostate. If he is of the nervous kind his worrying will soon give him additional symptoms that will confirm his suspicions. Probably one of the most familiar of phenomena, even to the non-medical man, is the ease with which worry and excitement causes frequent urination. Probably no system of organs in the body is so likely to be disturbed by the mind as the urinary system with the exception, of course, of the allied tract, the genital system, but the two are so one in union and sympathy that they cannot be separated in practice. The prostate is rather a genital than a urinary organ.

Urinary Worries.—When a man begins to worry about the possibility of bother from enlarged prostate and recalls that frequent urination is one of the symptoms of it, it will not be long before this symptom develops. Occasionally his first wakings to urinate at night or in the early morning are only due to passing conditions, either he drank freely shortly before bedtime or perhaps he did not drink enough. In the

257

one case the bladder is rather full; in the other a concentrated urine, especially with the patient lying on his back, makes itself felt over the sensitive area at the base of the bladder, waking him up. The rest of the symptoms may develop as a consequence of solicitude over a few such incidents.

Practically all men who reach sixty have some tendency to more frequent urination than before. Their bladder does not hold as much fluid with comfort and they are likely to have to get up in the early morning. This does not necessarily mean any enlargement of the prostate nor any pathological change. The physiological change that takes place seems to be rather conservative than otherwise. Old muscles are less capable of extension and thorough reaction than they were earlier in life and in order that the bladder may not be over-distended nature makes it more sensitive than before.

Emptying the Bladder.—In the study of these cases individual peculiarities in the emptying of the bladder must be remembered. There are some men who cannot urinate if anyone is near them, and who even have to step into a closed toilet if they are to succeed in emptying their bladders when others are in the room. Some who find no difficulty in the presence of others in open urinals find it difficult or impossible to urinate when it is expected of them. Under worry and excitement urination may become urgent or imperative, but on the other hand some men find it very difficult to empty their bladders under an emotional strain. Now that much more is written publicly with regard to symptoms from enlarged prostate and much more is heard of the affection, many old men got worried and lose some of the power that they had over their bladder before, not so much because of their enlarged prostate as from the {471} psychic loss of control over their bladder. The viscus consists of a series of muscles, the fibres of which must be rather nicely coordinated and controlled in order to secure that complete contraction necessary for thorough emptying. A certain amount of residual urine occurs occasionally at least in many other persons besides those who have prostatic obstruction.

The Question of Operation.—In recent years there has been a tendency to suggest operation even on comparatively small prostates when symptoms referable to them are noted. Operations on the prostate have become much more easy and successful, and there has been the same sort of feeling about them among surgeons as there was when operations for affections, real or supposed, of the ovaries came into general vogue twenty years ago. I have seen patients in whom an operation for the removal of the prostate had been suggested, though the only symptoms were somewhat increased frequency of urination during the day and the necessity for rising two or three times at night. Such a suggestion, by calling the patient's attention strongly to his condition, emphasizes the irritability of the vesical tissues and is almost sure to bring about a considerable increase in the symptoms. The first principle of any treatment of irritability of the bladder should be the setting of the patient's mind as free as possible from solicitude. Any over-attention is sure to lead to reflexes and often to what seems to be even imperative urination, though with a little care and discipline much can be done for the relief of such symptoms.

The necessity for operation must be judged entirely from the symptoms of the individual patient and not from any hard and fast rule with regard to the size of the prostate. Prostates are eminently individual organs, at least as individual as the human nose, and their projection into the rectum is dependent on the relations of other tissues in the neighborhood as well as on mere size. Men have been known to live with comparatively few or no symptoms for many years, though at autopsy they proved to have what would ordinarily be considered a pathologically enlarged prostate.

Operations upon the prostate are valuable and indeed often afford the only avenue of relief from an intolerable condition. The results are not so encouraging in all cases, however, as to make recourse to operation advisable until a thorough trial of palliative measures has been made. It is surprising how often the confident suggestion of assured relief when accompanied by the same amount of rest in bed and the special care that is required for an operation, brings about a disappearance of symptoms that seemed inevitably to demand surgical intervention. There may be much residual urine, there may even be, as a consequence of this, some fermentation with cystitis, and yet a course of rather simple remedial measures may serve to bring about a period of prolonged freedom from vesical symptoms. If these patients, however, have heard much of the trials and sufferings of a catheter life, the solicitude aroused with regard to their condition is sufficient of itself to disturb their urination to a marked degree. Unfavorable suggestion is particularly serious in its effects in these cases, while favorable suggestion frequently repeated will enable the patient very often to regain bladder control when the developments present might seem to put that almost out of the question.

Position Suggestions.—An important suggestion for treatment in prostatism with residual urine seems to be to teach the patient to urinate lying down, {472} especially with the hips somewhat elevated. This seems to be the element that proved capable of making many different operations, castration, the removal of one testicle, vasectomy, and other suggestions appear curative. My own experience is too limited to make my opinion of much weight; but I have seen certain patients greatly relieved of prostatic symptoms and their residual urine much diminished by the advice to urinate leaning well out of bed, lying prone with the head lower than the body. A small stool is brought to the side of the bed, a pillow placed on it and the patient leans over face down on this with the shoulders considerably lower than the pelvis. This allows gravity to assist rather than hamper the emptying of the bladder and after men have become a little used to it they are quite satisfied to take the trouble. Personally I feel sure that more generally applied this would put off the necessity for using a catheter a good deal and even save some cases from operation that now seem to need it. The principle is exactly the same as that by which patients suffering from bronchiectasis avail themselves of the help of gravity and get rid of the nocturnal accumulation of material in their dilated bronchi. They can thus be saved much trouble and exhausting effort.

So much, as we have said, is written in recent years with regard to prostatic symptoms that a body of unfavorable suggestion has been created. This must be neutralized as far as possible by calling the attention of patients who have initial symptoms of vesical disturbance to the ease with which mental influences act upon the urinary functions. Solicitude and anxiety will add to symptoms and may even bring about their continuance when the original, local and passing condition which has caused them has ceased. Very often if the patient's mind can be properly disposed a marked relief of symptoms will follow, especially if, at the same time, remedial measures of other kinds are employed to lessen the irritation that is being set up. While prostatism seems to be due to such purely mechanical difficulties that mental influences can mean very little, the history of the therapeutics of the condition for the last twenty years shows us clearly that if strong mental influences are aroused they bring so much relief that many patients consider themselves cured. This psychotherapy will not do away with the necessity for operation in many cases, but it will cure many of the sufferers from milder symptoms and will in not a few cases bring such relief as will prepare the patients to undergo operation, if it should be necessary, with more assurance of favorable results.

CHAPTER II

SEXUAL NEUROSES

Anything that disturbs the sexual sphere in either sex, no matter how trivial it may be, becomes a source of worry and depression quite beyond its real importance. It is not unusual for men and women to become so worried over some trifling affection of their sexual organs that they become convinced that serious pathological conditions are developing and that there is little hope of anything like a complete cure. This is particularly true of young patients, but holds also for those of older years. Slight discomforts are exaggerated into nagging aches and pains which produce extreme depression of spirits.

{473}

It is important, then, for the physician to recognize this and to treat the patient's mind by reassurance while conducting whatever other therapeutics may be required. There is danger always in these cases of either making too little or too much of the affection. If too much is made of it, an unfavorable influence is produced in the patient's mind and the discouragement leads to so much inhibition or even actual physical disturbance that the affection will not improve. If too little is made of it, patients get discouraged and are prone to think that the physician does not understand their cases. Then they go to the advertising specialist in men's diseases who works upon their fears and makes them feel much worse than before, though in the end he may lift the cloud of anxiety from their minds and pretend to have cured them. He always leaves them, however, with the impression that something serious has been the matter, and this acts as a nightmare and a source of dread in after time.

In men the unfavorable suggestions occur particularly as a consequence of affections of the external organs. In women the same suggestions are likely to make themselves felt with regard to the internal genital organs. We all recognize the exaggeration of feeling and even physical reaction that takes place with regard to slight sexual ailments in the male, because it is easy to recognize just exactly what pathological conditions are present and how trivial they may be and yet produce serious depression and all kinds of symptoms, reflexly referred to many other organs. There is a tendency to listen to the complaints from women more seriously because the actual pathological condition cannot be determined and there is always the fear that some serious affection may be at work. It must not be forgotten, however, that the complaints of pains and aches, the disturbance of sleep, of digestion and of the intestinal function, the mental and physical lassitude and the over-reaction to irritation which occur in both sexes as a consequence of sexual affections may be due entirely to mental solicitude and not to any real pathological change.

Trivial Afflictions—Varicocele.—It is curious what a little thing will sometimes set off the explosion of a train of sexual symptoms. Every physician has probably had some young man come to him with the look and the tone that there was something the matter that he knew was serious and would affect all his after life. The patient then goes on to say that he wants to know all and is brave enough to face it, and, though he has lost sleep for two or three nights and is not looking well for the present moment because his health has been disturbed by the loss of sleep, still he has the strength to know the worst and it is to be told him and he will bravely battle on in spite of the suffering that must come. Or he will submit to a serious operation if it is necessary for his relief. With a prelude like this, the inexperienced physician might expect strangulated hernia or some preliminary symptoms of brain tumor, but what he usually finds is a varicocele, and a small one at that. By chance the patient has discovered it and slept none the following night, went round in an agony of dread next day meaning to go to a physician, but too fearful to be told the worst, losing another night's sleep and then finally coming to a friend to be told all the ill that is in store for him.

There is no need for alarm in these cases; they merely illustrate the role of the mind disturbing the body. Nearly one-fourth of the male world carries its {474} varicocele around with it and never bothers about it. A few sensitive individuals are annoyed by a sense of weight and a feeling of distention from congestion in connection with it. In a few, because of special pathological conditions or congenital defects, the varicocele becomes so large that it has to be supported by a special bandage. In people who ride horseback, in athletes, and those who indulge in severe exercise, this sort of a bandage may be necessary or at least may make the wearer more comfortable even in slighter forms of the affection. Severe cases may be much relieved by it.

On first discovery of his varicocele nearly every young man, because of concentration of attention on it, is so much annoyed that he thinks he must wear a bandage. After a time, however, he often finds that the bandage itself is a source of more annoyance than the varicocele, and then he learns to forget it and its feelings—and that is all about it.

I have dwelt on this succession of events that takes place so often with regard to varicocele, because it is typical of the effect that an affection of the sexual organs has upon the mind. It exerts an unfavorable influence entirely disproportionate to the physical cause that is at work. If, as sometimes happens, a young man hesitates to confide in some one capable of undeceiving him with regard to the supposed significance of his affection, he may work himself into a decided nervous condition and lose much weight before he discovers his mistake.

This physical running down confirms his exaggerated notion of the significance of the affection. He is sure that it constitutes the reason why he is losing weight and declining in health and he rather congratulates himself on the fact that he discovered the cause so shortly before the serious effects began.

If under these conditions he places himself in the hands of any of the men who advertise themselves as curing "men's diseases," or as relieving the "awful" symptoms that are likely to follow varicocele, instead of being reassured he will be told that he has come just in time and that while his cure will require a long time and will cost a great deal of money, yet it can surely be effected. In nothing can men or women be more easily imposed upon than with regard to affections involving their sex organs. They lose their power of judgment and their control over their feelings and so plunge sometimes into profound depression. Every year we have a number of suicides among young men, the most important element in whose depression is due to unrelieved occupation of mind with the thought that they are suffering from some incurable sexual disease which will unsex them, and that even death is to be preferred to the alternative of being recognized generally—as they are sure they will be—as sexual defectives.

As a rule, these young men are suffering from only some slight ailment that could be easily cured if they were frank about their state of mind and described their symptoms to a reputable physician. Oftener than not their supposed ailment is something so common as to be of no significance, so far as any serious results may possibly be anticipated, and their only real ailment is the mental condition which has developed because of concentration of mind on this one phase of organic life and the consequent inevitable exaggeration of symptoms and feelings. It is sometimes not easy to disabuse them of their unfortunate notions, but there is probably no set of cases in medicine where psychotherapeutics means more than it does with regard to the curious {475} neurotic and psychic conditions which develop in those who are suffering from any sexual ailment, real or imaginary.

Long Prepuce.—Much has been said in recent years about the influence of a long prepuce in the male in producing various reflexes the effects of which may be seen in serious disturbance of even distant organs. The kidneys are sometimes said to be thus reflexly affected, and occasionally the digestion and the bowels—even, sometimes, mental processes are said to be influenced unfavorably by the diffusion of reflexes from the irritation consequent upon this sensitive structure being too long. A whole system of nosology exists in some minds due to an over-long prepuce. There are, of course, cases in which circumcision should be performed. There is a larger number of others, however, in which the redundant prepuce is neither adherent nor constricted and is only slightly longer than it should be. Occasionally something arouses the attention of the possessor of the redundant tissue and he gets the idea that it is the source of reflex irritation even for distant parts of his organism. It is an interesting study in suggestion to see how symptoms develop in various organs as a consequence of the cultivation of this thought. Urination becomes frequent, the patient even wakes at night to urinate and the urine, as in many neuroses, becomes more abundant and of lower specific gravity—the typical nervous urine of the hysterical, and there may be much worry and emotional disturbance.

These symptoms, however, are not effects of the long prepuce, but are results of the neurotic influence of concentration of mind on it. It will often be advisable, in young men particularly, to have circumcision performed, but in most cases this is unnecessary, and if the patient can be made to understand how the symptoms have developed he will learn a precious lesson in not interfering with his functions by over-attention to them. Of course, there are many surgeons who will continue to hold, as they seem to now, that nature was quite at fault in the production of this organ and that it should be removed in nearly every human being. The majority of men, however, have lived their lives quite well and happily without such intervention and there are certain inconveniences attached to the condition which remains after operation that may in their way be quite as bothersome as the symptoms due to the long foreskin.

Psychic Impotence.—An important sexual neurosis, at least in the eyes of sufferers from it, is what physicians have come to know as psychic impotence. Young married men, because of over-anxiety with regard to themselves for a number of reasons, but without any physical factor to disturb them, find it impossible to complete the sexual act. Naturally this creates a serious disturbance of mind. The patient will either hurry to a physician at some place on his wedding tour, or his wedding tour will be shortened and he will return to consult a friend. He presents a lively picture of despair. He has not been sleeping, his appetite is disturbed, he feels lassitude and weakness, and if he has a lively imagination he is inclined to think that the fatal termination of some serious nervous disease of which he has heard, and which is accompanied by the symptom of sexual impotence, is impending over him. His condition is quite pitiable, though largely imaginary.

Reassurance.—The treatment of the condition is not so difficult as it might seem if the patient has a reasonable confidence in his physician. If he {476} goes to an advertising "specialist," as occasionally happens, because he concludes that the ordinary physician cannot know all the details of these intricately complex nervous diseases, he is sure to suffer severely in general health before cure is obtained. His morbid ideas will be fostered because he is ready to pay any amount of money in order to stop the progress of the presumed serious disease. An investigation of these "specialists" in New York, made a few years ago by a committee of the New York County Medical Society, showed to what an extent the terrors of these unfortunate patients are exploited for monetary reasons.

A physician of even a little experience in these matters, however, recognizes at once the entirely neurotic character of the case and by reassurance soon enables the young man to dispel many of his worst terrors. His general health can be regulated, his constipation, which so frequently exists, is relieved, and he can be told, what is very true, that the excitement consequent upon the preparations for his wedding and the exhaustion due to the overwork so frequently necessary in order to enable him to take the time off for his wedding journey, have made him so nervously irritable that the ordinary mechanism of the sexual act, which is extremely delicate and requires nice co-ordination for proper function, has been disturbed. Just as soon as this fatigue and the over-excitement of mind consequent upon the unfortunate experience are mitigated his potency will return. This assurance can be given almost at once.

His fears, however, will delay his recovery. His dread of incapacity will become an obsession. Probably the most effective means of treating this is to forbid him to attempt the sexual act for a definite length of time, say two or three weeks. This must be impressed upon him. There is a good reason for insisting that he shall not irritate his already excited sexual system by such attempts. Usually at the end of a week or ten days he will come back with a smiling look of confidence in himself and his physician, to confess that he has violated the injunction, but that he was not disappointed as before.

Subconscious Obsession.—In most of these cases the young men have been victims of sex habits of some kind or of drug addictions, and they have heard that occasionally individuals who have had such experiences may suffer from sexual impotence later in life. This is a strong suggestion to them and in some cases becomes a haunting obsession, and produces the unfavorable effect upon the organism. It is necessary to remove this obsession before a cure can be effected. The patient's confidence must be obtained and the physician's personality and persuasive powers used to change his point of view. Occasionally I have seen cases in which the patients themselves seem to be scarcely aware of this strong suggestion or obsession at work in them. It seemed to be more or less subconscious. An idea with regard to the evil effects of the old habit had been implanted and remained in their minds, occasionally making itself felt but more often apparently lying dormant. In these cases it is important that the physician should make this underlying factor clear to the patient. In some of these cases hypnosis is necessary. Usually the hypnoidal condition, with suggestions in the waking state, is all that is necessary and ordinary suggestions will often effect the purpose completely.

Organic Impotence.—Certain forms of sexual impotence are really preliminary signs of serious organic nervous disease. Sometimes it is the first {477} symptom of paresis or of locomotor ataxia. Oftener it is a very early symptom of syphilitic spinal myelitis. In practically all of these cases, however, there is a history of syphilis and the presence of this should always be a warning not to think of functional or psychic impotence until the possible influence of the syphilis itself or of some of the parasyphilitic diseases is thoroughly excluded. Unfortunately, not a few people who have had syphilis are nervous and anxious about themselves and by their very anticipation of possible developments may auto-suggest themselves into a state in which these symptoms will develop. It is cases of neurasthenia that develop after secondary syphilis in persons who have been studying syphilis and its possible effects, which present the most difficult problems in diagnosis that come to the nerve specialist. Many simulated symptoms are unconsciously developed and this makes differential diagnosis extremely hard. As a rule, the psychic impotence is merely functional and patients need reassurance more than anything else.

Nocturnal Emissions.—One of the sexual neuroses that gives rise to a high degree of solicitude centers around the question of involuntary seminal emissions. Young men who are living normal healthy lives and who are in robust health with no indulgence of sexuality are likely to experience more or less regular involuntary emissions. If for any reason they become nervous or anxious about their sexual functions, especially at times when they are under much mental strain, these phenomena of emptying the seminal vesicles may occur rather frequently. If they have been reading some of the literature, or hearing some of the exaggerated notions that are often expressed with regard to the evil effects that may come from this, they are likely to suffer much mental anxiety over it. Occasionally they lose sleep, frequently they feel so wearied and worried the day after the occurrence as to be disturbed at their work, sometimes they are sure they are so tired that they are unable to fulfill their ordinary duties, and I suppose every physician has known young men who were even sure that the loss of the seminal fluid was seriously interfering with health, hampering many physical functions and bringing them to an untimely grave. They had no appetite and in consequence of not eating enough they were constipated and then a whole round of physical troubles, headache, lassitude, over-fatigue, to which they are almost sure to add loss or disturbance of memory, began to annoy them.

In those cases it is not the physical effect of any loss of seminal fluid that is the disturbing factor of their health, but their worry over the losses. Just as soon as their minds can be taken off the subject, the supposed physical effects begin to disappear. So long as the solicitude continues the emissions themselves increase in number and the condition is made worse. These patients must be taught that in every normal healthy man in whom there is no regular occasion for the emptying of the seminal vesicles, nature provides for an evacuation about every ten days or two weeks. In some it is more frequent than this. In those who are much indoors and in whom oxidation processes are low this emptying takes place more frequently. In those who lead a sedentary life with the consumption of much proteid food the same thing seems to be true. Any anxiety about it is sure to cause frequent repetition of the evacuation processes. Over-solicitude about the bladder will have just the same effect. If the patient will take his mind off the subject, will eat normally, will get out in the air more than before, tiring himself thoroughly {478} if he is young and vigorous, and will not allow the sexual side of his being to be excited by stories or pictures, plays or voluntary thoughts, his affliction will soon disappear.

Prophylaxis.—Certain directions are helpful and by occupying the patient's mind will overcome certain physical factors that underlie the affection. It is important that the bladder should not be allowed to be full, above all, not to be over-distended at night. Some care should be exercised in not taking too much to drink shortly before going to bed and the bladder should be faithfully emptied before retiring. The weight of a large amount of urine in the bladder pressing down upon the seminal vesicles situated below and behind it causes them to contract rather easily. This is particularly true if the patient sleeps on his back and occasionally in certain over-irritable patients for a time at least an arrangement may have to be made by means of small pillows that will prevent him from sleeping on his back. On the other hand, it must not be forgotten that too great abstinence from fluid will cause the urine to be more concentrated and this will irritate the bladder and either wake the patient up at night, which of itself is undesirable, or else will cause congestion in the prostatic region which will irritate the seminal vesicles to the point of evacuation. While five or six glasses of water a day should be taken besides the ordinary fluid taken at meals, the only regulation necessary is of the amount of fluid taken in the evening after the last meal, that is, if more than three hours intervene before retiring for the night.

261

Besides the physical conditions in the bladder, an accumulation of fecal material in the rectum may cause irritation of the seminal vesicles. It is important, moreover, to remember that thoroughly free movements of the bowels, by preventing to a great extent the reabsorption of material from the intestines which may prove irritant when excreted through the kidneys and when present in the bladder, is of itself an excellent therapeutic measure in cases of irritability of the genital organs. The setting of the patient's mind to thinking about his rectum, his bowels, and his bladder instead of his genital tract is an excellent psychotherapeutic measure that will soon bear fruit.

The consumption of various foods, condiments and drinks enters into the underlying condition which produces frequent emissions. We have already suggested that the use of a large amount of proteid materials, especially in people who live a sedentary life, often predisposes to this condition. An abundance of the carbohydrates, however, by supplying more heat than is necessary may have a like effect. Certain spices seem to predispose to irritability of the sexual system. Red pepper has always seemed to those who saw much of these cases to be particularly at fault. Mustard, curries, peppers generally, however, and even other spices seem to have a corresponding effect. As a rule, young folks suffering from this disturbance or from the tendency to eroticism in other ways should be warned about this irritation of spices. In neurotic individuals tea and especially coffee has the same effect. Probably this is only an indirect influence of tea upon the nerve centers, making them more irritable, but coffee, by raising the blood pressure, seems to have a direct unfavorable effect.

All alcoholic drinks are contraindicated in these cases and must be forbidden. Certain of them seem to be more harmful than others. According to French tradition warm wine or mulled ale as it is used in England is {479} especially likely to excite sexuality. Warm alcoholic drinks of any kind are absorbed more rapidly than are cool drinks, which is the main reason in modern times for having these liquids cooled so that they will not be absorbed too rapidly and disturb the equilibrium. Champagne also has, by tradition, a special effect, sometimes said to be due to the increased hyperemia of the stomach induced by the carbonic acid gas and the consequent more rapid absorption.

The prohibition of spices and alcoholic drinks has a good effect in itself. It acts constantly as a suggestion to the necessity for care and guard over one's self. Besides the exercise of self-denial necessary to keep away from the use of such substances, especially under present social conditions, is of itself a good training that strengthens the will against certain tendencies to indulgence in sexual thoughts which predispose to the frequent emptying of the seminal vesicles.

Erotic Dreams.—Very often these nocturnal seminal emissions are associated with erotic dreams. Patients are inclined to attribute the occurrence of these dreams to some fault of their own or to consider that they are at least in some way responsible for them. This thought often becomes a source of serious worry, making their condition worse. A study of this question has convinced me that in most cases there is practically no responsibility in the matter. Pressure on the seminal vesicles by an over-full bladder, or a distended rectum, leads to the production of nervous stimuli around which the erotic dream-ideas gather. A straightforward explanation of this will relieve many patients' minds, and keep them from bothering about the subject in such a way as to make their genital tract even more sensitive than it is because of their concentration of attention on it.

Sexual Mental Troubles.—In our generation sex occupies a great deal of attention. Sexual tendencies are emphasized by suggestive reading of all kinds and by forced attention to sex matters. Most of the successful novels deal with the so-called sex problem, our plays are to a great extent sex problem plays and our newspapers are full of sex crimes and sexual divagations of many kinds. This acts as a strong incitement to sexuality and represents exactly the opposite of what nature intended in the matter. As a consequence, all the tendencies to over-solicitude with regard to sexual affections and all that instability of mind and over-reaction to all forms of irritation that comes in the midst of sexual excitation are noted. This seriously disturbs the minds of many patients and makes their health as well as their morals worse than they should be. The neurotic conditions seen in those who occupy their leisure with erotic subjects are fostered by this unfortunate over-attention to sexual matters. For general prophylaxis the physician needs to throw all the weight of his influence toward the correction of unfortunate tendencies in our present-day life and healthier subjects of thought should be encouraged.

We often hear it said in our time that the great fact of life is sex. Indeed, this has been insisted on *ad nauseam* in recent years. There is no doubt that without the sex element the race would not continue under the present dispensation. If sexual feelings did not mean so much to the generality of men and women it is doubtful whether marriage would be the success that it is, though so much is said nowadays about its failure. The analogy with all the beings lower in the scale than man shows how imperative and prominent {480} in life this instinct is and how much it signifies. Those who insist so much, however, on sex as the one great fact of life seem to forget that there are many other natural functions of quite as much importance to the individual at least, if not to the race. Without eating neither the individual nor the race could go on. Neither would the race go on without eliminating waste products. If there is one thing that our consideration of the problems of psychotherapy has made clear it is that whenever any of these animal facts of life is made much of and occupies attention to the exclusion of higher ideas, there is sure to be trouble. It matters not how apparently automatic and completely spontaneous a function may be, if exaggerated attention is given to it, it is sure to be disturbed in its functions and cause serious troubles in the organism.

There is no need further to illustrate this with regard to such physiological necessities as feeding and excretion. At present the world is much occupied with sex problems because, unfortunately, its attention has been focused on this subject. Physicians, particularly if they are paying attention to nervous patients, are likely to know many individuals who have food problems, diet problems, digestion problems, bowel problems, and many others of similar nature because they have been focusing their attention on these functions of their being.

The most distinguished psychiatrist of our generation, certainly the man whose works have done most to open up new vistas for us in mental diseases and who has added not only new knowledge but new possibilities of development, visited this country not long since and said, "Oh! here in America you are sex mad." He added, "I knew that we were madly following sex problems in Europe, but I thought that in this country, with so many other things to occupy the minds of men and women, you were not bothered so much with sex problems." What he said represents the impression of nearly every thoughtful foreigner who is surprised to find that wealth and luxury have brought to us this same degenerate interest in things sexual that occupies the so-called upper classes and their imitators in Europe.

Livy, the Roman historian, said long ago, "Whenever women become ashamed of the things they should not be ashamed of, it will not be long before they will begin not to be ashamed of the things they should be ashamed of." Whenever in history men and women have occupied themselves, not with the rearing of families, but with the suppression of families to as great an extent as possible, sex problems have always become emphasized. The woman who is a mother, and especially many times a mother, usually has no trouble at all about sex problems and no tendency to have "affinities." With her there is usually no question of sex as the central factor of life nor of any other of the curious nonsense that has been talked about this matter as the result of giving sex a place of importance that it does not deserve. Until there is a reform in this matter we can look for many "neurotic, erotic and tommy-rotic" tendencies, as they have been called, due to over-attention to one set of organs. Any organic system in the body would be disturbed by such attention, but the sexual system is particularly susceptible to suggestion.

The state of affairs thus emphasized is the result of interfering with an animal instinct. It will make itself felt properly and secure the due exercises of function if allowed to pursue the even tenor of its way under reasonable {481} control, but if it is fostered, thought about, discussed, excited in various ways, pampered by indulgence and perversion, it runs away with nature. The gourmet who constantly thinks about food, plans new modes of exciting the appetite, studies savors and odors in order to satisfy a palate that has been artificially stimulated, gets a certain animal enjoyment out of his food that other people do not; but he usually overeats, loses his appetite, and with it any real satisfaction in eating, and suffers from indigestion as a consequence of indulgence, so that the suffering much more than compensates for any slight additional pleasure that he has enjoyed. Besides, man is an essentially intellectual being, and occupation with the things of sense, that will manage themselves very well if let alone, takes up just so much of the precious time that should be devoted to other things to attain that satisfaction that makes life well worth living. Sexuality cultivated with the degree of attention that certain people devote to feeding, becomes a pest, ruins intellectual effort, hurts initiative, leads to the most serious disappointments in life and is the most fruitful cause of despondency and suicide that we have besides being the origin of many social evils that still further complicate life.

One great modern nation has debauched its literature to such an extent that probably the major portion of its books treat of sex and sex problems. Practically all of its esthetic expression has been seriously hurt by the same fault. Its painting, its sculpture, its dramatics, its art of all kinds, have all gone the same road. The result is seen in the lowered moral fiber of its people. A recent census report showed that the nation has reduced some 20,000 in numbers and that this was only the beginning of the race suicide. They have been thinking, talking, writing, painting, chiseling, acting sex problems, but in the only phase of life in which sex really counts it has been so pushed into the background or perverted that there it is failing utterly to accomplish its one legitimate purpose. The younger generation as they grow up are given the idea that they are missing the most wonderful thing in life unless they have memorable sex experiences. These experiences must be varied in order to satisfy the artificial appetite that has been created. As a consequence, family life and the real meaning of love and the affection of man for woman rooted in the depths of their nature is spoiled by mere animal passion and its passing expression.

Nature's own attitude with regard to over-attention to sex matters must not be forgotten. The purely sexual organs have been pushed into the background to as great an extent as possible and are intimately associated in both sexes with one of the two ugly excretory functions, urination, and placed in close relationship with the structures which subtend the other—defecation. Evidently nature intended that they should be the subject of as little attention as possible. Unfortunately, the paying of attention to them to any great extent lessens somewhat of the disgust naturally aroused by the excretory functions with which they are associated. Nature has provided as far as possible for deterrence from over-interest. One might expect that cleanliness and the cultivation of the feelings of refinement would serve as auxiliaries in the repression of sex indulgence. The lessons of history are that usually the great bathing nations have been most sexually divagant. Among the Greeks and the Romans the ugliest sex habits and proclivities found a place—among peoples who devoted themselves to the cleanliness of the body. The classes {482} who bathe most are often those with the strongest tendency to sexuality. Refinement instead of lessening the tendency to sexual indulgence rather increases it.

Education and the development of intellectuality, far from being a barrier to sexual divagations, seem to predispose to the exaggeration of the significance of sex in life, unless the individual has a well-balanced character or has been thoroughly grounded in ethical principles. The ugly stories of Greek love at a time when the Greeks were at the climax of culture, as well as what we know about the relations of the freedmen to their masters among the Romans during the classical period, is all confirmed by the revelations of corresponding tendencies in recent generations among the intellectual classes even at the universities. Development of mind apparently does not neutralize to any extent these sexual tendencies. Evidently the rule of life for health's sake must be to push sexuality as much into the background of the mind as nature has put the sex organs in the human body. Reason does not protect knowledge but increases suggestion. Only absorbing occupation of mind with other subjects that will bring about neglect of these functions, as of all other physiological functions, leaving them to nature, serves to keep them in their proper place and condition.

CHAPTER III

SEXUAL HABITS

As was emphasized in the preceding chapter, sexual symptoms are usually the subject of so much worry and disturbance of mind and become the center of so much unfavorable suggestion, that the only way to ameliorate the conditions which develop is by securing relaxation of the attention and diversion of mind. Mental influence is much more important than any other remedies that we have at our command in these cases, not only for their relief but for their ultimate cure.

263

A state of depression of mind similar to that which develops in patients frightened by seminal emissions is often seen in those who have for some time indulged in the habit of self-abuse. Rather frequently a physician, especially if he is known to be interested in nervous diseases, has to listen to the story of a patient who is sure that his health is completely undermined and that his future is the darkest possible, because of this habit in younger days. Usually the patient is a young man who has been reading some of the literature of the advertising "specialists" who distribute reading matter which pictures appalling and almost irretrievable effects from such sexual habits. The consequence is that the patient is in highly nervous condition, has lost his appetite, is not sleeping well, is avoiding society, because he fears that some one may recognize his condition and its cause, and he is really in a pitiable state. Such patients are usually sure that little can be done for them. Sometimes they have already been through the hands of several "specialists," particularly of the mail-order variety, and the literature provided for them and the letters written to them have all helped to make them worse and much more solicitous about themselves.

{483}

Unfortunately some of the exaggerated notions with regard to the effect of these habits that are so widely diffused by the exploiters of the young have been adopted by moralists with the idea that they can thus deter youth from certain practices and scare the victims of such habits out of them. It is extremely doubtful, however, whether self abuse of itself, unless practiced in very early years or indulged in to a degree that is possible only in those of unbalanced mind, ever works anything like the serious harm that is claimed. Certainly physicians who are most familiar with its results are not ready to confirm the opinions usually advanced as to the awful harmfulness of the practice. Personally, I have had a number of patients confess to me that they had indulged in the habit to some extent for twenty years and longer and yet had never suffered anything more than passing physical discomfort. It is unfortunate, then, that the exaggerations of the quack should by receiving the approval of the well-intentioned moralists, be emphasized so as to add to the neurotic disturbance of mind which makes these patients so miserable and for a time may seriously interfere with their health. Occasionally even suicides are reported in which the underlying motive seems to have been the dread on the part of a young man that a sexual habit has so undermined his health that cure is impossible and that physical and mental deterioration to a marked degree is inevitable. The opinions of conservative physicians tend to show that there is no good reason for thinking that in normal healthy persons such habits ever have the serious effects thus set forth.

Patients can be assured that whatever evil effects follow the practice will not remain after it has been given up. There are no serious enduring sequelae, with one or two exceptions in very special cases, that perhaps should be noticed. Most men of considerable experience in the matter are now decidedly of the opinion that self-abuse does not produce any more serious consequences than the same amount of ordinary sexual intercourse. It is possible for sexual intercourse indulged in excessively, as it sometimes is in early marital life, to produce the same feelings of exhaustion, lack of control over the vasomotor system and disturbance of the gastro-intestinal tract which are noted in self-abuse. In both cases the symptoms promptly disappear upon proper regulation of life. This is a very different opinion from that which used to be expressed in this matter and it is given only after due deliberation and consultation of many authorities both in writing and orally. Its expression, far from taking away one of the best deterrent motives against the practice, rather forces an appeal to the manliness of the individual. The motive of fear never accomplishes much, while a frank statement of the real condition may be greatly helpful.

While the habit of self-abuse as indulged in by the ordinary individual practically never has the awful consequences that have been sometimes pictured as resulting from it even long after its cessation, there is no doubt that it is productive of many physical symptoms during the time of its indulgence. There is almost sure to be a discouraging lassitude and a tendency to exhaustion after even comparatively small efforts. While this is true for ordinary muscular efforts it is also true for other bodily functions that involve muscular activity. In recent years we have learned that of the stomach functions the motor is more important than the chemical. In the bowels the motor function is extremely important. There are likely to be disturbances, then, in the gastro-intestinal tract as a consequence of the muscular condition that {484} develops in those patients. Probably more important even than the physical, however, are the psychic results of the habit. The patient feels discouraged and cast down at his inability to conquer himself and is likely to avoid such exercise and diversion of mind as would make normal healthy function possible.

Mental Disturbances.—It is the custom to say that mental deterioration almost surely follows the habit. Those familiar with mental cases often see self-abuse practiced with serious results by young folks whose mentality is deteriorated. In these cases the practice was indulged in with great frequency and with direct physical consequences, such as loss of sleep, of appetite and the like. It is not the habit, however, that has caused the mental deterioration. The young patients are going crazy, but not because of self-abuse. Their habit of self-abuse had originated and become exaggerated because they were already mentally unbalanced. Their extreme indulgence in it is especially due to their lack of control over themselves, because they are not possessed of strong will power with regard to any thing. A vicious circle is formed and the insane young man gradually deepens his insanity by hurting his physical condition through over-indulgence in the habit and all this further lessens his self-control; but were it not for the original mental weakness the habit would not have been indulged in to so great an extent.

Effect on Prostate.—There is one phase of the ill effects of self-abuse that it is well to recall as having the confirmation of men of large experience and conservative views. There is a definite impression among specialists in genito-urinary diseases that enlargement of the prostate in some cases is due to the frequently repeated irritation and the prolongation of that irritation of the prostate during the practice of self-abuse. When such men as Bangs and Keyes are agreed on a subject of this kind, then even though in a certain number of cases the changes in the prostate leading to its enlargement are evidently inflammatory, it is well to consider that the functional over-activity of the gland superinduced by the practice may lead at least to an enlargement of the glandular elements with the consequent interference with urination which so frequently comes in old age.

Physical Factors.—Besides mental elements that predispose to the formation of sexual habits there are physical factors that are important in these cases. They must be particularly looked for and treated carefully if found, or there can be little hope of relief for the conditions. The most prominent of these is the existence of a long foreskin, especially if its opening is small, thus leading to the retention of urine, the deposition of urinary salts with the formation of preputial concretions or so-called calculi. These are intensely irritant, cause frequent itching and thus predispose to these sexual habits. Even where the preputial opening is free and allows egress of urine without residue, the accumulation of smegma often causes considerable irritation and if the most scrupulous cleanliness with cleansing at least once a day is not maintained, irritative conditions arise, especially in hot weather, that may give occasions for sex habits.

Under these conditions the habit is sometimes seen in extremely early years. The youngest case I ever saw occurred in a child not quite nineteen months old whose mother said that for several months she had noticed certain curious actions that she could scarcely understand until finally the truth dawned on her. Then she was morbidly sensitive about it, sure that the habit was due {485} to a fault of her own and it was some time before she consulted a physician. This was her fourth child and, strange as it may seem, it was only at the conception of this child that she first knew what sexual pleasure was. She feared that her feeling had been in some way sinful and that as a consequence of her sin this curious habit had developed in such early years in her baby boy. As is usually the case in these instances, I found that the prepuce was very tight indeed, having scarcely more than a pinhole opening in it. During urination this ballooned and there remained in the pouch-like process at the end of the penis a certain amount of residual urine after every urination. From this urinary salts had been precipitated and had formed scaly concretions which remained in the preputial pouch and were extremely irritant. As a consequence of this irritation the baby had been very itchy and it was in the endeavor to relieve the itching by the natural process of scratching that the pleasure of the sensations aroused had been discovered and the sexual habit had been formed.

Not infrequently in young men a condition resembling this to some degree at least is found and then, of course, the question of its removal must be taken up at once. It is surprising how often in youths in their late teens concretions are seen. The constant irritation makes it practically impossible for the patient to keep his hands from the parts, and so circumcision is absolutely necessary. Not infrequently when the preputial condition is not nearly so bad this operation may also be at least advisable if not necessary. The matter of cleanliness must be attended to, preferably after getting up in the morning and not before going to bed at night, for the reaction after cold water may cause congestion of the organ. After a time the frequent use of cold water seems to make the parts much less reactive to irritation of any kind.

Physical Effects.—The super-excitation of nerves consequent upon the more or less general erethism that is induced, lessens resistive vitality. Victims of the habit are more liable to colds, to various infectious diseases, and are subject to fatigue and lassitude, with incapacity to work to their full power. They lose control over their vasomotor system to some extent as a result of this systemic erethism. They blush easily, they perspire easily, there is a tendency in many of them to flash as if of heat and cold, they become pale under excitement or anger more than formerly, they are likely to suffer from cold hands and feet, and the surface of the body is inclined to be cold and as a consequence patients are tremulous. This represents a waste of nervous energy and as a consequence sleep may be disturbed and digestion interfered with.

It is important, therefore, to consider these cases as really needing medical care. For their treatment the most important consideration is prophylaxis, not alone of the habit itself, but of each of the acts. Prophylaxis of the habit is an ethical question that we can scarcely do justice to here. Prophylaxis of the acts requires consideration of the physical and moral factors that predispose to their commission. While the habit may have secured such deep control that the patient almost despairs of relief from it, when care is taken to remove physical and moral predispositions the conquest of the habit becomes comparatively easy. Over and over again I have seen cases that have lasted for years in which the patients were surprised at the ease with which they were able {486} to drop the habit just as soon as they took the measures necessary to prevent predisposing conditions.

Breaking the Habit.—Once physical factors predisposing to it are removed, the habit is not so hard to break as it would seem to be from the suggestions to that effect made in sensational literature. It is neither so deleterious in its physical effects nor so deteriorating as regards character as is usually stated. Anyone with a reasonable amount of firmness can break it off if he really resolves to. Over and over again I have seen patients quite surprised at the ease with which they were able to avoid the practice for weeks once they made up their minds in the matter. Indeed this is one of the unfortunate features in completely conquering the habit. It is comparatively so easy to break it off when the mind is made up that there comes the feeling that now it must be absolutely facile to keep away from it. This is, however, never true. Relapses are extremely easy. If the patient allows himself to read vicious books, or suggestive literature of any kind, or permits himself an indulgence in the reading of several columns of the account of a sex murder trial, or goes to see a sex problem play with its suggestions, or exposes himself to sexually exciting conditions of any kind, he will be almost sure to lapse into the old habit.

Relapses are almost inevitable. But it is easier to break the habit the second time than it was the first and it becomes increasingly easy if the patient keeps up the effort of regulating his life so as to avoid the occasions of the habit. Relapses are quite as sure to occur as with regard to alcoholism if occasions for the taking of liquor are not sedulously avoided. The patient always seems to need a confidant—someone to whom he can go for help and who assures him of the ability that he has to overcome himself if he only will. The practice of confession in the Roman Catholic Church makes it comparatively easy for serious people of that faith to overcome the habit. The physician must be taken into confidence in the same way and for a time, at least once a week, the patient may have to be perfectly frank with regard to his condition in order to have the help afforded by such confidences. The physician can often, particularly at the beginning, make the physical conditions such as to help in the breaking of the habit. Bromides taken to the extent of a dram or more a day are almost a specific for superirritability of the nervous system, and if taken for two or three weeks the patient will usually have little or no difficulty in overcoming the habit. They are not of much avail after this time unless the patient's character has been aroused to determined helpfulness in the matter.

In obstinate cases it may be necessary to have a patient come every day, or at least every second day, for some time and give an account of how he has succeeded in resisting his habit in the interval. At least he must be asked to report whenever there is a lapse. It is surprising how much the anticipation of having to tell someone else of a drop back into the habit means in helping the patient eventually to overcome it. Very slight motives serve to cause relapses, but almost any external personal aid, if pursued with confidence, will avail effectually to break it. I talk from an experience of many cases and know how much can be accomplished even though patients insist that they have tried all the resources of their will power and of prayer without avail. They have really not tried, they have not willed in reality; sometimes they {487} have reached a point where they cannot will without the moral support of another personality. This can be readily supplied to them by a firm, sympathetic physician whom they respect. It will take time to overcome the tendency to relapse whenever the will is relapsed, but the habit itself can be broken without much difficulty in a few days.

Certain times are particularly dangerous for relapses into the habit. These are just before going to sleep at night and before getting out of bed in the morning. At these times the mind must be occupied or else the patient will almost surely find his habit recurring. Often the habit of reading in bed, properly supported by pillows and with abundant light at an angle that makes reading easy, seems to be good for these patients, because they may read until their eyelids get heavy, then pull the chain of their light to extinguish it and turn over to sleep. In the morning prompt rising after waking is important. Bed clothes that are too heavy and too great warmth of clothing predispose to sexual excitation and must be avoided. The room should be cool rather than warm and the mattress rather hard.

The more tired the patient is the less liability will there be to difficulty in these matters. But air is even more important than exercise in giving the tiredness which superinduces deep sleep. A lessening of the normal amount of oxygen seems to relax the inhibitory power of the higher centers over the sexual centers in the cord. People who are drowned, those who are hanged, and those whose supply of oxygen is shut off by the inhalation of the heavier gases are likely to have involuntary seminal emissions. These are probably consequent upon the shutting off of the air.

The important element in the treatment is to make the patient feel that, if he really wants to, he can conquer in this matter. The old motives of fear, and especially fear of physical consequences, were quite unworthy, and inasmuch as they had any effect rather produced a deterioration of character than a strengthening of it. The patient must understand that if he is a man he can overcome it. Religious motives will help much. I do not know that I have ever seen a case where religious motives were not the most important element in the cure, but that may be due to the conditions in which I have been placed. I have seen a number of these cases in men and women because clergymen have sent them to me in order that they might be helped in the work of reform, and while there are many relapses and some had apparently given up the effort in despair of their power to overcome themselves, nine out of every ten of those who have seriously faced the problem have succeeded in overcoming themselves, and as a result have a better knowledge of their own characters and more respect for themselves. They are better men in every way than if their improvement had come about through selfish fear of physical consequences.

After Cure.—After the habit of self-abuse has been conquered the seminal vesicles will have a tendency to evacuate themselves rather more frequently than before and as a consequence they will nag at certain sexual nerve endings. They are used to having their contents emptied and distention is followed by rather ready evacuation. During the course of this evacuation sexual thoughts are awakened in dreams and this may lead to dream states in which there seem to be lapses into the old habit. This constitutes a serious difficulty in getting rid of the habit entirely in young and vigorous men. They may even become disheartened by it. It should be explained to them that they must let {488} contrary habits form gradually and permit nature to accommodate herself to the new state of affairs. The bromides are a useful adjunct for body and mind.

Supposed After-effects.—At times a patient suffering from some exhausting or serious disease, consumption, heart disease or the various forms of Bright's disease, will be discouraged by remembrance of the fact that in earlier years he allowed himself for some time to fall into the habit of self-abuse. If he has read, and very few men have not, some of the literature issued by the advertising "specialists" and has heard the unfortunately exaggerated ideas commonly entertained with regard to the influence on health of this habit, he will become more or less disheartened by the idea that he thus undermined his constitution and that one reason why he is not able to react better against his affection is that he seriously diminished his resistive vitality. This idea must, of course, be overcome or it will act as a constant source of unfavorable suggestion, lessening appetite, tending to disturb sleep, banishing peace of mind to some extent and thus inhibiting the patient from releasing such stores of vital energy for his recovery as would surely be in his power under favorable conditions.

Female Habits.—The habit is more rare in women than in men, but when it occurs is a little harder to break. In men it usually develops in youth, but oftenest in women who are past thirty-five and unmarried. In these cases it is much harder for the patient to regain self-control, because the class of women patients who acquire such a habit have less character, as a rule, than the men who fall into the same condition. In all sex matters, once passion is aroused or habit formed, the woman is likely to lose control of herself more than is the man. Even in women, however, it is not only possible, but under favorable circumstances, quite easy to secure a break in the habit, though relapses are more frequent than in men. Certain occupations seem particularly to favor the development of the habit. These are mainly sedentary occupations that can be followed without the necessity for such attention as to prevent the mind from wandering off into thoughts that may prove provocative of sexual sensation. Dressmakers seem particularly likely to suffer from the affection, and those who run sewing-machines are predisposed by the movements involved in their occupation to the development or, at least, to the persistence of the habit.

For women even more than men religion and the motives it supplies are the most efficient factors for the ultimate cure of the habit. In general, the greater difficulty of overcoming it in them is due in no small degree to the fact that they live indoors much more than men, often have sedentary occupations, and are more frequently alone. These afford opportunities for introspection and for the harboring of thoughts that lead to relapses into the habit. Besides, women are more prone to read novels and stories relating to sex problems and the details of sex murder trials and the like which constitute ever-recurring sources of mental erethism. If their habits can be modified, especially if they can be made to realize the necessity for being out in the air as much as possible, and for keeping their windows open at night, as well as for thorough cleanliness—for every gynecologist notes the necessity for this and how frequently it happens that neglect of it leads to irritability of the external organs that is of itself a serious factor—then it would be no more difficult for women to overcome the habit and get beyond the relapses than it is for men. {489} Sometimes we have to overcome a morbid dread of touching themselves even for cleansing purposes which allows the accumulation of irritant material and predisposes to relapse.

Sexual Perversion.—Sexual perversions are sometimes considered as different from sexual neuroses, but such they really are. They are oftener due to habit than to anything deeper. Much has been said about the unfortunate natural inclination of some people to indulge in sexual perversion, but such talk partakes of the nature of similar remarks with regard to habits of other kinds. The alcohol habit, for instance, is formed by many men as the result of their environment and a weakness of character, with lack of resolution to support themselves in self-denial when they are tempted to drink. In recent years it has been only too often the custom to excuse or to justify many of these cases. There are a few persons in whom, owing to weakness of character, alcoholism is more or less inevitable if occasions for indulgence occur. And in the same way there has been much maudlin sentimentality wasted on sexual perverts, as if most of these men could not avoid the actions that the rest of humanity abominates. There are, perhaps, a few individuals who because of a failure on the part of nature to define sex in them properly—as if she had not quite made up her mind which sex they should belong to—are more to be pitied than held to account for their delinquencies in this matter. Compared to the whole number of sexual perverts, however, these are very few. Under the protection of the pity awakened for these, a large number of others find quasi-justification for their acts.

Anyone who knows much about these patients realizes that their story is, as a rule, very different from what it would be if they were inevitably impelled to the commission of the acts in question. Many of them had the greatest abhorrence for it at the beginning, were attracted to it out of curiosity and morbid sexualism, because they had allowed themselves to think and read and dream about sex matters overmuch. They are usually idle people who do not take life seriously and who have an inordinate curiosity about sex subjects. At the beginning the commission of the perverted sexual act was associated with an intensely deterrent rather than an attractive feeling, but gradually this was overcome and a contrary habit has been formed. It is difficult to break this habit and to get away from the morbid sexual ideas that have been allowed to develop and grow strong in connection with it.

This opinion is somewhat different from that held by many men who are recognized as authorities on this subject and who find many excuses in the nature of their patients for these perversions. If it is recalled, however, that whenever wealth has brought luxury to a people and luxury has brought over-refinement, such sex perversions have been particularly noted, it will be realized that not nature, but the ways of men are responsible for their development. Whenever men pay much attention to their bodies, exercise for the sake of their muscles, bathe not for cleanliness but for luxury, sex perversions become common in history. The story of Greek love is well known. Corresponding conditions developed at Rome under similar circumstances. According to good authorities, the English universities became tainted with it a generation ago. Our athletic clubs in this country have rightly or wrongly fallen under suspicion in this matter, though the tendency to exaggeration with regard to such things, and popular credulity in such matters must be recalled. {490} Some confirmatory evidence undoubtedly there was. Sexual perversions then would seem to be due in most cases to definite conditions and our knowledge suggests readily what should be the prophylaxis.

In the course of some studies with Professor Magnan at L'Asile Ste Anne in Paris I saw a number of these curious cases of sexual divagations, exhibitionism, sex perversions and similar conditions. Some of his cases were clearly curious examples of natural tendency, at least, to mental hermaphroditism. Occasionally men of normal development otherwise have a woman's waist and woman's torso above the waist, and many womanly coquettish ways that point to this curious mixture of sexes. Occasionally women are lacking in all the sex characteristics of the upper portion of the body, have no breasts and have the hirsute characteristics of men on the face and even on the chest. In such cases one may be tempted to let one's pity override one's better judgment and feel that resistance to the temptations to indulge in perverted sexual feelings may be so difficult for these people as to be almost impossible. Even in such cases, however, under Magnan's gentle tutelage, under his faithful care and sympathy, men and women lost most of the tendency to commit unnatural acts and certainly found it easier to live normal lives than before.

For the majority of these sexual perverts, however, it is as with regard to drug addictions, alcoholism, and obesity, just a question of willing not to indulge in certain appetites that serves to help them. There is no doubt that it is a difficult matter to break a habit that has become a second nature, and it is almost impossible that it should be accomplished without a number of relapses. If the patient really wishes to correct the evil habit, however, this is perfectly possible.

The talk of a third sex with homo-sexual inclinations is quite beside the mark. Certain of this class have a weakness of intellect and of will that is at the root of their trouble, but not a few of them pride themselves on their intellect and will power in most other things and must not be permitted to deceive themselves as to their weakness and its significance. It is not nature but self that is at fault and the disease can be completely eradicated.

{491}

SECTION XIII

SKIN DISEASES

CHAPTER I

PSYCHOTHERAPY IN SKIN DISEASES

The place of mental influence in the treatment of skin diseases will be best realized from the role that we know the mind plays in the production of various skin manifestations. There is a whole series of skin affections which depend to a considerable extent on mental conditions, worries, anxieties, shocks, frights and the like, and a number of skin affections that have been labeled hysterical which occur in nervous persons, due to over-attention to self and their conditions. It has been well said that it is possible to make the feet warm by thinking about them. Certainly attention to any part of the skin surface causes a tingling and hyperemia may follow. Blushing is an illustration of mental influence on the skin, and anything that would tend to make this endure for some time would give rise to erythematous conditions. We know the creepy, uncomfortable, hot feelings that come over us in times of suppressed excitement when we are waiting for something to happen; and, on the other hand, there is a pallor and tremor that accompanies fright or fear, which points to mental influences over the vasomotor system in the skin.

Urticarias.—Certain skin diseases, especially those allied to the urticaria group, are prone to occur in connection with excitement and worry. In the chapter on Neurotic Intestinal Affections attention is called to the fact that many patients who suffer from intestinal idiosyncrasies and have excessive reactions to special kinds of food, as cheese, strawberries, or the like, sometimes also suffer from skin lesions and intestinal disturbance through worry or excitement. While preparing for examinations or undergoing some physical trial or suffering from worry or anxiety such persons may have urticaria or even wheals on the skin. There may be some dietary disturbance to account for them, but they would not occur, or at least would not be so serious and annoying, but for the disturbed mental condition. Under these circumstances dermatographia is a common manifestation. It used to be considered a symptom of many physical conditions, but will occur in almost any nervous person during the course of an examination by a strange physician or when some important medical decision is pending.

Eczema.—Not only these passing conditions of the skin, however, but more lasting affections have been connected with mental disturbance. Probably every skin specialist has noted in a number of his cases that a first attack of eczema came after a period of worry or excitement, or sometimes followed directly on a fright. When relief from the condition has been brought about {492} by treatment, relapses occur during periods of business worry or family anxiety or mental stresses of one kind or another. Cabinet crises in England are found to be likely to be followed by the recurrence of eczematous conditions in older members of the Cabinet or by first attacks in some of those whose skin has been irritated by some internal condition. Unless business worries can be removed or family anxieties allayed the cure of eczema becomes a difficult matter. Men or women who worry about their eczematous condition apparently prolong it. This is particularly true if they have little to do and are likely to be much occupied with themselves and their condition.

Herpes.—Herpetic conditions resemble urticaria in their response to mental conditions. Herpes preputialis and herpes progenitalis occur particularly in people who worry over the possibility of some infection of the genitals. The lesions are likely to be indolent until the state of mind with regard to them is relieved by reassurance as to their comparatively innocuous character. Even herpes zoster is prone to come on after a period of worry and anxiety. It is due to infection, but the infection becomes more possible after a lowering of resistive vitality in the nervous system. This is particularly true as regards herpes facialis. It has been noted again and again that facial neuralgia is most likely to occur after fright, deep emotion, or prolonged anxiety. Treatment of these cases will only be successful if the mental state is set right. This is particularly true with regard to Bell's palsy. Patients who worry much about it and who fear that it may have lasting results are likely to prolong its course and to put off complete cure for a good while.

Vasomotor Disturbance.—There is a series of skin affections connected directly with the vasomotor system of the skin which are largely under the influence of emotional or mental factors. These represent particularly the milder forms of Raynaud's disease and the parallel forms of Weir Mitchell's disease. In the one case there is a spasm of the arterioles causing what the French call "dead fingers," and in the other paralysis of the vasomotor system with venous congestion in the parts. They are seen particularly in persons of highly nervous organization and especially after periods of emotional strain or stress. There is a series of affections related to these, characterized by numbness, paresthesiae, going to sleep of the fingers or members, tingling, and even milder forms of itchiness—sometimes dignified as pruritus—which are largely due to mental factors. Some physical condition will need to be corrected, but they will only disappear if the mind is set at rest and if the patient is kept from occupying his attention much with them. Concentration of attention will make them chronic.

Scurvy.—Scurvy is not usually thought of as a skin disease, though it has many local manifestations on the skin and mucous membrane. It is a deep nutritional disturbance of such nature that it would seem the mind could have but little influence over it. When scurvy was common, however, it was often noticed that any change of attitude of mind in affected persons brought amelioration or deterioration of condition. Scurvy develops with special virulence during discouragement; it gets better with the dawn of hope. It has been known to be much improved by the prospect of a naval engagement when all the sick men wanted to get into the fighting. The famous case of the Siege of Breda in 1625 is often quoted. The city was about to capitulate because so many of the soldiers were suffering from the disease. The

Prince of Orange, {493} however, sent word that a new and powerful remedy had been discovered that was sure to cure the affection, and that he had secured some of it and it would not be long before they would all be well. What he sent was a remedy that had been used with indifferent success for scurvy when taken in large doses. He could send only enough to give a few drops to each patient. This small dose was wonder-working in its effect and proved to have the healing virtue of a gallon of the liquor. Most of the patients got better and surrender was put off.

Warts.—A striking evidence of the influence of the mind upon the skin is given by what we know of warts. All sorts of charms have been not alone suggested for them but found to work in certain cases. Lord Bacon in his "Natural History" tells the story of the charming away of warts and exemplifies it by his own experience. When he was about sixteen a number of warts—at least 100—came out upon his hands. One of these had been there from childhood. The manner of their cure he details as follows:

The English Ambassador's lady, who was a woman far from superstition, told me one day she would help me away with my warts; whereupon she got a piece of lard with the skin on, and rubbed the warts all over with the fat side; and amongst the rest that wart which I had from my childhood. Then she nailed the piece of lard, with the fat towards the sun, upon a post of her chamber window, which was to the south. The success was that within five weeks' space all the warts went away, and that wart which I had so long endured for company. But at the rest I did not marvel, because they came in a short time, and might go away in a short time again; but the going away of that which had stayed so long doth yet stick with me.

Lucian, the Greek satirist, tells that warts were cured by magic in his time. Carpenter in his "Human Physiology," page 984, says: "The charming away of warts by spells of the most vulgar kind belonged to those cases which are real facts, however they may be explained." Dr. Hack Tuke in his "Influence of the Mind Upon the Body" says: "In visiting a county asylum some years ago my attention was directed to several of the patients who were pestered with warts and I solemnly charmed them away within a specified period. I had quite forgotten the circumstance until on revisiting the institution a few months afterwards I found that my practice had been followed by the desired effect and that I was regarded as a real benefactor." This feature of the method of removing warts, setting a date before which they shall disappear, is noted in most of the successful charms. Dr. Tuke tells of a case in which a gentleman on shaking hands with a young lady noticed that she had many warts. He asked her how many she had; she replied about a dozen, she thought. "Count them, will you," said the caller; and taking out a piece of paper he solemnly took down her counting, remarking: "You will not be troubled with your warts after next Sunday." Now it is fact that by the day named the warts had disappeared and did not return.

Neurotic Pigmentation.—Pigmentation occurs very commonly as the result of neurotic conditions. Dr. Champneys, in his article on "Pigmentation of the Face and Other Parts, Especially in Women," in St. Bartholomew's Hospital Reports, Volume XV, has illustrated this very thoroughly. The pigmentations of women during the phases of genital life, menstruation, pregnancy, the menopause and the fact that eunuchs are usually fair and fat, while deep pigmentation in the white race is usually associated with sexual irritability, all make interesting studies in this subject. From comparative {494} anatomy and physiology the influence of the nervous system over pigmentation has been very well illustrated. Brücke in 1851 established the influence of the nerves on the color of the chameleon and of the frog, and there have been many confirmations of his work. Pouchet, in 1876, in the *Journal de l'Anatomie et de Physiologie* proved that fish gained the power of changing color by practice and lost it by disuse. The influence in most cases, animal and human, which produces pigmentation is exerted by the nervous system through the vascular supply. The duskiness that sometimes comes with emotion, the pallor that accompanies strong mental disturbance, as well as the blushing states, show that the vasomotor system can be influenced in every part. Pigmentation often seems only a consequence of local continuance of such disturbance. Many of the feminine patients in whom even deep discolorations around the eyes occur in connection with menstruation are typical neurotic individuals. It is worry in combination with the physical disturbance that produces the pigmentation. There are some cases on record where emotional states have caused loss of pigment in the negro or other colored races, or in the hair, as when, in well-substantiated cases, people's hair has become white in a single night. In every case of pigmentary disturbance, then, the individual must be carefully studied and as far as possible all emotional disturbance must be eliminated. Without this other treatment usually fails.

Pruritus.—Pruritus in the old is often a bothersome symptom. All sorts of remedies, internal and external, are recommended for it and successes are reported with them. Whenever there are many remedies for a symptom complex, it usually means that the suggestive element in all of them is large. For pruritus the influence of the patient's mind is extremely important. Often it will be found that these old patients are getting out scarcely at all, but are living in close confinement in their rooms, the air of which is scarcely ever changed. I have known even the keyholes to be stuffed and arrangements made by which the cracks between the door and the frame were rendered impervious to air. In these cases the most important feature of any treatment is to secure a proper amount of air. Sir Henry Thompson, the great English surgeon, in his advice how to grow old successfully, written when he himself was over 80, suggested that the cells of the skin needed an air bath every day. He advised that men should make all their toilet arrangements for the day without any garments on. Washing, the preparation of clothing, shaving, and whatever else was done in the early morning was to be accomplished after the night clothes were taken off and before other clothes were put on. He lived to be well above eighty and was sure that this practice had been of help to him. Stimulating rubbings, if done gently and without the production of too much reaction, will always benefit these people.

If old people have no interest, nothing that attracts their attention, and if they once develop pruritus their mind gets concentrated on their cutaneous sensations and it will be impossible to relieve them by any treatment until their minds get occupied with something else. Anyone who wants to sit in a chair for a few minutes and think about his cutaneous sensations will soon realize how vividly these can be brought to mind and how annoying they can become. To sit and think of a portion of the body is to want to scratch it before long. Scratching produces a flow of blood to the surface that adds to the itchy feeling. The only way to get away from it is to get the mind {495} occupied with something else. Of course, where circulation is weak because of failing heart or disturbed because of arteriosclerosis, treatment directed to these conditions should be employed, but the influence of the mind on blushing and skin feeling must not be forgotten.

When pruritus develops in the old in connection with phases of arterial degeneration—its most intractable form—it is important to remember that diversion of mind is the most important therapeutic agent that we have. The old have few diversions. They have given up their ordinary occupations, they are often no longer interested in reading, friends whom they used to know have died, and they are left a great deal to themselves. Under these circumstances anything the matter with them brings about a concentration of attention. This is even more true if they have been very well in earlier life and have had practically no experience with sickness.

Hysterical Cutaneous Conditions.—There are certain cracks of the skin with ulcerative lesions which occur in hysterical patients in the neighborhood of the knuckles that represent a phase of unfavorable influence of the mind. When these patients begin to worry or be anxious they know that these skin lesions will follow. Expectancy seems to make it certain that the lesions will come and attention adds to their chronicity. It has been noted that "chapped hands," especially when accompanied by deep cracks in cold weather, are made worse by anxiety or worry. In many neurotic patients it is impossible to treat such conditions satisfactorily unless the patient's mind can be put at ease. It is surprising how intractable these conditions can be, but that is usually because all the physician's attention is devoted to the skin instead of a considerable portion of it being given also to the patient's mental and nervous condition.

Artefact Skin Lesions.—Of course artefact skin lesions produced by the application of carbolic acid or nitric acid or ammonia or some other chemical irritant, or by rubbing with pumice stone, or with the thumb as schoolboys make what in my schooldays were called "fox bites," are skin lesions connected with a special state of mind and so deserve a mention here. The physician finds them under the most unexpected circumstances at times and in patients apparently above all suspicion of their self-infliction. They can only be prevented by changing the patient's state of mind, though this is scarcely what is ordinarily thought of in psychotherapy. Where skin lesions are atypical it is well to bear in mind the possibility of this curious condition.

The Mind in Dermatotherapy.—I have had old dermatologists assure me that they felt that the mind influenced materially the course of many forms of skin disease. Younger dermatologists are prone to be localists; as they get older the treatment of the patient's general condition is felt to be more important; after twenty years of experience they realize the place of psychotherapy in the treatment of their cases. What is said here is only meant to be suggestive, but certainly sufficient data are supplied to make it quite sure that the mind greatly influences skin conditions and must always be treated if success, especially in chronic cases, is to be secured. I have seen confidence in a particular physician or remedy do much for even the most sloughing and obstinate psoriases. Eczema follows the same law. If psychotherapy can help in the treatment of conditions that are so often intractable, it must surely not be neglected in other cases.

{496}

SECTION XIV

DISEASES OF DUCTLESS GLANDS

CHAPTER I

DIABETES

Diabetes is an affection of metabolism definitely recognized as due to serious organic changes, though existing in several forms. We are not as yet absolutely sure whether there may not be quite different organic diseases in the various forms. Of one thing clinical experience has given us assurance, that the condition of the patient's nervous system is extremely important. While certain forms of diabetes are due to pancreatic changes and others perhaps to changes in the liver or other abdominal organs, the nervous system itself can affect the consumption and excretion of sugar within the body. Certain injuries, especially, as pointed out by animal experiments, irritation of the floor of the fourth ventricle may produce passing diabetes. The symptom may also occur in connection with states of the nervous system. Glycosuria, or the passage of sugar in the urine, may occur simply as alimentary glycosuria; and while this is usually due to an excess of sugar in the diet, the glycosuria itself is predisposed to by neurotic conditions in the patient. Diabetic patients are made worse by worry of any kind and particularly by solicitude about themselves and their ailment. Hence, the place that psychotherapy has in the treatment of the disease.

Unfavorable Suggestion.—In most cases of diabetes, however, probably the most important factor in the production of symptoms is the serious disturbance of mind. The patient has an incurable disease and is frankly told so. For the physician the word "incurable" means only that his remedies are as yet inefficient in preventing certain nutritional or metabolic disturbances, and that these will be likely to continue in spite of all he can do. For the patient "incurable" means that he has a disease for which the doctor confesses that he can do nothing—which is not true—and that it is almost surely progressive, while the many reports of death from diabetes of which he hears only confirm the impression that he has not long to live and that most of the time remaining will have to be spent in irksome care of himself and almost superhuman self-denial.

As a consequence of this train of unfavorable suggestions, the history of practically every case of the milder form of diabetes in older people contains a period in which, shortly after the discovery that they had the disease, they suffered more severely from it than at any other time. As a rule, the discovery was accidental. The occurrence of a succession of boils, the development of a {497} carbuncle, occasionally an intractable eczema or a great itchiness of the skin, or an irritation of the external urinary organs, the occurrence of cramps at night, or neuralgia pains, have led to an examination of the urine and the finding of a considerable quantity of sugar. As a rule, the patients are at once put on a diet containing little starch and no sugar, and after a short time most of the bothersome symptoms of the diabetes have ceased. Their own worry, however, the strictness of the regimen, the craving for starches, the decrease in weight from the limitation of diet, have made them profoundly miserable. Their feelings have been translated into the definite conclusion that the disease must still be making progress since they feel so miserable, and they have suffered more from their mental state than from their diabetes.

This is as true of physicians themselves when they are sufferers from diabetes as of ordinary patients. Indeed, it seems that physicians make themselves more profoundly miserable because of their supposed knowledge of the disease than other people do. I have had the confidences of more than a dozen physicians who were sufferers from diabetes, and all of them admitted that they had suffered more from their scare over the disease and from trying to maintain a sugar-free diet than from the effects of their ailment. The lowering of nutrition reacts upon the nervous system, already laboring under the strain of the persuasion that an incurable disease is present, and the consequence is a whole series of nervous and often mental symptoms, especially of the depressive kind, that still further disturbs digestion, interferes with peristalsis, causes constipation or alternate constipation and diarrhea, leads to wakefulness at night, inability to concentrate attention and a constant state of worry. All this reacts upon the system and further increases the diabetes, that is, the inability to use sugar properly, and adds to its elimination through the urine.

Favorable Suggestion.—Just as soon as these patients realize that people have often had considerable quantities of sugar—two per cent. or more—in their urine for years without serious consequences and that most diabetics die, not from the affection itself, but from intercurrent disease, the reassurance of mind which ensues makes their nervous system cease to be a factor in the further disturbance of metabolism and they are able to consume more starch and sugar without increasing the amount of sugar in their urine. This is not true, of course, for the severe diabetes that attacks young people. These run a rather rapid course and usually end in from one to two years in diabetic coma or some complication connected directly with the diabetes.

Danger of Over-treatment.—To strive to keep the urine of diabetic patients free or nearly free from sugar is practically always sure to produce a serious effect upon general nutrition and to disturb the patient's mind and nervous system. Very often, however, an attempt of this kind is made. Doctors who suffer from diabetes are too prone to watch their urine carefully from day to day and this only emphasizes their solicitude about themselves, impairs their digestion, and produces such preoccupation of mind that all their functions are sure to be disturbed. After a time they learn that their general condition is a more important question than the amount of sugar in their urine. If they can maintain their weight with reasonable freedom from the secondary symptoms of diabetes, then the primary symptom—the amount of sugar in the urine—may be almost or quite neglected.

{498}

Interval Treatment.—Van Norden has pointed out that if diabetic patients are occasionally made to observe for a couple of weeks at a time an absolute diet, these intervals seem to form a new starting-point for metabolism and enable the patient to increase his power of utilizing sugar and consequently to diminish his pathological elimination of it. Patients look forward with interest to these periods, provided that in the intervals they are allowed a certain amount of starch; and each one of them seems a landmark on the road to recovery. There is a strong element of suggestion in this that acts very favorably and greatly influences the actual power of such intermissions to help nature recover her lost metabolic faculties. This is certainly a better method of treatment than the attempt to keep up an absolute diet which so easily produces the other evil of nervousness that adds to the diabetes, so that there is question of choosing between two evils, and the lesser evil includes particularly the reassurance of the patient.

The Individual in Diabetes.—While diabetes is a question of glycosuria and usually of hyperglykemia, and the consumption of any form of cane sugar or of starch convertible into it, will usually increase the diabetic tendency, not all the forms of starch which may change into cane sugar have the same effect in all individuals or undergo the same modifications. Some patients, for instance, stand milk better than others and may take large quantities of it so that there is less craving for starchy foods. Most patients can take potatoes better than bread even when there is the same equivalent of starch in each. Those who have been accustomed to potatoes from their early years sometimes stand them well and may be able to take them almost with impunity. I have noted in several cases that the Irish and Scotch, accustomed to oatmeal from their early years, seem to be able to take notable quantities of this food when suffering from diabetes without having a marked increase of sugar in the urine.

There are forms of sugar that satisfy the craving of patients for sweets and may be taken in considerable quantities without seriously disturbing metabolism. Honey is one of these, its sugar occurring in the form of mannite, and there are other substances related to it that probably can be employed to advantage. It must not be forgotten that what seems to be sugar in the urine of certain patients, that is, grape sugar, has proved on more careful investigation to be one of the other chemical forms of sugar. We have a number of cases of pentosuria on record in which patients were excreting penatomic sugar, but had not glycosuria, though their urine responded to the ordinary tests for this.

It seems well not only to be sure of the diagnosis in these cases, but to use what we have learned to make patients feel that their condition though not curable is by no means hopeless. Care must be exercised to take advantage of every possible individual peculiarity for reassurance, for the extension of the diet in any possible way, and for the satisfaction of the cravings which are so likely to come to these patients. Some of their craving is really due to the suggestion that they cannot have a particular article of diet. Whenever any human being knows that he cannot have a thing, the liking for it grows by suggestion and then it may become an obsession. To be allowed even small quantities of it is often enough to enable patients to overcome this and at least put them in a better state of mind.

Physical Condition.—The most important element in the treatment of {499} the less severe cases of diabetes is exercise in the open air. Whatever the ultimate solution of the mystery of diabetes may be, there is no doubt but that the muscles are an important factor in our disposal of sugar within the body. The material which is burned up in the muscles during movement is a form of sugar derived directly from the starch and sugar ingested. When diabetics exercise freely much more of their sugar is consumed within the body and much less of it eliminated through the kidneys than when very little or no exercise is taken. It is interesting to note the difference in the amount of sugar in the urine when patients are taking abundant exercise and when they are taking practically none. Even on a much more liberal diet the percentage of sugar is likely to be less in the exercising patient. One of the results of the diabetic scare is likely to be almost a cessation of muscular exercise. This is partly due to the fact that one of the results of diabetes in many cases is a sense of fatigue in the muscles on comparatively little exertion. Indeed, this is sometimes the first symptom that is noted and that calls the attention of the patient to the fact that there is something seriously wrong with him.

This occurs when there is a serious disturbance of sugar metabolism so that the patient who consumes large amounts of starch and sugar is excreting most of it. Just as soon as the diet is made a little more rigid and the sugar metabolism improves, then exercise can be taken and will benefit the patient. This is particularly true of women suffering from diabetes whose depression on being told that they are suffering from an incurable disease tempts them to remain within doors; the frequent tendency to urination further adds to their disinclination to go out. Under these circumstances they lose their appetites, do not sleep well, and become highly nervous, thus increasing their diabetic tendency. If they are required to go out and take exercise in the open air and rather long riding or walking periods every day, their general health will at once improve and the diabetes will become more manageable. I have seen this happen without exception even in patients well beyond middle age, and I am convinced that it is the diversion of mind as well as the salutary tiredness and thorough oxidation consequent upon outdoor exercise that is the best possible remedial measure for these cases.

Solicitude.—It is important that diabetic patients should not be bothered by frequent reports upon their urine. Their improvement and the reduction of the amount of sugar excreted is at best but slow, and is subject to many variations. While improvements, especially at the beginning, are sources of great encouragement, the deteriorations that are likely to be rather more frequent are prone to overweigh the good effects and eventual discouragement results. It is not from the urine but from the general condition that the improvement in the diabetic condition is to be judged. So long as the patient feels strong, gains in weight (when they do not belong to the obesity type of diabetes), the diabetes itself is almost sure to be improving, even though there may be discouraging periods as regards the amount of sugar eliminated.

Dangers of Rigid Diet.—There are more dangers in a rigid diet than in a certain amount of liberty in the consumption of starches and sugars. The craving for these becomes so strong as to make life intolerable to many people unless a certain amount of these substances is allowed. It is rather easy to manage limitation while it is almost impossible to be sure that {500} patients will practice absolute denial. Besides, the almost complete absence of starches and sugars, even though their place is supplied by the fats, always seems to predispose patients to the development of the acid intoxication which results in the coma often so serious an incident of diabetes. It is for this reason particularly that mild diet regulations are clinically more judicious than the absolute denial which on chemical and physiological grounds seems to be the scientific ideal. A rather good therapeutic method is to have the patients maintain a rigid diet for some ten, fifteen or twenty days and then leave them practically without restrictions for the rest of the month. Continuous restriction of diet becomes appalling. Looking forward to a period when they can eat as other people do relieves the tedium, and makes it much easier to keep the restrictions. The mental influence of this moderate treatment is very favorable and encourages the patients in the thought that after all their disease is not so serious. This is the most important element in psychotherapy.

CHAPTER II

GRAVES' DISEASE

Graves' disease, sometimes called Basedow's disease, though the Irish physician has a right to the name by priority, is often called exophthalmic goitre, because this term is descriptive of the two most marked symptoms. It must not be forgotten, however, that there are cases in which there is no exophthalmos and even no goitre, at least no enlargement of the thyroid gland that can be demonstrated externally. It is said that in these cases there must be an enlargement of the thyroid bound down by fascia and concealed by other structures of the neck so that it does not appear externally. It is probable, however, that there are cases of true Graves' disease without enlargement of the thyroid yet with the characteristic tremor, rapid heart and the mental symptoms of the affection.

Etiology.—The symptoms of the affection often develop after a period of excitement or worry, or at critical times in life, if sorrow or misfortune proves a burden. Responsibility sometimes has a like effect. I have seen a woman patient on several occasions in the last fifteen years develop marked symptoms of Graves' disease when she was placed in a position of responsibility involving worry, while in the intervals when pursuing a simple ordinary life without trouble of mind no symptoms were present. Occasionally a fright seems to be at least a predisposing cause for the development of the symptoms. Emotional strains, mental stresses, play a large part in occasioning Graves' disease, though the cause of it is probably deeper in some structural defect. In recent years nearly all the medical attention has become concentrated on the idea that the disease is primarily due to hyperthyroidization. More detailed study, however, has shown that other ductless glands are probably also concerned in the etiology. The adrenals particularly seem to be associated closely with the thyroid and Graves' disease may be due to some disturbance of the co-ordination between these glandular systems. The thymus gland is usually {501} persistent in these cases and this must represent something in the affection and at one time the use of thymus substance for therapeutic purposes seemed to confirm this idea. The parathyroids have also been called into question and their use in therapeusis seems to justify this to some extent, though probably we know too little about them to be able to say anything definite in the matter.

Even though the affection may be due directly to hypersecretion of the thyroid, it is possible that the mental and nervous state may be closely concerned in the etiology. Some patients have had an enlarged thyroid for years, without any symptoms of Graves' disease. Then during a time of stress and worry or anxiety and responsibility symptoms of the affection develop. The circulation of the thyroid is under the control of the cervical sympathetic. It is possible that this may be affected by states of mind to such an extent as to cause an increase of the circulation in the thyroid and as a consequence more of the thyroid secretion may get into the blood stream and produce its effect. Under these circumstances anything that would allay the excited mental condition and thus neutralize the unfavorable effect of the cervical sympathetic would cure or at least relieve Graves' disease.

The affection is about five times as frequent among women as it is among men. This has sometimes been attributed to the fact that there seems to be some more or less direct correlation between the sex organs in women and the ductless gland systems. It has often been pointed out that the thyroid is likely to be engorged at the time of menstruation and, indeed, there are those who have attributed some of the symptoms of tremulousness, irritability, and tiredness at this time to over-functioning of the gland. In women who have borne a child the thyroid is usually somewhat enlarged. Good authorities in obstetrics have insisted that they could pick out of a group of women in evening dress, those who had borne children, from the appearance of their necks. Probably this is an exaggeration, but there is no doubt that the thyroid is intimately related to the genital functions in women. It has been said that a direct connection could be traced between disappointments in love or in sexual matters and the development of Graves' disease. To put much stress on this would easily lead to mistaken conclusions, though it represents a principle that should be recalled in certain cases of the affection. The frequency with which slighter disturbances of the thyroid occur in connection with the common genital incidents of female life and their comparative insignificance for health or strength, should make for the holding of a not too serious prognosis in the affection.

Symptomatology.—There are four cardinal symptoms of the disease: rapid heart action, tremor, enlargement of the thyroid, and exophthalmos. At least two of these are largely dependent on mental influences. There are certain accompanying symptoms that are of importance and supposed to be connected directly with the disease, though oftener they can be traced to the influence of the state of the patient's mind upon the organism. Emaciation is common. It is due to the fact that the appetite is likely to be seriously disturbed by anxiety and solicitude. Anemia develops as a consequence and there may be slight fever which is sometimes inanition fever. Attacks of vomiting and diarrhea occur intermittently and sometimes there is constipation. The disturbance of eating consequent upon the affections seems largely {502} responsible for these. The disturbance of the vascular system gives rise to flashes of heat and cold and often to profuse perspiration. Certain of the symptoms of the menopause can be compared rather strikingly with those of Graves' disease and have been attributed to the disturbance of the external secretion of the ovaries which are now known to act as ductless glands as well as genital organs.

With the exception of the enlargement of the thyroid and the exophthalmos, all of the symptoms of Graves' disease are of a kind that can be produced in states of excitement with nothing more present than a functional neurotic condition. It is true that the tremor is characteristic and differs from that of hysterical patients, being finer and at the rate of a little more than eight to the second. The rapid heart action, however, and the disturbance of the general circulation which causes flushing and pruritus and the sense of nervousness, as if the patients were in a constant state of fright, are always characteristically neurotic. The changes in disposition, often in the line of irritability, sometimes with severe mental depression, seem in many cases to be only a mental reaction to the patient's solicitude. The weakness of the limbs which sometimes amounts to a giving away of the legs, is connected with the tremor, but seems to be neurotic rather than of any more serious character. In spite of all our study of the affection its place among the neuroses must still be reserved for it, at least as regards many cases, and its treatment must be conducted with that idea in mind.

Diagnosis.—The disease is easy to recognize when fully developed. At the beginning of cases, however, and in certain abortive types of the affection which the French have called *formes frustes*, the diagnosis may be difficult. Usually the first symptom is tremor and this of itself will often serve, especially in association with general symptoms of nervousness, to make the diagnosis. Tremor with tachycardia puts the case beyond doubt, as a rule, though of course it must not be forgotten that hysteria may simulate rather closely this much of the disease.

The abortive types of the affection are important because they masquerade as forms of psychoneurosis, hysteria, and the like, though the patients are not suggestible, have very definite, not variable, symptoms and get better and worse according to the variations in the underlying affection. Occasionally they seem to be associated with certain other forms of neurotic conditions, especially those with vascular disturbances. There may be tinglings in the ends of the fingers, occasionally with suffusion, erythromelalgia—Weir Mitchell's disease—and even a tendency to the white "dead fingers" as the French call them, of Raynaud's disease. It seems not unlikely that further study will show that many of these affections involving disturbances of the vasomotor system are connected in some special way.

Prognosis in Young Patients.—Some of the cases, especially in young people, are likely to seem quite discouraging and apparently to justify even a serious operation. I have in mind a young woman seen some fifteen years ago when she was about seventeen. The prominence of the eyes, the enlargement of the thyroid, the tremor and the rapid heart were all marked. The symptoms had been growing worse for over a year and the outlook was serious. Ten years later I saw her in another city in perfectly normal health, married and happy and the mother of two healthy children. The only trace {503} apparently of the disturbance of the thyroid to be noted in the family was that her children got their teeth very late, her first child, a boy, not cutting his first tooth until after he was fifteen months old. In every other way, however, the boy was perfectly well, rugged and strong, having passed through his summers without any serious disturbance and not being a particularly nervous or excitable child. Such complete relief from symptoms after the condition had been so grave would ordinarily have seemed quite out of the question. It emphasizes the fact that for Graves' disease as it occurs among young growing people, where perhaps the thyroid does not grow in proper proportion to the rest of the body, but for some reason overgrows, the prognosis of the case may seem to be much worse than it really is.

Treatment.—The story of the various methods of treatment that have been reported as successful for Graves' disease serve to show very well how much the affection must depend upon psychic and neurotic conditions, for most of them have been positive in action at the beginning when their suggestive influence was strong, and quite inert after they had lost their novelty and their power to influence the mind. Sometimes even slight operations as on the nose, the removal of polyps, or of a spur on the septum, or an enlarged turbinate, have been found to bring relief of the symptoms of Graves' disease even in marked cases. Operations upon the tonsils have had a like effect and even shortening of the uvula has been reported as curative. A generation ago applications of iodin to the goiter were reported to have good effects. In lancing the goiter, sometimes evidently a cyst was punctured, but sometimes the lance was only followed by a slight issue of blood, yet the affection was favorably modified. More serious operations have followed by complete relief of symptoms for a time, though relapses are not infrequent and occasionally the patient was not relieved, though apparently all the conditions present were similar to those of other patients in whom the operation produced excellent results.

The medical treatment of Graves' disease demonstrates interestingly the power of suggestion. About fifteen years ago a distinguished English observer announced that he was getting good results in the treatment of Graves' disease by the administration of thyroid substance. At that time our present theories with regard to hyperthyroidization as the etiology of the affection had not been formulated, though some vague connection between the thyroid secretion and the symptoms had been accepted. A number of patients were improved by taking thyroid. Other observers found, however, that not only were their patients not improved, but they seemed to be worse as the result of the thyroid feeding. The English physician therefore was asked to say exactly how he obtained his material and prepared it for his patients. Organo-therapy was then new and it was found that the orders given to the butcher for thyroid had been filled by him according to the directions by furnishing portions of a large gland situated in the neck of the calf. This was the thymus, and not the thyroid. Thymus was then deliberately used for a while and there were some reported good successes while the treatment was new and strongly suggestive. After a time it proved to be of no avail.

A number of biological remedies were tried after this. Personally, after having made some studies of the parathyroids while in Virchow's laboratory, I resolved to try material from those glands. The first two patients to whom {504} the material was given, with a careful explanation of the theory on which it was administered, proceeded to obtain relief from their symptoms and an intermission in their disease. Just as soon as I purposely omitted to explain to patients how much might be expected from this new remedy and failed to make suggestions founded on the parathyroids, no improvement was noted. In the first two cases this had been more or less necessary in order to determine whether the patients could stand the doses suggested, which began very low and were gradually increased. The material seemed to have no ill effects, however, and a definite dosage could be used without the necessity of taking patients into one's confidence.

A number of serums of one kind or another were reported as beneficial for Graves' disease. It was admitted that they did not benefit all the cases, but that in certain cases they did much good. Practically all of these were strikingly more efficient in their discoverers' hands than when used by anyone else. Thyroids were removed from animals and after some time serum from these animals, supposed to be of lower thyroid content, was injected into human beings with the idea of reducing the hyperthyroidization or perhaps neutralizing it by some substance present in the serum. One very interesting observation on most of these cases deserves remark. The animals deprived of their thyroids, such as goats and sheep, lived on absolutely unhurt by the operation, and as one experimenter expressly noted, sold for more money after being kept for a year under observation than they had cost him before dethyroidization.

Most of our biological remedies for Graves' disease then are strongly reminiscent of the therapy of the affection in older times. It was particularly for Graves' disease, or at least for nervous symptoms closely resembling Graves' disease—those of fright, nervousness, irritability and tremor—that various more or less terrifying procedures and particularly deterrent substances were employed in medicine. These patients, for instance, were cured by the touch of a hanged criminal, and particularly by the touch of their goiter to the mark on his neck. It was especially for them that *Usnea*, the moss gathered from the skull of a criminal who had been hanged, was of benefit when administered internally. Mummy as a remedial substance remained in common use until well on into the latter half of the eighteenth century in England.

In older times a dead snake wrapped around the neck was said to be an excellent remedy for goiter and especially those cases of goiter that caused symptoms of fright and nervousness. Evidently anything that produces a strong effect upon the patient's mind may prove helpful. Perhaps the suggestion enables the mind to control the cervical sympathetic and by that means the circulation in the thyroid gland, thus lessening the amount of blood that flows through and therefore the amount of secretion that is carried out. There is no doubt but that the sympathetic is largely under the influence of the emotions and that through it very important effects may be worked out in various structures. There seems no other possible explanation for the uniformly reported success of remedies when their suggestive power is strong and their failure quite as invariably later even in the same cases.

Operations.—In recent years operations for the removal of portions of the enlarged thyroid have become popular and some very successful results have been reported. Those of us who know how easy it is to influence the minds of {505} patients in Graves' disease favorably hesitate as yet to pronounce definitely with regard to the indication for operation except under such conditions of pressure in the neck or projection of the eyeballs as may lead to serious symptoms. Not all the operators have been as successful as some who made a specialty of the affection. I have personal information which shows a number of unsuccessful cases after operation and the records of conservative surgeons as published indicate this. Unfortunately, a great many cases have been reported within a few months as cured; if they were comparatively without symptoms, surgical intervention is considered to have been eminently successful. For, be it noted, very few are entirely without symptoms, even after operation.

Dr. William H. Thompson in his book on "Graves' Disease" points out that even so good an operator and so thoroughly conservative a surgeon as Kocher reports cases of Graves' disease as cured, which are still exhibiting symptoms that would make the medical clinician hesitate to agree with him and, indeed, rather lead him to expect that under the stress of worry and excitement there may be redevelopment of the symptoms. As the number of cases operated upon has increased there has been a growing feeling that relapses might be expected in certain cases even after removal of large portions of the thyroid gland. The fact of the matter is that we do not understand as yet what is the underlying pathological significance of the symptoms grouped under the term Graves' disease. When there are severe symptoms, as extreme exophthalmos, greatly enlarged thyroid pressing upon the important neck structures, or serious disturbance of nutrition, an operation is always needed; but as yet we cannot be sure that it will produce even complete or lasting relief.

Many patients have been greatly benefited by operation, some of them perhaps permanently, but we need more of the after-history of these patients covering a long period of time, to be sure that the results flow entirely from the operation. There was a time when operations were reported as doing quite as much good for epilepsy as they are now for Graves' disease. As we have pointed out, a number of operative procedures that had nothing to do with the underlying basic pathology of the disease have proved the occasion for considerable improvement or sometimes what might be called a cure for a prolonged period. We can be sure, as a rule, that patients will be benefited immediately after operations. The rest, with care, the strong suggestion, the aroused feeling of expectancy, the confidence in the surgeon, all this would do much of itself. It remains to be seen how much more than this the operation does.

General Condition.—The treatment of patients suffering from Graves' disease consists largely in having them take up some occupation that, while reasonably absorbing, does not make too great a demand upon them. Often when they complain most of their symptoms they are below normal weight and the first indication is to have them brought back to it. I have seen such cases over and over again almost entirely without symptoms when they were up to normal weight and with a good many symptoms when they were below normal. It would be easy to theorize as to why this is so, but the observation is the most important consideration for practical purposes, and we are not yet in possession of enough scientific knowledge with regard to the thyroid or {506} its possible connection with other organs that have an internal secretion, to be able to say anything definite about it.

After weight and nutrition the most important indication is sleep. It is impossible for patients to get along with less than eight or nine hours of sleep. Most of them are much better if they have nine or ten every night. Late hours are particularly prejudicial to them. They are tired if they have been on their feet all day and they should be encouraged to take more sleep than others. Sleep is one of the most important considerations for sufferers from the abortive forms of Graves' disease and they must be encouraged to take it in the quantity that they need. This can only be decided by their feeling.

Diversion of Mind.—Much more than other nervous people these patients need encouragement and require diversion of mind. They are prone to be discouraged, rather tired, and easily tempt themselves into a routine in which there is little recreation and no diversion. For them more than for most other patients it is necessary to prescribe that twice every week they shall have some engagement different from their ordinary routine to which they look forward for several days. This looking forward to a break in the routine does much to make life more livable for them and must be encouraged in every way. As to what the diversion is to be must depend entirely on the character of the individual. Some find complete diversion of mind in the theater or even in vaudeville. Others are bored by this after a while and need other recreations. I have known people who were bored by the theater find an evening a week spent in helping a poor person or an afternoon devoted to a visit to a hospital ward or to an ailing friend an excellent diversion. Some of those who do not care for the theater like music and are helped by it. As a rule, however, one must be careful about the indulgence of music for neurotic people since it seems to exert a serious emotional strain on many of them and as the phrase goes "takes a good deal out of them." This is particularly true for younger people who have a passion for music. Older people may be trusted more in this matter and the attendance on concert and opera, which is looked upon as a social duty by some, giving them an opportunity to greet friends and to display their gowns and jewels, is a harmless diversion of mind.

Mental Treatment.—Graves' disease is, then, as we have said, especially likely to be influenced by the patient's state of mind. Nothing disturbs patients more than the declaration sometimes made by physicians that their condition is incurable or that they will have to doctor for it for many years. This must be avoided because our present knowledge does not justify any such positive declarations. Most cases of Graves' disease, while not particularly amenable to treatment by specific drugs, are very much improved if the patient's general health is brought up to the best standard and if all sources of worry and emotion are eliminated, as far as possible. Nothing is more serious for them, however, than the suggestion that they will not get well. Probably no one has ever seen a mild case of Graves' disease that did not improve so much as to be practically well after the lapse of some time. Recurrences take place, but if all sources of worry and irritation of the digestive tract and over-tiredness are removed, then patients will stay free from their symptoms for surprisingly long periods. Old people do not have these {507} favorable remissions so much as the young, but under twenty there can be, as a rule, definite promise of decided improvement and sometimes of results that seem like complete cure. For patients under thirty there is every reason to think that if they are in a run-down condition when the disease is first noted remissions of symptoms can be looked for lasting for long periods, during which they will be comparatively well.

Diet Suggestions.—The changes in diet necessary to bring improvement in Graves' disease are different for individual patients. Prof. Mendel, in Berlin, found in his extensive experience that meat does not seem to be disposed of well by these patients and acts somewhat as an irritant. He reduces the meat taken and usually allows it at but one meal. If patients get on well as vegetarians, meat is gradually eliminated from their diet. On the other hand, there are patients who seem to develop Graves' disease during a vegetarian diet. Very often it will be found that there is an intermittent constipation and diarrhea in these cases, and that the bowels will act much better if a certain amount of meat is given, and then the symptoms of Graves' disease remit, as a rule. As in most of the major neuroses, as is known so well in epilepsy, any irritative condition of the digestive tract will surely revive neurotic manifestations and make many of the major neuroses much worse than they were before.

{508}

SECTION XV

ORGANIC NERVOUS DISEASES

CHAPTER I

PSYCHOTHERAPY OF ORGANIC NERVOUS DISEASES

Since we know that the basis of many nervous diseases is an obliteration of certain cells of the brain or of the spinal cord, or certain tracts of the central nervous system through which impulses must pass if they are to be effective as motion, sensation or function in some other form, we realize that we cannot recreate these portions of highly organized tissue and that therefore organic nervous diseases are beyond the action of any remedies we now know or may even hope to discover.

The development of pathology has shown us that once there has been serious nephritis or cirrhosis of the liver certain portions of the glands are destroyed and therefore there cannot be any question of cure. There is no possibility of redintegration of destroyed tissues when they are of highly organized character, and so the patient will always be maimed. One might as well talk of causing an amputated finger to grow again as talk of curing diseases that involve destruction of specialized cells. When this first dawned on modern medicine as the result of the careful study of pathology a period of therapeutic nihilism developed during which physicians trained in the pathological schools were prone to distrust drugs entirely, or at least to a very great degree. The effect of this wave of nihilism has not entirely disappeared in our time, though we have learned that even where serious damage to an organ has been done by disease we may still hope to compensate for defect of tissue by stimulation of other organs and to replace its function by certain physiological remedies or biological products; and if we can do nothing more, we can at least alleviate the symptoms which develop as a consequence of the organic affection.

Nature's Compensation.—Physicians are prone to forget nature's wonderful powers of compensation. Apparently even some regeneration may take place in diseased organs of highly organized type if the patient's general condition is kept up to its highest point of nutritive efficiency. How far this may go we do not know, but observations show some marvelous examples of unexpected regeneration.

These counteracting processes can be stimulated sometimes by drugs, but oftener they can be best brought into play by keeping the patient in just as good condition of body and favorable condition of mind as possible for a prolonged period, so that nature accustoms herself to the defect and her powers of compensation have full play.

{509}

Unfavorable Suggestion.—What is true of organic diseases of all kinds is especially true of organic nervous diseases, and in spite of the fact that most of these are essentially incurable, so much can be done for patients that their condition is made more tolerable and indeed some of them improved to such an extent that they consider themselves quite relieved of their organic affection. One of the most serious burdens that the patient laboring under an organic nervous disease has to suffer is the consciousness drummed into him by successive physicians, by his reading, and by every possible means of suggestion, that his malady is incurable. This makes every symptom as severe in its effects as it can possibly be. Hope does not buoy up and discouragement weighs down every effort of the organism to compensate for the serious defect under which it is laboring. Nothing can be done for the disease itself, but much can be done for the patient. Many of the symptoms from which the patient suffers most are really due to his own discouragement, to that sluggish condition which develops in his body as a consequence of his lack of hope, to the absence of exercise and of air and of diversion of mind consequent upon the gloom that settles over him when he is told that his condition is incurable.

Adventitious Symptoms.—If the adventitious symptoms that are always present in cases of organic nervous disease are eliminated, if the conditions which develop from the unhygienic condition in which the patient lives because of his discouragement and retirement are removed, as a rule he feels so much better that it is hard to persuade him that some change has not come in his underlying nervous disease and that a process of cure is not at work. It is because of this that irregular practitioners so often succeed in apparently doing much more for these patients than the regular physician. The irregular does not insist on the incurability of the disease, but, on the contrary, he promises a cure. He then proceeds to relieve many bothersome symptoms that are quite extraneous to the underlying disease, but thus makes the patient ever so much more comfortable than before, gives a cheerful air to his life for a time, makes him sleep better as a consequence and it is not surprising that the patient thinks that his disease has been bettered, if not cured.

Suggestive Prophylaxis.—While we are optimistic just as far as possible since genuine nervous disease has declared itself, it must not be forgotten that we can by suggestion and warning often prevent or delay the development of nervous degenerations. This, too, is psychotherapy and must be employed wherever it seems advisable.

Post-syphilitic nervous conditions of so many kinds are likely to develop that it is important to warn the patients who are sufferers from this disease from taking up the more strenuous forms of existence. This may seem an exaggerated view of the condition, but it is amply justified by the results of the opposite rule of life in almost any physician's experience in city practice. A man who has had syphilis must be warned of the danger, one may almost say likelihood, if he takes up any of the professions in which there is much mental strain and nervous worry, that he will almost surely not live out the normal span of life without some serious nervous incident. Locomotor ataxia, and, above all, general paralysis develop, as a rule, in men who, having had syphilis, have some occupation in life that calls for considerable mental strenuosity, and involves excitement and worry. Actors, brokers, soldiers and sailors, speculators of all kinds, race-track gamblers, these are the classes from {510} which victims of paresis and locomotor ataxia are particularly recruited. People who have suffered from syphilis and who live the ordinary unemotional life of a teacher, or a merchant, or a writer, do not, as a rule, develop the postsyphilitic and parasyphilitic conditions.

Precocious apoplexy is especially likely to occur in patients who have had syphilis and who have then spent themselves at very hard work. I doubt if hard work alone, without some such antecedent condition, ever produces this result. Of course, it is not alone syphilis, but other serious conditions which affect the nervous system that ought to be guarded against in this same way. If there has ever been any affection of the kidneys, as a complication, for instance, of scarlet fever, then it has always seemed to me to be the duty of the family physician to warn such patients that their kidneys are more prone than those who have not suffered from such an incident to break down under any severe strain that may be put upon them by worry, especially worry following a period of strenuous work. In these cases the affection of the kidneys nearly always makes itself felt in the nervous system, and especially in the brain, and so this warning has a proper place here. Where there has been severe cerebro-spinal meningitis this warning seems also to be needful, though here our records have not been kept with sufficient care to enable us to speak positively of the necessity for the warning.

Treatment.—It is important to remember that as physicians we do not treat disease but patients. We *care* for patients, that is the real etymological significance of the Latin *curare*, we do not cure diseases in the modern sense that has come to be given to that term, of completely removing the *materies morbi* and setting the patient on his feet once more just as well as he was before his illness.

Relieving Incurable Disease.—A new cure for locomotor ataxia, for instance, is announced every now and then, and the evidence for its beneficial action is the testimony of patients who have been relieved of many symptoms that they thought connected directly with their spinal affection. All sorts of remedies have been employed with announced success. One man builds a particular kind of shoe for them and has a number of witnesses to his skill in curing them. Another does some slight operation on their nose or their throat or their urethra and straightway the patient feels so much better that he talks confidently about being cured. All the characteristic symptoms of the affection remain. Their knee-jerks are gone, their pupils do not react normally, they have some incoordination in their walk, but a number of other symptoms have disappeared and their walk is probably much improved because of their confidence and a certain amount of practice that they have gone through. The new hope born of confident assurance that they could be relieved gives them an appetite, makes their digestion better. This lessens the sluggishness of their bowels, gives them confidence to get out and see their friends, life takes on a new hope, they sleep better and it is no wonder they talk of having been helped or even cured.

There is a definite relation between the nervous affection in these cases and many visceral symptoms. There is no doubt, for instance, that certain cases of intractable dyspepsia are associated with tabes and that in nearly the same way obstinate constipation frequently develops. Notwithstanding the connection of these symptoms with an incurable condition of the spinal cord {511} that is no reason for thinking that they cannot be relieved even though no improvement of the spinal-cord lesions is expected.

Frequently, indeed, gastric dyspepsia is due more to worry over discomfort somewhere in the stomach region than to any real disturbance of the digestive functions. It may then be considerably ameliorated simply by the assurance that the trouble is local and is localized outside of the stomach itself, though there may be some sympathetic irritation of the gastric nerve supply. Probably Dr. Head and those who have studied reflexes so enthusiastically would not agree with this explanation of the relief of the gastric symptoms in some of the cases they have described, as due rather to suggestion than to the local treatment, and, as a matter of fact, we are not quite sure which factor may be the more important. Counter-irritation probably plays quite an important role in the relief of discomfort, but I am sure that the suggestive influence of acute sensory feelings at the surface produced by counter-irritation serves to divert the mind from the duller ache or the functional disturbance below. However, Dr. Head's paragraph should be given in his own words, for it furnishes a scientific basis for one aspect of these cases.

Throughout the study of cases of nervous diseases, evidence of the relation between pathological condition of certain viscera and sensory disturbances in the superficial structures of the body is constantly manifested. For instance, a man with caries of the spine suffered from a girdle sensation round the area of the eighth dorsal segment. At the same time he was greatly troubled by flatulent dyspepsia which was untouched by drugs. It was, however, greatly relieved by counter-irritation applied to the maximum tender point of the eighth dorsal area in the eighth space and mid-axillary line.

Optimistic Suggestions.—Our most prominent neurologists have in recent years insisted on the necessity for encouraging patients and for not permitting them to brood upon the worst side of what is to be expected from their ailment. Patients are entirely too prone to read up about their disease and the worst symptoms of the extreme cases impress their minds and are constantly recurring as suggestions of possible ills to come. Prof. Oppenheim in his "Letters to Nervous Patients" states in a striking way the optimistic view that it always seems advisable to give a patient in the initial stages of a serious, incurable or even progressive nervous disease. That letter is worth quoting:

I cannot conceal from you the fact, which you have already ascertained from other sources, that you show the premonitory symptoms of a disease of the spinal cord. This admission is not, however, as you fear, synonymous with the sentence "the beginning of the end." There is no reason for you to despair. We doctors regard and welcome it as a marked advance in our scientific knowledge that we are now in a position to diagnose a nervous disease of this kind in its first commencement. This is undoubtedly a great gain for the patient, as on account of this knowledge a judicious, experienced physician may, at least in many cases, by the timely regulation of the mode of life and the prescription of certain remedies, arrest the progress of the disease or retard its development. This advice may, however, and should as a general rule, be given without the patient himself being made aware of the diagnosis, for the ideas as to the nature of this disease which prevail in lay circles, and indeed among many doctors of the old school, arise from the knowledge of the disease in its advanced and fully established form, since it was only in this completely developed stage that it was recognized. Then, indeed, its very noticeable symptoms were obvious even to the uninitiated. This picture, sad enough indeed in itself, was rendered still gloomier by {512} the misery and despair which popular fancy has associated with the conception of locomotor ataxia.

Arteriosclerosis.—Even with regard to so serious a disease and, of course, absolutely fatal in its progress as arteriosclerosis, it must not be forgotten that much can be done for the patients and especially for the nervous symptoms that develop in connection with the condition. For the progressive hardening of the arteries on which the nerve symptoms depend absolutely nothing can be done. A man is as old as his arteries, and we cannot bring back the years even though the patient has become prematurely old. For the symptoms so frequently seen in connection with arteriosclerosis, the paresthesia, the burnings, the numbness, the pruritus, the pains around joints and the difficulties in connection with them, even for the intermittent claudication which develops, much can be done. Above all, the patient must not be allowed to cherish the notion that his disease is not only incurable, but that nothing can be done for it. It is inevitable and progressive, but then according to one definition, life is a progressive disease and every day brings us nearer death. "Life is a dangerous thing at best," as an American humorist once said, "and very few of us get out of it alive."

These patients can be relieved of many physical symptoms, they can be encouraged, their attention can be diverted from their symptoms, and it is concentration of mind on them that often makes them intolerable, while occupation with something, especially if it is interesting, will often prove an efficient remedy for the discomforts complained of. Old people who have no interests, who have retired from business, who did not have the opportunity when young to acquire tastes in art and literature, above all, those who have no interests in children, no grandchildren nor close relatives near them, are likely to become centered on their ills in the midst of their arteriosclerosis, and this more than the advancing degeneration of arteries itself is at the root of their symptoms. The ideal old age is that which is passed in the midst of younger people, with an occasional happy hour during the day with children in whom one is deeply interested. This is the best psychotherapeutic factor that we have.

Prof. Oppenheim has given the optimistic side of arteriosclerosis so suggestively that most patients suffering in this way should have the opportunity to read it. It occurs in his "Letters to Nervous Patients":

An eminent physician for whom I have much esteem has told you that your troubles, especially your vertigo, are caused by calcification of the arteries. You, sir, heard in this your death sentence, and since then the encyclopedia has revealed to you all the sufferings and terrors with which you may expect to be overtaken.

I would, however, explain to you, as the result of the most careful examination and the most absolute conviction on my part, that your anxiety is unfounded.

Since you have a certain amount of information and scientific knowledge, I may speak to you upon this matter almost as a colleague. One is certainly justified, when a man of your age complains of vertigo, in suspecting calcification of the arteries to be the cause of the trouble, since it constitutes the common senile change, and vertigo forms one of its most frequent symptoms. But—apart from the fact that in senile calcification of the vessels this vertigo is frequently a temporary and not always a serious sign—one is by no means justified in assuming that the appearance of this symptom in later life is in itself, and without further evidence, the sign of such a cause. This is an error which in my experience is {513} far too frequently made, to the detriment of the patient. It is first of all essential to closely examine and analyze the symptom in itself. . . . Two years ago, after having overloaded your stomach, you had a real attack of vertigo, which was repeated several times during the day, until, by vomiting and diarrhea, the contents of your stomach were evacuated. Since that time the fear of vertigo has overpowered you. In my experience it is neither new nor uncommon to find that a man who has shown his intrepidity and his contempt of death on many a battlefield, who is a hero in war, may be overcome by some dread of illness, by some anxiety, or even by some pain, and may be distressed by it in a way that is in sharp contrast to his whole personality. Your remembrance of that vertigo is so lively that the mere idea of it suffices to reawaken the symptom, or at least an imitation of it which very nearly approaches the reality. That this idea is present in your case is quite certain from the consideration of your symptoms. You admit that you almost never have vertigo at home, but as soon as you leave the house, and especially if you find yourself alone in the street far from home, the remembrance of the vertigo comes over you, puts you into a state of anxiety, and is followed by a sensation of tottering and swaying, so that you have to stand still; and at last it has gone so far that you no longer venture to go out alone. And so the hero of X sits like a timid woman in his arm chair, making life bitter for himself and for those around him.

Even were I to find that signs of arterial calcification were present, I should still be satisfied that your vertigo is not due to this cause, but that it is a vertigo of recollection and of fear.

CHAPTER II

CEREBRAL APOPLEXY

Cerebral apoplexy is an extremely serious organic disease that seems surely to be an affection for which psychotherapeutics can mean little or nothing. When an artery has burst in the brain and blood is either actually flowing out or has flowed out in damaging quantities into the delicate brain tissues, seriously injuring and perhaps destroying some of them forever, no amount of mental assurance will do any good for the organic lesions that have been produced. All that can be hoped is that the hemorrhage will not prove fatal and that the powers of nature will be sufficient to deal with it, and though not able to cure it in the sense of restoring tissues to former conditions, will compensate for the lesion in some way and dispose of its products so effectually that but little interference will result with nerve functions within the skull.

There is no pretence that by psychotherapy or any appeal to mental powers anything can be done for the underlying pathological process. And it may be frankly said that no remedy of any kind, physical or mental, will avail much, while some of those that have been suggested are just as likely to do harm as good. Position, with the head elevated and quiet of mind and body are the only remedial measures that promise definite help. Excitement greatly increases the danger. Reassurance does more than anything else to lessen blood pressure and lessen also the danger of a hemorrhage producing fatal effects. In nervous, excitable people the first stroke is often fatal. Occasionally the phlegmatic have three or more ruptures of brain arteries before death supervenes. Psychotherapy, then, has a definite role even at the time of the apoplexy.

{514}

The Mind Before and After.— Much can be accomplished for the patient by proper attention to his state of mind both before and after cerebral hemorrhage. There are many symptoms which point to the possible occurrence of the rupture of a cerebral artery, and older people are likely to know something about these and to dread them so much that to some extent they may by worrying precipitate the evil they fear. Many people, having read vaguely about apoplexy, having seen a case or two of it perhaps, and having heard of others, develop a dread of its occurrence in themselves that makes them miserable. Finally, the shock of a cerebral hemorrhage is very great and its after-effects likely to be very disturbing. It affects the whole personality and often makes a strong, vigorous, healthy man a decided hypochondriac. All of these associated mental states may be greatly benefitted by psychotherapy.

A number of neurotic symptoms are always added to whatever manifestations of mind and the somatic system may develop as a consequence of the cerebral apoplexy, and these are treated more effactually by mental reassurance than in any other way. Besides, apoplexy confines people to the house who have often been vigorous and active before, and this confinement with deprivation of exercise and air and consequent disturbance of appetite and digestive functions, acts as a serious factor in the production of neurotic symptoms. Tears and hysterical manifestation are not uncommon, and for these psychotherapy is the most important remedial measure.

In the period preceding true apoplexy there may be such symptoms as persistent headache with peculiar sensations in one hand. These sensations are variously described as creepy feelings or as of "pins and needles," and occasionally as if the fingers and sometimes the arm were asleep. The group of symptoms known as paresthesia are rather common as premonitory symptoms of cerebral apoplexy. When these are combined with headache patients often become seriously disturbed and begin to dread the occurrence of apoplexy. While these are premonitory symptoms of cerebral hemorrhage in those whose arteries are degenerated, patients must be made to understand that just because the fingers or hand or arm go to sleep occasionally, even though there may be complaint of headache, these are not indications of impending apoplexy unless other objective symptoms are present. Subjective symptoms alone can never mean much as regards organic disease. It is particularly neurotic individuals who are likely to exaggerate the significance of their subjective sensations, who are also prone to be so solicitous about apoplexy that they work themselves into a state of fear with regard to it. Even children have their hands go to sleep rather frequently, and at all ages if the arms or legs are placed in certain positions or under certain conditions of pressure, they are likely to develop that numbness which ends in the prickly "pins and needles" feeling that is spoken of as "going to sleep."

Diagnosing Arterial Sclerosis.—Unless, then, some of the arteries at the periphery of the body show signs of such degeneration as to indicate advanced arteriosclerosis, any subjective symptoms, no matter how bothersome, must not be allowed to depress the patient. Usually they mean nothing at all, and would pass quite unnoticed but for the patients' nervousness about themselves. If the temporal arteries are not prominent and visibly thickened and tortuous, and this may be seen at a glance, the patient may be assured almost without more ado. If his radial arteries on careful observation show no signs {515} of degeneration, then it is extremely doubtful if there is sufficient arterial change in the brain to justify a fear of arterial rupture. In examining the radial artery it must not be forgotten that the pulse

279

of nervous people, especially such as have exerted considerable mental control over themselves in order to come and see a physician about what they think is a serious condition, is likely to be of high tension. When the artery is rolled under the finger, then it may seem that there is some thickening in its walls, though it is only heightened blood pressure from emotion that causes the feeling. This high blood pressure may, of course, of itself be an indication of danger whenever there is heart or kidney disease, but it often occurs as a passing event in nervous patients whose vasomotor control is so capricious that arterial tension and blood pressure may change at very short intervals as the result of excitement.

It may not be easy to obliterate the pulse in the usual way in many of these cases and as a consequence the illusion of a thickened artery may remain even when the vessel is quite normal. The important rule is to ascertain whether the artery is tortuous. Whenever there is thickening of the arterial wall the artery is lengthened as well as thickened. If the artery is not lengthened the degenerative changes in it are so slight, as a rule, as to be negligible. Indeed, the very beginning of arteriosclerosis may thus be diagnosed. When this cannot be found, patients may be completely reassured that their suggestive symptoms have no significance as regards any possibility of cerebral hemorrhage from the ordinary causes of advancing years and arterial degeneration.

Differentiation.—Occasionally such paresthesiae as have been described especially when associated with headache, point to an intracranial growth, or to a developing syphilitic brain lesion, and these must be carefully eliminated, but they constitute quite separate problems which always present other accompanying symptoms that make diagnosis possible once a suspicion as to the nature of the lesion is aroused. Above all, these occur in much younger patients than are, as a rule, the subjects of cerebral apoplexy.

Symptoms.—*Dreads—Dizziness.*—There are other symptoms of which people have heard as preliminary signs of brain hemorrhage which occasionally disturb them to a great degree and set up a set of dreads that may be difficult to banish. Probably the one that is spoken oftenest of is dizziness. There is no doubt that under certain circumstances this may be a symptom of impending cerebral hemorrhage, especially if it is accompanied by headache and by objective signs in the arteries, but dizziness by itself is not enough to justify any anxiety in even elderly people. If, when a man stoops over and then straightens up rapidly everything becomes black before him and he must immediately take hold of something to keep himself from falling, it is probable that a pathological condition of his cerebral arteries is present. This interferes with brain circulation and may have seriously impaired the elasticity of the arteries which is so necessary to overcome the rapid variations of the influence of gravity on the blood current when there are sudden changes of position. Fits of dizziness that come on immediately on rising in the morning, or that attack the patient when he sits up suddenly in bed may have the same serious significance. None of these signs are significant, however, unless there are, as we have said, objective signs in the arteries.

{516}

But dizziness may come from many other causes besides degeneration of arteries. A very common cause of it is the presence of gas in the stomach which interferes with the heart action mechanically and so disturbs the circulation. The column of blood to the head is more easily affected than the rest of the circulation because it must be pumped up directly against gravity when we are in a standing position, and so any, even a slight, interference with the heart action is felt at once in this portion of the body. Besides, the brain is extremely sensitive to changes of circulation and even a slight disturbance of the blood supply to it may cause dizziness. There occurs also undoubtedly a feeling of dizziness that is entirely subjective. The patient for some reason loses confidence in himself and has a feeling of dismay, as if he could not support himself. Such a patient may complain that when he comes down stairs, at the first step or two, particularly of a high stairs, he has the dread that he may pitch forward. Such people have never actually fallen, but they have to grasp the railing and they have a dread of some accident of this kind. This is, however, rather a form of akrophobia than a true dizziness. Prof. Oppenheim has dwelt on vertigo as a dread (see preceding chapter).

Vertigo.—Besides, there are pathological conditions that cause dizziness yet have no connection at all with the dizziness that is a premonitory symptom of apoplexy. Menière's disease, for instance, even in its milder forms, causes at times a vertigo that is extremely annoying and that frequently gives rise to the fear that a serious brain lesion is either actually occurring or is impending. I have seen even comparatively young patients suffer so much from this dread that life became miserable to them and they were unable to do their work properly. A few words of explanation and reassurance literally work wonders for such patients. In one case the young woman assured me over and over again that my explanation meant a new lease of life for her. She still has occasional dizziness, but now she knows that it is due to her accompanying ear trouble and it does not worry her.

Motor Symptoms and Over-solicitude.—Besides dizziness, there are other symptoms of which patients complain and which may indicate that an apoplexy is impending or may mean only that a patient is occupying himself too much with himself and his symptoms. Not infrequently when there is degeneration of arteries in the brain there will be slight weaknesses of the limbs or awkwardness in the use of them. Occasionally women will complain of the fact that they do not button dresses as they used to. Sometimes men will complain that they do not button their collar or their suspenders at the back with facility, or that they are awkward and grow fatigued easily in such strained positions.

These symptoms may be indicative of some disturbance in the motor areas of the brain, but it must not be forgotten that all of these may be simulated by nervousness, especially if the person knows the meaning that is attached by doctors to these symptoms. In this matter particularly a little knowledge is a dangerous thing. We are only just getting a generation of trained nurses to the age when they are likely to suffer from dread of apoplexy and some of them are over-anxious patients because of their knowledge without the balance of complete practical experience with the meaning of such symptoms. Doctors themselves are prone to be disturbed by such thinking more than {517} almost anyone else. The delusion of thinking apoplexy is not at all uncommon in elderly physicians. In men it is important to insist that objective symptoms are the only details of real value and that subjective feelings are utterly illusory. If this cannot be brought home to them they make themselves extremely miserable and may even help to precipitate through worry the fatal complications they dread.

Prophylaxis.—There is no doubt but that heredity plays an important rôle in apoplexy. In certain families most of the members terminate existence by rupture of an artery in the brain, sometimes at comparatively early ages. Apparently the resistive vitality of their arteries is only sufficient to enable them to maintain themselves for a limited length of time against blood pressure. They are destined to have arterial degeneration that will predispose to arterial rupture sometime before they are sixty. Father, grandfather and great-grandfather had their apoplexies from fifty-five to sixty-five and the son must realize that he probably will go the same way. Even the delay of a year or two is important. Anything that will save the wear and tear of existence may bring about such a delay and it is not by drugs, nor even by dietetic precautions, so much as by attention to the patient's state of mind that this decided benefit can be best secured.

Over-indulgence.—People with such an unfortunate heritage should be made to understand reasonably early in life that they must save themselves from as much arterial wear and tear as possible. There are certain occupations involving intense emotion and excitement that are barred to them if they want to live out their lives, even to the extent usual in the family. There are three causes that weaken arterial walls. When the question of causation of aneurism is discussed it is usually said that it is especially the devotees of three pagan deities—Venus, Bacchus and Vulcan—who suffer from this form of arterial trouble. Just this same class suffer particularly from the tendency to early arterial rupture in the brain. Under the head of devotees of Vulcan, the hard workers, must now also be placed the advocates and exemplifiers of the strenuous life, who are perpetually doing, though often it is hard to see what they accomplish; the money-getters, who are really overworking as much as the forced laborers of olden time. People with an apoplectic heredity should not take up such professions as that of the actor, the broker, the speculator of any kind, the lawyer absorbed by the strain of trial work, perhaps not even that of the surgeon. Physicians generally are not long lived because of the irregularity of their hours of eating and sleeping and the responsibility of their professional life.

Many men will not be guided by such considerations and insist on living their lives in their own way in spite of the possibility of the family inheritance shortening their career in the late fifties. More than one has said that he would prefer to have the life of the salmon rather than that of the turtle. The strenuous life alone appeals to them.

"Better fifty years of Europe than a cycle of Cathay."

This would be an admirable response if what these men accomplished during their lives amounted to anything. Most of these who run out their existences in the midst of excitement, however, only do harm by adding to the swarm of speculators in life, or accomplish very little because of the intense {518} excitement under which they labor. It is the quiet lives, doing a few things and doing them well, outside of the strenuous current of the bustle of existence, that accomplish most for mankind. The others may attract attention for the moment, but they soon pass out, often having done rather harm than good.

Life-direction.—It is perfectly possible for the physician to make this clear to a young man with a dangerous heredity and perhaps change the current of life so as to make it effective in simplicity and serious patient work. The young man will usually be quite impatient to think that anything thirty years ahead should be expected to influence his decision as to how or what he shall do with life, yet this motive added to others may help to get at least some of this and the next generation from wasting their lives in an over-strenuous existence that at most merely accumulates money, often accumulates it only in order to lose it, with consequent disappointment and worry, and frequently leaves no real accomplishment but only the problem of the disposal of accumulated wealth for future generations. Where large wealth is left to the succeeding generation there is usually little use to give any advice with regard to the possibility of early apoplexy, because excitements of other kinds than those of business, of the heart rather than the mind, are likely to wear out existence even before the time when the family life of arteries ordinarily, though precociously, runs itself out.

Certain people have what is called the *apoplectic habitus*, that is, they are short in stature, rather stout, with short necks and florid complexions. It seems not unlikely that the mechanical arrangement within their bodies by which the distance from their heart to their brain is so much shorter than in ordinary persons is responsible for the tradition so generally accepted that there is a definite tendency in such people for apoplexy to occur at a comparatively early age. Such people should be warned gently but firmly of the danger that they incur if they subject themselves to a life of excitement or emotional stress or permit themselves to get into circumstances in which they will worry much. It may seem as though a warning of this kind would precipitate the worry of mind that it is meant to ameliorate, but in present-day publicity such people are likely to have heard of the meaning of their particular constitution of body and consequently worry about it, but usually after it is too late to do any good. In this matter, as in heart disease, the warning must come before there are any symptoms, or else must not be used at all.

Certain Abuses.—In most of these cases definite warnings with regard to habits of life and indulgence in stimulants and narcotics should be given. Both Prof. Von Leyden and Prof. Mendel of Berlin insist that for patients in whom there is any likelihood of the development of early apoplexy indulgence in alcoholic liquors is almost sure to be serious, but in addition to this generally accepted warning, both of them also insist that smoking has a tendency to produce serious, premature degeneration of arteries, especially in people who already have tendencies in that direction. Overeating and high living in general without moderate exercise causes a plethora of the circulation that must be avoided. On the other hand, violent exercise, running especially to catch trains or cars, haste in the ascent of stairs or hills, heavy lifting, straining at stool, and the like, are particularly prone to have serious consequences for such people. This warning is all the more needed because many a short, {519} stout man acquires the idea that gymnastic work and various exercises indoors may help him to reduce his weight and restore the activity of his earlier years. This is practically always a delusion and indoor gymnastic work is always of dubious value.

281

What these people need is not more muscle and the wearing off of fat but more air and the burning of it off by increased oxidation. Such patients must be taught to lead tranquil lives without any of the excitement and strenuosity that, after all, accomplishes so little. The sacrifice when first suggested, appears too great a one to make, but after a few years patients instead of feeling that it was a sacrifice at all pronounce it to be a blessing in disguise and are proportionately grateful to their physician. Life for many of these people may be prolonged not for a few years of hustle-bustle, but for many years of good work in quiet and peace, without hurting others by competition, but helping many because there is time in their considerate lives to see something of the sorrow and suffering around them and to relieve it.

Change of Occupation.—In the matter of prophylaxis it is particularly important to insist on the fact that when men have worked at hard manual labor when they are young and then, about middle life, have turned to intense intellectual labor, such as the management and administration of important affairs, they are a little more liable than are the general average of humanity to have an apoplectic seizure at sixty or a little later. Apparently inurement to a particular kind of labor when young makes for the capacity to stand it longer than would otherwise be the case. In this matter, however, the most important factor is heredity. Men who come from long-lived families are likely to live long—indeed far beyond the ordinary term of human life. Even in them, however, certain of these directions are helpful in securing the full measure of life.

After the Stroke.—After a stroke of apoplexy when it becomes clear that nature is about to reassert her control over the circulation in the brain and dispose of the remains of the old hemorrhage, psychotherapeutics is more important than anything else that we have for the treatment of these patients. As a rule, they have been active, vigorous men who are stricken and who suffer more from doing nothing and waiting to get better than from any pain they have to undergo. They know that another stroke may come at any time. It is no wonder that introspection plays its part, that every feeling that they have becomes exaggerated in significance, that their appetite fails them, that their bowels become sluggish, that they do not sleep, or that after having fallen asleep they wake up and then for hours lie awake thinking.

Lack of Air and Exercise.—As they usually have no exercise of any kind, do not get out into the air, and have very little diversion of mind, it is easy to understand that neurotic or hysterical symptoms develop, that they lose all confidence of recovery and make themselves even worse than they are by dwelling on their condition. The only way that this group of symptoms can be treated is by favorable suggestion, by encouragement, by mental reassurance and by occupation of mind.

I have always felt that the condition of affairs which developed in a family immediately after the occurrence of an apoplexy usually makes a very unfavorable environment for the treatment of these cases. It is practically impossible for those who come to visit the patient or for the members of the {520} family for some time to wear anything but the resigned air that indicates that they fear the worst.

Sympathetic Care.—After the stroke at once when survival is assured comes the question of the management of the patient. A devoted daughter seems to be able to do more for an apoplectic father than anyone else. Somehow her youth appeals to him sympathetically, and he has not that feeling of sadness mixed with a little envy that comes so readily to all men when they find themselves slipping out of life while their contemporaries and friends and relatives are left behind. It is as if the idea of his daughter being young and strong, even though he has lost vitality, docs not touch him poignantly because he has always expected that she should have health and strength after he was gone. On the other hand, a daughter is not always a good nurse for a mother. Just why, is hard to say. A hired nurse must take, as a rule, the place close to the mother which, in the case of the father, so naturally falls to the daughter. These ideas may be founded on too few cases to generalize very much about, but I have discussed them with many physicians, including some women physicians, and they agree with them, in general principle at least.

Trained Attendance.—As a rule, then, the first thing that has to be done for a patient who has had apoplexy and who is beginning to recover, is to have trained attendants near him who talk professionally to him and reassure him and do not make him feel constantly the possibility of an approaching end. If his improvement has begun his family must not be allowed to bother him, his affairs should not be talked over and, as far as possible, some occupation of mind should be secured for him. He needs new interests at once. These must be gradually awakened and he must be made to feel as early as possible that though he may be more helpless than before and most of his ordinary occupation in life may be cut off, there are still many interests in life which he may thoroughly enjoy. I shall never forget hearing Thomas Dunn English, the dear old poet to whom in his earlier years we owed "Sweet Alice, Ben Bolt," say at an alumni dinner of the University of Pennsylvania that he used to think that all the good things of life were somehow contained in its first eighty years, but that now since he had past his eightieth birthday (he was at the time in his eighty-third year) he was beginning to agree with Bismarck, who declared under similar circumstances that he had found many interests in the second eighty years of life. At the time English was quite blind, was almost completely deaf, had been seriously ill for several months, and had suffered a rather severe stroke some years before; and yet he made the best speech at the dinner that evening and had the youngest heart of us all—joyous, uplifting, encouraging, optimistic.

Outlook.—Men who have been great workers are prone to think that a stroke of apoplexy means the end of all serious work. Of course, it means nothing of the kind for the majority of patients. Many men find not only enjoyment in life after their recovery from even a serious stroke, but also possibilities of accomplishment sometimes better than they had done before. It has even been known that men who had been occupying themselves with things scarcely worth while, with the mere accumulation of money without any purpose, were awakened to a sense of their responsibilities to life and to their fellowmen by a stroke and planned in the after years institutions or aids to {521} existing institutions that did much to make life more livable for others. Nothing makes a man face life in a better mood to do really effective service for mankind than the prospect of possibly soon having to go out of life.

Encouraging Examples.—On the other hand, many men have been able in spite even of a severe stroke to go on after a time with the work they had been at before and, though feeling its effects, accomplish the best achievements of their lives. A typical example is the case of Pasteur, the great French bacteriologist, to whom we owe most of our modern preventive medicine and to whom Lord Lister frankly attributes the germ idea of the antiseptic theory. When little past fifty, Pasteur after years of hard work and worry suffered from a severe stroke of apoplexy followed by several of slighter character. It seemed absolutely the end of his labors. For more than a year he was able to do nothing. For all his after life he was seriously lame as a consequence of his stroke. In spite of this, which would seem to preclude the possibility of great intellectual work, Pasteur's most important discoveries were developed after this time and he continued for over twenty years to be the leader of biological science. Had he died at the age of fifty or given up his work we would scarcely know him for the great scientist that he afterwards proved.

It is worth while to be able to tell the stories of such lives as examples to patients who are dispirited and downhearted after a stroke. Of course, men must be prevented from doing hard work or from worrying during the time immediately following the hemorrhage of the brain, and, indeed, for some months. Work and worry, though worry much more than work, might easily hasten a recurrence of the seizure. It has always seemed to me, however, that it is impossible to keep the human mind utterly unoccupied. Men must think about something during their waking hours, and if they have not some interests close at heart they worry about themselves. Of the two things, worry is much harder on the tissues, raises blood pressure more, disturbs the circulation of the brain to a greater degree than does work. Anything that a man will interest himself in, then, should be allowed to him, provided, of course, that he is kept from getting into the state of mind which precipitated the rupture of the artery in his brain. It is a change of mental occupation above all that is needed and this is secured by deliberate attempts to interest his mind in various ways and keep him from dwelling on himself and his ills. This injunction cannot be repeated too often.

Change of Mental Interest.—I have already insisted in the chapter on Diversion of Mind that so far as we know at the present time different portions of the brain are occupied with different subjects in which we may interest ourselves. When a man by business worries, occupation with financial affairs, or with political troubles, has apparently worn out one portion of his brain, he may still use other portions to decided advantage. Hence the necessity for finding new interests for the apoplectic after their attack. The best interests for them are those associated in some way with their fellows, because these are accompanied by feelings of consolation, of encouragement, of desire to live and do good to others. These do more to take men out of their moodiness, their morbid introspection, and their self-centeredness, than anything else. With the help of a good nurse, herself of broad interests, this must become the main purpose of the physician's treatment.

{522}

Misplaced Sympathy.—After the first few days, when the shock is over, a strong, healthy man who has been suddenly taken down with apoplexy, then rendered helpless as a consequence of the lesion in his brain, rather resents the sympathy and, above all, the frequent expression of the feelings of his friends towards him. Time is needed for him to recover, there is no way of hastening it, he is already impatient at the delay and words of sympathy do him very little good and often add to his impatience. He is to be taken absolutely with professional calm, made to understand that time is the most important element in his cure, provided he will not worry and will have patience to wait and to help as far as he can. I nearly always feel that it is better for these patients to be away from home as soon as they can be moved with safety. This enables them to avoid without much difficulty what they are apt to consider the intrusive and obtrusive sympathy of friends. Especially is this true of business friends, themselves in good health, who come to offer their condolences.

Their hysterical condition is largely influenced by the fact that they are indoors and have so little diversion of mind. Just as soon as possible they must get out of doors. Over and over again I have found that patients did not care to expose themselves to the inquisitive gaze of neighbors and preferred to stay in the house, though the outing would be of much benefit to them. Hence the necessity for getting them away from home, among people whom they can observe without attracting too much attention themselves and, above all, without being the subjects of such obtrusive pity as will disturb them. None of us likes to be pitied and least of all the strong, vigorous man who often has had nothing the matter with him all his life and is now suddenly stricken. It requires years of experience to enable one to take sympathy properly and without resenting it.

Outings and Human Interests.—When patients care for carriage riding I have found that the city park is an excellent place for patients suffering from the effects of apoplexy, who require outdoor air and diversion of mind, yet without exercise or much exertion. The children in the park, if they play around, serve as a better diversion of mind than almost anything else for elderly people thus stricken, for they seem to renew their youth at the sight of the little ones. Grandchildren make the best possible consolers even when they seem to probe deep into old wounds by asking questions and by talking about death. The talk of death from young lips has not the same disturbing effect as from older people. The games of children interest the old once more, and if there is occasional music and the chance to see the passing throng of carriages and motor cars and the pleasure boats and all the rest there is refreshment and reinvigoration in it all that soon brings back to the patient deep, satisfactory, even dreamless uninterrupted sleep at night, and appetite and strength. At first there will usually be some objection to being thus treated as an invalid, but only a few days of experience are needed to convert even the most morbid to the idea that this outing will do them good. As a rule, friends must be warned not to spoil the effect of it by fearing lest the patient should be lonely and so go to the park to entertain him. If the drive, the lake and the children, as well as the passers-by, do not suffice to give the patient sufficient diversion of mind, the visits of friends will not have any favorable effect. As a rule, it is better for them to see the {523} patient at home and even that not too often unless they are of his immediate family.

Where people are able to go away and, above all, where they can have some pleasant companionship, a seaside resort is an ideal place for those recovering from apoplexy. The long ride in a wheel-chair on the boardwalk at least several hours in the morning and afternoon soon acts marvelously. There is constant diversion of mind at any season of the year, for there are lots of people to be seen in all sorts of costumes and the shops and the shows and the passing throng all have their interests. Then the sea air is bracing and tempts to sleepfulness and just as soon as sleep improves courage comes back. I have known patients so hysterical that they were crying every day and that seemed to have given up all hope, improve so much in two weeks at Atlantic City that it seemed little short of marvelous. What is needed, however, is not a stay of a few weeks but of several months.

Prognosis of Strokes.—While, of course, any single stroke may be fatal and no one can tell anything about the prognosis of a rupture of a brain artery, there are many favorable things that can be said to patients, and they are so prone to think of all the unfavorable things that this better side should be presented to them at once. The physician is tempted to present the worst side of the case lest it should be thought that he did not realize how serious the condition was. All the seriousness of it may be impressed upon friends, but the patient must be told all the possibilities of good. I have always felt that the tonic quality of hope was worth more in preventing further damage and in encouraging the beginning of repair than any drug that we have. If patients have been unconscious, just as soon as unconsciousness disappears, they should be told that very probably this is the beginning of recovery and that the great majority of people who have a stroke recover. The more rapidly the symptoms disappear the better is the ultimate prognosis. Many a man who has had a stroke has done years of good work afterwards and very few men who recover fail to accomplish something that is of supreme satisfaction to them. They have a new outlook on life as a consequence of the near vision of death.

Those who have had one stroke usually die in a subsequent one, though, of course, some intermittent disease such as pneumonia or some organic complication may anticipate the second stroke. Those who have had two strokes and survive are often much worried by the old tradition that a third stroke is always fatal. I am reasonably sure that many old men have not survived their third stroke when they felt its premonitory symptoms and knew just what was coming from their previous experience, because they had given up hope on account of this old tradition. Ignorant people or those of the lower classes who have not heard this axiom often survive their third stroke and I have seen a man who had suffered from seven apoplectic seizures.

Complications.—Occasionally a patient, especially if of the educated classes, may be much worried by the fact that while one side is distinctly lamed after his stroke, yet there is also a pronounced weakness on the other side of the body. This sometimes gives rise to the rather appalling thought that there was perhaps a simultaneous rupture on both sides of the brain. It needs to be explained to such patients that this slight weakness, sometimes quite distinct, however, on the side opposite that which is most affected is extremely {524} common. Ordinarily the rupture of an artery on one side of the brain causes a paralysis on the other side of the body. This paralysis or loss of control over muscular action is due to disturbance of the motor tracts of nerves through which muscular action is controlled and directed by the brain, and these normally cross to the other side on the way to the periphery. In nearly everyone the tracts remain uncrossed to some slight extent. In some so much of the pyramidal tract remains uncrossed that there may be decided weakness on the same side as the lesion in the brain.

CHAPTER III

LOCOMOTOR ATAXIA

How much can be done for organic nervous disease by attention to the individual patient and by favorable suggestion is illustrated in locomotor ataxia. This is, of course, an absolutely incurable disease. We know definitely that certain tracts of nerves in the spinal cord are entirely obliterated and their functions can never be restored. Occasionally the disease gives rise to severe localized pains called crises, for which even our strongest anodyne remedies are of little avail. As a rule, the patient grows more and more helpless and though he may live for twenty or thirty years after the beginning of the disease, and usually dies from some intercurrent affection rather than from any direct effect of his disease, the condition is burdensome and the outlook is most unfavorable and depressing. It is for locomotor ataxia, however, that the irregular practitioners have succeeded, apparently, in working wonders. Some of them, indeed, have made quite a reputation for the cure of the disease. This was not because they did the impossible and cured genuine cases, but because individual patients can, in many cases, be so much improved by attention to particular symptoms, and so much can be done to make life more livable for them, that it is no wonder that so many of them are ready to proclaim that they have been cured, though only certain symptoms, are bettered and their underlying disease remains in essence unchanged.

One thing that constantly happens in the progress of locomotor ataxia is a yielding of joint capsules and attachments so that there is more motion permitted in joints than is possible in the normal individual. As a consequence of this relaxation of tissues around the hip joint the leg may be stretched up along the trunk when the patient is lying down, the foot being placed over the shoulder almost as a gun is placed at carry-arms. Patients often walk with a distinct "back knee" because of the yielding of the tissues around the knee-joint. The ankle nearly always yields and a specially severe form of flat foot develops. This causes muscles to act at a disadvantage and produces great fatigue and even a painful muscular condition when the patient stands much on the feet. This form of flat foot is hopeless so far as cure is concerned, but it can be greatly relieved by the wearing of flat-foot braces or even, to a greater degree, by the wearing of specially fitted shoes. This does not seem much to do for a patient suffering from the serious organic nervous disease of locomotor ataxia, and yet a lot of patients for whom properly fitting shoes {525} were made, thought themselves so much improved and relieved by this simple measure that they allowed themselves to be persuaded that their locomotor ataxia was cured. In some cases, where the brunt of the disease was borne by the feet, this relief really did so much to afford the patients freedom from most symptoms of their affection that they thought themselves on the road to recovery.

Value of Favorable Suggestion.—If once the idea of the awful hopelessness of their cases is removed from locomotor ataxia patients they will suggest their own betterment so powerfully that they easily persuade themselves that their affection is considerably improved. It is evident, then, that the regular physician must take advantage of this wonderful power for the relief of human suffering and depression that proves so helpful to the irregular. We cannot cure the tabes of the spinal cord. We cannot re-create the nerve tracts that have been obliterated. We realize that there is no use trying to do so any more than there would be in trying to make an amputated finger grow to its full size again. We can treat the patient, however. We can remove many symptoms that sometimes bother him more than those necessarily connected with his spinal affection. We can relieve annoyances of all kinds that add to his misery and as a consequence we can give him hope, keep him from brooding about himself and thus perform the proper function of a physician. We shall not forget that we can only rarely cure, but we can almost always relieve pain and we can always help the patient in some way. The ataxic patient needs consolation, and this can be given without in any way deceiving him. The loss of sight seems an irreparable ill to those who see, yet the blind are quite happy, are much more cheerful than many seeing people, and have learned to stand their affliction not only with equanimity but really without much depression. In the olden times, before proper care was taken of the blind, they had little occupation, they had nothing to do with their hands, the future was blank and they suffered severely from depression. As a rule, they did not go out enough and their bodily health suffered and the disturbance of their functions still further heightened their depression. All of this happens now with the ataxic patient. A host of symptoms not at all necessarily connected with his spinal affection develop and prove sources of annoyance. Many of them can be removed entirely, all of them can be ameliorated. If, while doing this, we succeed in impressing a discouraged patient's mind with our power to benefit in spite of an underlying incurable disease, we have another triumph of psychotherapy.

Removing Unfavorable Suggestions.—The general experience with those suffering from locomotor ataxia has been that the depression consequent upon the announcement that they have the disease and the stigma that is supposed to attach to it in our day leads them to a great extent to avoid going out into the air. This adds woefully to their depressed condition. Take a healthy man, let him stay inside a great part of the time without any exercise, seeing no new faces, without any interests in life, and at the end of three months he will have a set of neurotic symptoms on a basis of depression that will make him supremely miserable. This will be true even though he has not the threat of an incurable disease hanging over his head. He must be made to realize that every neglect of any law of health in his condition is even more serious in its effect upon him than it would be were he in good health. Above {526} all, it must be made clear to him that while his neglect of hygiene may perhaps not shorten his life, it will greatly add to the mental suffering, much more unbearable in its way than the physical suffering which he will have to endure during the progress of his disease.

Treating Accessory Symptoms.—Nearly every ataxic patient who is not directly and almost constantly under the care of a physician, is a sufferer from two conditions that are so constantly present that they are sometimes thought to be consequences of the primary affection. These are loss of appetite with consequent loss of weight and constipation. Almost without exception neither of these symptoms or syndromes are at all connected with the locomotor ataxia. They are the result of the unhygienic life that the patient is living and of the depressed state of his mind and lack of diversion. They are mutually connected, for a man who does not eat enough will not have regular movements of his bowels, and constipation reacts to produce further depression. A vicious circle in pathogeny is formed and the patient is likely to get into a very debilitated and depressed condition. Both of these troublesome symptoms may be corrected to the manifest improvement of the patient by proper advice and ordinary care for his well being.

Appetite is largely a function, as the mathematicians say of something that depends on something else, not of exercise, as is often thought, but of fresh air. In the tuberculosis sanatoria patients with fever are not permitted to take exercise, yet if they are out in the air most of the day and if their rooms are well aired at night, they can eat heartily and digest their food well. Of course, appetite is largely a psychic matter and the thoroughly discouraged man will have no care for food in spite of abundance of air. A little persuasion, however, of the necessity for making the best of a bad job will usually arouse even a locomotor ataxia patient in the early stages of his disease to the necessity for eating a reasonable amount. If he has suffered from gastric crises and fears that eating normally may precipitate these, he must be persuaded that this is not the case, that the presence of food, or its amount, or quality, has nothing to do with the initiation of these painful attacks so far as we know, and that even though at the beginning of his affection before his locomotor ataxia was recognized, his gastralgia may have been declared by his physicians, as is so often the case, to be connected with some form of gastritis or indigestion, that idea may now be given up and he may eat plentifully with confidence that it will not increase his pains. On the contrary, limitation of food seems to have a distinctly unfavorable effect in increasing the number and severity of these attacks.

The same thing must be made clear to him as to intestinal and rectal crises. It seems likely that tendencies to constipation by irritating peripheral nerve endings may have some effect in bringing about the explosion in sensory nerves which have been called intestinal or rectal crises. In general, however, these are dependent on spinal and not peripheral conditions, and no thought of any connection must be allowed to disturb the consumption of a proper amount and variety of food. It seems clear that when patients are much run down, have lost considerable in weight and are in a generally depressed condition, their nervous system is much more irritable than it would otherwise be and they are likely to suffer more frequently from crises of various kinds. Once a patient is made to understand that his general {527} nutrition may affect not only the course but the occurrence of symptoms in the disease, as a rule it is not difficult to get him to eat enough and to do so with the definite feeling that it is going to do him good. Even though it should be necessary to use tonics, and often they will have to be prescribed, it is clear that this treatment of the patient's general condition is the physician's first duty, though it does not and cannot affect the specific disease.

285

Neurotic Complications.—There can, of course, be no doubt that the crises of locomotor ataxia represents extremely poignant attacks of pain. But on the other hand, anyone who has seen many of them is prone to think that not a few of them are really attacks of pain resembling those which occasionally develop in hysterical subjects. The pain of a gastric neurosis may, indeed, so simulate the gastric crises of locomotor ataxia as to make what is only a case of hysteria seem beyond doubt one of locomotor ataxic. Locomotor ataxia patients are prone to think much about themselves and to fear the recurrence of these painful crises once they have had experience with them. As a consequence they sometimes suffer from what are pseudo-crises, that is, from neurotic painful conditions which simulate genuine crises mainly in the amount of reaction they produce in the patient. True tabetic crises yield more readily to ordinary anodyne drugs than do these pseudo-crises. Nearly always the true crises are associated with and exaggerated by neurotic symptoms due to the depression of the patient, the yielding to his feelings, the conclusion that his pain is inevitable and is going to be worse each time, while successive crises are, as a matter of fact, often milder until they disappear for good, and this element in the case must always be borne in mind. Much can be done for the relief by psychotherapy, that is, by making the patient see the realities of his condition, suggesting to him that succeeding crises are less painful and that if his general condition is as good as it should be he becomes better able to stand the pain of his crises and the shock of them is not so disturbing to his system.

Mental Attitude.—Prof. Oppenheim, in one of his "Letters to Nervous Patients," advising a patient suffering from an incurable organic nervous disease, evidently locomotor ataxia, though that is not explicitly stated, outlines emphatically the favorable side of that disease. This is absolutely needed. Ever so many unfavorable suggestions with regard to his affection find their way to the patient. The very fact that it is pronounced absolutely incurable is disheartening. Prof. Oppenheim's words, then, may be a precious help and to have them repeated from time to time renews the suggestion:

Now, however, we neurologists know that that disease frequently runs a very mild course, that a man showing certain early symptoms of such a disease may for ten to twenty-five years and even longer retain his capacity for work and enjoyment. This for a man of thirty to forty years is almost tantamount to the expectation of a whole normal lifetime. But on the other hand, what danger to the peace of mind, what destruction of happiness in life may be caused if the knowledge that such a disease has begun to develop is imparted to the patient without being combined with the consoling information as to the nature and course of the benign forms of this trouble! In unceasing anxiety and fear, in daily expectancy of some fresh symptoms, of some increase or aggravation of his troubles, does the poor man waste his life; and I have frequently found that this wretched apprehension and excitement cause a nervousness and mental depression which in their effects are much more momentous than is the commencing spinal disease.

From this miserable condition I desire to protect you, and I would ask you to {528} take this advice deeply to heart: do not bear yourself as one who is condemned; as one who, affected by a progressive, incurable disease, will soon fall a victim to paralysis. On the strength of my own experience I give you the assurance that your condition of health will not necessarily in ten years' time be essentially different from what it is at present. But I would also strenuously exhort you to observe all the precautionary rules laid down for you, to avoid all unaccustomed strain or indulgence such as can only be undertaken with impunity by a man in full vigor and absolute soundness of health. I would advise you also to be thoroughly examined once a year by an experienced physician. But apart from these restrictions, you should as far as possible feel yourself and bear yourself like a healthy man, remaining attached to your work, and not withdrawing yourself from the pleasures of social intercourse.

Relearning Muscular Movements.—Perhaps the most interesting evidence of how much may be done for organic nervous disease in spite of the fact that the underlying lesion is absolutely incurable, may be obtained from what is accomplished by Frenkel's method of treating locomotor ataxia. As is well known, by reteaching the movements necessary for walking, ataxic patients regain control of the movements of their limbs to a marked extent. As a consequence, bed-ridden patients are enabled to walk once more even though they may have to carry a cane and be supported, and patients who have had to use two canes get along with only one, or may even eventually be able to walk without any artificial support.

Just how the improvement is brought about we are not quite sure. It seems probable that the eyes become trained to replace the muscle sense to a noteworthy degree, but there is in addition apparently a re-education of the muscle-sense. Perhaps there is also a transfer of the function of certain degenerated nerves to other tracts than those in which muscle impulses originally traveled. The improvement in muscular control originally obtained is a striking illustration of how much nature is able to compensate for even organic lesions and is a lesson in the necessity for never ceasing to try to do something even when the case seems hopeless. Certainly locomotor ataxic patients would seem the least likely to be benefited by training in movement and yet this movement therapy for tabes has had some wonderful results.

The story of how this mode of treatment came into existence is interesting and instructive as an illustration of how happy chance in our time, as so often with regard to drugs in the past, came to assist the rational development of therapeutics. A German professor wished to demonstrate to his class the varying inco-ordination of a series of tabetic patients. Some of them had their main inco-ordination in the legs, others in their hands. He went over the cases in his wards so as to arrange the demonstration for the next day. He told each patient that he would ask him to perform a particular set of movements before the class which would illustrate strikingly a particular phase of muscular inco-ordination. His patients were interested in the announced demonstrations and during the afternoon they went over the movements that they were expected to perform. They practiced them as assiduously as their condition permitted for the exhibition. As a consequence the most striking features of their inco-ordination disappeared. After having practiced the movement for a certain length of time they could do it ever so much better than before. The special feature of the professor's demonstration was spoiled, but a great contribution to our knowledge of nature's compensatory powers {529} was made and fortunately the hint of its significance for treatment was taken and developed.

Effect of Favorable Suggestion.—How much can be accomplished for the relief of the general symptoms of locomotor ataxia and for the placing of patients in an attitude of mind that makes most of their symptoms of vanishing importance, can be judged from some recent experiences with a new cure for the disease. This consisted only of some rather conventional treatment of the urethra by applications and dilatation, yet patients were relieved so much of the symptoms of locomotor ataxia, or at least persuaded themselves that they were, that both in this country and in Europe the discoverer of the new "cure" soon had scores of patients. The active therapeutic agent undoubtedly was the fact that patients who had been told that their disease was incurable and who had settled down in a state of discouragement and apathy in which their power over their muscles, their general health and their strength and vitality were at the lowest ebb, and their tendencies to discomfort emphasized and made poignant by the supposed hopelessness of their situation, became aroused to new vitality by the promise of cure and then, under the repeated suggestion of a treatment said to be sure to cure them and that had cured others, became so much better, that is, released so much latent energy, that they felt better, ate better, walked better, got out more and had their general health improved, and all to such a degree that their disease seemed cured.

Another interesting illustration of what would seem to be the power of suggestion over the symptoms of tabes occurs in a recent article in the Archivos Españoles de Neurologia Psyqiuatria y Fisioterapia of Madrid on the improvement of tabes dorsalis by antidiphtheritic serum. It is quite impossible that the serum should affect favorably any of the underlying lesions of the disease any more than that these should be ameliorated by the wearing of shoes of special character or operations on the urethra. The patient in this case, however, was distinctly improved in many ways *after* the antidiphtheritic serum was injected. There were some interesting sensory manifestations, pains in the arms and legs after the injection, but these were removed by santonin or methylene blue. Both of these drugs are eminently suggestive in their action, so that one would be prone to think the pains rather neurotic than actual. After a dozen injections had been given, the patient's sensations improved, his power to pick up small things was better, and the sense of walking on carpet had disappeared to a marked extent and he was able to walk much better than before and without support. Probably any attention given to him to the same degree would have produced like results.

We have had previous examples of this kind in the history of the treatment of locomotor ataxia. Certain drugs when given in the past with the definite promise of cure and pursued for a good while with frequently repeated favorable suggestions, have often seemed to benefit patients, though subsequent experience has shown their total lack of value to modify the disease. Nitrate of silver was one of these in the old days and many locomotor ataxia patients acquired an argyria as a consequence of the amount of silver absorbed and deposited in the skin. Arsenic was another and some of the aluminum {530} compounds were also used. When we recall the suspension treatment and its reported good effects—and failure, the over-extension treatment with the same history and many others in the past, the real place of the mental in the therapeutics of tabies is revealed. Once this is practically realized, we find that we have ready to hand and easy to use, the one really efficient factor in all these treatments—that is, the influence on the patient's mind. It is for the physician to devise thoroughly professional ways and means of using that in each particular case so that his patients may be benefited as much as possible. Certainly it would be foolish for us to leave to the irregular practitioner the use of this extremely valuable remedial measure, when we may do so much good with it, for the relief of symptoms at least.

CHAPTER IV

PARESIS

Paresis would seem to be one of the affections so inevitable in its course, so positively helpless as regards any medication, and so hopeless in its absolutely sure termination in idiocy and death, that nothing can possibly be done for it through the patient's mind, yet it is probably one of the diseases for which most can be accomplished by psychotherapy. Mental treatment for it naturally divides itself into three periods: that of prophylaxis, that of the early stage and that of the severer stage with remissions. Prophylaxis is much more important than is usually thought. It is very generally known at present that paresis is usually a parasyphilitic disease, that is, an affection not due directly to syphilis, but which develops by preference and perhaps exclusively in a soil prepared for it by an attack of syphilis. As a consequence of the diffusion of this knowledge men who have suffered from syphilis sometimes become supremely fatalistic as regards the development of locomotor ataxia or paresis in their cases. Worry is a prominent feature in the causation of paresis, and it is, therefore, extremely important to neutralize this.

I have had university graduates tell me their histories and ask whether I thought they had suffered from syphilis, and when I replied affirmatively have seen a look of despair come into their faces. One of them, a graduate of a large eastern university, said, after hearing my opinion, though it was given with every assurance that my experience with Fournier in Paris taught me the absolute curability of the disease, "Well, there are three men of my class who have already developed paresis, and I suppose I will go the same way." With a persuasion like this haunting him night and day, exhausting nervous energy and making his central nervous system less and less resistive, it would be almost a miracle if paresis did not develop. It is particularly in those who have had nervously exhaustive occupations—brokers, speculators, actors, and the like—that paresis does develop. The strain upon their nervous systems seem to be so great that the syphilitic virus still remaining in their system has a peculiarly degenerative effect upon nervous tissue. A man may be in the least worrisome of occupations, however, and if he is constantly brooding over the possibility of the coming of the hideous specter of paresis, {531} he puts himself in the condition most likely to encourage the development of the pathological changes that underlie the disease.

Prophylaxis.—As a rule patients who have had syphilis and who dread the development of paresis should be warned with regard to their occupations in life. After a patient has had tuberculosis which developed in particular surroundings, if it is at all possible, we no longer permit him to go back into the surroundings in which his disease developed. We are coming, more and more, to apply the principles of preventive medicine and this is as important in paresis as in anything else. Even though there may be many monetary or economic reasons in favor of certain occupations, the danger may overweigh these. Those who have had syphilis should be warned of the risk they run if they continue in occupations that require much mental excitement or the strain of anxiety and the speculative factor of uncertainty with the inevitable occurrence of disappointments. It is unjustifiable to permit a patient whose central nervous system is subjected to the deteriorating influence of the virus of syphilis, still in his body even after ten years, to submit to the nerve-racking irritation of occupations which require all the vigor of a healthy, undisturbed organism to survive their wear and tear.

Sources of Worry.—One of the symptoms which neurotic patients are sure must be a preliminary sign of paresis is a disturbance of memory. Patients have heard that paresis causes memory disturbances and fearing the development of the disease, they disturb themselves very much by finding real or supposed defects of memory. Most of them have had only a very vague idea of the sort of memory they possess and cannot tell whether it is worse than before, but finding a certain difficulty in recalling things they conclude that it is deteriorating. Occasionally their supposed defect of memory is founded on nothing more serious than the fact that they are paying so much attention to themselves, that they cannot concentrate their attention enough on what they wish to remember so as really to impress it on their memories. It is curious how persistent some patients are in making themselves believe they have serious lacunae in their memory when there are only certain conventional disturbances of it. The paretic has defects of memory, but he is, as a rule, quite unconscious of them. He has to have them pointed out to him. Patients who are supremely conscious of their supposed defects, by that very fact show their possession of good intellectual faculties.

Tremor is another symptom that may develop in the midst of the solicitude of those who dread paresis. The power to hold the limbs in a given position is due to a very nice balancing of flexor and extensor muscles. There are many people, especially those a little awkward in the use of their muscles, who lack this power to some extent. To stand without swaying is rather a difficult task in one who is nervous or anxious about himself. Patients who are worrying about paresis and its possible development will almost surely disturb their power over their muscles and cause at least a slight tremor or swaying.

In other words, in all of these cases a series of dreads, or mental obsessions which interfere with various functions which may cause tremor, or some stuttering, or at least some apparent difficulties of speech and which will surely revive any old-time difficulties of this kind, may develop in nervous persons and must not be allowed to pass as signs of developing paresis. The {532} diagnostic tests, of course, consist in the knee-jerks, the pupillary reactions, the difference in disposition, the delusions of grandeur, and, in general, the characteristic symptoms of a physical degeneration running parallel with a mental deterioration.

Prophylactic Reassurance.—The first point in psychotherapy, then, is to give just as much reassurance as can be given. Probably not one out of a thousand of those who have suffered from syphilis afterwards develops paresis. Nearly always there is something in the history besides syphilis that seems to be an essential etiological factor. A great many of the people who develop this disease have some hereditary taint of mental incapacity at least, if not of actual insanity. Very often there is a personal or family history that indicates some mental unevenness or at least some lack of intellectual vigor. When people are sanely intellectual and have no unfortunate hereditary tendencies they can be almost completely assured as to the possibility of the development of paresis, provided they take reasonable care of themselves.

Alcohol.—It is still an unsettled question whether alcoholism has anything to do, even in a subsidiary capacity, with the etiology of paresis. Probably it helps to predispose nerve tissues to degeneration by lowering their resistive vitality to the direct pathogenic action of the virus of syphilis. It seems clear, besides, that men who have acquired syphilis sometimes take to over-indulgence in alcohol, at least to a greater degree than would otherwise be the case, because of the discouraging dread that develops as a result of their worry over this constitutional taint. A warning in this matter of indulgence in intoxicants is important because there are many nerve specialists who insist that alcoholism is probably one of the prime factors in paresis.

Unconclusive Diagnosis.—When the first symptoms of paresis have developed so that the physician is almost certain that the disease is present—the cumulative experience of recent mistakes on the part of the most careful experts seems to show that he can never be entirely certain—then it is important not to announce the worst to the patient, but to let him learn the reality of his condition gradually, so that all the awfulness of it does not overwhelm him. What have seemed typical cases of paresis, so diagnosed by excellent authorities, have occasionally proved to be something else, or, at least, to be wayward and very irregular forms of that disease with a long course and marked remissions. There are forms of paranoia in the middle-aged which sometimes exhibit symptoms so strongly simulant of paresis as to deceive even the expert. There are forms of nervous weakness—neurasthenia—some of which are really cases of mental exhaustion or incapacity—the modern psychasthenia—which often lead even experienced physicians to think of and sometimes to diagnose paresis. There are cases of dementia praecox that only time can differentiate.

Prognosis.—*Seeing the Worst.*—There is a tendency in most physicians to see the worst side of the story rather than the better. This is not because of any desire to be a harbinger of evil tidings, nor, as is sometimes said, to show the patient, should he get better, from what a depth of affliction he has been rescued, but it is rather due to the very natural tendency existing in most of us to look on the worst side of things. Besides, we have found by experience that if patients are to be aroused to the necessity of care for themselves they must be scared a little, and so we have formed the habit, not of consciously {533} and deliberately telling the worst, but of stating the unfavorable possibilities of a group of symptoms, in order that a patient may take due precautions and that he may realize, if the worst does happen, that we were not ignorant of it. If he gets better he is correspondingly grateful for this. If the unfavorable happens and we had not warned him, he is more or less justifiably resentful.

Consoling Hesitancy of Final Judgment.—Patients suspected of suffering from paresis can then without any violation of truth be reassured that their cases may not be incurable until the epileptiform incidents of the disease bring on that happy obscuration of mentality, that either takes away all the terror of the disease or lessens so much its awful significance that the patient is spared the worst. There are cases of reported cures in the literature even after what seemed to be characteristic epileptiform attacks had occurred.

We cannot be sure, in any case, of the future course of an affection exhibiting symptoms resembling paresis. The patient can always be given the advantage of this doubt then and the awful word incurable or even the diagnosis paresis need not be mentioned to him. It is perfectly possible, as a rule, to take other means to prevent unfortunate incidents from tendencies to violence or serious loss from foolishness, without overwhelming the patient with an absolutely unfavorable prognosis, and the diagnosis of paresis, involving as it does, now that so much more is popularly known of the disease than before, the dread of inevitable idiocy. In this way much of the depression that constitutes so large a part of the really sane period of the early stage of paresis and which inevitably hastens the course of the disease may be avoided. On the other hand, failure to announce absolutely the diagnosis of paresis until there can be no particle of doubt, can do no harm and will do good to the patients themselves, as well as save their anxious friends from the trial of having to think of the awful possibilities of the disease. A single sensible member of the family may be selected as the confidant and the situation saved.

Rôle of Psychotherapy.—While it is important that someone closely connected with the patient should know the doctor's suspicions, he should be bound to absolute secrecy as regards the patient himself and especially as regards women friends and relatives. The attitude of mind assumed by women relatives, and especially those nearest and dearest, is sure to be communicated to the patient, if not directly at least indirectly and inadvertently, and makes for anything but relief from the depression that is sure to be his if he has any gleam of understanding of his condition. Indeed, so much of pain and suffering is needlessly inflicted on relatives of paretic patients in the early stages of the disease by a premature announcement of the diagnosis that it is especially important to insist on care in this matter. The family will usually clamor to know just what is the matter, but it is the physician's duty to care for his patient and save the sufferings of the patient's family, regardless of their unwitting insistence. Once the disease has developed and the patient's mind becomes affected it may be thought that psychotherapy is no longer of value. As a matter of fact, these patients as a rule become more childlike and are much more affected by suggestion than in their normal states. All this is worthy of careful attention on the part of the physician who feels that it is his duty to treat patients and not merely their disease.

The psychic care of the patient is the most important element in any {534} scheme of therapeutics during the longer remissions of paresis, which are sometimes so complete that it is difficult to understand that the patient, who is now as sensible as he ever was, only a few months before was doing the most foolish things under the influence of his delusions of grandeur and probably within a few months will be quite as insane as before and perhaps hopelessly demented. The brevity of these remissions in most cases seems to depend directly on how much the patient is persuaded that his disease will return without fail and run its inevitable course. It is well worth while to lengthen these remissions by setting the patient's mind just as much at rest as possible. Instead of the attitude which is so often assumed of absolute assurance on the part of the physician that the old condition will inevitably return, it is advisable always to give the opinion that the previous mental derangement was paranoiac rather than paretic, or was perhaps only a passing syphilitic condition and that the ultimate outlook is not as hopeless as might be thought. This opinion is thoroughly justified by certain surprising results in a number of recently reported cases. Some patients whose symptoms have been diagnosed as paresis by excellent diagnosticians, have, after a time, experienced a cessation of their symptoms which looked very much like a remission occurring in the midst of the inevitably progressive paretic degeneration and then to the surprise of their physicians have not exhibited any further symptoms of the affection. Syphilis of the nervous system sometimes simulates paresis to such an extent as to deceive the most expert, and proper antisyphilitic treatment will sometimes produce results that are little short of marvelous. It is beyond all question, then, for the good of the patient suspected of paresis that his physician should give him the benefit of every doubt.

CHAPTER V

EPILEPSY AND PSEUDO-EPILEPSY

EPILEPSY

With regard to the major neuroses generally, very much more therapeutic benefit can be secured than in any other way that we know by reassuring the patient's mind, by careful regulation of his life and by such modifications of his occupation as will take him out of a strenuous existence, so likely to be harmful to a nervous system laboring under these serious handicaps. In recent years we have come to realize that epilepsy, for instance, is more favorably influenced by a simple outdoor life in the country without worries and cares, with carefully regulated exercise in the open air and special attention to the digestive tract, than by any formal remedial measures or drug treatment. The fewer the emotional storms the less likelihood of repetitions of attacks of epilepsy. No medicine is so effective in prolonging the intervals between attacks as this placing of the patient in favorable conditions of mind and body. Our experience with the colony system has emphasized the fact that drug treatment is quite a subsidiary factor in this general care for the patient. The most important element in this treatment is the effect on the {535} patient's mind and the consequent gain in poise and in resistive vitality against emotional explosions which are so often the immediate occasion of attacks. This lessens their number and it is well known that frequent repetition is likely to be associated with that deterioration of the physical nature and mental condition which is most to be dreaded.

Mental Influences.—When living a quiet placid life without worry about himself or his concerns, the number of the epileptic attacks goes down in a noteworthy degree and the intervals between them become longer and longer. After years of quiet country living epileptics who had two or three attacks a week have scarcely more than one a month, if, indeed, that often, and their general condition is greatly improved. We have had many remedies for the affection, only a few of which have proved to be really therapeutic. The remainder have had their effect through the mental influence that went with them, the assurance of relief and the confidence that it aroused.

First attacks of epilepsy are not infrequently the result of an immediately preceding fright or sudden emotion of some kind or other. Gowers tells the story of a sentinel posted near a graveyard who was very much disturbed by his proximity to the dead and who, during the night, saw a white goat run past him, jump over a low wall and disappear. He was sure it was a ghost. He had his first attack of epilepsy shortly after. Children not infrequently have their first attack after a scare from a dog or a rough-looking stranger who has come near them. After the affection has established itself attacks of epilepsy follow vehement mental disturbances of any kind. Sometimes after a long interval of freedom from attacks a sudden strong emotion is followed by a fit and then the epileptic habit is reestablished. In order to be as free as possible from the affection patients must be protected from emotional storms.

Power of Suggestion.—-A strong proof of the favorable influence of suggestion upon epilepsy was given when operations for epilepsy became common about twenty years ago. A number of patients were operated on by trephining, even though almost nothing else was done except to open the dura and examine the brain, for often no definite pathological condition to justify surgical intervention was found. But these patients did not suffer from attacks of epilepsy for months and sometimes years afterwards. Many surgeons reported these cases as cured, as they apparently were when discharged from the hospitals, for no attacks had recurred; but physicians had to treat them later when their epilepsy redeveloped. The surgical procedure, as indeed might have been expected from the findings, had given only temporary betterment. The real therapeutic factor at work had probably been not any definite change within the skull, but the suggestive influence of the operation, the period of rest with favorable suggestion constantly renewed, and the confidence of recovery inspired during convalescence. Even in cases where adhesions were found between the dura and calvarium and these were broken up, the relief afforded was usually but temporary. The succession of events, the relief afforded and subsequent relapse, probably represented the same influence of suggestion as in the preceding cases with perhaps a slight physical betterment in addition.

An important factor in the psychotherapeutics of epilepsy is to relieve the patient as far as possible from the haunting dread of insanity, which, especially if he has read much of the disease, is so likely to hang over him as {536} a pall because of the absolutely bad prognosis which often occupies so prominent a place in older text-books and articles on epilepsy. There is no doubt that in a great many cases epilepsy is a progressive degenerative disease and that a state of lowered mentality will eventually develop. There are many cases, however, in which epilepsy is only a series of incidents which does not seem to affect the intellectual life and which is quite compatible not only with prolonged existence, but with mental achievements of a high order and, above all, with a personality that may be commanding in its power over others. This knowledge, which unfortunately is not usually given in text-books because they are studies in the pathology rather than in the psychology of epilepsy, is extremely important for the epileptic. This view is of special significance for those sufferers from the disease who are well educated and in whom mentality means so much.

The Individual in Epilepsy.—In epilepsy, indeed, the individual counts much more than his ailment, and even in severe cases of epilepsy there are individuals to whom the recurring convulsions are only annoying occurrences of life, somewhat dangerous because of the risks encountered during unconsciousness, but without any ulterior significance for degeneration of character or intellectual power. As a matter of fact, there are many men in history who were epileptics and who yet succeeded in great work of many kinds, even purely intellectual, unhampered by this condition, and some of them have proved to be leaders in achievement. In his paper read before the National Association for the Study of Epilepsy and the Care and Treatment of Epileptics, at its eighth annual meeting. Dr. Matthew Woods discussed what certain famous epileptics had accomplished in spite of epilepsy. He takes three typical examples—Julius Caesar, Mohammed and Lord Byron—the founders, respectively, of an empire, a religion and a school of poetry—with regard to whom there is convincing evidence that they were epileptics. A fourth name, that of Napoleon, might easily have been added. Greater accomplishments than these epileptics made in their various departments are not to be found in the history of the race.

Many other names of epileptics distinguished for achievement might well have been added to the list. The argument that would be founded on their lives is not that epileptics are necessarily or even usually of high intelligence, but that some of them, at least, retain in spite of the major neurosis, or even serious brain disorder, whichever it may be, all their intellectual qualities undisturbed. Lombroso, arguing from the other standpoint, has pointed out that there is a close relation between genius and insanity, and he sets down epilepsy as one of the forms of insanity (mental un-health) often associated with extraordinary mental qualities. A study of this subject is extremely reassuring to the epileptic who is prone to think from traditions with regard to the disease that his fate is almost sure to be a gradual lapse into imbecility. No epileptic is likely to be at all worried over the suggestion that epilepsy and genius are allied, for since he has the one he is quite willing that the other shall follow.

Treatment.—Reassurance is especially important when patients develop epilepsy in adult life. There is an unfortunate social stigma attached to the disease which adds to the unfavorable suggestions that are likely to run with it. This probably cannot be overcome, for it is a heritage, not alone of many {537} generations, but of many centuries. Our better knowledge of epilepsy, however, should gradually take the disease out of the sphere of suspected mystery in which it has been popularly placed and set it among the diseases to which human nature is liable, but which is surely as physical in its character as any other. If a favorable attitude of mind on the patient's part can be secured there is less necessity for many of the disturbing drugs that are used and there seems to be no doubt that even in producing the effect of these, such as it is, suggestion of a favorable character plays a large role. Over and over again in the history of the affection we have had remedies introduced which have seemed to be quite efficient in producing longer intervals between attacks, making the patient less nervous and putting him in better physical health. After a time, however, these have proved to be quite useless, or at most of but very slight value. It was suggestion that gave them their apparent value, and this suggestion must be used without the drugs whenever possible.

The bromides have done good in the treatment of epilepsy, but they are the only drugs that maintain the reputation they first had. All the others accomplished whatever benefit they conferred on the patient, and some of them for a time seemed to excellent authorities of large experience to give marvelous results, through their influence over the patient's mind. Nothing can produce more confidence in the physician who is using suggestion for epilepsy than this fact. Even the bromides, unless used carefully, easily do more harm than good and they have often worked mischief. Favorable suggestion cannot do harm. At the present time those of largest experience in the treatment of epileptics, the directors of farm colonies, as Dr. Shanahan of Craig Colony, insist that diet, hygiene, especially hydrotherapy, are of much more importance than drugs, but that the patient's attitude of mind towards himself and his malady and the future of it is even more important. He must have occupation of mind so as not to worry about himself. He must have recreation so as to relieve the gloom so likely to come in the disease. He must have outdoor air and proper exercise, which these patients are so prone to neglect.

Those who have studied the subject most in recent years agree that the great majority of cases of epilepsy are not primarily due to acquired causes, but to some congenital defect, so that there is an inherent instability of the nervous system. This makes the patient liable to explosions of nerve force, figuratively represented as boilings over of nervous energy, when not properly inhibited. Once such a paroxysm occurs it is likely to happen again, and very often it brings on gradual degeneration of the nervous system and of mentality. In many cases, however, this degeneration can be delayed or even completely kept off by putting the patient under favorable conditions. These patients need, above all, to realize that they cannot live the strenuous life nor even the ordinary busy life of most people. They are as cripples compelled to limit the sphere of their activities. If they will but take this to heart, however, and not attempt too busy occupations, they may live quite happy lives for many years, and if mentally content and without worrying anxieties they will have so few attacks as to incur only to a slight degree the dangers inevitably associated with fits of unconsciousness. To get the epileptic's mind into a condition of satisfaction with his condition must be the main portion of the treatment.

{538}

PSEUDO-EPILEPSY

There is a large and important field of psychotherapeutics in a class of cases so closely related to epilepsy that it is often extremely difficult to make the differential diagnosis between the two varieties of seizure. Fifteen years ago, while I was at the Salpêtrière, there was much discussion of a variety of attack called hystero-epilepsy, in which the patients' symptoms were such that it was difficult if not practically impossible to decide whether the case was true epilepsy or merely hysteria. Personally I do not think there is any third, intermediate variety deserving a separate term. The attacks are either hysterical, or, to use a less objectionable name, neurotic, or they are genuinely epileptic, that is, due to some as yet not well-defined change in the brain, and therefore not likely ever to be completely relieved. To decide whether a given case is neurotic or epileptic, however, is sometimes quite out of the question until long and careful study of it has been made. It is true that such signs as full loss of consciousness, biting of the tongue, the so-called epileptic cry, involuntary urination, dangerous falls and the like in the midst of an attack, have often been declared to be signs of true epilepsy, but there are cases in which one or other of these signs has been present, yet the subsequent course of the affection has shown them to be functional and not organic in origin.

Neurotic Simulation of Epilepsy.—Nearly every physician who has reasonably large experience with neurotic patients has seen cases in which there were recurrent attacks of loss of consciousness that came on sometimes at most inopportune moments, that rendered the patient quite incapable of caring for himself for the moment, yet lacked many of the signs of true epilepsy. Teachers sometimes complain of a complete lapse of memory that begins without warning and then recurs at intervals, making their work very difficult. Preachers sometimes bring the story of having lost the thread of their discourse and forgetting absolutely what they were talking about, there being a complete blank for some seconds at least. Occasionally such lapses are associated with falls that resemble fainting spells and seem to be accompanied by complete loss of consciousness. Usually after them there is a distinct tired feeling and an inclination to sleep, though, as a rule, there is a more marked tendency to want to get away from observation. Some of the cases are much more severe than those described and the conclusion that they are true epilepsy seems inevitable, yet they recover so completely that this conclusion is negatived.

Occasionally such attacks occur only when the patient has been strenuously exerting mind or body for a much longer period than usual. In teachers it is likely to occur toward the end of the year or in the midst of the hard work about examination time. In students this same period is likely to be a favorite starting point for the attacks and they recur oftener at this time than at others. Very often there is a story of some digestive disturbance in connection with the attacks. At times it seems possible to trace them to some interference with the cerebral circulation through a distended stomach pressing upward through the diaphragm and interfering with the heart action. In such cases stomach resonance will sometimes be found as high as the fifth rib {539} and the apex beat may be pushed out to the nipple line or beyond it. This may be true though there are no signs of valvular lesions and no symptoms or physical signs of dilatation or hypertrophy of the heart.

The Suggestive Element.—Analysis shows the real course of the trouble in these cases. The sufferer is usually following a sedentary occupation, not getting much exercise or diversion and prone to introspection. Many symptoms of themselves of no importance have been emphasized by concentration of attention on them. Especially is this true of any heart irregularity. The patient has dreaded for some time lest the feeling of pressure in the precordia and of discomfort in the heart might not sometime interfere with him in the midst of his teaching or preaching duties. Some day when he is feeling much worse than usual, in the midst of his work, there comes over him the feeling that now his intellect is going to stop action because there is something the matter with him. The sudden concentration of his attention on this with the fear of the consequences and the uncomfortable feeling that he will not be able to go on with his flow of ideas, cuts off the thread of what he is thinking about and puts but one single object before him—this possibility of failure of mental action. Usually the first attack is only such an interruption as is thus indicated. The fear of subsequent attacks, the worry over what has happened, the dread that some serious mental affection or nervous disease is at work emphasizes introspection and subsequent attacks are even more likely to be serious, and especially to last longer than the first.

The more the cases are studied the more the conclusion comes that in many of these instances it is nothing more than auto-suggestion that is responsible for the mental lapse. It is true that some physical condition may be the occasion, though the mental state is the active immediate cause. Suddenly concentrated attention on the dread of mental interruption inhibits mental action and what was dreaded follows almost necessarily. It is a sort of auto-hypnotism in which the patient's train of thought is interrupted by a momentary or longer hypnotic state the causes of which can be traced. Even when there is a real organic lesion of the heart, the lapses of memory and even of reasoning power that occasionally occur, have often seemed to me to be due rather to the patient's dread than to any real physical condition. I cannot think that there is a sufficient interruption of the cerebral circulation, even though only for a moment, to cause such a lapse. It is a question of nerve interferences rather than of blood supply. If the blood were diverted, even though only for a moment, or if there was a stoppage, the consequences would be more serious and more lasting than they are.

What evidently happens is some disturbance of neurotic connections within the brain brought on by sudden dread or emotion. The will has lost control or has seriously disturbed the conducting apparatus. The best proof that this is what happens and that it is not the result of organic change is found in the fact that when the physical occasion, that is, the digestive disturbance or the heart palpitation which is the initial factor in these states, is relieved, the attacks do not take place. Patients in whom they have occurred even for years cease to have them. This improvement does not begin, however, until their solicitude over their condition has been lessened by a confident declaration to them that they are suffering from merely functional and local reflex conditions apart from the brain itself. Usually it needs to be made clear {540} to them, too, that their anxiety in the matter means much more for the continuance of the attacks than any physical condition.

Almost invariably patients somewhat resent this suggestion. Their response to this explanation of their ailment usually is that the attacks come on them when they are not particularly expecting them and that there is first some physical symptom which might readily be taken for a sort of aura to a genuine epileptic attack and then the attack itself comes on. It is this preceding symptom, pain or discomfort, or whatever else it may be, that provokes the suggestive element and brings about the state of quasi-hypnosis, which is the main part of their attack.

Neurotic Syncopal Attacks.—Some of the cases of pseudo-epilepsy are very mild, though if the word epilepsy has been mentioned there naturally arises a feeling of dread in patient and friends with consequent unfavorable suggestion. A type not infrequently seen has for its main symptom a period, usually of but short duration, in which there is an intense tired feeling so that even the eyelids droop and require effort to lift them. During such attacks the respirations may slow down to fifteen or below, though usually the pulse is inclined to be rapid. The feeling of fatigue is almost entirely subjective, in the sense that, if patients are required to do something, they are able to accomplish it by a little urging, though a moment before they were sure that they could not. Such attacks are invariably functional, have no organic basis and do not deserve the name of epilepsy. If called hysterics this will cause the patient, who is often a woman, to rouse herself and so gradually overcome them. They are really a loss of confidence in one's power to do things and a passing astasia-abasia. The use of the word hysterics may cause the patient to lose the sympathy of her friends, though she may need it; for often there is an underlying pathological condition not in the nervous but in the somatic system. Sometimes the patients are anemic, sometimes they have an abortive form of Graves' disease, and sometimes they are low in nutrition.

These conditions give the indication for treatment. What is needed is, of course, improvement of the general condition, but, above all, a restoration of the patient's confidence in herself. Once it is made clear to her that the attacks are largely subjective, that is, are due to a feeling of prostration because of the fear that she is unable to do something, then the intervals between the attacks will gradually grow longer. It is important that long hours of sleep should be advised with plenty of fresh air, and that whatever disturbances of the digestive system are present should be carefully treated.

Pseudo-Epilepsy and the Menopause.—A number of these cases of pseudo-epilepsy occur at the menopause. They seem particularly likely to occur in women who have not much to occupy themselves with. Childless women who have no cares and enjoy every luxury sometimes seem to have these pseudo-epileptic attacks as equivalents for the flushings of the ordinary menopause. During "a rush of blood to the head" they lose control of themselves. Occasionally mothers who have two or three daughters and who get their menopause late in life, that is, well after fifty, are especially likely to suffer in the same way. The solicitude of those near them seems to eliminate some of their power of inhibition and makes them think overmuch of themselves. If then they keep much at home, as women at this time are prone to do, have few {541} diversions of mind, little fresh air and exercise, there is an accumulation of unused nervous energy which dissipates itself in explosive attacks very like epilepsy. It is with regard to these that the term hystero-epilepsy almost seems justified. Just as soon as occupation and diversion of mind and relaxation of the solicitude of friends for them is secured they begin to get better.

The differential diagnosis of these cases is made from the absence of certain of the pathognomic signs of true epilepsy. The tongue is not bitten, involuntary urination does not take place, and when the patient falls she does not hurt herself as a rule, though occasionally the fall may result in accidental abrasions or bruises, but these are quite trivial. If stress is laid upon the fact before these patients that they do not present any or all of the symptoms of epilepsy, some of them are likely to occur a little later. Slight abrasions on the tongue will be noted and the sputum will become a little bloody. Even very cleanly women will sometimes wet themselves. It is not a deliberate attempt at deception, but their curious psycho-neurotic condition causes suggestion to act upon them. Their attacks are really auto-hypnotic and during these the remarks made by the physician occur as suggestions and then are accomplished. If the suggestions in this matter have been carelessly made by previous physicians the attacks will so closely simulate true epilepsy that it will often be almost impossible to differentiate them with assurance.

In the preliminary diagnosis of these cases, as well as of all other cases of pseudo-epilepsy, we must, as far as possible, avoid the use of the word epilepsy, even of hystero-epilepsy. The unfavorable suggestion attached to such terms will have the worst possible effect. There is no need to fear that the patient will be any less taken care of, if the disease is called by some other name, for instance, neurotic paroxysms or nervous attacks.

Cure by Suggestion.—Such patients are often cured by remedial measures of one kind or another that are administered with the confident declaration that they will get well. A number of cases of epilepsy which were really of this character have been reported cured by Eddyism. A number also have been very favorably influenced by osteopathic treatment. Needless to say, the reports of such cured cases have not been diminished in significance by the publicity bureaus of these various cults. Mental healing has relieved a number more. Usually this relief has been afforded these cases after they had tried regular physicians who had treated them in the ordinary way with bromides, without doing anything more than causing them to miss a few attacks for a temporary period of relief, if even that, giving them bromism and further increasing their solicitude about themselves by unconsciously emphasizing their ideas as to how serious epilepsy can be. The cures of these cases are not due to the various treatments to which the patients proclaim their debt of gratitude, but to the confident assurance given them that their condition is not serious, and will be cured. After analysis of their attacks has shown them to be neurotic and not genuinely epileptic, the regular medical practitioner can readily do as much and even more; for psychotherapy has much more to do in affording relief in these cases than any other form of treatment. It must be applied with confidence and the results are often most favorable.

{542}

CHAPTER VI

PARALYSIS AGITANS

This is a chronic affection of the nervous system having for its most characteristic symptom a tremor, but with marked muscular rigidity and weakness. It is much more common in men than in women, in almost the reverse proportion of Graves' disease. It is usually a disease of the old, but may occur in early middle life and has been known to develop even early in the twenties. In the old days when malaria was a common diagnosis for many different conditions, paralysis agitans apparently followed malaria so often that there was thought to be some connection between the two diseases. The more we have learned of malaria the less likely this seems to be. Continuous exposure to cold for long periods and to dampness during the daily occupation for years, or repeated severe wettings, have been considered as causative elements. None of these physical factors, however, has been as directly connected with the occurrence of the affection as various emotional conditions, and the thought is suggested that even in cases of severe exposure the worry and fright and solicitude incident to the fear in an elderly person that this exposure will have serious consequences, is an important etiological element.

Psychic Factors.—*Fright.*—Practically all the authorities agree that mental conditions are prominent factors in the production of the disease. Serious business cares and worries and anxieties have often long preceded its development. Fright is mentioned by nearly all those who write on the subject as at least an occasion for the development of paralysis agitans if not a cause. One of my own most interesting cases occurred in the sheriff of a county of the Southwest who had earned for himself the deep enmity of an Indian by arresting him. Not long afterwards one Sunday morning when the sheriff quite unarmed came round a corner he found the Indian just in front of him wildly drunk and armed with a rifle. At once the rifle went to the Indian's shoulder, but he did not want to kill his man without having his revenge by torturing him, so he did not pull the trigger, but announced to him in vigorous though broken English that he had him now and was going to kill him. The sheriff tried to parley and for a moment the Indian permitted him to do so, apparently in order to prolong the agony. They were not more than two yards apart at the beginning, and the sheriff took his only chance and jumped and knocked the gun up. It went off just as he did so, the bullet singeing his hair. He succeeded in arresting the Indian and throwing him into jail, but the next day a tremor developed in the arm which had grasped the rifle. This spread and finally became typical of paralysis agitans. He was a man only slightly past fifty and there had been no preliminary symptoms.

Mental Control of Symptoms.—Many similar cases following fright or vehement emotion have been reported, so that it is easy to understand the feeling that the affection has a large psychic element in it, though evidently from its persistency and its continued

293

development, there is some underlying pathological condition. The tremor may be controlled in voluntary {543} movements, while emotion exaggerates it. There is no doubt, however, that concentration of will and the definite effort to control the symptoms enables the patient to rid himself of them to a great degree for a time at least. It has been noted frequently that when a consultant physician is called the patient will be better for the day of the consultation than he had been for months before. The visits of particular friends will often arouse a sufferer to such efforts as greatly lessen his rigidity, decrease his tremor and make him capable of getting around better than before. The state of mental depression that commonly develops in these cases exaggerates the symptoms, adds neurotic and even physical conditions that develop from lack of exercise and air, and makes the patient's general state much worse than it would otherwise be.

Pathology.—Our scanty but growing knowledge of the pathology of paralysis agitans makes it clear that the disease is, in typical cases, probably due to an overgrowth of connective tissue, the neuroglia cells, in the central nervous system. Just what causes this overgrowth of connective tissue is not clear. It is an exaggeration of a normal senile process. Apparently one of the processes of age in man is a decadence of the vitality of important higher tissues with a corresponding increase of vitality in the lower or connective tissues. When Flourens declared at a meeting of the French Academy of Sciences that such an overgrowth of connective tissue was natural with advancing years, he added that this probably accounted for the slowness with which older men come to conclusions. The old members of the Academy did not accept this new-fangled doctrine with equanimity. They were inclined to think that their conservatism and deliberateness were due to greater poise of intellect.

There seems to be no doubt that at least a comparative overgrowth of connective tissue is characteristic of the brain in advancing years. In some people this occurs to a greater extent and is more precocious than in others. Just what causes are responsible for individual differences we do not know. Paralysis agitans is seen often in those who have worked hard most of their lives, but, on the other hand, may occur in those who have lived sedentary lives, and in people of all occupations. Over-indulgence in alcohol, though this is often thought to predispose to the disappearance of the parenchyma of organs and to the overgrowth of connective tissue, does not seem to have any place in the etiology of this affection. Its occurrence is a part of that mystery by which the equilibrium of different kinds of cells in the body is maintained or diminished. In a mild way paralysis agitans represents such a change in the central nervous system.

Mental Influences.—With an overgrowth of connective tissue as the pathology of the disease there would seem to be no question of any relief of its symptoms or any benefit to be derived from psychotherapy. Anyone who has much to do with cases of paralysis agitans, however, knows that they are extremely susceptible to mental influences. Whenever there is anything that interests them, any business that they feel they must do, any special event that they look forward to, they will for days at a time be so much improved in general symptoms as to be greatly encouraged themselves and make their friends feel hopeful with regard to them. When they give in to their condition, however, and make no special effort at self-control and stimulation their symptoms increase very much. Their rigidity particularly increases, their {544} tremor becomes more marked and various inconveniences associated with these two cardinal symptoms are emphasized.

Methods of Treatment.—*The Vibrating Chair.*—It is interesting to recall some of the forms of treatment which have been reported as beneficial in paralysis agitans, because they illustrate how much the influence of the patient's mind has over his bodily condition and how much the interest aroused in any new and particularly in any unusual form of treatment has in mitigating symptoms and how often it seems to bring about remissions in the progress of the disease. Twenty years ago Charcot suggested the use of a mechanically vibrating arm-chair. He had noticed that patients who travelled by rail seemed to have their symptoms improved for the time at least by the shaking up in the train. This treatment undoubtedly made patients much less rigid and much less tremulous. The improvement lasted sometimes for hours and sometimes for days. It was tried rather extensively and everywhere with reported good results, when first tried at least. After a time it was found that it failed to have the desired effect. Apparently whatever therapeutic value it had was due to the interest aroused in the patient's mind and the consequent effort that was made to control his muscles.

The Suspension Treatment.—When the method of treatment by suspension became popular for cases of locomotor ataxia, the idea came to try the same thing for paralysis agitans. Accordingly suspension apparatuses of many kinds were used with reported good results. Patients were suspended by the neck for some minutes and some of them got used to the treatment and could stand it for a prolonged period. The effect was always a distinct mitigation of symptoms. The rigidity particularly became much less marked, but the tremor also was lessened and besides certain secondary symptoms were bettered. Constipation was improved, partly because patients were more cheerful, ate more heartily and, above all, were willing to make some effort in order to get out regularly into the air. There was a variety in life, different from the solitary sitting at home into which these patients so often drift. Sleep was better at night and the subjective sensations of heat and cold were lessened. Patients were encouraged to think of improvement and used all their available nervous energy. In the same way when overstretching of the spinal cord by forcibly bending of the body at the hips was tried with reported success in tabes it was also applied to paralysis agitans with similar improvement of symptoms. Both methods of treatment have gone out for both these affections and evidently their observed therapeutic efficiency at first was entirely due to their effect upon the mind.

Psychic Elements and Other Remedies.—When organo-therapeutics became the fad paralysis agitans was treated also by this method. Some cases were treated with reported good results by thyroid. Later when the parathyroids attracted attention they were administered with reported good success in even very severe cases. I think that there is a report of some cases of paralysis agitans being improved by injections of diphtheria serum. In other words, anything that was given to a patient with the promise that he would be better after it and that produced a definite effect upon his mind was likely to do him temporary good. If the remedy had some special theory behind it, if there was a story of some new scientific significance for the material employed or the method of giving it, then this improvement was sure to take

294

place. {545} In the drug treatment of the disease the same principles applied. Earlier, when nitrate of silver was the main recourse for organic nervous diseases, cases were reported improved by its administration. When the alterative properties of arsenic became a therapeutic fad this produced good effects. Atropin had for some time a reputation of relieving patient's symptoms. After a time all of them ceased to be used to any extent.

The Frenkel Method.—In recent years the application of the Frenkel directed movement method, modified somewhat from its application in tabes, has attracted attention in the therapeutics of paralysis agitans. It is interesting to note how often a mode of treatment that has been applied successfully to one of these diseases has also proved successful with the other. The two diseases are, of course, very different in etiology and pathology; but have one thing in common. The control over muscles has been lost to some degree in both cases in the progress of the disease, and a special effort of attention is required on the part of the patient in order to regulate movement. Anything that will arouse the patient to make this special effort will relieve the symptoms for a while and in tabes may bring about a lasting improvement, because the habit becomes easier after a time, though apparently this does not occur in paralysis agitans, except perhaps in the younger patients. It might very well be expected, then, that Frenkel's method in many cases would do good in paralysis agitans and it has proved to be another adjunct in the treatment of the affection. It must be used with great care not to exhaust the patient, but this is true also in tabes. The real source of its therapeutic quality seems to be the patient's interest in it and if this cannot be aroused it usually fails to do good. The success of these various mechanical methods makes it easy to understand why these patients often improve for a time under osteopathic treatment.

Psychotherapy.—It is clear, then, that the most important aid for these cases is the arousing of mental interest in some form of treatment that promises to be of benefit to them. New forms of treatment cannot always be invented and mental occupation must be secured by interest in other things. Patients suffering from paralysis agitans are prone to allow themselves to give up efforts to do things in which their interest would be aroused. They must be encouraged to do many things. Carriage riding, automobiling, train excursions, because of the effort required to resist vibration, are all helpful. They must not be allowed to drift into vacuous habits in which they make no effort for themselves. They can thus be made much more comfortable and most of their symptoms can be relieved to a marked degree. This requires constant attention and ever-renewed efforts to arouse the patient's mind and to have him make such efforts as will overcome rigidity and control the tremor to some extent; but with care an amelioration of the condition can always be brought about and can be maintained, at least to the extent of making the patient much more comfortable than would otherwise be the case.

{546}

CHAPTER VII

HEADACHE

In spite of the improvement in the general health of the community, due to more hygienic living, more healthy food and better ventilation, headache, instead of decreasing, has increased to a great degree. Any number of headache cures are advertised in the daily papers, in the street cars, on the signboards, even in medical journals, and besides these nearly every druggist has his own special preparation for headache, so it would seem as though literally many millions of doses of these headache cures must be taken every week. It would seem as though there must be some special unhygienic factor at work to produce headaches at a time when all other pathological conditions are being reduced in number and severity.

A study of the patients who are especially affected by headache seems to furnish evidence as to the special factor that has led to the increase of the affection. It occurs much more frequently in women than in men. It is complained of particularly by those who have less regular occupation, and the notable increase has come with the opportunity for leisure on the part of large numbers of the community due to the growth of wealth.

A feeling of discomfort in the head to which much attention is paid will become such a painful condition as to deserve the name of ache, if it develops in those who have no serious occupation in life and no interests that demand peremptory attention. With the noise of many children around them in the olden times women suffered comparatively little from headaches. Most of our grandmothers scarcely knew what it was to have a headache. Now most business men are likely to say the same thing. Very rarely do they suffer from headache. When they do, there is some specific reason and when this is removed the headache disappears. There are many women of leisure who have regular headaches for which they must have some remedy at hand or the pain becomes intolerable, but there are few women strenuously occupied with business affairs or with interests in which their attention is absorbed who find themselves under any such necessity.

It is evident that certain conditions predispose to headache. The principal of these is having sufficient time to advert to certain uncomfortable feelings in or around the head. Few people who stop to think of what their head feelings are but will find there is some unusual sensation somewhere in or outside the head which if dwelt upon becomes emphasized into an ache. If the mind can be diverted it disappears. If there has been some injury of the head or some pathological conditions set up by congestion or anemia, the feelings may become emphasized and occupy the center of attention, and even after the injury has disappeared or the pathological condition been ameliorated some sensations remain which with advertence produce achy feelings of discomfort. This is the history of a great deal of the increase of headache in our time. There are, of course, real headaches due to definite pathological conditions, but the great majority of

295

headaches complained of {547} are the result of over-attention to certain sensations, some of them normal, some of them only slightly abnormal, which are emphasized by concentration of attention on them until they become a torment.

Two main classes of headaches come to the physician for treatment. One class is seen in patients who suffer from real and even acute pain that cannot be distracted by diversion of mind, that is usually worse when they try to sleep, as toothache is, and is evidently due to definite physical disturbance. In the second class are the many queer feelings about the head called headaches, though the patient suffers rather from annoyance than from pain. It is said that the Chinese in olden times put criminals to a lingering death by fastening them in such a way that a drop of water fell every minute on their heads. It was impossible to avoid the falling drop, and its constant recurrence became an awful torture. Any feeling that engrosses consciousness will be followed by the same sense of torment. The constant exercise of function of any nerve without rest is of itself physically disturbing to a serious degree. This must be realized with regard to many forms of headache which, though trivial in origin, are the source of bitter complaint.

Attention Headaches.—Professor Oppenheim, in his "Letters to Nervous Patients," has a paragraph with regard to headache that is worth recalling for the benefit of patients who suffer from low-grade headaches. Doubtless these were at the beginning real aches due to some local condition. They are now due merely to exaggeration of more or less normal feelings within the head which have come into the realm of the conscious because of the attention attracted to them when the intracranial affection was first noted. Professor Oppenheim says:

Your headache also I ascribe to this source. Originally it may have been a real headache, the result of your nervous shock. There is no one who has not at some time had a transient feeling of pain in the head or in some other part of the body, quite apart from those caused by injuries or painful diseases. Out of a thousand various kinds of causes I will mention only an extremely common one: the pains which result from straining muscles or nerves. Every sudden awkward movement may in this way cause pain in different parts of the body, but very specially so in nervous persons, in whom the mechanical excitability of the nerves—that is, their sensitiveness to pressure and strain—is usually exaggerated. As a rule, however, this pain is quite transient. But here again the law of which I have been already speaking comes into force: under the stimulating influence of introspection the tiny, perishable seed-grain of pain grows into the firm, strong, enduring tree of neuralgia or psychalgia.

The first condition for the successful treatment of headache, then, must include the recognition of the possibility of some rather simple pathological condition being exaggerated by over-attention to a disturbing affection, or of some affection, now past, having produced a suggestion that, in a mind given to introspection, continues to have influence even to the inveteration of sensations for which there is no longer a physical cause.

These patients insist that their medical status is that of real pain. Hysterical patients describe a sensation as if a nail were being driven into the forehead—the so-called clavus hystericus. In nervous people the sense of pressure increases from one of mere discomfort to a positive pain, as a consequence of attention to it. In most cases of headache, however, what is most needed is a distraction of the attention from the ailment. Over and over {548} again I have found that when all remedies failed the deliberate search for an occupation of mind that would interest the patient during many hours of the day was the only thing that promised relief and in many cases the relief afforded was so complete that patients were effusive in their gratitude.

Power of Distraction.—The proof that these so-called headaches are really not aches is found in the comparative ease with which many of them may be suppressed. Almost any interesting occupation will make the sufferer forget them entirely and they will not return immediately after the occupation ceases, but usually only when the patient is alone and attention is once more directed to this symptom. These queer feelings about the head that are often raised to the dignity of headaches by attention and auto-suggestion may be distracted away completely. That they are not pain is shown by the fact that the ordinary remedies which ease pain so promptly often fail to relieve these or soon cease to have any effect on them.

Lack of Distractions.—The apartment hotel system has multiplied the victims of headaches. When a woman has nothing in the world to do except get her clothes fitted and attend to what she calls her "social duties," it is no wonder that her head bothers her. Blood is constantly going to the brain and interchange of nutritive elements is taking place, yet there is no real function of cells and no consumption of material, or at least function is so slight that consumption of material must be trivial. There is no reason why these women should get up in the morning. Their breakfast is brought to their rooms, and some of them do not get around until eleven o'clock. Women used to have a morning occupation in going out to market or else in planning the household day with housekeepers, but of course there is no more of that. In olden times, too, many of them had religious practices. Now women are likely to be unemployed until the afternoon, which must be occupied at most with so-called social duties that may be done if one wishes to do them, but that may be put off for many reasons and there are constantly recurring reasons for not making any special exertion. Also, the rooms these women live in must be kept at a high temperature because the poorer the air that we breathe the higher must be its temperature for comfort, while stimulating fresh air may be quite low in temperature and yet produce only a brisk reaction instead of chilly feelings.

Children used to be the best possible remedy for these non-occupation headaches, but either there are no children any more or there are but one or two and these are largely cared for by *bonnes* at home and by various schools once they have reached the age of three. The old idea that children should not leave home until six put upon the mother the burden of their early education, but since the coming of the kindergarten she is relieved of responsibility of this and the mother of one or two children might now almost as well be childless as far as any serious occupation from care of her children is concerned.

If patients are told all this bluntly there will be a vigorous protest from most of them, for to them their pains are very real. It must not be forgotten that a pain in the mind is often worse than in the body. Some of these women save themselves from having their unused mental faculties disturb them from very lack of something to do, by becoming interested in charities, in clubs, in social movements of various kinds, in art and in literature. It is {549} not to these that I refer. On the contrary, if women have nothing else to do I would insist that they

296

find some cause or movement in which they may become deeply interested. Their interest will save them from self-annoyance, though it may not exactly add to the gayety of nations in its effect upon other people. As a physician, however, I am only interested for the moment in the good of particular patients.

Source of Pain.—I would not be understood as saying that all headaches are not real aches nor pains in the most literal sense of the word, for some of them are agonizing tortures. With regard to all headaches, however, even the most genuine variety, there are certain considerations that are of value from the standpoint of psychotherapeutics. The most important of these is assurance as to the source or location of the pain. Most people think that it is the brain itself that is suffering pain and not a little of their suffering is due to the fact that they dread the effect of such pain upon the cerebral tissues and its possible consequences upon their mental state. These people will be much relieved to be told at once that the brain tissue itself is not sensitive, that when exposed it may be touched with impunity without causing any pain. It is the structures surrounding the brain that are sensitive. As a rule the lesion that causes pain is not progressive and all dreads with regard to serious after effects may be put aside.

Pressure Headaches.—It is important to insist on the fact that, as a rule, headaches and pains in the head are not due to the brain, but to extraneous structures within the skull. It is true that brain tumors, gliomatous and cystic and, above all, the overgrowth of the pituitary body in acromegaly give rise to agonizing pains. The cause of these headaches is undoubtedly pressure. It is not the pressure upon the brain tissue itself, however, that is the underlying cause of the pain, but pressure upon the sensitive structures connected with the brain. The same thing is true with regard to congestive headaches. Pain is produced not because vascular congestion presses on sensitive brain tissues, for we have no reason to think that any such exist, but because the congested brain exerts pressure upon sensitive filaments in its integuments. Neuralgia may be unbearable and yet it is borne with more equanimity, and less dread of results, because it is felt to be in a comparatively unimportant structure. One of the most serious elements in severe headache is the fear of lasting results in the brain tissues, that may lead to disturbance of mentality or to injury affecting mental processes. Patients find their pain much more bearable as soon as they are assured that headaches do not lead to mental disturbances and that, as a rule, even the growth of a tumor does not disturb mentality.

In the relation of the brain to the intellectual faculties that are so closely associated with it, we must remember that direct connection between the two has not been demonstrated and that the relations of the brain and the mind are almost as mysterious as they ever were. There are some who still think that the frontal convolutions are especially concerned in carrying out mental operations. All that we know about them in pathology, however, is that they are the silent convolutions. When a lesion occurs in other portions of the brain we see the effect of it practically always without delay, in some way, either in the sensory or motor functions of the body. Large lesions in the frontal region, however, often give no sign. Large tumors have been found {550} pushing frontal convolutions from their ordinary positions without any noticeable effect upon the individual.

Hard Study and Headache.—It is worth while to impart this knowledge to patients who suffer from headaches, because it at once improves their outlook on life. I have known hard students—men who had spent twenty or thirty years in work at a special subject—live in constant dread that sometime their minds would give way because they frequently suffered from headaches, or at least from some uncomfortable sensations in their heads, which they feared as a portent of ultimate mental breakdown. The assurance that such a thing is utterly unlikely and quite apart from the physician's ordinary experience, not only relieved their anxiety and made their headaches more bearable, but in a dozen of cases in my note-books the headache has gradually disappeared as certain habits of life were corrected and modified, as their habits of eating were varied, as bodily functions were controlled and as diversions of mind were introduced into lives that had before been too unvaried for healthy functions.

I do not think that I have ever seen a case, and I have been closely in touch with hard students for over twenty years, where I felt that the cause of a headache was mental overwork. I have known men who at the age of seventy or over have taken but four or five hours of sleep and who have worked at their favorite subjects for the better part of half a century. They never complained of headaches. Of course, there are others whose physical and mental power is less and who cannot be expected to stand a strain that for large-minded men is only the normal exercise of function. It has not been the mental work that they were doing, however, that was the source of whatever central nervous disturbance was to be found in lesser minds, but worry and anxiety and dread over what they were doing, anxiety as to what they were going to do that constituted the real pathological agents at work.

Local Conditions.—A striking case that impresses patients much more than the physician's declaration and is more likely to be remembered and is therefore of psychotherapeutic value, is that of Von Bülow, the German musician. He suffered for many years from excruciating headaches. They were so severe as almost to drive him crazy. His only relief was morphine and he and his friends lived in the midst of no little dread that sometime or other either the pain or the process which caused it would bring about a deterioration of mentality. After his death an autopsy was made. It was found to be a small nerve fiber pinched by a scar in the dura as a consequence of an injury received when Von Bülow was very young. Many other stories of this kind have been told.

It must not be forgotten that in many cases the pain is not within the skull itself or at least its cause is not and other sources should be carefully looked for. The connection of the eyes with headache has been so well worked out, owing to the initiative of S. Weir Mitchell, that nothing more need be said of it. One feature perhaps deserves to be mentioned. While strain of accommodation is a frequent source of headache and is at once looked for by ophthalmologists, there seems no doubt that some headaches, much fewer than accommodation cephalalgias, are due to muscle difficulties, that is, a lack of balance among the external muscles of the eye, whose full pathological significance has perhaps not yet been worked out. Headaches are {551} frequently due to sinus troubles, especially to disturbances in the frontal sinus and to intranasal difficulties. These must be eliminated before the patient can be helped. Sometimes these nasal and sinus

297

difficulties are signs of a deeper constitutional disturbance, due to lack of fresh air and exercise and are relieved promptly by the establishment of hygienic habits.

Congestion Headaches.—Some headaches require changes of habit and persuasion of the necessity for arranging the day's work so as to give proper intervals for relaxation. Much experience with persons whose absorption in their work causes them to miss a meal or delay taking it for seven or eight hours from the last time of eating has shown me that this disturbance of the routine of vegetative life is particularly likely to be followed by headache. This headache is not a mere dull ache and is much more than a sense of discomfort; it is often an excruciatingly painful condition that usually does not come on until toward the end of the day and then may seriously disturb sleep. An interesting thing about this class of headaches is that nearly always they are increased by lying down. Often only a faint preliminary symptom of it is apparent when the patients go to bed, though they may be wakened after two or three hours of disturbed slumber by a headache that prevents further sleep, and pass the remainder of the night in painful wakefulness.

Usually it becomes impossible to continue lying down. The head must be raised and much relief is afforded by sitting up. The headache does not disappear at once but it will gradually pass away and sleep may be resumed after a half an hour of sitting up, though the sleeper will have to be in a sitting posture. Older people get up and sit in an arm-chair. I have found that placing a chair with a rather long back beneath the mattress, the mattress slanting along the chair back at an angle of about forty-five degrees and then an arrangement of three or four pillows above that, will enable these patients to get to sleep better than anything else. The ordinary remedies for headache afford some relief, but even very large doses of the coal-tar products will not relieve the pain entirely unless some arrangement is made for keeping the head quite high and immovable.

The headache is evidently due to congestion. The reason for it is perhaps the failure of the blood to be recalled from the brain to do its usual physiological work at the digestive tract, with a consequent distention of arterioles in the brain so that a little later they do not react to prevent congestion. Usually with the headache there is some digestive disturbance, a feeling of unrest, flatulency with perhaps acid eructations. Accordingly the headache is often attributed to digestive disturbance. But both would rather seem to be effects of the same cause—the failure to supply the digestive apparatus with the proper amount of material to work on at the time when it expects it, while the mental absorption naturally attracts blood to the head. We know from delicate experiments made in physiological laboratories that at times of mental work there is an appreciably larger amount of blood in the head. A proof of the connection between the lack of a meal and the headache seems to be the fact that with most people even a glass of milk and a cracker, taken at the time when the meal is normally eaten, is sufficient to prevent the otherwise inevitable headache.

Whenever some such simple explanation as this for a headache is found and the patient made to realize its truth on his own observation, the {552} significance of the headache at once dwindles and it becomes much easier to bear it. Before the very real pains of it were emphasized by the dread of the consequences that would result from it. If it was really a brain ache patients would find it hard to understand how under its influence even serious changes might not take place in the brain. This is only a rational suggestion, but it is mental healing of the best kind.

Many of the aches which are spoken of as headaches are really forms of tenderness associated with the integuments of the skull. Certain of the muscles particularly are likely to suffer from achy feelings which are spoken of as headaches. This is true of certain feelings of discomfort in the frontal region and also of those that occur on the occipital region. External applications of many kinds relieve headaches in these regions, particularly in the frontal region. It is easy to understand that such applications do not affect the contents of the skull.

Some Occipital Aches.—Occasionally I have found that people who complained of a sense of weight at the back of the head, with some muscular tenderness, were sleeping on pillows that were too high. They were over-exerting these muscles and this gave a sense of fatigue, which when much attention was paid to it, became such an ache or at least discomfort as is often found in the occupation neuroses. I have seen schemata according to which headache complained of at the top of the head meant digestive disturbance, headache in the anterior portion of the head was referred to the eyes or the brain, and headache at the back of the head spinal exhaustion or severe neurasthenia, but these are at most very uncertain and I do not think that the tabulation of cases justifies any such diagram of absolute causes and effect. Usually there is some local condition that calls particular attention to a special part of the head and then the attention being concentrated complaint is made of that part.

Local Head Discomfort.—Usually a headache, accompanied by a localized sense of pressure or weight or constriction, occurs in highly neurotic people or those inclined to think much of themselves and whose attention becomes concentrated on some part. At all times we have sensations streaming up to our consciousness from every portion of the body and anyone who wants to think about them, or a particular set of them, can make them sources of considerable discomfort by concentration of attention. Sometimes there are special conditions that predispose to these localized sensory disturbances. I have known tight hats to produce such effects. It is sometimes surprising how tightly hats are worn. Nervous people are prone to overdo everything, and they overdo the pulling down of their hats. At times the wearing of a heavy hat will be the root of the trouble. I have known nervous men accustomed to wearing high hats all their lives who began to complain of headache when they were in the midst of busy worries and troubles of late life, find considerable relief by abandoning their high hats.

Toxic Headaches.—There are headaches that are due to the taking of stimulants, as is well known from common experience. The mistake is often made, however, of thinking that only alcoholic stimulation will cause a severe headache. Tea and coffee headaches may be quite as severe. Whenever people complain much of headache it is important to revise their dietary as to the consumption of tea and coffee. Of course, the headaches following {553} alcoholic stimulation are usually recognized as such, though occasionally a man accustomed to taking much alcohol without any such after effects is surprised in the midst of the worry incident to business stresses to find that he is having headaches. These are due to the combination of stimulants and congestion consequent upon an excess of alcohol with the increased brain work that is demanded, or even with the same amount of brain work from a tired brain. Gradually stopping the alcohol will do more to relieve these headaches than anything else. To advise the sudden stoppage of regular quantities of spirits that have been taken for some time, will sometimes produce an anemic headache and defeat the purpose of the advice.

When for some other reason tea or coffee or alcoholic stimulants are suddenly omitted after they have been taken to excess for some time, patients' complain of a headache. Some of this is probably imaginary, or at least is due to the idea that their craving for the stimulant, whatever it may be, must have a local manifestation, and the head sensation is exaggerated as a consequence. Tea and coffee cravings may here give more trouble than the longing for alcohol. Sometimes there may be a real disturbance of the circulation from the lack of the heart stimulant to which the system is accustomed and therefore an uncomfortable feeling in the head from brain anemia. This can be overcome by not cutting off the stimulant, whatever it may be, all at once, but by bringing about its gradual cessation. These patients, however, are very prone, even with the best of good will in the matter, to deceive themselves and find an excuse for not having their favorite tipple, be it tea or coffee or alcohol, taken from them, so that they readily create symptoms by auto-suggestion.

Direct Mental Treatment.—For both congestive and anemic headaches mental treatment is important. For those suffering from the congestive kind the physicians's business is not so much the cure of any one attack of headache (for this can be accomplished by various now rather familiar anodyne drugs as a rule), but the discovery and removal of the cause for the recurring attacks. These will be found in some habit of the patient which must be corrected. Drugs are seldom needed for the underlying condition which occasions the headache, for when it is due to such organic affections as brain tumors or other intracranial lesions, drugs can accomplish very little. In less serious conditions benefit may be obtained by having the patient change his attitude towards certain important details of his life, such as eating, sleeping, attention to business or to study and the like, so as to prevent the mistakes of daily habit that predispose to headache.

With regard to anemic headaches, especially those which occur in persons who are very much run down in weight, the most important element of treatment is to bring about an increase in weight. This can be accomplished much better through the mind than in any other way. Appetite is a function of the will, and patients should have an increase of diet dictated to them and then be persuaded to follow that. I have seen many a headache disappear among teachers, and religious workers particularly simply as the result of this measure.

As regards headaches for which no definite cause can be found mental treatment is the only efficient remedy. Practically nothing but a change of mental attitude towards the affection and its underlying causes, whether these {554} be neurotic or psychic, will bring about relief, and each patient is a problem quite distinct from any other.

There is no pretense that this use of mental healing for headache is new or even modern. Many stories show that in olden times headaches were often relieved by this means, and that suggestion was looked upon as an important element in the treatment for their relief. In the chapter on Great Physicians in Psychotherapy the quotation from Plato with regard to Socrates curing the headache of his young friend Charmides illustrates this very well.

In the old stories of Greek medicine there are a number of references to headaches cured by suggestion or at least by mental influence. Miss Hamilton, in her book on "Incubation," tells the story of Agestratos and his headaches and how they were cured at Epidaurus. Agestratos had a combination of headache and insomnia, the description of the ailments having a strangely modern air. Just as soon as he came to the Temple at Epidaurus he fell asleep and had a dream. The God of Medicine, AEsculapius, whose cult was practiced assiduously at Epidaurus, came to him in his sleep and promised him the cure of his headache and at the same time taught him wrestling and advised its practice. When day came he departed cured, and continued to practice wrestling. Not long after he competed at the Nemean Games and was victor in the racing. The suggestion that his headache would get better had come to him and at the same time he had been given a suggestion that provided him with occupation of mind and body. Many of the people who suffer from persistent headaches need this advice more than anything else. Probably every physician has had the experience of headaches being cured by some interesting exercise, especially if taken in the open air. The important factor is the change of mental attitude, though changes in exercise, diet, amount of sleep and the like are helpful auxiliaries.

{555}

SECTION XVI

NEUROSES

CHAPTER I

NERVOUS WEAKNESS (NEURASTHENIA)

Neurasthenia, from the Greek roots, *neur*, meaning nerve, and *sthenos*, strength, joined by the negative particle *a*, turning strength into weakness, means nothing more than nervous weakness. To tell a patient that he or she is nervously weak, or is suffering from nervous weakness is usually not satisfactory, but it may be absolutely true and may represent the limit of our knowledge with regard to the particular case. To tell them that they are sufferers from neurasthenia is satisfying as a rule, because then they have a nice, long, and imposing word with which to talk to their friends about their ailment. To discuss with friends one's own nervous weakness is just a little absurd; to talk over neurasthenia and its symptoms, however, adds importance to those symptoms and makes them seem manifestations of some interesting underlying condition.

The discussion of symptoms always does harm, but the internal complacency with its constant auto-suggestion of the underlying nervous disease is still more harmful. Neurasthenia seems to most people to signify a new and serious disease of the nervous system which has developed as the result of our high-pressure civilization and the modern strenuous life, and, therefore, has a special interest and an exaggerated importance. All of this makes for an unfavorable attitude of mind towards the affection and encourages the intensification of symptoms by attention to them. The opposite state of mind in which symptoms would be given their proper value by the term nervous weakness would act as a constant source of favorable suggestion. I believe that if the word neurasthenia must be used, it should be translated for the patient and the absolutely functional character of the affection insisted on in order to neutralize its suggestive influence.

Probably the most serious objection to the use of the word neurasthenia comes from the number of organic affections having vague nervous symptoms, including especially tiredness, a certain incapacity to do what was readily done before with tired feelings and a general feeling of unfitness, that have come to be grouped under this head. In this it resembles the word rheumatism rather strikingly. The diagnostic general principles seem to be: tired feelings equal neurasthenia; achy feelings (especially if worse on rainy days) equal rheumatism. So whenever either word is used, patients are apt to think of cases they have known which were labeled by one of these two terms, {556} rheumatism or neurasthenia and ended by developing some serious condition. The unfavorable suggestion consequent upon this has made many patients miserable and has prevented them from using their nervous energy to relieve their condition.

The use of the word neurasthenia has another decided disadvantage in that the facile recourse to it often keeps the physician from examining his patient sufficiently to detect an underlying pathological condition. The term can be made to cover so much that it has done great harm in this way. I feel, therefore, that in the discussion of what can be done for patients suffering from nervous weakness we should first of all describe and set aside a number of forms of disease that have sometimes masqueraded as "neurasthenia" and that have given the affection stronger unfavorable suggestiveness. Sir William Gowers, whom no one would suspect of either minimizing the significance of the word or of the affections that have come to be grouped under it, nor of wishing to attract attention by differing from others, has in one of his recent smaller medical works emphasized both of these unfortunate connotations of the word. Because his expressions as applied to other medical terms that are too general in their significance, will help physicians to get at the real meaning of them I venture to quote his opinion at some length:

The history of the word "neurasthenia" is noteworthy. ... I have to confess to the authorship of two words. One, "myotatic," was always a puny infant, and I doubt whether it still maintains an independent existence. The other, "knee-jerk," instantly attained universal use, and indeed, I think has seemed to most persons to have sprung spontaneously from the thing itself, without suggestion—perhaps the greatest compliment a word can pay its author. But the general use at once achieved by "neurasthenia" was in spite of a strong objection to it which was felt by many. The Royal College of Physicians of London could not include it in their "Nomenclature of Disease," and yet it is now one of the most common of medical words in every language. It would be instructive in more than one way to have a careful study of the forces which have influenced its career, but that I cannot attempt. We must, I think, admit that not only is it a satisfying word to those who suffer, but it has a certain convenience which has also compelled many to employ it who at first objected. If I may be pardoned for a partial paradox, its convenience is not the less real because this rests on features that are illusory. Remember that the word is a name which should have little meaning, even to those who use it. You may employ it to collect the symptoms of the case under a general designation, but do not let it cover them as a cloak.

Neurasthenia and Melancholia.—A serious mistake of diagnosis, though it is often not a mistake of knowledge but of medical judgment, is the confusion, apparent or real, of neurasthenia with melancholia. The word melancholia has come to have a definite serious significance, as it should, in the minds of many persons and as a consequence physicians sometimes hesitate to use it, and employ instead the all-embracing term neurasthenia, or neurasthenic depression. It is popularly well known that melancholies are likely to commit suicide if their condition is serious, while neurasthenia is not at all connected with the idea of suicide. As a consequence, patients are often not guarded as they otherwise would be and so we have suicides every {557} month of so-called neurasthenics who were really sufferers from melancholia. This sad state of affairs reflects in two ways to the detriment of medicine. First, it leaves melancholies without due protection. Second, it leads many of the neurotic patients whose ailments have been labeled neurasthenia and who read the stories of these supposed neurasthenics, to think that they, too, are tending toward suicide and so they are less capable of reacting against their neurotic condition and in general are much worse for the unfortunate dread of some such fatal termination.

Neurasthenia Simulation by Organic Disease.—Neurasthenia is especially a dangerous term since, like other words of this kind with wide connotation, many quite disconnected diseases may in early stages simulate it and give rise to the thought that there is only a functional nervous disease present, when the symptoms are really a manifestation of an underlying organic disease, heightened somewhat by a nervous organization or by worry on the patient's part. So-called neurasthenia in the old must always be looked upon with suspicion. Neurasthenia in the young may be a purely functional nervous disease, though it is probable that in most cases the nervous system is congenitally defective, or at least is unable to perform the functions which have been assumed by the patient. If a nervous organization has stood the strain of the trials of early and middle life, which are usually severe enough to try out individuals from the physical side, if they are in moderate circumstances, or from the mental side if they are wealthy, it will not, as a rule, be overborne by the burdens put upon it by age unless some organic disease has come to seriously disturb it.

Neurasthenia and Arteriosclerosis.—There are many serious conditions that masquerade as neurasthenia. Perhaps the most important is precocious arteriosclerosis. That a man is as old as his arteries is now recognized as an absolutely sure maxim of internal medicine. In many people the arteries wear out before their time and in all there is an inevitable wearing out in the course of years. With the beginning of degeneration of the arteries there are likely to be many symptoms that closely resemble neurasthenia. In the elderly these are nearly always symptoms of defective circulation because of lack of elasticity in the arteries and their failure to accommodate themselves to the variations of pressure in the circulation as the consequence of changes of position, variations in the barometer, heat and cold, and the like.

In these cases a study of the blood pressure will give the differential diagnosis when the actual thickening of the arteries cannot be felt, but it must not be forgotten that nervous excitement may greatly heighten blood pressure on occasions so that a number of observations have to be made.

Neurasthenia and Bright' s Disease.—Other general diseases almost inevitably produce nervous symptoms. It is curious how often a severe exacerbation of Bright's disease, which has been in existence for some time but has given no specific indication, is preceded by a series of neurotic symptoms thought to be due to nothing more than neurasthenia. Men of thirty-five to forty-five, the favorite time for the occurrence of the severe forms of Bright's disease, begin to complain of tiredness, especially on waking in the morning, of inordinate fatigue in the evening, of some stomach symptoms and occasionally a tendency to diarrhea. All of these are ascribed to a neurasthenic condition. Early in these cases an examination of the urine should be made {558} as a routine practice, because if there is nothing in it the patient will be just that much more reassured, while if it contains any pathological elements he need know no more about it than his physician deems proper, yet the real nature of the case and its indications will be appreciated. Without this a physician will often find himself suddenly confronted by serious symptoms in a patient when nothing of the kind was anticipated because the condition was thought to be entirely functional.

Occasionally the symptoms of Bright's disease seem to develop suddenly, as it were a storm in the organism out of a clear sky. As a matter of fact, however, there have been for some time before more or less indefinite symptoms pointing to some serious process at work, which if valued at their proper worth might have led to a much earlier diagnosis of the impending nephritis. Such patients are labeled as neurasthenics for months and at times even years before the serious conditions develop which make the recognition of their ailment comparatively easy. One case of this kind has come under my observation that is interesting in its lessons. A medical student had during the first year of his course exhibited every now and then what seemed to be neurotic symptoms. He was inclined to complain of headache for what seemed very slight reasons, and of pains and aches whenever there was a change in the weather and especially a fall in the barometer. He often had stomach symptoms and was anxious about his heart; in general he was looked upon as one of the nervous, complaining kind. During the course of a lesson in clinical pathology in his fourth year, he was asked to furnish a sample of urine which it was supposed would be normal, for comparison with an abnormal sample that was being investigated in the laboratory. To the surprise of the professor and to his own consternation, his urine was loaded with albumin. Up to that time there had been absolutely no objective symptoms and only the vague indefinite subjective symptoms mentioned. The next day his feet swelled. Even this for a time was considered to be rather an index of the neurotic tendency in him to react to very slight causes. It was hoped that the albuminuria was functional, as the examination was made in the full tide of digestion, and that it would pass off. Subsequent examinations, however, showed not only albumin but also casts. There was a slight intermission of symptoms and then an exacerbation. Within a month after the chance examination of his urine and its unexpected result he had a convulsion. Two weeks later, altogether six weeks after the albumin was first discovered, he died in nephritic coma.

Such cases are not so rare as they are thought, though they are seldom so fulminant. There is a story told of a professor at one of our American medical schools who, some twenty years ago, took a sample of his own urine in order to demonstrate the normal characteristics of healthy urine, and to his utter surprise he found albumin and casts in it. Within six months he was dead from Bright's disease.

Nervous Diarrhea and Organic Disease.—Other internal conditions may be called neurotic when they are really due to definite pathological entities. For instance, in three cases I have seen what had been pronounced by several physicians to be chronic diarrhea of nervous origin, proved to be due to quite other and serious pathological conditions of internal organs. In one of them a chronic diarrhea of several years' standing finally culminated in death in {559} early middle age from nephritis. After the event, there seemed to be no doubt but that the diarrhea, which no ordinary means of treatment had succeeded in benefiting more than temporarily, was really due to the effort of the intestinal mucosa to supplement the defective work of the kidneys. In this case apparently one of the strongest evidences that the affection was of nervous origin was the fact that whenever the patient was away from home, eating rather plentifully of a varied diet, his intestinal condition was better than when he was eating much more simple and unvaried food at home. The change of scene and surroundings proved a tonic to his kidneys and perhaps also to his skin, thus saving his intestines some of the extra work they had assumed.

Neurasthenia and Diabetes.—Another serious disease that may in its earlier stages be mistaken for neurasthenia is diabetes. There is no doubt that some patients have been passing sugar for a long time before any sure symptom can be noted in their general health, or, indeed, before there is anything to call attention to the possibility of glycosuria. In many of these cases, however, there is a feeling of muscular tiredness and a sense of inadequacy for occupations which were before easy, that may be attributed to neurasthenia. When this muscle tiredness changes to crampy feelings that should be enough to lead to an examination of the urine.

Undoubtedly one of the reasons why neurasthenia is sometimes called the American disease and is thought to be more frequent among us than it is in Europe is this confusion with the beginnings of serious organic disease because of failure to examine patients carefully in order

301

to detect underlying organic conditions. In recent years this neglect has become rarer and the consequence has been a reduction in the numbers of so-called neurasthenia cases. Our morbidity statistics of twenty years ago, for instance, seemed to show that we had only half as much diabetes to the population as they had in Europe. One of the reasons for this was undoubtedly the ease with which the diagnosis of neurasthenia might be made at the beginning of diabetes, and that the terminal stages of the affection were often masked by the development of the tuberculosis so frequent in diabetic conditions or of albuminuria with symptoms pointing to Bright's disease. Even at the present time it would be quite possible to reduce the number of neurasthenia cases by more careful attention to diagnosis.

Simulated Neurasthenia Due to Over-attention.—While there is danger of confusing neurasthenia on the one hand with more serious disease there is a distinct liability on the other hand to exaggerate the significance of certain minor symptoms by employing the word when it is only over-attention of mind to certain portions of the body that constitutes the disease in its literal sense. If something has particularly attracted a patient's attention to some part of his anatomy and if his attention is concentrated on it and allowed to dwell long on it, his feelings may be so exaggerated as to tempt him to think that they are connected with some definite pathological condition and he may even translate them into serious portents of organic disease. If a patient once begins to waste nervous energy on himself because of solicitude with regard to these symptoms then it will not be long before feelings of tiredness, incapacity for work, at times insomnia and certain disturbances of memory are likely to be noted. Then the neurasthenic picture seems to be {560} complete. This is the process so picturesquely called "short-circuiting" by which nervous energy exhausts itself upon the individual himself instead of in the accomplishment of external work. Many of the worse cases of so-called neurasthenia have their origin in this process. It is true that this set of events is much more likely to occur among people of lowered nervous vitality, but under certain conditions it may develop in those who are otherwise in good health up to the moment when the attention happened to be particularly called to certain feelings. The physician can start these patients off anew after improving their physical condition, if he can only bring them to see how much their concentration of mind upon themselves is the cause of their symptoms.

It has been well said, though to some it will doubtless seem an exaggeration, that we human beings are a regular boiler factory of sensations which, fortunately for our sanity, mental and physical, we have learned to neglect to a great extent. Wherever our clothing touches us, wherever the air touches us, wherever shoes or belts constrict us, there are definite sensations. These continue, but attract no attention unless they exceed a certain limit to which we are accustomed. Habit in this matter is very different in different individuals. After men and women have grown used to tight shoes or tight corsets these no longer produce disturbance. The chance visitor in a boiler factory or loom room of a cotton mill thinks he could not live in such din. But after a time people get so used to the din that silence and quiet may even become oppressive to them. City dwellers from the slums, especially children, find the peace of the country disturbing when they are first taken for vacations.

Over-attention to sensations, often scarcely abnormal, is indeed the real source of many of the symptoms that can so readily be exaggerated into pathological portents when attention is directed to them. Every portion of our body is connected with the central nervous system. Every square inch of surface touched either by clothing or the movement of the air producers a sensation at every moment of our waking life. Ordinarily we pay no attention at all to these sensations. We can recognize their presence by turning our attention for the moment to any portion of the body and recognizing at once that there are sensations coming from it, though the moment before we did not notice them. If we think of the point of our big toe on the right foot we find, though we were totally unaware of it a moment before, that a certain pressure is being exerted in it. If we continue to think of it queer feelings develop in it. We may get a sense of numbness that proceeds up along the tendons that lead to it. We can follow them up to the insertion of the muscles in the shin. If we dwell on the subject we have curious prickly sensations and numb feelings, all of which were there and were neglected a minute before but now are acutely felt.

This same thing is true of all the manifold sensations that come streaming into the brain. We learn almost to enjoy them though we are paying no attention to them. To be without them would mean very often a fright lest there should be something the matter. Usually we think of the outside of our body as the main source of sensation. It must not be forgotten, however, that our viscera have also certain sensitive nerves and while these are not as closely distributed as those on the surface they are there and their presence is often a source of pleasure or at least of satisfaction, but may be the source {561} of poignant discomfort. We are constantly disregarding ordinary messages from these, too. Something may easily call our attention to these sensations, however, and then we may translate them into pathological terms though they are really only physiological. Ordinarily man may put a couple of pounds of food and drink into his stomach and not feel it at all. If anything particularly calls attention to our stomachs, however, and we dwell on it, then this weighty feeling may seem to indicate serious indigestion because of the discomfort that is produced. This is what nervously weak persons, the so-called neurasthenics, are constantly doing. It is this habit that by suggestion and training they must be taught to break.

There is a tendency to the substitution of one neurotic symptom for another whenever by psychotherapy and mental discipline one condition is overcome. Often the substitution is of something just as bad or even worse. I have known cases where people when properly persuaded gave over paying too much attention to their stomachs and then proceeded to pay too much attention to their sleep with the result that insomnia developed. On the other hand, I have known patients to get over insomnia and then develop a series of complaints of queer feelings in their head which they usually spoke of as headache, though when asked to describe them carefully they confessed that they were at most a sense of pressure or of unusual feeling in some part of the head.

These curious substitutions take place particularly if for any reason special attention is called to another part of the body, either by accident or by some therapeutic manipulation or remedial measure. I have known a patient who complained of headache and was advised to take up exercise in the open air, do much stooping and lifting while cleaning snow from the sidewalk, develop a tired condition in the lumbar muscles and straightway this was thought to be rheumatic. Liniment was employed and the counter-irritation which developed attracted the patient's attention to that portion of the body for a week. The headache was no longer complained of, but lumbago was considered to have developed. I have known a person who suffered from headache develop what seemed to be a retention of urine for which unfortunately the doctor thought it necessary to use a catheter and after this there was no complaint of the headache, but the patient became almost unable to hold any amount of urine in her bladder and could not go out for social or other duties because of the fear of imperative urination.

CHAPTER II

CHOREA

This twitching affection, so familiar that it need not be described particularly, is sometimes classed as a pure neurosis, sometimes as a nervous disease with perhaps some organic basis and sometimes is placed among the ailments related to rheumatism and attributed to some pathological condition of the circulation.

Etiology.—Two elements must be considered in the problem of the etiology {562} of the disease—the predisposition and the direct occasion. The affection occurs particularly in nervous children who are made to occupy their intellects too much while their muscular systems are kept quiet for long hours. Often a preceding running down in weight is noticed, though sometimes the child only fails to increase in weight as it should in proportion to its growth. It occurs quite frequently among chlorotic girls just before or about the time of puberty. Anemia generally seems to predispose to it, but the affection may occur among children who seem to be in excellent physical health, though usually a distinct nervous heredity is found.

Immediate Causation.—Fright is one of the most frequent immediate causes or occasions of the development of chorea. Mental worry of any kind may have the same effect. Scolding has produced it; a sudden grief has seemed to be the occasion; a slight injury, and still more, a severe injury, or a surgical operation, even a slight one, may be the forerunner of it.

Pathology.—No definite lesions have been found to which the disease can be attributed, though a careful search has been made for them. Endocarditis is an extremely common accompaniment. It is probably present in three-fourths of the cases that have come to autopsy. Osler found it in sixty-two out of seventy-three cases in the literature. The association of the affection with rheumatism is insisted on by the French and English particularly, and certainly in a considerable number of cases there is a history of preceding or coincident rheumatism, that is, an acute rheumatic arthritis. Often these attacks are concealed under such names as "growing pains" or "colds in the joints" but it is not hard to elicit a history of a red and swollen joint with some fever. In children mild cases may occur of genuine acute rheumatism with the involvement of but a single joint and that not severely. These mild forms are often found in the history of cases of chorea.

It seems likely that the heart affection is often responsible for the symptoms and it is probably through the endocarditis that whatever connection there is between chorea and rheumatism exists.

All the elements in the disease point to the influence of the mind over it. The predisposition is caused by over-use of the mind at a time when many claims are being made on the nervous system because of the growth of muscles. There must, as a rule, be a pathological basis, natural or acquired, that is, something that tends to produce a defect in the circulation, but even without this certain children suffer from the affection. If the patient is an object of solicitude or of curiosity at home or at school, the symptoms rapidly become worse. At any time the consciousness of observation makes them worse. The symptoms do not occur during sleep, or at times when the patient's mind is much occupied with some absorbing interest. They lessen just to the degree that the patient's own attention is not called to them or the consciousness not allowed to be concentrated on them. Chorea often occurs in bright, intelligent children and always seems worse in them.

Treatment.—The story of the therapeutics of chorea in recent years strongly confirms the idea of the place of mental influence in the cure of the disease. We have had a whole series of remedies, introduced with a promise of cure by distinguished authorities, used for a time with apparent success by many physicians, and then gradually falling into innocuous desuetude. It was recognized that any remedy would have to be used over a rather {563} prolonged period, at least from five to ten weeks. It was appreciated, also, that the patient must be kept quiet, both in mind and body, emotional disturbances especially being avoided, that all physical functions have to be set right and that the nutrition particularly must be corrected if in anything it is abnormal. Where all this is done patients recover without any remedy quite as promptly in most cases as with any of the supposed specifics. Expectant treatment, supplemented by symptomatic treatment, has proved in many institutions to give excellent results without the necessity of troubling the patients with more or less dubious drugs. It was important that the patient should be given certain medicine and impressed with the idea that this medicine was expected to do them good, a suggestion automatically emphasized at every dose, but it is probable that few men of considerable clinical experience now hold the notion that we have any genuinely curative remedy for chorea, though we have certain tonic, alterative remedies which, in conjunction with the setting of the mind at rest, help to put the patient in a condition where the affection is gradually overcome.

The most important object in the treatment of chorea must be its prevention or its early recognition, and its immediate treatment; then there is little likelihood of relapses and, above all, the condition does not last long. Children who have had an attack of acute articular rheumatism or who have suffered from growing pains or any other of the rheumatic simulants of childhood should be watched carefully during their growing period and at certain critical times in early life. They should be especially regarded immediately after being sent to school. The first sign of involuntary twitchings should be taken to mean that the children are overborne and a period of rest from anxiety and study and over-exercise should be afforded them. Of course, all this watchful care must be exercised without attracting the little patient's attention, or the very purpose of the care will be defeated and the mind disturbed.

Rest does not mean that patients should be kept absolutely in bed even after chorea has frankly developed, but that there should be hygienic rest. Long hours of sleep, interesting occupations without much exercise, a period of lying down in the afternoon, but, above all, such occupation of mind with simple pleasant things as keeps their attention from themselves. Visitors should not be allowed to see them; above all, they should not be conscious objects of over-solicitous care on the part of father and mother or the relief of symptoms will be delayed and the condition will be made worse. As a rule, children do not worry about themselves nor their physical ailments, but they can be made to do so by seeing the over-anxiety of others. A good nurse of sympathetic nature with power to interest the child, is better than its mother for a constant companion, though family life, the playing with brothers and sisters and the regular routine of home is the best possible mental solace and occupation. Grandmothers are useful adjuvants in the treatment late in the affection. At the beginning their over-solicitude nearly always does harm.

Habit Following Chorea.—In certain nervous children after the chorea itself has subsided there remains a habit of twitching that often is almost more intractable than the chorea itself. This is particularly likely to be manifest in children who have an unfortunate nervous heredity or in those whose {564} nervous systems have been impaired by preceding infections disease as anterior polio-myelitis, syphilis or one of the forms of meningitis. Occasionally it is seen in children without nervous heredity, but they are usually children surrounded by solicitous relatives, made the centre of pathological interest and constantly fussed about. The habit is not surprising and would remind the observant physician of the whoop that by habit sometimes clings to children in any cough that they may have for months after they have had whooping cough. Often it will be found that these children are capricious eaters, that they take tea and coffee, that their diet instead of being the simple nutritious food that they should have consists of many things that their mothers obtain to tempt their appetites and that the children can really have anything they crave for and get it much oftener than is good for them. To continue any form of presumedly specific treatment in these cases does no good. If arsenic is used over long periods, or any of the salicylates because of the supposed connection of chorea and an underlying rheumatic diathesis they will certainly do harm. The patients' diet can be regulated, nerve stimulants of all kinds must be denied them, and their appetites must be brought into order by the proper care of a nurse who will not yield too readily to their caprices, and then the solicitous environment must be changed. These cases represent a good many of the so-called prolonged choreas and are really habits or tics due to concentration of mind and a certain hysterical tendency to continue to attract attention which may be noted.

CHAPTER III

TICS

Without any good reason in the etymology or the history of the word, the term "tics" has now been generally accepted to signify certain involuntary movements, frequently recurrent, of which, by habit, certain persons usually of diminished nervous control, become the victims. For the psychotherapeutist, however, they have an interest quite beyond that which they have for the ordinary student of nervous diseases. They represent the possibility of the formation of habits in the nervous system, originally quite under the control of the will, but which eventually become tyrannously powerful and quite beyond management by the individual. They deserve to be studied with particular care because it is probable that they represent objectively what occurs also on the sensory side of the system, but which not being manifest externally, is spoken of as entirely subjective. If nerve explosions of motor character can, through habit, get beyond the control of the patient, it is not unlikely that sensations, primarily of little significance, may, in persons of low nervous control, become by habit so likely to be repeated as to make the patient miserable. Hence the study of tics as here presented.

As a result of the studies of Gilles de la Tourette, we realize that there is an essential distinction between involuntary movements of various kinds, and that spasms and tics must be separated from one another. Tics consist of various movements of the voluntary muscles. Probably the most familiar {565} is that of winking. Everybody winks both eyes a number of times a minute quite unconsciously, though the unconscious movement accomplishes the definite and necessary purpose of keeping the conjunctiva free from irritant particles. When this same movement is done more frequently than is necessary, or is limited more to one eye than to the other, or is repeated exaggeratedly in both eyes, then it is a tic. There are many other facial tics. Most of them represent movements of the lips or of the nose or of the skin of the forehead and all of them are identical with movements that are occasionally performed quite voluntarily. There are movements of the lips as in sucking, or smacking sounds may be made, or such movements of the features as are associated with sensations of taste or smell. Sometimes changes of facial expression may be tics and without any reason there may be recurring expressions of emotion, of joy, or grief, or fright, or even pain. Sometimes the tics affect structures that are internal, as various motions of the larynx accompanied by the production of grunting or sighing sounds or sometimes even of particular words. In children the tendency is prone to manifest itself in the utterance of forbidden words, usually vulgar, sometimes indecent.

Besides these facial and throat tics any of the voluntary muscles of the body may be affected. There may be the gestures that accompany certain mental states, or there may be twisting or turning movements as if the patient were in an awkward position and wanted to get out of it, or as if the clothes were hampering movement and there was an effort to relieve some discomfort. The head may be lifted and lowered, or may be twisted from one side to the other and, indeed, various nodding tics are extremely common. Almost any ordinary movement may, in nervous people, come to be repeated so frequently as to be a tic.

Practically all of the convulsive or quasi-convulsive movements associated with respiration are likely to become the subject of tics. Yawning, for instance, involuntary to some degree, usually a reflex with a physical cause, but so readily the subject of imitation, may become so frequent as to be repeated a couple of times a minute and this repetition kept up for many days. Sneezing may also become a tic, though it is usually a definite reflex due to palpable physical causes. Hiccoughs may easily become the subject of a tic. The occurrence of a persistent hiccough is in popular medicine a sign of unfavorable prognosis in serious diseases, especially such as involve the abdominal region. In connection with neurotic affections of the abdomen, however, hiccoughs are not uncommon and are of no serious significance.

Varieties of Tics.—There are many more tics than are ordinarily supposed. Indeed, there are few of us who escape them entirely. Nearly all the curious phrases that people interlard so frequently into their conversation, usually quite unconscious of them, or of the ridiculous significance they often have, must be placed under the tics. Some men cannot say a dozen words without interpolating "don't you know." Others use some such expression as "in that way." I once knew a distinguished professor of elocution who by actual count used this phrase forty times in an hour. Some say "hum" or "hem" every sentence or so. Whenever there is a bit of obscurity in their thought these voluntary but unconscious expressions are sure to pop out. No one who has had much experience in public speaking ever succeeds in keeping entirely out of such bad habits. It is curious how phrases will insist on repeating {566} themselves. One year one set of words, or a pet phrase, or mode of expression, creeps unconsciously here and there into an address. Then either because the speaker has been reading dictated copy, or because some good friend has the courage to tell him of it, he finds out the bad habit and suppresses it.

Word formulas senselessly repeated are only one of many forms of tics that public speakers are prone to indulge in. Gesture which begins as an artificial adornment of speech, very appropriate in itself, after a while may settle down into certain forms that not only often lack elegance but that are really disturbing to an audience. Of these gestures and movements men are often quite unconscious. They have become habitual and in the absorption of mind with the thought and the words, they are reproduced quite involuntarily though they are all originally voluntary movements. Nearly every public speaker needs a mentor to correct him of such faults. It is rather difficult to break some of these habits and it requires no little concentration of effort and attention to be successful in eradicating them. It can be done, however, provided the habit is not too inveterate, and this is the best evidence that tics of other kinds can also be eradicated if the patient really takes the matter in hand and is not of a weakened will.

Teachers' Habits.—Indeed it is almost impossible for public speakers and teachers not to acquire certain habits irritating to their auditors at first but amusing as they grow used to them, and students particularly learn to look kindly at the ridiculous side of many of them. I remember an old professor of literature who used to lecture at some length on each of the important contributors to English prose and poetry. We soon observed that whenever he came to their deaths he took out his handkerchief and blew his nose. This was as inevitable and as invariable a rule as the laws of the Medes and the Persians. It was, as it were, his tribute of sympathetic condolence with humanity for the loss of a brilliant contributor to English literature.

Occasionally the effort to break up these habits will seriously interfere with modes of thought and habits of expression, for the time being at least. A professor at a certain university had a habit every now and then of plucking at a button on his coat. His students could tell when his hand was going to find this object of its occupation and knew from experience that he would twist it a certain number of times. He was not what would ordinarily be called a nervous person. One day he happened to take off his coat shortly before a lecture and one of the students surreptitiously removed the button. At the end of the first few minutes of his lecture his hand went up to find the button as usual but failed. For the moment there was a hesitancy in his speech; then he tried again. A little later his hand went up unconsciously and was disappointed; then he stammered and lost the thread of his discourse. The last half hour of that lecture was seriously impaired because of the absence of that button.

Tricks of Speech.—There are many other curious tricks of speech that are really tics. Women often indulge in them and sometimes even pretty women spoil their appearance by bad habits. All of us know the pretty woman who talks very fast, but who every now and then projects her tongue a little beyond her teeth. Occasionally there is a tendency to wrinkle the nose or the forehead. Most of us have seen the woman who sets her face into a definite smile of a particular kind whenever her company manners are in {567} use, though there is a vacancy behind the smile that is rather disturbing. Some people have habitual movements of the fingers that are really tics, and even positions assumed on sitting down that are very ungraceful, or that are very noticeable, sometimes partake of this character.

Fussiness.—A very common form of tic that is quite difficult to control is that tendency to be doing something with some of their muscles which characterizes many men. They must handle a pencil or a knife, or they must swing on their chair or tilt back on it, or keep one of their limbs swinging over the other, or twirl their moustaches or stroke their beards, or rumple their hair, and they cannot find it quite possible to sit still. The difference between men and women in this regard is remarkable. Women are conceded to be much more nervous than men, but men are ever so much more fidgety than women. The author of "The Life of a Prig" in his book "The Platitudes of a Pessimist" has some striking paragraphs with regard to this subject. He says:

To look nearer home, the British bar affords splendid examples of nervous fidget. Observe barristers pleading a cause. How they torture a piece of red-tape, how they twirl their eye-glasses or spectacles, and how they hitch at their garments, as if they momentarily expected them to desert their finely proportioned figures. But worse than the Queen's Counsellors, and even worse than the domestic peripatetic, is the villain who is abandoned to a performance vulgarly known as "the devil's tattoo"—drumming with the fingers.

Writers' Tics.—Writers, and above all writers for the daily press and such as have to do their writing in a rush and therefore get nervous and anxious about it, are especially prone to develop tics, though others who write leisurely may do so. Some of these are curious and others are only expressions of nervousness common to all people. Many of them chew their nails, some of them bite at their fingers round the nails and make them sore, many of them chew the ends of their pens and find it practically impossible to keep a pen with a long handle to it. Some of them run their hands through their hair until it is in a greatly rumpled condition, some of them pluck at their eyebrows. I have one patient who when he is going through a particular nervous strain plucks out the middle portion of his right eyebrow so that he has a distinct bald spot at this point.

The tradition in newspaper offices is that these curious expressions of the tendency of the body to occupy itself with something while the mind is occupied are more or less inevitable in nervous people. They continue for many, many years. They are only habits, however, that it would have been rather easy to break in the beginning, though they become extremely difficult to modify after they have once secured a firm hold. Occasionally I have fastened a piece of adhesive plaster over a much battered eyebrow, but that made it difficult for the man to go on with his work. His hand would go up involuntarily time after time and while plucking at his eyebrow would not disturb in the slightest his train of thought, just as soon as his fingers touched the unusual object a serious distraction occurred and work was not only slower, but much more difficult.

In Games.—The tendency to the formation of curious habits of associated movements can be seen very well in most games where skill is combined {568} to a certain degree with chance. It is most noticeable, perhaps, in bowling. Few men are able to restrain themselves from making some special movement just as the ball strikes the pin. This is sometimes a motion of the head, oftener it is a jerk of the trunk, sometimes it is an associated movement of the arms, occasionally it is a kick or a stamp. In billiards the same movements are noticeable if a man is much interested in making a difficult shot. Usually there is some movement of the body or of the hands or of the head that would indicate his desire to move the ball in a particular direction. Women who play these games do not usually have these associated movements to such a marked degree and this may be due either to their better restraint to movement in general, for as we have said men do not acquire the habit of self-restraint in small matters of deportment as women do, or to the fact that such associated movements might disarrange their clothes. Perhaps, also, they are not as much interested in the games as a rule as are the men. Of course, similar associated movements may be seen in outdoor sports that require skill yet have an element of chance in them. For it is, as it were, to overcome this that the additional movement is made.

Children's Tics.—Some tics consist of some very curious habits. Occasionally children hear some obscene or vulgar expression and repeat it. The repetition of it produces such a look of shock to propriety on the part of some of the other little ones who happen to be present that they repeat it in the spirit of bravado and then continue to utter it until it becomes a habit that is hard for them to break. After all, the use of blasphemy later on in life is really a tic, a habit of uttering words no longer expressive of any particular feeling, as a rule, unless in exceptional circumstances but just the result of a tendency for the speech organs to repeat certain words. They tell a good story of the Rev. Sydney Smith who, wishing to break an acquaintance of the habit of indulging in expletives, interlarded his speech with "fire tongs and sugar tongs" every ten words or so and when his auditor protested that that added nothing to the significance of what he said the Rev. Sidney suggested that that was also true of various blasphemous expressions that his acquaintance was accustomed to use.

At the Salpêtrière they tell the story of a little boy who had the habit of saying the French word which the corporal in Victor Hugo's "Les Miserables" made use of when anyone told him that it was because Wellington was a greater general than Napoleon that the French Emperor was defeated at Waterloo. Nothing seemed to be able to break the boy of the habit of interjecting this word into conversations sometimes in which he had no part and sometimes toward which he was expected to take only a respectful and childlike attitude of silence. He was sent to the Salpêtrière. The ordinary remedies had failed entirely. One day he was allowed to go outside of the hospital, or rather stole out of the gate and played marbles with some street gamins in front of it. During the game he used the word in question and they proceeded to give him a good thrashing. It is Charcot who tells that this broke him effectually of the habit.

One of the childish customs that sometimes disturbs parents very much because it seems to be such an unaccountable lapse into barbarism, though it is really nothing more than a tic in the strict sense of the word, is the habit that some children acquire of removing portions of hardened material {569} from their nose and then putting it into their mouth. Refined parents are apt to be so seriously disturbed by this that they fear for the child's mentality. Really the habit is not nearly so rare as is usually thought by some grown-ups who have forgotten about their own and others' childhood. In country places the habit is very common. It is not alone the dull children who do it but some very bright ones. Indeed, the tendency to the habit is so common that one wonders whether there is not something in nature that tempts to it. Parents who are fearful lest their children may be seriously hurt in health by the awfully insanitary habit may be reassured that after all a certain amount of the drainage of the nose is normally carried off through the posterior nares to the stomach and that no danger to health seems ever to have resulted from the practice. As a rule, the habit can be broken rather easily by a little judicious care and insistence, though I know of cases where relapses occurred and the habit continued surreptitiously.

Motor Tics.—Motor tics frequently develop as a consequence of some injury to a nerve or some intense overuse of it. Winking habits follow an herpetic involvement of the superior branch of the fifth nerve. Bell's palsy is sometimes followed in the face by a tendency to twitching on the unaffected side that makes the patient quite uncomfortable. Herpes zoster is sometimes followed by a catching of the breath, probably due to a little spasm in the muscles supplied by the nerve thus affected. Some of the yawning tics have this origin. Any neuritis may in the course of its betterment be followed by this curious tendency to explosion along the nerve that has been affected, as if the pathological process had more seriously interfered with inhibition than with the actual function of the nerve. Examples of over-exertion followed by twitchings are not rare. A scrubwoman who has seen better days and now has to carry a heavy bucket and use her right hand much with the brush may develop a twitching of the right arm. A janitor's wife who sweeps much may have a tendency to twitchings of the fingers as a consequence of the unusual exertion of holding the broom. Twitchings in the limbs of men who work at a foot lathe or other machine requiring foot power are not unusual though they are more often seen in the leg on which the workman habitually stands than in the other one and it seems to be oftener a strain on muscles than actual over-exercise that precedes the development of these tics.

Heredity.—Heredity plays as large a role in tics as it does in stuttering and other functional nervous disturbances. Occasionally the direct inheritance of some habit will be found, though there is nearly always more than a suspicion that a trick of speech or of act, which constitutes the tic, was learned by imitation rather than transferred directly. Besides, it is a case of a similarly constituted nervous system reacting in the same way to a similar environment, rather than any definite tendency existing by heredity in the nervous system. It is surprising what close observers children are and how easily they learn to imitate any habitual action of father or mother or, for that matter, of nurses or those who are close to them.

Mental Treatment.—The most important element in the psychotherapy of tics is their prophylaxis. They run in families, not by any inevitable hereditary influence, but as a consequence partly of imitation and of corresponding tendencies resulting from certain weaknesses in the family. Wherever they are known to be likely to occur, parents should be warned of the {570} possibility and the first symptom of any motor habit should be considered the beginning of a tic. As we have said, they are likely to begin in muscles that have been overstrained for any reason, especially when patients are run down. They are often seen after herpes and certain facial neuralgias.

There is probably no tic, no matter how long or how serious, that can not be eradicated, or greatly modified, if the patient will take the trouble and if the treatment is conducted so as gradually to get rid of it. Peculiar movements cannot be done away with at once. They can be lessened in intensity and in frequency and then gradually the patient will be encouraged by their becoming less noticeable than before to make renewed efforts. The habit must be gradually undone and this will take as long as it did to form it originally. The exercise of contrary muscular movements carefully carried out, and of gentle repression with definite times of exercise during the day, gradually increasing the length of the intervals of repression, in the end proves successful. Only a determined struggle will effect a cure. It depends on the patient's will. Like a drug addiction, or a tendency to overeat, or a craving for alcohol, it must be gradually overcome and then care must be exercised to prevent relapses; for when the condition is somewhat better, to relax vigilance and give up effort will allow the old condition to reassert itself with startling rapidity. People suffering from severe tics will often give up. Without the patient's hearty co-operation cure is impossible. With good will its gradual diminution gives the patient a confidence in self and an uplift in character that is extremely valuable, not only for physical but for mental conditions.

CHAPTER IV

STUTTERING, ATAXIA IN TALKING, WALKING, WRITING, ETC.

The difficulty of speech called stuttering has usually been considered rather as an unfortunate lack of control over the organs of articulation, somewhat corresponding to muscular awkwardness of any other kind, than as a pathological condition deserving the physician's attention. If anything was done for it formally, the first effort of the parents or the teacher was to correct the supposed bad habits and this failing the affection was relegated to someone who claimed to produce wonderful results by some special method. Perhaps, even oftener, stuttering was considered one of those affections, fortunately decreasing in number, that the child may be expected to outgrow. Often there was noted an hereditary element which was supposed to indicate incurability.

Stuttering deserves special treatment in a work on psychotherapy because it illustrates very strikingly one phase at least of mental influence over bodily function. While in the study of the etiology of the disease much has been made of anatomical features, nerves and muscles and anatomical anomalies of the speech organs and the respiratory tract, the sufferers from stuttering are certainly quite up to the average both in the physiology and anatomy of these regions. They are of all ranks and conditions of life, of all sizes and build, and it is evident that the trouble is not physical, but mental. They {571} pay too much attention to their speech and to the co-ordination of the many muscles engaged in speech production and the consequence is that they impair their power to use these organs. Practically all the cures recommended contain some element which distracts the attention from the speech to something else and so permits the function of the speech organs to proceed undisturbed.

A number of conditions develop in nervous individuals that resemble stuttering. There are disturbances of swallowing, disturbances of walking (astasia abasia), neurotic disturbances of writing, and of other uses of the hands and of the legs.

State of Mind.—It is perfectly clear to anyone who has closely observed the ways of stutterers that the state of mind is extremely important in these cases and indeed probably constitutes the underlying factor in the speech disturbance. Stuttering and all speech defects are much worse when the patient is laboring under excitement. This is so amusingly true that the impotence of a stutterer to say a word when he wants very much to say it is a commonplace in the cheap drama and never fails to raise a laugh. In ordinary conversation with friends the stutterer may have little difficulty. As soon, however, as he begins to talk with those with whom he is unfamiliar his speech defect becomes noticeable. When the others present are entire strangers and, above all, strangers whom he wishes to impress favorably, then his stuttering becomes pronounced. The mental element is the most important factor. Just as soon as consciousness of the task supervenes his power of co-ordination fails and stuttering begins.

Stuttering in Complex Activities.—There are many actions that become habitual and people are thus saved from the necessity of constantly performing them under the control of the will and the consciousness. Walking is a typical illustration of this and is seldom disturbed by consciousness, but there may be a stuttering in the gait of sensitive persons if they become overconscious when passing people who are watching them. Talking is even a more striking example of elaborate co-ordination without conscious effort. We have to bring into play more than a score of muscles whose movements are nicely and accurately co-ordinated, or else the effort at articulate speech is a failure. We have to change the positions of most of these muscles many times every minute, yet we do it without a thought of how it is done and most of us accomplish it with ease and perfection.

Stuttering Walk.—Stuttering, after all, comes most naturally under the head of dreads in the classification of the psychoses. Stuttering is not a physical difficulty so much as a nervous apprehension, and there may be a stuttering in any co-ordination as in speech. I have a patient under observation who, if people are looking at her, finds so much difficulty in walking because of a trembling that comes over her that she fears she may not be able to keep from falling. Boys at school whistle a certain air that requires a little halt in the gait to keep time with it, as their schoolgirl friends go by, and it is impossible for these not to drop into the peculiar gait indicated by the time of the tune.

Stuttering Writing.—There are many men who become so nervous about writing their signatures that they cannot sign while anyone is present. There are others whose penmanship becomes very irregular, or at least exhibits many signs of nervousness, whenever they think someone is watching them. Most of {572} the difficulties seen in speech may, indeed, be exhibited in writing. The same difficulty in beginning, the same elision of letters under stress of excitement, may occur.

Writer's cramp is, after all, much more of the nature of a stuttering in writing than a real cramp. Over-action, added motions, and, finally, incomplete power to act as desired are seen in both cases. It might be expected that this would not affect so simple and familiar a set of motions as those required for a personal signature, but it does, as many cases illustrate. A typical example was the treasurer of a large trust company who had to sign a number of bonds, some thirty thousand. At the rate of 200 an hour, over three a minute, as he did the first day with others making it easy for him, it looked as though he could complete the task, huge as it was, in a month. At the end of a week, however, the rate had fallen to 120 an hour and, toward the end of the second week, one a minute on the average was all that could be accomplished. At the end of the month his signature, while retaining certain of its original characteristics, had become very different from what it was at the beginning and signing had become an extremely difficult matter. He had to take a rest from business for several weeks after accomplishing this apparently mechanical procedure.

Emotional Ataxia.—Dr. S. Weir Mitchell in his article on "Motor Ataxia from Emotion" in the May number (1910) of *The Journal of Nervous and Mental Disease*, discusses some cases in which inability to write even a signature came as a consequence of nervousness and emotional disturbance.

In one of Dr. Mitchell's patients, other manifestations of ataxia occurred as the result of the consciousness that people were watching the patient. At times he is compelled to leave a dinner table, since with strangers it is almost impossible for him to eat. If there are two or three at the table with him, however, and especially if he is worried about himself, he may become almost helpless, requiring both hands to get a cup of coffee or a glass of water to his mouth. A patient of mine with like symptoms has described to me equivalents of various kinds to his own difficulties in his sisters. One of them cannot play the piano before strangers, though an excellent musician. The other cannot crochet with any success if any but intimate friends are present. How much of this family trait is due to suggestion or psychic contagion would be hard to say. The state that comes over amateur actors and which makes them forget their lines, stammer in their speech, walk awkwardly, and trip easily, are really manifestations of this same incapacity to control even familiar sets of actions when there is great self-consciousness and over-attention.

Mental Influence.—The correction of these conditions comes through soothing the mind of the patient and getting him or her not to be so self-conscious as to disturb action by thought about it. It is easy to say this and extremely difficult to do it. In certain nervous organizations it is quite impossible to overcome the tendency to this ataxia or inco-ordination of voluntary movements. Much can be accomplished, however, by proper training and discipline in all cases, and, while the patient can never be completely cured, great improvement may be brought about by patient habituation under favorable circumstances. In Dr. Mitchell's cases the taking of a glass of whiskey or of wine sometimes stimulated the patient so that co-ordination became possible where it was impossible before. In nearly all cases of writer's cramp {573} and writing difficulties the power to write is restored for a time by such stimulation. Strong coffee will sometimes serve the purpose as well as alcohol. It is easy to understand, however, how dangerous is the resort to such stimulation.

Practice in Self-Control.—The excitement and nervousness incident to appearance before an audience which make thought and speech so difficult and action so awkward and so exaggerated gradually disappear as the individual becomes habituated to appearing in public. In most people there is never a complete loss of self-consciousness with entire freedom from nervousness, but the conditions are much improved so that there is no noticeable interference with ordinary actions and speech. Whenever there is some reason for additional excitement, however, as when a new play is being put on, or when some special audience is being entertained, there is a reappearance of many of the old symptoms due to a self-consciousness.

Stuttering in the Young.—The prognosis of stuttering when it develops at a certain period is much better than at others. The stuttering of the very young can usually be overcome by a little careful training, if it is taken early and treated patiently by a competent teacher. Not infrequently a certain amount of stuttering develops at puberty when the voice changes, partly due to the inability of muscles and nerves to co-ordinate so easily as before upon the rapidly-enlarging vocal chords and larynx, and partly to that greatly increased self-consciousness amounting almost to painful bashfulness which develops in boys about this time. Breathing exercises and especially slow expiration is an excellent thing in these cases and distracts their attention from themselves and their speech.

The chest has usually developed rather rapidly at this time and the muscles have to some extent lost control over it, and it will be found on careful observation that the breathing is particularly superficial, that the descent of the diaphragm is quite limited and that the use of this important muscle of respiration requires practice in order that it may be controlled properly.

In Women.—Perhaps the most interesting thing about stuttering is that it is ever so much rarer in women than it is in men. Something less than one-fourth as many women suffer from it as men and this is true for all periods of life. Women are usually more bashful and self-conscious than men, but this rarely goes to the extent of disturbing their speech faculties. Ungallant observers have suggested that the sex quality of ready speech is too profoundly seated in nature to be disturbed by mere bashfulness, but there seems to be no doubt that the breathing of women has much to do with the difference between them and men in the matter of speech defects.

When stuttering occurs in women the defect is much less tractable and is usually dependent on a more serious disturbance of the psyche or of the central nervous system. The prognosis of cases of stuttering in women is not so good as in men, but remarkable cures are sometimes effected by mental treatment of the self-consciousness which causes the speech defect.

Correction of Respiratory Defects.—This last point, the correction of all pathological conditions in the respiratory tract, is especially important. Many stutterers are for one reason or another mouth breathers. If they are mouth breathers because they have adenoids, these must be removed. This must {574} be done early in life, certainly not later than the third or fourth year, or else there will come a serious deformation of the chest and that chicken-breastedness, which is not undesirable in itself, but which hampers to some extent the action of the diaphragm because that muscle cannot act as well in the deformed as in the natural chest. Not all who are chicken-breasted have any defect of speech, nor any tendency to stutter, but when there is a natural tendency to a lack of inco-ordination because of sub-normal nervous ability the presence of such a deformity makes the prospect of cure much less favorable than would otherwise be the case. If the mouth-breathing is due to stoppage of the nostrils, this must be relieved.

Realization of Allied Conditions.—A helpful suggestion for stutterers is found in the recognition of the fact that there are so many conditions allied to stuttering and so many people afflicted with them. Under the heading Neurotic Esophageal Stricture stuttering in swallowing is treated of. In the chapters on urinary symptoms stuttering in urination is discussed. Any set of muscles requiring careful co-ordination may thus be disturbed. The stutterer is apt to look upon his affliction as a very special individual annoyance. When he learns that in practically every set of muscles requiring nice adjustment for function like difficulties may occur, that in every action requiring careful co-ordination of muscles there may be a similar disturbance, and yet that in most of them careful mental discipline, especially training in self-control, proves a source of relief, he takes new courage to face the struggle necessary to overcome the self-consciousness which is the root of most of these troubles.

A striking form of inability to co-ordinate muscles so as to enable them to perform their ordinary function is aphonia, or mutism, sometimes spoken of as hysterical mutism. After some sudden emotion or fright or accident a neurotic person proves to be quite unable to talk. He cannot utter a sound. In Prof. Raymond's clinic at the Salpêtrière I once saw the classical case described by Charcot and presented at his clinics several times. It was a man whose wife had run away from him and been taken back three times. Each time on her disappearance he had an attack of aphonia, inability to utter a sound of any kind. It lasted for from several weeks to a few days. The cases are much commoner in women. After a disappointment in love or a scare the patients become unable to speak. Sometimes they can whisper but cannot phonate. The affection is entirely functional or neurotic, and if the patient's mind is properly predisposed speech returns without difficulty or delay. A little massage of the muscles of the throat or of the tongue by means of a tongue depressor or the use of Politzer's bag in the nose with the assurance that after proper swallowing movements the ability to speak will return, have proved successful. Occasionally hypnotism is recommended for these cases, but many of them are too highly neurotic to be readily susceptible to hypnotism and, besides, suggestion in the waking state proves just as effective.

After several days of speechlessness it seems little short of marvelous to make a patient talk readily after a little massage of the throat. It is all dependent, however, upon confident assurance and the suggestion to talk. The physician himself must possess absolute confidence in his power to bring this about, for the slightest sign of doubt or hesitation will make it impossible {575} to influence the patient and will completely destroy his psychotherapeutic efficiency.

Neurotic Esophageal Stricture.—A rare but interesting form of neurosis, which should be studied in connection with stuttering because of the light shed on both by their relations to each other, is that seen in the sufferers from so-called neurotic esophageal stricture. These patients are unable to swallow solids except after determined deliberate effort and occasionally the discomfort caused by this effort leads them to eat much less than is sufficient for their nutrition. The physician is sometimes tempted to overcome the spasmodic closure or partial closure of the esophagus by bougies and dilators, and these the patients learn to pass by themselves. I have never known any of these cases to be benefited more than temporarily by this treatment and I have seen two that were made distinctly worse. Forcible dilatation by concentrating attention on the affected parts hampers the proper flow of nervous impulses and the ordinary reaction to these which should occur.

309

To appreciate how closely related to stuttering this spasmodic closure of the esophagus is, it is necessary to see these patients swallow when they do not know that they are under observation. For when they are on exhibition for the physician, when their condition is intensified by the excitement of the occasion and by the definite purpose to make the doctor appreciate how serious is their case, they swallow with more difficulty. Nearly always they have more difficulty in eating in public than with friends, and it is only with those with whom the patient is on a footing of perfect familiarity that the best swallowing power is obtained.

In sufferers from esophageal stricture of the neurotic type the muscles by an unfortunate perversion of nerve force contract in front of the bolus instead of behind it. This contraction may be so complete as to prevent even the swallowing of liquids. Usually, however, liquids can be swallowed without much difficulty. Such patients, then, if they become much run down in weight, must be fed on milk and eggs and ice cream and the gruels and soups until they gain in weight. While they are much under weight their condition is distinctly worse and their power of co-ordination much less. It is, however, not hard to make them gain in weight. This gain in weight acts as a strong suggestion which persuades them that they are getting better and this of itself soon helps them to control their muscles. Local treatment does harm rather than good. Ice in small pieces swallowed shortly before a meal seems in some patients to have the effect of making the muscles less prone to follow the inco-ordinate nervous action and thus renders swallowing much easier. In some, and especially in nervous people, warm liquids have the same effect, while ice produces further irritation. Acids nearly always increase the spasmodic condition. Sucking a piece of hard candy for some time before a meal, especially if it is not too sweet nor flavored with acid, helps some people.

Nearly all of them when carefully questioned prove to have special foods that are more difficult of deglutition than others. Not infrequently these idiosyncrasies for food are found to follow ideas with regard to their digestibility. If the patient is hurrying for any reason and suddenly becomes conscious that he is not masticating sufficiently, swallowing at once becomes much more difficult.

{576}

The main element in the treatment, however, must be as far as possible to get the patient's mind off his condition. The more attention he gives to it the worse it will be. No treatment that we have will cure it any more than stuttering can be cured, though a deliberate effort to form a habit for the control of the swallowing muscles will often do much to lessen the discomfort and the inability to swallow.

It is important in all these cases to be sure that there has been no incident in childhood which might have caused the production of scar tissue in the esophagus with a consequent stricture. Sometimes it is many years before this manifests itself and, as in the case of the urethra, even ten to twenty years may pass before serious trouble comes. When the first symptoms are noticed, the actual stricture may be so slight as scarcely to be possible of diagnosis by the bougie. Occasionally the first symptom of a cancer of the esophagus is an inability to swallow, and cancers of the esophagus have been known to occur in quite young people, especially young men. I remember seeing a case at autopsy in Vienna where the first symptom had been the difficulty of swallowing and the man, at the recommendation of friends, swallowed a glass of beer with some black peppers in it and these stuck in his esophagus and produced death. Such cases are exceptional but must not be forgotten. Neurotic esophageal stricture is entirely benignant and its prognosis altogether favorable.

Treatment.—The treatment of stuttering presents the best example that we have of the influence of the mind over neurotic difficulties of any and every kind. Many forms of treatment have been announced as successful, most frequently in the hands of men who have themselves been stutterers and who have helped themselves by them. This would seem to make it clear beyond all doubt that discoveries in direct therapeutics had been found. As a matter of fact, however, when a review of all the methods is made, they are seen to be so different from one another and founded on such essentially diverse principles that the only common connecting link to be found is in the occupation of mind with something else besides speech which all these methods recommend. We have had successful cures announced by surgery, by discipline, by making speech more difficult by obstacles of various kinds, by special positions of the tongue—up against the palate or down against the floor of the mouth—by associated movements, by rhythmic speech, by special control of the muscles of respiration, and of many other structures much less related to speech. The interesting phase of all this is the uniform success claimed by different specialists using many different methods.

From the beginning of history cures have been suggested. That idea, still held among the non-medical, that the sufferer from a difficulty of speech is tongue-tied and needs to have the frenum cut, is as old as the history of medicine. Galen suggested cauterization of the tongue. Aetius, the first prominent Christian physician of whom we have any record, divided the frenum of the tongue. So did Paul of AEgina. Of course, in the Renaissance, when the old medical classics were revived, this became a favorite method of treatment. Hildanus is sure that it accomplishes great things. This idea has never been entirely given up, and recurs from time to time in the practice of those who do not reason much, but who look for some ready explanation and, above all, some direct method of treatment. Much more {577} serious surgical intervention has been suggested from time to time, however. Velpeau advised division of the extensor muscles of the tongue. Of course a number of surgeons have quite properly insisted on the removal of the tonsils, uvula, polyps in the nose and other obstructions of respiration.

Singing in Treatment.—A number of the stuttering cures employ singing as a method of training in forthright utterance. Few people stutter when they sing. Most people can be given confidence in themselves and their power to talk right on by being shown that as soon as they try to follow a set of notes there is little or no difficulty in utterance. The teaching of singing, then, is of distinct value in many cases. Taking advantage of this a number of those who correct stuttering endeavor to introduce a certain rhythm into speech. So long as the rhythm can be maintained stuttering does not occur. As Kussmaul has pointed out the rhythmus acts as an efficient will-regulator, so that nerve impulses go down regularly and are not interrupted by consciousness and by the sudden starts and stoppages due to fear and tremor and mental uneasiness. Undoubtedly the lesson of this method of teaching is extremely important as an index of how stuttering may be relieved.

Regulation of Respiration.—A number of systems to correct stuttering depend on the regulation of breathing. It has been shown over and over again, and notably by Prof. Gutzman of Berlin, that one of the most important differences between stutterers and those who talk naturally is that the normal individual talks during expiration as may be seen in Fig. 23, while the stutterer begins at the end of inspiration or at least where normally on the respiratory curve expiration is just about to begin, but instead of permitting his diaphragm to go up as in ordinary expiration, the stutterer makes it sink lower and lower in a forced inspiration.

Fig. 23.—Normal Diaphragm Curve in Normal Breathing. Expiration as we Talk Normally.

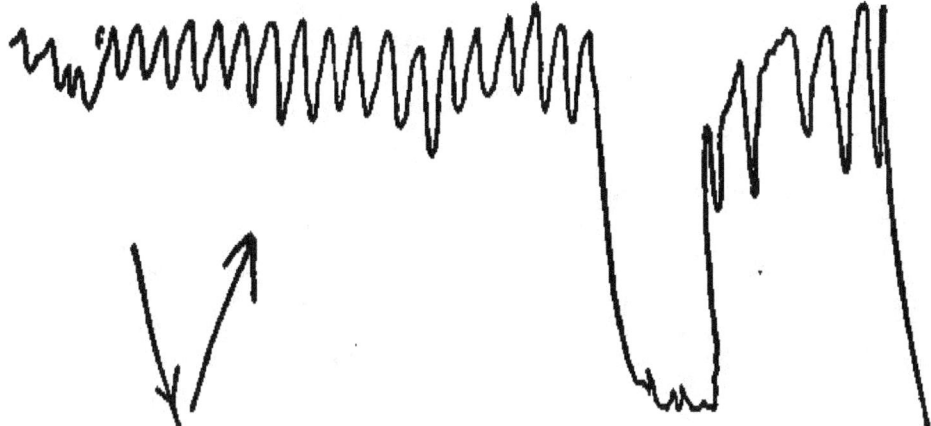

Fig. 24.—Curve in Diaphragm Before and During Talking by a Stutterer.

Attention to Something Besides Speech.—The attention must be centered on something besides speech itself. This is the important element in any method of treating stuttering. If it is allowed to occupy itself with that {578} nothing will save the individual from getting tangled in the efforts that he makes to co-ordinate the complex movements necessary, though if he would only allow them to proceed automatically, as do the rest of mankind, there would be no difficulty at all. Washington Irving, so ready with the pen, could not utter two successive sentences at a banquet without having to sit down, with expression absolutely inhibited from excitement. Expression, thought, utterance—all may be inhibited by overconscious attention, which may also disturb all other complex activities.

The most interesting methods of treatment for stuttering are those which involve the use of various hindrances to speech and which would seem to be least likely to make it possible for a person already laboring under speech difficulties to talk with more ease. The secret is, of course, that the added impediments so distract the attention of the patient that he is unconscious of the co-ordination necessary for speech and so accomplishes it without difficulty. It is because of over-attention to himself that the disturbance occurs. These methods developed very early in history. We all know the tradition of Demosthenes overcoming his impediment by placing pebbles in his mouth. One of the most earnest advocates of a similar method, who had himself suffered very seriously from stuttering was the Rev. Charles Kingsley, one of the most distinguished of English literary men. He cured himself, or at least greatly relieved his symptoms, by keeping a cork fast between his back teeth.

There have been many other curious suggestions for the cure of stuttering. What was known as the American method had great vogue in the early part of the nineteenth century. It was probably invented by Yeats of New York, though it came to be known as the Leigh method. Yeats, himself a physician, seemed to fear that he might fall into professional disrepute if he advertised the method in any way, so he had his daughter's governess, a Mrs. Leigh, open an institute for the cure of stuttering in which this method was practiced and it proved to be very successful. The entire secret of it was to have the patient raise the tip of the tongue to the palate and hold it there while speaking.

Another mode of treatment that attracted considerable attention consisted mainly of just exactly the opposite maneuver, that is, keeping the tongue as far as possible firmly placed on the floor of the mouth during speech. It is evident that neither of these suggestions does anything more than occupy the patient's attention with an additional activity, so that his speech function may be allowed to proceed automatically of itself, as it will if not disturbed by attention to it and by conscious attempts to regulate the various activities of it. Instruments were invented to help the patients to secure various positions of the tongue. Itard, for instance, during the second decade of the nineteenth century invented a golden or ivory fork to be placed beneath the tongue, so as to support it.

After the various methods of managing the tongue, the most popular curative maneuver has been that of regulating the breathing. During the nineteenth century there were at least a dozen different methods, all of which had a number of reported successes, of treating stuttering by means of breathing exercises.

Very simple methods of diverting the attention from speech are quite {579} sufficient in many cases to bring improvement. For instance, the insertion of extra letters that are themselves easy to say between words or preceding consonants that are hard to utter has been a favorite method among the specialists in stuttering. Johann Müller, as I said, suggested an e. Others have suggested an n. Occasionally stutterers themselves form the habit of using an m or a to and find that it aids their facility in uttering difficult sounds over which they would otherwise halt and stutter. A combination of these methods, as, for instance, an e between all words and the placing of an easy n before the most difficult sounds, has been repeatedly revived as an infallible method of treatment.

All this serves to show that in patients whose functions are being interfered with by over-attention diversion of mind must be the main remedy. If this can be secured, the function they are disturbing will be allowed to proceed unhampered. What will prove effective for one patient will fail with another, however. After the patient gets used to a particular form of diversion another must be tried. Simple methods are sometimes sufficient to secure good results. The one thing is not to be discouraged and to proceed from one effort to another, satisfied even if relief is obtained for a while, for after relapse another method of treatment may always be tried.

Suggestion for Stuttering.—There are many systems to train people out of the spasmodic inco-ordination that constitutes stuttering. All of these systems have their successes, but, as is well known, all of them have their failures. When the patient has confidence in the teacher and his method there is practically always quite a remarkable improvement, at the beginning. This improvement is more noticeable during the first month than at any other time. Not infrequently after this there is a tendency for patients to drop back into old habits, apparently discouraged, as a consequence of loss of confidence. It is the mental element that means more than anything else. It is the old, old story that we have to repeat with regard to every chronic ailment.

Distraction of Mind.—Each inventor is sure that his method is the best and his "cured cases" support his claim. Others who try his method, however, never succeed as well as he does and those who are interested invent methods of their own. I have on my desk, as I write, six different, infallible—to their authors—methods of treating stuttering. I am sure that none of them succeed absolutely, that is, none of them will cure every case and most of them will not succeed beyond a moderate degree, except where the enthusiasm and the confidence of the inventor or an immediate disciple of his is behind them to make them efficient. There are all sorts of elements in these cures, but most of them depend on their power to distract the patient from his over-attention to himself and what he is doing when he talks, so as to permit without hindrance the automatic movements which are so necessary for the complex function we call speech. Those who have spent most time in treating stutterers confess that the effect produced upon the patient's mind is an extremely important part of the treatment and that, if this cannot be secured, failure is almost certain. If the patient has no confidence that he can be cured and by this particular method, failure is inevitable from the very beginning and just as soon as a patient loses confidence improvement ceases.

{580}

CHAPTER V

TREMORS

Two types of tremors come to us for treatment: those that are quite involuntary and occur when muscles are at rest, and those that are associated with voluntary movements. The most common type of involuntary tremor is that seen in paralysis agitans to which a special chapter is devoted. After this, though coming for treatment much less frequently, is senile tremor which may, however, also be increased by voluntary movement. The tremors associated with voluntary movements are spoken of as intentional tremors. They may occur as the result of organic disease of the nervous system and the most characteristic type is that seen in multiple sclerosis. They are more frequent, however, with functional diseases of the nervous system and with emotional disturbances of various kinds. They are especially frequent as the result of dreads. Usually the idea of tremor is associated only with the head and the hands. Tremors may occur in other parts of the body, however, and tremors of the legs are particularly important. A familiar type is the tremor and unsteadiness of the legs which occur as a consequence of the dread of heights when a person unused to such situation attempts to walk across a narrow path a great distance above the ground.

Senile Tremor.—The most common of the involuntary tremors is that associated with old age. It develops in practically all very old people, but it comes to some who are comparatively young. Its occurrence at the age of fifty-five usually gives the sufferer a severe shock which is emphasized by the attitude of mind of friends toward the affection. They seem to be always sure that it is the index of rapidly advancing age and that it is practically a signal of approaching dissolution. As a matter of fact, when unassociated with gross pathological lesions, the senile tremor has no such significance. When associated with definite lesions it is the prognosis of the special condition and not any supposed significance of this particular symptom of tremor that expresses the genuine outlook in the case. Many people who live to a very old age develop tremor before they are threescore. Most of those who live to be eighty or more have some tremor that develops about or just after the age of seventy.

Significance.—Senile tremor is supposed to be due to, and in most cases probably is the result of, an overgrowth of connective tissue in the central nervous system which disturbs the ordinary conduction of nerve impulses, rendering them wavering and uncertain. This seems to indicate that it will not be long before the advancement of this sclerotic process will make serious inroads on the vigor of the individual. As a matter of repeated observation, however, the ordinary involuntary tremor of old people may last twenty years.

Reassurance.—The main principle in the treatment of tremors of the old is to make the patients realize that the symptom has no such bad prognosis as is usually attributed to it. Of course, they will find this out for themselves after a few years, but what they need is assurance at the beginning lest during the period of depression consequent upon the conclusion that the end is not far {581} off, which seems to be forced on them by their fears and the foolish sympathy of friends, their resistive vitality should be so lowered as to permit the invasion of some serious disease. In spite of apprehensions on the part of themselves and friends, tremor is rather a good sign than a bad one. It indicates the formation of connective tissue in the central nervous system, but this is always a slow process and is usually quite benign. As a matter of fact, most sclerotic processes are so chronic as to be compensatory in their action for many other degenerations. Those in whom tremor develops early often seem to be better protected against rupture of cerebral arteries, as if the growth of connective tissue was a conservative process here also. Information of this kind helps patients not to borrow trouble because of their condition.

Intention Tremors.—The tremors that occur in association with voluntary movements are often very troublesome and may be difficult to manage. The worst cases are entirely functional. They are typical neuroses and often develop as a consequence of some serious crisis through which the nervous system has passed. In older people they sometimes pass over into paralysis agitans or a close simulant of that affection. The incident of the Texas sheriff and the Indian related in the chapter on Paralysis Agitans illustrates how these tremors may be induced.

Tremors from Fright.—Frequently the tremors have no direct connection with any action, though they may be the result of fright. A little girl bitten by a dog and much shocked may, for some time afterwards, be quite unable to stand when she sees a dog on the street, so disturbing is the tremor that comes over her. Tremors of the same kind have been connected with horses after the patient had been run down in the street, and, in one case that I saw even when the patient was only thrown out of a carriage during a runaway. Occasionally fright by a burglar may cause a distinct tremulousness that supervenes whenever the patient thereafter is wakened suddenly at night.

Influence of Dread.—Tremors of all kinds can be made worse by the dread of them. In the chapter on Dreads we discuss the disturbance of function by dreads and especially the tendency to exaggeration of pathological conditions of any kind when the patient's mind becomes concentrated on it. Steadiness in any position is due to a nice balancing of extensor and flexor muscles requiring the sending down of a continuous stream of impulses. The equilibrium is attained and maintained in spite of the fact that, as a rule, the flexor muscles are stronger than the extensors and better situated to exert their mechanical force. If anything happens to disturb this balance even to a slight degree, the mind becomes attracted to it and there is a corresponding result as in stuttering, or other complex function when surveillance is too great. It is important to remember this at the beginning of all cases of tremor, for the patient nearly always exaggerates his tremor by attention to it and can be made so much better by reassurance and diversion of mind that he is much encouraged and his general health usually improves, making him feel, even though his affection is organic, that he is being cured.

Tremors may occur in connection with almost any set of actions requiring special co-ordination of muscles, but they are especially likely to occur when a feeling of dread disturbs the control over muscles. A typical example of this is noted in shaving. There are many men who cannot shave without trembling so as to cut themselves. The feeling that they have a sharp instrument in their {582} hand with which they may cut themselves sets up the tremor. There are others who cannot shave because they dread that while using the instrument over the important organs of the neck, and especially the blood vessels, they may be tempted to cut their throats. This is, of course, purely a dread and not a tremor. Some men find both the dread and the tremor much worse at times when they are tired and worried, and can shave very well at other times. Some men can shave very well when they are not under observation, but if anyone is looking at them they tremble and cut themselves. The safety razor usually does away with these troubles, large or small, but if it should happen that by particularly inexpert use they cut themselves even with a safety razor, especially in the throat region, the old dread and tremor reassert themselves and shaving becomes almost as difficult as before.

Self-consciousness.—Almost any position or action in which a man feels himself under observation may cause one of these tremors. As a consequence this particular set of actions may become the source of so much discomfort as to produce an intense sense of fatigue. It may, indeed, become quite impossible of accomplishment. Some teachers cannot do demonstrating work on a blackboard before a large unfamiliar class, at least not without serious efforts to control themselves, though they may be facile demonstrators before a small class. I have known men, however, who practically could not do blackboard work at all because of nervousness. Their writing went all askew and very often their thoughts would not follow one another in such order as to make demonstrations possible. Sometimes they were good talkers, so long as they did not turn their backs to the class and feel the eyes of all on them. The same thing is true of such religious services as Mass in the Catholic Church, where some of the clergymen have this feeling. I know of priests who have not said Mass publicly for years and others who can only say it in a small chapel before a few people because of the intense discomfort of the fatigue caused by this state of mind.

Stage Fright.—It is not alone the hands and the arms that tremors are likely to affect, for they may also occur in the legs. A typical and familiar case is the tremor that occurs upon the first appearance before large audiences of orators or actors or clergymen. Owing to excitement, they are unable to make flexor and extensor muscles exactly balance each other and the consequence is a tremulous movement that may be complicated by some swaying. Some people never lose this in spite of long experience in public appearance. Young people

313

may have it upon being introduced to persons of whom they think a great deal. This passes off with years, as a rule, but in some it persists, and any excitement causes tremor of the legs and swaying movements. The effort to control this is often severe and causes intense fatigue.

Any set of movements requiring even slight co-ordination of muscles may be the subject of disturbance by a tremor. Since the writing of the book on Pastoral Medicine, a text-book of medical information meant to be of assistance to clergymen, I have had some rather interesting tremors associated with the performance of clerical duties brought to my attention. One of these is a trembling of the legs which makes standing at a high altar almost impossible. Another troublesome tremor is that associated with the giving of communion. {583} Most priests find no difficulty in the performance of the rite. Some of them are much worried and anxious about it, however, and develop a slight tremor. Others become so nervous in performing the ceremony that they cannot succeed in placing the Host on the tongue of the communicant without certain false movements. These may cause them to touch the lips or the cheeks of the recipient and after this has happened a few times the giving of communion becomes practically impossible for them. Occasionally the men thus affected have no other nervous symptoms and often they are very intelligent, strong-minded men.

The General Health.—Tremor patients always complain more of this symptom when they are in a run-down condition. One of them is a wealthy merchant who, when he can be persuaded to take a vacation, comes back with nearly all the manifestations of his tremor latent or, at least, well under control. Another is a broker who at the end of a long winter of excitement and worry is at his worst, but who after a vacation in the North Woods is quite well again. Slight symptoms of this kind are not unusual in teachers, especially women, though I have seen them also in men, and are much more complained of at the end of the year when the individuals are in poorer general condition than at any other time. The symptom itself is annoying because of the notice that it attracts, but their dread that it may have some serious significance, indicating the development of a progressive lesion of the central nervous system, constitutes the worst part of their ailment. When the intentional tremor is intermittent and occurs only at times of excitement, or when the patients are under observation, they can be reassured that it is merely neurotic and that no ulterior development is to be anticipated.

Treatment.—The treatment of these conditions consists first in bringing the patient's health up to its normal condition as far as that is possible. Many of the sufferers from tremors are under weight. Whenever they are, a definite, determined effort must be made to bring them up to it. This must be done even though they insist that they have never been heavier and that to be rather underweight is a family trait. In many cases it will be found that this family trait, instead of being due to some inevitable hereditary tendency, is only the result of family habits in the matter of eating. Many of these people do not eat substantial breakfasts. Their tremor, too, is likely to be worse in the early morning than at any other time during the day, unless, of course, they have become overtired during the day, when the tremor will reassert itself with vigor. Most of them are much less disturbed in the afternoon than before. The drug treatment of the affection consists mainly in the use of nux vomica, but, not in the small doses of five or ten drops so often employed, but, according to the size of the individual, beginning with fifteen or twenty minims, thirty or forty drops, and gradually increased to physiological tolerance, when the dose should be set somewhat below that.

Mental Control.—The main treatment must consist, however, in enabling the patient to secure psychic control over himself and his muscles. This is not an easy matter. Most of them are quite discouraged, but their attitude of mind must be changed and the real significance of their affection made clear to them. As a rule, they have either heard or read or been told by a physician that their intentional tremor is significant of a serious pathological lesion of the central nervous system. Some of them have heard of multiple sclerosis {584} and are much disturbed. They must be reassured and it must be made clear to them that their disease is really due to over-consciousness and consequent lack of control. A good deal of reassurance can be given by telling them of patients who suffer from ailments not unlike theirs, showing how multiform the affection is. A man who has trouble with his signature may be told about the man who finds it difficult to drink when under observation, then, as a rule, he will better realize the neurotic character of his affection. With hysterical women this method must be used with care or the story of another patient will act as a suggestion and the physician will subsequently be treated to an exhibition of the symptoms which he has described.

Self-Discipline.—Persistent quiet discipline is the one thing that eventually does any good. When patients are first told of this and are persuaded to attempt it, they make such a determined effort to overcome the affection that they make themselves more conscious of it than before with the result that their tremor and spasmodic movements are emphasized. It is the old story of the man trying to stand so straight that he falls backwards. It must be made clear to them that discipline, to be of any value, must be carried out as much as possible without consciousness of it and with all available artificial aids. The man who has trouble with his signature may be shown that he can overcome much of the tendency to tremor and spasm of the forearm muscles that are at the root of his difficulty by sitting at a higher chair, so that his arm swings free of the table and so that, in Gowers' phrase, if a pen were attached to his elbow it would write the same thing as the pen in his hand. The man who trembles as he drinks may be taught for a time to raise a cup to his lips while resting his elbow on the table and bringing his head well down. Nearly always methods of performing particular actions that require less effort can be found, until the habit of over-consciousness and loss of control is overcome.

Hypnotism and Waking Suggestion.—Occasionally hypnotism is effective in these cases, but there is likely to be a relapse unless there is some discipline before and after its use. Suggestion in the waking state is often very effective. Patients need to be talked to and even though intelligent they need to be reminded at regular intervals for some time that their ailment is merely functional and not organic. Nearly always it will be found that they trace its beginning to some pathological event: occasionally there has been a severe accident, but sometimes only a slight accident seems to them a sufficient explanation. Sometimes it follows an attack of pneumonia, oftener still typhoid fever. In these cases the patients become convinced that this is one of the marks left after the accident or disease and so it is rather hard to persuade them that they can be cured. All such impressions, which act as auto-suggestions for the continuance of their tremor and lack of control, must be combated, otherwise there is very little hope of improvement. The preceding disease is not the direct cause, though the weakness consequent upon it may predispose to the tremor. Overhaste in attempting to resume their occupations before their strength has returned is often the real cause. It is the patient's mind more than his body that needs to be set in order, but this will not be possible unless the physical condition is normal and thorough reassurance can be given.

{585}

DISORDERS OF THE PSYCHE

SECTION XVII

PSYCHO-NEUROSES

CHAPTER I

PSYCHO-NEUROSES (HYSTERIA)

As the derivation of the name indicates, psycho-neuroses are functional nervous affections dependent on states of mind. They are not necessarily originated by the mind, though they may be. Their spontaneous occurrence as pure psychic phenomena, however, is rather rare. There is practically always some slight physical cause. This may be severe, for all diseases have neurotic accompaniments that disturb the nerves involved and exaggerate the original symptoms. In most cases the patient has no serious interest to divert his or her mind from this occupation with self, and as a consequence the particular feeling fills up the whole of consciousness, and as it is painful to begin with, the pain, following Cajal's law of avalanche, may become almost intolerable.

It is of primary importance to remember, however, that there is practically always a physical basis for these curiously interesting affections which are so difficult to treat and which have so often proved the despair of physicians. While the attitude of mind must be changed, the physical state itself must be corrected. These two things must be secured at the same time, however, for attention to the physical state without correction of mental attitude will usually only emphasize the condition by calling further attention to the symptoms. This is especially true of local treatment. The mind must, above all, be treated and diversion of attention secured. Psycho-neuroses may occur in connection with sensory or motor nerves. The patient may either complain of intense pain in some part of the body for which there is but a very slight basis, or may be unable to move certain muscles, or there may be a combination of sensory and motor symptoms with complaint of pain on movement. The painful conditions are most important because they prove a source of worry and anxiety to the patient's friends, as well as often of such annoyance at unsuitable hours as deprives those near them of rest to a degree that may undermine health.

{586}

FORMS OF NEUROTIC SIMULATION

Every possible painful condition is simulated by these psycho-neurotic conditions. They occur probably with more frequency in the abdomen than elsewhere; they may be thought to be colicky in nature and, as a rule, some accumulation of gas will be found. This gas is sometimes swallowed air and sometimes gaseous products that have been diffused apparently from the blood in the intestinal walls. This always produces discomfort but nothing like the discomfort that the patient complains of. The condition if treated by carminatives will nearly always be emphasized rather than relieved. Local treatment by heat will help oftener, but may exacerbate it. When chronic constipation is present, calomel in divided doses is suggestive as well as medicinal.

There may be gastric crises that recall those of tabes, and there may be vesical and rectal crises of a similar nature. I have seen a patient complain of every symptom of stone in the kidney. At the beginning the pains were vague, but after she had been to several physicians and had been asked certain questions intended to elicit pathognomonic signs of stone these questions were answered in the affirmative. Her attacks became strikingly like renal colic. After a consultation, at which two physicians and a surgeon were present, she was operated upon for stone in the left kidney. No trace of it was found. But after this she was well nearly a year. Then she had another crisis of pain in the early morning hours, a time when her painful condition always came on, apparently because it attracted more attention and caused more

315

disturbance at this time, and now all the symptoms pointed to the right kidney. She was treated on the principle that it was a neurosis, was made to gain some fifteen pounds in weight, has since then had no attacks, has not passed any stones, and there seems no doubt but that the whole case was merely neurotic. During her attacks instead of having suppression of urine, she had a free flow of urine and no blood. It is not unlikely that the physical basis of the attacks was that condition of the kidney which allows urine to flow through very freely during neurotic conditions and which somehow got into the sphere of her consciousness and being over-attended to became extremely painful.

Secretory Neuroses.—Lying between the pain and motor neuroses and dependent on psychic elements to some extent at least, there is a series of neuroses that have as their principal symptoms an increase or decrease of secretion. Occasionally, of course, they are complicated by motor neuroses, especially in connection with the viscera. There are various stomach affections, represented by an increase or decrease in stomach secretion, and accompanied by pain, discomfort, and decrease or increase of peristalsis. There are biliary neuroses accompanied by increase or inhibition of biliary secretions. There are gastric neuroses associated with vomiting, often very intractable, in which there seems to be sometimes a hypersecretion of gastric juice and sometimes a lessened secretion. All of these occur, as is said, spontaneously, but there will usually be found a history of some exhaustive work or worry during the weeks or months just before. Apparently nervous control is lost and then the secretory neurosis manifests itself sometimes in conjunction with painful or motor affections.

Neurotic Vomiting.—Persistent vomiting occurs in these cases but is not {587} so serious as it seems and patients do not lose weight, as might be expected. There is sometimes even a probability that some of the food ingested finds its way through the pylorus and is used for nutrition, though the vomiting may come on not long after ingestion. Practically always nature asserts herself and stops the vomiting when serious conditions seem about to develop. The solicitude of relatives may be calmed by this assurance, and just as soon, as a rule, as they show less anxiety about the patient, the first symptoms of improvement will be noted. The fasting girls exploited in the newspapers, in connection with these neurotic conditions are often frauds and investigation has shown on a number of occasions that they were obtaining food surreptitiously. It must not be forgotten, however, that, even though these cases have been discredited, we have a number of cases on record of men and women who have taken absolutely nothing nutritious and only water for from ten to forty or even fifty days. Until at least ten days have passed in one of these gastric neuroses, then, there is no need for urgent solicitude, and this of itself, when properly explained, makes an excellent favorable suggestion for these patients, and, above all, for their friends.

Simulant Appendicitis.—Some of these abdominal psycho-neuroses may simulate serious pathological conditions that, in recent years, have come to be looked upon as surgical. I have seen a number of cases, especially in women who have been constipated for some time, in which there was considerable discomfort in the right lower abdominal segment and occasionally surgeons thought that an operation should be performed. Usually in these cases there is no localized tenderness and no mass of any kind to be felt in this region. Sometimes tenderness is complained of, though when the patient's attention is diverted even deep pressure may be made without their wincing. Whenever there is no history of an acute attack, no temperature and no increase in pulse rate, unless there are very definitely localized symptoms, the question of operation is always to be answered in the negative. Disturbances of the pulse may mean little. The history must guide. I have seen these cases operated on, improved for a while, but relapse afterwards just as soon as there was a resumption of their constipation. As a rule, when the appendix has been removed, either because its function has something to do with the inhibition of putrefactive processes in the lower bowel, or because as the result of the operation and consequent adhesions, the colon was not so active in its peristalsis, the constipation seemed to be worse than before, unless special care was exercised. If there is relapse after an operation the patients' attacks are almost sure to be more frequent than before and their discomfort likely to be more pronounced.

Lest it be thought that such cases are mainly confined to women or that the most striking cases occur only in women, I may say that the most interesting case of this kind I ever saw was in a young, vigorous German soldier. He was admitted to Koenig's clinic in Berlin with a story of abdominal tenderness and pain, the tenderness being located in the right iliac region. There seemed even to be some distention of the abdomen after a time and the development of greatly increased diffuse tenderness. The pulse was considerably disturbed, but there was only a slight rise in temperature, and for a time it was thought that this might be a case of appendicitis without fever. A surprising feature of the case was the presence in the right iliac region of {588} a scar which, on careful investigation, proved to be double. Apparently the patient had been opened twice before in this region. His history was carefully investigated. He had had a fall from a horse about two years before and afterwards had considerable abdominal discomfort. He was quite sure that something serious had happened within his abdominal cavity as the result of the fall and his attention was concentrated on his right iliac region. At the time of the accident his symptoms were considered to be a psycho-neurosis or perhaps an exaggeration of symptoms with malingering tendencies.

Shortly after his term of service expired, however, some acute symptoms developed and there was swelling, or at least tympanitic distention of the abdomen with disturbance of the pulse, and he was operated on in the hospital and his appendix removed. There proved to be nothing the matter with it and no pathological condition was found within his abdomen. He seemed to recover completely. After six months he was admitted to another hospital with the same symptoms. He seemed to have the habit of swallowing air which found its way beyond his pylorus, or else gas leaked from the blood vessels in the walls of his intestines, producing a symptom-complex not unlike the tympanitic distention consequent upon general peritonitis. Once more this was taken to mean very probably a ruptured appendix and another operation was done. This operator went through the old scar, but to his surprise found no appendix and found everything within the abdomen normal. The third time the patient came to Koenig's clinic and, owing to his military record, his hospital experience was available and a third operation was not done. Instead, according to the story current at the time, the patient was tattooed with the legend "no appendix here." The case is interesting as an example of the extent to which an abdominal psycho-neurosis may simulate a ruptured appendix.

Pseudo Biliary Colic.—A similar state of affairs to that with regard to the appendix has developed in all that concerns the gall bladder and the biliary tract generally. Any complaint of discomfort in the right upper quadrant of the abdomen, if persisted in, is almost sure sooner or later to be diagnosed as due to a calculus. Now that operations for gallstones are more common than they used to be, it is probable that almost as many gall bladders are found without pathological conditions as appendices without justifiably operative lesions. In treating individuals who have a history of recurrent symptoms of intestinal reaction to various foods complicated by urticaria, it is important to remember that there may probably be lesions corresponding to those in the skin in portions of the intestinal tract which may functionally involve either the appendix or the biliary passages. Some of these cases are extremely difficult to handle because often there is pain, definite tenderness and some fever with the attacks, and very localized symptoms. The history, however, will be helpful. Operation will not relieve the patient from liability to recurrence. There are, however, other cases where the discomfort is much more vague, where there is no tenderness, no disturbance after jolting rides and where there has never been any severe pain. These should not be set down as biliary calculi without further developments. The possibility of a stone being present should not be hinted to the patient until some definite pathognomonic sign is discovered.

Other Simulated Conditions.—There are many painful conditions of the {589} head that are psycho-neurotic. Many forms of headache are due to sensations of pressure or tension or constriction, usually in the external integuments of the skull, which are dwelt on and then become painful achy conditions. This is particularly true of so-called headaches in the back of the head. As we emphasize in the chapter on Headache, probably most of the headaches of patients who have not much to occupy themselves with, are due rather to queer feelings in the head emphasized by the concentration of attention on them than to real pains. Earache may occur in the same way. Nearly always when one has been out in the wind, there is likely to be an uncomfortable sensation in the ear. By attention to it this may readily be exaggerated into an earache. Occasionally the physical basis of an ache in the region of the ear seems to be an unconscious performance of Valsalva's experiment while blowing the nose when catarrhal conditions are present.

All sorts of painful conditions of the arms and legs may develop in the same way. Unusual tiredness, or some special exertion of the muscles, may produce a sense of fatigue readily exaggerated by attention to it, into severe pain. This condition is not a voluntary simulation, but is due to lack of diversion and a certain inborn tendency in these people to pay attention to anything that is the matter with them. Very seldom does the physical condition need much treatment, though nearly always something can be done for it with advantage, but the mental state needs alteration and, above all, the patient needs to be diverted from over-concentration of mind.

Motor Neuroses.—As has been said, beside painful conditions, various forms of motor trouble may develop. These usually consist of inability to move certain groups of muscles. They have sometimes been spoken of as hysterical palsies or paralyses. The word hysterical, by its derivation connected with the Greek word for womb, apparently indicates that these conditions are limited to women. It is well known now that they are extremely common among men and especially among young men and have absolutely nothing to do with the genital system. As with painful psycho-neurotic conditions, there is practically always a physical basis. This sometimes requires careful questioning to locate exactly. There is some injury of the muscles of a particular region, or some over-use of them, or some employment of them under bad mechanical conditions with over-fatigue, and then attention to this leads to incapacity to use the muscles or inability to co-ordinate them properly.

Neurotic palsies, to use a term that carries much less unfavorable suggestion with it than the word paralysis or the word hysterical, may occur in any limb or group of muscles. They may occur in the legs with the production of complete paraplegia. One well-known form, astasia-abasia, inability to stand or to walk, affects the muscles of the trunk as well as of the lower limbs. These conditions often remain for long periods in spite of treatment, frequently recur, are often called by all sorts of names and continue to be a source of annoyance to the patient, until a definite successful effort is made to change the patient's mental state to one of less attention to the particular part.

There is, it seems to me, an unfortunate tendency to think that our observations upon these cases are comparatively recent. Sir Benjamin Brodie, nearly a century ago, insisted that at least four-fifths of the female patients among the higher classes of society supposed to suffer from diseased joints were really sufferers from neurotic conditions, or, as they called them then, {590} hysteria. Sir James Paget, in his Clinical Lectures and Essays, thinks that Brodie has exaggerated the proportion, for in his own practice, though, of course, he includes his hospital cases and the poor as well as the rich, he found less than one-fifth suffering from neurotic joints. The hip and the knee, which are the most frequent seats of genuine pathological conditions, are also most frequently the subject of neuroses. Next in order, but much more rarely, the metatarsal and metacarpal joints are affected and then the elbow and shoulder. In Sir James Paget's chapter on Nervous Mimicry or Neuro-Mimesis, he cites a number of cases which show how clearly psycho-neurotic affections were recognized in his time. He tells the story of a young man who had been overworking for examinations and who "after a three-hours' mathematical cram, fainted and when he rallied set up a very close mimicry of paraplegia which lasted many weeks." He insists that "such mimicry is found not only or chiefly in the silly selfish girls among whom it is commonly supposed that hysteria is rife, but even among the wise and accomplished, both men and women."

DIFFERENTIAL DIAGNOSIS

For the differential diagnosis of psycho-neuroses from definite organic conditions, the most important element is the patient's previous history and a knowledge of the condition of the nervous system. Where this is known the diagnosis is comparatively easy, but when the patient is seen for the first time it may often be extremely difficult. It is, above all, important not to jump to conclusions, for every nervous specialist knows of cases in which the diagnosis was considered to be surely a neurosis, yet a fatal termination showed that a serious organic condition was at work. It must not be forgotten either that neurotic patients may develop serious organic disease in the midst of their neurotic symptoms and care must be taken not to miss the significance of special symptoms. When the patient is not well known, the

317

presence of certain stigmata, as they have been called, enable the physician to recognize the probability that a neurotic condition is present. Patients who are subject to neuroses are likely to have certain areas of the skin surface and of the palpable mucous membranes more or less sensitive than normal. There are likely to be spots of hyperesthesia or hypesthesia or even complete anesthesia somewhere on the skin. These should be carefully looked for and in serious cases an examination of the whole skin surface should be made. Not infrequently anesthesia or a decided lack of sensitiveness to irritation will be found in the throat or in the nose. Occasionally the conjunctiva is much less sensitive than usual.

These used to be called hysterical stigmata. The word hysteria carries an innuendo of imaginativeness or occasionally of affection of the sexual organs that is unfortunate. It would be better, therefore, not to use the term in any way. The presence of these areas of hyperesthesia, hypesthesia and anesthesia indicates that association fibers are abnormally connected in the brain for the moment at least, and that as a consequence there is over-attention to certain portions of the body with lack of ordinary attention to others. This will account very readily for the occurrence of painful conditions in certain cases and palsies in others. When over-attention is paid, there may be a {591} hyperesthesia corresponding to that seen in the skin in any organ of the body. When, for any reason, there is a disturbance in a particular part, there may be a lack of motility due to nervous influences, just as there is a lack of sensation. In all of these cases the one essential element is to correct the nervous state through the mind as far as possible. Experience has shown that this can be done in nearly all cases. It must be the principal effort of the physician.

TREATMENT

Strong Mental Impression.—In the treatment of these affections two periods are to be considered, one during, the other after the attacks. During the attack a strong impression must be made upon the patient's mind so as to divert the concentrated attention. We have well authenticated stories of the various expedients resorted to by physicians who were confident of their diagnosis in order to secure such a strong mental impression. I once knew an old physician who was summoned to a childless wife whose adoring husband was in manifest agonies of solicitude over her and whose mother and mother-in-law had been caring for her for days with all anxiety, walk into the room of the patient, take one of her hands in his, slap her on the cheek, tell her to get up and walk and she would have no more of that supposed inability to walk which had caused the family so much anxiety. He succeeded. It can be imagined what would have happened had he not succeeded. We know of cases where an alarm of fire or a burglar scare or some sudden emotion has produced a like result. We cannot prescribe these things, however, and at the most, after one or two successes in a particular patient, they would fail.

The only thing that we can do as a routine practice is to relieve by direct treatment the slight physical condition that is usually present and then try and influence the patient's mind. If a thorough examination is made in the course of which the physician is able to show the patient that he understands the condition and that he can demonstrate for himself and them that there is nothing serious the matter with important organs, he can make them feel that their pain or disability is entirely due to concentration of attention on a particular nerve or set of nerves. With many patients this will succeed, not at once, but after two or three seances of positive suggestion, even in the waking state. If the patients are bothering their relatives very much it may be necessary to give some opium as an adjuvant. As a rule, the needle had better not be used, but a suppository given. This is not nearly so attractive to the patient's mind as the use of the needle and is not likely to be called for so often. Every physician has had the experience that after giving opium two or three times, either per rectum or hypodermically, almost anything can be given, provided the patient is persuaded that the drug is being given again. A reasonably large dose may be used the first time, but certainly after the second or third time a much smaller dose will produce the same effect and often a simple gluten suppository, provided it looks like the other, will work just as well as an opium suppository.

After Treatment.—The after treatment of these cases is directed mainly to such alterations of the mental attitude and physical condition as shall prevent {592} recurrences. The general condition of the patient must be improved in every case where there is indication for this. Many of these patients are under weight for their height. They must put on weight. Weir Mitchell's success with the "rest cure" consisted to a great extent in his power to cause these patients to put on weight. This supplies reserve energy, but, above all, replaces discouragement by hope and buoyancy. Gain in weight can be accomplished mainly by two methods. First, by seeing that the patient gets an abundance of air and, secondly, by dictating how much shall be eaten. In this matter details are important and it may be necessary to suggest the actual diet for each meal. This must be liberal and must consist of simple but particularly nutritious materials. Patients' dislikes need not be taken into much account, their likes are often helpful. When there is insistence on lack of appetite and decided objection to chewing, eggs and milk should be given in increasing quantities, until five or six eggs and some twelve glasses of milk are taken every day. Besides this, a good portion of meat should be eaten at one meal with some vegetables. By firm insistence, day after day, it will not be hard to get patients whose appetites are seriously inhibited to take this amount of food. To secure this, a good, firm, sensible nurse is invaluable. Appetite, as we have emphasized in the chapter on Appetite, is largely a matter of will, and anything that is eaten, provided it stays down, will do good unless there is organic disease.

A certain amount of exercise is important in these cases, but not nearly so important as an abundance of fresh air. Patients must not be allowed to overtire themselves. Riding in an open carriage or on the top of a bus, especially where there are distracting scenes and many human interests, is particularly beneficial. Automobiling is often likely to be more tiresome than is good for these patients when they are run down, though it is one of the best of therapeutic measures for those who are physically capable, that is, up to weight, even though they may complain of feeling weak.

Diversion of Mind.—It is in these cases particularly that diversion of mind is of prime importance. Many of these patients have either no serious interest or at most certain interests with which they may occupy themselves if they wish, but that are not engrossing and attention to which may be put off whenever they care to. Duties that are inevitable and that call for the occupation of so much time that the patient has little opportunity to think of herself are often the salvation of these patients. As I mention in the chapters on Occupation and Diversion of Mind, I have seen a number of cases and I am sure that every physician of reasonable large experience has seen similar cases, where women, particularly, who in the midst of prosperity have been constantly suffering from some form of psycho-neurosis, great or small, have, after some sudden turn of fortune, been completely relieved from their nervous symptoms by having to devote themselves seriously to some occupation for a livelihood.

Occupation, particularly with children, with the weak and the ailing, with the poor and those who are unable to help themselves, is specially likely to be helpful to such patients when they are women. Such interests affect them deeply and by the sympathy they arouse through contact with real physical suffering, they prevent over-attention to themselves. I have seen the care of a cancer patient, and especially of a relative affected by cancer, do more for {593} a psycho-neurotic sufferer than all that doctors had been able to accomplish in years. It is often difficult to find occupation and diversion of mind for these patients, but this is the therapeutic problem the physician must solve if he is going to secure relief from present conditions and prophylaxis against further attacks.

Oldtime Cures.—Many of the remedies for obscure abdominal conditions show how well the real character of the affection was duly recognized and appreciated in the past. It is in these cases particularly that the pillulae micarumpanis, the bread pills, of the olden times, were so commonly used with good effect. We have quoted examples in other chapters. Many of the drugs that are employed with reported success for these affections have a strong suggestive element in them. Valerian probably is a good tonic and yet there is no doubt that the suggestive quality of its nauseating smell and the almost inevitable eructations that occur after to emphasize it, are helpful in curing certain internal psycho-neuroses. Another drug that has been much used in the same way is asafetida, whose disgusting taste and odor have been excellent auxiliaries. Fresh pills of quinine and red pepper uncoated and therefore producing definite effects on the taste before swallowing and on the mucous membrane of the stomach after swallowing, often prove the best remedy for persistent vomiting or for enduring nausea. A drop of nux vomica, taken every half hour with the definite warning that the patient must by no means take more, and that the bottle must be carefully protected lest anyone else should be poisoned, is often very efficient. These remedies have a slight physiological action and a large psychic action, but that exactly corresponds with the etiology of the affection for whose treatment they are employed.

Dominant Ideas.—During the attack it is often possible to find either from the patient or from friends that there is some dominant idea which is bringing about the mental short-circuiting that leads to the concentration of attention. From the oldest times it has been recognized that in young women a disappointment in love may prove to be the occasion for a psycho-neurotic or, as they used to call it, hysterical attack. This is, however, not a specific cause. It is the disappointment much more than the sex element in the case, as a rule, that produces the unfavorable effect. It was easy to conclude that the sex factor was extremely important in older times when women's sphere of activity was largely limited to the home, and marriage was the one legitimate object of their ambition. Now that we have had more experience with the business woman, we know that serious disappointments of any kind have a tendency to initiate psycho-neurotic conditions in susceptible and especially suggestive individuals. A failure to secure promotion in a store, or to secure some position that is eagerly sought for, a loss of money in business, etc., especially when they have been preceded by weeks or months of solicitude and worry over the event that now happens, may lead to the development of a psycho-neurosis.

This is particularly notable with regard to educational interests of various kinds. Young women readily overdo application to study, or, rather, anxiety over it, and as a result get into a state of mind in which a failure to pass an examination, or to secure promotion, or even the failure to win a prize, may give rise to a highly nervous condition in which tears and laughter come unbidden and in {594} which further developments may bring on a typical psycho-neurotic attack. All sorts of pains and aches and motor incapacities may occur in these states. The supreme occupation with the single idea present in their minds at all times, waking and sleeping, while they try to study, or when they read or even when they are supposed to be diverting themselves, finally precipitates a nervous explosion along nerves that have been irritated for some reason, though the pathological condition present may be quite insufficient of itself to explain the affection that ensues. These are the popular nervous breakdowns, not difficult to treat once their real character is diagnosed.

Sorrows of various kinds may produce a like effect. Worry or anxiety about the serious illness of a near relative, especially an inevitably fatal illness, such as cancer or tuberculosis or the disturbing mental affections, may have a similar result, but usually not in those who are occupied with the actual care of the patients. The mental states constitute the psychic elements underlying the neurotic condition that develops.

Almost needless to say, successful treatment must include a faithful attempt to lessen the significance of the mental state that is so important in the case. Usually the mere obtaining of the patient's confidence is enough to lessen greatly the irritation produced by the mental condition. A sorrow shared is halved. It is, above all, secretive individuals who become depressed over their sorrows. While the patient who insists on constantly sharing them with everyone becomes a nuisance, it is always a little dangerous not to have a confidant to whom worries and anxieties are entrusted. If they are kept to one's self they are nearly always exaggerated—they are seen out of proper perspective and have a much more depressing influence. Calm, judicious reasoning with the patient over the significance of the condition as presented, is often of great help.

Often these ideas, so potent for mental and bodily disturbance, are almost entirely unconscious or exist in the patient's subconsciousness and are recalled only under such special conditions as remove the bonds of the patient's occupation with himself or herself at the present time and allow memories to come back without interference. There are many curious stories of such cases. A child is frightened or very much disturbed by having a cat kill a favorite bird. The cat becomes a deterrent object. Gradually this deterrence grows. As a consequence, there may develop one of those intense dreads of cats which makes life miserable if near that animal. There may even be physical effects produced by the continued presence of a cat in the same room. Often in these cases the beginning of this mental attitude, or at least its occasion in the incident of the killing of the bird is forgotten, or at least not consciously referred to as an etiological element in the dread.

Patients have been known to develop states of mind which made them object to certain figures or names because of earlier associations with them that were unpleasant. There is the story of a man who would never take a car with an odd number though this was sometimes a source of annoyance and delay and who could not explain to himself or his physician how this objection had developed, until his memory was searched and it was found that, years before, he had witnessed the death of a child under the wheels of a car with an odd number. He had completely lost the sense of the direct influence of this, but it existed in subconscious memory and proved the source of much {595} annoyance to him, for if with a friend he were not able to avoid taking an odd numbered car he would feel quite miserable during the ride. Frights of various kinds may produce this same effect. I have in my notes the case of a man who is unable to sleep at night without a light in his room, because of a fright. Once while asleep in the dark, he awoke conscious that someone was in the room and sat up and demanded who was there. The answer was a revolver shot and a bullet, passing not far away from him, pierced the head of the bed. As he sank back the burglar leaped from the window and escaped. He realized that this was the cause of his fear of the dark, but lesser incidents might easily become subconscious yet continue their influence.

Psycho-Analysis.—In recent years Freud has suggested that in many puzzling cases of psycho-neurosis, where, so far as is known, there seems to be no dominant idea bringing about the concentration of attention, careful analysis of the patients' memories will bring out the fact that there is a subconscious idea as the underlying substratum of these affections. Freud has developed what is called the process of psycho-analysis in order to bring out these ideas which are sometimes exerting their influence unconsciously to the patient. The subconscious is one of the fads of the hour, so that Freud's announcement attracted much attention. Psycho-analysis, however, is not advanced so confidently even by its inventor as a positively curative measure, as it was at the beginning. It has been found that after the dominant idea in the subconsciousness has been found and neutralized with a consequent amelioration of the psycho-neurotic symptoms, there may be a relapse, when another dominant idea will have to be found, and that there seems to be the possibility, in some cases at least, of an almost endless succession of such ideas to account for further and further relapses.

Undoubtedly psycho-analysis has its place in psychotherapy and is of great value in certain cases. There is no doubt, however, in my mind that in most of these cases reported as cured after psycho-analytic methods had been employed, what really happened is that the patient's mind became diverted to another idea—that of marvelous cure through mind searching which relieved the previous concentration of mind underlying the psycho-neurosis. These are the cases that used to be cured by hypnotism. Before hypnotism was developed they were cured by mesmerism. Before mesmerism they were cured by magnets or by the Leyden jar, and during the past century they have been cured by electrical methods or by osteopathy or by Eddyism. Many of the cures were effected by stroking and touches, the use of Perkins' tractors, or Greatrakes' methods, or anything else that attracted attention very strongly. They were given a new idea which occupied them very much and so saved them from that preoccupation with themselves and their feelings and whatever slight ailment might be present that was the physical occasion for psycho-neurotic symptoms. This happened with psycho-analysis. When it was absolutely new and the operator had great confidence in it, this confidence was imparted to the patients, with the consequent cure or decided amelioration of their psycho-neurosis, just as that used to be brought about by our previous method of treating such cases by some strong suggestion.

As I emphasize in the chapter on Dreams, the examination of the dreams in order to get a hint of the dominant idea, is particularly interesting, because it represents a return to the oldest methods of suggestion of which we have record. {596} The fact that sexual ideas seem to represent a great many of the dominant ideas in these cases is of interest for a similar reason. It represents the tendency constantly recurring to refer most nervous ailments, as indeed most other ailments, to something pathological in the sexual or genital sphere. The old idea embodied in the word hysterical exemplifies this very well. The "vapors" or "tantrums" or fits which were supposed to be due, to some extent at least, to suppressed sexuality by medical writers of three or four generations ago, have come back to us under another form and with other terms. Psycho-analysis gives occasion for instruction in so far as it helps the patient to get rid of old persuasions and exploded ideas as to disease and diet and the various functions of the body and the mind that have often almost unconsciously been acquired and secured a dominance. It is surprising how often it will be found that people are taking too much or too little water at meals, too many or too few vegetables, too much or too little of salt or of other condiments as the result of habits and notions acquired when they were young and under influences that they may now forget. In the same way habits of life with regard to bathing, clothing and the like may be the source of unfavorable conditions in mind and body that need only to be discovered to be corrected. Their correction will often bring about the relief of symptomatic conditions that have proved quite obstinate to treatment. We have emphasized this in the chapters on the Individual Patient and the necessity for acquiring just as much knowledge as possible about both his occupations and his mental attitude in order to be able successfully to treat chronic disease.

{597}

SECTION XVIII

DISORDERS OF MIND

CHAPTER I

MENTAL INCAPACITY (PSYCHASTHENIA)

In recent years we have come to realize that many of the so-called nervous diseases, or if they do not deserve the serious name of disease, nervous symptom-complexes, are really due to a deficiency of vital energy. Some people have a store of energy that enables them to accomplish many different things successfully. Some become exhausted from a few trivial occupations. What is noteworthy in the cases to be discussed in this chapter is that they show always certain symptoms of mental tiredness or, at least, of lack of capacity for affairs. Patients complain, for instance, that they cannot make up their minds so as to reach decisions because they doubt so much whether the decision they come to will be right or wrong. Others dread the outcome of any and every act and feel that something is hanging over them. Slight sources of irritation become so exaggerated by thinking about them and dwelling on their possibilities that they may even disturb sleep and appetite and, as a consequence, the general health. Fears come over patients lest various things should happen and they dread microbes, or infections, or dirt in general, or the approach of insanity, and all to such a degree as to incapacitate them for their ordinary occupations.

Many of these patients become quite incapable of willing effectively. They not only lose initiative, the power to undertake new enterprises, but they find it difficult to make up their minds as to details of the ordinary affairs of life. As we have stated elsewhere in Professor Grasset's expressive formula, these patients say that they cannot do things, their friends say "they will not," and the physician, taking the middle course, which, as usual in human affairs, has much more of truth than either of the extremes, says "they cannot will."

For these states Janet of Paris suggested the word psychasthenia. It is formed on the model of the word neurasthenia and unless it is used with discretion will have all the objections that attach to that other term. Above all, it shares the tendency pointed out by Sir William Gowers with regard to neurasthenia of being "too satisfying. Men are apt to rest on it as they would not on its English equivalent. Physicians, if they do not actually think that they have found the malady from which the patient is suffering, have an influence exerted on them of which they are often unconscious, which lessens the tendency to go farther in the search for the whole mental state." Much more can be said in defence of psychasthenia, however, than of neurasthenia, for the substitution for it of the translation of the Greek words of {598} which it is composed—"mind weakness" would be alarming. While it is important, then, to realize that the term may easily be made too general and prove, as such words as rheumatism has done in our time and malaria did in the past, a cloak for ignorance and an excuse for incomplete investigation for diagnostic purposes, it represents a satisfactory answer to the patient's question as to what is the matter without committing the physician to such definitely detailed opinions as to the patient's condition as would surely prove unfavorably suggestive.

Psychasthenia, Natural and Acquired.—There are two forms of the mental incapacity that underlies many of the curious symptom-complexes that have been studied under the term psychasthenia. One is natural, that is, inherent in the special character of the individual, and the other acquired through disease or exhausting labor, worry, or anxiety. Some people are born without sufficient mental energy to do the work they attempt to accomplish. This is true, also, in the physical order. It is often pitiable to see young men who have not the physical strength necessary for athletic exercises, or the dexterity required for them, faithfully trying to accomplish by effort what others do with ease. When there is some natural defect in the way they will usually fail, no matter how much they strive. Just in the same way some persons are not able to accomplish certain more serious purposes requiring special mental ability or power which they attempt. Their brothers, their friends, their schoolmates, may have the ability, and they cannot understand why they should not have it, but the fact remains that they are not possessed of it and if they try to make up for this defect by overwork they simply break down.

Differential Diagnosis.—Each of the two forms of mental incapacity, congenital and acquired, must be carefully differentiated and treated from a special standpoint. With regard to congenital lack of mental control, all that the doctor can do is to counsel against the assumption of duties and responsibilities that are too heavy for the patient. Some people have not enough nervous energy to run a business with many details, and some even find it difficult to try to do things involving much less responsibility. There is no use for a man five feet in height, weighing one hundred pounds, to try to be a stevedore. There is no use for men of delicate muscular build to try to make their living at heavy manual labor; they simply wear themselves out in a very short time. This inadaptability is recognized at once. Just the same thing is true with regard to many nervous systems, but the recognition is not so easy or immediate. Some cannot stand the strain of intricate business details or the burden of responsibility in important transactions. They must be taught to be satisfied, then, with quiet simple lives without what is for them, excessive responsibility and without strenuous business worries. A country life with regular hours, plenty of open air and as little responsibility as possible, is the ideal for them.

The most difficult problem in this matter is the question of diagnosis. As a rule, the history is the most helpful for this. The patient tells of having found difficulty all his life whenever anything of special significance was placed on his shoulders. He is one of those who were born tired and remain so all their lives. It has been the custom to blame these people; they are rather to be pitied. If they are born in circumstances that allow of their {599} living quietly in the country, they accomplish a certain amount of work quite successfully and live happy, contented lives. If they are born in the city where the hurry and bustle around them and the insistence of friends that they must take up responsibilities becomes poignant, they get discouraged and even despondent. It is from this class of patients that the "ne'er-do-wells" of modern life are recruited. They form the under-stratum of trampdom, the scions of good families with the wanderlust, the willing but incapable. Certain of them become vicious and criminal, either because they do not want to work or because their mentality is perverted in some way. Such patients cannot be treated with any hope of their becoming successful exemplars of the strenuous life, but they may be directed into the less exacting occupations of country life and so live quiet, useful and happy lives. For the congenital class we can do little except to prevent them from trying to do things that are beyond their mental capacity and helping them to see just what their limitations are.

Mental Exhaustion.—Many disturbances of mental energy are acquired. These may be either functional or organic. For the organic variety we cannot do much, since it is dependent on changes in organs that are permanent. We can, however, usually predispose the patient's mind to the recognition of the fact that he should no longer try to devote himself to occupations that constitute a special drain on his nervous energy. The man, for instance, who is already suffering from arterio-sclerosis must be warned that worry and work will surely hasten the process and that his nervous symptoms cannot be cured, but must be palliated. He must be advised to lessen his mental strain and to take up something which, while occupying his mind, does not make insistent calls on his vitality. In this matter it must be remembered that when a man over fifty develops nervous symptoms, as a rule there is no question of functional trouble but of organic change and usually heart or arteries or kidneys are at fault.

In recent years we have come to realize that typhoid fever often makes serious inroads upon a patient's vitality which can only be retrieved by care, not alone for some months but, if possible, even for some years, not to put an overstrain on the vital energy. Certain other diseases produce an even more lasting effect. A sufferer from well-developed tuberculosis will probably never be able to go back to the strenuous city life. If he attempts to do so, not only is there danger of a recurrence of his tuberculosis, but there may even be a development of neurotic symptoms. Syphilis is another disease that leaves patients in a condition in which it is dangerous for them to assume the serious responsibilities of an exacting occupation and especially anything that involves excitement and worry. Syphilitic patients should be warned of the danger of pursuing vocations that make such demands upon them. It is the actor, the broker, the speculator, and the strenuous business man generally, who is likely to suffer from parasyphilitic conditions, tabes, paresis and the like, much more than those who follow occupations that make less demands on them.

Functional Mental Incapacity.—In a large number of cases the incapacity to do things because of lack of mental energy is due to functional disturbances of the nervous system. These are the most important for the psycho-therapeutist because much can be accomplished for them. Nearly always the patient can be benefited by advice and suggestion, and very often some {600} unfavorable factor at work, using up his mental energy to no purpose, will be discovered. In order to do good, however, careful study of the individual patient is the most important element. The most frequent functional disturbance of the nervous system, leading to exhaustion of mental energy, is over-attention to one's self and to one's occupations. Men can do many complicated things quite naturally and easily, but when they carefully watch themselves doing them, accomplishment is not so ready and the task is double. They tire much easier, for, as a rule, what they are doing could be accomplished automatically and they are using up energy attending to it. This is probably one of the commonest causes for the rather frequent development of that state called nervous exhaustion in our time. People watch themselves too closely and by so doing they not only use up energy unnecessarily in the surveillance, but also they hamper their powers to do things and so consume additional energy in overcoming this inhibition.

Morbidly introspective people watch almost ceaselessly everything they do. They not only watch themselves work and worry about it, but they watch themselves play and grow solicitous that it will do them good; they watch themselves divert themselves to see if it is giving them real recreation and so spoil the diversion; they watch themselves eat and disturb their appetite, and watch themselves digest and hamper digestion; they even try at least to watch themselves sleep and so interfere with sleep. Many of the cases of insomnia are really due to this over-attention. They fear they will not sleep, they worry about it, they keep themselves awake hoping that they will sleep, and in the more serious cases even during sleep itself they are so solicitous that their dreams become very vivid and a form of unconscious cerebration goes on with surveillance of themselves. They do not rest even in sleep. They wake feeling not rested, they get up with a consciousness that they are beginning a long day without being properly refreshed and they exhaust enough energy to complete a good part of the day's work in wondering whether they will be able to go on with their occupation for the day, whatever it may be.

Inhibitory Surveillance.—People become afraid that they cannot or that they may not do things well and set a guard over themselves. This is illustrated very well in the doubts about accomplishment because of which they keep going back to see what they have done and how it was done, though usually it was accomplished quite well without any conscious attention. Dreads form another phase of this attitude of mind. For those who are affected with them they make a thing hard to do before it is begun, and harder to accomplish after it has been entered upon because of the suggestion that it may lead to some serious results, or they even inhibit their activities to a marked extent by their solicitude with regard to them. They worry about things before the event and thus consume energy uselessly. Worry has been defined as anxious solicitude about what we have to do next week at the same time that we occupy ourselves with what we are doing now and have to do in the next hour or two. The solicitude about next week is quite useless, as a rule, until the time comes, and it merely disturbs what we are doing now, making it harder to do and making errors in it almost inevitable, and so preparing ourselves for discouragement because of mistakes that have been made and still further adding to the difficulty of accomplishment.

{601}

Inhibition of Automatism.—These introspective people disturb themselves by over-attention to things that need no attention, that are accomplished automatically, and that are not done nearly so well if they are attended to. Not only is it true that it is harder to do work that ought to be accomplished automatically if much attention is given to it, but also nature resents the surveillance. Not only the brain does not work so well if watched to see whether perhaps it is working too much, or whether there are too many feelings in our head while we are doing things, but even the stomach resents being watched and does not do its work as well. The same thing is probably true for every one of our organic functions. In the chapters on the heart we call attention to the fact that surveillance makes a perfectly healthy though nervous heart miss beats. There is a dual waste of nervous energy then. We are employing our attention watching things done that need not be watched, and by that fact we are inhibiting natural processes and requiring that more energy shall be put into them for their accomplishment, and even then accomplishing them with discouraging imperfection.

Mental Short-Circuit.—The reflex mental process that particularly affects many individuals in our time and makes it hard for them to do their work, has been well described under the figure of a short-circuit in an electrical dynamo. The short-circuit diverts the current so that instead of acting outside the dynamo and performing useful work, it is discharged within the machine, brings about deterioration of its elements and soon leads to a reduction in the amount of electrical energy that that particular dynamo can develop.

Association Fibers Diversion.—Prof. Michael Foster in the Wilde Lecture for 1898, "The Physical Basis of Psychical Events," has many valuable suggestions with regard to the mechanism of mental operations on the neuron theory. He has particularly dwelt on the function of the association fibers in connection with mental operations, or with the raising of sensation to the plane of mentality. A portion of the brain that is originating impulses, instead of sending them down to the periphery, through the projection fibers, to lead to the accomplishment of external work, may have its messages diverted through the association fibers to other portions of the brain and thus do harm rather than good.

Occurrence of Psychasthenia.—It must not be thought that these curiously interesting conditions occur only among people of low intellectual caliber, or in those of narrow intellectual interests, mere specialists who may have acquired a reputation for doing one thing well. They are frequent among the most intellectual classes. Brain workers of all kinds, unless they are careful to vary the interests of life, unless, as suggested in the chapters on Occupation of Mind and Diversion of Mind, they have a hobby besides their usual occupations, are likely to suffer in this way. As a matter of fact, many intellectual people have had what are called nervous breakdowns of this kind. A biographical dictionary shows any number of them. Dr. Gould's Biographic Clinics furnish many documents for the study of these conditions. A typical instance, told by the sufferer himself, the distinguished Sir Francis Galton, is of special significance for the psychotherapeutist. I {602} quote because it illustrates the fact that such breakdowns do not portend a short or subsequently listless life, for Sir Francis, a most successful scientific investigator, lived well beyond fourscore years in the full possession of health of mind and body.

It was during my third year at Cambridge that I broke down entirely in health and had to lose a term and go home. I suffered from intermittent pulse and a variety of brain symptoms of an alarming kind. A mill seemed to be working inside my head; I could not banish obsessing ideas; at times I could hardly read a book, and found it painful to look at even a printed page. Fortunately I did not suffer from sleeplessness, and my digestion failed but little. Even a brief interval of mental rest did me good, and it seemed as if a long dose of it might wholly restore me. It would have been madness to continue the kind of studious life that I had been leading. I had been much too zealous, had worked too irregularly and in too many directions, and had done myself serious harm. It was as though I had tried to make a steam-engine perform more work than it was constructed for, by tampering with its safety-valve and thereby straining its mechanism. Happily the human body may sometimes repair itself, which the steam-engine cannot.

The physician with experience in such cases would be much more apt to say, "Happily we can learn to control our mental energy and not let it go to waste by foolish persistence at one set of ideas constantly, nor be dissipated in surveillance of functions that work automatically if left to themselves."

Etiological Factors.—This form of mental incapacity develops particularly in people after they have gone through a prolonged period of hard work and then have come to a time when they are much freer than they were before. They are prone to think that they exhausted their nerve force during the preceding period of labor and that now they are paying for it. Almost invariably what is really happening is that they now have much more time to occupy themselves with themselves and about themselves and to worry over their ills, real and imaginary. This is the typical nervous breakdown, as it used to be called, of elderly retired merchants or bankers. They have looked forward all their lives to a time when they could enjoy themselves doing nothing. They retire from business and then their troubles begin. It is no wonder that the old proverb, "A machine rusts out much sooner than it wears out" should have been so often quoted with regard to this condition. A man who has been working busily at something all his life cannot stop all at once and do nothing. He cannot learn to occupy himself with trivial things. Commonly, he has few, if any, interests apart from his business and he very soon wears the novelty off these and then introspection comes to make him exaggerate the significance of every feeling that he has, every stiffness that occurs, every muscle twinge due to change in the weather, until he becomes supremely miserable.

As a rule, these patients are simple, practical, common-sense, business men, and it is hard for the physician to think that there is nothing more than a functional neurosis present. It is even more difficult for the patient to be made to appreciate that his ills are mainly due to his own over-attention to himself in this idleness that he has looked forward to with so much pleasure. Ordinary medicines fail to relieve and the regular professional man seldom succeeds in doing these patients much good. They constitute the richest material for the quack and the charlatan. Much occupied with their ills they tell their friends all about them. Whenever a strong impression is produced {603} on their mind by a promise to cure them with some new wonderful remedy they are favorably influenced, often get better and then are walking advertisements for the particular quack who has happened to benefit them. It is this class of people that has given more trouble to legislative committees of medical societies than any other. Some of them appeal to legislators whenever a bill for the admission of some new form of practitioners of medicine comes up with the story of how much benefit they derived from the treatment. Since they have been successful business men their word carries weight. It is curious how little the making of money, though often presumed to be so, is a test of real intelligence. It is often the man of one idea with no intellectual breadth who is the best money-getter.

These conditions develop almost entirely in predisposed individuals who, for some reason, are trying to overdo the energy they possess, and who, as a consequence, have lost a certain control over themselves. At times, of course, they occur in persons who have so little occupation of mind that thoughts of various kinds along these lines become insistently suggestive and cannot be thrown off because the patients' interests are not sufficiently deep or sufficiently varied to occupy their attention. The rational treatment of them, then, must be founded on a careful study of individual cases, the recognition of the special cause, and also the occasions at work in each case, a neutralization of unfavorable suggestion and a provision of such favorable suggestions and occupation of mind as will enable the patient to rid himself of the annoyance occasioned by these and the physical symptoms that so often develop as a consequence. In a certain number of cases a history of corresponding or equivalent affections in preceding generations will be found. In many patients, however, there is no such history, though there is usually the story of symptomatic mental conditions of one or other of the types mentioned, earlier in life. When in good health physically the patient has very little bother from them. When run down in weight or when worried or anxious about business or from the stress of important responsibilities these symptoms may become bothersome mentally and physically. Often it will be impossible to obliterate them entirely, but always they can be greatly improved and the patient can be made to realize that they are not seriously significant, that in mild form they are rather common and that, above all, they are not so peculiar to the individual as he is likely to think, with consequent increase of the unfavorable suggestion.

CHAPTER II

HALLUCINATIONS

Hallucinations Differentiated from Illusions and Delusions.—Hallucinations are vivid impressions on the consciousness which appeal to their subject as strongly as if they were really the result of sensory impressions, though those who experience them know, either at the moment, or on investigation afterwards, that they had no objective reality, that is, were not due to any external physical cause. Illusions are deceptions of the senses, due to the imperfection of the senses or the conditions in which the perception occurs. {604} Delusions are mental states in which ideas are accepted, or conclusions drawn, or information assumed to be gained, though the whole process is mental and has no relation to reality. (For illustrations of illusions see chapter with that title in the Appendix.)

Hallucinations lie in between illusions and delusions as a mode of deception. They are mental occurrences, but they seem to come from the senses and probably the best explanation for them is that a previous sensory impression is vaguely aroused and then finds its way into the consciousness as if it were coming through the senses. It has been suggested that they might be due to a reversal of the nervous process by which a sensation reaches the brain. The external object produces the sensation, this travels along a nerve causing a perception, this perception is stored in the memory, and then, when very vividly reawakened, causes impulses to travel backward along the nerve to the periphery with the production of a feeling very like sensation.

Frequency.—While hallucinations are often supposed to be only incidents in the life of the insane, or at least of those who are in the danger zone near mental disequilibration, carefully collected recent observations show that many perfectly sane people have experienced them, and some of them have been much disturbed by them for fear they portended loss of mental control or some developing pathological condition. A certain number of men and women have seen things that either had no existence or existed only for them and for the moment, and that evidently were due to some state of mind rather than to their senses. They have heard things that were not said or that were not audible to others, or that were only reproductions of their memory of previous sounds and quite naturally such mysterious manifestations disquiet them. It was the rule in the past to dismiss such phenomena without serious consideration, or at most to consider that they were only subjective manifestations not worth discussing, or to go to the opposite extreme and say that they were due to mental disturbances.

Of course, as a rule, hallucinations are an index of mental disturbance. No matter how apparently sane the patient, this must be the first thought and must be carefully excluded before proceeding with the case. The subject of hallucinations is larger than that, however, and it is a mistake to brush it aside in every case as if it were either very serious or of no importance and that in either case nothing can be done to relieve solicitude about it. Physicians can often do much, first to prevent hallucinations by getting at the physical causes of them; second, to prevent them from disturbing patients seriously by showing them how common are such experiences and by indicating their possible physical significance; third, by securing such mental discipline and control as will render their recurrence much less frequent; and, fourth, they can make the almost inevitable unfavorable effect upon the mind of the patient and then reflexly upon his body, much less than it would otherwise be, by sympathetically discussing and entering into the details of them enough, at least, to explain their significance or throw some light on their origin in physical conditions.

Hallucinations of vision, the seeing of things and persons that have no real existence at the time and place they are seen, are usually considered to be rather uncommon and to occur only in those whose mentality is seriously disturbed. Careful studies of the subject, however, show that at least one in ten {605} of educated people consulted have had some hallucinations of vision. Either they have wakened up, or they have dreamt that they waked in the early morning, and have seen some one whom they knew, but knew to be at the moment at a distance, standing near them. Such visions have gradually faded away or suddenly disappeared. Occasionally these persons have in full light had some appearance, wraithlike or otherwise, some manifestation that appeals to vision, yet that they knew at the time or learned afterwards was non-existent.

Many people are backward about confessing that they have had such experiences, for they fear that it will make them ridiculous or even cause them to be suspected of disturbed mentality. Just as soon as it is made clear to them that their admissions will be taken as evidence for a phenomenon to be discussed seriously, many more than would otherwise be thought confess to such hallucinations. Most of these, it may be said at once, are quite sensible people, a great many of them belong to the educated classes; all of them are trustworthy witnesses as far as good will goes, and the circumstances of their hallucinations are such in many cases that there cannot be a mere mistake, or error of judgment.

The frequency with which hallucinations occur may be appreciated from the investigation made some years ago at the instance of the Congress of Experimental Psychology. The following question was put to 17,000 persons, mostly residents of Great Britain, and answers received: "Have you ever, when believing yourself to be completely awake, had a vivid impression of seeing or being touched by living beings or inanimate objects, or of hearing a voice, which impression, so far as you could discover, was not due to any external physical cause?" The answers showed that 655 out of 8,372 men and 1,029 out of 8,628 women had experienced a sensory hallucination at some time in their lives. Some of them had had a number of them. That is, one out of ten in the educated classes has had some hallucination, and nearly one out of every eight women. An analysis of the statistics, however, brings out some interesting suggestions. There were nearly twice as many hallucinations related as having occurred during the year before the question was asked as in the preceding years. There was a definite reduction in the number that had occurred in all the preceding years, except the fifth and tenth, and these were evidently due to uncertainties of memory, so that five- and ten-year periods seemed about the length of time that had passed since the event.

It is evident then that in spite of the fact that an hallucination would seem to be very important and surely startling enough to be well remembered, it is yet easily forgotten, since even a year's interval made so much difference in the number that were remembered. The committee, after considering this easy forgetfulness in the matter, considered that to arrive at the actual total of visual hallucinations experienced by this group of 17,000 persons during the ten-year period in question, the numbers in the table should be multiplied by four. That means that probably very nearly one in three people have had an hallucination of some kind within ten years. The great majority of the visual hallucinations consist of apparitions of human figures. Other forms that are seen are so few, as Mr. Podmore has insisted in his "Telepathic Hallucinations, The New View of Ghosts," that they are almost negligible. A frank {606} discussion of these details with a person who is much disturbed by having experienced an hallucination is the best possible remedy for the physical and mental disturbance that may result.

Sir Francis Galton, well known for his investigation of many subjects and who may well be called the father of biometrics or statistical biology, in his "Memories of My Life" tells of his own investigations of the visions of sane persons. The fact that he delivered a lecture on this subject at the Royal Institution of London shows how seriously his studies were made and how much value scientists placed on them. Galton's well-recognized training in the careful weighing of evidence and his ability to strip phenomena of everything that might divert their significance from what they really were, add to the worth of his conclusions. Those who care to study the subject further will find his discussion in the *Proceedings of the Royal Institution* (London, 1882).

There are few people beyond middle age who have not had one or more curious experiences in the matter of visions or appearances. Mostly these have been vague and have not proved a disturbing element in the minds of the subjects. Many more than are thought, however, have seen visions vividly and with a detail that makes it almost impossible for them to believe that what they saw was merely an externation of ideas already in their mind. In this matter it must not be forgotten that the dreams of many people, especially nervous people, often present themselves with marvelous vividness of detail. They see people or places in their dreams and reason about them quite rationally. Occasionally a dream will bring back details that have been forgotten. The dreaming state seems in some people to have wonderful power over the subconscious. Things that are not remembered at all in the waking state sometimes come back in dreams, and only then are recalled by the individual as representing past events in his life. He is apt to wonder where the details could possibly come from, since he had before no conscious memory of them. This same thing holds for the day-dreams or sudden visual appearances that come when the attention has been wrapped in something else.

A typical example of such visual hallucinations is the following incident told by a prominent London physician of himself:

One afternoon at tea time, before a meeting of the Royal Society, Sir Risdon Bennett (1809-1891, a well-known physician, President of the College of Physicians in 1876, and a fellow of the Royal Society), drew me apart and told me of a strange experience he had had very recently. He was writing in his study separated by a thin wall from the passage, when he heard the well-known postman's knock, followed by the entrance into his study of a man dressed in a fantastic medieval costume, perfectly distinct in every particular, buttons and all, who, after a brief time, faded and disappeared. Sir Risdon says that he felt in perfect health; his pulse and breathing were normal and so forth, and he was naturally alarmed at the prospect of some impending brain disorder. Nothing, however, of the sort had followed. The same appearance recurred; he thought the postman's knock somehow originated the hallucination. ... I heard the story at length, very shortly after the event, told me with painstaking and scientific exactness and in tones that clearly indicated the narrator's earnest desire to be minutely correct.

Those who are especially interested in this subject will find any number of similar stories, some apparently rich with meaning, most of them quite {607} meaningless, in the volumes of transactions of the English Psychic Research Society, in F. W. H. Myers' "Human Personality," in Podmore's "Naturalizing the Supernatural," in Flammarion's "The Unknown," or many other books published in recent years. It is quite easy to get sufficient material to bring reassurance to any patient that visual hallucinations, at least, mean nothing serious for the mind or body of the individual having the experience.

Hallucinations in the Past.—It must not be thought, however, that this subject of hallucinations is new. Literature is full of it and from the earliest times we find traces of it. Egyptian, Babylonian and Chaldean writers mention them. Nor indeed is the scientific consideration of the subject new. Aristotle speaks of them and it is evident that many of the old writers thought of them as psychic incidents on some physical basis, or at least due to some predisposition in the individual or in some special state of his senses. Two generations ago Johann Müller, the great German physiologist, discussed the whole subject at length in a monograph, and considered it of so much importance for physicians that he introduced a résumé of it into his great text-book of physiology. His explanation of the occurrence of visual hallucinations is not only a striking illustration of the thoroughly scientific character of his treatment of the subject, but it serves to show how well men considered these subjects long before the present fad for the study of abnormal psychology or mental influence came in. His discussion of the subject is sufficient of itself to make any patient understand his hallucinations and keep them from bothering him better than anything else I know:

The subjective images of which we are speaking have sometimes, however, both color and light; different particles of the retina, of the optic nerve, and of its prolongations to the brain, being conceived as existing in special states of action. This happens rarely in the state of health, but frequently in disease. These are the true phantasms which may occur to the sense of hearing and other senses as well as to that of vision. The process by which "phantasms" are produced, is the reverse of that to which the vision of actual external objects is due. In the latter case particles of the retina thrown into an active state by external impressions, are conceived in that condition by the sensorium; in the former case, the idea of the sensorium excites the active state of corresponding particles of the retina or optic nerve. The action of the material organ of vision, which has extension in space, upon the mind, so as to produce the idea of an object having extension, form and relation of parts, and the action of such an idea upon the organ of vision so as to produce a corresponding sensation, are both equally wonderful; and hence the spectral phenomena or visions are not more extraordinary than the ordinary function of sight. (Vol. II, p. 1393, Eng. transl., 1842.)

Apparitions and their Explanation.—In spite of suggested explanations on physical grounds, some of these apparitions that appear to people seriously disturb them. They cannot get them out of their minds. They are sure that they portend evil. Hence worries, and the more nervous the people are and the more worried already, the more likely is such a thing to recur and then to be made much of. Only through their minds can these people be treated, and it must be made clear to them not only how common are hallucinations, but that there is an easy psychic explanation of most of them. Sir Arthur Mitchell, K. C. B., in his book "About Dreaming, Laughing and Blushing," tells a story and then gives his explanation of it in such a way as to illuminate many of these occurrences:

{608}

Perhaps I should illustrate how I think that apparitions may be nothing more than dream hallucinations. A. B., a gentleman of culture and strong character, called one hot day, after a hearty lunch, on an ecclesiastic in a high position, who happened to be engaged in his library at the time of the call. A. B. was shown into a room opening off the library, and requested to wait. He sat down beside a table, and with his elbow resting on it, he leant his head on his hand. While in this position he saw a man in clerical costume come through the door communicating with the library, without any opening of the door. A. B. was absolutely certain that he had seen an apparition, and was surprised and hurt when I expressed a doubt. He called on me to explain, and I said that it was at least possible that he had been asleep for some moments, that if he had slept at all, however short the dream of the sleep, he must have had a dream, if I am right in thinking that there is no dreamless sleep, and that thus what he regarded as an apparition might be nothing more than a dream hallucination. He assured me persistently that he was continuously wide-awake, but I assured him that these moments of sleep often occurred without any consciousness that they had occurred. He refused to be deprived of his ghost, and I refused to believe in the supernormal when the normal was sufficient.

Such wraith-like appearances are supposed to occur especially in connection with the deaths of persons at a distance. Startling stories are told, particularly of those who are very near relatives, husbands and wives, mothers and sons, and, above all, twins, who have been very closely associated with one another during life. There are a large number of stories of this kind, however, that have been collected by the Psychic Research Society and other agents with strong evidence in their favor, in which the appearances have had no ulterior significance at all and have evidently been mere figments of the imagination, the externation of images from memory so vividly that they seem to be the reseen. Reassurances in this matter are the best possible source of relief from the sense of impending ill for many patients. The physician who wishes to relieve such symptoms must familiarize himself with some of the many stories that have been investigated and that serve to prove that these and like appearances must not be taken as significant of anything more than a definite tendency, that exists in human nature at moments of day dreaming or when one's attention is suddenly turned from a book in which one has been absorbed, to see externally what is really passing through the imaginative memory.

A Disappearance.—A very interesting commentary on some of these appearances is to be found in Mark Twain's story of a disappearance, which could probably be duplicated many times if experiences in this line were collected and collated. Mr. Clemens, sitting on the porch of his residence one day, saw a stranger of rather peculiar appearance come up the walk toward the front door and he expected to hear him ring the bell and have the servant come to the door and usher him in, and then perhaps be called to see him. About the middle of the walk, however, the stranger disappeared and Mr. Clemens was quite surprised to come to himself, rub his eyes and conclude that he had had one of these curious visions or hallucinations, in which the Psychic Research Society would surely be interested. He had plainly seen the stranger enter the gate, come up the walk, and then disappear. He was so impressed by the disappearance that he roused himself to go into the house to get his notebook, so as to make notes of what had happened before the details escaped him. To his surprise he found the stranger in conversation {609} with the servant in the house. There had simply been a lapse in Mr. Clemen's vision of him. He had had a disappearance phenomenon instead of an appearance. The story will be found to amuse patients who complain of appearances disturbing them, though Mr. Clemens always told his disappearance story very seriously, and it is as interesting a psychic phenomenon as any told of the wraith-like appearances.

Treatment.—Considering how frequent are such phenomena, the physician must be prepared to treat those who are disquieted by them. A wraith-like appearance, for instance, will disturb many people very seriously and often for days, sometimes for weeks, make them nervous, excitable, and impair their appetite, disturb their digestion and sleep and often such unfortunate occurrences are prone to come just when they are run down in weight and when they need the help of every factor that makes for improvement of health. Simply to dismiss such an appearance as if it were quite imaginary, that is, non-existent in some form of reality, or quite baseless and trivial, serves no good purpose, for, as a rule, the persons concerned are deeply impressed with what they have seen. The only way to remove the unfavorable impression produced by it is to discuss it straightforwardly on the basis of what we have come to know as the result of recent investigations and the collation of the literature which has been published by the various psychical research societies and authorities on the subject. We know now that while occasionally such wraith-like appearances seemed to have a definite significance, because of something that happened simultaneously or shortly afterwards, this is mere coincidence and there are literally thousands of such cases in which a well authenticated wraith-like appearance was followed by no serious consequence, was never shown to mean anything beyond a curious psychic phenomenon, and was evidently merely due to some personal subjective influence, some externation of an image in the memory, unusual, but not at all unique, or even very rare, and evidently due to a curious peculiar externalizing power with which certain intellects are gifted.

Auditory Hallucinations.—Hallucinations of hearing are more common than those of vision. Many people have had the experience of waking up thinking that someone was calling them. A great many people are sure that they have, at some time or other, heard a voice when no one was near enough to them to have said anything. They have even recognized the voice. Some people, when thinking deeply about a person, have the voice of that person occur to them so clearly that they cannot quite make out whether they have actually heard it or whether it has only been very vividly reproduced in their memory. Such experiences are so common as to be well known, though many people hesitate to tell the stories of them, for hearing voices is rightly looked upon as a frequent preliminary symptom of insanity.

Hallucinations of hearing are the most common early symptom of insanity. The hearing of voices must always arouse suspicion at once. It must not be forgotten, however, that a great many recognizedly sane people who have remained so for life, have thought that they heard voices. Of course, we have no definition for insanity, and it is difficult to draw the line. We have no definition for health either, yet we have a practical working standard for the recognition of it, as also for insanity. These hallucinations then, both of vision and hearing, deserve to be discussed seriously, and in {610} nearly every case, even though there is some mental disturbance, the physician can in this way benefit his patients and keep them from being overmuch distressed by their hallucinations.

There is an expression in such common use that it is evidently the result of an almost universal experience, according to which men sometimes explain, after having acted in a particular way, that "something told them to." What they mean, of course, is that a conclusion formed in their minds the reasons for which they could not understand, but which yet had force enough to cause them to follow it to a practical application. When we hear of Socrates being advised in life by a demon, a so-called familiar spirit, we are apt to wonder whether by this term is meant anything more than just this curious feeling of aloofness from ourselves that we sometimes have when we are trying to make up our minds, or, indeed, not infrequently when we are deeply engaged in any intellectual occupation. As discussed in the chapter on Unconscious Cerebration, our minds seem in a certain way to act independently of us. Occasionally they draw us to conclusions quite different from those which we previously expected to reach. There seems to be a something within us that works quite of itself and beyond our will. Whether under these circumstances there may not occasionally come so vivid a feeling of this power within us impressing itself upon us, that it seems to come from without, must always be taken into account in the effort to get at the real significance of these curious hallucinations. Only thus are we able to come to the relief of patients who are bothered by them.

Explanation by Sound Reproduction.—Auditory hallucinations are probably not more than reproductions of sounds heard before recalled vividly and apparently heard again at moments when attention is not attracted to actual auditory sensations and we are in receptive mood. Some of them are very startling because they are apparently warnings of future events, as is proved by their fulfillment. These, however, do not seem to be more than coincidences noted with regard to similar events connected with Premonitions, Dreads and Dreams (see chapters on these subjects). There is, for instance, a well authenticated story published by the English Psychic Research Society of a woman who was about to take a dose of what she thought was some ordinary home remedy, when she distinctly heard a voice telling her to taste it. The dose to be taken was a tablespoonful, and when she tasted it she found that by mistake she had placed her hands on a bottle containing a rather strong poison and a tablespoonful of it would almost inevitably have killed her. Unfortunately, such occurrences are so rare and the reason for them is so hard to find that their consideration as anything more than coincidences seems out of the question. Every medical journal almost brings the story of someone who has taken a dose of medicine that proves fatal, and there is no warning. If such warnings came with definite frequency, it would be easier to appreciate their significance.

There are similar stories with regard to other warnings. There is the story of the young man who in a storm drove under a shed for protection. Just as he did so he heard his mother's voice—she had been long dead—distinctly say "Drive out!" Ho drove out at once in the teeth of the storm, so deeply impressed was he, and was scarcely beyond the entrance when the shed fell, crushing everything within it. Similar warnings of impending {611} accidents are rather frequent in certain people's minds, yet it is hard to think of them as anything else than premonitions. These somehow take on the character of auditory hallucinations in certain sensitive minds. Compared to the whole number of accidents, however, such incidents are extremely rare and follow no law, and while there are those who like to think that perhaps such phenomena are due to the solicitude of some being in the other world, this is extremely doubtful. In that case, as St. Augustine suggested, they would be much more frequent and have a clearer significance than is at present the rule. St. Augustine, discussing the possibility, was sure that he would have had communications from his mother. Most men would re-echo his feeling.

Coincidences.—Most of these stories as they have been analyzed by careful investigators are indeed such trivial unmeaning things that it would be too bad to let people be bothered by them. They have occurred, however, from time immemorial. Veridical warnings are a commonplace in the literature of all countries. Undoubtedly some may suggest the action of a Higher Power, but the more one knows of the conditions in which they happened, the people to whom they came and their ultimate effects, the less will they seem providential. It is evident that under certain conditions they may be produced even at moments when men are not particularly excited and when they think

327

that they are perfectly calm and self-possessed. Each story must be discussed in its own merits. The only thing to do, then, is not to make too light of them and, above all, not to treat them as merely imaginary or as utterly illusory; for they are often natural phenomena, the reasons for which and the conditions of their production we do not as yet fully understand. If patients can be brought to this viewpoint, they may even become interested in searching out just what it was that caused each particular hallucination. Over and over again it has been found that a moonbeam or a peculiar unexpected reflection of the sun, or the light shining through an unnoted aperture, or any or several of these in connection with a mirror has been the main cause of the wraith-like appearance. When they happen during the day it is sometimes at the moment of passing from very bright light to a darker hall that the occurrence takes place and evidently there is some physical occasion for the appearances in the eye itself. Unusual noises of various kinds are responsible for the auditory hallucinations.

Dangers of Serious Considerations.—There is one serious aspect of these hallucinations and supposed warnings—they tend to paralyze action. If a person allows himself to become firmly persuaded that doubts and premonitory possibilities must be weighed and solved before he may dare to act with assurance, then action becomes almost impossible. Premonitions may serve to bring people into danger, or at least keep people from having such presence of mind as will enable them to get out of it, as they otherwise would. Doubts lead to inaction and make a state of mind that is eminently miserable. The patient's one hope is to put aside resolutely such hallucinations if they rise to the level of a disturbing doubt or a paralyzing premonition and to discipline himself against being influenced by them. In many persons this is a difficult matter, but it represents the only efficient path to the regaining of mental health and strength.

{612}

CHAPTER III

DREADS

In any discussion of the influence of mind over body, favorable and unfavorable, too much emphasis cannot be placed on the hold that dreads have over a great many people and how much they mean, not alone for the mental state, but also for the physical sense of well-being or of ill-feeling in the individual. The expression attributed to the old hermit who had lived to the age of one hundred and had spent some sixty years of existence in the solitude of the desert, with all the opportunities for introspection that this afforded, is the best illustration even in our day of what dreads signify in life: "I am an old man," he said to the young solitary who came to him for advice, "and I have had many troubles, but most of them never happened." We are nearly all of us, or at least those of us who spend most of our time in sedentary mental occupations, prone to fear that something untoward is preparing for us and in many cases to dread lest some serious ailment or other is just ahead of us. We are afraid that certain feelings, though we like to call them symptoms, due to some trivial cause or other as a rule that deserves no notice, may mean the insidious inroads of a constitutional disease destined to shorten existence. A little fatigue, over-tiredness of particular muscles, the straining of joints, the discomforts due to overeating and undersleeping, that are meant as passing warnings of nature for the necessity of a little more care in life, are exaggerated into symptoms that have a more or less serious significance.

DEFINITE DREADS

Besides these rather vague dreads, however, there are certain special disquietudes peculiar to individuals, even more groundless, if possible, than the generic apprehension just spoken of and that have been dignified in recent years by the name of phobias. Phobia means only "fear" in Greek, but the term is much more satisfying to nervous people than the shorter but too definite English term, dread, or fear. There is acrophobia, or the fear of looking down from a height; claustrophobia, or the fear of narrow places, as the dread of walking through a narrow street because of the sense of oppression that comes with the shut-inness of it. Then there is agoraphobia, market-place dread, or the fear to cross an open space because one has, as it were, grown accustomed to be near buildings and misses their presence. There are many others, indeed as many as there are dislikes in human nature, for any dislike apparently may be exaggerated into a dread. I mention a few at the beginning of the alphabet and some of special significance. There is aerophobia, dread of the air, a symptom sometimes mentioned in connection with hydrophobia; aichmophobia, the dread of pointed tools; ailurophobia, the dread of cats; anthrophobia or the dread of men; pathophobia or the fear of disease, microbophobia or bacillophobia; kenophobia or the dread of emptiness; phthisiophobia or the dread of consumption; zoophobia or the dread of animals; sitophobia or the dread of food, and even phobophobia, the dread of {613} dreading. Neuropsychologists seem to take a special pleasure in inventing some new phobia or at least giving us a fine long Greek name for a set of symptoms by no means new and that might well be explained in simpler terms. The most familiar examples are: the fear of lightning, which is more frequently brontophobia, the fear of thunder.

These learned words are all formed on the same etymological principle as hydrophobia, but they are entirely psychic in origin, while hydrophobia, as it is well to explain to patients who think of the word phobia in connection with their symptoms, is, of course, a misnomer for an infectious disease—rabies—which develops as the consequence of a bite of a rabid animal, and the principal symptom of which is not fear of water, but the impossibility of swallowing any liquid because of spasm of the esophageal muscles.

Almost any function of the body may become the subject of a dread or phobia that may interfere even seriously with it. Any disturbance of any function is likely to be emphasized by such dreads. The French have described the basophobia, which makes the patients suffering from beginning tabes dread so much walking that it becomes a much greater effort than it would otherwise be and often interferes with walking rather seriously. Then there is the fear of tremor which exaggerates a tremor due to some organic cause, but yet not necessarily of grave import, nor likely to increase rapidly. Many of the hysterical palsies are really due to dreads, consequent upon some incident, motor or sensory, which produced a profound effect upon the patient's mind. A patient who has been surprised by a digestive vertigo while descending a stairs, even though nothing more happened than the dizziness which required him to grasp the balustrade, will sometimes develop a fear of vertigo that will actually make it difficult for him to go down stairs without such an effort of will as is very exhausting. Even the slightest functions may be thus disturbed. Pitres and Regis described some ten years ago what they called the obsession of blushing, or erythrophobia, the fear of turning red. Patients make themselves extremely miserable in this way. Only training and self-control will help them.

These names are long and mouth-filling and consequently satisfying, and most people who are suffering from a particular phobia are almost sure to think that they have a very special affliction. When the word dread is used instead of the word phobia they are less likely to misunderstand the character of their affection and to realize that it is not a disease but only an unfortunate mental peculiarity that needs control and discipline, and not fostering care. Neurasthenia only means nervous weakness, as we have pointed out, but most people are rather rejoiced when informed that they have so high-sounding a disease as neurasthenia, while to be told that they are nervously weak or suffer from nervous weakness seems quite a come-down from their interesting Greek-designated affection. Most psychiatrists feel that it is better not to give the long Greek term, but to state in simple short Saxon words just what is the matter with the patient. They are suffering from the dread of a height, or the dread of a narrow street, or the dread of open spaces, or the dread of dirt, or of cats, or of whatever else it may be. This makes it easier for them to begin to discipline themselves against the state of mind into which they allow themselves to fall with regard to these various objects, and mental discipline is the only therapeutic adjuvant that is of any avail in {614} lessening these conditions. With reasonable perseverance most people can, if not cure themselves of these affections, at least greatly lessen the discomfort due to them. A consideration of particular dreads brings out the specific suggestions that may be made with regard to each and the directions that may be helpful to the patients. Probably the commonest is acrophobia, so that the detailed consideration of it shows the indications for other dreads.

Dread of Heights.—Almost without exception men have a sort of instinctive dread of looking down from a height. In most people this can be conquered to such a degree that almost anyone, if compelled by necessity, can learn to work on a skyscraper and continue to do good work without much bother about the height, though he may have to go up ten to twenty stories, or even more. When he takes up the work at first every workman finds it difficult. It gives most of us a trembly feeling even to sit in our chair and think of looking down from such a height. To see pictures of men standing on the iron frames of skyscrapers twenty or thirty stories up in the air looking down 300 to 500 feet below them gives one a series of little chilly feelings in the back and in many people a goneness or sense of constriction around the abdomen that is almost a girdle feeling. To sit at a window opposite where a skyscraper is going up and to see the men lean over the edge of a beam calling directions of various kinds to workmen below will give most people, even those who are not nervous or especially sensitive, creepy feelings with sometimes a little catch in the breath and an iciness in the hypochondria. It would seem absolutely impossible that we should ever be able to perform these feats of looking from a height, yet experience shows that most of us, after a little training, learn to do it without difficulty.

Even the men who work most confidently have some creepy feelings return to them whenever they stop and think about this and let their eyes wander to the distance below them. It is not difficult for us to walk across a plank raised a foot or two from the ground, though to walk across the same plank at a height of ten feet may be quite a trial and at thirty feet may become quite impossible. This is all due to lack of confidence on our part and there is no reason in the world why, if the plank is amply wide for us at two feet from the ground, it should not be just as wide and safe at 30 or 60 or even 100 feet. This is what the men who have learned to work on skyscrapers have disciplined themselves to. They have learned to disregard the wide vacant space around them and the yawning chasm beneath their feet; they keep their eyes fixed on something in the immediate vicinity, excluding thoughts of all that might happen if they should lose their balance.

Physical Basis.—There is a physical basis in many of these cases that constitutes the underlying occasion, at least, for the development of the psychic dread. Our eyes have grown accustomed to being fixed on near objects. Whenever they are not so fixed we get a feeling of trepidation. Even those who have done a little day-dreaming know that sometimes when they have been looking into space, objects around them have suddenly seemed to be transferred to a long distance and at the same time a curious sense of insecurity came over them. Anyone can get this feeling experimentally by making two large dots on a piece of paper about two inches apart and then gazing between the dots into vacancy beyond the paper as it were, until the dots have a tendency to become four because of the fact that each eye sees {615} each of the dots on a part of the retina not corresponding to that on which the other eye sees it (see Fig. 25).

Fig. 25.

When the experiment is successfully performed the dots begin to float before the eyes, then they may coalesce into one or become three, but any number up to four may readily be seen. This will give the sense of insecurity that comes from the eyes not having any fixed object to look at and illustrates the discipline of the eyes that must be learned in order that looking down from a height may not be productive of the usual dread.

329

Dread of Small Heights.—It is often thought that acrophobia, or the fear of a height, concerns only great heights and that ordinary elevations produce no discomfort. I have had patients, however, who, when compelled by circumstances over which they had no control or at least by social obligations that were hard to break, to sit on the front row of even a low balcony, have been extremely uncomfortable. There was a sense of tightness and oppression about the chest that made it difficult for them to breathe, that disturbed their heart action and gave them a general sense of ill-feeling. I have had a curiously interesting series of cases in clergymen who found it trying to say Mass or conduct services or to preach from the step of a high altar. One would be inclined at first to make little of their description of their utter discomfort. There is no doubt at all, however, of their real torture of mind and of the extreme effort required to enable them to support themselves in the trying ordeal. They are often so exhausted because of the effort required that only with difficulty can they do anything else during the day.

To most people such a state of mind is inexplicable. There are deeply intellectual men who, in my experience, are quite disturbed by apparently so simple a thing as having to say Mass on an altar that has three or four steps to it and is elevated five or six feet above the surrounding floor. As for higher altars, like the main altar of a cathedral, they usually find it quite impossible to conduct services unless they are in company with others, when their feelings are much relieved. This same thing is true of agoraphobia in some people. To go alone across an open place or square is agony, but even the company of a little child is sufficient to relieve them to a great degree. I told a distinguished American prelate of this curious dread in priests so often called to the physician's attention, and he said that he had never heard of it. To his surprise some of his clergymen present at the table told him that there were two examples of it in brothers in his own diocese.

Mental Discipline.—The lesson of the many men who, by discipline, have succeeded in conquering the aversion and the dread of heights that everyone has to some extent at least, shows the possibility there is for even those who are extremely sensitive in this matter to so lessen their timidity and the uncomfortable oppression that comes over them, as to make it possible to accomplish whatever is in their line of duty. It is no more difficult for the sensitive clergyman to learn by practice and discipline to walk with confidence on a reasonably high altar or platform, than it is for the workman to learn to {616} walk a beam on the top of a twenty-story building without a thought of the dangers of his position, or at least putting the thought away from him so that it does not interfere with his work. At the beginning he cannot do it, but he disciplines himself to form a habit that makes it easy. Yielding to his feelings makes it difficult to withstand the discomforts that come to him. After an accident on a high building, as a rule, men have to be sent home for the day to get their nerves settled by the night's sleep before they can work with sufficient confidence, and yet accomplish their usual amount of work.

So-called Misophobia—Dread of Dirt.—Misophobia, or the fear of dirt, has grown much more common in recent years, and the spread of the knowledge of the wide diffusion of bacteria has added to the unreasoning dread that possesses these people. Some of them wash their hands forty to fifty times a day, and one young man who was brought to me with the worst looking hands, because of irritation from soap and water, that I have ever seen, seemed to be always either just plunging his hands into water or wiping them dry. These people make themselves supremely miserable. They do not care to shake hands with friends and, above all, with physicians, and they invent all sorts of excuses so as to wait outside of doors till someone else opens them so as to avoid touching the knob or door pull, "which" with a poignant expression of repugnance they tell you "is handled by so many people." When the patients are women, getting on and off cars becomes a nightmare to them, because they do not want to touch the handle bars and unless they do they find it difficult to ascend and descend. The curious excuses they offer for their peculiar actions in avoiding the touch of objects around them are interesting.

Claustrophobia.—This sort of dread seems quite irrational to most people and many would probably conclude that individuals thus affected could not possibly be quite in their right minds, or must surely be rather weak-minded. On the contrary, many of the people who are affected by these curious dreads are above the average in intelligence and sometimes also in their power to do intellectual work. A typical example, for instance, of claustrophobia, or the fear of closed spaces, is found in the life of Philip Gilbert Hamerton. He was a distinguished painter and essayist, editor and novelist. Few men of his generation were able to do better intellectual work than he. His book on "The Intellectual Life" was more read perhaps than any work of its kind in the last generation. He was not a profound thinker, but he was a very talented practical man. The fact that besides being a writer whose books sold he was a painter whose works were in demand, shows a breadth of artistic quality that is quite unusual. His was not the sort of genius, however, that is so often supposed to be allied to insanity, for he was rather a worker who obtained his effects by plodding, than a brilliant genius that got his thoughts by intuition.

In a word, in spite of the fact that he was just the sort of man that one would not think likely to be affected by a phobia, he had a series of attacks of claustrophobia, some of which were intensely annoying to him and seriously disturbing to his friends. His wife has described some of them in his "Life and Letters." Once after crossing the English Channel, he had a severe attack in the railroad carriage on the way up to London. He had not been nervous {617} on the voyage and had not been seasick. He was returning from a vacation and was in the best of health and spirits, yet suddenly the feeling of inordinate dread that he was shut in came over him and he could scarcely control himself or keep from plunging out of the window in order to get into the open. His wife says that "His hands became cold, his eyes took on a far-reaching look, his expression became hard and set and his face flushed." He seemed "as if ready to overthrow any obstacle in his way; and indeed it was the case, for, unable to control himself any longer, he got up and told me hoarsely that he was going to jump out of the train. I took hold of his hand and said I would follow him, only I entreated him to wait a short time, as we were near the station. I placed myself quite close to the door of the railway carriage and stood between him and it. Happily the railway station was soon reached, when he rushed from the train and into the fields." His wife followed him like one dazed, and almost heart-broken. After half an hour he lessened his pace, turning to her and said, "I think it is going." For two hours they continued to walk, at the end of which Gilbert said tenderly in his usual voice, "You must be terribly tired, poor darling. I think I could bear to rest now. We may try to sit down."

Dread of Cats.—One of the most interesting of dreads, very frequently seen and producing much more discomfort than could possibly be imagined by anyone who had not seen striking cases of it, is the dread of cats which has been dignified and rendered more suggestively significant by the Greek designation ailurophobia. While the great majority of individuals suffering from this unreasoning dread of cats are women and usually of a delicate nervous organization, it must not be thought that it is by any means confined to them or has any necessary connection with hysterical symptoms. One of the most striking cases of this dread of which I know personally occurs in a large, rather masculine-looking woman, who cannot abide being in a room with a cat, and who is quite unable to do anything while one of these animals is within sight. Yet she is not at all what would be called timorous and she has more manly than womanly characteristics in every way. She once proceeded to thrash within an inch of his life a small burglar who entered her house and she rather prides herself on being able to protect herself. Nor is this dread necessarily associated with any other disturbances of mind or nervous system. Some of the patients I have seen, who confess to suffering from it, were thoroughly sensible, brave little women, able to stand suffering well, not at all hysterical in nature, and who in the midst of worries found time to be thoughtful of others and not to have that selfishness which, even more than physical symptoms, is so apt to characterize hysterical patients.

I have had men confess to me their dread of cats, and while, as a rule, they were of delicate constitution and inclined to be nervous and did not have the phobia to an inordinate degree, there was no doubt that they were extremely uncomfortable whenever a cat was near them. On the other hand, some of them were vigorous, husky men with strong aversions. One of the most marked cases of ailurophobia that was ever brought to my attention was in an army officer who had exhibited bravery in battle on many occasions, and what requires much more strength of mind, calm fortitude in difficult campaigning, yet for whom a cat had many more terrors than the battery of an enemy or even an ambuscade of Filipinos. More cases of this particular {618} aversion seem to occur in clergymen than in other men, yet one of the worst cases I ever saw was in a priest of great moral courage, who had served a pest-house over and over again in smallpox epidemics.

All that can be said about such a dread is that it exists, that it is unreasoning, that some patients have been known by discipline of mind to overcome the abhorrence to a great degree but never quite entirely. In this regard, however, it must not be forgotten that there are many things abhorrent to human nature that seem impossible to overcome the aversion for, yet discipline does much to relieve them. For instance, the handling of dead bodies so familiar to physicians brings with it an aversion that we never quite get over and which resumes most of its original strength with disuse, but that can be overcome to such an extent as to make pathological work produce very little aversion. Even Virchow, after all his years of occupation with pathological material, confessed toward the end of his life, that whenever he was away from his work for a few months his aversion had to be overcome anew.

The Spectator on Dreads.—There might be a tendency to think that these curious dreads came only as the result of the individualistic over-occupation with self and the introspective sophistication of the modern time, but the dread is not confined to our time nor special to it in any way, for we find Shakespeare talking of those who cannot bear a harmless, necessary cat. A number of other writers of different periods refer to it. As in so many other things *The Spectator* reflects his time in this and so we have a letter with regard to the dread of cats. It would not have been a subject for discussion in one of these popular communications only that the writer felt that a good many people would realize how like it was to things that they themselves knew of. In number 609 the following letter, supposed to be from a correspondent, seems worth giving in full, because it touches on other subjects in which uncontrollable, unreasoning feeling plays a role:

I wish you would write a philosophical paper about natural antipathies, with a word or two concerning the strength of imagination. ... A story that relates to myself on this subject may be thought not unentertaining, especially when I assure you that it is literally true. I had long made love to a lady, in the possession of whom I am now the happiest of mankind, whose hand I should have gained with much difficulty without the assistance of a cat. You must know then that my most dangerous rival had so strong an aversion to this species, that he infallibly swooned away at the sight of that harmless creature. My friend, Mrs. Lucy, her maid, having a greater respect for me and my purse than she had for my rival, always took care to pin the tail of a cat under the gown of her mistress, whenever she knew of his coming; which had such an effect that every time he entered the room, he looked more like one of the figures in Mrs. Salmon's wax-work than a desirable lover. In short, he grew sick of her company, which the young lady taking notice of (who no more knew why than he did), she sent me a challenge to meet her in Lincoln's Inn Chapel, which I joyfully accepted; and have, amongst other pleasures, the satisfaction of being praised by her for my stratagem.

Cat Fear and Furs.—This dread of cats is sometimes exhibited to a surprising degree under rather unexpected circumstances. For instance, it is not unusual, since the fashion for the longer-haired furs came in, to find that some of these patients cannot wear certain supposedly elegant furs, since they are really dyed catskin. At times this is not suspected until other possible causes for the discomfort have been eliminated. Some women cannot even bear to be near catskins in muffs and other such furs, though the imitation {619} may be so good as to deceive any but an expert, and they apparently had no suspicion at the beginning of the presence of cat fur near them. I have been told by a physician the story of a man, poignantly sensitive to cats, who purchased a fur-lined coat and found it quite impossible to wear it because of the sensations it produced in him, though he had no suspicion of any connection between cats and the fur when he purchased it.

Recognition of Presence.—Why this dread of cats occurs and, above all, the reason for the ability to know that a cat is near when the animal is concealed and others are not at all aware of its presence, or that its fur should produce a disagreeable sensation, is not easy to decide. Its discussion is suggestive for other forms of dreads, for there are probably like refinements of sensation, normal and abnormal, connected with them. Much has been said about this as a reversion to powers possessed by man in a savage state when there was necessity for guarding against animal attacks. Unfortunately for any such supposition as this, these people, who are most fearful of cats, that is, of the ordinary domestic animal, have no uneasiness in the presence of the huge cats in the menageries—the lions and the tigers. It is with regard to these that such a specialization of scent would be particularly valuable for men. There seems no doubt but that it is an odor or a sensation allied to an odor, though perhaps below the ordinary threshold of recognition as such, that enables these people to detect the presence of a

331

cat. Dr. Weir Mitchell in his article on "Ailurophobia and The Power to Be Conscious of the Cat as Near While Unseen and Unheard," in the *Transactions of the Association of American Physicians*, 1905, discusses odor in this connections as follows:

To be influenced by an olfactory impression of which (as odor) the subject rests unconscious, may seem an hypothesis worthy of small respect and beyond power of proof. Nevertheless it seems to me reasonable. There are sounds beyond the hearing of certain persons. If they ever cause effects we do not know. There are rays of which we are not conscious as light or heat, except through the effects to which they give rise. There may be olfactory emanations distinguished by some as odors and by others felt, not as odors, but only in their influential results on nervous systems unusually and abnormally susceptible. No other explanation seems to me available, and this gains value from certain contributory facts.

We must admit that all animals and human beings emit emanations which are recognizable by many animals and are in wild creatures protectively valuable.

This delicate recognition is commonly lost in mankind, but some abnormal beings like Laura Bridgeman and a perfectly normal lad I once saw, have possessed the power of distinguishing by smell the handkerchiefs of a family after they had been washed and ironed. In this lad I made a personal test of his power to pick out by their odor from a heap of clean handkerchiefs mine and those of others, the latter two belonging to his father and mother.

I have seen a woman, well known to me, who can distinguish by mere odor the gloves worn by relatives or friends. This lady, who likes cats as pets, is able to detect by its odor the presence of a cat when I and others cannot.

Two French observers believe that they have proved the sense of olfaction to be nine times more acute in women than in men.

So far as the present paper might serve in evidence, I should be inclined to say that the sense of smell was keener in women than in men, but as to this there is extreme diversity of opinion and the whole question awaits further investigation.

{620}

Dread of the Dark.—The discipline suggested with regard to overcoming the dread of heights must be applied to any of these dreads if patients are to be made comfortable. They can form the opposite habit and by refusing to yield to their fears can do much to lessen them. Nearly everyone who is unaccustomed to sleeping in a dark house alone has dreads that come over him when he first tries to do it. Every noise is exaggerated in significance and the creaking of stairs and rattling windows and doors and the wind through the trees are all made significant of something quite other than what they are. Nearly everyone knows, however, that this can be overcome simply by refusing to pay any attention to the idle fears that come over us as a consequence of the tension due to loneliness, and after a time, sleeping in a strange room and a strange house in the dark is not a difficult matter. It is harder for some people to accomplish than others, but it is impossible for none. Here is the lesson that all the sufferers from dreads must learn. Gradually, quietly, persistently, they must resist the dreads that come over them, must deliberately, without excitement, do the opposite to that suggested by their apprehension, until habits are formed that enable them to accomplish without discomfort what was before a source of even serious ill-feeling.

The dread of darkness that so many people have is usually supposed to be cowardice. It is not, however, in most cases, but is due to idiosyncrasy or to certain special physical factors in the environment. If children have been brought up so that when they were small a light has been constantly shining in their eyes, even though only a dim light, it will often be difficult to accustom them to be quite comfortable in the dark. Much depends on habit in this matter. I have known men, who, when they came from Ireland, feared the darkness of the coal mines very much and their dread was increased by the awful horror of possible ghostly appearances, since so many accidents had taken place where they worked. After some years, however, they were quite placid about it and would calmly go into the mine as fire bosses at three and four in the morning, long before others were to go in, examining absolutely dark passages by the mile, with no human being near them and with the creaking of the pillars, the dripping of water, the rumbling of the sides and the occasional fall of a small particle from the roof, besides the noises of rats to add to the disturbing factors. Like going up on a high building, one may get entirely accustomed to it so as scarcely to notice it at all.

When the fear is allowed to take hold of one, however, and no effort is made to overcome it, it may prove quite seriously disturbing. The unaccustomed, however, means more than anything else in this matter. Sometimes, {621} indeed, people have a dread of the dark that seems to be inborn and that apparently cannot be overcome, that, like the fear of cats or of lightning, may be quite beyond rational control. Hobbes, the English philosopher, was so perturbed by darkness that he kept a light in his bedroom all night. I know this to be the case in a clergyman who had been quite undisturbed about darkness until he was awakened one night by a burglar. He demanded "who's there?" and received as answer without further parley a bullet that fortunately struck only the head of the bed, but so close that it singed him. The burglar escaped, but the clergyman was never afterwards able to sleep without a light. Rousseau, the French philosopher, was also much afraid of darkness. Ordinarily it is presumed that superstition has something to do with this fear and that the victim of it has ghosts in mind or at least dreads spirit manifestations. Neither Hobbes nor Rousseau, however, was likely to be timorous about ghostly visitants. It was with them a physical idiosyncrasy.

Associated with dread of darkness is the fear of finding some one in a dark room whose presence may startle us. Sir Samuel Romilly, famous for his labors for the reform of the English criminal law, and who must be considered one of the great humanitarians of the nineteenth century, had this dread to an acute degree. It went so far that whenever he slept in a strange place he carefully examined all the possible hiding-places in the room and in wardrobes or closets connected with it and, as a last precaution, never failed to look under the bed. He did this even when he was in his own house. This, however, is not so unusual, even among men, as might be thought. Most women who sleep alone want to investigate under the bed and in a hotel closets and wardrobes and even bureau drawers are likely to be examined. Habit in this regard may make one quite miserable and over-solicitous. I have had patients whose sleep was seriously disturbed by the remembrance that they had not looked under the bed and who feared to get up and light a light to do so lest there should be someone there. Indeed, the idea of putting their feet on the floor before the light had come to reassure them seemed quite out of the question.

Dreads Connected with Water.—Strange as it may seem, water constitutes a source of dread for some people. We have the records of it in the peculiarities of great men and it is not unusual to meet it in common life. Dropping water is a source of disturbance for most people. It is quite impossible for the majority of men and women to go on writing or reading with any comfort if water is dropping near them. Dropping water, when one is trying to go to sleep, is one of the worst of awakeners. The Chinese are said to put people to death in horrible torture by having a drop of water fall at regular intervals on their heads. Robert Boyle, the great father of chemistry and a very sensible man in many ways, is said to have been thrown into convulsions by the sound of water dropping from a faucet. The splashing of water on some people is a poignant source of torture. I have had a woman patient who could not go to services where there was a sprinkling of water, for it seriously disturbed her and gave her a sense of depression that would not be overcome for some time. Peter the Great, though the father of the {622} Russian navy, and though he passed many years of his life in Holland, used to shudder at the sight of water, and if, when out driving, his carriage passed near a stream or over a bridge, he would close the windows and be overtaken with terror that brought the perspiration out all over him.

Dread of Death.—The fear of death is one of the dreads that bothers young as well as old, and, curiously enough, as its inevitable approach becomes more certain, men are prone to dread it more. Long ago Sophocles said:

None cleave to life so fondly as the old,

—and this has remained true for all the centuries since. A young man is quite ready to throw his life away, but the old man hesitates and even in the midst of suffering, if it is not absolutely continuous, craves that death shall not come. Sophocles' great rival, the elder Greek dramatic poet AEschylus, had said:

How far from just the hate men bear to death
Which comes as safeguard against many ills,

—but his message was only for those with the character to face the worst. One may reason with the dread of death, however, and patients can be given motives from philosophy, literature, religion and experience that will help to relieve, though it will not entirely cure them. Shakespeare said in "Julius Caesar":

Cowards die many times before their deaths.
The valiant never taste of death but once,

—and people may be aroused to appreciate this.

Fear of Early Death.—Many fear that if they have shown symptoms of delicacy of constitution at some time in life or suffered severely from some serious disease, that they are not likely to live long and, above all, that they are almost sure not to be able to accomplish anything worth while in life. The old proverb is "a healthy mind in a healthy body." This is, however, the ideal. There are very few ideals realized in life. Just because a man has a weak body is no argument at all that his mind may be weak and some of the world's finest work has been accomplished by men whose bodies were always delicate. Metchnikoff is the apostle of old age to our generation, but it is he, also, who has pointed out that many distinguished workers in science, in poetry, in art, men who have left a precious heritage in succeeding generations, were delicate all their lives. He cites such typical examples as Fresnel, the great French physicist; Giacomo Leopardi, the distinguished Italian poet; Weber and Schumann, the great German musicians, and Chopin, the Polish composer and pianist, all of whom did work that the world would not willingly miss, in spite of delicacy of health and weakness of body which shortened their lives. Intellectual power is not dependent on bodily energy and accomplishment is not a question of years of work, but intensity of work.

It would not be difficult to add many other names to those mentioned by Metchnikoff. Naturally his thoughts recurred to men of distinction on {623} the Continent, but in English-speaking countries we have a number of typical examples of strong minds doing fine work in weak bodies. Robert Louis Stevenson is the best remembered by our generation. Elizabeth Barrett Browning, delicate all of her life, a neurasthenic during the precious adolescent years that are supposed to mean so much for future accomplishment, always an invalid to some degree at least, did some of the best work that was given to any woman to do during the nineteenth century. J. Addington Symonds, the historian of the Renaissance and of Italian literature, is another striking example of a man who had to do his work under great physical difficulties, yet who left a long bookshelf of large volumes after him as the product of the hours that he could cheat from caring for his health. Henry Harland, whose recent death all too young was a blow to the English-speaking world, is another striking example. The names of such men and women and their stories must be made familiar to people who are themselves delicate in health and who fear for their future and, above all, are despondent about the possibility of ever doing anything worth while.

Dread of Insanity.—People who have relatives who are already sufferers from such severe forms of insanity as require asylum treatment are often likely to be much disturbed over the possibility that they themselves should become insane. Of course, there is no doubt but that these people are much more liable to suffer from insanity than others, but their worrying over the matter is sure to do them harm rather than good. There are quite enough sources of worry in life without the additional one of dread of a future event that may not occur, and this must be made as clear to them as possible. The people who have no obligations on them, who have nothing to do that they feel they have to do, are especially likely to suffer from such obsessions. The best possible relief for them is afforded, not by the effort not to worry about their dread, which usually has exactly the opposite effect and emphasizes their fear by the constant effort which they make to put it aside, but by getting something else to interest them. This must not be merely a passing interest, if possible, but a serious attraction of some kind that fully occupies the mind. A hobby is an excellent thing for this, but alas! a hobby must be cultivated for many years, as a rule, to become powerful enough to bring relief in such serious matters.

Occasionally the thought of the insane asylum or the sight of an institution of this kind passed even at a distance in the train is enough to give some people a fit of depression that may last for some time. The thought of going to visit their ailing relatives is enough to make them even more depressed. I have sometimes found that in chosen cases, especially among women and those of sympathetic disposition, the apparently heroic remedy of making them visit their relatives in the asylum was excellent for them. It is the usual rule for people who are themselves sane to consider that it is the greatest hardship of asylum confinement for the patients to be associated with those whom they recognize to be insane. Exactly the opposite effect is the usual result. To be among people, many of whom are more irrational than themselves and some of whom are quite beside themselves, proves a stimulus and an encouragement. Contentment has been defined by a cynic as the feeling that things might be worse.

{624}

DREADS OF MEN OF GENIUS

The insane are particularly prone to suffer from dreads, so that some people argue from their dreads to the thought of insanity. It is quite a mistake, however, to think of dreads as necessarily connected with insanity in any way. They are irrational though they will commonly be found to be dependent on some special physical condition. This is usually some exaggeration of attention to a sensation natural enough in itself but disturbing when dwelt on to such a degree that it produces a much greater reaction in these individuals than in other people. These dreads have existed in all sorts of people. It is said that they are more frequent in the highly intellectual, especially in the class known as geniuses, and they are often said to represent the definite evidence of a relationship between genius and insanity. I have always felt, however, that they are quite as common among ordinary people who have no genius and no signs of it as among the so-called geniuses. They are not so much spoken of by ordinary people, however, because they are rather ashamed of them. Genius, on the contrary, is quite willing, as a rule, to exploit its peculiarities for the benefit of the public, or what is even more true, its peculiarities are remembered and commented on as details of history.

With this in mind the following paragraph from Dr. Dorland's book on "The Ages of Mental Virility" deserves to be recalled. He has gathered a number of examples that are very interesting:

Fear has played an important rôle in the development of the antipathies of the great—fear that was often groundless in its origin and inexplicable in its manifestation. The unaccountable fear of dogs is not so common as ailurophobia, although it is said that De Musset cordially detested them, and Goethe despised them, notwithstanding, forsooth, he kept a tame snake. Much more frequent is the fear of spiders, centipedes, and other insects. Charles Kingsley, thorough naturalist though he was, entertained an unconquerable horror of spiders, even the common house spider; Turenne became weak when he saw a spider; while the author of the "Turkish Spy" once asserted that he would far prefer, with sword in hand, "to face a lion in his desert lair than to have a spider crawl over him in the dark." Lord Lauderdale, on the contrary, while declaring that the mewing of a cat was "sweeter to him than any music," had a most intense dislike for the flute and the bag-pipe; and Dr. Johnson was so fond of his cats that he would personally buy oysters for them, his servants being too proud to do so.

There are curious contradictions to be found in these matters. Montaigne confesses that he did his best writing and was in the best humor for keeping at his Essays while stroking his favorite cat with his left hand, his other being occupied with his writing. This would be seriously disturbing to many people, but apparently occupied certain distracting sensory tendencies and enabled him to concentrate his mental energies. To many people the very thought of doing anything like this would put all ideas for writing out of their mind. Other of Montaigne's peculiarities are quite as interesting. He always refused to sit down with thirteen at table, his liking for odd numbers was so great that he made all sorts of excuses in order not to use {625} even numbers and his aversion for Friday made the quota of work that he could do on that day much less than any other day of the week.

OBSESSIONS

There are many curious obsessions that disturb people and that are often extremely difficult of explanation even by themselves. Dr. Johnson, one of the most sensible men in many ways in his time in England, could not, it is said, pass a post on the street without touching it. At least if he did so he felt that somehow he had omitted to do something that he ought to have done and it would make him uncomfortable. There are many people who have some idea that it is lucky to touch posts as they pass along and the number of people who do things like this is larger than might be imagined. Many people put themselves out of the way in order to avoid letting a post come between the person with whom they are walking and themselves because it is said to be unlucky. Most of them will laugh at it, but still they continue the practice in spite of the bother it may occasion them. Occasionally there is some incident in their past life which accounts for such obsessions, though the patients themselves are occasionally not quite conscious of them. Dr. Boris Sidis tells the story of a man who could not take a car with an odd number. Psycho-analysis showed that he had once seen a child run down by an odd-numbered car.

In such cases there has been a long series of suggestions that have created a dominant state of mind. The only way to overcome this when it becomes a serious annoyance is to undo the influence of the suggestions by a continued series of counter-suggestions, and by such discipline of mind as will prevent the former suggestion from exerting itself. The cure can be accomplished in this way, though, as a rule, the patient will need the help of someone else.

FORGOTTEN FRIGHTS AND DREADS

Dreads founded on terrifying or seriously disturbing incidents of the past, the details of which at times have gone out of the patient's mind, are not infrequent. It is probable that many of the unreasoning dreads have some such foundation and occasionally, if patients' memories are carefully searched, the whole story can be reconstructed. All that is needed, as a rule, is to get the patients interested in conjunction with the physician in tracing the origin of their affliction and not infrequently an interesting story will turn up. Hypnosis used to be considered of great value for such reconstructions, but unfortunately patients then become so suggestible that it is often difficult to decide how much of what is brought out by questioning is due to the suggestive quality that cannot well be kept out of questions, and how much to a true redintegration of memory.

Frights in children may for a time be forgotten and yet the memory of them may come back, or a dread connected with them develop, that will make the patient profoundly miserable. One of my patients slipped and fell on a smooth steel plate at the head of a coal breaker and was only saved by good fortune from falling a long distance. This happened when he was a {626} boy of ten. There were times when the memory of this recurred so vividly as to set him all atremble and he could not look down from a height without something of the feeling of goneness coming over him that he felt at the time of the accident. The calling of his attention to the fact that his memory probably exaggerated the danger he had been in as a boy led him to go back and have another look at the conditions in which he had fallen some thirty years before. He found that they were not so dangerous as he thought and that while he would have been scratched and his clothes would probably have been soiled and torn, he would not have been seriously injured. This has greatly diminished his dread of heights.

Various physical manifestations may be due to dreads which are often supposed to be the result of some physical process in the nervous system. Occasional fits of trembling, for instance, are, in sensitive people, due to more or less forgotten memories of dangers or frights. Occasionally even slight convulsive seizures may follow such recurrent dreads. Not a few of the cases of so-called hystero-epilepsy in the borderland between hysteria and epilepsy but always one or the other, are due to such mental states rather than to any physical conditions. Such incomplete memories are sometimes spoken of as subconscious. The word subconscious has been so much abused, however, that I prefer not to use it. The reminiscences have been obscured by an accumulation of other facts but may with an effort of attention and concentration of mind be recalled. Hypnosis, or the milder form of it spoken of as the hypnoidal state, may enable the patient to recall them more vividly by enabling him to concentrate his attention, but there are always risks that suggestion will vitiate the old story in these cases. With care all the details can usually be recalled and the patient is thus given renewed confidence in himself and his own powers and does not learn to lean on someone else in the process.

TREATMENT

The most important psychotherapeutic factor for the relief of the discomfort due to dreads is the knowledge that there are so many and such different varieties of them and that so many people suffer from them. Many of those afflicted are inclined to think that their cases are almost unique. To have them know that there are all forms and phases of these curious aversions is to make them laugh a little at their own because they laugh so readily at others, and it gives them new courage for the attempt to conquer them. The aversion cannot be entirely overcome, but it can be prevented from seriously influencing sleep or appetite or occupation. This is after all the important feature of the case from the standpoint of psychotherapy. Besides, patients are encouraged not only to take up, but, above all, to continue, the practice of that mental discipline and self-control which will enable them to lessen their natural aversion, if not to remove it entirely. I have many cases in which patients' aversions have been entirely overcome. Curiously enough, there are rather often relapses when the patients are run down in weight, or are in an irritable condition from worry or emotional stress, and then something of the former mental discipline has to be reinstituted to make them once more free from disturbance.

{627}

I have sometimes found that the recommendation to patients suffering from dreads to read Mary Wollstonecraft Shelley's "Frankenstein" has proved an excellent therapeutic agent. This is particularly true when the patients are women, for it is likely to bring them close to the sad lives of the Shelleys. The circumstances in which the book was written add to the appeal. "Frankenstein" itself is interesting, so that the mood created by this combination of interests is excellently therapeutic. It will be recalled that in "Frankenstein" the inventor seeking to make a man does make an automaton that is able to move and to talk, but that then haunts its inventor, demanding of him a soul. It proves a plague to him, but he cannot escape from it. Fly where he will his creation follows him and bothers the life out of him, killing a friend, strangling his bride, and making existence intolerable. The symbol is complete and to the point. The things that bother us in life are to a great extent of our own invention. The dreads that make so many people miserable are practically always without any groundwork in reality, figments of our imagination without the soul of real life, but capable, as was Frankenstein's monster, of making their creators intensely miserable and with them, to an even greater degree, their friends.

CHAPTER IV

HEREDITY

There are so many false and, indeed, from a scientific standpoint, utterly groundless notions with regard to heredity which, as a result of the popularization of science, have become widely diffused, that notions about inheritance are a most copious source of dreads and discouragement and even produce inhibition of resistive vitality against disease on the part of many patients. At first it seemed to me as though the subject should be treated in the chapter on Dreads. It is so much more important than the other dreads, however, and there are so many people with so many different notions as to the evil influence of heredity that it seems advisable to devote a special chapter to it in which to provide contrary suggestion. Many patients are constantly suggesting to themselves that, because they are suffering from certain symptoms due to real or supposed hereditary conditions, there is little or no hope of their recovery or of any effective relief. In the old days, when tuberculosis was considered to be hereditary, it was almost hopeless to try to rouse patients into a state of vital resistance to their disease because of this overhanging dread. Such a prepossession of mind must be overcome.

In spite of all that has been said about the power for evil of heredity, and in this as in every other phase of pseudo-science, the reason why there are false popular notions is because the medical profession first cherished them and then they spread popularly, we now know that it means comparatively little in pathology. The false notions will continue, however, to be popularly diffused probably for another generation, at least, and will have to be combated. Their force must be lessened, for they are a heavy incubus on the patient's mind, imposing a burden on vitality that inhibits normal, vital reaction. This can only be done by a frank and complete statement of {628} our present knowledge of heredity, which is even yet not nearly so definite as we would like to have it, but which contradicts entirely most of the older impressions. In the matter of disease what we know of heredity, instead of being a source of distress and discouragement for patients, provides rather new incentives for vigorous reaction, since nature helps rather than hampers the effort of the individual to throw off disease from generation to generation.

False Impressions and Expression.—Probably the commonest expressions that the physician hears from his patients, though we hear many stereotyped phrases in our time when patients so freely discuss their ills and their physicians' opinions among themselves, are such as: "My father suffered from rheumatism, and I suppose I must expect to be bothered by the same ailment." "My mother died of heart disease and I think I have a weak heart; I suppose that we have weak hearts in the family." "I have had three relatives die of cancer in the last three generations, so I presume that cancer is in the family, or at least we are much more liable to cancer than the generality of people." And, finally, what used to be the commonest of all, but fortunately we have changed that at least, though we sometimes hear it still: "Tuberculosis runs in our family, my mother and an uncle died of it and one of my brothers is suffering from it, so I suppose I must just make up my mind that I, too, am sure to get it." Even the rarer affections, like kidney disease, liver disease, various nervous troubles, stomach and intestinal disturbances of many kinds, flatulence, constipation or diarrhea, are all supposed to be hereditary and patients explain their ill feelings by an appeal to the supposed principle of heredity and its application to themselves and their families.

In many chapters in this book the subject of heredity has been considered with regard to specific affections. We have no evidence at all, or the evidence is so trivial as to be quite negligible, that anything acquired by the individual, be it for good or evil, is ever transmitted to the next generation. That acquired characters are not transmitted is now almost a universally accepted principle among biologists. The more a biologist knows of recent biological research and investigation the more will he be likely to consider this principle of the non-transmission of acquirements as definitely settled. According to this, then, no disease is ever transmitted to the next generation. This is such a complete reversal of former opinions, such an open contradiction of popular beliefs, that the subject merits thorough discussion from this newer standpoint for medical applications. We must not forget that popular medicine, even when egregiously wrong, is founded on opinions held by the medical profession aforetime and, indeed, on this subject of heredity many of the medical profession still cling to the former opinion.

Tuberculosis, which used to furnish the most serious argument in this matter, has now come to be the best possible explanation that we have for the fallacy of the transmission of anything acquired. The disease followed families so constantly that it seemed impossible to explain it unless the principle of its heredity was conceded. Now that we know its contagiousness, however, it is comparatively easy to explain its occurrence in families. When we recall how carelessly people coughed and even expectorated around the house, while children crept on the floors and carried the germs of the disease to their mouths on their hands, the wonder is, not that so many members of the family acquired the disease seeing the manifold opportunities for contagion, but that {629} any of them ever escaped. We know now that practically every adult above the age of thirty either has or has had tuberculosis. Careful autopsies show us remains of the disease even in the bodies of those who, without any history of tuberculosis, die from other diseases. One out of eight of the population dies of tuberculosis, but the remaining seven are quite capable of resisting the disease and so we find healed lesions at autopsies in this proportion of cases.

Family History Favorable.—It is certain, then, that tuberculosis is not hereditary. On the contrary, as we have learned more about the disease in recent years, it has been recognized by specialists that patients who have a family history of tuberculosis are notably less likely to succumb to the disease early than those who have no such history. An acute case of tuberculosis with considerable loss of weight has a very unfavorable prognosis unless there is a history of the disease in the preceding generation, when at once the outlook becomes more hopeful. This newer view is confirmed by what we have learned from the ethnological pathology of the disease. Peoples exposed to the disease for the first time rapidly succumb to it. This is practically true for all the infectious diseases. Our American Indians succumbed in large numbers not only to tuberculosis but also to smallpox and even to measles when each was first introduced among them. The same thing was true in the South Sea Islands. Where nations have been exposed to the disease for some time they have acquired not an immunity, but at least they possess a greater resistive vitality to its ravages and while they still may be susceptible they are not so subject to the fatal forms of the disease, and even if they acquire it they live on for many years.

Many people may insist that this immunity or comparative immunity to tuberculosis and increased resistive vitality against the disease is transmitted and illustrates the principle of heredity. The reaction of the system to the disease increases in each generation and this increase is an acquired character which passes down with the family strain. This immunity should be viewed from another standpoint, however. Certain families possess a resistive vitality to the disease; others lack it. The resistant families do not succumb to it, and propagate themselves. The others gradually die out. What caused the resistant families originally to possess this quality we do not know. We have no trace of its being acquired. Like so many other characters by which men differ from one another, we do not know the beginning of it. Once it comes in as a family trait it is transmitted. In successive generations we have no evidence that it is stronger, only the danger is recognized from experience and better precautions are taken; the consequence is that the original resistive vitality has a better chance to make itself felt and so the family is preserved. This is as true with regard to the conquest of the tendency to excess in the taking of toxic substances, as alcohol and opium, as with regard to disease. It is not the transmission of an acquired character, but the descent of a family trait the origin of which we do not know.

Hereditary Syphilis.—Many physicians will protest that, at least, we have ample evidence for the transmission of syphilis by heredity. We have for many years talked of hereditary syphilis as if it were absolutely sure that its transmission by inheritance took place. There is no doubt, of course, that the disease is conveyed from mother to child. If a mother is actively syphilitic, {630} then her child will surely have syphilis when it is born. This, however, is no argument for the hereditary transmission of syphilis. We know now that if a mother is tuberculous, in an active stage of that disease, her child will almost surely have the disease, but this is a question of contagion not of inheritance. If a mother with active tuberculosis nurses her child she is likely to give it tuberculosis. Usually the idea is that the milk is not infective unless there are tuberculous lesions in the breasts, and in cattle it is well known that such lesions in the milk apparatus inevitably bring tubercle bacilli into the milk. The demonstration of tubercle bacilli in the blood of patients in the active stage of the disease is now much more frequent than used to be the case and there seems no doubt that the bacillus can pass through glandular structures into the secretions.

In the same way syphilitic nurses are likely to infect nurslings, though, of course, in this case there are usually syphilitic sores on the nipples which directly communicate the disease. It is almost impossible for a syphilitic woman to nurse a child, if she is in an active stage of the disease, without the production of such infective sores on her nipples. When children are born with syphilis it means only that in the process of feeding the child through the placental tissues, a mother has infected her child quite as she might infect it by nursing afterwards, in case she acquired syphilis after the birth. Lesions corresponding to those on the nipple occur in placental tissues and can be demonstrated without much difficulty. Congenital syphilis, however, can always be traced to contagion and the being born with the disease or having the manifestations of it occur shortly after birth is no argument for heredity at all. It merely emphasizes the danger of contagion.

Mothers of Syphilitic Children.—But there are some cases in which the child who shows symptoms of syphilis after birth is born from a mother who never had any manifestations of syphilis and therefore it has been supposed that the infection must have come from the sperm, and that in these cases, at least, there is a true heredity. It is perfectly possible, however, that syphilitic infective material may accompany the spermatozoon and so bring about the occurrence of syphilis in the offspring. Even this would be infection, however, and not heredity. Much more frequently it would seem that the disease in the infant was contracted from the mother while suffering from a latent form of syphilis, rather than from the paternal contributory particle to its existence. The mother gives no sign of the disease, but Colles' Law is that the mother of a syphilitic child may, without danger to herself, be allowed to nurse her own infant even though she herself has never had any symptoms. This can only mean that she is thoroughly protected against the disease. We would not think for a moment of allowing an ordinarily healthy women to nurse a syphilitic child. Such immunity in the mother of the syphilitic child can only come, so far as the present state of our knowledge goes, from her having had the disease. It has been said that as the result of the intimate communication with her child in utero she has acquired an immunity by the passage across the placental membrane which separates maternal and fetal blood of protective substances of various kinds due to the reaction against the disease already beginning in the child. As a matter of fact, however, there is no evidence of any such reactive substances in the blood of the child which after birth proceeds to have a series of acute lesions that are, as a rule, indicative {631} of almost complete lack of resistive vitality. Maternal immunity is evidently due to the occurrence of the disease in some form within the maternal tissues which produces the usual protection against the disease in a briefer time than usual. This certainly seems to be a more satisfactory explanation than that of a transmission of an immunity from the child to the mother which the child itself does not possess. It is easier to understand the transmission of an infection that does not manifest itself externally than of an immunity which there has been no time to acquire. Both explanations leave a mystery, but the mystery in the second case can be explained more in consonance with what we know about syphilitic transmission and immunity than in the other case. It does away with the transmission directly from the father almost completely, of course, leaves practically no ground for the heredity of syphilis, but it accords much better than older explanations with biological principles.

Late Lesions and Heredity.—Many physicians will be likely to insist that the late developments of syphilis in children, in which not only three or five years afterwards, but even fifteen or twenty years after birth, there are syphilitic manifestations, are beyond all doubt examples of heredity. In the last twenty-five years, however, our ideas with regard to the after-effects of syphilis have been entirely modified by what we have learned of such diseases as locomotor ataxia, paresis and the like. These are undoubtedly parasyphilitic diseases in most cases, yet they not infrequently develop from ten to twenty years after any manifestation of syphilis and they seem to occur, by preference almost, in cases where the preliminary symptoms have been very mild. In not a few cases, indeed, the symptoms of syphilis have been so transient in

337

these patients that the true significance of them was missed until the later developments showed their real character. Krafft-Ebing, at the International Medical Congress at Moscow in 1897, detailed some experiments that he had made on paretics in Vienna. They were patients in whom no history of syphilis could be found, yet they were suffering from typical paresis. As they were in the ultimate stage of the disease it did not seem unjustifiable to inoculate them with syphilis, and in most cases it was found that they would not take the disease, showing that they were probably protected by a previous attack, though there was no history of it.

The development of the late symptoms of syphilis in the second generation can then be much more satisfactorily explained on the basis of a mild infection with very few primary symptoms, almost lacking in secondary symptoms, yet followed by subsequent symptoms of great severity consequent upon the deterioration of vitality produced by the disease. As for the manifestations in the third generation, they are not directly syphilitic, but are, whenever they occur, due to conditions consequent upon the degeneration that had been effected in the preceding generation and which directly weakened the offspring—on the same principle that weak parents give birth to weak children, and starving parents cannot have strong, healthy children—but not because of any direct influence of the disease. It is worth while to discuss this subject from this standpoint, since it disposes of the only supposed evidence left for the hereditary transmission of disease that we now have, though only a few years ago most diseases were supposed to be hereditary.

Heredity in Cancer.—With regard to other diseases, the evidence for any inheritance has been founded entirely on coincidence. All the human race {632} dies and must die some way, and so in families a certain number will die of the same disease. The argument for heredity in cancer is extremely weak. When all the relatives of a person afflicted with cancer as far out as the third generation are taken into account, only about one in five of them are found to have suffered from cancer. When we remember, however, that more than one in thirty of all those who die, die of cancer and that the death-rate of this disease is greater than that of typhoid fever, smallpox, scarlet fever, measles, and all other infectious diseases put together, it is easy to understand how large a role coincidence plays in any such set of statistics, and how little the significance of the occurrence of cancer in different members of the same family means, unless possibly there is an occasional element of contagiousness which must not be left out of the reckoning.

Heredity in Other Affections.—Other ailments present much less possibility or probability of any element of heredity. For instance, over-indulgence in meat or drink may readily bring about various ailments of the gastro-intestinal tract. These are, of course, definitely acquired conditions, some of them temporary and some persistent, that will continue to give trouble so long as the patient continues to produce irritation of them. They may, of course, lead to permanent pathological conditions. To say that any of these are likely to be inherited would be quite as absurd as to say that a corn could be inherited, or the permanent deformities produced in toes by wearing badly-fitting shoes could be transmitted to the next generation. We do not think for a moment that because a man has lost a finger his children are likely to be born without a finger, and still less if by some accident or abuse he has been deprived of the use of an arm or leg, that that is likely to be transmitted to the next generation. Yet people calmly talk of the heredity of similarly produced conditions within the body, and even physicians are not entirely free from the superstition, for such it is, of the influence of heredity in producing pathological conditions.

Habits of various kinds, physical and mental, are calmly accepted by many people as influenced by or having their origin in heredity. Under Alcoholism and Drug Addictions we have discussed this phase of the subject, but a word or two more may make it clearer. A tendency to form the same habits may be a family trait and descend from one generation to another. That a specific habit should be the subject of heredity or transmission is as much out of the question as that a facility for doing anything should be transmitted. The son of an acrobat must practice quite as faithfully as did his father in order to secure his father's skill. He may inherit from his father that particular constitution of body, that specific combination of muscle and sinew and bone that enables him to become an acrobat by practice, though with a different kind of body it would be impossible, but his father's acquired facility influences in no way the son's ability. We often hear of a man being the descendant of a series of generations each of whom has gone to the university, as if that somehow assured him a readier and better facility for education, but we know very well that this is not true and that the boys straight from the soil are often the best students and far ahead of the scions of long-time academic families.

Inheritance of Defects.—Acquired characters are not transmitted, though family traits are the subject of inheritance. Disease is not hereditary, but {633} defect is. Crossed eyes occur very commonly in families and are evidently a subject of transmission. Family noses are often very peculiar and may be traced for many generations. The Hapsburg lip has been noted in sixty per cent. of the Hapsburgs since the family came into prominence in the thirteenth century. Features of all kinds are inherited, as anyone who has ever spent some time in a family portrait gallery where the ancestors were genuine and the paintings reasonably true to life, knows very well. Certain features of European families can be traced for many generations. The tendency to have six toes or to have an extra finger runs in certain families. So small a thing as a patch of white hair in a particular part of the head may be the subject of hereditary transmission. Moles on a particular part of the body are inherited. All these, however, are characters with regard to the acquisition of which we know nothing, but that have somehow found their way into the family strain and have become subjects of transmission from generation to generation. They provide no evidence, however, as to the transmission of acquired characters.

Variation.—What is even more surprising in biology, however, is that there is another marvelous force at work quite as incomprehensible in its way, perhaps even more so, than that of heredity. This is variation. All creatures have a tendency to vary from their parents. A very small proportion of the offspring resemble parents so closely as to be quite similar. The great majority of them, however, have noteworthy, individual, distinctive qualities. Occasionally these qualities may be traced to the less immediate ancestors and then we talk about reversion. Occasionally there appears in a child some trait or anomaly supposed to be remotely ancestral and it is spoken of as atavism. Whenever there is a tendency of the offspring of exceptional parents to regress toward the racial average, we talk of regression.

Tall parents often have tall children, some of them may, by a special tendency of heredity, be taller even than themselves. Most of them will be shorter, however, and tend to regress toward the racial average.

Few people understand what a wonderful power among living things is exerted by this very opposite of heredity—variation. All the possibility of improvement not only in humanity but among all living things is dependent on variation. It does not seem difficult to understand how offspring resemble parents. They are of them, therefore they are like them. When we analyze the problem of heredity, however, and find that the connecting link between offspring and parents is always only a single cell of less than one one-hundredth of an inch in diameter, the mystery of heredity looms up in all its immensity. This minute bit of protoplasm, so small that it requires a rather strong power of the microscope to see it, somehow contains compressed within itself all the qualities that characterize the parent and are to be transmitted to the offspring. Among animals, the color of the eyes and hairy covering, the form and height of the animal, its generic characteristics, and its individual characters—all are contained within this minute spherule. The white blaze on the horse's hind leg, the black blotch on the puppy's face, the white lock on a human head, are all carried over from one generation to another with all the other qualities in this small package. That is the mystery of heredity.

To this must be added another mystery quite as great and even more {634} difficult to understand—variation. This tendency to vary is the basis for whatever evolution there is in the world. Some living things vary in such a way as to be better suited to their environment than they were before and then these outlive others because more favorably situated, and natural selection brings about a maintenance of the favorable variation. Instead, then, of patients being impressed with the unfavorable influence of heredity, they should rather be made to feel the weight of the idea that whatever evil tendencies the parent has the child is more likely to have less of them than more, so that variation tends to make the race better. We have had too much stress laid on the heredity of unfortunate qualities and entirely too little made of the variation tendency, which is constantly lifting the race up. It is, of course, only what happens in everything else, unfavorable are likely to have more weight than favorable suggestions, and unless these latter are emphasized their influence becomes swamped. This has happened with regard to variation. It is quite as important a biological element as heredity and it makes for the removal of unfortunate qualities, yet it has never become a popular idea and is little appreciated even by physicians.

Patients who are worried about their heredity will, after a frank discussion of our present knowledge of heredity and its co-ordinate factor of variation, lose most of their dread of this specter of supposed evil influence which so often proves the source of discouragement and failure to react properly against pathological conditions. There is probably no phase of modern biology in which the so-called popularization of science has done more harm by providing an abundant source ol unfortunate suggestions. Whatever influence heredity has in relation to disease is favorable to the human race. It is true that this is exerted by the elimination of the unfit, yet the very consequence of this is that the children of parents who have suffered from a particular disease are likely to have greater average resistance to it than the generality of mankind, since their parents passed the age up to reproductive activity without succumbing to it. For cancer, tuberculosis and syphilis this teaching is of special value and is probably more effective than any other single means could be to prevent the ravages of the disease if it should occur, since it keeps the patient from interfering with his own resistive vitality by the discouraging conviction that there is no possible hope for him because his parents also suffered from the disease.

CHAPTER V

PREMONITIONS

A state of mind that disturbs many people seriously, sometimes even producing physical results, because of the burden of dread that hangs over them, is that in which attention is paid to premonitions of evil. There are two of these general conditions to be considered. In the one there is a definite feeling that some special evil, occasionally very particularly outlined in the mind, as a railroad accident, fire, or a street accident of some kind, is to occur. In another mental condition there is a generic premonition of evil, {635} as if the worst were sure to happen and the patients must be constantly preparing for it. Occasionally this takes on some such form as an assurance of early breakdown in health, or of death at an untimely age, or of some crippling infirmity. This represents, of course, only one form of lack of control over the mind, but it is surprising how much physical suffering it may occasion. Only those who have had much to do with patients who suffer from this state of mind realize it. Sympathetic knowledge of the conditions that bring it about and of the real significance of premonitions will do more to help patients than anything else.

Every now and then newspapers tell the story of someone who had an impending sense of danger, perhaps of a particular form of accident or misfortune, which he could not shake off and which finally came true. Sometimes it is a fire that was anticipated, though without any reason except the dread, and precautions that eventually proved life-saving to the patient were taken, or at least friends were told of it so that the person seemed actually to have had some warning beforehand of the danger that was to come. Sometimes it is the story of a railroad accident, which some particularly fortunate individual escaped, because of a premonition that made him take another train or make a happy change of cars. Nothing is said of the times when premonitions failed, nor of the disappointments of such dreads. Most people laugh at the stories, but a few individuals become seriously impressed with the possibility of such warnings and then make themselves miserable by having frequent premonitions.

Etiology.—As to the origin of these premonitions it is hard to say. They occur more frequently on dark days than in bright weather and are complained of much more in spring and fall than during the cold brisk winter or during the summer time. A succession of very hot days, however, brings a series of premonitions, especially with regard to accidents by heat, that is not surprising since the newspapers have many accounts of sunstrokes and there is every suggestion of the possibility of danger of this kind. How large a role suggestion plays in the matter can be realized from the fact that after some particularly serious railroad accident many people have premonitions that they may be hurt and occasionally they put themselves to considerable inconvenience in choosing the car in which they will sit, if the last serious preceding accident of which they have heard happens to have brought death mainly in a particular car of a train. It is always suggestible people who are likely to have premonitions. The thought comes very simply at first, they dwell on it a little unwillingly, then they find it impossible to banish it and finally it may become a positive obsession. The soil and the seed for suggestion are both needed to produce premonitions.

Royce suggests that many of the supposedly fulfilled premonitions are really only pseudo-presentiments and represent an instantaneous and irresistible hallucination of memory, which may give rise to the impression that there has been a previous dream or other warning presaging the facts, though no such phenomenon actually took place. In other words, there would be an auto-suggestion consequent upon the hearing of other fulfilled presentiments that sometime some such thing must also occur to us, and then when a happening that reminds us of something in the previous stories of {636} presentiments comes there is the sudden responsive feeling "why, this is what I saw or must have seen in my dream."

Podmore suggests an illusion of memory magnifying or rearranging the details of a recent dream or premonitory impression, so as to make it fit into the happenings. Dreams are so vague that unless they have been written down we are not quite sure of them an hour after they occurred and a day or two later we have only the merest hint of what they were. If this can be made to have any connection with a casualty of any kind that happens subsequently we may very readily recreate the dream with its details concordant to the event. Certainly no reliance can be placed on a story of a dream fulfilled unless the dream was told before the happening.

Premonitions of Death.—Certain premonitions are common and are frequently brought to the physician's notice. Among old people it is not unusual to find that a premonition of death will hang over them for days, seriously disturbing them and their friends, hampering often a healthy reaction against disease and always lowering resistive vitality. Many of them have heard stories which make them credit the belief that such premonitions are likely to come true and therefore they cannot shake them off. They have heard stories of people who have become convinced that they were going to die at a particular time on a particular day and whose conviction has been proven by the event. Like all the other premonitions, whatever truth there may appear to be in them, is due entirely to the fact that nearly everybody has premonitions and occasionally, therefore, one of them must come true. Those that are fulfilled create such an impression that they are remembered, while those that fail are forgotten, until, though it is not realized, it becomes true that fulfilled premonitions represent exactly that much misunderstood principle that the exception proves the rule. The rule is that premonitions fail. Exceptionally, however, a premonition comes true. Instead of proving that premonitions mean anything, the rarity of their fulfillment proves the rule of their non-significance and demonstrates that they are merely coincidences.

Persuasion of Short Life.—Much mental suffering occurs in nervous people as a consequence of a premonition or persuasion which comes to them in middle life that they are destined not to live very long. This is a commoner impression than is usually thought and comes to nearly everyone at some time in life. Especially is it likely to come to those who have suffered some severe illness and who know how weak they were during their convalescence and, in spite of their thorough recovery of strength, cannot quite persuade themselves but that an ailment which made them so weak must surely have sapped their vitality so as to make long life for them impossible. It is, of course, one of the vague dreads that men always seem to be harboring, but there are times that it becomes so prominent and so influential in the production of depressive feelings that it is worth while to have the means at hand to counteract it as far as possible. In the last ten years I have made it a practice to ask, not only all my patients but most of my acquaintances above 70 years of age whether they had ever experienced such a premonition. I have particularly asked what were their feelings with regard to the hope of long life for them when they were in their forties and fifties. Without exception I have been told by all those who had the education and leisure to {637} be at all introspective, that they had felt sure that they would not have long life.

Most of the men consulted took out life insurance in such a way as to benefit their families after their death rather than themselves during life. Indeed it seems not an unusual thing for men to have some experience with an ailment between 40 and 55 which makes them realize their mortality much more than the deaths of their friends around them had succeeded in doing. Premonitions and impressions, then, of this kind evidently mean nothing, so far as the prospect of long life is concerned. Practically everyone has them, and since, of course, the great majority of men do not live to die of old age, it would seem that their premonition of comparatively short life was fulfilled. Occasionally a man will be found at the age of fifty unwilling to take up further work or develop his business because of the dread that has come over him that he may not live long enough to make it worth the while. Where there is serious kidney or heart trouble such an abstention from business is commendable, but in many cases it leaves a man without occupation or with insufficient occupation and he becomes short-circuited on himself with more serious results from worry than would have come from work.

Publication of Fulfilled Premonitions.—The publication of fulfilled premonitions has always seemed to me to be an especially fertile source of premonitions for other people. Every now and then someone goes to bed in a hotel having communicated to friends the idea that he fears there may be fire before morning. I do not suppose that one out of ten people who sleep in a strange hotel fail to have some such thought, they do not consider it a premonition, however, but only a suggestion for the taking of proper precautions so as to know where exits and fire escapes and other means of escape are situated, so that in the excitement of the fire they may not have to do any thinking, but may have already made up their minds what they shall do. This sort of premonition, if we call it by that name, has a definite useful purpose. Occasionally it seems marvelously provident. The other makes its possessor toss sleepless a portion of the night, does no good and much harm. If, however, the premonition has been communicated to someone else and then a fire should occur, the reporting of the fulfilled premonition comes to a lot of weak-minded people as a confirmation of their worst fears. It is, of course, only a question of coincidence in a succession of events by no means connected in any causal relation, yet by the unthinking set down as showing the possibility of such premonitions being supremely significant. If we had all the stories of unfulfilled premonitions also published then the true significance of the others would be clear.

An Unfulfilled Premonition.—There is an excellent story of a strong but unfulfilled premonition told by Carl Schurz in his "Recollections," which seems to me such a good antidote to the influence of supposed premonitions, that every physician should know its details for their psychotherapeutic value with patients prone to be troubled in this way. The ease with which the depression consequent upon the premonition was relieved as soon as another forcible suggestion that the danger was past took possession of him, shows how such states of mind can be altered with no more real reason for the alteration than there was for the original depression.

{638}

On the morning of the battle of Chancellorsville General Schurz awoke with the absolute persuasion that at last his time had come and he was to be killed that day. He had never had such a premonition before. He had heard of many cases in which such premonitions proved the forerunner of death. He realized how ridiculous was the idea that he should know anything about what the future held for him, even vaguely, and he tried to shake it off. He found it impossible to do so. He thought that after he took up the routine work of the day the force of the premonition would be lost. It was not, but, on the contrary, seemed to increase in power over him. Finally the idea became so imperative that he sat down and wrote letters of farewell to his wife and friends, telling them that he had been tempted to do so because of this premonition of danger. When he went into battle—and it may be recalled that the Eleventh Corps did some fighting at Chancellorsville that day—he was sure that now the end was not far off. It did not take away his courage, however, and though he was well in the zone of danger, he issued his orders and kept his troops well in hand as we know from the history of the battle.

Finally his aide-de-camp, riding toward the front of the line beside him, was killed by a cannon ball. All in an instant the thought came over him that this was the only danger that was likely to be near him for the day. The burden of premonition lifted from him as if the fact that a friend had been killed beside him gave him an assurance that he himself was not to be taken. There was absolutely no reason for his thinking so, but his feelings of solicitude with regard to himself and his fate faded completely and at once. He continued in the thick of the fight and of danger and was untouched. He himself called attention to the fact that if his premonition had come true, as well it might in the midst of the very serious danger which he faced, it would have seemed a strong confirmation of the impression that premonitions have a meaning other than that of coincidence. It was, however, a magnificent example of a failed premonition quite as striking as any of the stories that are told about premonitions that came true.

Rôle of Coincidence.—This must be remembered in many of our arguments in medical and other scientific matters. Most diseases are self-limited, therefore anything that is given as a remedy for them just about the time that nature has succeeded in conquering the virulence of the disease and bringing about the cure of the patient, seems to be curative. Such cures, often remedies of supposed wonderful potency, come and go in medicine by the hundred every ten years. Such curious doctrines as that of the influence of maternal impressions in producing deformities and defects in the unborn child are founded on nothing better than these coincidences. They are often very startling, but the rule by which they must be judged is the number of times in which in spite of similar conditions no premonition takes place. Literally thousands of people go to bed every night who are to be waked by the danger of fire before morning and yet have no premonition of it. Literally millions of people have gone to bed in recent years without any premonition of earthquake, yet have been wakened before morning with their houses tumbling around them. If a few people have premonitions in these cases it is easy to understand that it is coincidence and not anything else, for these are exceptions, and this again is a case of the exception proving the rule.

{639}

Premonitions and Superstitions—Thirteen.—Occasionally premonitions are connected with certain events that are themselves, even though happening quite accidentally, supposed to be portentous. How many people, for instance, feel quite uncomfortable if they sit down thirteen at a table. The very fact of the gathering of thirteen is supposed to be a spontaneous or automatic premonition that is a forewarning of evil that has to come to some of them. Unfortunately, this superstition continues to have a vogue and an influence over people's minds because stories are told that are supposed to confirm it. Needless to say, when these stories are true, they are merely coincidences. Out of any baker's dozen of people who sit down to dinner it is not surprising if one should die or be killed during the year. Some of the stories, however, are merely sensational inventions worked up to be given to the public because a number of people are interested in this sort of thing. Probably one of the stories that has gone the rounds most and that has served to confirm many people in their uneasiness over the number 13 is that which is told as happening to Matthew Arnold and some friends, supposedly the year the great English litterateur died.

The story runs that just as Mr. Arnold and his friends were about to sit down to the table it was discovered that there were thirteen present. According to the old tradition in the matter it is the one who first gets up from table under these circumstances that is likely to be affected by the malignant influence. When the end of the dinner had arrived, by previous arrangement Mr. Arnold and two very healthy friends, brothers, arose simultaneously. According to the widely diffused newspaper account of years afterward, Mr. Arnold himself died within the year and one of the brothers was lost in the wreck of an English passenger vessel off the coast of Australia in six months, while the other brother committed suicide before the end of the year. Careful investigation of the details has shown, however, that the story was made out of whole cloth. Mr. Arnold himself, who was suffering from heart trouble towards the end of his life, was not likely to take part in any such arrangement because of the constant danger, well-known to himself, of sudden death in his case. This might happen at any time and might seem to confirm the superstition. The dates of the story, moreover, are all wrong. Matthew Arnold's death and the loss of the English passenger vessel in Australian waters, referred to, do not occur within five years of each other. The story has gone round the world. The correction will never reach so far. The story is startling; the explanation commonplace. Many people will continue to believe that here, at least, was one striking confirmation of their superstition.

341

It is curious how the force of this "13" superstition has continued in spite of education and enlightenment. Most passenger vessels now built have no staterooms numbered thirteen. On certain streets in large cities one finds the number 12-1/2 (until this year it was so on my own) substituted for thirteen. Sometimes one finds "twelve a" or something similar. In the large hotels, where they have immense banquet halls with the tables numbered so that guests may be able to find their places, I have often noted that there was no table number thirteen. It is said that in some of the new skyscraper buildings twenty stories and more in height there has been question of skipping the thirteenth floor as a designation, because while most {640} people would be quite undisturbed about it, some do not care to have an office on the thirteenth floor, giving as an excuse that clients or patrons do not care to come to the thirteenth floor. In automobile races men are willing to risk their lives by going a hundred miles an hour on roads never intended for such performances, but they refuse to race behind the fell number thirteen. This, after all, can be readily understood. The slightest thing that takes away a man's complete confidence in himself may be serious in an automobile going as fast as these. Men must not think of fear or they lose some of their power and control over themselves and their machine. They must simply forget everything except the task before them.

The belief in the thirteen superstition is one form of acceptance of premonitions. That of itself should be enough to enable sensible people to throw them off. Above all, it must be remembered that such supposed malignant influence, when allowed to affect people, impairs their presence of mind and may thus lead up to the accident or mishap which it is supposed to foreshadow. This is the serious feature of such premonitions and dreads. Unless people can be persuaded sensibly to be rid of them they handicap themselves whenever they are placed in danger that causes them to recur to the thought of the premonition or dread. While there is absolutely nothing but coincidence in even the supposed true stories, and many of the stories are merely sensational inventions, yet people need to be persuaded to rid themselves of the incubus that settles over them because of such ideas.

Premonitions and Telepathy.—There are many people who think that premonitions have something to do with telepathy. Somehow the future event is supposed to be able to send some message to specially susceptible minds. Either that, of course, or there is some being in another world whose interest is sufficient to convey some inkling of the future. A little consideration of this subject, however, shows the utter lack of rationality in any such opinion. Future events, having as yet no existence, cannot in any way influence intelligence. Such future events, when dependent on human free will, are quite impossible of being foretold and, as has been said, no being except the Creator Himself knows anything about them. It would be only from Him, then, that information might be supposed to come and it would be hard to think such information would be so vague and indefinite as to leave room for doubt and, besides, often defeat its purpose of protection by seriously disturbing patients and lessening their presence of mind. There is no reasonable explanation by which a human being can be supposed to obtain knowledge of a future event unless there is a complete overturning of the ordinary laws of nature and then it would be reasonably supposed that no doubt of the significance of the event would be left.

Nearly all of us have premonitions that fail. Only a few especially introspective people who are constantly afraid of what will happen to them, and who are sure that the worst is always preparing for them, have their premonitions come true more than once or twice in life. The striking fulfillments of a few premonitions could be paralleled by an endless number of just as striking failures, only that most people dismiss the idea completely from their minds as too foolish to be further talked about. It is quite the same with dreams. All the world dreams and there would be a serious violation of the theory of probabilities if some dreams did not come true. The great {641} majority of mankind, especially after the age of thirty, is fearful lest something ill is going to happen to them and their premonitions are rather frequent. If some of these did not come true then the mathematics of coincidences as based on the theory of probabilities would prove false.

CHAPTER VI

PERIODICAL DEPRESSION

Fits of periodical depression, familiarly known as "the blues," occur in the experience of practically everyone. In some people they are only slight and passing. In others they last for hours and make the individual quite miserable. In still others, without actually running into melancholia, they produce serious discouragement and continuous discomfort which persists even for days and makes life intolerable. They come and go quite unaccountably. During their occurrence all vitality is lowered, appetite lessened, aches and pains are emphasized, sleep may be disturbed, exercise becomes distasteful, and they usually present an interval when health is at a low ebb. Ordinarily when described as "the blues" they have no definite connection with any known physical cause. They are passing incidents which seem to recur at irregular intervals. When connected with physical ills they are thought of directly as symptoms of these ills. All forms of disease may be associated with such fits of depression and many physical symptoms seem to be due to the fact that during these periods there is a distinct lowering of physical vitality so that the nerve impulses which ordinarily enable functions to be performed without interference are interrupted, or at least are inhibited, to a noteworthy degree. While to a certain extent the condition is a mental disease, it may be modified by the correction of physical derangements, by stimulation and, above all, by suggestion and a change in the point of view.

Serious Pathological Conditions.—Of course, such periodical fits of depression are associated with various serious progressive ailments and then are primarily physical, and are only secondarily psychic. From the standpoint of psychotherapy it is important to remember that certain serious organic lesions may show their first signs in the patient's mental state. It is not unusual, for instance, for the disposition of a patient suffering from kidney disease to change so materially that the attention of friends is called to the change before any physical symptom of the nephritis has been noted. Sometimes for a year there will be a progressive clouding of what had previously been a rather happy disposition. Decisions will be made more slowly than before. The judgment will be impaired. There are some striking examples of this in history, of which the unfortunate Athenian general, Nicias, put to death for incapacity that was undoubtedly pathological, is one. Pleasures will be taken half-heartedly; men who have been bright and jovial will now become saturnine. Men who have been the life of parties will try to hold the place they acquired before, though all around them will perceive how difficult it is for them to maintain the role they have set for themselves. Whenever there is a notable change in disposition, it is well not to attribute it to some passing mental condition and, above all, not to dismiss {642} it as a peculiarity unamenable to treatment, but to look for the underlying pathological basis of the new condition.

In this way physical disease will sometimes be discovered long before it otherwise would be. This must be particularly noted when there have been a series of worries. Occasionally it seems enough to many people to ascribe a change of disposition to the troubles that have come over a patient. If a business man fails or passes through a crisis in his affairs in which failure is very near, or he has many business worries over a prolonged period, these are sometimes thought to be quite enough to explain a change of disposition. They are, but not to the degree that is often noted, for, in excess, melancholic tendencies are always pathological, that is, they have some basis in a serious mental or physical change. If there is an insidious nephritis already at work, its symptoms will be much exaggerated and its progress accelerated by the worries and disquietude of such a time. If a wife loses her husband, or an only son, or a favorite child, the occurrence of a prolonged period of depression should lead to a careful investigation of physical conditions and of the underlying mental state in the hope of guarding against serious developments.

Heart Disease.—Periods of depression are also common in heart disease and are often the first symptom of the beginning of a break in compensation. This effect is not so simple and direct, however, as in the case of the kidneys. Probably the first physical symptom of a break in compensation, where there is real valvular heart disease, is a decrease in the amount of urine. This points to an insufficient elimination of the products of metabolism and to the retention in the circulation of toxic substances. The reason for this is the lessened circulation through the kidneys because of the diseased heart. There is also a lessened circulation through the brain. This impairs the function of the brain and quite naturally leads to mental depression, slowness of decision, and unwillingness to occupy one's self with many things. Besides, because of the lessened function of the kidney the circulating blood not only does not nourish so well but it tends still further to depress the brain cells by the toxic substances that are in it. Depression in such cases is rather to be expected and at the beginning is not continuous but comes in ever longer periods with shortening intervals as the disturbance of the circulation progresses. At first, like other diminutions of function, it is conservative in order to spare the heart work.

Respiratory Affections.—Very curiously an affection of the lungs has exactly the opposite effect and is likely to create in the patient an artificial sense of well-being. *Spes phthisica*, the characteristic hope of consumptive patients, is well known, and has been described by many a careful observer from Hippocrates and Galen to our own time. A lessened amount of oxygen in the blood produces a certain sleepiness, but this seems to be preceded by a period of slight excitation. The most familiar example of this occurs at the beginning of the inhalation of laughing gas. Practically the only direct physical effect of the inhalation of nitrous-dioxide is to shut off our oxygen and it is a slight period of deoxygenation that produces the anesthesia by this agent. Whether we have not in this the explanation of the feeling of the consumptive, so that often on the day before his death he plans a number of things that he is going to do next year, may require more careful {643} investigation, but the suggestion may serve to show how much disposition, both lively and serious, depends on physical factors as well as on the natural state of mind.

MENTAL STATES OF DISAPPOINTMENT

Quite apart from these serious ailments, however, there are passing phases of depression that come to nearly everyone after adult life is reached that are likely to be somewhat more frequent as years go on, but that are not entirely unknown even in early years. They are more likely to come to those who feel that life has been somewhat of a failure and that they have accomplished very little in spite of all that they have tried to do. Not infrequently they come, however, to those who in the estimation of other people have made a magnificent success of life. The rich man, after he has made his fortune, unless he continues to engross himself with some time-taking and interest-claiming work, may be the subject of repeated attacks of mental depression. Social leaders among women who begin to feel something of the emptiness of social striving, after they have made what is called a success in society and at the time when they are the envy of many on the social ladder below them, are particularly likely to be subject to attacks of "the blues." The only men and women who are free from them to a great extent, and even they not absolutely, are those who are busily engaged with some occupation not entirely selfish in which they can see that what they are doing is accomplishing something for the people around them.

Very often an attack of depression is ushered in by some small disappointment. As a rule, however, this is not the causative factor but is only an occasion which makes manifest the depressed state that has existed for some time and that now declares itself openly. In the same way only a slight occasion is necessary apparently to dispel clouds that hang over a person in the milder attacks of depression, because, for some time before, relief has been preparing itself and a livelier phase of existence has been gradually coming on. Relief can be promised with absolute assurance, but freedom from relapse cannot be assured and the only true source of consolation that is helpful is the frank recognition of the fact that these are successive phases of existence quite as likely to be periodic as certain physical facts in life. Depression is likely to be a little more manifest in the morning than at other times, partly because the interests of the day have not yet come to occupy the mind, but mainly because the physical life as indicated by the pulse and the temperature is lower during the morning hours than in the

343

afternoon and evening. Just as soon as people realize the physical nature of certain dispositional changes they give much less depressive significance to them.

Occupation of Mind.—The most important feature of the treatment of depression of mind is to secure somehow such occupation as will catch the attention and arouse the interest. This is not always an easy matter. How effective it is, however, can be best judged from what one notes of the effect of such things as physical pain or great solicitude for someone else besides themselves. I have known a mother, whose fits of "the blues" were getting deeper and the intervals growing shorter to be roused from her condition when all means had failed by the elopement of a daughter who had been partly pushed into leaving because things had become so unpleasant around home {644} during her mother's depression, and any change seemed welcome. On the other hand, I had a doctor friend who felt quite alarmed about his growing depression and who even had some fears lest, if it continued to deepen, he might commit suicide. He was completely lifted out of his increasing depression by the occurrence of pneumonia in his boy of sixteen. The pneumonia did not end by crisis but by lysis and for weeks he had very little sleep. He confessed that the intense preoccupation of mind had completely driven away his blues and had even done much to relieve him of various digestive symptoms to which he had previously attributed his depression.

Again and again I have known men who, in the midst of prosperity, found life dull and rather hard to bear, and who just as soon as a crisis in their affairs compelled them to pay attention to other things than themselves and the state of their feelings, grew better mentally and physically. It seems almost a contradiction in terms to say that it is the man of little occupation, as a rule, or at least of occupations that are not insistent, who is likely to be troubled with insomnia, while the very busy man, especially the man busy not about one or two narrow interests, but about a number, is seldom so bothered. Nothing contributes more to the depression of mind than loss of sleep or supposed loss of sleep. Even women who, while living in ease and comfort, had much to complain of as regards depression, often lose entirely their tendencies to "the blues" or have fits of them at much longer intervals, when necessity compels them either to earn their own living or, at least, to occupy themselves much more with absolutely necessary duties.

Provision of Occupation.—It is a hard matter to create such occupation of mind as will be satisfactory. Patients have to be tried by various suggestions. The tendency to periodic fits of depression deep enough to be called to the physician's attention is much more noticeable in recent years than it used to be, and seems to me at least to bear a corresponding ratio to the decrease of home life. Home duties usually mean joys and of late there has been a neglect of the joys of life while seeking its pleasures. Certain phases of city life are responsible for much dissatisfaction with existence and depression of spirits. Most of the women who live in apartment hotels have practically no serious occupation of mind. They need not get up if they do not feel quite right or quite rested—and who after the age of forty ever does feel quite all right in the morning hours unless sleep has been in the open air? Nothing is so likely to start a day of depression than failure to get up promptly, lounging around with forty winks here and there, reading in bed, and the like. If breakfast is taken in bed, then some reading indulged in, and then some sleeping, and only an hour or two of dawdling around comes before lunch, that meal is not properly enjoyed and the afternoon is started badly; unless there is some special diversion of mind depression is almost sure to get the upper hand.

Place of Children in Psychotherapy.—Where there are children the interests are much more urgent and there is little time for such preoccupation with self as gives one "that tired feeling." We are very interesting to ourselves, but just as soon as we have no other subject to occupy us than ourselves we soon grow very tired of the subject. Children are the best interest that one can think of, for women particularly. When they have none of their own an interest in orphan asylums, in day nurseries, in various children's {645} institutions, and, above all, in the adoption of a child, will do more than anything else to relieve the tendency to blues. Of late years the adoption of children has been much less frequent than used to be the case in childless families, and doctors see the result in mental depression. Children are a great care, but they are a great blessing to women, and while the present trend of social life eliminates them as far as possible, this elimination, beginning with their relegation to nurses when they are infants, to nursemaids as they grow a little older, and then to the kindergarten up to six years of age, far from adding to comfort rather increases the discomfort of many mothers. Nature takes her revenge. The reason why the mothers of past generations could stand the suffering that they must have borne with patience before gynecology developed to relieve them, was that they had their children around them, and their minds and their hearts and their hands were so full that they had no time to think of themselves, to brood over their ills, and consequently these troubled them much less than would otherwise have been the case.

Delicate mothers really interested in their children undoubtedly suffer very little compared to delicate women who are alone in life, and what is thus true of the mother is true also of those who have the care of children. It is not alone a satisfaction of the maternal instinct, but it is an occupation of mind and heart with cares for little ones. Other people's children serve just as good a therapeutic purpose, if only their necessities are imposed on the attendant. The reason why women in religious orders have such happy peaceful lives and are happier in spite of a routine of life that would seem to be fatal to happiness, is that their minds are filled with the interests of others, every moment of their time is occupied, and, above all, they have to care for children, the ailing, the poor, sometimes the vicious, who make many demands on them, many calls on their sympathies and keep them from thinking about themselves.

Occupation with Living Things.—After occupation with human beings the most important therapeutic factor against periods of depression is occupation with living things of various kinds. Horseback riding is an excellent remedy for the blues and the outside of a horse in the old axiom is literally very good for the inside of man or woman. There is a sympathy between man and animal that in itself means much, but the most important element is the absolute impossibility of preoccupation with oneself and one's little troubles and worries while one is trying to manage a somewhat restive animal. If the horse, however, is old and very quiet—so that one can throw the reins on his neck and allow him to jog on for himself, then horseback riding may mean very little. Where the care of the animal is entirely taken off the rider's shoulders by a groom who brings him to a particular place and takes him afterwards, then, also, much of the benefit of horseback riding is lost. Care for other animals as well as the horse is of great service and especially is this true if the owners feel the duty of exercising the animals. Many a downhearted person finds that to take an animal out for a stroll will do much to lift the clouds of depression.

With the disappearance of children from the families of the better-to-do classes, pet dogs have grown in favor mainly because of this influence. They awaken sympathies and so keep people from thinking too much about themselves. For many an elderly woman who is alone in the world her dogs or her {646} cats or a combination of both are the best possible remedies for depression. At times it will be found necessary to prescribe them. There is no better way to get an elderly person to go out at certain times than to have them feel that their pets need exercise.

Garden Cures.—After animals the next best thing is the care of a garden. Here once more human sympathies with living things are aroused and it is easier to cultivate a forgetfulness of self while cultivating flowers and plants. Growing plants do not arouse the interest that growing animals do, but still they have advantages over things that do not vary, and their growth is a subject of day-to-day interest and the effect on them of vicissitudes of the weather arouses feelings of solicitude which help to dissipate the little insistent cares for self that depress. The care of a garden is the very best thing for the "pottering old." Younger people are too impatient to get much benefit out of a garden, but after middle life many an hour of depression will be saved in the care of plants.

Intellectual Occupations.—It might be expected that intellectual occupations would serve to brush away "the blues" for educated people. They are perfectly capable of doing so, but they must be of the kind that grip attention and must be undertaken seriously, usually with an appeal quite apart from mere cultural interests. Hobbies of various kinds, especially the making of collections, even of such trivial things as stamps, will often serve the purpose of distraction from gloomier thoughts. Unfortunately, a hobby cannot be created all at once and usually does not take a strong enough hold to be available for mental therapeutic purposes unless it was acquired when the person was comparatively young and has been indulged in for many years. Reading and study utterly fail unless there is some end in view apart from the reading and study itself. The reading of novels and newspapers is particularly likely to be a failure. The gloomier thoughts obtrude themselves in the midst of the reading and very often what is read proves suggestive of melancholic thoughts and all the time the mind and the person are not occupied seriously enough to push away the state of depression which exists. The mind must be interested, not merely occupied superficially, or the depression will continue.

It might be thought that the reading of books that concerned human suffering might have a similar appeal to that to be obtained from real touch with human suffering. This is true to a certain extent when the books concern real and not fictitious suffering. For this reason the trials and hardships of travelers at the North and South poles or in the heart of tropical Africa—Nansen and Peary and Stanley and Livingston—have all been excellent therapeutic agents. The stories of mountain climbers have something of the same effect. Adventures in Alaska and in the Far North, especially, come in the same category. Novels, however, even though they use the same material, soon fail to have a corresponding effect. Even when the novel does touch the emotions deeply it is prone to make the reader forget the suffering around him and does not prove a good diversion from his own feelings. In his play, "The Night Asylum," Maxim Gorky, the Russian novelist and playwright, brings this out very well. One of his characters, a young scrubwoman, wears her fingers to the bone during the day for a miserable pittance and sleeps in a squalid night lodging house, yet this comparatively young creature, {647} crouched near the only light in the room, sheds tears over the imaginary sufferings of the fictitious people that she reads about, while the real human suffering around her fails entirely to arouse her sympathy or affect her emotions, except to anger her if lodgers come in between her and the light or when the complaints made by some of those who are suffering around her annoy and distract her from her reading.

In younger folks, study, provided there is some definite object to be attained by it, is often helpful. Correspondence schools are of value by setting a definite purpose before the mind. In a number of cases I have found that the suggestion to make translations from a foreign language when the patient knew that language even tolerably well, afforded excellent relief from that over-occupation with self which was the real cause of the depression. There are many people who know enough French to be able to translate fairly well and there are many articles and books a translation of which may at least be submitted to editors and often proves available for publication. To have some such end as this in view is of itself one of the best means that can be provided for these people to relieve their tendency to depression. Occasionally even the suggestion to write stories may prove helpful. One hesitates to add to the number of story-writers in this country, but it may be remembered as a last resort. I know at least two people saved from themselves by even a very moderate success as writers of short stories.

Consolation from History.—Perhaps the most serious thing about depression is the feeling of those afflicted by it that they are singular in this respect and that other people who seem gay never have depressed states. There is probably no one who has not periods of depression. They may not be very deep and "the blues" may be only of a light tinge, but they are there. The higher the intelligence, as a rule, the more tendency there is to feelings of discouragement and depression at intervals when one is not occupied. Those who have the artistic temperament and the striving after the expression of the beautiful as they see it, whether it be in art or in letters or in the betterment of humanity, usually suffer more than others because they realize poignantly their failure to reach their ideals. This is well illustrated by the experience of writers and artists. As a rule, most men and women look forward to the completion of any intellectual work with confidence that after it is finished they will have a period of rest and peace. Commonly just the opposite is true. The completion of any work leaves one with a sense of dissatisfaction with what has been done, for no man of real intelligence ever thinks that he has so realized his ideals as to be satisfied, and only the foolishly conceited fail to feel the many defects that there are in their work.

There is abundance of evidence, however, that it is not alone artists and writers who thus feel the hollowness of life and the tears there are in things. Many of the men who have accomplished great things in science and in politics have been prone to times of depression. Virchow told me there were moments when life seemed very empty to him and that he had to shake off feelings of depression in order to be able to go on with his work. At one time in the sixth decade of his life he suffered considerably from what we would now call neurasthenic symptoms, gave up his medical work and spent a long time with Schliemann in the Troad. His presence was valuable to the excavator in his work at Troy, and the change gave Virchow back his health.

{648}

Even more striking is what we know of Von Moltke, who seemed in many ways to have an ideally happy life. He had had the fulfillment of all his desires or, at least, the fruition of all his hopes, and the successful accomplishment of what he worked for beyond what is usually given to man. He had come to be one of the most highly respected men of Europe and was the subject of veneration on the part of his own German people and of intimate affection from his sovereign, who loaded him with honors. He was a man who had probably no enemies and many, many firm friends. It was said that "he could keep silence in eleven languages" and so he had avoided most of the pitfalls of life. His domestic life was ideally happy and his letters to his wife for over fifty years read like those of a lover, before all his great battles his last thought and written word was for her, after them his first thought and message was for her. In spite of this, towards the end of his life, when the question of reincarnation was a subject of discussion in Berlin and it was brought particularly to his attention, he declared that looking back on his career, in spite of all its good fortune, there seemed to him to be so many chances in life, so many possible sources of failure, so many springs of discouragement, that he would prefer not to have to live again. Surely, if anyone, he might be expected to be ready to take the chances of re-incarnation after such happy experiences of life, yet he was not. Such an expression could only come from a man who had looked depression often in the face, who had shaken off the blue devils and who knew that even the joy of success was followed by the gloom of uncertainty as to the future and solicitude as to the real significance of accomplishment.

Literature and Life.—We have many examples of this tendency to depression that come to the literary man in the lives and letters of distinguished writers that have been published so frequently in recent years. Perhaps one of the most striking is to be found in the life of Robert Bulwer Lytton, the second Lord Lytton, so well known as a diplomatist in European circles and throughout the English-speaking world as a poet, under the pen name of "Owen Meredith." It might be thought that Lytton would be one of the men safely harbored from storms of depression and discouragement, for his life seemed ideally situated to enable him to get the best out of himself without worry or dissipation of energy in occupation with mere personal matters. His father had made a distinguished success as a literary man and a politician, had been raised to the peerage and the son began life with every possible advantage. He made a distinguished success in literature so that he even converted his father to praise him and as a diplomatist he occupied nearly every important post in English diplomacy and had hosts of friends all over the world.

It is all the more surprising, then, to have many passages in his letters refer to periodic attacks of depression. He says, for instance, "My physical temperament has a great tendency to beget blue devils and when those imps lay siege to my soul they recall those words of Schopenhauer's and say to me 'thou art the man.'" Perhaps the price that the artistic temperament pays for the satisfaction that it gets out of life in other directions is this occasional tendency {649} to depression because achievement does not equal aspiration. Certainly the price often seems excessive to those who have to pay it. In the same letter to his daughter, Lytton continues:

When my blue devils are cast out, and I recover sanity of spirits, then I say to myself just what you say to me in your letter—that the main thing is not to do but to be; that the work of a man is rather in what he is than in what he does; that one may be a very fine poet yet a very poor creature; that my life has at least been a very full one, rich in varied experiences, touching the world at many points; that had I devoted it exclusively to the cultivation of one gift, though that the best, I might have become a poet as great at least as any of my contemporaries, but that this is by no means certain to me for my natural inclination to, and unfitness for, all the practical side of life are so great that I might just as likely have lapsed into a mere dreamer; that the discipline of active life and forced contact with the world has been specially good for me, perhaps providential, and that what I have gained from it as a man may be more than compensation for whatever I may have lost by it as an artist.

It is surprising to think of a man of this kind becoming so depressed by the death of a son that all the world and the meaning of life took on a somber hue for him. In 1871 Lord Lytton lost a young boy by a very painful illness which had probably been more painful for sympathetic onlookers than for the patient himself. The incident proved sufficient, however, to make the father think that there could not be a beneficent Providence ruling over the world. He felt sure that somehow God's power must be shortened, if such suffering, for which he could see no reason, had to be permitted. He was much depressed after this and never was quite the same in his outlook upon the world and the significance of life. It was easy to understand that this was due rather to his character than his intellect, but it illustrates forcibly how much a deeply intelligent man may be affected by something that seems after all, only the course of nature.

It is sometimes surprising to find from the life stories of men how often those who would be thought least likely to suffer from periodical depression were victims of it. Few Americans in our time have apparently had a more satisfying career than that of James Russell Lowell, a successful author as a young man, then a successful editor, a teacher whom his students appreciated very much, and in later life the subject of many honors and such honors as provided him with splendid opportunities for the exhibition of his special genius. He would seem to be the last who should suffer from depression. His post as Minister to Spain gave him an opportunity which he took magnificently to study the great Spanish authors and to store up material for writing about them. As Minister to England few men were so popular. He was constantly in demand for occasional addresses and his special style enabled him to respond to these demands with brilliant success. Here in America no great occasion was complete without Lowell. In spite of all this that would surely seem ample to satisfy the aspirations of any man, Lowell was often depressed and sometimes even talked about the possibility of suicide. Life seemed at times very empty to him. The story of the lives of such men, if made familiar to patients, proves a source of consolation, for it makes them realize that they are not alone in their experiences, that depression at some times is the lot of man, and that very few people are without the sphere of its influence.

{650}

346

Depression an Incident, not a State.—This suggestion may, in the case of some of those inclined to longer periods of depression, lead to indulgence in the luxury of being depressed and so putting off the doing of things. It must be pointed out, however, that just inasmuch as depression has this effect it is pathological. It seems to be natural to man to suffer from periods of discouragement and depression which keep him from devoting himself too persistently to lines of work that may be insignificant and make him take cognizance of the real values of what he is doing. Depression, however, that continues after the recognition of this takes place is morbid and must be actively resisted. Just inasmuch as depression precedes and prepares patients for a reaction, it is an incident in practically all lives. Indulged in as a luxury, it is abnormal.

Suggestive Treatment.—The most important thing for patients who suffer from periodic depression is to make them understand that this state of mind, far from being personal to them or very rare, or even uncommon, is an extremely frequent experience of men and women. There are certain men and a few women eminently occupied with the external life, busy with many things, though often they are trivial enough, and even when they are important, significant only in a financial or a social way, but meaning nothing for the great realities of life, who seem during their younger active years to escape the periodical attacks of depression that come to most people and come almost without exception to people who think seriously. Some of the best thoughts and inspirations of men come to them as the result of the serious mood that follows an attack of depression. A butterfly existence lacks these sources of inspiration. Far from being objectionable then, attacks of depression, if not allowed to proceed too far, and if kept from paralyzing activity, prove to be intervals when life values are seriously weighed and when a proper estimation of such values is come to. Men are prone without such interruptions to get too interested in trivial concerns that seem to them important because they are occupied with them to the exclusion of other ideas, but that prove to be of no real import when seen on the background of a certain hollowness that there is in human life, if lived merely for its own sake.

The occurrence of periodical depression is a part of the mystery of life and it affords us a better opportunity to get a little closer to the heart of the mystery than almost anything else. It is out of such periods that men have risen "on stepping-stones of their dead selves to higher things" and have even risen to the highest that there is in life. Geniuses have nearly always had deep periods of depression, but in the midst of them have read new meanings into life and have read the lessons of humanity in their own souls better than at any other time. Depression throws a man back on himself and makes him think deeper than in his mind—in what has been called his heart. "The fascination of trifles obscures the good things in life" are words of old-time wisdom and men are weaned from this by fits of depression that are really moods of precious dissatisfaction with their work inasmuch as it falls short of the best accomplishment. Without periodic depression, apparently, a man never gets as close to the heart of life as he otherwise would. Far from being an unwelcome visitant, it should be rather welcome as a stimulus to the possibility of further study of self and the realities of life.

{651}

CHAPTER VII

INSOMNIA

To the minds of many people insomnia is one of the most serious ills to which human nature is heir. Most of this quite false impression is due to the sensational cultivation of dreads with regard to insomnia by newspapers and in general conversation. If we were to credit such impressions, there is a certain number of unfortunates who, for some unknown reason, find it impossible to sleep and who, night after night, drag out the weary hours wooing sleep that does not come, until when daylight dawns they are in despair, distracted by lack of rest. This is presumed to occur night after night, until finally the worn-out mind succumbs to the intolerable anguish of being kept constantly on the rack of wakefulness and the patient becomes insane or saves himself from that by suicide. No wonder, then, that many a one of these patients takes to the use of habit-forming drugs to produce sleep. These, though effective only to a small degree, soothe him for the time, but finally render him such a wreck that there is not even will power enough for him to take his own life and end his intolerable suffering.

Such gruesome pictures of the awful effects of insomnia run rife and produce dreads in the community until just as soon as the ordinary nervous supersensitive person loses an hour or two of sleep two or three nights in a month, he begins to conjure up the specter of insomnia with its awful terrors and still more awful possibilities, and begins to bewail the fate that has chosen him as an unfortunate victim. This exaggerated dread that slight losses of sleep, for which there are often excellent reasons, will develop into an incurable condition of persistent wakefulness has more to do than any other single factor with the production of the state called insomnia which is, however, never half as bad as it is pictured.

Absolute Sleeplessness.—A certain number of patients insist that they sleep very little at night and some tell their friends and even their physicians quite ingenuously that they sleep none at all, and that this has been the case with them for a prolonged period. Practically every physician has heard such stories, and at the beginning of his professional career has usually wondered how the patients continued to live and enjoy reasonably good health in spite of the lack of absolutely necessary brain cell rest. After the physician has the opportunity to investigate some of these stories he understands them better. Patients in hospital, who insist that they are wakeful all the night, prove usually when faithfully watched by a nurse to be wakeful for an hour or two at the beginning of the night and then to sleep for hours at a time, and all of them sleep for intervals more or less prolonged, though they may wake a number of times during the night and may think that they have not been asleep because they hear the clock regularly or some other recurring noise. It is improbable that patients ever spend several nights in succession without sleep and their story is only an index of the persuasion that they are under that they do not sleep, though they are having so many thoroughly restful intervals that their brain cells suffer but little from {652} the need of sleep. *Indeed, the principle source of nervous wear and tear for them consists in their persuasion that they do not sleep and the resultant impelling suggestion that a breakdown must before long be inevitable.*

Individual Differences.—There are too many safeguards in nature's ordinary dealings with human beings for us to think that people can pass many nights absolutely without rest. Brain cells may apparently be very wakeful, they may be quite ready to take up at once and seemingly without a break trains of thought interrupted sometime before, yet somehow they succeed in obtaining their needed rest. In this matter, as is well known, though it needs to be emphasized again for the benefit of nervous individuals, different people have very different needs. Some require many continuous hours of sleep or they soon begin to have symptoms of nervous exhaustion. Others live on only with snatches of sleep at intervals, or with interrupted sleep during a limited portion of the twenty-four hours, yet enjoy good health for many years. A few seem to be able to live in health and strength with but a few hours of sleep. It may possibly be thought that those who are living their lives with a small amount of sleep are drawing drafts on their future vital powers, and that what they make up in intensity of activity now by shortening sleep, they will discount by shortness of life. How utterly untrue this impression is, however, will be best understood from the fact that many of the men who have worked hardest and slept the least number of hours in the day, have lived to be eighty or even ninety years of age and some of them have even been centenarians.

Cell Rest.—The great differences in the brain cells of different individuals in what concerns sleep becomes more readily intelligible when we recall the extreme differences as regards the need of rest of the various cells in the same individual. While the brain cells seem to require for healthy life, as a rule, nearly one-third of the time, and a man who is constantly taking much less than eight hours of sleep is probably hindering rather than helping his productiveness, especially if his work is intellectual, there are cells in the body that need no such amount of rest as this. Peristaltic movements occur in the digestive tract almost constantly, with only short intervals, and these cells get their rest between their movements. Pulmonary cells and tissues must do the same thing, and are able to do it without any special strain being put on them. The extreme example of the lack of need for prolonged rest is found in the heart. Two-fifths of every second the cells of this organ have a rest during the diastole, but during the remaining three-fifths of every second for all of life they must not only be ready to work but actually engaged in it or serious symptoms ensue. The cells in the brain that subtend cardiac and respiratory activity must be even more able to do without rest, since their action is ceaseless during life. By analogy with these it is not difficult to understand that the brain cells which are involved in consciousness should on occasion be able to stand prolonged periods of activity, or at least of wakefulness. Persistent wakefulness does not appeal to us as so surely destructive after this consideration.

Solicitude Over Sleep.—For those who are much disturbed by the loss of even slight amounts of sleep and who are prone to complain rather bitterly if they are not able to get more than five or six hours a night, I find it a useful preliminary to any more formal treatment of their so-called insomnia {653} to recall the examples of some of the great workers who succeeded in accomplishing marvelously good work though they took much less sleep than the amount the patient secures, yet seems to think inadequate. In spite of such lack of sleep, these workers lived to advanced old age. There are many well-authenticated illustrations of this in recent times. Perhaps the most striking testimony to the power of the human mind to continue work without requiring the refreshment of sleep, except for very short periods, is that of Humboldt, the great traveller, scientist writer and diplomat. Max Müller, in his autobiography tells the story. It was when he himself was about forty. Humboldt said to him: "Ah! Max, when I was your age I had time to accomplish something, now I find that I must take at least five hours of sleep every night." At the moment Humboldt was over eighty. Müller said to him: "But, Your Excellency, how much sleep, then, did you take when you were my age?" "Oh!" he said, "I used to turn the light down, throw myself on the lounge for a couple of hours, and then get up and go on with my work again." Humboldt, after a life full of the hardest kind of work of many kinds, lived well past ninety in the full vigor of his intellectual powers.

There are many other examples that might readily be quoted. The traditions of the University of Berlin contain many illustrations of men who did very little sleeping, yet succeeded in accomplishing an immense amount of work and lived far beyond the Psalmist's limit. Virchow, whom I knew very well, did not take more than four or five hours of sleep on most nights in the year. He would be in the Lower House of the Prussian Legislature, which, like the House of Commons, holds its meetings late at night, until one A. M. or later and would be at his laboratory shortly after seven. There was a tradition at the University of Berlin in my time there of one of the older professors in the theological department who went to bed only every alternate night. He had a forty-eight-hour day for work with a seven-hour break. He lived to the age of eighty-five. I know one of our most distinguished workers in medicine here in America who was so busy and so tired at the end of his day that he could not write his book. He would fall asleep on his chair at his desk to wake up only when the milkman came in the morning. He had constructed for himself a special stool without back or sides, shaped like a bench, so that whenever he fell asleep on it he fell off. The fall would wake him up and he would then go on with his work for some hours. He did this sort of thing for many years, and yet he is alive and in the full possession of intellectual health at the age of eighty-three. He learned this expedient from a German professor of medicine who told him of it and at the same time told him that it was no uncommon practice among German professors. Indeed, most of the famous long-livers of the nineteenth century were also well known for the small amount of sleep they required, and apparently there is no need of being anxious lest loss of sleep should prove serious, unless one is adding to whatever detriment to health it may be by worrying about it find so setting two damaging factors at work.

TREATMENT

Probably the most important immediate assurance that can be given to those who come complaining of insomnia is that practically no one has ever {654} been seriously hurt by the wakefulness called insomnia. Patients suffering from brain tumors, from serious disturbance's of cerebral circulation that give objective signs, from various organic diseases, as of the heart or liver, or certain constitutional diseases, have been made worse by the wakefulness induced by their affections. In the cases where there were no definite objective signs and wakefulness was the only symptom we have no cases on record of serious injury resulting. Men have come complaining of wakefulness for days or weeks and sometimes, though it is strange to understand it, for months or even years, and yet have lived their lives without serious developments and have neither gone into insanity nor into any premature loss of vitality, much less a fatal termination. It is not subjective symptoms but objective signs that are of value for the diagnosis of the serious organic conditions. This reassurance lifts a load from patients' minds at once and does more than anything else to relieve them of the burden of solicitude which is the main factor in the continuance of their insomnia.

Suggestive Treatment.—The psychotherapy of sleep consists in changing the patient's attitude of mind toward his sleep. It is quite impossible for him to sleep normally and regularly if he worries much about it and if the afternoon and evening hours are mainly spent in wondering whether he will sleep, anxious as to when he is going to sleep like other people, marvelling how long he will last in health and sanity if his tendency to wakefulness continues. There is no factor so strong in insomnia as getting one's self on one's mind. It weighs as an intolerable burden, an incubus that is sure to keep its subject awake. Insomnia is a mental and not a physical ailment in much more than nine out of every ten cases. It is not the brain but the mind that is at fault. Patients must be made to realize that if they go quietly to bed, confident that if they do not sleep the early part of the night they will sleep later, and that in case they should lose considerable sleep, so long as they lie quietly for eight hours in bed, their physical organism is not likely to come to any serious trouble. They must be quiet, peaceful and unworried. They must not begin to toss at the first sign of not going promptly to sleep for by so doing they may put off completely the possibility of falling to sleep. Finally they must prepare for sleep by passing a quiet evening, as a rule, occupied with diversions of various kinds.

There are many factors which inhibit sleep that must be removed or at least obviated. These are very different in different individuals and the suggestion of getting them out of the way helps a great deal in making people realize that they are better prepared for sleep than before. They have been keeping themselves awake by contrary unfavorable suggestions. They must be taught to aid themselves in going to sleep by a series of favorable suggestions attached to the doing of certain things that are helpful and, above all, avoiding acts of various kinds that have an unfavorable suggestive influence. In this way an accumulation of suggestions can be secured that will prove helpful.

Drugs.—Of course, patients must be warned with regard to the taking of drugs. Certain drugs may be taken for an occasional loss of a night's sleep, where the loss of sleep is regular and frequent, however, drugs are sure to do more harm than good. Opium leads to a serious habit, chloral is dangerous because it must be increased, most of the coal-tar somnifacients produce {655} serious after results and their physical effect is in the end probably more deleterious than would be the loss of the sleep which they are supposed to counteract. This is true for even the vauntedly least harmful of them, and it is important to make patients understand it.

External Conditions to be Inhibited.—In the treatment of insomnia two sets of inhibitory conditions are particularly to be looked to, those external to the patient, and those internal. Unless every possible obstacle is removed there can be no assurance of the relief of sleeplessness, while very often the careful regulation of a few conditions that are disturbing the patient will bring sleep fully and promptly. It is curious what small annoyances will sometimes prove disturbing.

No Pillow.—I have found patients who had heard somewhere the idea that it was natural for man to sleep without a pillow. The pillow in this theory was supposed to be an added refinement of men in a state of luxury, but a real degeneration opposed to nature, and the many presumed benefits of sleeping on a perfectly level mattress with the head no higher than the rest of the body was emphasized. While in ordinary health these patients had found that after the preliminary discomfort of getting used to sleeping without a pillow, they were apparently the better for it. People will feel better for almost anything if they are only persuaded that they ought to. After a certain length of time, however, worry or work had a tendency to keep them more or less wakeful and then insomnia came on, that is, for several hours at the beginning of the night they did not go to sleep and became very much worried about it.

In several of these cases I have found one of the most helpful adjuncts to more direct treatment of their wakefulness was the restoration of the pillow. Just how the hygienic theory of pillowless sleep originated, or on what it is supposed to be founded, I do not know. The only theory of sleep that seems to have many adherents at present is that it is due to brain anemia. With the head a little higher than the rest of the body the force of gravity tends to help in the production of this brain anemia. The experience of mankind seems to confirm this. Certainly, from the earliest records of history men have slept with something under their head, even though they could find nothing better than a log or a stone. To sleep without a pillow is, owing to the conformation of the head and neck and shoulders, almost inevitably to sleep mainly on the back. From the anatomical relations of the internal organs it is easy to understand that sleeping on the side is more comfortable and healthy than sleeping on the back and hence most people naturally take this position. Relaxation is much more complete and comfort is greater. What the majority of men do is almost surely dictated by instinct, and instinct is the most precious guide we have in the natural functions of life. We are not so differently formed from the animals that the analogy from their habits should not have some weight for us. Patients should then be advised always to sleep with a reasonably firm pillow, not too low, so that the head is a little higher than the body and the lateral position perfectly comfortable.

Too high Pillow.—There is an abuse in the other direction of too high a pillow that deserves to be noted. Occasionally the physician hears complaints of waking up with tired feelings in the large muscles of the back of the neck near their insertion into the occiput. This is sometimes complained of {656} as an occipital headache. Not infrequently it will be found that these people are sleeping on pillows that are too large, or that they pile up several of them. Most physicians have found in their experience that having the head quite a little higher than the rest of the body materially aided sleep, especially in elderly people. This is true even when there is no distinct heart lesion, but this favorable position is best secured not by means of one or more high pillows, but by raising the head of the bed, or by the insertion of bolsters beneath the mattress, so that there is a gentle slope upward from the hips to the head. High pillows should, as a rule, be discouraged, especially in young folks where the assumption of the strained positions which they cause, may encourage various deformities in the anatomy of the head and shoulders so that stoop shoulders or a craned neck result. On the other hand, before attempting to give drugs to elderly people, the arrangement of the mattress so as to put the head a foot, or even more, higher than the body should be tried and will often be found to give relief where other things fail.

Discomfort Due to Cold.—In order to sleep well patients must be thoroughly comfortable in bed. In recent years as the very hygienic practice of having a window in the sleeping apartment open has become a rule among intelligent people, sleeping rooms have been much colder than they used to be. Care must be taken lest the active factor in causing wakefulness should be cold. Over and over again I have found that patients who complain of wakefulness, in the latter part of the night particularly, that is, in the early morning, were awakened by the increasing cold because they were insufficiently clothed. Whenever the sleeping room becomes very cold, then, the patient should not sleep between cotton or linen sheets which are likely to induce sensations of chilliness, but in a light woolen nightgown. It is curious what a difference in the patient's feelings is produced by the touch of wool to the skin in cold weather as compared with cotton. Thin, anemic patients are especially likely to suffer from chilliness. It must not be forgotten, however, that some stout people, in spite of an accumulation of fat, are really anemic. Their red blood corpuscles and hemoglobin are distinctly below normal. These constitute some of that large class of stout women in whom reduction cures fail because of the anemic tendency. They must be as carefully protected from cold as thinner persons, yet they need fresh air for their comfort and health almost as much as tuberculosis patients. The experience of sanatoria in the Adirondacks and at altitudes generally shows that for quiet, undisturbed sleep, if the room becomes distinctly cold during the night because of an open window, a hood or night-cap and gloves, as well as the wearing of woolen underclothing, even to stockings, is almost indispensable. In older times, when houses were not well heated, many persons very sensibly wore night caps. Now that a return to cold fresh air in the sleeping room has come many will have to resume the old night-cap habit in spite of cosmetic objections to it. These may seem little things, but they count very much in relieving disturbed sleep. The curious thing about them is that patients themselves seldom realize that certain common-sense regulations are more important for sleep than formal remedies. They want to be "cured" of their insomnia, not relieved by suggestion.

Cold Feet.—A large number of people have their sleep at the beginning of the night seriously disturbed by cold feet. Some cannot get to sleep for {657} an hour or more, because their feet are cold. If the patients become worried over this loss of sleep, a real insomnia may develop. It is for these people that the old-fashioned warming-pan was invented and it should not be forgotten that the symptom can be relieved very promptly by means of a hot-water bag or a hot brick wrapped in flannel at the foot of the bed. An excellent practice for very sensitive persons, is to have the sheets warmed thoroughly for a couple of hours before bedtime. This is especially important in damp weather.

The distinguished English surgeon. Sir Henry Thompson, who lived well beyond eighty years of age (when surely he would seem to have some right to do so), wrote a little book on how to be well and grow old and describes a habit which he had acquired and that I have often recommended to patients and friends as well as used myself with advantage when there is a tendency to cold feet, either habitually or occasionally. It is, moreover, useful whenever there is a tendency to insomnia because some exciting occupation has preceded going to bed. Before retiring Sir Henry used to sit beside his bath tub and let the hot water flow into it over his feet, gradually becoming warmer and warmer, until he could no longer stand the heat. A temperature well above 120 degrees may be borne with comfort after a while, though at the beginning it would seem entirely too hot. The feet are kept in the hot water at least five minutes. When taken out they should be thoroughly red and show evidence of a good deal of blood having been attracted to them. If they are now carefully wiped and rubbed vigorously there will usually be no further tendency to cold feet that night and sleep will come naturally. Sir Henry said that when he had been out at meetings where he had to make an address or had to take part in business of any kind that inclined to make him wakeful, he found this an excellent method of preparing himself for immediate sleep.

It must not be forgotten that the worst forms of cold feet are found among those suffering from flatfoot. The dropping of the arch interferes with the return circulation and also with lymphatic circulation. These individuals feel very tired because of their foot condition, yet their cold feet often disturbs their sleep at the beginning of the night. The only effective relief for this is afforded by proper treatment of the feet. (See the chapter on Foot Troubles3.)

Lack of Air.—On the other hand, occasionally it happens in spite of all that has been said in recent years about fresh air in sleeping rooms, windows are hermetically sealed and even then people cover themselves with many thicknesses of bed clothing and are too warm. I have found over and over again that where people could not be persuaded to leave a window open all night (and when they are old and deeply prejudiced in the matter I do not insist, for the suggestion of possibly catching cold would almost surely keep them awake), the thorough airing of rooms before retiring made a great difference in the sleep of elderly people. When patients are young, I simply insist on the window being wide open for some time before they go to bed and slightly during the night, except in extreme cold weather. Many a patient who complains of waking several times during the night and being awake for some time on each occasion will begin to have longer periods of sleep without a break if such a change in the ventilation of the room is effected. {658} Anyone who has seen fever patients who had been restless, disturbed and wakeful, sink into a quiet slumber after the room has been thoroughly aired and the temperature of it reduced ten or fifteen degrees, will realize how helpful this same method of treatment will be in nervous, wakeful irritability.

How important air is for the obtaining of the power to sleep for many hours every day can be best understood and appreciated from the habits insisted on for patients in tuberculosis sanatoria as a result of experience. When there is any tendency to a rise in temperature in these patients they are kept absolutely without exercise. They are either in bed or on a lounging chair all day, but they are out in the air or at least close to an open window. As a rule, they sleep some in the morning and then they sleep again in the afternoon. This would ordinarily be fatal to sleep at night in even healthy people taking considerable exercise and therefore presumably tired and more likely to sleep than these patients who had made no exertion during the twenty-four hours; but it is not often, after patients have been for ten days or two weeks at the sanatorium, that there is any complaint of lack of sleep at night. This is true in spite of the fact that patients are often wakened by coughing during the night, yet after a comparatively short interval they go to sleep again and sleep until morning. This is not true when patients do not pass most of their time in the open air and when their rooms are not well aired.

Sleep at Sea.—I know nothing that is more effective in doing away with insomnia than a sea voyage. The passengers sit on their lounging chairs all the morning in the open air, usually sleeping for some time, often for several hours. During the afternoon this is repeated. In spite of this extra sleep they turn in, not long after ten, and sleep well until morning. There is practically no exercise and the air usually excites such an appetite that five and even six meals a day are consumed. There is no disturbance of digestion unless some special excess is indulged in, and, above all, sleep is rather favored than impaired by the large amount of food taken. This experience which is so common, is very valuable as indicating just what is the best pre-requisite for sleep. It is not exercise and tiredness to such a degree that one fairly drops from fatigue, but such an oxidation of all tissues by the breathing of pure air that there are no toxic waste products left in the system to act as excitants for disturbance of sleep.

Cold Water.—In summer, when wakefulness is due to heat, a cool bath, or at least a rub down with cold water and going to bed without drying is an excellent method of inviting sleep. Under these circumstances the sheet acts as a soothing cool pack and people who have been wakeful for hours before, or at least have found considerable difficulty in getting to sleep, sleep promptly. The mechanism of sleep-production is easy to understand. There is less blood to go to the brain when the little capillaries at the surface are pretty well extended and after the application of cool water the reaction which follows the closing of the capillaries in response to cold leaves them of sufficient size to accommodate a large amount of the blood of the body. Of course, in both cases there is the suggestive value of a proceeding of this kind so well calculated to predispose the patient's mind to go to sleep without solicitude.

{659}

Diet.—As has already been outlined in the hints that precede, the first thing in the treatment of insomnia is to remove any causes that may be at work in producing wakefulness. Among the most common of these in our modern life is the taking of coffee or tea, important in the order mentioned. Every physician has frequent experiences of people who complain of insomnia, yet who take a cup of coffee late at night. A large proportion of humanity cannot do this with impunity and expect to go to sleep promptly. Occasionally one finds that patients complaining of sleeplessness are taking three to five cups of coffee a day. This must be stopped. A physician may be told by such patients that they cannot get along without their coffee. I have only one answer for this and it is meant to show patients that if they want to sleep they must take the means to secure it and, above all, must remove all disturbing factors. I tell them that if they cannot do without coffee they may continue to do without sleep. If they want to sleep they must give up coffee or at least must limit the amount. I have found it comparatively easy to get people to limit coffee-taking by the suggestion that there should be one tablespoonful of strong coffee taken to a cup of hot milk. This gives the taste, or rather the aroma of coffee, for coffee has properly no taste to speak of, and while, at first, patients crave the stimulation they have been accustomed to, it takes but a few days to overcome this craving entirely.

Usually it is easy to get people to confess that they are taking too much coffee. For some reason not easy to understand it is harder to get them to acknowledge that they are taking too much tea. Coffee is taken with a certain amount of deliberation. Tea may be and often is taken at odd intervals for friendliness' sake and sometimes patients do not know how much they are taking. Six or seven cups a day may be their usual quota, yet they do not realize it and at first are inclined to answer that they take it only two or three times a day, forgetting the little potations between meals. Tea is not so prone to cause wakefulness as coffee, yet the toxic irritant principle in both is the same and when the amount of tea and its strength are sufficient, the same results follow. The tea habit must always be given up if there is complaint of lack of sleep, especially early in the night.

There is a very common persuasion that the eating of food in any quantity shortly before going to bed, and especially the eating of certain materials, will keep people awake. It is well known, however, that there are a great many people who can eat anything and sleep well after it and young children sleep best when their stomachs are full. There are undoubtedly idiosyncrasies in this matter that must be respected, but many patients are deceiving themselves. They are eating too little and their wakefulness is more due to the mental state than to anything else. As this contradicts a very prevalent impression, I may say that it is said deliberately and only after much experience with people inclined to be over-solicitous about their diet and their health generally and who were actually producing wakefulness or at least very light dreamful sleep, by their elimination from their diet, and especially from their evening meal, of many nutritious substances. I make it a rule to insist with patients that if it is more than five hours since their last meal they must take a glass of milk and some crackers or a cup of cocoa and something to eat before going to bed. This is particularly important if they have been out in the air much between their last meal and bedtime.

{660}

The Evening Hours.—The use of the hours after the evening meal is an extremely important factor with regard to insomnia. If the patient tries to read the paper or some conventionally interesting magazine or book, thoughts of the possibility of his not sleeping will surely obtrude themselves and he will fail to get to sleep when he lies down. As a matter of fact, he will have so disturbed himself as to

351

predispose to insomnia. Some quiet occupation, interesting yet not too interesting, that diverts the mind from the thoughts about itself and about sleep possibilities, yet does not excite it, is the best possible auxiliary and preparation for sleep. Prof. Oppenheim has, as usual, said this very well in his "Letters to Nervous Patients," to which we have turned so often:

A great deal depends upon the right use of the evening hours. On no account let yourself occupy them with anxious forebodings about the night. But, on the other hand. It is not at present wise to take up your mind with too exciting thoughts, as the strong after-impression of feeling and fancy may counteract the tendency to sleep. You must find out for yourself whether a quiet game (cards, halma, chess, or patience), the reading of a serious or an amusing book, the perusal of an illustrated paper, or a chat with a friend will be most certain to give you that tranquillity of mind through the vestibule of which you will pass into the temple of sleep.

Direct Sleep Suggestions.—Many plans are suggested by which people are supposed to be able to get to sleep. A favorite and very old suggestion is that of counting sheep go over a fence or something of that kind that is merely mechanical, yet takes the mind from other thoughts. As a rule, any plan involving mental occupation that is meant to produce sleep is likely to react and do harm rather than good. Sleep must not be wooed deliberately but must be allowed to come of its own sweet will. It is extremely important that exciting thoughts and bothering interests be put aside, not at the moment when we want to go to sleep, but some considerable time before. This is not always an easy matter and often requires careful planning. It is worth while doing it, however, in order to secure sleep promptly and not allow a prolonged period to pass while one is lying awake, for if nervous irritability ensues wakefulness is still further prolonged and the patient may begin to toss and so disarrange the bedclothing and disturb himself as to prepare for several hours of sleeplessness which would not have occurred if there had been an appropriate interval given to preparing the mind for sleep.

Diminishing Solicitude.—Patients must not be too anxious for sleep. If they worry themselves over the possibility of not sleeping then they will almost surely disturb their sleep, or at least delay its coming. The ideal state of mind is not to bother one's head about it, to lie down habitually at a given hour, compose one's self to sleep with assurance and then wait its coming without solicitude. Many people will say this is not easy to do, but habit makes it easy. Most of our animal life is lived by habit. We are hungry at certain times by habit. Our bowels move at a particular time by habit. We can sleep by habit. If we try to use our intellect solicitously with regard to any of these habitual functions we do much more harm than good. The more anxiety there is about sleep the more likely it is to be disturbed. When the habit of sleep at a particular hour has been broken the best way to regain it is to lie down at that particular hour and then wait patiently for {661} the advent of sleep. If impatience gets the better of us sleep is kept off and will not come for hours. If the patient can lie down feeling "Well, if I do not sleep now I will to-morrow morning" then there is usually little difficulty about sleep.

Dread of Consequences.—Many people who suffer from insomnia fear that their loss of sleep will injure their intellectual capacity or make them prematurely aged, or drain their vitality so that they will not have health and strength of mind and body when they grow old. This adds to their solicitude about themselves and inveterates their condition. There is only one answer to this dread, which has no foundation in what we know of actualities, and that is, to tell them the experience of certain persons which absolutely contradicts such a notion. One distinguished physician who, at the age of seventy-five, is writing books that are attracting widespread attention and is doing an amount of work that many a younger man might envy, has told me of all that he suffered from insomnia between the ages of thirty and fifty-five. His mental productivity was much hampered at that time by his wakefulness and anxiety with regard to it. He feared the worst as regards advancing years, yet he is in the full possession of mental and bodily strength well beyond the Psalmist's limit. His is not an exceptional case, for there are many others in my own personal knowledge. Virchow once told me of years when he suffered from insomnia, yet he lived to be well past eighty and then died, not from natural causes, but from an injury. A man who accomplished an immense amount of work in his day in the organization of a great university suffered from insomnia in his younger years to such a degree that his friends and even he himself feared for his mental stability, eventually overcame this symptom completely and went on to years of great active work, dying in the end, not from his head, but his heart. We have records of a number of such cases. Few of the hard students of the world went through life without having some bother from insomnia. It is well-known, however, that many of the great thinkers, investigators and discoverers in philosophy and in science have lived long lives well beyond the age of the generality of mankind.

Mental Diversion.—The main thing is to banish the thoughts of one's ordinary occupation as far as that can be accomplished without laboring so intently at this as to give the mind another bothersome occupation. Many people find that a game of cards just before going to bed takes their thoughts off business and worry almost better than anything else. Something like this is needed in many people. Most people must not write for some time before retiring, because writing proves so absorbing an occupation, as a rule, that the mind becomes thoroughly awake and then remains so for some time afterwards. Reading is better, but the reading must be chosen with proper care. An exciting story, for instance, may serve to keep one awake for hours, as everyone knows who has tried and found himself still reading at three in the morning after having begun an interesting book. The reading of works of general information, of travels, of description of places, where it is comparatively easy to stop at any place, of short stories which do not hold the interest beyond a brief period, is much better. Osler's recommendation to have a classic author beside one's bed to be read for a few minutes every night after retiring as a preparation for sleep is an excellent remedy for the milder forms of insomnia, as well as a stepping-stone to scholarship.

{662}

William Black in one of his books has a description of an old man who had suffered from insomnia very severely until he discovered a plan of his own to enable him to get to sleep. This consisted in reading the Encyclopedia Britannica. He began at the beginning and read straight ahead, article after article, and volume after volume. He never even by any chance departed from this routine either to look up cross references, or read anything further about men who were mentioned in the article he was going through at the moment and whose names occurred in another volume. He read straight on until his eyes got heavy and then he went to sleep. At the time he was introduced into the story he had already read the whole work through twice and was, I think, at "D" on the third reading. He had had considerable bother about getting to sleep before he adopted this plan, but it proved an always efficient somnifacients. There is a story about an old American farmer who said that he read the dictionary over and over again for the same purpose. The stories were short and disconnected, but they never bothered his sleep, while his wife and daughters were sometimes kept up more than he thought was good for them by their interest in the story paper.

Treatment of Early Morning Wakefulness.—With regard to the disturbance of sleep in the early morning hours there are certain instructions to patients that have always seemed to me extremely important. Most of the patients who complain of wakefulness in the early morning hours are really suffering from hunger at that time. This is especially true with regard to those who stay up rather late at night. They have their last regular meal about seven or a little earlier, they get to bed at eleven or even later, and some of them, following the old maxim that eating before sleep is likely to disturb it, go to bed on an empty stomach. Whenever more than four hours have passed since the last meal the stomach is quite empty, and after the preliminary fatigue has worn off and the sleep has become lighter and the lack of nourishment more pronounced a vague sense of discomfort in the abdominal region wakes them, though most of them do not realize that they are disturbed by a craving for food. In a large number of these cases I have found that the recommendation of a glass of milk and some crackers, or some simple cake, just before retiring does more than anything else to lengthen sleep and prevent what has been learnedly called matutinal vigilance.

After emptiness of the digestive tract, the most prominent cause of wakefulness in the early morning is anxiety about the hour of rising or about some engagement that has to be kept in the early morning. I have known patients who worked themselves up so much thinking over the necessity for rising at a particular hour to catch a train, that they were awake for several hours before they needed to be. Some are much more inclined to this over-anxiety than others. If they move to the country where trains have to be caught regularly, their sleep may be seriously disturbed by this circumstance. If the trouble becomes acute they must simply change their residence. If it is absolutely necessary that they stay, then they must have someone to wake them at a definite time. This must be someone on whom they can absolutely depend, otherwise the old solicitude will reassert itself. This seems a small matter, yet I have known serious cases of neurasthenia with annoying digestive symptoms due to nothing else than this morning wakefulness consequent upon overanxiety with regard to trains and other morning engagements.

{663}

Habits.—In the correction of troubles of sleep one of the difficulties that the physician has to contend with when patients have grown accustomed to staying up late and finally have so disturbed their sleep mechanism that symptoms of insomnia develop, is the declaration that there is no use for them going to bed early since they cannot sleep. If a man has been accustomed for a long period to go to bed between midnight and 2 a. m. and his habits are suddenly changed so that he goes to bed at ten or even eleven, it is very likely that for some time after retiring he will not sleep. If he grows over-anxious he may toss and become somewhat feverish and then, even when the accustomed time for sleep comes, he may not secure it. Besides, the depression consequent upon failure to sleep when he has fulfilled his physician's directions and when he knows that this is considered an important adjuvant in his treatment, acts as a distinctly discouraging factor. Under these circumstances it is important to recall to him that one habit can only be removed by the making of another. It may be necessary to send him to bed for awhile only an hour earlier than before until he has grown accustomed to going to sleep somewhat sooner, and then this habit, in turn, be changed to an earlier hour so as to secure all the sleep that is necessary.

In a word, insomnia is not a definite affection to be treated by giving one or the other of one's favorite drugs, or if these should fail trying still others, but it is a condition of mind very often predisposed to by certain conditions of body. If this condition of mind can be adjusted by careful attention to the correction of whatever may be physically out of order, then there is every reason to look for definite improvement very soon and complete cure without any delay. Insomnia is not the awful ailment that it is sometimes pictured, nor all that it appears to the excited imagination of the young person who loses a few hours' sleep; but a manifold condition to be dealt with very differently in different individuals, according to the indications of the case. If the patient's confidence can be secured that means more than almost anything else that can be done. If a little patience is exercised in obtaining such definite details of the mental state and of certain physical factors as may seem quite trivial to the patient yet are really predisposing elements for his affection, the therapeutics become comparatively simple. It is the use of tact and judgment in this matter that means most, however, and then very few drugs will be required. Between the habits consequent upon the opiates and certain of the serious hemolytic conditions due to the abuse of coal-tar products, this is a consummation that may well be worked for assiduously.

CHAPTER VIII

SOME TROUBLES OF SLEEP

Certain annoying incidents in connection with sleep annoy those affected by them so much as to arouse them very completely from sleep and make them wakeful for a time. Nothing disturbs most people so much as the thought that some passing incident, a little out of the common, is quite individual and peculiar to them. If they are at all nervous they are likely to think that it portends some serious ailment, either present or about to {664} develop. Nothing reassures them more than to learn that these incidents are not so uncommon as they imagine, indeed that many of them are quite frequent, and, above all, that many people who have had them are still alive and well beyond threescore and ten, and laughing at the fears of their earlier years.

Starting.—Perhaps one of the most annoying of these incidental troubles is starting in sleep. It occasionally happens that just about the time a person is dozing off he suddenly starts and, almost before he realizes it, is fully awake, his heart beating emphatically and there may even be a little feeling of oppression on the chest. The cause is not the same in all cases and individual differences are worth investigating. In most people this starting means that there is, for the moment, some mechanical interference with the action of the heart and that a systole has been delayed and has been pushed through with more force than usual because of this delay. A full stomach will occasionally cause this, especially if patients lie on their left sides. In some people even a drink of water taken just before retiring will be sufficient weight to cause this interference with heart action. An accumulation of gas in the stomach will do it by pushing up against the diaphragm. Where there is a distinct tendency to the accumulation of gas in the stomach I have sometimes been sure that the expansion of the gas consequent upon the cozy warmth of the patient in bed, or its greater effect upon the stomach because the relaxation of sleep affected even the stomach walls slightly, was the cause of it. It happens more frequently in the old than it does in the young, but it is observed at all ages and patients are usually quite disturbed about it, as, indeed, they are likely to be with regard to anything that affects their hearts.

The thought that this forcible beat must mean some serious pathological condition will obtrude itself on many people, and if it does sleep is sure to be disturbed. Even though there may be no discoverable lesion of the heart, these patients often, though they are physicians, will worry lest some underlying condition should be developing. The first patient who ever described this symptom to me told me of it while I was a medical student and he is still alive and in good health, though he is past seventy. At the time I went over him rather carefully with the idea that there might be an organic heart lesion, but found none. The prognosis of these cases is always favorable, for there are many who suffer yet live long. I have found it to occur particularly in elderly people when they were a little overtired on going to bed, or in anemic young people when they had had somewhat more exertion than usual during the day. Unless there is really some demonstrable heart lesion the start does not mean anything and patients can be reassured at once. They should be counselled against lying on the left side, though in some of them it will occur even while lying on the right side and then the mechanism of its production seems to be the gaseous over-distention of the stomach. Patients may be told at once that it occurs in a large number of people and then, instead of lying awake and worrying about it as they often do, they learn simply to place themselves in a more comfortable position and go to sleep again without solicitude. They would learn this for themselves in the course of time, but the physician's reassurance will enable them to anticipate the lessons of experience and they will thus be saved worrying.

At times this starting from sleep seems due to some unusual noise. In {665} certain nervous states even slight noises produce an exaggerated reaction and there seems to be a surprising, almost hypnotic, acuity of hearing just at the moment when all the other senses are going to sleep. Any of the small noises that sound so loud in the stillness of the night may serve to wake the patient so thoroughly after a preliminary doze that sleep is disturbed for some time. As a rule, however, such noises would not disturb people if they were in normal healthy condition, or at least the disturbance would be only momentary. The solicitous effort that some people make to get away from every possible noise is an attempt in the wrong direction. We have heard of people building special houses, or noise-proof rooms in the center of houses where they hoped it would be impossible to be disturbed. What is needed is not so much an effort to secure absolutely noiseless surroundings, which is almost impossible in any circumstances, be it city or country, but to change the patient's physical condition so that slight noises are not reacted to so explosively. There are many general directions for this and certain drugs, as the bromides, are of distinct service. On the other hand, the taking of cinchona products seems often to emphasize it.

I have found that two classes of nervous patients particularly were likely to be disturbed by these starts in their sleep. The first class is perhaps the larger. They are the patients who do not eat enough. They will usually be found to be underweight and to be nursing some thought with regard to their digestion, or some supposed idiosyncrasy towards food that is keeping them below the normal weight for their height. Nothing makes sleep lighter than a certain amount of hunger. This hunger may be disguised so completely, or so covered up by the patient's persuasion that more food cannot be taken without serious gastric disturbance, that it may pass utterly unnoticed. When such patients are disturbed early in the night, it usually means that besides taking a not quite sufficient amount of food they are taking more tea or coffee or some stimulant than is good for them. I say some stimulant because in several cases that I investigated rather carefully the cause seemed to be the alcohol taken with one of the largely advertised patent medicines, a supposed digestive tonic, consisting mainly of dilute alcohol, and really about as strong as whiskey. When the tendency to be startled occurs in the early mornings, then people need to eat something simple just before they go to bed.

The other class of cases who are likely to start at night in their sleep are those who do not get out into the air enough during the day or who sleep in rooms insufficiently ventilated. At the beginning of the night the lack of ventilation makes the sleep light and easily disturbed. After a certain number of hours have been spent in a badly ventilated room the patient sinks into a rather deep sleep, which is likely to be dreamy, however, and then he is rather hard to waken, but wakes not feeling rested, but on the contrary often heavier and more tired than on retiring. In these cases an investigation of the amount of air the patient is allowing to enter his sleeping room or that his circumstances provide him with is extremely important. As for those who do not get out enough during the day, it is easy to understand that their sleep may be light. To them, as a rule, it will be a surprise to find how much depth is added to their sleep by an additional hour or two in the air. Commonly, people who do not get out much during the day are shivery and {666} suffer from cold, especially in the winter time, and so they are likely to keep their rooms rather tightly closed. In this case they have two reasons for a tendency to be wakeful, which is emphasized if there are noises near them or if there is anything that disturbs their sleep.

In young children, of course, it must not be forgotten that starting in sleep may be due to the twitching pains of a beginning tuberculous joint disease. At times the children are so young, or the symptoms so vague and the tenderness, if there is any, so deep, that the real significance of this may not be recognized. The most successful treatment for these starting pains in children that has thus far been found, forms a striking commentary on what we have just been saying with regard to fitful sleep when ventilation is insufficient or when the patient has not been out of doors enough during the day. The children from the New York hospitals who in recent years were taken down to

Sea Breeze during the autumn and winter and made to live in wards, the windows of which were constantly open so that the temperature was often below fifty, so that doctors and nurses had to wrap themselves up warmly and sometimes cover their heads and their hands, had all been sufferers from these starting pains before this experience, but gradually they lessened in frequency until after a few months the crying of a child at night because of these pains was extremely rare. The lesson is evident, and abundance of air not only cures tuberculous conditions, but also makes the nervous system so much less irritable that starting pains do not so easily affect it.

Noise.—Slight noises often make it impossible for nervous people to sleep. This is much more a question of personal sensitiveness and anxious expectancy and over-irritability than anything else. One distinguished physician whom I knew was extremely sensitive to noise and would be awake for hours if wakened up early in the night by the slamming of a door or a call in the street or anything of the kind. He suffered from insomnia to a noteworthy degree and found to his surprise that he could sleep better on a train than anywhere else. After he had lost two or three nights of sleep he actually used to make arrangements to take a berth on an express train going out of his city, ride until the morning and then come back. He usually slept well amidst all the noise and jar of the train, though he would be quite sleepless at home as the result of even slight noises. I have known people suffering from insomnia who took a long ocean trip on a slow vessel and who slept well amidst all the noises of shipboard, but were light sleepers after landing, and felt that they missed the noise and bustle. Of course, in these cases the rocking movements sometimes predispose to sleep. It is not the custom now to rock infants to sleep and a very definite agreement seems to have been come to among pediatrists to forbid the practice as harmful. It is probable, however, that the instinct of the race in the matter was not at fault. Rocking seems to relax a certain tension of muscles that of itself prevents the brain anemia which is the physiological basis of sleep. It is extremely difficult for nervous people to relax themselves completely, and the rocking movements, by tending to help them in this matter, are excellent predisposing factors. A rocking chair or a hammock furnish abundant proof of this.

Noise in general, as regards its relation to sleep, is an extremely individual matter. Habit plays the largest role in the matter. We all know the {667} stories of men who have gone to great expense in order to build noise-proof rooms and yet have found afterwards that they did not sleep well. The rustle of the bedclothes as their thoraxes rose and fell in respiration was enough to disturb them when they allowed themselves to become over-sensitive about noise. We all know how impossible sleep becomes with a rustle of a mouse in the wastepaper basket, or the scratching of one on the wainscoting. On the other hand, anyone who has lived in a large city where past hundreds of thousands of homes the elevated trains thunder every few minutes all during the night, or the trolley goes rolling by within a few feet of the bed, knows, too, that a great many people become accustomed to noises so as to be utterly undisturbed by them, though at the beginning any such insensitiveness to noise seemed out of the question.

I remember having a patient who insisted that he could not sleep so near the elevated. At the end of a week he had lost so many nights of sleep that he was almost in despair. If he did get sound asleep he said he used to hear the thunder of the elevated train coming toward him in his dreams and he would begin to pull his feet up so as to get them out of the way of the train, yet always with the feeling that he could not get them quite far enough, until his knees were almost to his chin. Under the influence of a little bromides, two hours more of outdoor air than he had been accustomed to before, and some reassurance that noise need not disturb sleep at all if taken philosophically, he learned in the course of two weeks to sleep quite peacefully and now has lived for ten years where the elevated passes within ten feet of his window, which is wide open for seven months in the year and always at least slightly open, except in the most stormy weather. It is a question, then, of the individual much more than his surroundings. The problem is to predispose the mind to sleep and then the senses will not disturb it except under special circumstances.

As a matter of fact, noises usually disturb people very little at night. The most surprising things can happen between 12 and 3 o'clock and attract no attention. Burglars calmly blow up a safe in a hotel confident that if there is no one awake when the explosion occurs there will be no investigation, because even though people wake up at the noise, they will wait for its repetition in order to see what it means, will not get up to investigate, especially in cold weather, and usually promptly go to sleep again.

Lying Awake.—There are many people to whom lying awake carries with it a sense of discouragement and dread. They seem to forget that lying awake and occupation with pleasant thoughts may be made a very agreeable pastime by those who are not over-anxious to sleep and who let the pleasant thoughts that may be suggested by the environment or the noises that are heard flow through consciousness. Everyone knows how pleasant it is or may be to listen to the rain patter on the roof of a country house, or to hear the murmur of the ocean or of the wind through the trees when there is not too much anxiety about to-morrow and to-morrow's occupations and the necessity for sleep to be ready for them. Stewart Edward White, in his series of essays on "The Forest," has a chapter on Lying Awake at Night that can well be recommended to the attention of those who complain bitterly of an hour of sleeplessness. Of course, in his case the lying awake is in the midst of the forest with all the witchery of wind in the trees and the {668} unusual sounds of forest life, while ordinary lying awake is in the rather monotonous environment at home, but still there is much that can be said for his insistence that in peaceful brooding, faculties revive while soft velvet fingers are laid on the drowsy imagination and you feel that in their caressing vaster spaces of thought are opened up. The impatience that comes to so many almost at once if they fail to go to sleep promptly only serves to keep them awake just that much more surely.

Very often, as suggested by Mr. White, this wakefulness occurs just when a good night's rest is surely expected. There is sometimes even a preliminary period of drowsiness. Then some little noise that ordinarily would not be noticed at all floats into the consciousness with a vigor that indicates that one sense is thoroughly awake. The very surprise of it wakes up the other senses with a start and then comes the thought that there is to be no sleep for some time. If this is resented, the period of wakefulness will be all the longer. If, when it has proved to be inevitable, one sits up quietly, reads a book for a time, plays a quiet game of solitaire, it may be on a board kept beside the bed for such purposes, or in some quiet way succeeds in bothering away the thought of insomnia, then almost surely sleep will come after a time, quietly and restfully, and the lost period will not prove harmful. If nature does not want to sleep she must not be forced into it, but gently led and after a time the wakefulness will disappear.

Night Terrors.—One of the troubles of sleep that is more often called to the attention of the physician than almost any other, is the so-called "night terrors" of children. Little ones wake with a scream, sit up in bed, evidently terrified, usually trembling, and ready to seek refuge from something that has seriously disturbed them. Under Dreams we have called attention to the fact that usually these terrors are due to a dream. Sometimes the dreams are the ordinary experience of supposed falling in sleep, from which the patients wake very much startled, or they are repetitions of exciting scenes through which they have passed, or of stories that they have heard, or, above all, plays that they have seen. Ghost stories, for instance, told shortly before they go to bed will often disturb children. Fairy stories and the ordinary myths of childhood, usually with a happy ending and without any serious terrors in them, are not so likely to disturb them. Melodramatic theatrical performances to which children lend themselves and their attention with great concentration of mind, have nearly as much effect on them as if they passed through the actual scenes. Every physician knows how much a fright is likely to disturb a child and cause it to wake many a night afterwards in a state of terror.

Respiratory Interference.—It is particularly important to remember that any interference with breathing will almost surely wake the child in a seriously startled condition. Adults are often affected by this same sort of dream, due very often to some pathological condition in the throat around which a series of dream ideas collect with somewhat poignant results. I have known a man suffering from elongated uvula wake up thinking that he was suffocating because, as he thought, he had nearly swallowed his tongue, or at least had been trying to do so. The sensation was so startling that it brought him to his feet at once. I have known a patient traveling a long five-days' railroad journey and suffering severely from train catarrh, come to the {669} persuasion that he might suffocate during sleep because his nose was completely stopped up and he had not the habit of sleeping with his mouth open. As a result his sleep was as much disturbed by his mind as his breathing. If these affect adults so strongly, it is easy to understand why children should be so frightened by them. Children who are mouth-breathers from adenoids or nasal obstruction, and still more those whose nasal breathing apparatus is not completely stopped up, but who are frequent intermittent mouth-breathers, are especially likely to be troubled in this way. The neurosis known as nervous croup, due to a spasm of the vocal cords, occurs oftenest in this class of children and is an associated phenomenon to that of night terrors.

Sleeping in the Light.—The habit of accustoming children to sleep with a light in the room nearly always lessens the depth of their sleep. They are more easily wakened and their sleep is not so refreshing. Besides, if they do not grow accustomed to the dark when they are young, they may always retain a dread of the dark and will require some light in the room where they sleep. Nature intended that the eyes and the optic nerve should have as complete a rest as possible and even with the lids lowered some light stimulus, if it is present, finds its way to the nerve fibers. Hence the desirability of having as far as possible an absolutely dark room. For some very timorous children, this may seem impossible. Many mothers will recall how awful the dark seemed to them and what shadowy shapes loomed up in it. It will usually be found on inquiry, however, that in these cases the children, after having been accustomed to sleep with some light and after having had all sorts of exciting pictures shown them and stories told them, were asked to sleep in the dark. From the very beginning they should be accustomed to sleeping in the dark and then it has none of the terrors thus pictured.

CHAPTER IX

DREAMS

Dreams, that is, thoughts and illusions and mental phenomena of various kinds that occur during sleep, have always been interesting to the psychologist, and have usually been related to physicians by patients either because they were thought to have a significance related to disease, or because something in them disturbed the patient's mind. This is almost as true in the modern time as it was long ago. It is curiously interesting to note that the very latest development of psychotherapy includes the use of hints obtained from dreams in order to determine the origin of psycho-neurotic conditions and certain of the minor psychic disturbances, and also as a foundation for treatment. The oldest stories of therapeutics that we have are those of patients waited on by the priest physicians of the olden times in the temples, who were supposed to be greatly helped by information obtained from the patient's dreams. It is interesting to read such recent studies as that of "Incubation in the Old Temples," by Miss Ingersoll, with the thought in mind that we are once more analyzing dreams in order to accomplish a similar purpose.

{670}

Dreams are so often a source of disturbance of mind for patients, lead to such disturbed sleep, or even so affect the bodily health that it is important for anyone who wants to influence patients through their minds to know the significance attributed to dreams by the most recent studies of them. This is all the more important because dreams are such a universal phenomenon. From our earliest years we dream. The night terrors of children are probably due to dreams and show that even as early as the age of three we dream vividly. Doubtless some of the terrifying dreams of childhood are similar to those that we experience later. Dreams of falling, dreams of being cold, of being out of breath, with vivid repetitions of exciting scenes through which they have gone during the day, or which they have seen in picture or been told in story, form the substance of these dreams. Children are likely to be much disturbed by them. They wake in a terror of anxiety, in cold sweat, and crying bitterly because of their dream visions. Older people are not so much disturbed at the moment, but often brood over dreams and may be seriously affected by them.

It is difficult, however, to persuade many people that their dreams have no special significance, either of present or of future evil, and to many the fact that they dream much becomes a suggestion of wakefulness that disturbs sleep and makes them quite unequal to the next day's work, because they have the feeling that, as they have been dreaming all night, they must be quite tired. Tiredness in nervous people is often a matter of the mental state rather than of physical exhaustion or genuine mental weariness. The actual place of dreams in psychology, then, becomes an important consideration in psychotherapeutics.

Our real advances in the knowledge of the significance of dreams have come from the study of the dreams that are common to most people. These show us exactly how and why dreams occur and just what their meaning is. Probably the most familiar dream common to all the human race is that of falling from a height. Everyone has been wakened with a startled sense of intense relief that the sensation of falling was illusory. The waking came just before the bottom was reached. There is a tradition that if one ever did strike the bottom in one's dream it would be the end and that death would result as surely as if the fall were real. So far we have had no one come back to tell us of that, and the tradition is reasonably safe from direct contradiction. It serves without any reason, however, to disturb timorous people and make them dread to fall asleep again. Often this dream-falling so seriously affects sensitive individuals that they do not get to sleep for an hour or more and occasionally those with an inclination to insomnia may even suffer for the rest of the night from the effect of it. It is important to explain, then, what we know about the causation of the dream. In nearly all cases the subject on waking finds himself on his back, and then the inclination is at once to turn over to the side with a sigh of relief. Commonly the dream occurs rather early in the night, when a rather heavy meal has been taken shortly before retiring. The weight in the stomach, particularly if considerable liquid has been taken, seems to press upon the abdominal aorta and interferes, to some extent at least, with the circulation to the legs. This deprives little nerves at the periphery of the body of some of their nutrition and causes a tingling feeling in them. This is quite different from pressure {671} on nerves, which gives the sensation termed "being asleep" to a limb. This tingling feeling resembles that which we experience when going down rapidly in an elevator. It is the falling sensation. This sensation tries to force its way into the consciousness and in this process does not completely wake consciousness up, but brings about an association of ideas connected with falling—hence the dream of being on a height and of falling therefrom out of which we wake so startled. The whole process instead of being injurious is really conservative. It is important that the aorta should not be pressed upon and this is the mode by which awakening is brought about and the position shifted so that further interference is stopped, though we ourselves are quite unconscious of the real purpose that has been accomplished. An explanation of this kind usually makes people who suffer from such dreams and have been disturbed by them much more tolerant of the phenomenon and more ready to go to sleep again, since evidently nature can be trusted to care for them even during sleep.

After the sensation of falling probably the commonest dream that humanity has, at least in the civilized state, is that of being out in some public place without sufficient clothing. Usually we wake just to find that some portion of our anatomy has been exposed to the air and that it is cold. It is this sensation gradually forcing its way into consciousness that has gathered around it a group of ideas that form our dream.

Among men, a familiar dream is that of running for a car, or away from something, or to catch someone, and finding that it is almost impossible to move. We are so out of breath that we are scarcely able to drag one foot after another and, indeed, sometimes we seem to be actually rooted to the spot. We cannot move at all. When we wake after this dream we find that, because of a cold in the head, our nose is stopped up by the secretion and that our mouths are shut and consequently we were getting no air. When that sensation tries to break into the consciousness there gather around it certain familiar ideas usually associated with being out of breath and hence we have the dream of trying to run without being able to move.

Frequency of Dreams.—Nervous people often complain that they dream all night or else very frequently, and that as a consequence their sleep is not restful. It is probable that there are always ideas in the mind and that literally we dream without ceasing. These ideas, however, do not get into our consciousness except just during the process of waking. All those who have investigated the subject of dreams are practically agreed on this. In subsequent paragraphs we quote a number of good observers on this subject. Certainly this is what we should expect from what we all know about day-dreaming. We can never catch ourselves during the day without finding some thought wandering through our minds. If we want to understand dreaming during sleep this day dreaming is instructive. We jump from one idea to another, apparently without a connection; yet there is always some connecting link. We have just read in the paper of someone in Cairo, and we think of old Egypt, and then of old Babylonia, and the Code of Hammurrabi, and the laws of the Medes and the Persians, and Xenophon and our school days, and of an old schoolmaster now a missionary in Japan, and of Japanese art and of an American artist much influenced by it, and of one of his great windows in a church in New York and of social work in connection with that church, {672} and of settlement houses and then Hull House, Chicago, and then of the Adamses in Massachusetts, and so on.

Thus, also, do our minds go flitting round apparently during the night. We remember only such things as are brought into our consciousness directly and emphatically during the process of wakening. During our day dreaming we recall only those things which for some reason led us to think consciously about them and then follow out our thoughts to definite conclusions. It is an interesting study to follow back our day dreams through their wanderings to the origin. As a rule, however, we lose track of the connections and after a time remember only some of the wonderful transformations and transmigrations of thought; and so it is in our dreams.

With regard to the frequency of dreaming. Sir Arthur Mitchell in his book "Dreaming, Laughing, and Blushing" (London, 1905), insists on the great probability of the constancy of our dreaming during sleep. He says:

It seems to me that there is no such thing as dreamless sleep. During the whole continuance of sleep, the mind, I believe, is occupied with a certain kind of thinking which works round what I have called hallucinations. I do not expect to be able to prove the correctness of this opinion as to the persistence of dreams all through sleep, but I think that it can easily be shown to be possibly correct. I go further, and say that many things show that it is probably correct. I may not be able to prove absolutely its correctness, but it is proper to bear in mind that it is quite as difficult to prove absolutely that it is not correct. My difficulty is frankly avowed. Many things, however, are taught in biology as being certainly true. In regard to which a like avowal could be made but is not made. There is what has been called a "conjectural biology."

We do not and we cannot remember much of what we have been thinking about while we are awake. This is unquestionably true in a large sense. But, nevertheless, we do not doubt that we have been thinking continuously. We do not suppose that at any time all thinking had ceased, though we may be completely unable to recall what it was about.

He shows further that many writers on dreams and careful students of the subject in the past have come to the same conclusion. Robert Dale Owen, for instance, deliberately endeavored to find out whether he had always been dreaming just before he awoke. After months of observation he records that in every instance he was conscious of having dreamed. Hazlitt, a century ago, tried the same thing for a prolonged period and notes that whenever he was waked, and immediately recollected himself as to possible dreaming, he was always aware that he had been dreaming. Sir Arthur Mitchell himself has tried this same experiment on himself and for a considerable time has scarcely ever failed to put to himself this question about dreaming when he awoke and always got a satisfying affirmative answer. Personally, for several years, I have been interested enough in this subject to recur frequently to it immediately on awaking and I cannot say that I have ever, under those circumstances, failed to find that there had been some vague dream fancies at least running through my mind before I was fully awake. This opinion as to the constancy of dreaming during sleep has many authorities in its support. Sir Arthur Mitchell has quoted a number, some of them distinguished physicians, who add the weight of their testimony to this view:

It is not a new thing to hold that there is no sleep without dreaming—in other words, that dreaming goes on unceasingly all through sleep. I have stated my own {673} opinion strongly, but the same opinion has been nearly as strongly expressed by others. Sir Benjamin Brodie, for instance, may be said to express it when he writes, "I believe that I seldom if ever sleep without dreaming." Sir Henry Holland expresses it still more plainly when he says: "No moment of sleep is without some condition of dreaming." Goodwin says much the same thing when he asserts that "sleep is not a suspension of thought"—in other words, that dreaming is sleep-thinking. Dr. John Reid still more clearly holds the opinion, though he does not furnish me with a short apt quotation. Hazlitt, too, may be taken as holding that there is no such thing as dreamless sleep.

Descartes and his followers may, perhaps, be regarded as holding that the mind is unceasingly at work in sleep—even in the "profoundest sleep," though "the memory retains it not," and Isaac Watts says that "the soul never intermits its activity," and that we may "know of sleeping thoughts at the moment they arise, and not retain them the next moment."

Hippocrates, Leibnitz, and Abercrombie have also been quoted as holding that there is no dreamless sleep, and so far as they express themselves on the subject they appear to do so.

A strong weight of opinion in all ages favors the view that during sleep dream-thoughts are constantly running through our mind, though we recollect only those which are impressed upon us at the moment of awaking. We do not even recall those unless, for some reason, we have paid special attention to them. That is just exactly what is true of day dreaming. After it is over we have no idea at all of the thoughts that occupied our minds for hours, though we are all aware that at any given moment, if we turned our consciousness inwards we found that there was something that we were thinking about.

Short Duration of Dreams.—This view of the constant occurrence of dreams during sleep is confirmed by other things that we have come to know as to dreams and dream states. Probably the most interesting of these is with regard to the length of dreams. As our memory of dreams is only such as we have from the thoughts of sleep getting into our consciousness just at the moment of awaking, dreams are never as long as they sometimes seem to be. As a matter of fact, they occupy but a few moments, though in that time a long story may seem to unroll itself. Probably nothing gives more assurance to people who are persuaded that they are losing much rest because of their dreams than this explanation of the brevity of the phenomena. Nervous people wake frequently. Whenever they wake they find themselves dreaming. As a consequence, they acquire the persuasion that they have been dreaming "all the night long," and it is not hard for them to suggest to themselves in the early morning that they are not rested. Nervous people seldom feel rested in the early morning, it is their worst time, and with the occurrence of dreams as a suggested reason for this, they exaggerate the feeling of tiredness with which they get up. A frank discussion of this question of the duration of dreams is often the best possible therapeutic auxiliary for such cases. It gives them a new series of suggestions and, above all, relieves them of unfavorable suggestions.

Prof. Maury of the University of Paris tells a striking story of a very brief dream of his own which shows how short may be the time occupied by what seems surely a long dream. He had been reading before going to bed a very striking book on the Reign of Terror. He dreamt that he himself was arrested during the Terror, taken to prison, that his name was called on the list of the condemned, that he was carried to the guillotine, fastened to the {674} board, pushed beneath the knife and that he woke just as the knife struck his neck. Of course he awoke with the usual sense of thankfulness and relief that comes at such times. When he awoke he found that a light curtain rod had fallen from the bed above him and had struck just across his neck. His dream evidently had all come to him during the extremely short time necessary for him to become fully awake after the rod had hit him. His mind was occupying itself with the history that he had read before going to bed. When the rod struck him the long story of his arrest and imprisonment, the journey to the place of the guillotine and the preparations for execution, all came to him as a series of rapid ideas during his coming to consciousness.

It is probable that most of our dreams are not much longer than this. One of my earliest recollections is of an old gentleman coming into the country school during my first year as a pupil and telling us the story of a dream of his of the night before quite as brief as that of Professor Maury. He had fallen asleep after dinner in his chair and, having a cold that stopped up his nose and his mouth being shut, he had the usual dream of being out of breath from running. It took him back to the story of the massacre of Wyoming, near the scene of which the school was situated. He dreamt that for hours he had been running away from the Indians and seemed at last utterly unable to escape them because he was out of breath. He made such efforts in his chair that his wife awakened him and then he found that he had been asleep altogether only a very few minutes.

Significance of Dreams.—Many people are quite sure that their dreams have a definite significance quite apart from any mere wandering of the mind or the suggestion of half-waking and the ideas that gather round sensations not fully in the consciousness. A number of people, for instance, have dreams of events that are happening at a distance at the moment that they dream. The Psychic Research Society of England has gathered a number of these and it is indeed difficult to understand many of them. There seems no doubt, however, that in many cases there is an illusion of memory, by which, after an event, dreams that might be taken to refer in some vague way to the happening, are clothed with a wealth of detail which appears to make them wonderful premonitory representations of future events or repetitions of simultaneous events. One of the most familiar of this form of dreams is what has been called a phantasm of the dying. People dying at a distance seem to have some wonderful power of making themselves appear to very near friends, especially brothers and sisters, and, above all, twins, and to friends with whom they have been very intimately associated. Occasionally such phantasms are seen during waking hours, or what are supposed to be waking hours, though it must not be forgotten that dreams may come very easily and almost unconsciously in short naps, but much more frequently in what are known to be dreams.

Nearly always these partake of the nature of the ordinary dream, as can be seen by a careful analysis of their conditions, and are mere coincidences occupying a very brief space of time. A typical example of this is to be found in one of the stories told by Camille Flammarion, the French astronomer, in his book "The Unknown." A young man who had fallen in love with a young woman was deeply grieved to be parted from her by the injunction of parents. Separated by a long distance, they kept up a clandestine {675} correspondence for more than a year. For a considerable period, however, he had not heard from her, and he was beginning to be anxious lest anything had happened to her. One night she appeared to him in a dream in his room in white garments with a pale face and, placing her cold hand in his, she bade him good-bye. He awoke with a start. He found it difficult to sleep and was very anxious about her. The next day he learned that she had died the night before and concluded that his dream was a last message from her. The end of the story, however, as it is told, spoils this nice sentimental conclusion. When he awoke he found he had in his hand a glass of ice water which had been standing on the table beside him. The grasping of this had awakened him. During the awakening process the thoughts of her in his mind gathered round the cold sensation in his hand and gave him the dream of her and the last farewell.

There are many instances in which dreams of future events seem to come true. Indeed, so many of these stories have been told that it is hard to persuade some people that dreams have no meaning and can have no meaning. By this we mean that they can by no possibility represent prophetic foresight. What patients need to be made to understand is that dreams represent only straggling sensations trying to get into our consciousness, just barely succeeding, and then arousing trains of ideas unconnected in themselves, but which we connect afterwards when we recollect our dreams. This whole subject has been studied so thoroughly in Maury's work on *"Le Sommeil et les Rêves"* about the middle of the last century and Freud *"Ueber den Traum"* and Sante de Sanctis' *"I Sogni"* Turin, 1899, at the end of the century, that there can be no further doubts about the matter for those who are open to conviction. Most people, however, want to believe that their dreams mean something. They like to think that they are in some way picked out from the multitude and that their dreaming has a significance more than is accorded to other people. It is, indeed, this self-centeredness that makes for the belief in premonitions and prophetic dreams and, as in all cases, these feelings work out their own revenge.

If they will listen to reason, however, most people may be rather readily convinced that their dreams cannot have any serious significance. In the chapter on Premonitions we have already called attention to the situation that exists with regard to the possibility of future events giving information of themselves in advance of their happening. Simultaneous events may perhaps in some way give warnings. The possibility of action on the mind at a distance, especially where minds are involved, has been discussed and admitted. The cases in which it is supposed to have happened are, to my mind, all dubious and are mere coincidences. For future events, however, there is no possible physical explanation. When we turn to explanations in the borderland between spirit and matter we find nothing satisfactory. The future event exists nowhere. No spirit even knows it; it is dependent on human free will. To the Creator it is known only as a contingent possibility dependent on free will. The information does not come from Him, for then there would be more design in these incidents. Such dreams would effect some serious purpose, while usually they have but minor significance in the stories as told and they often concern only the most trivial things.

What is thus true of premonitions can readily be applied to dreams. {676} There is no reasonable source of information with regard to future events. What, then, are we to say of the dreams that come true? There is no doubt that dreaming is extremely common. Probably, as was said, we never sleep without dreams. There are a billion dreams at least, probably many billions of dreams every night, then, in this little world of ours. When these are startling they cling to us. It would be surprising if some of them did not come true. Indeed, it is inevitable, according to the theory of probabilities, that some of them will connect themselves directly with future events. We have a few thousands of such startling coincidences in the history of the race. Out of these have been made all the data supposed to underlie the teaching that dreams have a prophetic significance. It is much easier to understand with regard to dreams than even with regard to telepathy coincidence explains all the supposedly wonderful warnings of events that actually happen after we have had apparently premonitory dreams.

An interesting example of a premonition that did not come true, the subject of which was sure that it was a waking premonition and not a dream, though it seems more likely that it was as suggested by the narrator a sleep vision, is told by Sir Arthur Mitchell in his "Dreaming, Laughing, Blushing" (London, 1905). A number of scientists who discussed the story declared that if it had only come true it would have been one of the most startling manifestations of premonition and of the clairvoyant power of dreams, or at least of their telepathic significance, that we have ever had. It involved so many distinguished scientists that there could have been no doubt about it. It was so detailed and those details were known to so many authorities in science, that it would have carried great weight and it would have been extremely difficult to have people accept it as a mere coincidence. It is easy to see now after the event that, if it had been fulfilled, it would have been, in spite of its startlingness, a mere coincidence. Since it was not fulfilled, however, it represents one of the best evidences that we have for the insignificance of premonitory or telepathic dreams.

Sir William T. Gairdner, K. C. B., whose interesting typhus delirium experience appears in the paper by Professor Coates on "Sleep, Dreams and Delirium" (*Glas. Med. Jour.*, Vol. xxxviii, 1892, pp. 241-261), has written to me about his dreams generally, and he concludes his letter with the narrative of a dream, which, as he correctly says, "if it had only fulfilled itself, might have become famous." He prefaces the narrative by this statement: "In all my individual experience, now extending over more than the usual term of life, I have never met with anything suggestive in the remotest degree of telepathy or second sight, or of dream prophecies or any other fact bearing on the marvellous." He then goes on to tell the dream to which I have referred. "In crossing the Atlantic In 1891," he says, "in delightful weather and perfect bodily health, and without a shade of anxiety on my mind so far as I was aware (in waking consciousness), I was suddenly aroused in the very early morning, say, three or four a. m., out of a perfectly sound, and, as I should call it, dreamless sleep, by the apparition of a telegram written on the usual paper, and presumably from home, in these words: 'Miss Dorothea died at ——,' all the rest being blurred and indistinct, but these words having a startling distinctness and a vivid sense of reality. I was not, I think, in the least degree alarmed at first, and certainly had no superstition about it on discovering that it was only a dream; but, failing to get any more sleep, I rose early, took my bath as usual, and went on deck, where I had to repeat the story of my dream to each one of some three or four companions who were on board, of whom I will only mention Sir. John Batty Tuke, Professor Young of Owens College, and Professor {677} Cunningham, then of Trinity College, Dublin. Any of these gentlemen will confirm my saying that I attached no special importance to this dream in the way of a scare or a superstition, but in this way it got abroad to a certain extent within a small circle on board in such a way as would have ensured it a widespread fame had it only come true. In discussing the matter at breakfast I remarked (alluding to telepathy) that the telegram was clearly, judging from its terms, not from my wife or any member of my immediate family, and could only have been despatched by a servant or some one with whom I could not be supposed to be in telepathic rapport. From this point of view it clearly refuted itself, and yet the effect upon my mind was such that, upon arriving at New York, I at once despatched a telegram announcing my arrival and making inquiry, the reply to which showed that the family were pursuing a quite undisturbed course at St. Andrews."

Sir William describes himself as aroused out of sound sleep by the apparition of a telegram, but I think this only means that he became suddenly awake on seeing the telegram during sleep. He does not say whether he knew in his dream that he was a passenger on a great ship on the mid-ocean, but he says that the telegram was written on the usual paper by which I take it that he means the paper used here on shore.

If it happened that the death of Miss Dorothea took place about the time of the appearance of the telegram to so distinguished a man as Sir William in his sleep, I scarcely think there would be any more startling record of a so-called telepathic message. But most happily the death did not take place, so that the story of the dream will be forgotten. Tens of thousands of similar dream stories have that fate.

Children's Dreams.—There is an old tradition that to tell our dreams causes them to come back, or at least to recur in some other form. This tradition is so old and so universal that probably there is more in it than might at first be thought. This emphasizing of certain forms of unconscious cerebration probably encourages their repetition, or, at least, the repetition of further processes of the same kind. There seems to be no doubt, too, that the reading of certain kinds of imaginative writing and the looking at exciting pictures sometimes leads to dreams about them. Certainly children should not be told terrifying stories and the more nervous they are and the more affected they are by such stories, which to some people make renewed temptations to tell them, the more should they be avoided.

Any physician who has had much experience with city children, especially in New York City, is likely to know how exciting, tragic and, above all, melodramatic scenes serve as the basis for disturbing dreams and night terrors. They will not, of course, in vigorous, healthy and strong-minded children, but these are the ones who are most prone to play out of doors and so are likely to be less bothered. Just the nervous, old-fashioned, delicate children who prefer the theater to sports of other kinds, are likely to be most affected in this unfortunate way. The scenes become so real to children that they impress them very deeply and are readily rehearsed in the unconscious cerebration of sleep. Many a child sees in its dreams someone, often a near relative, fastened on the carriage of a sawmill and inevitably approaching a buzz-saw, or fastened inextricably to the rails while an express train thunders down on them. That they should wake up with a start and a scream of terror and lose most of their night's sleep and disturb that of others, is not surprising. It is well known how witnessing actual danger, as of an automobile accident, or a railroad wreck, disturbs a child's imagination for long after; and its theater experiences are almost as actual as the reality.

{678}

Many of the colored supplements of Sunday newspapers seem to be particularly undesirable literature for children in this respect, though, of course, there are many other reasons why children should not be encouraged to look at them. It is not unusual for the newspapers to give lurid pictures of wonderful dreams or things that happen in dreams. This is undoubtedly a suggestion that acts in causing nearly all children, but especially those of nervous organization, to dream much more than would ordinarily be the case. It recalls the old warning about telling dreams. These sets of pictures certainly serve to develop the imagination of the child along undesirable lines. Possibly some of them which emphasize the fact that after eating certain very undesirable foods, dreams are much more likely to come than at other times may not be without their prophylactic sanitary value, but this is a doubtful advantage compared to the psychic harm that they bring. I am not of those who would limit the fairy stories and other pleasant essays in imagination which delight children so much and form a desirable part of their education, but artistic effort that is terrifying or deterrent, whether with pen or brush, should be kept away from them until after their mental control is well established. Children will probably dream anyhow, and, therefore, should have a pleasant fund of imaginative material as a basis for their dreams.

CHAPTER X

DISORDERS OF MEMORY

Many patients suffering from various nervous symptoms insist that they are losing their memory or that it is becoming notably deficient in some ways. If they are a little on in years they are sure that their memory is not as good as it used to be and that they now forget many things that were formerly remembered without difficulty. Especially are they likely to assert that the names of people and certain words will not come to them when they want them, that they often have to seek for facts and dates that should be quite familiar, that they fail to remember acquaintances and the like. These symptoms of which they complain are often sources of considerable worry and serve to emphasize in them the idea that there is something serious the matter with their general health, or some pathological condition developing in their brain. They have heard much of loss of memory as a sign of degenerative nervous diseases and they are prone to think that their own special loss of memory, be it real or imaginary, must be a forerunner, or perhaps even an early symptom, of some important organic lesion.

This idea of progressive memory disturbance as a preliminary of nervous breakdown often becomes so firmly fixed as to be of itself a profound source of anxiety to patients, and an almost unspeakable dread. So it is important to make them understand what the real nature of their condition is and what their loss of memory, supposed or real, is due to. As a matter of fact, what many of these patients need is not treatment for a diseased memory, but reassurance from what we know about the psychology of memory, that their troubles are only quite natural incidents in the life history of their particular memory {679} faculty. Many a man who is worrying about his supposed loss of memory or, at least, impairment of it in some way, is not suffering from a true pathological condition, but is usually the victim only of some functional disturbance of the nervous system with the neurotic anxiety and heightened introspection that accompanies such a condition.

Reasons for Memory Difficulties.—Nervous patients particularly complain that they do not remember what they wish to as easily as they used to a few years before. They say that it is much more difficult for them to impress things upon their memories and, in addition, that it is much easier for them to forget. There are three quite natural reasons for these phenomena as far as they actually exist, which should be pointed out to these patients. The first and most important is that they are incapable of that concentration of mind which they had in earlier years and which enabled them to give themselves up so completely to the consideration of a particular subject that it could not help but be impressed on their minds. They are now so much occupied with many other things, and, above all, most of these patients are so preoccupied with themselves that they cannot hope to have the concentration of mind that was comparatively easy when they were younger and is now impaired, but which is so necessary for the enduring remembrance of things. Secondly, their over-anxiety to remember things sometimes acts as an inhibitory motive in securing that deep, impression that will enable them to remember details very well. Thirdly, their supposed impairment of memory is due to a false judgment with regard to themselves. They are not comparing their power of memory now with what they used to have, but owing to anxiety about themselves they have taken to comparing themselves with others and, after all, the faculty of memory acts very differently for different people and it is well known that what one man remembers with ease another recalls with difficulty, or only because of special attention.

Attention and Memory.—The first of these causes for supposed impairment deserves to be discussed further. It is often said that as we grow older our memory is not so retentive as it used to be, and that while we remember the events of boyhood and the things we learned in the early years of school life, our recollection of recent events and things learned in later years is much less vivid. This is all very true, but the reason usually given, that in the meantime our memories have failed in power is inconclusive. What we learned in early childhood came to us with the surprise of novelty and for this reason we paid close attention, it was new and impressed us with its importance, it was dwelt upon for long periods and often, because there was little else to think about, has been frequently recalled since and, of course, is indelibly impressed upon our memories. The same thing is true with regard to early acquaintances. We got to know them so well that, of course, we cannot forget them. What we have learned in later life, however, has come in the midst of many other things, has not been dwelt on very long, has not been often recalled and, of course, occupies much less place in the memory than the things of earlier life. That is not, however, because of any defect in memory, but because of lack of attention and repetition that means so much for memory.

Age and Memory.—It is often said that people do not learn so readily when they get older. This is, of course, a truth of common experience, but {680} it is not because of dullness of the faculty of memory, but failure to concentrate the attention sufficiently for memorizing. I have known old men who could learn things just as well as any young man and indeed better than most of them. They were men who had been accustomed all their lives to concentrate attention on the subject they had in hand and who did not allow the cares and worries of life to intrude on their studies. Cato learning Greek at eighty is often quoted as an exceptional example, but I have had some dear old friends who could learn things quite as readily as younger men and whose minds were just as bright and clear. Whenever they devoted as much attention to anything that they wanted to remember as they did when they were younger men, I am sure that they remembered quite as well. It is a question of attention and not of any loss of faculty that makes the difference between the memory of the young and the old until, of course, senile impairment actually comes.

Solicitude and Memory.—Everyone who has had to depend much on his memory knows that over-anxiety with regard to the recollection of anything may seriously inhibit the power to recall it. Public speakers know that to hesitate is to be lost. If they want a particular name or word which they know often escapes them, they must with confidence begin the sentence in which it is to occur, though perhaps wondering all the time whether the word will be on hand or not for them to use it. Occasionally it will not come, but as a rule it turns up just in time. If they allow themselves to be disturbed by the thought that the word or expression may not come, then they know the hopeless vacant blank that stares them in the face when they want it. They have to make a circumlocution in the hope that it may turn up. Some let it go at that, but many start another sentence in the hope to tempt it to come and often it will eventually come, but sometimes it persistently refuses to come. That is not a loss of memory but a failure of neuron connections. There are some of us who know that certain words will always do that with us. Archimedes has bothered me for years and his name will often not come when I want it. Then there are certain words with regard to which transposition is likely to take place. We involuntarily and unconsciously substitute one word for another. We call one man by another's name. We have done it before and we know that we are likely to do it again. Somehow the connections in memory exist along these wrong lines and are constantly mismade. The name of something a man has written comes up instead of his name. This heterophemia is often noted in men of excellent memory.

Peculiarities of Memory.—Memory is an illusive and elusive function at best. All of us have had the sensation of having a word, and particularly a name, on the tip of our tongues. We often know the first letter and sometimes the first syllable of it. What memory brings to us, however, may not always be the first syllable of a word or name, though we are prone to think it must be, and we may go looking for it in the dictionary of names only to discover after a time that we are many letters away from its beginning. Very often we have to give up seeking in sheer inability to get a hint of it and then of itself it will come a little later. Sometimes it will come when we no longer want it. As a rule, words that have escaped us once in this way are prone to do so again. Over and over again the experience will be that {681} a particular word or group of words escapes our memory, or at least fails to be at our command, as most other things are. Those of us who are not much given to introspection take no notice of these difficulties which are common-place experiences enough, but the man or the woman who is looking for symptoms, who is prone to believe for some reason or other that his or her memory is failing, will take these hints of the more or less natural fallacy of memory as confirmations, strong as direct proof of the fact that memory is seriously deteriorating.

Such pauses and lapses of memory are much more likely to occur if we are nervous and over-anxious about possible loss of memory. I was once asked to attend for a few hours before the time fixed for his oration one of the greatest orators of this country, who was about to talk at a university commencement. What surprised me was that this practiced speaker, who had often appeared before very large audiences, took a very light meal in considerable trepidation, immediately after asked to have certain books brought to him and certain facts looked up for him, took notes in a hurried, feverish way and generally displayed all the over-excitement of the schoolboy about to make his first oration. He was a magnificent occasional speaker, often called upon, yet he assured me that it was always thus with him and that the reason for it was that in spite of previous preparation—and the finish of his orations made it clear that he had devoted much thought to them beforehand—certain of his facts and names and dates had the habit of slipping from him in the midst of the development of his theme, unless he had refreshed his memory with regard to them immediately before, and that he feared that sometime he would find himself in the midst of an address with an absolute blank before him and that he would be compelled to sit down in disgrace. He had never done so and never did in the many years that he, lived afterwards, though always with this dread, never trusting his memory as most people do.

Name Memory.—There are certain circumstances in which memory may fail and yet no significance of a pathological nature can be attributed to the fact. All of us probably have had the disturbing experience of undertaking to introduce two friends whom we had known for many years and yet having to ask at least one of them for his name before we could make the introduction. It is not that we did not know the name, but at the moment we were utterly unable to recall it. After this has happened once or twice it is prone to happen again, because when we set about introducing people the thought of the previous unfortunate occurrences of this kind comes to our mind and acts as an inhibition of memory, making it impossible for us to recall names. Not infrequently if we are brought to the pass of having to ask one of the parties for his name we have to ask the other, though it was on the tip of our tongue a moment before, because in the meantime the disturbance of mind incident to having to ask has interfered with the train of recollection. Men have been known to forget their own names under circumstances of great excitement and such a forgetting is not pathological, but only a physiological disturbance of function because of secondary trains of association set to work in the brain which disturb ordinary recollection. Of course, some people have an excellent memory for names and never have such experiences, but they are very rare, though practice in recalling names does much to keep {682} people from such embarrassing situations. On the other hand, there are some people especially gifted with name memories. Napoleon could recall all his soldiers' names.

Fatigue and Memory.—Occasionally it happens quite normally that when we are very tired certain portions of our memory at least become vague and indefinite and may even fail to respond to any excitation on our part. Under these circumstances we seem to be able only with considerable effort to exert the effort necessary to bring about such connections of brain cells as will facilitate recollection and reproduction and we may fail entirely. In a foreign country it is, as a rule, much more easy to talk the language in the morning when we are fresh than in the evening when we are tired. Especially is this true if we are asked to pass from one foreign language to another, which always requires a special effort. Everyone who has traveled must have had the experience that on crossing the frontier suddenly to be addressed in German after he has been talking French for weeks, may quite nonplus the traveler, even though he knows German as well or even better than French. This is especially true if much depends on the answers, if he has been addressed by a railway official or customs inspector. Apparently there must be a momentary wait until some shifting operation takes place in the brain before the German memory can get to work to establish the connections necessary to enable him to talk German. After a man has been talking to a number of people in one foreign tongue he is likely to be quite lost for words for a moment if he has to use another. The effects of fatigue and excitement and unusualness upon memory then must be remembered in order to be able to reassure patients who pervert the significance of the phenomena.

Ribot gives an excellent personal illustration of this peculiarity of memory in his "Diseases of Memory," which is worth recalling here. He says:

I descended on the same day two very deep mines In the Hartz Mountains, remaining some hours underground in each. While in the second mine, and exhausted both from fatigue and inanition, I felt the utter impossibility of talking longer with the German inspector who accompanied me. Every German word and phrase deserted my recollection; and it was not until I had taken food and wine, and been some time at rest, that I regained them again.

Sensations and Memory.—Just as soon as people compare their memories with others, as they do when they worry and begin to grow introspectively self-conscious, they find noteworthy differences and because of differences they will be prone to think that their memory is pathologically defective when it is only different, or, still more, that because they are not able to remember some things, as others do, their memory must be failing. It is well known that some people have a good memory for things seen, others for things heard, and still others only for things in which they have taken actual part. These are spoken of as visual, auditory and action memories. Memories for things seen are divided into special classes. Some people remember forms very well, while others remember colors. It is evident that our memories are somehow dependent on the special mode in which sensation affects us and that our acutest sensations are the sources of our longest and best memories. Color vision defectives are not affected much by colors and easily forget them. The tone-deaf have no memory for tunes. Every sense defect affects the memory. Sense defects are often unconscious. Their effect on memory may {683} only be noted when introspection begins to bring out the special sensation and memory qualities of the individual. Nature, not disease, may be the basis of some memory troubles thus brought to recognition. All these curious phenomena with regard to memory need to be recalled whenever there is question of a supposed deterioration of it, for it is not easy to decide such a question.

Limits of Normal Forgetfulness.—Curious instances of forgetfulness may occur in the experience of men with excellent memories, which, when they happen to persons morbidly inclined to test their every act, are interpreted to signify something much more serious than they really mean. Nearly everyone has had more than once the experience of telling a story to a particular group of people and then forgetting all about having told it and coming back a few days later to tell it over again. Occasionally a teacher hears the same lesson a week apart and yet does not remember that he went over it before, though the class is almost sure to do so. A man may repeat a lecture that he has given before to the same audience without realizing it. The story has been told more than once of a clergyman delivering the same sermon on two Sundays in succession and, though such lapses are very rare, they do not necessarily indicate a failing memory, but may only mean a lack of concentration of attention on the part of the human mind. Prof. Ribot in his "Diseases of Memory" tells the story of one such case in which the subject was quite alarmed lest it should indicate that he was beginning to suffer from some serious memory disturbance due to brain disease, though there was no ground for his fears:

A dissenting minister, apparently in good health, went through the entire pulpit service one Sunday morning with perfect consistency—his choice of hymns and lessons and extempore prayer being all related to the subject of the sermon. On the Sunday following he went through the service in precisely the same manner, selecting the same hymns and lessons, offering the same prayer, giving out the same text, and preaching the same sermon. On descending from the pulpit he had not the slightest remembrance of having gone through precisely the same service on the preceding Sunday. He was much alarmed and feared an attack of brain disease, but nothing of the kind supervened.

Attention not Memory.—When patients come with complaints of the loss of memory, the most important thing is to analyze their symptoms carefully. This will usually enable us to give patients ample reassurance. I have known men who were convinced that they were losing their memories because of their failure to recall important details in their business affairs in the midst of much hurry and bustle in the winter time, find that when they were living a simpler life in the course of travel or life in the country during the summer time under conditions different from the ordinary, their memory could be absolutely depended on for trains and travel details and all important matters to which they were now devoting attention.

Cultivating Looseness of Memory.—Many people complain of loss of memory in the sense that they do not now remember when things took place as well as they used to. For instance, I have had men of fifty tell me that they were sure that their memories were growing weaker than they used to be because a number of times within a year they had found that events which they thought had taken place only a year or two ago really dated four or {684} five or even more years in the past. Some are considerably disturbed by this. As a matter of fact it is only another instance of lack of attention. Most of what we read in newspapers attracts so little of our serious attention that it is no wonder that we do not recall with exactness when events took place. Events crowd each other out of memory. Newspaper reading is, indeed, the best possible cultivation of looseness of memory that we could have. We do not expect to remember what we read. We would probably grow distracted if we did. At the end of the day if you ask a man what he read in the morning paper he will have no idea at all, unless something especially startling or particularly interesting to him has turned up. After a week we could no more separate Monday's from Tuesday's news of the week before than we could recall a random list of events, having heard it but once. We cultivate looseness of memory with great assiduity. Let us not be surprised if, to some extent, we succeed.

Memories Individual.—People are often much worried over children's memories and may communicate this worry and anxiety to the children themselves, making them solicitous. It is probable that our memories are like our stature. They are what they are. By thinking we cannot add a cubit to the one nor facility to the other. The training of the memory is a very small element compared to the natural faculty. It must not be forgotten, however, that many distinguished men have been noted for rather bad memories when they were young and yet these faculties have developed quite enough to enable them to accomplish good work afterwards. The memory is, after all, a comparatively unimportant faculty in itself and other intellectual faculties surpass it in significance. It is the faculty that first develops, however, and so a child is often thought to be intellectually slow when it has not so bright a memory as its companions, though a little later its other faculties may develop so as to put it on a plane above its fellows. Memories, too, are very individual and may not retain any of the ordinary subjects, while they may be very attentive for certain special lines of thought. This form of the faculty is better, for the encyclopedic memory is usually of little use and, except in high degrees, encourages superficiality rather than real knowledge.

As a matter of fact, few of our greatest thinkers have had what would be called brilliant memories and it would almost seem as though the diversion of mental energy to this faculty rather disturbed the development of the others. Many a distinguished man has been rather notorious as a child for bad memory, so that in the early days when memory was the only faculty called upon at school he was set down as a dunce. Perhaps the most striking example of this was Sir Isaac Newton, who was actually called a dunce, and yet the world would welcome a few other such dunces. Thomas of Aquin, the great medieval writer on philosophy and theology, who still influences philosophy so much, was so slow as a young man that he was called by his fellow pupils "the dumb ox." His great teacher, Albertus Magnus, recognized the depth of mind that his fellow students could not see and declared that the bellowings of that "ox" would be heard throughout the world. Sir Walter Scott was spoken of as a very backward child. This is all the more surprising to those who know and appreciate the wealth of information that he put into his Waverley Novels. Goldsmith, than whom we have no more brilliant writer in English, seemed not only a dunce as a child, but all his {685} life, so far as outward appearance went, was a numbsknll. This was due to a lack of readiness rather than any lack of wit.

Tricks of Memory.—Some tricks of memory may be very disturbing to those who are over-occupied with themselves and with the possibility of losing their memory. For their consolation it is well for the physician who hears their complaints to have at hand some stories that illustrate certain of these curious tricks of memory. I had been trying to persuade a literary woman for some time that it was not her memory that was playing her false, but merely her habit of attention and lack of concentration of mind on things because she is occupied with a great many interests, when one day she came to me with what she thought was absolutely convincing proof that her memory was going. She had read a passage in a newspaper the day before which she liked very much, but after reflection it sounded strangely like some of the things that she had thought along these lines herself. It was a quotation, but there was no indication to tell whence it came. A little inquiry, however, showed that the quotation was from an article of her own written only two years before. Here was definite proof of a failure of memory. Strange as it may seem, however, this experience is quite common. I feel sure that there is not a single writer for periodical literature who has not had similar experiences. Anyone who writes much editorially, where the articles are unsigned, finds it rather difficult two or three years later, as a rule, to be absolutely sure which editorials are his. Occasionally it happens that even by the time the proof comes back for monthly periodicals, say six weeks or two months, some at least of what was written may seem quite unfamiliar. This will be particularly true if phases of the same subjects have been treated in successive articles and thus repetitions are caused.

There is plenty of good warrant for such occurrences in the lives of distinguished writers. Scott once heard a song in a drawing-room that he did not care for very much and he said rather contemptuously, "Oh! that's some of Byron's stuff." His attention was called to the fact that he was the author of the stuff himself. Carlyle confessed to Froude when Froude went over some of the passages of Carlyle's own autobiography with him, that he had quite forgotten some of the things written down there. Manzoni, the distinguished Italian writer, whose "I Promessi Sposi" has probably been more read throughout Europe than any novel written during the nineteenth century, except possibly some of Scott's, tells some stories of his own lapses of memory and, above all, of having once quoted a sentence of his own to confirm something that he was saying, though he confessed that he did not know by whom the quotation had been written.

Memory and Low Grade Intelligence.—There are many people who complain of their memory and of their inability to recall many things which others recall without difficulty. They are prone to think that this is some defect in them and not infrequently, as a consequence of comparisons, they persuade themselves that their memory was better and that it has lost some of its qualities. Until they became familiar with some of the feats of memory possible of performance by others, they were quite satisfied, but now they find in every instance of forgetting a new symptom of an increasingly deficient memory. I have found in these cases, that setting before such people some of the curiosities of memory, and especially the fact that memory is by no {686} means necessarily connected with profound intelligence, so that, indeed, its presence is quite compatible with a low grade of intelligence or even with what is practically idiocy, will do much to rob these gloomy forebodings of their terrors with regard to their own supposed deterioration of intellect. Ribot, in his "Diseases of Memory" has an excellent passage in which he sums up a number of these peculiarities of memory that are likely to be especially consolatory to people of ordinary memory who are worrying about themselves.

It has long been observed that in many idiots and imbeciles the senses are very unequally developed; thus, the hearing may be of extreme delicacy and precision, while the other senses are blunted. The arrest of development is not uniform in all respects. It is not surprising, then, that general weakness of memory should co-exist in the same subject with evolution and even hypertrophy of a particular memory. Thus certain idiots, insensible to all other impressions, have an extraordinary taste for music, and are able to retain an air which they have once heard. In rare instances there is a memory for forms and colors, and an aptitude for drawing. Cases of memory of figures, dates, proper names, and words in general, are more common. An idiot "could remember the day when every person in the parish had been buried for thirty-five years, and could repeat with unvarying accuracy the name and age of the deceased, and the mourners at the funeral. Out of the line of burials he had not one idea, could not give an intelligible reply to a single question, nor be trusted even to feed himself." Certain idiots, unable to make the most elementary arithmetical calculations, repeat the whole of the multiplication table without an error. Others recite, word for word, passages that have been read to them, and cannot learn the letters of the alphabet. Drobisch reports the following case of which he was an observer: A boy of fourteen, almost an idiot, experienced great trouble in learning to read. He had, nevertheless, a marvelous facility for remembering the order in which words and letters succeeded one another. When allowed two or three minutes in which to glance over the page of a book printed in a language which he did not know, or treating of subjects of which he was ignorant, he could, in the brief time mentioned, repeat every word from memory exactly as if the book remained open before him. The existence of this partial memory is so common that it has been utilized in the education of idiots and imbeciles. It is worth noting that idiots attacked by mania or some other acute disease frequently display a temporary memory. Thus, an idiot in a fit of anger told of a complicated incident of which he had been a witness long before, and which at the time seemed to have made no impression upon him.

Training Memory.—In recent years in many departments of therapeutics training has been found to be of value. This is especially true with regard to nervous defects. Probably one of the greatest surprises that nervous specialists have had in the last twenty-five years in the domain of therapeutics came from the introduction of Frenkel's methods of retraining the muscles in locomotor ataxia. This idea of retraining has been found useful in such distinct departments as the use of the eye muscles, the co-ordination of the muscles of speech, so as to get rid of stuttering and stammering, and the muscles of the hand for writing. We are only just beginning to realize that retraining can be of great value in psychic affections also. Patients may be disciplined against their dreads and tremulousness due to over-apprehension and against even certain defective uses of their intellect. Urbantschitsch of Vienna showed that by training defective hearing it might in many cases be very much improved. What he accomplished, however, was not {687} any better use of the external auditory apparatus, but a more intense attention of mind which enabled the patient to catch and understand sounds which had hitherto been so vague that their significance was lost.

In a number of cases of complaint of loss of memory I have deliberately set patients to retrain their memories and have at least relieved their apprehensions if I have not always succeeded in increasing their actual memory power. It has even seemed, however, that in old people some actual improvement of the memory faculties was thus brought about. Under the head of Occupation of Mind I have referred to the exercise of memory in younger people as representing an excellent form of mental diversion. When the idea first suggested itself it seemed as though patients would not take to it at all, and yet I have found that with a little persuasion they become much interested and find a great deal of pleasure in their gradually increasing power to recall the great thoughts of great authors in the literal original words. A reference to that chapter will tell more of my experience. This made me more confident of the possibilities there were of making people understand that if they were losing their memories they could bring them back by proper exercise. In this way many of the modern evils of lack of attention and of failure of concentration of mind can be corrected.

My rule now is to tell patients who come complaining of loss of memory that if there is any real loss of memory it is due to their improper use of the faculty, or perhaps to their failure to exercise it sufficiently, for the proper performance of function depends on adequate exercise. They are then instructed to take certain simple classical bits of literature and commit them to memory. At the beginning such short poems with frequently repeated rhymes of the modern poets as are comparatively easy to learn are set as memory exercises. Later Goldsmith's "Traveler" and "Deserted Village" are suggested. Then passages from Shakespeare are given. Just as soon as the patient finds that he can commit to memory as he used to, if he only gives himself to the task, a change comes over his ideas with regard to the loss of memory. For many of these people the occupation of mind is an excellent therapeutic measure. Besides selections can be made in such a way as to keep before their minds the thoughts they most need in the shape of memory lessons. It is a discipline of memory that revives it and also a constant exercise in favorable suggestion.

Gregor in the *Monattschrift für Psychiatrie und Neurologie*, Band XXI, has detailed some of his experiences with the retraining of the memory of patients suffering from Korsakoff's Psychosis—alcoholic neuritis with psychic disturbances, especially of memory. The patient was required to learn words and then after a certain length of time was tested to see if he could learn a similar series with fewer repetitions than at first. The memory increased in capacity with the exercises and there was evidently a definite gain in the faculty. In this disease patients have also lost the power to some degree at least of recognizing objects. After exercises in recognition they are much more capable in this matter, however, and it is evident that in every way the memory can be improved. This experience, with a serious form of disease that gravely impairs the memory, shows how much can be accomplished in circumstances far more unfavorable than are those which usually bring patients to the physician complaining of deficiencies of memory.

{688}

CHAPTER XI

PSYCHIC CONTAGION

The term psychic contagion is often thought of as merely figurative. It is, however, quite literal. Many minds are influenced by what they see happening round them and induced to imitate the activities of others. The term psychic contagion is so thoroughly descriptive of what happens that it deserves the place that it has secured.

Everywhere and at all times we find historical traces of psychic contagion compelling people to perform in crowds or groups the most curious and inexplicable and sometimes the most horrible things. Even in the old myths before the times of the Trojan War, we have the story of hysteria spreading among the daughters of King Proteus, so that the famous old physician, Pelampus, had to administer white hellebore in goat's milk in order to relieve them. It is probable that this rather heroic remedy with its definite effect upon the bowels produced such a revulsion of feeling as to cure the hysteria. Anyone who has read the awful tragedy that Euripides has written in the

Bacchae will have had brought home to him a typical example of psychic contagion. The queen mother in the midst of one of the Bacchic orgies kills her own son in the frenzy that has come from the religious excitement exaggerated by the association of a number of women in the religious rites of the god Bacchus. It is well understood that this was not a case of drunkenness, but of psychic intoxication.

Phrygian Bacchantes are described as overcome from time to time by paroxysms of curious uncontrollable automatic movements with or without disturbance of consciousness. This represents the earliest form of what came to be known afterwards as St. Vitus Dance when it spread among a number of people. Such manifestations were not at all uncommon in the East in the earlier days and they have continued during all history. In Hindustan epidemics of automatic movements, evidently choreic in character, have been known for many centuries under the name of *lapax*. Outbreaks of this kind were common in the Middle Ages and Paracelsus has described them as happening early in the sixteenth century. At any time the occurrence of an hysterical seizure in a crowded hall, and especially in a schoolroom, will lead to other hysterical manifestations. A case of chorea will induce imitative movements in susceptible bystanders that may be quite uncontrollable. Tics of various kinds are readily picked up by children and special care must be exercised to prevent their spread. In general the state of mind is extremely important in all these conditions and they can be influenced favorably only through the mind.

Contagions Trifles.—Perhaps the extent to which psychic contagion influences us can be seen better in little things than anywhere else. Everyone knows how contagious yawning is. Again and again observations have been made while actors were yawning upon the stage. Nearly everyone in the theater begins to yawn in a few minutes and, in spite of the most determined {689} efforts, every now and then even the most serious-minded elderly gentleman in the audience finds himself unconsciously joining in. It seems foolish and to an onlooker appears almost prearranged. It is only necessary, however, to yawn a few times in a street car, especially at night, to have many imitators. Nearly the same thing is true of all respiratory phenomena. Sighing, for instance, is quite contagious. Coughing is often as much the result of imitation as anything else. At certain pauses in church services a preliminary cough is heard and then some scattering coughs here and there, like the musketry of scouts, and then a whole battery of coughs is let off, especially if it is in the winter time, because nearly everybody within hearing is tempted to cough. To talk about yawning or coughing or sighing before some people is almost sure to produce a tendency to these manifestations. These apparently trivial happenings help to explain many phenomena of human imitation in more serious things.

Most of the phenomena associated with expression are liable to be initiated as the result of imitation. Laughing, for instance, is particularly contagious among young folks and is especially likely to be insuppressible when they wish to be particularly solemn. At religious services it takes but little to make people laugh and giggle, no matter how much they may wish to be dignified and reverential. A few giggling girls will sometimes disturb a serious service. Extremes are particularly prone to meet in this matter and the sublime easily becomes the ridiculous. A titter will set off even the best intentioned of young folks in spite of resolutions to the contrary. Crying has something of the same contagious nature, though it is not quite so strong, but among women tears are particularly likely to evoke tears. The epidemic of curious manifestations of expression, usually of an hysterical nature, that we know by tradition to have spread in communities in the Middle Ages and much later, are only typical examples of this tendency for modes of expression to be contagious to an exaggerated degree.

Expectoration is largely dependent on imitation, sometimes conscious, of course, but often quite unconscious. In the recent crusade organized to prevent the spread of tuberculosis the question of expectoration as a diffusing agent of the bacilli has given a new importance to observations on this subject. It is recognized that we have "a spitting sex" and that men spit from force of habit, boys imitate them, while women and girls almost never spit. There is no reason in the world why when men and women are engaged in the same occupations there should be any difference in this regard between them, yet employers know how hard it is to keep corners and by-places in the rooms where men work free from expectoration, while no such difficulty is found where women work. We have a spitting sex because of psychic contagion, and in spite of the fact that there are serious dangers connected with the habit. What is true of spitting may also be true of other habits relating to the respiratory passages. Hawking and blowing the nose more frequently than is needed are spread by psychic contagion and certain habits in these matters that are injurious to the respiratory apparatus often require considerable effort to break.

Fads and Health.—Enlightened as we think ourselves, we have many more examples of psychic contagion in the present than we would perhaps care to admit, unless the facts were called to our special attention. {690} At a particular period in the modern time it becomes the fad to do things in a special way. We write alike, we build our houses after a common type. We take our recreation in a particular fashion. Bicycling comes in and goes out; roller skating attacks nearly every one of the young folks and then is abandoned. There are fashions in everything and fashions, after all, are recurring instances of psychic contagion. The mental influence spreads from one to another. It may be that a particular fashion, as in houses or in clothes, is especially ugly. That makes no difference. After a time taste revolts against it, but in the meantime the psychic contagion is enough to overturn the canons of taste. There are fashions in literature, or at least what is called literature. The nature novel comes and goes, then the novel of adventure has its place, then the detective novel, after a time the little-country prince or princess and their romance comes into fashion. After a time we realize that these are passing fancies, but in the meantime they have influenced many people.

Some of these fashions bring conditions that are deleterious to health. The moving-picture show in places that almost never have a stime of sunlight in them and are, in their way, quite as bad, especially for respiratory troubles, as the dust-laden atmosphere of the roller-skating rink, become the fad of the moment in spite of knowledge or ignorance of hygiene. Just now we are in the midst of a fad for fresh air, that, unfortunately, goes and comes with the centuries and we have no guarantee that people will not learn again to live in closely sealed houses. High heels come and go, as do corsets of various kinds, more or less injurious, in spite of the admonition of the physician. In fact, one of the most interesting studies in psychic contagion is the history of the fashions. A particular fashion, especially in its exaggerated forms, will probably look well on about one-fifth of the women at a given time. About four-fifths of them, however, adopt it in spite of the fact that on three-fifths it emphasizes certain qualities that it would be well to keep in the background. It is woman's principal desire to please, yet this is completely perverted by the psychic epidemic of fashion which causes people to follow after others quite as much as did the medieval people in various fads that attracted attention and have come down to us.

Our enlightenment, at least in as far as that word means general diffusion of the ability to read, has rather added to the power of psychic contagion. People accept ideas from others almost as unconsciously as they catch disease from those suffering from it. The psychology of advertising shows how easy it is to make people accept things just by insisting on them and by frequent repetitions of statements. The psychology of the proprietary medicine business in modern times is about as typical an example of psychic contagion induced deliberately as one could well imagine. Those who stop to reason do not fall victims. Most people, however, do not stop to reason. They have not the mental resistive vitality to render them immune to the influence of certain irrationalities and so literally hundreds of millions of dollars have been spent on perfectly useless, oftentimes harmful drugs, which people had become persuaded through the psychic contagium of printer's ink were sure to do them good. The psychology of the mob has been studied somewhat in recent years and it shows how clear it is that men follow after one another in doing foolish things even more than in doing wise ones. Psychic contagion is a prominent factor in life, it always has been, is now, and evidently always {691} will be, and must be reckoned with by anyone who wishes to recognize the principles that underlie psychotherapy.

Suicide Contagions.—It is with regard to much more serious things than fashions, however, that psychic contagion is most manifest. For instance, there is no doubt that suicide is frequently the result of such psychic influence. Seldom does it happen that a very queer suicide is reported without there being certain imitations of it more or less complete in various parts of the country afterwards. There is no doubt that the reporting of suicides has a serious effect in this matter. Perhaps the most striking example of this that we have ever had in America was the well-known suicidal epidemic at Emporia, Kansas, which reached its height just about the middle of June, 1901. Two or three well-known people in town committed suicide at the end of May and the beginning of June. A veritable epidemic of suicide broke out as a consequence. Nothing seemed to stop it and the authorities were much disturbed. Finally it was agreed that the most potent influence in bringing about the imitation of the epidemic was the publication of the details of the suicides in the papers. The Mayor of the city, after consulting with the Board of Health, decided to issue the following proclamation:

I have consulted the Board of Health, and if the Emporia papers do not comply with my request I shall have a right to stop, and I will stop summarily, the publication of these suicide details, under the law providing for the suppression of epidemics. There is clearly an epidemic in this city, and although it is mental, it is none the less deadly. Its contagion may be clearly shown to come from what is known in medicine as the psychic suggestion found in the publication of the details of suicides. If the paper on which the local Journals are printed had been kept in a place infected with smallpox, I could demand that the Journals stop using that paper, or stop publication. If they spread another contagion—the contagious suggestion of suicide—I believe the liberty of the press is not to be considered before the public welfare, and that the courts would sustain me in using force to prevent the publication of newspapers containing matter clearly deleterious to the public health.

Murder.—In almost the same way murders prove contagious. Especially is this true of murder and suicide together. These occur notably in groups. A man who is downhearted and for whom the future looks blank, will, out of a sense of pity for those who are dependent on him, murder them and himself; then the brutal story is reported and another tottering intellect gives way and a similar story has to be told within a few days. A mother who is melancholic about her health and includes her children in her gloomy outlook makes away with them and herself. Within a few days a similar story is reported because of the influence of psychic contagion. Very often there are distinct imitations of the methods employed in the first case. Often, however, it is only the idea itself that has proved contagious. There is no doubt that this suggestion brings about subsequent cases when otherwise such an awful thought might not occur. The connection is too clear for us to doubt the reality of it or to think that it is mere coincidence. As in Emporia, doubtless the suppression of the description of such events would have a beneficial effect. There are many disequilibrated minds, apparently just tottering on the verge of an insane act of this kind, that are pushed over by the suggestion furnished by the details of another story.

{692}

Place of Psychic Contagion.—The physician who would treat nervous patients successfully and use psychotherapeutics to advantage must recognize the place that psychic contagion has in influencing the generality of mankind. We know that direct suggestions are profoundly influential. It must be constantly kept in mind, however, that indirect suggestion, suggestion that does not come by any formal method, but that is represented by the examples of those around, also has great weight.

Favorable Influence.—Fortunately it is not alone for evil that psychic contagion is manifest. People in a crowd stand fatigue better than when alone. Soldiers marching in step do not notice their tiredness to such a degree and even forget their sore feet. People suffering from hunger, so long as there is a good spirit among them, will help each other to bear it. The accidents in coal mines in recent years in which men have been imprisoned for considerable periods have shown that in groups they stand the hardships of confinement and of lack of food and water better than they do when alone, men live longer, they do not suffer so much or at least their suffering is not so insistent, and they bear up better.

This has been particularly noticed in the cures at various watering places. The very air of the place takes on a favorable suggestion that is helpful to patients. The routine, the hopefulness of those who are completing the cure, the stories of improvement, the evident betterment, all these things combine to give a psychic contagion of health. Health is, in this sense, quite as contagious as disease. This must be taken advantage of just as far as possible for the advantage of patients. On the other hand, ideas are contagious for ill and patients may derive from their environment notions that prove auto-suggestive and against which it is extremely difficult to work. Ideas derived from the general feelings of those around, without any direct suggestion, may become obsessions. The physician, therefore, must be ready to secure prophylaxis against psychic contagion and then by counter-suggestion relieve the patient, who has become afflicted by it, of the resulting

367

disturbance of mind. It must not be forgotten that, instead of being less susceptible as education and civilization progress, people really become more susceptible.

Psychology of the Mob.—The most interesting instance of psychic contagion is the tendency just hinted at for crowds to run away with the sober judgment of serious sensible people that happen to be among them and do things that may be extremely regrettable. A mob always follows the suggestions of the worst elements in it unless perchance there is some extremely strong character who asserts himself and imposes his views on the rest. The tendencies to panic, to cowardly flight, sometimes to destructiveness, that come over crowds represent the power of psychic contagion to override reason. An alarm of fire will, if a few persons lose their heads, lead to the most serious consequences. Persons trample over one another, pull and maul one another, sometimes even pulling out hair or pulling off ears in their insane efforts to escape what is often an imaginary danger, though a few moments before they were rational beings and they will be quite reasonable a short time after. It is possible, however, to overcome even the worst tendencies in human nature by the suggestive power of discipline. Fire drills in schools enable children to get out in a few minutes without confusion when without them the most serious results could be looked for. Discipline and training, {693} following commands and observing tactics, helps an army almost more than the individual courage of soldiers. The suggestive influence of the thought that now is the time to do something that has often been done before at the word of command is enough to enable the soldier to control his panicky feelings. The difference between the trained soldier and the raw recruit is great, but it consists only in this mental discipline and self-control.

Prevention.—Evidently, then, in the many circumstances in life in which psychic contagion manifests itself it is perfectly possible to overcome its influence by such discipline and mental training as gives the individual control over himself. In children corporal punishment is often not effective in breaking up habits and tendencies and the motive of fear often lessens self-control and makes conditions worse. In older people the fear of punishment is likely to be forgotten, whereas the suggestion of discipline will assert itself powerfully. Psychic contagion can be neutralized by psychotherapy, but its force in life must be recognized and its unfavorable influence guarded against. While it concerns mainly the less serious things of life, it may affect the most serious and imitation leads even to such serious criminal acts as suicide and murder. The modes of psychic contagion, then, must be constantly under surveillance.

With this before us it is extremely interesting to realize how unfavorably suggestive for human health and happiness are our newspapers. They are constantly suggesting disease and suicide and murder and sex crimes and crimes against property, by giving all the details available with regard to these subjects. Such news can do no good, only excites morbid curiosity which requires still further satisfaction in the same line, and keeps thoughts with regard to these things constantly before the mind. We have had many burglaries and holdups and stealings of various kinds as a consequence of boys and even girls seeing the pictures of crimes in the moving-picture show. The saturation of mind with disease and crime produced by daily reading of unsavory and sensational newspaper accounts is sure to produce evil effects. There seems to be consolation for some people in reading of the crimes and punishments of others because they feel that, bad as is their own state, there are others who are worse. This *schadenfreude*, "harm-joy" as the Germans call it, is not satisfying to think of for human nature and it has an inevitable reaction through the unfavorable suggestion of these crimes.

I have found over and over again that the prohibition of reading the newspapers for a time did many nervous people much good. This is particularly true for sufferers from such forms of psychasthenia as bring down on them dreads and premonitions of evil in fears for the development of disease and in general a sense of instability with regard to the future, lest dreadful things should happen to them. At first patients object strenuously and seem to be deprived of a great satisfaction. After a time, however, they are invariably persuaded of the fact that the absence of mental contact with human misfortune, in this morbid way, is doing them good and that their dreads and premonitory feelings of evil drop from them.

{694}

SECTION XIX

DISORDERS OF WILL

CHAPTER I

ALCOHOLISM

In recent years so much has been said about addiction to alcohol as a disease rather than as a habit that the treatment of it frankly as a disease in psychotherapeutics, even though there be not entire readiness to agree with those who emphasize exclusively the pathological interest of these cases, will not seem surprising. It is with regard to the various habits, drug and alcoholic, occurring in neurotic subjects that psychotherapy proves most effective and has secured some of its real triumphs. As a matter of fact, it has long been conceded that all of the so-called cures for alcoholism are dependent for their success upon the mental effect produced upon the patient. Most of them emphasize the necessity for building up the physical condition of the patient as a necessary preliminary to any lasting cure. There is no doubt that the powers of resistance of a man whose physical health has been seriously impaired by over-indulgence in alcohol and the lack of food and irregular sleep and exposure to the elements that so frequently accompany it, will not be sufficient to enable him to break off the alcohol habit, nor afford him the ability to inhibit the craving for stimulants, that he would have in a state of health. On the other hand, even in good health, unless his moral character is braced up, there will surely be a return to his old habit.

Historical Résumé of Cures.—We have had many different cures for alcoholism exploited during the last half century. The older method of the first inebriate asylums founded in this country was to give a man a disgust for liquor, as it was then called, by putting a small amount of alcohol into practically everything that he consumed. This did not give him enough to satisfy his craving, but it did create in him an intense distaste for it by constantly keeping the flavor before him. There was a drop or two of whiskey in his tea, there was some whiskey in his milk, there was a taste of it in the water that he drank, there was some of it mixed even in the gravy of his meat, and he always had weak brandy sauce on his dessert. The consequence was, in most cases, such a complete disgust for liquor that men were sure that they would never touch it again. Of course, in the meantime they were fed well and heartily, they were kept in an environment free from temptations to excessive indulgence in alcoholic drinks, they had brought home to them what a mess they were making of their lives and their health, they had time to reflect what ruin they were bringing on themselves and their families and usually they {695} recognized that they were the kind of men who must stay away from alcohol absolutely, for whom there could be no such thing as a moderate indulgence in stimulants. This, with the intense distaste for alcohol, amounting almost to nausea at the sight of it, acquired from the system in vogue, started them well on the road to reform.

Moral Cures.—It was the moral elements in the cure, however, that were the most important, though its inventors were sure that the physical elements played the largest role. The physical disgust for alcohol consequent upon having its taste constantly recur in everything at table passed off in a few weeks or at the most a few months. It was then that the moral uplift came in and had to be effective if the patient was to be preserved for the future from his old habit. If he was of a weak and flabby character, if, unfortunately, he was placed in circumstances where temptations were frequent, if, owing to the enforced absence in the inebriate asylum his business affairs had become involved and he was subject to many worries, then almost surely he dropped back. As a result his case was even more hopeless than before and, indeed, second cures were seldom of much benefit, for the man's confidence in himself was gone.

All in all, however, this old-time, simple method probably produced as large a proportion of "real cures" as any other method, even the much advertised and discussed scientific discoveries of modern times. All of us have heard stories of men who had seemed to be hopeless drunkards, who were thus reformed and hundreds of men who appeared to be drifting into hopeless inebriety were reformed to such an extent that they became not only useful members of society and supports to their families where they had before been a drain, but even became leaders in the work of uplifting the character of others to resist the temptation of over-indulgence in stimulants.

Modern Cures.—Of late we have had a number of "cures" for alcoholism widely exploited by well-directed advertising in the hands of men who realized what a fortune there was in this sort of thing and who actually have made immense sums of money out of them. Needless to say these "cures," though supposed to be secret, did not long remain so. Perhaps the most famous of them, the one whose institutes were found all over the country, was said to have used only two drugs, strychnin and apomorphin. The strychnin was given as a needed and well-chosen tonic for the physical condition of the patients who came to the institution usually in a rather seriously broken down condition. When patients began the treatment they were distinctly told that if they wanted whiskey at any time they could have it, but that the next injection of the "cure" after they took the whiskey would show how directly opposed to alcohol the ingredients of it were, by producing vomiting and prostration.

As a rule, the patients came in perfectly confident of the effect of the remedy they had heard so much of. The strychnin injections made an excellent tonic for these nervous wrecks, bracing them up at once so that they felt better from the very beginning and this betterment was confirmed by the growing assurance from the physician and the patients around them that now, at last, they were to be relieved of their degrading habit. To those whose craving for alcohol returned in spite of the favorable condition in which they were placed and the stimulation of the strychnin, which made up so well, as a {696} rule, for the absence of their accustomed alcohol, whiskey was actually allowed. When the next time for their injection came, however, these patients who had been given whiskey on their request did not now receive an injection of strychnin but instead a small injection of apomorphin. The apomorphin acted promptly in making the stomach relieve itself and produced a complete and immediate sense of prostration. The limpness and discomfort of seasickness is as nothing compared to the state that, as a rule, develops after such treatment. Anyone who has ever had to handle, in a hospital, a wildly drunk, longshoreman, whose brute strength in his irrational condition made him a dangerous object for patients and physicians, who has seen even large doses of morphin fail to produce quiet, and then has felt bound for the patient's sake as well as those around him, to administer a tenth of a grain of apomorphin with the result of having an eminently tractable patient in a few minutes, will have a good idea of what happened to the poor alcoholic who got apomorphin instead of strychnin.

After that the inebriate knew that any further indulgence in liquor would be followed by this extremely unpleasant result and so he had a new argument for avoiding it. After a month or six weeks of careful treatment, the preliminary rest that would restore physical health and strength being followed by a course of exercise in the open air with plenty of good food, pleasant surroundings, and hope constantly held out to them, it is no wonder that these patients went out of the sanitariums as a rule confident that their habit was conquered for good. In many cases this proved to be true. It was soon found, however, that there were many relapses. This hurt the prestige of the "cure" and the gradual diffusion of this idea spoiled its effectiveness. It still continued to do good, however, and though it has been modified in various ways, and, indeed, in various parts of the country is said to be applied quite differently, there are still many reformations worked by these

369

cures every year and they undoubtedly do good. The secret of its success, however, is not any marvelous drug or other mode of treatment that is employed, but is because the victims of alcoholism are given an opportunity to retrieve their physical condition and then to brace up their moral characters so as to resist their craving for alcohol.

Mental Influence.—Other so-called cures and treatments have followed almost exactly similar lines. The main element in the cure has been the producing in the mind of the patient a definite idea that he can stay away from liquor if he really wishes to and then helping his run-down physical condition so that he craves stimulants less than before. Whenever such "sure cures" are used on the worst forms of alcoholic patients as we see them in the large general hospitals of our greater cities, the bums of the streets, the drunkards of a score of years or more, they have practically no effect. The man must have moral stamina, he must have some character left, besides, as a rule, he must have some good reasons in worldly interest to help him to brace up and then he may get away from alcoholism if he sincerely wills to reform. The important element, however, is the will to do so. If he is firmly convinced that he cannot stay away from liquor, if he feels in spite of all that has been done for him that he cannot resist his craving, then, of course, he will not reform. Men, however, who have sunk to the lowest depths, who, according to their own and others' testimony, have scarcely drawn a {697} sober breath for ten or even twenty years, sometimes have something happen to them, often it seems very trivial to everyone but themselves, that stiffens their relaxed moral fiber, that wakens their sense of manhood, that serves quite beyond expectation to give them a new purpose in life, and they reform and never drink again.

It is this successful phase of the cure of alcoholism, however it may be explained, that is most interesting. It represents the most encouraging aspect of the whole question. Probably nothing more harmful has ever been done than the public proclamation that alcoholism is often an hereditary disease against which it is hopeless to struggle, and that the poor victims of it are to be pitied and not blamed. Except in those of low mentality, whether of intellect or will, or in the actually insane, there never was a case of alcoholism that did not deserve at least as much blame as is usually accorded to it. This is said after making due allowances for temperament. It is quite clear that for one man alcohol has no attractions at all, while for another the craving for it is almost an insuperable temptation. It is idle to say that these two contrasted men are equally free as to whether they shall take alcohol or not. Of course they are not equally free. If the man who has no craving for alcohol prides himself on his power of resistance against the vile habit, he is simply fooling himself. He probably knows nothing about the real nature of the temptation of alcohol. The Spaniards have a proverb: "He who doesn't drink wine and doesn't smoke, the devil gets by some other way." There is probably something else with regard to which the non-alcoholic has quite as little freedom as the poor victim of alcoholism and the great law of compensation comes in to make up to both of them, for their failings. Man has the defects of his virtues.

Supposed Inheritance.—No man is such a slave to the habit, however, that he cannot correct it if he will. We have heard much about the inheritance of this disease. We have heard even more about its essentially morbid character, though people used to think it a moral defect. It must still be considered a moral defect, however, even though we all concede that there is an element of the pathological in it. We are getting away entirely from the ordinary idea of inheritance of disease. There is no inheritance of acquired characters. The fact that a man's father acquired the drinking habit because he was placed in circumstances where it was easy for him to indulge himself and because he did not have the moral stamina to resist, is no reason why his son should have an unconquerable or even a very strong craving for alcohol. One might as well say that because a father lost a finger when he was young his son would be born without that finger. Alcohol destroyed certain cells in the father's body and injured certain others, but produced no change deep enough to lead to hereditary influences.

Contagion More than Heredity.—Perhaps some tendency to take alcohol runs in a family, that is, perhaps there is lessened resistance to the craving for stimulants that awakens in every human being if it is once aroused. This is what is true in tuberculosis. Some people have less resistive vitality to it than others. Careful autopsies show that practically every man who lives to be over thirty has or has had living tubercle bacilli in his tissues. Seven-eighths of us are thoroughly able to resist them. The other eighth succumbs. Their lack of resistive vitality may in some degree be due to hereditary taint, {698} but that is doubtful and we know that they acquire the disease by contact with others who have it already and, as a rule, it is able to work its ravages because they are not living in conditions that would help them to resist it. If they live in the free open air and have plenty of good, simple food, the disease will not run its fatal course, but nature will cure it. If the craving for alcohol is lighted up by association, aroused by indulgence, rendered strong by environment and by exposure to temptations of all kinds with regard to it, then the resistive power of the individual is so lowered that the alcoholic habit rules him instead of his being able to command it.

Inherited Resistance.—The most curious fact that has come out in our studies of heredity in recent years has been that far from heredity working its will in causing degeneration and deterioration of mankind, immunity, for the race at least, is acquired in the course of subjection to disease and to various morbid habits. Nations, for instance, that have been subjected to diseases for long periods no longer display the susceptibility to them which they formerly possessed. After a disease has been endemic among a people for many generations that people gradually becomes quite insusceptible to its effects and suffers much less from it than before.

Just this same thing is true of alcoholism. Nations that have been the longest in a position to be subject to the temptation to use alcohol in its stronger forms suffer least from the ravages of alcoholism. The southern nations of Europe using wine daily and knowing well the process of distillation to help them to make stronger drink for many hundreds of years, now exhibit much less tendency to over-indulgence in strong drink than the northern nations whose ancestors have only in comparatively recent times been subjected to the temptation of craving for strong alcoholic liquors. The attitude of any nation toward alcohol is a function of the length of time that nation has had a chance to procure strong drink easily. Our American Indians discovered, as has every people at some time, that intoxicating liquor could be made by allowing solutions of starch and sugar to ferment. It was only with the coming of the European, however, that they were provided with "fire water"—strong drink—in quantities. Its effect on them is a matter of history. Two things the white man brought his Indian brother to which the Indians were unaccustomed and that gradually obliterated the original inhabitants of this country—infectious diseases and strong alcoholic liquors. They proved equally fatal because of Indian susceptibility to them.

From these considerations it is clear that just such an immunity to the effect of alcohol is produced in a people exposed to its effects in concentrated form for a long time as with regard to an infectious disease when they have been correspondingly exposed to it. Heredity, then, instead of playing a role that brings about deterioration in the race, on the contrary, carries on the higher qualities and gives us, as might be expected in the course of evolution, a better, that is, a more resistant, race. Most of what is commonly said as to alcoholism, and unfortunately most of the recent so-called popular scientific articles on this subject, seem to point to just the opposite conclusion to this. Men are supposed to be condemned by heredity to an inevitable craving to take alcoholic drinks that, in certain of them at least, cannot be overcome by any natural power of resistance. At this stage of our western civilization this is not true for anyone, as the more susceptible families have been long {699} since eliminated and it is a personal weakness and not a family characteristic that leads people to indulge this appetite to their own destruction.

Unfavorable Suggestion of Heredity Idea.—An alcoholic patient, or even a man with only a moderately strong tendency to take alcohol to excess, who harbors any such notion as this, has a serious impediment to the full exercise of his will in overcoming the difficulties that he encounters in any attempt at reform. In going counter to so much that has been written and still more that has been said and generally accepted on this subject I feel it necessary to quote a good recent authority on the matter and so here insert these passages from "The Principles of Heredity" by Dr. Archdall Reid. He says (p. 157):

Formerly all the world believed in the transmission of acquirements, and consequently all the world was constantly finding conclusive evidence of its constant occurrence. To-day there is hardly a rag of that evidence left, and, with rare exceptions, only certain French medical observers are able to discover fresh evidence. It is a remarkable fact, however, that the problem of evolution—of adaptation—has excited singularly little interest in France, and it is equally curious that these French observations relate almost entirely to laboratory work which it is not easy to repeat. In Great Britain or Germany, you may cut off the tails of a thousand dogs, or amputate the limbs of a thousand men, or observe the non-infected offspring of a thousand tuberculous patients, and get no evidence of transmission.

With regard to alcohol Dr. Reid in the same volume insists on the proposition that alcohol does not cause degeneration of a race, creating, as is claimed, ever more and more a tendency for people to take it because their immediate ancestors have taken it, but, on the contrary, there is a distinct evolution against it, and that what is hereditary, not by acquisition, but by family trait, is an immunity against the disease which eventually protects the nations that have been longest exposed to the effects of alcohol from the evil consequences of the substance. He says (p. 196):

How, then, has alcohol affected the races that have used it? Are the Jews and the races inhabiting the South of Europe the most degenerate on earth? Are North Europeans only less degenerate? Are the races that have never used alcohol, the Terra del Fuegians, the Esquimaux, and the Australian blacks, for instance, mentally and physically the finest in the world? We have only to state the proposition to see its absurdity. There is no evidence that the hereditary tendencies of any race have been altered by alcohol circulating in the blood and acting directly on the germ plasm. Once again the sufferings of the peoples have produced no effect, but the deaths among the peoples have produced an immense effect. Every race that has had experience of alcohol is temperate in the presence of an abundant supply in proportion to the length and severity of its past experience of the poison. The South Europeans and the Jews are the most temperate peoples in the world. West Africans also are very temperate. North Europeans are not drunken. Those savages, and those only, who have had little or no experience of alcohol—Esquimaux, Red Indians, Patagonians, Terra del Fuegians, Australian blacks—are beyond all the peoples the most drunken on earth.

Lest it should be thought that this discussion of the subject is only of significance with regard to nations and does not touch the individual, and, therefore, has but little significance for the problem that we are treating here. Dr. Reid's succeeding paragraph deserves attention:

{700}

Stated in this brief and direct way, the thesis is apt to excite incredulity. It is sharply opposed to popular beliefs, though that need not trouble us. Popular notions on abstruse points of science are occasionally erroneous. Of more importance is the fact that a mass of statistics purporting to prove that the children of drunkards tend to be degenerate has been compiled, especially by medical men in charge of lunatic asylums. But no "control" observations appear to have been made. We know that many drunken parents have normal children; certainly, therefore, parental drunkenness is not invariably a cause of filial degeneration. We know also that many temperate parents have defective children. There is nothing to show that the proportion is greater in the one case than in the other. Even were it established that the proportion of defective children is higher in the case of drunken parents, it would still have to be proved that the relation is one of cause and effect. People who have an inborn tendency to mental defect, who are abnormally depressed, nervous, restless or irritable, are often so constituted as to find solace in drink. Their children are liable to inherit their inborn mental defects with spontaneous variations—that is, to inherit the defect to a greater or lesser extent. The unborn child of a drunken and pregnant mother is practically another drunken person, as liable, or more liable to suffer from the effects of drink; but in such a case the resulting defect, though a mere acquirement, is tolerably certain to be regarded as a congenital (i. e. inborn) defect by the medical man who sees it. Mere acquirements, also, are the defects due to the ill-treatment, want and neglect to which the children of drunken parents are particularly exposed. Indeed, were it fully established that drunken parents, other than pregnant mothers, tend to have an excessive number of their children "congenitally defective," it would still be a question whether the filial defects were not mere acquirements. Prof. Cossar Ewart's observations on diseased pigeons renders this not unlikely. All these sources of error render the success of a statistical inquiry peculiarly difficult, if not impossible, but there is no indication that they ever occurred to the minds of the compilers.

371

Warnings as Suggestions.—I have a case in my notes in which a rather prominent professional man insists that he is quite sure that the alcoholism from which he suffered during the ten years between twenty-five and thirty-five was entirely due to suggestion. As a boy of sixteen he had gone off to boarding school, but not until his mother had taken him aside, told him that his father had drunk himself to death, had done it by secret tippling, and that they had found that for many years he had been accustomed to have whiskey near him in his office and take it rather frequently. He had never tasted spirituous liquor at this time and his mother begged him not to, for she felt sure that if he did his father's craving would awaken in him and would become uncontrollable. The day that he went away his father's eldest brother took him aside and said practically the same thing to him. A maiden aunt was not quite so emphatic, but she, too, pleaded with him to understand all the dangers. For his first year at school he did not touch liquor, but in his second year he tasted it once or twice but had no particular craving aroused in him. By chance when he was home at Christmas time some college mates who were visiting him gave his mother the impression that he belonged to a rather jovial set. Once more he was warned by mother and uncle. Above all they told him never to keep strong drink near him because that was what his father used to do. During his college years the fear of this hung over him. He resented it and probably took more liquor than he would have so far as actual craving went. After getting out into active life once more he suggested himself into the habit of taking an occasional glass of whiskey by himself. After a time he was constantly taking too much. For {701} ten years he hurt all of his prospects, broke his mothers heart, and was looked upon as a hopeless alcoholic. Then one day the thought came to him that it was not that he craved alcohol so much, but that his thoughts turned on it constantly and at first he dreaded it overmuch, then wondered what attraction there could be and then acquired a habit by suggestion. Once this train of thought worked itself out in his mind, he quit spirituous liquors for good. For ten years he has not touched them, he does not care for them, they do not constitute a temptation.

It must not be forgotten that many warnings may so preoccupy the mind with regard to a danger as to constitute temptations by suggestion. This is eminently true of alcoholism, the drug habits, sex habits and the like, in spite of the foolish present-day notion that information and warning must necessarily be helpful. In all these, teaching may be suggestively harmful.

Prophylaxis.—The most important part of the treatment of alcoholism through mental influence is by prophylaxis, and that, to be effective, must begin very early. Just as with regard to overeating, as I have pointed out in the chapter on Obesity, it is extremely important not to permit children to acquire habits with regard to alcohol when they are young. During the growing years the system, indeed one may say all the systems of the body—the nervous, the muscular, the digestive and the mental systems—are all more or less unstable. Deep impressions may be produced on them then, and if children are allowed, much less encouraged, during their growing years (and this includes practically all the years up to twenty-five) to indulge in alcohol, then one can look for the development of a craving very hard to eradicate later in life. Many of them will be able to conquer the desire thus awakened, but a great many of them will not. We have some very definite evidence on this point and some of it collected here in America is very valuable. Dr. Alexander Lambert of New York made a study of over 250 cases of alcoholism seen in the wards at Bellevue Hospital, paying special attention to the age at which the patients remembered they had begun the use of alcoholic liquors. If anyone doubts the influence of youth in this matter, then his statistics should be read:

Of 259 instances where the age of beginning to drink was known, four began before six years of age; thirteen between 6 and 12 years; sixty between 12 and 16; one hundred and two between 16 and 21; seventy-one between 21 and 30; and eight only after 30 years of age. Thus nearly seven per cent. began before 12 years of age, or the seventh school year; thirty per cent. began before the age of 16; and over two-thirds—that is, sixty-eight per cent.—began before 21 years of age.

Dr. Henry Smith Williams, commenting on Dr. Lambert's study of this subject in his article on "The Scientific Solution of the Liquor Problem," states emphatically the conclusion so inevitable from these statistics that more than anything else alcoholism is the result of habits and occasions created in early years. He adds some remarks that are worth noting for those who are interested in the prevention and cure of alcoholism, not only in particular cases, but also for the community:

{702}

In the light of such facts, it is clear that the drink problem is essentially a problem of adolescence. The cumulative effects of alcoholic poisoning frequently fail to declare themselves fully until later in life; but the youth who does not taste liquor till his majority minimizes the danger of acquiring the habit in its most insistent form; and the man who does not drink until he is thirty is in no great danger of ever becoming a drunkard. As to the man who has passed forty—well, according to the old saw, he must be either a fool or his own physician. His habits of mind and body are formed, and if he becomes a drinker now he can at most curtail by a few years a life that is already entering upon the reminiscent stage. As factors in racial evolution, the youth of each successive generation, not its quadragenarians, are of interest and importance.

Treatment.—The conclusions that naturally flow from the historical introduction to this chapter which show mental influence as the basis of all cures, simplify very much the treatment of alcoholism on psychotherapeutic principles. There is no doubt that moral means are the only really effective remedies in this matter. They fail often, not because of any lack of power, but because of lack of co-operation on the part of the patient. There are men whose mentality and responsibility is breaking down, and who are on the way to the insane asylum for various causes, who cannot be thus influenced. They are, however, not alcoholics, but incipient insane patients likely to go to excess in any line. There is no pretense that psychotherapy will cure mental disorder that rises to the height of real insanity. On the other hand, just as after several relapses of tuberculosis due to the foolishness of the patient, further improvement by sanatorium treatment is usually out of the question, so each relapse of the alcoholic patient makes it increasingly difficult to bring about noteworthy improvement. There are examples, however, which demonstrate that even after seventy times seven relapses men may still encounter something that rouses their dormant wills to real activity and then their alcoholism is a thing of the past, for good and all.

Sanitarium Question.—There always comes the question whether these cases need to be sent to a sanitarium or can be treated at home. The answer to this question is the same for alcoholism as it is for tuberculosis or, indeed, for any of the exhaustive diseases. It all depends on the individual's physical condition and his circumstances. If tuberculosis is discovered, as it should be, at a very early stage in the disease—not when the patient is coughing up bacilli in large numbers and already has many physical signs in his lungs, but when he has a slight unproductive cough and over-rapid pulse and some prolongation of expiration at one apex—then he may be cared for at home, if the physician is confident that he can make his patient feel the absolute necessity for following instructions and can make him realize the seriousness of his condition in spite of the few symptoms that are present. If his environment is unfavorable, in a crowded tenement house or where an abundance of fresh air cannot be readily obtained, the patient may have to go to a sanitarium for proper treatment even at this early stage, or at least he will have to change his living conditions.

This question has received a very different answer in recent years from what used to be given to it. Formerly the physician hesitated to say "tuberculosis" to his patient until the disease was well advanced and then he advised the distant West or some other change of climate, though, as a rule, this brought only a palliation of symptoms, the case being too far advanced, and {703} the fatal termination came in the course of two or three years. Now the careful physician diagnoses tuberculosis much earlier, detects the disease in its incipiency, and is able to treat the patient at home quite successfully, if conditions are at all favorable. It is true he has to make him give up fatiguing occupations, and especially those in dusty places; he has to insist on his living out of doors a good part of the day, even though there should be no better means of securing this than the roof or a fire-escape, and on keeping his windows open all night. He has to watch his nutrition carefully and see that he gains in weight. If all this can be accomplished, however, there is no reason why a tuberculosis patient in the incipient state should not get better at home almost as well as he would at a sanitarium. The only difference between the two methods of treatment is that in a sanitarium the patient realizes that his one duty in life is to care for his health and he does not bother about other things, as he is likely to do if he remains at home.

If this precious development of teaching with regard to tuberculosis, which is founded on such thorough-going common sense and the application of good therapeutic principles to the treatment of the disease, be transferred to the sphere of alcoholism, then the answer to the question whether there shall be sanitarium treatment or not is practically arrived at. If the patient is in an early stage of his alcoholism, if the pathological character of his tendency to take intoxicants has been recognized and made clear to him early, then there is little difficulty in treating him at home. The crux of the problem is just that which occurred with regard to tuberculosis years ago. The physician does not take the early symptoms of the affection seriously enough. He does not want to disturb his patient's equanimity by the suggestion that he is in the incipient stage of alcoholism any more than a few years ago the family physician cared to suggest the awful thought of tuberculosis until the condition had reached a serious stage. But this is the essential preliminary to the successful treatment of alcoholism just as it is to the successful treatment of tuberculosis.

It is almost useless to send advanced cases of tuberculosis, in which cavity formation has already occurred, to a sanitarium. The course of their disease may be delayed for a while, but scarcely more than that. Their resistive vitality has been so overcome by the ravages of the disease that their ultimate cure seems beyond hope, yet not infrequently wonderful results are obtained even in these cases. Just this same thing is true with advanced cases of alcoholism. No one can do anything with them, though careful treatment in a sanitarium may, on a number of occasions, afford them opportunity to brace up and be themselves, i.e., their better selves, for several months. Just as with tuberculosis, however, even the quite advanced cases will sometimes be so much bettered by sanitarium treatment that, though their prognosis seemed absolutely hopeless and was so pronounced by good authorities, all the symptoms are relieved and the patients get a new lease of life that may last for many years.

In the same way some apparently hopeless cases of alcoholism will brace up after sanitarium treatment and have many years of useful sober life without a break. In alcoholism, as in tuberculosis, the will of the individual is the all-important consideration. Someone has said that tuberculosis takes away mainly the quitters. Those who have the courage to insist that they {704} *will live* in spite of everything being apparently against them, pull through crises that seem absolutely hopeless and survive for years. Robert Louis Stevenson bravely doing his work, living on in spite of fate and disease, is the typical example. Alcoholism completely overcomes only the quitters. If a man wants to give up drinking even when he seems practically a hopeless wreck from the effects of alcohol, he can do so if he has a physician in whom he has confidence, who will relieve him from depressing symptoms due to previous excess, who will lift him up and strengthen him by food and stimulation, and, above all, by faithful, unending, never discouraged assurance that he can conquer the craving which has such a hold of him, if he only persists a little and does not give up the struggle. The victory is worth while and it is not hard to lift a man up if he has any remnants of character left.

Confidence.—In the treatment of alcoholism, then, just two things are necessary. One of these is that the patient has confidence in himself, the other that he has confidence that his physician can help him over the hard spots on the road. There is no doubt that many drugs can be used that will lessen the patient's irritability, increase his nerve force, stimulate organs which are depressed by the reaction against over-stimulation, arouse appetite and correct disturbed functions. All these things must be done. It is no use laying down any set of rules as to how they shall be done, for they must be done differently in individual patients. It is not alcoholism that is treated nor the effects of alcoholism, but an individual alcoholic patient, and a set of symptoms that are very different in every individual. The more physiological disturbance can be relieved by proper drug, dietetic, hydropathic and remedial measures, the more chance is there for the patient to get over his habit without trouble. Every ill feeling that he has tempts him to think of alcohol. Above all, he must be made to sleep, his bowels must be thoroughly regulated, and he must be made to eat heartily. For stimulation full doses of nux vomica, not less than thirty drops three or four times a day or even oftener, are probably best.

For cases of alcoholism in the earlier stages there is but little difficulty. Those who try the effect of favorable suggestion, of confident assurance, of constantly repeated encouragement on individuals who have begun to be afraid that they cannot break the habit, will frequently have the most gratifying results. The important point to remember is that men are suffering from alcoholism who are indulging in alcohol every day and to whom it has become more or less of a necessity, though even as yet its effect upon their business is not marked and they are not known, even among their acquaintances, as drunkards. Whenever a man must have three or four whiskeys a day or he cannot do his business and his appetite fails him and he does not sleep well, he is an alcoholist. He has the cellular craving that later may become an absolute tyrant. If we can educate the community generally to realize this as we are gradually educating them to the knowledge that tuberculosis must be caught in its incipient stage and that pulmonary consumption begins in very mild symptoms after a person has been exposed to it, we shall have little difficulty in curing tuberculosis or in treating alcoholism successfully by suggestion.

For alcoholism, as for the drug habits and also the sex habits, moral influences are all-important. Hence the necessity for exercising them {705} frequently. It is probable that the best way to break any of these habits is to have the patient come regularly to the physician's office, at least once, and at the beginning twice a day. In cases of alcoholism the method of giving for the first week, at least, the dose of the stimulant drug which replaces the alcoholic stimulation directly to the patient is often of great service. It seems a good deal to ask the patient to come three times a day just to get a drug (tonic), but it is comparatively easy to resist the craving for liquor for four or five hours, that is, until the doctor is seen again, while sometimes twenty-four hours will seem a long while. The personal element in this matter is extremely valuable. It is this that has made the efficiency of all forms of cures, and it is only this that can be successfully used.

How much can be accomplished for even the worst forms of drunkenness and under extremely unfavorable circumstances once a really strong impression is made on the individual's mind and his will is aroused to help himself seriously may be readily learned from the lives of any of the great temperance advocates. Their experience is illuminating. It shows clearly that strong personal influence will do more than anything else for these sufferers. Sometimes their efforts are supposed to affect only certain classes of individuals who have character but who, for some reason, have fallen into an unfortunate habit. A little investigation will show, however, that they affect all classes and kinds of individuals and, indeed, may reform a whole community. The story of Father Matthew is very interesting in this regard because there is some striking testimony as to his reformation of whole neighborhoods that had been given over to drink before and that among a people especially emotional and susceptible. The movement that he initiated still lives in the temperance societies of the English-speaking peoples everywhere which help by prophylaxis in youth and the moral force of association in later life.

After-Treatment.—In alcoholism the most important feature of the treatment is what has come to be known in our time as the after-treatment. This department of therapeutics has taken on great importance in recent years in every form of disease. For early and middle life most diseases have a definite tendency to get better, though many of them leave distinct pathological tendencies. The after-treatment, then, has become much more important than the cure for the patient during the existence of the acute or sub-acute stage. Even in children's diseases it is now generally recognized that while measles and whooping cough are not dangerous affections as a rule, they may prove the forerunners of tuberculosis, because of the weakened pulmonary resistance consequent upon their invasion. For scarlet fever, the possibilities of injury to the kidneys after the great irritation to which they have been subjected, is now recognized and convalescence is prolonged. In typhoid fever we realize that not weeks but many months of convalescence are needed to put the patient beyond the risk of various degenerative processes that may be serious. There is even question in the minds of many observant physicians whether the weakness incident to typhoid fever may not, if a premature return to work is allowed, prove a potent cause of precocious arterio-sclerosis.

In a word, after-treatment has become one of the most interesting subjects of modern therapeutics. It will not be surprising, then, if we insist that the after-treatment of the alcoholic is the most important part of the remedial methods to be employed. If a man who has suffered from tuberculosis because {706} he was working in one of the many dusty trades and living in a badly ventilated tenement house is restored to health or at least has all his symptoms disappear as a consequence of sanitarium treatment, it is almost needless to say that he must not be allowed to return to the conditions in which his disease originally developed. If he does, he is absolutely certain to have a relapse. This phase of tuberculosis has been much discussed in recent years. It is often said that it is impossible to keep working people from a return to their occupations. Just so far as that is impossible, so far will any real hope of keeping their tuberculosis in abeyance be reduced. They are much more likely to suffer from the disease, as a rule, after their return from the sanitarium than they were before they originally contracted it, because apparently some of their immunity has been destroyed by the invasion of the bacillus.

It is only recently that we have thus planned for the after-treatment of tuberculosis. If we are to be successful in the after-treatment of alcoholism, at least some of this same thoughtfulness must be exercised. The victims must be discouraged from going back into the conditions in which their habit developed. It is comparatively easy, especially at the beginning of his alcoholism, to stimulate a man back to normal physical condition, to reduce his craving for intoxicants, give him back his appetite and set him on his feet again. The affection is quite curable. If a man returns to the conditions in which it originally developed, however, it will develop again quite as inevitably as tuberculosis does under similar conditions. We do not blame the sanitarium if, after having given a man a new lease of life in spite of tuberculosis, he resumes the unsanitary life in which his disease originally developed and has a relapse. It is not the fault of the system of treatment for alcoholism if men relapse, but the blame is upon them that they do not take their danger of relapse seriously enough, permit themselves to get into an unfavorable environment, and, as a consequence, suffer once again from their affection.

Religious Motives.—More and more we are realizing the place of the higher motives of life in the reform of alcoholic patients. Religious motives probably form the best possible source of suggestions that enable a patient to lift himself out of the slough of despond of chronic alcoholism. Many of the best workers for the reform of the drunkard were themselves drunkards for many years. The motive of helping others is particularly important in its effects upon any alcoholic. Some motive apart from himself is more helpful than any appeal to his selfishness or even to what he can do for his children and his wife. It is the newer motive that appeals most strikingly. In recent years certain church movements have done much for alcoholic patients. In this they are only repeating the effect of other great church movements and the effect of the lives of apostles of temperance in recent generations. Without these higher motives cure is probably impossible in many cases. With them it not only becomes possible but even comparatively easy in the most hopeless-looking cases.

In the light of what we have heard recently of the success of the Emanuel movement in the treatment of alcoholism, it is interesting to recur to what was said in this relation by Prof. Forel of Zurich on the treatment of alcoholism, in a communication read to the South German Neurologists and Psychiatrists at its meeting in Freiburg over twenty years ago. Prof. Forel, who is not what {707} would be called a particularly religious-minded man, insisted that "an inebriate asylum can only with great difficulty be successful without religious auxiliaries, since most inebriates, and especially at the beginning of their reformation, are entirely too weak to get along without religious consolation. To secure this, however, the nicest tact is required in order to permit the practice of all the different nuances of faith that men have, in peace and comfort. This can only be secured if in practice faith is subjected to charity for one's neighbor as the basis for religion."

Many such expressions have been used before and since in practically every country in Europe. The assertion that physicians have failed to recognize the part that religion plays in such cases is entirely without foundation and can only be made by those who are quite ignorant of our medical literature.

CHAPTER II

DRUG ADDICTIONS

Much of what has been said with regard to alcoholism finds ready application to the treatment of drug addictions. At the very beginning it must be realized that there is no specific remedy that will enable the patient to overcome his craving for a drag to which he has become habituated. There is no method of treatment that will infallibly and without serious and prolonged and determined effort on his part enable him to overcome his craving. The first and most important thing in any system of treatment is the patient's good will. If the patient is not ready to give up the drug, then nothing that a physician can do for him will make him do so, or will turn him against it; above all, nothing will make the process of cure so easy that there will be no trouble involved or only a passing period of struggle required to accomplish it. There have been many claims made in this matter. We have wanted such remedies and methods of treatment so much that it has been rather easy to persuade us sometimes that they have been discovered. It is like the question of specifics in medicine. For centuries men devoted themselves to trying to find a specific remedy for each disease. It was thought they must exist in nature. Now we know that they probably do not exist, though those who claim to discover them find an easy livelihood exploiting the credulity of those who still cherish the belief in them. Scientific students of medicine have practically given over the search for them in order to devote themselves to strengthen the patient to resist the disease rather than spend more time trying to find something to give him that cures it.

Treating the Patient rather than the Habit.—This principle holds with special force with regard to drug addictions. We do not treat the patient's habit, but we treat the patient. He must be braced up, must be made to understand that if he wants to quit the habit, no matter how slavishly he is addicted to it, he can do so. He must be told of men who had habits like his, often of longer duration and to a greater degree, yet gave them up when firmly resolved and properly stimulated. It is not hard to find such examples, since medical and even ordinary literature abound with them and every physician's experience furnishes him with instances. The first and {708} most absolutely necessary preliminary of the treatment is to lift up the patient in his own eyes and make him understand that, low as he has sunk, his case is not hopeless, that his degradation is not at all uncommon nor so rare as he might think, and that men and women have succeeded in lifting themselves out of conditions worse than his. The psychotherapeutist must, above all, not be of those who insist that human nature is degenerating and that people are much weaker physically and morally than they used to be, though of course he must be thoroughly aware that drug habits are more frequent than they were and are quite alarmingly on the increase. This is not due to any deterioration in human nature, however, but mainly to the excitement of modern life and its inevitable reaction, the strenuousness with which men now take existence and the consequent craving for artificial relief from over-activity, and then, above all, the facility with which the habit-forming drugs can be obtained.

Prophylaxis.—This last point accounts for the frequency of drug habits in our time more than anything else. Men have always been ready to do something for the sake of novelty and excitement. Everyone is curious to experience for himself the effects produced by drugs that can make people such slaves to them. We hear too often of the intense pleasure that the drug habitué gets from his use of drugs. The curiosity thus aroused constitutes the suggestion that has led many to try the effect, confident that he or she would be able to resist any craving just before it became seriously tyrannous. Psychiatrists agree that one of the worst elements in modern social conditions is the impression generally maintained that there is such intense pleasure in the taking of drugs. A clear statement of the reality of the case is eminently desirable. It is not positive pleasure that the drug habitué has, but mere negative pleasure, as a rule. His "dope" does not so much add to his good feeling as take away the bad feelings that he has because of depression or ennui at the beginning and later because of the craving for the drug.

Physicians to whom many drug habitués have told their experience frankly are not at all inclined to think that the usually accepted opinion of pleasure in drug taking is true. It is not that it is heaven to have the drug so much as it is hell to be without it. The patient's system has learned to crave it so much because of the surcease of painful consciousness of self it gives and this it is that compels these unfortunates to go back to ever-increasing doses. The pleasant side is a very dubious affair at all times, accompanies only the earliest steps of the formation of the habit at most, and usually whatever agreeable feelings there are are accompanied by such a nightmare of solicitude and anxiety as a background that the pleasure is more poignant than agreeable. As a prophylactic against the formation of drug habits this aspect of the experience of drug habitués deserves to be emphasized and knowledge of it widely diffused. Of course, the morphin fiend brightens up after his dose of morphin, his eye lightens, his expression becomes happy, and his nerves get steadier, but that is only because the depression in which he was sunk before has now been stimulated away, the struggle with his worst feelings is over and the consequent reaction has developed. Of course, the cocain-taker is pitiably helpless and downcast without his "dope," but it is only by contrast with this previous state that his succeeding condition can be said to be pleasant or agreeable, even to himself.

{709}

Favorable Suggestion.—One of the most helpful sources of favorable suggestion for these patients is to be found in the stories of cured drug habitués. These may be used tactfully to bring confidence to patients that they, too, can be broken of their habit if they are willing to take the pains to do so. De Quincey, taking his thousand drops of laudanum a day, represents one of the most encouraging examples of this since he succeeded eventually in breaking away from his habit. Coleridge succeeded, also, in breaking his habit more than once, but unfortunately returned again and again, and illustrates the danger of the almost inevitable tendency to relapse, if the patient permits himself to think that now that he has once conquered the habit he is too strong ever to let it get hold of him again. If he ventures to think complacently of his self-control and that consequently he may with impunity—always for some good reason—take a dose or two of his favorite drug in order to tide him over some crisis of mental worry or some spell of physical pain, relapse is certain. The tendency of patients to fool themselves in this way is too well known to need special emphasis, but it is as well to say that there is scarcely a single cured case that does not relapse. The relapse is due not so much to craving for the drug, as to the memory of its previous effects in relieving discomfort and the unfortunate confidence that the patient has developed that now, knowing the dangers, he will be able to resist the formation of the habit before it gets a strong hold of him.

It is curious how even highly intelligent patients will slip back into their old habits, sometimes deeper than before, on this reasoning, in spite of the lessons of experience, even their own as well as others. Like the drunkard, they persuade themselves that just this once will not count, and when it would have been comparatively easy for them to say no they yield once or twice and make self-denial for the future increasingly difficult. This is especially true if patients have the drug near them, so that it is not difficult for them to have recourse to it. Hence doctors and nurses are not hard to cure of such habits, as a rule, provided they are away from their professional duties, but they almost inevitably relapse when they go back to work. Every time the relapse is due to the fact that tired feelings, because of irregular hours or some physical pain, prompt them to seek relief and they yield to the temptation of taking the old drug, sure that they need it, only for the moment. They will all assert that they could just as well resist as not, that, indeed, had not the drug been so handy, they would not have taken it, and that if anyone had been near to help them by a word in the matter even then they would not have indulged in it.

If patients are to be kept from relapsing, all this must be set before them frankly. After they have been told once or perhaps twice or perhaps many times and yet relapse into their habits, they must simply be told it again a little more emphatically, more encouragingly, up to seventy times seven, if necessary. Patience is needed more than anything else in taking care of these cases. Over and over again their confidence in their power to overcome their habit, if they really wish to do so, must be reawakened. Without this confidence in themselves success is hopeless. It matters not how often they have relapsed, they can still break off the habit, and if they will not fool themselves into over-confidence in their power to keep away, they need never be slaves to the habit again. There will be quite as many disappointments in {710} treating drug addiction as in the treatment of alcoholism. Those who have most experience insist that there are even more, but there are some wonderfully encouraging examples of men and women who have broken from their habit, even after a number of bad relapses, and have for many years lived absolutely without any of their drug and, though still not over-confident in their power to resist if once they should yield (such confidence, it cannot be repeated too often, is always fatal), do actually keep away from the drug without any other bother than the necessity of living a regular hygienic life and exercising a little self-control.

In drug addictions as in alcoholisms, the question of sanitarium treatment comes up in every case. Much more rarely than in the case of the alcohol habit is it necessary to send a drug habitué to a sanitarium. Here once more, however, the patient's circumstances and the possibility of diversion of mind with reasonable freedom from temptations to take the drug and from ready access to it, are the most important considerations. If a patient really wants to break off the use of a drug, it can be done gently and without much bother in the course of three or four weeks. I have seen cocain fiends who have tried many remedies and many physicians completely cured in five or six weeks without serious trouble. The important thing is perseverance in the effort and in the treatment and the definite persuasion of the patient that it is not only perfectly possible to get rid of the habit, but that it is even easy with good will on his part. If certain other milder stimulants are supplied for a time so that all the symptoms due to the physiological effects of the excessive use of the drug are minimized, the physical trial need not be severe. The patient's mind, however, must be occupied. Time must not be allowed to hang heavy on his hands and all physical symptoms must be treated promptly. Drug addictions are indeed more curable than alcoholism and the danger of relapse is not quite so imminent. The social temptations do not exist for drug habitués as they do for alcoholics. As I have said, however, in the cases of nurses and physicians almost a corresponding state of affairs obtains and in them the danger of relapse is great.

Early Treatment.—It is quite as important for drug victims as it is for alcoholics that the case should be taken under treatment early. Every physician knows how curiously easy it is for some people, indeed for most people, to acquire a drug habit. I have seen one of the solidest men I ever knew, with plenty of character that had been tried by many a crisis in life, recommended cocain for a toothache when he was past fifty years of age and in the course of ten days acquire a thorough beginning of the cocain habit, so that he was taking several grains a day. He had no idea that he was unconsciously slipping into a drug habit. When the druggist refused any longer to supply the cocain solution without a prescription he was quite indignant. It was not until he had forty-eight hours of nervous symptoms and craving that he realized that he had created a need for stimulation of his nervous system by the mere taking of cocain by application on his gums. This habit was broken up at once and there has never been any tendency to its recurrence. He had his warning, fortunately, without evil effects.

If the cocain habit can be formed as unconsciously as this, there should be little difficulty in treating it. It is not a profound change in the organism, but only a habit. It is not the habit itself that is hard to break, but the effects {711} upon the nervous system of the patient are such as to create a series of symptoms that can only be soothed by the drug. It is these symptoms of depression, irritation, sleeplessness, lack of appetite, constipation and the rest that it is the physician's duty to treat in order to help the patient. The patient breaks the habit by his will-power when properly persuaded and when it is made clear to him that it is neither so difficult as he thought, nor is he so likely to fail in the matter as he has imagined, and as has perhaps been suggested to him even by physicians. The mental treatment consists in making him realize that he can do it and that if he wants to get rid of his habit he must do it for himself. With this must come the assurance that every annoying symptom will be met, that he need not recur to his favorite drug for this purpose, that his appetite will be gradually restored and that, though perhaps for a week he will have considerable inconvenience to bear, after that it will be plain sailing. Usually three days can be set as the term at which his craving ceases to be so disturbing as to make the possibility of his relapsing into the habit a positive danger. As in alcoholic and sex habits, the patient to be helped in breaking the habit should be seen once a day at least, usually oftener. If he can be made to understand that whenever the old tendency seems about to get the upper hand is the time to see his physician, and if something physical as well as moral is done for him, the breaking of the habit is comparatively simple.

This method of treatment looks too simple to be quite credible to those who have so often tried and failed in the cure of drug habits. It is not the doctor, however, who fails, but the patient. We cannot put new wills into a patient, but we can so brace up even an old and tottering will as to make it possible for the worst victims of drug habits to reform. The doctor, too, easily becomes discouraged. He has not confidence enough in his own methods to make assurance doubly sure for the patient as to his cure. This is what many of the pretended specific purveyors of drug habit cures have as their principal stock in trade. They assure patients with absolute confidence, while the physician only too often says the same thing, but half-heartedly. A half-hearted physician makes a hesitant patient, and success is then very dubious from the beginning. Every patient can be cured. They may relapse, but then they can be cured again. This is the essence of the psychotherapy of drug habits, but it is also the only successful element in any treatment of the drug habit that is really effective. Specifics come and go. Sure cures cease to have their effect. The only really effective element in any cure is the absolute trust of the patient.

In his "Drugs and the Drug Habit" (Methuen, London) Dr. Harrington Sainsbury, Senior Physician to the Royal Free Hospital of London, has emphasized all these points that can only be touched on very briefly here. He has called particular attention to the fact that the victim of one drug habit is rather prone to acquire another if by any chance he should once begin to take another habit-forming drug. The original drug habit has broken down the will. It is not so much the craving for a particular drug as the lack of will power that proves unfortunate for the patient. He suggests "incidentally, if this explanation hold good, it proves the solidarity of the will that it works as a whole and not by compartments." He has dwelt on recoveries from the most discouraging depths and insists "we must teach that {712} no one is ever so enslaved by a habit as to be incapable of relief—this alone is *right* teaching, justifiable moreover by records well substantiated of recoveries from desperate plights."

Heredity and Unfavorable Suggestion.—As to the suggestion, sometimes encountered, of the influence of heredity and its all-powerful effect in making it practically impossible for the son of a man who has taken drugs to keep from doing the same thing, we must recall very emphatically here the principles discussed elsewhere. So far as concerns heredity, opium and the other drugs are exactly in the same position as alcohol in their effect upon the human race. Instead of being justified in saying that by heredity individuals of succeeding generations are rendered more susceptible to them, just the opposite is true and, if anything, an immunity is produced. This is not only racial and general but is personal and actual. In recent years we have come to realize that individuals born of tuberculous parents who care for themselves properly are much better able to resist the invasion of the tubercle bacilli than those who come from stocks that were never affected by the disease. They are the patients who, in spite of the fact that their disease reaches an advanced stage, sometimes live on for years with proper care. Just this is true for drug addictions so far as we know anything about it. The whole subject is as yet obscure, but heredity rather favors than hurts the patient in these cases.

Hereditary Resistance.—Instead of being discouraged by the fact that his father took a drug to excess and that therefore he is weaker against this than other people, a man should rather be encouraged by the thought that a certain amount of resistance to the craving has probably been acquired by the particular line of cells through which his personality is manifested. Dr. Archdall Reid has said that "the facts concerning opium are very similar" (to those that concern alcohol). Then he continues:

That narcotic has been used extensively in India for several centuries. It was introduced by the English into China about two centuries ago. Quite recently the Chinese have taken it to Burma, to various Polynesian Islands, and to Australia. There is no evidence that the use of opium has caused any race to deteriorate. Indeed it happens that the finest races in India are most addicted to its use. According to the evidence given before the late Royal Commission on Opium, the natives of India never or very rarely take it to excess. When first introduced into China it was the cause of a large mortality; but to-day most Chinamen, especially in the littoral provinces, take it in great moderation. On the other hand, Burmans, Polynesians and Australian natives take opium in such excess and perish of it in such numbers that their European governors are obliged to forbid the drug to them, though the use of it is permitted to foreign immigrants to their countries. In exactly the same way alcohol is forbidden to Australians and Red Indians in places where it is permitted to white men.

After-Cures.—I have said so much about the after-cure of alcoholism that applies directly to drug addictions also, that it does not seem necessary to repeat it here. Patients must be warned that if they become overtired, if they lose sleep, if they are subject to much excitement, if they put themselves in conditions of anxiety and worry, if any form of recurrent pain develops—headache, toothache, stomach-ache—they are likely to be tempted to take up their old habit. If they are in a position where they can easily get the drug it is almost inevitable that something will happen to make them feel that {713} they are justified in taking one or two doses and from this to the reestablishment of the habit is only a small step. Often these patients need a change of occupation. Some of them are over-occupied, some of them have not enough to do. In either case it is the doctor's duty to know enough about his patient to be able to give directions. We do not treat a drug addiction with the hope of curing it, but we treat a patient suffering from a particular drug habit and we try so to modify that patient's life that after we have succeeded in getting him away from his habit, which is never difficult, he will not relapse into it. The after-cure is the more important of the two.

CHAPTER III

SUICIDE

In spite of the gradual increase of comfort in life and its wide diffusion—far beyond what people enjoyed in the past—there has been a steady progressive increase in the number of suicides in recent years. It is as if people found life less worth living the more of ease and convenience there was in it. This increase in suicide is much greater (over three times in the last twenty years) than the increase in the population. Surprising as it may seem, prosperity always brings an addition to the number of suicides. Stranger still, during hard times the number of suicides decreases to a noteworthy degree. It is not those who are suffering most from physical conditions who most frequently commit suicide. Our suicides come, as a rule, from among the better-to-do classes of people. While suicide might seem to be quite beyond the province of the physician, it is a duty of the psychotherapeutist to prevent not only the further increase of suicides in general but to save particular patients from themselves in this matter. A careful study of the conditions as they exist, moreover, will show that he can accomplish much—more than is usually thought—and that it is as much a professional obligation to do so as, by the application of hygienic precautions and regulations, to lessen disease and suffering of all kinds and prevent death.

The same two modes of preventive influence that we have over disease in general can be applied to suicide. The physician can modify the mental attitude in individual cases and thus save people from themselves and then he can, by his influence in various ways upon public opinion, lessen the death rate from suicide. For this purpose, just as with regard to infectious disease, it is important for him to appreciate the social and individual conditions that predispose to suicide, as well as the factors that are more directly causative. The more he studies the more will he be convinced that what we have to do with in suicide is a mental affliction not necessarily inevitable in its results and that may be much influenced by suggestion. Indeed, unfavorable suggestion is largely responsible for the increase in suicide that has been seen in recent years. Favorable suggestion might be made not only to stop the increase, but actually to reduce the suicide rate. For this purpose it is important to know just what are the conditions and motives that predispose to suicide and, above all, to realize that it is not the result of insufferable pain {714} or anguish, but rather of the concentration of mind on some comparatively trivial ailment, or exaggeration of dread with regard to the consequences of physical or moral ills.

Suicides are often said to be irrational; in a certain sense they are. No one who weighs reasonably all the consequences of his act will take his own life. This irrationality, however, is nearly always functional and passing, not of the kind that makes the commission of suicide inevitable, but only produces a tendency to it. This tendency is emphasized by many conditions of mind and body that the physician can modify very materially if he sets about it. Many of the supposed reasons for suicide are founded on the complete misunderstanding of the significance of symptoms and dread of the future of his ailments, often quite unjustified by what the individual is actually suffering. Indeed, the desperation that leads to suicide is practically always the result of a state of mind and not of a state of body. It is exactly the same sort of state of mind which sometimes proves so discouraging in the midst of diseases of various kinds as to make it impossible for patients to get over their affections until a change is brought about in their ideas. This makes clear the role of psychotherapy with regard to suicide, and there is no doubt that many people on the verge of self-murder can be brought to a more rational view and then live happy, useful lives afterwards. For this purpose, however, it is important that the physician should come to be looked upon as a refuge by those to whom the thought of suicide has become an obsession.

A well-known social religious organization not long since established a suicide bureau, that is, a department to which those contemplating suicide may apply with the idea that they would there find consolation and perhaps some relief for their troubles and thus the idea of suicide might be dissipated. Many a suicide would be avoided if the reasons that impelled to it had been known to one or two other people beforehand, so that some relief might have been afforded to what seemed an intolerable condition. This suicide bureau is said to have done much good. There is no doubt that the mere act of giving one's confidence to another is quite sufficient of itself to diminish to a marked degree a burden of grief and trial. If anything in the world is true, it is that sorrows are halved by sharing them with another, while joys are correspondingly increased. The fact that there is someone to whom they might go, who would look sympathetically at their state of mind, who would appreciate the conditions, who had been accustomed to dealing with such cases, would be enough to tempt many people from that awful introspection and concentration of mind on themselves which, more than their genuine sufferings and trials, whatever they may be, make their situation intolerable.

There has always been a suicide bureau, however, in the office of every physician who really appreciates the genuine responsibilities of his profession. More than any others we have the opportunity to alleviate physical sufferings, to lessen mental anguish and to make what seemed unbearable ill at least more or less tolerable. Unfortunately in recent years the change in the position of the physician in his relations to the family has somewhat obscured this fact in the minds of the public. The old family physician occupied to no slight extent the position of a father confessor, to whom all the family secrets were told, from whom indeed, as a rule, it was felt that they should not be kept; to whom father went with regard to himself and mother, to whom mother {715} went with regard to all the family as well as herself, to whom the boy confided some of his sex trials and the girl some of the secrets that she hid from almost everyone else, so that to go to him for anything disturbing became the first thought. We must restore something of this old-fashioned idea of the doctor's place in life if all our professional duties are to be properly fulfilled. If those contemplating suicide learn to think of us as persons to be appealed to when all looks so black that life is no longer tolerable, we shall soon be in a position to confer increased benefits on this generation that needs them so much.

Physical Factors.—As a rule there is a physical element as the basis for nearly all suicides. With the unfortunate, unfavorable suggestion that has come from the supplying of details of pathological information—the half-knowledge of popular medical science—without the proper antidote of the wonderful compensatory powers of the human body for even serious ailments, a great many nervous people are harboring the idea that they have or soon will have an incurable disease. Physicians have abundant evidence of this. All sorts of educated people come to us to be reassured that some trivial digestive disturbance does not mean cancer of the stomach, or, when they are between forty and fifty, come to make sure that some slight disturbance of urination is not an enlarged prostate. Brain workers of all classes come over and over again to be reassured that they are not breaking down because of organic brain disease, of which they show absolutely no sign. Sometimes they have been making themselves quite miserable for a long period by such thoughts. It is easy to understand, then, how many less informed people, yet provided with the opportunities of quasi-information that modern life affords, are apt to think the worst about themselves.

So-called Insomnia.—The correction of such preconceived notions will always greatly alleviate the mental sufferings of these patients. For this purpose there are many chapters of this book which point out how various symptoms and syndromes that are often amongst the factors in the production of suicide may be managed. Perhaps one of the most frequent of these is so-called insomnia. Most people are insomniac, mainly because they are overanxious about their sleep. A few of them are wakeful because of bad habits in the matter of work and the taking of air and exercise. Essential insomnia is extremely rare and symptomatic; insomnia is not mental, but is usually due to some definite physical condition that can be found out and, as a rule, treated successfully. There is always some other symptom besides loss of sleep. If men will live properly and rationally there is no reason why insomnia should be a bane of existence, nor even any reason why the morphin or other drug habit should be formed which is so likely to come if inability to sleep is treated as if it were an independent ailment. In the forms in which it incites to suicide it owes its origin to a nervous superexcitement with regard to sleep in people whose daily life in some way does not properly predispose them for the greatest of blessings on which there is no patent right. Additional suggestions as to these insomniac conditions are made in the chapters on Insomnia and Some Troubles of Sleep which make it clear that suicide, because of insomnia is due to a delusion.

Headache.—Persistent supposedly incurable headache is another prominent feature of the stories of suicides and here once more we have to deal rather {716} with a delusion of over-attention of mind and concentration of self on a particular part than a real physical ailment. Most of the so-called headaches that are supposed to be so intractable are really not headaches but pressure feelings and other queer sensations in the head originally perhaps partaking of the nature of an ache but continued through over-advertence. Severe pain within the head occurs in cases of congestion and brain tumor, and without the head in cases of neuralgia, but most of these are only temporary and long-continued headaches are rather neurotic than neuritic or due to any real disturbance of the nervous system. This is discussed in the chapter on Headaches. People commit suicide who have for a long time been sufferers from headache because they fear that they may go crazy. There is absolutely no reason in the world to think this probable, and in the one case of continuance of severe intermittent headaches for years already mentioned—that of von Bülow, the Austrian pianist and composer, in which we have the autopsy record—it was found, after a long life, that his severe intracranial headaches were due to the pinching of a nerve in the dura and not to any organic change in the brain itself.

Mental Factors.—While physical factors enter into the suicide problem to a marked degree, it would be a great mistake to think that physical conditions or material circumstances are the main causes or occasions in suicide. It is supposed, as a rule, to be due to depression produced by incurable disease, oppressive weather, financial losses and the like. There is no doubt that these are contributing causes, but the physical conditions have very little influence compared with the attitude of the patient's mind toward himself. As a rule, it is not those who are in absolutely hopeless conditions who turn to this supposed refuge of a voluntary exit from life in order to get out of trouble, but rather those who are momentarily discouraged and who have not sufficient moral stamina to face the consequences of their acts. There was a time when it was considered brave to fight a duel and cowardly to refuse to do so. Looking back now, we know that they were the real brave men who dared to refuse when a barbarous civilization would force them into a false position and who, in spite of disgrace, ventured to be men and not fools. There are those who used to say that it was brave to take one's own life rather than bring disgrace on loved ones, but the mitigation, if there be any, of the disgrace that suicide brings with it, comes from that lowest of all motives, pity for the survivors, and the cowardly suicide leaves to others the thankless task of making up for his faults.

Suicide and the Weather.—An investigation of suicide records shows, as we have said, that it is not nearly so often bodily or material hardships that lead men to it as mental states. These mental states are not mental diseases, but passing discouragements in which men are tempted beyond their strength and do irretrievable things for which there is no rational justification. It is not in dark damp weather that men commit suicides most, though this was supposed to be a commonplace in our knowledge of suicide. Recent investigations show that quite the contrary is true. Professor Edwin T. Dexter of the University of Illinois published a very important study of this question in a paper entitled "Suicide and the Weather." He followed out the records of nearly 2,000 cases of suicide reported to the police in the City of New York {717} and placed beside them the records of the weather bureau of the same city for the days on which these suicides occurred. According to this, which represents the realities of the situation, the tendency to suicide is highest in spring and summer and the deed is accomplished in the great majority of cases on the sunniest days of these seasons.

His conclusions are carefully drawn and there is no doubt that they must be accepted as representing the actual facts. All the world feels depressed on rainy days and in dark, cloudy weather, but suicides react well, as a rule, against this physical depression, yet allow their mental depression to get the better of them on the finest days of the year. Prof. Dexter said:

The clear, dry days show the greatest number of suicides, and the wet, partly cloudy days the least; and with differences too great to be attributed to accident or chance. In fact there are thirty-one per cent. more suicides on dry than on wet days, and twenty-one per cent. more on clear days than on days that are partly cloudy.

What is thus brought out with regard to the influence of weather can be still more strikingly seen from the suicide statistics of various climates. The suicide rate is not highest in the Torrid nor in the Frigid zones, but in the Temperate zones. In the North Temperate zone it is much more marked than in the South Temperate zone. Civilization and culture, diffused to a much greater extent in the North Temperate zone than in the South, seem to be the main reason for this difference. We make people capable of feeling pain more poignantly, but do not add to their power to stand trials nor train character by self-control to make the best of life under reasonably severe conditions. With this in mind it is not surprising to find that the least suicides occur in the month of December, when the disagreeable changes so common produce a healthy vital reaction, though the many damp dark days that occur would usually be presumed to make this the most likely time for suicides. On the contrary, it is the month of June, the pleasantest in the North Temperate zone, that has the most suicides. It is important to remember this in estimating the role of physical influences on the tendency to suicide.

Social Factors that Restrain Suicides.—*War.*—A most startling limitation of suicide is brought about by war. For instance, our Spanish-American war reduced the death rate from suicide in this country over forty per cent. throughout the country and over fifty per cent. in Washington itself, where there was most excitement with regard to the war. This was true also during the Civil War. Our minimum annual death rate from suicide from 1805 (when statistics on this subject began to be kept) was one suicide to about 24,000 people, which occurred in 1864 when our Civil War was in its severest phase. There had been constant increase in our suicide rate every year until the Civil War began, then there was a drop at once and this continued until the end of the war. In New York City the average rate of suicide for the five years of the Civil War was nearly forty-five per cent. lower than the average for the five following years. In Massachusetts, where the statistics were gathered very carefully, the number of suicides for the five-year period before 1860 was nearly twenty per cent. greater than for the five-year period immediately following, which represents the preliminary excitement over the war and the actual years of the war. This experience in America is only in accordance {718} with what happens everywhere. Mr. George Kennan in his article on "The Problems of Suicide" (*McClure's Magazine*, June, 1908), has a paragraph which brings this out very well. He says:

In Europe the restraining influence of war upon the suicidal impulse is equally marked. The war between Austria and Italy in 1866 decreased the suicide rate for each country about fourteen per cent. The Franco-German War of 1870-71 lowered the suicide rate of Saxony 8 per cent., that of Prussia 11.4 per cent. and that of France 18.7 per cent. The reduction was greatest in France, because the German invasion of that country made the war excitement there much more general and intense than it was in Saxony or Prussia.

Great Cataclysms.—Even more interesting than the fact that war reduces the suicide rate is the further fact that a reduction of the number of suicides takes place after any severe cataclysm. The earthquake at San Francisco, for instance, had a very marked effect in this way. Before the catastrophe suicides were occurring in that city on an average of twelve a week. After the earthquake, when, if physical sufferings had anything to do with suicide, it might be expected that the self-murder rate would go up, there was so great a reduction that only three suicides were reported in two months. Some of this reduction was due to inadequate records, but there can be no doubt that literally hundreds of lives were saved from suicide by the awful catastrophe that levelled the city. Men and women were homeless, destitute, and exposed to every kind of hardship, yet because all those around them were suffering in the same way, everyone seemed to be reasonably satisfied. Evidently a comparison with the conditions in which others are has much to do with deciding the would-be suicide not to make away with himself, for by dwelling too much on his own state he is prone to think that he is ever so much worse off than others.

If life were always vividly interesting, as it was in San Francisco after the earthquake, and if all men worked and suffered together as the San Franciscans did for a few weeks, suicide would not end ten thousand American lives every year, as it does now.

Individual Restraints.—*Religion.*—It seems worth while to call to attention certain factors that modify the tendency to suicide and limit it very distinctly, because it is with the limitation of it that the physician must be mainly occupied. There seems to be no doubt that certain religious beliefs, which affect the individual profoundly and occupy his thoughts very much, furnishing, both by tradition and heredity as it were, sources of consolation for evils in this life by the thought of a future life, notably lessen the suicide rate. All over the world the Jews who cling to their old-time belief have perhaps the lowest suicide rate of any people. This is true in spite of racial differences. People who retain the confidence in prayer, that used to characterize members of all religions a century or more ago, are likely to be able to resist the temptation to suicide. This is true particularly for the more or less rational suicide. Oppenheim has recalled attention to the power of prayer against depression and in the insane asylums of England its efficiency in this way is well recognized.

It is well-known that Roman Catholics the world over have much less tendency to suicide than their Protestant neighbors living in the same {719} communities. It is true that where the national suicide rate is high many Catholics also commit suicide, but there is a distinct disproportion between them and their neighbors. The suicide rate of Protestants in the northern part of Ireland, as pointed by Mr. George Kennan, is twice that of Roman Catholics in the southern part. He discusses certain factors that would seem to modify the breadth of the conclusion that might be drawn from this, but in the end he confesses that their faith probably has much to do with it and that, above all, the practice of confession must be considered as tending to lessen the suicide rate materially. It is the securing of the confidence of these patients that seems the physician's best hope of helping them to combat their impulse and Mr. Kennan's opinion is worth recalling for therapeutic purposes:

In view of the fact that the suicide rate of the Protestant cantons in Switzerland is nearly four times that of Catholic cantons, it seems probable that Catholicism, as a form of religious belief, does restrain the suicidal impulse. The efficient cause may be the Catholic practice of confessing to priests, which probably gives much encouragement and consolation to unhappy but devout believers and thus induces many of them to struggle on in spite of misfortune and depression.

Disgrace as a Restraint.—It is curious what far-fetched motives, that appear quite unlikely to have any such influence, sometimes prove able to affect favorably would-be suicides and prevent their self-destruction. Plutarch tells the story, in his treatise on "The Virtuous Actions of Women," of the well-authenticated instance of the young women of Milesia. Disappointed in love, they thought life not worth living. Accordingly there was an epidemic of suicide among the young women and it even became a sort of distinction to prefer death to matrimony. Some perverted sense of delicacy entered into the feeling that prompted the suicides, as if sex and its indulgence were something belittling to the better part of their nature. The authorities in Milesia must have been psychologists. They issued a decree that the body of every young woman who committed suicide would be exposed absolutely naked in the market-place for a number of days after her death. This decree, once put into effect, immediately stopped the suicides. The young women shrank from this exposure of their bodies, even though it might be after death, and the suicide fashion came to an end.

It might be thought perhaps that this incident represented ancient feeling and that a similar condition in the modern times would not have a corresponding effect. It so happens that something similar has been tried. In some of the cities of South Central Europe in which the suicide rate is almost the highest in the world, it was decided about a generation ago by the Church authorities of the towns that suicides would not thereafter be buried in the cemeteries near the bodies of those who died in the regular course of nature, but must be interred in a separate portion reserved for themselves. Strange as it may seem, just as in the case of the young women of Milesia, this proved a great deterrent to suicide. The suicide rate was reduced one-half the next year.

As a matter of fact, it only takes some reasonably forceful countervailing notion to set a train of suggestions at work that will prevent suicide. If those contemplating suicide are made acquainted with some of these curious facts we know, then the notion of suicide loses more than half its terrible {720} attraction by being stripped of all of its supposed inevitableness. Almost any motive that attracts attention, even apparently so small a thing as disgrace after death, makes these people realize the littleness and the cowardice of the act.

Favoring Factors.—*Psychic Contagion.*—A prominent factor in suicides that must constantly be borne in mind is the influence of example or, as we have come to call it learnedly in recent years, psychic contagion. It is discussed more in detail in the chapter on Psychic Contagion, but its place here must be emphasized. It has often been noted that certain peculiar suicides are followed by others of the same kind. If a special poison has been used, others obtain it and put an end to their lives in that way. Even such horrible modes of death as eroding the jugular vein by drawing the neck backward and forward across a barbed-wire fence have been imitated. If the story of jumping off a high building is told with lurid details, special care has to be taken in permitting unknown people to go up to the same place for some time afterwards. The imitative tendency is evidently a strong factor. Plutarch's story of the young women of Milesia brings this out, and it has been noted all down the centuries.

In any discussion of the prophylaxis of suicide the effect of newspaper descriptions of previous suicides must be looked upon as very important. The influence of suggestion of this kind on people who have been thinking for some time of suicide is very strong. There comes to them the impelling thought that the suicide's miseries are over and they wish they were with him. From the wish to the resolve and then to the deed itself are only successive steps when suggestion is constantly prodding the unfortunate individual. If we are going to reduce the suicide rate materially or, indeed, keep it from increasing beyond all bounds, this question must be squarely faced. Accounts of suicides are not news in the ordinary sense of the word and while they might find a place for legal and other purposes in a few lines of an obituary column, the present exploitation of them by the papers makes them a constantly recurring source of strong suggestion to go and do likewise. These suggestions come to persons already tottering on the edge of disequilibration in this matter, and it is like tempting children to do things that they know are wrong, but that look irresistibly inviting when presented under certain lights. The very fact that their death will produce a sensation and will give them so much space in the newspapers attracts many morbidly sensation-loving people. Physicians must work as much for this prophylaxis as we have for the prevention of infectious diseases.

Child Suicides.—Probably the worst feature of the suicide statistics of recent times in all countries is the great increase of self-murder among children. Arthur MacDonald in discussing the "Statistics of Child Suicide" has shown that there is a special increase of young suicides everywhere. In France there are nearly five times as many suicides at the end of the nineteenth century as there were at the beginning of it. In England there is almost as startling an increase. Though the statistics are not as well kept, child suicide has increased not only in proportion to the increase of suicide among adults, but ever so much more. In Prussia the condition is even worse.

{721}

The French child suicide rate is especially interesting and disheartening. In the Paris Thesis for 1906 Dr. Moreau discusses the subject of suicide among young people and shows how rapid has been the growth of the number of such suicides in the last 100 years. The first statistics available for the purpose that, in his opinion, are exact enough to furnish a basis for scientific conclusions, are from 1836 to 1840. Altogether during that period in France there were 92 suicides under the age of seventeen years, 69 of whom were boys and 23 girls. In 1895 this number had increased to such a degree that in a single year there were almost as many suicides (90) as there had been in five years, only fifty years before. In 1895 the proportion of suicides less than ten years of age was a little more than one in twenty of the total number of suicides in France. There are countries in Europe in which the suicide rate among such children is even higher than it is in France. In every country it has gone on increasing and the awful thing is that the suicide rate is increasing more rapidly among children than it is among adults, though among adults it doubles every twenty years.

Causes at Work.—The causes for the increase in suicide among children were pointed out even by Esquirol, the great French psychiatrist, nearly a century ago. They are the same to-day, only emphasized by the conditions of our civilization. He attributed it to a false education which emphasizes all the vicious side of life, makes worldly success the one object of life, does not properly prepare the child for constancy in the midst of hardships, nor make it appreciate that suffering is a precious heritage to the race, that has its reward in forming character and fixing purpose. He thought that there were two very serious factors for the increase of suicide among children not usually realized. They were in his time literature and the theater. He said: "When the theater presents only the triumphs of crime, the misfortunes of virtue, when the books that are in common circulation because of the low price at which they are issued, contain only declarations against religion, against family ties and duties towards our neighbor and society, then they inspire a disdain of life and it is no wonder that suicide rapidly increases even among the very young." He was commenting on the case of a child of thirteen who had hanged himself, leaving this written message: "I bequeath my soul to Rousseau and my body to the earth."

Cowardice of Suicide.—Of course, the strongest motive for dissuasion from suicide is the utter cowardice of the act. As a rule, the man who contemplates suicide is not a sufferer from inevitable natural causes, but one who for some foolish act has put himself into what seems to him an intolerable position out of which escape without disgrace is impossible, and he is afraid to face the consequences of his own acts. It is from the fear of mental worry and of the condemnation of others rather than from any dread of physical suffering and pain that men commit suicide. The suicide leaves those who are nearest and dearest to him to face the battle of life alone, with all the handicaps that have been created by their foolishness. Running away in battle is as nothing compared to the cowardice of the suicide. The deserter is deservedly held in deepest dishonor, and if there is some little pity for the suicide, it is because of the supreme foolishness of his act and the feeling that it only can have been dictated by some defect of mental equilibrium. A frank recognition of these conditions in their real significance probably will do more than anything {722} else to make the prospective suicide realize the true status of his act better than anything else.

Men sometimes seem to persuade themselves that it is a brave thing thus to face death. The shadowy terrors of what may come after death are too little realized to deter a man from his act when compared with the real disgrace that he is so familiar with and that he has often witnessed in actual life. It is the man, as a rule, who has most condemned others when something has gone wrong, who has found no sympathy in his heart for the slips of his fellows, who discovers no courage in himself when he has to face disgrace. He does not realize that for most men there are so many extenuations of any evil that a man may do, that the large-minded man is ready to forgive and eventually to forget almost anything that happens. "To know all is to forgive all," and the more we know of men the readier we are to forgive them. Little men do not forgive and cannot forget the failings of their fellows and they think that everyone else looks upon men's failings in the same way. It is only the small, narrow man who contemplates suicide as a refuge from disgrace, and the fact that he can complacently plan the abandonment of others not only to the disgrace which he himself is not ready to face, but to all the suffering consequent upon it, is the best proof of his littleness of soul. The utter pusillanimity of suicide is the best mental antidote for the temptation to it.

Besides, the thought that deterred Hamlet may well be urged:

```
                         There's the rub;
   For in that sleep of death what dreams may come.
   When we have shuffled off this mortal coil,
   Must give us pause;
        . . . who would fardels bear,
   To grunt and sweat under a weary life;
   Cut that the dread of something after death.—
   The undiscovered country, from whose bourn
   No traveller returns.—puzzles the will;
   And makes us rather bear those ills we have.
   Than fly to others we know not of?
```

It is sometimes said that this is the argument of a coward, but such cowardice is as reasonable as the dread of touching a wire that may be carrying a high charge of electricity. Besides it is only such an argument that will properly suit the man who, in his cowardice, is ready to let others bear the brunt of his disgrace, flying from it himself.

There has sometimes been an erroneous tendency to confuse suicide and heroism, but Chesterton, in "Orthodoxy," has well expressed the difference:

{723}

A soldier surrounded by enemies, if he is to cut his way out, needs to combine a strong desire for living with a strange carelessness about dying. He must not merely cling to life, for then he will be a coward, and will not escape. He must not merely wait for death, for then he will be a suicide, and will not escape. He must seek his life in a spirit of furious indifference to it; he must desire life like water and yet drink death like wine. No philosopher, I fancy, has ever expressed this romantic riddle with adequate lucidity, and I certainly have not done so. But Christianity has done more: it has marked the limits of it in the awful graves of the suicide and the hero, showing the distance between him who dies for a great cause and him who dies for the sake of dying. And it has held up ever since above the European lances the banner of the mystery of chivalry: the Christian courage, which is a disdain of death; not the Chinese courage, which is a disdain of life.

The feature of incidents in life that bring with them disgrace and punishment which needs to be insisted on for those to whom the thought of suicide comes, is that the sensation which the revelation of such acts causes is but a passing phase of present-day publicity, and that after all it is not even a nine-days' wonder, but a two- or three-days' wonder, and then it is forgotten and replaced by something else. The facing of the condemnation for the moment may seem an extremely severe trial. The world's blame, however, is largely a bogey, a dread that is phantom-like and that disappears, or at least diminishes, to a great degree as soon as it is bravely faced. Besides, as practically every man who has been carrying around a guilty secret with him for years is free to confess, there is an immense sense of relief once the worst is known. At last the effort at concealment, the nervous tension, the fear of the moment of exposure are all past and a new set of thoughts can be allowed to come. Those may be unpleasant and yet they are not so bad as the dread of discovery that hung over the unfortunate. If a man can be braced up to meet exposure, usually he will find in a very few days that there are sources of consolation that make it much easier for him to live than he thought possible before.

Real Suffering a Tonic.—Probably the best remedy for a man or a woman who talks of suicide and seems to fear lest the temptation should overcome them is, if possible, to give them an opportunity to see some real suffering. I have on a number of occasions had the opportunity to note the effect on a discouraged man or woman of the sight of a cancer patient suffering severely, yet bearing the suffering patiently, wishing that the end might come, yet ready to wait until it shall come in the appointed order of nature. Suffering, like everything else, becomes much more bearable with inurement to it. The old have learned the lesson of not only not looking for pleasure in life, but of being quite satisfied with their lot if no pain comes to them, and they even grow to consider that they have not much right to murmur if their pain is not too severe. It is not among those who have to suffer severe pain that one finds suicides as a rule. It is true that young, strong, healthy persons who suddenly find that pain is to be their lot for a prolonged period may grow so discouraged and moody over it as to take their lives. The patients that I have seen suffering from incurable diseases have expressed no desire at all that their life should be shortened, except during the paroxysms of their pain, unless they feel that they are a serious burden on others when they may express the wish to be no more.

Euthanasia.—Every now and then there is a discussion in the newspapers {724} of the justifiableness of euthanasia, that is, the giving of a pleasant death to those who are known to be incurably ill and who are doomed to suffer pain for most of what is left of their existence. The question usually discussed is whether patients have the right to shorten their own existence and then, also, whether their physician might have the right or, even as some people say, the duty, to lessen human suffering by abbreviating existence for such incurable cases. The discussion has always seemed to me beside the realities of things, because physicians do not see many patients, I might almost say any patients, who really want to shorten their lives or would want to have them shortened. I have known many physicians die of cancer, but very seldom is it that one tries to shorten his own existence, or that even his best friend in the profession would consider that he was justified in doing this for him. This, it seems to me, should be the test of the problem. It is true that not infrequently, in the midst of their paroxysms of pain, patients wish they were dead, but there come intervals of surcease from discomfort to some degree at least that make life quite livable for a time again and even occasionally there is real happiness in these intervals, deep, human, natural happiness in heroic forbearance and example.

We can recall Æsop's fable of the old man who, gathering wood for the fire in the winter that he needed so much, finds the burden of his labor and the wood too much for him and calls loudly for death to come to him. Promptly Death makes his appearance and asks what the old man wants. "Oh! nothing," is the reply; "only I would like you to help me to carry this bundle of sticks." This is the attitude of mind of practically all who have grown old in suffering. They have learned to bear with patience, and that patience gives even something of satisfaction. After all, it is not so often the pleasant things in life that we look back on and recall with most satisfaction as the difficulties and trials. Virgil said long ago, *"Forsan et hoc olim meminisse juvabit"*—perhaps at some future time we shall recall these, our trials and pains, with pleasure. It is the conquering of difficulty that means most for men and even the standing of pain is not without an aftermath, if not of pleasure, at least of broad human satisfaction. When we talk about euthanasia, then, it would be well to ask some of these old people whether they want it or not. Seldom will the answer be found to be that which is so often presumed, by those in good health and strength, to be inevitable under such conditions.

Physicians have all seen incurable cancer patients who were approaching their end inevitably and with the fatal termination not far off, have hours and days of alleviation of suffering and even of enjoyment that made up for the prolongation of life almost in the midst of constant agony. The distinguished New York surgeon who had the pleasure a few years ago of listening once more to his favorite singer and fairly seemed to get renewed life from the inspiration of her voice and who for days after had the pleasant consciousness of smooth running life in improvement so characteristic of convalescence, is a typical example of what may happen under such circumstances. I shall not soon forget Dr. Thomas Dunn English, the well-known author of "Sweet Alice, Ben Bolt," saying at an Alumni dinner of the University of Pennsylvania, that, like Bismarck, he used to think that all the joys of life's existence were in the first eighty years of life, but of late years he had found {725} that many of them were also in the second eighty years of life. He was at the time 83. He made the most joyous and happiest speech on that occasion. He was quite blind, was almost deaf, had been reported dying some months before, and had gone through prolonged suffering, yet he was by his cheeriness and whole-hearted gaiety on that occasion a joy and inspiration to all the younger men at the table.

Dread of Suicide.—There are patients who come to the physician worked up because they fear they may commit suicide. Every now and then the thought comes to them that some time or other they will perhaps throw themselves out of a window, or be tempted to drop in front of a passing train, or over the side of a steamboat, or impulsively take poison. Some nervous people become quite disturbed by these thoughts. Every physician is sure to have some patients who must be reassured, every now and then, that they are not likely to commit

383

suicide. Their nervousness over the fear of this may serve to make them supremely miserable and it evidently becomes the doctor's duty to reassure them. It is not difficult to do this, as a rule, provided the physician will be absolutely confident and unhesitating in his declaration that there is no danger that they will commit suicide, since it has almost never been known that patients who dread it very much and, above all, those who dread it so much that they take others into their confidence in the matter, take their own lives. The very fact that the thought produces so much horror and disturbance in them is the best proof that they will not impulsively do anything irretrievable in this way.

Prof. Dubois has discussed this subject in his usual thoroughly practical way and his words serve as an authoritative confirmation of what has been already said, though as a matter of fact the expressions and experience of nearly every nervous specialist thoroughly justify the position here assumed. Besides, it must be realized that this confident assurance is the best possible prop that doubting patients can have with regard to the actions they dread, and by positive declarations the physician will accomplish more than in any other way.

There are patients who are subject to strange obsessions. They are afraid that they will throw themselves out of the door of a car, or climb over the parapet of a bridge. They are afraid that they will throw their relatives out of a window, or will wound somebody with a knife or a gun. There are some with a strong impulse to open their veins. But if there is a certain attraction in such things, it is really a phobia. It tends to make one shrink back and not to act.

Nothing quiets these patients like the frequently repeated statement that they will not do anything. It is necessary to show them the vast distance there is between the impulse toward suicide and murder and the phobia which, however distressing it may be, is a safeguard. One must keep at this education of the mind with imperturbable persistence and use the most forceful and convincing arguments that one can think of to correct the judgment of his patient, in order to make the strings of moral feeling and reason vibrate in unison.

It is through lack of courage and perseverance that we err in the treatment of these psychoneuroses. We wait too long to distinguish the morbid entities that bear on a certain etiology or a different prognosis. We do not see clearly enough the bond which unites these different affections.

It may seem to some physicians as though they would be assuming too much responsibility in giving patients such positive assurance that their dreads {726} will not be fulfilled, but as a matter of fact the experience of physicians is quite sufficient to justify the confident statements here suggested. It is true that occasionally a person who afterwards commits suicide talks the matter over and hints at the possibility of taking his own life. He does not, as a rule, speak of it with dread, however, but as one of the alluring solutions of his difficulties that he sees ahead of him. He is much more likely to write a letter to his physician telling him that all his arrangements are made and that by the time this letter reaches him he will be already dead. The prospective suicide is usually quite secretive about this purpose, not only to friends, lest he should be prevented from accomplishing it, but even with his physician, in whom he has had absolute confidence and to whom he has told practically everything else. The patients who fear the possibility of committing suicide, who tell how much they dread the horror of it, and who rush to consult the physician to help them against themselves, show by the very fact the unlikelihood of action on their part.

The Physician and Suicide.—By mental influence, then, the physician may lessen the tendency to suicide in the individual and in the community. To do this is to save suffering and to help in the solution of one of the most serious social problems in modern times. It can only be accomplished by a sympathetic attitude towards the whole subject and a tactful understanding of each individual case. Every effort in the matter, however, is well worth while, for there is no more hideous blot on our modern civilization than the startling increase of suicide. It is particularly important to bring about improvement in this regard among young suicides, and fortunately it is here that the influence of the physician for good is likely to be most felt. The saving of life is the noblest part of the mission of the physician and nowhere, perhaps, can this be accomplished more successfully than with regard to some of these patients whom a rash resolution, due to a momentary fit of depression and a sense of suffering exaggerated out of all proportion to their actual pain, is hurrying out of life.

CHAPTER IV

GRIEF

Grieving would seem at first glance to be one of the conditions for which the physician, especially if the etymology of the name of his profession be taken strictly, should not be called upon to minister, nor his remedies be expected to relieve. Grief is usually supposed to be due to moral ills and, therefore, at most to come under the care of the alienist, with the feeling that even he can accomplish very little for what is an affective rather than a true mental disorder. There is no doubt at all, however, that grieving, especially in the excess that shows it to be pathological, is always associated with certain physical and mental conditions for which the physician can accomplish much. Indeed more often than not the physical condition of the grief-stricken person is a prominent factor in the production of the state of feeling which causes grief to be exaggerated, while, on the other hand, this state of mind {727} itself reacts upon the physical being so as to make it more sluggish in all its functions, and as a consequence a vicious circle of cause and effect is formed affecting unfavorably both the mental and physical conditions. It is when patients are run down in health that grief becomes extremely difficult or apparently impossible to bear and grief itself still further brings about a deterioration of health that makes the mind's reactionary power against its gloomy feelings still weaker than they were.

Viewed in this way, grief is an ailment that should properly come to the physician for treatment and with regard to which that important principle is eminently true that the physician cannot always cure, but he can nearly always relieve, and he can always console his patients. On the one hand, an improvement in the general health always make grief easier to bear because it increases the resistive vitality of both mind and body. On the other, any diversion of mind that lifts the burden of grief even to some degree, releases new stimuli and physical powers for the restoration of bodily function to the normal and this brings about an immediate lessening of the depressive condition. In a word, for the vicious circle of unfavorable influences ever pushing the victim farther into depression, a virtuous circle, in the Latin sense of the word virtue, meaning courage, favoring strength, must be formed, that brings about an immediate improvement in the patient's mental and physical well-being. This is not a pretty bit of theory but is the result of the experience of every physician who has ever taken seriously the problems of caring for the grief-stricken.

Natural and Pathological Grief.—It is, of course, not easy to distinguish between grief that may be called morbid in the sense of a melancholy, that is, more than natural—a true mental disease—and that which represents only an affective state accompanied by depression from which there will be complete reaction. A mother loses a favorite, it may be an only son, and is plunged into grief. For days, even weeks, she refuses to take any interest in life, she thinks moodily about the awful affliction that has come to her and how blank the future is, and she cannot be aroused to attend either to her own affairs or to the duties of life around her. Such a grief is, in many cases, not more than the normal depression incident to such a loss. If after months, however, the mother still continues to refuse to take interest in life and the things around her, especially if, besides, she now talks of having been visited with this punishment because of some unpardonable sin in her own life, or because the Deity has been offended beyond all hope of propitiation, then the case verges over into one of true melancholy in which the mental depression is not merely a symptom of a passing condition, but partakes of the nature of a mental disease, or is the consequence of a profound neurotic condition.

It must not be forgotten that there is always the danger that exaggerated grief, as it seems for the moment to be, may be only the first symptom of a true melancholic condition. Only too often friends and physicians have been deceived by this. Some of the sad cases of self-destruction and a few cases of homicide and suicide have followed a condition that seemed to be only abnormal grief for the loss of a relative.

Etiology.—The cause of exaggerated, prolonged grief is, in a considerable proportion of the cases, a melancholic tendency, that is, a failure on the {728} part of the mind to react against depression. The weakness of mind that predisposes to this may be inherent or acquired. Sometimes no special loss is needed to produce melancholia in susceptible individuals, while occasionally it is precipitated by some misfortune, inasmuch as this is a mental disease, very little can be done directly, and yet the patient can be helped and diversion of mind may bring a good measure of relief. More often, however, the reason for persistent grieving is that before the disturbing loss came into the life of the individual there had been a serious deterioration in health. This was due to the conditions preceding the unfortunate event. Wives sometimes have worn themselves out physically and mentally while nursing husbands, or mothers their children, and this has produced a lack of physical force which prevents them from reacting with healthy mentality against the subsequent shock of loss.

Prophylaxis.—For the melancholic tendency prophylaxis cannot be special, but must be general. We cannot prevent people from suffering serious losses, but we can foresee the possibility of a loss proving very depressing, and can, therefore, try to keep the individual in reasonably good physical condition. If this is done the subsequent depression will be much less than it otherwise would be. Very often there is little or no recognition of the fact that there is a definite tendency in some patients to too great an inclination toward melancholic thoughts, and it is not until an exaggerated manifestation of it comes that the danger is realized. It is not easy to make patients realize the dangers, but where the physician talks with assurance and points out definite things to do in order to prevent serious developments, patients, or at least their friends, can be made to appreciate the dangers.

The best demonstration that I know of the value of work as a remedy for grief is my experience with members of religious orders. For them, as a rule, there is no interruption in life no matter what the loss may be. Their work goes on the day after the funeral just as before. This is the most precious possible arrangement, time and occupation of mind are the two factors that will dull the edge of grief and while humanly we may resent the consolation that is thus brought by such conventional things as the passage of time and humdrum occupations, they represent nature's resources. Above all, patients must be given something to do and if that something concerns other suffering human beings, there is every reason to expect relief.

Treatment.—The most important element in the treatment of grief cases is to prevent physical running down as far as possible and to build up the physical condition. Depression that comes to patients who have lost considerable weight, even though it may show some of the signs of melancholia, is always hopeful. Where patients are twenty or thirty pounds under weight the recovery of weight up to the normal condition will often mean the relief of their depressed condition. The one hope lies in this physical improvement. Mental treatment by diversion of mind must, of course, be practiced. This does not mean getting the patients interested once more in trivial things, but to be successful it means arousing the deeper feelings of their nature. Above all, the solace of tears will often save depressed and grieving persons from themselves. An interest in the sufferings of other people that awaken their sympathy will do the most to end exaggerated grieving over their own loss. The self-centeredness of their grief is the principal reason for its exaggeration. {729} It is because of overestimation of their own importance and of the importance of their loss that these people suffer severely.

Motives of Consolation.—The main resource of the physician who would employ psychotherapy for the treatment of those who are grieving beyond the limit of what is normal, is to supply motives by which they can understand the real significance of their loss. Very often, especially in young folks, there is no proper estimation of values in life and no recognition of the fact that human life was evidently not meant for happiness since that comes to but few, while suffering and partings are inevitable. They come to all, and apparently will always continue to do so. It is the young or, at least, those under middle age, who are most likely to be affected by exaggerated depression over losses and disappointments. Older folks have grown more accustomed to such incidents. These patients must be made to see how many motives there are to take their grief philosophically and while permitting themselves the luxury of sorrow, not to let this interfere either with their physical condition or their mental state to such a degree as to prevent them from taking the proper interest in their duties in life.

The ethical motives that may be urged to keep people from grieving over-much are many, but there is sometimes the feeling in the physician's mind that it is scarcely his business to emphasize them in any way. It is supposed that to the clergyman must be committed the task of consoling people for losses in life. This has always seemed to me a serious mistake. As physicians we know how much the mind influences the body and since it is our duty to care for the body, we must, above all and first of all, care for the mind as far as we can. *Mens sana in corpore sano* is a very old motto and is usually taken only in the sense that to have a healthy mind one must have a healthy body. In its Latin form, however, it might very well also be taken to mean that to have a healthy body one must have a healthy mind. Since grief has an untoward influence on the body, physicians are bound to learn what to do for it in any and every possible way and to exercise every faculty they have for its relief. This is all the more true because in recent years many persons have no regular religious attendant who would come to offer them consolation or to whom they would go in their trouble. It is not at all with the idea of infringing on the rights of the clergy or invading his territory that I would insist not only on the right of the medical man, but even his duty, to afford consolation to the mind as well as relief for the body.

The Family Physician.—In older times the family physician was a friend of the family to whom people turned in all troubles where he might possibly be of aid, with just as much confidence and as promptly as they did to their religious attendant. Unfortunately, in the progress of medicine, though still more because of the social vicissitudes that have taken place in recent years, this relationship of the family physician has been largely diminished, but that constitutes only one more reason why every physician, to whose attention the grief of a patient for any loss is presented as a cause of ill-health, should know all the means and be ready to employ them for the amelioration of the condition. As a matter of fact, there is often a feeling on the part of patients that it is more or less the business of the clergyman to afford consolation and that the performance of his duty in this matter is somewhat conventional, not {730} as if he performed it less thoroughly because of this, but as if the feeling of the routine practice detracted from its effectiveness. Some of the motives for consolation advanced by the clergyman, then, lose in significance, in some persons' minds at least, because of this feeling, while motives presented by the physician rather gain in weight because of the impression that he is a thoroughly practical man, deeply interested in life's problems from a common-sense standpoint, and who knows the motives for consolation because he has realized that losses are inevitable, suffering unavoidable, and grief sure to come, though somehow we must learn to bear up bravely under life as we find it.

Physicians have always done this in the past, but in more recent years either they have lost the habit, or have considered it unworthy of their profession, or else, perhaps, only too often they themselves have had no motives to offer that might seem sources of consolation for those in suffering and especially those who are grieved for the loss of friends. If life were a mere chance, if there were not an evident purpose in it, if, as Lord Kelvin insisted, science did not demonstrate (not "suggest" but "demonstrate" is the word he used) the existence of a Creator and a Providence, Who, while caring for the huge concerns of the universe, can just as well employ Himself with the little details of human life, then there would be some reason for physicians thinking that their science kept them from seeking consolation from the ordinary motives. Even if they occupy an advanced agnostic position, however, they may still find sources of consolation that, if not so effective as those attached to the old beliefs, at least will provide something for the forlorn to take hold of, that will mitigate their grief and sense of loss and make the present and the future look not all too blank.

Few men have been so thoroughly agnostic as Prof. Huxley, yet on the death of his wife he found that some of the thoughts of the old beliefs might prove a source of consolation. Huxley had loved his wife very dearly and their separation by death meant very much. The epitaph that he wrote for her sums up his doubts yet plucks out of them something to console, expressed in old Scriptural language:

```
And if there be no meeting past the grave.
If all is darkness, silence, yet 'tis rest.
Be not afraid, ye waiting hearts that weep.
For God still giveth His beloved sleep;
And if an endless sleep He wills, so best.
```

Attitude Toward Death.—The ordinary attitude of people toward death is a very curious one. Death is the one absolutely certain thing in life after birth, yet most of us live our lives without much regard to it, and whenever it comes and under whatever circumstances, at whatever age, it is always a shock to us. No matter how old people are it always comes a little before it is expected. When death comes it is always a shock and all that can be said of it is what Hamlet resents when the commonplace consolations for the loss of his father, who also lost a father and so on all down the course of history, are offered to him. Perhaps, however, as much the reason for his resentment was the person who offered the consolation as the form of the consolation itself, which, after all, exhausts nearly all that we can say in this matter for grief for near and dear ones:

{731}

```
King.
  'Tis sweet and commendable in your nature, Hamlet,
  To give these mourning duties to your father:
  But, you must know, your father lost a father;
```

```
That father lost, lost his; and the survivor bound
In filial obligation, for some term
To do obsequious sorrow: but to persevere
In obstinate condolement, is a course
Of impious stubbornness: 'tis unmanly grief:
     . . . Fie! 'tis a fault to heaven,
A fault against the dead, a fault to nature.
To reason most absurd, whose common theme
Is death of fathers, and who still hath cried,
From the first corse, till he that died to-day,
"This must be so."
```

Death and Pain.—One of the most effective consolations in our day for all classes of people, quite apart from religious affiliations or beliefs, is the sociological import of death and suffering in the world. Life, without suffering and death in it, would be a riot of selfishness. Men, as a rule, would not care for others at all, the weak would go to the wall, the individuals who possess less efficiency than others would simply have to make out as best they could, and bad as social conditions are now, they would be intolerably worse. As it is the young and strong and vigorous have very little of true sympathy. Nothing makes a man feel for others like having gone through some suffering himself. On the other hand, nothing makes him feel the impotence of struggling ceaselessly for vain success and the futile rewards of life than to lose near and dear friends whose share in that success and joy over the rewards would constitute their only real value and justification. As a man grows older and has gone through some of the sufferings and has had to bear the losses of life, he learns more and more to feel for others, he is ready even to make sacrifices that others may not have to suffer as he has suffered, he has charity for them for the sake of his own suffering and that of near and dear ones, and things are much better than they could possibly be without suffering and death.

Therapy by Example.—Many men have taken losses so seriously as to think that life held no more for them, and have foolishly given up their occupations, yet have found that Time, the great healer, could work his marvels in their case as well as in most others and that new interests and, above all, their life work, could arouse them to a sense of duty and bring them back to the old routine of life. Dr. Mumford, in his "Sketch of Sir Astley Cooper," tells the story of how even that veteran surgeon gave up everything at the death of his wife and yet found, after a year of idleness, that he had to come back to the old life again. Dr. Mumford says: "Sir Astley Cooper was an emotional man. In 1827 his wife died, and the event prostrated him with grief. He felt that all the interests of life were over for him. He fell into an acute physical decline, sold his town house, threw up his practice and other professional employments, and retired to his country place to pass his last days. Within a year of the sad event he had returned to town, taken another house, resumed practice with increased vigor, and married again. He was then sixty years old, he lived on until 1841, and died in his seventy-fourth year."

{732}

A typical example of how much a strong man whose diplomatic ability had stamped him as one of the large men of his generation may yet be afflicted beyond measure by a loss of this kind is to be found in the life of the second Lord Lytton. I have told it somewhat in detail in the chapter on Periodic Depression. After the death of his boy Lord Lytton, who for more than a week of anguish had watched unceasingly at the death-bed of his dying son, came to the conclusion that God was not in His world or, at least, that the arm of Providence was shortened if such (as it seemed to him) needless suffering was permitted. The boy had probably suffered much less than the bystanders thought and much less than he seemed to, for in these cases nearly always there is a merciful deadening of the senses that to a great extent eliminates suffering, but Lord Lytton could not understand and refused ever to look at life from the same standpoint afterwards. This is, of course, only what happens in many cases, but it represents an exaggeration of grief since death and suffering have always been in the world and sometimes they will come to those near and dear to us, much as we may resent it.

Neither profound intelligence nor the sympathetic genius of the poet or artist is sufficient to safeguard men against the severer forms of griefs for loss. Louis, the distinguished French physician (to whom we in America are indebted so much as the Master of the Boston and Philadelphia schools of diagnosis, and, above all, for his teaching of the differentiation between typhoid and typhus fever), suffered so much from the loss of his son that he could scarcely be consoled. Dante Gabriel Rossetti was so much affected by the death of his wife that he put into her coffin the only manuscript copy of his poems that he possessed. It is interesting to learn that some years later he had the coffin exhumed and took out his manuscript at the urging of friends, and published the poems. Many other examples of this kind might be given, for exaggeration of grief affects all classes and conditions in life. They are practically always pathological, usually on a basis of somewhat disturbed mentality, though often the real underlying and predisposing condition is the physical exhaustion that has preceded the loss and which makes patients unable to bear the strain of it after weeks of care, solicitude, anxiety and neglect of eating and sleep.

CHAPTER V

DOUBTING

In recent years the attention of physicians has been called to the fact that many people are made profoundly miserable by an unconquerable tendency to doubt about nearly everything that has happened to them, or is happening, or is about to happen. This is not a new phenomenon, but introspection has emphasized it, leisure gives more opportunity for it, and so physicians hear more of it now than they did in the past. This doubting tendency sometimes makes serious inroads on the peace of mind of sufferers from it because they cannot make up their minds to do things, even to take exercise, to eat as {733} they should in quantity or quality, and to share the ordinary life around them sufficiently to get such diversion of mind as will keep their physical functions normal. The state used to be described as a neurasthenia (nervous weakness), but in recent years has come better to be designated as in the class of psychasthenias (lack of mental energy). It is always a mental trouble in the sense that it is difficult for these patients to make up their minds about things, yet it is not a mental disease in the ordinary sense of the term, and these people are often eminently sane and thoroughly intellectual when their attention has been once profoundly attracted. They may even, under favorable circumstances, be active and useful helpers in great causes, yet there is always to be observed in them a certain noteworthy difference in mentality from the normal. The physician can do more for an affection of this kind than is usually thought, and he is probably the only one who can thoroughly appreciate and sympathize and, therefore, be helpful in the condition.

Sufferers are often laughed at by their friends and relatives and are likely to be the subjects of at least a little ridicule if they take their troubles to their physician. As a matter of fact, however, doubting is a typical case for psychotherapeutics and not only can much be done for its relief, but it can be kept from disturbing the general health, which it is prone to do if neglected, and by mental discipline and acquired habits of self-control, the doubting habit may be almost completely eradicated.

Exaggeration of Ordinary State of Mind.—The first thing absolutely necessary to impress upon the minds of these victims of their own doubts is that their condition is by no means unique, it is not even very singular, but is only an exaggeration of that hesitancy and tendency to put off making decisions that practically every person finds in a lifelong experience. This frame of mind is rather cultivated by education and by a large accumulation of knowledge. The less one knows the easier it is to come to decisions about difficult problems and to form conclusions without hesitancy. The young man will decide anything under the sun, and a few other things besides, almost without a moment's hesitation, and after but slight consideration. Twenty years later he looks back and wonders how he did it, and having done it, how he succeeded in turning the practical conclusions to which he came to advantage. The scholar is eminently a doubter and a hesitater, and we recognize that he loses certain of the qualities that would make him a practical man of affairs, though he gains so much more that broadens and deepens life's significance that there can be no doubt about the value of his liberal education.

"Hamlet" is just the story of one of these doubters and hesitaters. He saw his duty clearly and that duty was imperative. In spite of cumulative evidence, however, he refused to go on to the performance of that duty, urging to himself now one and now another reason of delay, until finally he wonders whether it would not be worth the while to take his own life, rather than try any longer to solve the problems that lie around him demanding solution. When he finally does something, his hand is forced and circumstances have so arranged themselves that instead of one clean-cut punishment for a great crime, there is the tragedy that involves six lives, including his own. The play seems to involve such exceptional characters and to be written around such an unusual set of circumstances that it might be thought {734} that it would prove uninteresting for men and women generally. As a matter of fact, however, "Hamlet" is the most popular of Shakespeare's plays and probably the most popular play, both for readers and auditors, that was ever written. There are commentaries by the hundred on it in nearly every modern language. Men have been more interested in this figment of Shakespeare's imagination than in any man that ever lived. Caesar and Napoleon have not attracted so much attention. Only Homer and Dante have been perhaps more written about than Hamlet.

Shakespeare has emphasized the condition of Hamlet by showing us an eminently well educated man. His deep interest in literature, and especially in dramatic literature and all that relates to the stage, can be appreciated very readily from his speech to the players. No one but a man of profound critical ability and deep intellectual interests could have so summed up the actors' relation to the drama. Of course, this is Shakespeare himself talking and unthinking people have said that this was a purple patch fastened on the play because it gave the author an opportunity to express his views with regard to actors and their ways. Instead of that, it is of the very essence of the development of Hamlet's character and shows us the scholarly amateur who knows so much about many things that he has become quite unable to make up his mind about the practical problems that lie before him. James Russell Lowell says that Shakespeare sent Hamlet to Wittenberg, though Wittenberg was not founded until centuries after Hamlet existed—and Shakespeare probably knew that very well—because Wittenberg in Shakespeare's time, on account of its connection with Luther and the religious revolt in Germany, had the widespread repute of occupying men's minds with doubts about many of the things that had been deemed perfectly settled before, and its popular reputation serves to give an added hint as to the character of Hamlet as the dramatist saw it.

Once those who are perturbed by doubts learn that the reason for the universal human interest in Hamlet is that there is a large capacity for doubt of self in every man and woman, that we all put off making decisions whenever possible, sometimes refuse to open letters when they come if we fear that they will contain some disturbing news, put off writing letters because we have to state ideas definitely, apparently hope that the day and the night will bring us counsel and that somehow the decision will be made for us without the trouble of making up our minds, then they lose their sense of discouragement over their condition and appreciate that they are suffering only from an exaggeration, probably temporary and quite eradicable, of a state of mind that comes to practically every human being.

This is the important thing, because on it can be founded the only really hopeful therapy of the condition. Doubting is a habit that may be increased by yielding to it, but that can be diminished to a very great extent by constant discipline, which refuses to permit doubts and hesitancy and bravely makes decisions, even though there may be the feeling that they may prove to be wrong.

Extent of Affection.—If such discipline is not instituted, then the lengths to which the doubting hesitant habit may go are almost incredible. I have had patients tell me that they doubted about nearly everything in the past. A very dear friend once confided to me that it was always a source of bother {735} to him that he was not quite sure whether he was married or not. His marriage I knew had been a public ceremonial, and he had led his bride down the aisle to the strains of the "Wedding March" in quite conventional style, but he was hesitant of speech, especially under excitement, and he was not sure that he had ever said "I will" to the question of the clergyman, for there was a constriction at his throat at the moment and he could utter no sound. The absence of any audible sound from the groom is not so unusual as to attract attention and, of course, his intention and his bodily presence and everything else gave the assent without the necessity for the word, but he could not get out of his mind the thought that possibly he was not married and at times it gave him poignant discomfort. He was a thoroughly intelligent man, a teacher and a writer, with no abnormalities that attracted attention, and his tendency to doubt was only known to very near friends who laughed at it and had no idea at all of the annoyance that it often gave its unfortunate victim.

I have a clergyman friend who has had some serious scruples with regard to his ordination. He is a Catholic priest and at a certain part of the ceremonial of ordination it is considered necessary for the candidate for orders to touch at the same moment the paten, the small metal plate on which the Host is placed, and the chalice. This clergyman is not sure that he had done this simultaneously. As a rule, great care is exercised in seeing that all the details of the ordination ceremonies are carried out very exactly and as there are a number of attendants on the altar whose duty it is to see that the absolutely necessary details are properly fulfilled, it is quite improbable that any mistake in this matter was made. The young clergyman, however, had not made an act of conscious attention at the moment when he was supposed to do this, and consequently he could not be sure afterwards whether he had done it or not. He thought of it as the very essence of his ordination and he feared that all his subsequent acts as a clergyman might be impaired by this negligence.

Trivial Doubts.—It is not alone with regard to important things, however, that people may doubt and are disturbed by doubts, but with regard to every trivial thing in life, if they permit the habit to grow on them. Doubting is, after all, one of the phobias, that is to say, it is the fear that something may happen if the decision they make is wrong, that causes people to hesitate so much. There is a tendency in all of us which, if undisciplined, may make us put off the doing of things until the last moment. It is easy to resolve the night before that we will do certain things the next day, but when the next day comes we find excuses to put them off. I have already suggested as a symptom that some people put off the opening of letters. There are probably more who do this than anyone has any idea of. Delay in answering letters is probably much more often due to hesitancy of decision than to actual laziness. We doubt as to what we should say about certain things, and we do not care to take the trouble of making up our minds, and we fear if we do make up our minds it may be wrong, so we adjourn the whole matter to another time and keep on adjourning it. Many people are quite ready to confess that they do not do things until they have to, though few are ready to acknowledge that it is due to hesitancy or doubting about themselves and their decisions.

{736}

Of course, the man who doubts whether he has locked the door of his house after he gets to bed can only satisfy himself by getting up and actually investigating the state of affairs. Then there is the man who doubts whether he has locked his safe at the office. He may get his doubts just as he reaches the foot of the elevator and then if he is wise he will go back and determine the matter. If he is wise with experience he will also deliberately determine while he is there whether the office window is closed and locked and will make a conscious act when he comes out as to the locking of the office door. If he does not do all this he will have further doubts on the way up town and at his home during the evening which will make the doing of anything else a matter of discomfort and he will spoil the restfulness of his after-dinner hours. Some men conquer their first doubt, make their way home only to be beset by so many doubts that at the end of an hour they go back to their office and determine whether the safe is locked or not. Finding it locked they may forget to notice other things about the office and then they will surely have doubts about these, and they may have to go back again and see about them.

Then there is the man who doubts whether he posted a letter or if he did post it, who doubts whether it found its way down to the bottom of the mail box, or whether it may not have caught on a projecting screw or bolt or some portion of the upper part of the box and so fail of collection; he may go back several times to determine this. Doubts about even more trivial matters than this, however, annoy some people. I have known widows on whom the responsibility of managing the financial affairs of the household had been thrown for the first time after their husbands' death, who constantly doubted whether they could afford to spend this or that, though they were regularly saving money from their income. Over and over again they would have to go over all their recent expenditures to decide whether they could afford certain expenses. Such little things as the sort of paper to use in their correspondence, the wages they paid their servants, the amount of waste in the food in the household, all aroused in them doubts and set them to calculating once more just what was the relation of their income to expenditure, all to no purpose, for they would have the same doubts the next week or month.

Then there are people who doubt whether their friends really think anything of them. They think that though they treat them courteously this may be only common politeness and they may really resent their wasting their time when they call on them. They hesitate to ask these people to do things for them, though over and over again the friends may have shown their willingness and, above all, by asking favors of them in turn, may have shown that they were quite willing to put themselves under obligations. They doubt about their charities. They wonder whether they may really not be doing more harm than good, though they have investigated the cases or have had them investigated and the object of their charity may have been proved to be quite deserving. They hesitate about the acquisition of new friends, and doubt whether they should give them any confidence and whether the confidences that they have received from them are not really baits. This is, of course, a verging on suspicion as well as hesitancy and doubt, but the stories of how these people try to conquer themselves, yet have to

389

make decision after decision, each one requiring time and a certain resolution of mind, are quite {737} pitiable. It gets worse rather than better unless a definite discipline of opposition and control is organized.

What ordinary people do habitually and easily and without any effort of mind, these people must waste time and mental energy over so that it is extremely difficult for them to accomplish anything. Training of mind, as of hand, consists in making certain actions so habitual that they are accomplished quite automatically. If we have decided that we are to get up at a certain hour we get up at that hour and do not have to make up our minds about it again, though this is one of the actions in which we all have the most lapses and the most need of renewal of resolution and habit. We make up our mind what we are going to eat and gradually acquire the habit of eating a certain quantity and a certain variety at meals and then we do not have to make up our minds about it every time. We go out, to do whatever must be done in our occupation quite automatically and there is no need of wasting mental energy over decisions about it. It is this that the doubter cannot do. He or she calls every trifling act before the supreme court of last decision, the bar of intellect, to decide whether it is worth while doing, whether it is to be done or not, how it is to be done, and then there is a doubt whether after it is done it may not prove to be quite the wrong thing to have done. This adds so much to the friction of life that all the surplus energy is used up in the settling of trivial matters, and nothing worth while is accomplished.

Sir James Paget once expressed all the realities of the situation of many of these people in a few terse phrases. It is probably the best explanation of its kind that we have and it deserves to be in the notebook and often before the mind of physicians who treat neurotic patients. Sir James said: "The patient says 'She cannot'; her friends say 'She will not'; the truth is she cannot will."

The expression, of course, applies to many other phases of so-called nervous disease besides doubting and especially to the psychasthenias. It represents, indeed, the keynote of many of these puzzling affections. The fact that it was uttered more than half a century ago shows how much better these affections were understood two generations before ours than we are likely to think, and how well physicians then got to the heart of them. From this to the re-education of will, that mental discipline and relearning of self-control which constitutes the essence of the treatment of them, is but a short step.

Prophylaxis.—*Serious Occupation.*—Of course, the real way out of the trouble is to have to do certain important things that occupy the mind and require the doing of many other things as subsidiaries which must be accomplished in order to carry out the greater resolution. Men who have important affairs on their hands seldom are bothered by doubts and hesitancy. Women who have not much to do make mountains out of the molehills of their little occupations and every trifle must be adjudged. The larger interests must be cultivated, the smaller ones must be turned over to the automaton which every one of us can develop in our persons if we only set about it resolutely. Each thing that comes up must be settled at once and action must replace contemplation. The Hamlet in us all must be put down and resolution must not be allowed to be sicklied over with the pale cast of thought. We must do {738} things and not think about them too much. The doubters can learn this lesson. They will never be entirely without hesitancy, but they can remove many of their difficulties, and live to accomplish much in spite of their make-up.

Physical Treatment.—The physical treatment of the doubting state consists, of course, in bringing the individual's physical condition as near as possible up to the normal. When the state occurs in people who are under weight its betterment is rather easy. The special feature of the physical condition that needs seeing to is an ample supply of fresh air. People who live in ill-ventilated places, or who do not get out into the air enough, are almost sure to suffer from the tendency to avoid the making of decisions. The man of decision usually is a vigorous outdoor-air individual. Even the perfectly healthy man who has been in the house for some reason for days together gets into a state of mind where the making of decisions becomes objectionable. He wants to push things away from him. In individuals who already have a natural tendency this way this is greatly exaggerated by confinement. Arrangements must be made, therefore, that will ensure getting out for some time, not once but twice every day. The regular making of decisions for this purpose is of itself a good mental discipline. It must not be omitted even for rain or snow, unless there are additional reasons of some kind. An abundance of fresh air in the sleeping-room is extremely important and must be secured.

Mental Treatment.—The mental treatment consists in diversion of mind. Usually the doubters have no interests that appeal to them deeply and in which they have to make prompt regular decisions. If possible, these must be secured. They must form habits of doing things regularly and of making up their minds to do them, and then not have to repeat the adjudication and resolution. In recent years people realize, quite apart from its religious significance, the value of what older religious writers called examination of conscience. Regularly before they go to sleep these people must be told to call up what they have done during the day and to note their faults in the matter of putting off doing things and making decisions slowly. They must, however, not only realize their faults, but they must make up their mind to correct them during the following day. They must not leave the arrangement of what they shall do next day to chance, but must decide just how and when they shall do things and then, as far as possible, keep to this program. The program must, of course, be sensible and considerate. This preliminary arrangement can be made to mean much more than might be thought. Some people thus learn to correct entirely their tendency to doubt whether they should do things or not and lessen greatly the difficulties they have in making decisions.

CHAPTER VI

RESPONSIBILITY AND WILL POWER

The development of science (meaning by that term knowledge with regard to physical nature in contradistinction to philosophy or the relation of nature to man) in modern times has brought about in some minds a hesitant, if {739} not frankly contradictory attitude towards the question of free will. There are many scientists who not only doubt the existence of free will, but insist that there cannot be such a thing. For them, man like the animals is determined to do things from without rather than from within. The stronger motive compels him. There may be a weighing in the balance of motives, but that is a question of intellect and not of will. It is true that the stronger motive may be one that is less alluring to nature or to sense than some of the others which clamor for a hearing, but it is eventually the stronger motive that compels. A man may desire something that does not belong to him very much, but the consciousness that it does not belong to him and that to take things that do not belong to him is unworthy of him will override his covetousness and so he remains honest if he has been trained to regard things that way. After all, the old maxim, "Honesty is the best policy," is founded on some such reasoning as this, since only one who is at heart dishonest would consider men as swayed by the thought that to be honest is the most profitable, instead of being the right, and therefore the only proper thing.

The argument for free will that appeals to most men is the consciousness that we are free and that at any given moment we can do a thing or not do it, just as suits us. If two things are presented to us we can do that one which seems right to us to do, or we can do both of them, or we can permit ourselves to be led into the wrong, though always acknowledging to ourselves that it is the wrong and feeling downcast, or at least disturbed, that we should let ourselves be led away from higher motives. Even in this case the determinist insists that we are determined from without by motives due to our training, to our education along certain lines with the influence of the environment in which we live, to the special sentiment that we have within us as a consequence of the influences of preceding life. Such determination, however, does not come from without us, but from within. It is the result of the formation of our wills in a particular direction. The argument is, therefore, a begging of the question. A man may have formed the habit of doing evil things and then finds it easy to do them without compunction. On the other hand, the exercise of his will in doing what he considers right, in spite of the fact that it may not be pleasant at the moment, is a training of the will founded on its essential freedom. There is an essential distinction between right and wrong, and we have it in our power, as many a man has done, to follow the right even though it costs our life.

Bad Temper.—A typical example of supposed determinism, which proves exactly the opposite of what is sometimes urged, may be noted with regard to exhibitions of temper. As Clouston declares in his "Unsoundness of Mind" (Methuen, London, 1911), "an uncontrollable temper is in many cases very like and nearly allied to an unsoundness of mind. It is certain that bad temper may gradually pass into technical insanity and that a considerable number of persons who are passing or have passed into insanity exhibit as the most marked symptom morbidness and violence of temper. 'It's just temper. Doctor,' is one of the most common remarks that I have heard made to me by patients' friends. I think that it is quite certain that in most cases much might be done in youth to establish a reasonable control over temper where it is inclined to be uncontrolled, so preventing serious discomforts in life both to its possessor and to others. In many cases I am satisfied that {740} this education would have the effect of preventing unsoundness of mind also, arising out of uncontrolled temper." There are many examples in the literature of hagiology particularly, from which it is clear that men have learned to control even violent tempers and by self-discipline and training in self-control have even become rather quiet, gentle individuals. The truth of such examples is attested too well to be discredited. This question of training, then, is extremely important.

It has been pointed out that the consciousness of freedom to which an appeal is made in this argument for free will is shared with us by the insane even in the performance of many acts that we know are compelled in certain ways. Insane persons reason themselves into a peculiar state of mind, in which they represent to themselves that they have been persecuted, for instance, by a particular person and then they become persecutors in turn and do harm. As they see their act, it is often a species of self-defense. They themselves have no consciousness, or, at most, a very dim and hazy realization of the inner compulsion to which they are subjected at the time of the act and sometimes talk quite rationally and discuss the motives which impelled them to do things, just as if they were free. We recognize, however, the distinction between this delusion of the insane and the rational state of mind of the sane. We have no definition for insanity, that is, no formula of words, which will absolutely include all the insane and at the same time exclude all the sane, but we have a practical working knowledge that enables us to judge rather well between those who are compelled to do things by delusions, and those who do them from motives that are rationally weighed and that influence a will that is free to follow them as it pleases. We hold the rational man responsible for his acts because he knows he was free not to do them. We punish him partly because he should not have done them and partly because we want him not to do them again, and we know that punishment will help him to keep from committing crime, because it will support his free will against his inclinations, when the time of trial comes again.

Above all, we are conscious of our own responsibility. We know that when we do wrong we are worthy of blame. We know that when we allow covetousness to lead us into the appropriation of what does not belong to us we are deserving of punishment, because we need not have done it, but we yielded to unworthy motives. We know that while anger may be blind we can control it, at least those of us who are fully in possession of our intellectual and voluntary powers, so as to keep from doing violence, even in the heat of it. This dealing with ourselves is the best proof that we have of our recognition of our freedom of will. We are responsible, and what we genuinely do not will to do is not accomplished. Our will may be bent by many attractions, but we know that these motives are not compelling unless we allow them to be. When a child tells us that he did something because he could not help it, we either feel sorry for him because he is not yet in possession of his full faculties or else we laugh at this excuse. There is a tendency to admit this excuse as having a meaning, but only by those who themselves come into court with hands assoiled in some way and who are looking for pardon from others for offenses, and who, above all, want to feel that they can pardon, or at least excuse, themselves.

In recent years we have seriously impaired the idea of responsibility in {741} the minds of the general public by a foolishly sentimental mercifulness to criminals. If a man under indictment for murder can show that he has ever previously in his life acted even slightly irrationally, or if he has been peculiar in certain ways, provided, of course, he has money enough to pay for the opinions, there will be an abundance of expert testimony to declare that he is irresponsible and should not be punished. As a consequence, in many cases justice fails. We are reaping the harvest of this pseudo-scientific invasion of law. Human life is cheaper in no country in the world than it is in America. Our murder rate is going up by leaps and bounds, while that of Canada remains almost stationary, and the reason is that while nine out of ten of all our murderers do not receive the death penalty and many of them escape serious punishment of any kind, nearly as large a proportion of Canadian murderers are punished by death. A man may have his responsibility somewhat impaired and yet retain sufficient free will so that he deserves to be punished for serious crimes. It is hard to decide in certain cases, but in most cases the decision is not difficult if, with the right sense of justice, morbid sentimentality is put aside.

While the doctrine of free will is so clear it is still true that the question of responsibility for actions, and above all for criminal actions, is not so simple as many people used to proclaim it in the past. No two men are free to perform an act or not to perform it in quite the same way. Familiar examples are ready to hand: One man finds no difficulty at all in resisting the inclination to take spirituous liquor to excess; another finds it a most difficult feat, often apparently impossible for him to refrain from indulging to excess almost whenever the opportunity offers, or at least whenever he gets a taste of liquor. This difference between the two men is founded in their very nature. It would be utterly a mistake to praise the one for his abstinence or to blame the other under certain circumstances for his indulgence. Between these two classes there are others quite different individually. Some of them have a slight tendency, and, fearing the worst, do not indulge in it; some of them have a marked tendency which they are able to resist under most circumstances without very much difficulty once they have made up their minds; some are sorely tempted, fall occasionally, yet never become habitual drunkards. For each of these men there is a different responsibility, and so far as they are to be punished a different punishment must be meted out, for it is our effort in the modern time to make the punishment fit the criminal and not the crime.

This same thing holds true for many other forms of crime. Some men readily lose sight of the distinction between mine and thine, and possess themselves of their neighbors' goods almost without realizing that they have done wrong. They are rare, and we have been accustomed to call these people kleptomaniacs. Between these and the man who hesitates to steal, even when starving or for his starving children, there are many degrees of inclination and disinclination toward stealing. The same thing is true to a more noteworthy degree with regard to anger. Anger, the old saw says, is a brief madness. In America we say very frankly that a man who is very angry is mad. In this brief madness he may be led to do things which he would not do at all in his sober senses. Some men easily get into one of these awful fits of anger in which their responsibility is lessened, while others have a calm phlegmatic disposition from which they are scarcely aroused even by the worst forms of abuse or injury, or even physical suffering.

It is evident in all these cases that in order to measure how much of punishment ought to be meted out for acts committed it is more necessary to know the individual than his act. This often becomes an extremely difficult matter, for {742} after the commission of crime every effort is made to make out as little responsibility as possible for the criminal. The easiest way to do this has been to use the insanity plea. As already stated, we have no definition of insanity. It is easy to understand then that there will be a disagreement among physicians as to who is or is not insane, and the result is almost sure to create doubt which tends to obscure the principles on which are based the proper punishment of crime. Now this system is founded on certain wrong principles as regards the administration of Justice. While it is difficult to decide with regard to a man's insanity or sanity, it is not difficult to decide with regard to his punishment when the ordinary purposes of punishment are kept well in view.

The old idea of punishment used to be that of revenge. A man had done a wrong, and what would ordinarily be held a wrong had to be done to him in order that the scales of Justice should be maintained level. At the present time we have no such idea at all. Punishment has two main purposes—the prevention of further disturbance of social order by the particular criminal, and the deterrence of others from like acts. If a man takes away the life of another we do not take away his because thus Justice will be obtained, but we take it away to prevent him from ever doing anything of the same kind again. A man who has committed murder is more likely to do it again than another. He has committed one breach of social order; we shall prevent him forever from committing another of the same kind. This is the very best deterrent to such crimes that there is. It will be said, of course, that these men could not refrain from doing their acts. It is doubtful, however, whether this contention is true in the great majority of cases, and the proper punishment of such as occur furnishes the best possible motive to help others from the commission of like acts.

This holds true for children at a time when their sense of responsibility for their acts is as yet undeveloped. They can be taught, even very early in life, by properly applied punishment, that need not be severe, that they must not do certain things, and then they will not do them, or at least, will do them much less. This is true not only for perfectly rational children, but also for those that are to some degree irrational. Punishment is of great importance in the training of children of low grade intelligence, and there is scarcely any child, however wanting it may be in intellect, that cannot be disciplined into conduct that makes it much less bothersome than would ordinarily be the case. This is well known and it is also well known that the attempt to manage such children without punishment would be extremely difficult, not to say impossible. They do not reason about the thing, they are not quite responsible for their acts; but they do connect punishment with what they have done, and are in many cases deterred from doing it again, especially while they realize that authority is near them and that punishment is inevitable. These are the principles on which the adjudication of punishment for crime must be measured. There is nothing else that can be done if society would preserve itself and its members from those who are irresponsible even in minor degrees.

In this matter practical experience is well worth the while. The lower order of creatures, the animals, we do not consider responsible for their acts in the same way as human beings. We know the value, however, of punishment in deterring them. A dog, for instance, by being whipped a few times when he is young, can be taught not to steal things to eat, and taught that there is an inevitable connection between the taking of such things and the infliction of such punishment. I shall not soon forget my first lesson in philosophy from a dear old professor, who, talking of the memory of animals, demonstrated that they had a memory, from the ordinary experience of mankind with regard to them. "If a cat does something naughty in your room," he said, "you rub its nose in it, and it will not do it again." The cat had no idea that it was doing wrong. According to its way of life it was not doing wrong. It learned, however, from sensory experience that it must not do this sort of thing under special circumstances, and after the lesson has been once thoroughly learned there is no more trouble of this kind.

392

Individuals who are of less mental stability than normal require, indeed, more careful discipline than average men. The rational may be managed by sweet reasonableness. The defective child must be made to realize that certain actions {743} will surely be followed by painful punishment, though, of course, the main purpose of modern care for such children is to watch over them so diligently as to prevent them getting into mischief. This is after all what we do with the animals, and we realize the necessity for it. Defective human beings approach the animal in their lessened power to resist impulses, and they must be treated in the same way. If we were to save the animals in an excess of tenderness toward them, because we held to the notion either that they did not know any better or else could not resist their impulses, and then permitted them to do things without punishment, we should either have to get rid of animals entirely, or else life would be one continuous readjustment of things to animal ways. Since defectives occur in the general population, it must be realized that far from being less rigid with them in the matter of meting out punishment for things they do that are harmful to others, we must be even more strict with them. Otherwise, we will have to take the bitter consequences of our own foolishness.

It does not make so much difference if the thoroughly rational individual occasionally escapes punishment for something done, but whenever the subrational escapes, he is encouraged to do it again. More than that, the example of his punishment is needed for others. So far as possible, punishment must inevitably follow crime in the world, in order to impress the subrational and deter them from yielding to impulses. Far from being less deserving of punishment in every sense in which a modern penologist cares to inflict punishment, these individuals are more impressed by it, and, above all, need to be more impressed by it. When the subrational know that they can do things without being severely punished for them, they will always abuse that state of affairs. The thoroughly rational man may be depended on to do his duty as a rule without the need of punishment hanging over him. This is not true for the others, and hence the greater increase in crime, and above all in murder, which has made human life cheaper in this than in any other country in the world, as the direct consequence of recent abuses in our penal system.

It has become very clear now that in recent years we have come to take entirely too lenient a view in these matters, and that many criminals who deserved to be punished, both because in this way they would be prevented from future crime and others deterred by the knowledge of their punishment, have been allowed to escape Justice. The tendency is toward too great mercifulness, which spoils the character of the nation, just as leniency to the developing child spoils individual character. Men may very well be insane, in the broad meaning of that term, in the sense that they have done irrational things, but then there is almost no one who has not. The responsibility of most men for a definite action is quite clear in the sense that if they are punished they will not do it again, or will be less likely to do it again, while if they are not punished their escape becomes a suggestion to themselves and to others to repeat such acts. It is for the subrational that we most need to insist on punishment. The cunning of the insane is proverbial, and this extends also to the subrational, and many of these folk realize that their difference from others, their queerness, as their folks call it, is quite enough to make a verdict of insanity in their case assured with the present lax enforcement of law. If the present state of affairs continues in this matter, we are simply allowing ourselves to be led by the nose by these cunning people into the perpetuation of a state of affairs in which they may do what they like because we have become foolishly oversensitive in the matter of inflicting punishment.

On the principle that punishment deters, a man who has killed another man, even under conditions that seriously impaired his responsibility for the act and with evidence of previous lowered mentality, must never again be free to live the ordinary life of men. He must be under surveillance, and should be confined for life in an institution for the criminally insane. For the subrational such a sentence, if known to be inevitable, would usually be more deterrent than even imprisonment in an ordinary prison for life with all the possibilities for freedom which are presented by executive clemency, pardoning boards, and the like. It is absurd to say that a man may have such an attack of mental unsoundness as will lead him to do so serious an act as taking away human life, and then be expected to get over his mental condition so as not to be likely to do the same thing again. {744} Every alienist knows that this is not true. Such acts, when really due to mental instability, occur either in depressed or maniacal conditions, and these, as is now well known from carefully collected statistics, inevitably recur, or in weakened toxic conditions in susceptible subjects, and a return to the old mode of life may at any time bring recurrences.

It is in the treatment of disorders of the will of various kinds that the physician is brought to realize how much harm is done by the teaching that determinism and not free will rules life. It is true that we often find cases in which men and women cannot use their wills or at least seem not to be able to use them. They are lacking in some essential quality of human mentality. We find many human beings, however, doing things that are harmful for them and that are so inveterated by habit that it is extremely difficult to get away from them. In every case the sane person can conquer and break the habit, no matter how much of a hold it may have obtained.

We have heard much of the born criminal and of the degenerate and his inevitable tendencies, but most of the theories founded on this phase of criminal anthropology have gradually been given up as a consequence of more careful and, above all, more detailed observation. Many criminals bear the stigmata of so-called degeneration. Many of them have irregular heads, uneven ears, some fastened directly to the cheek and some with the animal peak, many have misshapen mouths and noses, but, on the other hand, many people having these physical qualities are good men and women, perfectly capable of self-control, honest, efficient members of society, and it is evident that the original observations were founded too exclusively on the criminal classes, instead of on the whole population. It is important, then, to get away from the notion of irresponsibility in these cases.

While men are free, yet each in a different way and the freedom of their wills is as individual as their countenances, it must not be forgotten that the freedom of the will is a function of the human being, and, like all other functions, can be increased or decreased by exercise or the lack of it. The old idea of "breaking the will" was as much of a mistake as that other old-fashioned notion contemporary with it of "hardening" children by exposing them to inclement weather and severe physical trials. The will may be strengthened, however, by the exercise of it and if not exercised it may not be expected, by analogy, at least, to be as weak and flabby as muscles would be under similar circumstances. The training of the will by self-denial and self-control is extremely important. When there is an hereditary influence, a family trait and not merely an acquired character, by which the will rather easily passes out of control, there is all the more need for the training of it in early youth. Without such training men may find it impossible to make up their minds to deny themselves indulgence of many kinds, but this is not because they have not free will, but because this function has never been exercised sufficiently to enable them to use it properly. A man who attempts to do gymnastic feats without training comes a cropper. A man who is placed in circumstances requiring hard muscle exertion will fail if his muscles have not been trained to bear it. The same thing will happen with the will.

Unfortunately this training of the will has been neglected to a considerable extent in modern education, and, above all, in modern families, where the presence of but one or two children concentrates attention on them, {745} over-stimulating them when young, leading to self-centeredness and, above all, discouraging self-denial in any way and preventing that development of thorough self-control which comes in the well-regulated large family. Besides, unfortunately it is just the neurotic individuals who most need thorough training in self-control and whose parents suffer from the same nervous condition (for, while disease is not inherited, defects are inherited), that are deprived of such regular training in self-control because of the inability of their parents to regulate either themselves or others properly. Here is the secret of the more frequent development of neurotic symptoms in recent years. It is not so much the strenuous life as the lack of training of the will so that the faculty of free will can be used properly. Lacking this, hysterical symptoms, unethical tendencies, lack of self-control become easily manifest. The training that would prevent these should come early in life, and when it does not it is very difficult to make up for it later. Just as far as possible, however, it is the duty of the psychotherapeutist to supply by suggestions as to training and discipline for the education of the will that has unfortunately been missed.

{746}

SECTION XX

PSYCHOTHERAPY IN SURGERY

CHAPTER I

PSYCHOTHERAPY IN OLD-TIME SURGERY

Surgery, a name derived from chirurgy—handwork—might seem to be dependent almost entirely on mechanical and technical skill, yet there has always been the conviction that the patient's attitude of mind towards an operation is almost as important a factor in the success of surgery as the surgeon's skill.

Astrology in Surgery.—From the earliest history of surgery we, find that astrology was mainly employed in order to determine what days were likely to be favorable, and what unfavorable, for the practice of such surgical procedures as were in vogue at that time. Certain conjunctions of the planets were declared to be particularly unfavorable, and some of them, indeed, were declared almost absolutely fatal; others were said to be especially favorable. As astronomical and anatomical knowledge grew, more and more details were added in this matter. Definite portions of the body were supposed to be under the occult influence of certain constellations. It was only with careful reference to these constellations then that surgical procedures or, indeed, the application of remedies of any kind, might be undertaken. All remember the picture in old almanacs of a man with the signs of the zodiac around him, and the indications that referred certain of these signs and the corresponding constellations to the different parts of the body.

Venesection and the Stars.—When venesection became a frequently used remedy, the question of the favorable and unfavorable influence of the stars was an important element in it. In old Babylonia, noted for its knowledge of astronomy, which was then called astrology without any of our derogatory meaning in the word, certain positions of the planets were absolute contraindications for the performance of venesection. Indeed, astrology often furnished the best possible excuses for the failure of what were thought to be absolutely specific remedies. When the remedies did not succeed, their failure was attributed to their being taken at unfavorable times and not to the remedies themselves. These astrological ideas continued to influence medicine, and, above all, surgery, down almost to our own time. Galileo and Kepler made horoscopes, and Mesmer wrote a thesis on the influence of the stars on human constitutions. In fact, very few important patients of the seventeenth and even eighteenth centuries were treated medically or surgically without due reference to the stars at the time. All this had a profound influence on {747} the patient's mind. He felt that every precaution was being taken to preclude the possibility of failure and assure favorable results, and he, therefore, submitted to the operation absolutely confident that so far as human knowledge could go, everything was favorably disposed in his regard.

Mental Influence in Old Hospitals.—It is rather interesting to realize how much the history of medicine illustrates the profound attention that was given in the old times to the question of the occupation of patients' minds as an eminently helpful factor in the treatment of disease and, above all, in convalescence. In the great health resorts, the temple hospitals like that at Epidaurus, or even the city hospital, the AEsculapeum at Athens, the question of recreation of mind was evidently considered very important. At Athens, the two city theaters, the larger one seating perhaps 50,000, and the smaller, Odeon, were not far from the hospital. At Epidaurus, a theater seating probably 12,000, in which the great Greek classic plays were given; a Stadium, seating nearly 10,000, in which athletic contests were conducted, and a Hippodrome, seating 6,000, in which animal performances might be witnessed, were all in connection with the temple hospital. Outdoor sleeping apartments were provided; that is, the patients slept under a colonnade, and, in general, the mental and physical hygiene of modern times was thoroughly anticipated. All of this was considered particularly important for convalescents. Patients were occupied, while in bed, with various interests. Just as soon as they could be moved, their minds were occupied with all sorts of interests external to themselves, and especially such as had the readiest appeal to humanity. (See bird's-eye view, facing p. 9.)

Medieval Hospitals and the Mind.—It is not difficult to trace the development of similar conditions in the hospitals of the Middle Ages. While we are inclined to think of these older hospitals as surely lacking in everything that we have developed in our modern hospitals, they prove, on the contrary, to have anticipated most of our hospital improvements. They were of single story construction, with large windows high up in the wall so that there could be no drafts, with a balcony on which patients could sit in the sun, with arrangements for procuring privacy rather easily by means of sliding partitions, with tiled floors, and, above all, with pictures on the walls, some of them the products of the brush of the great artists of the old time and which would serve to occupy patients' minds. Probably nothing is worse for patients who are convalescing from illness or operation than to be left to their own thoughts. Often they must not be talked to overmuch, or permitted the exertion of conversation or of reading, yet they must have some occupation of mind. The frescoes painted directly on the walls of the old hospitals were eminently psychotherapeutic in this respect, and we shall probably have to imitate them. Besides, the patients had the opportunity every morning to hear Mass, which was said at an altar at an end of the ward, and certain religious exercises were conducted by the sister nurses each afternoon. How much of consolation this was to believing patients at a time when all were believers is rather easy to understand.

Medieval Surgeons and Mental Influence.—Some of the insistence on this favorable state of mind for operations during the Middle Ages is extremely interesting. One of the great surgeons of the fourteenth century was Mondeville, whose text-book has recently been published in both France and {748} Germany. I have translated in "Old-time Makers of Medicine" some of his emphatic expressions, which show how important he deemed it to keep the patient in as favorable a state of mind as possible before and after operations. He went so far as to suggest that someone should be deliberately called in to tell him jokes. He said, "Let the surgeon take care to regulate the whole regimen of the patient's life for joy and happiness by promising that he will soon be well, by allowing his relatives and special friends to cheer him, and by having someone to tell him jokes, and let him be solaced also by music on the viol or psaltery. The surgeon must forbid anger, hatred, and sadness in the patient, and remind him that the body grows fat from joy and thin from sadness. He must insist on the patient obeying him faithfully in all things." He repeats with approval the expression of Avicenna that "often the confidence of the patient in his physician does more for the cure of his disease than the physician with all his remedies."

Mondeville was but one of the great surgeons of the medieval period who dwelt on this. It would not be hard to find corresponding expressions in the books of such men as Guy de Chauliac, Hugh of Lucca, Theodoric, or even earlier among the great Arabian physicians and surgeons. Rhazes, for instance, declared that "physicians ought to console their patients even if the signs of impending death seem to be present, for the bodies of men are dependent on their spirits." He considered that the most valuable thing for the physician to do was to increase the patient's natural vitality. Hence his advice: "In treating a patient, let your first thought be to strengthen his natural vitality. If you strengthen that, you remove ever so many ills without more ado. If you weaken it, however, by the remedies that you use, you always work harm." Another of his aphorisms seems worth while quoting: "The patient who consults a great many physicians is likely to have a very confused state of mind." For him a confused state of mind evidently meant a lessened tendency to recovery.

Surgical Lesions Influenced.—The King's touch in England, which so often proved beneficial for scrofulous patients, illustrates very well how much strong mental influence may avail even in cases where surgery seems surely indicated. Many cases of epilepsy were also greatly benefited by the King's touch, and, indeed, in this matter there are probably many more cases of the cure of epilepsy, or at least relief of the worst symptoms of the affection, reported as following the King's touch than after operation in the modern time. In both sets of cases we are now confident that the good effects produced came through the minds of the patients. When, during the eighteenth century, Mesmerism began to attract attention, investigators and experimenters on the subject were able to show that many pains and aches could be greatly benefited by psychic treatment. The painful conditions following fractures and sprains proved to be particularly amenable to mental influence exerted in this special way. As we approach the modern time, there comes to be a definite recognition of the fact that the mind may produce many pains and aches which seem due to purely physical conditions that might be expected to yield only to physical treatment. A corresponding recognition of the power of the mind to lessen and even suppress actual physical pain is almost a corrollary of this.

{749}

Sir Benjamin Brodie declared, as I have quoted in the section on "Diseases of the Muscular and Articular System" that a large proportion of the painful joint conditions that he saw among his better-to-do patients were of the hysterical or neurotic type. Sir James Paget thought this expression of Brodie an exaggeration, but acknowledged that one-fifth to one-fourth of all his cases in both hospital and private practice were due to hysteria. In those days most of the painful conditions were considered to belong rather to surgery than to medicine, so that these opinions represent very well the practice of medicine in these cases during the early nineteenth century.

During the nineteenth century great practical surgeons, and especially those who have taught us how to treat individual patients rather than their diseases—for it is quite as true in surgery as in medicine that the patient is more than his disease—have made distinct contributions to the department of psychotherapy in surgery. Dr. Hilton's great book on "Rest and Pain" is full of psychotherapy. His cases illustrate the fact that when patients' minds and bodies are set at rest, all sorts of serious conditions proceed to get better. The rest of mind, the cessation of worry, the presence of a feeling of confidence in recovery, is quite as important as the physical measures. Young surgeons particularly probably could not do better than follow the advice of the old Scotch surgical professor at Edinburgh who suggests to his pupils that they should read Hilton's "Rest and Pain" at least once a year.

CHAPTER II

MENTAL INFLUENCE BEFORE OPERATION

Much may be done during the preparation for operation to put the patient in the most suitable condition for the manifestation of healthy reaction of tissue and of normal convalescence. Many patients do not come for operation until their health has been somewhat impaired at least by the condition requiring operation. Not infrequently a good proportion of this impairment of health is due not so much to the lesion that is present as to the worry over it and the anxiety and solicitude which its development has occasioned. If the lesion is in connection with the digestive tract, this is particularly likely to be true, and nutrition will often have been sadly interfered with, not so much by direct influence of the pathological condition as by the unfavorable mental influence developing in connection with it. We know now that it is perfectly possible for an indigestion which is entirely above the neck to make rather serious inroads upon the health of the patient, by producing dislike for food or at least such loss of appetite as leads to considerable reduction in weight. In such cases there are often complications, such as tendencies to constipation, that still further impair health or at least reduce vitality and therefore hamper that healthy reaction which should occur after operation in order to assure normal convalescence.

Accessory Neuroses.—In many of these cases, even where there is a definite lesion present, the patient can be brought up to normal weight, or at least his condition can be greatly improved by medical treatment accompanied {750} by such attention to his state of mind as will neutralize its unfavorable influence. If he can be made to understand that a definite effort to increase weight and to bring back his strength will be of assistance in recovery from the operation, and that the reestablishment of certain habits of eating and caring for himself will do much to help in this, very desirable changes for the better in his general health may be brought about. This is illustrated very well by what happens in certain incurable cancer cases. The patients often have lost considerable weight, even thirty to forty pounds, before an operation is decided on, and then when the operation is performed their cancer is found to be inoperable. After the exploration the patient is not told this, but is mercifully spared and is assured that now he ought to get better, since an operation has been performed. Such patients have been known to gain twenty, thirty, and in one case I believe over forty pounds as the result of the mental influence of this suggestion and the resumption of former habits of life to some extent at least, consequent upon the neutralization of the unfavorable state of mind into which they had sunk before through over-solicitude about themselves. If even the depressing effect of the toxins of cancer can thus be overcome, it is easy to understand how much can be accomplished when there is no such physical factor at work.

Dominant Ideas.—As a general rule, it must be recognized that patients may be, and indeed frequently are, besides their definite pathological conditions, under the influence of dominant ideas which must be recognized and as far as possible neutralized. Some of them have persuasions with regard to food and the amount that they can eat, others have removed many important nutritious articles from their diet and are quite sure that any attempt on their part to take such articles is sure to be followed by indigestion, and still others have habits with regard to the amount and the kind of fluids that they take at meals and between meals and, above all, the lack of fluids in their diet which need to be overcome. Unless such ideas are counteracted there is difficulty even in convalescence, and very often they have brought patients into physical conditions in which whatever pathological condition is present is emphasized by that over-attention which the nervous system is so prone to give to even slight sensations when the organism is in a state of lowered nutrition.

In not a few of these cases the bringing of the patient up to the normal condition of weight and health, and the removal of the influence of dominant ideas, will perhaps also remove many of the indications for operation. There are many patients, and especially such as are reasonably educated and have some leisure, who get certain of their organs on their minds and produce symptoms or emphasize such symptoms as are present until it seems as though an operation is the only thing that can lift their burden of discomfort and permit them to go on again with their work. We have all known of physicians who felt sure that they ought to be operated on for such conditions as gastric ulcer or duodenal ulcer, though subsequent developments in the case, when they were persuaded to put off operation and made to reform certain ill-advised habits, proved that no such lesion as they suspected had ever been present. Indeed, some of these physicians and even surgeons have insisted so much that surgical friends occasionally have operated on them and have found nothing to justify the operation.

{751}

Some of these states in connection with discomfort of various kinds in the abdomen have been discussed in the chapter on Abdominal Discomfort, and some illustrations of useless operations given. We must not forget that there is a constant stream of pathological suggestion in the air at the present time, not only in medical journals, but even in the secular press, and that this concentrates the attention of patients on comparatively slight discomforts and leads to the exaggeration of them until even an operation seems a welcome relief for them.

Operative Persuasions.—While surgical operations are in practically all cases mutilations, they are absolutely necessary under certain circumstances, are often, indeed, life-saving, and there is no doubt that they have saved mankind a great deal of discomfort. Surgeons are agreed, however, that they are not to be performed unless they hold out a definite promise of physical relief. It is extremely important, then, that patients must not become persuaded of the need of an operation in their cases unless surgical intervention is really necessary. This is as true for physicians and even surgeons themselves, as I have said, as it is for the general public. Women are much more susceptible than men to operation suggestions, and since it has become fashionable to talk about *their* operations, not only has the deterrent idea of surgical mutilation been greatly lessened, but there has actually developed in many of them a morbid fascination for a similar experience with all its attraction of attention and promised occupation of mind for the woman of leisure.

This phase of the necessity for favorable mental influence has been especially emphasized in the chapters on Gynecology. Unless, therefore, there are very definite indications, operations must not be performed, for they will relieve, as a rule, only for the time being, and further operations may have to be done to no purpose. Any physician of reasonably large experience has seen such cases. Patients get the idea of an operation as their one hope, and then nothing less than that will produce such diversion of mind as will bring relief of symptoms. It is important in these cases that such patients should not have operations suggested to them. Once the suggestion takes hold, they do not use their reserve energy in such a way as to help out effectively other remedies that may be given. They distrust all remedial measures, think that at most they can be only palliative, and so do not add to other forms of therapeutics the power of psychotherapy to cure them.

Besides the abdominal conditions, there are certain tuberculous conditions with regard to which this seems to be particularly true. I have seen enlarged cervical glands disappear without discharge when patients have taken up the outdoor life, and, above all, when they have gone out of the city and have lived the regime proper for those in whom tubercle bacilli are growing. If such patients, however, once become persuaded that their glands must be operated on, they are likely to need, if not active intervention, at least the discharge of material from their tuberculous lesions before they get well. Operations of a radical character for tuberculosis used to be much more popular than they are now, when we are likely to think that nature can do more for tuberculous lesions in nearly all cases than the most skillful surgery.

Fractures and the Mind.—In such surgical conditions as fractures and dislocations, a change has come about in the mode of treatment, at least in many hands, that seems entirely physical in its effect, yet has undoubtedly {752} exerted important psychic influences favorable to recovery which deserve to be noted. In dislocations and fractures, and particularly the latter, it was the custom in the past to do the fractured limb up in bandages and then leave it until knitting of the bones, or, in dislocations, healing of the soft tissues, had taken place. Apparently it was forgotten that this eminently artificial condition was not conducive to that healthy reaction of tissues for reparative purposes which must be expected in these cases. Circulation was not so good because of the constrictive effect of the bandages; vitality not so high because of failure of nervous activity in absolute immobility; the return venous circulation was somewhat hampered because there were no contractions of muscles; and all the conditions were distinctly unfavorable, though nature was expected not only to maintain the health of the part, but bring about the added functions of repair. In spite of the more or less unfavorable conditions, nature was able, as a rule, to do so. Prof. Lucas Championére reintroduced the older method of treating fractures and dislocations more openly and of even using certain manipulations, passive movements, and massage in order to encourage the circulation and the natural vitality of the limb.

There is another phase of the influence of this mode of treatment that deserves to be recalled. When the fracture is hidden away for many days and the patient is not absolutely sure whether it is getting on well or not, solicitude or anxiety is awakened in some minds that prevents, or at least delays, normal healthy repair. It is well known by surgeons that fractures do not heal so well after accidents in which there has been considerable shock, or in which the simultaneous death of a friend seriously disturbs the patient's mind. Nor do fractures heal so well if the patient is worried about business affairs or seriously disturbed over family matters. Among sensitive patients, a state of mind not unlike that produced by worry or shock may develop as a consequence of the dread that the fracture may not heal properly, or that there may be deformity, or that when the surgeon removes the bandages he may find it necessary either to break it again or do something that would involve considerable discomfort. These patients need reassurance. If the surgeon sees the broken limb occasionally, and, by manipulation and passive movements such as may properly be used, assures himself as to its condition, the patient's mind is much better satisfied and that inhibition of trophic processes which otherwise sometimes occurs is prevented.

Incisions and Suggestion.—Something of this same psychotherapeutic influence is noted with regard to the healing of incisions when these are not left without inspection too long. The newer surgical customs of comparatively few dressings, so that the wound may easily be inspected and the patient may be completely assured with regard to it, has undoubtedly had a good influence in bringing about more rapid repair. Air is the best environment for a healing as well as a healthy skin, and mental trust is best for the patient's power of repair. In vigorous individuals such repair will occur anyhow. It is in those of delicate health, neurotic disposition, and psychoneurotic tendencies, that reassurances are needed. Often their physical condition is such that they need every possible aid in bringing about complete repair. Their state of mind, then, must be noted carefully, and any inhibitory ideas that may be present because of over-anxiety as to how the incision is getting on must be removed. This does not mean that patients' whims should be yielded {753} to in the matter of over-solicitude about their condition, but that proper care should be taken to prevent inhibition of trophic influences through unfavorable mental states just as far as is possible. Most surgeons of experience do these things in the proper way by instinct from the beginning, or by a tactful habit, which develops in their surgical experience of adapting themselves to individual patients. It is well to realize, however, that such mental attitudes are extremely important and must be deliberately treated by the surgeon.

Pseudo-rabies.—Certain conditions usually treated of as surgical have mental relations that are very interesting. There seems no doubt that in a certain number of cases pseudo-rabies occurs; that is, persons are bitten by a dog, become seriously disturbed over the possibility of rabies developing, and after brooding over this for a time their mind gives way and there is either a neurosis simulating many symptoms of true rabies, or a state of collapse from fright in which even death may take place. These cases are not frequent. Their occurrence is taken by some of those who are opposed to animal experimentation as a proof that rabies is always some such delusion, and that it is due to the exaggeration of the significance of dog-bites by the medical profession that the symptom complex known as rabies has come into existence. This is, of course, nonsense, and many true cases of rabies occur. Since, however, these other cases provide the opportunity for argument in the matter, it is all the more necessary that they should be recognized for what they are. When a patient has been bitten by a dog that has not died from rabies within three weeks after the bite, there is practical certainty that the animal did not have and could not communicate rabies. The cases of hydrophobia with long incubation periods are rather dubious, and the general impression now is that there has been subsequent infection. Patients who are in the midst of overwhelming dread of the development of rabies must be taken seriously and their cases treated by mental influence. Suggestion, instruction, and the neutralization of wrong ideas by reference to authorities in the matter, must be used to overcome the unfortunate state of mind which may, if allowed to continue and, above all, to develop, prove serious for the individual.

Pseudo-rabies is but a type, though the most serious and perhaps most frequent of what may be called surgical psycho-neuroses. There are others. Imaginary syphilis is an affection that often causes worry and trouble to patient and physician. *Herpes preputialis* with mental symptoms is almost as bad. These are mental infections of various kinds. There are many neoplastic persuasions and toxic suggestions that must be treated with tact and firmness.

CHAPTER III

MENTAL INFLUENCE IN ANESTHESIA

Nowhere in the domain of surgery is the influence of the mind more important than in the production of anesthesia for surgical purposes. It is well known that intense preoccupation of mind will make an individual completely anesthetic even for very severe injuries. In battle men frequently are severely wounded, yet do not know it, or at least have no idea of the extent of the wound and of the pain that ordinarily would be inflicted by it. In the {754} midst of panics, as during fires, or when crowds are trying to get out of buildings rapidly, people often suffer severe injuries and know nothing about them. The story of the woman who lost her ear in the theater panic and was quite unaware of it until her attention was called to it, is only one of many striking examples. Men have been known to walk round even with a broken leg, or with a dislocation with which it proved quite impossible for them to move, once their mental preoccupation for others ceased and they had time to think about themselves. Anesthetic incidents under conditions in which great pain might well be expected are not uncommon. It is evidently possible so completely to occupy the mind that pain sensations cannot find their way into the consciousness.

Pain and Diversion of Mind.—From very old times, attempts have been made to use this power of the mind to prevent pain, and often with some results. In preanesthetic surgery, minor operations were performed rapidly, beginning just after the patient's attention had been attracted to something else besides the thought of the operation. Pain is, of course, much less tolerable and seems to the sufferer at least to be much more severe whenever the attention is concentrated on it. Specialists in nervous diseases, during the process of eliciting complaints of pain or tenderness while employing movements or manipulations, usually try to attract the patient's attention as much as possible to something else, in order to determine just how much genuine pain or tenderness is present. Often it is found that, while a part of the body is complained of as exquisitely tender or it is averred that a joint cannot, be touched or a limb moved without severe pain, when the patient's attention is attracted strongly to something else, deep palpations may be practiced and rather extensive manipulations can be made without complaint. In these cases very often the pain is not imaginary, but is slight, due to some physical basis, and has been very much increased by the concentration of attention on it. This part, at least of the pain, may be removed by an appeal to the mind. The principle is valuable when there is question of minor operations.

Surgeons have often taken advantage of this power of distraction of attention to relieve pain in surgical manipulations. The story is told of the French surgeon, Dupuytren, that he was called one day to see a lady whom he knew very well in order to determine the form of injury from which she was suffering. He found that she had a dislocation of the shoulder, and during the manipulations, in order to make his diagnosis, he almost inevitably inflicted considerable pain. She complained very bitterly and told him that she understood that he was very rough with his hospital patients, but he must not be rough with her. He had hold of her hand at the moment, and, just before grasping the arm in such a way as to make the manipulations necessary to reduce the dislocation, he slapped her face and told her that she must not talk to him while he was treating her. Needless to say, she was deeply shocked. Before her shock had passed away, Dupuytren had completed the reduction of the dislocation, and in her preoccupation of mind she felt almost no pain. She remarked afterwards, however, that she had suffered so much mental anguish from his unexpected roughness that she was not sure whether, after all, she had been really spared in her feelings.

Hypnotic Anesthesia.—When, in the first half of the nineteenth century, {755} scientific attention was seriously attracted to hypnotism, it was hoped that this would prove an effective means of producing anesthesia during surgical operations or at least of greatly lessening pain. The hope was not disappointed. There was a discussion on the subject before the Medical Chirurgical Society of London in 1840, and in 1843 Dr. Eliotson wrote a work with the title, "Numerous Cases of Surgical Operations Without Pain in the Mesmeric State." In 1846 Sir John Forbes wrote in his Review that "the testimony as to the value of hypnotism as an anesthetic is now of so varied and extensive a kind as to require an immediate and complete trial of the practice in surgical cases." At the end of that same year, ether as an anesthetic was introduced into England, and the first case was reported under the caption "Animal Magnetism Superseded," which shows how much attention the previous attempts at hypnotic anesthesia had attracted. After this, hypnotism was given up for anesthetic purposes except by a few enthusiastic students of it. These, however, succeeded in accomplishing much with it. Dr. Esdaile, in India, succeeded in doing all sorts of operations under hypnotism. Dr. Milne Bramwell, in "Hypnotism, Its History, Practice and Theory" (London, 1906), lays down the rules for hypnosis for anesthetic purposes. They are eminently practical.

While hypnotism can be used to produce anesthesia, it has many disadvantages. The length of the hypnosis cannot always be arranged so as to assure anesthesia during the whole of an operation, while in some cases it will continue after the operation for some time in spite of every effort on the part of the hypnotist to bring the patient to himself. Besides, the depth of the hypnosis cannot always be assured, and sometimes some sensation remains. Patients will groan and wince and move, though, of course, under ether or chloroform such manifestations may take place, yet the patient afterwards will give every assurance that not the slightest pain was felt. In some cases, however, even where the pain sensation is not severe during an operation under hypnosis, it may, nevertheless, prove sufficient, when continued for some time, to bring the patient out of the hypnotic state.

For short operations of minor character, undoubtedly hypnosis can be employed successfully. As we explain in the chapter on Hypnotism, anyone can produce hypnosis who has confidence in his own power and in whom the patient has trust. There is no need of a special hypnotist, and there is no special faculty required. There should be some familiarity with procedures, but any man has just as much hypnotic power as another. The influence does not pass from the operator to the subject, but is due to the subject's concentration of his attention so that there is a short circuiting of association tracts within the brain very probably, which does not permit the entrance into consciousness of sensations through any path except one or two, usually that of hearing, and sometimes of sight, less frequently of other sensations.

Concentration of Attention.—In a great many cases of minor operations, such as the opening of a boil of a small abscess, the pulling of a tooth, the lancing of a gum, or other such procedures, a surgeon who is confident in his own mental power over his patient can rather easily produce a state of mind in which the discomfort of the surgical procedure is greatly minimized. There are certain physical helps for this. For instance, if patients are asked to breathe rapidly and deeply for a few minutes, there is a hyperoxygenation {756} of the blood which seems to obtund sensibility. If patients are told of this, and then made to breathe rapidly for a half a minute in order that they may continue consciously their deep, rapid breathing even when pain is noted, a state of mind is produced from concentration of attention on their breathing in which painful sensations are greatly obtunded. The effect is probably more mental than physical, and is well worth while trying because of the amount of pain it often saves.

Waking Suggestion.—Without resort to hypnotism, much can be accomplished by mental suggestion in the waking state to lessen the pain of surgical operations and maneuvers. This is particularly true as regards nervous persons, who will otherwise emphasize their discomfort, and for those of lesser intelligence, children, and the like. Esdaile's experiences in India show how much can be done in this way. Often the hypnosis was so slight that the patients were perfectly cognizant of everything that went on around them, yet under the compelling influence of the assurance of Dr. Esdaile, whom they trusted completely, they did not complain of pain nor wince even when considerable surgical intervention was practiced, and they always assured their friends afterwards that they had felt nothing. I know an American physician who has an almost similar power over negroes. Ordinarily it requires more of an anesthetic to produce insensitiveness to pain in the negro than in a white person. By personal assurance, by the absolute securing of their confidence, and through their trust in him, this man is able to produce anesthesia without the use of more than a minimum quantity of the anesthetic. He is able to do the same thing with children, and, of course, it is well known that mental influence over them is extremely important in limiting the amount of anesthetic that will be necessary.

Personality of Anesthetist.—Some anesthetists by their personal influence are able to bring patients under the influence of an anesthetic with much less excitement and, as a consequence, with the use of much less of the anesthetic than others. It is the same question of personal influence that extends through all medicine. Some men seem to have it naturally, and others not, though to some extent, at least, it may be cultivated. Of course, it is now well understood that, under no circumstances, should a patient be forced to take an anesthetic. This is as true for a child as for any other patient. Only a little management is required to secure the cooperation of even a young child. Above all, there must be no struggling, and while there may be a passing stage of excitement, which cannot be entirely controlled, this can be eliminated by those who are skillful. It may be necessary, especially in the case of children, for the little patients to become familiar with the anesthetist. They should see him on several occasions and should be made to feel that they know him. The presence of a stranger is enough of itself to excite children and make them suspicious and resentful of any manipulations. It may be well for them to have breathed through the cone on several occasions and to play a sort of game with it. In this way children will often go under an anesthetic without any struggle or excitement.

It seems a little childish to suggest similar procedures with grown patients, but even surgeons of long experience with the older methods who have insisted on the trial being made on their patients have found much benefit from it. Familiarity with the anesthetist and even with the inhaler {757} and the breathing through it on several occasions beforehand, when no anesthetic is being administered, helps many patients not a little. This preliminary is particularly of help with regard to nervous patients and especially women. It is very seldom necessary to use nitrous oxide as a preliminary to ether if this mode of procedure is practiced.

Mental Diversion.—It is well to concentrate the mind of the patient on something else besides his sensations. One element that is extremely important for anesthesia is deep breathing. The patient must then have his attention called to the necessity for deep breathing and should frequently have the suggestion to this effect repeated in his ear as he comes under the anesthetic. There should be some practice in deep breathing deliberately beforehand, with the idea of accustoming the respiratory mechanism to take deep breaths by habit even when not entirely under the control of the will. This may be done with the inhaler on a few occasions at least. The occupation of attention necessary for deep breathing during the taking of the anesthetic lessens the concentration of mind on the feelings, and actually makes the discomfort much less. Besides, deep breathing distributes the anesthetic over the lungs, leads to its absorption more rapidly, and makes the irritation of the anesthetic less by diffusing it over a larger surface. On the contrary, short, rapid breaths lead to an intensity of irritation and much slower absorption.

Skilled anesthetists have found it of decided advantage to keep the patient's mind fixed on something else besides the breathing. Perhaps the easiest recommendation is that of locking the hands over the abdomen just above the umbilicus and asking the patient to hold tight. This gives something very definite to think about and to occupy the mind with. I have seen patients of rather nervous organizations go under the influence of even a very small quantity of an anesthetic when required to hold their hands thus and when the command was constantly repeated, "Hold your hands tight," whenever there was the slightest sign of struggle or excitement. Where this was done tactfully and regularly, I have seen patient after patient go into anaesthesia without struggle or excitement and usually without any noise or even a loud word. I realize how much the personality of the anaesthetist means in such cases, and I feel sure that anyone who is confident in his own power in the matter will produce a corresponding feeling of confidence in the patients.

Fright in Anesthesia.—There seems good reason to think that occasionally the deaths reported from anesthesia have really occurred from fright or at least have been greatly influenced by emotional factors. It has often been noted that these deaths occurred particularly at the beginning of the administration of an anesthetic and before anything like a sufficient quantity to produce a toxic effect had been administered. In other cases it has been noted that patients were allowed to come out partially from under the anesthetic, and as they recovered consciousness were disturbed by some incident. Sometimes the pain seems to act as an inhibitory agent on the heart. In more than one reported case the patient told afterwards of hearing very distinctly some remark that seemed to be of bad omen. In one case in my own experience the breathing and heart stopped (though the patient fortunately was resuscitated) as a consequence of hearing a series of rather loud goodbyes said at the door of the elevator leading to the operating room during the {758} course of an operation just at a moment when the anaesthetic influence was very much lessened for a while. In some cases where there has been great fear of the anesthetic which has been talked over beforehand by the patient, even a few whiffs of the ether or chloroform have given rise to serious symptoms from stoppage of the heart. It is evident that it is extremely important properly to predispose such patients.

The well-known surgical warning not to make remarks during the course of an operation that might prove disturbing to the patient, needs to be emphasized. By a very curious psychological anomaly some patients, though thoroughly anesthetic as regards pain, are able to hear and understand very well remarks that are made near them. Fortunately, such patients are few in number, but they are sometimes rather seriously disturbed by chance observations that for the moment at least seem to have an unfavorable bearing on their case. Besides, certain patients sometimes have their special senses come out from under the influence of the anesthetic before their sense of pain. They may also hear and be disturbed. These cases illustrate very well the place of mental influence and how much deliberate attention should be given to this phase of the treatment of surgical cases coming out of anesthesia, as well as while more or less under its influence.

Local Anesthesia.—In local anesthesia it has come to be generally recognized in recent years that the personality of the operator is one of the most important factors for success. A number of local anesthetics have been introduced, and in some hands only comparatively small quantities of them are needed in order to produce complete absence of pain during operations. In other hands, however, considerable and even toxic quantities may have to be employed and sometimes without entire satisfaction. Infiltration anesthesia depends for its success largely on the personal influence of the administrator over the patient. It is extremely important that the patient should have complete confidence and not have that confidence disturbed in any way. For instance, he needs to be warned that he will feel the slight prick of the needle when it is first introduced, for otherwise he will be disturbed by even so slight a pain at the very beginning and will magnify subsequent feelings until satisfactory local anesthesia becomes impossible. Without thorough command over the patient and complete trust, local anesthesia never succeeds except in very minor operations. There are some men, however, who can do even severe and extensive operations with comparatively small amounts of local anesthesia. Others cannot perform satisfactorily even minor operations with large amounts. It is the operator, his personality, and mental influence over the patient that counts.

Vomiting After Anesthesia.—The vomiting that comes after anesthesia, especially with ether, often constitutes not only an annoying but sometimes a seriously disturbing complication. It must not be forgotten that vomiting in neurotic individuals, and especially women, may be largely due to a neurosis. In the section on Psychotherapy in Obstetrics we discuss the vomiting that occurs in connection with pregnancy and suggest that it is nearly always neurotic in character. The best-known European obstetricians are now agreed in this. While ether produces a tendency to vomit in everyone, in some the actual vomiting is very slight or completely absent. If patients expect that there is to be vomiting, if they are of the neurotic temperament that not only {759} vomits easily but has a tendency to secure sympathy by fostering this symptom unconsciously perhaps, then the vomiting may become even a dangerous complication. If there is no expectancy in the matter, however, but if, on the contrary, it is made clear to these patients before the anesthetic is administered that, while there may be some nausea, there need be no vomiting unless they yield too readily to their feelings, much can be done to lessen the vomiting. A single suggestion may not mean much in this matter, but a series of suggestions properly given beforehand, especially if the patient has seen others vomiting after operations and is worrying about it, may prove of excellent contrary suggestive value.

If there is no expectancy, the physician must be careful not to arouse it by over-solicitous anxiety in the matter. A plain statement should be made on several occasions, however, so that the patient will have in mind a good basis for contrary suggestion when coming out of the anesthetic. Many remedies have been suggested for this post-anesthetic vomiting, but, just as with regard to the vomiting of pregnancy, the most important element in all the cures that have been reported has been the influence upon the patient's mind. Whenever we have a number of remedies for an affection, it is almost sure that it is not their physical but their psychic effect that is of most importance.

CHAPTER IV

MENTAL INFLUENCE AFTER OPERATION

Every surgeon feels the necessity of having his patients as quiet and restful as possible after operation. Any unfavorable mental influence will surely hamper the curative reaction of tissues and delay convalescence. We all know how fear blanches tissues, and anxiety causes hyperemia, and how solicitude with regard to any part of the body interferes with the normal control of the sympathetic nervous system and sets up vasomotor disturbances. Either a lessening or surplus of blood in a particular part interferes with the normal and healthy curative reaction of tissues. The patient's mind should therefore be as much as possible diverted from attention to the part that has been operated on in order to leave nature to pursue its purposes without disturbance. For this, of course, pain must be relieved and every possible measure taken that will add to the comfort of the patient. In spite of the fact that opium may interfere with certain natural processes, it is always useful after severe operations, because it represents the lesser of two evils. The pain of itself would produce more detriment than does the opium which relieves the pain. There are, of course, other anodynes which may be used and that have less disturbing sequelae. In this matter, routine is unfortunate, for individual patients react very differently to opium and its derivatives, the disturbing effect upon the mind being greater than the quieting effect on the body. Many patients stand the coal-tar derivatives much better because of their lack of effect on the mind.

Removal of Worries.—Worries of all kinds not associated with the operation must have been thoroughly removed beforehand and must not be allowed {760} to obtrude themselves afterwards until convalescence is well established. Business is quite another matter. Whenever it does not imply worry but only means occupation of mind and distraction of the attention of the patient from himself, it may very well be permitted, after only a comparatively brief interval after operation. Within a few days a business man may certainly be allowed to dictate letters for an hour or so, and an author may even be allowed to dictate notes of some of the fancies that came to him during anesthesia. When a man has the opportunity to look forward to even a short interval during the day when he can do something that is useful, it serves as an excellent distraction for many hours beforehand and as a satisfactory memory for hours afterwards.

Pleasant Visits.—It used to be the custom to keep visitors from patients after operation much longer than is at present the custom. There has come the realization, however, that short visits from pleasant friends may mean much for the patient. It is hard to make the selection, for certain friends and especially relatives disturb and annoy rather than help the patient. Anyone who shows much solicitude and, above all, fussy over-anxiety, must be excluded, no matter how nearly related he or she may be.

Psychic Conditions of Hospitals.—The atmosphere of the hospital must all conduce to peace and quiet of mind. It is surprising the differences that may be noted in this respect. I have been in a hospital where only a dozen of operations were done a week and have scarcely ever been there without hearing complaints of pain and discomfort that were surely disturbing to others. On the other hand, I have been in a hospital where twenty capital operations a day were done, and have heard no complaint, and at nine o'clock at night have found in it the peace of a religious community. I knew that it was all due to the personality of the surgeons and their lack of power in one case to impress their patients' minds and a very marvelous power in the other of impressing patients favorably. The success of many a surgeon in a material way depends on this power to impress his patients. It is they who send others to him, and in general there is a feeling that if he cannot cure them no one can.

Of course, it is extremely important that circumspection should be employed as regards chance remarks that may be seriously misinterpreted and prove unfavorably suggestive. Patients should not, as a rule, be allowed to see their own charts whenever there are disturbing developments in pulse and temperature. During dressings the conversation should be cheerful, distracting to the patient, and should not contain remarks that may be disturbing. The surgeon and his assistants must know how to control their expressions so as not to reveal any solicitude that may be occasioned by the patient's progress or by the state of his wound when these are not satisfactory.

Surgeon's Visits.—Practically every time that a surgeon visits a patient after operation there is something that the patient has to ask or have explained. A good deal depends, as far as regards the comfort and peace of mind during the interval until the coming of the surgeon again, on the satisfaction derived from the surgeon's explanation. He should be prepared, therefore, to answer in such a way as will leave no haunting doubts in the patient's mind. Some patients are very prone to find unfavorable suggestions in even simple expressions of the physician. He must be prepared for {761} this, therefore, and be sure to say nothing that can possibly be misunderstood. In spite of this, at times patients will draw unfavorable inferences and then the nurse should have the confidence of the patient sufficiently to set the matter right or at least to give reassurance that will keep the patient's anxiety from disturbing until the next visit of the surgeon. All of this seems trivial from a certain standpoint, but even surgery is as yet an art and not a science. Art depends on personality and the influence of it and the power to express itself. The personality of the surgeon must be felt in the patient, and the more he can make it felt the better the convalescence and the less discomfort even though there should be more of pain. The amount of pain actually felt depends on how much of it gets above the threshold of consciousness.

Almost any surgical patient, especially if he has gone through a serious convalescence, will tell you how much good the visits of his physician used to do him, though a glum and over-serious surgeon may have exactly the opposite effect. Sometimes busy surgeons neglect to visit their patients daily, and nearly always this has an unfortunate effect. In serious cases, the seeing of the surgeon several times a day, when it is well understood that his visits are not due to over-anxiety with regard to the patient, may hasten convalescence materially.

Comfort, Mental and Physical.—Everything must be done to make the patients as physically comfortable as possible. It must be well understood, however, that comfort lies much more in variety and response to feeling than in any continuous condition. Patients will have little complaints and there must be always something novel to do for them. This does not necessarily imply medicine or even troublesome external applications, but the rearranging of bed clothing, the use of a hot-water bag or of an ice bag, the relief of pressure, sometimes mild applications of pressure, the lifting of the head, slight turning, even small changes of position and the like. Whenever a patient can be relieved by some means so simple as these external trifling remedial measures, confidence is awakened that the discomfort they feel is not due to any serious condition, but is only such achy tiredness as comes from confinement to bed. Without relief afforded in this way, they are likely to let unfavorable suggestion accumulate until their dread of something serious may inhibit convalescence or at least interfere with sleep and greatly enhance their discomfort generally. It is the state of mind that develops as a consequence of continued trifling discomforts and not the physical results of those discomforts that must be carefully looked to in post-operative patients.

Nursing.—In the general management of patients after operations it would be eminently helpful to the surgeon if surgical nurses were supposed to read at least once a year, Florence Nightingale's "Notes on Nursing." written half a century ago, and if the surgeon himself should have read it through once at least and dip into it occasionally afterwards. In her chapter on Noise there are many remarks that I should like to quote, but the whole chapter is so valuable that it is hard to know where it stops, and so only a few expressions may be given here. For instance, "Never to allow a patient to be waked intentionally or accidentally, is a *sine qua non* of all good nursing. If he is aroused out of his first sleep he is almost certain to have no more sleep." "The more sleep patients get the better will they be able to sleep." "I have often {762} been surprised at the thoughtlessness (resulting in cruelty, quite unintentionally) of friends or of doctors who will hold a long conversation just in the room or passage adjoining the room of the patient, who is either every moment expecting them to come in, or who has just seen them, and knows they are talking about him." "Everything you do in a patient's room after he is 'put up' for the night increases tenfold the risk of his having a bad night. Remember, never to lean against, sit upon, or unnecessarily shake or even touch the bed in which a patient lies."

Miss Nightingale, as might be expected, insists emphatically on the state of the room, the arrangement of the furniture and the cheerfulness of surroundings as important factors for the cure of patients. One of the most important elements is, of course, the nurse. She must be gentle, patient, quick to understand, often ready to anticipate wishes, and always as noiseless as possible. Slowness may be neither gentle nor noiseless. Patients, particularly men, often grow impatient at the slowness with which things are done for them.

Chattering Hopes.—There is scarcely an element of mind in the patient's environment that Miss Nightingale has not thought of and touched with very practical wisdom. She deprecates, as does anyone who knows anything about the care of patients, the "chattering hopes" of those who try to cheer patients by simply telling them that they ought to be more cheerful, that of course they will get well and that they must not be anxious. She says: "I would appeal most seriously to all friends, visitors, and attendants of the sick to leave off this practice of attempting to 'cheer' the sick by making light of their danger and by exaggerating their probabilities of recovery." Cheerfulness and kindness towards the sick are one thing and foolish attempts at encouragement not founded on good reasons quite another.

Variety of Thoughts.—From the chapter on Variety the following quotations show the very practical character of Miss Nightingale's persuasion as to the value of influencing the patient's mind:

"To any but an old nurse or an old patient the degree would be quite inconceivable to which the nerves of the sick suffer from seeing the same walls, the same ceilings, the same surroundings, during a long confinement to one or two rooms." "The nervous frame really suffers as much from this lack of variety as the digestive organs from long monotony of diet." "The effect in sickness, of beautiful objects, of variety of objects, and especially of brilliancy of color is hardly at all appreciated."

As Miss Nightingale insists, flowers are remedies of great value for the ailing and especially for those who are confined to their room for a long period. She pleads for having the bed placed near a window in order that they may see out into the fields and the scenery around them, to which I would add with emphasis, and so that, if it is possible, they may see the occupations of human beings. Miss Nightingale adds: "Well people vary their own objects, their own employments many times a day; and while nursing (!) some bedridden sufferer then, they let him lie there staring at a dead wall without any change of object to enable him to vary his thoughts." Quite needless to say, variety is more important for the ailing than the well.

Pain Psychic Conditions.—Pain after operation is an extremely common symptom and often causes much disturbance. Every surgeon knows how {763} individual are patients in this respect, and how much depends on the personal reaction to pain. There are men and women who have very serious lesions, from which much pain might be expected, who complain very little. There are, on the other hand, many men as well as women who complain exaggeratedly after even trifling surgical intervention. We have probably had some of the most striking examples of the influence of mind over body in these cases. Many a patient who complained bitterly of torment that made it impossible to rest has, after being given a preliminary dose of morphine hypodermically, subsequently been given less and less of that drug, until finally, after a few days, he was getting injections of only distilled water. Without their injection he was in agony. After it he settled down to a quiet, peaceful night. Very often it is noted that these pains are worse at night and there is a tendency for such patients to attract attention only at such times as may be productive of considerable disturbance of the regular order and as may call special attention to them. We used to call such conditions hysteria, though, of course, they have nothing to do with the uterus and must be looked for in men quite as well as women.

Psychoneuroses.—These neurotic conditions, to use a term that carries no innuendo with it, may affect other functions besides that of sensation. Occasionally a neurologist is asked to see a patient in whom, following an operation, usually not very serious, some paralytic symptoms have developed. There is an inability to use one or more limbs, and the suspicion of thrombosis is raised. It is rather easy, however, to differentiate thrombotic conditions from neurotic palsies. The ordinary symptoms of the psychoneurosis are present. There is likely to be considerable disturbance of sensation, with patches of anesthesia and hyperesthesia, some narrowing of the fields of vision, and anesthesia of the pharynx, sometimes even of the conjunctiva. Often there is something in the history that points to the possible occurrence of a neurotic condition. Sometimes it is extremely difficult to get such patients over the mental persuasion that is the basis of their palsy, but usually it can be accomplished by suggestion in connection with certain physical means. Electricity is often of excellent effect in demonstrating to these patients that their muscles react properly under stimulus and that it is only a question of inability to use them because of mental inhibition. Such conditions as astasia-abasia may develop quite apart from surgery, but there is always some "insult," as the Germans say, that is some physical basis for them, and so they are often considered to be surgical.

Psychic Disturbance of Function.—Besides motion and pain, other functions may be affected through the mind. After operations within the abdomen it is sometimes difficult to move the bowels when it is desired to do so. It must not be forgotten that not infrequently in these cases the patient's mental attitude of extreme solicitude with regard to his intestines is inhibiting peristalsis. Such constipation will sometimes not yield to even rather strong purgatives, and yet will promptly be bettered by something that alters the mental state. It must not be forgotten that it is in cases of neurotic constipation that *pittulae micarum panis* have proven particularly useful. In the chapter on Constipation there is a discussion of this subject that will often prove suggestive to surgeons.

This same thing is true with regard to post-operative urination. In women, {764} particularly, there may be difficulty of urination after vaginal operations, which may be attributed to some lesion of the urinary tract and yet only be due to failure of the patient properly to control muscles in these cases. As in obstetrical cases, position, the presence of others, and the mental disturbance, may inhibit urination. The subject is discussed more fully in the section on Psychotherapy in Obstetrics. Surgeons are not so inclined now to insist on absolute post-operative immobility, and even a slight change of position may enable patients to gain control over their bladders without the necessity for the use of the catheter, which always carries an element of danger with it.

The influence of the mental attitude with regard to both of these functions—intestinal and vesical evacuation—must not be forgotten. There are many persons who find it extremely difficult to bring about such evacuations in the lying position. Everything is unusual, and their exercise of the coordination of muscles necessary to accomplish these functions is interfered with. It is somewhat like stuttering and the incapacity of an individual who may be able to talk very well to close friends and yet stammers just as soon as strangers are present or he is placed in unusual conditions. It has even been suggested that there should be some exercise of these functions in the lying position before operation, in order to accustom patients to the conditions that will obtain afterwards. They thus become used to their surroundings and the newer methods required, and, above all, if there should be any post-operative difficulty, they realize that it is not due directly to the operation, but rather to the unaccustomed conditions. This proves helpful in saving them from solicitude and consequent unrest and adds to the rapidity of convalescence.

Food Craving.—When food is to be given in small quantities and there is likely to be craving for it, much can be done to save the patient disquietude and disturbance by giving small portions rather frequently, rather than distributing it over three times a day, as the routine of life sometimes suggests. When water has to be denied, small pieces of ice may occasionally be used with excellent advantage. Patients learn to look forward to breaks at the end of comparatively short intervals in their craving, and the accumulative effect is greatly lessened. It is well understood that whenever people are absolutely denied anything, they are likely to let their minds dwell on that fact and crave it much more than would otherwise be the case. If they can look forward to having even the minutest quantities of anything that they want, however, craving is much less likely to be insistent, and the state of mind is much easier to manage. In all of these cases the confidence of the patient and the lessening of neurotic tendencies by suggestion means more than most of the physical remedies that have been recommended. There are some patients who respond almost in a hypnotic way to suggestion from a physician in whom they have great confidence.

Position and Peace of Mind.—The patient's general comfort is very important for the maintenance of a favorable state of mind. It used to be the custom to keep patients rigidly in one position for days, sometimes more than a week, after operation. We know now that this is almost never necessary, and that, of course, it is most fatiguing to the patient. Keep the ordinary well person absolutely in one position, without the opportunity to change from side to side even during a single night, and there will be justifiable {765} complaint of tired and achy feelings as a consequence. To enforce such a state for forty-eight hours in those who are well will produce a highly nervous state, consequent upon the fatigue and soreness of muscles induced. Hence, the importance of taking every possible means to provide even slight changes of position for those who have been operated upon. A number of regular-sized pillows should be provided so that the head may be raised and lowered, and a number of smaller pillows should be at hand which can be so placed as to relieve pressure at various parts and permit the patient to make at least slight changes of position during the first forty-eight hours. After this, usually definite alterations of position may be allowed without danger. The surgeon must think of these elements in the treatment and insist on them with his nurses, or they will not be carried out. It is possible now to permit patients to sit up much sooner than before, and, indeed, in pelvic operations, this is said to be definitely beneficial by preventing the spread of any infectious material that may be present into the general peritoneal cavity, and in older people it prevents the development or, at least, greatly facilitates the dispersion of congestion or such beginning pneumonic areas from hypostatic congestion as may be present.

{766}

APPENDIX I

ILLUSIONS

A physician who wishes to use psychotherapy effectively should know something about physiological psychology, or analytical or experimental psychology, as it is variously called, because of the help that he will derive from it in understanding many of his patients' symptoms. Fortunately this branch is now being taught in some of the medical schools, and the greater requirements for preliminary training bring to the medical school men who have already had a course in this subject. The chapter on Illusions is particularly important because it affords many illustrations of how easy it is to be deceived by the senses and, therefore, how many precautions have to be taken in order to be sure that impressions produced on patients' minds that seriously disturb them may not merely be due to exaggeration of the significance of information brought them by their senses.

These illusions are of special interest because they represent not only failures of the senses to convey truth, but because they illustrate how easy it is for the mind to be led astray by the senses. People often declare that they have seen things with their own eyes or in some other way have definite sensory knowledge of them, yet these illusions make it clear that it is perfectly possible for such sensory phenomena to convey quite mistaken information. People who are suffering from many symptoms are persuaded that they must pay attention to their sensations. The main purpose of the psychotherapeutist often is to have them neglect their sensations and correct them by means of information gathered from other sources. We do this with regard to our sensory illusions, why not also with regard to many sensations which are probably quite as mistaken, in certain individuals at least, as these universal illusions of mankind. The argument from analogy holds very well and can be used to decided advantage in many cases.

A startling illusion which makes it clear that care is needed in interpreting our sensations, is the so-called tube illusion or experiment. If a sheet of note paper be rolled into a tube of something less than an inch in diameter and then held close to one eye, both eyes being kept open, while the hand opposite to the eye before which the tube is held is placed palm faceward against the side of the tube about its middle, a hole will be seen, as it were, through the palm of the hand. This false vision is as clear as can be and persists after any number of repetitions of the experiment. It merely illustrates two-eyed vision. We have a picture in each eye and we combine them. When the pictures cannot be combined for any reason, optical illusions result. There are many more optical illusions than we think and there are many reasons besides two-eyed vision for them.

Other illusions of two-eyed vision may be illustrated rather easily. If {767} two dots are made on a sheet of paper about two inches apart and the eyes look at them in a dreamy way, looking far beyond the paper, with vision more or less fixed between them, after a few moments a number of things happen. Usually the two dots exhibit a tendency to float together.

Fig. 26

After an interval four dots will be seen—each of the dots having a picture in each eye. Then only one dot may be seen because the pictures combine. Sometimes three dots will be seen. When the dots swim toward one another, a curious feeling of insecurity comes over the experimenter, showing how much our sense of stability is dependent on vision and illustrating why vision from a height is so disturbing because objects cannot be properly fixed on the distant background.

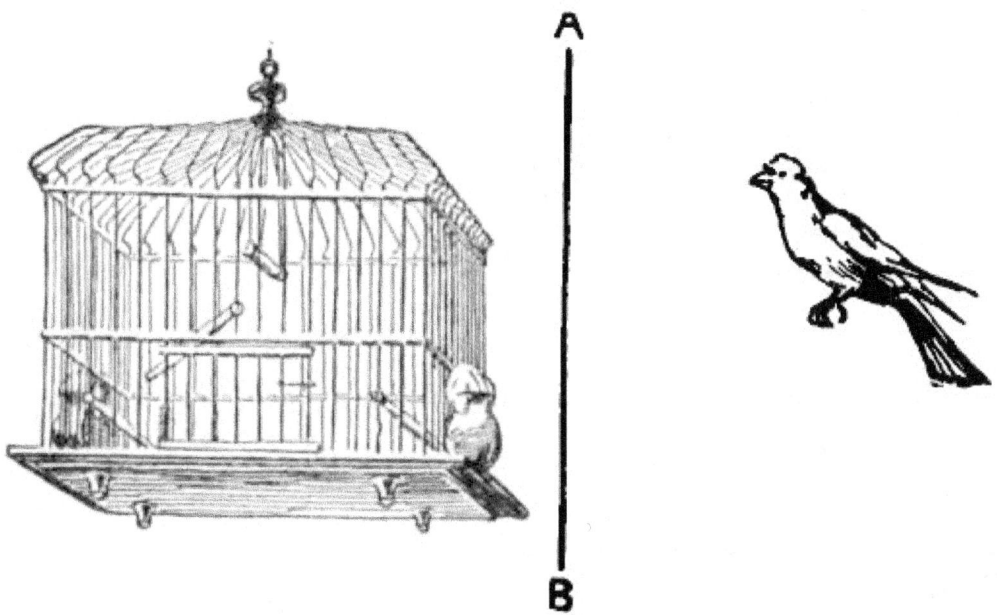

Fig. 27

Just as the two dots may be made to come together, so, after a little practice, a bird may be made to go into a cage (Fig. 27) or an apple made to go onto a plate (Fig. 28),

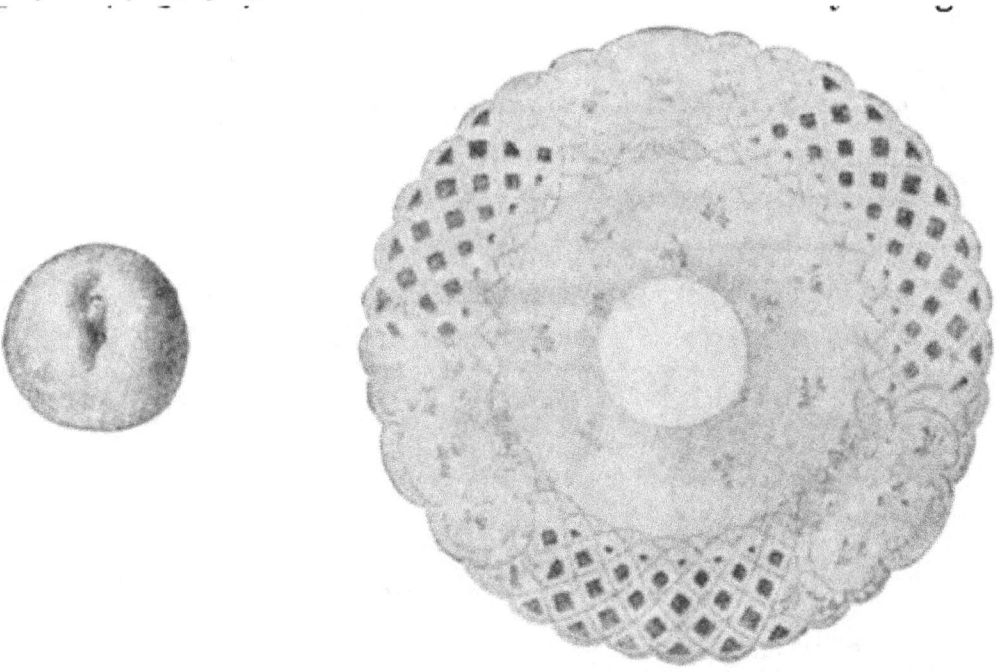

Fig. 28

These illusions show how many things that people {768} "see with their own eyes" are not so. All depends on the attention and the state of mind at the time when the seeing is done. In day-dreams these illusions often occur and may be the basis of delusions.

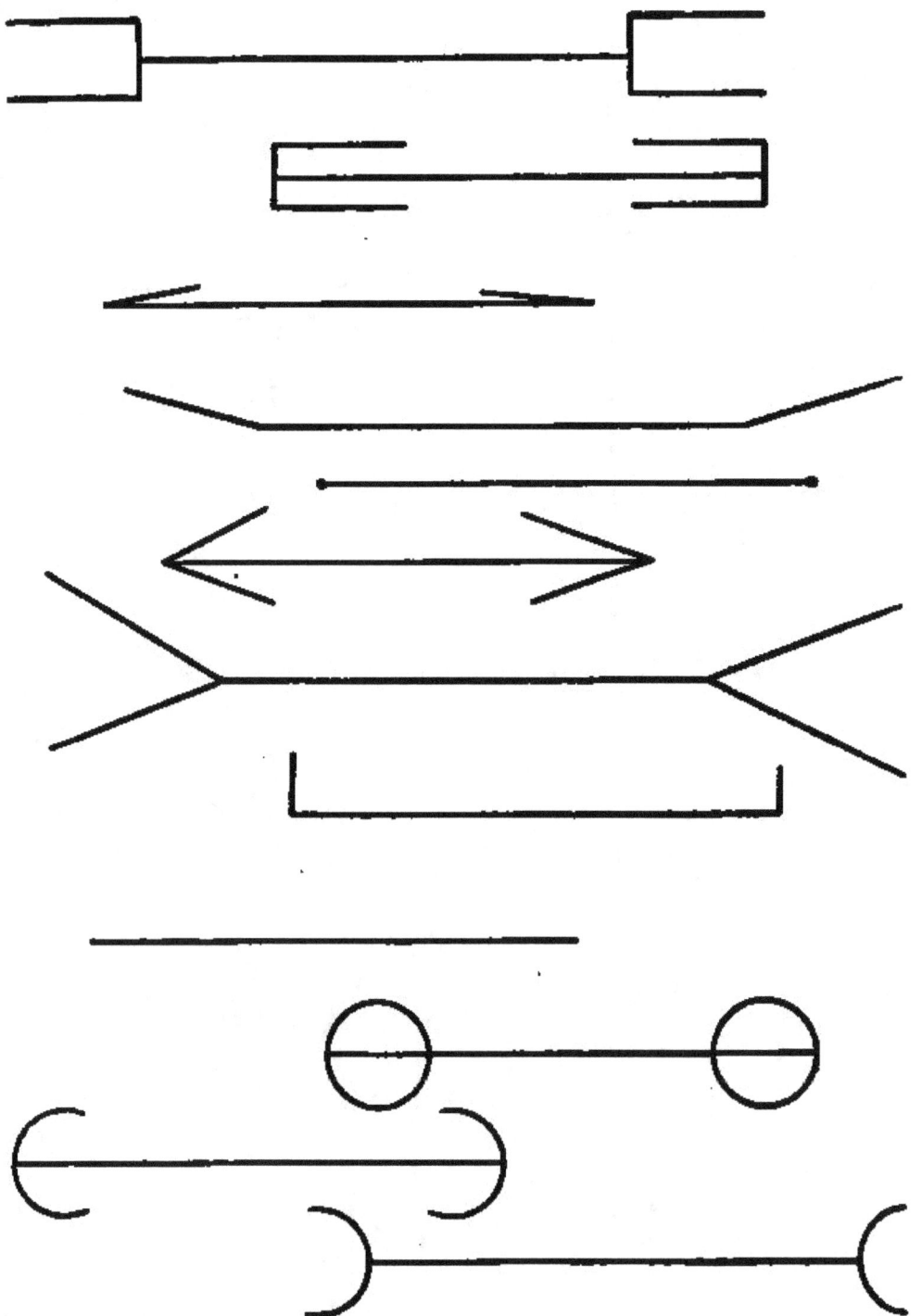

Fig. 29

There are, however, a number of optical illusions which illustrate certain defects of our vision that cannot be corrected, no matter how much we may desire to see correctly. We continue to see them not as they are but as they seem, and we must correct our vision by information from other sources. The Müller-Lyer lines are familiar and are given here (Fig. 29) because {769} they show how easily the senses may deceive us, even that most acute of our senses, vision, as to the sizes of things.

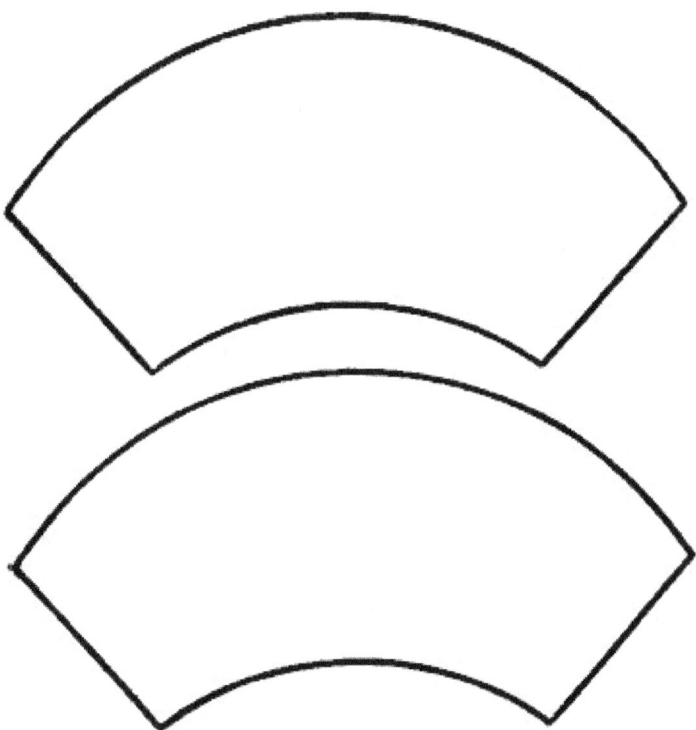

Fig. 30

Figure 30 illustrates how easy it is to be deceived by the juxtaposition of different portions of objects. I have had a woman who had cut out high collars for children and who happened to put them in the juxtaposition of the sketch here given think that she was either losing her sight or her judgment was being affected by the nervous condition in which she was. Nothing would persuade her that some serious development was not taking place until I showed her this illustration. In this illusion the juxtaposition of the short curved line to the long curved line of the other figure produces all the disturbance of judgment of size.

The illusions of filled and unfilled space are interesting and are quite inevitable. They are due to physiological visual effects and are very strikingly illustrated by what is known as the sun and moon illusion. Both these luminaries seem larger at the horizon than they are at the zenith. This is entirely an optical illusion. The horizon seems farther away than the zenith because vision to it is interrupted. The heavens appear not to be a half sphere, but more like an old-fashioned watch glass.

Fig. 31

Since the sun and moon occupying the same space on the retina are, because of this apparent difference of distance, judged to be farther away at the horizon than they are at the zenith, we are inevitably forced to the conclusion that they are larger in size than when in the other position. The over-estimation of filled space as compared with {770} the unfilled is mainly due to the interrupted muscular action of the eyes in traveling over the space requiring more effort. This makes it seem longer. Probably physiological processes on the retina also contribute to the illusion. A series of objects, even dots, will cause a greater physiological excitation of the retina than an equal amount of space, the boundaries of which alone are brought to our attention.

Illusions of size are even more startling than illusions of distance. It is perfectly possible to take three spaces, each exactly a square inch, and by drawing lines in two of them in different directions to make the figures appear of {771} very different size. This is a rather disturbing illusion, particularly for women who are apt to think that perpendicular lines make them appear tall and thin, while horizontal lines have the opposite effect. This is true if the lines are not placed quite close together. The reason why women wear many ribbons, however, whether they themselves recognize it or not, is that the attraction of attention to these makes the space in which they are seem longer. Hussars are dressed in uniforms with many rows of gilt cord or braid running across their chests in order to increase their apparent height. As a rule, a cavalry man must not weigh over 140 pounds or his horse will break down in long, forced marches. Such men are often

407

of small stature and their apparent height must be increased by their uniform, so as to make them look formidable. Advantage is taken of this optical illusion of filled space to produce this effect.

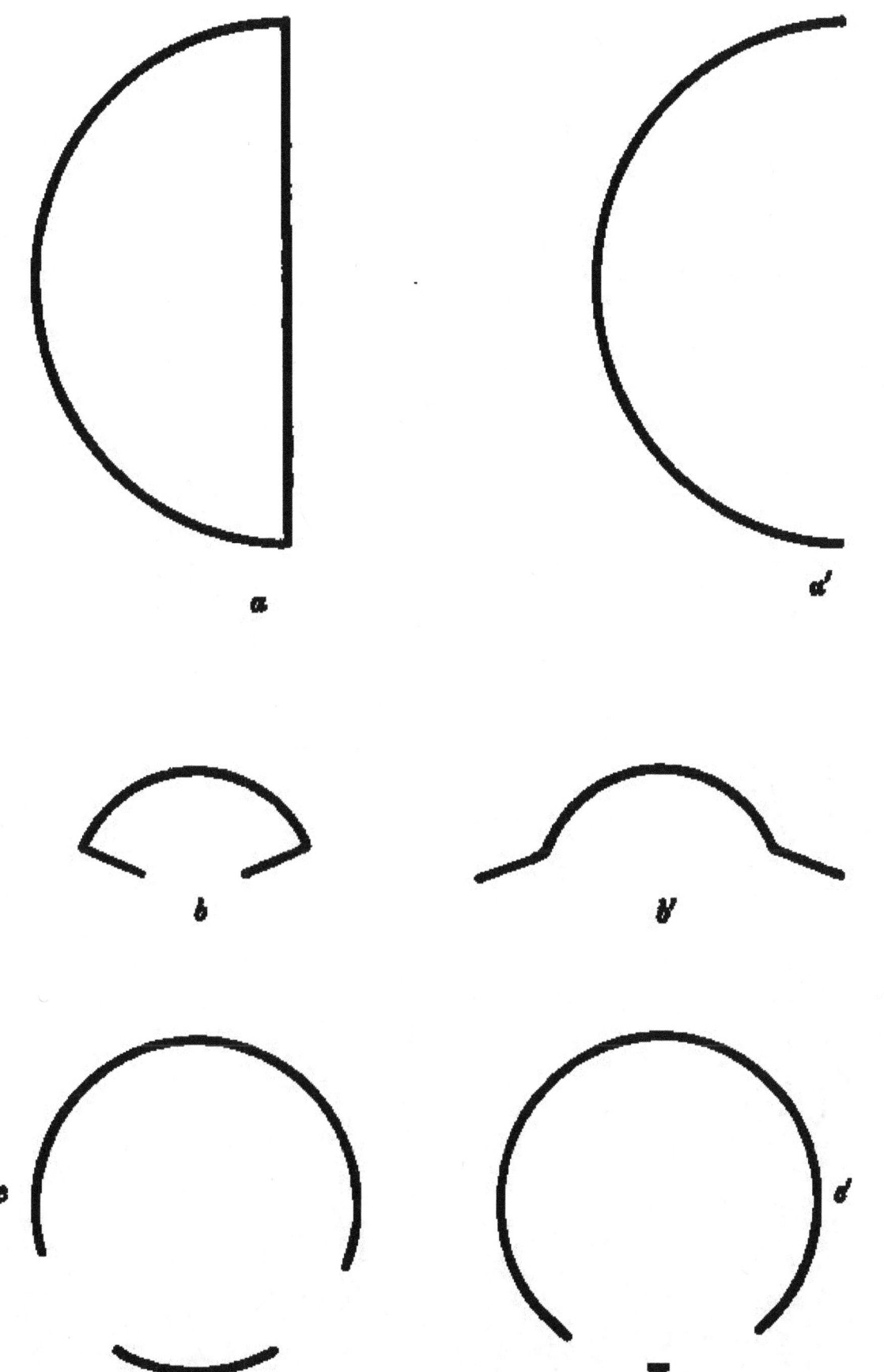

Fig. 32

Other illusions of size are quite frequent. It is rather hard for the ordinary observer to think that the half circles, *a* and *a'* (Fig. 32), are the same size, or that *b* and *b'* in the same chart are the same curve. The interruption in the circles *c* and *c'* produce very curious erroneous impressions which require a knowledge of this illusion to correct.

Optical illusions with regard to directions of lines are extremely common. Quite unconsciously we translate directions into special meanings. This is what enables perspective to be effective in drawings. It has many disturbing features, however. Some of these are striking illustrations of the defects of our vision.

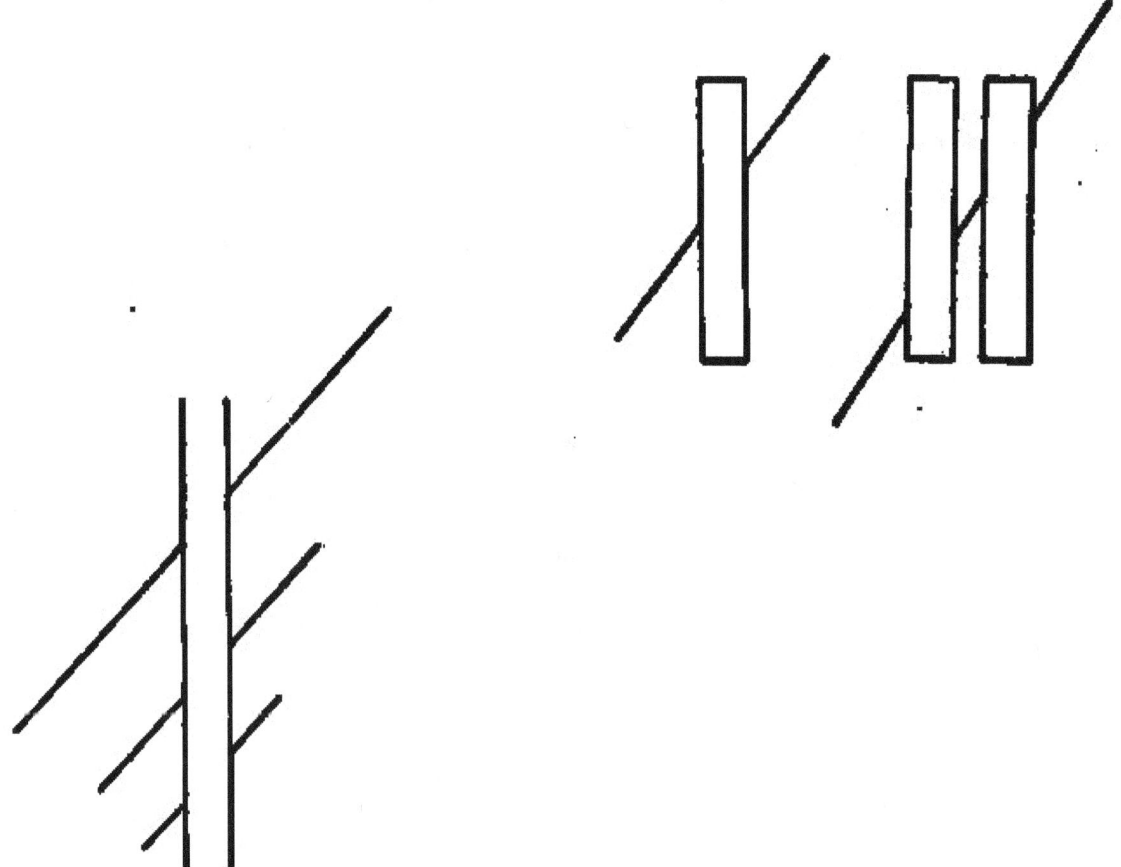

Fig. 33

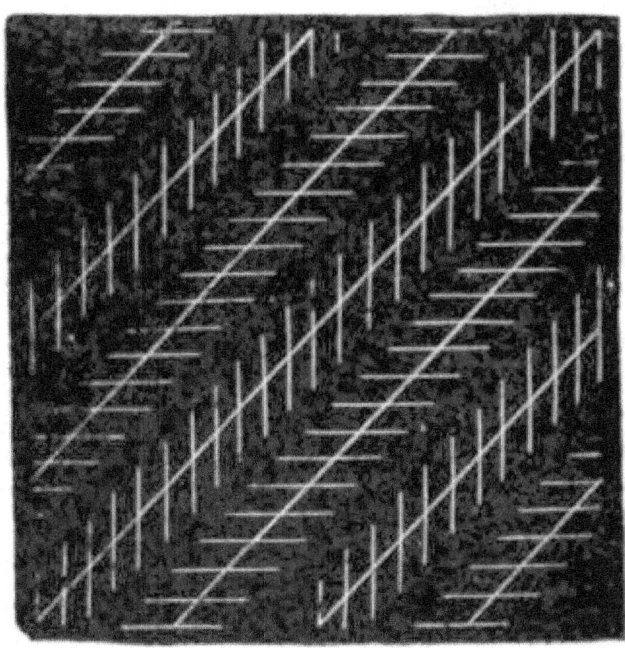

Fig. 34

Poggendorf's illustration of the displacement of oblique lines (Figure 33) {772} and Zöllner's distortion of parallel lines as illustrated by Figure 34, make it very clear that our judgment of direction must depend on many factors besides our vision, if we are not to make serious mistakes.

These optical illusions might seem to be of little significance, but the Greeks thought them of so much importance and recognized so thoroughly that they could not be corrected, and that the distortions and displacements would inevitably take place, that they deliberately put certain optical corrections into their great architectural monuments in order to avoid these false appearances. These have been traced very accurately in the Parthenon, for instance. In a word, the Greeks, knowing of these optical illusions, in order to make the lines of their buildings appear correct, deliberately made them wrong to a sufficient degree to correct the optical illusion; This frank mode of yielding to a limitation of human nature is a fine lesson for patients to learn if they can only be made to learn it from these illustrations.

It is with regard to colors, however, that we have the best examples of optical illusions depending on the individual and his special anatomy and physiology. Color-blind people are quite sure that they see color, just as other people do, until their defect is demonstrated to them. A man who is color blind for red thinks that he sees that color as other people do, while all that he sees is a particular shade of brightness which, because other people call it red, he has come to call red. When asked to pick out red from a series of other colors he may often succeed. When asked, however, to take a skein of red wool selected for him to a basket containing a number of different colored wools, and to bring back all those that are of the same color, he will select grays and browns and sometimes greens as well as reds, and present them as all matched colors. A man who is color blind for all colors will still think that he sees colors as other people do. The ingenious illustration of the American flag as it appears to people suffering from different forms of color blindness, though they are all persuaded that they see the same kind of flag, is an interesting example of how different may be people's sensations, though their conclusions are the same. It may be seen in many of the text books of analytical or experimental psychology.

{773}

Dalton, to whom we owe the atomic theory, was himself color blind for red and made the first investigations in that subject. He was of Quaker origin and found that a great many of his brethren were deficient in color vision. It becomes much easier from this to understand why they resolved to wear nothing but gray. They did not see colors as other people do and therefore could not understand nor sympathize with the joy of other people in color. Dalton tells the story of a Quaker prominent in his sect who once went to town to buy a gray waistcoat and purchased instead one of bright red. When he appeared at meeting in this he was promptly tried for heresy and violation of church regulations.

There is an interesting tendency on the part of people who are themselves defective in certain faculties of sensation, to conclude that when other people are wrapt in admiration of something that they cannot perceive, it is because these other people have some mental defect that leads them to enthuse too easily over their sensations. A story is told of a newspaper man who used to insist that all that was said about the beauty of the song of birds was due to the vivid imagination of the writers, for he could find nothing to admire about the songs of birds. He was placed in a room with a number of fine song birds all round him and it proved that he could not hear any of the higher notes at all. It was easy, then, to understand his condemnation of the enthusiasm of others as hysterical and imaginative. Nearly this same thing is true of many quite intelligent people with regard to music. They hear ordinary sounds, as did the newspaper man, very well. They are tone-deaf however, that is, they are quite unable to hear and appreciate combinations of sounds or even to catch melodious successions of single notes. They cannot recognize one tune from another and often do not know "Yankee Doodle" from the "Doxology," or, at most, know only

411

the most familiar tunes, but they set themselves up very calmly as judges of the intellects of others and conclude that music lovers are really a hysterical set of people who go into ecstasies over certain quite insignificant sensations.

These interesting tendencies are helpful in enabling the physician to understand his patients better. They often serve as texts from which the physician can explain curious things to patients who are prone to draw wrong conclusions from them and often suggestions unfavorable to their health.

These illustrations and their discussion serve to make very clear the distinction between illusions, delusions and hallucinations, which are often confounded. Illusions are deceptions of the senses. If a man walking along a country road where he fears the presence of snakes sees in the gathering twilight a piece of rope coiled, he will almost surely mistake it for a snake. This is an illusion produced by the conditions in which the object is seen. If walking along the same road the next day, more timorous than ever as to snakes, he should see in broad daylight the same coil of rope, he might in his fright not stay long enough to decide whether it was a snake or not, and his illusion would continue, though it would partake somewhat of the nature of a delusion due to fright disturbing his judgment. If, in spite of careful examination, however, of it, such as would satisfy any ordinary mind that it was a coil of rope and not a snake, he should still insist in believing that it was a snake, this would be a delusion. There is always a mental element in delusions. If, having seen nothing, he should insist, owing to fright and {774} nervousness or to some other cause, that he sees a snake where there is nothing at all resembling a snake and where evidently whatever is the basis of his idea of the presence of the snake, is within his own mind, then he is suffering from an hallucination.

Illusions may be quite inevitable. Most of the optical illusions continue to appeal to us as truths even when we know that they represent errors of vision. In spite of the fact that we know that the sun and moon are not larger at the horizon than they are at the zenith, by optical illusion we continue to see them of larger size. It is our duty to correct such illusions by information gathered from other sources. To follow an illusion, that is, to give it credit, when we should correct it, is a delusion. To think that because we cannot see red that therefore there is no red, or because we do not hear the sounds of notes of birds that they do not utter any notes, in spite of the fact that we have the testimony of nearly the whole human race to the contrary, is a delusion. When, using the verb in its broadest sense, as "perceive," we seem to see things very differently from the generality of people around us, there is every reason to suspect that there is some specific or individual limitation of our senses which makes us fail to perceive these things as others do. We have to suspect our sources of information then and to correct them by what we can learn from the experience of others. These are important considerations for many of the ideas that patients cherish with regard to themselves and their ills.

Hallucinations are entirely mental. But the phenomena that sometimes appear to be hallucinations may be due to illusions of the senses within the organism. For instance, those who indulge in cocaine often have the feeling of having a veil over the face, or of having run into a cobweb or something of that kind. The presence of the veil or the cobweb on the face is probably not an hallucination, but is due to certain disturbances in the circulation, or perhaps in the nerves themselves, which affect the nerve endings of the face, causing them to tingle in a particular way, and this sensation is translated as coming from without in terms of something that has been felt before. Some of the appearances of *muscae volitantes*, or of specks before the eyes, or occasionally of wavy lines, are due to disturbances of the circulation within the eyeball which cause corresponding disturbances of the optic nerve, with consequent apparent visions. When the eyeball is pressed upon, the sensation first produced is that of light and not of pain, because whenever a nerve of special sense is irritated, it produces its own specific sensation in the brain.

The chilly stage in malaria is a typical example of a physical condition having an effect upon sensory nerves that more or less necessarily produces a delusion. The patient is actually at the height of his fever when the chilliness and shivering come on and when he demands a larger amount of covers in order to protect himself from the cold he will often have a temperature of 104 degrees Fahrenheit, or even higher. What has happened is that the little blood vessels at the surface of the body are shut up by the effect of the plasmodium upon the system. Whenever we are cold these little blood vessels shut up in order to protect the blood from being chilled by the external atmosphere. The shutting up of the little blood vessels deprives, for the time being, the terminal nerves in the neighborhood of some of their nourishment. Their response is to set up a tremor or shivering, which will mechanically tend {775} to open the blood vessels so that they may have their nourishment once more. Whenever we have a set of sensations that correspond to this connected set of events, we translate them as feeling cold. The outer air does feel cold to the body because the blood is not flowing through to the surface as it would normally in order to warm it. Hence the chilliness. This is not an hallucination; but an illusion with something of a delusion in it; until we know how things are. Nervousness may set our teeth chattering just as it may cause tremor through our sympathetic nervous system, disturbing the flow of blood through muscles and so disturbing control of them. Vehement emotion, anger, fright, and even those of less violence may cause similar effects. All these phenomena illustrate the close relation between mind and body.

{776}

APPENDIX II

RELIGION AND PSYCHOTHERAPY

Religion and psychotherapy have, of late, come to have many relations to each other and many interests in common, at least in the minds of a number of clergymen, and in popular estimation. There is no doubt but that religion can do much to soothe troubled men and women, even when their troubles are entirely physical in nature and origin. It at least lessens the unfavorable effect of worry in exaggerating such pathological processes as are at work. All diseases, functional and organic, are rendered worse by solicitude, while many troublesome symptoms become quite bearable if only the patient does not dwell on them too much but takes them as they come, carefully refraining from emphasizing them by over-attention. That is the very essence of psychotherapy. Religion, in the sense of trust in divine wisdom, can do much to originate and maintain this imperturbed frame of mind. People who are without religion, that is, without the feeling that somehow all their ills are a part of the great plan of the universe, the mystery of which is insoluble, but the recognition of which is demanded by reason, and who lack the assurance that somehow, in Browning's phrase:

```
"God's in His Heaven-
All's right with the world!"
```

—are more prone to give way to over-anxiety and consequently to make themselves suffer more in all their ills, than is necessary or even likely in the more favorable state of mind of those whose trust in Providence is thorough and efficient.

In recent years there has been in the general population a distinct loss of faith in the great religious truths that are so helpful in engendering a peaceful state of mind in suffering. Many have come, if not to doubt of the Providence of the Creator, at least to feel that we do not know enough about it to place any such supreme dependence on it in the trials of life as would make it a source of relief, or at least consolation, in suffering. This same spirit of doubt has paralyzed faith in the hereafter and in all that trust in it brings, to sufferers, of consolation to come for their ills if these are borne as becomes rational creatures whose suffering has a purpose, though we may not comprehend it. Some people are destined by their physical make-up or by accidental conditions to considerable suffering. There are many ailments that are incurable and are definitely known to be incurable. Some of these entail great suffering of body and even more suffering of mind. Such suffering becomes quite unbearable unless the patient is of a very stoic disposition, or unless the thought of a hereafter in which the sufferings of this life will have a meaning is present to console.

{777}

Great scientists in the midst of all our advance in science—one need but mention here such men as Lord Kelvin, Clerk Maxwell, Johann Müller, Laennec, Pasteur, Claude Bernard, though the number might easily be multiplied—have insisted that the existence of a Creator is absolutely demanded by what we know of the physical universe. "Science demonstrates the existence of a Creator," is Lord Kelvin's expression. The existence of a Creator implies, also, the existence of laws made by Him, by which His universe is regulated in every detail, nothing being left to chance. Chance is indeed only a term which indicates that we do not know the causes at work. If somehow the Creator's power has been sufficient to bring the manifold things of the universe into existence according to a plan in which there is no such interference with one another as would cause serious disturbance of the universal order around us, then He can be trusted also to care for even the minutest details of creation and of human life.

In the gradual disintegration of the religious sense which has come as a consequence of certain materialistic tendencies in nineteenth century education and science, these religious sources of consolation have been shut off from a great many people. They have come to the feeling of being portions of a machine that moves hopelessly on, somehow, on the old principle, "The mills of the gods grind slow, but they grind exceeding fine." The sufferings of humanity then, are, for these people, only a portion of a great universe of suffering that is constantly going on but for which they can see no reason and no purpose. Lucretius's lines which make human sufferings the butt of the jokes of the gods who look gleefully on from their Elysian happiness, would represent the feelings of these doubters better than any religious expression. We have come back in this age, when evolution has so much influenced the thought of the time, after the curious cyclic fashion in which human thought repeats itself from era to era, to the attitude of mind of the old Roman poet who almost singly among his contemporaries, had been deeply affected by the same doctrine of evolution. The pessimism he was prone to as to the significance of human life has become once more the fashion.

Such pessimistic thoughts do not come, as a rule, while people are in good health, but they assert themselves with double emphasis in moments of trial and suffering. Lucretius himself is said to have committed suicide. The result of the diffusion of this materialistic pessimism in our time has been a gradual preparation for a revulsion of feeling in many minds. One manifestation of this reaction has been seen in a form of religion which denies entirely the existence of evil. God the Creator is good and therefore there can be no evil in His world. Whatever of evil there is, is only due to man's failure to see the entirety of things. Evil is an error of mortal mind—only that and nothing more. In spite of the manifest absurdity of the underlying principle, if people can only be brought to persuade themselves that there is no such thing as evil or suffering, then many of their discomforts disappear, all of their symptoms grow less and a sense of well-being results. It is, indeed, surprising how many even physical ills will be relieved by this state of mind if sincerely accepted. It is the highest possible tribute to psychotherapy and the curative influence of mind over body.

Another phase of this revulsion of feeling has been the institution of a church movement that would make sufferers realize once more all the {778} consolations there are in religion. The sufferer is brought to a renewed lively sense of the presence of the Creator in the universe and of His care for His creatures. The great purpose of suffering in making people better and stripping them of their meanness and selfishness is brought out. Anyone who has ever had called to his attention the difference between two brothers, one of whom has been chastened by suffering above which he has risen by character development, and another who has enjoyed good health and prosperity all his life, will realize how much of good suffering means in the world. Pain is not in itself an evil, but a warning, and most of the trials of life can rather readily be shown to partake of this character. A man who can be made to submit himself, then, to the will of the Creator and be persuaded to acknowledge that somehow we must try to work out our part in the great scheme of things behind which the Creator stands, is somewhat like the soldier ready even when tired and worn out, to go in on a forlorn hope, because he has confidence that he is executing a part of the plan of his general for his country's welfare, though he does not know how, and he is quite well aware that it is going to cost him much in pain and suffering, and perhaps his life.

There is no doubt that an abiding sense of religion does much for people in the midst of their ailments and, above all, keeps them from developing those symptoms due to nervous worry and solicitude which so often are more annoying to the patient than the actual sufferings he or she may have to bear. While religion is often said to predispose to certain mental troubles, it is now well appreciated by psychiatrists that it is not religion that has the tendency to disturb the mind, but a disequilibrated mind has a tendency to exaggerate out of all reason its interests in anything that it takes up seriously. Whether the object of the attention be business, or pleasure, or sexuality, or religion, the unbalanced mind pays too much attention to it, becomes too exclusively occupied with it, and this over-indulgence helps to form a vicious

413

circle of unfavorable influence. While many people in their insanity, then, show exaggerated interest in religion, this is only like other exaggerated interests of the disequilibrated, and religion itself is not the cause but only a coincidence in the matter.

Clouston, in his book on "Unsoundness of Mind" (Methuen, London, 1911), put this very well when he said, "It is true that religion, touching as it does, in the most intense way the emotional nature, and the spiritual instincts of mankind, sometimes appears to cause and is often mixed up with insanity. But in nearly all such cases the brain of the individual was originally unstable, specially emotional, over-sensitive, hyperconscientious, and often somewhat weak in the intellectual and inhibitory faculties and, if looked for, other causes will usually be found." He had said just before, "To talk of 'religious insanity' as if it were a definite and definable form is in my judgment a mistake."

On the contrary, there is now a growing conviction that a deep religious feeling, a sense of dependence on and trust in the Almighty, will do more than anything else to keep people from those neurotic manifestations which so often are seen in our day and are growing more and more frequent as life becomes more strenuous and more attention is paid to the material side of things, to the exclusion of the spiritual. How true this is may be judged from expressions that have been used in recent years by well-known specialists in {779} nervous diseases and in psychology. These have included men who were often not believers in religion themselves but who recognized its influence for good for others. Such expressions are to be found in the writings of men of every nationality. Not infrequently, in spite of their own religious affiliation, they acknowledge what a profound influence certain forms of religion have over people. These testimonies have been multiplying in our medical literature in recent years, because apparently physicians have come to appreciate much better by contrast the influence for good of religion over some of their patients, since so many of the sufferers from nervous diseases they see have not this source of consolation to recur to.

In America we have a number of such testimonies. In his "Self Help for Nervous Women" Dr. John K. Mitchell of Philadelphia, who may be taken to represent in this matter the Philadelphia School of Neurologists, to which his father has lent such distinction, said:

It is certainly true that considering as examples two such widely separated forms of religious belief as the Orthodox Jews and the strict Roman Catholics, one does not see as many patients from them as from their numbers might be expected, especially when it is remembered that Jews as a whole are very nervous people and that the Roman Church includes in this country among its members numbers of the most emotional race in the world.

Of only one sect can I recall no example. It is not in my memory that a professing Quaker ever came into my hands to be treated for nervousness. If the opinion I have already stated so often is correct, namely that want of control of the emotions and the over-expression of the feelings are prime causes of nervousness, then the fact that discipline of the emotions is a lesson early and constantly taught by the Friends, would help to account for the infrequency of this disorder among them and adds emphasis to the belief in such a causation.

Prof. Münsterberg, who may be fairly taken to represent the German school, but whose long years of residence in America have made him a cosmopolitan, is quite as positive in his declaration of the place that religion may hold in making human suffering less. In his "Psychotherapy" he devotes considerable attention to the subject. The religious discipline, that is, the training of human beings from their earliest years to recognize that there is a higher law than their own feelings and that they must suppress many of their desires and take evil as it comes as a portion of human life, is of itself, he insists, an excellent preparation to enable the individual to bear up under the physical and mental trials of life and to make many symptoms that would otherwise be almost intolerable, quite bearable. It is from earliest years that this training must make itself felt, and Prof. Münsterberg insists that from early childhood the self-control has to be strong and the child has to learn from the beginning to know the limits to the gratification of his desires and to abstain from reckless self-indulgence. A good conscience, he says, a congenial home and a serious purpose, are, after all, the safest conditions for a healthy man, and the community does effective work in preventive psychotherapy whenever it facilitates the securing of these factors.

Self-denial has always been one of the main elements of religious training, and indeed was declared a chief source of merit for the hereafter. The modern psychotherapeutist, however, preaches self-denial almost as strenuously as the religious minister of the olden time, only now not for any religious {780} merit or reward, but because it makes life more pleasant and by that much happier. When men and women have learned to deny themselves in their younger years, it is not hard to stand even pain when they grow older, and pain is inevitable in every human life and the training to stand it is therefore worth while. Pain borne with equanimity is lessened by one-half if not in its intensity then at least in its power to disturb, and since religion will do this it possesses an important remedial value. Here is where religion is particularly valuable and the passing of it from many minds has thrown them back on themselves and left them without profound interests, so that they occupy themselves overmuch with the trivial incidents of life within them and disturb the course of many of their functions by giving exaggerated thought to them. Religion adds a great purpose to life and such a purpose keeps men and women to a great extent from being disturbed about trifles.

Of course, it would be too bad if religion should do no more than this. This, however, is the only phase of it with which we are concerned here. We may think very strongly with Prof. Münsterberg, that it would be quite wrong to assign to it only this place in life. He says: "The meaning of religion in life is entirely too deep that it should be employed merely for the purpose of lessening the pains and aches of humanity and the dreads that are so often more imaginary than real." He insists that "It cheapens religion by putting the accent of its meaning in life on personal comfort and absence of pain." He adds, "If there is one power in life which ought to develop in us a conviction that pleasure is not the highest goal and that pain is not the worst evil, then it ought to be philosophy and religion." Present-day movements, however, tend to subordinate religion to this-worldliness rather than to other-worldliness, and by just that much they take out of religion its real significance. We are here on trial for another world is the thought that in the past strengthened men to bear all manner of ills, if not with equanimity, at least without exaggerated reaction. It has still the power to do so for all those who accept it simply and sincerely.